W9-CZS-220

PRENTICE HALL

Algebra 2

with Trigonometry

Stanley A. Smith

Randall I. Charles

John A. Dossey

Marvin L. Bittinger

Prentice Hall

Glenview, Illinois
Needham, Massachusetts
Upper Saddle River, New Jersey

REVIEWERS

Donald R. Price
Alvarado Intermediate School
Rowland Heights, California

Joyce F. Henderson
Millikan High School
Long Beach, California

CONTENT CONSULTANTS

Elizabeth Cunningham
Mathematics
Prentice Hall National Consultant
Mansfield, Texas

Shawyn Jackson
Mathematics
Prentice Hall National Consultant
Bayshore, New York

Bridget Hadley
Mathematics
Director, Prentice Hall National Consultants
Hopkinton, Massachusetts

Sandra Mosteller
Mathematics
Prentice Hall National Consultant
Anderson, South Carolina

Loretta Rector
Mathematics
Prentice Hall National Consultant
Foresthill, California

ISBN 0-13-051968-5
4 5 6 7 8 9 10 04 03 02 01

AUTHORS

Stanley A. Smith
Formerly, Coordinator,
Office of Mathematics
Baltimore County Public Schools
Baltimore, Maryland

Randall I. Charles
Professor Emeritus
Department of Mathematics &
Computer Science
San Jose State University
San Jose, California

John A. Dossey
Distinguished University Professor
of Mathematics Emeritus
Department of Mathematics
Illinois State University
Normal, Illinois

Marvin L. Bittinger
Professor of Mathematics Education
Indiana University - Purdue University
Indianapolis, Indiana

PRENTICE HALL

Algebra 2
with Trigonometry

About the Cover:
The cover shows the skyline and inner harbor of Baltimore, Maryland. Baltimore is located just off the Chesapeake Bay along the Patapsco River. It has been an active port since the 1730s. Fort McHenry, which was under attack in 1814 when Francis Scott Key wrote "The Star-Spangled Banner," was built to prevent enemy ships from sailing into Baltimore.

Smith ♦ Charles ♦ Dossey ♦ Bittinger

Table of Contents

CHAPTER 1

Real Numbers, Algebra, and Problem Solving

REVIEW

ASSESSMENT

CHAPTER

2 Equations and Inequalities

REVIEW

ASSESSMENT

Relations, Functions, and Graphs

REVIEW

ASSESSMENT

Systems of Equations and Problem Solving

REVIEW

ASSESSMENT

CHAPTER 5

Polynomials and Polynomial Equations

REVIEW

ASSESSMENT

Rational Expressions and Equations

REVIEW

ASSESSMENT

CHAPTER 7

Powers, Roots, and Complex Numbers

REVIEW

ASSESSMENT

CHAPTER

8 Quadratic Equations

REVIEW

ASSESSMENT

CHAPTER 9

Quadratic Functions and Transformations

REVIEW

ASSESSMENT

CHAPTER

10 Equations of Second Degree

REVIEW

ASSESSMENT

CHAPTER

11 Polynomial Functions

REVIEW

ASSESSMENT

CHAPTER 12

Exponential and Logarithmic Functions

REVIEW

ASSESSMENT

CHAPTER 13

Matrices and Determinants

REVIEW

ASSESSMENT

Sequences, Series, and Mathematical Induction

REVIEW

ASSESSMENT

Chapter 15 Counting and Probability

REVIEW

ASSESSMENT

CHAPTER 16

Statistics and Data Analysis

REVIEW

ASSESSMENT

CHAPTER 17

Trigonometric Functions

CHAPTER 18

Trigonometric Identities and Equations

CHAPTER 

What You'll Learn in Chapter 1

- How to identify, and distinguish between, rational and irrational numbers and add, subtract, multiply, and divide real numbers
- How to evaluate algebraic expressions, and write equivalent expressions
- How to use the distributive property to multiply and factor, and to collect like terms
- How to use the addition and multiplication properties to solve equations
- How to use the rules for integer exponents, and apply them to scientific notation
- How to use axioms and properties to justify statements and write proofs

Skills & Concepts You Need for Chapter 1

Write fractional notation for each number.

1. 3.2 **2.** 5.15 **3.** 0.04 **4.** 1.001

Write decimal notation for each number.

5. $\frac{11}{20}$ **6.** $\frac{18}{25}$ **7.** $3\frac{3}{5}$ **8.** $4\frac{1}{7}$

Calculate.

9. $31.3 + 6.07$ **10.** $6.79 + 3.4$ **11.** $3 - 1.53$ **12.** $4.055 - 3.889$

13. 16×0.8 **14.** 2.21×1.8 **15.** $0.6 \div 0.24$ **16.** $2.7 \div 7.2$

17. $\frac{3}{5} + \frac{1}{3}$ **18.** $1\frac{2}{3} + 3\frac{1}{4}$ **19.** $\frac{5}{7} - \frac{9}{14}$ **20.** $8\frac{3}{4} - 7\frac{5}{6}$

21. $\frac{1}{6} \times \frac{5}{8}$ **22.** $3\frac{3}{8} \times \frac{2}{3}$ **23.** $\frac{4}{5} \div \frac{3}{4}$ **24.** $1\frac{9}{16} \div \frac{5}{8}$

Find each percent.

25. 36% of 92 **26.** 25% of 25 **27.** 130% of 64 **28.** $\frac{1}{2}$% of 400

Write the correct symbol =, <, or >.

29. 3.5 □ 3.36 **30.** 0.074 □ 0.703

31. $\frac{3}{13}$ □ $\frac{3}{16}$ **32.** $\frac{12}{25}$ □ $\frac{36}{75}$

Write each ratio. Simplify if possible.

33. 28 astronauts for 4 missions **34.** 52 weeks in 12 months

35. 92 kilometers in 8 hours **36.** 16 runs in 44 innings

Real Numbers, Algebra, and Problem Solving

The Statue of Liberty ("Liberty Enlightening the World") was a gift from the people of France to the people of the United States of America, recognizing the love of liberty inherent in both countries' revolutions. Sculptor Auguste Bartholdi's creation was presented in Paris on July 4, 1884. It then was shipped to the United States in early 1885 in 250 crates containing 350 pieces. It was finally assembled and placed on its pedestal in 1886. You will learn more about the statue and its dimensions in Lesson 1-6.

1-1 Real Numbers and Operations

What You'll Learn

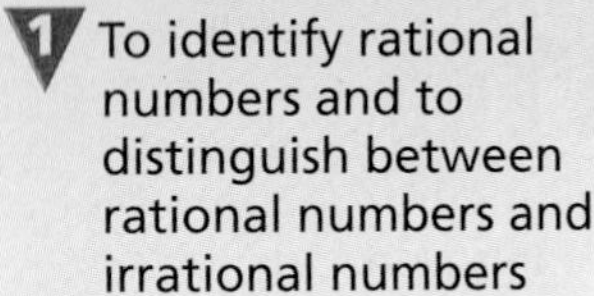

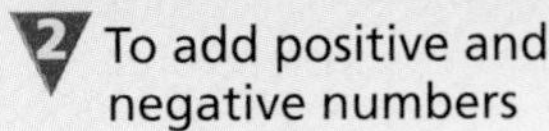

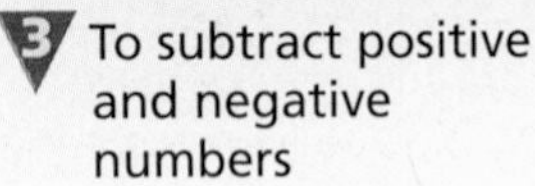

. . . And Why

To use real numbers in solving problems

The most important set of numbers in algebra is the set of **real numbers.** There is exactly one real number for each point on a number line.

The positive numbers are shown to the right of zero, and the negative numbers to the left. Zero is neither positive nor negative. The sets of **natural numbers** $\{1, 2, 3, 4, \ldots\}$, **whole numbers** $\{0, 1, 2, 3, 4, \ldots\}$, and **integers** $\{\ldots, -3, -2, -1, 0, 1, 2, 3, \ldots\}$ are all subsets of the set of real numbers.

PART 1 Rational and Irrational Numbers

Objective: Show that a number is rational and distinguish between rational and irrational numbers.

The real numbers consist of the **rational** and **irrational** numbers.

Definition

Rational numbers are those that can be expressed as a ratio $\frac{a}{b}$, where a and b are integers and $b \neq 0$.

These are rational numbers: $-\frac{2}{7} \quad 4 \quad 9.6 \quad 0 \quad 0.\overline{6}$

Since they can be written as: $\frac{-2}{7} \quad \frac{4}{1} \quad \frac{96}{10} \quad \frac{0}{1} \quad \frac{2}{3}$

If a real number cannot be expressed as a ratio of integers $\frac{a}{b}$, $b \neq 0$, then it is called *irrational*. For instance, we can prove that there is no rational number that is a square root of 2. That is, we cannot find integers a and b for which $\frac{a}{b} \cdot \frac{a}{b} = 2$. We can come close, but there is no rational number whose square is *exactly* 2. Thus $\sqrt{2}$ is not a rational number. It is irrational. Unless a whole number is a perfect square, its square root is irrational. The following numbers are irrational.

$$\sqrt{3} \qquad \sqrt{8} \qquad -\sqrt{45} \qquad \sqrt{11} \qquad \pi$$

Decimal notation for a rational number either ends or repeats. Decimal notation for an irrational number never ends and never repeats.

EXAMPLES Determine which are rational and which are irrational.

1 8.974974974 . . . (numerals repeat) Since the numerals repeat, the number is rational. We can express it as $8.\overline{974}$. The bar indicates that those digits repeat.

2 3.12112111211112 . . . (numerals do not repeat) Since the numeral does not end and numerals do not repeat, the number is irrational.

3 4.325 Since the numeral ends, the number is rational.

4 $\sqrt{17}$ Since 17 is not a perfect square, the number $\sqrt{17}$ is irrational.

Try This Which of the following are rational and which are irrational?

a. 7.42 **b.** $\sqrt{49}$ **c.** 0.47646464 . . . (numerals repeat)

d. $-\sqrt{32}$ **e.** $\frac{59}{37}$ **f.** 2.5734107656631 . . . (numerals do not repeat)

The **absolute value** of a number is its distance from 0 on a number line. We denote the absolute value of x as $|x|$.

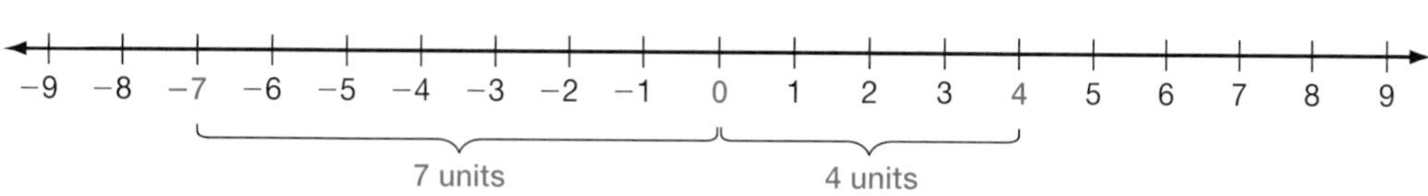

Since 4 is four units from 0, $|4| = 4$. Since -7 is seven units from 0, $|-7| = 7$. The absolute value of 0, $|0|$, is 0. We will define absolute value algebraically in Chapter 2.

Reading Math

There is no quick way to read 8.974974974 . . . or $8.\overline{974}$. Even calling the digits *974* the *repetend*, or the *block of numerals that repeats*, does not help much. "Eight point nine seven four, with repetend 974," "eight point nine seven four, repeat the block of numerals 974," and "eight point nine seven four, nine seven four, nine seven four, and so on" are common ways to read the number.

PART 2 Addition of Real Numbers

Objective: Add positive and negative numbers.

Recall the rules of signs for adding real numbers.

Rules for Addition of Real Numbers

1. To add when there are like signs, add the absolute values. The sum has the same sign as the addends.
2. To add when there are unlike signs, subtract the absolute values. The sum has the sign of the addend with the greater absolute value.

EXAMPLES Add.

5 $-5 + (-9) = -14$ Adding absolute values; the sum is negative.

6 $23 + (-11) = 12$ Subtracting absolute values; the positive addend has greater absolute value.

7 $-9.2 + 3.1 = -6.1$ The negative addend has greater absolute value.

8 $-\frac{5}{4} + \frac{1}{7} = -\frac{35}{28} + \frac{4}{28} = -\frac{31}{28}$ The negative addend has greater absolute value.

Try This Add.

g. $-8 + (-9)$ **h.** $-8.9 + (-9.7)$ **i.** $-\frac{6}{5} + \left(-\frac{23}{10}\right)$

j. $14 + (-28)$ **k.** $-4.5 + (7.8)$ **l.** $\frac{3}{8} + \left(-\frac{5}{6}\right)$

Subtraction of Real Numbers

Objective: Subtract positive and negative numbers.

Every real number has exactly one **additive inverse** or **opposite.** The additive inverse of a number is the number added to it to get 0. The additive inverse of a number x is symbolized by $\mathbf{-x}$.

The Property of Additive Inverses

For each real number a, there is exactly one number b for which $a + b = 0$.

The additive inverse of a number is the number opposite it, with respect to 0, on a number line.

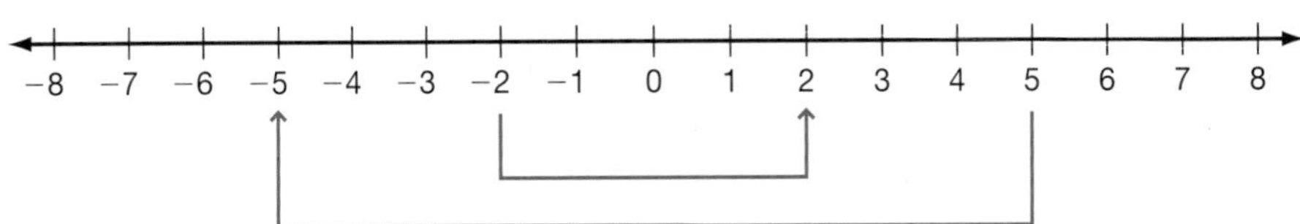

To find the additive inverse of 5, we reflect to the opposite side of 0. The additive inverse of 5 is -5. (We read -5 as "the additive inverse of 5" or "negative 5.") The additive inverse of -2 is $-(-2)$, or 2.

To find the additive inverse of a number quickly, merely change its sign.

Subtraction is defined in terms of addition. Subtraction and addition are inverse operations.

Definition

Subtraction

The **difference** $a - b$ is the number c such that $c + b = a$.

We can always subtract by adding an inverse. This fact can be proved, and we shall prove it later. If a statement can be proved, we call it a **theorem.**

Theorem 1-1

The Subtraction Theorem

For all real numbers a and b, $a - b = a + (-b)$.
(To subtract, we can add the inverse.)

The number subtracted is called the **subtrahend.** To subtract, we can change the sign of the subtrahend and then add it to the other number.

EXAMPLES Subtract by adding an inverse.

9 $5 - (-4) = 5 + 4 = 9$ Adding the inverse of the subtrahend, or changing the sign and adding.

10 $-\frac{4}{3} - \left(-\frac{2}{5}\right) = -\frac{4}{3} + \frac{2}{5} = -\frac{20}{15} + \frac{6}{15} = -\frac{14}{15}$

Try This Subtract by adding an inverse.

m. $8 - (-9)$ **n.** $23.7 - 5.9$ **o.** $-\frac{11}{16} - \left(-\frac{23}{12}\right)$

1-1 Exercises

Internet Connection
Extra Help On the Web
Look for worked-out examples at the Prentice Hall Web site.
www.phschool.com

A

Mental Math Determine which of the following are rational and which are irrational.

1. $\frac{3}{17}$ **2.** -13.91 **3.** -25 **4.** 42

5. $\sqrt{36}$ **6.** $\sqrt{19}$ **7.** $-\sqrt{16}$ **8.** $-\sqrt{37}$

9. $-12.3333\ldots$ (numerals repeat)

10. $5.101101110\ldots$ (numerals do not repeat)

Add.

11. $-12 + (-16)$ **12.** $9 + (-4)$ **13.** $-23 + 8$

14. $-24 + 0$ **15.** $-8.4 + 9.6$ **16.** $-5.83 + (-7.43)$

17. $-\frac{2}{7} + \frac{3}{7}$ **18.** $-\frac{5}{6} + \frac{1}{6}$ **19.** $-\frac{11}{12} + \left(-\frac{5}{12}\right)$

Subtract.

20. $5 - 7$ **21.** $15.8 - 27.4$ **22.** $-5 - 7$

23. $-6 - (-11)$ **24.** $10 - (-5)$ **25.** $-18.01 - 11.24$

26. $-\frac{21}{4} - \left(-\frac{7}{4}\right)$ **27.** $-\frac{16}{5} - \left(-\frac{3}{5}\right)$ **28.** $-\frac{1}{2} - \left(-\frac{1}{12}\right)$

29. ***Error Analysis*** Pac and Tim each simplified $-1(-1 - 3) - (-4)$ incorrectly. Pac got 0. Tim got 2. What errors did they make?

B

The number 3 can be represented by the symbols 3, III, $\sqrt{9}$, $\frac{36}{12}$, $(\sqrt{3})^2$, $\sqrt[3]{27}$, and so on.

Write five different representations for each of the following numbers.

30. 2 **31.** 10 **32.** 0.5 **33.** -3

34. ***Critical Thinking*** What patterns do you find in the decimal notation for $\frac{1}{13}, \frac{2}{13}, \frac{3}{13}, \ldots, \frac{12}{13}$?

Challenge

35. Suppose that $n = 0.\overline{8}$. We can find rational notation for n by finding $10n$ and then finding $10n - n$ as follows.

$$10n = 8.\overline{8}$$
$$n = 0.\overline{8}$$
$$10n - n = 8 \qquad 9n = 8, n = \frac{8}{9}$$

Find rational notation for each of the following.

a. $0.\overline{6}$ **b.** $0.\overline{7}$ **c.** $0.8\overline{2}$ (Hint: Find $100n$, $10n$, and $100n - 10n$.)

36. Write a decimal for an irrational number using only the digits 0 and 9.

37. ***Mathematical Reasoning*** A set of numbers is said to be *densely ordered* if between any two numbers there is another that is also in the set. Which of the following sets are densely ordered?

a. natural numbers **b.** integers **c.** multiples of 10
d. even integers **e.** rational numbers **f.** real numbers

Quick Review

A counterexample is one instance where a rule is false.

38. Vecha says $-x - y$ is always a negative number. Find a counterexample.

Mixed Review

Calculate. **39.** $\frac{5}{12} - \frac{1}{8}$ **40.** $1.103 + 2.908$ **41.** $\frac{7}{10} + \frac{3}{8}$

42. $38.9 + 17.6$ **43.** $12.7 \cdot 20.4$ **44.** $\frac{2}{7} \cdot \frac{7}{11}$ **45.** $\frac{1}{2} \cdot \frac{2}{3} \cdot \frac{3}{4}$

46. $\frac{1}{2} + \frac{2}{3} + \frac{3}{4}$ **47.** $\frac{2}{3} \div \frac{1}{3}$ *previous course*

Find the greatest common factor (GCF) for each pair of numbers.

48. 8 and 20 **49.** 27 and 64 **50.** 256 and 512
previous course

Find the least common multiple (LCM) for each pair of numbers.

51. 6 and 20 **52.** 15 and 35 **53.** 11 and 36
previous course

Multiplication and Division of Real Numbers

1-2

Multiplication of Real Numbers

Objective: Multiply positive and negative numbers.

When multiplying real numbers, we multiply the absolute values. Use the following rules to determine the sign of the product.

Multiplication of Real Numbers

1. If numbers are both positive or both negative, their product is positive.
2. If one number is positive and the other is negative, their product is negative.

EXAMPLES Multiply.

1 $6(-7) = -42$ Multiplying absolute values; the product is negative.

2 $-5.2(-10) = 52$ Multiplying absolute values; the product is positive.

3 $-8 \times -7 \times 6 = 56 \times 6 = 336$

Try This Multiply.

a. $-4 \cdot 6$ **b.** -8.1×-3.5 **c.** $9.1(-4.7)$ **d.** $\left(-\frac{3}{4}\right)\left(-\frac{5}{6}\right)$

PART 2 Division of Real Numbers

Objective: Divide positive and negative numbers.

Every nonzero real number has a **multiplicative inverse** or **reciprocal.** The reciprocal of a number is the number we multiply it by to get 1.

The Property of Multiplicative Inverses

For each nonzero number a, there is exactly one number b for which $ab = 1$.

To find the reciprocal of a number, we divide 1 by that number. The reciprocal of 8 is $\frac{1}{8}$, or 0.125 because $8\left(\frac{1}{8}\right) = 1$. If the number is in rational notation, we can find the reciprocal by inverting. The reciprocal of $-\frac{2}{3}$ is $-\frac{3}{2}$ since $\left(-\frac{2}{3}\right)\left(-\frac{3}{2}\right) = 1$. Note that the reciprocal of a negative number is negative.

What You'll Learn

1. To multiply positive and negative numbers
2. To divide positive and negative numbers
3. To recognize that division by zero is impossible

. . . And Why

To use real numbers to solve problems

Writing Math

The multiplication symbol × looks similar to the variable x. To avoid confusion, you can use the symbol · or parentheses.

Division and multiplication are inverse operations. In fact, division is defined in terms of multiplication.

Definition

Division

The **quotient** $\frac{a}{b}$, where $b \neq 0$, is the number c such that $c \cdot b = a$.

To subtract, we can add the additive inverse. To divide, we can multiply by the multiplicative inverse. The following theorem parallels the subtraction theorem.

Theorem 1-2

The Division Theorem

For all real numbers a and b, $b \neq 0$,

$$\frac{a}{b} = a \cdot \frac{1}{b}$$

(To divide a by b, we multiply a by the reciprocal of b.)

When dividing real numbers, we divide the absolute values. Use the following rules to determine the sign of the quotient.

Division of Real Numbers

1. If numbers are both positive or both negative, the quotient is positive.
2. If one number is positive and the other is negative, the quotient is negative.

EXAMPLES Divide.

4 $\frac{10}{-2} = -5$ The quotient is negative.

5 $\frac{-5.6}{-7} = 0.8$ The quotient is positive.

Try This Divide.

e. $\frac{24}{-8}$ **f.** $-\frac{10}{5}$ **g.** $\frac{-10}{-40}$

EXAMPLES Divide.

6 $\frac{1}{4} \div \frac{3}{5} = \frac{1}{4} \cdot \frac{5}{3}$ Using the division theorem

$= \frac{5}{12}$ Multiplying numerators and denominators

7 $\frac{2}{3} \div \left(-\frac{4}{9}\right) = \frac{2}{3} \cdot \left(-\frac{9}{4}\right)$ Using the division theorem

$= -\frac{18}{12} = -\frac{3}{2}$ Multiplying and simplifying

Try This Divide.

h. $-\frac{3}{4} \div \frac{7}{8}$

i. $-\frac{12}{5} \div \left(-\frac{7}{15}\right)$

PART 3 Division and Zero

Objective: Recognize division by zero as impossible.

We can divide zero by any nonzero number. The answer is always zero. On the other hand, we can never divide by zero. By the definition of division, we would have $\frac{n}{0} = c$ such that $c \cdot 0 = n$. But $c \cdot 0 = 0$ for any number c, so the only possible number that n could be is 0. Let's consider what $\frac{0}{0}$ might be.

$\frac{0}{0}$ might be 5 because $0 = 0 \cdot 5$.

$\frac{0}{0}$ might be 267 because $0 = 0 \cdot 267$.

It looks as if $\frac{0}{0}$ could be any number. Thus we cannot define and must exclude division by 0. Zero is the only real number that does not have a reciprocal.

EXAMPLES Which of the following divisions are possible?

8 $\frac{7}{0}$ It is not possible to divide by zero.

9 $\frac{0}{7}$ Possible; zero divided by 7 equals zero.

10 $\frac{4}{x - x}$ Not possible; $x - x = 0$, and it is not possible to divide by zero.

Try This Which of the following divisions are possible?

j. $\frac{0}{8}$ **k.** $\frac{0}{0}$ **l.** $\frac{8}{0}$ **m.** $\frac{17}{2x - 2x}$

Finding Reciprocals

Many scientific calculators have a reciprocal key 1/x .

Find the reciprocal of 63.

63 1/x → 0.015873

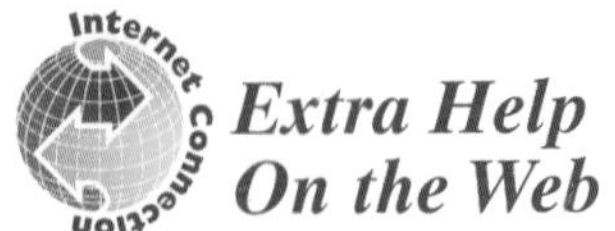

Extra Help On the Web

Look for worked-out examples at the Prentice Hall Web site.
www.phschool.com

1-2 Exercises

A

Mental Math Multiply.

1. $3(-7)$
2. $5(-8)$
3. $-2 \cdot 4$
4. $-5 \cdot 9$
5. $(-8)(-2)$
6. $(-7)(-3)$

Multiply.

7. $(-9)(-14)$
8. $(-8)(-17)$
9. $(-6)(5.7)$
10. $(-7)(-6.1)$
11. $-4.2(-6.3)$
12. $-7.4(9.6)$
13. $-3\left(\frac{2}{-3}\right)$
14. $-5\left(-\frac{3}{5}\right)$
15. $-3(-4)(5)$
16. $-6(-8)(9)$
17. $4(-3) \cdot (-2)(1)$
18. $-3 \cdot (-6)(8)(0)$
19. $-\frac{3}{5} \cdot \frac{4}{7}$
20. $-\frac{5}{4} \cdot \frac{11}{3}$
21. $-\frac{9}{11} \cdot \left(-\frac{11}{9}\right)$
22. $-\frac{13}{7} \cdot \left(-\frac{5}{2}\right)$
23. $-\frac{2}{3} \cdot \left(-\frac{2}{3}\right) \cdot \left(-\frac{2}{3}\right)$
24. $-\frac{4}{5} \cdot \left(-\frac{4}{5}\right) \cdot \left(-\frac{4}{5}\right)$
25. $-\frac{1}{2}\left(\frac{2}{3}\right)\left(-\frac{3}{4}\right)\left(\frac{4}{5}\right)$

Divide.

26. $\frac{-8}{4}$
27. $-\frac{16}{2}$
28. $\frac{56}{-8}$
29. $\frac{-28}{7}$
30. $\frac{-5.4}{-18}$
31. $\frac{-8.4}{-12}$
32. $18.6 \div (-3.1)$
33. $39.9 \div (-13.3)$
34. $(-75.5) \div (-15.1)$
35. $(-12.1) \div (-0.11)$
36. $\frac{2}{7} \div \left(-\frac{4}{3}\right)$
37. $\frac{3}{5} \div (-6)$
38. $-\frac{12}{5} \div \left(-\frac{3}{10}\right)$
39. $-\frac{5}{6} \div \left(-\frac{2}{3}\right)$
40. $-\frac{8}{3} \div \left(\frac{4}{7}\right)$
41. $\frac{6}{7} \div \left(-\frac{9}{14}\right)$

Which of these divisions are possible?

42. $\frac{9}{0}$
43. $\frac{0}{16}$
44. $\frac{(a - a)}{28}$
45. $\frac{(2x - 2x)}{(2x - 2x)}$

B

Find the reciprocal of each number.

46. $|-8|$
47. $\frac{|7-19|}{-6}$
48. $-\frac{|25|}{|-9|}$
49. $-\left|\frac{1}{-2}\right|$

50. Are 0.025 and -40 reciprocals?
51. Are 6 and $0.1\overline{6}$ reciprocals?
52. ***Critical Thinking*** Describe how you would perform the following multiplication:

$$\left(-\frac{1}{6}\right)\left(\frac{1}{5}\right)\left(\frac{1}{4}\right)\left(-\frac{1}{3}\right)\left(-\frac{1}{2}\right)(-1)(2)(-3)(-4)(5)(-6)$$

Challenge

53. *Mathematical Reasoning* Is it *sometimes*, *always*, or *never* true that, if x is a real number, $(-x)(-x)$ is negative?

54. Find the product of any nonzero number and the reciprocal of its additive inverse.

55. Is the reciprocal of a nonzero rational number rational or irrational? Explain.

56. **a.** How might you define the reciprocal of a percent?

b. What would be the reciprocal of 40%?

c. What would be the reciprocal of 125%?

57. Find the number, which when multiplied by the reciprocal of $-\frac{1}{8}$ gives a product that is the absolute value of -2.

Mixed Review

Write decimal notation for each number. **58.** $7\frac{7}{8}$ **59.** $\frac{81}{16}$ **60.** $-4\frac{2}{3}$

previous course

Determine which numbers are rational and which are irrational.

61. $\sqrt{24}$ **62.** $-\sqrt{25}$ **63.** 0.0013 *1-1*

Simplify. **64.** $3 + (-6)$ **65.** $-5.1 + (-4.3)$ **66.** $8 - 11$

67. $3 - (-4)$ **68.** $\frac{2}{9} + \left(-\frac{7}{9}\right)$ **69.** $-\frac{2}{3} - \left(-\frac{2}{3}\right)$ **70.** $\frac{3}{5} - \frac{1}{10}$

71. $\frac{2}{3} + \left(-\frac{1}{6}\right)$ **72.** $|-37| + |12|$ **73.** $-\frac{5}{6} + \frac{2}{3}$

74. $|0| - |1| - |2|$ **75.** $-\frac{1}{2} + \frac{1}{3} - \frac{1}{4} + \frac{1}{5}$ *1-1*

Find each percent. **76.** 90% of 90 **77.** 180% of 45

78. Tickets for the state fair cost \$5.75 for adults and \$3.50 for children. Children under 3 are admitted free. What would it cost a family of two adults, an 18-month-old child, and twin 10-year-olds to enter the fair?

previous course

Many state fairs have Ferris wheels. George Ferris created this Ferris wheel for the World Columbian Exhibition in Chicago in 1893. The wheels and cars weighed 2100 tons. A full load of passengers added 150 tons. If the average weight of a passenger was about 130 pounds, about how many people could ride at one time?

Connections: Operations Theory

A **binary operation** assigns to each pair of numbers of a set another number of the set. The operations of addition and multiplication are examples of binary operations on the set of real numbers. Addition assigns a **sum** to a pair of numbers and multiplication **a product.** A **unary operation** takes a single number and assigns another number to it.

How can a calculator be thought of as an operation machine? What unary operations can be performed using your calculator?

1-3 Algebraic Expressions and Properties of Numbers

What You'll Learn

1. To evaluate algebraic expressions
2. To write equivalent expressions

. . . And Why

To solve problems algebraically

In algebra we use letters to represent numbers. For example, in the formula for the area of a circle

$$A = \pi r^2$$

A stands for the area and r stands for the radius. The Greek letter π stands for the ratio of circumference to diameter of a circle. A and r can represent various numbers, so they are called **variables.** The letter π represents only one number, so it is called a **constant.**

PART 1 Algebraic Expressions

Objective: Evaluate algebraic expressions.

Algebraic expressions consist of numerals, variables, and other mathematical symbols such as + or $\sqrt{\ }$. Here are some examples of algebraic expressions.

$$x + 5 \qquad |y - 8| \qquad \sqrt{x + 6} \qquad y^2 - 2y + 9$$

When we **substitute** numbers for the variables in an expression and then calculate, the number we get is the **value** of the expression for those replacements. We say that we are **evaluating** the expression.

EXAMPLE 1 Evaluate $2y + x$ for $x = 3$ and $y = 5$.

$2y + x = 2 \cdot 5 + 3$ Substituting 3 for x and 5 for y
$= 10 + 3$ Calculating
$= 13$

The value of the expression is 13.

EXAMPLE 2 Evaluate $-(-x)$ for $x = -7$.

$-(-x) = -(-(-7))$ Substituting −7 for x
$= -(7)$ Calculating within the parentheses
$= -7$ Finding the inverse of 7

The value of the expression is −7.

EXAMPLE 3 Evaluate $|x| + 2|y|$ for $x = 15$ and $y = -10$.

$|x| + 2|y| = |15| + 2|-10|$ Substituting 15 for x and −10 for y
$= 15 + 2 \cdot 10$ Finding absolute values
$= 15 + 20 = 35$

The value of the expression is 35.

Try This Evaluate each expression.

a. $5x - y$ for $x = 10$ and $y = 5$

b. $-(-y)$ for $y = -8$

c. $|x| - 2|y|$ for $x = -16$ and $y = -4$

Expressions and Number Properties

Objective: Use number properties to write equivalent expressions.

The subtraction theorem tells us that the expressions $m-n$ and $m + (-n)$ will always have the same value whenever we make the same substitutions in both expressions. **Equivalent expressions** always have the same value for all acceptable replacements.

EXAMPLES Use the subtraction theorem to write equivalent expressions.

4 $4y - x = 4y + (-x)$ Adding an inverse

5 $3p + 5q = 3p - (-5q)$ Using the subtraction theorem in reverse

Try This Use the subtraction theorem to write equivalent expressions.

d. $-5x - 3y$

e. $17m - 45$

f. $-6p + 5t$

A number that does not give us a value when substituted in an expression is not an *acceptable* replacement. For example, the number 1 is not an acceptable replacement for x in the expression

$$\frac{4 + x}{x - 1}$$

because it gives us a divisor of 0, and division by 0 is undefined.

Number properties help us identify equivalent expressions. The **commutative properties** tell us that we can change order when adding or multiplying and obtain an expression equivalent to the original one.

The Commutative Properties

Addition

For any real numbers a and b, $a + b = b + a$.

Multiplication

For any real numbers a and b, $a \cdot b = b \cdot a$.

The **associative properties** tell us that we can change grouping when adding or multiplying and obtain an equivalent expression.

The Associative Properties

Addition

For any real numbers a, b, and c, $a + (b + c) = (a + b) + c$.

Multiplication

For any real numbers a, b, and c, $a \cdot (b \cdot c) = (a \cdot b) \cdot c$.

EXAMPLE 6 Use the commutative property of addition to write an expression equivalent to $3x + 4y$.

$$3x + 4y = 4y + 3x \quad \text{Changing order}$$

EXAMPLE 7 Use the associative property of multiplication to write an expression equivalent to $3x(7y \cdot 9z)$.

$$3x(7y \cdot 9z) = (3x \cdot 7y) \cdot 9z \quad \text{Changing grouping}$$

We can use both the commutative and associative properties to write equivalent expressions.

EXAMPLE 8 Use the commutative and associative properties of addition to write an expression equivalent to $\left(\frac{5}{x} + 2y\right) + 3z$.

$$\left(\frac{5}{x} + 2y\right) + 3z = \frac{5}{x} + (2y + 3z) \quad \text{Using the associative property}$$

$$= \frac{5}{x} + (3z + 2y) \quad \text{Using the commutative property}$$

Try This

g. Use the associative property of addition to write an expression equivalent to $(8m + 5n) + 6p$.

h. Use the commutative property of multiplication to write an expression equivalent to $(17x)(-9t)$.

i. Use the commutative and associative properties of multiplication to write an expression equivalent to $9p(4q \cdot 16r)$.

We can use the identity properties of addition and multiplication to write equivalent expressions.

The Identity Properties

Addition

For any real number a, $a + 0 = a$.

Multiplication

For any real number a, $a \cdot 1 = a$.

The number "0" is the **additive identity,** and the number "1" is the **multiplicative identity.** Recall that the ratio $\frac{b}{b}$ is equivalent to 1 for any nonzero number b. Also, the difference $b - b$ is equivalent to 0 for any number b.

EXAMPLE 9 Write an expression equivalent to $\frac{x}{3y}$. Use $\frac{8}{8}$ for 1.

$$\frac{x}{3y} = \left(\frac{x}{3y}\right)\left(\frac{8}{8}\right) \qquad \text{Multiplying by 1}$$
$$= \frac{8x}{24y} \qquad \text{Multiplying numerators and denominators}$$

The expressions $\frac{x}{3y}$ and $\frac{8x}{24y}$ are equivalent. They will represent the same number for any acceptable replacements for x and y.

Try This

j. Write an expression equivalent to $\frac{19t}{3x}$. Use $\frac{9}{9}$ for 1.

EXAMPLE 10 Write an expression equivalent to $\frac{6xy}{2x}$ by simplifying.

$$\frac{6xy}{2x} = \frac{2 \cdot 3 \cdot xy}{2x} \qquad \text{Factoring the numerator}$$
$$= \left(\frac{2x}{2x}\right) \cdot \frac{3y}{1} \qquad \text{Factoring the rational expression}$$
$$= 1 \cdot \frac{3y}{1}$$
$$= 3y$$

The expressions $\frac{6xy}{2x}$ and $3y$ are equivalent. They will represent the same number for any acceptable replacements for x and y.

Try This

k. Write an expression equivalent to $\frac{10yz}{5z}$ by simplifying.

EXAMPLE 11 Write an expression equivalent to $4x - 2$ by adding 0. Use $7y - 7y$ for 0.

$$4x - 2 = 4x - 2 + (7y - 7y) \qquad \text{Adding 0}$$
$$= 4x + 7y - 2 - 7y \qquad \text{Rearranging}$$

The expressions $4x - 2$ and $4x + 7y - 2 - 7y$ are equivalent.

Try This

l. Write an expression equivalent to $8a - b$ by adding 0. Use $x - x$ for 0.

Extra Help On the Web

Look for worked-out examples at the Prentice Hall Web site.
www.phschool.com

1-3 Exercises

A

Evaluate each expression.

1. $3x + y$ for $x = 16$ and $y = 6$

2. $5y - x$ for $x = 8$ and $y = -11$

3. $2p + 3t$ for $p = -20$ and $t = 17$

4. $5s - 3t$ for $s = -14$ and $t = 13$

5. $3x + 5y + z$ for $x = 18$, $y = 9$, and $z = 4$

6. $8x + 4y - 2z$ for $x = 5$, $y = 17$, and $z = -8$

7. $-y$ for $y = 4$

8. $-x$ for $x = -8$

9. $-(-x)$ for $x = -17$

10. $-(-m)$ for $m = 12$

11. $-(y + 4a)$ for $y = 2$

12. $-(y + 20)$ for $y = -6$

13. $-(x - 2)$ for $x = 17$

14. $-(y + 2)$ for $y = 1$

15. $3|x + 2|$ for $x = -4$

16. $|p| + |q|$ for $p = -31$ and $q = -12$

17. $5|y|$ for $y = -23$

18. $|p + q|$ for $p = 21$ and $q = -9$

19. $|p| + |q|$ for $p = 21$ and $q = -9$

20. $|p - q|$ for $p = 31$ and $q = -6$

Use the subtraction theorem to write equivalent expressions.

21. $8y - 9x$ **22.** $16m - 56$ **23.** $t - 34s$ **24.** $-18x - 5y$

25. $9x + 7$ **26.** $23x + 12y$ **27.** $-18m + n$ **28.** $-65k + 15h$

29. Use the commutative property of addition to write an expression equivalent to $9y + 73x$.

30. Use the associative property of multiplication to write an expression equivalent to $9a \cdot (6b \cdot 12c)$.

31. Use the associative property of addition to write an expression equivalent to $12x + (9y + 89z)$.

32. Use the commutative property of multiplication to write an expression equivalent to $(32a)(-12b)$.

33. Use the commutative and associative properties of addition to write an expression equivalent to $\left(\frac{y}{8} + 90\right) + 6x$.

34. Use the commutative and associative properties of multiplication to write an expression equivalent to $(9x \cdot 12y)8z$.

Write an expression equivalent to each of the following. Use the ratio given for 1.

35. $\frac{12x}{23y}$; $\frac{8}{8}$ **36.** $\frac{19a}{b}$; $\frac{9}{9}$ **37.** $\frac{102}{5xy}$; $\frac{7}{7}$ **38.** $\frac{90z}{16y}$; $\frac{x}{x}$

Write an expression equivalent to each of the following by simplifying.

39. $\frac{4y}{4x}$ **40.** $\frac{8xy}{16y}$ **41.** $\frac{5y}{-2xy}$ **42.** $\frac{3(y + 1)}{21(y + 1)}$

B

Write as an algebraic expression.

43. five more than the absolute value of a number

44. the sum of the additive inverse of a number and its absolute value

45. the additive inverse of the absolute value of twice some number

46. the absolute value of the sum of two numbers

47. the sum of the absolute values of two numbers

48. The absolute value of the difference of x and y is greater than 5.

49. Three times the absolute value of a number is 8.

50. The absolute value of the sum of two numbers is less than the square of their sum.

51. ***Critical Thinking*** Write an algebraic expression in x and y that has a value of 20 when $x = 2$ and $y = -6$.

Quick Review

Remember that *the difference of* a *and* b is "a − b."

Challenge

52. ***Mathematical Reasoning*** Suppose we define a new operation @ on the set of real numbers as follows: $a @ b = 3a - b$. Thus $9 @ 2 = 3(9) - 2 = 25$. Is @ commutative? That is, does $a @ b = b @ a$ for all real numbers a and b?

53. ***Mathematical Reasoning*** Suppose we define a new operation $\oplus$ on the set of real numbers as follows: $a \oplus b = a^2 + b^2$. Thus $4 \oplus 2 = 4^2 + 2^2 = 16 + 4 = 20$. Is $\oplus$ commutative?

Mixed Review

Simplify. **54.** $4.2 + (-6.8)$ **55.** $6(-9)$ **56.** $-3.2(-4.1)$

57. $-8 \div 2$ **58.** $-4 - 9$ **59.** $-9(-3)$ **60.** $40 \div (-5)$

61. $-8 + 27$ **62.** $7 - 11$ **63.** $-\frac{3}{16} + \frac{8}{16}$ **64.** $\frac{3}{5} - \frac{3}{10}$ **65.** $-\frac{4}{5} \cdot \frac{1}{2}$ *1-1, 1-2*

Express as a ratio of integers. **66.** -5 **67.** 9.1 **68.** $\frac{2.8}{4.5}$ **69.** $-\frac{0.2}{0.05}$ *1-1*

Determine which of the following are rational and which are irrational.

70. $\sqrt{25}$ **71.** $3.454554555\ldots$ **72.** 3.45455 **73.** $-\frac{1}{7}$ **74.** $\sqrt{8}$ *1-1*

Connections: Limits of $\frac{1}{x}$

a. Evaluate the expression $\frac{1}{x}$ for $x = 0.1$, $x = 0.01$, $x = 0.001$, $x = 0.0001$, and so on. What happens as the value of x gets smaller and smaller?

b. Evaluate the expression $5\left(\frac{1}{n}\right)$ for $n = 0.001$, $n = 0.01$, $n = 0.1$, $n = 1$, and so on. What happens as the value of n gets larger and larger?

1-4 The Distributive Property

What You'll Learn

1. To use the distributive property to multiply
2. To use the distributive property to factor expressions
3. To use the distributive property to collect like terms
4. To write the inverse of a sum
5. To simplify expressions using the distributive property

. . . And Why

To solve more difficult equations

PART 1 Multiplying

Objective: Use the distributive property to multiply.

The **distributive property** tells us that when multiplying a number by a sum, we can add first and then multiply, or multiply first and then add.

The Distributive Property of Multiplication Over Addition

For any real numbers a, b, and c, $a(b + c) = ab + ac$.

In stating this property, we have used an agreement about parentheses. Parentheses show us which calculations are to be done first. We agree to omit them around products, however. Thus the expression $ab + ac$ is equivalent to $(ab) + (ac)$, since multiplications are performed before additions.

The following theorem can be proved by using the subtraction theorem.

Theorem 1-3

For any real numbers a, b, and c, $a(b - c) = ab - ac$.

We can also use the distributive property to write equivalent expressions.

EXAMPLES Multiply.

1 $4(x + 2) = 4x + 4 \cdot 2$ Using the distributive property
$= 4x + 8$ Simplifying

2 $b(s - t + f) = bs - bt + bf$

3 $-3(y + 4) = (-3)(y) + (-3)(4)$
$= -3y - 12$

4 $-2x(y - 1) = -2x \cdot y - (-2x) \cdot 1$
$= -2xy + 2x$

Try This Multiply.

a. $5(x + 9)$ **b.** $8(y - 10)$ **c.** $a(x + y - z)$

PART 2 Factoring

Objective: Use the distributive property to factor expressions.

The reverse of multiplying is **factoring.** To **factor** an expression is to find an equivalent expression that is a product. The parts of an expression like $3x + 4y + 8z$, separated by plus signs, are called **terms** of the expression. In this expression the terms are $3x$, $4y$, and $8z$. In the term $3x$, 3 and x are **factors.** The **coefficient** of x is 3.

If all the terms of an expression have factor in common, we can factor it out using the distributive property. We usually factor out the greatest common factor of all the terms.

EXAMPLES Factor.

5 $cx - cy = c(x - y)$ Using the distributive property

6 $9x + 27y = 9x + 9 \cdot (3y) = 9(x + 3y)$

7 $P + Prt = P \cdot 1 + Prt = P(1 + rt)$

Try This Factor.

d. $2l + 2w$ **e.** $ac - ay$ **f.** $6x - 12$ **g.** $-25y + 15w + 5$

PART 3 Collecting Like Terms

Objective: Collect like terms.

Terms whose variables are the same, such as $9y$ and $23y$, are called **like terms.** Similarly, $8a^5$ and $17a^5$ are like terms. Terms such as $23x$ and $9x^2$ are not like terms. Using the distributive property, we can simplify by collecting like terms. An expression with like terms collected is equivalent to the original expression.

EXAMPLES Collect like terms.

8 $x - 3x = 1 \cdot x - 3 \cdot x = (1 - 3)x = -2x$

9 $2x + 3y - 5x - 2y$

$= 2x + 3y + (-5x) + (-2y)$ Adding an inverse to subtract

$= 2x + (-5x) + 3y + (-2y)$ Using the commutative and associative properties

$= (2 - 5)x + (3 - 2)y$ Using the distributive property

$= -3x + y$

Try This Collect like terms.

h. $9x + 11x$ **i.** $5x - 12x$ **j.** $22x - 2.5 + 1.4x + 6.4$

PART 4 Inverses of Sums

Objective: Write the inverse of a sum.

When we multiply a number by -1, we get the additive inverse of that number.

Theorem 1-4

The Multiplicative Property of -1

For any real number a, $-1 \cdot a = -a$.

(Negative 1 times a is the additive inverse of a. Multiplying any number by -1 changes its sign.)

Using the multiplicative property of -1, we can replace an inverse sign by -1.

EXAMPLES Simplify.

10 $-(-9y) = -1(-9y)$ Using the property of -1
$= [-1(-9)]y$ Using the associative property
$= 9y$

11 $-(3x - 2y + 4) = -1(3x - 2y + 4)$ Using the property of -1
$= -1(3x) - (-1)(2y) + (-1)(4)$ Using the distributive property
$= -3x - (-2y) + (-4)$ Using the property of -1
$= -3x + 2y - 4$ Using the subtraction theorem

Try This Simplify.

k. $-(7x)$ **l.** $-(y + 10)$ **m.** $-(-3x - 2y + 1)$

Example 11 illustrates another important property of real numbers.

Theorem 1-5

The Inverse of a Sum Property

For any real numbers a and b, $-(a + b) = -a + (-b)$.

(The inverse of a sum is the sum of the inverses.)

This property also holds when there is a sum of more than two terms. It holds for differences because any difference is equivalent to a sum. The property leads us to another rule: to find the additive inverse of an expression with more than one term, change the sign of every term.

EXAMPLES Simplify.

12 $-(3x - 4y + 59) = -3x + 4y - 59$ Changing the sign of each term

13 $-\left(-9t + 7z - \frac{1}{4}w\right) = 9t - 7z + \frac{1}{4}w$ Changing the sign of each term

Try This Simplify.

n. $-(-2x - 5z + 24)$ **o.** $-\left(\frac{1}{4}t + 41w - rd + 23\right)$

PART 5 Using the Distributive Property

Objective: Use the distributive property to simplify expressions.

When a sum or difference is being subtracted, we can subtract by adding an inverse. We can simplify, using the distributive property to remove parentheses.

EXAMPLES Simplify.

14

$$\begin{aligned} 6x - (4x + 2) &= 6x + [-(4x + 2)] && \text{Adding an inverse} \\ &= 6x + [(-4x) + (-2)] && \text{Using the inverse of a sum property} \\ &= 6x - 4x - 2 && \text{Using the subtraction theorem} \\ &= 2x - 2 && \text{Collecting like terms} \end{aligned}$$

When an expression in parentheses is preceded by a subtraction sign or additive inverse sign, the sign of each term inside the parentheses is changed.

15

$$\begin{aligned} x - 5(x + y) &= x + [-5(x + y)] && \text{Adding the inverse of } 5(x + y) \\ &= x + [-5x - 5y] && \text{Using the distributive property} \\ &= x - 5x - 5y && \\ &= -4x - 5y && \text{Collecting like terms} \end{aligned}$$

When parentheses are needed within parentheses, we may use other grouping symbols. Computations are done within the innermost symbols first.

16

$$\begin{aligned} &6y - \{4[3(y - 2) - 4(y + 2)] - 3\} \\ &= 6y - \{4[3y - 6 - 4y - 8] - 3\} && \text{Multiplying to remove the innermost parentheses} \\ &= 6y - \{4[-y - 14] - 3\} && \text{Collecting like terms in the brackets} \\ &= 6y - \{-4y - 56 - 3\} && \text{Multiplying to remove the brackets} \\ &= 6y + 4y + 59 = 10y + 59 \end{aligned}$$

Try This Simplify.

p. $6x - (3x - 8)$ **q.** $x - 2(y + x)$
r. $3x - 5(2y - 4x)$ **s.** $15x - \{2[2(x - 5) - 6(x + 3)] + 4\}$
t. $9a + \{3a - 2[(a - 4) - (a + 2)]\}$

lp
eb

e

1-4 Exercises

A

Mental Math Multiply.

1. $3(a + 1)$ **2.** $4(x - y)$ **3.** $-5(2a + 3b)$

4. $2a(b - c + d)$ **5.** $2\pi r(h + 1)$ **6.** $\pi r(1 + s)$

Factor.

7. $8x + 8y$ **8.** $9p - 9$ **9.** $7x - 21$ **10.** $xy + x$

11. $2x - 2y + 2z$ **12.** $3x + 3y - 3z$ **13.** $3x + 6y - 3$

14. $4a + 8b - 4$ **15.** $ab + ac - ad$ **16.** $xy - xz - xw$

17. $\pi rr + \pi rs$ **18.** $\frac{1}{2}ah + \frac{1}{2}bh$

Collect like terms.

19. $4a + 5a$ **20.** $8b - 11b$ **21.** $14y + y$

22. $12a - a$ **23.** $15x - x$ **24.** $t - 9t$

25. $x - 6x$ **26.** $5x - 3x + 8x$ **27.** $3x - 11x + 2x$

28. $9a - 10b + 4a$ **29.** $7c + 8d - 5c + 2d$

30. $12a + 3b - 5a + 6b$ **31.** $4x - 7 + 18x + 25$

32. $13p + 5 - 4p + 7$ **33.** $17a + 17b - 12a - 38b$

Error Analysis Identify the error made in simplifying each of these expressions.

34. $3(4 + 3a) = 21a$ **35.** $5x - x = 5$

36. $6p - (-2p - 5p) = -p$ **37.** $2[(-3)(-1 - 5)] = 72$

Simplify.

38. $-(-4b)$ **39.** $-(-5x)$ **40.** $-(a + 2)$ **41.** $-(b + 9)$

42. $-(b - 3)$ **43.** $-(x - 8)$ **44.** $-(t - y)$ **45.** $-(r - s)$

Find the additive inverse.

46. $a + b + c$ **47.** $x + y + z$

48. $8x - 6y + 13$ **49.** $9a - 7b + 24$

50. $-2c + 5d - 3e + 4f$ **51.** $-4x + 8y - 5w + 9z$

Simplify.

52. $a-(2a + 5)$ **53.** $x - (5x + 9)$

54. $4m - (3m - 1)$ **55.** $5a - (4a - 3)$

56. $3d - 7 - (5 - 2d)$ **57.** $8x - 9 - (7 - 5x)$

58. $-2(x + 3) - 5(x - 4)$ **59.** $-9(y + 7) - 6(y - 3)$

60. $5x - 7(2x - 3)$ **61.** $8y - 4(5y - 6)$

62. $9a - [7 - 5(7a - 3)]$

63. $12b - [9 - 7(5b - 6)]$

64. $5\{-2 + 3[4 - 2(3 + 5)]\}$

65. $7\{-7 + 8[5 - 3(4 + 6)]\}$

66. $2y + \{7[3(2y - 5) - (8y + 7)] + 9\}$

67. $-3[9(x - 4) + 5x] - 8\{3[5(3y + 4)] - 12\}$

68. **TEST PREP** Which of the following is the solution of $7b - \{6[4(3b - 7) - (9b + 10)] + 11\}$?

A. $-119b + 217$ **B.** $-63b - 217$ **C.** $-11b + 217$ **D.** $11b + 217$

B

Simplify.

69. $-[-(-(-9))]$

70. $-\{-[-(-(-10))]\}$

71. $-\{-[-(-(-(-8)))]\}$

72. $\frac{2}{3}[2(x + y) + 4(x + 4y)]$

73. Is it *sometimes*, *always* or *never* true that, if x is a real number, $-(-(-(-x)))$ is negative?

The expression $P + Prt$ gives the value of an account of P dollars principal, invested at a rate r (in percent) for a time t (in years). Find the value of an account under the following conditions.

74. $P = \$120$ $r = 12\%$ $t = 1$ yr

75. $P = \$500$ $r = 14\%$ $t = \frac{1}{2}$ yr

76. ***Critical Thinking*** Decide whether finding the absolute value is distributive over addition. That is, can we add first and then find the absolute value or find the absolute values and then add?

The charter of the First Bank of the United States was signed by President Washington in 1791 to handle the colossal debt from the Revolutionary War, and to create a standard form of currency. The First Bank was in business for only 20 years. It cost $110,168.05 to build. If that amount had been invested at 7% interest for 200 years, what would the value of the account have been in 1991? See Exercises 74 and 75.

Challenge

Simplify.

77. $[-(7a - b) - (a + 5b)] - [2(a + \frac{1}{2}b) + 3(7a - \frac{5}{3}b)]$

78. $0.01\{0.1(x - 2y) - [0.001(3x + y) - (0.2x - 0.1y)]\} - (x - y)$

79. ***Mathematical Reasoning*** Find a rule for simplifying problems like 69–71.

80. Show that $(x - y)(y - x)$ is equivalent to $-(x - y)^2$.

Mixed Review

81. Evaluate $-(s - 4t)$ for $s = -4$ and $t = 15$. *1-3*

82. Use the commutative property of addition to write an expression equivalent to $-3x + 6y$. *1-3*

83. Use the commutative and associative properties of multiplication to write an expression equivalent to $8x(9y \cdot 17z)$. *1-3*

Write decimal notation. **84.** 12% **85.** 50% **86.** $\frac{2}{5}$ **87.** $\frac{1}{0.7}$ *previous course*

Write rational notation. **88.** 10% **89.** 0.45 **90.** 10.5 **91.** 125% *previous course*

1-5 Solving Equations

What You'll Learn

1 To solve equations using the addition and multiplication properties

. . . And Why

To solve problems using equations

Introducing the Concept: Equation

A scale has several weights on one side and an object on the other. The scale is balanced. Suppose we add a two-pound weight to each side of the scale. Must the scale still balance?

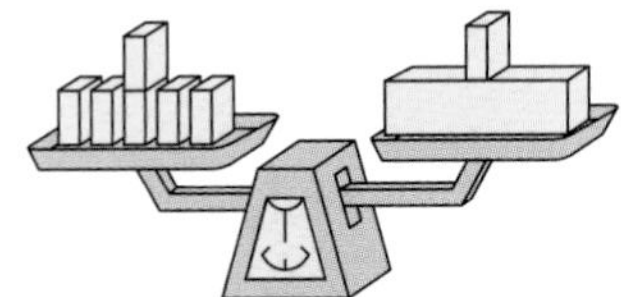

PART 1 Solving Equations

Objective: Solve equations using the addition and multiplication properties.

A mathematical sentence $A = B$ says that the symbols A and B are equivalent. Such a sentence is an **equation.** The set of all acceptable replacements is the **replacement set.** The replacements that make an equation true are its solutions. The set of all solutions is the **solution set.** Unless otherwise stated, the replacement set we will use for solving equations and inequalities is the set of real numbers.

When we have found all the solutions of an equation, we say that we have **solved** the equation. One approach to solving an equation is to transform it to a simpler equation whose solution set is obvious. The addition and multiplication properties of equality can be used when transforming equations.

Theorem 1-6

The Addition Property of Equality

If $a = b$, then $a + c = b + c$ for any real number c.

Using the addition property, we can assume that the scale above will balance. Suppose we triple the weight on each side of the scale. Will the scale balance?

Theorem 1-7

The Multiplication Property of Equality

If $a = b$, then $a \cdot c = b \cdot c$ for any real number c.

Using the multiplication property, we can assume that the scale will balance.

We often need to use the addition and multiplication properties together. We usually use the addition property first.

EXAMPLE 1 Solve.

$$3x - 4 = 13$$

$$3x - 4 + 4 = 13 + 4 \quad \text{Using the addition property; adding the inverse of } -4$$

$$3x = 17$$

$$\frac{1}{3} \cdot 3x = \frac{1}{3} \cdot 17 \quad \text{Using the multiplication property; multiplying by the reciprocal of 3}$$

$$x = \frac{17}{3} \quad \text{Simplifying}$$

Check:

$3x - 4$	$= 13$
$3\left(\frac{17}{3}\right) - 4$	13
$17 - 4$	13
13	13 ✓

The solution is $\frac{17}{3}$.

Try This Solve.

a. $13 = -25 + y$ **b.** $-4x = 64$ **c.** $9x - 4 = 8$ **d.** $-\frac{1}{4}y + \frac{3}{2} = \frac{1}{2}$

If there are like terms in an equation, they should be collected first. If there are like terms on opposite sides of an equation, we can get them on the same side using the addition property and then collect them.

EXAMPLE 2 Solve.

$$-12y + 22 = -y$$

$$-12y + y + 22 + (-22) = -y + y + (-22) \quad \text{Adding } -22 \text{ and } y \text{ to both sides}$$

$$-11y = -22$$

$$-\frac{1}{11}(-11y) = \frac{1}{11}(-22) \quad \text{Multiplying both sides by } -\frac{1}{11}$$

$$y = \frac{22}{11}, \text{ or } y = 2$$

Check:

$-12y + 22$	$= -y$
$-12(2) + 22$	-2
-2	-2 ✓

EXAMPLE 3 Solve.

$$8x + 6 - 2x = -12 - 4x + 5$$

$$6x + 6 = -7 - 4x \quad \text{Collecting like terms}$$

$$6x = -13 - 4x \quad \text{Adding } -6 \text{ to both sides and simplifying}$$

$$10x = -13 \quad \text{Adding } 4x \text{ to both sides and simplifying}$$

$$x = -\frac{13}{10} \quad \text{Multiplying both sides by } \frac{1}{10} \text{ and simplifying}$$

Check:

$$\begin{array}{r|l} \multicolumn{2}{c}{8x + 6 - 2x = -12 - 4x + 5} \\ \hline 8\left(-\frac{13}{10}\right) + 6 - 2\left(-\frac{13}{10}\right) & -12 - 4\left(-\frac{13}{10}\right) + 5 \\ \left(-\frac{52}{5}\right) + 6 + \left(\frac{13}{5}\right) & -12 - \left(-\frac{26}{5}\right) + 5 \\ -\frac{39}{5} + 6 & -7 + \frac{26}{5} \\ -\frac{9}{5} & -\frac{9}{5} \checkmark \end{array}$$

The solution is $-\frac{13}{10}$.

Try This Solve using the addition and multiplication properties.

e. $5y - 8 = -8 - 4y - 4$ **f.** $5x - 12 - 3x = 7x - 2 - x$

Extra Help On the Web

Look for worked-out examples at the Prentice Hall Web site.
www.phschool.com

1-5 Exercises

A

Solve using the addition and multiplication properties.

1. $y + 11 = 8$ **2.** $t + 13 = 4$

3. $x - 18 = 22$ **4.** $p - 15 = 11$

5. $x + 9 = -6$ **6.** $p + 14 = -42$

7. $t - 9 = -23$ **8.** $y - 7 = -3$

9. $x - 26 = 13$ **10.** $5x = 20$

11. $3x = 21$ **12.** $8y = -72$

13. $9t = -81$ **14.** $-24x = -192$

15. $-13y = 117$ **16.** $\frac{1}{5}y = 8$

17. $\frac{1}{4}x = 9$ **18.** $\frac{2}{3}x = 27$

19. $4x - 12 = 60$ **20.** $4x - 6 = 70$

21. $5y + 3 = 28$ **22.** $7t + 11 = 74$

23. $2y - 11 = 37$ **24.** $3x - 13 = 29$

25. $-4x - 7 = -35$ **26.** $-9y + 8 = -91$

27. $5x + 2x = 56$ **28.** $3x + 7x = 120$

29. $9y - 7y = 42$ **30.** $8t - 3t = 65$

31. $-6y - 10y = -32$ **32.** $-9y - 5y = 28$

33. $7y - 1 = 23 - 5y$ **34.** $15x + 20 = 8x - 22$

35. $5 - 4a = a - 13$ **36.** $8 - 5x = x - 16$

37. $3m - 7 = -7 - 4m - m$ **38.** $5x - 8 = -8 + 3x - x$

39. $5r - 2 + 3r = 2r + 6 - 4r$ **40.** $5m - 17 - 2m = 6m - 1 - m$

B

Mental Math Solve.

41. $0x = 0$

42. $4x = 0$

43. $0x = 5$

44. $7y = 7y$

45. $7w = -7w$

46. $4x - 2x - 2 = 2x$

Solve.

47. $2x + 4 + x = 4 + 3x$

48. $-\frac{3}{4}x + \frac{1}{8} = -2$

49. $y - \frac{1}{3}y - 15 = 0$

50. $\frac{3x}{2} + \frac{5x}{3} - \frac{13x}{6} - \frac{2}{3} = \frac{5}{6}$

51. $3x + 2^2 = x + 3^2$

52. $2^3 \cdot x + 9 = 2^2 \cdot x - 23$

53. *Critical Thinking* Determine whether the following statement is true or false. If true, tell why. If false, give a counterexample.
If a statement $a \neq b$ is true, then $a + c \neq b + c$ is true for any real number c.

Challenge

An **identity** is an equation that is true for all acceptable replacements. Determine which of the following are identities.

54. $2(x - 3) + 5 = 3(x - 2) + 5$

55. $3(x - 4) = 3x - 4$

56. $\frac{3y - 1}{y^2 - y} - \frac{2}{y - 1} = \frac{1}{y}$

57. $7(x - 3) \cdot \frac{1}{7} = x - 3$

Mixed Review

Simplify.

58. $4a - 7(3a - 9)$

59. $[5(a + 2) + 6a] - \{8[2(5a - 4)] + 17a\}$ *1-3, 1-4*

Factor.

60. $9c + 12b - 3a$

61. $8n - 8m$

62. $14t - 7$

63. $6n + 12$ *1-4*

Evaluate.

64. $2m + 4n$ for $m = -6, n = 2$

65. $4(m + 3) - 15$ for $m = 2$

66. Use the commutative and associative properties of multiplication to write an expression equivalent to $\left(\frac{1}{2}x \cdot 5y\right)\left(\frac{1}{5}y \cdot 2x\right)$.

67. Use the commutative and associative properties of addition to write an expression equivalent to $\left(\frac{1}{2}x + 5y\right) + \left(\frac{1}{5}y + 2x\right)$. *1-3*

1-6 Writing Equations

What You'll Learn

1 To solve simple algebraic problems

. . . And Why

To increase efficiency in solving problems by applying algebraic reasoning skills

PART 1 Solving Simple Algebraic Problems

Objective: Become familiar with and solve simple algebraic problems.

In your studies of mathematics, you have had considerable experience solving problems. The following guidelines can help to solve many algebra problems.

PROBLEM-SOLVING GUIDELINES

- **Phase 1: UNDERSTAND the problem**

  What am I trying to find?
  What data am I given?
  Have I ever solved a similar problem?

- **Phase 2: Develop and carry out a PLAN**

  What strategies might I use to solve the problem?
  How can I correctly carry out the strategies I selected?

- **Phase 3: Find the ANSWER and CHECK**

  Does the proposed solution check?
  What is the answer to the problem?
  Does the answer seem reasonable?
  Have I stated the answer clearly?

EXAMPLE 1

The time that a traffic light remains yellow is 1 second more than 0.05 times the speed limit. What is the yellow time for a traffic light on a street with a speed limit of 30 mi/h?

- **UNDERSTAND the problem**

Question: What is the time that the traffic light remains yellow?
Clarifying the question

Data: The yellow time is 0.05 times the speed limit plus 1 second.
Identifying the data

Usually the time a traffic light remains red is less than 50 seconds. See Example 1.

Develop and carry out a PLAN

Choose the strategy *Write an Equation.*

Yellow time	is	1 second	more than	0.05	times	the speed limit.
y	$=$	1	$+$	0.05	$\cdot$	s

$y = 1 + 0.05s$ — Translating to an equation

For a speed limit of 30 mi/h, s will be 30. Thus we have the following.

$$y = 1 + 0.05(30)$$
$$y = 1 + 1.5$$
$$y = 2.5$$

Solving the equation

Find the ANSWER and CHECK

On a 30 mi/h street, 2.5 seconds is a reasonable time for the light to remain yellow.

The yellow time is 2.5 seconds. — Stating the answer clearly

EXAMPLE 2 It has been found that the world record for the men's 10,000-meter run has been decreasing steadily since 1950. The record is approximately 28.87 minutes minus 0.05 times the number of years since 1950. Assume the record continues to decrease in this way. Predict what it will be in 2010.

UNDERSTAND the problem

Question: What will the record probably be in 2010? — Clarifying the question

Data: The record was 28.87 min in 1950. It decreases 0.05 times the number of years since 1950. — Identifying the important data

Develop and carry out a PLAN

Record	is	28.87 minutes	minus	0.05	times	the number of years since 1950.
R	$=$	28.87	$-$	0.05		$(2010 - 1950)$

$R = 28.87 - 0.05(2010 - 1950)$ — Translating to an equation

$R = 28.87 - 0.05(60) = 25.87$ — Solving the equation

Find the ANSWER and CHECK

The number checks in the equation.

It is less than the original record and makes sense in the problem.

We predict that the record in 2010 will be 25.87 min. — Stating the answer clearly

Try This

a. The County Cab Company charges 70¢ plus 12¢ per $\frac{1}{4}$ kilometer for each ride. What will be the total cost of a 14-km ride?

b. It has been found that the world record for the 800-m run has been decreasing steadily since 1930. The record is approximately 1.82 min minus the product of 0.0035 and the number of years since 1930. Predict what the record will be in 2010.

EXAMPLE 3

An insecticide originally contained $\frac{1}{2}$ ounce of pyrethrins. The new formula contains $\frac{5}{8}$ oz of pyrethrins. What percent of the pyrethrins of the original formula does the new formula contain?

UNDERSTAND the problem

Question: What percent of the original amount of pyrethrins does the new formula contain? — Clarifying the question

Data: The original formula contained $\frac{1}{2}$ oz, the new formula is $\frac{5}{8}$ oz. — Identifying the data

Develop and carry out a PLAN

We may translate to an equation and solve.
What percent of $\frac{1}{2}$ oz is $\frac{5}{8}$ oz?

$$y \times \frac{1}{100} \cdot \frac{1}{2} = \frac{5}{8}$$ Translating percent to "$\times \frac{1}{100}$"

$$y \times \frac{1}{200} = \frac{5}{8}$$ Multiplying

$$y = \frac{5}{8} \times 200$$ Multiplying by the reciprocal of $\frac{1}{200}$

$$y = 125$$ Simplifying

Find the ANSWER and CHECK

We must find out whether 125% of $\frac{1}{2}$ is $\frac{5}{8}$.

$$\frac{125}{100} \times \frac{1}{2} = \frac{125}{200} = \frac{5}{8}$$

The number checks. This is reasonable, since $\frac{5}{8}$ is greater than $\frac{1}{2}$, the percent must be greater than 100.

The amount of pyrethrins in the new formula, $\frac{5}{8}$ oz is 125% of the original amount of $\frac{1}{2}$ oz. — Stating the answer clearly

Try This

c. A public television station set a goal of \$350,000 in pledges during a certain month. The total pledged was \$525,000. What percent of the station's goal was reached?

d. A bread recipe calls for $\frac{2}{3}$ cup of rye flour. You only have $\frac{3}{4}$ cup on hand. What percent of your original amount of rye flour will remain after baking the bread?

Extra Help On the Web

Look for worked-out examples at the Prentice Hall Web site.
www.phschool.com

1-6 Exercises

A

1. Tony's Baby-Sitting Service charges \$8.50 per job plus \$6.75 per hour. What is the cost of a 7-hour baby-sitting job?
2. Renting a rug shampooer costs \$5.25 per hour plus \$4.25 for the shampoo. Find the cost of shampooing a rug if the time required is 3.5 hours.
3. The Jalopy Car Rental charges \$32 per day plus \$0.23 per mile. Find the cost of renting a car for a 3-day trip of 320 miles.
4. A phone company charges 40¢ per long distance call plus 20¢ per minute. Find the cost of an 18-minute long distance phone call.
5. The distance from Earth to the moon is about 240,000 mi. That is about 0.005 the distance from Earth to Mars. Find the approximate distance from Earth to Mars.
6. Jamie gave Laura \$3 more than Laura already had. Now Laura has \$19. How much did Jamie give her?
7. The height of the Statue of Liberty is 93 m. This is about 0.27 the height of the Hancock Building in Chicago. What is the approximate height of the Hancock Building?
8. The area of the Red Sea is about 18% of the area of the Mediterranean Sea. The area of the Red Sea is about 453,000 km. Find the approximate area of the Mediterranean Sea.
9. The melting point of aluminum is 1220 degrees Fahrenheit. This is 1.96 times the melting point of lead. What is the melting point of lead?
10. The area of the Pacific Ocean is about 239,000,000 km^2. This represents 46% of Earth's area. What is the approximate area of Earth?
11. The Olympic time for men's 500-m speed skating has been decreasing by about 0.1 seconds per year since 1924, when the record was 44.0 seconds. Predict what the time will be in 2010.
12. The Olympic time for women's 500-m speed skating has been decreasing by about 0.2 seconds per year since 1920, when the record was 54 seconds. Predict what the time will be in 2010.
13. The Olympic time for men's 400-m hurdles has been decreasing by about 0.09 seconds per year since 1930, when the record was 52 seconds. Predict what the time will be in 2010.

In a 50 mi/h wind, the statue's crown sways 3 in. while the torch's tip sways 5 in. How many inches does the crown sway per meter of height from the base of the pedestal?

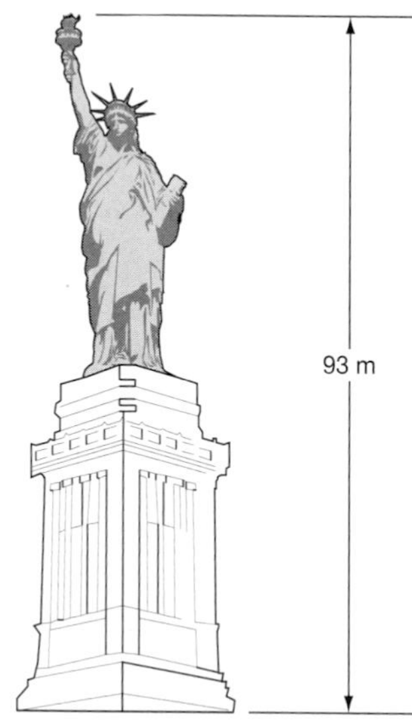

14. The number of physicians in the United States has been rising at the rate of about 17,000 per year since 1980, when there were about 467,700 physicians. Predict how many physicians there will be in the year 2010.
15. A person invested in stock selling for $\$26\frac{3}{8}$ per share. The stock value is now $\$22\frac{1}{2}$ per share. What percent of the original investment is the current stock value?
16. In 1995 the average American ate 48.8 lb of chicken. This was 6.3 lb more than the average in 1990. What was the percent of increase in chicken consumption from 1990 to 1995?
17. Between 1970 and 1980, the population of Sierra Vista, Arizona, grew from 6689 to 25,968. By what percent did the population increase?
18. The price of a computer was cut in half. Then it was cut another $34. The new price was $338. What was the original price?

B

19. On Monday, Ramon bought five Zip disks. Two days later the price of the disks was decreased by $1.50 per disk. Leticia bought ten disks at the sale price and paid $22 more than Ramon paid for five disks. What was the original price of a disk?
20. Kirra is two years older than Reggie. Reggie is six times as old as Delia. The average of their ages is nine years and four months. How old is each of them?
21. A gallon of one brand of paint covers approximately $\frac{2}{5}$ of the total wall area of a room. A gallon of a different brand will cover about $\frac{1}{3}$ of the total wall area. After the first gallon is used, what percent of the remaining wall area will the second gallon cover?
22. ***Critical Thinking*** Write a problem that can be solved by using the equation $y = \frac{1}{2}x + 10$.

Challenge

23. At 6:00 A.M., the Wong family left for a vacation trip and drove south at an average speed of 40 mi/h. Their friends, the Heisers, left two hours later and traveled the same route at an average speed of 55 mi/h. At what time could the Heisers expect to overtake the Wongs?
24. The tens digit of a two-digit number is three greater than the ones digit. The difference between twice the original number and half the number obtained after reversing the digits is 108. What is the original number?

Check your progress. Look for a self-test at the Prentice Hall Web site.
www.phschool.com

Mixed Review

Collect like terms. **25.** $11t + 4t$ **26.** $3c + 4c - 9c$ **27.** $x - 9x$ *1-3*

Solve. **28.** $y + 6 = 14$ **29.** $2m + 5 = 4$ **30.** $34t - 7 = 10$

31. $\frac{1}{2}r + 13 = 20$ **32.** $6a + 18 = 54$ **33.** $-9w = 27$

34. $5(n - 2) = -65$ **35.** $9c + 4 = 31 + 18c$ **36.** $4w + 5 = 6w + 1$

37. $8 - 5y = 11y - 8$ **38.** $7c + 15 = 16c - 3$ *1-5*

Exponential Notation

1-7

What You'll Learn

1 To use integer exponents

. . . And Why

To use scientific notation and solve problems involving exponents

Introducing the Concept: Exponents

The ability to write numbers in different forms is a powerful problem-solving tool. For example, 81 can be written as $8(10) + 1$ or as 3^4. The first form is **standard form,** the second is **exponential notation.** In exponential notation a^n, a is the **base** and n is the **exponent.** We say 3^4 is a **power** of 3 because it can be written as a product where all the factors are 3: $81 = 3^4 = 3 \cdot 3 \cdot 3 \cdot 3$. How might we define an integer exponent? Consider the following table of equivalencies. What is the pattern?

10^3	10^2	10^1	10^0	10^{-1}	10^{-2}	10^{-3}
1000	100	10	1	?	?	?

PART 1 Using Integer Exponents

Objective: Simplify expressions with integer exponents.

First we define whole number exponents.

Definition

Whole number exponents

Exponential notation a^n, where n is an integer greater than 1, means

$$\underbrace{a \cdot a \cdot a \cdot \ldots \cdot a \cdot a}_{n \text{ factors}}$$

Exponential notation a^1 means a.

Exponential notation a^0 means 1, provided $a \neq 0$.

EXAMPLES Simplify.

1 $(-6)^2 = (-6)(-6) = 36$

2 $-6^2 = -(6 \cdot 6) = -36$

3 $(4x)^2 = 4x \cdot 4x = 16x^2$

4 $(-3y)^3 = (-3y)(-3y)(-3y) = -27y^3$

5 $-5^3 = -(5^3) = -125$

6 $7(2x)^2 = 7(2x)(2x) = 7(4x^2) = 28x^2$

Try This Simplify.

a. $(8x)^3$ **b.** $(-3m)^4$ **c.** 9^2 **d.** $9(3y)^3$

At the beginning of the lesson, you looked for a pattern in the table. As each exponent decreased by 1, each value was multiplied by $\frac{1}{10}$. So for the pattern to continue, the missing values in the table are $\frac{1}{10}$, $\frac{1}{100}$, and $\frac{1}{1000}$. This suggests the following definition.

Reading Math

Read b^{-n} as "b to the additive inverse of n" or "b to the opposite of n."

Definition

Integer Exponents

For any nonzero real number b and integer n, b^{-n} means $\frac{1}{b^n}$.

This definition tells us that b^n and b^{-n} are reciprocals.

EXAMPLES Write equivalent expressions without negative exponents.

7 $(-2)^{-3} = \frac{1}{(-2)^3}$, or $-\frac{1}{8}$

8 $(3x)^{-2} = \frac{1}{(3x)^2}$, or $\frac{1}{9x^2}$

Try This Write equivalent expressions without negative exponents.

e. 10^{-4} **f.** $(-4)^{-3}$ **g.** $(5y)^{-3}$ **h.** $(-5)^{-4}$

EXAMPLES Write equivalent expressions using negative exponents.

9 $\frac{1}{5^2} = 5^{-2}$

10 $\frac{1}{(3x)^5} = (3x)^{-5}$

Try This Write equivalent expressions using negative exponents.

i. $\frac{1}{4^3}$ **j.** $\frac{1}{(-5)^4}$ **k.** $\frac{1}{(2x)^6}$ **l.** $\frac{1}{(-8x)^5}$

Internet Connection

Extra Help On the Web

Look for worked-out examples at the Prentice Hall Web site.
www.phschool.com

1-7 Exercises

A

Simplify.

1. $(3y)^3$ **2.** $(-2x)^4$ **3.** $(-6)^0$ **4.** -3^4

5. $3(2m)^1$ **6.** $5(-6x)^2$ **7.** -5^3 **8.** -8^2

Write equivalent expressions without negative exponents.

9. 9^{-5} **10.** 16^{-2} **11.** 11^{-1} **12.** $(-4)^{-3}$

13. $(6x)^{-3}$ **14.** $(-5y)^{-2}$ **15.** $(3m)^{-4}$ **16.** x^2y^{-3}

17. $2a^2b^{-5}$ **18.** $a^2b^{-3}c^4d^{-5}$ **19.** $\frac{x^2}{y^{-2}}$ **20.** $\frac{a^2b^{-3}}{x^3y^{-2}}$

Write equivalent expressions using negative exponents.

21. $\frac{1}{3^4}$ **22.** $\frac{1}{9^2}$ **23.** $\frac{1}{(-16)^2}$ **24.** $\frac{1}{(-8)^6}$

25. $\frac{1}{(5y)^3}$ **26.** $\frac{1}{(5x)^5}$ **27.** $\frac{1}{3y^4}$ **28.** $\frac{1}{4b^3}$

B

Write an equivalent expression without rational notation.

29. $\frac{x^2y}{z^7}$ **30.** $\frac{20}{4xy}$ **31.** $\frac{b^{-10}}{x^{10}y^{10}}$ **32.** $\frac{a^2b^{-3}}{x^3y^{-2}}$

Evaluate each of the following.

33. x^{-4} for $x = 2$ **34.** $m^{-3} + 7$, for $m = -0.25$

35. $x^3 + y^{-2}$, for $x = -3$ and $y = 4$

36. *Critical Thinking* Find several pairs of numbers such that the second power of the first is the same as the fourth power of the second.

Challenge

Simplify.

37. $(-2)^0 - (-2)^3 - (-2)^{-1} + (-2)^4 - (-2)^{-2}$

38. $2(6^1 \cdot 6^{-1} - 6^{-1} \cdot 6^0)$ **39.** $\frac{(-8)^{-2} \cdot (8 - 8^0)}{2^{-6}}$

40. Evaluate $(x - y)(x^{y-x} - y^{x-y})$ when $x = 1$ and $y = -2$.

41. *Write a Convincing Argument*

a. About 3500 years ago, this problem appeared in one of the earliest known arithmetic books. Solve the problem. Then write an argument to convince a classmate your solution is correct.

Each of 7 persons owns 7 cats, each cat eats 7 mice, each mouse eats 7 ears of barley, each ear of barley yields 7 measures. How many measures is this?

b. Then write a problem similar to this one.

If each of 6 persons owns 6 cats, and so on, how many fewer measures of barley are eaten? (See Exercise 41.)

Mixed Review

Factor. **42.** $ab + mb - xb$ **43.** $17 - 51y^2$ **44.** $20k^3a^2 - 16k^2a^3$

45. $\frac{2abc}{3dx} - \frac{8bcd}{15ax} + \frac{4acd}{9bx}$ *1-4*

Solve. **46.** $9 - 3y = 5y - 23$ **47.** $5c + 3c = 16$ **48.** $-21t = 21$

49. $\frac{5}{x-1} = \frac{3}{x+2}$ *1-5*

1-8 Properties of Exponents

What You'll Learn

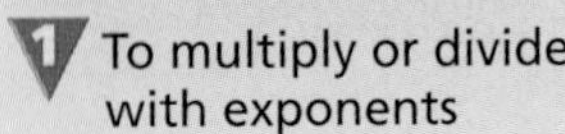

1. To multiply or divide with exponents
2. To raise powers to powers
3. To use the rules for order of operations to simplify expressions

. . . And Why

To use scientific notation, and to solve algebraic problems involving exponents

PART 1 Multiplication and Division

Objective: Multiply or divide with exponents.

To multiply using exponential notation when we have the same base, we add the exponents. For example, $x^3 \cdot x^2 = x^{3+2} = x^5$. Let us consider a case in which one exponent is positive and one is negative.

$$b^5b^{-2} = b \cdot b \cdot b \cdot b \cdot b \cdot \frac{1}{b \cdot b} \quad \text{Using the definition of exponents}$$
$$= \frac{b \cdot b}{b \cdot b} \cdot b \cdot b \cdot b \quad \text{Using the associative property}$$
$$= 1 \cdot b \cdot b \cdot b$$
$$= b \cdot b \cdot b \quad \text{Using the identity property of multiplication}$$
$$= b^3$$

Notice that adding the exponents gives the correct result.

Theorem 1-8

For any nonzero real number a and integers m and n, $a^m a^n = a^{m+n}$.

(We can add exponents if the bases are the same.)

EXAMPLES Multiply and simplify.

1 $4^5 \cdot 4^{-3} = 4^{5+(-3)} = 4^2 = 16$ Adding exponents

2 $(-2)^{-3}(-2)^7 = (-2)^{-3+7} = (-2)^4 = 16$

3
$$(8x^4y^{-2})(-3x^{-3}y) = 8 \cdot (-3) \cdot x^4 \cdot x^{-3} \cdot y^{-2} \cdot y^1$$
$$= -24(x^{4-3})(y^{-2+1})$$
$$= -24xy^{-1}, \text{ or } \frac{-24x}{y}$$

4
$$(4x^a \cdot y^b)(2x^2y^3) = 4 \cdot 2(x^{a+2})(y^{b+3})$$
$$= 8(x^{a+2})(y^{b+3})$$

Try This Multiply and simplify.

a. $8^{-3}8^7$

b. $(-3x^{-4})(25x^{-10})$

c. $(5x^{-3}y^4)(-2x^{-9}y^{-2})$

d. $(5x^my^n)(6x^7y^4)$

We now consider division using exponential notation.

$\frac{8^5}{8^3}$ means $\frac{8 \cdot 8 \cdot 8 \cdot 8 \cdot 8}{8 \cdot 8 \cdot 8}$. This simplifies to $8 \cdot 8$, or 8^2.

We can obtain the result by subtracting exponents. This is always true, even if exponents are negative or zero.

Theorem 1-9

For any real number $a \neq 0$ and integers m and n, $\frac{a^m}{a^n} = a^{m-n}$.

(We can subtract exponents if the bases are the same.)

EXAMPLES Divide and simplify.

5 $\frac{5^7}{5^{-3}} = 5^{7-(-3)}$ Subtracting exponents

$= 5^{7+3}$

$= 5^{10}$

6 $\frac{9^{-2}}{9^5} = 9^{-2-5}$

$= 9^{-7}$, or $\frac{1}{9^7}$

7 $\frac{7^{-4}}{7^{-5}} = 7^{-4-(-5)}$

$= 7^{-4+5} = 7^1 = 7$

8 $\frac{16x^4y^7}{-8x^3y^9} = \frac{16}{-8} \cdot \frac{x^4}{x^3} \cdot \frac{y^7}{y^9} = -2xy^{-2}$, or $-\frac{2x}{y^2}$

9 $\frac{14x^4y^7}{4x^5y^{-5}} = \frac{14}{4} \cdot \frac{x^4}{x^5} \cdot \frac{y^7}{y^{-5}} = \frac{7}{2}x^{-1}y^{12}$, or $\frac{7y^{12}}{2x}$

10 $\frac{18x^{5a}}{2x^{3a}} = \frac{18}{2} \cdot \frac{x^{5a}}{x^{3a}} = 9x^{5a-3a} = 9x^{2a}$

We do not define 0^0. Notice the following.

$$0^0 = 0^{1-1} = \frac{0^1}{0^1} = \frac{0}{0}$$

We have seen that $\frac{0}{0}$ is undefined, so 0^0 is also undefined.

Try This Divide and simplify.

e. $\frac{5^4}{5^{-2}}$ **f.** $\frac{10^{-2}}{10^{-8}}$ **g.** $\frac{42y^7x^6}{-21y^{-3}x^{10}}$

h. $\frac{33a^5b^{-2}}{22a^7b^{-4}}$ **i.** $\frac{56y^{ab}}{-7y^{ab}}$

Journal

Write a paragraph explaining why "A whole number exponent tells how many times to multiply a number by itself." is not a good definition of a whole number exponent.

PART 2 Raising Powers to Powers

Objective: Use exponential notation in raising powers to powers.

Consider the expression $(5^2)^4$. It means $5^2 \cdot 5^2 \cdot 5^2 \cdot 5^2$, or 5^8. We can obtain the result by multiplying the exponents.

$$5^{2\cdot 4} = 5^8$$

Consider $(8^{-2})^3$. It means $\frac{1}{8^2} \cdot \frac{1}{8^2} \cdot \frac{1}{8^2}$, or $\frac{1}{8^6}$, which is 8^{-6}.

Again, we could obtain the result by multiplying the exponents.

Theorem 1-10

For any nonzero real number a and integers m and n, $(a^m)^n = a^{m\cdot n}$.

(To raise a power to a power, we can multiply exponents.)

EXAMPLES Simplify.

11 $(3^5)^7 = 3^{5\cdot 7} = 3^{35}$ Multiplying exponents

12 $(x^{-5})^4 = x^{-5\cdot 4} = x^{-20}$, or $\frac{1}{x^{20}}$

Try This Simplify.

j. $(3^7)^6$ **k.** $(x^2)^{-7}$ **l.** $(t^{-3})^{-2}$

When there are several factors inside the parentheses, we can use the next theorem.

Theorem 1-11

For any nonzero real numbers a and b and integers m, n, and p, $(a^m b^n)^p = a^{m\cdot p} \cdot b^{n\cdot p}$

(To raise an expression with several factors to a power, raise each factor to the power by multiplying exponents.)

EXAMPLES Simplify.

13 $(3x^2y^{-2})^3 = 3^3(x^2)^3(y^{-2})^3 = 3^3x^6y^{-6} = 27x^6y^{-6}$, or $\frac{27x^6}{y^6}$

14 $(5x^3y^{-5}z^2)^4 = 5^4(x^3)^4(y^{-5})^4(z^2)^4 = 625x^{12}y^{-20}z^8$, or $\frac{625x^{12}z^8}{y^{20}}$

Try This Simplify.

m. $(2xy)^3$ **n.** $(-2x^4y^2)^5$ **o.** $(10x^{-4}y^7z^{-2})^3$

We now consider raising a quotient to a power. Consider $\left(\frac{5^5}{3^4}\right)^3$.

$$\left(\frac{5^5}{3^4}\right)^3 = \frac{5^5}{3^4} \cdot \frac{5^5}{3^4} \cdot \frac{5^5}{3^4} \cdot = \frac{5^{15}}{3^{12}}$$

Once more, we can obtain the result by multiplying the exponents. This is true in general, for positive, negative, or zero exponents.

Theorem 1-12

For any nonzero real numbers a and b and any integers m, n, and p, $\left(\frac{a^m}{b^n}\right)^p = \frac{a^{m \cdot p}}{b^{n \cdot p}}$.

To raise a quotient to a power, raise both the numerator and denominator to the power by multiplying exponents.

EXAMPLES Simplify.

15 $\left(\frac{x^2}{y^{-3}}\right)^{-5} = \frac{x^{2(-5)}}{y^{-3(-5)}} = \frac{x^{-10}}{y^{15}} = x^{-10}y^{-15}$, or $\frac{1}{x^{10}y^{15}}$

16 $\left(\frac{2x^3y^{-2}}{3y^4}\right)^5 = \frac{(2x^3y^{-2})^5}{(3y^4)^5} = \frac{2^5x^{15}y^{-10}}{3^5y^{20}}$

$$= \frac{2^5x^{15}}{3^5y^{30}} = \frac{32x^{15}}{243y^{30}}, \text{ or } \frac{32}{243}x^{15}y^{-30}$$

Try This Simplify.

p. $\left(\frac{x^{-3}}{y^4}\right)^{-3}$ **q.** $\left(\frac{3x^2y^{-3}}{2y^{-1}}\right)^2$

PART 3 Order of Operations

Objective: Use the rules for order of operations to simplify expressions.

When several operations, including raising to powers, are to be done in a calculation, we must decide in what order they are to be done. The agreements made about such calculations are given by the following rules.

Order of Operations

1. Calculate within innermost parentheses first.
2. Evaluate exponential expressions.
3. Multiply and divide in order from left to right.
4. Add and subtract in order from left to right.

EXAMPLES Simplify.

17 $3^2 - 9 \cdot 6$

$= 9 - 9 \cdot 6$ Evaluating the exponential expression first
$= 9 - 54$ Multiplying
$= -45$ Subtracting

18 $[2(8 - 13 + 2)^3 \div 6 + 2]^2$

$= [2(-3)^3 \div 6 + 2]^2$ Calculating within parentheses
$= [2(-27) \div 6 + 2]^2$ Simplifying the exponential expression
$= [-54 \div 6 + 2]^2$ Calculating within brackets
$= [-9 + 2]^2$ Dividing
$= [-7]^2$ Adding
$= 49$ Simplifying the exponent

Try This Simplify.

r. $3 \cdot 2^2 + 4$ **s.** $3 \cdot (2^2 + 4)$ **t.** $\{[(3 + 2)^2 - 3 + 2^2 + 1] \div 9\}^3$

Using Exponents

Scientific calculators have an exponential key y^x

Calculate 5^7.

5 y^x 7 = → 78125

Calculate 3^{-4}.

3 y^x 4 +/– = → 0.012345679

Extra Help On the Web

Look for worked-out examples at the Prentice Hall Web site.
www.phschool.com

1-8 Exercises

A

Multiply and simplify.

1. $5^6 \cdot 5^3$ **2.** $6^2 \cdot 6^6$ **3.** $8^{-6} \cdot 8^2$ **4.** $9^{-5} \cdot 9^3$
5. $8^{-2} \cdot 8^{-4}$ **6.** $9^{-1} \cdot 9^{-6}$ **7.** $b^2 \cdot b^{-5}$ **8.** $a^4 \cdot a^{-3}$
9. $a^{-3} \cdot a^4 \cdot a^2$ **10.** $x^{-8} \cdot x^5 \cdot x^3$ **11.** $(2x^3)(3x^2)$ **12.** $(9y^2)(2y^3)$
13. $(14m^2n^3)(-2m^3n^2)$ **14.** $(6x^5y^{-2})(-3x^2y^3)$
15. $(-2x^{-3})(7x^{-8})$ **16.** $(6x^{-4}y^3)(-4x^{-8}y^{-2})$
17. $(5x^ay^b)(-6x^5y^9)$ **18.** $(-9x^my^6)(-8x^ny^p)$

Divide and simplify.

19. $\frac{6^8}{6^3}$ 20. $\frac{4^3}{4^{-2}}$ 21. $\frac{10^{-3}}{10^6}$ 22. $\frac{9^{-4}}{9^{-6}}$

23. $\frac{a^3}{a^{-2}}$ 24. $\frac{y^4}{y^{-5}}$ 25. $\frac{9a^2}{(-3a)^2}$ 26. $\frac{24a^5b^3}{-8a^4b}$

27. $\frac{-24x^6y^7}{18x^{-3}y^9}$ 28. $\frac{14a^4b^{-3}}{-8a^8b^{-5}}$ 29. $\frac{-18x^{-2}y^3}{-12x^{-5}y^5}$ 30. $\frac{-14a^{14}b^{-5}}{-18a^{-2}b^{-10}}$

31. $\frac{20x^{6a}}{-2x^a}$ 32. $\frac{-18x^{5y}}{-3x^{-6y}}$ 33. $\frac{36x^ay^b}{-12x^2y^5}$ 34. $\frac{-100x^{3a}y^{-5}}{-25x^{-a}y^6}$

Simplify.

35. $(4^3)^2$ 36. $(8^4)^{-3}$ 37. $(6^{-4})^{-3}$ 38. $(3x^2y^2)^3$

39. $(-2x^3y^{-4})^{-2}$ 40. $(-3a^2b^{-5})^{-3}$ 41. $(-6a^{-2}b^3c)^{-2}$ 42. $(-8x^{-4}y^5z^2)^{-4}$

43. $\left(\frac{4^{-3}}{3^4}\right)^3$ 44. $\left(\frac{5^2}{4^{-3}}\right)^{-3}$ 45. $\left(\frac{2x^3y^{-2}}{3y^{-3}}\right)^3$ 46. $\left(\frac{-4x^4y^{-2}}{5x^{-1}y^4}\right)^{-4}$

47. $3 \cdot 2 + 4 \cdot 2^2 - 6(3 - 1)$ 48. $3[(2 + 4 \cdot 2^2) - 6(3 - 1)]$

49. $4(8 - 6)^2 + 4 \cdot 3 - 2 \cdot 8 \div 4$ 50. $[4(8 - 6)^2 + 4] \cdot (3 - 2 \cdot 8) \div 4$

51. Find a counterexample to show that generally $(x^{-3})^{-3} \neq x^{-6}$. Is there a value of x for which this is true?

B

Simplify.

52. $\frac{(2^{-2})^{-4}(2^3)^{-2}}{(2^{-2})^2(2^5)^{-3}}$ 53. $\left[\frac{(-3x^2y^5)^{-3}}{(2x^4y^{-8})^{-2}}\right]^2$ 54. $\left[\left(\frac{a^{-2}}{b^7}\right)^{-3} \cdot \left(\frac{a^4}{b^{-3}}\right)^2\right]^{-1}$

55. $\left[\frac{(-4x^2y^3)(-2xy)^{-2}}{(4x^4y^2)(-2x^5y)}\right]^{-2}$ 56. $\frac{(3xy)^2(6x^2y^2) \times 4x^4y^4}{(4xy)^2 \times 13x^2y^2}$

57. *Critical Thinking* How can you use the definition of a negative exponent to make Theorem 1-12 a special case of Theorem 1-11?

Challenge

Simplify.

58. $(x^y \cdot x^{2y})^3$ 59. $(y^x \cdot y^{-x})^4$ 60. $(a^{b+x} \cdot a^{b-x})^3$

61. $(m^{a-b} \cdot m^{2b-a})^p$ 62. $(x^by^a \cdot x^ay^b)^c$ 63. $(m^{x-b}n^{x+b})^x(m^bn^{-b})^x$

64. $\left[\frac{(2x^ay^b)^3}{(-2x^ay^b)^2}\right]^2$ 65. $\left[\left(\frac{x^r}{y^s}\right)^2\left(\frac{x^{2r}}{y^{3s}}\right)^{-2}\right]^{-2}$

Mixed Review

Evaluate. 66. $t(3t + 5)$, for $t = 4$ 67. $-3x + 7 + 2x$, for $x = 5$ *1-3*

Simplify. 68. $\left(-\frac{1}{2}\right)\left(-\frac{2}{3}\right)\left(-\frac{3}{4}\right)\left(-\frac{4}{5}\right)$ 69. $(200)(-4)\left(-\frac{3}{2}\right)(0)(0.974)$ *1-2*

70. $3(x + 17) - 3(17 + x)$ 71. $7(14x - 15x) + 4(x + x)$ *1-3*

1-9 Scientific Notation

What You'll Learn

1. To convert between scientific and standard notation
2. To use scientific notation in multiplication and division
3. To use scientific notation in approximating and estimating

. . . And Why

To work problems involving large numbers easily

Scientific notation is useful for calculating with very large or very small numbers. It is also helpful for estimating. Scientific notation for 2,800,000,000 miles, the distance from the planet Neptune to the sun, is 2.8×10^9; for 0.000000022 cm, the diameter of a helium atom, it is 2.2×10^{-8}; and for 100 it is 1×10^2.

Definition

Scientific notation for a number is notation of the form $a \times 10^n$ where $1 \leq a < 10$ and n is an integer.

PART 1 Conversions

Objective: Convert between scientific and standard notation.

We can convert to scientific notation by multiplying by 1, choosing $10^b \cdot 10^{-b}$ for the number 1, where b is the number of decimal places to be moved.

EXAMPLE 1 Write scientific notation for 20,000,000 degrees Kelvin, the temperature near the sun's center.

We need to move the decimal point 7 places to the left, so that it is between the digits 2 and 0, so we choose $10^7 \times 10^{-7}$ for 1 and then multiply.

$20{,}000{,}000 \times (10^7 \times 10^{-7})$ Multiplying by 1
$= (20{,}000{,}000 \times 10^{-7}) \times 10^7$ Using the associative and commutative properties
$= 2.0 \times 10^7$

EXAMPLE 2 The wavelength of a certain red light is 0.000066 cm. Write scientific notation for this number.

We need to move the decimal point 5 places to the right. We choose $10^5 \times 10^{-5}$ for 1, and then multiply.

$0.000066 \times (10^5 \times 10^{-5})$ Multiplying by 1
$= (0.000066 \times 10^5) \times 10^{-5}$ Using the associative property
$= 6.6 \times 10^{-5}$

EXAMPLE 3 Light travels about 9,460,000,000,000 km in one year. Write scientific notation for this number.

$9{,}460{,}000{,}000{,}000 \times 10^{-12} \times 10^{12}$ Multiplying by 1
$= 9.46 \times 10^{12}$ 10^{-12} moved the decimal point 12 places to the left.

Try This

a. Convert 460,000,000,000 to scientific notation.
b. Convert 0.000000001235 to scientific notation.
c. The mass of a hydrogen atom is 0.0000000000000000000000017 grams. Write scientific notation for this number.
d. The distance from Earth to the sun is about 150,000,000 km. Write scientific notation for this number.

You should try to make conversions between standard and scientific notation mentally.

EXAMPLES Convert to standard notation.

4 $7.893 \times 10^5 = 789{,}300$ Moving the decimal point 5 places to the right

5 $4.7 \times 10^{-8} = 0.000000047$ Moving the decimal point 8 places to the left

Try This Convert to standard notation.

e. 7.893×10^{11} **f.** 5.67×10^{-5}

PART 2 Multiplying and Dividing

Objective: Use scientific notation in multiplication and division.

To multiply and divide using scientific notation, we use the commutative and associative properties and then use the properties of exponents to simplify the powers of ten.

EXAMPLE 6 Multiply and write scientific notation for the answer.

$$(3.1 \times 10^5)(4.5 \times 10^{-3})$$

We apply the commutative and associative properties.

$$\begin{aligned}(3.1 \times 10^5)(4.5 \times 10^{-3}) &= (3.1 \times 4.5)(10^5 \times 10^{-3})\\ &= 13.95 \times 10^2\end{aligned}$$

We convert 13.95 to scientific notation and then simplify.

$$\begin{aligned}13.95 \times 10^2 &= (1.395 \times 10^1) \times 10^2\\ &= 1.395 \times 10^3\end{aligned}$$

EXAMPLE 7 Divide and write scientific notation for the answer.

$$\begin{aligned}\frac{7.2 \times 10^{-7}}{8.0 \times 10^6} &= \frac{7.2}{8.0} \times \frac{10^{-7}}{10^6} && \text{Factoring}\\ &= 0.9 \times 10^{-13} && \text{Dividing}\\ &= (9.0 \times 10^{-1}) \times 10^{-13} && \text{Converting 0.9 to scientific notation}\\ &= 9.0 \times 10^{-14}\end{aligned}$$

Try This Multiply or divide and write scientific notation for the answer.

g. $(9.1 \times 10^{-17})(8.2 \times 10^{3})$ **h.** $\frac{4.2 \times 10^{5}}{2.1 \times 10^{2}}$ **i.** $\frac{1.1 \times 10^{-4}}{2.0 \times 10^{-7}}$

PART 3 Estimating and Approximating

Objective: Use scientific notation in approximating and estimating.

Scientific notation is helpful in estimating or approximating. Such estimating is an important skill in problem solving.

EXAMPLE 8 Estimate $780{,}000{,}000 \times \frac{0.00071}{0.000005}$.

$$\frac{(7.8 \times 10^{8})(7.1 \times 10^{-4})}{(5 \cdot 10^{-6})} \quad \text{Converting to scientific notation and multiplying}$$

$$= \frac{7.8 \times 7.1}{5} \times \frac{(10^{8})(10^{-4})}{10^{-6}} \quad \text{Regrouping}$$

$$\approx \frac{8 \times 7}{5} \times 10^{8+(-4)-(-6)} \quad \text{Rounding}$$

$$\approx \frac{56}{5} \times 10^{10}$$

$$\approx 11 \times 10^{10} \quad \text{Rounding}$$

$$\approx 1.1 \times 10^{11} \quad \text{Converting to scientific notation}$$

We now have an approximation of 1.1×10^{11}.

Try This Estimate. Answer may vary depending on how you round.

j. $830{,}000{,}000 \times \frac{0.0000012}{3{,}100{,}000}$

Computing with Scientific Notation

Many calculators switch their displays automatically to scientific notation when results are greater than the capacity of the display. If we multiply 20,820,000 by 5000 on a calculator, the display may show 1.041 11. This means 1.041×10^{11}. Calculators with keys EXP or EE allow you to enter numbers in scientific notation. To enter 0.0035698 in scientific notation, press

3.5698 EXP 3 +/–

Calculate $34{,}700{,}000 \times 5000$ using scientific notation.

3.47 EXP 7 × 5 EXP 3 = → 1.735 11

1-9 Exercises

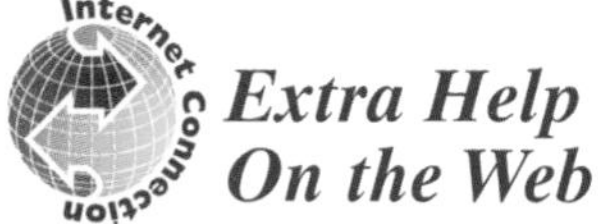

Extra Help On the Web

Look for worked-out examples at the Prentice Hall Web site.
www.phschool.com

A

Convert to scientific notation.

1. 47,000,000,000
2. 2,600,000,000,000
3. 863,000,000,000,000,000
4. 957,000,000,000,000,000
5. 0.000000016
6. 0.000000263
7. 0.00000000007
8. 0.00000000009

Write scientific notation for the number.

9. The mass of an electron is 0.000000000000000000000000000911 g.
10. The population of the United States is about 273,000,000.
11. An electron carries a charge of 0.00000000048 electrostatic units.
12. The volume of a grain of sand is about 0.0000000013 ft^3.
13. An oxygen atom is about 0.000000001 times the size of a drop of water.
14. The distance from the sun to Pluto is 3,664,000,000 miles.
15. The weight of a blue whale is 306,990 pounds.
16. The gross national product (GNP) of the United States in 1996 was $7,567,100,000,000.

Convert to decimal notation.

17. 4×10^{-4}
18. 5×10^{-5}
19. 6.73×10^{8}
20. 9.24×10^{7}
21. 8.923×10^{-10}
22. 7.034×10^{-2}

Multiply or divide, and write scientific notation for the answer.

23. $(2.3 \times 10^{6})(4.2 \times 10^{-11})$
24. $(6.5 \times 10^{3})(5.2 \times 10^{-8})$
25. $(2.34 \times 10^{-8})(5.7 \times 10^{-4})$
26. $(3.26 \times 10^{-6})(8.2 \times 10^{-6})$
27. $(3.2 \times 10^{6})(2.6 \times 10^{4})$
28. $(3.11 \times 10^{3})(1.01 \times 10^{13})$

Divide, and write scientific notation for the answer.

29. $\dfrac{8.5 \times 10^{8}}{3.4 \times 10^{5}}$
30. $\dfrac{5.1 \times 10^{6}}{3.4 \times 10^{3}}$
31. $\dfrac{4.0 \times 10^{-6}}{8.0 \times 10^{-3}}$
32. $\dfrac{7.5 \times 10^{-9}}{2.5 \times 10^{-4}}$
33. $\dfrac{12.6 \times 10^{8}}{4.2 \times 10^{-3}}$
34. $\dfrac{3.2 \times 10^{-7}}{8.0 \times 10^{8}}$

Estimation Simplify.

35. $\dfrac{(6.1 \times 10^{4})(7.2 \times 10^{-6})}{9.8 \times 10^{-4}}$
36. $\dfrac{(8.05 \times 10^{-11})(5.9 \times 10^{7})}{3.1 \times 10^{14}}$
37. $\dfrac{780{,}000{,}000 \times 0.00071}{0.000005}$
38. $\dfrac{830{,}000{,}000 \times 0.12}{3{,}100{,}000}$
39. $\dfrac{43{,}000{,}000 \times 0.095}{63{,}000}$
40. $\dfrac{0.0073 \times 0.84}{0.000006}$

B

Convert to scientific notation.

41. 3,871.5403 **42.** 510.0036 **43.** 20,000,000.029 **44.** $71.\overline{428571}$

45. The distance light travels in 100 years is about 5.8×10^{14} miles. How far does light travel in 13 weeks?

46. The average distance of Earth from the sun is around 9.3×10^{7} miles. About how far does Earth travel in its yearly orbit about the sun? (Hint: Assume the orbit is circular.)

47. *Critical Thinking* Scientific notation for a number is $a \times 10^n$, where a is an odd prime number that is a factor of 845 and n is the greatest multiple of 4 that is less than 11. Find standard notation for the number.

Challenge

48. Compare $8 \cdot 10^{-90}$ and $9 \cdot 10^{-91}$. Which is larger and by how much? Write scientific notation for the difference.

Use the table below for Exercises 49–55. Write the answers using scientific notation.

Feet in a mile	5.28×10^3	Minutes in an hour	6×10^1
Yards in a mile	1.76×10^3	Hours in a day	2.4×10^1
Sec in a minute	6×10^1	Days in a year	3.6525×10^2

49. One foot per second is how many miles per hour?

50. Find miles per hour for a speed of 25 feet per second.

51. The men's outdoor world record for the mile in 1999 was 3 minutes 43.13 seconds. Find the record in feet per second.

52. The men's outdoor world record for the 400 m run was 43.18 seconds. Find the average speed in feet per second. (1m $\approx$ 3.28 ft)

53. What percent faster was the record for the 400 m run than for the mile?

54. The speed of light is about 186,282 miles per second. A light year is the distance light travels in one year. How many feet does light travel per day?

55. How many seconds does it take for light to travel 100 yards?

Mixed Review

Simplify. **56.** $6y - [8 - 11(9y + 4)]$

57. $[9(y + 2) + 8y] - \{6[(3y - 5) - (6y + 11)] + 16\}$ *1-3* **58.** $\left(\frac{5^{-6}}{3^2}\right)^4$ *1-7*

59. $[6(9 - 4) + 3] \cdot (4 - 3 \cdot 8) \div 5$ *1-2*

60. $(4t)^3$ **61.** $(-t)^2$ **62.** $5(-3m)^2$ *1-7*

Collect like terms. **63.** $4a - 5b - 6a + 3b$ **64.** $9m - 5n + 3n - 12m$ *1-4*

Factor. **65.** $\frac{wx}{2} - \frac{yx}{2}$ *1-4*

Field Axioms, Theorems, and Proofs

Field Axioms and Properties

Objective: Use axioms and properties to justify algebraic statements.

What You'll Learn

1. To use axioms and properties to justify algebraic statements
2. To write column proofs

. . . And Why

To easily construct proofs

Properties that we accept without proof are called **axioms.** We try to choose the more obvious and acceptable properties as axioms. Different mathematicians may make different choices. Here are properties accepted as axioms in this text.

Axioms for Real Numbers

The Properties of Closure

Addition: For every real number a and b, $a + b$ is a real number.
Multiplication: For every real number a and b, ab is a real number.

The Commutative Properties of Addition and Multiplication
For any real numbers a and b, $a + b = b + a$; $a \cdot b = b \cdot a$.

The Associative Properties of Addition and Multiplication
For any numbers a, b, and c, $a + (b + c) = (a + b) + c$; $a(bc) = (ab)c$.

The Distributive Property of Multiplication over Addition
For any numbers a, b, and c, $a(b + c) = ab + ac$.

The Identity Properties
Addition: For any number a, $a + 0 = a$.
Multiplication: For any number a, $a \cdot 1 = a$.

The Properties of Inverses
Addition: For each real number a, there is one and only one additive inverse b for which $a + b = 0$.
Multiplication: For each nonzero number a, there is one and only one multiplicative inverse b for which $ab = 1$.

The following properties hold for equality.

Properties of Equality

For any real numbers a, b, and c,
Reflexive Property $a = a$.
Symmetric Property if $a = b$, then $b = a$.
Transitive Property if $a = b$ and $b = c$, then $a = c$.

EXAMPLES Which axioms or properties of equality, if any, justify the following statements?

1 $6(x + 3) = 6x + 18$ — Distributive property

2 $5y - x = 5y - x$ — Reflexive property of equality

3 $3x^2 \cdot 1 = 3x^2$ — Identity property of multiplication

4 If $2 + 3 = 5$ and $5 = 4 + 1$, then $2 + 3 = 4 + 1$ — Transitive property of equality

Try This Which axioms or properties of equality, if any, justify the following statements?

a. $5 + (a + b) = (5 + a) + b$

b. $5(x - 2) = 5x - 10$

c. $5y^3 + 0 = 5y^3$

d. $(x + 2)\left(\frac{1}{x + 2}\right) = 1$

Any number system with two operations defined in which the axioms on page 49 hold is called a **field.** The axioms are known as **field axioms.** The set of real numbers with addition and multiplication form a field.

EXAMPLE 5 Does the set of integers with addition and multiplication form a field?

The set of integers does not satisfy the property of multiplicative inverses. It is not a field.

Try This Tell whether each of these sets with addition and multiplication form a field. If not, tell why.

e. the set of whole numbers

f. the set of rational numbers

Proofs

Objective: Write column proofs.

Number properties that can be proved by using axioms and definitions are called **theorems.** The following theorem may be called an "extended distributive property."

Theorem 1-13

An Extended Distributive Property

For any real numbers a, b, c, and d, $a(b + c + d) = ab + ac + ad$.

To prove a theorem, we write a sequence of statements. Each must be supported by an axiom, definition, or previously proved statement. Proofs are sometimes written in columns to make sure that every statement is supported.

EXAMPLE 6 Prove Theorem 1-13.

An Extended Distributive Property

For any real numbers a, b, c, and d, $a(b + c + d) = ab + ac + ad$.

1. $a(b + c + d) = a[(b + c) + d]$	1. Associative property of addition
2. $\quad = a(b + c) + ad$	2. Distributive property
3. $\quad = ab + ac + ad$	3. ?
4. $a(b + c + d) = ab + ac + ad$	4. Transitive property of equality

Try This

g. Supply the reason for step 3 of the proof in Example 6.

Here are some further number properties, stated as theorems.

Theorem 1-14

The Multiplicative Property of 0

For any real number a, $a \cdot 0 = 0$.

Theorem 1-15

Additive Inverses of Products

For any real numbers a and b, $-(ab) = -a \cdot b = a(-b)$.

(The additive inverse of a product of two numbers is equivalent to the product of either number and the additive inverse of the other).

Theorem 1-16

Products of Additive Inverses

For any real numbers a and b, $(-a)(-b) = ab$.

(The product of the inverses of two numbers is the same as the product of those numbers.)

Extra Help On the Web

Look for worked-out examples at the Prentice Hall Web site. www.phschool.com

1-10 Exercises

A

Which axioms or properties of equality, if any, justify each statement?

1. $a(-b + b) = a \cdot 0$

2. $-1 \cdot 3x = -3x = (-3) \cdot x$

3. $\frac{2}{x+1} = 2 \cdot \frac{1}{x+1}$

4. $\frac{1}{2}(x + y) = \frac{1}{2}x + \frac{1}{2}y$

5. If $2 = x$, then $x = 2$.

6. $a + b = a + b$

7. $x^2 + y^2 = y^2 + x^2$

8. $(a + b) + c = a + (b + c)$

9. $x^3 - y^3 = x^3 + (-y^3)$

10. If $-1 \cdot x = -x$ and $-x = y$, then $-1 \cdot x = y$.

11. **TEST PREP** Applying the commutative property of multiplication to $x(a + b) - c$ gives which of these expressions?

A. $x(a + b) + (-c)$

B. $-c + x(a + b)$

C. $(xa + xb) - c$

D. $(a + b)x - c$

Mathematical Reasoning Tell whether each of these sets with addition and multiplication forms a field. If not, tell why.

12. The set of natural numbers

13. The set of even numbers

14. The set of rational numbers

15. The set $\{0, 1\}$

16. Complete the proof of Theorem 1-1, the subtraction theorem:

For any real numbers a and b, $a - b = a + (-b)$.

To prove the subtraction theorem, we will use the definition of subtraction. It says that $a - b$ is the number c such that $c + b = a$. We will show that $a + (-b)$ represents the number c.

1. $[a + (-b)] + b = a + [(-b) + b]$	1. ?
2. $= a + 0$	2. Property of additive inverses
3. $= a$	3. ?
4. $[a + (-b)] + b = a$	4. Transitive property of equality
5. $a + (-b) = a - b$	5. Definition of subtraction

17. Is this a valid proof? Why or why not?

$$2(-x + y) - 4[3 - (x + 2)]$$
$$= 2(y - x) - 4[3 - x + 2]$$
$$= 2y - 2x - 12 + 4x - 8$$
$$= 2y - 2x - 20$$

18. Is this a valid proof? Why or why not?

$$(3x^2)^{-2}\left(\frac{9x^{-2}}{4x^{-3}}\right)^2$$
$$= \frac{1}{(3x^2)^2}\left(\frac{9x}{4}\right)^2$$
$$= \frac{1}{9x^4}\left(\frac{81x^2}{16}\right)$$
$$= \frac{9}{16x^2}$$

B

Prove the following

19. For any real numbers a and b, $-(a - b) = b - a$.

20. For any real number a, $-(-a) = a$.

21. Theorem 1-2, the division theorem

22. Theorem 1-5, the inverse of a sum

23. For any nonzero real number a, $\frac{a}{a} = 1$.

24. ***Critical Thinking*** A set is *closed* under an operation if, whenever the operation is performed on elements within the set, the result is also in the set. Determine which of the following sets are closed under the given operation.

a. the set of whole numbers; addition

b. the set of whole numbers; subtraction

c. the set of odd integers; addition

d. the set of even integers; multiplication

e. the set of rational numbers; multiplication

Challenge

25. ***Mathematical Reasoning***
A number system consists of $\{0, 1, 2\}$ and the operation of $+$ and $\times$ defined by these tables. For example, in this system, $1 + 2 = 0$, and $2 \times 2 = 1$.

+	0	1	2
0	0	1	2
1	1	2	0
2	2	0	1

×	0	1	2
0	0	0	0
1	0	1	2
2	0	2	1

Determine whether this number system is a field.

Mixed Review

Multiply. **26.** $5x(y + 3z)$ **27.** $3a(2b - 3c)$ **28.** $2w(1 - 3x)$ *1-4*

Simplify. **29.** $6^2 \cdot 6^4$ **30.** $m^{-8} \cdot m^5$ **31.** $y^3 \cdot y^{-7} \cdot y^2$ **32.** $x^{13} \cdot x^{-9}$ *1-8*

Solve. **33.** $m - 31 = 19$ **34.** $z - 64 = 241$ **35.** $23x = 368$ *1-5*

36. $-\frac{7}{16}y = \frac{7}{4}$ *1-4*

37. Alfredo has saved \$714 to buy a racing bicycle. This represents 85% of the cost of the bike. Find the cost of the bike. *1-6*

38. The fine for speeding in one town is \$10 plus \$2 for each mile per hour exceeding the speed limit. What is the fine for a driver stopped for driving 44 miles per hour in a 25-mile-per-hour zone? *1-6*

Divide and write scientific notation for the answer.

39. $\frac{1.28 \times 10^{-3}}{6.4 \times 10^{-1}}$ **40.** $\frac{7.29 \times 10^2}{8.1 \times 10^4}$ **41.** $\frac{10^4}{8 \times 10^4}$ *1-9*

1-11 Reasoning Strategies

What You'll Learn

1 To solve nonroutine problems

. . . And Why

To increase efficiency in solving problems by applying reasoning skills

PART 1 Draw a Diagram

Objective: Solve nonroutine problems using the strategy *Draw a Diagram.*

PROBLEM-SOLVING GUIDELINES
■ UNDERSTAND the problem
■ Develop and carry out a PLAN
■ Find the ANSWER and CHECK

Problem-Solving Guidelines were introduced in this chapter to help you solve problems. The three phases in the guidelines can be helpful in solving all problems.

The planning phase involves selecting and implementing *strategies* for solving problems. The problem-solving strategy called *Write an Equation* is the one you will work with often in your study of algebra.

There are many other strategies you can use to solve problems in mathematics. Usually, some combination of strategies is used. For example, the strategy called *Draw a Diagram* can often be used to help you understand a problem for which you will also write an equation to find a solution.

EXAMPLE 1

The average rainfall in May in one western city is 0.5 in. This amount is only 20% of the average amount of rainfall in one midwestern city in May. How much rainfall does the midwestern city average in May?

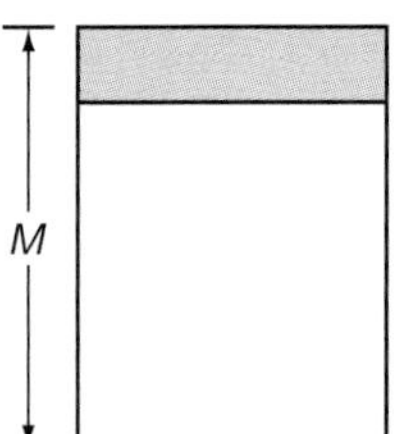

Drawing a diagram helps show the relationship between the numbers in the problem and the unknown quantity.

20% of the midwestern city's average rainfall is 0.5 in.
The midwestern city's average rainfall is unknown.

From the diagram, we can see that the equation $20\% \times M = 0.5$ expresses the relationship between the total amount of rainfall in the midwestern city and the 20%, or 0.5 in. of rainfall in the western city. Solve the equation to finish carrying out your plan.

$$0.20 \times M = 0.5 \qquad \text{Writing 20\% as 0.20}$$
$$M = \frac{0.5}{0.20} = 2.5$$

The average amount of rainfall in the midwestern city is 2.5 in. The answer checks.

EXAMPLE 2

A professional decorator can hang wallpaper on a square wall with sides of 10 feet in 30 minutes. How long would it take this person to cover a square section of wall with sides of 5 feet? Assume the wallpaper was hung at the same rate of speed.

An incorrect assumption is that it will take half as long to cover the smaller wall, since the side of the square is half the side of the larger square. Drawing a picture shows why this is incorrect and helps show the correct answer.

The diagram shows the information given in the problem. The square is 10 ft on each side, and it takes 30 min to cover this square.

10 ft
10 ft
30 minutes to cover

We can use the original diagram to show that a square with sides of 5 ft is $\frac{1}{4}$ the area of the original square. Thus it will take only $\frac{1}{4}$ as long to cover this section.

5 ft
5 ft

It will take $7\frac{1}{2}$ min to cover the square section with sides of 5 ft.

Reasoning Strategies

Write an Equation	Draw a Diagram	Try, Test, Revise
Make an Organized List	Make a Table	Look for a Pattern
Use Logical Reasoning	Simplify the Problem	Work Backward

1-11 Problems

Solve using one or both of the strategies presented so far.

1. How many spokes does a wheel have if there are 16 spaces between the spokes?
2. An adult dosage of a medicine uses 280 grams of one ingredient. A child's dosage uses 125 grams. What percent of the adult dosage is needed for the child's dosage?
3. Two train shipments reached the same factory from different cities. The distance from each city to the factory was 900 miles. One train traveled 600 miles in the same time that the other traveled only 400 miles. How much of a head start, in miles, was the slower train given if both trains arrived at the same time?
4. The population in a certain city is 35% greater than it was 10 years ago. If the population in this city today is 105,000, what was the population 10 years ago?
5. ***Multi-Step Problem*** A chemical compound evaporates in a predictable way. In the first hour, $\frac{1}{2}$ of the amount in the jar at the beginning of the hour evaporates. In the second hour, $\frac{1}{3}$ of the amount in the jar at the beginning of the second hour evaporates. In the third hour, $\frac{1}{4}$ of the amount in the jar at the beginning of the third hour evaporates, and so on. If a container started with 60 L of compound, after how many hours would the amount of the compound be less than 10 L?

1 Chapter Wrap Up

Key Terms

absolute value (p. 5)
Addition Property of Equality (p. 26)
additive identity (p. 17)
additive inverse (p.6)
Additive Inverses of Products (p. 51)
algebraic expressions (p. 14)
Associative Properties (p. 15)
axioms (p. 49)
base (p. 35)
binary operation (p. 13)
coefficient (p. 21)
Commutative Properties (p. 15)
constant (p. 14)
difference (p. 6)
Distributive Property (p. 20)
division (p. 10)
Division Theorem (p. 10)
equation (p. 26)
equivalent expressions (p. 15)
evaluating (p. 14)
exponent (p. 35)
exponential notation (p. 35)
Extended Distributive Property (p. 50)
factor (p. 21)
factoring (p. 21)
factors (p. 21)
field (p. 50)
field axioms (p. 50)
identity (p. 29)
Identity Properties (p. 16)
integer exponents (p. 36)
integers (p. 4)
Inverse of a Sum Property (p. 22)
irrational numbers (p. 4)
like terms (p. 21)
Multiplication Property of Equality (p. 26)
multiplicative identity (p. 17)
multiplicative inverse (p. 9)

1-1

A **rational number** can be expressed as a ratio $\frac{a}{b}$, where a and b are integers and $b \neq 0$.

1. Is -3 a natural number? a whole number? an integer? a rational number?

Determine which are rational and which are irrational.

2. $-\sqrt{49}$ **3.** -0.733 **4.** $6.5\overline{27}$

To add when there are like signs, add the absolute values. The sum has the same sign as the addends. To add when there are unlike signs, subtract the absolute values. The sum has the sign of the addend with the greater absolute value.

Add.

5. $-\frac{7}{5} + \left(-\frac{13}{10}\right)$ **6.** $8.7 + (-7.9)$ **7.** $-\frac{7}{8} + \frac{5}{6}$

To subtract a rational number, add its inverse.

Subtract.

8. $-\frac{6}{7} - \left(-\frac{2}{5}\right)$ **9.** $-13.8 - 5.9$ **10.** $16.56 - (-15.72)$

1-2

When multiplying or dividing rational numbers, multiply or divide their absolute values. If both numbers are positive or both are negative, then the answer is positive. If one number is positive and the other is negative, then the answer is negative.

Multiply.

11. $-4(2.1)$ **12.** $-\frac{5}{6}\left(-\frac{18}{7}\right)$ **13.** $(-6.01)(-1000)$

The **quotient** $\frac{a}{b}$ is the number c such that $c \cdot b = a$.

Divide.

14. $\frac{-18.72}{3.6}$ **15.** $-\frac{7}{8} \div \left(-\frac{3}{4}\right)$ **16.** $\frac{2}{3} \div \left(-\frac{8}{5}\right)$

1-3

The **commutative properties,** $a + b = b + a$ and $ab = ba$, and **associative properties,** $a + (b + c) = (a + b) + c$ and $a(bc) = (ab)c$, are used to write equivalent expressions.

17. Use the commutative property of multiplication to write an expression equivalent to $4x \cdot 7y$.

18. Use the associative property of addition to write an expression equivalent to $\left(\frac{x}{3} + 5\right) + 2y$.

19. Write an equivalent expression by simplifying $\frac{10(x - 2)}{24(x - 2)}$.

Evaluate each expression for $x = 3$ and $y = -2$.

20. $2x + 1 - 3y$ 21. $-(x - 1 - y)$ 22. $2|x - 4| - |y|$

1-4

The **distributive property,** $a(b + c) = ab + ac$, tells us that when multiplying a number by a sum, we can add first and then multiply, or multiply first and then add.

Multiply.

23. $6(x - y + z)$ 24. $-3(k - 2t + w)$ 25. $12\left(\frac{a}{2} - \frac{b}{3} + \frac{c}{4}\right)$

Factor.

26. $ax - ay$ 27. $-20x + 5y - 10z$ 28. $2ab - 6ac - 8ad$

Combine like terms.

29. $-6y - 8z - 4y + 3z$ 30. $2.3y - 8 - 4y + 7.6x - 5.8x$

Simplify.

31. $-(r - t)$ 32. $-(-4x + 3y)$

Simplify.

33. $2a - (3a - 4)$ 34. $y - 3(2y - 4x)$

35. $5x - [2x - (3x + 2)]$ 36. $8x - \{2x - 3[(x - 4) - (x + 2)]\}$

1-5

We use the **addition property of equality** (if $a = b$, then $a + c = b + c$) and the **multiplication property of equality** (if $a = b$, then $ac = bc$ for any real number c) to solve equations.

Solve.

37. $5x - 3 = 27$ 38. $6y + 3 = y - 12$ 39. $3t - 8 - t = 7t - 8 + 2t$

1-6

The three phases of the Problem-Solving Guidelines are: UNDERSTAND the problem, develop and carry out a PLAN, and find the ANSWER and CHECK.

40. Ace Car Rental charges $27 per day plus $0.35 per mile to rent a car. Find the cost of renting a car for a 7-day trip of 840 miles.

1-7

For any nonzero number b and integer n, b^{-n} means $\frac{1}{b^n}$.

Write equivalent expressions using negative exponents.

41. $\frac{1}{8^3}$ 42. $\frac{1}{(-3)^2}$ 43. $\frac{1}{3y^5}$ 44. $\frac{1}{(3y)^5}$

Internet Activity On the Web

Look for extension problems for this chapter at the Prentice Hall Web site.
www.phschool.com

Write equivalent expressions without negative exponents.

45. $(-4)^{-3}$ **46.** $\frac{x^3}{y^{-4}}$ **47.** $3a^3c^{-5}$ **48.** $w^3x^{-2}y^5z^{-6}$

1-8

For any real number $a \neq 0$, and integers m, n, and p, $a^m \cdot a^n = a^{m+n}$, $\frac{a^m}{a^n} = a^{m-n}$, and $(a^m b^n)^p = a^{m \cdot p} b^{n \cdot p}$.

Simplify.

49. $(7x^3y^{-1})(-2x^{-4}y)$ **50.** $\frac{a^{-2}}{a^{-4}}$ **51.** $-\frac{54x^{-5}y^4}{18x^3y^{-1}}$

52. $(-3x^2y^3)^4$ **53.** $(-2x^3)^{-3}$ **54.** $\left(-\frac{2x^3y^{-6}}{3y^4}\right)^2$

1-9

Scientific notation for a number is notation of the form $a \times 10^n$ where $1 \leq a < 10$ and n is an integer.

Write scientific notation.

55. 80,000,000 **56.** 0.00000074

57. $(1.8 \times 10^{12})(2.1 \times 10^{-3})$ **58.** $\frac{6.25 \times 10^{-6}}{2.5 \times 10^3}$

1 Chapter Assessment

Which of the following numbers are rational and which are irrational?

1. $\sqrt{5}$ **2.** $0.\overline{153846}$ **3.** 0.1121231234 . . .

4. 0 **5.** $\sqrt{10}$ **6.** $\frac{1.7}{2.9}$

7. 3.14159265 . . . (numerals do not repeat)

8. $3.\overline{142857}\,\overline{142857}$ . . . (numerals repeat)

Add.

9. $-4.9 + (-3.08)$ **10.** $\frac{9}{16} + \left(-\frac{7}{10}\right)$ **11.** $-\frac{4}{9} + \frac{7}{12}$

Subtract.

12. $-0.74 - (-11.8)$ **13.** $\frac{8}{9} - \left(-\frac{5}{6}\right)$ **14.** $-30.7 - 6.1$

Multiply.

15. $-0.9(3.1)$ **16.** $-\frac{2}{7}\left(-\frac{10}{3}\right)$ **17.** $0.43(-100)$

Divide.

18. $\frac{4}{3} \div \left(-\frac{8}{15}\right)$ 19. $-\frac{6.09}{0.29}$ 20. $\frac{-7.2}{-0.4}$

21. Use the associative property of multiplication to write an expression equivalent to $(x \cdot 2y) \cdot 8z$.

22. Use the commutative property of addition to write an expression equivalent to $5y + 3x$.

23. Write an equivalent expression by simplifying $\frac{12xyz}{8y}$.

Evaluate each expression for $x = -1$ and $y = 5$.

24. $3x - y + 7$ 25. $-(y - x + 1)$ 26. $3|x + 1| - |y|$

Multiply.

27. $-4(x - y + 8)$ 28. $a(3b - c - d)$ 29. $6\left(3x - \frac{y}{2} - \frac{z}{4}\right)$

Factor.

30. $2xy - xz$ 31. $6ab - 8bc - 4bd$ 32. $3xy - 6xyz$

Combine like terms.

33. $9x - 5x - 6x + 7x$ 34. $3.2y - 9 - 5y + 4.8x - 5.7x$

Simplify.

35. $-(-2t)$ 36. $-(-5 - 3x)$ 37. $-(6 - 5y)$

Simplify.

38. $3t-(5t - 6)$ 39. $9y - [4y - (2y - 5)]$ 40. $2x - 5(3 - 2x) - 5$

Solve.

41. $3 - 2x = 7$ 42. $5y - 2 = y - 10$ 43. $5x - 2 + 3x = 9 - 2x - 11$

44. A housecleaning service charges \$10.00 a visit plus \$7.50 an hour. How much would this service charge if it took $3\frac{1}{2}$ hours to clean a house?

Write using negative exponents.

45. $\frac{1}{a^3}$ 46. 3^2 47. x^n 48. $\frac{1}{3x^2}$

Write without negative exponents.

49. $(-2)^{-2}$ 50. $x^{-2}y^3$ 51. $2a^{-2}c^4$ 52. $\frac{1}{-x^{-5}}$

Simplify using positive exponents.

53. $(-5x^3)(-6x^5)$ 54. $\frac{63y^4z^9}{9y^2z^{-3}}$ 55. $\frac{2x^{-4}}{8x^{-2}}$

56. $(-4x^2y^4)^3$ 57. $(-3x^4y)^{-3}$ 58. $\left(\frac{3x^2y^3}{12x^{-1}y^{-6}}\right)^2$

Write scientific notation.

59. 90,400,000 60. 0.00000752 61. $\frac{2 \times 10^{-4}}{5 \times 10^3}$

CHAPTER

What You'll Learn in Chapter 2

- How to use equations to solve problems
- How to solve inequalities, compound inequalities, and absolute value equations
- How to prove some statements and their converses

Skills & Concepts You Need for Chapter 2

1-1 Write the correct symbol =, <, or >.

1. $-8.09 \square -8.11$ **2.** $-0.001 \square -\frac{1}{1000}$ **3.** $-\frac{2}{7} \square \frac{6}{7}$

1-1 Add.

4. $3.8 + (-3.8)$ **5.** $-4.8 + 1.2$ **6.** $-\frac{3}{8} + \left(-\frac{1}{6}\right)$

1-1 Subtract.

7. $8 - (-5)$ **8.** $-18.2 - 4.7$ **9.** $-\frac{2}{3} - \left(-\frac{4}{7}\right)$

1-2 Multiply.

10. $3 \cdot (-8)$ **11.** $-4.7 \cdot 10$ **12.** $-8 \cdot \left(-\frac{3}{4}\right)$

1-4 Factor.

13. $3x - 18$ **14.** $5x - 10y + 15$

15. $4x - 8 + 6y$ **16.** $12ab + 4ac - 16ad$

1-4 Multiply.

17. $5(y - 4)$ **18.** $a(2 - b)$

19. $c(x + y - z)$ **20.** $-3(x - y + 1)$

1-4 Collect like terms.

21. $x + 3x - 5x$ **22.** $2y + 3 + 5y - 1$

Equations and Inequalities

Bowling is one of many sports that require specialized equipment. Some balls have the holes drilled to fit the bowler's hand precisely, thus adding to the cost of the ball. In Lesson 2-2 you will find the original cost of a discounted bowling ball.

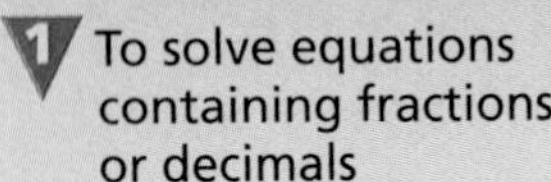

2-1 More on Solving Equations

What You'll Learn

1. To solve equations containing fractions or decimals
2. To solve equations containing parentheses
3. To use the principle of zero products

. . . And Why

To solve more difficult equations

PART 1 Clearing Fractions or Decimals

Objective: Solve equations containing fractions or decimals.

When an equation contains fractions or decimals, we can use the multiplication property to eliminate them. The process is called **clearing the equation** of fractions or decimals.

EXAMPLE 1 Solve.

$$\frac{3}{4}x + \frac{1}{2} = \frac{3}{2}$$

We multiply both sides of the equation by the **least common denominator,** in this case 4.

$4\left(\frac{3}{4}x + \frac{1}{2}\right) = 4 \cdot \frac{3}{2}$ Multiplying by 4

$4 \cdot \frac{3}{4}x + 4 \cdot \frac{1}{2} = 4 \cdot \frac{3}{2}$ Using the distributive property

$3x + 2 = 6$ Simplifying

$3x = 4$

$x = \frac{4}{3}$

Check:

$\frac{3}{4}x + \frac{1}{2}$	$= \frac{3}{2}$
$\frac{3}{4}\left(\frac{4}{3}\right) + \frac{1}{2}$	$\frac{3}{2}$
$1 + \frac{1}{2}$	$\frac{3}{2}$
$\frac{3}{2}$	$\frac{3}{2}$ ✓

The solution is $\frac{4}{3}$.

EXAMPLE 2 Solve.

$$12.4 - 3.64x = 1.48$$

We multiply both sides of the equation by a power of ten.

$$\begin{aligned} 100(12.4 - 3.64x) &= 100 \cdot 1.48 \quad \text{Multiplying by 100} \\ 1240 - 364x &= 148 \\ -364x &= 148 + (-1240) \\ -364x &= -1092 \\ x &= 3 \end{aligned}$$

Since $12.4 - 3.64(3) = 1.48$, the solution is 3.

Try This Solve.

a. $\frac{2}{3} - \frac{5}{6}y = \frac{1}{3}$

b. $6.3x - 9.6 = 3$

Equations with Parentheses

Objective: Solve equations containing parentheses.

When an equation contains parentheses, we first use the distributive property to remove them. Then we proceed as before.

EXAMPLE 3 Solve.

$3(7 - 2x) = 14 - 8(x - 1)$	
$21 - 6x = 14 - 8x + 8$	Using the distributive property
$21 - 6x = 22 - 8x$	
$8x - 6x = 22 + (-21)$	Using the addition principle
$2x = 1$	Collecting like terms and simplifying
$x = \frac{1}{2}$	The number checks, so the solution is $\frac{1}{2}$.

Guidelines for Solving Equations

1. Use the distributive property to remove parentheses, if necessary.
2. Clear fractions or decimals, if necessary.
3. Collect like terms on both sides of the equation.
4. Use the addition and multiplication properties to solve for the variable.

Try This Solve.

c. $3(y - 1) - 1 = 2 - 5(y + 5)$

The Principle of Zero Products

Objective: Use the principle of zero products to solve equations.

When we multiply two numbers, the product will be zero if one of the factors is zero. Furthermore, if a product is zero, then at least one of the factors must be zero.

A statement that A and B must be both true or both false can be abbreviated as ***A* if and only if *B*.** This is equivalent to *if A then B, and if B then A.*

Writing Math

The expression "if and only if" is sometimes abbreviated "iff."

Theorem 2-1

The Principle of Zero Products

For any real numbers a and b, $ab = 0$ if and only if $a = 0$ or $b = 0$.

EXAMPLE 4 Solve.

$$(x + 4)(x - 2) = 0$$
$$x + 4 = 0 \quad \text{or} \quad x - 2 = 0 \qquad \text{Using the principle of zero products}$$
$$x = -4 \quad \text{or} \quad x = 2 \qquad \text{Solving each equation separately}$$

Check:

$(x + 4)(x - 2) = 0$	
$(-4 + 4)(-4 - 2)$	0
$0 \cdot (-6)$	0
0	0 ✓

$(x + 4)(x - 2) = 0$	
$(2 + 4)(2 - 2)$	0
$6 \cdot 0$	0
0	0 ✓

There are two solutions, -4 and 2. We can show the solutions as a set by listing them inside braces. The solution set is $\{-4, 2\}$.

EXAMPLE 5 Solve.

$$7x(4x + 2) = 0$$
$$7x = 0 \quad \text{or} \quad 4x + 2 = 0 \qquad \text{Using the principle of zero products}$$
$$x = 0 \quad \text{or} \quad 4x = -2$$
$$x = 0 \quad \text{or} \quad x = -\tfrac{1}{2} \qquad \text{Solving each equation separately}$$

The solutions are 0 and $-\frac{1}{2}$. The solution set is $\left\{0, -\frac{1}{2}\right\}$.

EXAMPLE 6 Solve.

$$(-2x + 5)(5x + 1) = 0$$
$$-2x + 5 = 0 \quad \text{or} \quad 5x + 1 = 0$$
$$-2x = -5 \quad \text{or} \quad 5x = -1$$
$$x = \tfrac{5}{2} \quad \text{or} \quad x = -\tfrac{1}{5}$$

The solution set is $\left\{\frac{5}{2}, -\frac{1}{5}\right\}$.

Try This Solve.

d. $(x - 19)(x + 5) = 0$ **e.** $x(3x - 17) = 0$ **f.** $(9x + 2)(-6x + 3) = 0$

Extra Help On the Web

Look for worked-out examples at the Prentice Hall Web site.
www.phschool.com

2-1 Exercises

A

Solve.

1. $\frac{1}{4} + \frac{3}{8}y = \frac{3}{4}$
2. $\frac{1}{5} + \frac{3}{10}x = \frac{4}{5}$
3. $-\frac{5}{2}x + \frac{1}{2} = -18$
4. $0.9y - 0.7 = 4.2$
5. $0.8t - 0.3t = 6.5$
6. $1.4x + 5.02 = 0.4x$
7. $2(x + 6) = 8x$
8. $3(y + 5) = 8y$
9. $80 = 10(3t + 2)$
10. $27 = 9(5y - 2)$
11. $180(n - 2) = 900$
12. $210(x - 3) = 840$

13. $5y - (2y - 10) = 25$

14. $8x - (3x - 5) = 40$

15. $0.7(3x + 6) = 1.1 - (x + 2)$

16. $0.9(2x + 8) = 20 - (x + 5)$

17. $\frac{1}{8}(16y + 8) - 17 = -\frac{1}{4}(8y - 16)$

18. $\frac{1}{6}(12t + 48) - 20 = -\frac{1}{8}(24t - 144)$

19. $a + (a - 3) = (a + 2) - (a + 1)$

20. $0.8 - 4(b - 1) = 0.2 + 3(4 - b)$

21. $(x + 2)(x - 5) = 0$

22. $(x + 4)(x - 8) = 0$

23. $(y - 8)(y - 9) = 0$

24. $(t - 3)(t - 7) = 0$

25. $(2x - 3)(3x - 2) = 0$

26. $p(p - 5) = 0$

27. $m(m - 8) = 0$

28. $(3y - 4)(4y - 1) = 0$

B

Solve.

29. $x(x - 1)(x + 2) = 0$

30. $y(y - 4)(y + 2) = 0$

31. $\frac{1}{7}(a - 3)(7a + 4) = 0$

32. $24\left(\frac{x}{6} - \frac{1}{3}\right) = x - 24$

33. $0.5(x - 2) - 2(x - 5) = 0.4(x - 5) - 5(x - 2)$

Solve for x.

34. $8x + 3 = c$

35. $16x - 4 = f$

36. $cx + 3h = 5a$

37. $7x - 3 = ax + 5b$

38. $ax - bx = 12$

39. $5x + ax = 19$

40. Contrast solving $0.8y - 1.2 = -1.6y$ by first clearing decimals with solving without first clearing decimals. Which would you do using a calculator? Why?

41. ***Critical Thinking*** Write an equation that has both 7 and -8 as solutions.

Challenge

Solve.

42. $x \cdot x = 1$

43. $x \cdot x = x$

44. $x(x - 1) = x$

45. $x(x - 1) = x(x + 1)$

46. What is the solution set for each equation?

a. $x(x - 1)(x - 2)(x - 3) \cdots = 0$

b. $(x - 1)(x - 2)(x - 3) \cdots = 0$

c. $(x + 1)(x + 2)(x + 3) \cdots = 0$

d. $x(x - 2)(x - 4)(x - 6) \cdots = 0$

e. $x(x - 10)(x - 20)(x - 30) \cdots = 0$

f. $\cdots (x + 3)(x + 2)(x + 1)x(x - 1)(x - 2)(x - 3) \cdots = 0$

Mixed Review

Simplify. **47.** $4^2 \cdot 4^3 \cdot x^0$ **48.** $(-y)^3(-y)^2$ **49.** $x^3 \cdot x^{-5}$ **50.** $(3c^2)^3$ *1-7, 1-8*

Convert to scientific notation. **51.** 390,040 **52.** 0.000421 **53.** 24.072 *1-9*

Convert to standard notation. **54.** 4.03×10^{-6} **55.** -8.22×10^6 *1-9*

2-2 Using Equations

What You'll Learn

1 To translate problems to equations

. . . And Why

To solve problems algebraically

PART 1 Using Equations to Solve Problems

Objective: Solve problems by translating to equations.

PROBLEM-SOLVING GUIDELINES
■ UNDERSTAND the problem
■ Develop and carry out a PLAN
■ Find the ANSWER and CHECK

Many problems can be solved by translating them into mathematical language. Often this means translating a problem into an equation. When appropriate, drawing a diagram usually helps us to understand the problem.

EXAMPLE 1 A 28-ft rope is cut into two pieces. One piece is 3 ft longer than the other. How long are the pieces?

■ **UNDERSTAND the problem**

Question: What are the lengths of the two pieces of rope? — Clarifying the question

Data: The total length of the rope is 28 ft. One piece of rope is 3 ft longer than the other piece. — Identifying the data

A diagram can help translate the problem to an equation.

28 ft

One piece — 3 ft longer piece — Drawing a diagram

■ **Develop and carry out a PLAN**

Here is one way to translate.

Length of one piece plus length of other is 28. — Translating to an equation

$$x + (x + 3) = 28$$ Using x for the length of one piece and $x + 3$ for the other

$$2x + 3 = 28$$
$$2x = 25$$
$$x = \frac{25}{2}, \text{ or } 12\tfrac{1}{2}$$ Solving the equation

■ **Find the ANSWER and CHECK**

One piece is $12\frac{1}{2}$ ft long, and the other piece is 3 ft longer, or $15\frac{1}{2}$ ft long. The sum of the lengths is 28 ft. — The answer checks in the problem.

Try This

a. A 23-ft cable is cut into two pieces, one three times as long as the other. How long are the pieces?

EXAMPLE 2 Five plus twice a number is seven times the number. What is the number?

5	plus	twice a number	is	seven	times	the number.	Translating
↓	↓	⏟	↓	↓	↓	⏟	
5	$+$	$2x$	$=$	7	$\cdot$	x	

We have used x to represent the unknown number.

$$
\begin{aligned}
5 + 2x &= 7x \\
5 &= 7x - 2x \\
5 &= 5x \\
x &= 1
\end{aligned}
$$

Twice 1 is 2. If we add 5, we get 7. Seven times 1 is also 7. This checks, so the answer to the problem is 1. Checking

Try This

b. If seven times a certain number is subtracted from 6, the result is five times the number. What is the number?

c. Chris bought a baseball card in 1975. By 1985, the value of the card had tripled. Since 1985, the value has increased by another $30. The card is now worth 5 times its original value. How much was the card worth when Chris bought it?

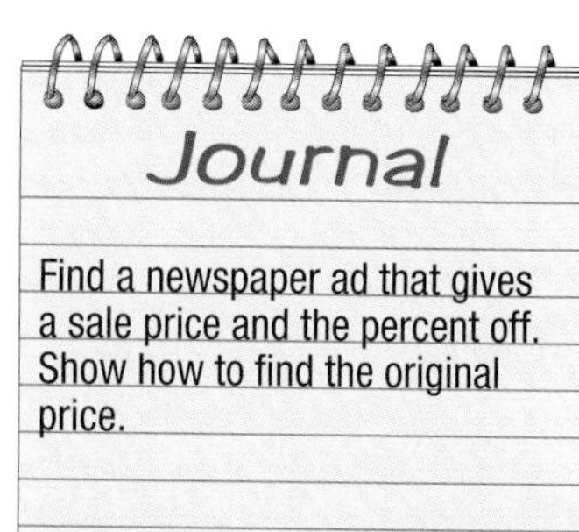

EXAMPLE 3 The price of a mobile home was cut 11% to a new price of $48,950. What was the original price?

Original price	minus	11%	of	original price	is	new price.	Translating
⏟	↓	↓	↓	⏟	↓	⏟	
x	$-$	11%	$\cdot$	x	$=$	$48{,}950$	

We have used x to represent the original price.

$$
\begin{aligned}
x - 0.11 \cdot x &= 48{,}950 && \text{Replacing 11\% by 0.11} \\
1x - 0.11x &= 48{,}950 \\
(1 - 0.11)x &= 48{,}950 && \text{Factoring} \\
0.89x &= 48{,}950 \\
x &= 55{,}000
\end{aligned}
$$

The solution of the equation is 55,000. Check: 11% of 55,000 is 6050. Subtracting from 55,000 we get 48,950. The number checks, so the original price was $55,000.

The first factory-built mobile home was made in 1926. By 1943, the average trailer was 8 ft wide by 22 ft long. Now some double-wide modular homes are 24 ft wide by 50 ft long. How many times as great as the area of the average 1943 trailer is the area of a current double-wide modular home?

Try This

d. A clothing store drops the price of a suit 25% to a sale price of \$93. What was the original price of the suit?

e. An investment is made at 12% simple interest. It grows to \$812 at the end of 1 year. How much was invested originally? (Hint: Recall the expression $P + Prt$ regarding the return on a principal of P dollars.)

EXAMPLE 4 The sum of two consecutive integers is 35. What are the integers?

$$\underbrace{\text{First integer}} + \underbrace{\text{second integer}} = 35$$
$$x + (x + 1) = 35 \qquad \text{Translating}$$

Since the integers are consecutive, we know that one of them is 1 greater than the other. We call one of them x and the other $x + 1$.

$$\begin{aligned} x + (x + 1) &= 35 \qquad \text{Solving the equation} \\ 2x + 1 &= 35 \\ 2x &= 34 \\ x &= 17 \end{aligned}$$

Since x is 17, then $x + 1$, the second integer, is 18. The answers are 17 and 18. These are both integers and consecutive. Their sum is 35, so the answers check in the problem.

Guidelines for Writing Numbers in Algebraic Problems

1. If two numbers are consecutive, call one x and the other $x + 1$.
2. If two numbers are consecutive even numbers, call one $2x$ and the other $2x + 2$.
3. If two numbers are consecutive odd numbers, call one $2x + 1$ and the other $2x + 3$.
4. If a number x is increased by $n\%$, the new number can be written $x + \frac{1}{100}n \cdot x$.

Try This

f. The sum of two consecutive odd integers is 36. What are the integers?

g. Field goals in basketball count two points each. In one game, Harold had one less field goal than Gunther. Together they scored 46 points on field goals.

(1) How many points did each player score on field goals?

(2) How many field goals did each player make?

2-2 Exercises

Extra Help On the Web

Look for worked-out examples at the Prentice Hall Web site. www.phschool.com

A

Solve.

1. A 12 cm piece of tubing is cut into two pieces. One piece is 4 cm longer than the other. How long are the pieces?
2. A piece of rope 5 m long is cut into two pieces so that one piece is three fifths as long as the other. Find the length of each piece.
3. The product of 6 and nine times a number is the same as the difference of ten times the number and 2. What is the number?
4. Find three consecutive odd integers such that the sum of the first, two times the second, and three times the third is 82.
5. A pro shop in a bowling alley drops the price of bowling balls 24% to a sale price of \$134.20. What was the original price?
6. An appliance store drops the price of a certain type of TV 18% to a sale price of \$410. What was the original price?
7. Money is borrowed at 11% simple interest. After 1 year, \$721.50 pays off the loan. How much was borrowed originally?
8. Money is borrowed at 12% simple interest. After 1 year, \$896 pays off the loan. How much was borrowed originally?

See Exercise 5.

For Exercises 9 and 10, remember that the sum of the measures of a triangle is 180°.

9. The second angle of a triangle is three times the first and the third is 12° less than twice the first. Find the measures of the angles.
10. The second angle of a triangle is four times the first and the third is 5° more than twice the first. Find the measures of the angles.

For Exercises 11 and 12, remember that the area of a rectangle is $l \times w$ (the product of the length and the width), and the perimeter is $2l + 2w$.

11. The perimeter of a college basketball court is 96 m and the length is 14 m more than the width. What are the dimensions?
12. The perimeter of a certain soccer field is 310 m. The length is 65 m more than the width. What are the dimensions?
13. A 20% raise in salary gives a new salary of \$18,000. What was the old salary?
14. A 7.5% raise brings a salary to \$46,225. What was the salary before the raise?
15. **TEST PREP** *Error Analysis* The sentence "Given two consecutive even integers, two times the first plus three times the second is 76." is ambiguous. Which of the following equations could NOT represent the sentence?

    A. $(2[2x + 3])(2x + 2) = 76$ **B.** $2(2x) + 3(2x + 2) = 76$

    C. $2(2x)(2x + 2) = 76$ **D.** $2(2x + 3[2x + 2]) = 76$
16. *Write a Convincing Argument* Write an argument to convince a classmate of your answer to Exercise 15.

17. The total cost for tuition plus room and board for one quarter at Southern State University is \$6584. Tuition costs \$704 more than room and board. What is the quarterly tuition fee?

18. The cost of a private pilot course is \$4250. The flight portion costs \$1500 more than the ground school portion. What is the cost of each?

B

19. A student's scores on five tests are 93%, 89%, 72%, 80%, and 96%. What must the student score on the sixth test so that the average will be 88%?

20. The yearly changes in the population of a city for three consecutive years are, respectively, 20% increase, 30% increase, and 20% decrease. What is the total percent change from the beginning to the end of the third year?

21. Three numbers are such that the second is the difference of three times the first and 6 while the third is the sum of 2 and $\frac{2}{3}$ the second. The sum of the three numbers is 172. Find the largest number.

22. An appliance store is having a sale on 13 VCR models. They are displayed left to right in order of increasing price. The price of each VCR differs by \$60 from that of each adjacent VCR. For the price of the VCR at the extreme right, a customer can buy both the second and the sixth models. What is the price of the least expensive VCR?

23. *Multi-Step Problem* A tank at a marine exhibit contains 2000 gallons of sea water. The sea water is 7.5% salt. How many gallons, to the nearest gallon, of fresh water must be added to the tank so that the mixture contains only 7% salt?

24. Is it *sometimes*, *always*, or *never* true that the sum of two consecutive odd integers is an odd integer?

25. The perimeter of a square is 12 cm greater than that of another square. Its area exceeds the area of the other by 39 cm^2. Find the perimeter of each square.

26. *Critical Thinking* Rewrite the problem of Example 1 so that in the solution the shorter piece of rope has a length of $16\frac{1}{2}$ feet.

Challenge

27. Diophantus spent one sixth of his life as a child, one twelfth as a young man, and one seventh as a bachelor. Five years after he was married he had a son who died 4 years before his father at half his father's final age. How long did Diophantus live?

Mixed Review

Collect like terms. **28.** $x^2 + 3 + (-2x^2) + 4$ **29.** $x^4 + x^2y + 2x^4 + 2yx^2 - xy^2$ **30.** $a^3b + 2a^2b - 6ab^2 - 3a^3b + 2ab^2 - a^2b$ **31.** $3x - [2x - 3 - (-x - 4)]$ **32.** $a^2 + b^2 + c^2 - (-a^2 - b^2 - c^2)$ *1-4*

Factor. **33.** $2x^2 + 2x$ **34.** $3a^2b^2 - 9ab^2$ **35.** $30x^2y + 6xy^2 - 12x^3y$ *1-4*

Multiply. **36.** $(8.2 \times 10^{-3})(2 \times 10^5)$ *1-9*

Solving Formulas

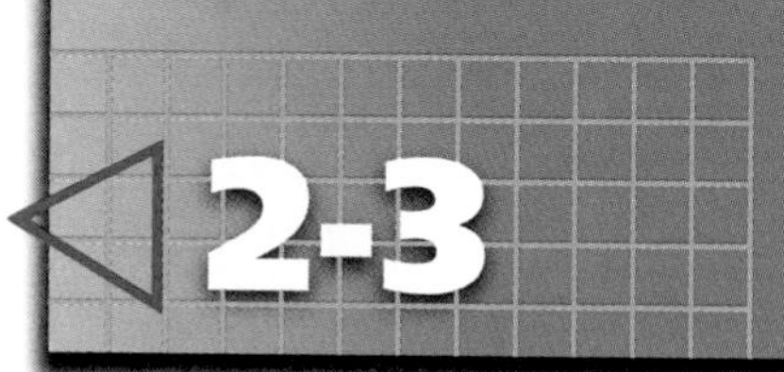

Solve a Formula

Objective: Solve a formula for a specified letter.

What You'll Learn

1 To solve a formula for a particular variable

... And Why

To be prepared to use formulas in various ways

A **formula** is a rule for doing a specific calculation. Formulas are often given as equations. A formula for finding wattage is $W = EI$ where E represents voltage and I represents resistance. Suppose we know the wattage and voltage and want to find the resistance. We can solve the formula for a specific variable, following the same steps we use to solve an equation.

EXAMPLE 1 Solve the formula $W = EI$ for I.

$W = EI$ — We want the letter I alone.

$\frac{1}{E} \cdot W = \frac{1}{E} \cdot EI$ — Multiplying both sides by $\frac{1}{E}$

$\frac{W}{E} = I$

EXAMPLE 2 Solve for b.

$A = \frac{5}{2}(b - 20)$

$\frac{2}{5}A = b - 20$ — Multiplying both sides by $\frac{2}{5}$

$\frac{2}{5}A + 20 = b$ — Adding 20 to both sides

Try This Solve.

a. $A = \frac{1}{2}bh$, for b **b.** $P = \frac{3}{5}(c + 10)$, for c

c. $H = 2r + 3m$, for m **d.** $Q = 3r + 5p$, for p

EXAMPLE 3 Solve for P.

$A = P + Prt$ — An interest formula

$A = P(1 + rt)$ — Factoring

$A \cdot \frac{1}{1 + rt} = P(1 + rt) \cdot \frac{1}{1 + rt}$ — Multiplying on both sides by $\frac{1}{1 + rt}$

$\frac{A}{1 + rt} = P$ — Simplifying

Try This Solve.

e. $T = Q + Qiy$, for Q **f.** $x = G - Gr^2p$, for G

Extra Help On the Web

Look for worked-out examples at the Prentice Hall Web site.
www.phschool.com

2-3 Exercises

A

Solve.

1. $A = lw$, for l (an area formula)
2. $A = lw$, for w
3. $W = EI$, for I (an electricity formula)
4. $W = EI$, for E
5. $F = ma$, for m (a physics formula)
6. $F = ma$, for a
7. $I = Prt$, for t (an interest formula)
8. $I = Prt$, for P
9. $E = mc^2$, for m (a relativity formula)
10. $E = mc^2$, for c^2
11. $P = 2l + 2w$, for l (a perimeter formula)
12. $P = 2l + 2w$, for w
13. $c^2 = a^2 + b^2$, for a^2 (a geometry formula)
14. $c^2 = a^2 + b^2$, for b^2
15. $A = \pi r^2$, for r^2 (an area formula)
16. $A = \pi r^2$, for π
17. $C = \frac{5}{9}(F - 32)$, for F (a temperature formula)
18. $W = \frac{11}{2}(h - 40)$, for h
19. $V = \frac{4}{3}\pi r^3$, for r^3 (a volume formula)
20. $V = \frac{4}{3}\pi r^3$, for π
21. $A = \frac{1}{2}ha + \frac{1}{2}hb$, for h (an area formula)
22. $A = \frac{1}{2}ha + \frac{1}{2}hb$, for b
23. $F = \frac{mv^2}{r}$, for m (a physics formula)
24. $F = \frac{mv^2}{r}$, for v^2

B

Solve.

25. $s = v_i t + \frac{1}{2}at^2$, for a
26. $A = \pi rs + r^2$, for s

27. In Exercise 7, you solved the formula $I = Prt$ for t. Use it to find how long it will take a deposit of \$75 to earn \$3 when invested at 10% simple interest.

28. In Exercise 8, you solved the formula $I = Prt$ for P. Use it to find how much principal would be needed to earn \$6 in two thirds of a year at 12% simple interest.

29. ***Critical Thinking*** In Exercises 13 and 19 you solved for a^2 and r^3, respectively. Tell how you could use a calculator to find a and r.

Challenge

30. A gas formula from physics is $\frac{P_1V_1}{T_1} = \frac{P_2V_2}{T_2}$. Solve it for V_1.

31. Solve the gas formula of Exercise 30 for T_2.

Mixed Review

Simplify. **32.** $(x^2)^2$ **33.** $(6^3)^{-2}$ **34.** $(2m^2n)^2$ **35.** $(8^{-2})^{-3}$ *1-8*

36. $0.4n + 2.7 = 5.1$ **37.** $\frac{3}{5} + \frac{t}{2} = \frac{5}{4}$ **38.** $\frac{11}{2}m - 3 = \frac{13}{2}$ **39.** $-\frac{1}{8}t + \frac{1}{6} = -\frac{1}{12}$

40. $4n - (3n + 6) = -1$ **41.** $(x - 4)(x + 5) = 0$ *1-5, 2-1*

Solving Inequalities

2-4

PART 1 Solutions and Graphs

Objective: Determine if a number is a solution of an inequality and graph the solution set.

The order of the real numbers is often pictured on a number line.

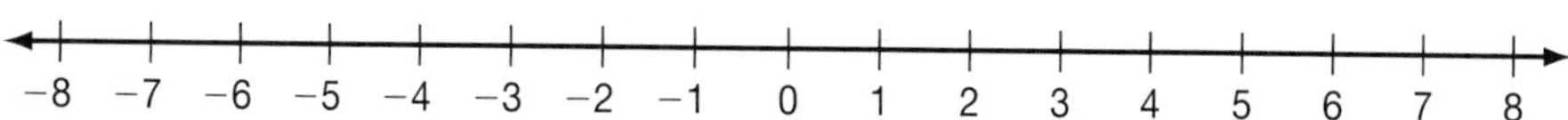

If a number occurs to the left of another on the number line, the first number **is less than** the second, and the second **is greater than** the first. We use the symbol $<$ to mean "is less than" and $>$ to mean "is greater than."

The symbol $\leq$ means "is less than or equal to," and the symbol $\geq$ means "is greater than or equal to."

Mathematical sentences containing $<$, $>$, $\leq$, or $\geq$ are called **inequalities.** A solution of an inequality is any number that makes it true. The set of all solutions is called the **solution set.** When we have found all solutions of an inequality, we say we have **solved** the inequality.

What You'll Learn

1. To determine if a number is a solution of an inequality, and graph the solution set
2. To solve inequalities using the addition property
3. To solve inequalities using the multiplication property
4. To solve inequalities using both the addition and multiplication properties

. . . And Why

To solve more difficult inequality problems

EXAMPLES Determine whether the given number is a solution of the inequality.

1 $x + 3 < 6; 5$

We substitute and get $5 + 3 < 6$, or $8 < 6$, a false sentence. Thus, 5 is not a solution.

2 $2x - 3 > -3; 1$

We substitute and get $2(1) - 3 > -3$, or $-1 > -3$, a true sentence. Thus, 1 is a solution.

3 $4x - 1 \leq 3x + 2; 3$

We substitute and get $4(3) - 1 \leq 3(3) + 2$, or $11 \leq 11$, a true sentence. Thus, 3 is a solution.

Try This Determine whether the given number is a solution of the inequality.

a. $3 - x < 2; 4$ **b.** $3y + 2 > -1; -2$ **c.** $3x + 2 \leq 4x - 3; 5$

A graph of an inequality is a drawing that shows all of its solutions on a number line. The graph is a picture of the solution set.

EXAMPLE 4 Graph $x < 2$ on a number line.

The solutions consist of all numbers less than 2, so we shade all numbers less than 2. Note that 2 is not a solution. We indicate this by using an open circle at 2.

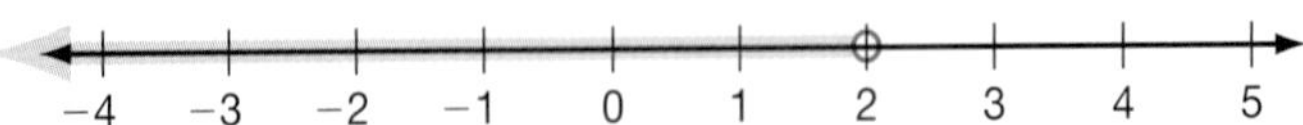

The solution set graphed in Example 4 can be written $\{x|x < 2\}$. This is called **set-builder notation**. The notation is read "the set of all x such that x is less than 2." Set notation of this type is written using braces. The symbol | is read "such that."

EXAMPLE 5 Graph $x \geq -3$ on a number line.

We draw a picture of the solutions $\{x|x \geq -3\}$.

This time the solution set consists of all the numbers greater than −3, including −3. We shade all numbers greater than −3 and use a solid circle at −3 to indicate that it is also a solution.

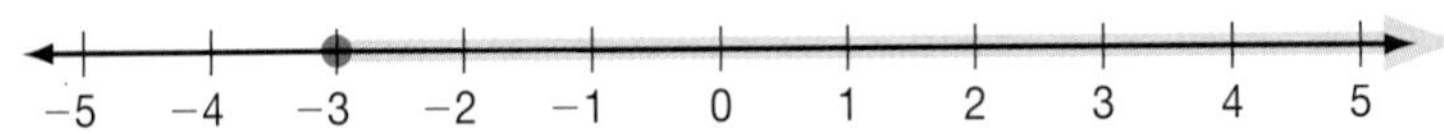

Try This Graph on a number line.

d. $x < -2$ **e.** $x \geq 1$ **f.** $x \leq 5$

The Addition Property

Objective: Solve and graph inequalities using the addition property.

There is an addition property for inequality similar to the one for equality.

Theorem 2-2

Addition Property of Inequality

If $a < b$ is true, then $a + c < b + c$ is true for any real number c.

Similar statements hold for $>$, $\leq$, and $\geq$.

If any number is added to both sides of a true inequality, another true inequality is obtained.

To solve an inequality using the addition property, we transform the inequality into a simpler one by adding the same number to both sides, as we do in solving equations.

EXAMPLE 6 Solve. Then graph.

$$x + 4 > 7$$
$$x + 4 + (-4) > 7 + (-4) \quad \text{Using the addition property, adding } -4$$
$$x > 3$$

The solution set is $\{x | x > 3\}$.
The graph is as follows.

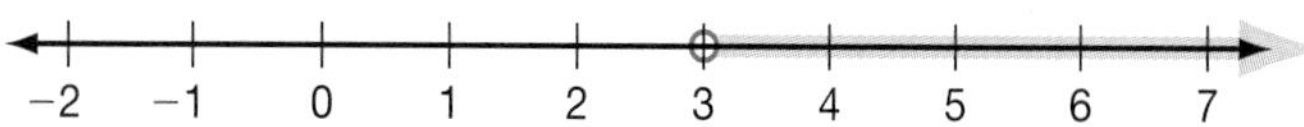

In Example 6, every number greater than 3 was a solution. Because there are many solutions to an inequality, we cannot check all the solutions by substituting into the original inequality as we do for equations. We can check our calculations by substituting for the variable in the original inequality at least one number from the proposed solution set.

Quick Review

Remember that if $a < b$, it is also true that $b > a$.

Try This Solve. Then graph.

g. $x + 6 > 9$ **h.** $10 \geq x + 7$ **i.** $3x - 1 \leq 2x - 3$

PART 3 The Multiplication Property

Objective: Solve inequalities using the multiplication property.

Consider the true inequality $4 < 9$.

If we multiply both numbers by 2, we get the true inequality $8 < 18$.

If we multiply both numbers by -3, we get the false inequality $-12 < -27$.

If we reverse the inequality symbol, we get the true inequality $-12 > -27$.

If we multiply both sides of a true inequality by a positive number, we get another true inequality. If we multiply by a negative number and reverse the inequality symbol, we get another true inequality.

Theorem 2-3

Multiplication Property of Inequality

If $a < b$ is true, then

$ac < bc$ is true for any positive real number c, and

$ac > bc$ is true for any negative real number c

Similar statements hold for $>$, $\leq$, and $\geq$.

When we solve an inequality using the multiplication property, we can multiply by any number except zero.

EXAMPLES Solve.

7

$$3y < \frac{3}{4}$$

$$\frac{1}{3} \cdot 3y < \frac{1}{3} \cdot \frac{3}{4} \quad \text{Multiplying by } \frac{1}{3}$$

$$y < \frac{1}{4}$$

Any number less than $\frac{1}{4}$ is a solution. The solution set is $\left\{y \middle| y < \frac{1}{4}\right\}$.

8

$$-4x < \frac{4}{5}$$

$$-\frac{1}{4} \cdot (-4x) > -\frac{1}{4} \cdot \frac{4}{5} \quad \text{Multiplying by } -\frac{1}{4} \text{ and reversing the inequality sign}$$

$$x > -\frac{1}{5}$$

Any number greater than $-\frac{1}{5}$ is a solution. The solution set is $\left\{x \middle| x > -\frac{1}{5}\right\}$.

Try This Solve.

j. $5y \leq \frac{3}{2}$ **k.** $-2y > \frac{5}{6}$ **l.** $-\frac{1}{3}x \leq -4$

PART 4 Using the Properties Together

Objective: Solve inequalities using both the addition and multiplication properties.

We use addition and multiplication properties together in solving inequalities in much the same way as for equations.

EXAMPLE 9 Solve.

$$16 - 7y \geq 10y - 4$$

$$-16 + 16 - 7y \geq -16 + 10y - 4 \quad \text{Adding } -16$$

$$-7y \geq 10y - 20$$

$$-10y - 7y \geq -10y + 10y - 20 \quad \text{Adding } -10y$$

$$-17y \geq -20$$

$$-\frac{1}{17} \cdot (-17y) \leq -\frac{1}{17} \cdot (-20) \quad \text{Multiplying by } -\frac{1}{17} \text{ and reversing the inequality sign}$$

$$y \leq \frac{20}{17} \quad \text{The solution set is } \left\{y \middle| y \leq \frac{20}{17}\right\}.$$

Try This Solve.

m. $6 - 5y \geq 7$ **n.** $3x + 5x < 4$ **o.** $17 - 5y \leq 8y - 5$

2-4 Exercises

Extra Help On the Web

Look for worked-out examples at the Prentice Hall Web site.
www.phschool.com

A

Mental Math Determine whether the specified number is a solution of the inequality.

1. $2y - 5 > -10; 3$ **2.** $5y - 2 > 3y + 8; 8$ **3.** $6 - y < 9; -3$

Graph.

4. $x \leq 4$ **5.** $y < -1$ **6.** $x > 5$ **7.** $x \geq 3$

Solve.

8. $x + 8 > 3$ **9.** $x + 5 > 2$ **10.** $y + 3 < 9$ **11.** $t + 14 \geq 9$

12. $x - 9 \leq 10$ **13.** $y - 8 > -14$ **14.** $8x \geq 24$ **15.** $0.5x < 25$

16. $-9x \geq -8.1$ **17.** $-8y \leq 3.2$ **18.** $-\frac{3}{4}x \geq -\frac{5}{8}$ **19.** $-\frac{5}{6}y \leq -\frac{3}{4}$

20. $2x + 7 < 19$ **21.** $5y + 13 > 28$ **22.** $5y + 2y \leq -21$

23. $-9x + 3x \geq -24$ **24.** $2y - 7 < 5y - 9$ **25.** $8x - 9 < 3x - 11$

26. $0.4x + 5 \leq 1.2x - 4$ **27.** $0.2y + 1 > 2.4y - 10$

28. ***Error Analysis*** Jadranko says the solution to $y - 9 > -18$ is $y < -9$. What error has he made?

B

Solve.

29. $3x - \frac{1}{8} \leq -\frac{3}{8} + 3x$ **30.** $2x - 3 < \frac{13}{4}x + 10 - 1.25x$

31. $4(3y - 2) \geq 9(2y + 5)$ **32.** $4m + 5 \geq 14(m - 2)$

33. ***Critical Thinking*** Find two different inequalities whose solution sets contain all real numbers less than -5.

Challenge

Solve.

34. $(y + 3)(y - 3) < 0$ **35.** $y(y + 5) > 0$ **36.** $\frac{x + 3}{x - 3} > 0$ **37.** $\frac{x - 2}{x + 1} < 0$

38. Determine whether the statement is true. If false, give a counterexample.

a. For any real numbers a, b, c, and d, if $a < b$ and $c < d$, then $a - c < b - d$.

b. For any real numbers x and y, if $x < y$ then $x^2 < y^2$.

Mixed Review

Simplify. **39.** $a^5 \cdot a^{-3} \cdot a^2$ **40.** $(6x^3y^5)^2$ **41.** $(2m^5)^2$ **42.** $\frac{20n^{3t}}{5n^t}$ **43.** $\left(\frac{x^2}{y^2}\right)^3$ *1-8*

44. The sum of three consecutive integers is 65 more than twice the first integer. Find the three integers. *2-2*

2-5 Using Inequalities

What You'll Learn

1 To solve problems requiring inequalities

. . . And Why

To increase efficiency in solving problems by applying algebraic reasoning skills

PART 1 Using Inequalities to Solve Problems

Objective: Solve problems by translating to inequalities.

The Problem-Solving Guidelines can help when solving problems that translate to inequalities rather than to equations.

PROBLEM-SOLVING GUIDELINES

- Phase 1: UNDERSTAND the problem
  - What am I trying to find?
  - What data might I need?
  - Have I ever solved a similar problem?
- Phase 2: Develop and carry out a PLAN
  - What strategies might I use to solve the problem?
  - How can I correctly carry out the strategies I selected?
- Phase 3: Find the ANSWER and CHECK
  - Does the proposed solution check?
  - What is the answer to the problem?
  - Does the answer seem reasonable?
  - Have I stated the answer clearly?

EXAMPLE 1 In a history course there will be three tests. You must get a total score of 270 for an A. You get 91 and 86 on the first two tests. What score on the last test will give you an A?

UNDERSTAND the problem

Question: What test score will make the total 270 or more? — Clarifying the question

Data: The first two test scores are 91 and 86. — Identifying the given data

Develop and carry out a PLAN

Let x be your score on the last test. — Using a variable to represent what you are trying to find

$$\text{Total score} \geq 270$$ — Translating to an inequality

$$91 + 86 + x \geq 270$$ — Solving the inequality

$$177 + x \geq 270$$

$$x \geq 93$$

Find the ANSWER and CHECK

If the third score is 93, $91 + 86 + 93 = 270$ — Replacing x with 93

If the third score is greater than 93, say 95, $91 + 86 + 95 = 272$

The score on the third test must be at least 93 for you to receive an A. — The answer makes sense in the problem.

Quick Review

If the scores on 5 tests total 400 points, the average test score is $\frac{400}{5} = 80$.

Try This

a. In a chemistry course with five tests, a total of 400 points is needed to get a B. Your first four test scores are 91, 86, 73, and 79. What must you score on the last test to get a B?

EXAMPLE 2 On your new job you can be paid in one of two ways.

Plan A: A salary of \$1600 per month plus a commission of 4% of total sales

Plan B: A salary of \$1800 per month plus a commission of 6% of total sales over \$10,000

For what amount of total sales is Plan A better than Plan B, assuming that total sales are always more than \$10,000?

Understand the PROBLEM

Question: What total sales will make the pay for Plan A greater than the pay for Plan B? — Clarifying the question

Data: Plan A: \$1600/month salary plus 4% commission — Identifying the given data

Plan B: \$1800/month salary plus 6% commission on sales over \$10,000 — Interpreting the assumption

Develop and carry out a PLAN

Use x to represent the sales for the month.

Income from Plan A = $1600 + 4\%x$ — Writing an expression for the income from each plan

Income from Plan B = $1800 + (x - 10{,}000)6\%$

Income from Plan A > Income from Plan B — Translating to an inequality

$$1600 + 0.04x > 1800 + (x - 10{,}000)0.06$$
Recalling that % means times 0.01
$$1600 + 0.04x > 1200 + 0.06x$$
$$400 > 0.02x$$
$$20{,}000 > x$$

Find the ANSWER and CHECK

For total sales between \$10,000 and \$20,000, Plan A is better than Plan B. — The answer checks and makes sense in the problem.

Handymen are sometimes paid by the job and sometimes by the hour. See Try This **b.**

Extra Help On the Web

Look for worked-out examples at the Prentice Hall Web site.
www.phschool.com

Try This

b. A painter can be paid in two ways.
Plan A: \$500 plus \$45 per hour
Plan B: \$55 per hour
Suppose the job takes n hours. For what values of n is Plan A better for the painter?

2-5 Exercises

A

1. A car rents for \$23.95 per day, plus \$0.10 per mile. You are on a daily budget of \$76.00. Within what mileage must you stay to remain within budget?
2. You are taking a history course. There will be four tests. You have scores of 89, 92, and 95 on the first three. You must earn a total of 360 points to get an A. What score on the last test will give you an A?
3. You are going to invest \$25,000, part at 14% and part at 16%. What is the most that can be invested at 14% to make at least \$3600 interest per year?
4. You are going to invest \$20,000, part at 12% and part at 16%. What is the most that can be invested at 12% in order to make at least \$3000 interest per year?
5. In planning for a school dance, you find that one band will play for \$250, plus 50% of the total ticket sales. Another band will play for a flat fee of \$550. In order for the first band to produce more profit for the school than the other band, what is the highest price you can charge per ticket, assuming 300 people attend?
6. ***Multi-Step Problem*** On your new job, you can be paid in one of two ways.
Plan A: A salary of \$500 per month plus a commission of 4% of total sales
Plan B: A salary of \$750 per month plus a commission of 5% of total sales over \$8000
For what amount of total sales is Plan B better than Plan A, assuming that total sales are always more than \$8000?
7. ***Multi-Step Problem*** A chauffeur can be paid in two ways.
Plan A: \$500.00 plus \$9.00 per hour
Plan B: \$14.00 per hour
Suppose that the job takes n hours. For what values of n is Plan A better for the chauffeur than Plan B?
8. ***Estimation*** A mason can be paid in two ways.
Plan A: \$300.00 plus \$24.40 per hour
Plan B: \$38.80 per hour
Suppose that the job takes n hours. To the nearest 10 hours, estimate for what values of n plan B is better for the mason than Plan A.

B

9. An investment of P dollars made at the simple interest rate r for t years will grow to a total $T = P + Prt$. For an investment of \$10,000 to grow to at least \$12,000 in two years, what is the minimum interest rate at which it can be invested?

In a science course, you must average 89 for an A. Your first three tests were 75, 95, and 91.

10. If you have only one test remaining, what score do you need for an A?

11. If you have two tests remaining, what do you need to average on the two tests to receive an A?

12. After the first three tests, you find that you must average 90 or better on your remaining tests for an A. How many tests do you have left?

13. *Critical Thinking* Suppose that a machinist is manufacturing boxes of various sizes with rectangular bases. The length of a base must exceed the width by at least 3 cm, but the base perimeter cannot exceed 24 cm. What widths are possible?

Challenge

The formula $S = -16t^2 + v_0t + s_0$ tells the height at time t of a projectile fired vertically from height s_0 with initial velocity v_0.

Suppose a projectile is fired vertically from ground level at an initial velocity of 448 ft per second.

14. When will the projectile be higher than 3072 ft?

15. When, if ever, will the projectile's height exceed 10,000 ft?

A carpenter makes either a certain hourly rate of r dollars per hour, or a special rate that is \$5 per hour less if a fee of f dollars is paid first.

16. For what number of hours is the hourly rate cheaper?

17. Next year the fee will be doubled, but the discount will be \$7.50 per hour. For what number of hours will the special rate be cheaper?

18. *Error Analysis* A student gave "2, 4, 6" as the answer to the problem "Find three consecutive even integers such that 10 times the largest value exceeds the product of the other two by more than 40." Explain why the student's answer is not entirely correct.

Mixed Review

Solve. **19.** $2a + b = c$, for a

20. $x = \frac{1}{yz}$, for z

21. $ab + cd + ef = g$, for c

22. $A = 2\pi r + 2\pi rh$, for r 2-3

2-6 Compound Inequalities

What You'll Learn

1. To solve and graph conjunctions of inequalities
2. To solve and graph disjunctions of inequalities

. . . And Why

To solve more complex inequality problems

In mathematics and elsewhere, a **compound statement** may be composed of several shorter statements, each connected by the word *and* or the word *or*. A statement such as *The moon is red and the night is cold* may be true, depending upon whether the individual statements are true. Similarly, the **compound inequality** $x < 2$ *or* $x > 0$ may be true for a value of x, depending upon the truth of the individual statements.

PART 1 Conjunctions and Intersections

Objective: Solve and graph conjunctions of inequalities.

When two or more statements are joined by the word **and,** the new compound statement is called a **conjunction.** Here are some examples.

The moon is red *and* the night is cold.

$x + y = 5$ *and* $x - y = 2$

$-2 < x$ *and* $x < 1$

For a conjunction to be true, all of the individual statements must be true. Let's look at the solution sets of graphs of a conjunction and their individual statements.

$-2 < x$ *and* $x < 1$

$\{x \mid -2 < x\}$

−4 −3 −2 −1 0 1 2 3 4

$\{x \mid x < 1\}$

−4 −3 −2 −1 0 1 2 3 4

Reading Math

$\{x \mid x < 3\}$ is read "the set of real numbers x such that x is less than 3."

For a number to be a solution of the conjunction, it must be in both solution sets. The solution set of the conjunction contains the elements common to both of the individual solution sets.

$\{x \mid -2 < x \text{ and } x < 1\}$

−4 −3 −2 −1 0 1 2 3 4

The conjunction "$-2 < x$ *and* $x < 1$" can be abbreviated $-2 < x < 1$.

The set of common elements of two or more sets is called the **intersection** of the sets. For two sets A and B, we can represent the intersection by $A \cap B$. If sets have no common members, the intersection is the **empty set,** which can be represented by the symbol $\emptyset$.

The solution set of $-2 < x$ *and* $x < 1$ is the intersection of the solution sets.

$$\{x \mid -2 < x \text{ and } x < 1\} = \{x \mid -2 < x\} \cap \{x \mid x < 1\}$$

EXAMPLE 1 Graph $-3 \leq x < 4$.

The conjunction corresponds to an intersection of sets. The solution set is the intersection of the solution sets.

$$\{x \mid -3 \leq x\} \cap \{x \mid x < 4\}$$

The graph is the intersection of both individual graphs.

Graph of $\{x \mid -3 \leq x\}$

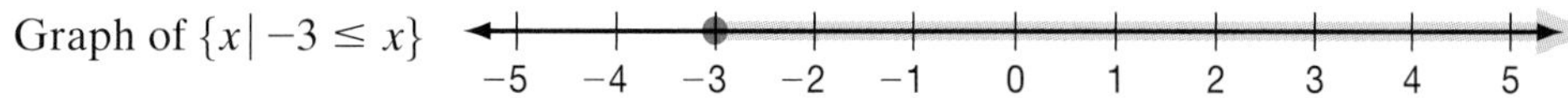

Graph of $\{x \mid x < 4\}$

−5 −4 −3 −2 −1 0 1 2 3 4 5

Graph of the intersection,

$\{x \mid -3 \leq x < 4\}$

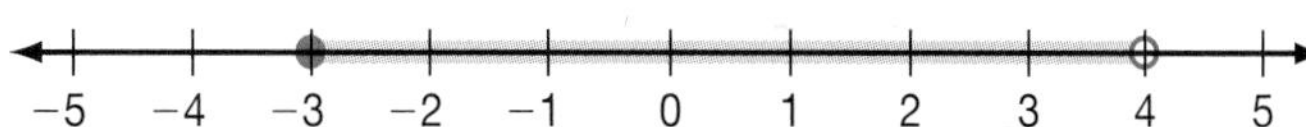

Try This Graph.

a. $-1 \leq x < 4$

b. $-2 < y < 5$

EXAMPLE 2 Solve.

$$-3 < 2x + 5 < 7$$

We write the conjunction with the word *and*

$$-3 < 2x + 5 \textit{ and } 2x + 5 < 7$$

We could solve the individual inequalities separately and abbreviate the answer.

$$\begin{array}{rcll} -3 < 2x + 5 & \text{and} & 2x + 5 < 7 & \\ -3 + (-5) < 2x + 5 + (-5) & \text{and} & 2x + 5 + (-5) < 7 + (-5) & \text{Adding } -5 \\ -8 < 2x & \text{and} & 2x < 2 & \\ -4 < x & \text{and} & x < 1 & \text{Multiplying by } \tfrac{1}{2} \\ & -4 < x < 1 & & \end{array}$$

Note that we did the same thing to each inequality in every step. We can simplify the procedure as follows.

$$\begin{array}{llll} -3 & < 2x + 5 & < 7 & \\ -3 + (-5) & < 2x + 5 + (-5) & < 7 + (-5) & \text{Adding } -5 \\ -8 & < 2x & < 2 & \\ -4 & < x & < 1 & \text{Multiplying by } \tfrac{1}{2} \end{array}$$

The solution set is $\{x \mid -4 < x < 1\}$.

Try This Solve.

c. $-2 \leq 3x + 4 \leq 7$

d. $4 \geq -x + 3 > -6$

Journal

Refer to Example 2 in Lesson 2-5. Test a value for *x*, and state what each plan would pay. Then write the complete solution as a conjunction.

PART 2

Disjunctions and Unions

Objective: Solve and graph disjunctions of inequalities.

When two or more statements are joined by the word **or** to make a compound statement, the new statement is called a **disjunction.** Here are some examples of disjunctions.

It is raining	*or*	the wind is blowing.
y is an even number	*or*	y is a prime number
$x < -3$	*or*	$x > 3$

For a disjunction to be true, *at least one* of the individual statements must be true. Let's look at the solution sets and graphs of a disjunction and its individual statements.

$x < -3$ *or* $x > 3$

$\{x|x < -3\}$

$\{x|x > 3\}$

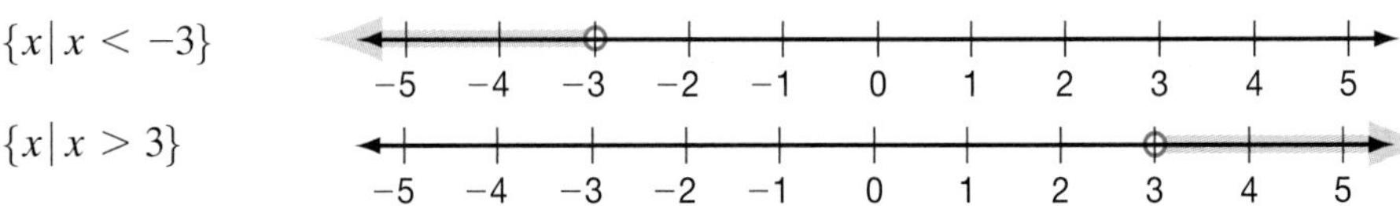

If a number is in *either* or *both* of the solutions sets, it is in the solution set of the disjunction. The solution set of the disjunction is the set we get by joining the other two sets.

$\{x|x < -3 \text{ or } x > 3\}$

The set obtained by joining two or more sets is called their **union.** For two sets A and B, we can name the union $A \cup B$. The solution set of $x < -3$ *or* $x > 3$ is the union.

$\{x|x < -3 \text{ or } x > 3\} = \{x|x < -3\} \cup \{x|x > 3\}$

EXAMPLE 3 Graph $x \leq 2$ or $x \geq 5$.

The graph consists of the union of their individual graphs.

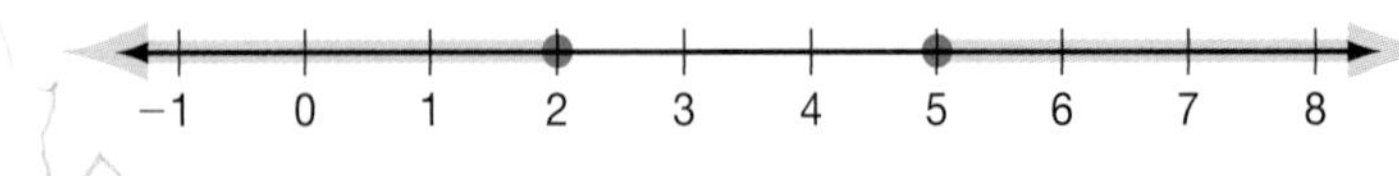

Try This Graph.

e. $x \leq -2$ or $x > 4$

f. $x < -4$ or $x \geq 6$

EXAMPLE 4 Solve $-2x - 5 \geq -2$ or $x - 3 > 2$.

We solve the individual inequalities separately, but we continue writing the word *or.*

$$-2x - 5 + 5 \leq -2 + 5 \quad \text{or} \quad x - 3 + 3 > 2 + 3$$
$$-2x \leq 3 \quad \text{or} \quad x > 5$$
$$x \leq -\frac{3}{2} \quad \text{or} \quad x > 5$$

The solution set is $\left\{x \middle| x \leq -\frac{3}{2} \text{ or } x > 5\right\}$.

Try This Solve.

g. $x - 4 < -3$ or $x - 4 \geq 3$

h. $-2x + 4 \leq -3$ or $x + 5 < 3$

2-6 Exercises

Extra Help On the Web
Look for worked-out examples at the Prentice Hall Web site.
www.phschool.com

A

Graph.

1. $1 < x < 6$

2. $0 \leq y \leq 3$

3. $-7 \leq y \leq -3$

4. $-9 \leq x < -5$

Solve.

5. $-2 < x + 2 < 8$

6. $-1 < x + 1 \leq 6$

7. $-10 \leq 3x - 5 \leq -1$

8. $-18 \leq -2x - 7 < 0$

9. $7 > -x + 7 > -7$

10. $-5 \geq -3x - 20 > -35$

Graph.

11. $x < -1$ or $x > 2$

12. $x < -2$ or $x > 0$

13. $x < -8$ or $x > -2$

14. $t \leq -10$ or $t \geq -5$

15. **TEST PREP** Which pair of numbers belongs to the solution set of $3 < 5x + 3 \leq 8$?

A. 0 and 8 **B.** $\frac{1}{2}$ and 1 **C.** $\frac{3}{5}$ and $\frac{8}{5}$ **D.** 0 and 1

Solve.

16. $x + 7 < -2$ or $x + 7 > 2$

17. $x + 9 < -4$ or $x + 9 > 4$

18. $2x - 8 \leq -3$ or $x - 8 \geq 3$

19. $x - 7 \leq -2$ or $3x - 7 \geq 2$

20. $3x - 9 < -5$ or $x - 9 > 6$

21. $4x - 4 < -8$ or $x - 4 > 12$

B

Solve.

22. $x \geq 2$ and $x > 5$

23. $x \geq 3$ and $x < -1$

24. $x \geq 4$ or $x > 1$

25. $x < 1$ or $x > -1$

26. $(x < 5$ or $x > 9)$ and $x < 0$

Solve.

27. $4a - 2 \leq a + 1 \leq 3a + 4$

28. $4m - 8 > 6m + 5$ or $5m - 8 < -2$

29. $-\frac{2}{15} \leq \frac{2}{3}x - \frac{2}{5} < \frac{2}{15}$

30. $2x - \frac{3}{4} < -\frac{1}{10}$ or $2x - \frac{3}{4} > \frac{1}{10}$

31. $3x < 4 - 5x < 5 + 3x$

32. $(x + 6)(x - 4) > (x + 1)(x - 3)$

Identify the following as *sometimes*, *always*, or *never* true for all real numbers a, b, and c.

33. If $b > c$ then $b \not\leq c$.

34. If $-b < -a$, then $a < b$.

35. If $c \neq a$, then $a < c$.

36. If $a < c$ and $c < b$, then $b \not\geq a$.

37. If $a < c$ and $b < c$, then $a < b$.

38. If $-a < c$ and $-c > b$, then $a < b$.

39. ***Critical Thinking*** Write a compound inequality that is the conjunction of two disjunctions.

Challenge

Solve.

40. $[4x - 2 < 8$ or $3(x - 1) < -2]$ and $-2 \leq 5x \leq 10$

41. $-2 \leq 4m + 3 < 7$ and $[m - 5 \leq 4$ or $3 - m > 12]$

42. $x + 4 < 2x - 6 \leq x + 12$

43. $x + \frac{1}{10} \leq -\frac{1}{10}$ or $x + \frac{1}{10} \geq \frac{1}{10}$

44. ***Mathematical Reasoning*** A certain conjunction is made up of p statements each separated by the word *and*.
    a. How many statements must be false for the conjunction to be false?
    b. How many statements must be true for the conjunction to be true?

45. ***Mathematical Reasoning*** A certain disjunction is made up of q statements, each separated by the word *or*.
    a. How many statements must be false for the disjunction to be false?
    b. How many statements must be true for the disjunction to be true?

Self-Test On the Web

Check your progress. Look for a self-test at the Prentice Hall Web site. www.phschool.com

Mixed Review

Evaluate. **46.** $-3t - 21$, for $t = -8$ **47.** $4|x + y|$, for $x = 3$, $y = -9$ *1-3*

48. $3(m - 5) + 2$, for $m = -1$ **49.** $3a(2b - 3c)$, for $a = 2$, $b = 3$, $c = -1$

Simplify. **50.** $(-3w)^2$ **51.** $-6(-4c)^2$ **52.** $(-4a^2b)^3$ **53.** $|-2048|$ *1-1, 1-8*

54. To run an ad in a local newspaper, you must pay \$100 for the design and \$25 per issue for each column inch. How much does it cost to run a 3-column-inch ad for 8 issues? *2-5*

Absolute Value

2-7

PART 1 Properties of Absolute Value

Objective: Simplify absolute value expressions.

We know that the **absolute value** of a number is its distance from 0 on a number line. We make our formal definition of absolute value as follows.

Definition

Absolute Value

For any real number x,

$|x| = x$ if x is nonnegative, and
$|x| = -x$ (the inverse of x) if x is negative.

The absolute value of a nonnegative number is the number itself. The absolute value of a negative number is the additive inverse of that number, which is always positive.

$$|5| = 5 \quad |0| = 0 \quad |-8| = 8$$

There are certain properties of absolute value that can be proved using the definition. They are stated in the next theorem.

Theorem 2-4

Properties of Absolute Value

A. For all real numbers a and b, $|ab| = |a| \cdot |b|$.

(The absolute value of a product is the product of the absolute values.)

B. $\left|\frac{a}{b}\right| = \frac{|a|}{|b|}$ assuming that $b \neq 0$.

(The absolute value of a quotient is the quotient of the absolute values.)

C. $|a^n| = a^n$ if n is an even integer.

(The absolute value of an even power is that power.)

Theorem 2-4 can be used to simplify expressions containing absolute value. To simplify, leave as little as possible within absolute value signs.

What You'll Learn

1. To simplify absolute value expressions
2. To use absolute value to find the distance between two points on the number line
3. To solve and graph absolute value sentences

. . . And Why

To solve problems involving absolute value

EXAMPLES Simplify.

1 $|5x| = |5| \cdot |x| = 5|x|$

2 $|x^2| = x^2$

3 $|x^2y^3| = |x^2y^2y| = |x^2| \cdot |y^2| \cdot |y| = x^2y^2|y|$

4 $\left|\frac{x^2}{y}\right| = \frac{|x^2|}{|y|} = \frac{x^2}{|y|}$

5 $|-5x| = |-5| \cdot |x| = 5|x|$

Try This Simplify.

a. $|7x|$ **b.** $|x^8|$ **c.** $|5a^2b|$ **d.** $\left|\frac{7a}{b^2}\right|$ **e.** $|-9x|$

PART 2 Distance on a Number Line

Objective: Find the distance between two points using absolute value.

On a number line, the number that corresponds to a point is called its **coordinate.** To find the **distance** between two points, we can subtract their coordinates and take the absolute value of the result, since distance is always nonnegative. For example, the distance from 2 to −3 on a number line is $|-3 - 2|$ or $|-5|$, which is 5.

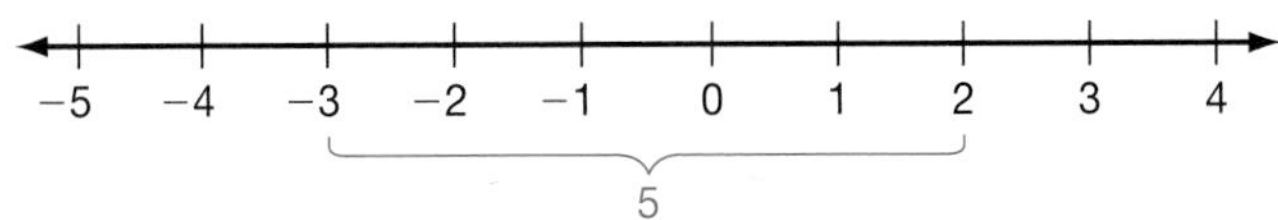

Note that we could have found this distance by subtracting in the reverse order, $|2 - (-3)| = |5| = 5$.

Definition

The **distance** between any two points on a number line having coordinates a and b is $|a - b|$ or $|b - a|$.

EXAMPLE 6 Find the distance between points having coordinates 10 and 3.

The distance is $|10 - 3|$, or $|7|$, which is 7.

EXAMPLE 7 Find the distance between points having coordinates −92 and −8.

The distance is $|-92 - (-8)|$, which is $|-84|$, or 84.

Try This Find the distance between points having the given coordinates.

f. −6, −35 **g.** 19, 14 **h.** −3, 17

PART 3 Equations and Inequalities with Absolute Value

Objective: Solve and graph equations and inequalities involving absolute value.

To solve equations or inequalities with absolute value, it may help to think about distance on a number line.

EXAMPLE 8 Solve $|x| = 4$. Then graph the solution set using a number line.

The solutions of the equation are those numbers x whose distance from 0 is 4. The solution set is $\{4, -4\}$. The graph consists of just two points as shown.

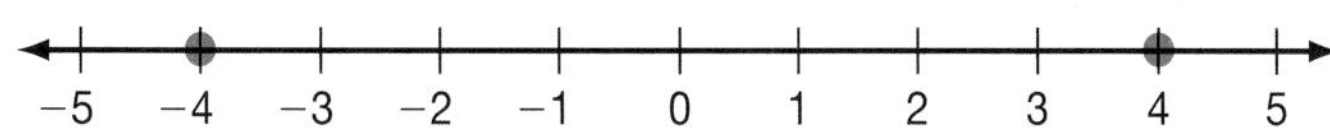

Try This Solve. Then graph using a number line.

i. $|x| = 6$ **j.** $|x| = \frac{1}{2}$

EXAMPLE 9 Solve $|x| < 4$. Then graph the solution set.

The solutions of $|x| < 4$ are those numbers whose distance from 0 is less than 4. The solution set is $\{x| -4 < x < 4\}$. The graph is as follows.

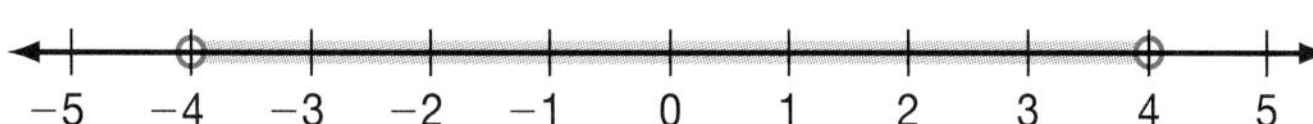

Try This Solve. Then graph.

k. $|x| < 5$ **l.** $|x| \leq 6.5$

EXAMPLE 10 Solve $|x| \geq 4$. Then graph the solution set.

The solutions of $|x| \geq 4$ are those numbers whose distance from 0 is greater than or equal to 4; in other words, those numbers x such that $x \leq -4$ or ≥ 4. The solution set is $\{x| x \leq -4 \text{ or } x \geq 4\}$. The graph is as follows.

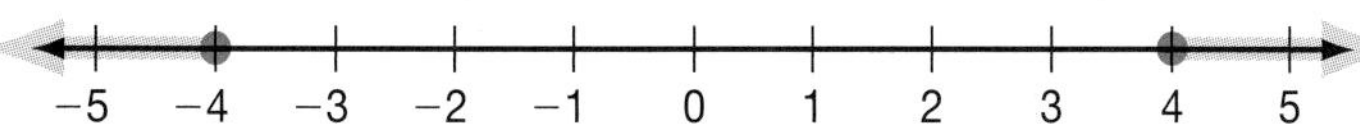

Try This Solve. Then graph the solution set.

m. $|y| \geq 8$ **n.** $|x| > \frac{1}{2}$

Examples 8–10 illustrated three cases of solving equations and inequalities with absolute value. The following theorem gives the general principles for solving.

Reading Math

Read "$-b$" as "the opposite of b" or "the negative of b" or "the additive inverse of b," not "minus b" or "negative b."

Theorem 2-5

Principles for Solving Absolute Value Sentences

For any positive number b and any expression $|N|$

A. The solutions of $|N| = b$ satisfy $N = -b$ or $N = b$.

B. The solutions of $|N| < b$ satisfy $-b < N < b$.

C. The solutions of $|N| > b$ satisfy $N < -b$ or $N > b$.

EXAMPLES Solve. Then graph.

11 $|5x - 4| = 11$ — $|N| = b$, where N is $5x - 4$ and b is 11.

$5x - 4 = 11$ or $5x - 4 = -11$ — Using Theorem 2-5A

$5x = 15$ or $5x = -7$ — Adding 4 to both sides

$x = 3$ or $x = -\frac{7}{5}$ — Multiplying both sides by $\frac{1}{5}$

The solution set is $\left\{3, -\frac{7}{5}\right\}$.

Here is the graph of the solution set.

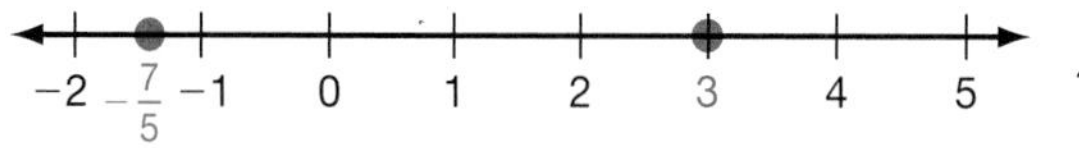

12 $|3x - 2| < 4$ — $|N| < b$, where N is $3x - 2$ and b is 4.

$-4 < 3x - 2 < 4$ — Using Theorem 2-5B

$-2 < 3x < 6$ — Adding 2

$-\frac{2}{3} < x < 2$ — Multiplying by $\frac{1}{3}$

The graph is as follows.

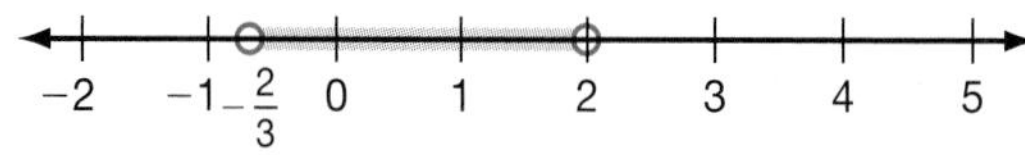

13 $|4x + 2| \geq 6$ — $|N| \geq b$, where N is $4x + 2$ and b is 6.

$4x + 2 \leq -6$ or $4x + 2 \geq 6$ — Using Theorem 2-5C

$4x \leq -8$ or $4x \geq 4$ — Adding -2

$x \leq -2$ or $x \geq 1$ — Multiplying by $\frac{1}{4}$

The graph is as follows.

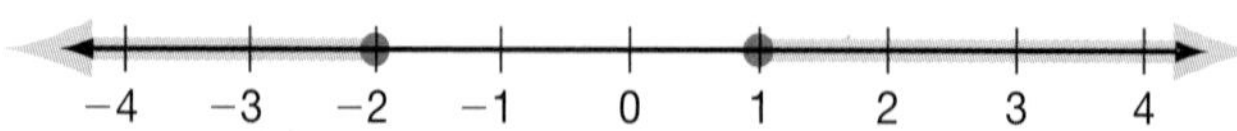

Try This Solve. Then graph.

o. $|3x + 4| = 9$ **p.** $|2x - 3| \leq 7$ **q.** $|2x - 4| > 7$

2-7 Exercises

Extra Help On the Web

Look for worked-out examples at the Prentice Hall Web site.
www.phschool.com

A

Mental Math Simplify, leaving as little as possible inside absolute value signs.

1. $|3x|$ **2.** $|4x|$ **3.** $|y^8|$ **4.** $|x^6|$

5. $|9x^2y^3|$ **6.** $|10a^4b^7|$ **7.** $\left|\frac{a^2}{b}\right|$ **8.** $\left|\frac{y^4}{m}\right|$

9. $|-16m|$ **10.** $|-9t|$ **11.** $|t^3|$ **12.** $|p^5|$

Find the distance between the points having the given coordinates.

13. $-8, -42$ **14.** $-9, -36$ **15.** $26, 15$ **16.** $54, 18$

17. $-9, 24$ **18.** $-18, -37$ **19.** $-5, 0$ **20.** $0, 23$

Solve. Then graph.

21. $|x| = 3$ **22.** $|x| = 5$ **23.** $|x| < 3$ **24.** $|x| \leq 5$

25. $|x| \geq 2$ **26.** $|y| > 8$ **27.** $|t| \geq 5.5$ **28.** $|m| > 0$

29. $|x - 3| = 12$ **30.** $|3x - 2| = 6$ **31.** $|2x - 3| \leq 4$

32. $|5x + 2| \leq 3$ **33.** $|2y - 7| > 10$ **34.** $|3y - 4| > 8$

35. $|4x - 9| \geq 14$ **36.** $|9y - 2| > 17$ **37.** $|10x + 8| > 2$

B

Solve.

38. $|m + 5| + 9 \leq 16$ **39.** $|t - 7| + 3 \geq 4$

40. $|g + 7| + 13 = 4$ **41.** $2|2x - 7| + 11 = 25$

42. ***Critical Thinking*** Determine whether the absolute value of a difference is *sometimes*, *always*, or *never* the same as the difference of the absolute values.

Challenge

Solve.

43. $|3x - 4| > -2$ **44.** $|x - 6| \leq -8$ **45.** $\left|\frac{5}{9} + 3x\right| < \frac{1}{6}$

46. $1 - \left|\frac{1}{4}x + 8\right| > \frac{3}{4}$ **47.** $|x + 5| > x$ **48.** $2 \leq |x - 1| \leq 5$

49. $|7x - 2| = x + 4$ **50.** $|x - 1| - 2 = |2x - 5|$

51. $|x + 1| \leq |x - 3|$

Mixed Review

Simplify. **52.** $n^{-8} \cdot n^{12}$ **53.** $\frac{m^3}{m^5}$ **54.** $\frac{y^5}{y^{-3}}$ **55.** $\frac{-56w^8}{7n^6}$ *1-8*

Solve. **56.** $1.8t = -3.6$ **57.** $12c + 6 = 9c$ **58.** $5a - (3a - 10) = 4a$ *2-1*

Use the commutative and associative properties to write three equivalent expressions for each. **59.** $ab + (c + d)$ **60.** $x^2(yz \times xy)$ *1-3*

2-8 Proofs in Solving Equations

What You'll Learn

1. To prove conditional statements
2. To write and prove converses of statements
3. To solve algebraic sentences by proving a statement and its converse
4. To recognize whether an operation will produce equivalent statements

. . . And Why

To justify solutions of algebraic sentences

PART 1 Conditional Statements

Objective: Prove conditional statements.

If-then statements are important in mathematics. Here are some examples.

If $x = 1$, then $x + 1 = 2$.
If $x < 5$, then $x < 10$.
If a figure is a square, then it has four sides.

In a statement *If P, then Q,*

P is a sentence that follows *if*, and *Q* is a sentence that follows *then*. The sentence *P* is called the **antecedent,** and the sentence *Q* is called the **consequent.** If-then statements are also called **conditionals.**

To prove the conditional, we *suppose* or *assume* that the antecedent *P* is true. Then we try to show that it leads to *Q*. That allows us to conclude that the statement *If P, then Q* is true. Solving equations provides a good example of proving conditionals.

EXAMPLE 1 Prove the statement: *If* $5x + 4 = 24$, *then* $x = 4$.

We first assume that $5x + 4 = 24$ is true. We call such an assumption a **hypothesis.** Then we use equation-solving principles to arrive at $x = 4$. We use a **column proof** to list each statement and the theorems or axioms that allow us to make this statement.

Statement	Reason
1. $5x + 4 = 24$	1. Hypothesis (assumed true)
2. $5x = 20$	2. Using the addition property
3. $x = 4$	3. Using the multiplication property
4. If $5x + 4 = 24$, then $x = 4$.	4. Statements 1–3

Quick Review

The *consequent* is also called the *conclusion.*

Here is a proof written in paragraph form, called a **narrative proof.**

Suppose that $5x + 4 = 24$ is true. Then, by the addition property, adding -4 to both sides, it follows that $5x = 20$. By the multiplication property, multiplying both sides by $\frac{1}{5}$, we obtain $x = 4$. Therefore, if $5x + 4 = 24$, then $x = 4$, which was to be shown.

Try This Prove the following statements.

a. If $3x + 5 = 20$, then $x = 5$.

b. If $-3x + 8 > 23$, then $x < -5$.

PART 2 Converses

Objective: Write and prove converses of statements.

From a statement *If P, then Q* we can make a new statement by interchanging the antecedent and consequent. We get *If Q, then P*. The two statements are called **converses** of each other.

EXAMPLES Write the converse of each statement.

2 If $x = 2$, then $x + 3 = 5$. The converse is: If $x + 3 = 5$, then $x = 2$.

3 If $x < 5$, then $x < 10$. The converse is: If $x < 10$, then $x < 5$.

4 If an animal is a cat, then it has four legs. The converse is: If an animal has four legs, then it is a cat.

Try This Write the converse of each statement.

c. If $3x + 7 = 37$, then $x = 10$.
d. If $x > 15$, then $x > 12$.

What does an if-then statement tell us? Consider the statement *If* $x < 5$, *then* $x < 10$. This statement is true. It tells us that any replacement for x that makes the antecedent true, also must make the consequent true. It does *not* tell us what happens if the antecedent is false. Let's try some substitutions.

	Antecedent	Consequent
x	$x < 5$	$x < 10$
3	$3 < 5$ true	$3 < 10$ true
6	$6 < 5$ false	$6 < 10$ true
15	$15 < 5$ false	$15 < 10$ false

Now let's look at the converse: *If* $x < 10$, *then* $x < 5$. This converse is false. For the replacement 7, we have a true antecedent and a false consequent. That can happen only when the conditional is *false*. Converses of true conditionals may not be true. We have just seen an example in which the converse is not true.

	Antecedent	Consequent
x	$x < 10$	$x < 5$
20	$20 < 10$ false	$20 < 5$ false
7	$7 < 10$ true	$7 < 5$ false
3	$3 < 10$ true	$3 < 5$ true

What is the converse of *If it is raining, then I use my umbrella*?

nsider the statement *If* $5x + 4 = 24$, *then* $x = 4$. We know this statement is true because we proved it in Example 1. Therefore, any number that makes $5x + 4 = 24$ true must also make $x = 4$ true. Let's prove the converse.

EXAMPLE 5 Prove: If $x = 4$, then $5x + 4 = 24$. We reverse the steps of Example 1.

1. $x = 4$	1. Hypothesis
2. $5x = 20$	2. Using the multiplication property
3. $5x + 4 = 24$	3. Using the addition property
4. If $x = 4$, then $5x + 4 = 24$.	4. Statements 1–3

Any number that makes $x = 4$ true must also make $5x + 4 = 24$ true.

Try This

e. In Try This **a**, you proved *if* $3x + 5 = 20$, *then* $x = 5$. Prove the converse.
f. In Try This **b**, you proved *if* $-3x + 8 > 23$, *then* $x < -5$.
(1) Prove the converse.
(2) Describe the solution sets of the antecedent and consequent.

PART 3 Solving Equations and Inequalities

Objective: Solve equations and inequalities by proving a statement and its converse.

When we solve an equation or inequality, in effect we write a proof. We start with the sentence to be solved, using it as a hypothesis. From that hypothesis, we try to obtain a very simple statement with an obvious solution set.

EXAMPLE 6 Solve.

$6x - 2 = 28$ Hypothesis
$6x = 30$ Using the addition property
$x = 5$ Using the multiplication property

The statement $x = 5$ has an obvious solution set, $\{5\}$. What about the solution set of $6x - 2 = 28$? We can prove the converse or we can check by substituting. For inequalities, we cannot check by substituting because the solution sets are infinite.

EXAMPLE 7 Solve $3x + 5 < 29$ by proving a statement and its converse.

(a) We prove this statement: *If* $3x + 5 < 29$, *then* $x < 8$. We abbreviate the writing as we ordinarily do in solving.

$3x + 5 < 29$ Hypothesis
$3x < 24$ Using the addition property
$x < 8$ Using the multiplication property

(b) We prove this statement: If $x < 8$, then $3x + 5 < 29$, also abb
the writing.

$x < 8$	Hypothesis
$3x < 24$	Using the multiplication property
$3x + 5 < 29$	Using the addition property

Since we have proved a statement and its converse, we know $3x + 5 < 29$ and $x < 8$ have the same solution set. Therefore, the solution set of $3x + 5 < 29$ is $\{x | x < 8\}$.

Try This

g. Solve $7x - 1 > 34$ by proving a statement and its converse.
h. Solve $9x - 5 = 103$
 (1) by proving a statement and its converse.
 (2) by proving a statement and then substituting.

PART 4 Equivalent Statements

Objective: Recognize whether an operation will produce equivalent statements.

Equivalent equations or **equivalent inequalities** have the same solution set. If in solving we know which manipulations give us equivalent statements, we can cut down on the work of proving converses.

Theorem 2-6

The use of the addition and multiplication properties of equality and inequality produces equivalent statements under the following conditions.
A. The expression added or multiplied must be defined for all replacements.
B. The expression by which we multiply must never have the value 0.

According to Theorem 2-6, whenever we add any constant or multiply by any nonzero constant, we obtain equivalent statements. Thus when solving simple equations or inequalities, we can depend on Theorem 2-6 and need not actually prove a converse.

EXAMPLE 8 To show that multiplying by 0 can be troublesome, "prove" that $x = 1$ and $x^2 = x$ are equivalent.

$x = 1$	
$x^2 = x$	Multiplying both sides by x

The solution set of $x = 1$ is $\{1\}$. The solution set of $x^2 = x$ is $\{0, 1\}$. The statements are *not* equivalent.

EXAMPLES Which of the following will be certain to produce an equivalent equation or inequality?

9 adding $\frac{1}{x}$ to both sides — No, x cannot be zero.

10 adding $3x - 3x$ to both sides — Yes

11 multiplying both sides by $x + 2$ — No, the expression could have the value 0.

12 multiplying both sides by $x^2 + 1$ — Yes, the expression will always be nonzero.

13 multiplying both sides by $\frac{3}{x} + 2$ — No, the expression could be undefined.

Try This Which of the following will be certain to produce an equivalent equation or inequality?

i. multiplying both sides by 5
j. multiplying both sides by $3x - 3x$
k. adding $\frac{x}{1} - x$ to both sides
l. adding 7 to both sides
m. multiplying both sides by $x + 5$
n. multiplying both sides by $\frac{1}{x} + 27$

Extra Help On the Web

Look for worked-out examples at the Prentice Hall Web site.
www.phschool.com

2-8 Exercises

A

Prove the following.

1. If $7x - 12 = 37$, then $x = 7$.
2. If $5y + 16 = 88 - 3y$, then $y = 9$.
3. If $15x - 5 \geq 11 - 2x$, then $x \geq \frac{16}{17}$.
4. If $13x + 12 < 15x - 7$, then $x > \frac{19}{2}$.

Write the converse of each statement.

5. If $3y = 5$, then $6y = 10$.
6. If $5x + 3 = 17$, then $2x + 5 = 14$.
7. If $x < 12$, then $x < 20$.
8. If $3y + 5 > 17 - y$, then $4y + 2 < 8y + 1$.

Write the converse of each statement, and then prove it. Compare with Exercises 1–4.

9. If $7x - 12 = 37$, then $x = 7$.
10. If $5y + 16 = 88 - 3y$, then $y = 9$.
11. If $15x - 5 \geq 11 - 2x$, then $x \geq \frac{16}{17}$.
12. If $13x + 12 < 15x - 7$, then $x > \frac{19}{2}$.

Solve by proving a statement and its converse.

13. $3x - 2 < 5x + 7$
14. $4y + 5 \geq 7y - 2$
15. $16x + 3 = 2x - 5$
16. $6y - 12 = 8y + 2$

Solve by proving a statement and then substituting.

17. $14x - 12 = 16x + 5$

18. $-5y + 7 = 10y - 14$

Which of the following will be certain to produce an equivalent equation or inequality?

19. multiplying both sides by x^2

20. adding $3 - x^2$ to both sides

21. adding $\frac{x - 2}{x + 3}$ to both sides

22. multiplying both sides by $\frac{1}{x^2 + 1}$

B

23. Prove the addition property of equality.

24. Prove the multiplication property of equality.

25. Prove the property of zero products.

26. *Critical Thinking* Write a conditional statement that has a true converse; a false converse.

Challenge

To prove the addition property and the multiplication property of inequality, we need another definition and an additional axiom for real numbers. We may also need to use the fact that $a > b$ and $b < a$ are equivalent statements.

Definition

For any real numbers a and b, $a < b$ is true if and only if $b - a > 0$.

Trichotomy

For any real number a, one and only one of the following is true.

a. $a > 0$ **b.** $a = 0$ **c.** $a < 0$

27. Prove the transitive property of inequality. (For any real numbers a, b, and c, if $a < b$ and $b < c$, then $a < c$.)

28. Prove the addition property of inequality.

29. Prove the multiplication property of inequality.

For each statement, rewrite in *if . . . then* form and then write the converse.

30. Integers are rational numbers.

31. Quitters never win.

32. Use the addition property to prove that $a > b$ and $-a < -b$ are equivalent.

Mixed Review

Evaluate for $m = \frac{1}{2}$. **33.** m^3 **34.** $m - \frac{4}{5}$ **35.** $\frac{m}{3}$ **36.** $\frac{1}{3} + 3m$ *1-3*

Solve. **37.** $16n + 8n = 312$ **38.** $-16 = 4c + 6$ **39.** $r - 16r = 645$ *2-1*

2-9  Reasoning Strategies

What You'll Learn

1. To solve problems using the strategy *Try, Test, Revise*

. . . And Why

To increase efficiency in solving problems by applying reasoning skills

PART 1 Try, Test, Revise

Objective: Solve problems using the strategy *Try, Test, Revise* and other strategies.

PROBLEM-SOLVING GUIDELINES
■ UNDERSTAND the problem
■ Develop and carry out a PLAN
■ Find the ANSWER and CHECK

Some problems can be solved by choosing a possible solution, testing it, and, if necessary, using information gained from the test to revise the possible solution. This strategy for solving problems is called *Try, Test, Revise.*

EXAMPLE 1 Use the *Try, Test, Revise* strategy to solve this problem.

A company received an electric bill of $109 for one month. The bill is shown at the left. The manager of the company told the employees that the electric bill needed to be cut exactly in half the next month. How many kilowatt hours did they need to use to have a bill half as large?

ELECTRIC BILL	
1st 600 kWh @ 4¢ each =	$ 24
Next 850 kWh @ 10¢ each =	$ 85
TOTAL =	$109

You can see that the number of kilowatt hours used must be greater than 600, since $24.00 is less than half of $109.00. Half of $109.00 is $54.50 ($109 \div 2 = 54.5$).

Try: 800 kWh	600 kWh @ 4¢ each = 600(0.04) = 24.00
	200 kWh @ 10¢ each = 200(0.10) = 20.00
	TOTAL = $44

Since $44.00 is less than $54.50, the possible solution of 800 kWh was too low. The next try should be higher.

Try: 1000 kWh	600 kWh @ 4¢ each = 600(0.04) = 24.00
	400 kWh @ 10¢ each = 400(0.10) = 40.00
	TOTAL = $64

Since $64.00 is greater than $54.50, the possible solution of 1000 kWh was too high. The next try should be less than 1000 but greater than 800.

If you continue this process of trying, testing, and revising, you can quickly find that the correct number of kilowatt hours used is 905.

Example 1 shows an important fact about solving problems in mathematics. The missing number in this problem was found using the *Try, Test, Revise* strategy. The missing number could also have been found using equation-solving techniques. Many problems in mathematics can be solved correctly in more than one way.

For some problems, there may be no solution. For others, several solutions are possible. In the following example, the strategy *Try, Test, Revise* is used to show that no solution is possible.

EXAMPLE 2 The cost of 3 different sandwiches on a menu are roast beef \$3.25, cheese \$2.75, and Reuben \$3.75. Carola bought 2 sandwiches with a \$10 bill and received \$4.25 change. Which sandwiches did she buy?

Try: 2 cheese sandwiches $2 \times \$2.75 = \$5.50$, $\$10 - \$5.50 = \$4.50$
\$4.50 is too much change. The next most expensive sandwich is roast beef.

Try: 1 cheese sandwich, 1 roast beef sandwich
$\$3.25 + \$2.75 = \$6$, $\$10 - \$6 = \$4$

\$4 is not enough change. Every other combination of sandwiches is more expensive, so less change than \$4 is returned. Thus there is no solution.

Reasoning Strategies

Write an Equation	Draw a Diagram	Try, Test, Revise
Make an Organized List	Make a Table	Look for a Pattern
Use Logical Reasoning	Simplify the Problem	Work Backward

2-9 Problems

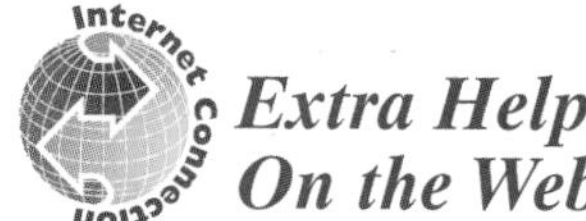

Look for worked-out examples at the Prentice Hall Web site.
www.phschool.com

Solve using one or more of the strategies presented so far.

1. Solve Example 1 above using the strategy *Write an Equation*.
2. Three computers were on sale. Model E computer was priced at $\frac{1}{3}$ the price of Model C, and Model P was priced at $\frac{1}{2}$ the price of Model E. One business bought one of each type of computer on sale and paid a total of \$1800, not including tax. What was the sale price of each computer?
3. The number of cable television subscribers in a particular city has been increasing at a rate of about 15% every 2 years. The company expects this rate to continue for at least the next 10 years. There are 275 subscribers in the city this year. About how many subscribers does the company predict there will be in 4 years?
4. ***Write a Convincing Argument*** Write an argument to explain to a classmate how to determine the greatest number of pieces into which a pie can be cut with four straight cuts. (The pieces may not be stacked.)
5. Two friends planned an 80-km walk/bike-a-thon. They wanted to start and arrive at the same time. The bike would only carry one person at a time. They decided that one of them would ride a certain distance, then leave the bike for the other and continue walking. Both walk at the same rate of speed and both ride at the same rate of speed. At what distances should the bicycle be left so that each person walks twice and rides twice?

Application

Helicopter Flight Time

This United States Coast Guard rescue helicopter can carry all sorts of cargo. For what distances is external loading preferable if the internal loading time is $\frac{1}{7}$ hr and the external loading time is $\frac{1}{10}$ hr?

Some helicopters can carry cargo internally, inside the body of the aircraft, or externally, strapped beneath or to the side of the body. When the cargo is carried externally, the airspeed is decreased because of drag on the helicopter. However, loading and unloading for cargo carried externally is much faster.

Suppose that cargo can be loaded by either of the two methods, but not by a combination. When transporting cargo, how can delivery time be minimized?

EXAMPLE

A load of medical equipment is to be carried a distance of 80 miles and delivery time is to be minimized. Assume the following data.

	Average Speed (mi/h)	**Loading Time** (hr)	**Unloading Time** (hr)
Internal Load	140	$\frac{1}{4}$	$\frac{1}{4}$
External Load	100	$\frac{1}{12}$	$\frac{1}{12}$

The average speed when carrying the load internally is 140 mi/h. Thus it will take $\frac{80}{140}$ hours to travel 80 miles with only an internal load.

The total delivery time for an inside load is

loading time + flight time + unloading time =

$$\frac{1}{4} \quad + \quad \frac{80}{140} \quad + \quad \frac{1}{4} \quad = \frac{15}{14} \approx 1.07 \text{ hr}$$

The average speed when carrying the load externally is 100 mi/h. Thus it will take $\frac{80}{100}$ hours to travel 80 miles with only an external load.

The total delivery time for an outside load is

loading time + flight time + unloading time =

$$\frac{1}{12} \quad + \quad \frac{80}{100} \quad + \quad \frac{1}{12} \quad = \frac{29}{30} \approx 0.97 \text{ hr}$$

Therefore, to ship this cargo 80 miles, external loading is preferable.

Suppose we want to ship this same cargo 200 miles. We then have the following.

	Loading Time	+	Flight Time	+	Unloading Time	=	Delivery Time
Internal	$\frac{1}{4}$	+	$\frac{200}{140}$	+	$\frac{1}{4}$	=	$\frac{270}{14} \approx 1.9$ hr
External	$\frac{1}{12}$	+	$\frac{200}{100}$	+	$\frac{1}{12}$	=	$\frac{13}{6} \approx 2.2$ hr

Therefore, to ship this cargo 200 miles, internal loading is preferable.

Problems

1. Determine the preferable loading for shipping this cargo 140 miles.

2. Determine the preferable loading for shipping this cargo 110 miles.

3. Determine the preferable loading for shipping this cargo 118 miles.

Suppose the helicopter is to carry this cargo D miles. For which distances is internal loading preferable? For which distances is external loading preferable?

Total delivery time for external load

$$\frac{1}{12} + \frac{D}{100} + \frac{1}{12}$$

Total delivery time for internal load

$$\frac{1}{4} + \frac{D}{140} + \frac{1}{4}$$

Therefore, external loading is preferable to internal loading whenever

$$\frac{1}{12} + \frac{D}{100} + \frac{1}{12} < \frac{1}{4} + \frac{D}{140} + \frac{1}{4}$$

Solving this inequality we have

$$\frac{D}{100} + \frac{1}{6} < \frac{D}{140} + \frac{1}{2}$$

$$21D + 350 < 15D + 1050$$

Multiplying both sides by 2100, the LCM of 100, 6, 140, and 4

$$6D < 700$$

$$D < \frac{700}{6} \approx 117 \text{ miles.}$$

Therefore, for distances less than 117 miles, external loading is preferable. For distances of 117 miles or greater, internal loading is preferable.

Problems

The following data are for a helicopter and forest firefighting equipment.

	Average Speed (mi/h)	**Loading Time** (hr)	**Unloading Time** (hr)
Internal Load	200	$\frac{1}{4}$	$\frac{1}{4}$
External Load	150	$\frac{1}{8}$	$\frac{1}{8}$

4. Determine the preferable loading for shipping this cargo 100 miles.

5. Determine the preferable loading for shipping this cargo 250 miles.

6. Suppose the helicopter is to carry this cargo D miles. For which distances is internal loading preferable? For which distances is external loading preferable?

2 Chapter Wrap Up

Key Terms

absolute value (p. 87)
addition property of inequality (p. 74)
and (p. 82)
antecedent (p. 92)
clearing an equation of fractions or decimals (p. 62)
column proof (p. 92)
compound inequality (p. 82)
compound statement (p. 82)
conditional statement (p. 92)
conjunction (p. 82)
consequent (p. 92)
converse (p. 93)
coordinate (p. 88)
disjunction (p. 84)
distance (p. 88)
empty set (p. 82)
equivalent equations (p. 95)
equivalent inequalities (p. 95)
formula (p. 71)
hypothesis (p. 92)
if and only if (p. 63)
if-then statement (p. 92)
inequalities (p. 73)
intersection (p. 82)
is greater than (p. 73)
is less than (p. 73)
least common denominator (p. 62)

2-1

When solving equations, use the distributive property to remove parentheses, clear fractions or decimals, collect like terms on both sides of the equation, and use the addition and multiplication properties to solve for the variable.

Solve.

1. $\frac{1}{4} + \frac{1}{2}x = \frac{5}{4}$ **2.** $\frac{2}{3}x + \frac{1}{6} = 9$ **3.** $0.6x + 1.5 = 2.1$

4. $2.9y - 4.6 = 0.6y$ **5.** $300(x + 7) = 350$ **6.** $\frac{1}{4}(3x - 5) = 10 - \frac{3}{4}(x - 1)$

The **principle of zero products** states that $ab = 0$, if and only if $a = 0$ or $b = 0$.

Solve.

7. $(x + 4)(x - 3) = 0$ **8.** $(2x - 5)(3x + 4) = 0$

2-2

Drawing a diagram often helps when solving problems.

9. One angle of a triangle is five times as large as the first angle. The measure of the third angle is 2° less than that of the first angle. The sum of the measures of the angles in a triangle is 180°. How large are the three angles?

10. A retail store decreases the price of suits 20% to \$120. What is the former price?

2-3

To solve a **formula** for a given letter, use the same methods as for solving any equation.

11. Solve $A = \frac{1}{2}bh$, for b **12.** Solve $V = ab + at$, for a

2-4

If we multiply both sides of a true inequality by a positive number, we get another true inequality; if we multiply by a negative number, we must reverse the inequality symbol.

Solve and graph on a number line.

13. $y + 3 \geq 4$ **14.** $2x + 7 > x - 9$ **15.** $\frac{1}{3}x \geq -9$

16. $-9y \geq -45$ **17.** $-\frac{2}{3}x \geq -20$ **18.** $3x - 8 \leq 7x + 5$

2-5

Use the Problem-Solving Guidelines to solve problems involving inequalities.

19. Find all sets of three consecutive positive odd integers whose sum is less than 20 but greater than 10.

2-6

For a **conjunction** to be true, all of its individual statements must be true. For a **disjunction** to be true, at least one of its statements must be true.

Graph on a number line.

20. $-3 < x < 5$ 21. $x < -5$ or $x > 3$

Solve. Then graph.

22. $-7 < 2x - 1 < 3$ 23. $x + 1 < -1$ or $x + 1 > 2$

Simplify.

24. $|y^3|$ 25. $|x^3y|$ 26. $|3x^2y^2|$

Find the **distance** between points having these **coordinates.**

27. -9 and 17 28. -23 and -40 29. -18 and 3

2-7

The solutions of $|N| = b$ satisfy $N = -b$ or $N = b$, the solutions of $|N| < b$ satisfy $-b < N < b$, and the solutions of $|N| > b$ satisfy $N < -b$ or $N > b$.

Solve. Then graph.

30. $|x| = 6$ 31. $|y| < 4$ 32. $|x| \geq 2$

33. $|x - 3| \geq 5$ 34. $|3x + 5| < 7$

multiplication property of inequality (p. 75)
narrative proof (p. 92)
or (p. 84)
principle of zero products (p. 63)
Principles for solving absolute value sentences (p. 90)
Properties of absolute value (p. 87)
solution set (p. 73)
solved inequality (p. 73)
trichotomy (p. 97)
union (p. 84)

Internet Connection

Internet Activity On the Web

Look for extension problems for this chapter at the Prentice Hall Web site. www.phschool.com

Chapter Assessment

Solve.

1. $r - 17 = 20$ 2. $-9n = 450$ 3. $3y + 10 = 16$

4. $-2z + 5 = 7$ 5. $0.8x - 3.7 = 0.3$ 6. $\frac{1}{5}y - \frac{2}{3} = 6$

7. $8(x + 9) = 112$ 8. $8y - (5y - 9) = -160$ 9. $(3x + 5)(2x - 6) = 0$

10. $y + 5 \geq 8$ 11. $4x \geq 28$ 12. $-8y \leq -40$

13. $4 + 7y \leq 39$ 14. $2x - 9 \leq 9x + 4$ 15. $-4x - 6 > 7x - 14$

16. A 14-m piece of cable is cut into 2 pieces. One piece is 4 m longer than the other. How long are the pieces?

17. Solve $Q = P - Prt$, for P. 18. Simplify $|x^5y^4|$.

19. You have made scores of 81, 76, and 82 on three quizzes. What is the least you can make on the fourth quiz to have an average of at least 80?

20. Find the distance between points with coordinates 33 and -12.

Solve. Then graph.

21. $-3 < x + 1 < 8$ 22. $|y| \geq 8$ 23. $|x - 2| \leq 6$ 24. $|2x + 7| < 9$

CHAPTER 

What You'll Learn in Chapter 3

- How to graph relations and functions
- How to write equations of lines
- How to find and use the slope of a line
- How to find the composite of two functions

Skills & Concepts You Need for Chapter 3

1-1 Add.

1. $-4 + 0$ **2.** $-2 + (-7)$

3. $-2.7 + (-3.5)$ **4.** $15 + (-8)$

5. $-8.1 + 2.4$ **6.** $\frac{2}{3} + \left(-\frac{3}{5}\right)$

1-3 Evaluate each expression when $x = -2$, $y = 3$, and $z = -4$.

7. $y - xz$ **8.** $3x + 2y - z$

2-1 Solve.

9. $x + 8 = -12$ **10.** $3x = 21$ **11.** $4x - 5 = 11$

12. $9x - 2x = 21$ **13.** $7x - 4 + 2x = -8 - 3x + 6$

14. $r + \frac{5}{6} = -\frac{3}{12}$ **15.** $5t = -12$ **16.** $\frac{2}{3}x = 16$

17. $-4y - 3y = 28$ **18.** $8 - 5x = x - 14$ **19.** $8a = 3(a + 5)$

2-4 Solve.

20. $x + 2 < 6$ **21.** $y - 8 \geq 0$

22. $4y \leq -8$ **23.** $-5x > 10$

24. $3x - 1 > 8$ **25.** $2 + 7y \leq 3$

26. $4y - 1 < y + 2$ **27.** $x - 6 \geq 3x - 10$

Relations, Functions, and Graphs

Crickets chirp, but the rate of chirping depends on the temperature. In Lesson 3-8 we will establish some rules for determining an equation that will allow you to compute how many chirps can be expected for a given temperature.

3-1 Relations and Ordered Pairs

What You'll Learn

1. To find a Cartesian product
2. To list elements of a relation
3. To list the domain and range of a relation
4. To use set-builder notation

. . . And Why

To prepare to graph sets

PART 1 Cartesian Products

Objective: Find the Cartesian product of two sets.

Consider the following sets:

$A = \{\text{Justin, Ramon, Yung Su}\}$ $\quad B = \{\text{jeans, tee shirt}\}$

From these sets we can form a set of **ordered pairs,** choosing the first element from set A and the second element from set B.

{(Justin, jeans), (Justin, tee shirt),
(Ramon, jeans), (Ramon, tee shirt),
(Yung Su, jeans), (Yung Su, tee shirt)}

The set of all ordered pairs formed as above is called the **Cartesian product** and is denoted $\boldsymbol{A \times B}$. We read $A \times B$ as "A cross B." In general, $A \times B$ will not produce the same set of ordered pairs as $B \times A$.

Definition

The **Cartesian product** of two sets A and B, symbolized $\boldsymbol{A \times B}$, is the set of all ordered pairs having the first member from set A and the second member from set B.

The two sets used to find a Cartesian product may be the same.

EXAMPLE 1 Find the Cartesian product $Q \times Q$, where $Q = \{2, 3, 4, 5\}$.

The Cartesian product $Q \times Q$ is as follows.

$$\{(2, 2), (2, 3), (2, 4), (2, 5), \\ (3, 2), (3, 3), (3, 4), (3, 5), \\ (4, 2), (4, 3), (4, 4), (4, 5), \\ (5, 2), (5, 3), (5, 4), (5, 5)\}$$

Try This Find the following Cartesian products.

a. $A \times B$, where $A = \{d, e\}$ and $B = \{1, 2\}$
b. $C \times C$, where $C = \{x, y, z\}$

PART 2 Relations

Objective: List ordered pairs from a Cartesian product that satisfy a given relation.

In some Cartesian products we can select ordered pairs that make up a common relation, such as $<$, as in the following example.

EXAMPLE 2 In the Cartesian product $\{(1, 1), (1, 2), (1, 3), (2, 1), (2, 2), (2, 3)\}$, list the set of ordered pairs for which the first member is less than the second member.

$\{(1, 2), (1, 3), (2, 3)\}$

This set of ordered pairs is the relation *less than.*

Try This

c. In the Cartesian product of Example 2, list the set of ordered pairs for which the first member is the same as the second member. This is the relation *equals*.

Any set of ordered pairs selected from a Cartesian product is a relation.

Definition

A **relation** from set A to a set B is any set of ordered pairs in $A \times B$.

PART 3 Domain and Range

Objective: List the domain and the range of a relation.

Definition

The set of all first members in a relation is the **domain** of the relation. The set of all second members in a relation is the **range** of the relation.

EXAMPLE 3 List the domain and the range of the relation $<$ in Example 2.

Domain: $\{1, 2\}$; Range: $\{2, 3\}$

Try This

d. List the domain and the range of the relation $\{(a, 1), (b, 2), (c, 3), (e, 2)\}$.
e. List the domain and the range of the relation $\{(2, 2), (1, 1), (1, 2), (1, 3)\}$.

Reading Math

The vertical line used in set-builder notation to separate the variable and the description is read, "such that." $\{x|x < 3\}$ is read, "the set of elements (or numbers), x, *such that* x is less than 3."

PART 4 Set-Builder Notation

Objective: Use set-builder notation to describe a relation.

In a set or relation, we often need to refer to those elements that satisfy a certain condition. With respect to the set $\{1, 2, 3, 4, 5, 6\}$, we may refer to the set of all x such that x is greater than 3. The numbers 4, 5, and 6 satisfy this condition. Thus we write $\{x|x > 3\} = \{4, 5, 6\}$. $\{x|x > 3\}$ is **set-builder notation.**

EXAMPLE 4 Use the set $\{1, 2, 3, 4, 5, \ldots, 10\}$. Find $\{x|2 < x < 8\}$.

The numbers 3, 4, 5, 6, and 7 satisfy both conditions, $x < 8$ and $x > 2$.

$$\{x|2 < x < 8\} = \{3, 4, 5, 6, 7\}$$

EXAMPLE 5 Use the relation $Q \times Q$, where $Q = \{2, 3, 4, 5\}$. Find $\{(x, y)|y > x + 1\}$.

We check each ordered pair to find those that satisfy $y > x + 1$.

$$\{(x, y)|y > x + 1\} = \{(2, 5), (2, 4), (3, 5)\}$$

Try This

f. Use the set $\{1, 2, 3, \ldots, 10\}$. Find $\{x|5 < x < 7\}$.
g. Use the set $Q \times Q$, where $Q = \{2, 3, 4, 5\}$. Find $\{(x, y)|x > 2 \text{ and } y > 3\}$.

Extra Help On the Web

Look for worked-out examples at the Prentice Hall Web site.
www.phschool.com

3-1 Exercises

A

Mental Math Find the following Cartesian products.

1. $A \times B$ where $A = \{\text{chili, pizza, salad}\}$ and $B = \{\text{cheese, onions, peppers}\}$

2. $A \times B$ where $A = \{\text{omelette, scrambled}\}$ and $B = \{\text{bacon, sausage}\}$

3. $B \times C$, where $B = \{x, y, z\}$ and $C = \{1, 2\}$

4. $B \times C$, where $B = \{5, 7, 10\}$ and $C = \{a, z\}$

5. $D \times D$, where $D = \{5, 6, 7, 8\}$

6. $E \times E$, where $E = \{-2, 0, 2, 4\}$

Consider the relation $E \times E$, where $E = \{-7, -3, 1, 2, 5\}$. List the set of ordered pairs determined by the relations.

7. $<$ (less than) **8.** $>$ (greater than) **9.** $\leq$ (less than or equal)
10. $\geq$ (greater than or equal) **11.** $=$ (equal) **12.** $\neq$ (not equal)

List the domain and the range for each of the following relations.

13. $\{(5, 6)\}$ **14.** $\{(5, 2), (6, 4), (8, 6)\}$ **15.** $\{(7, 1), (8, 2), (9, 5)\}$

16. $\{(7, -4)\}$ **17.** $\{(6, 0), (7, 5), (8, 5)\}$ **18.** $\{(8, 2), (10, 1), (6, 3)\}$

19. $\{(8, 1), (8, 1), (5, 1)\}$ **20.** $\{(6, 2), (2, 0), (-3, 0)\}$

Use the set C, where $C = \{2, 4, 6, 8, 10, 12\}$. Find the set indicated by each of the following.

21. $\{x | x > 7\}$ **22.** $\{x | 3 < x < 10\}$ **23.** $\{x | x > 6 \text{ or } x < 3\}$

Consider the relation $A \times A$, where $A = \{2, 3, 4, 5\}$. Find the sets indicated by each of the following.

24. $\{(x, y) | x \leq 2 \text{ and } y \leq 3\}$ **25.** $\{(x, y) | x > 4 \text{ and } y < 4\}$

26. $\{(x, y) | 2 \leq x \leq 3 \text{ and } y = 3\}$ **27.** $\{(x, y) | x < 4 \text{ and } 4 \leq y \leq 5\}$

28. $\{(x, y) | x = 3 \text{ and } y = 2\}$ **29.** $\{(x, y) | 2 < x < 4 \text{ and } 2 < y < 5\}$

B

30. **a.** Find the Cartesian product $D \times D$ where $D = \{-1, 0, 1, 2\}$.
b. Find the set of ordered pairs determined by the relation $\neq$.
c. List the domain and the range of this relation.
d. Find $\{(x, y) | x^2 = y^2\}$.

31. **a.** Find the Cartesian product $E \times E$, where $E = \{-1, 1, 3, 5\}$.
b. Find the set of ordered pairs determined by the relation $\leq$.
c. List the domain and the range of this relation.
d. Find $\{(x, y) \,|\, |x| < |y|\}$.

32. ***Critical Thinking*** List three different relations that have the same domain and range.

Challenge

Consider the set of all ordered triples (x, y, z) where x, y, and z are real numbers. Every subset of $R \times R \times R$ is called a relation in $R \times R \times R$.

33. List any five ordered triples in $A = \{(x, y, z) | x = 3, y > 0 \text{ and } z = y^2\}$.

34. List any five ordered triples in $B = \{(x, y, z) | x = 2y, y < 0 \text{ and } z = y^3\}$.

Mixed Review

Evaluate for $a = 3, b = -5$. **35.** $(a + b)^2$ **36.** $4a - 3b$ *2-1*

Evaluate for $a = 4, b = -1$. **37.** b^a **38.** $-a|2b|$ *2-1*

Simplify. **39.** $c^{-4} \cdot c^3 \cdot c^7$ **40.** $(-4x^2y^{-3})(2x^3y^2)$ *1-8*

Solve and graph. **41.** $\left(\frac{1}{3}\right)y + 5 > \left(\frac{3}{4}\right)y$ **42.** $-4 < x - 3 < 5$ *2-6*

Solve. **43.** $-5t - \frac{1}{8} < \frac{1}{2} - 3t$ *2-4*

3-2  Graphs

What You'll Learn

1. To graph ordered pairs
2. To determine whether an ordered pair is a solution of an equation
3. To graph equations by plotting several solutions

. . . And Why

To prepare to graph lines

PART 1 Graphing Relations

Objective: Graph the ordered pairs of a relation.

Most of the relations we will work with involve $R \times R$, where R is the set of real numbers. The set R is infinite. Thus relations involving R may be infinite and therefore cannot be indicated by listing the ordered pairs. We can indicate such relations with a **graph.**

On a number line, each point corresponds to a number. On a plane, each point corresponds to an ordered pair of numbers from $R \times R$. To represent $R \times R$, we draw an **x-axis** and a **y-axis** perpendicular to each other. Their intersection is called the **origin** and is labeled 0. The arrows show the positive directions. This is called the **Cartesian coordinate system.** The figure below shows the graph of the relation $\{(4, 3), (-3, 5), (-4, -2), (3, -4)\}$.

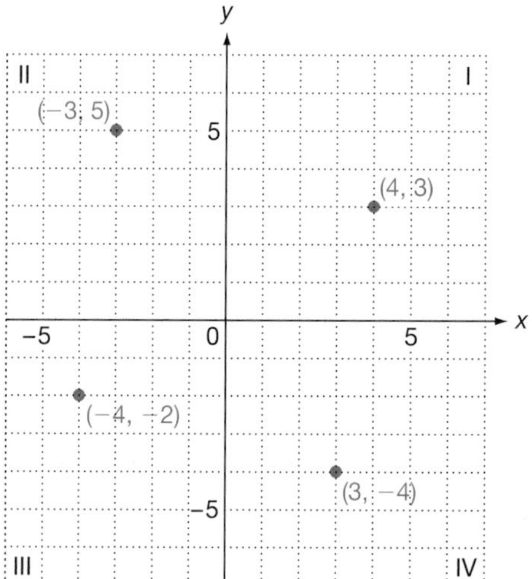

The first member of an ordered pair is called the **x-coordinate,** or **abscissa.** The second member is called the **y-coordinate,** or **ordinate.** Together these are called the **coordinates of a point.**

The axes divide the plane into four regions called **quadrants,** indicated by the Roman numerals numbered counterclockwise from the upper right.

To graph the relation, we plot the points that correspond to the ordered pairs in the relation.

EXAMPLE 1 Graph the relation $\{(-3, 2), (-1, -4), (4, 3), (5, 5)\}$.

For the ordered pair $(-3, 2,)$ the x-coordinate tells us to move 3 units to the left of the y-axis. The y-coordinate tells us to move 2 units up from the x-axis.

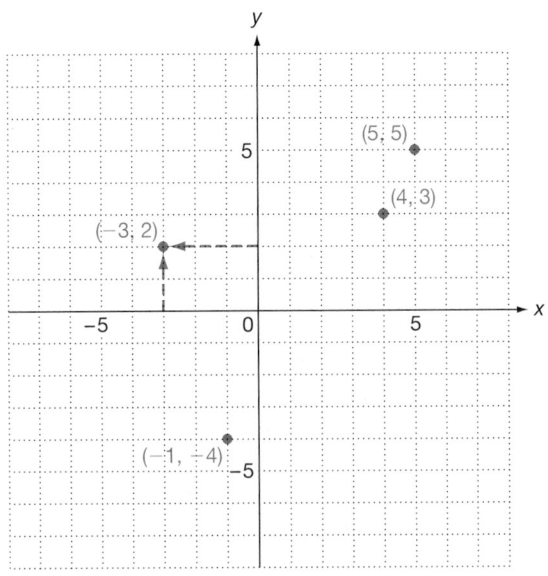

Try This Graph each relation.

a. $\{(-2, -2), (1, -4), (5, 6), (-3, 5), (0, 8)\}$
b. $\{(3, 2), (-5, 2), (-4, 3), (-4, 0), (3, -7)\}$

PART 2 Solutions of Equations

Objective: Determine whether an ordered pair is a solution of an equation.

If an equation has two variables, its solutions are ordered pairs of numbers. A **solution** is an ordered pair such that when the numbers are substituted for the variables, a true equation is produced.

EXAMPLE 2 Determine whether the given ordered pairs are solutions of this equation.

$(-1, -4)$ and $(7, 5)$; $y = 3x - 1$

y	$= \quad 3x - 1$	
-4	$3(-1) - 1$	Substituting -1 for x and -4 for y
-4	$-3 - 1$	
-4	-4 ✔	

The equation becomes true, so $(-1, -4)$ is a solution.

y	$=$	$3x - 1$	
5		$3 \cdot 7 - 1$	Substituting 7 for x and 5 for y
5		$21 - 1$	
5		20	

The equation becomes false, so $(7, 5)$ is not a solution.

Try This Determine whether the given ordered pairs are solutions of the indicated equation.

c. $(1, 7), (2, 9)$; $y = 2x + 5$
d. $(-1, 4), (0, 6)$; $y = -2x + 5$
e. $(-2, 5), (3, 9)$; $y = x^2$

PART 3 Graphing Equations

Objective: Graph equations by plotting several solutions.

The solutions of an equation with two variables are ordered pairs and thus determine a relation. Here are some general suggestions for graphing an equation.

Guidelines for Graphing

1. Use graph paper.
2. Label axes with symbols for the variables.
3. Use arrows to indicate positive directions.
4. Mark numbers on the axes for scale.
5. Plot solutions and complete the graph.
6. Label the equation or relation being graphed.

EXAMPLE 3 Graph $y = 3x - 1$.

Find some ordered pairs that are solutions. We can choose *any* number that is a possible replacement for x and then determine y.

Let $x = 0$.
Then $y = 3(0) - 1 = -1$.
So $(0, -1)$ is a solution.

Let $x = 1$.
Then $y = 3(1) - 1 = 2$.
So $(1, 2)$ is a solution.

Let $x = 2$.
Then $y = 3(2) - 1 = 5$.
So $(2, 5)$ is a solution.

Let $x = -1$.
Then $y = 3(-1) - 1 = -4$.
So $(-1, -4)$ is a solution.

Let $x = -2$.
Then $y = 3(-2) - 1 = -7$.
So $(-2, -7)$ is a solution.

We record the solutions in a table.

x	y
0	−1
1	2
2	5
−1	−4
−2	−7

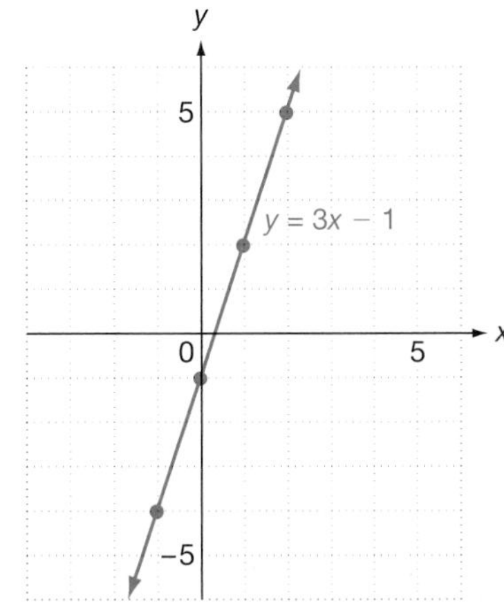

Next we plot these points. If we could plot all solutions, they would form a line. We can draw the line with a straightedge, and label it $y = 3x - 1$. The relation consists of all pairs (x, y) such that $y = 3x - 1$ is true. That is, $\{(x, y) | y = 3x - 1\}$.

Note that the equation $y = 3x - 1$ has an infinite set of solutions. The graph of the equation is a drawing of the solution set.

Try This Graph each of the following.

f. $y = -3x + 1$ **g.** $y = \frac{1}{2}x + 2$

Journal

Write a paragraph in which you explain how the idea of a Cartesian coordinate system allows us to think of a plane as an infinite sheet of graph paper.

EXAMPLE 4 Graph $y = x^2 - 5$.

We select numbers for x and find the corresponding values for y. The table gives us the ordered pairs $(0, -5)$, $(-1, -4,)$ and so on.

x	y
0	−5
1	−4
2	−1
3	4
−1	−4
−2	−1
−3	4

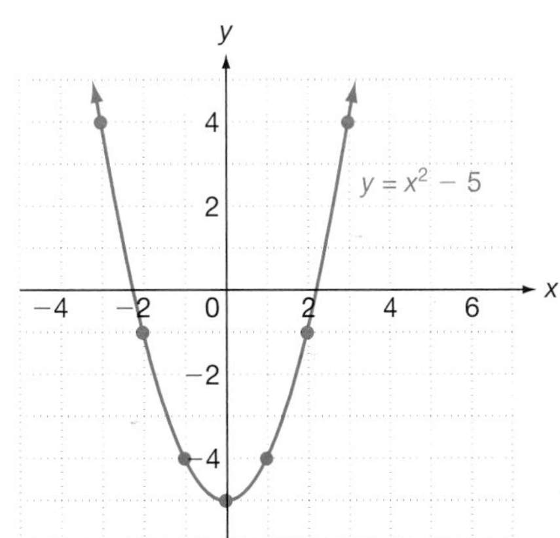

Next we plot these points. We note that as the absolute value of x increases, $x^2 - 5$ also increases. Thus the graph is a curve that rises gradually on either side of the y-axis, as shown above. This graph shows the relation $\{(x, y) | y = x^2 - 5\}$.

Try This Graph each of the following.

h. $y = 3 - x^2$

i. $x = y^2 - 5$ (Hint: Select values for y.)

Extra Help On the Web

Look for worked-out examples at the Prentice Hall Web site.
www.phschool.com

3-2 Exercises

A

Graph each relation.

1. $\{(3, 0), (4, 2), (5, 4), (6, 6)\}$

2. $\{(1, 1), (2, 3), (3, 5), (4, 7)\}$

3. $\{(3, -4), (3, -3), (3, -2), (3, -1), (3, 0)\}$

4. $\{(-2, 1), (-2, 2), (-2, 3), (-2, 4), (-2, 5)\}$

5. $\{(4, 3), (4, 2), (3, 2), (3, 3), (5, 2), (5, 3)\}$

6. $\{(2, -2), (3, -2), (2, -3), (3, -3), (2, -4), (3, -4)\}$

7. ***Mathematical Reasoning*** When you analyze a set of ordered pairs to determine whether it is a function, would you *always, sometimes,* or *never* look at the x-coordinates? Explain your answer.

8. ***Mental Math*** What points do you need to discover in order to determine that a relation is not a function?

Determine whether the given ordered pairs are solutions of the indicated equation.

9. $(1, -1), (0, 3);\ y = 2x - 3$

10. $(2, 5), (-2, -7);\ y = 3x - 1$

11. $(3, 4), (-3, 5);\ 3s + t = 4$

12. $(2, 3), (-5, 15);\ 2p + q = 5$

13. $(3, 5), (-2, -15);\ 4x - y = 7$

14. $(2, 7), (-1, 8);\ 5x - y = 3$

15. $\left(0, \frac{3}{5}\right), \left(-\frac{1}{2}, -\frac{4}{5}\right);\ 2a + 5b = 3$

16. $\left(0, \frac{3}{2}\right), \left(\frac{2}{3}, 1\right);\ 3f + 4g = 6$

17. $(2, -1), (-0.75, 2.75);\ 4r + 3s = 5$

18. $(2, -4), (2.4, -5);\ 5w + 2z = 2$

19. $(3, 2), (22, 31);\ -3x + 2y = -4$

20. $(1, 2), (-40, 14);\ 2x - 5y = -6$

Graph each of the following.

21. $y = x$

22. $y = 2x$

23. $y = -2x$

24. $y = -\frac{1}{2}x$

25. $y = x + 3$

26. $y = x - 2$

27. $y = 3x - 2$

28. $y = -4x + 1$

29. $y = -2x + 3$

30. $y = x^2$

31. $y = -x^2$

32. $y = x^2 + 2$

33. $y = x^2 - 2$

34. $x = y^2 + 2$

35. $x = y^2 - 2$

B

36–41. Indicate the domain and range for each relation in Exercises 30–35.

42. Draw a triangle with vertices at (1, 1), (4, 2,), and (3, 6). Shade the triangle and its interior.

a. Shade (on the x-axis) the domain. Describe the domain.

b. Shade (on the y-axis) the range. Describe the range.

43. Draw a circle with radius of length 2, centered at (4, 3). Shade its interior.

a. Shade (on the x-axis) the domain. Describe the domain.

b. Shade (on the y-axis) the range. Describe the range.

Graph each relation. All relations are in $R \times R$, where R is the set of real numbers.

	First Coordinate	Second Coordinate
44.	any real number	2
45.	-3	any real number
46.	any real number	1 more than the first coordinate
47.	any real number	1 less than the first coordinate
48.	any real number	twice the first coordinate
49.	any real number	the square of the first coordinate
50.	the second coordinate squared	any real number

Consider $M \times M$, where $M = \{-5, -4, -3, \ldots, 4, 5\}$. Graph each relation.

51. $\{(x, y) | y > 2x\}$

52. $\{(x, y) | -3 < x < 3 \text{ and } y = 0\}$

53. $\{(x, y) | x^2 + y^2 > 25\}$

54. $\{(x, y) | x \cdot y = 0\}$

55. ***Critical Thinking*** Find and graph three equations that have $(-2, 1)$ as a solution.

Challenge

Graph the following relations in $R \times R$.

56. $\{(x, y) | 1 \leq x \leq 4 \text{ and } -3 \leq y \leq -1\}$

57. $\{(x, y) | -1 \leq x \leq 1 \text{ and } -4 \leq y \leq 4\}$

Graph using 20 values of x between -5 and 5. (Use a calculator.)

58. $y = \frac{1}{3}x^3 - x + \frac{2}{3}$

59. $y = \frac{1}{3}x^3 - \frac{1}{2}x^2 - 2x + 1$

Mixed Review

Solve. **60.** $|a - 11| - 7 = -2$ **61.** $2(y^2 - y) = \frac{1}{2}(4y^2 + 10)$ *2-7, 2-1*

62. The sum of three consecutive odd integers is 41 more than twice the smallest. Find the three integers.

63. A $2\frac{1}{2}$-ft ribbon is cut in two so that the shorter piece is $\frac{1}{4}$ the length of the longer piece. How long is each piece of ribbon?

64. Rae invested \$500. The money she deposited in account A earned 6% annual interest, while the amount in account B earned 8%. At the end of the year, she had a total of \$535 in the two accounts. How much had she invested in each account? *2-2*

3-3 Functions

What You'll Learn

1. To recognize functions and their graphs
2. To use function notation to find function values
3. To find the domain of a function given its formula

. . . And Why

To work with special functions

The number of innings credited to a baseball pitcher is based upon the number of outs recorded. One out corresponds to $\frac{1}{3}$ inning, two outs to $\frac{2}{3}$ inning, three outs to 1 inning, and so on. The number of innings is thus a function of the number of outs recorded. Relations in which each member of the domain is matched with exactly one member of the range are called **functions.**

PART 1 Recognizing Functions

Objective: Recognize functions and their graphs.

In a function, no two ordered pairs can have the same first coordinate and a different second coordinate. Thus each member of the domain determines exactly one member of the range.

The relation $A = \{(2, 3), (5, 9), (1, 0), (10, -2)\}$ is a function because no two ordered pairs have the same first coordinate and different second coordinates.

The relation $B = \{(4, 5), (4, 0), (-1, 9)\}$ is not a function because the ordered pairs (4, 5) and (4, 0) have the same first coordinate and different second coordinates.

EXAMPLE 1 Which of the following relations are functions?

$$R = \{(9, 1), (-5, -2), (2, -1), (3, -9)\}$$
$$S = \{(6, a), (8, f), (6, b), (-2, p)\}$$
$$T = \{(z, 7), (y, -5), (r, 7), (z, 0), (k, 0)\}$$
$$M = \{(2, 3), (4, 3), (7, 3), (0, 3), (17, 3), (-3, 3)\}$$

Relations R and M are functions. Relations S and T have ordered pairs with the same first coordinate and different second coordinates, and thus are not functions.

Try This

a. Which of the following relations are functions?

$$A = \{(9, 0), (3, 8), (5, 8), (9, -1)\}$$
$$B = \{(0, t), (9, e), (-2, q), (-5, b)\}$$
$$C = \{(-3, 5), (7, -2), (4, -6)\}$$
$$D = \{(0, 1), (1, 0), (-1, 1)\}$$
$$E = \{(5, -5), (5, -5)\}$$

Suppose a relation has two ordered pairs with the same first coordinate, but different second coordinates. The graphs of these two ordered pairs would be points on the same vertical line. This gives us a method to test whether a graph is the graph of a function.

The Vertical Line Test

If it is possible for a vertical line to intersect a graph at more than one point, then the graph is not the graph of a function.

EXAMPLE 2 Which of the following are graphs of functions?

(a)

(b)

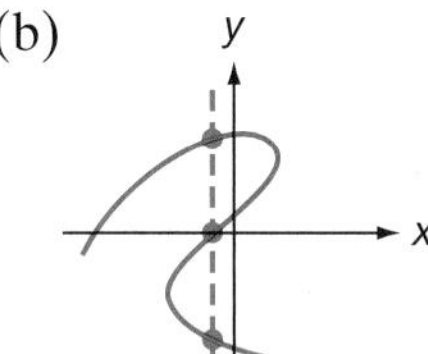

(c)

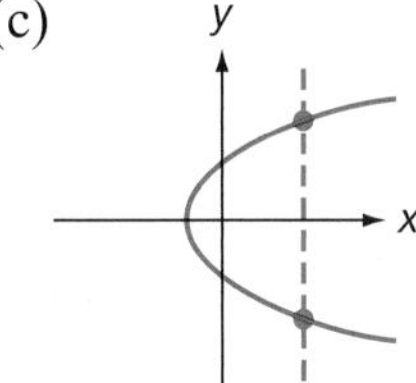

(d)

(e)

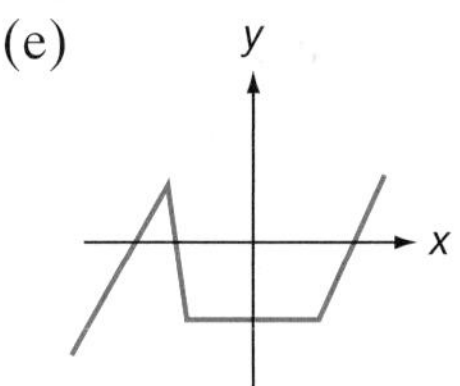

(f)

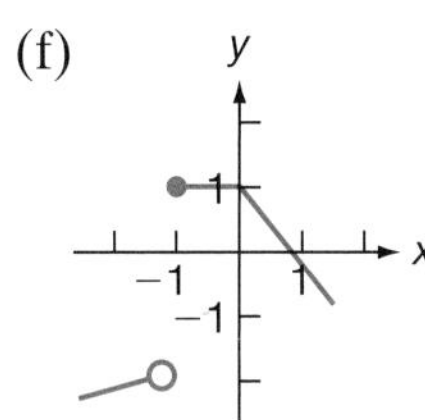

In graph f, the solid dot shows that $(-1, 1)$ belongs to the graph. The open dot shows that $(-1, -2)$ does not belong to the graph.

Examples a, e, and f are graphs of functions. Graphs b, c, and d fail the vertical line test.

Try This

b. Which of the following are graphs of functions?

(1)

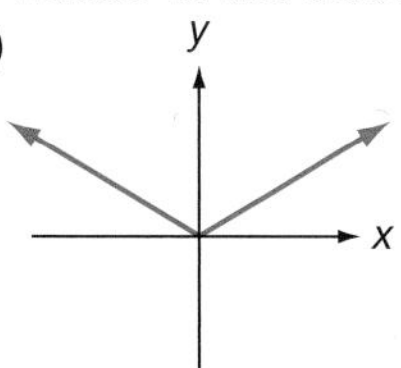

(2)

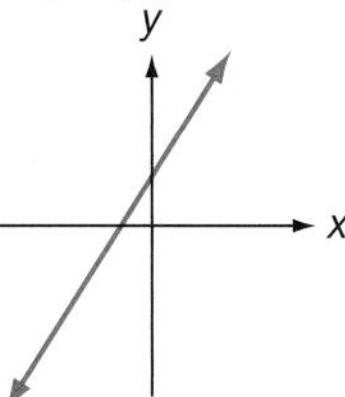

(3)

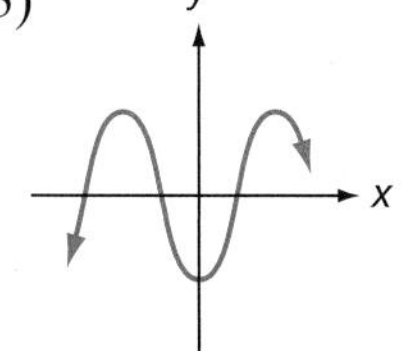

(4)

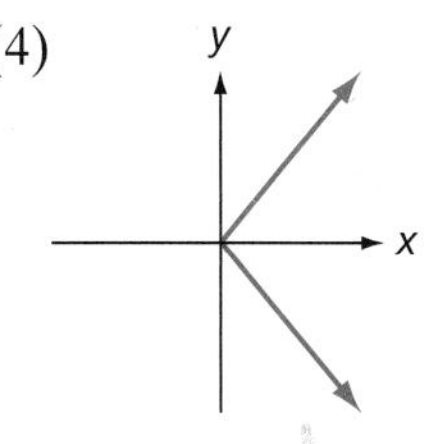

PART 2 Function Notation

Objective: Use function notation to find function values.

Functions are often named by letters. Since a function is a relation, a function f is thus a set of ordered pairs. We can represent the first coordinate of a pair by x, the second coordinate y by $f(x)$.) The ordered pair is then $(x, f(x))$. The symbol $f(x)$ is read "f of x." The number represented by $f(x)$ is called the **value of the function** at x.

EXAMPLE 3 Find $g(2)$ and $g(5)$ for $g = \{(1, 4), (2, 3), (3, 2), (4, -8), (5, 2)\}$.

Since we have the ordered pair $(2, 3)$, $g(2) = 3$. Similarly, $(5, 2)$ gives us $g(5) = 2$.

Try This

c. Consider the function $h = \{(-4, 0), (9, 1), (-3, -2), (6, 6), (0, -2)\}$. Find $h(9)$, $h(6)$, and $h(0)$.

Some functions can be defined by formulas or equations. Function values can be obtained by making substitutions for the variables.

EXAMPLE 4 $f(x) = 2x^2 - 3$. Find each of the following.

	$f(x) = 2x^2 - 3$
(a) $f(0)$	$f(0) = 2 \cdot 0^2 - 3 = -3$
(b) $f(-3)$	$f(-3) = 2(-3)^2 - 3 = 18 - 3 = 15$
(c) $f(5a)$	$f(5a) = 2(5a)^2 - 3 = 2(25a^2) - 3 = 50a^2 - 3$

Try This Find each of the following for $f(x) = 3x^2 + 1$.

d. $f(0)$ **e.** $f(1)$ **f.** $f(-1)$ **g.** $f(2a)$

PART 3 Finding the Domain of a Function

Objective: Find the domain of a function, given a formula for the function.

When the function in $R \times R$ is given by a formula, the domain is understood to be all real numbers that are acceptable replacements.

EXAMPLE 5 What is the domain of f for $f(x) = \frac{x - 4}{x + 3}$?

To find the domain of f, we must determine whether there are any unacceptable replacements. Notice what happens when $x = -3$.

$$f(-3) = \frac{-3 - 4}{-3 + 3} = \frac{-7}{0}$$

Since we cannot divide by 0, the replacement -3 is not acceptable. When a replacement is not acceptable, that number is not in the domain of the function. Thus the domain of f is $\{x \mid x \neq -3\}$.

Try This

h. $g(x) = \frac{x}{(x - 1)(x + 3)}$. What is the domain of g?

i. $h(x) = 3x + 9$. What is the domain of h?

j. $p(x) = \frac{x - 2}{3} - \frac{1}{3x}$. What is the domain of p?

3-3 Exercises

Extra Help On the Web

Look for worked-out examples at the Prentice Hall Web site. www.phschool.com

A

Mental Math Which of the following relations are functions?

1. $K = \{(1, 2), (2, 3), (3, 4), (4, 1)\}$
2. $L = \{(3, -5), (0, 0), (-5, 3), (-3, -5)\}$
3. $T = \{(-4, -4), (-1, -6), (-4, 4), (-6, -1)\}$
4. $V = \{(2, -9), (4, 2), (0, 5), (4, -9)\}$
5. $B = \{(6, -6), (-2, 2), (0, 0), (2, -2), (-6, 6)\}$
6. $F = \{(0, a), (1, a), (-1, a), (1, -1), (-1, -1)\}$

Which of the following are graphs of functions?

7.

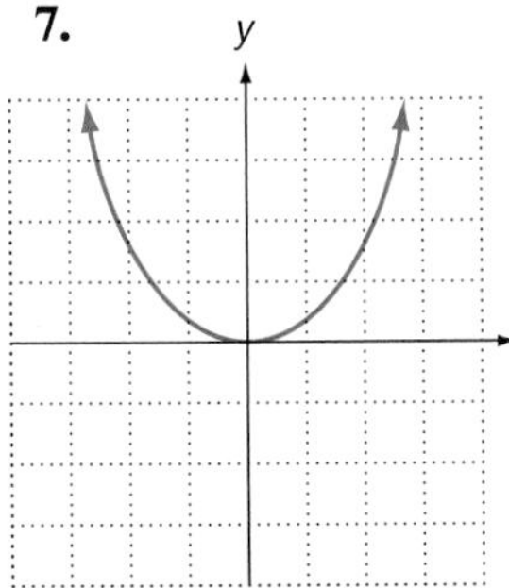

8.

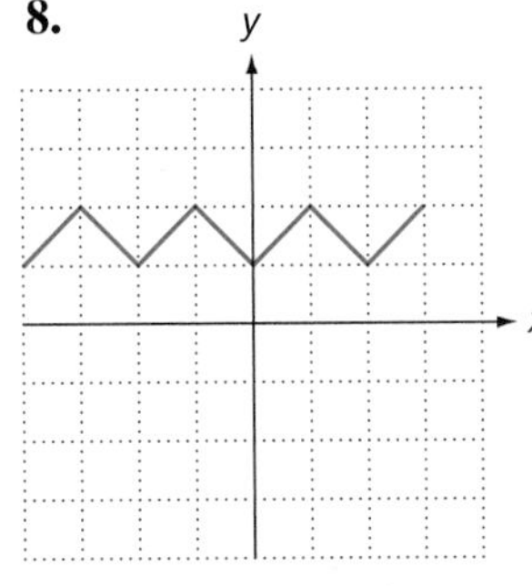

9.

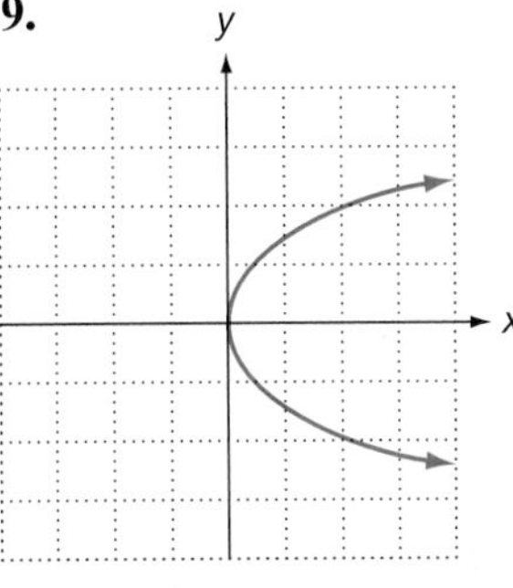

10.

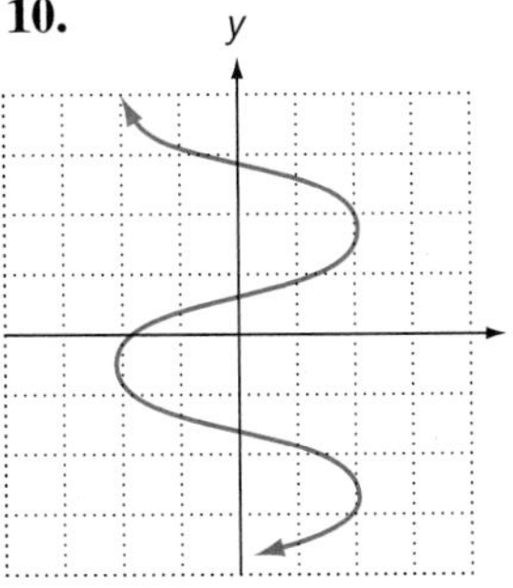

11.

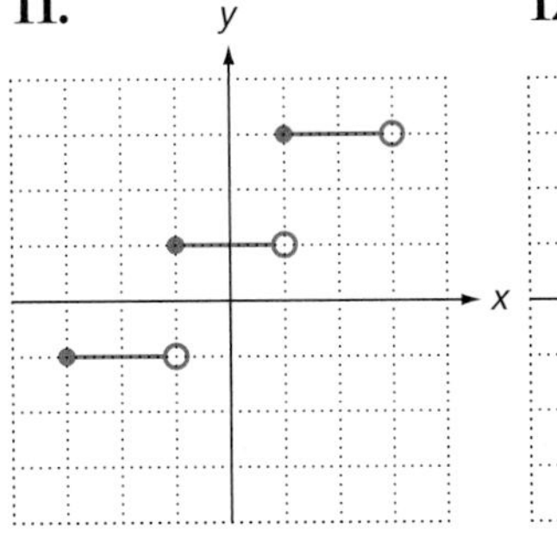

12.

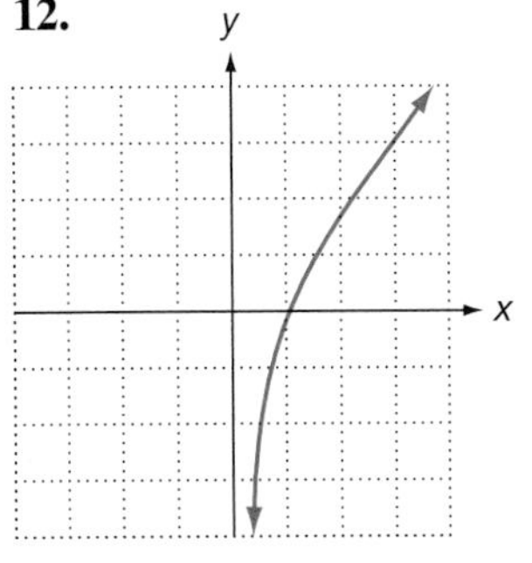

Consider the following functions. Find the indicated function values.

13. $g(x) = x + 1$
   a. $g(0)$ b. $g(-4)$ c. $g(-7)$ d. $g(8)$

14. $h(x) = x - 4$
   a. $h(4)$ b. $h(8)$ c. $h(-3)$ d. $h(-4)$

15. $f(x) = 5x^2 + 4x$
   a. $f(0)$ b. $f(-1)$ c. $f(3)$ d. $f(t)$

16. $g(x) = 3x^2 - 2x$
   a. $g(0)$ b. $g(-1)$ c. $g(3)$ d. $g(t)$

17. $f(x) = 3x^2 + 2x - 1$
   a. $f(2)$ b. $f(3)$ c. $f(-3)$ d. $f(1)$

18. $h(x) = 4x^2 - x + 2$
   a. $h(3)$ b. $h(0)$ c. $h(-1)$ d. $h(-2)$

19. $f(x) = \dfrac{x^2 - x - 2}{2x^2 - 5x - 3}$
   a. $f(0)$ b. $f(4)$ c. $f(-1)$ d. $f(3)$

20. $s(x) = \dfrac{3x - 4}{2x + 5}$
   a. $s(10)$ b. $s(2)$ c. $s\left(-\frac{5}{2}\right)$ d. $s(-1)$

What is the domain of each of the following functions?

21. $f(x) = 7x + 4$

22. $f(x) = |3x - 2|$

23. $f(x) = 4 - \dfrac{2}{x}$

24. $f(x) = \dfrac{1}{x - 3}$

25. $f(x) = \dfrac{1}{5x + 8}$

26. $f(x) = \dfrac{1}{(3 - x)(x + x)}$

27. $f(x) = \dfrac{4x^3 + 4}{x(x + 2)(x - 1)}$

28. $f(x) = x^3 - x^2 + x - 2$

B

Think of a function as a machine. *Inputs* are entered into the machine. The machine then gives the *output*. The inputs that are acceptable to the machine are the elements of the domain of the function. The outputs of the machine are the elements of the range of the function.

29. Find the indicated outputs.
   a. $f(2)$ b. $f(3)$ c. $f(-2)$ d. $f(0)$

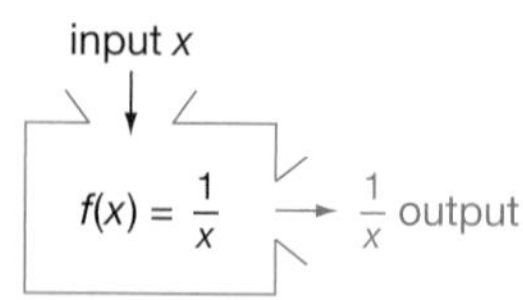

What inputs would not be accepted by the following machines?

30. **31.**

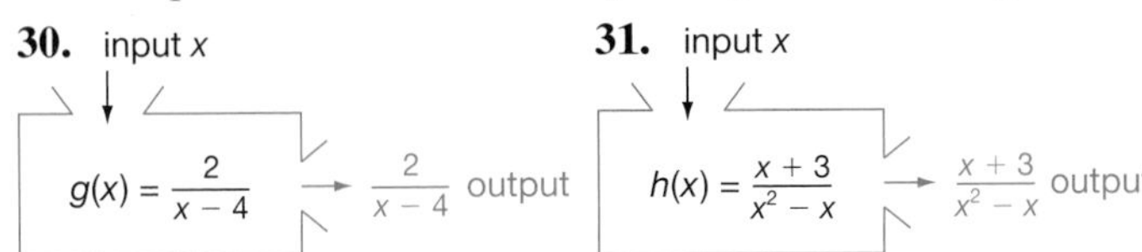

32.

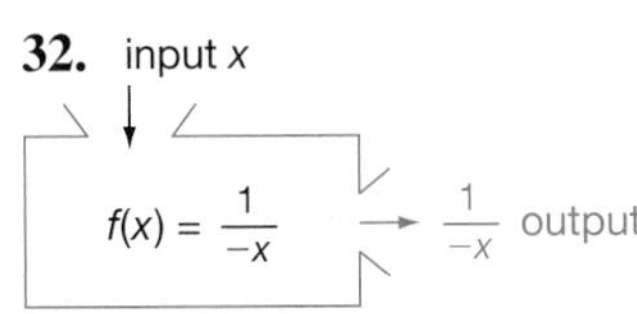

33. ***Critical Thinking*** The ordered pair (3, 2) is a solution to an equation describing a function from set A to set B. Is 3 in the domain of every function from set A to set B?

Challenge

The sum of two functions f and g (denoted by $f \oplus g$) is defined as $(f \oplus g)(x) = f(x) + g(x)$, for every x that is in the domain of f and the domain of g.

34. Suppose $f(x) = 2x + 3$ and $g(x) = x - 5$.

a. What is $(f \oplus g)(5)$? **b.** What is $(f \oplus g)(-6)$?

c. What is $(f \oplus g)(0)$? **d.** What is the domain of $(f \oplus g)$?

e. Is $(f \oplus g)(x) = (g \oplus f)(x)$ for all x in the domain of f and g?

35. Suppose $f(x) = \frac{1}{x}$ and $g(x) = \frac{1}{(x - 2)}$.

a. What is $(f \oplus g)(1)$? **b.** What is $(f \oplus g)(2)$?

c. What is $(f \oplus g)(0)$? **d.** What is the domain of $(f \oplus g)$?

36. ***Mathematical Reasoning*** How do you think the products of two functions would be defined?

Mixed Review

Find the distance between points on a number line having the given coordinates.

37. $-14, -22$ **38.** $-2, 8$ **39.** $0, 47.5$ **40.** $-24, -2$ *3-1*

Solve. Then graph. **41.** $-x + 2 < -1$ or $0.3x < 0.6$

42. $2x + 4 < 3x + 2 < 29$ **43.** $-\frac{9}{2} < -\frac{1}{2}x + 1 < -2$ *3-2*

For what replacements for x are the divisions possible? **44.** $x \div \frac{0}{x}$

45. $\frac{2(3x - 6)}{2(3x - 6) - 3(2x - 4)}$ **46.** $\frac{1}{x - 2} + \frac{1}{2 - x}$ *1-2*

3-4 Graphs of Linear Equations

What You'll Learn

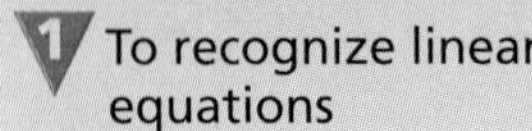
To recognize linear equations

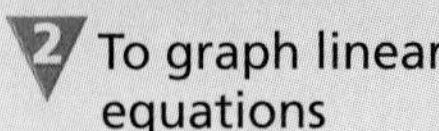
To graph linear equations

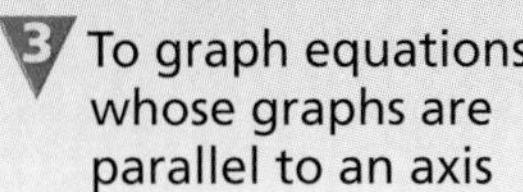
To graph equations whose graphs are parallel to an axis

. . . And Why

To solve linear equations in various formats

The equation $K = C + 273$, which gives the relationship between the Kelvin and Celsius temperature scales, has a graph that is a straight line. Such equations are called **linear** or **first-degree equations.**

PART 1 Recognizing Linear Equations

Objective: Recognize a linear equation.

An equation is linear if there are no products of variables, the variables occur to the first power only, and there are no variables in a denominator.

EXAMPLE 1 Which of the following equations are linear? If an equation is not linear, give the reason.

(a) $xy = 9$ (b) $2r + 7 = 4s$ (c) $4x^3 = 7y$

(d) $8x - 17y = y$ (e) $q = \frac{3}{p}$ (f) $4x = -3$

Equations b, d, and f are linear equations. Equations a, c, and e are not linear.

Equation a has a product of two variables. Equation c has a variable to the third power. Equation e has a variable in a denominator. It is equivalent to $q = 3p^{-1}$, which has a variable to a power other than 1.

Try This Which of the following equations are linear? If an equation is not linear, give the reason.

a. $5y + 8x = 9$ **b.** $7y = 11$ **c.** $5y^2x = 13$

d. $x = 4 + \frac{7}{y}$ **e.** $xy = 0$ **f.** $3x - 2y + 5 = 0$

PART 2 Graphing Linear Equations

Objective: Graph linear equations.

Theorem 3-1

The graph of any linear equation is a straight line.

Since two points determine a line, we can graph a linear equation by finding two points that belong to the graph. Then we draw a line containing those points. A third point should always be used as a check. Often the easiest points to find are the points where the graph crosses the axes.

Definition

The **y-intercept** of a graph is the y-coordinate of the point where the graph intersects the y-axis. The **x-intercept** is the x-coordinate of the point where the graph crosses the x-axis.

To find the y-intercept, let $x = 0$ and solve for y. To find the x-intercept, let $y = 0$ and solve for x.

EXAMPLE 2 Graph $4x + 5y = 20$.

First find the intercepts.

To find the y-intercept, let $x = 0$ and solve for y. We find $y = 4$, the y-intercept. We plot the point $(0, 4)$.

To find the x-intercept, let $y = 0$ and solve for x. We find $x = 5$, the x-intercept. We plot the point $(5, 0)$.

The point $\left(1, 3\frac{1}{5}\right)$ is used as a check.

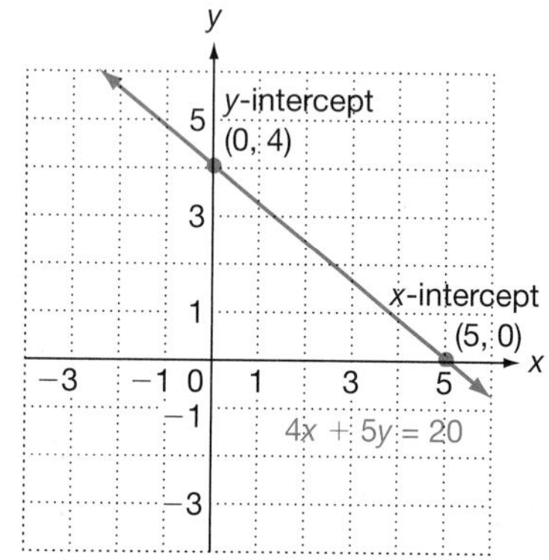

Try This Graph.

g. $2x - 6y = -2$ **h.** $3y = 2x - 6$

The graph of any equation of the form $y = mx$ contains the origin. The x-intercept and the y-intercept occur at the same point, $(0, 0)$. Another point will be needed in order to graph the equation.

EXAMPLE 3 Graph $y = 2x$.

x	y (or $2x$)
0	0
1	2
−1	−2

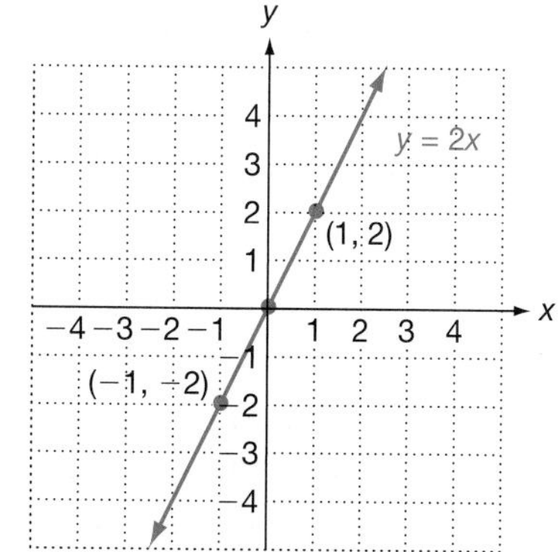

Try This Graph.

i. $y = -x$ **j.** $y = \frac{5}{2}x$

We have seen that the graph of $y = mx$ is a straight line containing the origin. Notice what happens if we add a number b to the right-hand side to get $y = mx + b$.

EXAMPLE 4

Graph $y = 2x - 3$ and compare it with the graph of $y = 2x$. First make a table of values. Then graph and compare.

x	y (or $2x - 3$)
0	−3
1	−1
3	3
−2	−7

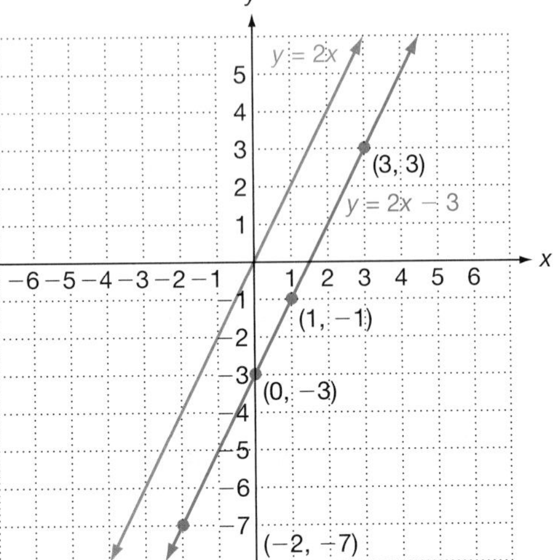

The graph of $y = 2x - 3$ is a line moved down 3 units from the graph of $y = 2x$.

Try This Graph and compare with the graph of $y = 2x$.

k. $y = 2x + 1$ **l.** $y = 2x - 4$

Theorem 3-2

The graph of $y = mx$ is a line containing the origin. The graph of $y = mx + b$ is a line parallel to $y = mx$ and has b as the y-intercept.

Quick Review

Recall that parallel lines are coplanar lines that do not intersect. Perpendicular lines are coplanar lines that form a 90°, or right, angle.

PART 3 Lines Parallel to the Axes

Objective: Graph equations whose graphs are parallel to the x-axis or y-axis.

Consider the equation $y = 4$, or $y = 0 \cdot x + 4$. No matter what number we choose for x, the value of y is 4. Thus, $(x, 4)$ is a solution of the value chosen for x.

Theorem 3-3

For constants a and b, the graph of an equation of the form $y = b$ is a line parallel to the x-axis with y-intercept b. The graph of an equation of the form $x = a$ is a line parallel to the y-axis with x-intercept a.

EXAMPLES

5 Graph $y = 4$.
Any ordered pair $(x, 4)$ is a solution. Thus the line is parallel to the x-axis, and the y-intercept is 4.

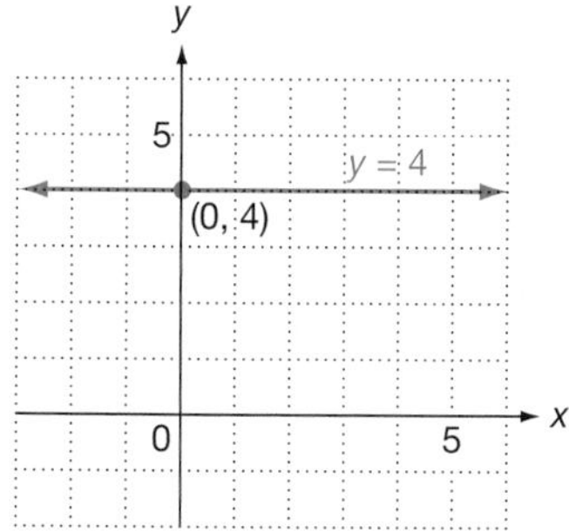

6 Graph $x = -2$.
Any ordered pair $(-2, y)$ is a solution. Thus the line is parallel to the y-axis, and the x-intercept is -2.

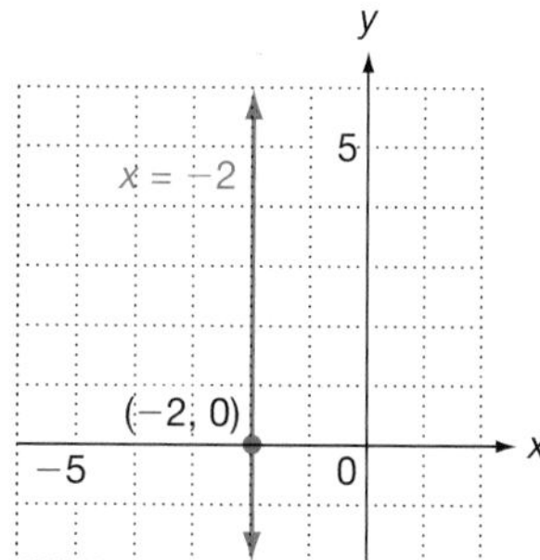

Try This Graph these equations.

m. $x = 4$ **n.** $y = -3$ **o.** $y = 0$

Graphing Linear Equations

1. If there is a variable missing, solve for the other variable. The graph will be a line parallel to an axis.
2. If no variable is missing, find the intercepts. Use the intercepts to graph.
3. If the intercept points are too close together, or are the same point, choose another point farther from the origin.
4. Use a third point as a check.

3-4 Exercises

Extra Help On the Web

Look for worked-out examples at the Prentice Hall Web site.
www.phschool.com

A

Mathematical Reasoning Which of the following equations are linear? If an equation is not linear, give the reason.

1. $3x - 4 = y$

2. $x = 9$

3. $4r^2 = 2r + 1$

4. $2 + 3pq = -9$

5. $y = 7$

6. $3x^2 + 4y^2 = 16$

7. $4x - 5y = 20$

8. $5 = \frac{1}{x}$

9. $3p - 4 = q - 1$

10. $5 = r + 4t$

Graph each of the following linear equations.

11. $x + 3y = 9$ **12.** $-x + 4y = 8$ **13.** $-x + 2y = 6$

14. $3x + y = 6$ **15.** $3y - 3 = 6x$ **16.** $2y - 6 = 4x$

17. $y = -\frac{5}{2}x - 4$ **18.** $y = -\frac{2}{5}x + 3$ **19.** $3x + 6y = 18$

20. $x - 2 = y$ **21.** $5x - 4y = 20$ **22.** $3x - 5y = 15$

23. ***Estimation*** Graph $2x + 3y = 7$. Look at the graph and estimate the value of y when $x = .906$.

Graph and compare.

24. $y = 3x + 3$ and $y = 3x$ **25.** $y = -2x - 4$ and $y = -2x$

26. $y = \frac{1}{2}x + 1$ and $y = \frac{1}{2}x$ **27.** $y = \frac{5}{8}x$ and $y = -\frac{8}{5}x$

Graph.

28. $x = 2$ **29.** $x = 4$ **30.** $y = -6$ **31.** $y = -3$

32. $3y - 9 = 0$ **33.** $3x + 15 = 0$ **34.** $2x - 10 = 0$ **35.** $6y + 24 = 0$

B

Find the coordinates of the intercept points for the following equations.

36. $2x + 5y + 2 = 5x - 10y - 8$ **37.** $\frac{1}{8}y = -x - \frac{7}{16}$

38. $0.4y - 0.004x = -0.04$ **39.** $x = -\frac{7}{3}y - \frac{2}{11}$

40. ***Critical Thinking*** Which of the graphs in Exercises 28–35 are graphs of functions?

41. ***Write a Convincing Argument*** Solve the problem below. Then write an argument to convince a classmate that your solution is correct. What is the equation of the line which has the x-axis as its graph?

Challenge

42. Consider the equation $y - 2 = k(x - 3)$. The set of all lines that results from replacing k with different values is a **family of lines,** and k is the **parameter** of the family.

a. Replace k with any four numbers and graph the resulting equations.

b. What do you observe about these lines?

c. Graph four lines containing the point $(-5, 3)$. Write an equation with parameter k that describes these lines.

Mixed Review

Simplify. **43.** $(-2x^3y^2)^2(-xy)^4(x^{-2}y^{-1})^{-2}$ **44.** $\left(\frac{1}{a^{-2}}\right)^3$ **45.** $b^3\left(\frac{b}{b^{-2}}\right)^{-1}$ *1-8*

Consider $A = \{a, b, c\}$, $B = \{0, 1\}$, and $C = \{-1, 0, 1\}$. Find the following.

46. $A \times B$ **47.** $B \times A$ **48.** $<$ for $C \times C$ *3-1*

Slope

3-5

The **grade** of a road is a measure of its steepness. The grade is the ratio of the rise of the road to every 100 feet of distance.

It is usually given as a percent. For instance, a road can have a 2% grade. In much the same manner we can describe the steepness of a line.

What You'll Learn

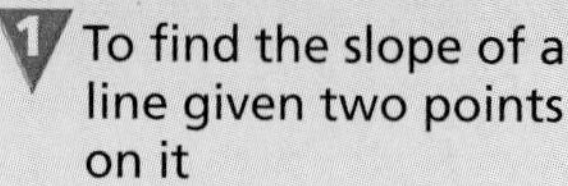

1 To find the slope of a line given two points on it

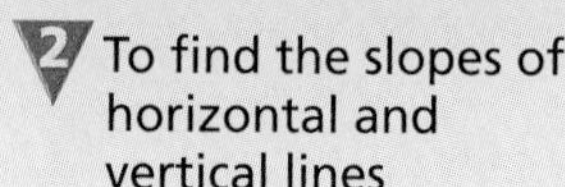

2 To find the slopes of horizontal and vertical lines

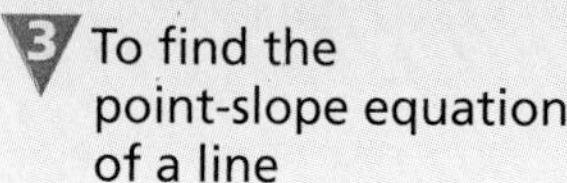

3 To find the point-slope equation of a line

. . . And Why

To determine characteristics of lines, such as perpendicularity

PART 1 Finding the Slope of a Line

Objective: Find the slope of a line containing a given pair of points.

Here is a line with two points marked. As we go from P_1 to P_2, the change in x is $x_2 - x_1$. Similarly, the change in y is $y_2 - y_1$.

The ratio of the change in y to the change in x is called the **slope** of the line.

We usually use the letter m to designate slope.

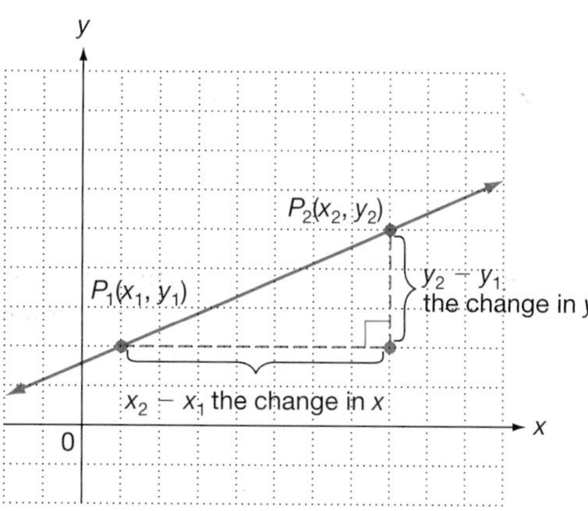

Definition

The **slope** m of a line is the change in y divided by the change in x, or

$$m = \frac{y_2 - y_1}{x_2 - x_1}$$

where (x_1, y_1) and (x_2, y_2) are any two points on the line, and $x_2 \neq x_1$.

To find the slope of a line, use the coordinates of any two points to determine the change in y and the change in x. Then divide the change in y by the change in x.

EXAMPLE 1 The points (1, 2) and (3, 6) are on a line. Find its slope.

$$\begin{aligned} \text{The slope, } m &= \frac{y_2 - y_1}{x_2 - x_1} \quad \frac{\text{change in } y}{\text{change in } x} \\ &= \frac{6 - 2}{3 - 1} \\ &= \frac{4}{2}, \text{ or } 2 \end{aligned}$$

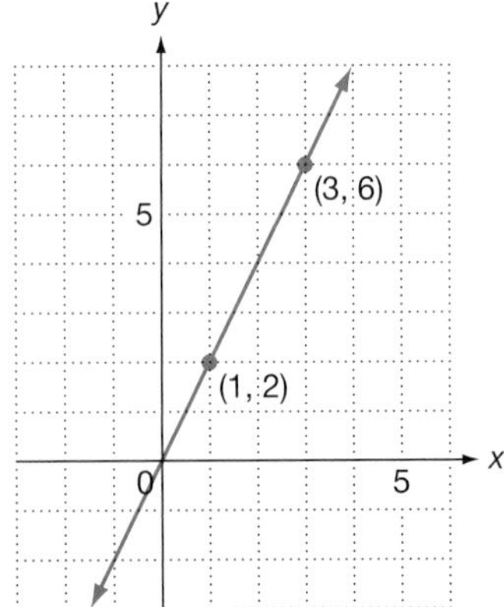

If we use the points (1, 2) and (3, 6) in opposite order, we find that the change in y is negative and the change in x is negative. We get the same number for the slope.

$$m = \frac{2 - 6}{1 - 3} = \frac{-4}{-2}, \text{ or } 2$$

When we compute slope, the order of the points does not matter as long as we take the same order for finding the differences.

The points (0, 0) and (−1, −2) are also on the line. If we use those points to compute the slope, we get the following.

$$m = \frac{-2 - 0}{-1 - 0} = 2$$

The slope will be the same no matter what pair of points we use.

Try This Find the slope of the line containing each pair of points.

a. (1, 1) and (12, 14)
b. (3, 9) and (4, 10)
c. (0, −4) and (5, 7)
d. (7, 2) and (6, 3)

If a line slants up from left to right, it has positive slope, as in Example 1. If a line slants down from left to right, it has negative slope.

These graphs show the relative positions of lines with different positive slopes.

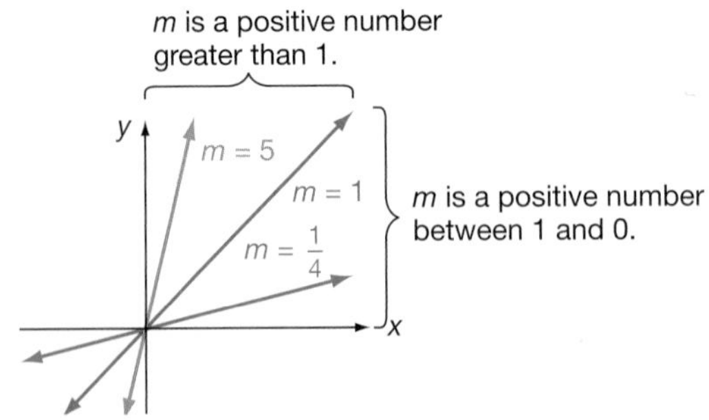

These graphs show the relative positions of lines with different negative slopes.

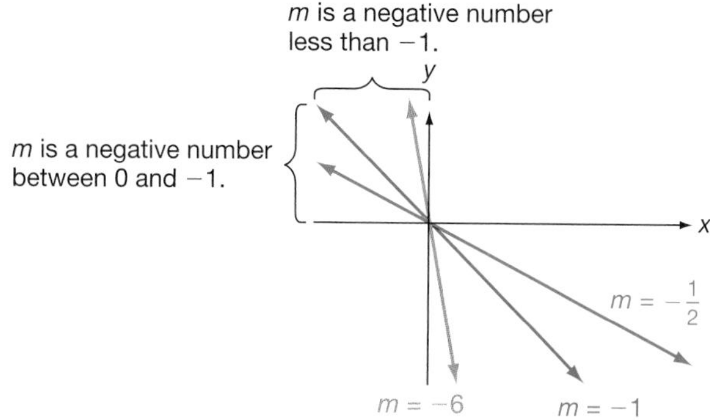

PART 2

Horizontal and Vertical Lines

Objective: Find the slopes of horizontal and vertical lines.

Vertical and horizontal lines do not slant. Let us apply the definition of slope to them.

EXAMPLE 2 Find the slope of the line $y = 3$.

$$
\begin{aligned}
m &= \frac{y_2 - y_1}{x_2 - x_1} \\
&= \frac{3 - 3}{-2 - 4} \\
&= \frac{0}{-6} \\
&= 0
\end{aligned}
$$

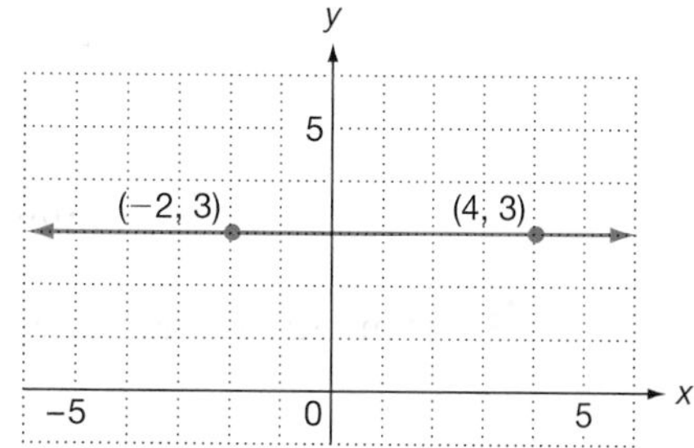

Any two points on a horizontal line have the same y-coordinate. The change in y is 0, so the slope is 0.

EXAMPLE 3 Find the slope of the line $x = -4$.

$$
\begin{aligned}
m &= \frac{y_2 - y_1}{x_2 - x_1} \\
&= \frac{-2 - 3}{-4 - (-4)} \\
&= \frac{-5}{0}
\end{aligned}
$$

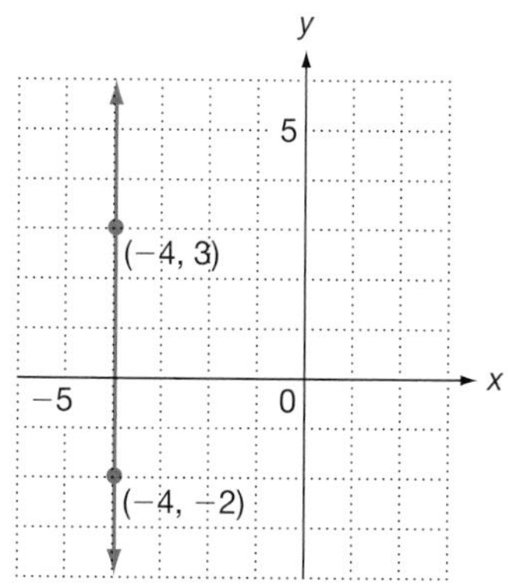

Since division by 0 is not defined, we say that this line has *no slope.*

Any two points on a vertical line have the same x-coordinates. The change in x is 0, so the denominator in the formula for slope is 0. Thus a vertical line has no slope.

Theorem 3-4

A horizontal line has slope 0. A vertical line has no slope.

Try This Find the slope, if it exists.

e. $y = -5$ **f.** $x = 17$

Point-Slope Equations of Lines

Objective: Use the point-slope equation to find an equation of a line.

If we know the slope of a line and the coordinates of a point on the line, we can find an equation of the line, the **point-slope equation.**

Theorem 3-5

The Point-Slope Equation

A line containing (x_1, y_1) with slope m has an equation $(y - y_1) = m(x - x_1)$.

EXAMPLE 4 Find an equation of a line containing $\left(\frac{1}{2}, -1\right)$ with slope 5.

$$(y - y_1) = m(x - x_1)$$

$$y - (-1) = 5\left(x - \frac{1}{2}\right) \quad \text{Substituting}$$

$$y + 1 = 5\left(x - \frac{1}{2}\right)$$

$$y = 5x - \frac{7}{2} \quad \text{Simplifying}$$

EXAMPLE 5 Find an equation of the line with y-intercept 4 and slope $\frac{3}{5}$.

$$(y - y_1) = m(x - x_1)$$

$$y - 4 = \frac{3}{5}(x - 0) \quad \text{Substituting}$$

$$y = \frac{3}{5}x + 4 \quad \text{Simplifying}$$

Try This

g. Find an equation of the line containing the point $(-2, 4)$ with slope -3.

h. Find an equation of the line containing the point $(-4, -10)$ with slope $\frac{1}{4}$.

i. Find an equation of the line with x-intercept 5 and slope $-\frac{1}{2}$.

3-5 Exercises

Extra Help On the Web

Look for worked-out examples at the Prentice Hall Web site.
www.phschool.com

A

Find the slope, if it exists, of the line containing each pair of points.

1. (5, 0) and (6, 8)
2. (4, 0) and (7, 3)
3. (0, 7) and (−2, 9)
4. (0, 8) and (3, 8)
5. (4, −3) and (6, −4)
6. (5, −7) and (8, −3)
7. (0, 0) and (−4, −8)
8. (0, 0) and (−5, −6)
9. (−2, −4) and (−9, −7)
10. (−3, −7) and (−8, −5)
11. $\left(\frac{1}{2}, \frac{1}{4}\right)$ and $\left(\frac{3}{2}, \frac{3}{4}\right)$
12. $\left(\frac{3}{5}, \frac{1}{2}\right)$ and $\left(\frac{1}{5}, -\frac{1}{2}\right)$
13. $\left(\frac{1}{8}, \frac{1}{4}\right)$ and $\left(\frac{3}{4}, \frac{1}{2}\right)$
14. $\left(\frac{1}{3}, -\frac{1}{8}\right)$ and $\left(\frac{5}{6}, -\frac{1}{4}\right)$
15. (3.2, −12.8) and (3.2, 2.4)
16. (−16.3, 12.4) and (8.3, 12.4)

Find the slope, if it exists, of each line.

17. $x = 7$
18. $x = -4$
19. $y = -3$
20. $y = 18$
21. $x = 6$
22. $x = -17$
23. $y = 20$
24. $y = -31$
25. $5x - 6 = 15$
26. $-12 = 4x - 7$
27. $5y = 6$
28. $19 = -6y$
29. $y - 6 = 14$
30. $12 - 4x = 9 + x$
31. $15 + 7x = 3x - 5$
32. $3y - 2x = 5 + 9y - 2x$

Find the equation of the line containing the given points and the indicated slope.

33. (3, 2); $m = 4$
34. (4, 7); $m = -2$
35. (−5, −2); $m = -1$
36. (−2, −4), $m = 3$
37. (−6, 4); $m = \frac{1}{2}$
38. (3, −1), $m = -\frac{4}{3}$
39. (0, −7); $m = 0$
40. (3, 0); $m = 0$

B

Use a calculator to find the slope of the line containing the given pair of points.

41. (0.04, 0.08) and (0.47, 0.83)
42. (0.02, 0.8) and (−0.2, −0.04)

Use a calculator to find an equation of each line.

43. The line containing the point (3.014, −2.563) with slope 3.516
44. The line containing the points (1.103, 2.443) and (8.114, 11.012)
45. ***Multi-Step Problem*** Determine whether these three points are on a line. (Hint: Compare the slopes of $\overline{AB}$ and $\overline{BC}$. $\overline{AB}$ refers to the segment from A to B.)

    $A(9, 4), B(-1, 2), C(4, 3)$

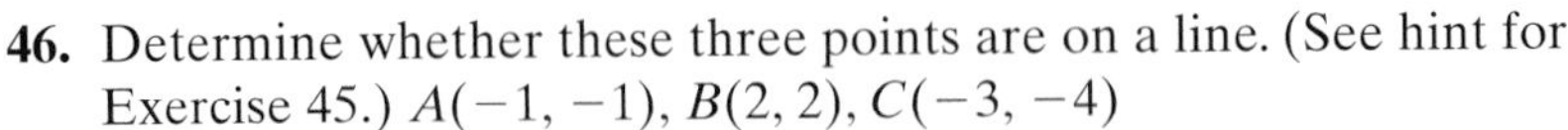

46. Determine whether these three points are on a line. (See hint for Exercise 45.) $A(-1, -1)$, $B(2, 2)$, $C(-3, -4)$

47. Determine a so that the slope of the line containing this pair of points has the given value. $(-2, 3a)$, $(4, -a)$; $m = -\frac{5}{12}$

48. Find the slope of the line that contains the given pair of points.

a. $(5b, -6c), (b, -c)$ **b.** $(b, d), (b, d + e)$

c. $(c + f, a + d), (c - f, -a - d)$

49. A line contains the points $(-100, 4)$ and $(0, 0)$. List four more points of the line.

Find two solutions of each equation. Use these to find the slope.

50. $2x + 3y = 6$ **51.** $2x + 5y + 2 = 5x + 10y - 8$

52. ***Critical Thinking*** Suppose that the product of the slopes of two lines through the origin is positive. What can you say about the location of the lines?

On steep roads there are often warning signs, and some give the grade of the road. Runaway trucks are not uncommon, so on some curves, sand exit roads are constructed. If a truck's brakes fail, the driver exits onto the sand and slows to a stop. How much does this road rise in this 7-mile stretch where the grade is 6%? See Exercise 55.

Challenge

53. Plot the points $A(0, 0)$, $B(8, 2)$, $C(11, 6)$ and $D(3, 4)$. Draw $\overline{AB}, \overline{BC}, \overline{CD}$, and $\overline{DA}$. Find the slopes of these four segments. Compare the slopes of $\overline{AB}$ and $\overline{CD}$. Compare the slopes of $\overline{BC}$ and $\overline{DA}$.

54. Plot the points $E(-2, -5)$, $F(2, -2)$, $G(7, -2)$, and $H(3, -5)$. Draw $\overline{EF}, \overline{FG}, \overline{GH}, \overline{HE}, \overline{EG}$, and $\overline{FH}$. Compare the slopes of $\overline{EG}$ and $\overline{FH}$.

55. Numbers like 2%, 3%, and 6% are often used to represent the *grade* of a road. Such a number tells how steep a road is. For example, a 3% grade means that for every horizontal distance of 100 ft, the road rises or descends 3 ft. In each case, find the road grade and an equation giving the height y of a vehicle in terms of a horizontal distance x.

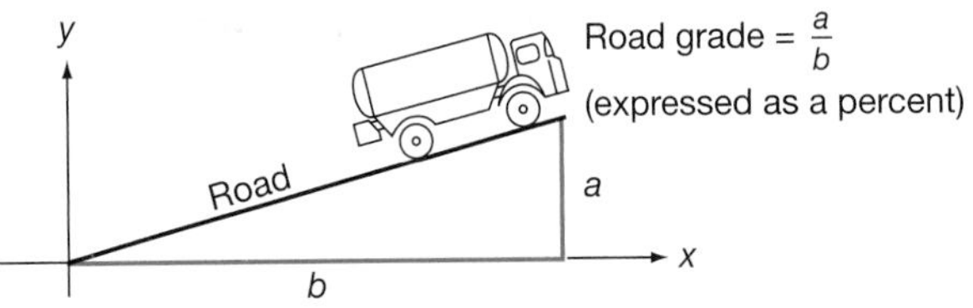

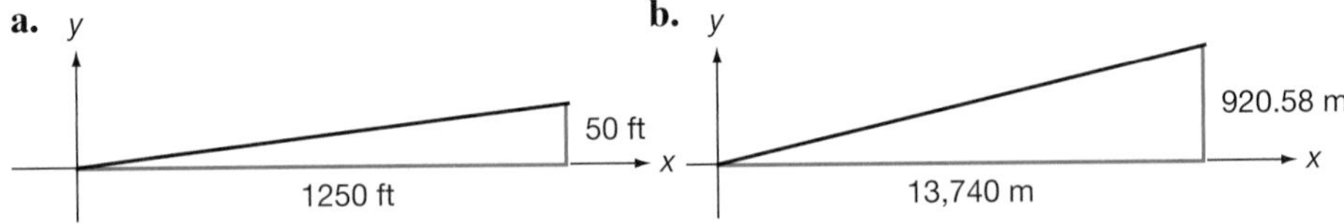

Mixed Review

Find the domain of each function. **56.** $f(x) = 12 + \frac{3}{x}$ **57.** $f(x) = |x + 2|$ *3-3*

Evaluate for $n = 4$. **58.** $5(n + 2) + 12$ **59.** $n(6 - n) + 7$ **60.** $(3n)^2$ *1-3*

Solve. **61.** $c + \frac{2}{3} = \frac{1}{2}$ **62.** $r - \frac{1}{2} = \frac{2}{5}$ **63.** $-\frac{k}{9} = \frac{4}{5}$ **64.** $9c = \frac{2}{5}$ *2-1*

More Equations of Lines

3-6

PART 1 Two-Point Equations of Lines

Objective: Use the two-point equation to find an equation of a line, given two points on the line.

Given two points, we can find an equation of the line containing them. If we find the slope of a line by dividing the change in y by the change in x and substitute this value for m in the point-slope equation, we obtain the **two-point equation.**

Theorem 3-6

The Two-Point Equation

Any nonvertical line containing the points (x_1, y_1) and (x_2, y_2) has an equation

$$y - y_1 = \frac{y_2 - y_1}{x_2 - x_1}(x - x_1)$$

EXAMPLE 1 Find an equation of the line containing the points (2, 3) and (1, −4).

We find the slope and then substitute in the two-point equation. We take (2, 3) as (x_1, y_1) and (1, −4) as (x_2, y_2).

$$y - 3 = \frac{-4 - 3}{1 - 2}(x - 2) \quad \text{Substituting}$$

$$y - 3 = \frac{-7}{-1}(x - 2) \quad \text{Simplifying}$$

$$y - 3 = 7(x - 2)$$

$$y - 3 = 7x - 14$$

$$y = 7x - 11$$

In Example 1, we could have taken (1, −4) as (x_1, y_1) and (2, 3) as (x_2, y_2) and arrived at the same equation.

$$y - (-4) = \frac{3 - (-4)}{2 - 1}(x - 1)$$

$$y = 7x - 11 \quad \text{Simplifying}$$

Try This Find an equation of the line containing the following pairs of points.

a. (1, 4) and (3, −2)

b. (3, −6) and (0, 4)

What You'll Learn

1. To find the two-point equation of a line
2. To find the slope and y-intercept of a line from the slope-intercept equation
3. To graph equations in slope-intercept form
4. To find the standard form of a linear equation

. . . And Why

To use linear equations for understanding problems

PART 2 Slope-Intercept Equations of Lines

Objective: Find the slope and y-intercept of a line, given the slope-intercept equation for the line.

If we know the slope and y-intercept, we can find an equation for the line. Suppose a line has slope 4 and y-intercept -2. From the point-slope equation we have

$$y - (-2) = 4(x - 0)$$
$$y + 2 = 4x$$
$$y = 4x - 2$$

This is the **slope-intercept equation** of the line.

Theorem 3-7

The Slope-Intercept Equation

A nonvertical line with slope m and y-intercept b has an equation $y = mx + b$.

From any equation for a nonvertical line, we can find the slope-intercept equation by solving for y. There is no slope-intercept equation for a vertical line because the line has no slope.

EXAMPLE 2 Find the slope and y-intercept of the line whose equation is $y = 2x - 3$.

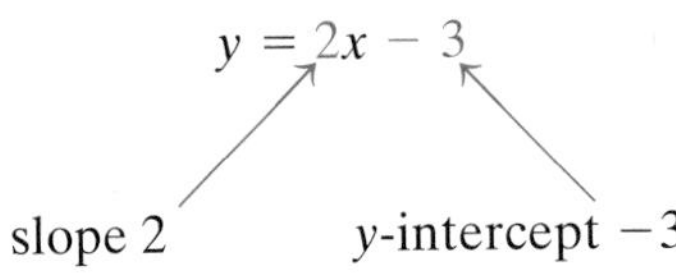

EXAMPLE 3 Find the slope and y-intercept of the line whose equation is $3x - 6y - 7 = 0$.

First solve for y. This puts the equation into slope-intercept form.

$$-6y = -3x + 7$$
$$-\frac{1}{6} \cdot (-6y) = -\frac{1}{6} \cdot (-3x) + \left(-\frac{1}{6}\right) \cdot 7$$
$$y = \frac{1}{2}x - \frac{7}{6}$$

The slope is $\frac{1}{2}$, the y-intercept is $-\frac{7}{6}$.

Try This Find the slope and y-intercept of each line.

c. $y = -5x + \frac{1}{3}$ **d.** $-2x + 3y - 6 = 0$ **e.** $2y - 6 = 0$

PART 3 Graphing Using Slope-Intercept Form

Objective: Graph linear equations in slope-intercept form.

EXAMPLE 4 Graph $5y - 20 = -3x$.

Solving for y, we find the slope-intercept form $y = -\frac{3}{5}x + 4$. Thus the y-intercept is 4 and the slope is $-\frac{3}{5}$.

We plot (0, 4) and then find another point by moving 5 units to the right and 3 units down. The point has coordinates (5, 1). We can then draw the line.

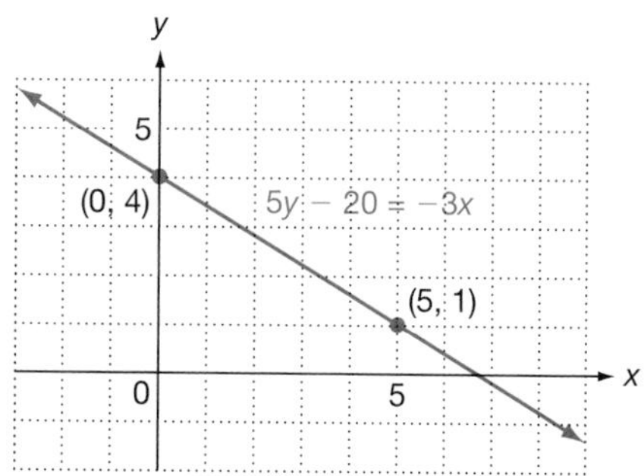

Graph each equation using slope-intercept form.

f. $y = 3x - 1$ **g.** $7y = -4x - 21$ **h.** $6x = -5y - \frac{5}{2}$

PART 4 Finding the Standard Form

Objective: Find the standard form of a linear equation.

Any linear equation can be written so that 0 is on the right side. This is called **standard form** of a linear equation.

Definition

The **standard form** of a linear equation is $Ax + By + C = 0$, where A and B are not both zero.

In standard form, A, B, and C represent constants.

We can change the standard form of a linear equation to the slope-intercept equation by solving for y. This leads to the following theorem.

Theorem 3-8

The slope of a line whose equation is $Ax + By + C = 0$ is $-\frac{A}{B}$ if $B \neq 0$.

EXAMPLE 5 Find the standard form and slope of the equation
$$7x = \frac{1}{4} - 5y.$$

$$7x = \frac{1}{4} - 5y$$
$$7x + 5y - \frac{1}{4} = 0 \quad \text{Using the addition principle, adding } 5y - \tfrac{1}{4}$$

This equation is of the form $Ax + By + C = 0$, where $A = 7$, $B = 5$, and $C = -\frac{1}{4}$. The slope is $-\frac{A}{B} = -\frac{7}{5}$.

Try This Find the standard form and slope of each equation.

i. $5y = \frac{1}{2} + 5x$ **j.** $8x = 10 + 5y$

Extra Help On the Web

Look for worked-out examples at the Prentice Hall Web site.
www.phschool.com

3-6 Exercises

A

Find an equation of the line containing the following pairs of points.

1. $(1, 4)$ and $(5, 6)$
2. $(2, 6)$ and $(4, 1)$
3. $(-1, -1)$ and $(2, 2)$
4. $(-3, -3)$ and $(6, 6)$
5. $(-2, 0)$ and $(0, 5)$
6. $(6, 0)$ and $(0, -3)$
7. $(3, 5)$ and $(-5, 3)$
8. $(4, 6)$ and $(-6, 4)$
9. $(0, 0)$ and $(5, 2)$
10. $(0, 0)$ and $(7, 3)$
11. $(-4, -7)$ and $(-2, -1)$
12. $(-2, -3)$ and $(-4, -6)$

Find the slope and y-intercept of each line.

13. $y = 2x + 3$
14. $y = 3x + 4$
15. $y = -4x + 9$
16. $y = -5x - 7$
17. $y = 6 - x$
18. $y = 7 - x$
19. $2y = -6x + 10$
20. $-3y = -12x + 6$
21. $3x - 4y = 12$
22. $5x + 2y = -7$
23. $6x + 2y - 8 = 0$
24. $3y - 2x + 5 = 0$
25. $-7x - 3y - 9 = 0$
26. $-8x - 5y - 7 = 0$
27. $y = 7$
28. $y = 9$
29. $3y + 10 = 0$
30. $4y + 11 = 0$

Graph each equation using slope-intercept form.

31. $y = -x + 4$
32. $6x - 6 - y = 0$
33. $-2y = -3x + 2$
34. $4x = -5y + 40$
35. $7x - 6y + 42 = 0$
36. $3y = -8x - 5$

Find the standard form and slope, if it exists, of each equation.

37. $4x - 8 = y$ **38.** $y = 6x - 2$ **39.** $y = 2x + 3$

40. $x = 2y - 1$ **41.** $x = 6$ **42.** $y = 9$

43. $5x = -5y + 10$ **44.** $y + 4 = 4x + 8$ **45.** $3x - 8 = x - 2$

46. $9x + 7 = 9x + 7 + y$ **47.** $3(x + 2y) = \frac{1}{2}(6x + 12y)$

B

Find an equation of a line with the given slope and y-intercept.

48. $m = -4$; y-intercept 3 **49.** $m = \frac{2}{5}$; y-intercept -4

50. $m = 75$; y-intercept -18 **51.** $m = -0.36$; y-intercept 10

Find an equation of the line containing each pair of points.

52. $(-0.2, 0.7)$ and $(-0.7, -0.3)$ **53.** $\left(\frac{1}{11}, \frac{1}{2}\right)$ and $\left(-\frac{10}{11}, -2\right)$

54. Find an equation of the line containing $(2, -3)$ and having the same slope as the line $3x + 4y = 10$.

55. Find an equation of the line containing $(3, -4)$ and having slope -2. If the line contains the points $(a, 8)$ and $(5, b)$, find a and b.

56. Write an equation of the line that has x-intercept -3 and y-intercept $\frac{2}{5}$.

57. *Critical Thinking* Consider the following equations. Tell which equation does **not** belong in the group and why.

a. $y = 5x + 3$ **b.** $2x + 3 = 5y - 9 + 4x$

c. $3x - 5y + 9 = 0$ **d.** $3(x + 9) = 4y - 7$

Challenge

58. Prove that $\frac{x}{a} + \frac{y}{b} = 1$ has x-intercept a and y-intercept b.

Use the result of Exercise 58 to find a, b, and the slope of each line.

59. $5x - 4y - 7 = 0$ **60.** $2y - 3x = 4$

61. $1.25y + 7.8x = 4.2x - 18$

62. Prove Theorem 3-8.

Mixed Review

Which of the following relations are functions?

63. $\{(0, 0), (1, 7), (2, 0), (-1, 7)\}$ **64.** $\{(1, 6), (1, 2)\}$

65. $\{(x, y) | y = 2x + 1\}$ **66.** $\{(x, y) | y = 3\}$ **67.** $\{(x, y) | x = 2\}$ *3-3*

68.–72. List the domain and the range for each of the above relations. *3-1*

73. Lucinda needed an average score of 9.45 to win a jump competition. The first 3 judges gave her 9.35, 9.40, and 9.25. What score did she need from the fourth judge to win? *2-2*

3-7 Parallel and Perpendicular Lines

What You'll Learn

1. To use equations to determine if two lines are parallel
2. To write the equation of a line through a given point, parallel to a given line
3. To use equations to determine whether two lines are perpendicular
4. To write the equation of a line through a given point, perpendicular to a given line

. . . And Why

To prepare for using equations

PART 1 Parallel Lines

Objective: Use equations to determine whether two lines are parallel.

When we graph a pair of linear equations on the same axes, there are three possibilities.

1. The equations have the same graph.
2. The graphs intersect at exactly one point.
3. The graphs are **parallel lines.**

Theorem 3-9

Two nonvertical lines are **parallel** if and only if they have the same slope and different y-intercepts.

EXAMPLE 1 Determine whether the graphs of $y = -3x + 5$ and $4y = -12x + 20$ are parallel.

We find the slope-intercept equations by solving for y.

$y = -3x + 5$ is already in slope-intercept form.

For $4y = -12x + 20$ we have

$$y = -\frac{12x}{4} + \frac{20}{4}$$

$$y = -3x + 5$$

The second equation is now in slope-intercept form. The two slope-intercept equations are the same. This tells us that the graphs are the same line. Thus the lines are not parallel.

EXAMPLE 2

Are the graphs of $y - 3x = 1$ and $-2y = 3x + 2$ parallel?

First find the slope-intercept form for each equation.

$$y = 3x + 1,\ y = -\frac{3}{2}x - 1$$

The slopes are different. Thus the lines are not parallel.

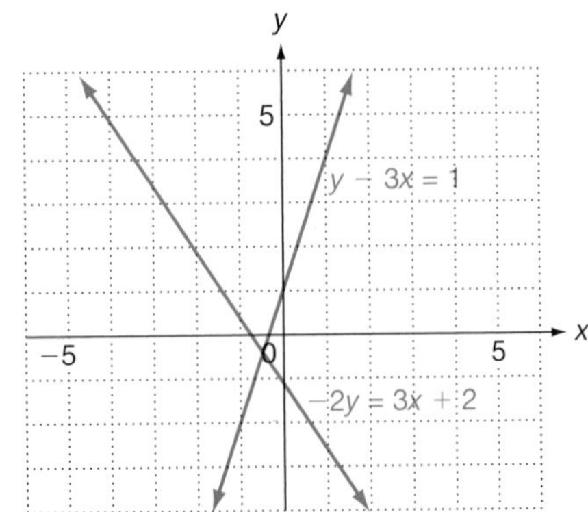

EXAMPLE 3 Determine whether the graphs of $3x - y = -5$ and $y - 3x = -2$ are parallel.

Solving for y in the equations

$$y = 3x + 5 \text{ and } y = 3x - 2.$$

The slopes are the same, but the y-intercepts are different. Thus the lines are parallel.

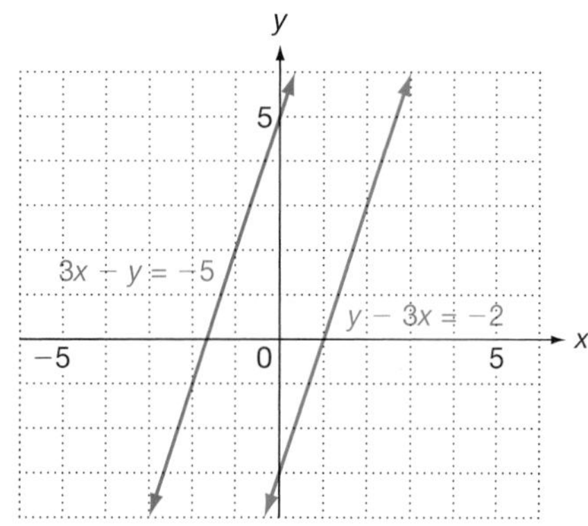

Try This Determine whether the graphs of each pair of equations are parallel.

a. $x + 4 = y$
$y - x = -3$

b. $y + 4 = 3x$
$4x - y = -7$

c. $y = 4x + 5$
$2y = 8x + 10$

PART 2 Finding Equations of Parallel Lines

Objective: Write an equation that contains a given point and is parallel to a given line.

EXAMPLE 4 Write an equation of the line containing the point $(-1, 3)$ and parallel to the line $2x + y = 10$.

We first find the slope-intercept equation.

$$y = -2x + 10$$

Now we see that the parallel line must have slope -2.

Next we find the point-slope equation of the line with slope -2 and containing the point $(-1, 3)$.

$y - y_1 = m(x - x_1)$	Theorem 3-5
$y - 3 = -2[x - (-1)]$	Substituting
$y = -2x + 1$	Simplifying

The equations $y = -2x + 10$ and $y = -2x + 1$ have the same slope and different y-intercepts. Hence their graphs are parallel.

Try This

d. Write an equation of the line containing the point $(-2, -4)$ and parallel to the line $2y + 8x = 6$.

PART 3 Perpendicular Lines

Objective: Use equations to determine whether two lines are perpendicular.

If two lines meet at right angles, they are **perpendicular.**

Theorem 3-10

Two nonvertical lines are **perpendicular** if and only if the product of their slopes is -1.

EXAMPLE 5 Determine whether the graphs of lines $5y = 4x + 10$ and $4y = -5x + 4$ are perpendicular.

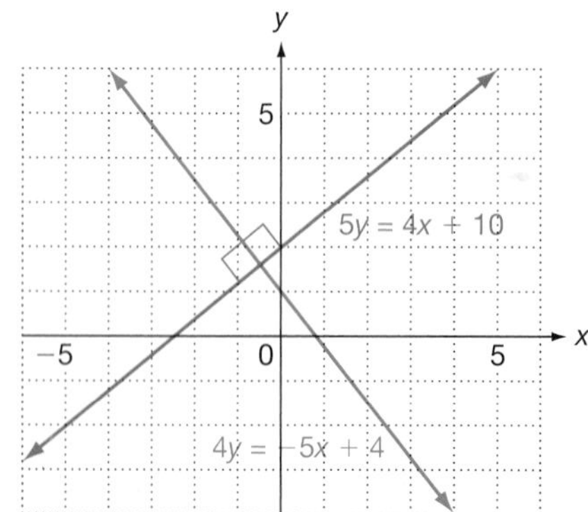

We find the slope-intercept equations by solving for y.

$y = \frac{4}{5}x + 2, \qquad y = -\frac{5}{4}x + 1$

The product of the slopes is -1; that is, $\frac{4}{5} \cdot \left(-\frac{5}{4}\right) = -1$.

The lines are perpendicular.

Proof of Theorem 3-10

Consider the line $\overleftrightarrow{AB}$ as shown, with slope $\frac{a}{b}$. Then think of rotating the entire figure 90° to get a line perpendicular to $\overleftrightarrow{AB}$. For the new line the roles of a and b are interchanged, but a is now negative. Thus the slope of the new line is $-\frac{b}{a}$. Let us multiply the slopes $\frac{a}{b}\left(-\frac{b}{a}\right) = -1$.

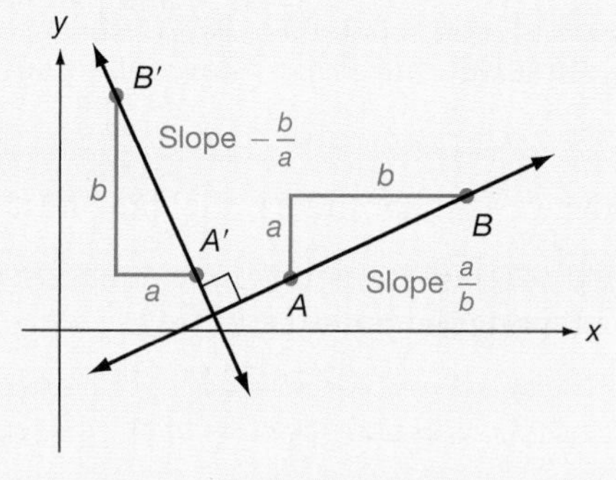

This is the condition under which lines will be perpendicular.

Try This Determine whether the graphs of each pair of equations are perpendicular.

e. $2y - x = 2$ and $y + 2x = 4$

f. $3y = 2x + 15$ and $2y = 3x + 10$

PART 4 Finding Equations of Perpendicular Lines

Objective: Write an equation of the line that contains a given point and is perpendicular to a given line.

EXAMPLE 6 Write an equation of the line perpendicular to $4y - x = 20$ and containing the point $(2, -3)$.

We find the slope-intercept equation for $4y - x = 20$.

$$y = \frac{1}{4}x + 5$$

We know that the slope of the perpendicular line must be -4 because $\frac{1}{4}(-4) = -1$. Next we find the point-slope equation of the line having slope -4 and containing the point $(2, -3)$.

$y - y_1 = m(x - x_1)$	Theorem 3-5
$y - (-3) = -4(x - 2)$	Substituting
$y = -4x + 5$	Simplifying

Try This Write an equation of the line containing the given point and perpendicular to the given line.

g. $(-1, 2);\ y = \frac{7}{8}x - 3$ **h.** $(3, 4);\ 4 - y = 2x$

3-7 Exercises

Internet Connection ***Extra Help On the Web***

Look for worked-out examples at the Prentice Hall Web site. www.phschool.com

A

Determine whether the graphs of each pair of equations are parallel.

1. $x + 6 = y$; $y - x = -2$

2. $2x - 7 = y$; $y - 2x = 8$

3. $y + 3 = 5x$; $3x - y = -2$

4. $y + 8 = -6x$; $-2x + y = 5$

5. $y = 3x + 9$; $2y = 6x - 2$

6. $y = -7x - 9$; $-3y = 21x + 7$

Multi-Step Problems Write an equation of the line containing the given point and parallel to the given line.

7. $(3, 7);\ x + 2y = 6$

8. $(0, 3);\ 3x - y = 7$

9. $(2, -1);\ 5x - 7y = 8$

10. $(-4, -5);\ 2x + y = -3$

11. $(-6, 2);\ 3x - 9y = 2$

12. $(-7, 0);\ 5x + 2y = 6$

Determine whether the graphs of each pair of equations are perpendicular.

13. $y = 4x - 5$ and $4y = 8 - x$

14. $2x - 5y = -3$ and $2x + 5y = 4$

15. $x + 2y = 5$ and $2x + 4y = 8$

16. $y = -x + 7$ and $y = x + 3$

Write an equation of the line containing the given point and perpendicular to the given line.

17. $(2, 5); 2x + y = -3$

18. $(4, 0); x - 3y = 0$

19. $(3, -2); 3x + 4y = 5$

20. $(-3, -5); 5x - 2y = 4$

21. $(0, 9); 2x + 5y = 7$

22. $(-3, -4); -3x + 6y = 2$

B

23. Find an equation of the line containing $(4, -2)$ and parallel to the line containing $(-1, 4)$ and $(2, -3)$.

24. Find an equation of the line containing $(-1, 3)$ and perpendicular to the line containing $(3, -5)$ and $(-2, 7)$.

25. Use slopes to show that the triangle with vertices $(-2, 7)$, $(6, 9)$, and $(3, 4)$ is a right triangle.

26. Write an equation of the line that has y-intercept $\frac{5}{7}$ and is parallel to the graph of $6x - 3y = 1$.

27. Write an equation of the line that has x-intercept -1.2 and is perpendicular to the graph of $6x - 3y = 1$.

28. *Critical Thinking* Two lines are perpendicular, and neither is vertical. How many quadrants must the lines pass through?

29. *Error Analysis* Jessie rewrote Theorem 3-10 as follows: "Two nonvertical lines are perpendicular if and only if their slopes are negative reciprocals of each other." Is Jessie's statement equivalent to the statement on page 140?

Challenge

30. Line l is perpendicular to line m, and line m is perpendicular to line n. Lines l and n do not coincide.

a. What is the relationship between the slopes of lines l and n?

b. How many points do lines l and n have in common?

c. If line l has an equation $y = mx + b$, write an equation for line n.

31. Find a so that the graphs of $5y = ax + 5$ and $\frac{1}{4}y = \frac{1}{10}x - 1$ are parallel.

32. Find k so that the graphs of $x + 7y = 70$ and $y + 3 = kx$ are perpendicular.

Self-Test On the Web

Check your progress. Look for a self-test at the Prentice Hall Web site. www.phschool.com

Mixed Review

Determine whether the following ordered pairs are solutions of $y = 3x + 5$.

33. $(5, 0)$ **34.** $(-1, 2)$ **35.** $(0, 8)$ **36.** $(-50, -145)$ **37.** $(50, 145)$ 3-2

Consider the function $f(x) = 3x^2 - 2x + 6$. Find each function value.

38. $f(0)$ **39.** $f(-2)$ **40.** $f(3)$ **41.** $f(1)$ **42.** $f(-6)$ **43.** $f(6)$ 3-3

Mathematical Modeling: Using Linear Functions

PART 1 Determining Linear Functions

Objective: Find a linear function and use the equation to make predictions.

What You'll Learn

1 To determine a linear equation from a table and make predictions

. . . And Why

To find a graph to represent data

Crickets are known to chirp faster at higher temperatures and slower at lower temperatures. The number of chirps is thus a function of the temperature.

The following data were collected and recorded in a table.

Temperature °C	6	8	10	15	20
Number of chirps per min	11	29	47	75	109

If a cricket chirps 38 times per minute, use the formula of Example 1 to determine the approximate temperature.

Can we predict the number of chirps per minute for a temperature of 18°C? If a linear equation fits the data reasonably well, we can develop a **linear function** as a **mathematical model** of the situation. We can then use the model (the linear function) to make predictions.

EXAMPLE 1 Use the data collected in the table to predict the number of chirps per minute when the temperature is 18°C.

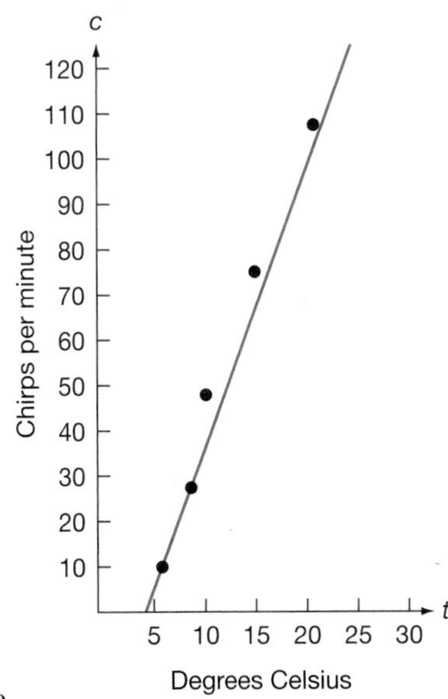

UNDERSTAND the problem

Question: Can a linear function fit the data, and, if so, what is the approximate number of chirps per minute for a temperature of 18°C?

Data: Crickets chirp 11 times per minute at 6°C, 29 times per minute at 8°C, and so on, as listed in the table.

Develop and carry out a PLAN

First, we plot the data to determine whether a linear equation gives an approximate fit. We make a graph with a t-axis (temperature) and a c-axis (chirps per minute), and plot the data. We see that they lie approximately on a straight line. Thus, we can use a linear function to model the situation.

The line is placed so that some points are above and some are below the line, and so that each is close to the line.

We can use two of the **data points** that are close to the line to find a two-point equation. We choose the points given by (6, 11) and (20, 109) since the line through these points is very close to the line we fit, over the domain of the data.

$$c - c_1 = \frac{c_2 - c_1}{t_2 - t_1}(t - t_1)$$ Using the two-point equation, c is chirps, t is temperature.

$$c - 11 = \frac{109 - 11}{20 - 6}(t - 6)$$ Substituting

$$c - 11 = 7(t - 6)$$

$$c = 7t - 31$$

■ Find the ANSWER and CHECK

Using this equation as a formula, we find that when $t = 18$, $c = 7(18) - 31 = 95$. When the temperature is 18°C, crickets chirp about 95 times per minute. The answer is reasonable, since 95 falls between 75 and 109, and is closer to 109.

EXAMPLE 2

Wind tunnel experiments are used to test the wind friction, or resistance, of an automobile at various speeds. If resistance is a linear function of speed, predict the resistance of an automobile traveling 50 km/h.

Speed (km/h)	Resistance (kg)
10	3.2
21	4.8
34	7.2
40	8.0
45	15.1
52	30.0

Use the graph in Example 2 to predict the resistance of an automobile traveling 30 km/h.

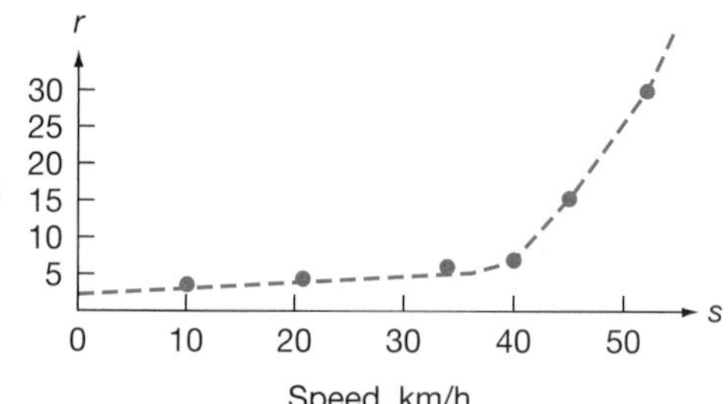

When graphed, the data do not approximate one straight line. However, there appear to be two linear parts to the graph: for speeds up to 40 km/h and for speeds of 40 km/h and above. We use (10, 3.2) and (40, 8.0) to find $r = 0.16s + 16$ for $s \leq 40$, and use (40, 8.0) and (52, 30) to find $r = 1.83s - 65.3$ for $s \geq 40$.

For $s = 50$, $r = 1.83(50) - 65.3 = 26.2$. Thus the resistance at 50 km/h is approximately 22.4 kg. Note that a nonlinear function might fit the data better.

Try This

a. It has been found that certain running records have changed with time, according to linear functions. In 1920 the record for the 100-m dash was 10.43 seconds. In 1983 it was 9.93 seconds. Let R represent the record in the 100-m dash and t the number of years since 1920.

1. Fit a linear function to the data points.

2. Use your function to predict the record in 2005; in 2050.

3. In what year will the record be 9.0 seconds?

b. A chemistry experiment generated the following temperatures for a solution over time.

Time (minutes)	5	15	25	30	32
Temperature °F	75	130	175	200	210

If a linear function fits the data, determine the function, predict the temperature of the solution after 8 minutes, and predict the time it takes for the temperature to reach 60°F.

Guidelines for Finding Linear Functions

1. Graph the data.
2. If the data lie approximately on a straight line, a linear function can be used.
3. Graph a line so that approximately half the points are above and half are below the line.
4. Find the coordinates for two of the data points on or close to the line.
5. Apply the two-point equation to find a linear function.

3-8 Exercises

Extra Help On the Web

Look for worked-out examples at the Prentice Hall Web site. www.phschool.com

A

Solve.

1. In 1950 the life expectancy of women was 72 years. In 1970 it was 75 years. Let E represent the life expectancy and t the number of years since 1950 ($t = 0$ gives 1950 and $t = 10$ gives 1960).

a. Fit a linear function to the data points. [They are (0, 72) and (20, 75).]

b. Use the function to predict the life expectancy of women in 2003; in 2018.

2. In 1950 the life expectancy of men was 65 years. In 1970 it was 68 years. Let E represent the life expectancy and t the number of years since 1950.

a. Fit a linear function to the data points.

b. Use the function to predict the life expectancy of men in 2003; in 2017.

3. In 1950 natural gas demand in the United States was 20 quadrillion joules. In 1960 the demand was 22 quadrillion joules. Let D represent the demand for natural gas t years after 1950.

   a. Fit a linear function to the data points.

   b. Use the function to predict the natural gas demand in 2004; in 2015.

4. In 1930 the record for the 1500-m run was 3.85 minutes. In 1950 it was 3.70 minutes. Let R represent the record in the 1500-m run and t the number of years since 1930.

   a. Fit a linear function to the data points.

   b. Use the function to predict the record in 2006; in 2021.

   c. When will the record be 3.3 minutes?

5. In 1930 the record for the 400-m run was 46.8 seconds. In 1970 it was 43.8 s. Let R represent the record in the 400-m run and t the number of years since 1930.

   a. Fit a linear function to the data points.

   b. Use the function to predict the record in 2003; in 2012.

   c. When will the record be 40 seconds?

6. The cost of a taxi ride for the first $\frac{1}{5}$ mi is \$2.10. For 3 mi the cost is \$5.20.

   a. Fit a linear function to the data points.

   b. Use the function to find the cost of a 7-mi ride.

   c. How far could a person ride for \$20?

7. If you rent a car for 1 day and drive it 100 mi, the cost is \$40.00. If you drive it 150 mi, the cost is \$48.00.

   a. Fit a linear function to the data points.

   b. Use the function to find how much it will cost to rent the car for 1 day if you drive it 200 mi.

8. An accountant located five different city tax returns for a specific year. These were the city taxes for some different incomes.

Income (in \$000)	8	15	25	40	75
Taxes (in dollars)	24	70	180	300	560

   If a linear function fits the data, determine the function, predict the taxes for an income of \$55,000, and predict the income for taxes of \$240.

9. An instant espresso coffee comes in several size jars. These were the prices for each size at one supermarket.

Ounces	2	6	10	16	32
Price	\$1.65	\$4.15	\$5.29	\$7.89	\$12.99

   If a linear function fits the data, determine the function, predict the price of a 24-oz jar, and predict the size of a jar that would sell for \$17.99.

B

Solve, assuming a linear function fits the situation.

10. The value of a copy machine is \$5200 when it is purchased. After 2 years its value is \$4225. Find its value after 8 years.

11. Water freezes at 32° Fahrenheit and at 0° Celsius. Water boils at 212°F and at 100°C. What Celsius temperature corresponds to a room temperature of 70°F?

12. A business determines that when it sells 7000 units of a product it will take in \$22,000. For the sale of 8000 units it will take in \$25,000. How much will it take in for the sale of 10,000 units?

13. For a linear function f, $f(-1) = 3$ and $f(2) = 4$.

a. Find an equation for f. **b.** Find $f(3)$. **c.** Find a such that $f(a) = 100$.

14. *Critical Thinking* Suppose in Example 1 that the temperature is actually determined by the number of times the crickets chirp. How could you quickly develop a linear function to determine the temperature for a specific number of chirps per minute?

Challenge

15. A person applying for a sales position is offered alternative salary plans.

Plan A: a base salary of \$600 per month plus a commission of 4% of the gross sales for the month

Plan B: a base salary of \$700 per month plus a commission of 6% of the gross sales of the month in excess of \$10,000

a. For each plan, formulate a function that expresses monthly earnings as a function of gross sales x.

b. For what gross sales values is Plan B preferable?

16. An anthropologist can use linear functions to estimate the height of a male or female, given the length of certain bones. A *humerus* is the bone from the elbow to the shoulder. The height, in centimeters, of a male with a humerus of length x is given by $M(x) = 2.89x + 70.64$. The height, in centimeters, of a female with a humerus of length x is given by $F(x) = 2.75x + 71.48$. A 45-cm humerus was uncovered in some ruins.

a. Assuming it was from a male, how tall was he?

b. Assuming it was from a female, how tall was she?

c. For what height would the lengths of a female humerus and a male humerus be equal?

Mixed Review

Find the slope, if it exists, of each line. **17.** $3y = -12$ **18.** $x = 4$ *3-5*

Find the equation of the lines containing the given points, with the indicated slopes.

19. $(-1, -4)$; $m = 1$ **20.** $(2, 3)$; $m = -1$ **21.** $(4, 2)$; $m = 0$ *3-6*

Simplify. **22.** $9c - 16c$ **23.** $4m + 2m - m$ **24.** $7x + 5 + (4 - 2x)$

25. $t + t + t$ **26.** $4(3r) - 12s + 2r$ **27.** $6(y + 4y) + 3y$ **28.** $(p^2 \cdot p^2)^2 \cdot p^{-4}$ *1-3, 1-7*

3-9 More about Functions

What You'll Learn

1. To graph special functions
2. To find the composite of two functions

. . . And Why

To use functions in solving problems

First class postage for letters or packages is a function of weight. For one ounce or less, the postage is 33¢. For each additional ounce *or fraction of an ounce*, 22¢ is due. Such a function is called a **step function** since at each integral ounce, the price steps to the next value. Another example of a step function is the **greatest integer function** $f(x) = [x]$.

PART 1 Special Functions

Objective: Graph special functions.

The greatest integer function, $f(x) = [x]$, is the greatest integer that is less than or equal to x. For example, $[4.5] = 4$, $[-1] = -1$, and $[-3.9] = -4$.

EXAMPLE 1 Graph $f(x) = [x]$.

For $0 \leq x < 1$, $f(x) = 0$.
For $1 \leq x < 2$, $f(x) = 1$.
For $2 \leq x < 3$, $f(x) = 2$,
and so on.

We can use the pattern above to graph $f(x)$ for x between any two integers, and thus graph the function for all real numbers.

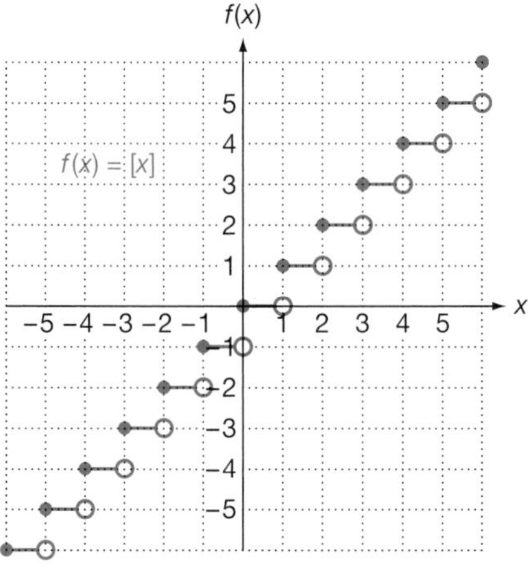

EXAMPLE 2 Graph $f(x) = |x|$.

Finding the absolute value of a number can also be thought of in terms of a function, the **absolute value function,** $f(x) = |x|$. The domain of the absolute value function is the set of real numbers; the range is the set of positive real numbers.

The graph has two parts,

For $x \geq 0$, $f(x) = x$.
For $x < 0$, $f(x) = -x$.

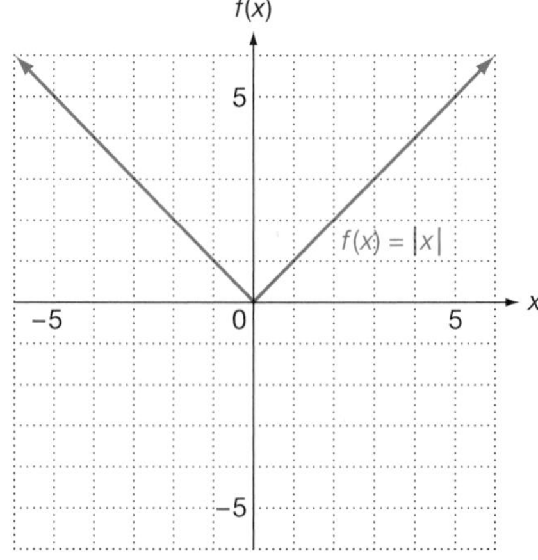

Try This Graph.

a. $y = [x] + 1$ **b.** $y = [x + 1]$ **c.** $f(x) = |x| + 1$ **d.** $f(x) = |x + 1|$

PART 2 Composition of Functions

Objective: Find the composite of two functions.

Functions can be combined in many ways. One such way is called **composition.**

Definition

Let f and g be any two functions such that the range of g is in the domain of f. The **composition** of f and g is the function given by $f(g(x))$.

Journal

Suppose a friend called asking how to graph a function that rounds a number to the nearest ten. Describe your instructions.

EXAMPLES Suppose $f(x) = x^2$ and $g(x) = x + 2$.

3 Find $f(g(3))$.

First find $g(3)$.

$g(3) = 3 + 2$ Substituting 3 for x in $g(x) = x + 2$
$= 5$

Then find $f(g(3))$.

$f(g(3)) = f(5)$ Substituting 5 for $g(3)$
$= 5^2$ Substituting 5 for x in $f(x) = x^2$
$= 25$

We can find compositions of functions by working within inner parentheses first.

4 Find $g(f(3))$.

$g(f(x)) = g(x^2)$ Substituting x^2 for $f(x)$
$g(f(3)) = g(3^2)$ Substituting 3 for x
$= g(9)$
$= 9 + 2 = 11$ Substituting 9 for x in $g(x) = x + 2$

Try This Suppose $f(x) = 2x$ and $g(x) = x - 7$.

e. Find $f(g(2))$. **f.** Find $g(f(2))$. **g.** Find $g(f(0))$. **h.** Find $f(g(-5))$.

We can find expressions that represent the composite of two functions.

EXAMPLES Suppose $f(x) = 4x$ and $g(x) = x + 3$.

5 Find an expression for $f(g(x))$.

$$\begin{aligned} f(g(x)) &= f(x + 3) && \text{Substituting } x + 3 \text{ for } g(x) \\ &= 4(x + 3) \\ &= 4x + 12 && \text{Using the distributive property} \end{aligned}$$

6 Find an expression for $g(f(x))$.

$$\begin{aligned} g(f(x)) &= g(4x) && \text{Substituting } 4x \text{ for } f(x) \\ &= 4x + 3 \end{aligned}$$

Try This Suppose $f(x) = -3x$ and $g(x) = x - 4$.

i. Find an expression for $f(g(x))$.
j. Find an expression for $g(f(x))$.
k. Find an expression for $f(f(x))$.
l. Find an expression for $g(g(x))$.

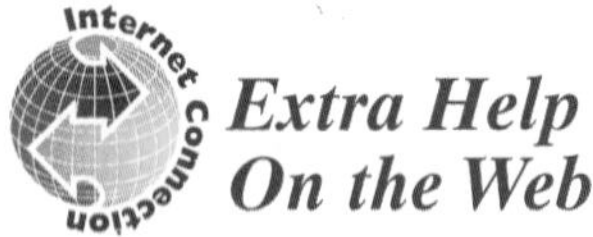

Extra Help On the Web

Look for worked-out examples at the Prentice Hall Web site.
www.phschool.com

3-9 Exercises

A

Graph.

1. $f(x) = [x - 2]$ **2.** $f(x) = [x] - 1$ **3.** $f(x) = [x - 1]$
4. $f(x) = |x - 1|$ **5.** $f(x) = |x - 2|$ **6.** $f(x) = |x| + x$
7. $f(x) = |x| - 1$ **8.** $f(x) = \frac{1}{2}|x|$ **9.** $f(x) = 2|x| - 2$

Find the following. For Exercises 10–25 suppose $f(x) = x^2$, $g(x) = x - 1$, and $h(x) = 4x$.

10. $f(g(2))$ **11.** $g(f(-1))$ **12.** $h(g(3))$ **13.** $f(h(-2))$
14. $h(g(0))$ **15.** $g(h(9))$ **16.** $f(g(-5))$ **17.** $h(g(-12))$

Find expressions for the following.

18. $f(g(x))$ **19.** $g(h(x))$ **20.** $f(h(x))$ **21.** $g(f(x))$
22. $g(g(x))$ **23.** $f(f(x))$ **24.** $h(f(x))$ **25.** $h(h(x))$

B

26. A person's bowling average is defined as follows. Bowling average $= \left[\frac{P}{n}\right]$ where P = total number of pins, and n = total number of games bowled. Find the bowling average.

a. 547 pins in 3 games **b.** 4621 pins in 27 games

27. Draw the graph of the postage step function described in the introduction to this lesson. What is the domain and the range of this function?

28. The **signum function, sgn,** is defined as follows: $\text{sgn}(x) = -1$ when $x < 0$, $\text{sgn}(x) = 0$ when $x = 0$, and $\text{sgn}(x) = 1$ when $x > 0$. Draw a graph of the signum function.

Suppose $f(x) = |x|$ and $g(x) = 2x$.

29. Find $f(g(-5))$. **30.** Find $g(f(-6))$. **31.** Find $f(g(-18))$.

The composite of two functions f and g is sometimes represented by $f \circ g$. Thus $(f \circ g) = f(g(x))$. Suppose $f(x) = -x$ and $g(x) = 7x$.

32. Find $(f \circ g)(-3)$. **33.** Find $(f \circ g)(7)$. **34.** Find $(g \circ f)(0)$.

Suppose $f(x) = -x^2$, $g(x) = x - 3$, and $h(x) = -2x$. Find the following.

35. $f(g(h(1)))$ **36.** $g(h(f(0)))$ **37.** $h(g(f(4)))$ **38.** $h(h(h(2)))$

Suppose $f(x) = 5x$, $g(x) = 2x - 1$, and $h(x) = x + 5$. Find expressions for the following.

39. $f(g(h(x)))$ **40.** $g(g(h(x)))$ **41.** $h(g(f(x)))$ **42.** $f(g(f(x)))$

43. ***Multi-Step Problem*** The temperature in degrees Kelvin is the number of degrees Celsius plus 273. The temperature in degrees Fahrenheit is $\frac{9}{5}$ times the number of degrees Celsius, plus 32.

a. Write a function for degrees Kelvin in terms of degrees Fahrenheit.

b. Find the Kelvin temperature for $-13°$F.

44. ***Critical Thinking*** The graph of a function is the reflection of $f(x) = |x|$ across the x-axis. Write an equation that defines this function.

45. **TEST PREP** If $f(x) = 3x + 2$ and $g(x) = -5x - 9$, find $f(g(3))$.

A. 74 **B.** -64 **C.** -70 **D.** 20

The average temperature of the human body is 98.6°F. What is the average temperature of the human body in °C? (See Exercise 43.)

Challenge

46. Graph $|x| - |y| = 1$.

47. Graph the relation $\{(x, y)|x| \leq 1 \text{ and } |y| \leq 2\}$.

48. Determine whether the relation $\{(x, y)|xy = 0\}$ is a function.

49. Graph the equation $[y] = [x]$. Is this the graph of a function?

50. $f(x) = 2x + 7$ and $g(x) = 3x + b$. Find b such that $f(g(x)) = g(f(x))$.

51. $f(x) = ax + b$. Find an expression for $f(f(x))$.

Mixed Review

For each pair of points, find the equation of the line containing them.

52. (1, 3) and (6, 13) **53.** $(-1, -1)$ and (3, 3) **54.** (0, 0) and $(2, -3)$ *3-6*

Write each expression without negative exponents.

55. 5^{-4} **56.** $(2w)^{-3}$ **57.** m^2n^{-9} *1-8*

Solve. **58.** $0.8a = -2.4$ **59.** $1.02 + c = -0.85$ **60.** $|3x - 5| = 19$ *2-1*

61. Valerie's mother loaned her $8700 interest-free. Valerie was to pay all but 25% of the money in equal monthly payments over 3 years and the remainder at the end of the loan. How much is her monthly payment? *2-2*

3-10  Reasoning Strategies

What You'll Learn

1 To make an organized list

. . . And Why

To solve problems using another strategy

PART 1 Make an Organized List

Objective: Solve problems using the strategy *Make an Organized List* and other strategies.

PROBLEM-SOLVING GUIDELINES
■ UNDERSTAND the problem
■ Develop and carry out a PLAN
■ Find the ANSWER and CHECK

Some problems can be solved by listing information from the problem in a systematic or organized way. This strategy for solving problems is called *Make an Organized List.*

EXAMPLE

A taxicab company was told that their license plates would consist of three letters followed by two numbers. The letters would be A, B, and C, and the numbers would be 3 and 5. No letter could be used twice in the same license plate, but a number could be used twice. How many choices did this company have for license plates?

We can solve this problem by making an organized list. First we can list the ways the letters can be arranged. There are 6 ways this could be done.

ABC BAC CAB
ACB BCA CBA

Next we can list the ways the numbers can be arranged. There are 4 ways.

33 35 53 55

Now we can list the ways the letters and numbers can be combined.

ABC33 BAC33 CAB33
ABC35 BAC35 CAB35
ABC53 BAC53 CAB53
ABC55 BAC55 CAB55

ACB33 BCA33 CBA33
ACB35 BCA35 CBA35
ACB53 BCA53 CBA53
ACB55 BCA55 CBA55

There are 24 choices for license plates. Notice that the list above was organized by first listing all possibilities with ABC in the license plate, then with BAC, and so on. Organizing the lists helps you know that you have listed all possibilities.

Reasoning Strategies

Write an Equation	Draw a Diagram	Try, Test, Revise
Make an Organized List	Make a Table	Look for a Pattern
Use Logical Reasoning	Simplify the Problem	Work Backward

3-10 Problems

Extra Help On the Web

Look for worked-out examples at the Prentice Hall Web site. www.phschool.com

Solve using one or more of the strategies presented.

1. A radio announcer had $48 to buy CDs. The $16 CDs were on sale for $6 and the $12 CDs were on sale for $4. In how many different ways could the announcer spend all of her money buying the CDs on sale?
2. The cost of a rectangular carpet for a certain room will be $858. Carpeting is sold with whole-number dimensions only, and then trimmed to fit the room. The cost is $6 per square foot. What are the dimensions of the carpet?
3. A designer had a poster board 36″ high by 48″ wide. She wanted to use 2″-high letters with 1″ of space between each line of words. She also wanted a 2″ border around the edge of the entire poster. How many lines of words can she get on this poster?
4. A basketball series between two teams is determined when one team wins three games. In how many ways could a team win the series?
5. At a banquet in a Chinese restaurant, 65 dishes were served. Every 2 guests shared a dish of rice between them; every 3 guests shared a dish of noodles; and every 4 guests shared a dish of meat. How many people were at the banquet?
6. *Mathematical Reasoning* Suppose you had an $8\frac{1}{2}$″ by 11″ sheet of paper. How could you use that paper to measure a line segment 6″ long?
7. Theo always carries lots of change in quarters, nickels, dimes, and pennies. Sonia needed change for a dollar. It turned out that Theo had the most change he could possibly have without having change for a dollar. How much did Theo have in change?
8. Avram forgot his four-digit ATM code. He knew that the four numbers were 2, 3, 5, and 8, but he could not remember the order. How many possible codes were there?
9. Three machines produce three pairs of headphones in three hours. How many pairs of headphones would nine machines produce in nine hours?

Write a function to show that an average of 15 chickens are cooked for every hour the Chinese restaurant is open during the day. See Exercise 5.

Application

Comparative Shopping

Whether you are buying or renting, you can save money by doing some comparative shopping. Consider car rentals. The rental fee may be a function of the number of days the car is rented, the number of miles driven, the amount of gasoline used, and the type of car rented.

EXAMPLE

Suppose you have a choice between the following companies for renting a particular car. You can assume that the gasoline costs will be equal.

Drive-Far Rent-A-Car	\$25/day and \$0.10/mile
Penguin Rent-A-Car	\$10/day and \$0.40/mile

Gasoline-burning cars create noise and pollution, but currently are about half as expensive to operate as battery-powered cars. In the future more cars will be solar cell or battery powered. The "filling station" of the future may be an electric "hitching post," tying the past in transportation to the future!

You need to consider your driving plans. If you'll be driving far, you may want to choose the lower mileage rate. If you plan to keep the car a long time, you may want to choose the lower daily rate. You can use equations to help make the decision. Compare the charges, assuming you need to rent a car for two days and drive it 60 miles.

Drive-Far: $2(\$25) + 60(\$0.10) = \$56$
Penguin: $2(\$10) + 60(\$0.40) = \$44$

In this case, Penguin is cheaper.

What if you planned to drive 300 miles in two days?

Drive-Far: $2(\$25) + 300(\$0.10) = \$80$
Penguin: $2(\$10) + 300(\$0.40) = \$140$

For this driving distance, Drive-Far is cheaper.

Problems

Choose which company you would use in each situation. Explain your decision.

Buckle-Up Car Rentals	\$30/day and \$0.10/mile
Rent-A-Roadster Car Rentals	\$14/day and \$0.15/mile

1. You need to rent a car for 3 days and drive 375 miles.
2. You need to rent a car for 3 days and drive 1200 miles.
3. You need to rent a car for 12 days and drive 3000 miles.
4. At what amount of mileage per day does one company become a better choice than the other?
5. Swift Car Rentals has a rate of \$25/day + \$0.20/mile, but the first 100 miles are free. For which situation in Problems 1–3 would Swift be cheapest?

3 Chapter Wrap Up

3-1

A **relation** from set A to set B is any set of ordered pairs in the **Cartesian product $A \times B$.**

1. Consider sets A and B, where $A = \{a, b, c\}$ and $B = \{1, 2\}$. List the set of ordered pairs in $A \times B$.
2. Consider the relation $C \times C$, where $C = \{-2, -1, 0, 1\}$. Find the set of ordered pairs determined by the relation $>$.
3. List the domain and the range of the relation $\{(1, 2), (-1, 4), (0, 5), (2, -4), (-6, 5), (2, 1)\}$.

3-2

If an equation has two variables, its solutions are **ordered pairs.** Each ordered pair, when substituted for the variables, produces a true equation.

4. Which of these ordered pairs $(-3, -3)$, $(0, 3)$, $(-1, 2)$ is a solution to the equation $y = 3 - 2x$?
5. Graph $y = -2x - 2$.
6. Graph $y = x^2 - 1$.

3-3

A **function** is a relation in which no two ordered pairs have the same first coordinate and different second coordinates.

Which of the following are graphs of functions?

7.

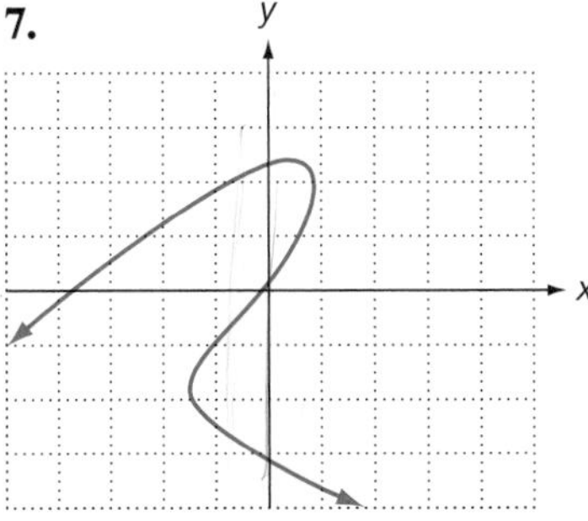

8.

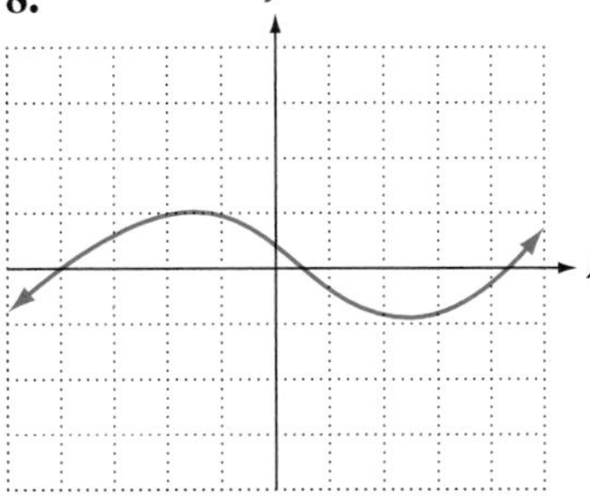

3-4

An equation is **linear** if the variables occur to the first power only, its graph is a straight line, and there are no variables in a denominator.

Which of these are linear equations?

9. $x - 5y = 8$ **10.** $3xy + y^2 = 0$ **11.** $2x = 5y - 9$ **12.** $y^2 - y = 9y$

Key Terms

$A \times B$ (p. 106)
abscissa (p. 110)
absolute value function (p. 148)
Cartesian coordinate system (p. 110)
Cartesian product (p. 106)
composition (p. 149)
coordinates of a point (p. 110)
data points (p. 144)
domain (p. 107)
family of lines (p. 126)
first-degree equation (p. 122)
function (p. 116)
grade (p. 127)
graph (p. 110)
greatest integer function (p. 148)
linear equation (p. 122)
linear function (p. 143)
mathematical model (p. 143)
ordered pair (p. 106)
ordinate (p. 110)
origin (p. 110)
parallel lines (p. 138)
parameter (p. 126)
perpendicular lines (p. 140)
point-slope equation (p. 130)
quadrant (p. 110)
range (p. 107)
relation (p. 107)
set-builder notation (p. 108)
(Key Terms continue on page 156.)

(Key Terms continued)
signum function (sgn) (p. 150)
slope (p. 127)
slope-intercept equation (p. 134)
solution (p. 111)
standard form (p. 135)
step function (p. 148)
two-point equation (p. 133)
value of a function (p. 118)
x-axis (p. 110)
x-coordinate (p. 110)
x-intercept (p. 123)
y-axis (p. 110)
y-coordinate (p. 110)
y-intercept (p. 123)

Internet Activity On the Web

Look for extension problems for this chapter at the Prentice Hall Web site. www.phschool.com

The **y-intercept** is the y-coordinate of the point where the graph crosses the y-axis. The **x-intercept** is the x-coordinate of the point where the graph crosses the x-axis.

13. Graph $-5x + 2y = 10$. **14.** Graph $x = 3$. **15.** Graph $y = -2$.

3-5

For a line containing, (x_1, y_1) and (x_2, y_2), the **slope** $m = \frac{\text{change in } y}{\text{change in } x}$, or $\frac{y_2 - y_1}{x_2 - x_1}$.

16. Find the slope of the line containing $(8, 2)$ and $(-4, -3)$.

A line containing a point (x_1, y_1) with slope m, has an equation $(y - y_1) = m(x - x_1)$.

17. Find the equation of the line containing $(-4, 2)$ with $m = \frac{1}{2}$.

3-6

A line containing (x_1, y_1) and (x_2, y_2) has an equation

$y - y_1 = \frac{y_2 - y_1}{x_2 - x_1}(x - x_1)$.

18. Find the equation of the line containing $(8, 2)$ and $(-4, -3)$.

The **slope-intercept equation** is $y = mx + b$ where m is the slope and b is the y-intercept.

19. Find the slope and y-intercept of $-5x + 2y = -4$.

The **standard form** for a linear equation is $Ax + By + C = 0$. Its slope is $-\frac{A}{B}$.

20. Find the standard form and the slope of $5x + 2y - 7 = 5y - 11$.

3-7

If two nonvertical lines are **parallel,** then they have the same slope. If two nonvertical lines are **perpendicular,** then the product of their slopes is -1.

21. Find an equation of the line containing $(-3, 7)$ that is

a. parallel to the line $5x + 3y = 8$.

b. perpendicular to the line $5x + 3y = 8$.

3-8

A **linear function** is a function f given by $f(x) = mx + b$.

In 1920 the record for the 200-m dash was 20.8 seconds. In 1945 it was 20.1 seconds. Let r represent the record in the 200-m dash and t the number of years since 1920.

22. Fit a linear function to the data points. **23.** Predict the record in 2004.

24. When would you predict that the record will be 18.5 seconds?

3-9

Two special functions are the **absolute value** and **greatest integer** functions.

25. Graph $y = |x - 3|$. **26.** Graph $y = [x] - 3$.

To find the **composition** $f(g(x))$, first find $g(x)$. Then substitute the value of $g(x)$ into $f(x)$.

If $f(x) = 2x$, $g(x) = x^2 - 1$, and $h(x) = x + 1$,

27. find $f(g(3))$. **28.** find $h(g(f(2)))$. **29.** find an expression for $f(g(h(x)))$.

3 Chapter Assessment

1. $A = \{-1, 1, 3, 7\}$ and $B = \{p, q\}$. List all ordered pairs in $A \times B$.
2. Consider the set $\{-4, -2, 0, 2\}$. Find the set of ordered pairs determined by the relation $\leq$ (is less than or equal to).
3. List the domain and the range of the relation $\{(-1, 4), (2, 3), (-2, -3), (1, -2)\}$.
4. Consider the set $\{-10, -5, 0, 5, 10\}$. Find the set indicated by $\{x | -7 < x < 5\}$.
5. Which of $(-2, 5)$, $(-2, 0)$, $(3, -1,)$ and $(0, -1)$ is a solution to $y = 2x - 7$?
6. Graph $y = -3x + 1$.
7. $y = 2x^2 + 1$.

Which of the graphs in the right column are graphs of functions?

8.

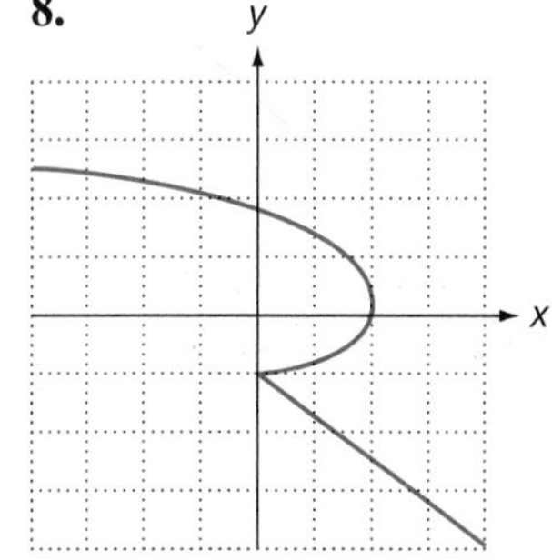

9.

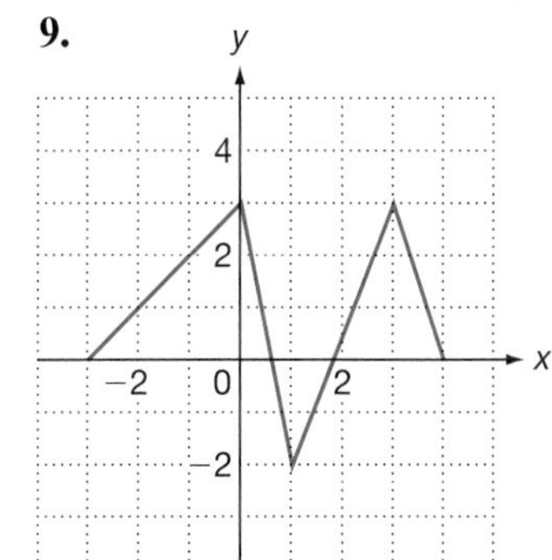

Which of these are linear equations?

10. $xy = 5$
11. $\frac{x}{y} = 4$
12. $2x = y$
13. $x = 7$
14. Graph $6x - 4y = 12$ using intercepts.
15. Graph $x = -4$.
16. Graph $y = 3$.
17. Find the slope of the line containing $(-3, 4)$ and $(5, -2)$.
18. Find the equation of the line containing $(-2, -3)$ with $m = -\frac{3}{4}$.
19. Find the equation of the line containing $(-3, -6)$ and $(2, -5)$.
20. Find the slope and y-intercept of the equation $-3x + 5y - 6 = 0$.
21. Find the standard form and the slope for $y = -\frac{3}{5}x - \frac{8}{5}$.

Find the equation of the line containing $(4, -3)$ that is

22. parallel to the line $6x - 4y = 1$.
23. perpendicular to the line $6x - 4y = 1$.
24. If you rent a car for one day and drive it 100 miles, the cost is \$40. If you drive it 150 miles, the cost is \$48.50.
    - **a.** Fit a linear function to the data points.
    - **b.** How much does it cost to rent the car for one day if you drive it 200 miles?
    - **c.** How far can you drive in one day for \$91?
25. Graph $y = |x| + 3$.
26. Graph $y = [x - 4]$.

If $f(x) = -2x + 1$, $g(x) = x^2$, and $h(x) = 2 - x$, find

27. $h(-2)$.
28. $g(f(2))$.
29. $f(h(g(-1)))$.
30. an expression for $g(h(f(x)))$.

CHAPTER

What You'll Learn in Chapter 4

- How to solve systems of equations in two variables by graphing and by substitution
- How to solve systems of equations in two or three variables by linear combinations
- How to solve problems by translating to a system of equations
- How to determine whether a system of equations has a solution and whether that solution is unique
- How to graph and solve systems of inequalities
- How to solve problems using linear programming

Skills & Concepts You Need for Chapter 4

1-1 Find the additive inverse of each number.

1. -8 **2.** 7 **3.** $\frac{3}{4}$ **4.** 0

1-1 Add.

5. $-\frac{3}{4} + \frac{1}{6}$ **6.** $\frac{4}{5} + \left(-\frac{4}{5}\right)$ **7.** $-8.6 + (-3.4)$

1-1 Subtract.

8. $8 - (-2)$ **9.** $-\frac{2}{3} - \frac{4}{5}$ **10.** $-3.2 - (-8.1)$

3-4 Graph.

11. $y - 3x = 2$ **12.** $2y = 3x + 2$ **13.** $\frac{1}{2}x = 4y - 3$

14. $4y - 4 = 2x$ **15.** $2y + 4 = 3x$ **16.** $y = -1$

2-5 Solve.

17. $3y - 1 > y - 3$ **18.** $2x - 3 > 5$

19. $|x + 2| \leq 6$ **20.** $-7 \leq 2x - 7 < 7$

3-7 Determine whether the lines are parallel.

21. $\frac{1}{2}x - 5y = 3$ and $-2x + 10y = 1$

Systems of Equations and Problem Solving

How does arc welding fuse pipes together? Arc welding uses an electric current or arc to melt a filler metal between the pipes along their circumference. Suppose three welders Todd, Don, and Carla, can weld 38 linear feet per hour working together. When working in pairs, Todd and Don can weld 23 linear feet per hour and Don and Carla can weld 29 linear feet per hour. How many linear feet per hour can each weld alone?

4-1 Systems of Equations in Two Variables

What You'll Learn

1 To visualize the solution of a system

. . . And Why

To solve real-world problems using algebraic reasoning skills

A set of two or more equations with the same variables is called a **system of equations.** The solution set of a system of equations in two variables consists of all ordered pairs that make all of the equations in the system true. If a system has only one solution it is the **unique** solution.

For example, $x + y = 11$, $3x - y = 5$ — (4, 7) is the unique solution of both equations.

Part 1 Solving a System Graphically

Objective: Solve a system of equations in two variables graphically.

One way to find solutions of a system is to graph the equations and look for points of intersection.

EXAMPLE Solve graphically.

$$y - x = 1$$
$$y + x = 3$$

The graph shows the solution set. The intersection appears to be the single ordered pair (1, 2). We check by substituting.

$y - x = 1$	
$2 - 1$	1
1	1 ✓

$y + x = 3$	
$2 + 1$	3
3	3 ✓

Since both are true, (1, 2) is the solution.

Try This Solve graphically.

a. $x + y = 11$
$3x - y = 5$

b. $2x - y = 7$
$-x + 2y = -5$

The graphs of two linear equations can be two intersecting lines, two parallel lines, or the same line.

Two intersecting lines
Unique solution

Parallel lines
No solution

Same line
Infinitely many solutions

4-1 Exercises

Extra Help On the Web

Look for worked-out examples at the Prentice Hall Web site.
www.phschool.com

A

Solve graphically.

1. $x + y = 4$
$x - y = 2$

2. $x - y = 3$
$x + y = 5$

3. $2x - y = 4$
$5x - y = 13$

4. $3x + y = 5$
$x - 2y = 4$

5. $4x - y = 9$
$x - 3y = 16$

6. $2y = 6 - x$
$3x - 2y = 6$

7. $a = 1 + b$
$b = -2a + 5$

8. $x = y - 1$
$2x = 3y$

9. $2u + v = 3$
$2u = v + 7$

10. $2b + a = 11$
$a - b = 5$

11. $y = -\frac{1}{3}x - 1$
$4x - 3y = 18$

12. $y = -\frac{1}{4}x + 1$
$2y = x - 4$

B

Solve graphically.

13. $3x - y = -5$
$y - 3x = -2$

14. $y = -3x + 5$
$4y + 12x = 20$

15. ***Critical Thinking*** Write systems of equations with the following solutions.

a. $(5, 1)$ **b.** $(-7, 3)$ **c.** no solution **d.** infinitely many solutions

Challenge

Solve graphically. (Hint: Make a table of values.)

16. $x - y = 0$
$y = x^2$

17. $x - y = 0$
$y = |x|$

18. A system of linear equations has solutions $(1, -1)$ and $(-2, 3)$.

a. Can you find another solution? **b.** How many solutions must exist?

Journal

Write a paragraph in which you explain how we can think of a system of equations as a conjunction of sentences. Include an example in your paragraph.

Mixed Review

Consider the function $f(x) = 2x^2 - x$ and find the following function values.

19. $f(3)$ **20.** $f(0)$ **21.** $f(-1)$
22. $f(1)$ **23.** $f(-3)$ **24.** $f(2)$ *3-3*

Find the slope and y-intercept of the line. **25.** $6x + 3y - 12 = 0$

Solve. **26.** $-9 < 3t < 6$ **27.** $|5a - 1| > 9$ **28.** $3.2(1.5 + m) = 19.2$ *3-6*

4-2 Solving Systems of Equations

What You'll Learn

1. To solve a system of equations in two variables by the substitution method
2. To solve a system of equations in two variables by linear combinations

. . . And Why

To solve problems using a system of equations in two variables

Graphing may not be an efficient or accurate method of solving a system of equations in two variables. We now consider more efficient methods.

PART 1 The Substitution Method

Objective: Solve a system of equations in two variables by the substitution method.

The **substitution method** is a useful technique for solving systems in which a variable has a coefficient of 1.

EXAMPLE 1 Use the substitution method to solve this system.

$$\begin{aligned} 2x + y &= 6 \\ 3x + 4y &= 4 \end{aligned}$$

We solve the first equation for y because its y-term has a coefficient of 1.

$$y = 6 - 2x$$

Thus y and $6 - 2x$ are equivalent. We can substitute $6 - 2x$ for y in the second equation.

$$\begin{aligned} 3x + 4y &= 4 \\ 3x + 4(6 - 2x) &= 4 \qquad \text{Substituting } 6 - 2x \text{ for } y \end{aligned}$$

This gives us an equation in one variable. We can then solve for x.

$$\begin{aligned} 3x + 24 - 8x &= 4 \qquad \text{Using the distributive property} \\ -5x &= -20 \\ x &= 4 \end{aligned}$$

Now we can substitute 4 for x in either equation and solve for y.

$$\begin{aligned} 2x + y &= 6 \qquad \text{Choosing the first equation} \\ 2 \cdot 4 + y &= 6 \\ y &= -2 \end{aligned}$$

We obtain $(4, -2)$. This checks, so it is the solution of the system.

Try This Use the substitution method to solve these systems.

a. $2y + x = 1$
$3y - 2x = 12$

b. $5x + 3y = 6$
$x - y = -1$

PART 2 Linear Combinations

Objective: Solve a system of equations in two variables by linear combinations.

If all variables have coefficients other than 1, we can use the multiplication and addition properties to find a combination of the linear equations that will eliminate a variable. This is called the method of **linear combinations.**

EXAMPLE 2 Use linear combinations to solve this system.

$$3x - 4y = -1$$
$$-3x + 2y = 0$$

The first equation tells us that $3x - 4y$ and -1 are equivalent expressions. We can use the addition property to add the same quantity to both sides of the second equation. Thus we can add $3x - 4y$ to the left side and -1 to the right side of the second equation.

$$-3x + 2y + (3x - 4y) = 0 + 1(-1) \quad \text{Using the addition property}$$

When we do this, we have actually added one multiple of the first equation to one multiple of the second equation. It is usually easier to add equations in column form.

$$\begin{array}{r} 3x - 4y = -1 \\ -3x + 2y = 0 \\ \hline -2y = -1 \end{array} \quad \text{Adding}$$

We can solve this equation easily, finding $y = \frac{1}{2}$. Next, we substitute $\frac{1}{2}$ for y in either of the original equations.

$$-3x + 2y = 0$$
$$-3x + 2\left(\frac{1}{2}\right) = 0 \quad \text{Substituting } \tfrac{1}{2} \text{ for } y \text{ in the second equation}$$
$$-3x + 1 = 0$$

Solving for x, we find $x = \frac{1}{3}$. Substitution will show that $\left(\frac{1}{3}, \frac{1}{2}\right)$ checks. The solution of the system is $\left(\frac{1}{3}, \frac{1}{2}\right)$.

Using this method we try to get an equation with only one variable, or to *eliminate* a variable. This method is thus also known as the **method of elimination.**

Note in Example 2 that a term in one equation and a term in the other were *additive inverses* of each other, thus their sum was 0. That enabled us to eliminate a variable.

We may need to multiply an equation by a constant in order to make two terms additive inverses of each other.

Writing Math

Sometimes this system of equations is written as

$$\begin{cases} 3x - 4y = -1 \\ -3x + 2y = 0 \end{cases}$$

The brace emphasizes that the two equations are a system of equations.

EXAMPLE 3 Use linear combinations to solve this system.

$$3x + 3y = 15$$
$$2x + 6y = 22$$

If we add the equations, no variables will be eliminated. We could eliminate the y-variable, however, if the $3y$ in the first equation were $-6y$. Therefore, we multiply both sides of the first equation by -2 and then add.

$$-2(3x + 3y) = -2(15) \quad \rightarrow \quad -6x - 6y = -30$$
$$2x + 6y = 22 \quad \rightarrow \quad 2x + 6y = 22$$
$$-4x = -8 \qquad \text{Adding}$$
$$x = 2 \qquad \text{Solving for } x$$

Substitute 2 for x in either of the original equations.

$$2x + 6y = 22$$
$$2(2) + 6y = 22 \qquad \text{Substituting 2 for } x \text{ in the second equation}$$
$$4 + 6y = 22$$
$$y = 3 \qquad \text{Solving for } y$$

Substitution will show that (2, 3) checks. The solution of the system is (2, 3).

Try This Use linear combinations to solve these systems.

c. $5x + 3y = 17$
$-5x + 2y = 3$

d. $6x + 2y = -16$
$-12x - 5y = 31$

Often we need to use linear combinations of both equations in order to make two terms additive inverses of each other.

EXAMPLE 4 Use linear combinations to solve this system.

$$5x + 4y = 11$$
$$3x - 5y = -23$$

We can multiply both sides of the first equation by -3 and both sides of the second equation by 5, in order to make the x-terms additive inverses of each other. Then we add and solve for y.

$$-3(5x + 4y) = -3(11) \quad \rightarrow \quad -15x - 12y = -33$$
$$5(3x - 5y) = 5(-23) \quad \rightarrow \quad 15x - 25y = -115$$
$$-37y = -148 \qquad \text{Adding}$$
$$y = 4 \qquad \text{Solving for } y$$

When we substitute 4 for y in either of the original equations, we find $x = -1$. The ordered pair $(-1, 4)$ checks, and is the solution of the system.

EXAMPLE 5 Use linear combinations to solve this system.

$$-0.3x + 0.5y = -0.1$$
$$0.01x - 0.4y = -0.38$$

We multiply the first equation by 10 and the second by 100 to clear the decimals.

$$10(-0.3x + 0.5y) = 10(-0.1) \quad \rightarrow \quad -3x + 5y = -1$$
$$100(0.01x - 0.4y) = 100(-0.38) \quad \rightarrow \quad x - 40y = -38$$

Solving this system, we obtain (2, 1) as a solution.

EXAMPLE 6 Use linear combinations to solve this system.

$$\frac{1}{2}x + \frac{2}{3}y = 1$$
$$\frac{3}{4}x - \frac{1}{3}y = 2$$

To clear fractions, we multiply both sides of the first equation by 6 and the second by 12.

$$6\left(\frac{1}{2}x + \frac{2}{3}y\right) = 6(1) \quad \rightarrow \quad 3x + 4y = 6$$
$$12\left(\frac{3}{4}y - \frac{1}{3}y\right) = 12(2) \quad \rightarrow \quad 9x - 4y = 24$$

Solving this system, we obtain $\left(\frac{5}{2}, -\frac{3}{8}\right)$ as a solution.

Try This Use linear combinations to solve these systems.

e. $3x + 5y = 30$
$5x + 3y = 34$

f. $0.2x + 0.3y = 0.1$
$0.03x - 0.01y = 0.07$

g. $\frac{3}{5}x + \frac{2}{3}y = 14$
$\frac{3}{4}x - \frac{1}{3}y = 14$

We summarize the steps for using linear combinations for systems of two equations.

Steps for Using Linear Combinations

1. Write both equations in the form $Ax + By = C$.
2. Clear any decimals or fractions.
3. Choose a variable to eliminate.
4. Make the chosen variable's terms additive inverses by multiplying one or both equations by a number.
5. Eliminate the variable by adding the equations.
6. Substitute to solve for the remaining variable.

Cramer's Rule for Two Equations

Gabriel Cramer (1704–1752) developed an algorithm to solve large systems of linear equations. The general system of two equations,

$$ax + by = c$$
$$dx + ey = f \quad \text{can be solved for } x \text{ and } y\text{:} \quad x = \frac{ce - bf}{ae - bd} \quad y = \frac{af - cd}{ae - bd}$$

Since the denominators are the same, $ae - bd$, it is helpful to find this value first and store the result.

Solve. $\quad 5x - 2y = 10$
$\qquad -8x + 0.4y = 40$

The denominator is $ae - bd$,

5 [×] 0.4 [−] 2 [+/−] [×] 8 [+/−] [=] −14 [STO]

Solving for x,

10 [×] 0.4 [−] 2 [+/−] [×] 40 [=] 84 [/] [RCL] [=] −6

Use this method to verify that $y = -20$, and the solution is thus $(-6, -20)$.

Solve these systems using the algorithm shown.

a. $0.2x + 1.2y = 3.1$
$2x + y = 9$

b. $-4.05x + 10y = -66.2$
$2x - 36.5 = 5.7y$

c. $x + 0.35y = 3.6$
$y + 0.22x = 4.484$

Extra Help On the Web

Look for worked-out examples at the Prentice Hall Web site.
www.phschool.com

4-2 Exercises

A

Use the substitution method to solve these systems.

1. $5m + n = 8$
$3m - 4n = 14$

2. $4x + y = 1$
$x - 2y = 16$

3. $4x + 12y = 4$
$5x - y = -11$

4. $3b - a = -7$
$5a + 6b = 14$

Use **linear combinations** to solve these systems. Clear decimals or fractions as needed.

5. $x + 3y = 7$
$-x + 4y = 7$

6. $x + y = 9$
$2x - y = -3$

7. $2x + y = 6$
$x - y = 3$

8. $x - 2y = 6$
$-x + 3y = -4$

9. $9x + 3y = -3$
$2x - 3y = -8$

10. $6x - 3y = 18$
$6x + 3y = -12$

11. $5x + 3y = -9$
$2x - 5y = -16$

12. $3x + 2y = 22$
$9x - 8y = -4$

13. $5r - 3s = 24$
$3r + 5s = 28$

14. $5x - 7y = -16$
$2x + 8y = 26$

15. $0.3x + 0.2y = 0.3$
$0.2x + 0.3y = -0.3$

16. $0.7x - 0.3y = 0.5$
$-0.4x + 0.7y = 1.3$

17. $5x - 9y = 7$
$7y - 3x = -5$

18. $a - 2b = 16$
$b + 3 = 3a$

19. $3(a - b) = 15$
$4a = b + 1$

20. $1.3x - 0.2y = 12$
$0.4x + 17y = 89$

21. $x - \frac{1}{10}y = 100$
$y - \frac{1}{10}x = -100$

22. $\frac{1}{8}x + \frac{3}{5}y = \frac{19}{2}$
$-\frac{3}{10}x - \frac{7}{20}y = -1$

B

Multi-Step Problems Each of the following is a system of equations that is *not* linear. Each is *linear in form* because an appropriate substitution (say u for $\frac{1}{x}$ and v for $\frac{1}{y}$) yields a linear system.

Solve for the new variable, and then solve for the original variable.

23. $\frac{1}{x} - \frac{3}{y} = 2$
$\frac{6}{x} + \frac{5}{y} = -34$

24. $\frac{2}{x} + \frac{1}{y} = 0$
$\frac{5}{x} + \frac{2}{y} = -5$

25. $3|x| + 5|y| = 30$
$5|x| + 3|y| = 34$

26. ***Critical Thinking*** Compare System A and System B shown below by graphing on the same set of axes. What is true of the two systems?

A: $2x - y = 10$
$x + 2y = -1$

B: $x = 3$
$y = -2$

Describe what happens when you solve System B by linear combinations.

27. ***Mathematical Reasoning*** If $f(x) = 4x + 1$ and $g(x) = \frac{1}{2}x - 1$, for what value of x does $f(x) = g(x)$?

Quick Review

Function notation was introduced on page 118.

Challenge

28. For $y = mx + b$, two solutions are $(1, 2)$ and $(-3, 4)$. Find m and b.

29. For $y = ax^2 + c$, two solutions are $(0, 3)$ and $(-2, 3)$. Find a and c.

Mixed Review

Write each equation in standard form.

30. $2x + 6 = y$

31. $y = -7$ *3-6*

State whether or not the graphs of the following equations are linear.

32. $y = \frac{3}{x} + 2$

33. $y = (x + 2)^2$

34. $y = 3xy + 1$

35. $y + x = 2x + 1$ *3-4*

36. Hideko invested \$5000 in two funds. After one year, fund A earned 10% interest and fund B earned 8% interest. She received at least \$435 interest from her investments. What is the most she could have invested in the B fund? *2-5*

4-3 Using a System of Two Equations

What You'll Learn

1. To solve problems by translating to systems of equations in two variables

. . . And Why

To solve real-world problems using algebraic reasoning skills

PART 1 Solving Problems

Objective: Solve problems by translating to systems of equations in two variables.

A delivery truck arrives at the Roberts' store with 8 small boxes and 5 large boxes. The total charge for the boxes, without tax or delivery charges, is \$184. A large box costs \$3 more than a small box. What is the cost of each size box?

PROBLEM-SOLVING GUIDELINES
■ UNDERSTAND the problem
■ Develop and carry out a PLAN
■ Find the ANSWER and CHECK

To solve the problems, we often translate to a system of equations in two variables. In this case the system becomes the mathematical model of the situation.

EXAMPLE 1 We can solve the problem above using the Problem-Solving Guidelines.

■ **UNDERSTAND the problem**

Question: What is the cost of each size box? — Clarifying the question

Data: 8 small boxes plus 5 large boxes cost \$184. A large box costs \$3.00 more than a small box. — Finding the relationships

■ **Develop and carry out a PLAN**

There are two statements in the problem. Translate each into an equation.

Let x represent the cost of a small box. Let y represent the cost of a large box.

$$\underbrace{\text{8 times the cost of a small box}}_{8x} \ \underset{+}{\text{plus}} \ \underbrace{\text{5 times the cost of a large box}}_{5y} \ \underset{=}{\text{is}} \ \underset{184}{\$184.}$$

Translating statement 1

$$\underbrace{\text{The cost of a large box}}_{y} \ \underset{=}{\text{is}} \ \underset{3}{\$3.00} \ \underbrace{\text{more than}}_{+} \ \underbrace{\text{the cost of a small box.}}_{x}$$

Translating statement 2

We now have a system of equations.

$$8x + 5y = 184$$
$$y = 3 + x$$

Substituting $3 + x$ for y in the first equation, we get $8x + 5(3 + x) = 184$. Solving for x, we find that $x = 13$. Since $y = 3 + x$, $y = 16$.

Find the ANSWER and CHECK

8 times \$13 (\$104) plus 5 times \$16 (\$80) is \$184. \$16 is \$3 more than \$13. Both conditions are satisfied. — Checking in the original problem

A large box costs \$16, a small box costs \$13. — Stating the answer clearly

Try This

a. One number is four times another number and their sum is 175. Find the numbers.

EXAMPLE 2

Solution A is 2% alcohol. Solution B is 6% alcohol. A service station owner wants to mix the two to get 60 liters of solution that is 3.2% alcohol. How many liters of each should the owner use?

UNDERSTAND the problem

Question: How many liters of each solution are needed for the mixture to be 3.2% alcohol? — Clarifying the question

Data: Solution A is 2% alcohol. Solution B is 6% alcohol. 60 L of mixture are needed. — Identifying the given data

Develop and carry out a PLAN

Organize the information in a *table*.

	Amount of solution	Percent of alcohol	Amount of alcohol in solution
A	x liters	2%	$2\%x$ or $0.02x$
B	y liters	6%	$6\%y$ or $0.06y$
Mixture	60 liters	3.2%	0.032×60, or 1.92 liters

If we add x and y in the first column, we get 60, the total amount of solution. This gives us one equation, $x + y = 60$.

We multiply each amount by the percent of alcohol to find the amount of alcohol in each solution and in the mixture. If we add the amounts in the third column, we get 1.92. This gives us a second equation, $0.02x + 0.06y = 1.92$.

We now have a system of equations.

$$x + y = 60$$
$$0.02x + 0.06y = 1.92$$

We clear the second equation of decimals.

$$x + y = 60 \quad \rightarrow \quad x + y = 60$$
$$100(0.02x) + 100(0.06y) = 100(1.92) \quad \rightarrow \quad 2x + 6y = 192$$

Multiplying by 100

The solution of the system is (42, 18).

■ **Find the ANSWER and CHECK**

Total number of liters of mixture — Checking in the original problem

$$x + y = 42 + 18 = 60 \text{ L}$$

Total amount of alcohol

$$2\% \times 42 + 6\% \times 18 = 0.02 \times 42 + 0.06 \times 18 = 1.92 \text{ L}$$

Percent of alcohol in mixture — The numbers check in the problem.

$$\frac{1.92}{60} = 0.032, \text{ or } 3.2\%$$

The owner should use 42 L of 2% solution and 18 L of 6% solution.

This is reasonable, since more of solution A than B is needed. (3.2% is closer to 2% than to 6%.)

Try This

b. A gardener has two solutions of weedkiller and water. One is 5% weedkiller and the other is 15% weedkiller. The gardener needs 100 L of a solution that is 12% weedkiller. How much of each solution should she use?

EXAMPLE 3

A train leaves Sioux City traveling east at 30 km/h. Two hours later, another train leaves Sioux City traveling in the same direction on a parallel track at 45 km/h. How far from Sioux City will the faster train catch the slower one?

To translate motion problems, we use the definition of speed

The French high-speed passenger trains, such as the ones shown, operate with a top average speed between 209 and 254 kilometers per hour.

$$\text{rate of speed} = \frac{\text{distance}}{\text{time}} \left(r = \frac{d}{t}\right)$$

or the equivalent equation $d = rt$.

To solve this problem, first *draw a diagram.*

Sioux City — 30 km/h — $t + 2$ hours — d kilometers

Sioux City — 45 km/h — t hours — d kilometers

Trains meet here

From the drawing we see that the distances are the same. Both distances can be represented by d. Let t represent the time for the faster train. Then the time for the slower train will be $t + 2$. We can organize the information in a table.

	Distance (km)	**Rate (km/h)**	**Time (hrs)**
Slow train	d	30	$t + 2$
Fast train	d	45	t

Using $d = rt$ in each row of the table, we get an equation. Thus we get a system of two equations.

$$d = 30(t + 2)$$
$$d = 45t$$

We solve using substitution.

$$45t = 30(t + 2) \quad \text{Substituting } 45t \text{ for } d \text{ in the first equation}$$
$$45t = 30t + 60$$
$$15t = 60$$
$$t = 4$$

Thus the time for the faster train should be 4 hours, and for the slower train 6 hours. The faster train would travel $45 \cdot 4$, or 180 km in 4 hours. The slower train would travel $30 \cdot 6$, or 180 km in 6 hours.

The faster train will catch the slower train 180 km from Sioux City.

Try This

c. A freight train leaves Tyler, traveling east at 35 km/h. One hour later a passenger train leaves Tyler, also traveling east on a parallel track at 40 km/h. How far from Tyler will the passenger train catch the freight train?

4-3 Exercises

Extra Help On the Web

Look for worked-out examples at the Prentice Hall Web site.
www.phschool.com

A

1. The sum of a certain number and a second number is -42. The first number minus the second is 52. Find the numbers.
2. The sum of two numbers is -63. The first number minus the second is -41. Find the numbers.

3. The difference between two numbers is 16. Three times the larger number is nine times the smaller. What are the numbers?
4. The difference between two numbers is 11. Twice the smaller number plus three times the larger number is 123. What are the numbers?
5. Soybean meal is 16% protein and corn meal is 9% protein. How many pounds of each should be mixed together to get a 350-lb mixture that is 12% protein?
6. A chemist has one solution that is 25% acid and a second that is 50% acid. How many liters of each should be mixed to get 10 L of a solution that is 40% acid?
7. One canned juice drink is 15% orange juice and another is 5% orange juice. How many liters of each should be mixed together to get a 10 L solution that is 10% orange juice?

8. Antifreeze A is 18% alcohol. Antifreeze B is 10% alcohol. How many liters of each should be mixed to get 20 L of a mixture that is 15% alcohol?

9. Two investments were made totaling $8800. For a certain year these investments yielded $1326 in simple interest. Part of the $8800 was invested at 14% and part at 16%. Find the amount invested at each rate.

10. Two investments were made totaling $15,000. For a certain year these investments yielded $1432 in simple interest. Part of the $15,000 was invested at 9% and part at 10%. Find the amount invested at each rate.

11. A total of $1150 was invested, part of it at 12% and part at 11%. The total yield was $133.75. How much was invested at each rate?

12. A total of $27,000 was invested, part of it at 10% and part at 12%. The total yield was $2990. How much was invested at each rate?

13. A train leaves a station and travels north at 75 km/h. Two hours later a second train leaves on a parallel track and travels north at 125 km/h. How far from the station will they meet?

14. Two cars leave town traveling in opposite directions. One travels at 80 km/h and the other at 96 km/h. In how many hours will they be 528 km apart?

15. Two motorcycles travel toward each other from Chicago and Indianapolis, which are about 350 km apart, at rates of 110 and 90 km/h. They started at the same time. In how many hours will they meet?

16. Two planes travel toward each other from cities that are 780 km apart, at rates of 190 and 200 km/h. They started at the same time. In how many hours will they meet?

17. One day a store sold 30 sweatshirts. White ones cost $9.95, and yellow ones cost $10.50. In all, $310.60 worth of sweatshirts were sold. How many of each color were sold?

18. One week a business sold 40 scarves. White ones cost $4.95, and printed ones cost $7.95. In all, $282 worth of scarves were sold. How many of each kind were sold?

19. One day a store sold 45 pens, one kind at $8.50 and another kind at $9.75. In all, $398.75 was taken in. How many of each kind were sold?

20. At a club play, 117 tickets were sold. Adults' tickets cost $1.25, and children's tickets cost $0.75. In all, $129.75 was taken in. How many of each kind of ticket were sold?

21. Carlos is 8 years older than his sister Maria. Four years ago Maria was two thirds as old as Carlos. How old are they now?

22. Paula is 12 years older than her brother Bob. Four years from now Bob will be two thirds as old as Paula. How old are they now?

23. The perimeter of a rectangular field is 628 m. The length of the field exceeds its width by 6 m. Find the dimensions.

24. The perimeter of a lot is 190 m. The width is one fourth the length. Find the dimensions.

25. The perimeter of a rectangle is 86 cm. The length is 19 cm greater than the width. Find the length and the width.

26. The perimeter of a rectangle is 384 m. The length is 82 m greater than the width. Find the length and the width.

B

27. Mr. Irwin and Mr. Lippi are mathematics teachers. They have a total of 46 years of teaching. Two years ago Mr. Irwin had taught 2.5 times as many years as Mr. Lippi. How long has each taught?

28. Nancy jogs and walks to school each day. She averages 4 km/h walking and 8 km/h jogging. The distance from home to school is 6 km, and she makes the trip in 1 hour. How far does she jog in a trip?

29. The tens digit of a two-digit positive integer is 2 more than three times the ones digit. If the digits are interchanged, the new number is 13 less than half the given number. Find the given integer. (Hint: Let $x =$ tens-place digit and $y =$ ones-place digit, then $10x + y$ is the number.)

30. A limited edition of a book published by a historical society was offered for sale to its members. The cost was one book for \$12 or two books for \$20. The society sold 880 books, and the total amount of money taken in was \$9840. How many members ordered two books?

31. The measure of one of two supplementary angles is 8° more than three times the other. Find the measure of the larger of the two angles.

32. ***Critical Thinking*** Write a problem that can be solved using the system

$$x + 2y = 25$$
$$2x + y = 20$$

Challenge

33. An automobile radiator contains 16 liters of antifreeze and water. This mixture is 30% antifreeze. How much of this mixture should be drained and replaced with pure antifreeze so that there will be 50% antifreeze?

34. A train leaves Union Station for Central Station, 216 km away, at 9 A.M. One hour later, a train leaves Central Station for Union Station. They meet at noon. If the second train had started at 9 A.M., and the first train at 10:30 A.M., they would still have met at noon. Find the speed of each train.

Mixed Review

Simplify. **35.** $|m^4|$ **36.** $|-3t|$ **37.** $|w^7|$ **38.** $|m^5n^4|$ **39.** $|75a^3|$ *2-7*

Find the slope of the line containing each pair of points.

40. $(-5, 2)$ and $(3, 2)$ **41.** $(1.9, 2.4)$ and $(1.1, 3.2)$ **42.** $(2, -3)$ and $(-2, 5)$ *3-5*

Write an equation of the line containing the given point and parallel to the given line. **43.** $(2, 1)$; $x + y = 1$ *3-7*

Suppose $f(x) = 2x - 1$ and $g(x) = \frac{1}{2}x + 1$.

44. Find $f(g(1))$. **45.** Find an expression for $f(g(x))$. **46.** Find $g(f(1))$.

47. Find an expression for $g(f(x))$. *3-9*

4-4 Systems of Equations in Three Variables

What You'll Learn

1 To solve a system of equations in three variables using linear combinations

. . . And Why

To solve problems using a system of equations in three variables

Introducing the Concept: Equations in Three Variables

Some basic geometric figures represent the graphs of algebraic equations.

On a number line, what geometric figure represents the equation $3x = 6$?

On a coordinate plane, what geometric figure represents the equation $3x + y = 6$?

Now suppose you have an equation with three variables, such as $3x + y + 2z = 6$. What kind of coordinate system would be used to graph it? What geometric figure would represent the graph?

A solution of a linear equation in three variables is an **ordered triple** (x, y, z) that makes the equation true. For instance, $\left(\frac{3}{2}, -4, 3\right)$ is a solution of the equation $4x - 2y - 3z = 5$. Thus, a solution of a system of equations in three variables is an ordered triple (x, y, z) that makes all of the equations in the system true. To show that $\left(\frac{3}{2}, -4, 3\right)$ is a solution of the following system, we substitute into all three equations, using alphabetical order. (Verify this on your own.)

$$\begin{aligned} 4x - 2y - 3z &= 5 \\ -8x - y + z &= -5 \\ 2x + y + 2z &= 5 \end{aligned}$$

The graph of a linear equation in two variables is a line. The graph of a linear equation in three variables is a plane. Thus, if a system of equations in three variables has a unique solution it is a point common to all of the planes.

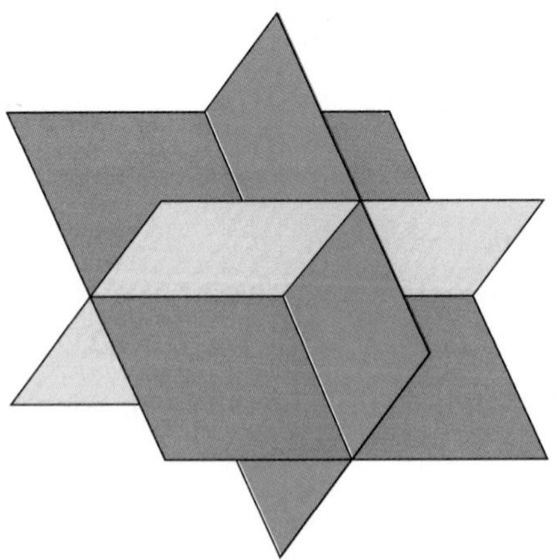

Solving a System in Three Variables

Objective: Solve a system of equations in three variables by linear combinations.

Graphical methods for solving linear equations in three variables are unsatisfactory because a three-dimensional coordinate system is required. Linear combinations followed by substitution is an effective method for solving systems of equations.

EXAMPLE 1 Solve.

$$\begin{aligned} x + y + z &= 4 \quad ① \\ x - 2y - z &= 1 \quad ② \\ 2x - y - 2z &= -1 \quad ③ \end{aligned}$$

① These numbers indicate ② the equations in the first, ③ second, and third positions, respectively.

We begin by multiplying ① by -1, and adding it to ② to eliminate x from the second equation. Equations ① and ③ are unchanged by this step.

$$\begin{aligned} -x - y - z &= -4 \quad \text{Multiplying ① by } -1 \\ x - 2y - z &= 1 \quad ② \\ \hline -3y - 2z &= -3 \quad \text{Adding} \end{aligned}$$

$$\begin{aligned} x + y + z &= 4 \quad ① \\ -3y - 2z &= -3 \quad ② \\ 2x - y - 2z &= -1 \quad ③ \end{aligned}$$

To eliminate x from the third equation, we multiply ① by -2 and add it to ③.

$$\begin{aligned} -2x - 2y - 2z &= -8 \quad \text{Multiplying ① by } -2 \\ 2x - y - 2z &= -1 \quad ③ \\ \hline -3y - 4z &= -9 \quad \text{Adding} \end{aligned}$$

$$\begin{aligned} x + y + z &= 4 \quad ① \\ -3y - 2z &= -3 \quad ② \\ -3y - 4z &= -9 \quad ③ \end{aligned}$$

Next we eliminate y from the third equation by multiplying ② by -1 and adding the result to ③.

$$\begin{aligned} 3y + 2z &= 3 \quad \text{Multiplying ② by } -1 \\ -3y - 4z &= -9 \quad ③ \\ \hline -2z &= -6 \quad \text{Adding} \end{aligned}$$

$$\begin{aligned} x + y + z &= 4 \quad ① \\ -3y - 2z &= -3 \quad ② \\ -2z &= -6 \quad ③ \end{aligned}$$

Since the third equation can be easily solved for z, we can use substitution to easily solve for the three variables.

First we solve ③ for z.

$$\begin{aligned} -2z &= -6 \\ z &= 3 \end{aligned}$$

Next we substitute 3 for z in ② and solve for y.

$$\begin{aligned} -3y - 2z &= -3 \quad ② \\ -3y - 2(3) &= -3 \\ -3y - 6 &= -3 \\ -3y &= 3 \\ y &= -1 \end{aligned}$$

Finally we substitute -1 for y and 3 for z in ①, and solve for x.

$$\begin{aligned} x + y + z &= 4 \qquad ① \\ x + (-1) + 3 &= 4 \\ x + 2 &= 4 \\ x &= 2 \end{aligned}$$

The solution is $(2, -1, 3)$. To be sure computational errors have not been made, check by substituting 2 for x, -1 for y, and 3 for z in the three original equations. If the ordered triple makes all three equations true, then it is a solution.

The algorithm we are using to solve systems of three equations is shown below. It can easily be extended to systems of more than three equations.

Triangularization Algorithm for Solving Systems of Linear Equations

For a system of three equations in three variables, our goal is to obtain an equivalent system of equations in the following **triangular form.**

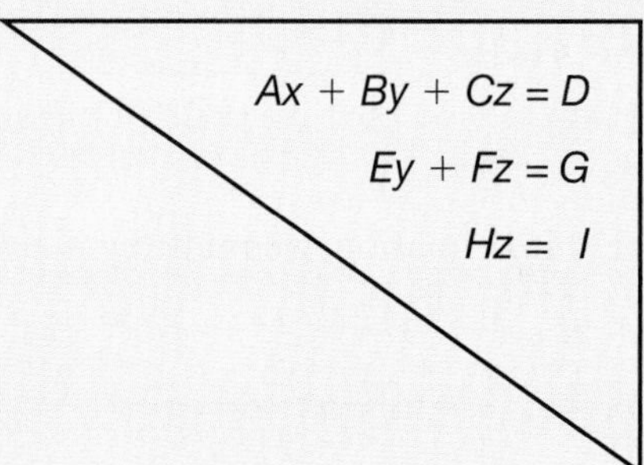

1. Use linear combinations to eliminate x-terms from the second and third equations.
2. Use linear combinations to eliminate the y-term from the third equation. The system will now be in triangular form.
3. Solve the third equation for z, substitute z in the second equation to find y, and then substitute y and z in the first equation to find x.

EXAMPLE 2 Solve.

$$\begin{aligned} 2x - 4y + 7z &= 24 \qquad ① \\ 4x + 2y - 3z &= 4 \qquad ② \\ 3x + 3y - z &= 4 \qquad ③ \end{aligned}$$

We begin by multiplying ③ by 2 to make each x-coefficient a multiple of the first.

$$\begin{aligned} 2x - 4y + 7z &= 24 \qquad ① \\ 4x + 2y - 3z &= 4 \qquad ② \\ 6x + 6y - 2z &= 8 \qquad 2③ \end{aligned}$$

Next we multiply ① by -2 and add it to ② to eliminate the x-coefficient in ②.

$$\begin{aligned} 2x - 4y + 7z &= 24 && ① \\ 10y - 17z &= -44 && -2①+② \\ 6x + 6y - 2z &= 8 && ③ \end{aligned}$$

We also multiply ① by -3 and add it to ③.

$$\begin{aligned} 2x - 4y + 7z &= 24 && ① \\ 10y - 17z &= -44 && ② \\ 18y - 23z &= -64 && -3①+③ \end{aligned}$$

Now we multiply the new ③ by -5 to make the y-coefficient a multiple of the y-coefficient in the new ②.

$$\begin{aligned} 2x - 4y + 7z &= 24 && ① \\ 10y - 17z &= -44 && ② \\ -90y + 115z &= 320 && -5③ \end{aligned}$$

Next we multiply ② by 9 and add it to ③.

$$\begin{aligned} 2x - 4y + 7z &= 24 && ① \\ 10y - 17z &= -44 && ② \\ -38z &= -76 && 9②+③ \text{ The system is in triangular form.} \end{aligned}$$

We can now solve ③ for z.

$$\begin{aligned} -38z &= -76 \\ z &= 2 \end{aligned}$$

Next we substitute 2 for z in ②, and solve for y.

$$\begin{aligned} 10y - 17(2) &= -44 && \text{Substituting in } 10y - 17z = -44 \\ 10y - 34 &= -44 \\ y &= -1 \end{aligned}$$

Finally we substitute -1 for y and 2 for z in ①.

$$\begin{aligned} 2x - 4(-1) + 7(2) &= 24 && \text{Substituting in } 2x - 4y + 7z = 24 \\ 2x + 4 + 14 &= 24 \\ x &= 3 \end{aligned}$$

The solution is $(3, -1, 2)$.

Try This Solve these systems.

a. $x + 2y - z = 5$
$2x - 4y + z = 0$
$3x + 2y + 2z = 3$

b. $x + y + z = 2$
$x - 2y - z = 2$
$3x + 2y + z = 2$

c. $x + y - z = 2$
$x - y - 2z = 2$
$2x + 3y + z = 9$

Extra Help On the Web

Look for worked-out examples at the Prentice Hall Web site.
www.phschool.com

4-4 Exercises

A

Solve these systems.

1. $x + y + z = 6$
$2x - y + 3z = 9$
$-x + 2y + 2z = 9$

2. $2x - y + z = 10$
$4x + 2y - 3z = 10$
$x - 3y + 2z = 8$

3. $2x - y - 3z = -1$
$2x - y + z = -9$
$x + 2y - 4z = 17$

4. $x - y + z = 6$
$2x + 3y + 2z = 2$
$3x + 5y + 4z = 4$

5. $2x - 3y + z = 5$
$x + 3y + 8z = 22$
$3x - y + 2z = 12$

6. $6x - 4y + 5z = 31$
$5x + 2y + 2z = 13$
$x + y + z = 2$

7. $3a - 2b + 7c = 13$
$a + 8b - 6c = -47$
$7a - 9b - 9c = -3$

8. $x + y + z = 0$
$2x + 3y + 2z = -3$
$-x + 2y - 3z = -1$

9. $2x + 3y + z = 17$
$x - 3y + 2z = -8$
$5x - 2y + 3z = 5$

10. $2x + y - 3z = -4$
$4x - 2y + z = 9$
$3x + 5y - 2z = 5$

11. $2x + y + z = -2$
$2x - y + 3z = 6$
$3x - 5y + 4z = 7$

12. $2x + y + 2z = 11$
$3x + 2y + 2z = 8$
$x + 4y + 3z = 0$

13. $x - y + z = 4$
$5x + 2y - 3z = 2$
$3x - 7y + 4z = 8$

14. $2x + y + 2z = 3$
$x + 6y + 3z = 4$
$3x - 2y + z = 0$

15. $4x - y - z = 4$
$2x + y + z = -1$
$6x - 3y - 2z = 3$

16. $a + 2b + c = 1$
$7a + 3b - c = -2$
$a + 5b + 3c = 2$

17. $2r + 3s + 12t = 4$
$4r - 6s + 6t = 1$
$r + s + t = 1$

18. $10x + 6y + z = 7$
$5x - 9y - 2z = 3$
$15x - 12y + 2z = -5$

B

Solve these systems.

19. $4a + 9b = 8$
$8a + 6c = -1$
$6b + 6c = -1$

20. $3p + 2r = 11$
$q - 7r = 4$
$p - 6q = 1$

21. $\frac{x+2}{3} - \frac{y+4}{2} + \frac{z+1}{6} = 0$
$\frac{x-4}{3} + \frac{y+1}{4} - \frac{z-2}{2} = -1$
$\frac{x+1}{2} + \frac{y}{2} + \frac{z-1}{4} = \frac{3}{4}$

22. $0.2x + 0.3y + 1.1z = 1.6$
$0.5x - 0.2y + 0.4z = 0.7$
$-1.2x + y - 0.7z = -0.9$

23. $w + x + y + z = 2$
$w + 2x + 2y + 4z = 1$
$w - x + y + z = 6$
$w - 3x - y + z = 2$

24. $w + x - y + z = 0$
$w - 2x - 2y - z = -5$
$w - 3x - y + z = 4$
$2w - x - y + 3z = 7$

Multi-Step Problems Solve.

(Hint: Let u represent $\frac{1}{x}$, v represent $\frac{1}{y}$, and w represent $\frac{1}{z}$. Solve for u, v, and w first.)

25. $\frac{2}{x} - \frac{1}{y} - \frac{3}{z} = -1$
$\frac{2}{x} - \frac{1}{y} + \frac{1}{z} = -9$
$\frac{1}{x} + \frac{2}{y} - \frac{4}{z} = 17$

26. $\frac{2}{x} + \frac{2}{y} - \frac{3}{z} = 3$
$\frac{1}{x} - \frac{2}{y} - \frac{3}{z} = 9$
$\frac{7}{x} - \frac{2}{y} + \frac{9}{z} = -39$

27. ***Critical Thinking*** Determine whether the following statement is true or false: For any ordered triple (x, y, z) there is a unique system of three equations in three variables that has (x, y, z) as a solution. If it is true, tell why. If it is false, give a counterexample.

Challenge

28. Determine a, b, and c if $(2, 3, -4)$ is a solution of the system.

$ax + by + cz = -11$
$bx - cy + az = -19$
$ax + cy - bz = 9$

In each case three solutions of an equation are given. Find the equation using a system of equations.

29. $Ax + By + Cz = 12$; $\left(1, \frac{3}{4}, 3\right)$, $\left(\frac{4}{3}, 1, 2\right)$, and $(2, 1, 1)$

30. $z = b - mx - ny$; $(1, 1, 2)$, $(3, -1, 6)$, and $\left(\frac{3}{2}, 1, 1\right)$

Mixed Review

Write an equation of the line containing the given point and perpendicular to the given line. **31.** $(5, 1)$; $y - 3x = 2$ *3-7*

Find the domain of each of the following functions.

32. $f(x) = -9x - 42$ **33.** $f(x) = \frac{3}{x} + \frac{1}{2}$ **34.** $f(x) = \frac{4}{x + 5}$ *3-3*

Write each equation in both standard form and slope-intercept form.

35. $4y = 2x - 8$ **36.** $x = 3y + 5$ *3-6*

37. To store material at one warehouse for six weeks costs \$42. For thirteen weeks it costs \$73.50.

a. Fit a linear function to the data.

b. How much would it cost to store the material for 26 weeks? *3-8*

4-5 Using a System of Three Equations

What You'll Learn

1 To solve problems by translating to a system of three equations in three variables

. . . And Why

To solve real-world problems using algebraic reasoning skills

PART 1 Solving Problems

Objective: Solve problems by translating to a system of three equations in three variables.

PROBLEM-SOLVING GUIDELINES
■ UNDERSTAND the problem
■ Develop and carry out a PLAN
■ Find the ANSWER and CHECK

Some problems can be solved by first translating to a system of three equations. Thus, the system of three equations becomes a mathematical model of the problem.

EXAMPLE

In a factory there are three machines, A, B, and C. When all three are running, they produce 222 suitcases per day. If A and B work, but C does not, they produce 159 suitcases per day. If B and C work, but A does not, they produce 147 suitcases per day. What is the daily production of each machine?

Let us use x, y, and z for the number of suitcases produced daily by the machines A, B, and C, respectively. There are three statements.

When all three are running, they produce 222 suitcases per day.

$$x + y + z = 222$$

When A and B work, they produce 159 suitcases per day.

$$x + y = 159$$

When B and C work, they produce 147 suitcases per day.

$$y + z = 147$$

We now have a system of three equations.

$$\begin{aligned} x + y + z &= 222 \\ x + y &= 159 \\ y + z &= 147 \end{aligned}$$

We solve and get $x = 75$, $y = 84$, $z = 63$. These numbers check, so the answer to the problem is that A produces 75 suitcases per day, B produces 84 suitcases per day, and C produces 63 suitcases per day.

Try This

a. There are three machines, A, B, and C, in a factory. When all three work, they produce 287 bolts per hour. When only A and C work, they produce 197 bolts per hour. When A and B work, they produce 202 bolts per hour. How many bolts per hour can each machine produce alone?

4-5 Exercises

Extra Help On the Web

Look for worked-out examples at the Prentice Hall Web site.
www.phschool.com

A

1. The sum of three numbers is 105. The third is 11 less than ten times the second. Twice the first is 7 more than three times the second. Find the numbers.
2. The sum of three numbers is 57. The second is 3 more than the first. The third is 6 more than the first. Find the numbers.
3. The sum of three numbers is 5. The first number minus the second plus the third is 1. The first minus the third is 3 more than the second. Find the numbers.
4. The sum of three numbers is 26. Twice the first minus the second is 2 less than the third. The third is the second minus three times the first. Find the numbers.
5. In triangle ABC, the measure of angle B is 2° more than three times the measure of angle A. The measure of angle C is 8° more than the measure of angle A. Find the angle measures.
6. In triangle PQR, the measure of angle Q is three times the measure of angle P. The measure of angle R is 30° greater than the measure of angle P. Find the angle measures.
7. In triangle TUV, the measure of angle U is twice the measure of angle T. The measure of angle V is 80° more than that of angle T. Find the angle measures.
8. In triangle FGH, the measure of angle G is three times that of angle F. The measure of angle H is 20° more than that of angle F. Find the angle measures.
9. Gina sells magazines part time. On Thursday, Friday, and Saturday, she sold \$66 worth. On Thursday she sold \$3 more than on Friday. On Saturday she sold \$6 more than on Thursday. How much did she take in each day?
10. Pat picked strawberries on three days. He picked a total of 87 quarts. On Tuesday he picked 15 quarts more than on Monday. On Wednesday he picked 3 quarts fewer than on Tuesday. How many quarts did he pick each day?
11. Kristin has a total of 225 on three tests. The sum of the scores on the first and second tests exceeds her third score by 61. Her first score exceeds her second by 6. Find the three scores.
12. In a factory there are three polishing machines, A, B, and C. When all three of them are working, 5700 lenses can be polished in one week. When only A and B are working, 3400 lenses can be polished in one week. When only B and C are working, 4200 lenses can be polished in one week. How many lenses can be polished in a week by each machine?
13. Sawmills A, B, and C can produce 7400 board feet of lumber per day. A and B together can produce 4700 board feet, while B and C together can produce 5200 board feet. How many board feet can each mill produce by itself?

Two metal pipes can be fused together by arc welding, which uses an electrical current or arc to melt a filler metal between the pipes along their circumference. See Exercise 14.

14. Todd, Don, and Carla can weld 37 linear feet per hour when working together. Todd and Don together can weld 22 linear feet per hour, while Todd and Carla together can weld 25 linear feet per hour. How many linear feet per hour can each weld alone?

B

15. Tammy's age is the sum of the ages of Carmen and Dennis. Carmen's age is 2 more than the sum of the ages of Dennis and Mark. Dennis's age is four times Mark's age. The sum of all four ages is 42. How old is Tammy?

16. Find a three-digit positive integer such that the sum of all three digits is 14, the tens digit is 2 more than the ones digit, and if the digits are reversed the number is unchanged.

17. *Critical Thinking* Abe gives Rafer as many raffle tickets as Rafer already had and Jorge as many as Jorge already had. Then Rafer gives Abe and Jorge as many tickets as each of them has. Similarly, Jorge gives Abe and Rafer as many tickets as each of them has. They each end up with 40 tickets. How many tickets did Rafer have originally?

Challenge

18. At a county fair, adults' tickets sold for \$5.50, senior citizens' tickets sold for \$4.00, and children's tickets sold for \$1.50. On the opening day, the number of children's and senior citizens' tickets sold was 30 more than half the number of adults' tickets sold. The number of senior citizens' tickets sold was 5 more than four times the number of children's tickets. How many of each type of ticket were sold if the total receipts from the ticket sales were \$14,970?

19. A bicyclist averages one speed uphill, one speed on level ground, and one speed downhill. She estimates the following mileage for her three previous rides:

Miles uphill	Miles level	Miles downhill	Total time
2	15	5	1.5 hours
6	9	1	1.4 hours
8	3	8	1.6 hours

What were her average speeds uphill, on level ground, and downhill?

Self-Test On the Web

Check your progress. Look for a self-test at the Prentice Hall Web site. www.phschool.com

Mixed Review

Consider $f(x) = x^2$, $g(x) = (x + 2)$, $h(x) = 2x$. Find each of the following.

20. $f(g(3))$ **21.** $g(f(3))$ **22.** $h(g(2))$ **23.** $g(h(2))$ 3-9

Determine whether the graphs of each pair of equations are parallel.

24. $y = 9 - 4x$ and $2y - 9 + 8x = 0$ **25.** $3y + 4 = 2x$ and $4y + 8 = 6x$ 3-7

Consistent and Dependent Systems

4-6

PART 1 Consistent Systems

Objective: Determine whether a system of equations is consistent or inconsistent.

What You'll Learn

1. To determine whether a system of equations is consistent or inconsistent
2. To determine whether a system of equations is dependent

. . . And Why

To use systems of equations in linear programming

Some systems of equations have no solution. Some systems of equations may have more than one solution. In order to classify various systems of equations we use the following terminology.

If a system of equations has at least one solution, we say that it is **consistent.**

If a system does not have a solution, we say that it is **inconsistent.**

We now consider such systems.

EXAMPLE 1 Determine whether this system is consistent or inconsistent.

$$x - 3y = 1 \quad ①$$
$$-2x + 6y = 5 \quad ②$$

We attempt to find a solution. We multiply ① by 2 and add it to ②.

$$x - 3y = 1 \quad ①$$
$$0 = 7 \quad 2① + ②$$

The last equation says that $0 \cdot x + 0 \cdot y = 7$. There are no numbers x and y for which this is true, so there is no solution. The system is inconsistent.

We can also consider the problem graphically. The slope-intercept forms of the original equations are

$$y = \frac{1}{3}x - \frac{1}{3} \quad ①$$
$$y = \frac{1}{3}x + \frac{5}{6} \quad ②$$

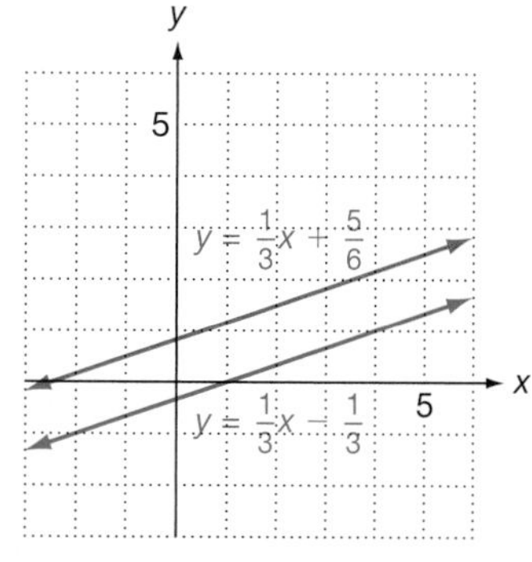

We can see that the lines are parallel. They have no point of intersection, so the system is inconsistent.

If when solving a system of equations we arrive at an obviously false equation, such as $0 = 7$, then the system is inconsistent.

Try This Determine whether these systems are consistent or inconsistent.

a. $3x - y = 2$
$6x - 2y = 3$

b. $x + 4y = 2$
$2x - y = 1$

EXAMPLE 2 Determine whether this system is consistent or inconsistent.

$$\begin{aligned} x + 2y + z &= 1 \quad ① \\ -x - y + 2z &= 0 \quad ② \\ y + 3z &= 4 \quad ③ \end{aligned}$$

We attempt to find a solution. We add equation ① to ②.

$$\begin{aligned} x + 2y + z &= 1 \quad ① \\ y + 3z &= 1 \quad ① + ② \\ y + 3z &= 4 \quad ③ \end{aligned}$$

We multiply our new second equation by -1 and add it to ③.

$$\begin{aligned} x + 2y + z &= 1 \\ y + 3z &= 1 \\ 0 &= 3 \quad -1\,② + ③ \end{aligned}$$

The system is inconsistent.

Try This Determine whether these systems are consistent or inconsistent.

c. $x + 2y + z = 1$
$3x + 3y + z = 2$
$2x + y = 2$

d. $x + z = 1$
$y + z = 1$
$x + y = 1$

PART 2 Dependent Systems

Objective: Determine whether a system of equations is dependent.

Consider this system.

$$\begin{aligned} 5x + 2y &= 3 \\ 10x + 4y &= 6 \end{aligned}$$

If we multiply the first equation by 2, we get the second equation. The graphs of the equations are the same line. Thus the system will have infinitely many solutions. We call the system **dependent.**

Dependent Systems

If a system of linear equations has infinitely many solutions, we say the system is **dependent.**

EXAMPLE 3 Determine whether this system is dependent.

$$2x + 3y = 1 \quad ①$$
$$4x + 6y = 2 \quad ②$$

We attempt to solve. We multiply ① by -2 and add it to ②.

$$2x + 3y = 1$$
$$0 = 0 \quad -2① + ②$$

The last equation says that $0 \cdot x + 0 \cdot y = 0$. This is true for all numbers x and y. The system is dependent.

We can also consider the problem graphically. The slope-intercept forms of the equations are

$$y = -\frac{2}{3}x + \frac{1}{3} \quad ①$$
$$y = -\frac{2}{3}x + \frac{1}{3} \quad ②$$

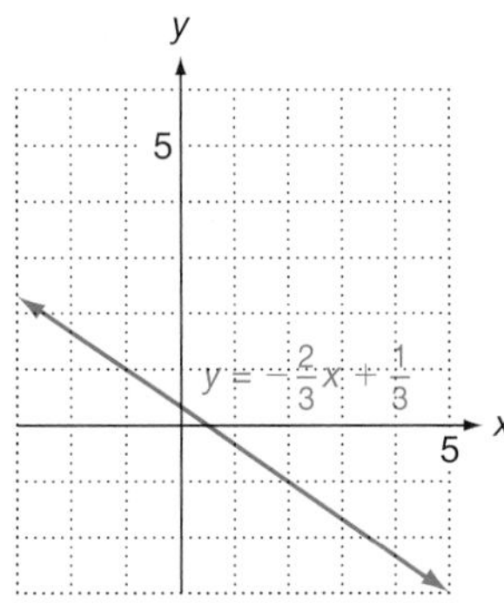

The slope-intercept equations of the lines are the same. This tells us that the graphs are the same. This system of equations has infinitely many solutions. Each point on the line $y = -\frac{2}{3}x + \frac{1}{3}$ has coordinates that constitute a solution. The system is dependent.

Try This Determine whether these systems are dependent.

e. $-6x + 4y = -2$
$3x - 2y = 1$

f. $x - y = 2$
$x + y = 4$

EXAMPLE 4 Determine whether this system is dependent.

$$x + 2y + z = 1 \quad ①$$
$$x - y + z = 1 \quad ②$$
$$2x + y + 2z = 2 \quad ③$$

We attempt to solve. We multiply ① by -1 and add it to ②.

$$x + 2y + z = 1$$
$$-3y = 0 \quad -1① + ②$$
$$2x + y + 2z = 2$$

We then multiply ① by -2 and add it to ③.

$$x + 2y + z = 1$$
$$-3y = 0$$
$$-3y = 0 \quad -2① + ③$$

Since the last two equations are identical, the system of three equations is equivalent to the following system of two equations.

$$\begin{aligned} x + 2y + z &= 1 \\ -3y \quad\quad &= 0 \end{aligned}$$

The system is dependent.

In solving a system, how do we know it is dependent? If, at some stage, we find that two of the equations are identical, or we obtain an obviously true equation such as $0 = 0$, then we can eliminate an equation. If we then have fewer equations than variables, the system is dependent. Be sure to check whether any inconsistent equations remain, however. An inconsistent system cannot be dependent, since it has no solution.

Try This Determine whether these systems are dependent.

g. $x + y + 2z = 1$
$x - y + z = 1$
$2x + 3z = 2$

h. $x + y + 2z = 1$
$x - y + z = 1$
$x + 2y + z = 2$

Extra Help On the Web

Look for worked-out examples at the Prentice Hall Web site.
www.phschool.com

4-6 Exercises

A

Determine whether these systems are consistent or inconsistent.

1. $x + 2y = 6$
$2x = 8 - 4y$

2. $y - 2x = 1$
$2x - 3 = y$

3. $y - x = 4$
$x + 2y = 2$

4. $y + x = 5$
$y = x - 3$

5. $x - 3 = y$
$2x - 2y = 6$

6. $3y = x - 2$
$3x = 6 + 9y$

7. $x + z = 0$
$x + y + 2z = 3$
$y + z = 2$

8. $x + y = 0$
$x + y = 1$
$2x + y + z = 2$

9. $x + z = 0$
$x + y = 1$
$y + z = 1$

10. $x - y = 0$
$y - z = 0$
$x - z = 0$

Determine whether these systems are dependent.

11. $x - 3 = y$
$2x - 2y = 6$

12. $3y = x - 2$
$3x = 6 + 9y$

13. $y - x = 4$
$x + 2y = 2$

14. $y + x = 5$
$y = x - 3$

15. $2x + 3y = 1$
$x + 1.5y = 0.5$

16. $15x + 6y = 20$
$7.5x - 10 = -3y$

17. $x + z = 0$
$x + y = 1$
$y + z = 1$

18. $2x + y = 1$
$x + 2y + z = 0$
$x + z = 1$

19. $x - y = 0$
$y - z = 0$
$x - z = 0$

20. **TEST PREP** Solve. $x + y + z = 1$
$-x + 2y + z = 2$
$2x - y = -1$

A. $(0, 0, 1)$ **B.** $(0, 1, 0)$ **C.** $(1, 0, 0)$ **D.** $(1, -1, 1)$

B

Solve. If a system has more than one solution, list three of them.

21. $x + 2y - z = -8$
$2x - y + z = 4$
$8x + y + z = 2$

22. $2x + y + z = 0$
$x + y - z = 0$
$x + 2y + 2z = 0$

23. $2x + 4y + 8z = 5$
$x + 2y + 4z = 13$
$4x + 8y + 16z = 10$

24. $x + y + z = 4$
$5x + 5y + 5z = 15$
$2x + 2y + 2z = 6$

25. Classify each of the systems in Exercises 21–24 as consistent and dependent, consistent and not dependent, or inconsistent.

26. *Critical Thinking* What happens when you use Cramer's Rule to solve an inconsistent system of two equations in two variables? What happens when you use Cramer's Rule to solve a dependent system? Explain your conclusions.

27. *Critical Thinking* Suppose when we graph a system of three equations in x and y in the coordinate plane, the lines form a triangle. How many solutions does the system have? Is the system consistent? Dependent? Explain.

Challenge

Determine the constant k such that each system is dependent.

28. $6x - 9y = -3$
$-4x + 6y = k$

29. $8x - 16y = 20$
$10x - 20y = k$

Consider the following dependent systems. For each system, find an ordered pair in terms of y that describes the solution set of the system.

30. $2x + 3y = 1$
$4x + 6y = 2$

31. $-6x + 4y = 10$
$3x - 2y = -5$

Mixed Review

Find the domain of each function. **32.** $f(x) = \frac{1}{2x - 4}$ **33.** $f(x) = \frac{1}{x(x - 1)}$ *3-3*

Find the slope and y-intercept of each line. **34.** $3x - 4y + 11 = 0$

35. $9y + 6x = 15$ **36.** $2y = 5x + 11$ *3-5*

Solve. **37.** $11 - 35m = -59$ **38.** $t + 4.2t = 156$ *3-8*

Connections: Geometry

The graph of an equation $ax + by + cz = d$ is a plane. Three equations in x, y, and z represent planes in space. Just as two lines on a plane may be parallel, intersect at one point, or coincide, three planes in space also may be related in several possible ways. What are the possible ways three planes may be related in space?

4-7 Systems of Inequalities

What You'll Learn

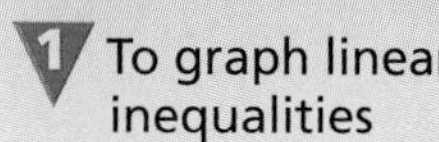

1. To graph linear inequalities

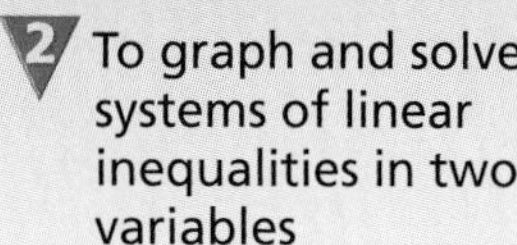

2. To graph and solve systems of linear inequalities in two variables

. . . And Why

To solve problems using linear programming

PART 1 Linear Inequalities

Objective: Graph linear inequalities.

An inequality in two variables is a **linear inequality.**

A solution of an inequality in two variables is an ordered pair of numbers that makes the inequality true. To show that an ordered pair (x, y) is a solution of a linear inequality, we substitute in the inequality in alphabetical order.

To determine whether $(-3, 2)$ is a solution of $5x - 4y \leq 13$, replace x by -3 and y by 2.

$$\begin{aligned} 5x - 4y &\leq 13 \\ 5(-3) - 4(2) &\leq 13 \\ -15 - 8 &\leq 13 \\ -23 &< 13 \end{aligned}$$

Since -23 is less than 13, the ordered pair $(-3, 2)$ makes the inequality true and is a solution.

The graphs of linear inequalities in two variables can be used to solve many problems, particularly those concerned with maximizing or minimizing quantities.

To graph a linear inequality, we first graph the corresponding linear equation.

EXAMPLE 1 Graph $y < x$.

We first graph the equation $y = x$. This line marks the **boundary** of points that satisfy the inequality and points that do not. We draw this line dashed, since the points on the line are not in the solution set of $y < x$.

For any point above the line, y is greater than x, or $y > x$. For any point below the line, y is less than x, or $y < x$. Thus the graph is the **half-plane** below the boundary line $y = x$. We show this by shading the lower half-plane.

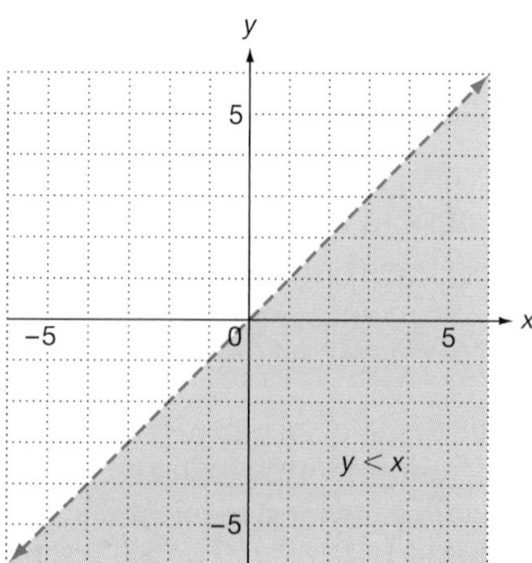

The graph of any linear inequality in two variables is either a half-plane or a half-plane together with its boundary (the line).

EXAMPLE 2 Graph $6x - 2y \leq 12$.

Method 1. Solve for y.

$$y \geq 3x - 6$$

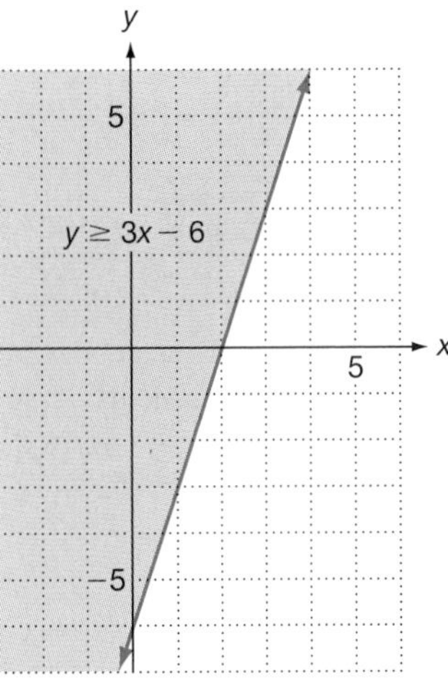

Graph the line $y = 3x - 6$. Since $y = 3x - 6$ is part of the solution, we draw the line solid this time. For any point above the line, the value of y is greater than $3x - 6$. Hence the graph of the inequality is the half-plane above the line, together with the line or boundary.

Method 2. Graph the line $6x - 2y = 12$, using any method.

This time we will use the intercept method. The intercepts are at $(0, -6)$ and $(2, 0)$. We plot them and draw the line.

To determine which half-plane is the solution, we test a point. The origin is an easy point to use if the line doesn't contain the origin. We try $(0, 0)$.

$$6 \cdot 0 - 2 \cdot 0 \leq 12$$
$$0 \leq 12$$

This gives us a true sentence. Hence $(0, 0)$ is a solution. We graph the half-plane containing $(0, 0)$.

Try This Graph.

a. $y > -2x$ **b.** $2x + y \geq 2$ **c.** $3x - y < -3$

EXAMPLE 3 Graph $-1 < y \leq 2$.

This is a conjunction of two inequalities.

$$-1 < y \text{ and } y \leq 2$$

It will be true for any y that is both greater than -1 and less than or equal to 2. Since our inequality is a conjunction, the graph is the intersection of the graphs of the two inequalities.

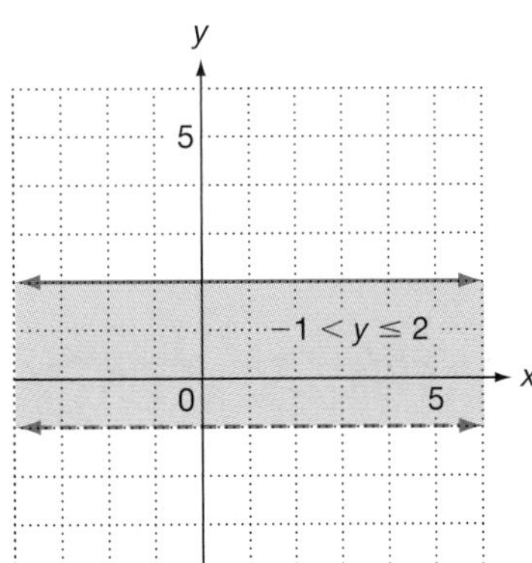

Try This Graph.

d. $-4 \leq x < 1$ **e.** $1 \leq y \leq 2\frac{1}{2}$

PART 2 Systems of Inequalities

Objective: Graph systems of inequalities in two variables in the plane, finding vertices, if they exist.

To graph the solution set of a system, or conjunction, of inequalities, graph the inequalities separately on the same axes and find their intersection.

EXAMPLE 4 Graph this system of inequalities.

$$2x + y > 5$$
$$3x - y > 2$$

Consider the graph of each inequality separately.

Graph $2x + y > 5$.

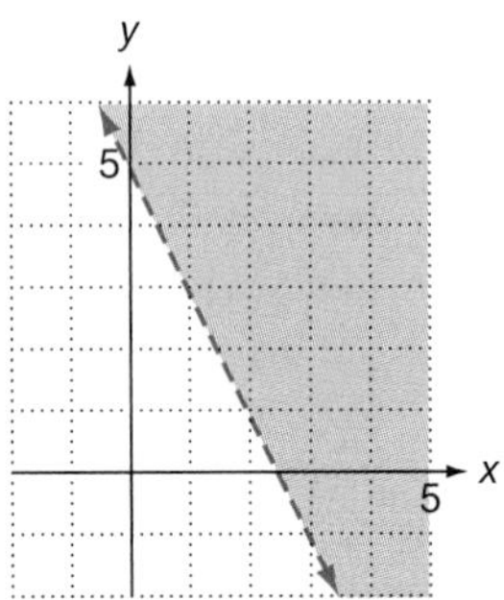

Graph $3x - y > 2$.

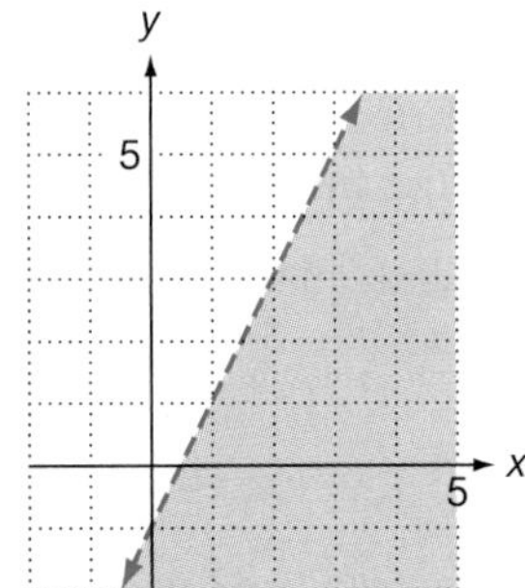

The intersection of the individual graphs is the graph of the system.

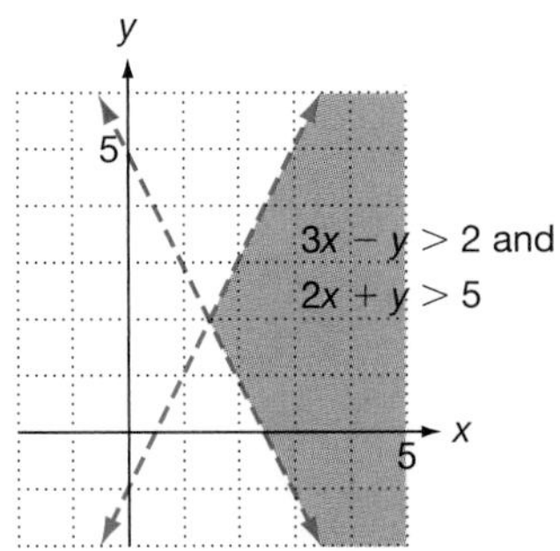

Try This Graph these systems of inequalities.

f. $y \geq 4$
$x - 2y \leq 3$

g. $x + y < 2$
$x - y \geq -3$

h. $x - 2y \geq 4$
$2x + 3y \leq 3$

A system of linear inequalities may have a graph that consists of a polygon and its interior. Some problems can be solved by finding the coordinates of the vertices.

EXAMPLE 5

Graph the inequalities. Find the coordinates of any vertices formed.

$$2x + y \geq 2$$
$$4x + 3y \leq 12$$
$$\frac{1}{2} \leq x \leq 2$$
$$y \geq 0$$

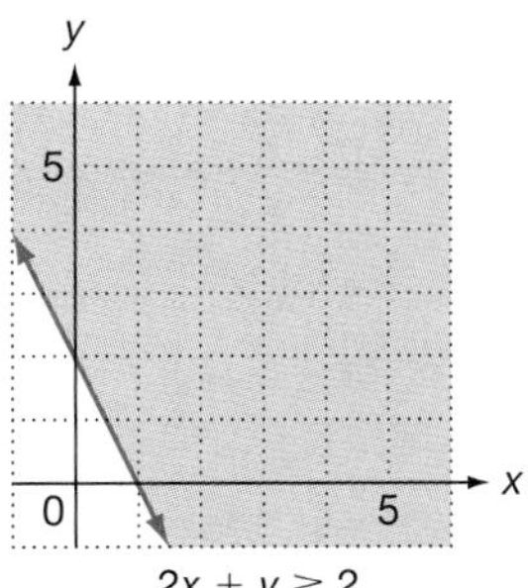

$2x + y \geq 2$

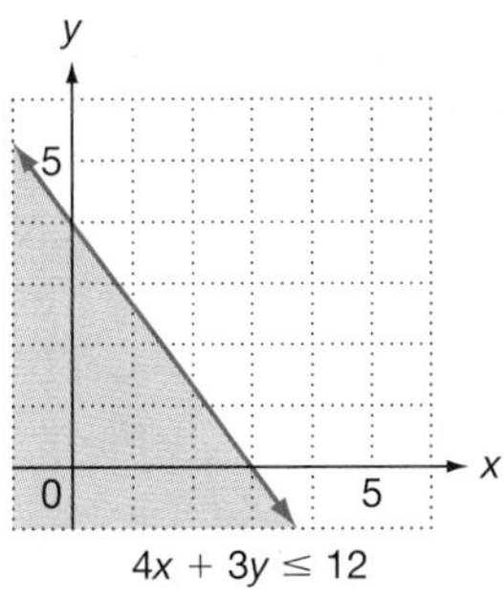

$4x + 3y \leq 12$

The separate graphs are shown at the right, and the graph of the intersection, which is the graph of the system, is shown below.

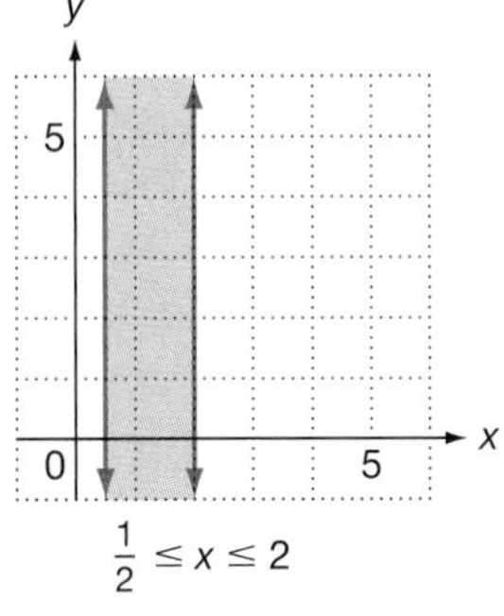

$\frac{1}{2} \leq x \leq 2$

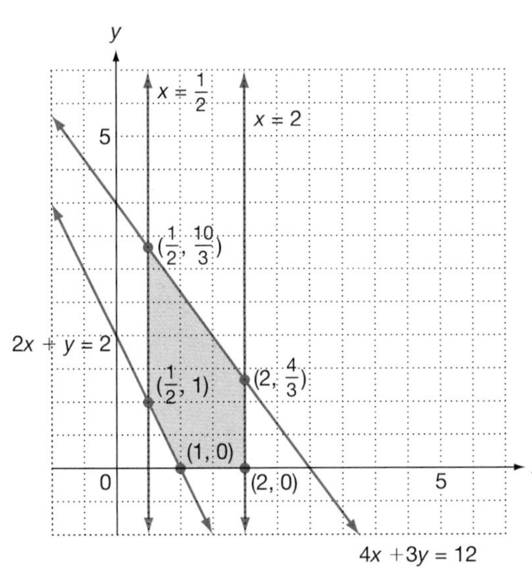

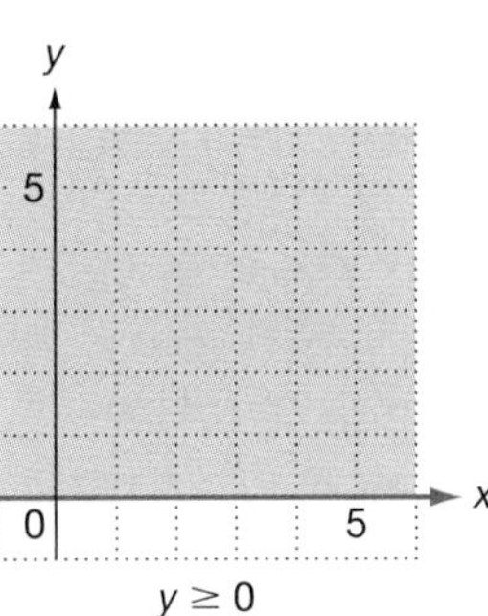

$y \geq 0$

We find the vertices $\left(\frac{1}{2}, 1\right)$ and $(2, 0)$ by solving these systems, respectively.

$$\begin{aligned} 2x + y &= 2 \\ x &= \frac{1}{2} \end{aligned} \quad \text{and} \quad \begin{aligned} x &= 2 \\ y &= 0 \end{aligned}$$

The vertices $\left(2, \frac{4}{3}\right)$ and $\left(\frac{1}{2}, \frac{10}{3}\right)$ were found by solving, respectively, the following two systems.

$$\begin{aligned} x &= 2 \\ 4x + 3y &= 12 \end{aligned} \quad \text{and} \quad \begin{aligned} x &= \frac{1}{2} \\ 4x + 3y &= 12 \end{aligned}$$

Try This Graph. Find the coordinates of any vertices formed.

i. $x + y \geq 1$
$y - x \geq 2$

j. $5x + 6y \leq 30$
$0 \leq y \leq 3$
$0 \leq x \leq 4$

Extra Help On the Web

Look for worked-out examples at the Prentice Hall Web site.
www.phschool.com

4-7 Exercises

A

Graph.

1. $y > 2x$ **2.** $y < 3x$ **3.** $y < x + 1$ **4.** $y \leq x - 3$
5. $y > x - 2$ **6.** $y \geq x + 4$ **7.** $x + y < 4$ **8.** $x - y \geq 3$
9. $3x + 4y \leq 12$ **10.** $2x + 3y < 6$ **11.** $2y - 3x > 6$ **12.** $2y - x \leq 4$
13. $3x - 2 \leq 5x + y$ **14.** $2x - 2y \geq 8 + 2y$ **15.** $-4 < y < -1$

Graph these systems of inequalities.

16. $y < x$, $y > -x + 3$ **17.** $y > x$, $y < -x + 1$ **18.** $y \geq x$, $y < -x + 4$ **19.** $y \leq x$, $y < -x + 2$

20. $y \geq -2$, $x > 1$ **21.** $y \leq -2$, $x > 2$ **22.** $x < 3$, $y \geq -3x + 2$ **23.** $x > -2$, $y \leq -2x + 3$

24. $y \geq -2$, $y \geq x + 3$ **25.** $y \leq 4$, $y \geq -x + 2$ **26.** $x + y \leq 1$, $x - y \geq 2$ **27.** $x + y < 3$, $x - y < 4$

28. $y - 2x > 1$, $y - 2x < 3$ **29.** $y + 3x > 0$, $y + 3x < 2$ **30.** $2y - x \leq 2$, $y - 3x \geq -1$

Graph. Find the coordinates of any vertices formed.

31. $4y - 3x \geq -12$, $4y + 3x \geq -36$, $y \leq 0$, $x \leq 0$

32. $8x + 5y \leq 40$, $x + 2y \leq 8$, $x \geq 0$, $y \geq 0$

33. $3x + 4y \geq 12$, $5x + 6y \leq 30$, $1 \leq x \leq 3$

B

Graph.

34. $y \geq |x|$ **35.** $y > |x| + 3$ **36.** $|x + y| \leq 1$
37. $|x| + |y| \leq 1$ **38.** $|x| > |y|$ **39.** $|x + y| \geq 2$

40. ***Critical Thinking*** Write a system of inequalities in two variables whose graphs will be the following geometric figures.

a. a square and its interior **b.** a triangle and its interior
c. a parallelogram and its interior **d.** a trapezoid and its interior

Challenge

41. Can a system of linear inequalities be inconsistent? If so, give an example.

Mixed Review

Write an equation of the line containing the point $(3, -2)$ with the given slope.

42. 3 **43.** -2 **44.** $\frac{1}{2}$ **45.** $\frac{4}{5}$ **46.** $-\frac{2}{3}$ *3-5*

Solve. **47.** $3m + 13 = 1 + m$ **48.** $4(4 - t) = 3(1 - t)$ *2-1*

Using Linear Programming

4-8

What You'll Learn

1 To solve problems using linear programming

. . . And Why

To solve real-world problems using algebraic reasoning skills

PART 1 Solving Problems

Objective: Solve problems using linear programming.

Mathematical models can be created to find optimal results based upon certain limits, or **constraints.** For example, a model may be created to maximize profits or minimize costs, given production limits, time constraints, or a specific allocation of resources. A field of mathematics where systems of linear inequalities are the basis of the model is called **linear programming.**

EXAMPLE 1

You are taking a test in which items of type A are worth 10 points and items of type B are worth 15 points. It takes 3 minutes to answer each item of type A and 6 minutes for each item of type B. The total time allowed is 60 minutes, and you may not answer more than 16 questions. Assuming all of your answers are correct, how many items of each type should you answer to get the highest score?

We can use a *linear programming* model to find the answer.

Let x = the number of items of type A, and y = the number of items of type B. The total score T is given by $T = 10x + 15y$. The set of ordered pairs (x, y) for which this equation makes sense is determined by the following *constraints.*

Total number of questions allowed, not more than 16: $x + y \leq 16$
Time, not more than 60 minutes: $3x + 6y \leq 60$
Number of items of type A, nonnegative: $x \geq 0$
Number of items of type B, nonnegative: $y \geq 0$

We now graph the system of inequalities and determine the vertices (if any).

The graph consists of a polygon and its interior. Under this condition, T has a maximum and a minimum value occuring at the vertices of the polygon. We need to find the vertices and substitute the coordinates in $T = 10x + 15y$.

Vertices: (x, y)	**Score:** $T = 10x + 15y$	
(0, 0)	0	Minimum
(16, 0)	160	
(12, 4)	180	Maximum
(0, 10)	150	

The maximum score is 180. To achieve this score, you would answer 12 of type A and 4 of type B.

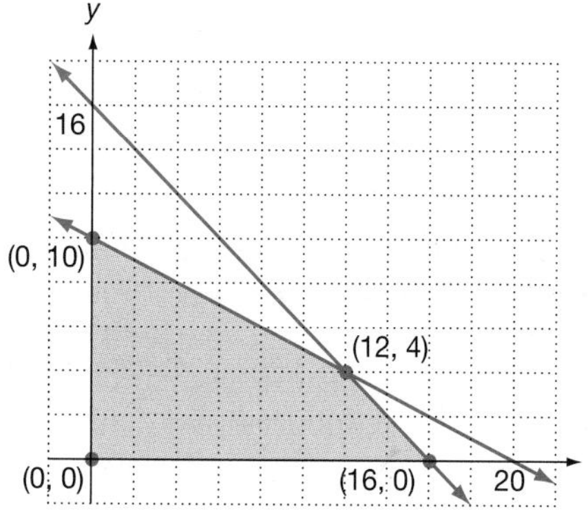

The following theorem is used to solve linear programming problems.

Theorem 4-1

Suppose a quantity F is given by a linear equation $F = ax + by + c$, and that the set of ordered pairs (x, y) for which the equation makes sense can be described by a system of linear inequalities. If the graph of this system consists of a polygon and its interior, then F has a maximum and a minimum value that occur at the vertices.

EXAMPLE 2

Wheels Inc. makes mopeds and bicycles. Experience shows they must produce at least 10 mopeds. The factory can produce at most 60 mopeds and 120 bicycles per month. The profit on a moped is \$134 and on a bicycle, \$20. They can make at most 160 units combined. How many of each should they make per month to maximize profit?

Businesses such as this factory, which produces mopeds and bicycles, use linear programming to maximize their profit. How do you suppose a business might use linear programming to help deliver its products to its retailers?

Let x = the number of mopeds to be produced
y = the number of bicycles to be produced

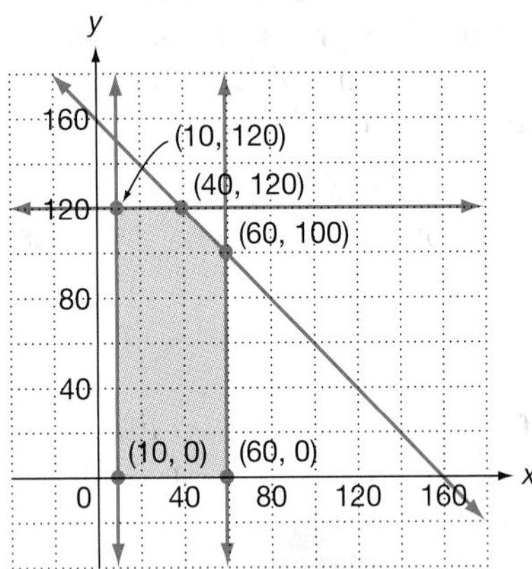

The profit $134x + 20y$ is subject to the constraints $10 \leq x \leq 60$, $0 \leq y \leq 120$, and $x + y \leq 160$.

Vertices: (x, y)	**Profit: $P = 134x + 20y$**
(10, 0)	1340
(60, 0)	8040
(60, 100)	10,040 Maximum
(40, 120)	7760
(10, 120)	3740

Wheels Inc. maximizes profit with 60 mopeds and 100 bicycles.

Try This

a. A snack bar cooks and sells hamburgers and hot dogs during football games. To stay in business, it must sell at least 10 hamburgers but cannot cook more than 40. It must also sell at least 30 hot dogs but cannot cook more than 70. The snack bar cannot cook more than 90 items total. The profit on a hamburger is 33¢ and on a hot dog it is 21¢. How many of each item should it sell to make the maximum profit?

4-8 Exercises

Extra Help On the Web

Look for worked-out examples at the Prentice Hall Web site.
www.phschool.com

A

1. You are about to take a test that contains questions of type A worth 4 points and of type B worth 7 points. You must answer at least 5 of type A and 3 of type B, but time restricts answering more than 10 of either type. In total, you can answer no more than 18. How many of each type of question must you answer, assuming all of your answers are correct, to maximize your score? What is the maximum score?
2. You are about to take a test that contains questions of type A worth 10 points and of type B worth 25 points. You must answer at least 3 of type A, but time restricts answering more than 12. You must answer at least 4 questions of type B, but time restricts answering more than 15. In total, you can answer no more than 20. How many of each type of question must you answer, assuming all of your answers are correct, to maximize your score? What is the maximum score?
3. A man plans to invest up to \$22,000 in bank X or bank Y, or both. He will invest at least \$2000, but no more than \$14,000, in bank X. He will invest no more than \$15,000 in bank Y. Bank X pays 6% simple interest, and bank Y pays $6\frac{1}{2}$%. How much should he invest in each to maximize income? What is the maximum income?

B

4. It takes a tailoring firm 2 hours of cutting and 4 hours of sewing to make a knit suit. To make a worsted suit it takes 4 hours of cutting and 2 hours of sewing. At most, 20 hours per day are available for cutting, and, at most, 16 hours per day are available for sewing. The profit on a knit suit is \$34 and on a worsted suit \$31. How many of each kind of suit should be made to maximize profit? What is the maximum profit?
5. *Critical Thinking* Suppose the profit on a bicycle and a moped were each \$100 in Example 2. How many of each should be produced? What is the maximum profit?

Challenge

6. An airline will provide accommodations for a minimum of 2000 first-class, 1500 business, and 2400 economy-class passengers. Airplane P-1 costs \$12,000 per mile to operate and can accommodate 40 first-class, 40 business, and 120 economy-class passengers. Airplane P-2 costs \$10,000 per mile to operate and can accommodate 80 first-class, 30 business, and 40 economy-class passengers. How many of each type of airplane should be used to minimize the operating cost?

Mixed Review

Solve. **7.** $19(c + 3) = 76$ **8.** $14 < 3r + 2$ **9.** $-4c + 2c > -18$ *2-1, 2-4*

Preparing for Standardized Tests

Systems of Equations

Some items on college entrance exams can be solved using the methods you learned in this chapter for solving systems of equations. Some items on these tests, however, can be solved more quickly using other methods.

EXAMPLE 1

If $3x + 2y = 17$ and $2x + y = 7$, then $\frac{5x + 3y}{2} =$

(A) 10 **(B)** 12 **(C)** 17 **(D)** 20 **(E)** 34

While linear combinations could be used to solve for x and y, this problem can be more easily solved by adding the two equations together and dividing by 2.

$$\begin{array}{r} 3x + 2y = 17 \\ 2x + y = 7 \\ \hline 5x + 3y = 24 \end{array}$$

Dividing by 2,

$$\frac{5x + 3y}{2} = 12$$

The answer is 12, choice B.

Another variation involves subtracting equations.

EXAMPLE 2

If $6x + 4y = 14$ and $3x + y = 8$, then $x + y =$

(A) 5 **(B)** 4 **(C)** 3 **(D)** 2 **(E)** 1

Subtracting equations results in the answer directly.

$$\begin{array}{r} 6x + 4y = 14 \\ -(3x + y = 8) \\ \hline 3x + 3y = 6 \end{array}$$

Multiplying by $\frac{1}{3}$,

$$\frac{1}{3}(3x + 3y) = \frac{1}{3}(6)$$

$$x + y = 2$$

The answer is 2, choice D.

Before solving, determine whether it would be easier to use substitution, linear combinations, or one of these variations.

EXAMPLE 3

If $8x - 7y = 14$ and $6x + 9y = -11$, then $7x + y =$

(A) $\frac{3}{2}$ **(B)** 3 **(C)** $\frac{49}{114}$ **(D)** 0 **(E)** $-\frac{2}{15}$

Adding the equations,

$$\begin{array}{r} 8x - 7y = 14 \\ 6x + 9y = -11 \\ \hline 14x + 2y = 3 \end{array}$$

Multiplying by $\frac{1}{2}$,

$$7x + y = \frac{3}{2}$$

The answer is $\frac{3}{2}$, choice A.

Problems

1. If $x + 2y = 6$ and $3x + y = 3$, then $8x + 6y =$

(A) 18 **(B)** 9 **(C)** 20 **(D)** 3 **(E)** 24

2. If $5x - 3y = 6$ and $x = \frac{4y}{5}$, then $y =$

(A) $\frac{4}{5}$ **(B)** $\frac{8}{5}$ **(C)** 6 **(D)** $\frac{8}{3}$ **(E)** 8

3. If $3x + 3y = 7$ and $x + 4y = 3$, then $\frac{4x + 7y}{5} =$

(A) 10 **(B)** 2 **(C)** 5 **(D)** 4 **(E)** 3

4. If $x + 4y = 5$ and $4x + 3y = 4$, then $10x + 14y =$

(A) 8 **(B)** 9 **(C)** 16 **(D)** 18 **(E)** 20

5. If $x + y = 3$ and $x - y = 2$, then $6x =$

(A) 15 **(B)** 14 **(C)** 30 **(D)** 12 **(E)** 5

6. If $4x - 3y = 10$ and $x = \frac{7y}{4}$, then $2y =$

(A) 2 **(B)** 10 **(C)** 4 **(D)** 5 **(E)** $\frac{5}{2}$

7. If $x + 2y = 3$ and $2x + y = 1$, then $9x + 9y =$

(A) 4 **(B)** 9 **(C)** 27 **(D)** 36 **(E)** 12

8. If $5x + 3y = 8$ and $3x + y = 4$, then $4x + 2y =$

(A) 5 **(B)** 4 **(C)** 3 **(D)** 6 **(E)** 12

9. If $3x + 5y = 44$ and $2x - 5y = -29$, then $5x + 5y =$

(A) 15 **(B)** 75 **(C)** 30 **(D)** 10 **(E)** 50

10. If $ax + by = c$ and $ax - by = d$, then $2x =$

(A) $\frac{c + d}{b}$ **(B)** $\frac{c - d}{a}$ **(C)** $\frac{c + d}{a}$ **(D)** $\frac{a}{c + d}$ **(E)** $\frac{2(c + d)}{a}$

4 Chapter Wrap Up

Key Terms

boundary (p. 188)
consistent systems (p. 183)
constraints (p. 193)
Cramer's Rule (p. 166)
dependent systems (p. 184)
half-plane (p. 188)
inconsistent systems (p. 183)
linear combinations (p. 163)
linear inequality (p. 188)
linear programming (p. 193)
method of elimination (p. 163)
ordered triple (p. 174)
substitution method (p. 162)
systems of equations (p. 160)
triangular form (p. 176)
unique solution (p. 160)

4-1

One way to solve a **system of equations** is to graph the equations and find points of intersection.

Solve graphically.

1. $-2x + y = 1$
$3x + y = 1$

2. $x = y$
$3x + y = 12$

4-2

The **substitution method** is a useful technique for solving systems in which a variable has a coefficient of 1.

Solve using the substitution method.

3. $2x - y = -9$
$3x - 8y = -7$

4. $x + y = 6$
$y = x + 2$

5. $y = 7 - x$
$2x - y = 8$

If all the variables have coefficients other than 1, **linear combinations** may be easier to use than the substitution method.

Solve using linear combinations.

6. $2x + 7y = 2$
$3x + 5y = -8$

7. $5x + 3y = 17$
$-5x + 3y = 3$

8. $-3a + 2b = 0$
$3a - 4b = -1$

4-3

Translating to a system of equations will often help when solving some problems.

9. On a recent trip, Ellie drove 264 km in the same length of time that Carol took to drive 198 km. Ellie's speed was 17 km/h greater than Carol's speed. Find the rate of each.

4-4

A solution of a system of equations in three variables is an **ordered triple** that makes all three equations true.

Solve.

10. $2x - y + z = 7$
$x + 2y + 2z = 3$
$7x - 3y - 3z = 4$

11. $2a + b - 4c = 0$
$a - b + 2c = 5$
$3a + 2b + 2c = 3$

4-5

Some problems can be best solved by translating to a system of three equations.

Solve.

12. Three assemblers, A, B, and C, can produce 86 circuit boards per hour. A and B together can produce 59 circuit boards per hour, while A and C together can produce 58 circuit boards per hour. How many circuit boards can each assembler produce in one hour?

Look for extension problems for this chapter at the Prentice Hall Web site.
www.phschool.com

4-6

If a system of linear equations has at least one solution, we say that it is **consistent.** If a system does not have a solution, we say that it is **inconsistent.** If a consistent system of linear equations has infinitely many solutions, we say the system is **dependent.**

Which system is inconsistent? Which is dependent?

13. $2x - y = 4$
$2x - y = 6$

14. $x - 2y = 3$
$4x - 8y = 12$

4-7

The solution set of an inequality in two variables is the set of all ordered pairs that make the inequality true.

Graph.

15. $y > x + 2$

16. $3x - 5y \leq 15$

Graph these systems of inequalities.

17. $y \geq 2x$
$y < -x + 3$

18. $y \leq 3$
$x \geq -5$

4-8

If the graph of a system of inequalities consists of a polygon and its interior, a linear function has a maximum and a minimum value satisfying the system. These occur at the vertices.

19. A woman wants to invest \$60,000 in mutual funds and municipal bonds. She does not want to invest more than 50%, or less that 20%, of her money in mutual funds. The minimum investment for municipal bonds is \$10,000, and they are only guaranteed up to \$40,000, so she will not invest more than \$40,000 in municipal bonds. The mutual funds should produce a return of 10%, and the municipal bonds a return of 12%. How much should she invest in each to maximize her income? What is her maximum income?

4 Chapter Assessment

Solve graphically.

1. $x + y = 2$
   $x - y = 4$

2. $x = 3y$
   $2x - 3y = 6$

Solve using the substitution method.

3. $2x - 3y = 0$
   $x + y = 5$

4. $2x = y - 5$
   $5x + 3y = 4$

Solve using linear combinations.

5. $x - 5y = 6$
   $3x + 4y = 18$

6. $4x - 7y = 23$
   $6x + 3y = -33$

7. Solve.

   The perimeter of a rectangular field is 606 m. The length is 42 m more than twice the width. Find the dimensions.

8. Solve.

   $$x + y - 3z = 8$$
   $$2x - 3y + z = -6$$
   $$3x + 4y - 2z = 20$$

9. Solve.

   When three printers, A, B, and C, are working together, they produce 4250 pages per hour. When only A and B are running, they produce 2900 pages per hour. When only B and C are running, they produce 3050 pages per hour. How many pages can each printer produce in one hour?

10. Is this system of equations inconsistent? Is it dependent?

    $$x = 3y + 4$$
    $$6y = 2x - 6$$

11. Graph $2y > 3x + 6$.

12. Graph this system of inequalities.

    $$y \geq 2x + 3$$
    $$3x + 5y < 0$$

13. Solve.

    A company produces a 16-oz jar of sunflower seeds and raisins. The jar cannot have more than 10 oz of raisins nor more than 12 oz of sunflower seeds. Each ounce of raisins costs 3¢ to package, while each ounce of sunflower seeds costs 5¢ to package. In order to make a satisfactory profit, the cost of packaging the mixture should be at most 60¢ per jar. Find the number of ounces of each to put into the mixture in order to maximize profit.

1–4 Cumulative Review

1-1 Subtract.

1. $-\frac{11}{13} - \frac{4}{5}$
2. $-18.9 - (-7.7)$
3. $17 - \left(-\frac{4}{31}\right)$

1-2 Multiply.

4. $-5\left(-\frac{3}{7}\right)$
5. $-2.3(-5.5)$
6. $-\frac{7}{8}\left(\frac{2}{3}\right)$

1-3 Evaluate each expression for $x = -1$ and $y = 4$.

7. $-(2x - y - 6)$
8. $2|y - 8| - |x|$
9. $-3|x + y|$

1-4 Simplify.

10. $3x - 2(5y - 4x)$
11. $8y - [2y - (5y - 7)]$
12. $xy - (3x + xy - 5y)$

1-5 Solve.

13. $6x - 7 = 23$
14. $-5y - 11 = -1$

1-6

15. A swim club requires a $120 membership, plus $4 each swim. How much would a person pay to swim 35 times?

1-7 Simplify.

16. $(5y)^3$
17. $(-3x)^4$
18. $\left(-\frac{1}{2}\right)^5$

1-8 Simplify.

19. $(2x^2y)(-5x^{-5}y^6)$
20. $-\dfrac{28x^{-3}y^2}{4x^5y^{-3}}$
21. $(8x^3)^{-2}$

1-9 Convert to scientific notation.

22. 676,000
23. 0.0015
24. 10.09

2-1 Solve.

25. $3(x - 5) = 18x$
26. $\frac{1}{8}x + \frac{3}{2} = \frac{1}{3} - \frac{1}{6}x$
27. $(x - 7)(2x + 1) = 0$

2-2

28. Monthly credit card interest is charged at a rate of 1.5%. After one month, total purchases plus interest equal $46.69. How much were the purchases?

2-3 Solve for the given letter.

29. $e = mc^2$, for m

30. $f = m\frac{M}{g^2}$, for M

2-4 Solve.

31. $3x - 8 > 2x - 1$

32. $-\frac{2}{3}y \leq 12$

33. $-3 + 7x < 2x + 9$

2-5

34. The sum of three consecutive odd integers is greater than 30. What are the least possible values for the integers?

2-6 Solve and graph.

35. $-3 < 4x + 1 < 6$

36. $2x + 1 < -1$ or $x - 3 > 4$

2-7 Solve.

37. $|x| < \frac{1}{2}$

38. $|14 - y| < 10$

39. $|-x + 7| \geq 3$

3-1 Consider the relation $A \times A$, where $A = \{-3, -2, -1, 0, 1, 2, 3\}$.

Find the sets indicated by the following relations.

40. $\{(x, y) | -3 \leq x < 0 \text{ and } 0 < y < 3\}$

41. $\{(x, y) | -2 < x \leq y\}$

3-2 Graph.

42. $-x + 2y = 1$

43. $2x - y = -4$

3-3 What is the domain of each function?

44. $f(x) = \frac{x - 2}{x + 3}$

45. $f(x) = -x^2 + \frac{x}{2}$

3-4 Graph using intercepts.

46. $5x - 3y = 15$

47. $-2x + 7y = 14$

3-5 Find an equation of each line. Write in standard form.

48. Line with slope $-\frac{1}{2}$ and containing $(-8, 0)$

49. Line containing $(-2, -1)$ and $(-3, 7)$

3-6 Find the slope and y-intercept.

50. $y = -4$

51. $5y - 3x + 8 = 0$

3-7 Write an equation of the line containing $(2, -3)$

52. parallel to $2y + x = 5$.

53. perpendicular to $2y + x = 5$.

3-8

54. The world land-speed record has been increasing linearly since 1898. In 1898 the record was 39.2 mi/h. In 1970 the record was 622.3 mi/h. Predict the record for the year 2008.

3-9

55. Suppose $f(x) = 1 + 3x$ and $g(x) = 2 - x^2$. Find $f(g(-3))$.

4-1–4-2 Solve each system

56. by graphing.
$3x - y = 6$
$x = \frac{1}{2}y + 3$

57. by substitution.
$2y + x = -8$
$4x - 3y = 1$

58. by addition.
$3x - 4y = 7$
$-12x + 4y = 20$

4-3

59. Judy bought $3\frac{1}{2}$ lb of rice and 4 lb of sunflower seeds for \$4.90. Margarite bought 2 lb of rice and $\frac{1}{2}$ lb of sunflower seeds for a total of \$1.05. What is the per pound price for each item?

4-4 Solve.

60. $2x - y - z = -11$
$x + 2y - 3z = -13$
$-x - y + 4z = 22$

61. $3x + y - 2z = 1$
$x - y - z = -6$
$-x + y - 3z = 10$

4-5

62. Virgil needs to buy 4 tablecloths. He picks one cotton, one linen, and one vinyl tablecloth, but he still needs a fourth. If the fourth is cotton, the total cost will be \$120. If it is linen, the total cost will be \$155, and if it is vinyl, the total cost will be \$105. Find the price of each kind of tablecloth.

4-6 Which system is inconsistent? Which is dependent?

63. $4x - 6y = 12$
$-6x + 9y = 18$

64. $-8x - 9y = -12$
$-2x - \frac{9}{4}y = -3$

4-7 Graph.

65. $-3x + y > 1$

66. $y > x - 1$
$2x + y < 5$

4-8

67. A glassmaker makes windows and doors. The profit per window is \$3 and per door is \$5. Each day he has enough glass to make no more than 4 windows, or no more than 6 doors. His daily allotment of 18 sheets of glass would be used up by producing 2 windows and 3 doors. How many of each should he produce daily to maximize profits?

CHAPTER

What You'll Learn in Chapter 5

- How to evaluate and simplify polynomial functions
- How to add, subtract, and multiply polynomials
- How to recognize and factor certain polynomials
- How to solve equations using the zero-product principle

Skills & Concepts You Need for Chapter 5

1-3

1. Evaluate $xy - xz$ for $x = -2$, $y = 4$, $z = 3$.

1-4 Factor.

2. $5x + 5y$ **3.** $10x + 15y - 5$

1-4 Multiply.

4. $3(y - 2)$ **5.** $4(x + 12)$ **6.** $c(t + s - f)$

1-4 Collect like terms.

7. $3y + 2y$ **8.** $a + 4a$ **9.** $b - 4b + 3b$

1-4 Remove parentheses and simplify.

10. $3x - (2x + 4)$ **11.** $7y - 2 - (8y - 4)$

1-8 Multiply and simplify.

12. $3^{-2} \cdot 3^5$ **13.** $(4a^7b^{-2})(2a^2b^3)$ **14.** $(8x^{-3}y^4)(3x^{-9}y^{-2})$

1-8 Simplify.

15. $(3a)^2$ **16.** $(-2y)^3$ **17.** $(2^{-3})^4$ **18.** $(x^{-2})^{-4}$

2-1 Solve.

19. $(x - 3)(x + 5) = 0$ **20.** $3x(2x + 10) = 0$

Polynomials and Polynomial Equations

The annual cost of operating an automobile is an important factor in a budget. In Lesson 5-1, you will study how to evaluate polynomials that will help you approximate this cost. If you drive a car at 50 km/h, will the operating cost be less than if you drive at 80 km/h? How can you verify your conclusion?

5-1 Polynomials and Functions

What You'll Learn

1. To evaluate polynomial functions
2. To simplify polynomials by collecting like terms

. . . And Why

To prepare for basic operations on polynomials

The polynomial $0.524hD^2 + 0.262hd^2$ can be used to find the approximate volume of a certain-shaped barrel given its height h, its greatest diameter D, and its smaller diameter d at the top and bottom.

In this chapter we will discuss polynomials. Here is a quick review of terms related to polynomials that you may recall from first-year algebra.

See page 208, Exercise 25.

PART 1 Polynomial Functions

Objective: Evaluate polynomial functions.

Expressions like these are polynomials in one variable.

$$5x^2 \quad 8a \quad 2 \quad -7x + 5 \quad 2y^2 + 5y - 3 \quad 5a^4 - 3a^2 + \frac{1}{4}a - 8$$

Expressions like these are polynomials in several variables.

$$5x - xy^2 + 7y + 2 \qquad 9xy^2z - 4x^3z + (-14x^4y^2) + 9 \qquad 15x^3y^2$$

The polynomial $5x^3y - 7xy^2 + 2$ has three **terms,** $5x^3y$, $-7xy^2$, and 2.

The **coefficients** of the terms are 5, −7, and 2. The **degree of a term** is the sum of the exponents of the variables in that term. The degree of $-7xy^2$ is 3 since the exponents are 1 and 2. The **degree of a polynomial** is the highest degree of its terms.

A polynomial with a single term is a **monomial.** A polynomial with two terms is a **binomial,** and one with three terms is a **trinomial.** Polynomials are usually arranged in order of increasing or decreasing powers of one variable (**ascending** or **descending order**). We now give a precise definition of a polynomial in one variable.

Definition

A **polynomial in *x*** is any expression of the form

$$a_nx^n + a_{n-1}x^{n-1} + \cdots + a_1x + a_0$$

where n is a nonnegative integer and the coefficients $a_0, \ldots, a_n$ are real numbers.

A **polynomial function** is a function that can be defined by a polynomial. For instance, $P(x) = 5x^7 + 3x^5 - 4x^2 - 5$ defines a polynomial function. To find values of a polynomial function, we substitute into the polynomial expression.

Reading Math

Read $P(x)$ as "P of x."

EXAMPLE 1 For the polynomial function $P(x) = 2x^2 - 3x + 4$, find the following function values.

$$P(x) = 2x^2 - 3x + 4$$

(a) $P(0) = 2 \cdot 0^2 - 3 \cdot 0 + 4$ Substituting

$= 4$

(b) $P(-10) = 2 \cdot (-10)^2 - 3(-10) + 4$

$= 200 + 30 + 4$

$= 234$

Try This

a. For $P(x) = 2x^3 - 3x^2 + 5$, find the following function values.
(1) $P(0)$ **(2)** $P(4)$ **(3)** $P(-2)$

PART 2 Collecting Like Terms

Objective: Simplify polynomials by collecting like terms.

If two terms of a polynomial have the same variables raised to the same powers, the terms are called similar or **like terms.** Like terms can be "combined" or "collected" using the distributive property.

EXAMPLES Collect like terms.

2 $3x^2 - 4y + 2x^2 = 3x^2 + 2x^2 - 4y$ Rearranging terms

$= (3 + 2)x^2 - 4y$ Using the distributive property

$= 5x^2 - 4y$

3 $3x^2y - 5xy^2 - 3x^2y - xy^2 = -6xy^2$

In Example 3, we collected like terms mentally, first recognizing that the two x^2y terms were additive inverses, and then collecting the two xy^2 terms.

Try This Collect like terms.

b. $5x^2 + 3x^4 - 2x^2 - x^4$
c. $5x^3y^2 - 2x^2y^3 + 4x^3y^2$
d. $3xy^2 - 4x^2y + 4xy^2 + 2x^2y + 3x^2 - y^2 + 2x^2y$

Extra Help On the Web

Look for worked-out examples at the Prentice Hall Web site.
www.phschool.com

5-1 Exercises

A

For each polynomial function, find the specified function values.

1. $P(x) = 4x^2 - 3x + 2$
Find $P(4)$ and $P(0)$.

2. $Q(x) = -5x^3 + 7x^2 - 12$
Find $Q(3)$ and $Q(-1)$.

3. $P(y) = 8y^3 - 12y - 5$
Find $P(-2)$ and $P\left(\frac{1}{3}\right)$.

4. $Q(y) = 9y^3 + 8y^2 - 4y - 9$
Find $Q(-3)$ and $Q(-1)$.

Collect like terms.

5. $6x^2 - 7x^2 + 3x^2$

6. $-2y^2 - 7y^2 + 5y^2$

7. $5x - 4y - 2x + 5y$

8. $4a - 9b - 6a + 3b$

9. $5a + 7 - 4 + 2a - 6a + 3$

10. $9x + 12 - 8 - 7x + 5x + 10$

11. $3a^2b + 4b^2 - 9a^2b - 6b^2$

12. $5x^2y^2 + 4x^3 - 8x^2y^2 - 12x^3$

13. $8x^2 - 3xy + 12y^2 + x^2 - y^2 + 5xy + 4y^2$

14. $a^2 - 2ab + b^2 + 9a^2 + 5ab - 4b^2 + a^2$

Quick Review

$1 \cdot x - 1 \cdot y$ is often written simply as $x - y$.

B

For each polynomial function find the specified function value.

15. $P(x) = -4x^3 + 2x^2 - 7x + 5$
Find $P(a)$.

16. $Q(x) = 6x^3 - 12x^2 - 8x - 3$
Find $Q(-b)$.

17. $P(x) = x^3 - 4x^2 + 3x - 7$
Find $P(2a)$.

18. $Q(x) = -7x^3 + 10x^2 + 6$
Find $Q\left(\frac{c}{2}\right)$.

For the polynomial functions $P(x)$ and $Q(x)$, find each of the following.

$$P(x) = 13x^5 - 22x^4 - 36x^3 + 40x^2 - 16x + 75$$
$$Q(x) = 42x^5 - 37x^4 + 50x^3 - 28x^2 + 34x + 100$$

19. $P(x) + Q(x)$

20. $P(x) - Q(x)$

21. $Q(x) - P(x)$

22. $4[P(x)] + 3[Q(x)]$

23. Evaluate $f(x, y) = 3xy^2 - 2x^2y$ for $x = 5$ and $y = -2$.

24. The cost, in cents per kilometer, of operating an automobile at speed s is approximated by the polynomial function $C(s) = 0.002s^2 - 0.21s + 15$. How much does it cost to operate the automobile at 50 km/h? 80 km/h?

25. The polynomial $0.524hD^2 + 0.262hd^2$ gives the approximate volume of certain barrels where d is the least diameter at the top and bottom, D is the greatest diameter at its bulge, and h is the height. Find the approximate volume of a barrel for which $h = 48$ inches, $d = 18$ inches, and $D = 24$ inches.

In Canada, highway distances are measured in kilometers. At 80 km/h, how long will it take to drive from Windsor, Ontario, to Toronto, a distance of 381 km? How many U.S. miles is this? (Consult an almanac or dictionary for a conversion factor.)

26. The polynomial $\pi(R^2 - r^2)$ gives the area of a ring with inner radius r and outer radius R. Find the area of a ring with outer radius 20 cm and inner radius 15 cm.

27. The polynomial $0.49W + 0.45P - 6.36R + 8.7$ gives an estimate of the percent of body fat of a man, where W is the waist circumference in centimeters, P is the skin fold above the pectoral muscle in millimeters, and R is the wrist diameter in centimeters. Find the percent of body fat for an 18-year-old male whose measurements are $W = 83.9$ cm, $P = 6.0$ mm, and $R = 7.1$ cm.

28. The polynomial $0.041h - 0.018A - 2.69$ gives the lung capacity in liters for a woman, where h is the height in centimeters and A is the age in years. Find the lung capacity for a woman with $A = 41$ and $h = 139.8$ cm.

29. *Critical Thinking* Write a trinomial in x and y of degree 6 in which all of the coefficients are negative even numbers.

Challenge

Find the value for a so that each term has degree n.

30. $x^n y^a$ **31.** $x^{(n-2)} y^a$ **32.** $x^a y^{\frac{n}{2}}$ **33.** $x^5 y^a z^a$

34. Using only the variables x, y, and z, how many different terms of degree 3 can you write?

35. Express the area of this box as a polynomial. The box is rectangular with an open top and dimensions as shown.

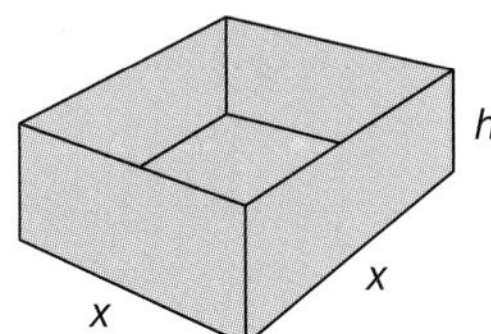

36. A box with an open top is to be made from a piece of cardboard 12 inches square. Corners are cut out and the sides are folded up. Express the volume of the box as a polynomial.

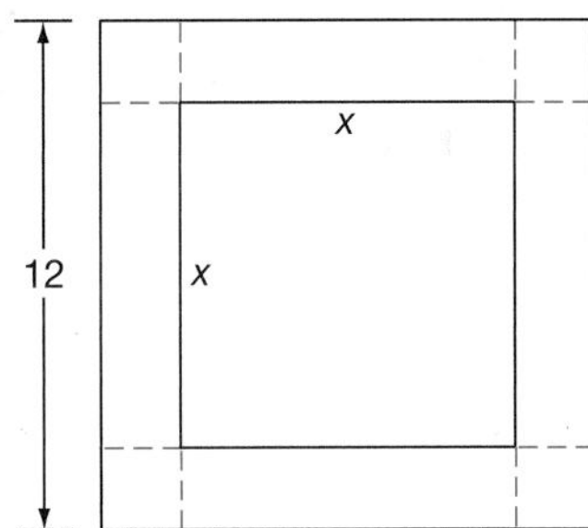

Mixed Review

Factor. **37.** $6m^2 + 3m$ **38.** $21n - 36m$ **39.** $2ab + 4ac$ *1-4*

For each pair of points, find an equation of the line containing them.

40. $(1, -2)$ and $(-1, 4)$ **41.** $(-2, -1)$ and $(6, 3)$ **42.** $(0, 2)$ and $(-2, 0)$ *3-6*

Solve. **43.** $4(1 - t) = 6$ **44.** $11a + 2 = 6a + 12$ *2-1, 1-5*

5-2 Addition and Subtraction of Polynomials

What You'll Learn

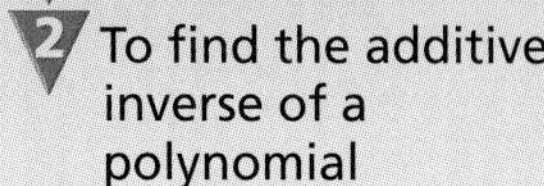

1. To add polynomials
2. To find the additive inverse of a polynomial

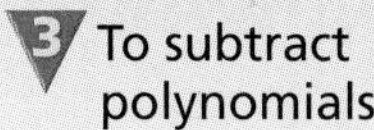

3. To subtract polynomials

. . . And Why

To prepare for multiplying and dividing polynomials

PART 1 Addition

Objective: Add polynomials.

The sum of two polynomials can be found by writing a plus sign between them and then collecting like terms.

EXAMPLES

1 Add $-3x^3 + 2x - 4$ and $4x^3 + 3x^2 + 2$.

The use of columns is often helpful. Write the polynomials one under the other, writing like terms under one another and leaving spaces for missing terms.

$$\begin{array}{rrrrr} & -3x^3 & & + 2x & - 4 \\ + & 4x^3 & + 3x^2 & & + 2 \\ \hline & x^3 & + 3x^2 & + 2x & - 2 \end{array}$$

2 Add $4ax^2 + 4bx - 5$ and $3ax^2 + 5bx + 8$.

$$\begin{array}{rrrr} & 4ax^2 & + 4bx & - 5 \\ + & 3ax^2 & + 5bx & + 8 \\ \hline & 7ax^2 & + 9bx & + 3 \end{array}$$

Addition of polynomials can also be done mentally.

3 Add.

$$(13x^3y + 3x^2y - 5y) + (x^3y + 4x^2y - 3xy + 3y)$$
$$= 14x^3y + 7x^2y - 3xy - 2y$$

4 Add.

$$\left(\frac{5}{6}dx^8 + \frac{2}{3}dx^4\right) + \left(-\frac{2}{3}dx^4 + \frac{1}{5}d\right)$$
$$= \frac{5}{6}dx^8 + \frac{1}{5}d$$

Try This Add.

a. $3x^3 + 4x^2 - 7x - 2$ and $-7x^3 - 2x^2 + 3x + \frac{1}{2}$

b. $5p^2q^4 - 2p^2q^2 - 3q + (-6pq^2 + 3p^2q^2 + 5)$

PART 2 Additive Inverses

Objective: Find the additive inverse of a polynomial.

The sum of a polynomial and its additive inverse is 0. The additive inverse of a polynomial can be found by replacing each term by its additive inverse.

EXAMPLE 5 Find the additive inverse of $7xy^2 - 6xy - 4y + 3$.

The additive inverse of $7xy^2 - 6xy - 4y + 3$ can be written as

$$-(7xy^2 - 6xy - 4y + 3)$$
$$= -7xy^2 + 6xy + 4y - 3. \quad \text{Replacing each term by its additive inverse}$$

Try This Find the additive inverse.

c. $5x^2t^2 - 4xy^2t - 3xt + 6x - 5$ **d.** $-3x^2y + 5xy - 7x + 4y + 2$

PART 3 Subtraction

Objective: Subtract polynomials.

Quick Review

For all real numbers a and b, $a - b = a + (-b)$.

Using Theorem 1-1, we can subtract by adding an inverse. Thus, to subtract one polynomial from another, we add its additive inverse. We change the sign of each term of the polynomial to be subtracted and then add.

EXAMPLE 6 Subtract.

$$(-9x^5 - x^3 + 2x^2 + 4) - (2x^5 - x^4 + 4x^3 - 3x^2)$$
$$= (-9x^5 - x^3 + 2x^2 + 4) + [-(2x^5 - x^4 + 4x^3 - 3x^2)] \quad \text{Adding the inverse}$$
$$= (-9x^5 - x^3 + 2x^2 + 4) + [-2x^5 + x^4 - 4x^3 + 3x^2]$$
$$= -11x^5 + x^4 - 5x^3 + 5x^2 + 4$$

EXAMPLE 7 Subtract the second polynomial from the first.

$$\begin{array}{rrrrr} (4x^2y & - 6x^3y^2 & & + x^2y^2 & - 5y) \\ -\ (4x^2y & +\ x^3y^2 & + 3x^2y^3 & & + 6y) \\ \hline & - 7x^3y^2 & - 3x^2y^3 & + x^2y^2 & - 11y \end{array}$$

Mentally changing signs and adding

Try This Subtract.

e. $(5xy^4 - 7xy^2 + 4x^2 - 3) - (-3xy^4 + 2xy^2 - 2y + 4)$

f.
$$\begin{array}{rrrrr} & 5x^2y & - 7x^3y^2 & & - x^2y^2 + 4y \\ -\ (& -2x^2y & + 2x^3y^2 & - 5x^2y^3 & - 5y) \\ \hline \end{array}$$

Extra Help On the Web

Look for worked-out examples at the Prentice Hall Web site.
www.phschool.com

5-2 Exercises

A

Add.

1. $5x^3 + 7x - 8$ and $-2x^3 - x^2 + 8$

2. $-9x^3 + 3x^2 - 6x$ and $7x^2 - 2x - 18$

3. $5x^2y - 2xy^2 + 3xy - 5$ and $-2x^2y - 3xy^2 + 4xy + 7$

4. $6x^2y - 3xy^2 + 5xy - 3$ and $-4x^2y - 4xy^2 + 3xy + 8$

5. $2x + 3y + z - 7$ and $4x - 2y - z + 8$ and $-3x + y - 2z - 4$

6. $2x^2 + 12xy - 11$ and $6x^2 - 2x + 4$ and $-x^2 - y - 2$

7. $1.23y^4 - 2.25y^3 - 3.4y - 5.2 + (8.23y^4 + 4.75y^3 - 8.4y + 2.1)$

8. $\frac{1}{3}x^5 - \frac{1}{5}x^3 - \frac{1}{2}x^2 - 8 + \left(\frac{1}{6}x^5 - \frac{1}{10}x^3 + \frac{1}{4}x^2 + \frac{2}{3}x - 11\right)$

9. $\frac{3}{4}x^3 + \frac{1}{8}x - \frac{1}{24} + \left(\frac{1}{4}x^2 - \frac{1}{16}x + 1\right)$

Find the additive inverse.

10. $5x^3 - 7x^2 + 3x - 6$

11. $-4y^4 + 7y^2 - 2y - 1$

12. $-6x^2y + 2xy^2 - 5y^3 + 10$

13. $20x^4y^4 - 12x^3y^3 + 5x^2y^2 - 3xy + 19$

Subtract.

14. $\begin{array}{r}(-x^3 + 3x^2 - 2x + 2)\\ -\,(-x^3 + 5x^2 - 8x + 4)\end{array}$

15. $\begin{array}{r}(-2x^3 \qquad\qquad - 7x + 8)\\ -\,(\qquad + 6x^2 - 6x - 3)\end{array}$

16. $\begin{array}{r}(3x^2 - 2x - x^3 + 2)\\ -\,(5x^2 - 8x - x^3 + 4)\end{array}$

17. $\begin{array}{r}(5x^2 + 4xy - 3y^2 + 2)\\ -\,(9x^2 + 4xy + 2y^2 - 1)\end{array}$

18. $5a^2 + 4ab - 3b^2 - (9a^2 - 4ab + 2b^2)$

19. $8x^4 - (2x^4 + 8x^2 - 9x + 4)$

20. $-5x^3 - (-3x^4 + 4x^3 - 7x + x^3y)$

21. $(0.09y^4 - 0.052y^3 + 0.93) - (0.03y^4 - 0.084y^3 + 0.94y^2)$

22. $\left(\frac{5}{8}x^4 - \frac{1}{4}x^2 - \frac{1}{2}\right) - \left(-\frac{3}{8}x^4 + \frac{3}{4}x^2 + \frac{1}{2}\right)$

23. $\left(\frac{4}{9}y^2 - \frac{10}{27}y + \frac{1}{3}\right) - \left(\frac{4}{9}y^3 - \frac{4}{3}y - \frac{1}{9}\right)$

B

Add.

24. $(2x^{2a} + 4x^a + 3) + (6x^{2a} + 3x^a + 4)$

25. $(47x^{4a} + 3x^{3a} + 22x^{2a} + x^a + 1) + (37x^{3a} + 8x^{2a} + 3)$

Add or subtract.

26. $(3x^{6a} - 5x^{5a} + 4x^{3a} + 8) - (2x^{6a} + 4x^{4a} + 3x^{3a} + 2x^{2a})$

27. $(2x^{5b} + 4x^{4b} + 3x^{3b} + 8) - (x^{5b} + 2x^{3b} + 6x^{2b} + 9x^{b} + 8)$

28. $(3x^2y + 5x^2z + 2y^2z - xyz) + (-5xy^2 - 11x^2z + 7xyz + z^2y)$

29. $(12x^3y^2z - 4x^2y^2z^2 + 16xy^2z^3 - 7x^3y^2z + 2xyz)$
$+ (-12x^3yz + 4x^2y^2z - 16xy^2z^3 - xyz^2 - 9)$

30. $(8ab^2c - 10ab^2 + 2ac + 15b^2c - 11ab^2c)$
$- (-2ab + ab^2c - 9b^2c - 10ab^2)$

31. $(17 - 24pq^2 + 4p^2q + p^2qr + 8pq^2r)$
$- (6q^2p + 8q^2pr + 4qp^2 - 7qp^2r - 3pqr)$

32. ***Critical Thinking*** Find two polynomials whose difference is $9x^3y^2 - 3x^2y^2 + 8xy^2 - 3xy$.

Challenge

33. ***Mathematical Reasoning*** Suppose $f(x) = 2x^2 + 3x + 5$ and $g(x) = 6x^2 - 9x - 11$. Find $f(2)$, $g(2)$, and $f(2) + g(2)$. Now find $h(x) = f(x) + g(x)$. Find $h(2)$. What do you observe?

34. ***Mathematical Reasoning*** Suppose $f(x)$ and $g(x)$ are defined as in Exercise 33. Find $f(3)$, $g(3)$, and $f(3) - g(3)$. Now find $p(x) = f(x) - g(x)$. Find $p(3)$. What do you observe?

35. For Exercise 30, suppose $a = b$ and $b = 2c$. Find the result in terms of a.

Mixed Review

Evaluate for $a = -2$.

36. $(3 - a)(a + 5)$ 37. $(4a)^a$ 38. $9a - (3a)^2$

Write each equation in standard form.

39. $6 - 4y = 2x$ 40. $2(x - y) = 4$

Solve.

41. $5x + 6 = 12 + 8x$ 42. $7a + 11a = 162$ 43. $25 = 4(m - 3) - 3$

44. 272 adults entered the amusement park one day. 183 paid the regular \$9 adult admission price, the rest had discount coupons. A total of \$2136.50 was collected on adults' tickets at the admissions gate. How much was a discount coupon worth?

45. Senior citizens at a local restaurant receive a 25% discount. Sunday brunch costs \$9.88 per person. Last Sunday, the restaurant collected \$2324.27 from 247 customers. How many customers were senior citizens?

5-3 Multiplication of Polynomials

What You'll Learn

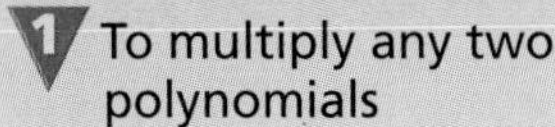

1. To multiply any two polynomials

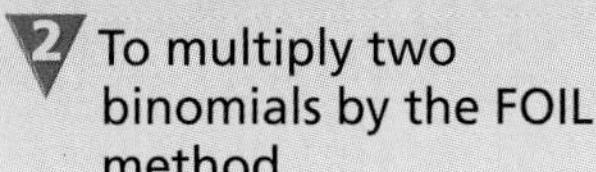

2. To multiply two binomials by the FOIL method
3. To square a binomial
4. To multiply the sum and difference of the same two terms
5. To cube a binomial

. . . And Why

To prepare for factoring polynomials

PART 1 Multiplication of Any Two Polynomials

Objective: Multiply any two polynomials.

Multiplication of polynomials is based on the distributive property. To multiply two polynomials, we multiply each term of one polynomial by each term of the other and then add the results.

EXAMPLE 1 Multiply.

$$\begin{array}{rrrrl} & 4x^4y & -\ 7x^2y & +\ 3y & \\ \times & & -\ 3x^2y & +\ 2y & \\ \hline -12x^6y^2 & +\ 21x^4y^2 & -\ 9x^2y^2 & & \text{Multiplying by } -3x^2y \\ & 8x^4y^2 & -\ 14x^2y^2 & +\ 6y^2 & \text{Multiplying by } 2y\text{, aligning like terms} \\ \hline -12x^6y^2 & +\ 29x^4y^2 & -\ 23x^2y^2 & +\ 6y^2 & \text{Adding} \end{array}$$

Try This Multiply.

a. $3x^2y - 2xy + 3y$ and $xy + 2y$
b. $p^2q + 2pq + 2q$ and $2p^2q - pq + q$

PART 2 Products of Two Binomials

Objective: Multiply two binomials using the FOIL method.

We can find a product of two binomials mentally. The procedure can be simplified as follows.

Multiplying Binomials

Multiply the **F**irst terms, then the **O**utside terms, then the **I**nside terms, then the **L**ast terms. We abbreviate this as **FOIL.**

$$(A + B)(C + D) = \overset{\textbf{F}}{AC} + \overset{\textbf{O}}{AD} + \overset{\textbf{I}}{BC} + \overset{\textbf{L}}{BD}$$

(1: $A \cdot C$; 2: $A \cdot D$; 3: $B \cdot C$; 4: $B \cdot D$)

EXAMPLES Multiply.

2 $(3xy + 2x)(x^2 + 2xy^2) = 3x^3y + 6x^2y^3 + 2x^3 + 4x^2y^2$ (F O I L; pairings 1, 2, 3, 4)

3 $(2x + 3y)(x - 4y) = 2x^2 - 5xy - 12y^2$

Try This Multiply.

c. $(2xy + 3x)(x^2 - 2)$ **d.** $(3x - 2y)(5x + 3y)$ **e.** $(2x + 20)(3y - 20)$

PART 3 Squares of Binomials

Objective: Square a binomial.

Note the following.

$$\begin{aligned}(A + B)^2 &= (A + B)(A + B) \\ &= A^2 + AB + AB + B^2 \quad \text{Using FOIL} \\ &= A^2 + 2AB + B^2\end{aligned}$$

Squaring Binomials

$$(A + B)^2 = A^2 + 2AB + B^2 \qquad (A - B)^2 = A^2 - 2AB + B^2$$

The square of a binomial is the square of the first expression, plus or minus twice the product of the expressions, plus the square of the second expression.

EXAMPLES Multiply.

4

$$(A - B)^2 = A^2 - 2\,A\,B + B^2$$

$$\begin{aligned}(y - 5)^2 &= y^2 - 2(y)(5) + 5^2 \\ &= y^2 - 10y + 25\end{aligned}$$

5

$$(A + B)^2 = A^2 + 2\,A\,B + B^2$$

$$\begin{aligned}(2x + 3y)^2 &= (2x)^2 + 2(2x)(3y) + (3y)^2 \quad A = 2x,\ B = 3y \\ &= 4x^2 + 12xy + 9y^2\end{aligned}$$

6

$$\begin{aligned}(a^2b^3 + a^3b^2)^2 &= (a^2b^3)^2 + 2(a^2b^3)(a^3b^2) + (a^3b^2)^2 \\ &= a^4b^6 + 2a^5b^5 + a^6b^4\end{aligned}$$

Try This Multiply.

f. $(4x - 5y)^2$ **g.** $(2y^2 + 6x^2y)^2$

PART 4 Products of Sums and Differences

Objective: Multiply the sum and difference of the same two terms.

Note the following. $(A + B)(A - B) = A^2 - AB + AB - B^2$ Using FOIL
$= A^2 - B^2$

Multiplying Sums and Differences

$$(A + B)(A - B) = A^2 - B^2$$

The product of the sum and difference of two expressions is the square of the first expression minus the square of the second.

EXAMPLES Multiply.

$(A + B)(A - B) = A^2 - B^2$

7 $(y + 5)(y - 5) = y^2 - 5^2$
$= y^2 - 25$

8 $(3xy^2 + 4y)(-3xy^2 + 4y) = (4y + 3xy^2)(4y - 3xy^2)$ Commutative property
$= (4y)^2 - (3xy^2)^2$
$= 16y^2 - 9x^2y^4$

9 $(5y + 4 + 3x)(5y + 4 - 3x) = (5y + 4)^2 - (3x)^2$
$= 25y^2 + 40y + 16 - 9x^2$

Try This Multiply.

h. $(4x + 7)(4x - 7)$

i. $(5x^2y + 2y)(5x^2y - 2y)$

j. $(2x + 3 + 5y)(2x + 3 - 5y)$

k. $(-2x^3y^2 + 5t)(2x^3y^2 + 5t)$

PART 5 Cubing a Binomial

Objective: Cube a binomial.

The following multiplication gives another useful pattern.

$(A + B)^3 = (A + B)(A + B)^2$
$= (A + B)(A^2 + 2AB + B^2)$ Squaring a binomial
$= (A + B)A^2 + (A + B)2AB + (A + B)B^2$ Distributive
$= A^3 + A^2B + 2A^2B + 2AB^2 + AB^2 + B^3$ property
$= A^3 + 3A^2B + 3AB^2 + B^3$ Collecting like terms

Cubing Binomials

$$(A + B)^3 = A^3 + 3A^2B + 3AB^2 + B^3$$

EXAMPLES Multiply.

$$(A + B)^3 = A^3 + 3A^2B + 3AB^2 + B^3$$

10 $(x + 2)^3 = x^3 + 3(x)^2(2) + 3(x)(2)^2 + 2^3$
$= x^3 + 6x^2 + 12x + 8$

11 $(x - 2)^3 = [x + (-2)]^3$ Writing in the form $(A + B)^3$
$= x^3 + 3(x)^2(-2) + 3(x)(-2)^2 + (-2)^3$
$= x^3 - 6x^2 + 12x - 8$

12 $(5m^2 - 4n^3)^3 = (5m^2)^3 + 3(5m^2)^2(-4n^3) + 3(5m^2)(-4n^3)^2 + (-4n^3)^3$
$= 125m^6 - 300m^4n^3 + 240m^2n^6 - 64n^9$

Note in Examples 11 and 12 that a separate formula for $(A - B)^3$ does not need to be memorized. We can think of $(A - B)^3$ as $[A + (-B)]^3$.

Try This Multiply.

l. $(x + 1)^3$ **m.** $(x - 1)^3$ **n.** $(t^2 + 3b)^3$ **o.** $(2a^3 - 5b^2)^3$

5-3 Exercises

Extra Help On the Web
Look for worked-out examples at the Prentice Hall Web site.
www.phschool.com

A

Multiply.

1. $2x^2 + 4x + 16$ and $3x - 4$
2. $3y^2 - 3y + 9$ and $2y + 3$
3. $4a^2b - 2ab + 3b^2$ and $ab - 2b + 1$
4. $2x^2 + y^2 - 2xy$ and $x^2 - 2y^2 - xy$
5. $(a - b)(a^2 + ab + b^2)$
6. $(t + 1)(t^2 - t + 1)$
7. $(2x + 3y)(2x + y)$
8. $(2a - 3b)(2a - b)$
9. $\left(4x^2 - \frac{1}{2}y\right)\left(3x + \frac{1}{4}y\right)$
10. $\left(2y^3 + \frac{1}{5}x\right)\left(3y - \frac{1}{4}x\right)$
11. $(2x^2 - y^2)(2x - 2y)$
12. $(3y^2 - 2)(3y - x)$
13. $(2x + 3y)^2$
14. $(5x + 2y)^2$
15. $(2x^2 - 3y)^2$
16. $(4x^2 - 5y)^2$
17. $(2x^3 + 3y^2)^2$
18. $(5x^3 + 2y^2)^2$
19. $(3x - 2y)(3x + 2y)$
20. $(3x + 5y)(3x - 5y)$
21. $(x^2 + yz)(x^2 - yz)$
22. $(2x^2 + 5y)(2x^2 - 5y)$
23. $(3x^2 - 2)(3x^2 + 2)$
24. $(5x^2 - 3)(5x^2 + 3)$
25. $(y + 5)^3$
26. $(t - 7)^3$
27. $(m^2 - 2n)^3$
28. $(2f + 3d)^3$

B

Multiply.

29. $\left(\frac{1}{2}x^2 - \frac{3}{5}y\right)^2$

30. $\left(\frac{1}{4}x^2 - \frac{2}{3}y\right)^2$

31. $(0.5x + 0.7y^2)^2$

32. $(0.3x + 0.8y^2)^2$

33. $(2x + 3y + 4)(2x + 3y - 4)$

34. $(x^2 + 3y + y^2)(x^2 + 3y - y^2)$

35. $(2x + y)(2x - y)(4x^2 + y^2)$

36. $(5x + y)(5x - y)(25x^2 + y^2)$

37. $[4x(x - 1)]^2$

38. $\left(3x^3 - \frac{5}{11}\right)^2$

39. $(x^a + y^b)(x^a - y^b)(x^{2a} + y^{2b})$

40. $(x^{a-b})^{a+b}$

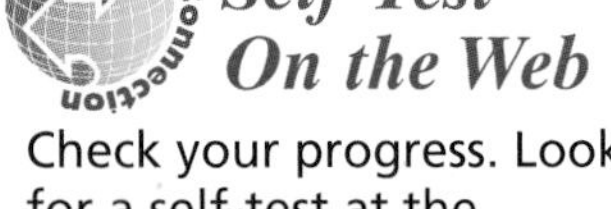

Self-Test On the Web

Check your progress. Look for a self-test at the Prentice Hall Web site. www.phschool.com

41. The amount to which \$1000 will grow in b years, with an interest rate (r) compounded annually, is given by the polynomial function A.

$$A(r) = \$1000(1 + r)^b$$

a. Find the amount to which \$1000 will grow in 2 years at 17%.
b. Find the amount to which \$1000 will grow in 3 years at 11%.
c. Find the amount to which \$1000 will grow in 4 years at 8%.
d. Find expanded forms of $A(r)$ for $b = 2, 3,$ and 4 years.

42. ***Critical Thinking*** The cube of a certain binomial is $8y^3 - 36y^2 + 54y - 27$. Find the binomial.

Challenge

Multiply.

43. $[(2x - 1)^2 - 1]^2$

44. $(x - 1)(x^2 + x + 1)(x^3 + 1)$

45. $[x + y + 1][x^2 - x(y + 1) + (y + 1)^2]$

46. $(y - 1)^3(y + 1)^3$

47. $(a - b + c - d)(a + b + c + d)$

48. $(4x^2 + 2xy + y^2)(4x^2 - 2xy + y^2)$

49. $y^3z^n(y^{3n}z^3 - 4yz^{2n})$

Vicki's car gets about 36 miles per gallon for highway driving. About how many gallons will be needed for a 600-mile round trip?

Mixed Review

Simplify. **50.** $\frac{x^3}{y^{-2}}$ **51.** $\frac{1}{8c^3}$ **52.** $\frac{xy^5}{a^2b^{-2}}$ *1-7*

53. $m^{-4} \cdot m^3$ **54.** $t^2 \cdot t^{-1}$ **55.** $(4x^3y^2)(-2x^ay^6)$ *1-8*

56. $(2.5 \times 10^4)(6 \times 10^{-6})$ **57.** $3c + 9 + (-6c) - 12$ *1-9, 1-4*

58. Vicki estimated the cost of operating her car for a year. If she drives 5000 miles, it will cost her \$2500. If she drives 15,000 miles, it will cost her \$4300. Fit a linear function to the data. *3-8*

Factoring

5-4

PART 1 Terms with Common Factors

Objective: Factor polynomials with a common factor.

Factoring is the reverse of multiplying. To **factor** an expression means to write it as an equivalent expression that is a product. When factoring a polynomial, first look for common factors.

EXAMPLE 1 Factor out a common factor.

$$4y^2 - 8 = 4 \cdot y^2 - 4 \cdot 2 \quad \text{4 is a common factor.}$$
$$= 4(y^2 - 2)$$

In some cases there is more than one common factor. In Example 2 below, 5 is a common factor, and x^3 is also a common factor.

EXAMPLES Factor out a common factor.

2 $5x^4 - 20x^3 = 5x^3(x - 4)$

3 $12x^2y - 20x^3y = 4x^2y(3 - 5x)$

4 $10p^6q^2 - 4p^5q^3 + 2p^4q^4 = 2p^4q^2(5p^2 - 2pq + q^2)$

We usually try to factor out all common factors. When we do this we say we have factored the **greatest common factor.**

Try This Factor out a common factor.

a. $3x^2 - 6x$ **b.** $9y^4 - 15y^3 + 3y^2$ **c.** $6x^2y - 21x^3y^2 + 3x^2y^3$

PART 2 Factoring Trinomial Squares

Objective: Identify and factor trinomial squares.

Squares of binomials are also called **trinomial squares.** They have the form $A^2 + 2AB + B^2$ or $A^2 - 2AB + B^2$. Here are some examples of trinomial squares.

$x^2 + 6x + 9$ This is the square of $x + 3$.
$y^2 - 22y + 121$ This is the square of $y - 11$.

We must first be able to recognize a trinomial square.

What You'll Learn

1. To factor polynomials with a common factor
2. To identify and factor trinomial squares
3. To factor differences of squares
4. To factor a polynomial by grouping

. . . And Why

To build skills for solving equations

Identifying Trinomial Squares

For a trinomial to be square, three conditions must be true.

1. Two of the terms must be squares (A^2 and B^2).
2. There must be no minus sign before A^2 or B^2.
3. If we multiply the square roots of A^2 and B^2 and double the result, we get the remaining term $2 \cdot A \cdot B$, or its additive inverse, $-2 \cdot A \cdot B$.

To factor trinomial squares, we use the following equations.

Factoring Trinomial Squares

$$A^2 + 2AB + B^2 = (A + B)^2$$
$$A^2 - 2AB + B^2 = (A - B)^2$$

EXAMPLES Factor as a trinomial square, if possible.

5 $x^2 - 10x + 25 = (x - 5)^2$

6 $16y^2 + 49 + 56y = 16y^2 + 56y + 49$ Rearranging terms
$= (4y + 7)^2$

7 $-20xy + 4y^2 + 25x^2 = 4y^2 - 20xy + 25x^2$ Rearranging terms
$= (2y - 5x)^2$

8 $36y^2 + 42y + 49$ Not a trinomial square, since $2AB$ is $2 \cdot 6y \cdot 7$, or $84y$

Try This Factor as a trinomial square, if possible.

d. $x^2 + 14x + 49$
e. $9y^2 + 25 - 30y$
f. $72xy + 16x^2 + 81y^2$
g. $100x^2 + 10xy + y^2$

Trinomial squares also occur in higher-degree polynomials.

EXAMPLES Factor.

9 $25x^4 + 70x^2y^3 + 49y^6 = (5x^2 + 7y^3)^2$

10 $-4y^2 - 144y^8 + 48y^5 = -4y^2(1 - 12y^3 + 36y^6)$ Removing a common factor first
$= -4y^2(1 - 6y^3)^2$

Try This Factor.

h. $16x^4 - 40x^2y^3 + 25y^6$
i. $-12x^4y^2 + 60x^2y^5 - 75y^8$

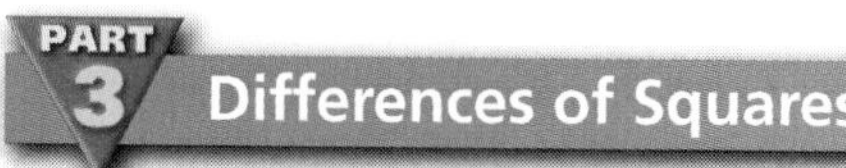

Differences of Squares

Objective: Factor differences of two squares.

To factor a difference of squares, we reverse the procedure for multiplying a sum and difference of two expressions.

Factoring Differences of Squares

$$A^2 - B^2 = (A + B)(A - B)$$

To factor the difference of two squares, write the square root of the first expression *plus* the square root of the second, times the square root of the first *minus* the square root of the second.

EXAMPLE 11 Factor $x^2 - 9$.

$$\begin{aligned} x^2 - 9 &= x^2 - 3^2 \\ &= (x + 3)(x - 3) \end{aligned}$$

EXAMPLE 12 Factor $25y^6 - 49x^2$.

$$\begin{array}{ccccc} A^2 & - & B^2 & = & (A + B)(A - B) \\ (5y^3)^2 & - & (7x)^2 & = & (5y^3 + 7x)(5y^3 - 7x) \end{array}$$

Try This Factor.

j. $y^2 - 4$ **k.** $49x^4 - 25y^{10}$ **l.** $36x^4 - 16y^6$

A difference of two squares can have more than two terms.

EXAMPLE 13 Factor.

$$\begin{aligned} x^2 + 6x + 9 - 25y^2 &= (x^2 + 6x + 9) - 25y^2 \\ &= (x + 3)^2 - (5y)^2 \end{aligned}$$

This is now a difference of two squares, one of which is a square of a binomial. When we factor, we get

$$(x + 3 + 5y)(x + 3 - 5y)$$

Try This Factor.

m. $x^2 + 2x + 1 - p^2$ **n.** $64 - (x^2 + 8x + 16)$

PART 4 Factoring by Grouping

Objective: Factor a polynomial of four or more terms by grouping.

Writing Math

By the commutative property, $(y + 4)(y + 3)$ may be written as $(y + 3)(y + 4)$.

Sometimes an expression of four or more terms can be grouped so that common factors can be found. The common factor may itself be a binomial.

In the following expression, we note that 4 is a factor of the last two terms and y is a factor of the first two terms.

$$y^2 + 3y + 4y + 12 = (y^2 + 3y) + (4y + 12)$$
$$= y(y + 3) + 4(y + 3) \quad \text{Factoring out } y \text{ and } 4$$
$$= (y + 4)(y + 3) \quad \text{Factoring out } y + 3$$

EXAMPLES Factor.

14 $4x^2 - 3x + 20x - 15 = x(4x - 3) + 5(4x - 3)$ Factoring out x and 5
$= (x + 5)(4x - 3)$ Factoring out $4x - 3$

15 $ax^2 + ay - bx^2 - by = ax^2 + ay + (-bx^2 - by)$
$= a(x^2 + y) - b(x^2 + y)$ Factoring out a and $-b$
$= (a - b)(x^2 + y)$ Factoring out $x^2 + y$

Try This Factor.

o. $x^2 + 5x + 4x + 20$ **p.** $5y^2 + 2y + 10y + 4$ **q.** $px + py - qx - qy$

Extra Help On the Web

Look for worked-out examples at the Prentice Hall Web site. www.phschool.com

5-4 Exercises

A

Mental Math Identify the common monomial factor.

1. $y^2 - 5y$ **2.** $4a^2 + 2a$ **3.** $6y^2 + 3y$ **4.** $y^3 + 9y^2$

5. $x^3 + 8x^2$ **6.** $3y^2 - 3y - 9$ **7.** $5x^2 - 5x + 15$ **8.** $6x^2 - 3x^4$

9. $8y^2 + 4y^4$ **10.** $4ab - 6ac + 12ad$ **11.** $8xy + 10xz - 14xw$

12. $4x^2y - 12xy^2$ **13.** $5x^2y^3 + 15x^3y^2$ **14.** $x^6 + x^5 - x^3 + x^2$

15. $y^4 - y^3 + y^2 + y$ **16.** $24x^3 - 36x^2 + 72x$ **17.** $10a^4 + 15a^2 - 25a$

Factor, if possible.

18. $y^2 - 6y + 9$ **19.** $x^2 - 8x + 16$ **20.** $x^2 + 14x + 49$

21. $x^2 + 16x + 64$ **22.** $x^2 + 1 + x$ **23.** $x^2 + 1 - x$

24. $a^2 + 4a + 4$ **25.** $a^2 - 4a + 4$ **26.** $y^2 + 36 - 12y$

27. $y^2 + 36 + 12y$ **28.** $-18y^2 + y^3 + 81y$ **29.** $24a^2 + a^3 + 144a$

30. $12a^2 + 36a + 27$ **31.** $20y^2 + 100y + 125$ **32.** $2x^2 - 40x + 200$

33. $32x^2 + 48x + 18$ **34.** $1 - 8d + 16d^2$ **35.** $64 + 25y^2 - 80y$

36. $x^2 - 16$ **37.** $y^2 - 9$ **38.** $9x^2 - 25$ **39.** $4a^2 - 49$

40. $4x^2 - 25$ **41.** $100y^2 - 81$ **42.** $6x^2 - 6y^2$ **43.** $8x^2 - 8y^2$

44. $3x^8 - 3y^8$ **45.** $5x^4 - 5y^4$ **46.** $4xy^4 - 4xz^4$ **47.** $9a^4 - a^2b^2$

48. $a^2 + 2ab + b^2 - 9$ **49.** $x^2 - 2xy + y^2 - 25$

50. $2m^2 + 4mn + 2n^2 - 50b^2$ **51.** $12x^2 + 12x + 3 - 3y^2$

52. $9 - (a^2 + 2ab + b^2)$ **53.** $16 - (x^2 - 2xy + y^2)$

54. $ac + ad + bc + bd$ **55.** $xy + xz + wy + wz$

56. $b^3 - b^2 + 2b - 2$ **57.** $y^2 - 8y - y + 8$

58. $t^2 + 6t - 2t - 12$ **59.** $2y^4 + 6y^2 + 5y^2 + 15$

60. **TEST PREP** To factor $y^3 - y^2 + 3y - 3$ completely, which expression represents a possible first step?

A. $y(y^2 - y + 3) - 3$ **B.** $y(y^2 - y) + 3(y - 1)$

C. $y^2(y - 1) + 3(y - 1)$ **D.** $y^2(y - 1) + 3(1 - y)$

B

Factor.

61. $\frac{4}{7}x^6 - \frac{6}{7}x^4 + \frac{1}{7}x^2 - \frac{3}{7}x$ **62.** $4y^{4a} + 12y^{2a} + 10y^{2a} + 30$

63. $0.25 - y^2$ **64.** $0.04x^2 - 0.09y^2$

65. $\frac{1}{25} - x^2$ **66.** $\frac{1}{36}y^4 - \frac{1}{81}x^2$

67. ***Critical Thinking*** Find two binomials whose product is a binomial; a trinomial; a four-term polynomial.

Challenge

Factor. Assume variables in exponents represent positive integers.

68. $a^{16} - 1$ **69.** $x^{2a} - y^2$ **70.** $y^{32} - 1$

71. $x^2 + ax + bx + ab$ **72.** $\frac{1}{4}p^2 - \frac{2}{5}p + \frac{4}{25}$

73. $bdx^2 + adx + bcx + ac$ **74.** $-225x + x^3$

75. $4x^{a+b} + 7x^{a-b}$ (assume $a > b$) **76.** $7y^{2a+b} - 5y^{a+b} + 3y^{a+2b}$

Mixed Review

Consider the function $f(x) = -3x + 1$ and find the function values.

77. $f(0)$ **78.** $f(-2)$ **79.** $f(3)$ **80.** $f(-9)$ **81.** $f(4)$ *3-3*

Find the slope and y-intercept. **82.** $y = -5x + 6$

83. $y = 3x - 1$ **84.** $3y = -6x + 9$ **85.** $2y = x$ *3-6*

Solve. **86.** $14 + a = 3a + 2$ **87.** $9m + 4m + 6 = 32$ *1-5*

5-5 More Factoring

What You'll Learn

1. To factor sums or differences of two cubes
2. To factor trinomials of the type $x^2 + bx + c$
3. To factor trinomials of the type $ax^2 + bx + c$

. . . And Why

To solve factorable polynomial equations

Introducing the Concept: The Sum or Difference of Two Cubes

Compute and compare. Look for patterns in the factors below.

$(4 + 5)(4^2 - 4 \cdot 5 + 5^2)$ and $4^3 + 5^3$
$(7 - 3)(7^2 + 7 \cdot 3 + 3^2)$ and $7^3 - 3^3$
$(3x + 2)[(3x)^2 - 3 \cdot 2 + 2^2]$ and $(3x)^3 + 2^3$
$(2y - 9)[(2y)^2 + (2y) \cdot 9 + 9^2]$ and $(2y)^3 - 9^3$

PART 1 Factoring Sums or Differences of Two Cubes

Objective: Factor sums or differences of two cubes.

Factoring Sums or Differences of Two Cubes

$$A^3 + B^3 = (A + B)(A^2 - AB + B^2)$$
$$A^3 - B^3 = (A - B)(A^2 + AB + B^2)$$

EXAMPLE 1 Factor.

$$x^3 + 125 = x^3 + 5^3$$

In one set of parentheses we write the cube root, x, of the first term plus the cube root, 5, of the second term. This gives us $x + 5$.

$$(x + 5)(\qquad\qquad)$$

To get the next factor, we do the following.

1. Square the first term: x^2.
2. Multiply the terms and then change the sign: $-5x$.
3. Square the second term: 25.

$$(x + 5)(x^2 - 5x + 25)$$

Note that we cannot factor $x^2 - 5x + 25$. A polynomial that cannot be factored is called a **prime polynomial.** The factors $x + 5$ and $x^2 - 5x + 25$ are **prime factors,** since neither can be factored.

Try This Factor.

a. $1000x^3 + 1$ **b.** $y^3 + 64x^3$

We can treat a difference of cubes as a sum in order to factor sums and differences of cubes using the same method.

EXAMPLE 2 Factor.

$$x^3 - 27y^3 = x^3 + (-3y)^3 \qquad A \text{ is } x, B \text{ is } -3y.$$
$$(A + B)(A^2 - AB + B^2)$$
$$= (x - 3y)(x^2 + 3xy + 9y^2)$$

Try This Factor.

c. $x^3 - 8$ **d.** $-8x^3 + 27y^3$

PART 2 Factoring Trinomials of the Type $x^2 + bx + c$

Objective: Factor trinomials of the type $x^2 + bx + c$.

Journal

In your own words, write a step-by-step set of instructions that tells how to factor the sum or difference of two cubes.

Consider this product.

$$\begin{aligned}(x + 3)(x + 5) &= \overset{F}{x^2} + \overset{O}{5x} + \overset{I}{3x} + \overset{L}{15} \\ &= x^2 + 8x + 15\end{aligned}$$

Note that the coefficient 8 is the sum of 3 and 5, and that the constant term 15 is the product of 3 and 5.

In general, $(x + A)(x + B) = x^2 + (A + B)x + AB$. To factor we can use this equation in reverse.

$$x^2 + (A + B)x + AB = (x + A)(x + B)$$

EXAMPLE 3 Factor $x^2 - 3x - 10$.

We look for pairs of integers whose product is -10 and whose sum is -3.

Pairs of factors	Sum of factors
−2, 5	3
2, −5	−3
10, −1	9
−10, 1	−9

The desired integers are 2 and -5.

$$x^2 - 3x - 10 = (x + 2)(x - 5)$$

We can check by multiplying.

$$\begin{aligned}(x + 2)(x - 5) &= x^2 - 5x + 2x - 10 \\ &= x^2 - 3x - 10\end{aligned}$$

Try This Factor.

e. $x^2 + 5x - 14$ **f.** $x^2 + 21 - 10x$

g. $y^2 - y - 2$ **h.** $y^2 + 18y + 32$

PART 3 Factoring Trinomials of the Type $ax^2 + bx + c$

Objective: Factor trinomials of the type $ax^2 + bx + c$.

In the trinomial $ax^2 + bx + c$, the x^2 term has a coefficient other than 1.

$$\begin{aligned}(2x + 3)(5x + 4) &= \overset{F}{10x^2} + \overset{O}{8x} + \overset{I}{15x} + \overset{L}{12} \\ &= 10x^2 + 23x + 12\end{aligned}$$

Factoring Trinomials

To factor $ax^2 + bx + c$ we look for binomials

$$(\_\_\_\_\_x + \_\_\_\_\_)(\_\_\_\_\_x + \_\_\_\_\_)$$

where products of numbers in the blanks are as follows.

1. The numbers in the *first* blanks have the product a.
2. The product of the numbers in the *outside* blanks and the product of the numbers in the *inside* blanks have a sum of b.
3. The numbers in the *last* blanks have the product c.

EXAMPLE 4 Factor $12x^2 + 34x + 14$.

We first note that the number 2 is a common factor, so we factor it out.

$$2(6x^2 + 17x + 7)$$

Now we consider $6x^2 + 17x + 7$. We first look for pairs of numbers whose product is 6. The positive numbers are 6, 1 and 2, 3. We then have these possibilities.

$$(6x + \_\_\_\_\_)(x + \_\_\_\_\_) \text{ or } (2x + \_\_\_\_\_)(3x + \_\_\_\_\_)$$

Next we look for pairs of numbers whose product is 7. The pairs are 7, 1 and $-7, -1$. By substituting and multiplying we find that

$$12x^2 + 34x + 14 = 2(2x + 1)(3x + 7).$$

EXAMPLE 5 Factor $x^2y^2 + 5xy + 4$.

In this case, we treat xy as if it were a single variable.

$$\begin{aligned}x^2y^2 + 5xy + 4 &= (xy)^2 + (4 + 1)xy + 4 \cdot 1 \\ &= (xy + 4)(xy + 1)\end{aligned}$$

Try This Factor.

i. $3x^2 + 5x + 2$

j. $4x^2 - 3 + 4x$

k. $24y^2 - 46y + 10$

l. $2x^4y^6 - 3x^2y^3 - 20$

5-5 Exercises

Extra Help On the Web

Look for worked-out examples at the Prentice Hall Web site.
www.phschool.com

A

Factor.

1. $x^3 + 8$ **2.** $c^3 + 27$ **3.** $y^3 - 64$

4. $z^3 - 1$ **5.** $w^3 + 1$ **6.** $x^3 + 125$

7. $8a^3 + 1$ **8.** $27x^3 + 1$ **9.** $y^3 - 8$

10. $p^3 - 27$ **11.** $8 - 27b^3$ **12.** $64 - 125x^3$

13. $64y^3 + 1$ **14.** $125x^3 + 1$ **15.** $343x^3 + 27$

16. $27y^3 + 64$ **17.** $a^3 - b^3$ **18.** $x^3 - y^3$

19. $a^3 + \frac{1}{8}b^3$ **20.** $b^3 + \frac{1}{27}a^3$ **21.** $8x^3 - 27y^3$

22. $x^2 + 9x + 20$ **23.** $y^2 + 8y + 15$ **24.** $y^2 - 8y + 16$

25. $a^2 - 10a + 25$ **26.** $x^2 - 27 - 6x$ **27.** $t^2 - 15 - 2t$

28. $m^2 - 3m - 28$ **29.** $x^2 - 2x - 8$ **30.** $14x + x^2 + 45$

31. $12y + y^2 + 32$ **32.** $y^2 + 2y - 63$ **33.** $x^2 + 3x - 40$

34. $t^2 - 11t + 28$ **35.** $y^2 - 14y + 45$ **36.** $3x + x^2 - 10$

37. $x + x^2 - 6$ **38.** $x^2 + 5x + 6$ **39.** $y^2 + 8y + 7$

40. $32 + 4y - y^2$ **41.** $56 + x - x^2$ **42.** $15 + t^2 + 8t$

43. $3b^2 + 8b + 4$ **44.** $9x^2 + 15x + 4$ **45.** $6y^2 - y - 2$

46. $3a^2 - a - 4$ **47.** $-7a + 6a^2 - 10$ **48.** $-35z + 12z^2 - 3$

49. $9a^2 + 6a - 8$ **50.** $4t^2 + 4t - 15$ **51.** $3x^2 - 16x - 12$

52. $6x^2 - 5x - 25$ **53.** $6x^2 - 15 - x$ **54.** $10y^2 - 12 - 7y$

55. $3a^2 - 10a + 8$ **56.** $12a^2 - 7a + 1$ **57.** $2t + 5t^2 - 3$

58. $4x + 15x^2 - 3$ **59.** $8x^2 - 16 - 28x$ **60.** $18x^2 - 24 - 6x$

61. $3x^3 - 5x^2 - 2x$ **62.** $18y^3 - 3y^2 - 10y$ **63.** $24x^2 - 2 - 47x$

64. $21x^2 + 37x + 12$ **65.** $10y^2 + 23y + 12$ **66.** $17x + 40x^2 - 12$

67. $2y + 24y^2 - 15$ **68.** $12a^2 - 17a + 6$ **69.** $20a^2 - 23a + 6$

B

Factor.

70. $x^4 + 11x^2 - 80$ **71.** $y^4 + 5y^2 - 84$ **72.** $x^2 - \frac{4}{25} + \frac{3}{5}x$

73. $y^2 - \frac{8}{49} + \frac{2}{7}y$ **74.** $y^2 + 0.4y - 0.05$ **75.** $t^2 + 0.6t - 0.27$

76. $-6xy + 8x^2 - 9y^2$ **77.** $-7ts + 2t^2 - 4s^2$ **78.** $7a^2b^2 + 6 + 13ab$

79. $9x^2y^2 - 4 + 5xy$ **80.** $rs^3 + 64r$ **81.** $ab^3 + 125a$

82. $5x^3 - 40z^3$ **83.** $2y^3 - 54z^3$ **84.** $x^3 + 0.001$

85. $y^3 + 0.125$ **86.** $64x^6 - 8t^6$ **87.** $125c^6 - 8d^6$

88. ***Critical Thinking*** Use the model to verify that $a^3 - b^3 = (a - b)(a^2 + ab + b^2)$.

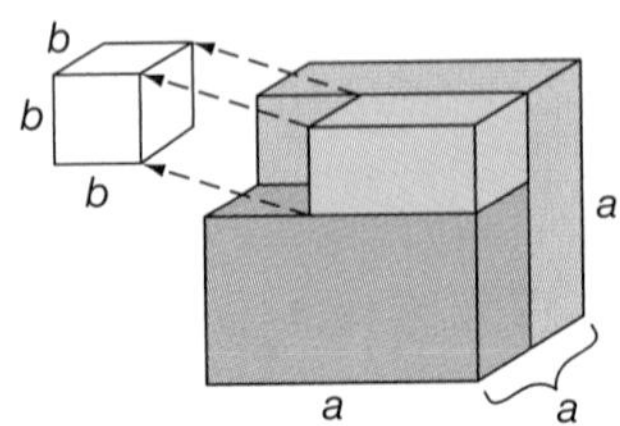

Challenge

Factor. Assume variables in exponents represent positive integers.

89. $3x^2 + 12x - 495$

90. $x^{6a} + y^{3b}$

91. $4y^3 - 96y^2 + 576y$

92. $3xy^2 - 150xy + 1875x$

93. $a^3x^3 - b^3y^3$

94. $12x^2 - 72xy + 108y^2$

95. $15t^3 - 60t^2 - 315t$

96. $216x + 78x^2 + 6x^3$

97. $x^{2a} + 5x^a - 24$

98. $4x^{2a} - 4x^a - 3$

99. $\frac{8}{27}x^3 + \frac{1}{64}y^3$

100. $\frac{1}{16}x^{3a} + \frac{1}{2}y^{6a}z^{9b}$

101. ***Write a Convincing Argument*** Factor $8x^2 - 10x - 3$. Then show why it is unnecessary to find the negative factors of 8.

Mixed Review

Solve these systems.

102.
$x - y - z = -5$
$3y + 2z = 22$
$3x - 2y - 3z = -7$

103.
$4a = 2c - 6$
$3a + 3b + c = -1$
$2(a - b) = c + 3$ *4-4*

Write an equation of the line containing the given point and perpendicular to the given line.

104. $(0, 3)$; $2x - 4y = 12$ *3-7*

Find the equation of the line containing the given point with the indicated slope.

105. $(3, -2)$; $m = -1$

106. $(0, 4)$; $m = 2$ *3-5*

107. ***Estimation*** $\frac{(3.7 \times 10^{-7})(4.1 \times 10^4)}{7.7 \times 10^{-2}}$ *1-9*

108. Yetta has dental insurance that pays 80% of all fees during the year after the first $75 deductible. Yetta's insurance company paid $168 of her dental fees this year. How much were her dental fees altogether? *2-2*

Factoring: A General Strategy

5-6

PART 1 Guidelines for Factoring

Objective: Factor polynomials using any of the methods learned previously.

What You'll Learn

1 To factor polynomials using any of the previously learned methods

. . . And Why

To solve equations and simplify rational algebraic expressions

The following guidelines summarize the factoring procedures we have studied.

Guidelines for Factoring

A. Always look first for a common factor.

B. Consider the number of terms.

Two terms Try factoring as a difference of two squares, or a sum or difference of two cubes.

Three terms Is it a trinomial square? If so, factor as a square of a binomial. If not, test the factors of the terms.

More than three terms
1. Try grouping.
2. Try differences of squares again.

C. Factor completely. Make sure that each remaining factor is prime.

EXAMPLES Factor.

1 $10a^2x - 40b^2x$

A. We look first for a common factor: $10x(a^2 - 4b^2)$.
B. The factor $a^2 - 4b^2$ has only two terms. It is a difference of squares. We factor it: $10x(a + 2b)(a - 2b)$.
C. Have we factored completely? Yes, because each factor with more than one term is prime.

2 $x^6 - y^6$

A. We look for a common factor. There isn't one.
B. There are only two terms. It is a difference of squares:

$(x^3)^2 - (y^3)^2$. We factor it: $(x^3 + y^3)(x^3 - y^3)$.

One factor is a sum of two cubes, and the other factor is a difference of two cubes. We factor them.

$$(x + y)(x^2 - xy + y^2)(x - y)(x^2 + xy + y^2)$$

C. We have factored completely because each factor is prime.

3 $10x^6 + 40y^2$

$$10x^6 + 40y^2 = 10(x^6 + 4y^2) \quad \text{Removing the largest common factor}$$

The sum of the two squares cannot be factored.

4 $2x^2 + 50a^2 - 20ax$

$$\begin{aligned} 2x^2 + 50a^2 - 20ax &= 2(x^2 - 10ax + 25a^2) \\ &= 2(x - 5a)^2 \end{aligned}$$

Removing the common factor and arranging; the trinomial is a square

5 $6x^2 - 20x - 16$

$$6x^2 - 20x - 16 = 2(3x^2 - 10x - 8)$$

Removing the largest common factor

The trinomial is not a square. We factor by testing factors of 3 and -8.

$$= 2(x - 4)(3x + 2)$$

We cannot factor further.

6 $y^2 - 9a^2 + 12y + 36$

There is no common factor (other than 1 or -1). There are four terms. Grouping to remove a common binomial factor is not possible. We try grouping as a difference of squares.

$$\begin{aligned} y^2 - 9a^2 + 12y + 36 &= (y^2 + 12y + 36) - 9a^2 \\ &= (y + 6)^2 - 9a^2 \\ &= (y + 6 + 3a)(y + 6 - 3a) \end{aligned}$$

Each factor is prime, so we have factored completely.

7 $x^3 - xy^2 + x^2y - y^3$

There is no common factor (other than 1 or -1). There are four terms. We try grouping to remove a common binomial factor.

$$\begin{aligned} x^3 - xy^2 + x^2y - y^3 &= x(x^2 - y^2) + y(x^2 - y^2) \\ &= (x + y)(x^2 - y^2) \\ &= (x + y)(x + y)(x - y) \\ &= (x + y)^2(x - y) \end{aligned}$$

Each factor is prime, so we have factored completely.

Try This Factor completely.

a. $2 - 32x^4$ **b.** $7a^6 - 7$ **c.** $3x + 12 + 4x + x^2$

d. $c^2 - 2cd + d^2 - t^2 - 8t - 16$ **e.** $5y^4 + 20x^6$

f. $6x^2 - 3x - 18$ **g.** $a^3 - ab^2 - a^2b + b^3$

h. $3x^2 + 18ax + 27a^2$ **i.** $a^2 + 2ab + b^2 - c^2$

5-6 Exercises

Extra Help On the Web

Look for worked-out examples at the Prentice Hall Web site. www.phschool.com

A

Factor completely. Remember to look first for a common factor.

1. $x^2 - 144$ **2.** $2x^2 + 11x + 12$ **3.** $3x^4 - 12$

4. $2xy^2 - 50x$ **5.** $a^2 + 25 + 10a$ **6.** $p^2 + 64 + 16p$

7. $2x^2 - 10x - 132$ **8.** $3y^2 - 15y - 252$ **9.** $4c^2 - 4cd + d^2$

10. $70b^2 - 3ab - a^2$ **11.** $-7x^2 + 2x^3 + 4x - 14$

12. $9m^2 + 3m^3 + 8m + 24$ **13.** $4x^2 - 27x + 45$

14. $3y^2 + 15y - 42$ **15.** $8m^3 + m^6 - 20$

16. $-37x^2 + x^4 + 36$ **17.** $ac + cd - ab - bd$ **18.** $xw - yw + xz - yz$

19. $m^6 - 1$ **20.** $64t^6 - 1$ **21.** $x^2 + 6x - y^2 + 9$

22. $t^2 + 10t - p^2 + 25$ **23.** $a^8 - b^8$ **24.** $2x^4 - 32$

25. $8p^3 + 27q^3$ **26.** $125x^3 + 64y^3$ **27.** $64p^3 - 1$

28. $8y^3 - 125$ **29.** $a^3b - 16ab^3$ **30.** $x^3y - 25xy^3$

31. $-23xy + 20x^2y^2 + 6$ **32.** $42ab + 27a^2b^2 + 8$

33. $2x^3 + 6x^2 - 8x - 24$ **34.** $3x^3 + 6x^2 - 27x - 54$

35. $250x^3 - 128y^3$ **36.** $16x^3 + 54y^3$

Choose the correct word.

37. The difference of two squares is (*sometimes, always, never*) factorable using only rational numbers.

B

Factor.

38. $(x - p)^2 - p^2$ **39.** $30y^4 - 97xy^2 + 60x^2$

40. $5c^{100} - 80d^{100}$ **41.** $3a^2 + 3b^2 - 3c^2 - 3d^2 + 6ab - 6cd$

42. $8(a - 3)^2 - 64(a - 3) + 128$ **43.** $-16 + 17(5 - y^2) - (5 - y^2)^2$

44. ***Critical Thinking*** Factor $x^6 - y^6$ by factoring first as a difference of cubes. How can you use the result of multiplying $(x^2 + xy + y^2)$ by $(x^2 - xy + y^2)$ to help you do this?

Challenge

Factor.

45. $(y - 1)^4 - (y - 1)^2$ **46.** $27x^{6s} + 64y^{3t}$ **47.** $c^{2w+1} + 2c^{w+1} + c$

Mixed Review

Find an equation of the line containing each pair of points.

48. $(1, 3)$ and $(4, 9)$ **49.** $(-2, 1)$ and $(1, -5)$ **50.** $(3, 11)$ and $(-2, -9)$ *3-6*

Consider the polynomial function $P(x) = 3x^3 - 4x^2 + 2x - 1$. Find the specified function values. **51.** $P(1)$ **52.** $P(-1)$ **53.** $P(0)$ **54.** $P(m)$ *5-1*

5-7 Solving Equations by Factoring

What You'll Learn

1. To solve equations by factoring and using the principle of zero products

. . . And Why

To solve problems that use equations with factorable expressions

PART 1 The Principle of Zero Products

Objective: Solve equations by factoring and using the principle of zero products.

The principle of zero products states that a product is 0 if and only if at least one of the factors is 0. To use this principle in solving equations, make sure that 0 is on one side of the equation. Then factor the other side.

EXAMPLE 1 Solve $x^2 - 3x - 28 = 0$.

First we factor the polynomial.

$$x^2 - 3x - 28 = 0$$
$$(x - 7)(x + 4) = 0 \qquad \text{Factoring}$$

We now have two factors whose product is 0. By the principle of zero products, one of the factors must be zero.

$$x - 7 = 0 \text{ or } x + 4 = 0 \qquad \text{Using the principle of zero products}$$
$$x = 7 \text{ or } \qquad x = -4$$

Check:

$x^2 - 3x - 28$	$= 0$
$7^2 - 3(7) - 28$	0
$49 - 21 - 28$	0
0	0 ✔

$x^2 - 3x - 28$	$= 0$
$(-4)^2 - 3(-4) - 28$	0
$16 + 12 - 28$	0
0	0 ✔

The solutions are 7 and -4.

Try This Solve.

a. $x^2 + 8 - 6x = 0$ **b.** $12y^2 - 3y = 9$ **c.** $25 + x^2 = -10x$

Here are some other examples of polynomial equations and their solutions.

EXAMPLES Solve.

		Factored	Using zero products	Solution
2	$5b^2 - 10b = 0$	$5b(b - 2) = 0$	$b = 0$ or $b - 2 = 0$	0, 2
3	$x^2 - 6x = -9$	$(x - 3)(x - 3) = 0$	$x - 3 = 0$ or $x - 3 = 0$	3

Try This Solve.

d. $8b^2 - 16b = 0$ **e.** $9x^2 + 27x = 0$ **f.** $x^3 + 3 = x + 3x^2$

5-7 Exercises

Extra Help On the Web

Look for worked-out examples at the Prentice Hall Web site.
www.phschool.com

A

Solve.

1. $x^2 + 3x - 28 = 0$ **2.** $y^2 - 4y - 45 = 0$ **3.** $x^2 - 12x + 36 = 0$

4. $y^2 + 16y + 64 = 0$ **5.** $9x + x^2 + 20 = 0$ **6.** $8y + y^2 + 15 = 0$

7. $x^2 + 8x = 0$ **8.** $t^2 + 9t = 0$ **9.** $x^2 - 9 = 0$

10. $p^2 - 16 = 0$ **11.** $z^2 = 36$ **12.** $y^2 = 81$

13. $y^2 + 2y = 63$ **14.** $a^2 + 3a = 40$ **15.** $p^2 - 11p = -28$

16. $x^2 - 14x = -45$ **17.** $32 + 4x - x^2 = 0$ **18.** $27 + 12t + t^2 = 0$

19. $8y^2 - 10y + 3 = 0$ **20.** $4x^2 + 11x + 6 = 0$ **21.** $12z^2 + z = 6$

22. $6x^2 - 7x = 10$ **23.** $5x^2 - 20 = 0$ **24.** $6y^2 - 54 = 0$

25. $2x^2 - 15x = -7$ **26.** $x^2 - 9x = -8$ **27.** $21r^2 + r - 10 = 0$

28. $12a^2 - 5a - 28 = 0$ **29.** $15y^2 = 3y$ **30.** $18x^2 = 9x$

31. ***Error Analysis*** Michael solved $4y^2 = 20y$ and checked his answer of $y = 5$. However, Juanita had two correct solutions. What did Michael forget to do?

B

Solve.

32. $x^2 - \frac{1}{25} = 0$ **33.** $y^2 - \frac{1}{64} = 0$ **34.** $16x^3 = x$ **35.** $9x^3 = x$

36. $x(x + 8) = 16(x - 1)$ **37.** $m(m + 9) = 4(2m + 5)$

38. $(a - 5)^2 = 36$ **39.** $(x - 6)^2 = 81$

40. $(x + 1)^3 = (x - 1)^3 + 26$ **41.** $(x - 2)^3 = x^3 - 2$

42. ***Critical Thinking*** Find two different equations whose solutions are 5 and −8.

Challenge

Solve for x.

43. $x^2 + 2ax - 3x - 6a = 0$ **44.** $2x^2 - 5bx + 4cx - 10bc = 0$

45. $x^3 + ax^2 - a^2x - a^3 = 0$ **46.** $x^2 + 10x + 25 - 9a^2 = 0$

Mixed Review

Solve these systems.

47. $3x + 5y = 2$, $x = 3y - 4$ **48.** $6x - y = 17$, $2x + y = -1$ **49.** $2x - y = 0$, $y + x = 3$ *4-3*

50. The average male grows from a height of 20 inches at birth to 51 inches at age 8. How tall would a male be at age 60 if growth continued at this rate? *3-8*

5-8 Using Equations

What You'll Learn

1 To solve problems that translate into factorable expressions equal to zero

. . . And Why

To solve problems by applying algebraic reasoning skills

PART 1 Translating Problems Into Factorable Equations

Objective: Solve problems by translating to equations and solving them by factoring.

The Schroeders are remodeling their square living room by tearing down one wall and extending the room by 3 meters. The room will then be rectangular with an area of 180 m^2. What are the current dimensions of the living room?

The new wall is to be 12 feet in height. About how many meters is this?

PROBLEM-SOLVING GUIDELINES
■ UNDERSTAND the problem
■ Develop and carry out a PLAN
■ Find the ANSWER and CHECK

EXAMPLE

Solve the problem stated above.

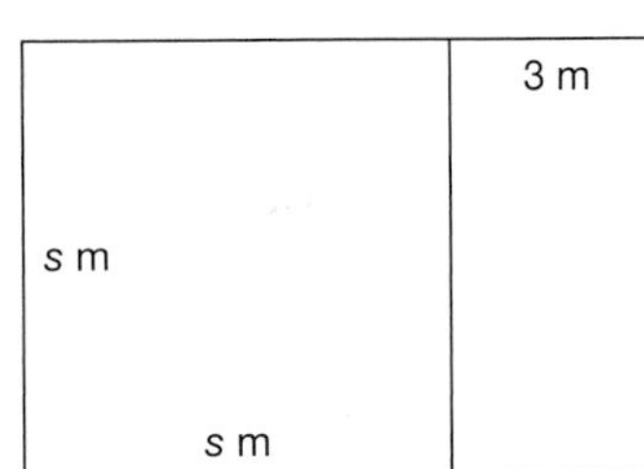

We can *draw a diagram* of the situation and use the Problem-Solving Guidelines to help solve the problem.

■ **UNDERSTAND the problem**

Question: What are the current dimensions of the living room? — Clarifying the question

Data: Increasing one side of the square room will give the room an area of 180 m^2. — Identifying the data

■ **Develop and carry out a PLAN**

Reword and translate to an equation.

The length of a side (s) times the length plus 3 is 180.

$$s \cdot (s + 3) = 180$$

Solve the equation.

$s(s + 3) = 180$
$s^2 + 3s - 180 = 0$ Adding -180 to both sides so that 0 is on one side
$(s + 15)(s - 12) = 0$ Factoring
$s = -15$ or $s = 12$ Using the principle of zero products

■ **Find the ANSWER and CHECK**

The solutions of the equation are -15 and 12. The solution -15 is not reasonable since the length of the room cannot be negative. Thus, the length is 12 m. Since the room is square, the dimensions are 12 m by 12 m.

Try This

a. The square of a number minus twice the number is 48. Find the number.
b. The width of a rectangle is 5 cm less than the length. The area is 24 cm^2. Find the dimensions.

5-8 Exercises

Extra Help On the Web

Look for worked-out examples at the Prentice Hall Web site.
www.phschool.com

A

Solve these problems.

1. Four times the square of a number is 21 more than eight times the number. What is the number?

2. Four times the square of a number is 45 more than eight times the number. What is the number?

3. The square of a number plus the number is 132. What is the number?

4. The square of a number plus the number is 156. What is the number?

5. The length of the top of a table is 5 ft greater than the width. Find the length and width if the area is 84 ft^2.

6. The length of the top of a workbench is 4 ft greater than the width. The area is 96 ft^2. Find the length and the width.

7. Sam Stratton is planning a garden 25 m longer than it is wide. The garden will have an area of 7500 m^2. What will its dimensions be?

8. A flower bed is to be 3 m longer than it is wide. The flower bed will have an area of 108 m^2. What will its dimensions be?

9. The sum of the squares of two consecutive odd positive integers is 202. Find the integers.

10. The sum of the squares of two consecutive odd positive integers is 394. Find the integers.

11. The base of a triangle is 9 cm greater than the height. The area is 56 cm^2. Find the height and base.

12. The base of a triangle is 5 cm less than the height. The area is 18 cm^2. Find the height and base.

13. **TEST PREP** Three consecutive even integers are such that the square of the third is 76 more than the square of the second. Which equation will determine the value of the first integer?

    A. $(2x + 4)^2 + 76 = (2x + 2)^2$ **B.** $(4x)^2 - (2x)^2 = 76$

    C. $(2x + 4)^2 - (2x + 2)^2 = 76$ **D.** $(2x + 2)^2 - (2x + 1)^2 = 76$

14. Find three consecutive integers such that the product of the first and third minus the second is one more than 10 times the third.

15. Find three consecutive integers such that four times the square of the third, less three times the square of the first, minus 41, is twice the square of the second.

B

16. A rectangular piece of tin is twice as long as it is wide. Squares 2 cm on a side are cut out of each corner, and the ends are turned up to make a box whose volume is 480 cm^3. What are the dimensions of the piece of tin?

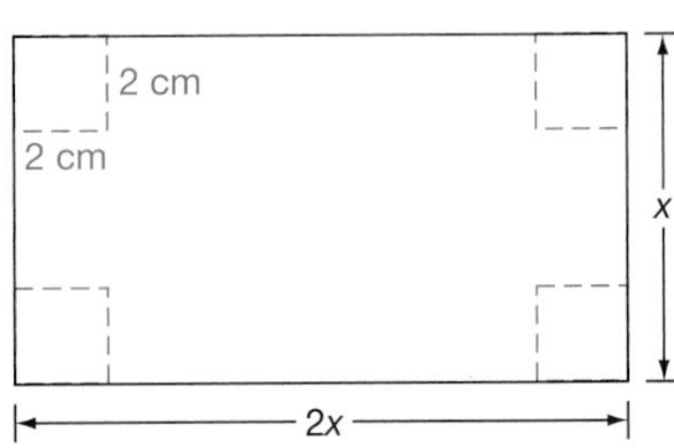

17. *Critical Thinking* Suppose the Schroeders' room in the Example is rectangular with an area of 180 m^2, but it will be square after the wall is torn down. What are the dimensions?

Challenge

18. The top and base of a fish tank are rectangles whose length is 10 in. more than the width. If the depth and the width of the tank total 50 in. and the combined area of the top and base is 400 $in.^2$ less than the total area of the four sides, what are the dimensions of the tank?

19. A rectangular swimming pool with dimensions of 11 m and 8 m is built in a rectangular backyard. The area of the backyard is 1120 m^2. If the strip of yard surrounding the pool is of uniform width, how wide is the strip?

20. The hypotenuse of a right triangle is 3 cm longer than one of its legs and 6 cm longer than its other leg. What is the area of the triangle?

A fish tank is 24 in. long, 12 in. wide, and 1 foot deep. What is the volume in cubic inches? In cubic feet?

Mixed Review

Simplify. **21.** $(5x^2y + 3xy - 6) + (4x^2y + 2xy^2 - 4xy - 9)$ 5-2

Factor. **22.** $y^2 + 7y$ **23.** $x^2 - 4$ **24.** $16y^2 + 4y$ **25.** $4y^2 - 2y$ 5-4

Solve. **26.** $3a - 5 = 19$ **27.** $-16 = 3x + 2$ **28.** $-6 = 0.75y + 3$ 1-5, 2-1

Preparing for Standardized Tests

Factoring

Some problems on college entrance exams can be solved using the skills you have learned related to *factoring.* Test items, however, will usually not tell you that factoring is a good approach to solving the problem. Your job is to look at a problem and decide whether factoring might be helpful in finding the solution. The reason for including these types of problems on exams is to determine whether you can apply algebraic skills to situations without being told to do so. Here are three factoring situations that often are encountered on college entrance exams.

$$a^2 - b^2 = (a - b)(a + b)$$
$$a^2 + 2ab + b^2 = (a + b)^2$$
$$a^2 - 2ab + b^2 = (a - b)^2$$

EXAMPLE 1

$0.85^2 - 0.75^2 =$

(A) 1.6 **(B)** 0.16 **(C)** 0.10 **(D)** 0.01 **(E)** 0.001

Here we factor and we can do the arithmetic mentally.

$$\begin{aligned} 0.85^2 - 0.75^2 &= (0.85 + 0.75)(0.85 - 0.75) \\ &= (1.60)(0.1) \\ &= 0.16 \end{aligned}$$

The arithmetic is simpler this way than directly squaring both numbers and subtracting. The answer is choice B.

EXAMPLE 2

If $x^2 - 9 = (15)(21)$, then x could be

(A) 16 **(B)** 17 **(C)** 18 **(D)** 19 **(E)** 20

Here we can factor $x^2 - 9 = (x - 3)(x + 3)$ and place the factors under (15)(21).

$$\begin{aligned} x^2 - 9 = {} & (15) \cdot (21) \\ & (x - 3)(x + 3) \end{aligned}$$

By inspection $x = 18$, so the answer is choice C.

EXAMPLE 3

If $x = 236.81$, then $\frac{x^2 + x - 12}{x + 4}$ rounded to the nearest whole number is

(A) 100 **(B)** 204 **(C)** 234 **(D)** 264 **(E)** 267

Factor and simplify before substituting.

$$\frac{x^2 + x - 12}{x + 4} = \frac{(x - 3)(x + 4)}{x + 4}$$
$$= x - 3 = 236.81 - 3 \approx 234$$

The answer is choice C.

EXAMPLE 4

$(59)^2 - 2(59)(49) + (49)^2 =$

(A) 10 **(B)** 71 **(C)** 100 **(D)** 108 **(E)** 1247

Here we recognize that this problem can be simplified to the form $(a - b)^2$, and instead of doing all of the arithmetic we can simplify first.

$$a^2 \quad - \quad 2ab \quad + \quad b^2 \quad = \quad (a - b)^2$$
$$(59)^2 - 2(59)(49) + (49)^2 = (59 - 49)^2 = 10^2 = 100$$

The answer is choice C.

Problems

1. If $(r - 3)\left(\frac{1}{r}\right) = 0$, what is r?

(A) 0 **(B)** 1 **(C)** 2 **(D)** 3 **(E)** Any nonzero integer

2. If $x - y = 7$ and $x + y = 5$, then $x^2 - y^2 =$

(A) 12 **(B)** 21 **(C)** 49 **(D)** 25 **(E)** 35

3. $0.53^2 - 0.47^2 =$

(A) 0.6 **(B)** 0.06 **(C)** 0.006 **(D)** 0.36 **(E)** 0.036

4. $(13)^2 - 2(13)(23) + (23)^2 =$

(A) 1296 **(B)** 698 **(C)** 100 **(D)** 46 **(E)** -100

5. If $x^2 - 16 = (12)(20)$, then x could be

(A) 14 **(B)** 15 **(C)** 16 **(D)** 17 **(E)** 18

6. If $ab = 2$ and $(a - b)^2 = 10$, then $a^2 + b^2 =$

(A) 14 **(B)** 18 **(C)** 6 **(D)** 8 **(E)** 12

7. If $m = 5$ and $n = 4$, then $\frac{m^2 - n^2}{m - n} =$

(A) 1 **(B)** 9 **(C)** 16 **(D)** 25 **(E)** 81

8. If $x + y = r$ and $x - y = \frac{1}{r}$, $(r \neq 0)$, then $x^2 - y^2 =$

(A) r **(B)** 1 **(C)** $\frac{1}{r}$ **(D)** $1 - \frac{1}{r}$ **(E)** Undefined

9. If $x^2 - y^2 = 60$ and $x + y = 10$, then $x - y =$

(A) 50 **(B)** $\frac{1}{6}$ **(C)** 6 **(D)** 9 **(E)** 10

5 Chapter Wrap Up

5-1

To find values of a **polynomial function,** substitute into the polynomial expression.

For each polynomial function, find the specified function value.

1. $P(x) = -3x^2 + 2x - 1; P(2)$ **2.** $P(y) = 2y^3 - 2y^2 - y - 33; P(-3)$

If two terms have the same variables raised to the same powers, the terms are similar or **like terms** and can be "combined" or "collected."

Collect like terms.

3. $2a + 7 - 3 + 9a + 3 - 7a$ **4.** $-3x^2y - 2xy + 5xy - 7xy^2$

5-2

The sum of two polynomials can be found by writing a plus sign between them and then collecting like terms. To subtract one polynomial from another, find the additive inverse of the second polynomial and then add it to the first polynomial.

Add.

5. $5x^2 - 8x^3 + 3x - 2$ and $4x^3 + 5x^2 + 9 - x$

6. $5a^4 + 7a^3 + 6a^2 - 7$ and $3a^4 - 5a^2 + 2 - a^3$

7. $p^3 - 5q^2 + 2pq$ and $3pq^3 - p^3 - 6$ and $4pq^2 + 5p^3 - pq + 6$

Find the additive inverse.

8. $x^5 - x^3 - 2x^2 + 18x - 1$ **9.** $-4y^4 - 16x^3y^3 + 13xy^2$

Subtract.

10. $(8y^2 + 3y + 6) - (-5y^2 + 4y - 3)$

11. $(8p - 5q + 7r) - (2p + 5q - 4r)$

12. $(8x^2 - 3xy - 7y^2) - (4x^2 - 6xy - 8y^2)$

13. $(15a - 5c + 4b) - (8b + 4c + 5a)$

5-3

To multiply any two polynomials, multiply each term of one by every term of the other and then add the results.

Multiply.

14. $(-8x^2y)(4xy^2)$ **15.** $(3xy + 4y)(x^2 - 2)$

16. $(3x - 2y + 5z)(-3x + 4z)$ **17.** $(5y^3 + 3y - 6)(6y^3 - 4y + 7)$

18. $(a - b)(a^2 + ab + b^2)$ **19.** $(-3x^2y^3 + 2t)(3x^2y^3 + 2t)$

20. $(7x - 5y)^2$ **21.** $(2x + 1)^3$

Key Terms

ascending order (p. 206)
binomial (p. 206)
coefficients (p.206)
degree of a polynomial (p. 206)
degree of a term (p. 206)
descending order (p. 206)
factor (p. 219)
FOIL (p. 214)
greatest common factor (p. 219)
like terms (p. 207)
monomial (p. 206)
polynomial function (p. 207)
polynomial in x (p. 206)
prime factors (p. 224)
prime polynomial (p. 224)
terms (p. 206)
trinomial (p. 206)
trinomial square (p. 219)

Internet Activity
On the Web

Look for extension problems for this chapter at the Prentice Hall Web site.
www.phschool.com

5-4–5-6

When factoring, always look first for a **common factor.** Then consider the number of terms. For two terms, try factoring as a **difference of two squares** or a **sum or difference of two cubes.** For three terms, is it a **trinomial square?** If so, factor as a square of a binomial. If not, **test the factors of the terms.** For more than three terms, try **grouping,** or try differences of squares again. Factor completely, making sure that each remaining factor is prime.

5-4

Factor.

22. $24x^2y - 40y^2$

23. $28t^4 - 35t^3 + 14t^2$

24. $49y^2 - 81$

25. $9y^2 - 64$

26. $4x^2y - xy^2$

27. $9x^2 - 9y^2$

28. $x^2 - 2xy + y^2 - 9$

29. $y^2 - 4y + 4 - 4x^2$

5-5

Factor.

30. $8a^3 - 1$

31. $25x^2 - 20xy + 4y^2$

32. $x^3 + y^6$

33. $a^2 - 10a + 24$

34. $a^2b^2 + 7ab + 12$

35. $72 - x - x^2$

36. $2y^2 - 3y - 2$

37. $8x^2 + 9 - 18x$

5-6

Factor.

38. $x^2 - 81$

39. $3x^2 - 27$

40. $8x^2 + 50 + 40x$

41. $4y^2 + 20y - 56$

42. $x^2y - 16y^3$

43. $8x^3 - 27y^3$

44. $5x^3 + 10x^2 - 45x - 90$

45. $kw - tw + ky - ty$

5-7

A product is zero if and only if one of the factors is 0. This is the **principle of zero products.**

Solve.

46. $x^2 - 8x = 0$

47. $2x^2 + 9x = -4$

5-8

Factoring can be used effectively when solving many problems.

48. The square of a number plus seven times the number is -12. Find the number.

49. The length of a rectangle is 3 cm more than the width, and the area is 54 cm^2. Find its dimensions.

5 Chapter Assessment

For each polynomial function, find the specified function value.

1. $Q(x) = 3x^3 - x + 3$
Find $Q(0)$ and $Q(-2)$.

2. $H(y) = -2y^4 + y^3 + 3y^2 - y - 6$
Find $H(2)$ and $H(-2)$.

Collect like terms.

3. $3x - 5 - 3 - 3x + 5 - 1$

4. $-3xy - 2x^2 + y^2 - xy + 3x^2$

Add.

5. $3x^2 - 4x^3 + 2x - 1$ and $5x^3 + 4x^2 + 3 - x$

6. $4y^2 - 3xy + 4x^2 + 7x^3$ and $5x^3 - 3x^2 - 2xy + 5y^2$

7. $-3x^2 - 2x - 6x^3$ and $x^3 - 7 + 2x^2 + 2x$

8. $x^2 - 3x - 2$ and $3x^2 - 2x + 5$ and $-2x^3 - 5x - 3$

Find the additive inverse.

9. $-3x^5 - x^3 + 2x^2 - 28x + 2$

10. $-4xy^4 + x^3y^3 - 23xy^2 + 16x^2$

Subtract.

11. $(7x^2 + 2x + 4) - (-2x^2 + 2x - 2)$

12. $(5r^2 - 2rs - 6s^2) - (3r^2 - 4rs - 7s^2)$

13. $(3x^4 - 2x^2 - 4) - (3x^3 - 2x^2 + 4)$

14. $(x^3 - x^2 + x - 1) - (-x^3 - x^2 + x - 1)$

Multiply.

15. $(14x^2y)(3xy^2)$

16. $(-3x^2y^2)(-2xy)(-x^2y)$

17. $(-4x + 3z)(2x - 3y + 4z)$

18. $(3x - 5)(3x + 5)$

19. $(x - 2)(x^2 + 2x + 4)$

20. $(5x + 2y)^2$

21. $(7x - 2y)(3x + y)$

22. $(9x - 5y)(2x - 7y)$

23. $(2x^2 - 3)^2$

24. $(y^2 - 3y + 9)(y + 3)$

Factor.

25. $9t - 27$

26. $16x^2 - 81$

27. $9x^2 + 24x + 16$

28. $3y^3 - 27y$

29. $x^2y^2 - 2xy - 15$

30. $6x^2 + 11x - 10$

31. $36 - 16x - x^2$

32. $y^6 - z^6$

33. $64p^3 - 125q^3$

34. $x^2 - 6x + 9 - a^2 + 2a - 1$

35. $x^3 + 4x^2 - 8x - 32$

36. $2a^2 + 4ab^2 - ab - 2b^3$

Solve.

37. $x^2 - 21 = 4x$

38. $y^2 - 9y = 0$

39. $2x^2 + 75 = 25x$

40. $x^3 + 2x^2 = 9x + 18$

41. The square of a number plus nine times the number is -8. Find the number.

42. The length of a rectangle is 5 cm more than the width, and the area is 84 cm^2. Find its dimensions.

CHAPTER

What You'll Learn in Chapter 6

- How to add, subtract, multiply, divide, and simplify rational expressions
- How to graph and analyze rational functions and solve rational equations
- How to divide one polynomial by another
- How to use synthetic division
- How to solve work, motion, and variation problems

Skills & Concepts You Need for Chapter 6

1-2 Add or subtract.

1. $\frac{2}{7} + \left(-\frac{7}{9}\right)$ **2.** $\frac{5}{3} - \left(-\frac{3}{5}\right)$

1-2 Multiply.

3. $7 \cdot \left(-\frac{2}{3}\right)$ **4.** $-\frac{3}{8} \cdot \left(-\frac{4}{7}\right)$

1-2 Divide.

5. $\frac{2}{3} \div \frac{3}{4}$ **6.** $-\frac{7}{3} \div \frac{1}{2}$ **7.** $\frac{3}{4} \div \left(-\frac{1}{4}\right)$

1-3

8. Evaluate $xy - xz$ for $x = 3$, $y = -2$, $z = 4$.

1-4 Factor.

9. $4x + 4y$ **10.** $3y + 6$ **11.** $cx - cr + cw$

1-8 Simplify.

12. $(7x^3y^{-2})(2x^{-2}y^4)$ **13.** $\frac{10x^5y^2}{2xy^4}$ **14.** $(2x^2y^{-4}z^3)^4$

2-2

15. Solve $8 - 3(a - 1) = 2 + 4(3 - a)$.

2-4

16. Solve $E = mc^2$, for m.

Rational Expressions and Equations

At the opening of the San Francisco Golden Gate Bridge on May 27, 1937, over 200,000 people walked across the bridge. On May 24, 1987, over 300,000 people walked the bridge to celebrate the 50th anniversary of this modern wonder of the world.

The 80,000 miles of steel wire in the suspension cables are enough to circle Earth more than 3 times, and the towers are 746 feet tall—191 feet taller than the Washington Monument. The bridge is engineered to withstand 100 mi/h winds and can sway up to 27 feet in the center. See Lesson 6-7.

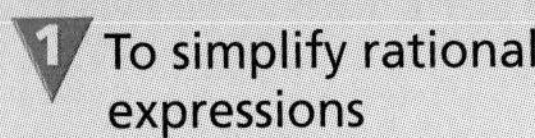

6-1 Multiplying and Simplifying

What You'll Learn

1. To simplify rational expressions
2. To multiply and simplify rational expressions
3. To divide and simplify rational expressions

... And Why

To solve formulas for a variable and to use rational expressions in solving problems

A **rational expression** is a quotient of two polynomials.

$$\frac{a}{b} \text{ means } a \div b, \text{ and } \frac{x^2 + 7xy - 4}{x^3 - y^3} \text{ means } (x^2 + 7xy - 4) \div (x^3 - y^3).$$

Since a rational expression indicates division, we cannot replace the variables in a denominator with numbers that make the denominator zero.

PART 1 Simplifying Rational Expressions

Objective: Simplify rational expressions.

To multiply rational expressions, we multiply numerators and denominators.

Theorem 6-1

Multiplication of Rational Expressions

For any rational expressions $\frac{a}{b}$ and $\frac{c}{d}$, where b and d are nonzero,

$\frac{a}{b} \cdot \frac{c}{d} = \frac{a \cdot c}{b \cdot d}$.

Any rational expression with the same numerator and denominator is equivalent to 1.

$$\frac{y+5}{y+5}, \quad \frac{4x^2-5}{4x^2-5}, \quad \frac{-1}{-1}$$

Each represents the number 1 for all acceptable replacements.

Any number multiplied by 1 is that same number, so we can multiply by 1 to get equivalent expressions.

EXAMPLE 1 Multiply $\frac{x+y}{5}$ by 1, using $\frac{x-y}{x-y}$ for 1.

$$\frac{x+y}{5} \cdot \frac{x-y}{x-y} = \frac{(x+y)(x-y)}{5(x-y)} \quad \text{Multiplying}$$

$$= \frac{x^2 - y^2}{5x - 5y}$$

The expressions $\frac{x+y}{5}$ and $\frac{x^2 - y^2}{5x - 5y}$ are equivalent. They represent the same number for all replacements, except those that make a denominator zero.

Try This Multiply.

a. $\frac{3x + 2y}{5x + 4y} \cdot \frac{x}{x}$ **b.** $\frac{2x^2 - y}{3x + 4} \cdot \frac{3x + 2}{3x + 2}$ **c.** $\frac{2a - 5}{a - b} \cdot \frac{-1}{-1}$

We can simplify a rational expression by reversing the procedure of multiplying by 1. First we factor both the numerator and denominator, then we remove a factor of 1.

Quick Review

Factoring is an application of the distributive property.

EXAMPLES Simplify.

2 $\frac{5x^2}{x} = \frac{5x \cdot x}{1 \cdot x}$ Factoring numerator and denominator

$= \frac{5x}{1} \cdot \frac{x}{x}$ Factoring the rational expression

$= 5x$ Simplifying

3 $\frac{4a + 8}{2} = \frac{2 \cdot 2a + 2 \cdot 4}{2 \cdot 1} = \frac{2(2a + 4)}{2 \cdot 1} = \frac{2}{2} \cdot \frac{2a + 4}{1} = 2a + 4$

Try This Simplify.

d. $\frac{7x^2}{x}$ **e.** $\frac{6a + 9}{3}$ **f.** $\frac{20y^2 + 32y}{4y}$

EXAMPLES Simplify.

4 $\frac{x^2 - 1}{2x^2 - x - 1} = \frac{(x - 1)(x + 1)}{(2x + 1)(x - 1)}$ Factoring numerator and denominator

$= \frac{x - 1}{x - 1} \cdot \frac{x + 1}{2x + 1}$ Factoring the rational expression

$= 1 \cdot \frac{x + 1}{2x + 1}$

$= \frac{x + 1}{2x + 1}$ Simplifying

5 $\frac{9x^2 + 6xy - 3y^2}{12x^2 - 12y^2} = \frac{3(x + y)(3x - y)}{12(x + y)(x - y)}$ Factoring

$= \frac{3(x + y)}{3(x + y)} \cdot \frac{3x - y}{4(x - y)}$

$= \frac{3x - y}{4(x - y)}$ Simplifying

After removing all possible factors of 1, we usually leave the numerator and denominator in factored form.

Try This Simplify.

g. $\frac{6x^2 + 4x}{2x^2 + 4x}$ **h.** $\frac{y^2 + 3y + 2}{y^2 - 1}$ **i.** $\frac{10x^2 - 25xy + 15y^2}{7x^2 + 7xy - 14y^2}$

PART 2 Multiplying and Simplifying

Objective: Multiply and simplify rational expressions.

We can simplify products of rational expressions by first factoring numerators and denominators, then removing factors of 1.

EXAMPLES Multiplying and simplifying.

6

$$\frac{x+2}{x-2} \cdot \frac{x^2-4}{x^2+x-2} = \frac{(x+2)(x^2-4)}{(x-2)(x^2+x-2)}$$ Multiplying numerators and denominators

$$= \frac{(x+2)(x-2)(x+2)}{(x-2)(x+2)(x-1)}$$ Factoring numerator and denominator

$$= \frac{(x+2)(x-2)}{(x+2)(x-2)} \cdot \frac{x+2}{x-1}$$

$$= \frac{x+2}{x-1}$$ Simplifying

7

$$\frac{a^3-b^3}{a^2-b^2} \cdot \frac{a^2+2ab+b^2}{a^2+ab+b^2} = \frac{(a^3-b^3)(a^2+2ab+b^2)}{(a^2-b^2)(a^2+ab+b^2)}$$

$$= \frac{(a-b)(a^2+ab+b^2)(a+b)(a+b)}{(a-b)(a+b)(a^2+ab+b^2)}$$

$$= \frac{(a-b)(a^2+ab+b^2)(a+b)}{(a-b)(a^2+ab+b^2)(a+b)} \cdot \frac{a+b}{1}$$

$$= \frac{a+b}{1}$$

$$= a+b$$

Try This Multiply and simplify.

j. $\frac{(x-y)^2}{x+y} \cdot \frac{3x+3y}{x^2-y^2}$

k. $\frac{a^3+b^3}{a^2-b^2} \cdot \frac{a^2-2ab+b^2}{a^2-ab+b^2}$

PART 3 Dividing and Simplifying

Objective: Divide and simplify rational expressions.

Two expressions are **reciprocals** of each other if their product is 1. The reciprocal of a fraction $\frac{a}{b}$ is the fraction $\frac{b}{a}$. This is also true for rational expressions.

Theorem 6-2

Reciprocals of Rational Expressions

For any rational expression $\frac{a}{b}$ that is nonzero, its reciprocal is $\frac{b}{a}$.

EXAMPLES Find the reciprocal.

8 $\frac{x + 2y}{3x^2y + 7}$ The reciprocal of $\frac{x + 2y}{3x^2y + 7}$ is $\frac{3x^2y + 7}{x + 2y}$.

9 $y - 8$ The reciprocal of $y - 8$ is $\frac{1}{y - 8}$.

10 $\frac{1}{x^2 + 3}$ The reciprocal of $\frac{1}{x^2 + 3}$ is $x^2 + 3$.

Try This Find the reciprocal.

l. $\frac{x + 3}{x - 5}$ **m.** $x + 7$ **n.** $\frac{1}{y^3 - 9}$

Recall that we can always divide by multiplying by the reciprocal. This is also true for rational expressions.

Theorem 6-3

Division of Rational Expressions

For any rational expressions $\frac{a}{b}$ and $\frac{c}{d}$ for which $\frac{c}{d}$ is nonzero,

$$\frac{a}{b} \div \frac{c}{d} = \frac{a}{b} \cdot \frac{d}{c}.$$

(We can divide by multiplying by the reciprocal.)

EXAMPLES Divide and simplify.

11
$$\frac{x - 2}{x + 1} \div \frac{x + 5}{x - 3} = \frac{x - 2}{x + 1} \cdot \frac{x - 3}{x + 5}$$ Multiplying by the reciprocal
$$= \frac{(x - 2)(x - 3)}{(x + 1)(x + 5)}$$ Multiplying numerators and denominators

12
$$\frac{a^2 - 1}{a + 1} \div \frac{a^2 - 2a + 1}{a + 1} = \frac{a^2 - 1}{a + 1} \cdot \frac{a + 1}{a^2 - 2a + 1}$$ Multiplying by the reciprocal
$$= \frac{(a + 1)(a - 1)}{a + 1} \cdot \frac{a + 1}{(a - 1)(a - 1)}$$ Factoring numerators and demominators
$$= \frac{(a + 1)(a - 1)}{(a + 1)(a - 1)} \cdot \frac{a + 1}{a - 1}$$
$$= \frac{a + 1}{a - 1}$$ Simplify

Try This Divide and simplify.

o. $\frac{x^2 + 7x + 10}{2x - 4} \div \frac{x^2 - 3x - 10}{x - 2}$ **p.** $\frac{a^2 - b^2}{ab} \div \frac{a^2 - 2ab + b^2}{2a^2b^2}$

Extra Help On the Web

Look for worked-out examples at the Prentice Hall Web site.
www.phschool.com

6-1 Exercises

A

Multiply to obtain equivalent expressions. Do not simplify.

1. $\frac{3x}{3x} \cdot \frac{x+1}{x+3}$
2. $\frac{4-y^2}{6-y} \cdot \frac{-1}{-1}$
3. $\frac{t-3}{t+2} \cdot \frac{t+3}{t+3}$
4. $\frac{p-4}{p-5} \cdot \frac{p+5}{p+5}$

Simplify.

5. $\frac{3a-6}{3}$
6. $\frac{4y-12}{4y+12}$
7. $\frac{8x+16}{8x-16}$
8. $\frac{t^2-16}{t^2-8t+16}$
9. $\frac{p^2-25}{p^2+10p+25}$
10. $\frac{x^2+7x-8}{4x^2-8x+4}$
11. $\frac{y^2+4y-12}{3y^2-12y+12}$
12. $\frac{x^4-4x^2}{x^3+2x^2}$
13. $\frac{a^3-b^3}{a^2-b^2}$
14. $\frac{x^3+y^3}{x^2-y^2}$

Multiply or divide and simplify.

15. $\frac{x^2-16}{x^2} \cdot \frac{x^2-4x}{x^2-x-12}$
16. $\frac{y^2+10y+25}{y^2-9} \cdot \frac{y+3}{y+5}$
17. $\frac{y^2-16}{2y+6} \cdot \frac{y+3}{y-4}$
18. $\frac{m^2-n^2}{4m+4n} \cdot \frac{m+n}{m-n}$
19. $\frac{x^2-2x-35}{2x^3-3x^2} \cdot \frac{4x^3-9x}{7x-49}$
20. $\frac{y^2-10y+9}{y^2-1} \cdot \frac{y+4}{y^2-5y-36}$
21. $\frac{x^2-y^2}{x^3-y^3} \cdot \frac{x^2+xy+y^2}{x^2+2xy+y^2}$
22. $\frac{4x^2-9y^2}{8x^3-27y^3} \cdot \frac{4x^2+6xy+9y^2}{4x^2+12xy+9y^2}$
23. $\frac{3y+15}{y} \div \frac{y+5}{y}$
24. $\frac{6x+12}{x} \div \frac{x+2}{x^3}$
25. $\frac{y^2-9}{y} \div \frac{y+3}{y+2}$
26. $\frac{x^2-4}{x} \div \frac{x-2}{x+4}$
27. $\frac{4a^2-1}{a^2-4} \div \frac{2a-1}{a-2}$
28. $\frac{25x^2-4}{x^2-9} \div \frac{5x-2}{x+3}$
29. $\frac{x^2-16}{x^2-10x+25} \div \frac{3x-12}{x^2-3x-10}$
30. $\frac{y^2-36}{y^2-8y+16} \div \frac{3y-18}{y^2-y-12}$
31. $\frac{x^3-64}{x^3+64} \div \frac{x^2-16}{x^2-4x+16}$
32. $\frac{8y^3+27}{64y^3-1} \div \frac{4y^2-9}{16y^2+4y+1}$

B

Simplify.

33. $\frac{x(x+1)-2(x+3)}{(x+1)(x+2)(x+3)}$
34. $\frac{2x-5(x+2)-(x-2)}{x^2-4}$
35. $\frac{m^2-t^2}{m^2+t^2+m+t+2mt}$
36. $\frac{a^3-2a^2+2a-4}{a^3-2a^2-3a+6}$
37. $\frac{x^3+x^2-y^3-y^2}{x^2-2xy+y^2}$
38. $\frac{u^6+v^6+2u^3v^3}{u^3-v^3+u^2v-uv^2}$
39. ***Critical Thinking*** Write three different rational expressions that, when simplified, are equivalent to $\frac{x+3}{x-1}$.

Challenge

Simplify.

40. $\dfrac{x^5 - x^3 + x^2 - 1 - (x^3 - 1)(x + 1)^2}{(x^2 - 1)^2}$

Prove the following theorems.

41. Theorem 6-1 **42.** Theorem 6-2 **43.** Theorem 6-3

44. ***Mathematical Reasoning*** For any rational expressions a and b, $(ab)^{-1} = a^{-1}b^{-1}$. Prove this theorem by showing that the product of $a^{-1}b^{-1}ab$ is 1.

Mixed Review

Arrange in decreasing degrees of x. **45.** $2xy^2 + 4x^3y^3 - x^7 + x^4 - \frac{1}{2}$ *5-1*

Factor. **46.** $81x^4 - 16$ **47.** $x^2 - 4x + 4 - y^2$ **48.** $ab - bc + 2ad - 2cd$ *5-4*

Connections: Calculus

The slope of a linear function does not change. For any two points, the slope is the same. For a curve, the slope is constantly changing. The slope is a function of x, and is the slope of the line tangent to $f(x)$ at any point on the curve.

We can find the **slope function, $f'(x)$,** by first finding the slope of a line through any two points P and Q of $f(x)$ that are h units apart on the x-axis, $(x, f(x))$, and $(x + h, f(x + h))$.

$$m = \frac{f(x + h) - f(x)}{(x + h) - x} = \frac{f(x + h) - f(x)}{h}$$

As the distance h approaches 0, this expression approaches the slope of the tangent line P.

Example: Find the slope function $f'(x)$ for $f(x) = x^2$.

$$m = \frac{f(x + h) - f(x)}{h} = \frac{(x + h)^2 - x^2}{h} = \frac{x^2 + 2hx + h^2 - x^2}{h} = \frac{2hx + h^2}{h} = 2x + h$$

When h approaches 0, $2x + h$ approaches $2x$. Thus the slope function of $f(x) = x^2$ is given by $f'(x) = 2x$. So when $x = 0$, the slope of $f(x)$ is 0; when x is 5, the slope is 10; and so on.

Find the slope function $f'(x)$.

a. $f(x) = x^3$ **b.** $f(x) = x^4$ **c.** $f(x) = x^5$ **d.** $f(x) = \frac{1}{x}$

6-2 Addition and Subtraction

What You'll Learn

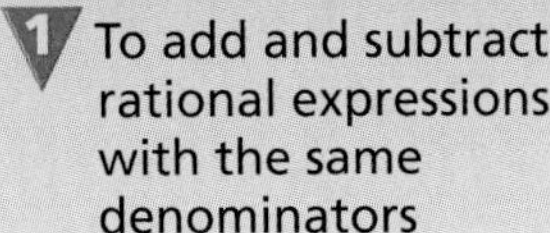

1. To add and subtract rational expressions with the same denominators
2. To add and subtract rational expressions with different denominators

. . . And Why

To solve formulas for one variable, and to solve equations and problems involving rational expressions

PART 1 Addition with Like Denominators

Objective: Add or subtract rational expressions when the denominators are the same.

When we add or subtract rational expressions with the same denominator, we add or subtract the numerators and keep the same denominator.

Theorem 6-4

Addition of Rational Expressions

For any rational expressions $\frac{a}{c}$ and $\frac{b}{c}$ for which c is nonzero,

$$\frac{a}{c} + \frac{b}{c} = \frac{a+b}{c} \quad \text{and} \quad \frac{a}{c} - \frac{b}{c} = \frac{a-b}{c}.$$

EXAMPLE 1 Add.

$$\frac{3+x}{x} + \frac{4}{x} = \frac{3+x+4}{x} = \frac{7+x}{x}$$ Adding numerators

Example 1 shows that $\frac{3+x}{x} + \frac{4}{x}$ and $\frac{7+x}{x}$ are equivalent expressions. This means that both expressions represent the same number for all replacements except 0.

EXAMPLE 2 Subtract.

$$\frac{4x+5}{x+3} - \frac{x-2}{x+3} = \frac{4x+5-(x-2)}{x+3}$$ Subtracting numerators

$$= \frac{4x+5-x+2}{x+3} = \frac{3x+7}{x+3}$$

Try This Add or subtract.

a. $\frac{5+y}{y} + \frac{7}{y}$

b. $\frac{2x^2+5x-9}{x-5} + \frac{x^2-19x+4}{x-5}$

c. $\frac{a}{b+2} - \frac{b}{b+2}$

d. $\frac{4y+7}{x^2+y^2} - \frac{3y-5}{x^2+y^2}$

When one denominator is the additive inverse of the other, we first multiply one expression by $\frac{-1}{-1}$. This will give us a common denominator.

EXAMPLE 3 Add.

$$\frac{9}{2a} + \frac{a^3}{-2a} = \frac{9}{2a} + \frac{-1}{-1} \cdot \frac{a^3}{-2a} \quad \text{Multiplying by } \frac{-1}{-1}$$

$$= \frac{9}{2a} + \frac{-a^3}{2a} = \frac{9 - a^3}{2a} \quad \text{Adding numerators}$$

Try This Add or subtract.

e. $\frac{3x^2 + 4}{x - 5} + \frac{x^2 - 7}{5 - x}$

f. $\frac{4x^2}{2x - y} - \frac{7x^2}{y - 2x}$

PART 2 Addition with Unlike Denominators

Objective: Add or subtract rational expressions when denominators are different.

When we add or subtract rational expressions with different denominators that are not additive inverses of each other, we must first find the **least common denominator** or **LCD.** The LCD is the **least common multiple,** or **LCM,** of the denominators.

To find the LCM of two or more algebraic expressions, we first factor each expression. Then we use each factor the greatest number of times it occurs in any of the factorizations.

To find the LCM of $x^2 - y^2$, $x^3 + y^3$, and $x^2 - 2xy + y^2$, we first factor.

$$x^2 - y^2 = (x + y)(x - y)$$
$$x^3 + y^3 = (x + y)(x^2 - xy + y^2)$$
$$x^2 - 2xy + y^2 = (x + y)(x + y)$$

The LCM is $(x - y)(x + y)(x + y)(x^2 - xy + y^2)$.

In finding LCMs, if factors that are additive inverses occur, we do not use them both. For example, if $(a - b)$ occurs in one factorization and $(b - a)$ occurs in another, we do not use them both, since $b - a = -(a - b)$.

EXAMPLE 4 Add.

$$\frac{7a}{8} + \frac{5b}{12a}$$

First find the LCD.

$$8 = 2 \cdot 2 \cdot 2$$
$$12a = 2 \cdot 2 \cdot 3 \cdot a \quad \text{The LCD is } 2^3 \cdot 3 \cdot a\text{, or } 24a.$$

Now we multiply each expression by 1. For each expression we choose a ratio equivalent to 1 that will give us the least common denominator.

$$\frac{7a}{8}\cdot\frac{3a}{3a}+\frac{5b}{12a}\cdot\frac{2}{2}=\frac{21a^2}{24a}+\frac{10b}{24a} \qquad \text{Multiplying each factor by 1}$$

$$=\frac{21a^2+10b}{24a}$$

Multiplying by $\frac{3a}{3a}$ in the first term gave us a denominator of $24a$.

Multiplying by $\frac{2}{2}$ in the second term also gave us a denominator of $24a$.

EXAMPLE 5 Add.

$$\frac{1}{2x}+\frac{5x}{x^2-1}+\frac{3}{x+1}$$

We first factor the denominators and find the LCD.

$$2x = 2\cdot x$$
$$x^2-1=(x-1)(x+1) \qquad \text{The LCD is } 2x(x-1)(x+1).$$
$$x+1=x+1$$

Now we multiply by 1 to get the LCM in each denominator. Then we add and simplify. We leave the result in factored form.

$$\frac{1}{2x}\cdot\frac{(x-1)(x+1)}{(x-1)(x+1)}+\frac{5x}{(x-1)(x+1)}\cdot\frac{2x}{2x}+\frac{3}{x+1}\cdot\frac{2x(x-1)}{2x(x-1)} \qquad \text{Multiplying by 1}$$

$$=\frac{(x-1)(x+1)}{2x(x-1)(x+1)}+\frac{10x^2}{2x(x-1)(x+1)}+\frac{6x(x-1)}{2x(x-1)(x+1)} \qquad \text{Multiplying in the numerator}$$

$$=\frac{x^2-1}{2x(x-1)(x+1)}+\frac{10x^2}{2x(x-1)(x+1)}+\frac{6x^2-6x}{2x(x-1)(x+1)}$$

$$=\frac{17x^2-6x-1}{2x(x-1)(x+1)}$$

EXAMPLE 6 Subtract.

$$\frac{2y+1}{y^2-7y+6}-\frac{y+3}{y^2-5y-6}=\frac{2y+1}{(y-6)(y-1)}-\frac{y+3}{(y-6)(y+1)}$$

The LCD is $(y-6)(y-1)(y+1)$.

$$=\frac{2y+1}{(y-6)(y-1)}\cdot\frac{y+1}{y+1}-\frac{y+3}{(y-6)(y+1)}\cdot\frac{y-1}{y-1}$$

$$=\frac{(2y+1)(y+1)-(y+3)(y-1)}{(y-6)(y-1)(y+1)}$$

$$=\frac{2y^2+3y+1-(y^2+2y-3)}{(y-6)(y-1)(y+1)}$$

$$=\frac{2y^2+3y+1-y^2-2y+3}{(y-6)(y-1)(y+1)}$$

$$=\frac{y^2+y+4}{(y-6)(y-1)(y+1)}$$

Try This Add or subtract.

g. $\frac{3x}{7} + \frac{4y}{3x}$ **h.** $\frac{4y - 5}{y^2 - 7y + 12} - \frac{y + 7}{y^2 + 2y - 15}$ **i.** $\frac{a}{a + 3} - \frac{a - 4}{a}$

EXAMPLE 7 Calculate.

$$\frac{2x}{x^2 - 4} + \frac{5}{2 - x} - \frac{1}{x + 2}$$

$$= \frac{2x}{(x - 2)(x + 2)} + \frac{-5}{x - 2} - \frac{1}{x + 2}$$ Factoring and multiplying by $\frac{-1}{-1}$

$$= \frac{2x}{(x - 2)(x + 2)} + \frac{-5}{x - 2} \cdot \frac{x + 2}{x + 2} - \frac{1}{x + 2} \cdot \frac{x - 2}{x - 2}$$ The LCD is $(x - 2)(x + 2)$.

$$= \frac{2x - 5(x + 2) - (x - 2)}{(x - 2)(x + 2)} = \frac{2x - 5x - 10 - x + 2}{(x - 2)(x + 2)}$$

$$= \frac{-4x - 8}{(x - 2)(x + 2)} = \frac{-4(x + 2)}{(x - 2)(x + 2)}$$

$$= \frac{-4}{x - 2}$$

Try This Calculate.

j. $\frac{8x}{x^2 - 1} + \frac{2}{1 - x} - \frac{4}{x + 1}$ **k.** $\frac{7y}{y^2 - y} + \frac{8}{2 - y} - \frac{3}{y + 2}$

6-2 Exercises

Extra Help On the Web

Look for worked-out examples at the Prentice Hall Web site. www.phschool.com

A

Mental Math Add or subtract.

1. $\frac{3y}{x} + \frac{5y}{x}$ **2.** $\frac{-8x}{3y} + \frac{6x}{3y}$ **3.** $\frac{-9y}{x + y} + \frac{16y}{x + y}$

4. $\frac{3a^2}{a - b} + \frac{-4a^2}{a - b}$ **5.** $\frac{25xy}{x^2 + y^2} - \frac{16xy}{x^2 + y^2}$ **6.** $\frac{37a^2b}{a^2 - b} - \frac{42a^2b}{a^2 - b}$

Add or subtract.

7. $\frac{a - 3b}{a + b} + \frac{a + 5b}{a + b}$ **8.** $\frac{x - 5y}{x + y} + \frac{x + 7y}{x + y}$ **9.** $\frac{a^2}{a - b} + \frac{b^2}{b - a}$

10. $\frac{r^2}{r - s} + \frac{s^2}{s - r}$ **11.** $\frac{3}{x} - \frac{8}{-x}$ **12.** $\frac{2}{a} - \frac{5}{-a}$

13. $\frac{2x - 10}{x^2 - 25} - \frac{5 - x}{25 - x^2}$ **14.** $\frac{y - 9}{y^2 - 16} - \frac{7 - y}{16 - y^2}$

15. $\frac{4xy}{x^2 - y^2} + \frac{x - y}{x + y}$ **16.** $\frac{5ab}{a^2 - b^2} + \frac{a + b}{a - b}$

17. $\frac{9x + 2}{3x^2 - 2x - 8} + \frac{7}{3x^2 + x - 4}$ **18.** $\frac{3y + 2}{2y^2 - y - 10} + \frac{8}{2y^2 - 7y + 5}$

Add or subtract.

19. $\frac{4}{x+1}+\frac{x+2}{x^2-1}+\frac{3}{x-1}$

20. $\frac{-2}{y+2}+\frac{5}{y-2}+\frac{y+3}{y^2-4}$

21. $\frac{x-1}{3x+15}-\frac{x+3}{5x+25}$

22. $\frac{y-2}{4y+8}-\frac{y+6}{5y+10}$

23. $\frac{5ab}{a^2-b^2}-\frac{a-b}{a+b}$

24. $\frac{6xy}{x^2-y^2}-\frac{x+y}{x-y}$

25. $\frac{3y+2}{y^2+5y-24}+\frac{7}{y^2+4y-32}$

26. $\frac{3y+2}{y^2-7y+10}+\frac{2y}{y^2-8y+15}$

27. $\frac{3x-1}{x^2+2x-3}-\frac{x+4}{x^2-9}$

28. $\frac{3p-2}{p^2+2p-24}-\frac{p-3}{p^2-16}$

29. $\frac{1}{x+1}-\frac{x}{x-2}+\frac{x^2+2}{x^2-x-2}$

30. $\frac{2}{y+3}-\frac{y}{y-1}+\frac{y^2+2}{y^2+2y-3}$

31. **TEST PREP** Which of the following is a simplification of

$\frac{4x}{(x^2-1)}+\frac{3x}{(1-x)}-\frac{4}{(x-1)}$?

A. $\frac{(-3x^2-3x-4)}{(x^2-1)}$ B. $\frac{(-3x^2-3x+4)}{(x^2-1)}$

C. $\frac{(-3x^2+3x+4)}{(x^2-1)}$ D. $\frac{(-3x^2+3x-4)}{(x^2-1)}$

32. Nu says that, in adding or subtracting fractions with two or more terms, the resulting denominator is always the product of the denominators of the terms. Find a counterexample.

B

Perform the indicated operations and simplify. Write without negative exponents.

33. $2x^{-2}+3x^{-2}y^{-2}-7xy^{-1}$

34. $5(x-3)^{-1}+4(x+3)^{-1}-2(x+3)^{-2}$

35. $4(y-1)(2y-5)^{-1}+5(2y+3)(5-2y)^{-1}+(y-4)(2y-5)^{-1}$

Simplify each of the following, using $A=x+y$ and $B=x-y$.

36. $\frac{A+B}{A-B}-\frac{A-B}{A+B}$

37. $\left(\frac{1}{A}+\frac{x}{B}\right)\div\left(\frac{1}{B}-\frac{x}{A}\right)$

38. Prove the first part of Theorem 6-4.

39. Prove the second part of Theorem 6-4.

40. ***Critical Thinking*** Find three rational expressions whose LCD is $(x-y)(x-y)(x+y)(x^2+xy+y^2)$.

Challenge

Consider the following polynomial functions.

$$g(x)=x^2-16,\ h(x)=x^2+x-20,\ d(x)=x^2-25$$

Find a simplified expression for each *rational function* given below.

41. $R(x)=\frac{h(x)}{d(x)}$

42. $R(x)=\frac{g(x)}{h(x)}$

43. $R(x)=\frac{d(d(x))}{h(g(x))}$

Find the LCM.

44. $x^8 - x^4, x^5 - x^2, x^5 - x^3, x^5 + x^2$

45. ***Mathematical Reasoning*** The LCM of two expressions is $8a^4b^7$. One of the expressions is $2a^3b^7$. List all the possibilities for the other expression.

Mixed Review

Solve each system of equations.

46. $x + \frac{1}{3}y = 19$
$-\frac{1}{2}x - 4y = -67$

47. $0.25x + 1.25y = 0.84$
$6x + 30y = 20.16$

48. $x - y + z = 6$
$2x + y - z = 0$
$3x - 2y - 4z = -2$ *4-2, 4-4*

Solve. **49.** $2x^2 - 24x + 22 = 0$ **50.** $256x^4 = 16$ **51.** $2x^3 = 6x^2 + 8x$ *5-7*

Graphing Rational Functions

Functions can be defined by rational expressions. Consider the function $f(x) = \frac{1}{x - 2}$. We can see that this function is not defined when $x = 2$. (Why?) It is interesting to see how the graph of this function behaves when the value of x is close to 2. We first make a table of values and then graph.

Exercises

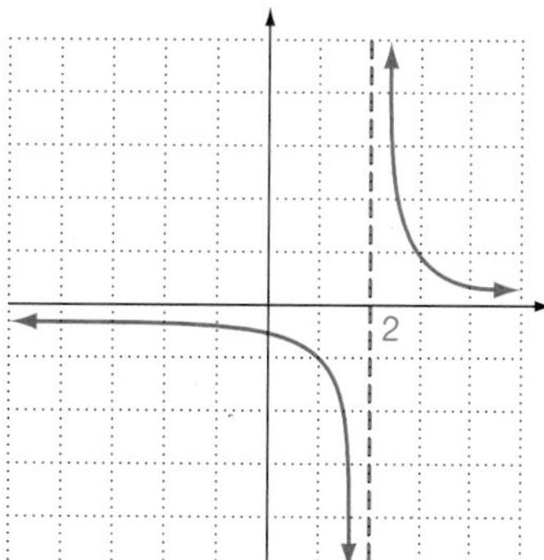

1. What happens to $f(x)$ as x approaches 2?
2. Will the graph of this function ever cross the x-axis? Why or why not?
3. Graph these rational functions. Use your calculator to make a table of values. Observe what happens to $f(x)$ as x approaches any unacceptable value.

   a. $f(x) = \frac{2}{x + 3}$ **b.** $f(x) = \frac{1}{x + 3}$

4. Graph $f(x) = \frac{x + 1}{x^2 - x - 2}$. (Hint: Factor the denominator first. Compare the graph of this rational function with the graph at the right.)

6-3  Complex Rational Expressions

What You'll Learn

1 To simplify complex rational expressions

. . . And Why

To solve algebraic problems using complex rational expressions

PART 1 Simplifying Complex Rational Expressions

Objective: Simplify complex rational expressions.

A **complex rational expression** is one that has a rational expression either in its numerator, its denominator, or both. Here are some examples of complex rational expressions.

$$\frac{x}{x - \frac{1}{3}}, \quad \frac{2x - \frac{4x}{3y}}{\frac{5x^2 + 2x}{6y^2}}, \quad \frac{a^{-1} + b^{-1}}{a^{-3}b^{-3}}, \quad \frac{\frac{5}{x}}{\frac{x}{y}}$$

Complex rational expressions can be simplified. One method is to find the LCD of *all* denominators appearing in the expression, then multiply both the numerator and denominator by the LCD.

EXAMPLE 1 Simplify $\dfrac{1 + \frac{1}{x}}{1 - \frac{1}{x^2}}$.

$$\frac{1 + \frac{1}{x}}{1 - \frac{1}{x^2}} = \frac{x^2}{x^2} \cdot \frac{\left(1 + \frac{1}{x}\right)}{\left(1 - \frac{1}{x^2}\right)}$$ The LCD is x^2.

$$= \frac{x^2 + \frac{x^2}{x}}{x^2 - \frac{x^2}{x^2}}$$ Using the distributive property

$$= \frac{x^2 + x}{x^2 - 1}$$ Simplifying

$$= \frac{x(x + 1)}{(x - 1)(x + 1)}$$ Factoring the numerator and denominator

$$= \frac{(x + 1)}{(x + 1)} \cdot \frac{x}{(x - 1)}$$ Factoring the rational expression

$$= \frac{x}{x - 1}$$ Simplifying

Try This Simplify.

a. $\dfrac{y + \frac{1}{2}}{y - \frac{1}{7}}$

b. $\dfrac{1 - \frac{1}{x}}{1 - \frac{1}{x^2}}$

Another method for simplifying complex rational expressions is to simplify the numerator and denominator separately, then treat the result as a division.

EXAMPLE 2 Simplify $\dfrac{\dfrac{x^2 - 9}{x^2 + 5x + 4}}{\dfrac{x^2 + 6x + 9}{x^2 - 1}}$.

$$\frac{\dfrac{x^2 - 9}{x^2 + 5x + 4}}{\dfrac{x^2 + 6x + 9}{x^2 - 1}} = \frac{\dfrac{(x + 3)(x - 3)}{(x + 1)(x + 4)}}{\dfrac{(x + 3)(x + 3)}{(x + 1)(x - 1)}}$$ Factoring numerators and denominators

$$= \frac{(x + 3)(x - 3)}{(x + 1)(x + 4)} \cdot \frac{(x + 1)(x - 1)}{(x + 3)(x + 3)}$$ Using Theorem 6-3 (multiplying by the reciprocal)

$$= \frac{(x + 3)(x + 1)}{(x + 3)(x + 1)} \cdot \frac{(x - 3)(x - 1)}{(x + 4)(x + 3)}$$ Factoring the rational expression

$$= \frac{(x - 3)(x - 1)}{(x + 4)(x + 3)}$$ Simplifying

Try This Simplify.

c. $\dfrac{\dfrac{c^2 - 1}{4c + 4}}{\dfrac{c - 1}{c + 1}}$ **d.** $\dfrac{\dfrac{a^3 + b^3}{a^2 - b^2}}{\dfrac{a^2 - ab + b^2}{a^2 - 2ab + b^2}}$

When simplifying rational expressions that have negative integers as exponents, first rename the expression to remove the negative exponents and then simplify the new complex rational expression.

EXAMPLE 3 Simplify $\dfrac{1 - 3a^{-1}}{1 - 2a^{-1} - 3a^{-2}}$.

$$\frac{1 - 3a^{-1}}{1 - 2a^{-1} - 3a^{-2}} = \frac{1 - \dfrac{3}{a}}{1 - \dfrac{2}{a} - \dfrac{3}{a^2}}$$ Writing without negative exponents

The denominators are a and a^2, so the LCD is a^2.

$$= \frac{a^2}{a^2} \cdot \frac{\left(1 - \dfrac{3}{a}\right)}{\left(1 - \dfrac{2}{a} - \dfrac{3}{a^2}\right)} = \frac{a^2 - 3a}{a^2 - 2a - 3}$$

$$= \frac{a(a - 3)}{(a + 1)(a - 3)} = \frac{a}{a + 1}$$

Try This Simplify.

e. $\dfrac{x^{-1} + y^{-1}}{x^{-1} + 3y^{-1}}$ **f.** $\dfrac{(x - 2)^{-2}(x + 2)}{\dfrac{1}{(x^2 + x - 2)^{-1}(x^2 - 4)}}$

Reading Math

Writing a complex fraction is easier than reading one unambiguously. For example, $\dfrac{\left(\frac{5}{x}\right)}{\left(\frac{x}{y}\right)}$ should be read "the quotient of the quotient of 5 and x and the quotient of x and y."

Extra Help On the Web

Look for worked-out examples at the Prentice Hall Web site.
www.phschool.com

6-3 Exercises

A

Simplify.

1. $\dfrac{\frac{1}{x} + 4}{\frac{1}{x} - 3}$ **2.** $\dfrac{\frac{1}{y} + 7}{\frac{1}{y} - 5}$ **3.** $\dfrac{x - \frac{1}{x}}{x + \frac{1}{x}}$ **4.** $\dfrac{y + \frac{1}{y}}{y - \frac{1}{y}}$ **5.** $\dfrac{\frac{3}{x} + \frac{4}{y}}{\frac{4}{x} - \frac{3}{y}}$

6. $\dfrac{\frac{2}{y} + \frac{5}{z}}{\frac{1}{y} - \frac{4}{z}}$ **7.** $\dfrac{\frac{x^2 - y^2}{xy}}{\frac{x - y}{y}}$ **8.** $\dfrac{\frac{a^2 - b^2}{ab}}{\frac{a + b}{b}}$ **9.** $\dfrac{a - \frac{3a}{b}}{b - \frac{b}{a}}$ **10.** $\dfrac{1 - \frac{2}{3x}}{x - \frac{4}{9x}}$

11. $\dfrac{\frac{1}{a} + \frac{1}{b}}{\frac{a^2 - b^2}{ab}}$ **12.** $\dfrac{\frac{1}{x} - \frac{1}{y}}{\frac{x^2 - y^2}{xy}}$ **13.** $\dfrac{x^{-3} - x}{x^{-2} - 1}$ **14.** $\dfrac{y^{-3} + y}{y^{-2} + 1}$ **15.** $\dfrac{\frac{y^2 - y - 6}{y^2 - 5y - 14}}{\frac{y^2 + 6y + 5}{y^2 - 6y - 7}}$

16. $\dfrac{\frac{x^2 - x - 12}{x^2 - 2x - 15}}{\frac{x^2 + 8x + 12}{x^2 - 5x - 14}}$ **17.** $\dfrac{\frac{x}{1 - x} + \frac{1 + x}{x}}{\frac{1 - x}{x} + \frac{x}{1 + x}}$ **18.** $\dfrac{\frac{y}{x - y} + \frac{x + y}{y}}{\frac{x - y}{x} + \frac{y}{x + y}}$

19. $\dfrac{5x^{-1} - 5y^{-1} + 10x^{-1}y^{-1}}{6y^{-1} + 12x^{-1}y^{-1}}$ **20.** $\dfrac{\frac{4}{x - 5} + \frac{2}{x + 2}}{\frac{2x}{x^2 - 3x - 10} + \frac{3}{x - 5}}$

B

Find the reciprocal.

21. $\frac{1}{x} + 1$ **22.** $x^2 - \frac{1}{x}$ **23.** $\dfrac{1 - \frac{1}{a}}{a - 1}$ **24.** $\dfrac{a^3 + b^3}{a + b}$

25. ***Critical Thinking*** Find a complex rational expression whose reciprocal is $x + 1$.

Challenge

26. Simplify $1 + \dfrac{1}{1 + \dfrac{1}{1 + \dfrac{1}{1 + \frac{1}{x}}}}$.

27. For $f(x) = \frac{1}{1 - x}$, find $f(f(x))$ and $f(f(f(x)))$.

28. Find and simplify $\dfrac{f(x + h) - f(x)}{h}$ for the rational function $f(x) = \frac{x}{1 + x}$.

Self-Test On the Web

Check your progress. Look for a self-test at the Prentice Hall Web site.
www.phschool.com

Mixed Review

29. The sum of a number and its square is 42 more than twice the number. What is the number?

30. Jeremy received a 14% raise, bringing his salary to $25,080. What was Jeremy's salary before he received the raise? *5-8*

Division of Polynomials

6-4

PART 1 Dividing Polynomials by Monomials

Objective: Divide a polynomial by a monomial.

What You'll Learn

1. To divide a polynomial by a monomial
2. To divide two polynomials when the divisor is not a monomial

. . . And Why

To solve problems involving division of polynomials

Remember that rational expressions indicate division. In some cases, it is useful to carry out that division. Division by a monomial can be done by first writing a rational expression.

EXAMPLE 1 Divide $12x^3 + 8x^2 + x + 4$ by $4x$.

$$\frac{12x^3 + 8x^2 + x + 4}{4x} \qquad \text{Writing a rational expression}$$

$$= \frac{12x^3}{4x} + \frac{8x^2}{4x} + \frac{x}{4x} + \frac{4}{4x} \qquad \text{Using Theorem 6-4}$$

$$= 3x^2 + 2x + \frac{1}{4} + \frac{1}{x} \qquad \text{Simplifying each rational expression}$$

Try This Divide.

a. $\dfrac{x^3 + 16x^2 + 6x}{2x}$

b. $(12x^3 + 3x^2 + 6x) \div 3x$

c. $(4x^7 + 3x^6 + 6x^5 + 12x^4 + 2x^3 + x^2 + 2x) \div 2x$

EXAMPLE 2 Divide $(8x^4 - 3x^3 + 5x^2)$ by x^2.

$$\frac{8x^4 - 3x^3 + 5x^2}{x^2} = \frac{8x^4}{x^2} - \frac{3x^3}{x^2} + \frac{5x^2}{x^2}$$

$$= 8x^2 - 3x + 5$$

Dividing a Polynomial by a Monomial

To divide a polynomial by a monomial, divide each term by the monomial.

Try This Divide.

d. $(15y^5 - 6y^4 + 18y^3) \div 3y^2$

e. $(x^4 + 10x^3 + 16x^2) \div 2x^2$

f. $\dfrac{16y^4 + 4y^3 + 2y^2}{4y}$

Quick Review

In long-division notation, the dividend is inside the division symbol, the divisor is to the left of it, and the quotient is above it. (Note that, as with any fraction, the rational fraction representing the division may also be called a quotient.)

PART 2 Dividing Two Polynomials

Objective: Divide two polynomials when the divisor is not a monomial.

When the divisor is not a monomial, we use a procedure very much like long division.

EXAMPLE 3 Divide $x^2 + 5x + 8$ by $x + 3$.

$$\begin{array}{r l} x & \leftarrow \text{Dividing the first term of the dividend by the first term of the divisor: } \frac{x^2}{x} = x \\ x + 3\overline{)x^2 + 5x + 8} & \\ x^2 + 3x & \text{Multiplying the divisor by } x \\ \hline 2x & \text{Subtracting} \end{array}$$

We now "bring down" 8, the next term of the dividend.

$$\begin{array}{r l} x + 2 & \text{Dividing the first term by the first term of the divisor: } \frac{2x}{x} = 2 \\ x + 3\overline{)x^2 + 5x + 8} & \\ x^2 + 3x & \\ \hline 2x + 8 & \\ 2x + 6 & \text{Multiplying the divisor by 2} \\ \hline 2 & \text{Subtracting} \end{array}$$

The quotient is $x + 2$, the remainder is 2. To check, we multiply the quotient by the divisor and add the remainder to see if we get the dividend.

Quotient · Divisor + Remainder = Dividend

$$(x + 2) \cdot (x + 3) + 2 = (x^2 + 5x + 6) + 2 = x^2 + 5x + 8$$

The answer checks.

Try This Divide and check.

g. $x - 2\overline{)x^2 + 3x - 10}$

Always remember to arrange polynomials in descending order and to leave space for missing terms in the dividend (or write them with 0 coefficients).

EXAMPLE 4 Divide $(125y^3 - 8)$ by $(5y - 2)$.

$$\begin{array}{r l} 25y^2 + 10y + 4 & \\ 5y - 2\overline{)125y^3 + 0y^2 + 0y - 8} & \text{Writing zero coefficients for missing terms} \\ 125y^3 - 50y^2 & \\ \hline 50y^2 + 0y & \\ 50y^2 - 20y & \\ \hline 20y - 8 & \\ 20y - 8 & \\ \hline 0 & \end{array}$$

The quotient is $25y^2 + 10y + 4$.

EXAMPLE 5 Divide $(x^4 - 9x^2 - 5)$ by $(x - 2)$.

$$
\begin{array}{r}
x^3 + 2x^2 - 5x - 10 \\
x - 2\overline{)x^4 + 0x^3 - 9x^2 + 0x - 5} \\
\underline{x^4 - 2x^3} \qquad\qquad\qquad \\
2x^3 - 9x^2 \qquad\qquad \\
\underline{2x^3 - 4x^2} \qquad\qquad \\
-5x^2 \qquad\qquad \\
\underline{-5x^2 + 10x} \qquad \\
-10x - 5 \\
\underline{-10x + 20} \\
-25
\end{array}
$$

The first subtraction is $x^4 - (x^4 - 2x^3)$.

The second subtraction is $(2x^3 - 9x^2) - (2x^3 - 4x^2)$.

The quotient is $x^3 + 2x^2 - 5x - 10$ and the remainder is -25.

This can be written as $x^3 + 2x^2 - 5x - 10$, R -25, or

$$x^3 + 2x^2 - 5x - 10 - \frac{25}{x - 2}$$

The expression in red is the remainder over the divisor.

Try This Divide and check.

h. $(9y^4 + 14y^2 - 8) \div (3y + 2)$

i. $(y^3 - 11y^2 + 6) \div (y - 3)$

When dividing, we continue until the degree of the remainder is less than the degree of the divisor. The answer can be written as a quotient and remainder, or as a polynomial plus a rational expression.

EXAMPLE 6 Divide $(x^3 + 9x^2 - 5)$ by $(x^2 - 1)$.

$$
\begin{array}{r}
x + 9 \qquad\qquad \\
x^2 - 1\overline{)x^3 + 9x^2 \qquad - 5} \\
\underline{x^3 \qquad\quad - x \quad} \\
9x^2 + x - 5 \\
\underline{9x^2 \qquad - 9} \\
x + 4
\end{array}
$$

Leaving space for the missing term

The degree of the remainder is less than the degree of the divisor, so we are finished.

The quotient is $x + 9$, R $x + 4$, or

$$x + 9 + \frac{x + 4}{x^2 - 1}$$

Checking,

$$
\begin{aligned}
(x + 9)(x^2 - 1) + x + 4 &= x^3 - x + 9x^2 - 9 + x + 4 \\
&= x^3 + 9x^2 - 5
\end{aligned}
$$

The answer checks.

Try This Divide and check.

j. $(y^3 - 11y^2 + 6) \div (y^2 - 3)$

Extra Help On the Web

Look for worked-out examples at the Prentice Hall Web site. www.phschool.com

6-4 Exercises

A

Divide.

1. $\dfrac{30x^8 - 15x^6 + 40x^4}{5x^4}$

2. $\dfrac{24y^6 + 18y^5 - 36y^2}{6y^2}$

3. $(9y^4 - 18y^3 + 27y^2) \div 9y$

4. $(24a^3 + 28a^2 - 20a) \div 2a$

5. $(a^2b - a^3b^3 - a^5b^2) \div a^2b$

6. $(6p^2q^2 - 9p^2q + 12pq^2) \div (-3pq)$

7. $(x^2 + 10x + 21) \div (x + 3)$

8. $(y^2 - 8y + 16) \div (y - 4)$

Mental Math For each division state whether or not there is a remainder.

9. $(16y^4z^2 - 8y^6z^4 + 12y^8z^3) \div 4y^4z$

10. $(18y^7 - 27y^4 - 3y^2) \div (-3y^2)$

11. $(a^2 - 8a - 16) \div (a + 4)$

12. $(a^2 - 81) \div (a - 9)$

13. $(8x^3 + 27) \div (2x + 3)$

14. $(x^4 - x^2 - 42) \div (x^2 - 7)$

Divide and check.

15. $(y^2 - 10y - 25) \div (y - 5)$

16. $(y^2 - 25) \div (y + 5)$

17. $(y^3 - 4y^2 + 3y - 6) \div (y - 2)$

18. $(x^3 - 5x^2 + 4x - 7) \div (x - 3)$

19. $(a^3 - a + 12) \div (a - 4)$

20. $(x^3 - x + 6) \div (x + 2)$

21. $(64y^3 - 8) \div (4y - 2)$

22. $(y^4 - y^2 - 54) \div (y^2 - 3)$

23. $(8x^4 - 6x^2 - 2x + 2) \div (2x^2 - 1)$

24. $(y^4 - y^2 - y + 3) \div (y + 1)$

25. $(10y^3 + 6y^2 - 9y + 10) \div (5y - 2)$

B

Divide.

26. $(x^4 - x^3y + x^2y^2 + 2x^2y - 2xy^2 + 2y^3) \div (x^2 - xy + y^2)$

27. $(4a^3b + 5a^2b^2 + a^4 + 2ab^3) \div (a^2 + 2b^2 + 3ab)$

28. $(x^4 - y^4) \div (x - y)$

29. $(a^7 + b^7) \div (a + b)$

30. ***Critical Thinking*** When two rational expressions are divided, the quotient is $5x^2 + 3x + 12 + \frac{7}{x + 5}$. What are the two polynomials?

Challenge

31. ***Mathematical Reasoning*** Find k so that $x^3 - kx^2 + 3x + 7k$ divided by $x + 2$ has remainder 0.

32. ***Mathematical Reasoning*** When $x^2 - 3x + 2k$ is divided by $x + 2$, the remainder is 7. Find the value of k.

Mixed Review

Simplify. **33.** $\dfrac{-16n^5m^{-7}}{-4n^{-3}m^6}$ **34.** $\dfrac{25w^2}{(-5w)^2}$ **35.** $\left(\dfrac{3m^2n^3}{4mn}\right)^2$ **36.** $\left(\dfrac{n^3}{2m^2}\right)^3$ *1-8*

Convert to decimal notation. **37.** 1.04×10^3 **38.** 6.34×10^{-4} *1-9*

Factor. **39.** $y^2 + 12y + 36$ **40.** $16x^2 + 16xy + 4y^2$ **41.** $x^2 - 7x$ *5-4*

Synthetic Division

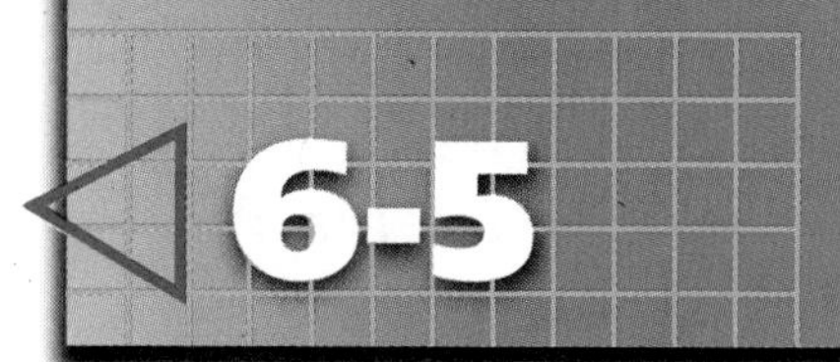

Dividing Using Synthetic Division

Objective: Use synthetic division to find the quotient of certain polynomials.

An **algorithm** is a systematic procedure for doing a certain computation. The division algorithm of the preceding section can be shortened if the divisor is a **linear polynomial** of the form $x - a$.

EXAMPLE 1 Divide $4x^3 + x + 7$ by $x - 2$.

To streamline division, we can arrange the work so that duplicate writing is avoided. Note that we can divide using only the coefficients. Compare B to A.

A.

$$\begin{array}{r}
4x^2 + 8x + 17 \\
x - 2\overline{)4x^3 + 0x^2 + x + 7} \\
\underline{4x^3 - 8x^2} \qquad\qquad \\
8x^2 + x \qquad \\
\underline{8x^2 - 16x} \qquad \\
17x + 7 \\
\underline{17x - 34} \\
\text{Remainder} \qquad 41
\end{array}$$

B.

$$\begin{array}{r}
4 \quad 8 \quad 17 \\
1 - 2\overline{)4 + 0 + 1 + 7} \\
\underline{4 - 8} \qquad\quad \\
8 + 1 \quad \\
\underline{8 - 16} \quad \\
17 + 7 \\
\underline{17 - 34} \\
41
\end{array}$$

We can shorten the division process further by using the additive inverse of -2 in the divisor. The following algorithm, called **synthetic division,** uses addition rather than subtraction and also avoids repeating numbers.

C. Synthetic Division

Divisor Dividend

$$\begin{array}{r|rrrr}
2 & 4 & 0 & 1 & 7 \\
 & \downarrow & & & \\ \hline
 & 4 & & &
\end{array}$$

Writing the 2 of $x - 2$ and the coefficients of the dividend

Bringing down the first coefficient

$$\begin{array}{r|rrrr}
2 & 4 & 0 & 1 & 7 \\
 & & 8 & & \\ \hline
 & 4 & 8 & &
\end{array}$$

Multiplying 4 by 2 to get 8

Adding 0 and 8

$$\begin{array}{r|rrrr}
2 & 4 & 0 & 1 & 7 \\
 & & 8 & 16 & \\ \hline
 & 4 & 8 & 17 &
\end{array}$$

Multiplying 8 by 2 to get 16

Adding 1 and 16

$$\begin{array}{r|rrrr}
2 & 4 & 0 & 1 & 7 \\
 & & 8 & 16 & 34 \\ \hline
 & 4 & 8 & 17 & 41
\end{array}$$

Multiplying 17 by 2 to get 34

Adding 7 and 34

Quotient Remainder

What You'll Learn

1. To divide polynomials by using synthetic division

. . . And Why

To make dividing by a linear factor more efficient

The last number, 41, is the remainder. The other numbers are the coefficients of the quotient, with that of the term of highest degree first. Since the divisor is of the first degree, the degree of the quotient is one less than the degree of the dividend.

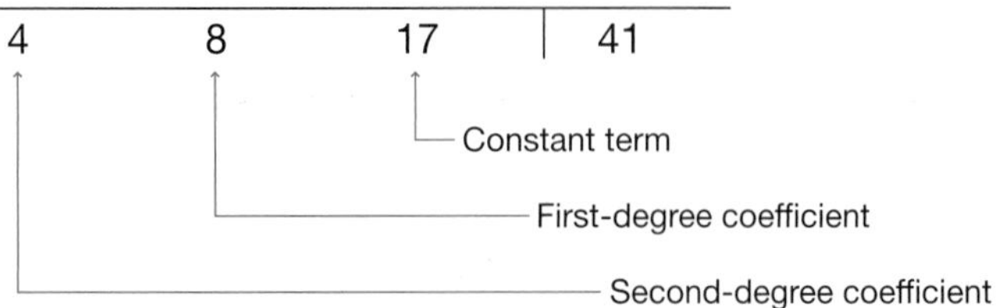

The quotient is $4x^2 + 8x + 17$; the remainder is 41.

Remember that for this method to work, the divisor *must* be in the form $x - a$.

Journal

The synthetic division below represents division of a cubic polynomial $C(x)$ by a linear polynomial $L(x)$. Write the algebraic sentence that represents $C(x) =$ Quotient $\cdot L(x) +$ Remainder and explain your reasoning.

$$\begin{array}{r|rrrr} -2 & 1 & 0 & 1 & 0 \\ & & -2 & 4 & -10 \\ \hline & 1 & -2 & 5 & -10 \end{array}$$

EXAMPLE 2 Use synthetic division to find the quotient and remainder.

$(x^3 + 6x^2 - x - 30) \div (x - 2)$

$$\begin{array}{r|rrrr} 2 & 1 & 6 & -1 & -30 \\ & & 2 & 16 & 30 \\ \hline & 1 & 8 & 15 & 0 \end{array}$$

Writing the 2 of $x - 2$ and the coefficients of the dividend

Using synthetic division

The quotient is $x^2 + 8x + 15$, the remainder is 0.

Try This Use synthetic division to find the quotient and remainder.

a. $(x^3 + 5x^2 - 9x - 45) \div (x - 3)$
b. $(8x^2 - 12x + 4) \div (x - 3)$

EXAMPLES Use synthetic division to find the quotient and remainder.

3 $(2x^3 + 7x^2 - 5) \div (x + 3)$

There is no first degree x-term in the dividend, so we must write a 0 for that coefficient. To write the divisor $x + 3$ as a difference, we write $x - (-3)$.

$$\begin{array}{r|rrrr} -3 & 2 & 7 & 0 & -5 \\ & & -6 & -3 & 9 \\ \hline & 2 & 1 & -3 & 4 \end{array}$$

The quotient is $2x^2 + 1x - 3$, the remainder is 4.

4 $\dfrac{8x^5 - 6x^3 + x - 8}{x + 2}$

$$\begin{array}{r|rrrrrr} -2 & 8 & 0 & -6 & 0 & 1 & -8 \\ & & -16 & 32 & -52 & 104 & -210 \\ \hline & 8 & -16 & 26 & -52 & 105 & -218 \end{array}$$

Note: We must write 0s for missing terms.

The quotient is $8x^4 - 16x^3 + 26x^2 - 52x + 105$, the remainder is -218.

Try This Use synthetic division to find the quotient and the remainder.

c. $(x^3 - 2x^2 + 5x - 4) \div (x + 2)$ **d.** $(y^3 + 1) \div (y + 1)$

6-5 Exercises

Extra Help On the Web

Look for worked-out examples at the Prentice Hall Web site.
www.phschool.com

A

Use synthetic division to find the quotient and remainder.

1. $(x^3 - 2x^2 + 2x + 5) \div (x - 1)$ **2.** $(x^3 - 2x^2 + 2x + 5) \div (x + 1)$

3. $(a^2 + 11a - 19) \div (a + 4)$ **4.** $(a^2 + 11a - 19) \div (a - 4)$

5. $(y^3 - 3y + 10) \div (y - 2)$ **6.** $(x^3 - 2x^2 + 8) \div (x + 2)$

7. $(9x^3 - 15x^2 + 4x) \div (x - 3)$ **8.** $(6y^4 + 15y^3 + 6) \div (y + 3)$

9. $(x^3 - 27) \div (x - 3)$ **10.** $(x^5 - 32) \div (x - 2)$

11. $(5x^2 - 7x) \div (x - 3)$ **12.** $(3x^4 - 5x^2 + 10) \div (x - 7)$

Error Analysis Are these synthetic divisions correct? If not, explain why not, and write the work correctly.

13.

$$\begin{array}{r|rrrr} 4 & 4 & -4 & 4 & -9 \\ & & 16 & -80 & -304 \\ \hline & 4 & -20 & -76 & -313 \end{array}$$

14.

$$\begin{array}{r|rrrrr} -5 & 1 & 0 & 0 & 5 & 0 \\ & & -5 & 25 & -125 & 600 \\ \hline & 1 & -5 & 25 & -120 & 600 \end{array}$$

B

Use synthetic division and a calculator to find the quotient and remainder.

15. $(3x^4 - 24x^2 - 13) \div (x - 2.41)$ **16.** $(5x^5 + 11x^3 + 217) \div (x + 17.07)$

17. ***Critical Thinking*** $P(x) = 8x^5 - 3x^4 + 7x - 4$.

a. Find the remainder using synthetic division. $P(x) \div (x - 2)$; $P(x) \div (x + 4)$.

b. Find $P(2)$; $P(-4)$.

c. Compare the answers and the algorithms.

Challenge

18. Devise a procedure to use synthetic division when the divisor is a linear polynomial $ax + b$ with a leading coefficient different from 1. Use the procedure to divide $12x^4 - 30x^2 + 30x - 12$ by $6x + 12$.

19. Use synthetic division to divide $7x^9 - 15x^6 - 3x^3 + 10$ by $x^3 - 3$.

Mixed Review

Give the domain of each of the following functions. **20.** $f(x) = x^2$

21. $f(x) = \frac{7}{x + 3}$ **22.** $f(x) = \frac{2}{x + 2x}$ **23.** $f(x) = \frac{6}{x(x + 3)}$ **24.** $f(x) = \frac{1}{2 + x^2}$ 3-3

Factor. **25.** $8x^2 - 8xy + 2y^2$ **26.** $9y^2 - x^2 - 2x - 1$ **27.** $27x^3 - 1$ 5-6

6-6 Solving Rational Equations

What You'll Learn

1. To solve rational equations

. . . And Why

To solve problems using rational equations

PART 1 Solutions of Rational Equations

Objective: Solve rational equations.

A **rational equation** is an equation that contains one or more rational expressions. These are rational equations.

$$\frac{2}{3} + \frac{5}{6} = \frac{1}{x}, \qquad \frac{x-1}{x-5} = \frac{4}{x-5}$$

To solve a rational equation, we multiply both sides by the LCD to clear fractions.

EXAMPLE 1 Solve $\frac{2}{3} - \frac{5}{6} = \frac{1}{x}$.

The LCD is $6x$.

$$\begin{aligned} 6x\left(\frac{2}{3} - \frac{5}{6}\right) &= 6x\left(\frac{1}{x}\right) && \text{Multiplying by the LCD} \\ 6x\left(\frac{2}{3}\right) - 6x\left(\frac{5}{6}\right) &= 6x\left(\frac{1}{x}\right) && \text{Multiplying to remove parentheses} \\ 4x - 5x &= 6 && \text{Simplifying} \\ -x &= 6 \\ x &= -6 \end{aligned}$$

Check:

$\frac{2}{3} - \frac{5}{6}$	$= \frac{1}{x}$
$\frac{2}{3} - \frac{5}{6}$	$\frac{1}{-6}$
$\frac{4}{6} - \frac{5}{6}$	$-\frac{1}{6}$
$-\frac{1}{6}$	$-\frac{1}{6}$ ✓

When clearing fractions, be sure to multiply every term in the equation by the LCD. This yields an equation without rational expressions, which can be solved directly.

Try This Solve.

a. $\frac{2}{3} + \frac{5}{6} = \frac{1}{x}$ **b.** $\frac{1}{8} - \frac{2}{5} = \frac{3}{x}$

When we multiply both sides of an equation by an expression containing a variable, we may not get an equivalent equation. The new equation may have solutions that the original one does not. Thus we must *always* check possible solutions in the *original* equation.

EXAMPLE 2 Solve $\frac{x-1}{x-5} = \frac{4}{x-5}$.

The LCD is $x - 5$. We multiply by $x - 5$ to clear fractions.

$$(x-5)\cdot\frac{x-1}{x-5} = (x-5)\cdot\frac{4}{x-5}$$
$$x - 1 = 4$$
$$x = 5$$

Check: $\frac{x-1}{x-5} = \frac{4}{x-5}$

$\frac{5-1}{5-5}$	$\frac{4}{5-5}$
$\frac{4}{0}$	$\frac{4}{0}$

5 is not a solution of the original equation because it results in division by 0. Since 5 is the only possible solution, the equation has no solution.

Try This Solve.

c. $\frac{y-2}{5} - \frac{y-5}{4} = -2$

d. $\frac{x-7}{x-9} = \frac{2}{x-9}$

EXAMPLE 3 Solve $\frac{x^2}{x-2} = \frac{4}{x-2}$.

The LCD is $x - 2$. We multiply by $x - 2$.

$$(x-2)\cdot\frac{x^2}{x-2} = (x-2)\cdot\frac{4}{x-2}$$
$$x^2 = 4$$
$$x^2 - 4 = 0$$
$$(x+2)(x-2) = 0$$
$$x = -2 \text{ or } x = 2 \quad \text{Using the principle of zero products}$$

Check: For -2: $\frac{x^2}{x-2} = \frac{4}{x-2}$

$\frac{(-2)^2}{-2-2}$	$\frac{4}{-2-2}$
$\frac{4}{-4}$	$\frac{4}{-4}$
-1	-1 ✔

For 2: $\frac{x^2}{x-2} = \frac{4}{x-2}$

$\frac{2^2}{2-2}$	$\frac{4}{2-2}$
$\frac{4}{0}$	$\frac{4}{0}$

The number -2 is a solution, but 2 is not since it results in division by 0.

EXAMPLE 4 Solve $x + \frac{6}{x} = 5$.

The LCD is x. We multiply both sides by x.

$$x\left(x + \frac{6}{x}\right) = 5 \cdot x \quad \text{Multiplying both sides by } x$$
$$x^2 + x \cdot \frac{6}{x} = 5x$$
$$x^2 + 6 = 5x \quad \text{Simplifying}$$
$$x^2 - 5x + 6 = 0 \quad \text{Using the addition principle}$$
$$(x - 3)(x - 2) = 0 \quad \text{Factoring}$$
$$x = 3 \text{ or } x = 2 \quad \text{Using the principle of zero products}$$

Check: $x + \frac{6}{x} = 5$

$2 + \frac{6}{2}$	5
5	5 ✔

$x + \frac{6}{x} = 5$

$3 + \frac{6}{3}$	5
5	5 ✔

The solutions are 2 and 3.

Try This Solve.

e. $\frac{x^2}{x + 3} = \frac{9}{x + 3}$

f. $x - \frac{12}{x} = 1$

g. $1 + \frac{1}{x} = 2x$

h. $2 - \frac{1}{x^2} = \frac{1}{x}$

EXAMPLE 5 Solve $\frac{2}{x + 5} + \frac{1}{x - 5} = \frac{16}{x^2 - 25}$.

The LCD is $(x + 5)(x - 5)$. We multiply both sides of the equation by $(x + 5)(x - 5)$.

$$(x + 5)(x - 5) \cdot \left[\frac{2}{x + 5} + \frac{1}{x - 5}\right] = (x + 5)(x - 5) \cdot \frac{16}{x^2 - 25}$$
$$(x + 5)(x - 5) \cdot \frac{2}{x + 5} + (x + 5)(x - 5) \cdot \frac{1}{x - 5} = (x + 5)(x - 5) \cdot \frac{16}{x^2 - 25}$$
$$2(x - 5) + (x + 5) = 16$$
$$2x - 10 + x + 5 = 16$$
$$x = 7$$

This checks in the original equation, so the solution is 7.

Try This Solve.

i. $\frac{2}{x - 1} = \frac{3}{x + 2}$

j. $\frac{2}{x^2 - 9} + \frac{5}{x - 3} = \frac{3}{x + 3}$

6-6 Exercises

Extra Help On the Web

Look for worked-out examples at the Prentice Hall Web site.
www.phschool.com

A

Solve.

1. $\frac{2}{5} + \frac{7}{8} = \frac{y}{20}$ **2.** $\frac{1}{3} - \frac{5}{6} = \frac{1}{x}$ **3.** $\frac{5}{8} - \frac{2}{5} = \frac{1}{y}$

4. $\frac{x}{3} - \frac{x}{4} = 12$ **5.** $y + \frac{5}{y} = -6$ **6.** $\frac{y+2}{4} - \frac{y-1}{5} = 15$

7. $\frac{x+1}{3} - \frac{x-1}{2} = 1$ **8.** $\frac{4}{3y} - \frac{3}{y} = \frac{10}{3}$ **9.** $\frac{x-3}{x+2} = \frac{1}{5}$

10. $\frac{y-5}{y+1} = \frac{3}{5}$ **11.** $\frac{y-1}{y-3} = \frac{2}{y-3}$ **12.** $\frac{3}{y+1} = \frac{2}{y-3}$

13. $\frac{x+1}{x} = \frac{3}{2}$ **14.** $\frac{y+2}{y} = \frac{5}{3}$ **15.** $\frac{2}{x} - \frac{3}{x} + \frac{4}{x} = 5$

16. $\frac{4}{y} - \frac{6}{y} + \frac{8}{y} = 8$ **17.** $\frac{1}{2} + \frac{2}{x} = \frac{1}{3} + \frac{3}{x}$ **18.** $-\frac{1}{3} - \frac{5}{4y} = \frac{3}{4} - \frac{1}{6y}$

19. $\frac{60}{x} - \frac{60}{x-5} = \frac{2}{x}$ **20.** $\frac{50}{y} - \frac{50}{y-2} = \frac{4}{y}$ **21.** $\frac{7}{5x-2} = \frac{5}{4x}$

22. $\frac{1}{2t} - \frac{2}{5t} = \frac{1}{10t} - 3$ **23.** $\frac{x}{x-2} + \frac{x}{x^2-4} = \frac{x+3}{x+2}$

24. $\frac{3}{y-2} + \frac{2y}{4-y^2} = \frac{5}{y+2}$ **25.** $\frac{a}{2a-6} - \frac{3}{a^2-6a+9} = \frac{a-2}{3a-9}$

26. $\frac{2}{x+4} + \frac{2x-1}{x^2+2x-8} = \frac{1}{x-2}$ **27.** $\frac{2x+3}{x-1} = \frac{10}{x^2-1} + \frac{2x-3}{x+1}$

B

Equations that are true for all acceptable replacements of the variables are *identities*. Determine which equations are identities.

28. $\frac{x^2+6x-16}{x-2} = x + 8$ **29.** $\frac{x^3+8}{x^2-4} = \frac{x^2-2x+4}{x-2}$

30. *Critical Thinking* Write a rational equation that cannot have 2 or -7 as solutions.

Challenge

Solve.

31. $\frac{x^3+8}{x+2} = x^2 - 2x + 4$ **32.** $\frac{(x-3)^2}{x-3} = x - 3$

33. $\frac{x+3}{x+2} - \frac{x+4}{x+3} = \frac{x+5}{x+4} - \frac{x+6}{x+5}$ **34.** $\left(\frac{y+3}{y-1}\right)^2 - 2 = \frac{y+3}{y-1}$

Mixed Review

Simplify. **35.** $\frac{25y^2}{10y}$ **36.** $\frac{6x+12}{6}$ **37.** $\frac{3x+9}{3x-9}$ **38.** $\frac{x^2-y^2}{x^3-y^3}$ *6-1*

Evaluate for $a = 2.5, b = 3$. **39.** $2(a-b)$ **40.** $b(b^2-a)$ **41.** $(a+b)(a-b)$ *1-3*

6-7 Using Rational Equations

What You'll Learn

1. To solve work problems using rational equations
2. To solve motion problems using rational equations

. . . And Why

To apply algebraic models to real-world situations

PART 1 Work Problems

Objective: Solve work problems using rational equations.

Tom knows that he can mow a golf course in 4 hours. He also knows that Perry takes 5 hours to mow the same course. Tom must complete the job in $2\frac{1}{2}$ hours. Can he and Perry get the job done in time? How long will it take them to complete the job together?

If Perry gets a larger mower so that he can mow the course alone in $3\frac{1}{4}$ hours, how long will it take Tom and Perry to complete the job together?

Solving Work Problems

If a job can be done in t hours, then $\frac{1}{t}$ of it can be done in one hour. (The above condition holds for any unit of time.)

EXAMPLE 1 Tom can mow a lawn in 4 hours. Perry can mow the same lawn in 5 hours. How long would it take both of them, working together with two lawn mowers, to mow the lawn?

■ **UNDERSTAND the problem**

Question: How long will it take the two of them to mow the lawn together? — Clarifying the question

Data: Tom takes 4 hours to mow the lawn. Perry takes 5 hours to mow the lawn. — Identifying the data

■ **Develop and carry out a PLAN**

Let t represent the total number of hours it takes them working together. Then they can mow $\frac{1}{t}$ of it in 1 hour.

We can now translate to an equation.

$\frac{1}{4} + \frac{1}{5} = \frac{1}{t}$ Translating to an equation

We solve the equation.

$$20t\left(\frac{1}{4} + \frac{1}{5}\right) = 20t\left(\frac{1}{t}\right)$$ Multiplying on both sides by the LCD to clear fractions

$$\frac{20t}{4} + \frac{20t}{5} = \frac{20t}{t}$$

$$5t + 4t = 20$$

$$9t = 20$$

$$t = \frac{20}{9}, \text{ or } 2\tfrac{2}{9} \text{ hours}$$

Find the ANSWER and CHECK

Tom can do the entire job in 4 hours, so he can do *just over half* in $2\frac{2}{9}$ hours. Perry can do the entire job in 5 hours, so he can do *just under half* the job in $2\frac{2}{9}$ hours. It is reasonable that working together they can finish the job in $2\frac{2}{9}$ hours.

It will take them $2\frac{2}{9}$ hours together, so they will finish in time.

Try This

a. Carlos can do a typing job in 6 hours. Lynn can do the same job in 4 hours. How long would it take them to do the job working together with two typewriters?

EXAMPLE 2

At a factory, smokestack A pollutes the air twice as fast as smokestack B. When the stacks operate together, they yield a certain amount of pollution in 15 hours. Find the time it would take each to yield that same amount of pollution operating alone.

Let x represent the number of hours it takes A to yield the pollution. Then $2x$ is the number of hours it takes B to yield the same amount of pollution.

$\frac{1}{x}$ is the fraction of the pollution produced by A in 1 hour.

$\frac{1}{2x}$ is the fraction of the pollution produced by B in 1 hour.

Together the stacks yield $\frac{1}{x} + \frac{1}{2x}$ of the total pollution in 1 hour. They also yield $\frac{1}{15}$ of it in 1 hour. Now we have an equation.

$\frac{1}{x} + \frac{1}{2x} = \frac{1}{15}$ This is the translation.

Solving for x we get $x = 22\frac{1}{2}$ hours for smokestack A, and $2x$ or 45 hours for smokestack B. This checks.

Try This

b. Pipe A can fill a tank three times as fast as pipe B. Together they can fill the tank in 24 hours. Find the time it takes each pipe to fill the tank.

PART 2 Motion Problems

Objective: Solve motion problems using rational equations.

Recall from Chapter 4 the formula for distance, $d = rt$. From this we can easily obtain rational equations for time and for the rate of speed.

$$t = \frac{d}{r} \text{ and } r = \frac{d}{t}$$

We can use these equations to solve motion problems.

If a plane flies 430 mi/h with the wind and 214 mi/h against the same wind, how long will it take to travel 500 mi with no wind?

EXAMPLE 3

An airplane files 1062 km with the wind. In the same amount of time it can fly 738 km against the wind. The speed of the plane in still air is 200 km/h. Find the speed of the wind.

■ **UNDERSTAND the problem**

Question: What is the speed of the wind? — Clarifying the problem

Data: An airplane has a speed of 200 km/h. The airplane flies 1062 km with the wind. The airplane can only fly 738 km against the wind in the same time. — Identifying the data

■ **Develop and carry out a PLAN**

First *draw a diagram.* Let r represent the speed of the wind and organize the facts in a *chart.*

1062 km — t hours
$200 + r$ (The wind increases the speed.)

t hours — 738 km
$200 - r$ (The wind decreases the speed.)

	Distance	Rate	Time
With wind	1062	$200 + r$	t
Against wind	738	$200 - r$	t

The times are the same, so we write the equations in the form $t = \frac{d}{r}$.

$$t = \frac{1062}{200 + r} \text{ and } t = \frac{738}{200 - r}$$ This is the translation.

Using substitution, we obtain $\frac{1062}{200 + r} = \frac{738}{200 - r}$.

Solving for r, we get 36.

■ **Find the ANSWER and CHECK**

The number 36 checks in the equation. A 36 km/h wind also makes sense in the problem. With the wind, the plane has a speed of 236 km/h. If it travels 1062 km, it must fly for 4.5 hours. Against the wind, the plane travels at 164 km/h. It will travel 738 km, also in 4.5 hours.

Thus, the speed of the wind is 36 km/h. Stating the answer clearly

Try This

c. A boat travels 246 mi downstream in the same time it takes to travel 180 mi upstream. The speed of the current in the stream is 5.5 mi/h. Find the speed of the boat in still water.

6-7 Exercises

Extra Help On the Web

Look for worked-out examples at the Prentice Hall Web site.
www.phschool.com

A

1. Antonio, an experienced shipping clerk, can fill a certain order in 5 hours. Brian, a new clerk, needs 9 hours to do the same job. Working together, how long would it take them to fill the order?

2. Leslie can paint a room in 4 hours. Fran can paint the same room in 3 hours. Working together, how long would it take them to paint the room?

3. Sheila can frame in a room in 5 hours. David can do the same job in 4 hours. Working together, how long would it take them to frame in a room?

4. Andrew can complete a plumbing job in 6 hours. Vivian can do the same job in 4 hours. Working together, how long would it take them to complete the job?

5. **TEST PREP** ***Mathematical Reasoning*** If Jacob takes x hours to do a job and Rebecca takes y hours to do the same job, and $x > y$, then how many hours working together will it take them to do the job?

A. $x + y$ hours **B.** $x - y$ hours

C. less than y hours **D.** between x and y hours

6. A swimming pool can be filled using either a pipe, a hose, or both. Using the pipe alone it takes 12 hours. Using both it takes $8\frac{4}{7}$ hours. How long does it take using the hose alone?

7. A tank can be filled using pipes A, B, or both. It takes pipe A, running alone, 18 hours to fill the tank. It takes both pipes, running together, 9.9 hours to fill the tank. How long does it take pipe B, running alone, to fill the tank?

8. Ally can clear a lot in 5.5 hours. Her partner can do the same job in 7.5 hours. How long would it take them to clear the lot working together?

9. One printing press can print an order of booklets in 4.5 hours. Another press can do the same job in 5.5 hours. How long would it take if both presses are used?

10. The speed of a stream is 3 km/h. A boat travels 4 km upstream in the same time it takes to travel 10 km downstream. What is the speed of the boat in still water?
11. The speed of a stream is 4 km/h. A boat travels 6 km upstream in the same time it takes to travel 12 km downstream. What is the speed of the boat in still water?
12. The speed of train A is 12 km/h slower than the speed of train B. Train A travels 230 km in the same time it takes train B to travel 290 km. Find the speed of each.
13. The speed of train X is 14 km/h faster than the speed of train Y. Train X travels 400 km in the same time it takes train Y to travel 330 km. Find the speed of each.
14. Manuel has a boat that can move at a speed of 15 km/h in still water. He rides 140 km downstream in a river in the same time it takes to ride 35 km upstream. What is the speed of the river?
15. A paddleboat can move at a speed of 2 km/h in still water. The boat is paddled 4 km downstream in a river in the same time it takes to go 1 km upstream. What is the speed of the river?
16. ***Multi-Step Problem*** Sue Chin has just enough money to rent a canoe for 1.5 hours. How far out on a lake can she paddle and return on time if she paddles out at 2 km/h and back at 4 km/h?
17. ***Multi-Step Problem*** Kelly has just enough money to rent a canoe for 2.5 hours. How far out on the lake can she paddle and return on time if she paddles out at 3 km/h and back at 2 km/h?
18. One car travels 25 km/h faster than another. While one travels 300 km the other travels 450 km. Find their speeds.
19. One car travels 30 km/h faster than another. While one travels 450 km the other travels 600 km. Find their speeds.
20. The sum of the reciprocal of 5 and the reciprocal of 7 is the reciprocal of what number?
21. The sum of the reciprocal of 3 and the reciprocal of 6 is the reciprocal of what number?
22. The sum of a number and 6 times its reciprocal is -5. Find the number.
23. The sum of a number and 21 times its reciprocal is -10. Find the number.

B

24. In a rational numeral the numerator is 3 more than the denominator. If 2 is added to both numerator and denominator, the result is $\frac{3}{2}$. Find the original numeral.
25. In a rational numeral the denominator is 8 more than the numerator. If 5 is subtracted from both numerator and denominator, the result is $\frac{1}{2}$. Find the original numeral.

Average speed is defined as a total distance divided by total time.

26. Wayne drove 3 hours on a freeway at 55 mi/h and then drove 10 miles in the city at 35 mi/h. What was his average speed?
27. For the first 100 miles of a 200 mile trip, Deborah drove at a speed of 40 mi/h. For the second half of the trip, she drove at a speed of 60 mi/h. What was the average speed for the entire trip? (It was not 50 mi/h.)

28. Donna drove half the distance of a trip at 40 mi/h. At what speed would she have to drive for the rest of the distance so that the average speed for the entire trip would be 45 mi/h?

29. *Critical Thinking* Trucks A, B, and C, working together, can move a load of sand in t hours. When working alone, it takes truck A one extra hour to move the sand; B, six extra hours; and C, t extra hours. Find t.

30. At what time after 4:00 will the minute hand and the hour hand of a clock first be in the same position?

31. At what time after 10:30 will the hands of a clock first be perpendicular?

Challenge

Write a Convincing Argument Solve the two problems below. Write an argument to convince a classmate that your solutions are correct.

32. An employee drove to work on Monday at 45 mi/h and arrived one minute early. The employee drove to work on Tuesday, leaving home at the same time driving 40 mi/h and arriving one minute late.

a. How far does the employee live from work?

b. At what speed should the employee drive to arrive five minutes early?

33. The *point of no return* for an airplane, flying over water from point A on land to point B on land, is that distance into the trip for which it takes just as much time to go on to B as it does to return to A. The distance from San Francisco to Honolulu is 2387 miles. A plane leaves San Francisco at a speed, in still air, of 400 mi/h. There is a 50 mi/h tail wind.

Shown is the Golden Gate Bridge in San Francisco. (See Exercise 33.)

a. Find the point of no return.

b. After traveling 1042 miles, the pilot of the plane determines that it is necessary to make an emergency landing. Would it require less time to continue to Honolulu or to return to San Francisco?

Mixed Review

Simplify. **34.** $\dfrac{\frac{1}{x} + 2}{\frac{1}{x} - 5}$ **35.** $\dfrac{y - \frac{2}{y}}{y + \frac{2}{y}}$ **36.** $\dfrac{\frac{3}{x} + \frac{2}{y}}{\frac{2}{x} - \frac{3}{y}}$ 6-3

Factor. **37.** $8x^2 + 12x - 8$ **38.** $2x^2 + x - 3$ **39.** $x^3 + 27$ 5-5, 5-6

Solve. **40.** $x^2 + 3x + 2 = 0$ **41.** $y^2 + 12y + 36 = 0$ **42.** $6 = 0.8m$ 5-7

6-8 Formulas

What You'll Learn

1. To solve rational formulas for a specified variable
2. To use formulas to solve problems

. . . And Why

To make solving problems easier

In 1994, Greg Maddux pitched 202 innings for an earned-run average of 1.56. In 1999 his ERA was 3.57 when he pitched 219.1 innings. How many more earned runs were scored against him in 1999 than in 1994?

PART 1 Solving Rational Formulas

Objective: Solve rational formulas for a specified variable.

The formula for calculating a pitcher's earned run average (ERA) is $A = \frac{9R}{I}$ where A is the ERA, R is the number of earned runs, and I is the number of innings pitched. If we know the ERA and the number of earned runs we can find the number of innings pitched by solving the formula for I. To solve a rational formula for a specific letter we can use the same techniques as we use to solve rational equations.

EXAMPLE 1 Solve the formula $A = \frac{9R}{I}$ for I.

$$I \cdot A = I \cdot \frac{9R}{I} \quad \text{Clearing fractions}$$
$$I \cdot A = 9R$$
$$I = \frac{9R}{A}$$

From the formula solved for I, you can calculate the number of innings a pitcher pitched if you know the pitcher's ERA and the number of earned runs the pitcher gave up.

Try This

a. The formula $\frac{PV}{T} = k$ relates the pressure, volume, and temperature of a gas. Solve it for T.

PART 2 Solving Problems by Using Formulas

Objective: Solve problems involving the use of a formula.

It may be necessary to look up a formula or a definition to understand a problem fully. You may then need to solve a formula for a certain variable.

EXAMPLE 2

Two electrical resistors are connected in parallel. The resistance of one of them is 6 ohms and the resistance of the combination is 3.75 ohms. What is the resistance of the other resistor?

UNDERSTAND the problem

In a book on electricity or physics, we find that resistors in parallel are diagrammed as at the right.

Using a reference to find missing information

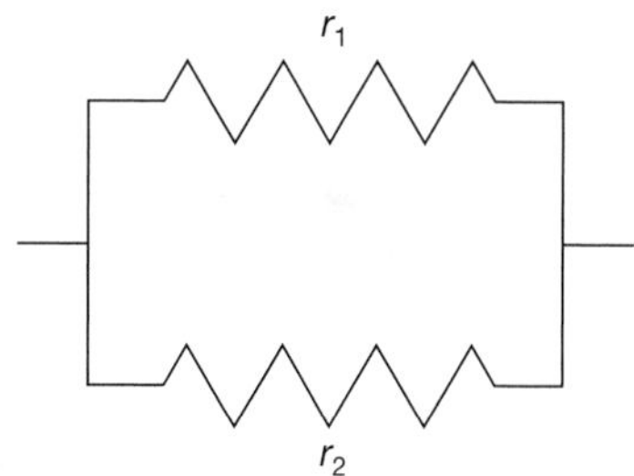

The rule for finding the resistance of a combination is given by the formula $\frac{1}{R} = \frac{1}{r_1} + \frac{1}{r_2}$, where r_1 and r_2 are the resistances of the individual resistors, and R is the resistance of the combination. In this problem we know $R = 3.75$ ohms and $r_1 = 6$ ohms. We want to find r_2.

Develop and carry out a PLAN

We solve the formula for the unknown resistance r_2.

$$\frac{1}{R} = \frac{1}{r_1} + \frac{1}{r_2}$$

$$Rr_1r_2\left(\frac{1}{R}\right) = Rr_1r_2\left(\frac{1}{r_1} + \frac{1}{r_2}\right)$$ Multiplying by Rr_1r_2

$$r_1r_2 = Rr_2 + Rr_1$$ Simplifying

$$r_1r_2 - Rr_2 = Rr_1$$ Adding $-Rr_2$ to both sides

$$r_2(r_1 - R) = Rr_1$$

$$r_2 = \frac{Rr_1}{r_1 - R}$$

We now substitute into the formula.

$$r_2 = \frac{3.75(6)}{6 - 3.75} = \frac{22.5}{2.25} = 10$$

Find the ANSWER and CHECK

The resistor has a resistance of 10 ohms.

10 ohms checks in the original formula.

Try This

b. The formula $\frac{1}{p} + \frac{1}{q} = \frac{1}{f}$ applies to a lens. The distance from an object to the lens and from the image to the lens are represented, respectively, by p and q. The focal length of the lens is represented by f. Find the focal length of a lens that forms an image 15 cm from the lens when an object is placed 10 cm from the lens.

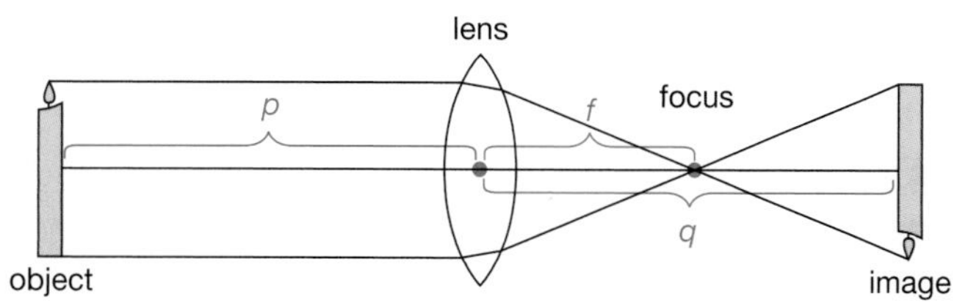

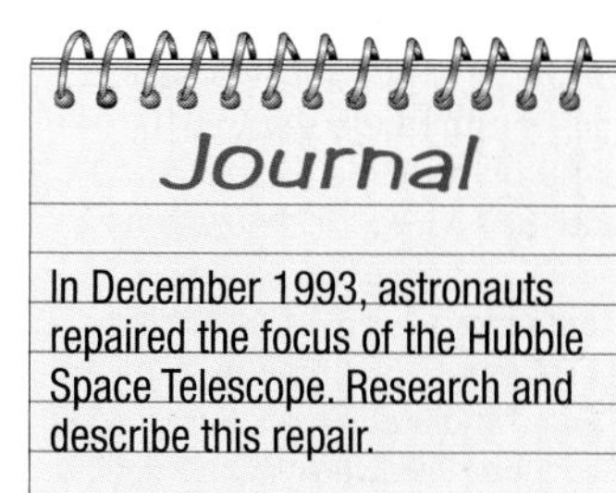

Extra Help On the Web

Look for worked-out examples at the Prentice Hall Web site.
www.phschool.com

6-8 Exercises

A

Solve each formula for the given letter.

1. $\frac{W_1}{W_2} = \frac{d_1}{d_2}$; d_1
2. $\frac{W_1}{W_2} = \frac{d_1}{d_2}$; W_2
3. $S = \frac{1}{2}v_1t + \frac{1}{2}v_2t$; t
4. $S = \frac{1}{2}v_1t + \frac{1}{2}v_2t$; v_1
5. $\frac{1}{R} = \frac{1}{r_1} + \frac{1}{r_2}$; r_2
6. $\frac{1}{R} = \frac{1}{r_1} + \frac{1}{r_2}$; R
7. $R = \frac{gs}{g + s}$; s
8. $R = \frac{gs}{g + s}$; g
9. $I = \frac{2V}{R + 2r}$; r
10. $I = \frac{2V}{R + 2r}$; R
11. $I = \frac{nE}{R + nr}$; r
12. $I = \frac{nE}{R + nr}$; n
13. $S = \frac{H}{m(t_1 - t_2)}$; H
14. $S = \frac{H}{m(t_1 - t_2)}$; t_1
15. $\frac{E}{e} = \frac{R + r}{r}$; e
16. $\frac{E}{e} = \frac{R + r}{r}$; r
17. $S = \frac{a - ar^n}{1 - r}$; a
18. $S = \frac{a}{1 - r}$; r
19. Two resistors are connected in parallel. Their resistances are 8 ohms and 15 ohms. What is the resistance of the combination?
20. A resistor has a resistance of 30 ohms. What size resistor should be put with it, in parallel, to obtain a resistance of 3 ohms?
21. A lens with a focal length of 8 cm forms an image of an object that is 24 cm away from it. How far from the lens is the image?
22. A pitcher's earned run average is 2.40, and he has pitched 45 innings. How many earned runs were given up?

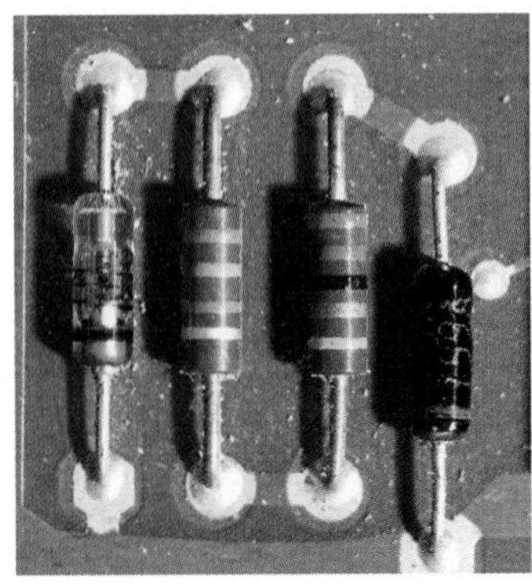

The color bands around a resistor are a code indicating its resistance. For example, the colors on the resistor second from the left are coded as red, white, red, and silver, and so its resistance is $29 \times 10^2\ \Omega \pm 10\%$. Its resistance falls in the range from 2610 to 3190 ohms. (See Exercises 19 and 20.)

B

23. Working alone, Pam can do a certain job in a hours while Elaine can do the same job in b hours. Working together, it takes them t hours to do the job.
    a. Find a formula for t.
    b. Solve the formula for a.
    c. Solve the formula for b.
24. *Critical Thinking* The harmonic mean of two numbers, a and b, is a number M, such that the reciprocal of M is the average of the reciprocals of a and b. Find a formula for the harmonic mean.

Challenge

25. In a physics book, find the formula for *centripetal force.* Solve the formula for r. Find the length of a string fastened to a 5-kg mass being spun at a speed of 3 meters per second (m/s) and that has a centripetal force of 22.5 newtons acting upon it.

Mixed Review

Find the least common multiple. **26.** $24xy, 6x^3, 8y^2$ **27.** $3a, 6b, 7a$ 6-2

Solve. **28.** $x^2 + x - 12 = 0$ **29.** $x^2 + 10x + 21 = 0$ **30.** $x^2 - 25 = 0$ 5-7

Variation and Problem Solving

6-9

PART 1 Direct Variation

Objective: Find the constant of variation and an equation of variation for direct variation problems.

What You'll Learn

1. To find the constant and an equation of variation for direct variation problems
2. To find the constant and an equation of variation for inverse variation problems
3. To solve direct and inverse variation problems

. . . And Why

To apply algebraic models to real-world situations

An apprentice plumber earns \$35 per hour. In 2 hours \$70 is earned. In 3 hours \$105 is earned, and so on. This pattern results in a set of ordered pairs of numbers, all having the same ratio.

$$(1, 35), (2, 70), (3, 105), (4, 140), \ldots$$

The ratio of earnings to time is $\frac{35}{1}$ in every case.

Whenever a situation results in pairs of numbers in which the ratio is constant, we say that there is **direct variation.** Here the earnings **vary directly** with the time, t.

$$\frac{E}{t} = 35 \text{ (a constant), or } E = 35t$$

Definition

Whenever a situation translates to a linear function $f(x) = kx$, or $y = kx$, where k is a nonzero constant, we say that there is **direct variation,** or that y **varies directly** with x. The number k is the **constant of variation.**

EXAMPLE 1

Find the constant of variation and an equation of variation where y varies directly with x, and where $y = 32$ when $x = 2$.

We know that $(2, 32)$ is a solution of $y = kx$.

$$32 = k \cdot 2 \qquad \text{Substituting}$$
$$\frac{32}{2} = k, \text{ or } k = 16 \qquad \text{Solving for } k$$

The constant of variation is 16.
The equation of variation is $y = 16x$.

Try This

a. Find the constant of variation and an equation of variation where y varies directly with x, and $y = 8$ when $x = 20$.

PART 2 Inverse Variation

Objective: Find the constant of variation and an equation of variation for inverse variation problems.

A bus is traveling a distance of 20 km. At a speed of 20 km/h it will take 1 hour. At 40 km/h it will take $\frac{1}{2}$ hour. At 60 km/h it will take $\frac{1}{3}$ hour, and so on. This pattern results in a set of ordered pairs of numbers, all having the same product.

$$(20, 1), \left(40, \tfrac{1}{2}\right), \left(60, \tfrac{1}{3}\right), \left(80, \tfrac{1}{4}\right), \ldots$$

Whenever a situation results in pairs of numbers whose product is constant, we say that there is **inverse variation.** Here the time **varies inversely** with the speed.

$$rt = 20 \text{ (a constant), or } t = \frac{20}{r}$$

Writing Math

Sometimes *as* is used instead of *with* in variation equations. If the sentence is "y varies directly as x," the equation is still $y = kx$.

Definition

Whenever a situation translates to a rational function $f(x) = \frac{k}{x}$, or $y = \frac{k}{x}$, where k is a nonzero constant, we say that there is **inverse variation,** or that y **varies inversely** with x. The number k is the **constant of variation.**

EXAMPLE 2

Find the constant of variation and an equation of variation where y varies inversely with x, and $y = 32$ when $x = 0.2$.

We know that $(0.2, 32)$ is a solution of $y = \frac{k}{x}$.

$$32 = \frac{k}{0.2} \quad \text{Substituting}$$

$$(0.2)32 = k \quad \text{Solving}$$

$$6.4 = k$$

The constant of variation is 6.4.
The equation of variation is $y = \frac{6.4}{x}$.

Try This

b. Find the constant of variation and an equation of variation where y varies inversely with x, and $y = 0.012$ when $x = 50$.

Solving Problems Using Variation

Objective: Solve problems using direct variation and inverse variation.

PROBLEM-SOLVING GUIDELINES
■ UNDERSTAND the problem
■ Develop and carry out a PLAN
■ Find the ANSWER and CHECK

Equations of direct and inverse variation can serve as mathematical models of many situations. We can then use the Problem-Solving Guidelines to solve problems related to them.

EXAMPLE 3

The volume of water produced from melting snow varies directly with the volume of snow. Meteorologists found that 150 cm^3 of snow in one watershed melted to 16.8 cm^3 of water. Suppose 200 cm^3 of snow melts there. Predict the resulting volume of water.

This photo is of Matanuska Glacier, in Alaska. Glaciers are formed when more snow falls than melts.

■ **UNDERSTAND the problem**

Question: Into how many cm^3 of water will 200 cm^3 of snow melt? — Clarifying the question

Data: 150 cm^3 of snow melted to 16.8 cm^3 of water. — Identifying the data

The volume of snow varies directly with the volume of water produced when snow melts.

■ **Develop and carry out a PLAN**

First find the constant of variation using the data, and then find an equation of variation.

$W = kS$	*W* is the volume of water, *S* is the volume of snow.
$16.8 = k \cdot 150$	Substituting
$\frac{16.8}{150} = k$	Solving for *k*
$0.112 = k$	This is the constant of variation.

The equation of variation is $W = 0.112S$.
Next use the equation to predict how many cm^3 of water will result from melting 200 cm^3 of snow.

$$W = 0.112S$$
$$W = 0.112(200) = 22.4$$

■ **Find the ANSWER and CHECK**

22.4 cm^3 of water is reasonable, since it is about $\frac{1}{9}$ the volume of snow, just as 16.8 is about $\frac{1}{9}$ of 150. Thus, 200 cm^3 of snow will melt to 22.4 cm^3 of water.

Try This

c. Ohm's law states that the voltage in an electric circuit varies directly as the number of amperes of electric current in the circuit. If the voltage is 10 volts when the current is 3 amperes, what is the voltage when the current is 15 amperes?

EXAMPLE 4

The time (t) required to do a job varies inversely with the number of people (P) who work on the job. It takes 4 hours for 12 people to erect some football bleachers. Predict how long it would take for 3 people to do the same job.

UNDERSTAND the problem

Question: How long would it take 3 people to erect the bleachers? — Clarifying the question

Data: It takes 4 hours for 12 people to do the job. The time required varies inversely with the number of people. — Identifying the data

Develop and carry out a PLAN

First find the constant of variation using the data, and then find an equation of variation.

$$t = \frac{k}{P}$$

$$4 = \frac{k}{12} \quad \text{Substituting}$$

$$48 = k \quad \text{Solving for } k\text{, the constant of variation}$$

The equation of variation is $t = \frac{48}{P}$. Next use the equation to find the time it would take 3 people to do the job.

$$t = \frac{48}{P}$$

$$t = \frac{48}{3} = 16$$

Find the ANSWER and CHECK

The time is reasonable since it would take 3 people four times as long as it takes 12 people. It would take 3 people 16 hours.

Try This

d. The time (t) required to drive a fixed distance varies inversely as the speed (r). It takes 5 hours at 60 km/h to drive a fixed distance. How long would it take to drive that same distance at 40 km/h?

6-9 Exercises

Extra Help On the Web

Look for worked-out examples at the Prentice Hall Web site.
www.phschool.com

A

Find the constant of variation and an equation of variation, where y varies directly as x.

1. $y = 24$ when $x = 3$ **2.** $y = 5$ when $x = 12$ **3.** $y = 16$ when $x = 1$

4. $y = 2$ when $x = 5$ **5.** $y = 15$ when $x = 3$ **6.** $y = 1$ when $x = 2$

7. $y = 1$ when $x = 1$ **8.** $y = 0.6$ when $x = 0.4$

Find the constant of variation and an equation of variation, where y varies inversely as x.

9. $y = 6$ when $x = 10$ **10.** $y = 16$ when $x = 4$ **11.** $y = 12$ when $x = 3$

12. $y = 9$ when $x = 5$ **13.** $y = 27$ when $x = \frac{1}{3}$ **14.** $y = 81$ when $x = \frac{1}{9}$

15. The electric current (I), in amperes, in a circuit varies directly as the voltage (V). When 12 volts are applied, the current is 4 amperes. Predict the current when 18 volts are applied.

16. Hooke's law states that the distance (d) a spring is stretched by a hanging object varies directly as the weight (w) of the object. The distance is 40 cm when the weight is 3 kg. Predict the distance when the weight is 5 kg.

17. The current (I) in an electrical conductor varies inversely as the resistance (R) of the conductor. The current is $\frac{1}{2}$ ampere when the resistance is 240 ohms. What is the current when the resistance is 540 ohms?

18. The time (t) required to empty a tank varies inversely as the rate (r) of pumping. A pump can empty a tank in 45 minutes at the rate of 600 kiloliters per minute. How long will it take the pump to empty the tank at the rate of 1000 kL/m?

19. The number (N) of plastic straws produced by a machine varies directly as the amount of time (t) the machine is operating. The machine produces 20,000 straws in 8 hours. How many straws can it produce in 50 hours?

20. The time (T) required to do a job varies inversely as the number of people (P) working. It takes 5 hours for 7 bricklayers to complete the certain job. How long would it take 10 bricklayers to complete the job?

21. The volume (V) of a gas varies inversely as the pressure (P) upon it. The volume of a gas is 200 cm^3 under a pressure of 32 kg/cm^2. Predict its volume under a pressure of 40 kg/cm^2.

22. The weight (M) of an object on the moon varies directly as its weight (E) on Earth. A person who weighs 95 kg on Earth weighs 15.2 kg on the moon. How much would a 105-kg person weigh on the moon?

23. The amount of pollution (A) entering the atmosphere varies directly as the number of people (N) living in an area. 60,000 people result in 42,600 tons of pollutants entering the atmosphere. Predict how many tons enter the atmosphere in a city with a population of 750,000.

24. The time (t) required to drive a fixed distance varies inversely as the speed (r). It takes 5 hours at 80 km/h to drive a fixed distance. How long would it take to drive the fixed distance at 60 km/h?

25. The number (N) of aluminum cans used each year varies directly as the number of people using the cans. 250 people use 60,000 cans in one year. Predict the number of cans used each year in a city with a population of 850,000.

26. A wavelength (W) of a radio wave varies inversely as its frequency (F). A wave with a frequency of 1200 kilohertz per second has a length of 300 meters. Predict the length of a wave with a frequency of 800 kilohertz per second.

27. The number of kilograms of water (W) in a human body varies directly as the total weight. A person weighing 96 kg contains 64 kg of water. How many kilograms of water are in a person weighing 75 kg?

B

28. To determine the number of deer in a forest, a conservationist catches 612 deer, tags them, and releases them. Later, 244 deer are caught, 72 of which are tagged. Predict how many deer are in the forest.

29. It is known that it takes 60 oz of grass seed to seed 3000 ft^2 of lawn. At this rate, how much would be needed for 5000 ft^2 of lawn?

30. ***Critical Thinking*** Consider these graphs. Describe each as a graph of direct variation, inverse variation, or neither. Tell how you made your decisions.

a.

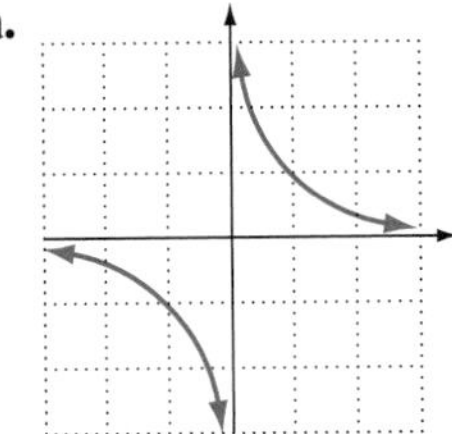

b.

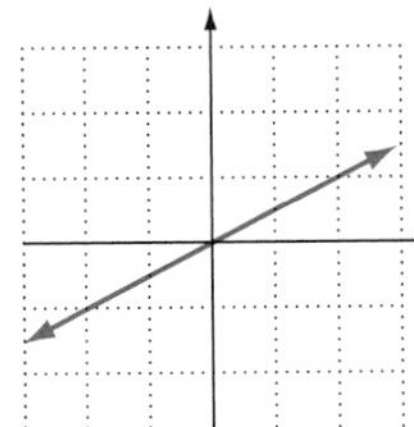

c.

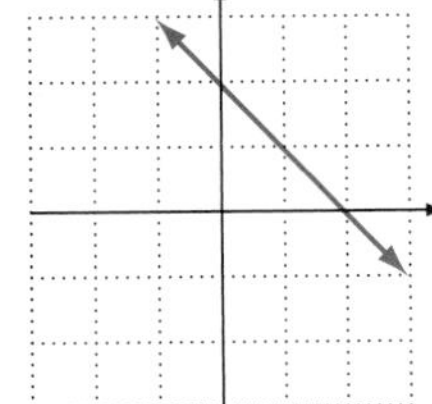

Challenge

31. ***Mathematical Reasoning*** Is it *sometimes*, *always*, or *never* true that if P varies directly as Q, then Q varies directly as P?

32. ***Mathematical Reasoning*** Is it *sometimes*, *always*, or *never* true that if A varies inversely as B, then B varies inversely as A and $\frac{1}{A}$ varies directly as B?

Mixed Review

Simplify. **33.** $\frac{21a^5b^3}{3a^2b^2}$ **34.** $\frac{64w^{-2}v^2}{8w^{-2}v}$ **35.** $4.6 \times \frac{10^5}{2.3} \times 10^{-7}$ *1-8, 1-9*

36. $(3.4 \times 10^{10})(5.5 \times 10^{-4})$ **37.** $(-4x^2y^{-3})(2x^3y^2)$ **38.** $(-5x^2y^5)(-8x^ay^{-3})$

Factor. **39.** $x^3 - 27$ **40.** $16x^2 - 36$ **41.** $6x^4 - 3x^3 + 18x^2$ *5-4, 5-5*

Reasoning Strategies

6-10

PART 1 Make a Table, Look for a Pattern

Objective: Solve problems using the strategies *Make a Table, Look for a Pattern,* and other strategies.

The problem-solving strategies called *Make a Table* and *Look for a Pattern* are helpful when solving problems involving numerical relationships. When data are organized in a table, numerical patterns are easier to recognize.

What You'll Learn

1 To solve non-routine problems using the strategies *Make a Table* and *Look for a Pattern*

. . . And Why

To increase efficiency in solving problems by applying reasoning skills

EXAMPLE 1

How many steps would there be if 55 blocks were used?

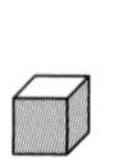
1 step

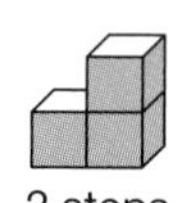
2 steps

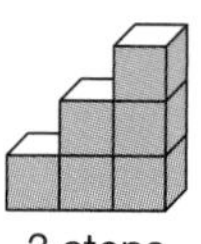
3 steps

You can *make a table* showing the number of steps and the number of blocks used.

Number of steps	0	1	2	3	4	5	6	7	8	9	10
Number of blocks	0	1	3	6	10						

+1 +2 +3 +4

You can use this pattern to extend the table to 55 blocks for 10 steps. Notice another pattern in the number of blocks.

Number of Steps	**Number of Blocks**
1	1
2	$1 + 2 = 3$
3	$1 + 2 + 3 = 6$
4	$1 + 2 + 3 + 4 = 10$
10	$1 + 2 + 3 + 4 + \ldots + 10 = 55$

Note the following for when there are 5 steps.

$$\begin{array}{r} 1 + 2 + 3 + 4 + 5 \\ + 5 + 4 + 3 + 2 + 1 \\ \hline 6 + 6 + 6 + 6 + 6 = 5(6) \end{array}$$

The number of blocks for 5 steps
Also the number of blocks for 5 steps

The sum $5(6)$ represents *twice* the number of blocks for 5 steps, so $\frac{5(6)}{2}$ blocks are used for 5 steps. For n steps, $\frac{n(n + 1)}{2}$ blocks are used.

If this square pyramid of 30 oranges had two more layers, how many oranges would there be? Describe the pattern.

Reasoning Strategies

Write an Equation	Draw a Diagram	Try, Test, Revise
Make an Organized List	Make a Table	Look for a Pattern
Use Logical Reasoning	Simplify the Problem	Work Backward

Extra Help On the Web

Look for worked-out examples at the Prentice Hall Web site.
www.phschool.com

6-10 Problems

Solve using one or more of the strategies.

1. ***Write a Convincing Argument*** Given the following pattern, explain how to find the total number of dots in B_{10}.

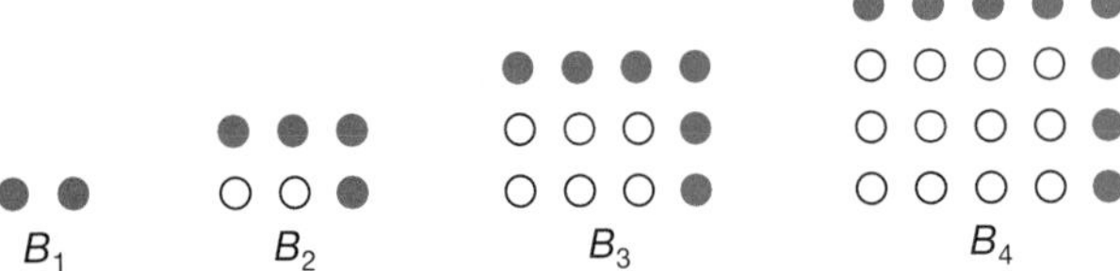

2. Some pages were torn out of a book by mistake. The person repairing the book noticed that the number on one of the facing pages was 11 more than twice the number on the other facing page, and the difference of the page numbers was 23. How many sheets of paper were torn out of this book?
3. Grass seed was sold in 3 lb and 5 lb bags. An order came in for exactly 48 lb of this grass seed. How many bags of each size could be sent to fill this order?
4. A biologist has a mixture made up of two types of cells, type A and type B. Every 2 hours each B cell produces one A cell and one B cell. Type A cells do not produce additional cells. Assume there was one cell of each type to start. How many cells of each type would accumulate after 1 day?
5. A waiter earned an average of \$15 a day in tips working at a restaurant. His friend earned an average of \$10 a day in tips working at another restaurant. At the end of the first pay period, the one earning less had worked 5 more days than the other, and they both had earned the same amount in tips. How many days did each work?
6. Each piece of art in an art show had to be assigned its own number. The art projects had to be numbered consecutively starting at 1. The person responsible for doing this had to place on the display table a sticker for each digit in the number given each piece of art. Each digit sticker cost 25¢. A total of 882 stickers were used and none was wasted. The total cost of the stickers had to be shared equally by the people who entered projects. How much did each person pay for stickers?
7. A football team scored 34 points in its last victory. All the points were scored on touchdowns (6 points), extra points after touchdowns (1 point), and field goals (3 points). In how many ways could the points have been scored?

6 Chapter Wrap Up

6-1

To multiply two **rational expressions,** multiply the numerators and denominators. To simplify rational expressions, first factor the numerator and denominator. To divide two rational expressions, multiply by the reciprocal.

Multiply.

1. $\frac{y}{y} \cdot \frac{4y - 3}{2y + 5}$

2. $\frac{4x - 3}{x + 5} \cdot \frac{x^2 - 1}{x^2 - 1}$

Simplify.

3. $\frac{3a^2 - 3b^2}{4a^2 + 8ab + 4b^2}$

4. $\frac{3x^2 - 4x - 4}{4x^2 - 3x - 10}$

5. $\frac{x^3 - 64}{8x^3 + 1} \cdot \frac{4x^2 - 1}{x^2 + 4x + 16}$

6. $\frac{6y^2}{y^2 - 9} \div \frac{3y^2}{2y^2 + 7y + 3}$

6-2

To add or subtract rational expressions, first find the **least common denominator.**

Add or subtract. Simplify if possible.

7. $\frac{a + 9}{a + 3} + \frac{12 - 5a}{a + 3}$

8. $\frac{y + 2}{y - 3} + \frac{y}{3 - y}$

9. $\frac{7}{x^2 - 81} - \frac{x - 4}{3x^2 - 25x - 18}$

10. $\frac{1}{3y} + \frac{4y}{y^2 - 1} + \frac{7}{y - 1}$

6-3

To simplify a **complex rational expression,** simplify the numerator and denominator separately and divide, or multiply the numerator and denominator by the LCD.

Simplify.

11. $\frac{\frac{1}{a} + \frac{1}{b}}{\frac{1}{a} - \frac{1}{b}}$

12. $\frac{\frac{x^2 - 16}{x^2 - 6x + 9}}{\frac{x^2 - 3x - 4}{x^2 - 2x - 3}}$

13. $\frac{a^{-1} - b^{-1}}{a^{-2} - b^{-2}}$

6-4

To divide a polynomial by a monomial, divide each term by the monomial. When the divisor is not a monomial, use a procedure similar to long division in arithmetic. Be sure to account for missing terms in the dividend.

Divide and check.

14. $(10y^4 - 8y^3 + 12y^2) \div 2y^2$

15. $(2x - 3)\overline{)4x^4 - 5x^2 + 2x - 10}$

Key Terms

addition of rational expressions (p. 250)
algorithm (p. 263)
complex rational expression (p. 256)
constant of variation (pp. 279, 280)
direct variation (p. 279)
dividing a polynomial by a monomial (p. 259)
division of rational expressions (p. 247)
f′(*x*) (p. 249)
graphing rational functions (p. 255)
inverse variation (p. 280)
LCD (p. 251)
LCM (p. 251)
least common denominator (p. 251)
least common multiple (p. 251)
linear polynomial (p. 263)
multiplication of rational expressions (p. 244)
rational equation (p. 266)
rational expression (p. 244)
reciprocal (p. 246)
reciprocals of rational expressions (p. 246)
slope function (p. 249)
solving work problems (p. 270)
synthetic division (p. 263)
vary directly (p. 279)
vary inversely (p. 280)

Internet Activity On the Web

Look for extension problems for this chapter at the Prentice Hall Web site. www.phschool.com

6-5

Synthetic division is an algorithm that simplifies polynomial division.

Divide.

16. $(x^4 - 3x^3 - 2x + 4) \div (x - 2)$ **17.** $(3x^3 + 5x^2 - 3) \div (x + 1)$

6-6

To solve a **rational equation,** first multiply both sides by the LCD of all the denominators, then solve the resulting equation.

Solve.

18. $\frac{x^2}{x + 3} = \frac{9}{x + 3}$ **19.** $\frac{15}{y} - \frac{15}{y - 2} = -2$ **20.** $\frac{2}{y + 4} + \frac{2y - 1}{y^2 + 2y - 8} = \frac{1}{y - 2}$

6-7

Work and motion problems can be solved using rational expressions and the Problem-Solving Guidelines.

21. One car travels 90 km in the same time that a car going 10 km/h slower travels 60 km. Find the speed of each.

22. Sue can paint a chair in 3 hours. Jerry can paint the same size chair in $2\frac{1}{2}$ hours. Working together, how long would it take them to paint 10 chairs?

23. An airplane flies 560 miles against the wind. In the same amount of time, it can fly 840 miles with the wind. The speed of the plane in still air is 420 miles per hour. Find the speed of the wind.

6-8

To solve **rational formulas,** use the same techniques used to solve rational equations.

24. Solve $T = Rn + \frac{mn}{p}$, for p. **25.** Solve $\frac{1}{p} + \frac{1}{q} = \frac{1}{f}$, for q.

6-9

If $y = kx$, then y is said to **vary directly** with x, and k is called the **constant of variation.**

26. Find the equation of direct variation, where y varies directly as x, and $y = 36$ when $x = 8$.

27. The weight (M) of an object on the moon varies directly as its weight (E) on Earth. A person who weighs 75 kg on Earth would weigh 12 kg on the moon. How much would a person who weighs 27 kg on the moon weigh on Earth?

If $y = \frac{k}{x}$, then y is said to **vary inversely** with x.

28. Find the equation of inverse variation, where y varies inversely as x, and $y = 36$ when $x = 8$.

29. The time required to build a house varies inversely as the number of workers. It takes 8 workers 25 days to build a house. How long would it take 5 workers?

6 Chapter Assessment

Multiply.

1. $\frac{y+1}{2y-3} \cdot \frac{y^2}{y^2}$

Simplify.

2. $\frac{5x^2+38x+21}{3x^2+22x+7}$ 3. $\frac{y^3+27}{9y} \cdot \frac{3y}{y+3}$ 4. $\frac{8t^5}{t^2-25} \div \frac{4t^2}{7t^2-34t-5}$

Add or subtract. Simplify if possible.

5. $\frac{t+9}{t-5} + \frac{2t}{5-t}$

6. $\frac{4}{5x-15} + \frac{x+8}{4x^2-11x-3}$

7. $\frac{8}{y^2-64} - \frac{y-5}{2y^2-15y-8}$

8. $\frac{1}{2x} + \frac{4x}{x^2-1} - \frac{2}{x+1}$

Simplify.

9. $\dfrac{\frac{b^2+3b-10}{b^2-5b+6}}{\frac{b^2-25}{b^2-4b-5}}$

10. $\frac{(3a)^{-1}-4}{(2a)^{-1}-1}$

Divide.

11. $(-6x^3+4x^2-10x) \div -2x$

12. $3x-1\overline{)15x^4-5x^3+3x^2-4x+2}$

Use synthetic division to find the quotient and remainder.

13. $(x^4-2x^3+3x^2-x+2) \div (x-2)$

14. $(2x^4-x^3-2x^2-2x-3) \div (x+1)$

Solve.

15. $\frac{x}{x-1} = \frac{7}{1-x}$

16. $\frac{12}{x-1} - \frac{8}{x} = 2$

17. Kaya can ride her bike 3 mi/h faster than Josh can ride his bike. If Kaya and Josh ride their bikes at the same time, Kaya will travel 60 mi and Josh will travel 12 mi less. How fast can Josh and Kaya ride their bikes?

18. Chan can mow a lawn in 4 hours. When Tao helps him, they can mow the lawn in $2\frac{1}{2}$ hours. How long would it take Tao to mow the lawn?

19. Solve $\frac{E}{e} = \frac{T+r}{r}$ for T.

20. Find the equation of direct variation where y varies directly as x, and $y = 5$ when $x = 16$.

21. Find the equation of inverse variation where y varies inversely as x, and $y = 5$ when $x = 16$.

22. The time (t) required to make a car varies inversely with the number of people (p) working on it. Twelve auto workers can produce a new car in 18 working hours. How long would it take if there were only 8 auto workers?

23. The time (t) required to drive a car at a fixed speed varies directly as the distance (d). It takes 8 hours to drive 380 mi at a fixed speed. How long would it take to drive 475 mi at that same fixed speed?

CHAPTER

What You'll Learn in Chapter 7

- How to factor and rationalize radical expressions
- How to add, subtract, multiply, divide, and factor radical expressions
- How to use rational exponents
- How to define, add, subtract, multiply, divide, find absolute values of, and graph imaginary and complex numbers
- How to solve equations using radicals, imaginary numbers, and complex numbers

Skills & Concepts You Need for Chapter 7

1-1 Simplify.

1. $|-8|$ **2.** $|0|$ **3.** $|\sqrt{3}|$

1-8 Simplify.

4. $y^7 \cdot y^3$ **5.** $8^3 \cdot 8^{-2}$ **6.** $(3x^2y^{-4})(4x^3y^2)$

7. $\frac{4^8}{4^2}$ **8.** $\frac{3^{-4}}{3^{-6}}$ **9.** $\frac{32x^3y^{10}}{4x^4y^4}$

1-8 Simplify.

10. $(4^2)^4$ **11.** $(a^{-3})^{-4}$ **12.** $(4xy^{-3})^3$ **13.** $(10x^3y^{-2}z^{-4})^2$

2-1 Solve.

14. $2(8 - 3x) = 3 - 5(x - 1)$ **15.** $9x + 7 - 2x = -12 - 4x + 5$

16. $(x - 5)(x + 3) = 0$ **17.** $(x + 5)(x - 7) = 0$

5-3 Multiply.

18. $(2 - 3y)(1 + 4y)$ **19.** $(3x + 8)^2$ **20.** $(2x - 3)(2x + 3)$

5-4–5-6 Factor.

21. $x^2 - 1$ **22.** $16x^4 - 40x^2y^4 + 25y^8$

23. $-27x^2 + 36x - 12$ **24.** $x^2 - 13x + 36$

Powers, Roots, and Complex Numbers

Galileo, the 17th-century Italian physicist, studied and discovered the laws of the pendulum. He thought a pendulum could regulate time. Dutch scientist Christiaan Huygens patented the first pendulum clock in 1657, 15 years after Galileo died. Galileo found that the period (T) of a pendulum varies directly as the square root of its length (L). See Lesson 7-3 to apply the formula $T = 2\pi\sqrt{\frac{L}{980}}$.

7-1 Radical Expressions

What You'll Learn

1 To find principal square roots of numbers

2 To find odd and even *k*th roots

... And Why

To prepare for multiplication and division of radical expressions

PART 1 Square Roots

Objective: Find principal square roots of numbers.

A **square root** of a number a is a number c such that $c^2 = a$.

25 has a square root of 5 because $5^2 = 25$.
25 has a square root of -5 because $(-5)^2 = 25$.
-16 does not have a real-number square root because there is no real number c such that $c^2 = -16$.

Later in this chapter we shall see that there is a number system in which negative numbers do have square roots.

Theorem 7-1

Every positive real number has two real-number square roots. The number 0 has just one square root, 0 itself. Negative numbers do not have real-number square roots.

EXAMPLE 1 Find the two square roots of 64.

The square roots are 8 and -8 because $8^2 = 64$ and $(-8)^2 = 64$.

Try This Find the square roots of each number.

a. 9 **b.** 36 **c.** 121

Definition

The **principal square root** of a nonnegative number is its nonnegative square root. The symbol $\sqrt{a}$ represents the principal square root of a. The negative square root of a is written $-\sqrt{a}$.

EXAMPLES Simplify. Remember, $\sqrt{}$ indicates the principal square root.

2 $\sqrt{25} = 5$ **3** $-\sqrt{64} = -8$ **4** $\sqrt{\frac{25}{64}} = \frac{5}{8}$ **5** $\sqrt{0.0049} = 0.07$

Try This Simplify.

d. $\sqrt{1}$ **e.** $-\sqrt{36}$ **f.** $\sqrt{\frac{81}{100}}$ **g.** $-\sqrt{0.0064}$

These are **radical expressions.**

$$\sqrt{5} \qquad \sqrt{a} \qquad -\sqrt{5x} \qquad \sqrt{\frac{y^2 + 7}{\sqrt{x}}}$$

Definition

The symbol $\sqrt{}$ is a **radical sign.** An expression written with a radical sign is a **radical expression.** The expression written under the radical sign is the **radicand.**

In the expression $\sqrt{a^2}$, the radicand is a perfect square.

Suppose $a = 5$. Then we have $\sqrt{5^2}$, which is $\sqrt{25}$, or 5.

Suppose $a = -5$. Then we have $\sqrt{(-5)^2}$, which is $\sqrt{25}$, or 5.

Suppose $a = 0$. Then we have $\sqrt{0^2}$, which is $\sqrt{0}$, or 0.

The symbol $\sqrt{a^2}$ does not represent a negative number. It represents the principal square root of a^2. Note that if $a \geq 0$, then $\sqrt{a^2} = a$. If $a < 0$, $\sqrt{a^2} = -a$. In all cases the radical expression $\sqrt{a^2}$ represents the absolute value of a.

Theorem 7-2

For any real number a, $\sqrt{a^2} = |a|$. The principal (nonnegative) square root of a^2 is the absolute value of a.

EXAMPLES

6 $\sqrt{(-16)^2} = |-16| = 16$

7 $\sqrt{(3b)^2} = |3b| = 3|b|$

8 $\sqrt{(x - 1)^2} = |x - 1|$

9 $\sqrt{x^2 + 8x + 16} = \sqrt{(x + 4)^2} = |x + 4|$

Try This Find the following. Assume that variables represent any real number.

h. $\sqrt{(-24)^2}$ **i.** $\sqrt{(5y)^2}$

j. $\sqrt{16y^2}$ **k.** $\sqrt{(x + 7)^2}$

PART 2 Odd and Even *k*th Roots

Objective: Find odd and even *k*th roots.

The number c is the **cube root** of a if $c^3 = a$.

2 is the cube root of 8 because $2^3 = 2 \cdot 2 \cdot 2 = 8$.
-5 is the cube root of -125 because $(-5)^3 = (-5)(-5)(-5) = -125$.

Every real number has *exactly one* cube root in the system of real numbers. The symbol $\sqrt[3]{a}$ represents the cube root of a.

EXAMPLES Simplify.

10 $\sqrt[3]{8} = 2$

11 $\sqrt[3]{-27} = -3$

12 $\sqrt[3]{-\frac{216}{125}} = -\frac{6}{5}$

13 $\sqrt[3]{-8y^3} = -2y$

No absolute value signs are needed when finding cube roots because a real number has just one real cube root. The real cube root of a positive number is positive. The real cube root of a negative number is negative.

Try This Simplify.

l. $\sqrt[3]{-64}$ **m.** $\sqrt[3]{27y^3}$ **n.** $\sqrt[3]{-\frac{343}{64}}$

There are also 4th roots, 5th roots, 6th roots, and so on. If $\sqrt[4]{a} = c$, then we know $c^4 = a$. If $\sqrt[k]{a} = c$, then we know $c^k = a$. We say c is the **kth root** of a.

Similarly, if $\sqrt[9]{a} = c$, then $c^9 = a$, and c is the 9th root of a.

Reading Math

When we write $\sqrt{9}$, we read it as "The square root of 9." For numbers greater than 2, an index number is added. For example, $\sqrt[5]{32}$ is read as "The fifth root of 32." If we use an algebraic index, then $\sqrt[k]{8}$ is read as "The *k*th root of 8."

EXAMPLES Rewrite using exponential notation.

14 $c = \sqrt[7]{b} \rightarrow c^7 = b$

15 $y = \sqrt[6]{100} \rightarrow y^6 = 100$

16 $t = \sqrt[11]{22} \rightarrow t^{11} = 22$

Try This Rewrite using exponential notation.

o. $b = \sqrt[5]{a}$ **p.** $c = \sqrt[12]{63}$ **q.** $\sqrt[9]{16a} = n$

The number k in $\sqrt[k]{}$ is called the **index.** If k is an odd number, we say that we are finding an **odd root.**

When finding any odd root of a number, there is just one answer. If the number is positive, the root is positive. If the number is negative, the root is negative. Absolute value signs are never needed when finding odd roots.

EXAMPLES Find the following.

17 $\sqrt[5]{-32} = -2$

18 $-\sqrt[5]{32} = -2$

19 $\sqrt[7]{x^7} = x$

20 $\sqrt[9]{(x-1)^9} = x - 1$

Try This Find the following.

r. $\sqrt[5]{-243}$ **s.** $-\sqrt[5]{243}$ **t.** $\sqrt[5]{-32x^5}$ **u.** $\sqrt[7]{(3x+2)^7}$

When the index k in $\sqrt[k]{}$ is an even number, we say that we are finding an **even root.** Every positive real number has two kth roots when k is even. One of those roots is positive and one is negative. Negative numbers do not have real-number kth roots when k is even. When finding even kth roots, absolute value signs are sometimes necessary.

EXAMPLES Find the following.

21 $\sqrt[4]{16} = 2$

22 $-\sqrt[4]{16} = -2$

23 $\sqrt[4]{-16}$ No real root

24 $\sqrt[4]{81x^4} = 3|x|$

25 $\sqrt[6]{(y+7)^6} = |y+7|$

Theorem 7-3

For any real number a, the following statements are true.

A. $\sqrt[k]{a^k} = |a|$ when k is even. B. $\sqrt[k]{a^k} = a$ when k is odd.

We use absolute value when k is even unless a is nonnegative. We do not use absolute value when k is odd.

Try This Find the following.

v. $\sqrt[4]{81}$ **w.** $-\sqrt[4]{81}$ **x.** $\sqrt[4]{-81}$ **y.** $\sqrt[4]{16(x-2)^4}$ **z.** $\sqrt[8]{(x+3)^8}$

7-1 Exercises

Extra Help On the Web

Look for worked-out examples at the Prentice Hall Web site.
www.phschool.com

A

Mental Math Find the square roots of each number.

1. 16 **2.** 144 **3.** 9 **4.** 81 **5.** $\frac{49}{36}$ **6.** $\frac{81}{144}$

Find the following.

7. $\sqrt{225}$ **8.** $\sqrt{400}$ **9.** $-\sqrt{\frac{361}{9}}$

10. $-\sqrt{\frac{16}{81}}$ **11.** $\sqrt{0.09}$ **12.** $-\sqrt{0.0049}$

13. $\sqrt{16x^2}$ 14. $\sqrt{(-6b)^2}$ 15. $\sqrt{25t^2}$ 16. $\sqrt{(-7c)^2}$

17. $\sqrt{(a+1)^2}$ 18. $\sqrt{(5-b)^2}$ 19. $\sqrt{x^2-4x+4}$

20. $\sqrt{4x^2+28x+49}$ 21. $\sqrt[3]{-64x^3}$ 22. $\sqrt[3]{-125y^3}$

23. $-\sqrt[3]{-1000}$ 24. $\sqrt[3]{-64x^3y^6}$

25. $\sqrt[3]{0.343(x+1)^3}$ 26. $\sqrt[3]{0.008(y-2)^3}$

Rewrite using exponential notation.

27. $p = \sqrt[4]{10}$ 28. $\sqrt[8]{56} = k$ 29. $r = \sqrt[28]{500h}$ 30. $a = \sqrt[x]{y}$

Simplify.

31. $\sqrt[4]{625}$ 32. $-\sqrt[4]{256}$ 33. $\sqrt[5]{-1}$ 34. $-\sqrt[5]{-32}$

35. $\sqrt[5]{-\frac{32}{243}}$ 36. $\sqrt[5]{-\frac{1}{32}}$ 37. $\sqrt[6]{x^6}$ 38. $\sqrt[8]{y^8}$

39. $\sqrt[4]{(5a)^4}$ 40. $\sqrt[4]{(7b)^4}$ 41. $\sqrt[5]{(x-2)^5}$ 42. $\sqrt[9]{(2xy)^9}$

B

43. The number (N) of temporary stalls needed for waiting cars before parking lot attendants can park them is given by $N = 2.5\sqrt{A}$ where A is the number of arrivals during peak hours. Find the number of spaces needed for the given average number of arrivals during peak hours.

a. 25 **b.** 36 **c.** 49 **d.** 64

Find the domain of each function.

44. $f(x) = \sqrt{x}$ 45. $f(x) = \sqrt[3]{x}$ 46. $f(x) = \sqrt{2x+8}$

47. $f(x) = \sqrt{4-3x}$ 48. $f(x) = \sqrt{-3x^2}$ 49. $f(x) = \sqrt{x^2+1}$

50. ***Critical Thinking*** Find several pairs of numbers such that the square root of the first is the same as the fifth root of the second.

Challenge

Find the domain of each function.

51. $f(x) = \dfrac{\sqrt{x}}{2x^2-3x-5}$ 52. $f(x) = \dfrac{\sqrt{x+3}}{x^2-x-2}$ 53. $f(x) = \dfrac{\sqrt{x+1}}{x+|x|}$

Mixed Review

Solve. 54. $\frac{1}{3} + \frac{2}{5} = \frac{x}{6}$ 55. $y - \frac{4}{y} = 3$ 56. $\dfrac{2}{x-2} = \dfrac{5}{x+4}$ *6-6*

57. The square of a number minus the number is 6. Find the number. *5-8*

58. Ervin ran for 3416 yards during his three years playing college football. During his senior year, he ran for as many yards as in his sophomore and junior years combined. He also ran for 426 more yards in his junior year than in his sophomore year. How many yards did he gain each year? *6-10*

Multiplying and Simplifying

7-2

Introducing the Concept: Multiplication and Radicals

Simplify and compare your answers.

$\sqrt{4} \cdot \sqrt{25}$ and $\sqrt{4 \cdot 25}$ $\qquad$ $\sqrt[3]{27} \cdot \sqrt[3]{8}$ and $\sqrt[3]{27 \cdot 8}$

What You'll Learn

1. To multiply radical expressions
2. To simplify radical expressions by factoring
3. To multiply and simplify radical expressions

. . . And Why

To solve algebraic equations involving radical expressions

PART 1 Multiplying

Objective: Multiply radical expressions.

The results of the introductory work suggest the following theorem.

Theorem 7-4

For any nonnegative numbers a and b, and any natural-number index k,

$\sqrt[k]{a} \cdot \sqrt[k]{b} = \sqrt[k]{ab}.$

EXAMPLES Multiply.

1 $\sqrt{x+2}\sqrt{x-2} = \sqrt{(x+2)(x-2)} = \sqrt{x^2-4}$ $\qquad$ Using Theorem 7-4

2 $\sqrt[3]{4}\sqrt[3]{5} = \sqrt[3]{4 \cdot 5} = \sqrt[3]{20}$

3 $\sqrt[4]{\frac{y}{5}}\sqrt[4]{\frac{7}{x}} = \sqrt[4]{\frac{y}{5} \cdot \frac{7}{x}} = \sqrt[4]{\frac{7y}{5x}}$

Try This Multiply.

a. $\sqrt{19}\sqrt{7}$ $\quad$ **b.** $\sqrt{x+2y}\sqrt{x-2y}$ $\quad$ **c.** $\sqrt[4]{403}\sqrt[4]{7}$ $\quad$ **d.** $\sqrt[3]{8x}\sqrt[3]{x^4+5}$

PART 2 Simplifying by Factoring

Objective: Simplify radical expressions by factoring.

Applying the symmetric property of equality to Theorem 7-4, we have $\sqrt[k]{ab} = \sqrt[k]{a} \cdot \sqrt[k]{b}$. This shows a way to factor and thus simplify radical expressions. Consider $\sqrt{20}$. The number 20 has 4, a perfect square, as a factor.

$\sqrt{20} = \sqrt{4 \cdot 5}$ $\qquad$ Factoring the radicand (4 is a perfect square)

$= \sqrt{4} \cdot \sqrt{5}$ $\qquad$ Factoring into two radicals

$= 2\sqrt{5}$ $\qquad$ Finding the square root of 4

To simplify a radical expression by factoring, look for factors of the radicand that are perfect kth powers, where k is the index. Remove those factors by finding the kth root.

EXAMPLES Simplify by factoring.

4 $\sqrt{50} = \sqrt{25 \cdot 2} = \sqrt{25} \cdot \sqrt{2} = 5\sqrt{2}$ Finding a perfect-square factor

5 $\sqrt[3]{32} = \sqrt[3]{8 \cdot 4} = \sqrt[3]{8} \cdot \sqrt[3]{4} = 2\sqrt[3]{4}$ Finding a perfect-cube factor

6
$$\begin{aligned} \sqrt{2x^2 - 4x + 2} &= \sqrt{2(x-1)^2} \\ &= \sqrt{(x-1)^2} \cdot \sqrt{2} \\ &= |x-1| \cdot \sqrt{2} \end{aligned}$$

Try This Simplify by factoring.

e. $\sqrt{32}$ **f.** $\sqrt[3]{80}$ **g.** $\sqrt{300}$ **h.** $\sqrt{3x^2 + 12x + 12}$
i. $\sqrt{12ab^3c^2}$ **j.** $\sqrt[3]{16}$ **k.** $\sqrt[4]{81x^4y^8}$ **l.** $\sqrt[3]{(a+b)^4}$

PART 3 Multiplying and Simplifying

Objective: Multiply and simplify radical expressions.

After we multiply, we can often simplify by factoring.

EXAMPLES Multiply and simplify.

7 $\sqrt{15}\sqrt{6} = \sqrt{15 \cdot 6} = \sqrt{90} = \sqrt{9 \cdot 10} = 3\sqrt{10}$

8
$$\begin{aligned} 3\sqrt[3]{25} \cdot 2\sqrt[3]{5} &= 6 \cdot \sqrt[3]{25 \cdot 5} && \text{Multiplying radicands} \\ &= 6\sqrt[3]{125} \\ &= 6 \cdot 5, \text{ or } 30 \end{aligned}$$

9
$$\begin{aligned} \sqrt[3]{18y^3}\sqrt[3]{4x^2} &= \sqrt[3]{18y^3 \cdot 4x^2} \\ &= \sqrt[3]{2 \cdot 3^2 \cdot y^3 \cdot 2^2 \cdot x^2} && \text{Factoring the radicand} \\ &= \sqrt[3]{2^3 \cdot y^3 \cdot 3^2 \cdot x^2} && \text{Using the commutative and associative properties} \\ &= 2y\sqrt[3]{9x^2} && \text{Simplifying} \end{aligned}$$

Try This Multiply and then simplify by factoring.

m. $\sqrt{3}\sqrt{6}$ **n.** $\sqrt{18y}\sqrt{14y}$ **o.** $\sqrt[3]{3xy^2}\sqrt[3]{36x}$ **p.** $\sqrt{7a}\sqrt{21b}$

7-2 Exercises

Extra Help On the Web

Look for worked-out examples at the Prentice Hall Web site.
www.phschool.com

A

Multiply.

1. $\sqrt{3}\sqrt{2}$
2. $\sqrt{5}\sqrt{7}$
3. $\sqrt[3]{2}\sqrt[3]{5}$
4. $\sqrt[3]{7}\sqrt[3]{2}$
5. $\sqrt[4]{8}\sqrt[4]{9}$
6. $\sqrt[4]{6}\sqrt[4]{3}$
7. $\sqrt{\frac{6}{x}}\sqrt{\frac{y}{5}}$
8. $\sqrt{2x}\sqrt{13y}$
9. $\sqrt[5]{9t^2}\sqrt[5]{2t}$
10. $\sqrt[5]{8y^3}\sqrt[5]{10y}$
11. $\sqrt{x-a}\sqrt{x+a}$
12. $\sqrt{y-b}\sqrt{y+b}$
13. $\sqrt[3]{0.3x}\sqrt[3]{0.2x}$
14. $\sqrt[3]{0.7y}\sqrt[3]{0.3y}$

Simplify by factoring.

15. $\sqrt{24}$
16. $\sqrt{20}$
17. $\sqrt{180x^4}$
18. $\sqrt{175y^6}$
19. $\sqrt[3]{54x^8}$
20. $\sqrt[3]{108m^5}$
21. $\sqrt[4]{32}$
22. $\sqrt[4]{80}$
23. $\sqrt[4]{162c^4d^6}$
24. $\sqrt[4]{243x^8y^{10}}$
25. $\sqrt[3]{(x+y)^4}$
26. $\sqrt[6]{(a+b)^7}$

Multiply and simplify by factoring.

27. $\sqrt{3}\sqrt{6}$
28. $\sqrt{5}\sqrt{10}$
29. $\sqrt{2}\sqrt{32}$
30. $\sqrt{6}\sqrt{8}$
31. $\sqrt{2x^3y}\sqrt{12xy}$
32. $\sqrt[3]{y^4}\sqrt[3]{16y^5}$
33. $\sqrt[3]{5^2t^4}\sqrt[3]{5^4t^6}$
34. $\sqrt[3]{(b+3)^4}\sqrt[3]{(b+3)^2}$
35. $\sqrt[3]{(x+y)^3}\sqrt[3]{(x+y)^5}$

B

Estimation The speed that a car was traveling can be estimated by measuring its skid marks. The formula $r = 2\sqrt{5L}$ can be used, where r is the speed in mi/h and L is the length of the skid marks in feet. Estimate the speed of a car that left skid marks of

36. 20 ft
37. 70 ft
38. 156.8 ft

39. ***Critical Thinking*** Find two radical expressions whose simplified product is $5\sqrt{10}$.

A police officer measures skid marks after an accident to determine the speeds of the cars and trucks involved. See Exercises 36–38.

Challenge

Here is a formula for finding *windchill temperature,* when T is the actual temperature given in degrees Celsius and v is the wind speed in m/s. Find the windchill temperature for the given actual temperatures and wind speeds.

$$T_w = 33 - (10.45 + 10\sqrt{v} - v)(33 - T) \div 22$$

40. $T = 7°\text{C}, v = 8$ m/s
41. $T = 0°\text{C}, v = 12$ m/s
42. $T = -23°\text{C}, v = 15$ m/s

Mixed Review

Factor. 43. $4x^2 + 6x + 2$ 44. $3y^2 - 14y - 5$ 45. $9a^2 - 3a$ *5-2, 5-4*

Divide. 46. $(x^2 + 10x + 21) \div (x + 3)$ 47. $(3y^2 - 13y - 12) \div (y - 5)$ *6-4*

7-3 Operations with Radical Expressions

What You'll Learn

1. To find roots of quotients
2. To divide radical expressions
3. To add and subtract radical expressions

. . . And Why

To increase efficiency in solving algebraic equations and problems with radicals

The *period* of a pendulum is the time it takes to complete one cycle, swinging side to side and back to the original position. If a pendulum consists of a ball on a string, the period (T) is given by the formula $T = 2\pi\sqrt{\frac{L}{980}}$. T is in seconds and L is the length of the pendulum in centimeters.

Find the period of a pendulum on a string 8820 cm long. The constant 980 in the formula is the acceleration due to gravity acting on the pendulum, in cm/s².

PART 1 Roots of Quotients

Objective: Find roots of quotients.

Consider the following.

$$\sqrt{\frac{16}{9}} = \frac{4}{3} \text{ and } \frac{\sqrt{16}}{\sqrt{9}} = \frac{4}{3}; \text{ also } \sqrt[3]{\frac{27}{8}} = \frac{3}{2} \text{ and } \frac{\sqrt[3]{27}}{\sqrt[3]{8}} = \frac{3}{2}$$

These examples suggest the following theorem.

Theorem 7-5

For any natural-number index k and any real numbers a and b, $(b \neq 0)$, where $\sqrt[k]{a}$ and $\sqrt[k]{b}$ are real numbers, $\sqrt[k]{\frac{a}{b}} = \frac{\sqrt[k]{a}}{\sqrt[k]{b}}$.

From Theorem 7-5, we have the following rule.

Finding kth Roots

To find the kth root of a quotient, find the kth roots of the numerator and denominator separately.

EXAMPLES Simplify by finding roots of the numerator and denominator.

1 $\sqrt[3]{\frac{27}{125}} = \frac{\sqrt[3]{27}}{\sqrt[3]{125}} = \frac{3}{5}$ Finding the cube root of the numerator and denominator

2 $\sqrt{\frac{25}{y^2}} = \frac{\sqrt{25}}{\sqrt{y^2}} = \frac{5}{|y|}$ Finding the square root of the numerator and denominator

3 $\sqrt{\frac{16x^3}{y^4}} = \frac{\sqrt{16x^3}}{\sqrt{y^4}} = \frac{\sqrt{16x^2 \cdot x}}{\sqrt{y^4}} = \frac{4|x|\sqrt{x}}{y^2}$

4 $\sqrt[3]{\frac{27y^5}{343x^3}} = \frac{\sqrt[3]{27y^5}}{\sqrt[3]{343x^3}} = \frac{\sqrt[3]{27y^3 \cdot y^2}}{\sqrt[3]{343x^3}} = \frac{\sqrt[3]{27y^3} \cdot \sqrt[3]{y^2}}{\sqrt[3]{343x^3}} = \frac{3y\sqrt[3]{y^2}}{7x}$

Try This Simplify by finding roots of the numerator and denominator.

a. $\sqrt{\frac{25}{36}}$ **b.** $\sqrt[3]{\frac{1000}{27}}$ **c.** $\sqrt{\frac{x^2}{100}}$ **d.** $\sqrt{\frac{4a^3}{b^4}}$

PART 2 Dividing Radical Expressions

Objective: Divide radical expressions.

Applying the symmetric property of equality to Theorem 7-5, we have

$$\frac{\sqrt[k]{a}}{\sqrt[k]{b}} = \sqrt[k]{\frac{a}{b}}.$$

This gives us a rule for dividing radical expressions.

Dividing Radical Expressions

To divide radical expressions with the same index, divide the radicands. Simplify, if possible.

EXAMPLES Divide. Then simplify by finding roots, if possible.

5 $\frac{\sqrt{80}}{\sqrt{5}} = \sqrt{\frac{80}{5}}$ Dividing radicands

$= \sqrt{16}$

$= 4$

6 $\frac{5\sqrt[3]{32}}{\sqrt[3]{2}} = 5\sqrt[3]{\frac{32}{2}}$ Dividing radicands

$= 5\sqrt[3]{16}$

$= 5\sqrt[3]{8 \cdot 2}$ Finding a perfect cube factor

$= 5\sqrt[3]{8}\sqrt[3]{2}$ Factoring

$= 5 \cdot 2\sqrt[3]{2} = 10\sqrt[3]{2}$ Simplifying

7 $\frac{\sqrt[4]{32a^5b^3}}{\sqrt[4]{2b^{-1}}} = \sqrt[4]{\frac{32a^5b^3}{2b^{-1}}} = \sqrt[4]{16a^5b^4} = \sqrt[4]{16a^4b^4 \cdot a} = \sqrt[4]{16a^4b^4}\sqrt[4]{a} = 2|ab|\sqrt[4]{a}$

Reading Math

The symmetric property of equality allows us to express Theorem 7-5 as either "The square root of the quotient is the quotient of the square roots," or "The quotient of the square roots is the square root of the quotient."

Try This Divide. Then simplify by finding roots, if possible.

e. $\dfrac{\sqrt{75}}{\sqrt{3}}$ **f.** $\dfrac{14\sqrt{128xy}}{2\sqrt{2}}$ **g.** $\dfrac{4\sqrt[3]{250}}{7\sqrt[3]{2}}$ **h.** $\dfrac{\sqrt[3]{8a^3b}}{\sqrt[3]{27b^{-2}}}$

PART 3 Addition and Subtraction

Objective: Add or subtract radical expressions.

Any two real numbers can be added. For example, the sum of 7 and $\sqrt{3}$ can be expressed as $7 + \sqrt{3}$. We cannot simplify this sum. However, when we have like radical terms (radical terms having the same index and radicand), we can use the distributive property to simplify, then collect like radical terms.

EXAMPLES Add or subtract. Collect like radical terms, if possible.

8 $6\sqrt{7} + 4\sqrt{7} = (6 + 4)\sqrt{7} = 10\sqrt{7}$ Using the distributive property

9 $8\sqrt[3]{2} - 7x\sqrt[3]{2} + 5\sqrt[3]{2} = (8 - 7x + 5)\sqrt[3]{2}$ Factoring out $\sqrt[3]{2}$

$= (13 - 7x)\sqrt[3]{2}$

10 $6\sqrt[5]{4x} + 4\sqrt[5]{4x} - \sqrt[3]{4x} = (6 + 4)\sqrt[5]{4x} - \sqrt[3]{4x} = 10\sqrt[5]{4x} - \sqrt[3]{4x}$

Try This Add or subtract. Simplify by collecting like radical terms, if possible.

i. $5\sqrt{2} + 8\sqrt{2}$ **j.** $7\sqrt[4]{5x} + 3\sqrt[4]{5x} - \sqrt{7}$

Sometimes we need to factor in order to have like radical terms.

EXAMPLES Add or subtract. Simplify by collecting like radical terms, if possible.

11 $3\sqrt{8} - 5\sqrt{2} = 3\sqrt{4 \cdot 2} - 5\sqrt{2}$ Factoring 8

$= 3\sqrt{4} \cdot \sqrt{2} - 5\sqrt{2}$ Factoring $\sqrt{4 \cdot 2}$ into 2 radicals

$= 3 \cdot 2\sqrt{2} - 5\sqrt{2}$ Finding the square root of 4

$= 6\sqrt{2} - 5\sqrt{2} = \sqrt{2}$ Collecting like radical terms

12 $5\sqrt{2} - 4\sqrt{3}$ No simplification possible

13 $5\sqrt[3]{16y^4} + 7\sqrt[3]{2y} = 5\sqrt[3]{8y^3 \cdot 2y} + 7\sqrt[3]{2y}$ Factoring the first radical

$= 5\sqrt[3]{2^3y^3} \cdot \sqrt[3]{2y} + 7\sqrt[3]{2y}$

$= 5 \cdot 2y \cdot \sqrt[3]{2y} + 7\sqrt[3]{2y}$ Finding the cube root

$= 10y\sqrt[3]{2y} + 7\sqrt[3]{2y}$

$= (10y + 7)\sqrt[3]{2y}$ Collecting like radical terms

Try This Add or subtract. Simplify by collecting like radical terms, if possible.

k. $7\sqrt{45} - 2\sqrt{5}$ **l.** $3\sqrt[3]{y^5} + 4\sqrt[3]{y^2} + \sqrt[3]{8y^6}$

m. $\sqrt{25x - 25} - \sqrt{9x - 9}$ **n.** $\sqrt[3]{54} - \sqrt{54}$

7-3 Exercises

Extra Help On the Web

Look for worked-out examples at the Prentice Hall Web site.
www.phschool.com

A

Mental Math Simplify by finding roots of the numerator and denominator.

1. $\sqrt{\frac{16}{25}}$ **2.** $\sqrt{\frac{100}{81}}$ **3.** $\sqrt[3]{\frac{64}{27}}$ **4.** $\sqrt{\frac{49}{y^2}}$ **5.** $\sqrt{\frac{121}{x^2}}$

Simplify.

6. $\sqrt[3]{\frac{343}{512}}$ **7.** $\sqrt{\frac{25y^3}{x^4}}$ **8.** $\sqrt{\frac{36a^5}{b^6}}$ **9.** $\sqrt[3]{\frac{8x^5}{27y^3}}$ **10.** $\sqrt[3]{\frac{64x^7}{216y^6}}$

Divide. Then simplify by finding roots, if possible.

11. $\frac{\sqrt{21a}}{\sqrt{3a}}$ **12.** $\frac{\sqrt{28y}}{\sqrt{4y}}$ **13.** $\frac{\sqrt[3]{54}}{\sqrt[3]{2}}$ **14.** $\frac{\sqrt[3]{40}}{\sqrt[3]{5}}$

15. $\frac{\sqrt{40xy^3}}{\sqrt{8x}}$ **16.** $\frac{\sqrt{56ab^3}}{\sqrt{7a}}$ **17.** $\frac{\sqrt[3]{96a^4b^2}}{\sqrt[3]{12a^2b}}$ **18.** $\frac{\sqrt[3]{189x^5y^7}}{\sqrt[3]{7x^2y^2}}$

19. $\frac{\sqrt{72xy}}{2\sqrt{2}}$ **20.** $\frac{\sqrt{75ab}}{3\sqrt{3}}$ **21.** $\frac{\sqrt{x^3 - y^3}}{\sqrt{x - y}}$ **22.** $\frac{\sqrt{r^3 + s^3}}{\sqrt{r + s}}$

Add or subtract. Simplify by collecting like radical terms, if possible.

23. $6\sqrt{3} + 2\sqrt{3}$ **24.** $8\sqrt{5} + 9\sqrt{5}$ **25.** $9\sqrt[3]{5} - 6\sqrt[3]{5}$

26. $14\sqrt[5]{2} - 6\sqrt[5]{2}$ **27.** $4\sqrt[3]{y} + 9\sqrt[3]{y}$ **28.** $6\sqrt[4]{t} - 3\sqrt[4]{t}$

29. $8\sqrt{2} - 6\sqrt{2} + 5\sqrt{2}$ **30.** $2\sqrt{6} + 8\sqrt{6} - 3\sqrt{6}$

31. $4\sqrt[3]{5} - \sqrt{3} + 2\sqrt[3]{5} + \sqrt{3}$ **32.** $5\sqrt{7} - 8\sqrt[4]{11} + \sqrt{7} + 9\sqrt[4]{11}$

33. $6\sqrt{8} + 11\sqrt{2}$ **34.** $2\sqrt{12} + 5\sqrt{3}$ **35.** $8\sqrt{27} - 3\sqrt{3}$

36. $9\sqrt{50} - 4\sqrt{2}$ **37.** $8\sqrt{45} + 7\sqrt{20}$ **38.** $9\sqrt{12} + 16\sqrt{27}$

39. $18\sqrt{72} + 2\sqrt{98}$ **40.** $12\sqrt{45} - 8\sqrt{80}$ **41.** $3\sqrt[3]{16} + \sqrt[3]{54}$

42. $\sqrt[3]{27} - 5\sqrt[3]{8}$ **43.** $5\sqrt[3]{32} - 2\sqrt[3]{108}$ **44.** $9\sqrt[3]{40} - 7\sqrt[3]{135}$

45. $2\sqrt{128} - \sqrt{18} + 4\sqrt{32}$ **46.** $5\sqrt{50} - 2\sqrt{18} + 9\sqrt{32}$

47. $2\sqrt[3]{125a^4} - 5\sqrt[3]{8a}$ **48.** $9\sqrt[3]{16x^5y} - 2\sqrt[3]{128x^2y}$

49. $\sqrt{8y - 8} + \sqrt{2y - 2}$ **50.** $\sqrt{12t + 12} + \sqrt{3t + 3}$

51. $\sqrt{x^3 - x^2} + \sqrt{9x - 9}$ **52.** $\sqrt{4x - 4} - \sqrt{x^3 - x^2}$

B

Estimation Use the formula at the beginning of the lesson to find the period of a pendulum for each length given. Use 3.14 for π. Round your answer to the nearest hundredth.

53. 65 cm **54.** 98 cm **55.** 120 cm

56. ***Mathematical Reasoning*** What conditions must be satisfied for the following equation to be true? $\sqrt{a} + \sqrt{b} = \sqrt{a + b}$

57. What conditions must be satisfied for the following equation to be true? $\sqrt[3]{a} + \sqrt[3]{b} = \sqrt[3]{a + b}$

58. ***Critical Thinking*** Find three different pairs of radical expressions whose sum is $2\sqrt{7}$.

Challenge

59. **TEST PREP** $\dfrac{12\sqrt{68x^5y^3}}{\sqrt{4x^2y^2}} - \dfrac{9\sqrt{85x^7y^5}}{\sqrt{5x^4y^4}} =$

A. $3\sqrt{17x^3y}$ **B.** $6\sqrt{68x^3y} - 9\sqrt{17x^3y}$ **C.** $21x\sqrt{17y}$ **D.** $3|x|\sqrt{17xy}$

Simplify.

60. $\frac{2}{3}\sqrt{4\frac{1}{2}} + \frac{3}{2}\sqrt[3]{16} + \frac{1}{4}\sqrt{72}$

61. $x\sqrt[3]{2y} - \sqrt[3]{16x^3y} + \frac{x}{3}\sqrt[3]{54y}$

62. ***Mathematical Reasoning*** Without using a calculator, determine which is larger, $5\sqrt[3]{2}$ or $2\sqrt[3]{31}$.

Mixed Review

Find the variation constant and an equation of variation where y varies directly as x and the following are true.

63. $y = 3$ when $x = 6$ **64.** $y = -4$ when $x = 2$ **65.** $y = 4$ when $x = 7$ 6-9

Simplify. **66.** $\dfrac{5.2 \times 10^{-3}}{2.6 \times 10^4}$ **67.** $\dfrac{3.78 \times 10^7}{2.7 \times 10^8}$ **68.** $\dfrac{5.95 \times 10^8}{1.7 \times 10^5}$ 1-9

Solve. **69.** $x^2 - 2x = 8$ **70.** $y^2 - 4y = 21$ **71.** $4a^2 = 25$ 5-7

72. Six yards of fabric cost \$11.00, and 15 yards cost \$24.50.

a. Fit a linear function to the data points.

b. Use the function to find the cost of 11 yards of fabric. 3-8

73. Canned juice A contains 70% apple juice; canned juice B contains 55% apple juice. How many liters of each should be mixed together to get 12 liters of juice that contains 60% apple juice? 2-2

More Operations with Radical Expressions

7-4

What You'll Learn

1. To multiply radical expressions
2. To rationalize the denominators of radical expressions

. . . And Why

To simplify radical expressions when solving algebraic equations containing radicals

PART 1 Multiplying

Objective: Multiply radical expressions.

To multiply radical expressions in which some factors contain more than one term, we use the same procedures as for multiplying polynomials.

EXAMPLES Multiply.

1 $\sqrt[3]{y}\left(\sqrt[3]{y^2} + \sqrt[3]{2}\right) = \sqrt[3]{y} \cdot \sqrt[3]{y^2} + \sqrt[3]{y} \cdot \sqrt[3]{2}$ Using the distributive property

$= \sqrt[3]{y^3} + \sqrt[3]{2y}$ Multiplying radicals

$= y + \sqrt[3]{2y}$ Simplifying $\sqrt[3]{y^3}$

2 (F O I L)

$\left(4\sqrt{3} + \sqrt{2}\right)\left(\sqrt{3} - 5\sqrt{2}\right) = 4\left(\sqrt{3}\right)^2 - 20\sqrt{3} \cdot \sqrt{2} + \sqrt{2} \cdot \sqrt{3} - 5\left(\sqrt{2}\right)^2$

$= 4 \cdot 3 - 20\sqrt{6} + \sqrt{6} - 5 \cdot 2$

$= 12 - 20\sqrt{6} + \sqrt{6} - 10$

$= 2 - 19\sqrt{6}$

3 $\left(\sqrt{5} + \sqrt{7}\right)\left(\sqrt{5} - \sqrt{7}\right) = \left(\sqrt{5}\right)^2 - \left(\sqrt{7}\right)^2$ Multiplying as the sum and difference of two expressions

$= 5 - 7$

$= -2$

Try This Multiply.

a. $\sqrt{2}\left(5\sqrt{3} + 3\sqrt{7}\right)$ **b.** $\left(\sqrt{a} + 2\sqrt{3}\right)\left(3\sqrt{b} - 4\sqrt{3}\right)$

c. $\left(2\sqrt{5} - y\right)^2$ **d.** $\left(8 - 5\sqrt{x}\right)\left(8 + 5\sqrt{x}\right)$

PART 2 Rationalizing Denominators

Objective: Rationalize denominators of radical expressions.

When calculating with radical expressions, we usually write the result without radicals in the denominator. This is called **rationalizing the denominator.** When rationalizing a denominator, we multiply by 1 to make the denominator a perfect power.

EXAMPLE 4 Rationalize the denominator.

$$\sqrt[3]{\frac{7}{9}} = \sqrt[3]{\frac{7}{3 \cdot 3} \cdot \frac{3}{3}}$$ Multiplying the radicand by 1 to make the denominator a perfect cube

$$= \sqrt[3]{\frac{21}{3 \cdot 3 \cdot 3}} = \frac{\sqrt[3]{21}}{\sqrt[3]{3^3}} = \frac{\sqrt[3]{21}}{3}$$

In Example 4, we multiplied by 1 inside the radical sign. We can also multiply by 1 outside the radical sign.

EXAMPLE 5 Rationalize the denominator.

$$\sqrt{\frac{2a}{5b}} = \frac{\sqrt{2a}}{\sqrt{5b}}$$ Converting to a quotient of radicals

$$= \frac{\sqrt{2a}}{\sqrt{5b}} \cdot \frac{\sqrt{5b}}{\sqrt{5b}}$$ Multiplying by 1

$$= \frac{\sqrt{10ab}}{\sqrt{25b^2}}$$ The radicand in the denominator is a perfect square.

$$= \frac{\sqrt{10ab}}{5|b|}$$ Finding the square root of $25b^2$

Try This Rationalize the denominator.

e. $\sqrt{\frac{2}{3}}$ **f.** $\sqrt{\frac{10}{7}}$ **g.** $\sqrt[3]{\frac{3}{6}}$ **h.** $\sqrt{\frac{4a}{3b}}$ **i.** $\frac{\sqrt{4x^5}}{\sqrt{3y^3}}$

EXAMPLE 6 Rationalize the denominator.

$$\frac{\sqrt[3]{a}}{\sqrt[3]{9x}}$$

To choose the symbol for 1, we look at the radicand $9x$. This is $3 \cdot 3 \cdot x$. To make it a perfect cube we need another 3 and two more x's. Thus, we multiply by $\frac{\sqrt[3]{3x^2}}{\sqrt[3]{3x^2}}$.

$$\frac{\sqrt[3]{a}}{\sqrt[3]{9x}} = \frac{\sqrt[3]{a}}{\sqrt[3]{9x}} \cdot \frac{\sqrt[3]{3x^2}}{\sqrt[3]{3x^2}}$$ Multiplying by 1

$$= \frac{\sqrt[3]{3ax^2}}{\sqrt[3]{27x^3}}$$

$$= \frac{\sqrt[3]{3ax^2}}{3x}$$ Simplifying

Try This Rationalize the denominator.

j. $\frac{\sqrt[3]{7}}{\sqrt[3]{2}}$ **k.** $\sqrt[7]{\frac{3x^5}{2y}}$

When the denominator to be rationalized has two terms, we choose a symbol for 1 as illustrated below.

Expression	Symbol for 1	Expression	Symbol for 1
$\frac{3}{2+\sqrt{7}}$	$\frac{2-\sqrt{7}}{2-\sqrt{7}}$	$\frac{4+\sqrt{3}}{\sqrt{3}-\sqrt{11}}$	$\frac{\sqrt{3}+\sqrt{11}}{\sqrt{3}+\sqrt{11}}$

Multiplying by such symbols for 1 produces a difference of two squares in the denominator. Expressions such as $2 + \sqrt{7}$ and $2 - \sqrt{7}$ are **conjugates** of each other.

EXAMPLES

7 Rationalize the denominator.

$$\frac{3}{2+\sqrt{7}} = \frac{3}{2+\sqrt{7}} \cdot \frac{2-\sqrt{7}}{2-\sqrt{7}}$$ Using the conjugate of the denominator to multiply by 1

$$= \frac{3(2-\sqrt{7})}{(2+\sqrt{7})(2-\sqrt{7})}$$ Multiplying numerators and denominators

$$= \frac{3(2-\sqrt{7})}{(2)^2-(\sqrt{7})^2}$$ Multiplying as the sum and difference of two expressions

$$= \frac{3(2-\sqrt{7})}{4-7}$$ Simplifying

$$= \frac{3(2-\sqrt{7})}{-3}$$

$$= -2 + \sqrt{7}$$

8 $$\frac{4+\sqrt{2}}{\sqrt{5}-\sqrt{2}} = \frac{4+\sqrt{2}}{\sqrt{5}-\sqrt{2}} \cdot \frac{\sqrt{5}+\sqrt{2}}{\sqrt{5}+\sqrt{2}}$$ Using the conjugate of the denominator to multiply by 1

$$= \frac{(4+\sqrt{2})(\sqrt{5}+\sqrt{2})}{(\sqrt{5}-\sqrt{2})(\sqrt{5}+\sqrt{2})}$$ Multiplying numerators and denominators

$$= \frac{4\sqrt{5}+4\sqrt{2}+\sqrt{2}\sqrt{5}+(\sqrt{2})^2}{(\sqrt{5})^2-(\sqrt{2})^2}$$ Using FOIL

$$= \frac{4\sqrt{5}+4\sqrt{2}+\sqrt{10}+2}{5-2}$$ Squaring in the denominator

$$= \frac{4\sqrt{5}+4\sqrt{2}+\sqrt{10}+2}{3}$$

Try This Rationalize the denominator.

l. $\frac{5}{1-\sqrt{2}}$ **m.** $\frac{1}{\sqrt{2}+\sqrt{3}}$ **n.** $\frac{\sqrt{5}+1}{\sqrt{3}-1}$ **o.** $\frac{2\sqrt{3}-3}{3\sqrt{3}-3}$

Extra Help On the Web

Look for worked-out examples at the Prentice Hall Web site.
www.phschool.com

7-4 Exercises

A

Multiply.

1. $\sqrt{6}(2 - 3\sqrt{6})$ **2.** $\sqrt{3}(4 + \sqrt{3})$ **3.** $\sqrt{2}(\sqrt{3} - \sqrt{5})$

4. $\sqrt{5}(\sqrt{5} - \sqrt{2})$ **5.** $\sqrt{3}(2\sqrt{5} - 3\sqrt{4})$ **6.** $\sqrt{2}(3\sqrt{10} - 2\sqrt{2})$

7. $\sqrt[3]{2}(\sqrt[3]{4} - 2\sqrt[3]{32})$ **8.** $\sqrt[3]{3}(\sqrt[3]{9} - 4\sqrt[3]{21})$

9. $\sqrt[3]{a}(\sqrt[3]{2a^2} + \sqrt[3]{16a^2})$ **10.** $\sqrt[3]{x}(\sqrt[3]{3x^2} - \sqrt[3]{81x^2})$

11. $(\sqrt{3} - \sqrt{2})(\sqrt{3} + \sqrt{2})$ **12.** $(\sqrt{5} + \sqrt{6})(\sqrt{5} - \sqrt{6})$

13. $(\sqrt{a} + \sqrt{b})(\sqrt{a} - \sqrt{b})$ **14.** $(\sqrt{x} - \sqrt{y})(\sqrt{x} + \sqrt{y})$

15. $(3 - \sqrt{5})(2 + \sqrt{5})$ **16.** $(2 + \sqrt{6})(4 - \sqrt{6})$

17. $(\sqrt{3} + 1)(2\sqrt{3} + 1)$ **18.** $(4\sqrt{3} + 5)(\sqrt{3} - 2)$

19. $(2\sqrt{7} - 4\sqrt{2})(3\sqrt{7} + 6\sqrt{2})$ **20.** $(4\sqrt{5} + 3\sqrt{3})(3\sqrt{5} - 4\sqrt{3})$

21. $(\sqrt{a} + \sqrt{2})(\sqrt{a} + \sqrt{3})$ **22.** $(2 - \sqrt{x})(1 - \sqrt{x})$

23. $(2\sqrt[3]{3} + \sqrt[3]{2})(\sqrt[3]{3} - 2\sqrt[3]{2})$ **24.** $(3\sqrt[4]{7} + \sqrt[4]{6})(2\sqrt[4]{9} - 3\sqrt[4]{6})$

25. $(2 + \sqrt{3})^2$ **26.** $(\sqrt{5} + 1)^2$

27. $(3\sqrt{2} - \sqrt{3})^2$ **28.** $(5\sqrt{3} + 3\sqrt{5})^2$

29. **TEST PREP** Multiply. $(2\sqrt{5} - 3\sqrt{7})(4\sqrt{5} + 11\sqrt{7})$

A. $40 - 231$ **B.** $8\sqrt{5} - 33\sqrt{7}$ **C.** $10\sqrt{35} - 191$ **D.** $6\sqrt{5} + 8\sqrt{7}$

Rationalize the denominator.

30. $\sqrt{\frac{6}{5}}$ **31.** $\sqrt{\frac{11}{6}}$ **32.** $\sqrt{\frac{10}{7}}$ **33.** $\sqrt{\frac{22}{3}}$

34. $\frac{6\sqrt{5}}{5\sqrt{3}}$ **35.** $\frac{2\sqrt{3}}{5\sqrt{2}}$ **36.** $\sqrt[3]{\frac{16}{9}}$ **37.** $\sqrt[3]{\frac{3}{9}}$

38. $\frac{\sqrt[3]{3a}}{\sqrt[3]{5c}}$ **39.** $\frac{\sqrt[3]{7x}}{\sqrt[3]{3y}}$ **40.** $\frac{\sqrt[3]{2y^4}}{\sqrt[3]{6x^4}}$ **41.** $\frac{\sqrt[3]{3a^4}}{\sqrt[3]{7b^2}}$

42. $\frac{1}{\sqrt[3]{xy}}$ **43.** $\frac{1}{\sqrt[3]{ab}}$ **44.** $\frac{5}{8 - \sqrt{6}}$

45. $\frac{7}{9 + \sqrt{10}}$ **46.** $\frac{-4\sqrt{7}}{\sqrt{5} - \sqrt{3}}$ **47.** $\frac{-3\sqrt{2}}{\sqrt{3} - \sqrt{5}}$

48. $\frac{\sqrt{5} - 2\sqrt{6}}{\sqrt{3} - 4\sqrt{5}}$ **49.** $\frac{\sqrt{6} - 3\sqrt{5}}{\sqrt{3} - 2\sqrt{7}}$ **50.** $\frac{\sqrt{x} - \sqrt{y}}{\sqrt{x} + \sqrt{y}}$

51. $\frac{\sqrt{a} + \sqrt{b}}{\sqrt{a} - \sqrt{b}}$ **52.** $\frac{5\sqrt{3} - 3\sqrt{2}}{3\sqrt{2} - 2\sqrt{3}}$ **53.** $\frac{7\sqrt{2} + 4\sqrt{3}}{4\sqrt{3} - 3\sqrt{2}}$

B

Rationalize the numerator.

54. $\frac{\sqrt{7}}{\sqrt{3}}$ **55.** $\sqrt{\frac{14}{21}}$ **56.** $\frac{4\sqrt{13}}{3\sqrt{7}}$ **57.** $\frac{\sqrt[3]{7}}{\sqrt[3]{2}}$ **58.** $\sqrt{\frac{7x}{3y}}$

59. $\frac{\sqrt[3]{5y^4}}{\sqrt[3]{6x^5}}$ **60.** $\frac{\sqrt{3}+5}{8}$ **61.** $\frac{\sqrt{3}-5}{\sqrt{2}+5}$ **62.** $\frac{\sqrt{5}-\sqrt{2}}{\sqrt{2}+\sqrt{3}}$

Multiply.

63. $(\sqrt{x+3}-3)(\sqrt{x+3}+3)$ **64.** $(\sqrt{x+h}-\sqrt{x})(\sqrt{x+h}+\sqrt{x})$

65. ***Critical Thinking*** Find two different pairs of conjugates whose product is 8.

Challenge

Simplify.

66. $\frac{\sqrt[3]{c^3+3c^2d+3cd^2+d^3}}{\sqrt{c^2-d^2}\cdot\sqrt{c^2-d^2}}$ **67.** $\frac{1+\sqrt{y}}{\sqrt{x}+\sqrt{xy}}\cdot\frac{1-\sqrt{y}}{1-y}\cdot\frac{x-xy}{\sqrt{x}-\sqrt{xy}}$

68. $\frac{\sqrt{x}}{\sqrt{x}-\sqrt{x+1}}$

69. $\frac{\sqrt{p-4q}}{\sqrt{3q^2+4pq+p^2}}\cdot\frac{\sqrt{p+3q}}{\sqrt{p^2+6pq+8q^2}}\div\frac{1}{\sqrt{p^2+3pq+2q^2}}$

Mixed Review

Find the variation constant and an equation of variation where y varies inversely as x and the following are true.

70. $y = -4$ when $x = 2$ **71.** $y = 4$ when $x = 7$ *6-9*

Factor.

72. $2x^2 + 4x + 2$

73. $9y^2 - x^2 - 2x - 1$

74. $8y^3 - 27$ *5-7*

Suppose $f(x) = x^2 + 1$ and $g(x) = \frac{1}{2}x - 3$.

75. Find $f(g(10))$. **76.** Find $g(f(10))$.

77. Find an expression for $f(g(x))$. **78.** Find an expression for $g(f(x))$. *3-9*

79. The sum of the squares of two consecutive even integers is 52. Find the integers.

80. The Looksnice Painting Company charges \$125 plus \$85 per room to paint interiors. Find the cost of painting a six-room house.

81. A telethon has raised \$1250 so far. That is about 2.5% of its goal. Find the amount the telethon is trying to raise. *5-8*

7-5 Rational Numbers as Exponents

What You'll Learn

1. To calculate radical expressions of the form $\sqrt[k]{a^m}$ in two ways
2. To write expressions with rational exponents as radical expressions and vice versa
3. To simplify expressions containing negative rational exponents
4. To use rational exponents to simplify radical expressions

. . . And Why

To simplify more-involved radical expressions when solving algebraic equations and problems

Introducing the Concept: Exponents with Radicals

Simplify and compare your answers.

$$\sqrt[3]{8^2} \text{ and } \left(\sqrt[3]{8}\right)^2 \qquad \sqrt{4^2} \text{ and } \left(\sqrt{4}\right)^2$$

PART 1 Combinations of Powers and Roots

Objective: Calculate expressions of the form $\sqrt[k]{a^m}$ in two ways.

The results of the introductory work suggest the following theorem.

Theorem 7-6

For any nonnegative number a, any natural-number index k, and any integer m, $\sqrt[k]{a^m} = \left(\sqrt[k]{a}\right)^m$.

We can raise to a power and then take a root, or we can take a root and then raise to a power. One method of simplifying may be easier than the other.

EXAMPLES Simplify as shown. Then use Theorem 7-6 to simplify another way.

1

$$\sqrt[3]{27^2} = \sqrt[3]{729} = 9$$
$$\left(\sqrt[3]{27}\right)^2 = (3)^2 = 9$$

2

$$\sqrt[3]{2^6} = \sqrt[3]{64} = 4$$
$$\left(\sqrt[3]{2}\right)^6 = \sqrt[3]{2} \cdot \sqrt[3]{2} \cdot \sqrt[3]{2} \cdot \sqrt[3]{2} \cdot \sqrt[3]{2} \cdot \sqrt[3]{2} = 2 \cdot 2 = 4$$

3

$$\begin{aligned}\left(\sqrt{5x}\right)^3 &= \sqrt{5x} \cdot \sqrt{5x} \cdot \sqrt{5x}\\ &= \sqrt{5^3x^3}\\ &= \sqrt{5^2x^2}\sqrt{5x} = 5|x|\sqrt{5x}\\ \sqrt{(5x)^3} &= \sqrt{125x^3}\\ &= \sqrt{25x^2} \cdot \sqrt{5x} = 5|x|\sqrt{5x}\end{aligned}$$

Try This Simplify as shown. Then use Theorem 7-6 to simplify another way.

a. $\sqrt[3]{8^2}$ **b.** $\left(\sqrt{6y}\right)^3$

PART 2 Rational Exponents

Objective: Write expressions with rational exponents as radical expressions and vice versa.

To extend the idea of an exponent to include rational exponents, consider $a^{\frac{1}{2}} \cdot a^{\frac{1}{2}}$. If the usual properties of exponents are to hold, then $a^{\frac{1}{2}} \cdot a^{\frac{1}{2}}$ should equal a^1, or a. We also know that $\sqrt{a} \cdot \sqrt{a} = a$. Thus $a^{\frac{1}{2}}$ should be defined as $\sqrt{a}$. Similarly, $a^{\frac{1}{3}} \cdot a^{\frac{1}{3}} \cdot a^{\frac{1}{3}} = a^1$, or a. Thus, $a^{\frac{1}{3}}$ should be defined as $\sqrt[3]{a}$.

Definition

For any nonnegative number a and any natural-number index k, $a^{\frac{1}{k}}$ means $\sqrt[k]{a}$ (the nonnegative kth root of a).

When working with rational exponents, we will assume that variables in the base are nonnegative.

EXAMPLES Write without rational exponents.

4 $x^{\frac{1}{2}} = \sqrt{x}$ **5** $27^{\frac{1}{3}} = \sqrt[3]{27}$, or 3 **6** $(abc)^{\frac{1}{5}} = \sqrt[5]{abc}$

Radical expressions can also be rewritten with rational exponents.

EXAMPLES Write with rational exponents.

7 $\sqrt[5]{7xy} = (7xy)^{\frac{1}{5}}$ **8** $\sqrt[7]{\frac{x^3y}{9}} = \left(\frac{x^3y}{9}\right)^{\frac{1}{7}}$

Try This Write without rational exponents.

c. $y^{\frac{1}{4}}$ **d.** $(3a)^{\frac{1}{4}}$ **e.** $16^{\frac{1}{4}}$

Write with rational exponents.

f. $\sqrt[4]{a^3b^2c}$ **g.** $\sqrt[5]{\frac{x^2y}{16}}$

How should we define $a^{\frac{2}{3}}$? If the usual properties of exponents are to hold, we have $a^{\frac{2}{3}} = \left(a^{\frac{1}{3}}\right)^2$, or $\left(\sqrt[3]{a}\right)^2$, or $\sqrt[3]{a^2}$.

Definition

For any natural numbers m and k, and any nonnegative number a, $a^{\frac{m}{k}}$ means $\sqrt[k]{a^m}$.

Thus, $a^{\frac{m}{k}}$ represents the principal kth root of a^m. Since by Theorem 7-6 we know that $\sqrt[k]{a^m} = \left(\sqrt[k]{a}\right)^m$, it follows that $a^{\frac{m}{k}}$ also represents $\left(\sqrt[k]{a}\right)^m$.

EXAMPLES Write without rational exponents.

9 $(27)^{\frac{2}{3}} = (\sqrt[3]{27})^2$, or $(27)^{\frac{2}{3}} = \sqrt[3]{27^2}$

$= (3)^2 \qquad = \sqrt[3]{729}$

$= 9 \qquad = 9$

10 $4^{\frac{3}{2}} = (\sqrt[2]{4^3})^3$, or $4^{\frac{3}{2}} = \sqrt[2]{4^3}$

$= 2^3 \qquad = \sqrt{64}$

$= 8 \qquad = 8$

EXAMPLES Write with rational exponents.

11 $\sqrt[3]{8^4} = 8^{\frac{4}{3}}$

12 $(\sqrt[4]{7xy})^5 = (7xy)^{\frac{5}{4}}$

Try This Write without rational exponents.

h. $x^{\frac{3}{2}}$

i. $8^{\frac{2}{3}}$

Write with rational exponents.

j. $(\sqrt[3]{7abc})^4$

k. $\sqrt[5]{6^7}$

l. $\sqrt[4]{x^2y^3}$

PART 3 Negative Rational Exponents

Objective: Simplify expressions containing negative rational exponents.

Negative rational exponents have a meaning similar to that of negative integer exponents. Changing the sign of an exponent amounts to finding a reciprocal.

Definition

For any rational number $\frac{m}{n}$ and any positive real number a, $a^{-\frac{m}{n}}$ means $\frac{1}{a^{\frac{m}{n}}}$.

$a^{\frac{m}{n}}$ and $a^{-\frac{m}{n}}$ are reciprocals.

EXAMPLES Rewrite with positive exponents.

13 $4^{-\frac{1}{2}} = \frac{1}{4^{\frac{1}{2}}}$ $\quad$ $4^{-\frac{1}{2}}$ is the reciprocal of $4^{\frac{1}{2}}$.

Since $4^{\frac{1}{2}} = \sqrt{4} = 2$, the answer simplifies to $\frac{1}{2}$.

14 $(5xy)^{-\frac{4}{5}} = \frac{1}{(5xy)^{\frac{4}{5}}}$ $\quad$ $(5xy)^{-\frac{4}{5}}$ is the reciprocal of $(5xy)^{\frac{4}{5}}$.

Try This Rewrite with positive exponents.

m. $5^{-\frac{1}{4}}$ **n.** $(3xy)^{-\frac{7}{8}}$

The properties of exponents that hold for integer exponents also hold for rational exponents.

EXAMPLES Use the properties of exponents to simplify.

15 $3^{\frac{1}{5}} \cdot 3^{\frac{3}{5}} = 3^{\frac{1}{5}+\frac{3}{5}} = 3^{\frac{4}{5}}$ Adding exponents

16 $\frac{7^{\frac{1}{4}}}{7^{\frac{1}{2}}} = 7^{\frac{1}{4}-\frac{1}{2}} = 7^{\frac{1}{4}-\frac{2}{4}} = 7^{-\frac{1}{4}}$ Subtracting exponents

17 $(7.2^{\frac{2}{3}})^{\frac{3}{4}} = 7.2^{\frac{2}{3}\cdot\frac{3}{4}} = 7.2^{\frac{6}{12}} = 7.2^{\frac{1}{2}}$ Multiplying exponents

Try This Use the properties of exponents to simplify.

o. $7^{\frac{1}{3}} \cdot 7^{\frac{3}{5}}$ **p.** $\frac{5^{\frac{7}{6}}}{5^{\frac{5}{6}}}$ **q.** $(9^{\frac{3}{5}})^{\frac{2}{3}}$

PART 4 Simplifying Radical Expressions

Objective: Use rational exponents to simplify radical expressions.

Rational exponents can be used to simplify some radical expressions. The procedure is as follows.

1. Convert radical expressions to exponential expressions.
2. Use the properties of exponents to simplify.
3. Convert back to radical notation when appropriate.

EXAMPLES Use rational exponents to simplify.

18 $\sqrt[6]{x^3} = x^{\frac{3}{6}}$ Converting to an exponential expression

$= x^{\frac{1}{2}}$ Simplifying the exponent

$= \sqrt{x}$ Converting back to radical notation

19 $\sqrt[6]{4} = 4^{\frac{1}{6}} = (2^2)^{\frac{1}{6}} = 2^{\frac{2}{6}} = 2^{\frac{1}{3}} = \sqrt[3]{2}$

Try This Use rational exponents to simplify.

r. $\sqrt[4]{a^2}$ **s.** $\sqrt[4]{x^4}$ **t.** $\sqrt[6]{8}$

EXAMPLE 20 Use rational exponents to simplify.

$$\begin{aligned}\sqrt[8]{a^2b^4} &= (a^2b^4)^{\frac{1}{8}}\\ &= a^{\frac{2}{8}} \cdot b^{\frac{4}{8}}\\ &= a^{\frac{1}{4}} \cdot b^{\frac{2}{4}}\\ &= (ab^2)^{\frac{1}{4}}\\ &= \sqrt[4]{ab^2}\end{aligned}$$

Try This Use rational exponents to simplify.

u. $\sqrt[4]{x^4y^{12}}$ **v.** $\sqrt[12]{x^3y^6}$

We can use properties of rational exponents to write a single radical expression for a product or quotient.

EXAMPLES Write as a single radical expression.

21 $$\begin{aligned}\sqrt[3]{5} \cdot \sqrt{2} &= 5^{\frac{1}{3}} \cdot 2^{\frac{1}{2}}\\ &= 5^{\frac{2}{6}}2^{\frac{3}{6}}\\ &= (5^2 \cdot 2^3)^{\frac{1}{6}}\\ &= \sqrt[6]{5^2 \cdot 2^3}\\ &= \sqrt[6]{200}\end{aligned}$$

22 $$\begin{aligned}\sqrt{x-2} \cdot \sqrt[4]{3y} &= (x-2)^{\frac{1}{2}}(3y)^{\frac{1}{4}}\\ &= (x-2)^{\frac{2}{4}}(3y)^{\frac{1}{4}}\\ &= [(x-2)^2(3y)]^{\frac{1}{4}}\\ &= \sqrt[4]{(x^2-4x+4) \cdot 3y}\\ &= \sqrt[4]{3x^2y - 12xy + 12y}\end{aligned}$$

23 $$\frac{\sqrt[4]{(x+y)^3}}{\sqrt{x+y}} = \frac{(x+y)^{\frac{3}{4}}}{(x+y)^{\frac{1}{2}}} = (x+y)^{\frac{3}{4}-\frac{1}{2}} = (x+y)^{\frac{1}{4}} = \sqrt[4]{x+y}$$

Try This Write as a single radical expression.

w. $\sqrt[4]{7} \cdot \sqrt{3}$ **x.** $\dfrac{\sqrt[4]{(a-b)^5}}{a-b}$

EXAMPLE 24 Write as a single radical expression.

$$\begin{aligned}a^{\frac{1}{2}}b^{-\frac{1}{2}}c^{\frac{5}{6}} &= a^{\frac{3}{6}}b^{-\frac{3}{6}}c^{\frac{5}{6}} && \text{Rewriting exponents with a common denominator}\\ &= (a^3b^{-3}c^5)^{\frac{1}{6}} && \text{Using the properties of exponents}\\ &= \sqrt[6]{a^3b^{-3}c^5} && \text{Converting to radical notation}\end{aligned}$$

Try This Write as a single radical expression.

y. $x^{-\frac{2}{3}}y^{\frac{1}{2}}z^{\frac{5}{6}}$ **z.** $\dfrac{a^{\frac{1}{2}}b^{\frac{3}{8}}}{a^{\frac{1}{4}}b^{\frac{1}{8}}}$

We now have seen four different methods of simplifying radical expressions.

Simplifying Radical Expressions

1. **Simplifying by factoring** Factor the radicand, looking for factors that are perfect powers.
2. **Rationalizing denominators** Multiply the radical expression by 1 to make the denominator a perfect power. Then simplify the expression.
3. **Collecting like radical terms** Use the distributive laws to collect terms with the same radicand and index.
4. **Using rational exponents** Convert to exponential notation; use the properties of exponents to simplify. Convert back to radical notation.

7-5 Exercises

Look for worked-out examples at the Prentice Hall Web site.
www.phschool.com

A

Simplify as shown. Then use Theorem 7-6 to simplify another way.

1. $\sqrt{(6a)^3}$ **2.** $\sqrt{(7y)^3}$ **3.** $(\sqrt[3]{16b^2})^2$ **4.** $(\sqrt[3]{25r^2})^2$

5. $\sqrt{(18a^2b)^3}$ **6.** $\sqrt{(12x^2y)^3}$ **7.** $(\sqrt[3]{12c^2d})^2$ **8.** $(\sqrt[3]{9x^2y})^2$

Write without rational exponents.

9. $x^{\frac{1}{4}}$ **10.** $y^{\frac{1}{5}}$ **11.** $(8)^{\frac{1}{3}}$ **12.** $(16)^{\frac{1}{2}}$ **13.** $(a^2b^2)^{\frac{1}{5}}$

14. $(x^3y^3)^{\frac{1}{4}}$ **15.** $a^{\frac{2}{3}}$ **16.** $b^{\frac{3}{2}}$ **17.** $16^{\frac{3}{4}}$ **18.** $4^{\frac{7}{2}}$

19. $(a^5t^3)^{\frac{1}{2}}$ **20.** $m^{\frac{5}{6}}$ **21.** $y^{\frac{7}{2}}$ **22.** $32^{\frac{3}{5}}$ **23.** $(m^3n^5)^{\frac{1}{4}}$

Write with rational exponents.

24. $\sqrt[3]{20}$ **25.** $\sqrt[3]{19}$ **26.** $\sqrt{17}$ **27.** $\sqrt{6}$

28. $\sqrt[4]{cd}$ **29.** $\sqrt[5]{xy}$ **30.** $\sqrt[5]{xy^2z}$ **31.** $\sqrt[7]{x^3y^2z^2}$

32. $(\sqrt{3mn})^3$ **33.** $(\sqrt[3]{7xy})^4$ **34.** $(\sqrt[7]{8x^2y})^5$ **35.** $(\sqrt[6]{2a^5b})^7$

36. $(\sqrt[4]{16xy})^5$ **37.** $(\sqrt[6]{12ab})^3$ **38.** $(\sqrt[8]{2x^4y^6})^3$ **39.** $(\sqrt[7]{3a^4b^3})^4$

Write with positive exponents.

40. $x^{-\frac{1}{3}}$ **41.** $y^{-\frac{1}{4}}$ **42.** $(2rs)^{-\frac{3}{4}}$ **43.** $(5xy)^{-\frac{5}{6}}$

44. $\left(\frac{1}{10}\right)^{-\frac{2}{3}}$ **45.** $\left(\frac{1}{8}\right)^{-\frac{3}{4}}$ **46.** $\frac{1}{x^{-\frac{2}{3}}}$ **47.** $\frac{1}{x^{-\frac{5}{6}}}$

Use the properties of exponents to simplify.

48. $5^{\frac{3}{2}} \cdot 5^{\frac{1}{8}}$ **49.** $11^{\frac{2}{3}} \cdot 11^{\frac{1}{2}}$ **50.** $\frac{7^{\frac{5}{8}}}{7^{\frac{3}{8}}}$ **51.** $\frac{9^{\frac{9}{11}}}{9^{\frac{7}{11}}}$

52. $\frac{8.3^{\frac{3}{4}}}{8.3^{\frac{2}{5}}}$ **53.** $\frac{3.9^{\frac{3}{5}}}{3.9^{\frac{1}{4}}}$ **54.** $(10^{\frac{3}{5}})^{\frac{2}{5}}$ **55.** $(5^{\frac{5}{4}})^{\frac{3}{7}}$

Write an exponential expression. Then simplify, if possible. Write radical notation for the answer, if appropriate.

56. $\sqrt[6]{a^4}$ **57.** $\sqrt[6]{y^2}$ **58.** $\sqrt[3]{8y^6}$ **59.** $\sqrt{x^4y^6}$

60. $\sqrt[5]{32c^{10}d^{15}}$ **61.** $\sqrt[4]{16x^{12}y^{16}}$ **62.** $\sqrt[6]{\frac{m^{12}n^{24}}{64}}$ **63.** $\sqrt[5]{\frac{x^{15}y^{20}}{32}}$

Write as a single radical expression.

64. $\sqrt{x}\sqrt[3]{x-2}$ **65.** $\sqrt[4]{3x}\sqrt{y+4}$ **66.** $\frac{\sqrt[3]{(a+b)^2}}{\sqrt{(a+b)}}$ **67.** $\frac{\sqrt[3]{(x+y)^2}}{\sqrt[4]{(x+y)^3}}$

68. $a^{\frac{2}{3}} \cdot b^{\frac{3}{4}}$ **69.** $x^{\frac{1}{3}} \cdot y^{\frac{1}{4}} \cdot z^{\frac{1}{6}}$ **70.** $\frac{s^{\frac{7}{12}} \cdot t^{\frac{5}{6}}}{s^{\frac{1}{3}} \cdot t^{-\frac{1}{6}}}$ **71.** $\frac{x^{\frac{8}{15}} \cdot y^{\frac{4}{5}}}{x^{\frac{1}{3}} \cdot y^{-\frac{1}{5}}}$

B

Simplify. Write without rational exponents.

72. $\frac{1}{x^{\frac{1}{2}}} \cdot \frac{1}{y^{\frac{1}{2}}}$ **73.** $\frac{(a+b)^{\frac{1}{2}}}{(a-b)^{-\frac{1}{2}}}$ **74.** $(x^2 + 2xy + y^2)^{\frac{1}{3}}(x+y)^{\frac{1}{3}}$

75. $(x+y)^{\frac{1}{2}}(x-y)^{\frac{1}{2}}$ **76.** $\left(\frac{1}{a^{-2}} + 4ab + \frac{4}{b^{-2}}\right)^{-\frac{1}{2}}$ **77.** $(a^3 - 3a^2b + 3ab^2 - b^3)^{-\frac{1}{3}}$

Simplify. Write without rational exponents.

78. *Critical Thinking* Explain each step to simplify $\sqrt[5]{\sqrt[4]{x}}$.

79. $\frac{\sqrt{x^2 + 7x + 6}}{\sqrt{x+1}}$ **80.** $\frac{1}{\sqrt{x+y}} + \frac{1}{\sqrt{x-y}}$

81. *Write a Convincing Argument* Look at the problem below. Then write an argument to convince a classmate that your reasoning is correct. Prove that $a^{\frac{m}{n}}$ and $a^{-\frac{m}{n}}$ are reciprocals.

Challenge

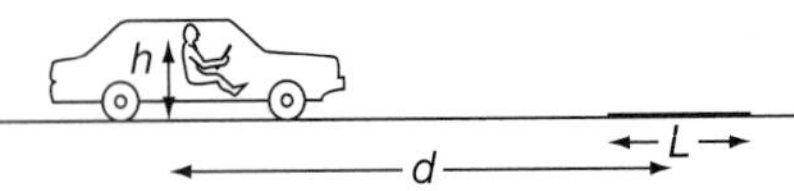

The optimal length (L) of the letters of a message printed on pavement is given by the following formula, where d is the distance of a car from the lettering and h is the height of the eye above the surface of the road. Find L, given the values of d, h, and $L = \frac{(0.00252)d^{2.27}}{h}$.

82. $h = 2.4$ m, $d = 80$ m **83.** $h = 0.9906$ m, $d = 75$ m

Mixed Review

Determine whether these systems are dependent.

84. $3x + y = 5$
$2y = 10 - 6x$

85. $2y = x - 3$
$x = 2y - 3$

86. $2x + 4y = 6$
$-2y = 3 - x$ *4-6*

Simplify. **87.** $x^2 + x^3 + 2x^2 + 3x^3$ **88.** $x^2 \cdot x^3 \cdot 2x^2 \cdot 3x^3$ *5-1*

Solving Radical Equations

7-6

The formula $V = 1.2\sqrt{h}$ is a **radical equation** that can be used to approximate the distance (V) in miles that a person can see to the horizon from a height of h feet.

What You'll Learn

1. To solve radical equations
2. To solve problems containing radicals

. . . And Why

To increase efficiency in solving problems

PART 1

The Principle of Powers

Objective: Solve radical equations.

Suppose the equation $a = b$ is true. When we square both sides we still get a true equation, $a^2 = b^2$.

Theorem 7-7

The Principle of Powers

For any natural number n, if $a = b$ is true, then $a^n = b^n$ is true.

EXAMPLES Solve.

1 $\sqrt{x} - 3 = 4$

$\sqrt{x} = 7$ Adding 3 to both sides

$x = 7^2$, or 49 Squaring both sides

Check:

$\sqrt{x} - 3$	4
$\sqrt{49} - 3$	4
$7 - 3$	4
4	4 ✓

The solution is 49.

2 $\sqrt{x} = -3$

$(\sqrt{x})^2 = (-3)^2$ Using the principle of powers

$x = 9$

Check:

$\sqrt{x}$	-3
$\sqrt{9}$	-3
3	-3

The number 9 does not check because the principal square root of a number is never negative. Hence the equation has no solution.

Try This Solve and check.

a. $\sqrt{x} - 7 = 3$ **b.** $3 - \sqrt{x} = 12$

To solve a radical equation, isolate a radical term on one side of the equation.

EXAMPLE 3 Solve $x = \sqrt{x + 7} + 5$.

$$x - 5 = \sqrt{x + 7} \quad \text{Isolating the radical}$$
$$(x - 5)^2 = (\sqrt{x + 7})^2 \quad \text{Using the principle of powers; squaring both sides}$$
$$x^2 - 10x + 25 = x + 7$$
$$x^2 - 11x + 18 = 0$$
$$(x - 9)(x - 2) = 0 \quad \text{Factoring}$$
$$x = 9 \text{ or } x = 2 \quad \text{Using the principle of zero products}$$

Check: $x = \sqrt{x + 7} + 5$

x	$\sqrt{x + 7} + 5$
9	$\sqrt{9 + 7} + 5$
9	$\sqrt{16} + 5$
9	$4 + 5$
9	9 ✓

$x = \sqrt{x + 7} + 5$

x	$\sqrt{x + 7} + 5$
2	$\sqrt{2 + 7} + 5$
2	$\sqrt{9} + 5$
2	$3 + 5$
2	8

Since 9 checks but 2 does not, the solution is 9. Note that 2 is a solution to the equation that resulted from squaring both sides. It is not a solution of the *original* equation. Such numbers are **extraneous roots.**

A radical term may remain after squaring both sides. The same procedures may be used again when this occurs.

EXAMPLE 4 Solve.

$$\sqrt{2x - 5} = 1 + \sqrt{x - 3} \quad \text{One radical is already isolated.}$$
$$(\sqrt{2x - 5})^2 = (1 + \sqrt{x - 3})^2 \quad \text{Squaring both sides}$$
$$2x - 5 = 1 + 2\sqrt{x - 3} + (x - 3)$$
$$x - 3 = 2\sqrt{x - 3} \quad \text{Isolating the remaining radical}$$
$$(x - 3)^2 = (2\sqrt{x - 3})^2 \quad \text{Squaring both sides again}$$
$$x^2 - 6x + 9 = 4(x - 3)$$
$$x^2 - 10x + 21 = 0$$
$$x = 7 \text{ or } x = 3 \quad \text{7 and 3 check and are the solutions.}$$

Try This Solve.

c. $\sqrt{x} - \sqrt{x - 5} = 1$ **d.** $\sqrt{3x + 1} = 1 + \sqrt{x + 4}$

PART 2 Problem Solving

Objective: Solve problems with radicals.

EXAMPLE 5 The formula $V = 1.2\sqrt{h}$ is a radical equation that approximates the distance (V) in miles that a person can see to the horizon from a height of h feet. Find a formula to approximate height. How high is a person who can see 72 miles to the horizon?

$$V = 1.2\sqrt{h}$$
$$V^2 = (1.2\sqrt{h})^2 \quad \text{Squaring both sides}$$
$$V^2 = 1.44h$$
$$\frac{V^2}{1.44} = h \quad \text{Solving for } h$$

Substituting 72 for V, $h = \frac{72^2}{1.44} = \frac{5184}{1.44} = 3600$. The person is at a height of 3600 feet.

Using the formula on page 318, a person overlooking the ocean from a hill or mountain can determine the distance they can see if the height is known or can be estimated.

Try This

e. The formula $S = \pi r\sqrt{r^2 + h^2}$ gives the surface area of a cone, given its radius and height. Solve the formula for h. What is h when $S = 15\pi$ and $r = 3$?

7-6 Exercises

Extra Help On the Web

Look for worked-out examples at the Prentice Hall Web site.
www.phschool.com

A

Solve.

1. $\sqrt{2x - 3} = 1$ **2.** $\sqrt{x + 3} = 6$ **3.** $\sqrt{y + 1} - 5 = 8$

4. $\sqrt{x - 2} - 7 = -4$ **5.** $\sqrt[3]{x + 5} = 2$ **6.** $\sqrt[3]{x - 2} = 3$

7. $\sqrt[4]{y - 3} = 2$ **8.** $\sqrt[4]{x + 3} = 3$ **9.** $\sqrt{3y + 1} = 9$

10. $\sqrt{2y + 1} = 13$ **11.** $3\sqrt{x} = 6$ **12.** $8\sqrt{y} = 2$

13. $\sqrt[3]{x} = -3$ **14.** $\sqrt[3]{y} = -4$ **15.** $\sqrt{y + 3} - 20 = 0$

16. $\sqrt{x + 4} - 11 = 0$ **17.** $\sqrt{x + 2} = -4$ **18.** $\sqrt{y - 3} = -2$

19. $8 = \frac{1}{\sqrt{x}}$ **20.** $3 = \frac{1}{\sqrt{y}}$

21. $\sqrt[3]{6x + 9} + 8 = 5$ **22.** $\sqrt[3]{3y + 6} + 2 = 3$

23. $\sqrt{3y + 1} = \sqrt{2y + 6}$ **24.** $\sqrt{5x - 3} = \sqrt{2x + 3}$

25. $2\sqrt{1 - x} = \sqrt{5}$ **26.** $2\sqrt{2y - 3} = \sqrt{4y}$

27. $2\sqrt{t - 1} = \sqrt{3t - 1}$ **28.** $\sqrt{y + 10} = 3\sqrt{2y + 3}$

29. $\sqrt{y - 5} + \sqrt{y} = 5$ **30.** $\sqrt{x - 9} + \sqrt{x} = 1$

31. $3 + \sqrt{z - 6} = \sqrt{z + 9}$ **32.** $\sqrt{4x - 3} = 2 + \sqrt{2x - 5}$

33. $\sqrt{20 - x} + 8 = \sqrt{9 - x} + 11$ **34.** $4 + \sqrt{10 - x} = 6 + \sqrt{4 - x}$

35. $\sqrt{x + 2} + \sqrt{3x + 4} = 2$ **36.** $\sqrt{6x + 7} - \sqrt{3x + 3} = 1$

37. $\sqrt{4y + 1} - \sqrt{y - 2} = 3$ **38.** $\sqrt{y + 15} - \sqrt{2y + 7} = 1$

39. $\sqrt{3x - 5} + \sqrt{2x + 3} + 1 = 0$ **40.** $\sqrt{2m - 3} = \sqrt{m + 7} - 2$

Studying atomic nuclei was made easier by using the Van de Graaff generator. It is a source of charged particles. A belt inside the dome contains ions that get brushed to the surface of the dome. A person can conduct the ions and become a "human magnet;" the hair is "attracted" to the air around it. See Exercise 42.

41. The formula $v = \sqrt{2gs}$ represents the velocity (v) of an object that has fallen a distance of s feet, where g is acceleration due to gravity. Solve the formula for s, and find s for a falling object with velocity $32g$.

42. The radius of a Van de Graaff generator that can collect a maximum charge of Q coulombs on its surface is given by $R = 1.826 \times 10^{-2}\sqrt{Q}$. Solve the formula for Q, and find Q for a generator with a radius of 1.5 m.

B

Solve.

43. $x^{\frac{1}{3}} + 5 = 7$

44. $(x - 5)^{\frac{1}{3}} - 3 = 7$

45. $(x - 5)^{\frac{2}{3}} = 2$

46. $\dfrac{x + \sqrt{x + 1}}{x - \sqrt{x + 1}} = \dfrac{5}{11}$

47. $\sqrt{x + 2} - \sqrt{x - 2} = \sqrt{2x}$

48. $2\sqrt{x + 3} = \sqrt{x} + \sqrt{x + 8}$

49. $\sqrt[3]{2x - 1} = \sqrt[6]{x + 1}$

50. ***Critical Thinking*** Consider the equation $x = \sqrt{6 + \sqrt{6 + \sqrt{6 + \sqrt{6 + \ldots}}}}$ where the radicals continue infinitely. Design a plan for estimating or finding the solution.

Challenge

51. Prove Theorem 7-7.

Solve.

52. $\sqrt{y + \sqrt{2y}} = 2$

53. $\sqrt{\sqrt{x + 25}} - \sqrt{x} = 5$

Self-Test On the Web

Check your progress. Look for a self-test at the Prentice Hall Web site.
www.phschool.com

Mixed Review

Simplify. 54. $\sqrt[3]{216}$ 55. $\sqrt{12y^2}$ 56. $\sqrt[3]{(y - 5)^4}$ 57. $\sqrt{2} \cdot \sqrt{8}$ *7-2*

Finding Roots

If your calculator has an $\sqrt[x]{y}$ key, you can find the kth root of a number.

To find $\sqrt[9]{0.01}$, press:

0.01 $\sqrt[x]{y}$ 9 = → 0.5994843

You can also find kth roots using rational exponents and the y^x key.

To find $\sqrt[5]{83}$, recall that $\sqrt[5]{83} = 83^{\frac{1}{5}}$. Press:

83 y^x (1 ÷ 5) = → 2.4200014

Imaginary and Complex Numbers

7-7

What You'll Learn

1. To express the square roots of negative numbers and their products using *i*
2. To define complex numbers and add or subtract with them

... And Why

To solve and graph quadratic equations

Part 1 Imaginary Numbers

Objective: Express the square root of negative numbers and their products in terms of *i*.

In the set of real numbers, negative numbers do not have square roots. An equation like $x^2 = -1$ has no solution. **Imaginary numbers** were invented so that negative numbers would have square roots and certain equations would have solutions. These numbers were devised using an imaginary unit named ***i*** and the agreement that $i^2 = -1$, or $i = \sqrt{-1}$.

We assume that *i* acts like a real number in other respects. Square roots of all negative numbers can then be expressed as a product of *i* and a real number.

EXAMPLES Express these numbers in terms of *i*.

1 $\sqrt{-5} = \sqrt{-1 \cdot 5}$ — Factoring the radicand

$= \sqrt{-1}\sqrt{5}$ — Using Theorem 7-5

$= i\sqrt{5}$, or $\sqrt{5}i$ — Using the definition of *i*

2 $-\sqrt{-7} = -\sqrt{-1 \cdot 7} = -\sqrt{-1}\sqrt{7} = -i\sqrt{7}$

3 $\sqrt{-99} = \sqrt{-1 \cdot 9 \cdot 11} = i\sqrt{9}\sqrt{11} = 3i\sqrt{11}$

Try This Express each number in terms of *i*.

a. $\sqrt{-7}$ **b.** $-\sqrt{-36}$ **c.** $\sqrt{-160}$

Definition

The **imaginary numbers** consist of all numbers bi, where b is a real number and i is the imaginary unit, with the property that $i^2 = -1$.

The first four powers of *i* establish an important pattern and should be memorized.

Powers of *i*

$i^1 = i \quad i^2 = -1 \quad i^3 = -i \quad i^4 = 1$

To multiply imaginary numbers or an imaginary number by a real number, it is important first to express the imaginary numbers in terms of i.

EXAMPLES Multiply.

4 $47i \cdot 2 = 94i$

5 $\sqrt{-5} \cdot 2i = i\sqrt{5} \cdot 2i = 2i^2\sqrt{5} = -2\sqrt{5}$

6 $-\sqrt{-3} \cdot \sqrt{-7} = -i\sqrt{3} \cdot i\sqrt{7} = -i^2\sqrt{21} = -(-1)\sqrt{21} = \sqrt{21}$

Try This Multiply.

d. $6i \cdot 3i$ **e.** $\sqrt{-3} \cdot 3i$ **f.** $\sqrt{-3} \cdot \sqrt{-6}$

Complex Numbers

Objective: Add or subtract complex numbers.

To construct a complete number system, we shall define sums of real and imaginary numbers. We call these **complex numbers.**

Definition

The **complex numbers** consist of all sums $a + bi$, where a and b are real numbers and i is the imaginary unit. The real part is a, and the imaginary part is bi.

Every real number a is a complex number because $a = a + 0 \cdot i$. Thus, the complex numbers are an extension of the real number system. All imaginary numbers bi are also complex because $bi = 0 + bi$. We show these relationships with the following diagram.

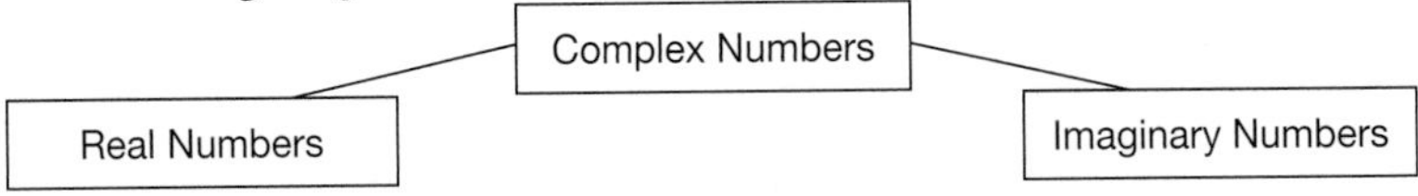

We assume that i acts like a real number, obeying the commutative, associative, and distributive properties. Thus to add or subtract complex numbers, we can treat i as we would treat a variable. We combine like terms.

EXAMPLES Add or subtract.

7 $7i + 9i = (7 + 9)i = 16i$

8 $(-5 + 6i) + (2 - 11i) = -5 + 2 + 6i - 11i = -3 - 5i$

9 $(2 + 3i) - (4 + 2i) = 2 + 3i - 4 - 2i = -2 + i$

Try This Add or subtract.

g. $(-2 + 3i) + (2 - 3i)$ **h.** $3i - 4i$ **i.** $(-4 + 10i) - (-2 + 3i)$

7-7 Exercises

Extra Help On the Web

Look for worked-out examples at the Prentice Hall Web site. www.phschool.com

A

Mental Math Express these numbers in terms of i.

1. $\sqrt{-2}$ **2.** $\sqrt{-3}$ **3.** $\sqrt{-36}$ **4.** $\sqrt{-25}$

5. $-\sqrt{-9}$ **6.** $-\sqrt{-16}$ **7.** $\sqrt{-128}$ **8.** $\sqrt{-12}$

9. $\sqrt{-\frac{9}{16}}$ **10.** $\sqrt{-\frac{25}{4}}$ **11.** $-\sqrt{-80}$ **12.** $-\sqrt{-75}$

Multiply.

13. $23i \cdot 4$ **14.** $-12i \cdot (-3)$ **15.** $\sqrt{-3} \cdot 4i$

16. $\sqrt{-5} \cdot 6i$ **17.** $\sqrt{-2}\sqrt{-3}$ **18.** $\sqrt{-5}\sqrt{-3}$

19. $-\sqrt{-2}\sqrt{-18}$ **20.** $-\sqrt{-3}\sqrt{-15}$ **21.** $\sqrt{-3}\sqrt{-15}$

22. $\sqrt{-10}\sqrt{-2}$ **23.** $-\sqrt{-10}(-\sqrt{-10})$ **24.** $-\sqrt{-7}(-\sqrt{-7})$

Add or subtract.

25. $-7i + 10i$ **26.** $4i + (-10i)$ **27.** $(3 + 2i) + (5 - i)$

28. $(-2 + 3i) + (7 + 8i)$ **29.** $(4 - 3i) + (5 - 2i)$ **30.** $2i - (4 - 3i)$

31. $3i - (5 - 2i)$ **32.** $(3 - i) - (5 + 2i)$ **33.** $(-2 + 8i) - (7 + 3i)$

B

Simplify. (Hint: $i^{31} = i^{28} \cdot i^3 = (i^4)^7 \cdot i^3 = 1^7 \cdot i^3 = i^3$)

34. i^{13} **35.** i^{20} **36.** i^{18} **37.** i^{27}

38. i^{99} **39.** $i^{71} - i^{49}$ **40.** $i^{68} - i^{72} + i^{76} - i^{80}$

41. ***Critical Thinking*** Write a formula for all powers of i that are equal to 1, to -1.

Challenge

Simplify.

42. i^{-1} **43.** i^{-2} **44.** i^{-3} **45.** i^{-4} **46.** i^{-99} **47.** i^{-27}

For any integer n, find i^{4n+a} when a takes on the following values.

48. 3 **49.** 2 **50.** 1 **51.** 0 **52.** -1 **53.** -2 **54.** -3

Mixed Review

Simplify. **55.** $\sqrt[3]{7} \cdot \sqrt[3]{5}$ **56.** $\sqrt{m + n} \cdot \sqrt{m - n}$ **57.** $\sqrt[4]{112m^5n^2}$ *7-2*

Divide. **58.** $\frac{x^2 + x - 6}{x^2 + 3x - 10}$ **59.** $\frac{y^2 - 5y + 4}{y - 4}$ **60.** $\frac{x^2 - 4}{4x^2 + 13x + 3} \div \frac{x + 2}{x + 3}$ *6-4*

Solve. **61.** $x + \frac{8}{x} = 6$ **62.** $\frac{x + 2}{3x + 1} = \frac{2x - 3}{2x}$ **63.** $3x - \frac{2}{x} = 1$ *6-6*

7-8 Complex Numbers and Graphing

What You'll Learn

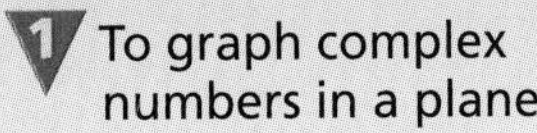
1. To graph complex numbers in a plane

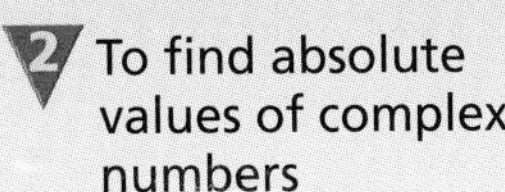
2. To find absolute values of complex numbers

. . . And Why

To increase efficiency in using complex numbers

PART 1 Graphing Complex Numbers

Objective: Graph complex numbers in a plane.

The real numbers are graphed on a line. We graph a complex number, $a + bi$, in the same way we graph ordered pairs of real numbers, (a, b). In place of an x-axis we have a **real axis,** and in place of a y-axis we have an **imaginary axis.**

EXAMPLE 1 Graph.

A: $3 + 2i$
B: $-4 + 5i$
C: $-5 - 4i$
D: i (or $0 + i$)
E: 5 (or $5 + 0i$)

Horizontal distance corresponds to the real part of a complex number. Vertical distance corresponds to the imaginary part.

Try This Graph.

a. $5 - 3i$ **b.** $-3 + 4i$ **c.** $-5 - 2i$ **d.** $-5i$ **e.** -5

PART 2 Absolute Value

Objective: Find absolute values of complex numbers.

We know the absolute value of a real number can be thought of as its distance from 0. We can think of the **absolute value of a complex number** in a similar manner.

From the graph at the right, we see that the length of the segment drawn from the origin to $a + bi$ is $\sqrt{a^2 + b^2}$. Note that this quantity is a real number. It is called the absolute value of $a + bi$ and is denoted $|a + bi|$.

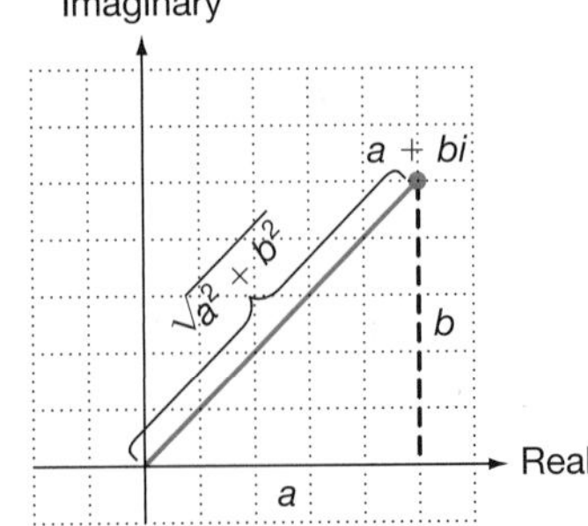

Definition

The **absolute value of a complex number** $a + bi$ is denoted $|a + bi|$ and is defined as $\sqrt{a^2 + b^2}$.

EXAMPLE 2 Find $|-3 + 4i|$.

$$|-3 + 4i| = \sqrt{(-3)^2 + 4^2} = \sqrt{9 + 16} = \sqrt{25} = 5$$

Try This Find the absolute value.

f. $|4 - 3i|$ **g.** $|-12 - 5i|$ **h.** $|1 + i|$

7-8 Exercises

Internet Connection
Extra Help On the Web
Look for worked-out examples at the Prentice Hall Web site.
www.phschool.com

A

Graph.

1. $3 + 2i, 2 - 5i, -4 - 2i$
2. $3 - 4i, -5 + 3i, -2 - 3i$
3. $-4 + 2i, -3 - 4i, 2 - 3i$
4. $-5 + 4i, 3 - 2i, -5 + 5i$

Find the absolute value.

5. $|-4 - 3i|$ **6.** $|-3 - 4i|$ **7.** $|8 + 15i|$ **8.** $|7 - 24i|$
9. $|3i|$ **10.** $|-2i|$ **11.** $|c - di|$ **12.** $|-c + di|$

B

13. Graph.
a. $\{a + bi \mid a \leq 3 \text{ and } b \leq 2\}$ **b.** $\{a + bi \mid |a + bi| \leq 3\}$
c. $\{a + bi \mid a = 3 \text{ and } |b| \geq 2\}$

14. Let $G = \{a + bi \mid |a + bi| \leq 4\}$. Which of these numbers are in G?
a. $3 + 3i$ **b.** $3i$ **c.** $-4 + 3i$ **d.** i^5 **e.** $2 - 4i$ **f.** $6 + 2i$

15. *Critical Thinking* What happens to the absolute value of a complex number $a + bi$ if it is multiplied by i? Describe what happens to its graph.

Challenge

16. Show that for any complex number z, $|z| = |-z|$. (Hint: Let $z = a + bi$.)

Mixed Review

Simplify. **17.** $\sqrt{27}$ **18.** $\sqrt{45m^2}$ **19.** $\sqrt[3]{16a^3}$ **20.** $\sqrt[8]{(-2)^8}$ *7-2*
Factor. **21.** $a^3 + 27$ **22.** $m^3 - 8$ **23.** $x^3 - 12x^2 + 48x - 64$ *5-5, 5-4*

7-9 More About Complex Numbers

What You'll Learn

1. To solve equations with complex numbers
2. To multiply complex numbers
3. To find conjugates of complex numbers
4. To divide and find reciprocals of complex numbers

... And Why

To use complex numbers more efficiently

PART 1 Equality for Complex Numbers

Objective: Solve equations with complex numbers.

Equality for complex numbers is the same as equality for real numbers. A sentence $a + bi = c + di$ says that $a + bi$ and $c + di$ represent the same number. For this to be true, a and c must be the same and b and d must be the same. Thus, $a + bi = c + di$ when $a = c$ and $b = d$.

EXAMPLE 1 Solve for x and y.

Suppose that $3x + yi = 5x + 1 + 2i$. Find x and y.

We equate the real parts.

$$3x = 5x + 1$$
$$x = -\frac{1}{2} \quad \text{Solving}$$

We equate the imaginary parts.

$$yi = 2i$$
$$y = 2 \quad \text{Solving}$$

Check: $3x + yi = 5x + 1 + 2i$

$3\left(-\frac{1}{2}\right) + (2)i$	$5\left(-\frac{1}{2}\right) + 1 + 2i$
$-\frac{3}{2} + 2i$	$-\frac{5}{2} + 1 + 2i$
$-\frac{3}{2} + 2i$	$-\frac{3}{2} + 2i$ ✔

Try This Solve for x and y.

a. Suppose $3x + 1 + (y + 2)i = 2x + 2yi$.

PART 2 Multiplying

Objective: Multiply complex numbers.

We multiply complex numbers as we would multiply monomials or binomials, treating the imaginary parts as like terms. Remember that $i^2 = -1$.

EXAMPLES Multiply.

2 $3i \cdot 4i = (3 \cdot 4)i^2 = 12(-1) = -12$

3 $(7i)^2 = 7^2 i^2 = 49(-1) = -49$

4 $(4 + 3i) \cdot (7 + 2i) = 28 + 8i + 21i + 6i^2$
$= 28 + (8i + 21i) + 6(-1)$ Since $i^2 = -1$
$= 28 + 29i - 6$
$= 22 + 29i$

Try This Multiply.

b. $5i \cdot 6i$ **c.** $(10i)^2$ **d.** $(-2 - 3i)(6 + 5i)$

PART 3 Complex Conjugates

Objective: Find conjugates of complex numbers.

Definition

The **conjugate** of $a + bi$ is $a - bi$, and the conjugate of $a - bi$ is $a + bi$.

EXAMPLES Find the conjugate of each number.

5 $3 + 4i$ The conjugate of $3 + 4i$ is $3 - 4i$.

6 $-4 - 7i$ The conjugate of $-4 - 7i$ is $-4 + 7i$.

7 $5i$ The conjugate of $5i$ is $-5i$, since $0 - 5i$ is the conjugate of $0 + 5i$.

8 6 The conjugate of 6 is 6, since $6 - 0i$ is the conjugate of $6 + 0i$.

Journal

Write a paragraph to explain why multiplying a complex number by its conjugate has the same result as squaring the absolute value of either the complex number or its conjugate.

Try This Find the conjugate of each number.

e. $6 + 3i$ **f.** $-9 - 5i$ **g.** $-7i$ **h.** -8

The product $(A + B)(A - B) = A^2 - B^2$ applies to complex numbers.

Theorem 7-8

The product of a nonzero complex number $a + bi$ and its conjugate $a - bi$ is the positive real number $a^2 + b^2$.

EXAMPLES Multiply.

9 $(5 + 7i)(5 - 7i) = 5^2 - (7i)^2$
$= 25 - (49i^2)$
$= 25 + 49$
$= 74$

10 $(a + bi)(a - bi) = a^2 - (bi)^2$
$= a^2 - b^2i^2$
$= a^2 + b^2$

Try This Multiply.

i. $(7 - 2i)(7 + 2i)$ **j.** $(-3 + i)(-3 - i)$ **k.** $(3p - 2qi)(3p + 2qi)$

Division and Reciprocals

Objective: Divide and find reciprocals of complex numbers.

To divide complex numbers, we multiply by 1 using the same techniques as when rationalizing a denominator with two terms. In choosing a symbol for 1, we use the conjugate of the divisor.

EXAMPLES Divide.

11

$$\begin{aligned}\frac{-5 + 9i}{1 - i} &= \frac{-5 + 9i}{1 - i} \cdot \frac{1 + i}{1 + i}\\ &= \frac{-14 + 4i}{1 - i^2}\\ &= \frac{-14 + 4i}{2}\\ &= -7 + 2i\end{aligned}$$

12

$$\begin{aligned}\frac{2 - 3i}{3 + 5i} &= \frac{2 - 3i}{3 + 5i} \cdot \frac{3 - 5i}{3 - 5i}\\ &= \frac{-9 - 19i}{9 - 25i^2}\\ &= \frac{-9 - 19i}{34}\\ &= -\frac{9}{34} - \frac{19}{34}i\end{aligned}$$

Try This Divide.

l. $\frac{6 + 2i}{1 - 3i}$ **m.** $\frac{2 + 3i}{-1 + 4i}$

The reciprocal of a number $c + di$ is, of course, that number by which we multiply $c + di$ to get 1. By definition of division this is $\frac{1}{c + di}$. To express $\frac{1}{c + di}$ in the form $a + bi$, we can divide.

EXAMPLE 13 Find the reciprocal of $2 - 3i$ and express it in the form $a + bi$.

The reciprocal of $2 - 3i$ is $\frac{1}{2 - 3i}$.

$$\begin{aligned}\frac{1}{2 - 3i} &= \frac{1}{2 - 3i} \cdot \frac{2 + 3i}{2 + 3i}\\ &= \frac{2 + 3i}{2^2 - 3^2i^2}\\ &= \frac{2 + 3i}{4 + 9}\\ &= \frac{2}{13} + \frac{3}{13}i\end{aligned}$$

Thus, $\frac{2}{13} + \frac{3}{13}i$ is the reciprocal of $2 - 3i$ in $a + bi$ form.

Check: Does the number multiplied by the reciprocal equal 1?

$$\begin{aligned}&(2 - 3i)\left(\frac{2}{13} + \frac{3}{13}i\right)\\ &= \frac{4}{13} + \frac{6}{13}i - \frac{6}{13}i - \frac{9}{13}i^2\\ &= \frac{4}{13} + 0 - \frac{9}{13}(-1)\\ &= \frac{4}{13} + \frac{9}{13} = \frac{13}{13} = 1\end{aligned}$$

Indeed, the number times its reciprocal is 1. The answer checks.

Try This

n. Find the reciprocal of $3 + 4i$ and express it in the form $a + bi$.

7-9 Exercises

Extra Help On the Web

Look for worked-out examples at the Prentice Hall Web site.
www.phschool.com

A

Solve for x and y.

1. $4x + 7i = -6 + yi$ **2.** $8 + 8yi = 4x - 2i$ **3.** $-5x - yi = 10 + 8i$

Multiply.

4. $7i \cdot 9i$ **5.** $3i \cdot i$ **6.** $(9i)^2$ **7.** $(-5i)^2$

8. $(3 + 2i)(1 + i)$ **9.** $(4 + 3i)(2 + i)$ **10.** $(5 - 2i)^2$ **11.** $(-2 + 2i)^2$

Find the conjugate of each number.

12. $-4 + 8i$ **13.** $7 - i$ **14.** $\sqrt{2} - \frac{1}{2}i$ **15.** $-m + ni$

Multiply or divide.

16. $(1 - i)(1 + i)$ **17.** $(6 + 3i)(6 - 3i)$ **18.** $(3 - i\sqrt{2})(3 + i\sqrt{2})$

19. $\frac{3 + 2i}{2 + i}$ **20.** $\frac{8 - 3i}{-2 + 7i}$ **21.** $\frac{5 - 10i}{-3 + 4i}$ **22.** $\frac{\sqrt{2} + i}{\sqrt{2} - i}$

Find the reciprocal of each number and express it in the form $a + bi$.

23. i **24.** $-i$ **25.** $2 - 4i$ **26.** $-3 - 5i$ **27.** $-4 + 7i$

28. *Error Analysis* Mario said that 8 has only one cube root. Of what number was he thinking? Karen had cubed $(-1 + i\sqrt{3})$ and $(-1 - i\sqrt{3})$ and said he was mistaken. Cube Karen's binomials to show why Mario's statement is in error.

B

Express in the form $a + bi$.

29. i^{-3} **30.** i^2 **31.** $\frac{1 - i}{(1 + i)^2}$ **32.** $\frac{1 + i}{(1 - i)^2}$

33. Let $z = a + bi$. Find the general expression for $\frac{1}{z}$.

34. Show that $\sqrt{a \cdot b} = \sqrt{a} \cdot \sqrt{b}$ does not hold for all real numbers.

35. *Critical Thinking* Find the complex number whose reciprocal is $5 + 6i$.

Challenge

Simplify to the form $a + bi$.

36. $(1 + \sqrt{-3})^{-2}$ **37.** $(\sqrt{-2} + 2\sqrt{-6})^2$ **38.** $(1 + i)^{-3}(2 - i)^{-2}$

Mixed Review

Rationalize the denominator.

39. $\sqrt{\frac{9}{2}}$ **40.** $\frac{3\sqrt{3}}{2\sqrt{5}}$ **41.** $\frac{\sqrt{m} - \sqrt{n}}{\sqrt{m} + \sqrt{n}}$ *7-4*

42. Find an equation of the line containing $(2, 3)$ and $(-1, -6)$. *3-7*

7-10 Solutions of Equations

What You'll Learn

1. To determine if a complex number solves an equation
2. To find an equation that has given complex numbers as solutions
3. To solve first-degree equations with complex numbers as solutions
4. To verify and find square roots of complex numbers

. . . And Why

To solve problems involving complex numbers

PART 1 Complex Numbers as Solutions of Equations

Objective: Determine whether a complex number is a solution of an equation.

EXAMPLE 1 Determine whether $1 + i\sqrt{7}$ is a solution of $x^2 - 2x + 8 = 0$.

$x^2 - 2x + 8 = 0$	
$(1 + i\sqrt{7})^2 - 2(1 + i\sqrt{7}) + 8$	0
$1 + 2(i\sqrt{7}) + (i\sqrt{7})^2 - 2 - 2i\sqrt{7} + 8$	0
$1 + 2i\sqrt{7} - 7 - 2 - 2i\sqrt{7} + 8$	0
0	0 ✔

$1 + i\sqrt{7}$ is a solution.

Try This

a. Determine whether $1 - i$ is a solution of $x^2 + 2x + 1 = 0$.

PART 2 Writing Equations with Given Solutions

Objective: Find an equation that has given complex numbers as solutions.

The principle of zero products for real numbers also holds for complex numbers, thus we can find equations having given solutions.

EXAMPLE 2 Find an equation having $4 + 3i$ and $4 - 3i$ as solutions.

$$x = 4 + 3i \text{ or } x = 4 - 3i$$
$$x - (4 + 3i) = 0 \text{ or } x - (4 - 3i) = 0$$
$$[x - (4 + 3i)][x - (4 - 3i)] = 0 \quad \text{Using the principle of zero products}$$
$$[x - 4 - 3i][x - 4 + 3i] = 0$$
$$x^2 - 8x + 16 - 9i^2 = 0$$
$$x^2 - 8x + 16 + 9 = 0$$
$$x^2 - 8x + 25 = 0 \quad \text{Simplifying}$$

Quick Review

Shortcuts in multiplication can be used. In Example 2, $[x - 4 - 3i][x - 4 + 3i]$ may be recognized as $(x - 4)^2 - (3i)^2$.

Try This Find an equation having the given numbers as solutions.

b. $1 + i, 1 - i$ **c.** $2 - 3i, 2 + 3i$

Solving Equations

Objective: Solve first-degree equations that have complex numbers as solutions.

First-degree equations in complex numbers are solved very much like first-degree equations in real numbers.

EXAMPLE 3 Solve $3ix + 4 - 5i = (1 + i)x + 2i$.

We begin by getting all x terms to one side of the equation.

$3ix - (1 + i)x = -4 + 7i$ — Adding $-(1 + i)x$ and $-(-4 - 5i)$ to both sides

$(-1 + 2i)x = -4 + 7i$ — Simplifying

$x = \frac{-4 + 7i}{-1 + 2i}$ — Dividing

$x = \frac{-4 + 7i}{-1 + 2i} \cdot \frac{-1 - 2i}{-1 - 2i}$ — Multiplying by 1

$x = \frac{18 + i}{5}$

$x = \frac{18}{5} + \frac{1}{5}i$

Try This Solve.

d. $3 - 4i + 2ix = 3i - (1 - i)x$

Linear equations always have solutions. Complex numbers were invented so that certain other equations would have solutions. How many solutions, if any, does a polynomial equation have? The answer depends upon a very important theorem.

Theorem 7-9

Every polynomial with complex coefficients and of degree n (where $n > 1$) can be factored into n linear factors.

The factors of a polynomial are not always easy to find, but they exist.

EXAMPLE 4 Show that $(x + i)(x - i)$ is a factorization of $x^2 + 1$.

$$\begin{aligned}(x + i)(x - i) &= x^2 - ix + ix - i^2 \quad \text{Multiplying}\\ &= x^2 + 1\end{aligned}$$

Try This

e. Show that $(x + 2i)(x - 2i)$ is a factorization of $x^2 + 4$.

Writing Math

In this lesson you find equations with given solutions. Remember that those equations are usually written in standard form or $ax^2 + bx + c = 0$, where a, b, and c are integers.

We can now answer the question about solutions of polynomial equations.

Theorem 7-10

Every polynomial equation of degree n ($n \geq 1$) with complex coefficients has at least one solution and at most n solutions in the system of complex numbers.

Proof of Theorem 7-10

Consider a polynomial equation of degree n, $P(x) = 0$. The polynomial $P(x)$ is either of degree 1, in which case there is a solution, or, by Theorem 7-9, it can be factored into n linear factors. We then have

$$(x - a_1)(x - a_2) \ldots (x - a_n) = 0$$

By the principle of zero products, we have

$$x = a_1 \text{ or } x = a_2 \text{ or } x = a_3 \text{ or} \ldots \text{ or } x = a_n$$

Thus, the equation has solutions $a_1, a_2, \ldots, a_n$. Some of these may be the same. Therefore, there is at least one solution, and there are not more than n solutions.

PART 4 Square Roots of Complex Numbers

Objective: Verify one square root of a complex number and find the other square root.

Theorem 7-9 can be used to prove Theorem 7-11.

Theorem 7-11

Every nonzero complex number has two square roots. They are additive inverses of each other. Zero has just one square root.

EXAMPLE 5 Show that $1 + i$ is a square root of $2i$. Find the other square root.

We square $(1 + i)$ to show that we get $2i$.

$$(1 + i)^2 = 1 + 2i + i^2 = 1 + 2i - 1 = 2i$$

By Theorem 7-11, the other square root of $2i$ is the additive inverse of $1 + i$, so it is $-1 - i$.

Try This

f. Show that $(-1 + i)$ is a square root of $-2i$. Then find the other square root.

7-10 Exercises

Extra Help On the Web

Look for worked-out examples at the Prentice Hall Web site.
www.phschool.com

A

Determine whether the given numbers are solutions of the equation.

1. $2i, -2i; x^2 + 4 = 0$ **2.** $4i, -4i; x^2 + 16 = 0$

3. $i\sqrt{2}, -i\sqrt{3}; x^2 + 3 = 0$ **4.** $i\sqrt{3}, -i\sqrt{2}; x^2 + 2 = 0$

5. $-1 + i, -1 - i; z^2 + 2z + 2 = 0$ **6.** $2 - i, 2 + i; z^2 - 4z + 5 = 0$

Find an equation having the specified numbers as solutions.

7. $5i, -5i$ **8.** $7i, -7i$ **9.** $2 + 3i, 2 - 3i$

10. $4 + 3i, 4 - 3i$ **11.** $i\sqrt{3}, -i\sqrt{3}$ **12.** $2 - i\sqrt{2}, 2 + i\sqrt{2}$

13. $6 + i\sqrt{6}, 6 - i\sqrt{6}$ **14.** $1 - i\sqrt{8}, 1 + i\sqrt{8}$ **15.** $3 - i\sqrt{17}, 3 + i\sqrt{17}$

Solve.

16. $(3 + i)x + i = 5i$ **17.** $(2 + i)x - i = 5 + i$

18. $2ix + 5 - 4i = (2 + 3i)x - 2i$ **19.** $5ix + 3 + 2i = (3 - 2i)x + 3i$

20. $(1 + 2i)x + 3 - 2i = 4 - 5i + 3ix$

21. $(5 + i)x + 1 - 3i = (2 - 3i)x + 2 - i$

22. $(5 - i)x + 2 - 3i = (3 - 2i)x + 3 - i$

23. Show that $(2x + i)(2x - i)$ is a factorization of $4x^2 + 1$.

24. Show that $(2x + 2i)(2x - 2i)$ is a factorization of $4x^2 + 4$.

25. Show that $(2 + i)$ is a square root of $3 + 4i$. Then find the other square root.

B

Find an equation having the specified numbers as solutions.

26. $5, i$ **27.** $1, 3i, -3i$ **28.** $2, 1 + i, i$ **29.** $i, 2i, -i$

30. ***Critical Thinking*** $3 + 5i$ is a square root of a certain complex number. Find the number.

Challenge

31. Show that $(a + bi)^2 = (a + b)(a - b) + 2abi$.

32. Find the square roots of $3 - 4i$. (Hint: Use the result of Exercise 31.)

Mixed Review

Convert to standard notation. **33.** 5.023×10^{-5} **34.** 4.441×10^6 *1-9*

Simplify.

35. $\dfrac{\frac{2}{x} + 3}{\frac{2}{x} - 5}$ **36.** $\dfrac{m - \frac{3}{m}}{m + \frac{3}{m}}$ **37.** $\dfrac{\frac{2}{x} + \frac{5}{y}}{\frac{5}{x} - \frac{2}{y}}$ **38.** $\dfrac{3c + \frac{2}{c}}{3c - \frac{2}{c}}$ *6-3*

Preparing for Standardized Tests

High school students take standardized exams for college placement. Many state tests also use a standardized "multiple-choice" test to determine how well material has been learned. Problems 1–11 on page 335 test the topics of averages and weighted averages.

Averages

College entrance exams often require that the **average,** or **mean,** of a set of numbers be found. These test items usually do not tell you to find the average. Many of these problems can be solved using the *Try, Test, Revise* strategy. Most are solved more efficiently, however, using the definition of average and the equation-solving techniques you have learned.

EXAMPLE 1

Tony's scores on five tests are 60, 80, 55, 75, and 65. What must his score be on the next test to raise his average to 70?

(A) 70 **(B)** 75 **(C)** 80 **(D)** 85 **(E)** 90

Since we know the average we want is 70, and the number of tests is 6, we can write the following equation.

$$70 = \frac{(\text{sum of the 6 numbers})}{6}$$

$$70 \cdot 6 = \text{sum of the 6 numbers}$$

$$420 = \text{sum of the 6 numbers}$$

The sum of the 5 test scores is $60 + 80 + 55 + 75 + 65 = 335$.

Thus, he needs $420 - 335 = 85$ points on the last test to get an average of 70. The correct answer is (D).

Example 2 involves **weighted average** because the groups are of different sizes.

EXAMPLE 2

If the average of three numbers is 5, and the average of seven other numbers is 15, then the average of all the numbers is

(A) 8 **(B)** 10 **(C)** 9.6 **(D)** 12 **(E)** 13

Using the formula for average, we know that the following are true.

$$5 = \frac{\text{the first sum}}{3} \rightarrow \text{the first sum} = 3 \cdot 5 = 15$$

$$15 = \frac{\text{the second sum}}{7} \rightarrow \text{the second sum} = 7 \cdot 15 = 105$$

To find the mean for all numbers, we divide the *total sum* by 10, the total number of numbers.

$$\begin{aligned} \text{total sum} &= \text{the first sum} + \text{the second sum} \\ &= 15 + 105 \\ &= 120 \end{aligned}$$

$$\text{Average} = \frac{120}{10} = 12, \text{ so the correct answer is (D).}$$

Problems

1. If Nick's first three test grades are 79, 85, and 90, what grade does he need on the next test to average 85?

   (A) 87 **(B)** 86 **(C)** 85 **(D)** 84 **(E)** 83

2. If Esperanza's first two test grades are 80 and 71, what grade must she make on her third test for the average of the three to be 70?

   (A) 59 **(B)** 58 **(C)** 57 **(D)** 56 **(E)** 55

3. The average of three numbers is greater than 50. If two of them are 47 and 48, then the third number could be

   (A) 56 **(B)** 55 **(C)** 54 **(D)** 53 **(E)** either **A** or **B**

4. In an algebra class there are 20 boys and 15 girls. If the 20 boys have an average score of 50 and the 15 girls have an average score of 57, then what is the average score for all 35 students?

   (A) 55 **(B)** 54 **(C)** 53 **(D)** 53.2 **(E)** Cannot be determined

5. If the average of three numbers is between 8 and 12, then the sum of the three numbers could be any one of the following except

   (A) $20\frac{1}{2}$ **(B)** $24\frac{1}{2}$ **(C)** 26 **(D)** 28 **(E)** 35

6. The average of two numbers is A, and one number is N. The other number is

   (A) $2N$ **(B)** $2A - 2$ **(C)** $2A$ **(D)** $A - N$ **(E)** $2A - N$

7. If two students averaged 75 on a test and three other students averaged 90, find the average of all five students.

   (A) 85 **(B)** 84 **(C)** 83 **(D)** 82 **(E)** 81

8. If the average of the first 5 numbers on a list is equal to the average of the first 4 numbers on the list, then the fifth number must be equal to

   (A) the average of the first 4 numbers.
   (B) zero.
   (C) a negative number.
   (D) a number greater than the average of the first 4 numbers.
   (E) a number less than the average of the first 4 numbers.

9. The average of five positive numbers is 26. If three of the numbers are 25, 28, and 22, which of the following could *not* be one of the other two numbers?

   (A) 8 **(B)** 30 **(C)** 36 **(D)** 43 **(E)** 56

10. A class of 30 students took a test that was scored from 0 to 60. Exactly 10 students received scores less than or equal to 30. If A is the class average score, what is the greatest possible value of A?

    (A) 30 **(B)** 40 **(C)** 48 **(D)** 50 **(E)** 52

11. The average of M numbers is A, and the average of N numbers is B. What is the average of all the numbers?

    (A) $A + B$ **(B)** $\frac{A + B}{2}$ **(C)** $\frac{AM + BN}{2}$ **(D)** $\frac{AM + BN}{M + N}$ **(E)** $\frac{AM + BN}{A + B}$

Chapter Wrap Up

Key Terms

absolute value of a complex number (pp. 324, 325)
complex numbers (p. 322)
conjugate (p. 307)
cube root (p. 294)
even root (p. 295)
extraneous roots (p. 318)
i (p. 321)
imaginary axis (p. 324)
imaginary numbers (p. 321)
index (p. 294)
*k*th root (p. 294)
odd root (p. 294)
principal square root (p. 292)
Principle of Powers (p. 317)
radical equation (p. 317)
radical expressions (p. 293)
radical sign (p. 293)
radicand (p. 293)
rational exponents (p. 311)
rationalizing the denominator (p. 305)
real axis (p. 324)
square root (p. 292)

7-1

A ***k*th root** of a number a is a number c such that $c^k = a$. When k is even, every positive real number has two roots, one positive and one negative. When k is odd, every real number has one root that has the same sign as the number.

Simplify.

1. $\sqrt{(-36)^2}$ **2.** $\sqrt{16x^2}$ **3.** $\sqrt[3]{\frac{-8x^3}{27}}$ **4.** $\sqrt[5]{-243}$ **5.** $\sqrt[4]{(-2x)^4}$

7-2

For any nonnegative real numbers a and b, and any index k,

$$\sqrt[k]{a} \cdot \sqrt[k]{b} = \sqrt[k]{ab}$$

To simplify a **radical expression,** find the kth root of factors that are perfect kth powers. Assume variables represent nonnegative numbers.

Multiply and simplify.

6. $\sqrt{18x} \cdot \sqrt{12x}$ **7.** $\sqrt[3]{a^2b} \cdot \sqrt[3]{a^4b^6}$ **8.** $\sqrt[3]{3c^2d^5} \cdot \sqrt[3]{16c^2d^2}$

7-3

For any nonnegative number a, any positive number b, and any index k,

$$\sqrt[k]{\frac{a}{b}} = \frac{\sqrt[k]{a}}{\sqrt[k]{b}}$$

Divide and simplify.

9. $\frac{\sqrt[3]{32}}{\sqrt[3]{2}}$ **10.** $\sqrt{\frac{12a^3}{b^7}}$ **11.** $\frac{\sqrt{40x^7}}{\sqrt{32x^3}}$

Like radical terms can be combined.

$$a\sqrt[k]{x} + b\sqrt[k]{x} = (a + b)\sqrt[k]{x}$$

Add or subtract.

12. $2\sqrt{32} - \sqrt{50} + \sqrt{162}$ **13.** $\sqrt[3]{24} - \sqrt[3]{81}$ **14.** $5\sqrt{3y^3} - \sqrt{12y}$

7-4

To multiply radical expressions with more than one term, use the FOIL method for multiplying polynomials.

Multiply and simplify.

15. $(7 - 4\sqrt{3})(7 + 4\sqrt{3})$ **16.** $(3\sqrt{6} + 2)^2$

17. $(2\sqrt[3]{2} + \sqrt[3]{3})(\sqrt[3]{2} + 3\sqrt[3]{3})$

When **rationalizing a denominator,** multiply the numerator and denominator by the same expression to make the denominator a perfect power.

Rationalize the denominator.

18. $\frac{\sqrt{8}}{\sqrt{3}}$ **19.** $\frac{6}{3 - \sqrt{17}}$ **20.** $\frac{\sqrt{3} + 5}{7 + \sqrt{3}}$

Internet Activity On the Web

Look for extension problems for this chapter at the Prentice Hall Web site. www.phschool.com

7-5

For any nonnegative number a, any natural-number index k, and any integer m,

$$\sqrt[k]{a^m} = (\sqrt[k]{a})^m$$

Simplify.

21. $(\sqrt[3]{16})^2$ **22.** $(\sqrt{3x})^3$ **23.** $\sqrt{(a^3b^2)^2}$ **24.** $\sqrt[3]{\left(\frac{3}{a^2}\right)^3}$

For any natural number m, integer k, and any nonnegative number a,

$$a^{\frac{m}{k}} \textbf{ means } \sqrt[k]{a^m}$$

Write without rational exponents.

25. $x^{\frac{2}{3}}$ **26.** $27^{\frac{1}{3}}$ **27.** $32^{\frac{2}{5}}$ **28.** $(8x)^{\frac{5}{2}}$

Write with rational exponents.

29. $\sqrt[3]{15}$ **30.** $\sqrt[3]{32}$ **31.** $\sqrt[3]{x^3y^4z^5}$ **32.** $\sqrt[4]{8x^3y^2}$

For any rational number $\frac{m}{n}$ and any positive real number a, $a^{-\frac{m}{n}}$ **means** $\frac{1}{a^{\frac{m}{n}}}$.

Rewrite with positive exponents.

33. $x^{-\frac{1}{2}}$ **34.** $\frac{1}{x^{-4}}$ **35.** $\left(\frac{1}{16}\right)^{-\frac{1}{2}}$ **36.** $\frac{1}{8^{-\frac{2}{3}}}$

Use rational exponents to write in simplest radical form.

37. $\sqrt[4]{x^2}$ **38.** $\sqrt[3]{16y^6}$ **39.** $\sqrt[4]{\frac{x^{-8}y^{12}}{16}}$ **40.** $\sqrt[10]{\frac{64x^6}{y^8z^{-4}}}$

7-6

For any natural number n, if an equation $a = b$ is true, then the equation $a^n = b^n$ is true. To solve an equation containing radical signs, isolate a radical term, then use the **principle of powers.** If a radical term remains, repeat this procedure. Always check your solutions.

Solve.

41. $\sqrt{5 - 3x} - 6 = 0$ **42.** $\sqrt{7 - 4x} - \sqrt{3 - 2x} = 1$

Solve the formula for the given variable.

43. $T = 4\pi\sqrt{\frac{L}{g}}$; L **44.** $\sqrt{\frac{E}{m}} = c$; E **45.** $A = \sqrt{\frac{w_1}{w_2}}$; w_2

7-7

Remember that the **imaginary number** $i = \sqrt{-1}$, and $i^1 = i$, $i^2 = -1$, $i^3 = -i$, and $i^4 = 1$.

Express each number in terms of i.

46. $\sqrt{-49}$

47. $-\sqrt{-25}$

Simplify.

48. $\sqrt{-6} \cdot 6i$

49. $(6 + 2i) + (-4 - 3i)$

50. $(3 - 5i) - (2 - i)$

7-8

To graph a **complex number** $a + bi$, replace the x-axis with a real axis and replace the y-axis with an imaginary axis.

Graph.

51. $4 - 2i$

52. $-3 + 5i$

The **absolute value of a complex number** $a + bi$ is denoted by $|a + bi|$ and is defined as $\sqrt{a^2 + b^2}$.

Find the absolute value.

53. $|5 - 3i|$

54. $|-4 + 3i|$

7-9

Multiply complex numbers as you would multiply monomials or binomials, treating real and imaginary parts as unlike terms.

Multiply and simplify.

55. $(2 - 2i)(3 + 4i)$

56. $(2 - 3i)(3 + 2i)$

57. $(3 - 2i)(3 + 2i)$

58. $(2 + 6i)(2 - 6i)$

To divide complex numbers, rationalize the denominator by multiplying both numerator and denominator by the **conjugate** of the denominator.

59. $\frac{3 - 2i}{2 - i}$

60. $\frac{4 - 2i}{4 + 2i}$

The reciprocal of $c + di$ is $\frac{1}{c + di}$.

Find the reciprocal and express it in the form $a + bi$.

61. $2 + 4i$

62. $1 - i$

7-10

First-degree equations in complex numbers are solved very much like first-degree equations for real numbers.

Solve.

63. $2ix - 5 + 3i = (2 - i)x + i$

7 Chapter Assessment

Simplify. Assume variables represent any real number.

1. $-\sqrt{121}$

2. $\sqrt[3]{-0.027}$

3. $\sqrt{x^2 - 10x + 25}$

4. $\sqrt{49y^2}$

5. $\sqrt[3]{-y^3}$

6. $\sqrt[8]{x^8}$

7. $\sqrt{20}\sqrt{18}$

8. $\sqrt[3]{x^2y^4}\sqrt[3]{x^5y^2}$

9. $\sqrt{12x^5}\sqrt{6x^2y}$

10. $\dfrac{\sqrt{8x^2}}{\sqrt{2x}}$

11. $\dfrac{\sqrt[3]{750}}{\sqrt[3]{3}}$

12. $\sqrt[4]{\dfrac{64x^5y^7}{36xy^2}}$

Add or subtract.

13. $\sqrt{27} + \sqrt{108}$

14. $\sqrt[3]{40} - \sqrt[3]{135}$

Multiply.

15. $(8 + 5\sqrt{6})(8 - 5\sqrt{6})$

16. $(2\sqrt{7} - 3\sqrt{5})(\sqrt{7} - \sqrt{5})$

Rationalize the denominator.

17. $\dfrac{\sqrt{5}}{\sqrt{7}}$

18. $\dfrac{\sqrt{3} + 7}{8 - \sqrt{5}}$

Simplify. Assume variables represent nonnegative numbers.

19. $\sqrt[3]{9a^2b^4}$

20. $\sqrt[3]{\dfrac{n^{24}}{a^8}}$

21. $\sqrt[4]{81x^8y^8}$

Write in simplest radical form with positive exponents.

22. $x^{-\frac{2}{3}}$

23. $\sqrt[3]{\dfrac{81x^8y^{-3}}{z^2}}$

24. $\sqrt[4]{9x^6}$

Solve.

25. $x - 5 = \sqrt{x + 7}$

26. $\sqrt{2x - 5} = 1 + \sqrt{x - 3}$

27. Solve $c = \sqrt{a^2 + b^2}$ for b. Find b if $a = 5$ and $c = 13$.

Add or subtract.

28. $(3 + 2i) + (2 - 3i)$

29. $(9 - 4i) - (3 + 2i)$

30. Graph $2 + 3i$.

31. Find $|4 + 2i|$.

Multiply or divide.

32. $(1 + 2i)(2i - 1)$

33. $(2 + 5i)(2 - 5i)$

34. $\dfrac{1 - 3i}{2 + i}$

35. Find the reciprocal of $1 + 2i$ and express it in the form $a + bi$.

36. Solve $-5ix + 8i - 4 = (7 + i)x + 10i$.

What You'll Learn in Chapter 8

- How to solve equations of the type $ax^2 + bx + c = 0$ by factoring, completing the square, or using the quadratic formula
- How to solve problems by translating to quadratic equations
- How to determine the nature of the solutions of a quadratic equation with real coefficients
- How to find a quadratic equation given its solutions
- How to solve equations that are reducible to quadratic form
- How to find equations and solve problems involving direct, indirect, and joint quadratic variation
- How to solve problems using logical reasoning

CHAPTER

Skills & Concepts You Need for Chapter 8

5-5 Solve.

1. $x^2 - 5x - 14 = 0$

2. $4x^2 - 8x = 0$

3. $x^2 + 10x + 25 = 0$

4. $x^2 - 9 = 0$

6-9 Find the constant of variation and an equation of variation.

5. y varies directly as x, and $y = 8$ when $x = 20$

6. y varies inversely as x, and $y = 20$ when $x = 8$

7-4 Rationalize the denominator.

7. $\sqrt{\frac{8}{7}}$

8. $\frac{1}{2\sqrt{2}}$

9. $\frac{1}{3 - \sqrt{3}}$

7-7 Express in terms of i.

10. $\sqrt{-7}$

11. $\sqrt{-20}$

Quadratic Equations

The volume (V) of wood in a tree varies jointly as the usable height (h) and the square of the girth (g), the circumference of the tree at $4\frac{1}{2}$ feet above the ground. The volume of a tree is 18.8 ft^3 for a usable height of 32 ft and a girth of 5 ft. What is the usable height of a tree whose volume is 46.06 ft^3 and girth is 7 ft?

8-1 Introduction to Quadratic Equations

What You'll Learn

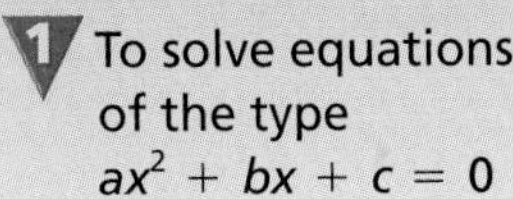

1 To solve equations of the type $ax^2 + bx + c = 0$

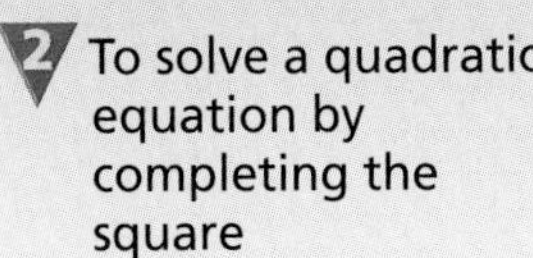

2 To solve a quadratic equation by completing the square

... And Why

To solve problems using quadratic equations

The second-degree or **quadratic equation** $16t^2 + v_0t - h = 0$ models projectile motion by relating the time t an object is in the air to the initial velocity v_0 and the height h of the object.

Definition

An equation of the type $ax^2 + bx + c = 0$, where a, b, and c are constants and $a \neq 0$, is called the **standard form** of a quadratic equation.

PART 1 Equations of the Type $ax^2 + bx + c = 0$

Objective: Solve equations of the type $ax^2 + bx + c = 0$.

Every quadratic polynomial $ax^2 + bx + c$ with complex coefficients can be factored into two linear factors.

EXAMPLE 1 Solve $3x^2 + 5x = 0$.

This is an equation of the type $ax^2 + bx + c = 0$, where $c = 0$. Quadratic equations in standard form where $c = 0$ can be easily solved by factoring.

$$x(3x + 5) = 0 \quad \text{Factoring}$$

$$x = 0 \text{ or } 3x + 5 = 0 \quad \text{Using the principle of zero products}$$

$$x = 0 \text{ or } x = -\frac{5}{3}$$

These numbers check, so the solutions are 0 and $-\frac{5}{3}$.

A quadratic equation of this type will always have 0 as one solution.

Sometimes it helps to find standard form before factoring.

EXAMPLE 2 Solve $(x - 1)(x + 1) = 5(x - 1)$.

$$x^2 - 1 = 5x - 5 \quad \text{Multiplying}$$

$$x^2 - 5x + 4 = 0 \quad \text{Finding standard form}$$

$$(x - 4)(x - 1) = 0 \quad \text{Factoring}$$

$$x = 4 \text{ or } x = 1 \quad \text{Using the principle of zero products}$$

These numbers check, so the solutions are 4 and 1.

Try This Solve.

a. $5x^2 + 8x = 0$ **b.** $14x^2 + 2 = 11x$ **c.** $(x + 2)(x - 2) = 2 - x$

Consider any quadratic equation in standard form $ax^2 + bx + c = 0$, where $b = 0$, that is, an equation of the form $ax^2 + c = 0$. We can use the multiplication and addition principles to obtain an equation of the form $x^2 = k$, where $x = \sqrt{k}$ or $x = -\sqrt{k}$.

EXAMPLE 3 Solve $3x^2 - 6 = 0$.

$$3x^2 = 6 \quad \text{Using the addition property}$$
$$x^2 = 2 \quad \text{Multiplying both sides by } \tfrac{1}{3}$$
$$x = \sqrt{2} \text{ or } x = -\sqrt{2}$$

We can abbreviate this as $x = \pm\sqrt{2}$.

Sometimes we get solutions that are complex numbers.

Quick Review

To rewrite the square root of a negative number, you may factor the radicand:

$$\sqrt{-a} = \sqrt{-1 \cdot a}$$
$$= \sqrt{-1} \cdot \sqrt{a} = i\sqrt{a}$$

EXAMPLE 4 Solve $4x^2 + 9 = 0$.

$$4x^2 = -9 \quad \text{Adding } -9 \text{ to both sides}$$
$$x^2 = -\frac{9}{4} \quad \text{Multiplying both sides by } \tfrac{1}{4}$$
$$x = \sqrt{-\frac{9}{4}} \text{ or } x = -\sqrt{-\frac{9}{4}} \quad \text{Finding square roots}$$
$$x = \frac{3}{2}i \text{ or } x = -\frac{3}{2}i$$
$$x = \pm\frac{3}{2}i$$

Try This Solve.

d. $7x^2 - 5 = 0$ **e.** $2x^2 + 1 = 0$ **f.** $49x^2 + 4 = 0$

PART 2 Solving Equations by Completing the Square

Objective: Solve a quadratic equation by completing the square.

The trinomial $x^2 + 10x + 25$ is the square of a binomial, because $x^2 + 10x + 25 = (x + 5)^2$. Given the first two terms of a trinomial, we can find the third term that will make it a square. This process is called **completing the square.**

EXAMPLE 5 Complete the square for $x^2 + 12x$.

What must be added to $x^2 + 12x$ to make it a trinomial square? We take half the coefficient of x and square it.

$x^2 + 12x$
↓
Half of 12 is 6, and $6^2 = 36$. We add 36.

$x^2 + 12x + 36$ is a trinomial square. It is equal to $(x + 6)^2$.

EXAMPLE 6 Complete the square for $y^2 + \frac{3}{4}y$.

Half of $\frac{3}{4}$ (the coefficient of y) is $\frac{1}{2} \cdot \frac{3}{4} = \frac{3}{8}$.

$$\left(\frac{3}{8}\right)^2 = \frac{9}{64}$$

Thus, $y^2 + \frac{3}{4}y + \frac{9}{64}$ is a trinomial square. It is $\left(y + \frac{3}{8}\right)^2$.

Try This Complete the square.

g. $x^2 + 14x$

h. $y^2 - 11y$

i. $x^2 - \frac{2}{5}x$

j. $x^2 + 2ax$

We can solve quadratic equations of the form $ax^2 + bx + c = 0$ by completing the square.

Reading Math

A convenient way to read the expression $1 \pm \sqrt{6}$ is "one, plus or minus the square root of six," or "one, plus or minus radical six."

EXAMPLE 7 Solve by completing the square.

$$x^2 - 2x - 5 = 0$$

$$x^2 - 2x = 5 \quad \text{Adding 5 to both sides}$$

$$x^2 - 2x + 1 = 5 + 1 \quad \text{Adding 1 to complete the square, } \left(\frac{-2}{2}\right)^2 = 1$$

$$(x - 1)^2 = 6$$

$$x - 1 = \sqrt{6} \text{ or } x - 1 = -\sqrt{6}$$

$$x = 1 + \sqrt{6} \text{ or } x = 1 - \sqrt{6}$$

Check:

$x^2 - 2x - 5$	0
$(1 + \sqrt{6})^2 - 2(1 + \sqrt{6}) - 5$	0
$1 + 2\sqrt{6} + 6 - 2 - 2\sqrt{6} - 5$	0
0	0 ✓

$x^2 - 2x - 5$	0
$(1 - \sqrt{6})^2 - 2(1 - \sqrt{6}) - 5$	0
$1 - 2\sqrt{6} + 6 - 2 + 2\sqrt{6} - 5$	0
0	0 ✓

The numbers check, so they are the solutions. The solutions can be abbreviated as $x = 1 \pm \sqrt{6}$.

Try This Solve by completing the square.

k. $x^2 + x - 1 = 0$

l. $x^2 - \frac{1}{2}x - \frac{1}{2} = 0$

For many quadratic equations the leading coefficient is not 1, but we can use the multiplication principle to make it 1.

EXAMPLE 8 Solve by completing the square.

$$4x^2 + 12x - 7 = 0$$
$$x^2 + 3x - \frac{7}{4} = 0 \quad \text{Multiplying both sides by } \tfrac{1}{4}$$
$$x^2 + 3x = \frac{7}{4}$$
$$x^2 + 3x + \frac{9}{4} = \frac{7}{4} + \frac{9}{4} \quad \text{Adding } \tfrac{9}{4} \text{ to complete the square}$$
$$\left(x + \frac{3}{2}\right)^2 = 4$$
$$x + \frac{3}{2} = 2 \text{ or } x + \frac{3}{2} = -2$$
$$x = \frac{1}{2} \text{ or } x = -\frac{7}{2}$$

Try This Solve by completing the square.

m. $8x^2 - x - 1 = 0$ **n.** $9x^2 + 9x - 10 = 0$

8-1 Exercises

Extra Help On the Web

Look for worked-out examples at the Prentice Hall Web site.
www.phschool.com

A

Solve.

1. $7x^2 - 3x = 0$ **2.** $14x^2 + 9x = 0$ **3.** $19x^2 + 8x = 0$

4. $x^2 + 8x + 15 = 0$ **5.** $x^2 + 9x + 14 = 0$

6. $6x^2 - x - 2 = 0$ **7.** $2x^2 + 13x + 15 = 0$

8. $9t^2 + 15t + 4 = 0$ **9.** $3y^2 + 10y - 8 = 0$

10. $6x^2 + 4x = 10$ **11.** $3x^2 + 7x = 20$

12. $2x(4x - 5) = 3$ **13.** $t(2t + 9) = -7$

14. $(p - 3)(p - 4) = 42$ **15.** $16(t - 1) = t(t + 8)$

16. $4x(x - 2) - 5x(x - 1) = 2$ **17.** $14(x - 4) - (x + 2) = (x + 2)(x - 4)$

Solve.

18. $4x^2 = 20$ **19.** $3x^2 = 21$ **20.** $2x^2 - 3 = 0$

21. $3x^2 - 7 = 0$ **22.** $-3x^2 + 5 = 0$ **23.** $-2x^2 + 1 = 0$

24. $25x^2 + 4 = 0$ **25.** $5x^2 + 1 = 0$ **26.** $2x^2 + 14 = 0$

27. $3x^2 + 15 = 0$ **28.** $\frac{4}{9}x^2 - 1 = 0$ **29.** $\frac{16}{25}x^2 - 1 = 0$

Fill in the missing term to complete a perfect-square trinomial.

30. $x^2 + x + \_\_\_$ **31.** $2x^2 + \_\_\_ + 4$ **32.** $x^2 + \frac{b}{a}x + \_\_\_$

Mental Math Complete the square.

33. $x^2 + 8x$ **34.** $y^2 - 20y$ **35.** $a^2 - 7a$

36. $y^2 - \frac{1}{5}y$ **37.** $x^2 + \frac{1}{2}x$ **38.** $x^2 - 2.2kx$

Solve by completing the square.

39. $x^2 - 3x + 2 = 0$ **40.** $y^2 + 7y + 12 = 0$ **41.** $x^2 + x + 1 = 0$

42. $x^2 - 4x + 1 = 0$ **43.** $y^2 + 6y - 3 = 0$ **44.** $3x^2 - 5x - 10 = 0$

45. $2y^2 + 7y - 9 = 0$ **46.** $\frac{1}{2}y^2 - 3y + 9 = 0$ **47.** $2d^2 + 2d + 4 = 0$

B

Solve.

48. $(3x^2 - 7x - 20)(2x - 5) = 0$ **49.** $x(2x^2 + 9x - 56)(3x + 10) = 0$

Solve for x.

50. $\left(x - \frac{1}{3}\right)\left(x - \frac{1}{3}\right) + \left(x - \frac{1}{3}\right)\left(x + \frac{2}{9}\right) = 0$ **51.** $ax^2 - b = 0$

52. $ax^2 - bx = 0$

Mental Math Use the result of Exercise 52 to find the nonzero solution for each of the following quadratic equations.

53. $2x^2 - 3x = 0$ **54.** $\frac{1}{2}x^2 + 7x = 0$ **55.** $10x = x^2$ **56.** $\frac{x^2}{2} + kx = 0$

Solve by completing the square.

57. $\frac{1}{2}(1 + m)(1 - m) = 10m$ **58.** $a^2 - 2\sqrt{3}a + 2 = 0$

59. ***Critical Thinking*** Show the geometrical representation of completing the square for $x^2 + ax$ by providing the missing labels. What is the resulting binomial square?

	x	?
x	x^2	?
?	?	?

Challenge

Solve for x.

60. $ax^n + bx^{n-1} = 0$ **61.** $ax^n + b = 0$

62. How do the solutions of $ax^2 + h = 0$ compare to the solutions of $ax^2 = h$, where a and h are positive?

Mixed Review

Multiply. **63.** $\sqrt[5]{(m + 4)^6} \cdot \sqrt[5]{(m + 4)^4}$ **64.** $\sqrt{6a} \cdot \sqrt{10a^5}$

65. $\sqrt{6m^3n^5} \cdot \sqrt{8m^2n^3}$ **66.** $\sqrt{2}(1 - 4\sqrt{5})$ **67.** $(\sqrt{m} + \sqrt{n})(\sqrt{m} - \sqrt{n})$

68. $(\sqrt{7} + \sqrt{2})(\sqrt{7} - \sqrt{3})$ *7-2*

Graph. **69.** $2 + 5i; 3 - 4i; -1 + 5i; -3 - 2i; -5 + 1; 1 + 2i$ *7-8*

Find the absolute value. **70.** $|12 + 5i|$ **71.** $|4 - 3i|$ **72.** $|4i|$ *7-8*

73. Linessa's credit card interest was 1.5% per month, compounded monthly. She paid \$400 for an item with her credit card. Assuming she made no payments, how much did she owe after two months? *2-9*

Using Quadratic Equations

8-2

PART 1 Solving Problems

Objective: Solve problems by translating to quadratic equations.

What You'll Learn

1 To solve problems by translating to quadratic equations

. . . And Why

To solve real-world problems that involve quadratic equations

PROBLEM-SOLVING GUIDELINES
■ UNDERSTAND the problem
■ Develop and carry out a PLAN
■ Find the ANSWER and CHECK

For some problems a quadratic equation will serve as a mathematical model. Problem-solving strategies such as *write an equation, draw a diagram,* and others may be used together, as with a linear model.

EXAMPLE 1 A rectangular lawn is 60 m by 80 m. Part of the lawn is torn up to install a pool, leaving a strip of lawn of uniform width around the pool. The area of the pool is $\frac{1}{6}$ of the old lawn area. How wide is the strip of lawn?

■ **UNDERSTAND the problem**

Question: Find the width of the strip of lawn. Clarifying the question

Data: The lawn is 60 m by 80 m.

The pool is $\frac{1}{6}$ of the total area. Identifying the important data

■ **Develop and carry out a PLAN**

First *draw a diagram.*

Let x represent the width of the strip of lawn

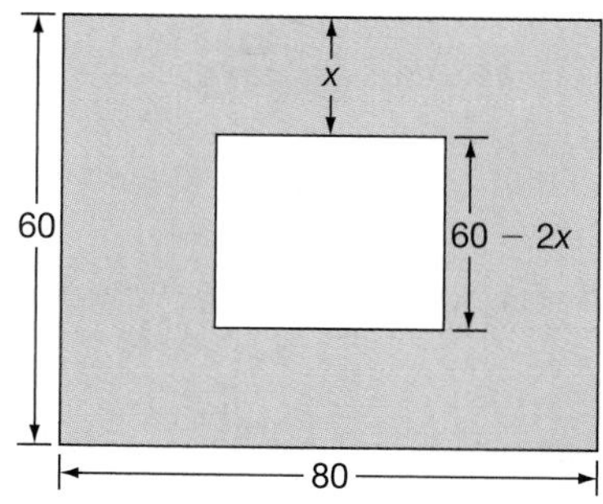

$$\text{Total area} = 60 \cdot 80$$
$$\text{Area of pool} = (60 - 2x)(80 - 2x)$$

The area of the pool is $\frac{1}{6}$ the original area of the lawn. Therefore,

$$(60 - 2x)(80 - 2x) = \frac{1}{6} \cdot 60 \cdot 80$$
$$4800 - 160x - 120x + 4x^2 = 800 \quad \text{Solving the equation}$$
$$4x^2 - 280x + 4000 = 0$$
$$x^2 - 70x + 1000 = 0$$
$$(x - 20)(x - 50) = 0$$
$$x = 20 \text{ or } x = 50$$

Find the ANSWER and CHECK

We see that 50 cannot be a solution because when x is 50, $60 - 2x$, which is the width of the pool, is -40. But the width of the pool cannot be negative. A 20-meter wide strip checks in the problem. Since the width must be smaller than 60, it is a reasonable answer.

Try This

a. An open box is to be made from a 10 cm by 20 cm rectangular piece of cardboard by cutting a square from each corner. The area of the bottom of the box is 96 cm^2. What is the length of the sides of the squares that are cut from the corners?

The following theorem is helpful for solving problems involving quadratic equations.

Theorem 8-1

The Pythagorean Theorem

In any right triangle, if a and b are the lengths of the legs and c is the length of the hypotenuse, then $a^2 + b^2 = c^2$.

EXAMPLE 2 Bicyclists A and B leave the same point P at the same time at right angles. B travels 7 km/h faster than A. After 3 hours they are 39 km apart. Find the speed of each.

We first make a *drawing*, letting r be the speed of A and $r + 7$ be the speed of B. Since they both travel 3 hours, their distances from P are $3r$ and $3(r + 7)$, respectively.

$$[3(r + 7)]^2 + (3r)^2 = 39^2 \quad \text{Using the Pythagorean theorem}$$
$$9(r + 7)^2 + 9r^2 = 1521$$
$$(r + 7)^2 + r^2 = 169 \quad \text{Multiplying by } \tfrac{1}{9}$$
$$r^2 + 14r + 49 + r^2 = 169$$
$$2r^2 + 14r + 49 = 169$$

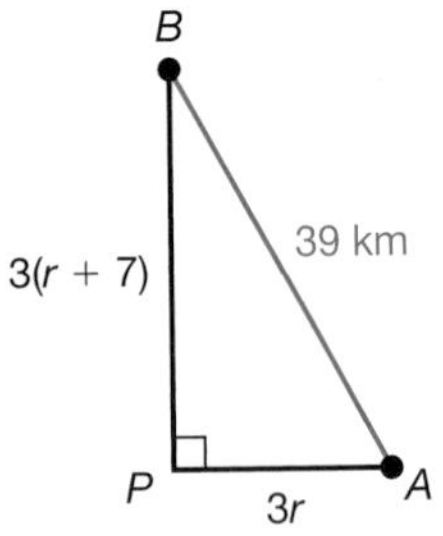

$$2r^2 + 14r - 120 = 0 \quad \text{Finding standard form}$$
$$r^2 + 7r - 60 = 0 \quad \text{Multiplying by } \tfrac{1}{2}$$
$$(r + 12)(r - 5) = 0 \quad r = -12 \text{ or } r = 5$$

B

39 km

3(r + 7)

P 3r A

The solutions of the equation are -12 and 5. Since speed cannot be negative, -12 is not a solution. The speed of A is 5 km/h and the speed of B is 12 km/h.

Try This

b. Runners A and B leave the same point P at right angles. A runs 4 km/h faster than B. After 2 hours they are 40 km apart. Find the speed of each.

8-2 Exercises

Extra Help On the Web

Look for worked-out examples at the Prentice Hall Web site. www.phschool.com

A

1. A picture frame measures 14 cm by 20 cm. 160 cm^2 of the picture shows inside the frame. Find the width of the frame.
2. A picture frame measures 12 cm by 20 cm. 84 cm^2 of picture shows inside the frame. Find the width of the frame.

Find the length and width. Assume the shapes are rectangular.

3. The width of a dock is 4 m less than the length. The area is 12 m^2.
4. The width of a photo is 5 cm less than the length. The area is 24 cm^2.
5. The hypotenuse of a right triangle is 26 m long. One leg is 14 m longer than the other. Find the lengths of the legs.
6. The hypotenuse of a right triangle is 25 km long. The length of one leg is 17 km less than the other. Find the lengths of the legs.
7. Boats A and B leave the same point at the same time at right angles. B travels 7 km/h slower than A. After 4 hours they are 68 km apart. Find the speed of each boat.

B

8. Find three consecutive integers such that the square of the first plus the product of the other two is 46.
9. A bicyclist traveled 280 km at a certain speed. If the speed had been increased 5 km/h, the trip could have been made in 1 hour less time. Find the actual speed.
10. Airplane A travels 2800 km at a certain speed. Airplane B travels 2000 km at a speed that is 50 km/h faster than Plane A in 3 hours less time. Find the speed of each.
11. ***Critical Thinking*** Write a consecutive integer problem that can be solved by using a quadratic equation.

Challenge

12. Find three consecutive integers such that the sum of their squares is 149.
13. Two open boxes are made by cutting squares from each corner of a 20″ by 15″ piece of cardboard, and from an 18″ by 18″ piece. The same size squares are cut from the corners of both pieces, and the flaps created are folded up. Is it possible for the boxes to have equal volumes? If so, find the length of a side of the square.

Passenger jetliners travel at a speed of 600 mi/h. What is the speed of a Concorde SST (supersonic transport) that can cover 1000 miles 52 minutes faster than a jetliner traveling 600 mi/h?

Mixed Review

Solve. **14.** $\sqrt[3]{x + 3} = 2$ **15.** $\sqrt{2x - 1} - 3 = 0$ **16.** $\sqrt[4]{x} - 2 = 0$ 7-6

Solve. **17.** $\frac{x}{4} - \frac{x}{5} = 5$ **18.** $\frac{(x + 2)}{2} - \frac{(x - 2)}{4} = 3$ **19.** $\frac{5x}{8} - \frac{15}{6} = \frac{x}{2}$ 6-6

8-3 The Quadratic Formula

What You'll Learn

1. To solve quadratic equations using the quadratic formula
2. To find approximate values for solutions to quadratic equations

. . . And Why

To solve problems requiring solutions to quadratic equations

PART 1 Solving Equations Using the Quadratic Formula

Objective: Solve quadratic equations using the quadratic formula.

Some quadratic equations cannot be solved by factoring. Here is a formula for finding the solutions of any quadratic equation.

Theorem 8-2

The Quadratic Formula

The solutions of any quadratic equation with complex coefficients, $ax^2 + bx + c = 0$, are given by the quadratic formula.

$$x = \frac{-b \pm \sqrt{b^2 - 4ac}}{2a}$$

EXAMPLE 1 Solve $3x^2 + 5x = -1$.

First find the standard form and determine a, b, and c.

$$3x^2 + 5x + 1 = 0$$
$$a = 3, b = 5, c = 1$$

Then use the quadratic formula.

$$x = \frac{-b \pm \sqrt{b^2 - 4ac}}{2a}$$

$$x = \frac{-(5) \pm \sqrt{(5)^2 - 4 \cdot 3 \cdot 1}}{2 \cdot 3} \quad \text{Substituting}$$

$$x = \frac{-5 \pm \sqrt{25 - 12}}{6} = \frac{-5 \pm \sqrt{13}}{6}$$

The solutions are $\frac{-5 + \sqrt{13}}{6}$ and $\frac{-5 - \sqrt{13}}{6}$.

When using the quadratic formula, the solutions obtained are always solutions of the original equation unless a computational error has been made.

Try This Solve using the quadratic formula.

a. $3x^2 + 2x = 7$ **b.** $5x^2 + 3x = 9$

When the expression under the radical sign is negative, we obtain complex solutions.

EXAMPLE 2 Solve $x^2 + x + 1 = 0$.

$$a = 1, b = 1, c = 1$$

$$x = \frac{-b \pm \sqrt{b^2 - 4ac}}{2a}$$

$$x = \frac{-1 \pm \sqrt{1^2 - 4 \cdot 1 \cdot 1}}{2 \cdot 1} \quad \text{Substituting}$$

$$x = \frac{-1 \pm \sqrt{1 - 4}}{2}$$

$$x = \frac{-1 \pm \sqrt{-3}}{2}$$

$$x = \frac{-1 \pm i\sqrt{3}}{2}$$

The solutions are $\frac{-1 + i\sqrt{3}}{2}$ and $\frac{-1 - i\sqrt{3}}{2}$.

Quick Review

The expressions $a + bi$ and $a - bi$, where $b \neq 0$, are referred to as complex conjugates.

Try This Solve using the quadratic formula.

c. $x^2 - x + 2 = 0$ **d.** $3x^2 + 2x + 2 = 0$

PART 2 Approximating Solutions

Objective: Find approximate values for solutions to quadratic equations.

A calculator or square root table can be used to find rational-number approximations to the exact solutions given by the formula.

EXAMPLE 3 Approximate the solutions of the equation in Example 1. Use a calculator or Table 1.

$$\frac{-5 + \sqrt{13}}{6} \approx \frac{-5 + 3.6055513}{6} \quad \text{Using a calculator to find } \sqrt{13}$$

$$\approx \frac{-1.3944488}{6}$$

$$\approx -0.23 \quad \text{Rounding to the nearest hundredth}$$

$$\frac{-5 - \sqrt{13}}{6} \approx \frac{-5 - 3.6055513}{6}$$

$$\approx \frac{-8.6055513}{6}$$

$$\approx -1.43 \quad \text{Rounding to the nearest hundredth}$$

Try This

e. Approximate the solutions to $3x^2 + 2x = 7$. Round to the nearest hundredth.

Proof of Theorem 8-2

Consider any quadratic equation in the form $ax^2 + bx + c = 0, (a > 0)$. Let's solve by completing the square.

$$x^2 + \frac{b}{a}x + \frac{c}{a} = 0 \qquad \text{Multiplying by } \tfrac{1}{a}$$

$$x^2 + \frac{b}{a}x = -\frac{c}{a} \qquad \text{Adding } -\tfrac{c}{a}$$

Half of $\frac{b}{a}$ is $\frac{b}{2a}$. The square is $\frac{b^2}{4a^2}$. We complete the square.

$$x^2 + \frac{b}{a}x + \frac{b^2}{4a^2} = -\frac{c}{a} + \frac{b^2}{4a^2} \qquad \text{Adding } \tfrac{b^2}{4a^2} \text{ to both sides}$$

$$\left(x + \frac{b}{2a}\right)^2 = -\frac{4ac}{4a^2} + \frac{b^2}{4a^2} \qquad \text{The LCD is } 4a^2.$$

$$\left(x + \frac{b}{2a}\right)^2 = \frac{b^2 - 4ac}{4a^2}$$

$$x + \frac{b}{2a} = \sqrt{\frac{b^2 - 4ac}{4a^2}} \text{ or } x + \frac{b}{2a} = -\sqrt{\frac{b^2 - 4ac}{4a^2}}$$

$$x + \frac{b}{2a} = \frac{\sqrt{b^2 - 4ac}}{2a} \text{ or } x + \frac{b}{2a} = -\frac{\sqrt{b^2 - 4ac}}{2a} \qquad \text{Since } a > 0, |a| = a.$$

$$x = -\frac{b}{2a} + \frac{\sqrt{b^2 - 4ac}}{2a} \text{ or } x = -\frac{b}{2a} - \frac{\sqrt{b^2 - 4ac}}{2a}$$

The solutions are given by $x = \dfrac{-b \pm \sqrt{b^2 - 4ac}}{2a}$.

Extra Help On the Web

Look for worked-out examples at the Prentice Hall Web site.
www.phschool.com

8-3 Exercises

A

Solve.

1. $x^2 + 6x + 4 = 0$
2. $x^2 - 6x - 4 = 0$
3. $x^2 + 4x - 5 = 0$
4. $x^2 - 2x - 15 = 0$
5. $y^2 + 7y = 30$
6. $y^2 - 7y = 30$
7. $2t^2 - 3t - 2 = 0$
8. $5m^2 + 3m - 2 = 0$
9. $3p^2 = -8p - 5$
10. $3u^2 = 18u - 6$
11. $x^2 - x + 1 = 0$
12. $x^2 + x + 2 = 0$
13. $1 + \frac{2}{x} + \frac{5}{x^2} = 0$
14. $1 + \frac{5}{x^2} = \frac{2}{x}$
15. $x^2 - 2x + 5 = 0$
16. $x^2 - 4x + 5 = 0$
17. $x^2 + 13 = 4x$
18. $x^2 + 13 = 6x$
19. $t^2 + 3 = 0$
20. $h^2 + 4 = 6h$
21. $3x + x(x - 2) = 0$
22. $4x + x(x - 3) = 0$
23. $5x^2 + 2x + 1 = 0$
24. $3x^2 + x + 2 = 0$
25. $(2t - 3)^2 + 17t = 15$
26. $2y^2 - (y + 2)(y - 3) = 12$
27. $(x - 2)^2 + (x + 1)^2 = 0$
28. $(x + 3)^2 + (x - 1)^2 = 0$
29. $x + \frac{1}{x} = \frac{13}{6}$
30. $\frac{3}{x} + \frac{x}{3} = \frac{5}{2}$

31. ***Error Analysis*** Given $x^2 - 2x + 3 = 1$, use the quadratic formula to determine if the following solution is correct. If not, explain where the error occurred.

$$x = \frac{2 \pm \sqrt{4 - 4(1)(3)}}{2(1)} = \frac{2 \pm \sqrt{-8}}{2}$$
$$= 1 \pm i\sqrt{2}$$

Approximate solutions to the nearest hundredth.

32. $x^2 + 6x + 4 = 0$ **33.** $x^2 - 6x + 4 = 0$ **34.** $x^2 - 4x + 1 = 0$

35. $2x^2 - 3x - 7 = 0$ **36.** $3x^2 - 3x - 2 = 0$

B

Solve.

37. $x^2 + x - \sqrt{2} = 0$ **38.** $x^2 - x - \sqrt{3} = 0$ **39.** $\sqrt{2}x^2 + 5x + \sqrt{2} = 0$

40. $x^2 + \sqrt{5}x - \sqrt{3} = 0$ **41.** $x^2 + 3x + i = 0$ **42.** $ix^2 - 2x + 1 = 0$

43. $\frac{1}{x^2 - x} = \frac{1}{2}$ **44.** $\frac{1}{x^2 - x} = 2$

45. ***Multi-Step Problem*** The difference between two positive numbers is 3 and the product is 28. Write and solve a quadratic equation to find the smaller of the two numbers.

46. A boat travels 2 km upstream and 2 km downstream. The total time of the trip is 1 hour. The speed of the stream is 2 km/h. What is the speed of the boat in still water?

47. ***Critical Thinking*** Write a quadratic equation whose solutions are not real numbers.

48. ***Critical Thinking*** For what values of c does the quadratic equation $x^2 + c = 0$ have no real solutions?

49. ***Critical Thinking*** For what values of c does the quadratic equation $x^2 + 2x + c = 0$ have no real solutions?

Challenge

50. Solve $3x^2 + xy + 4y^2 - 9 = 0$ for x in terms of y.

51. One solution of $kx^2 + 3x - k = 0$ is -2. Find the other solution.

52. Prove that the solutions of $ax^2 + bx + c = 0$ are the reciprocals of the solutions of $cx^2 + bx + a = 0$.

Mixed Review

Divide and simplify. **53.** $\frac{\sqrt{35x}}{\sqrt{7x}}$ **54.** $\frac{\sqrt[3]{216}}{\sqrt[3]{8}}$ **55.** $\frac{\sqrt{42x^2y^2}}{\sqrt{7x}}$ *7-3*

Find the reciprocal of each number and express it in the form $a + bi$.

56. i **57.** $1 - 3i$ **58.** $3 + i$ **59.** $3 - 4i$ *7-9*

Solve. **60.** $2x - 19 + 4i = 5ix$ **61.** $x^2 + 9 = 0$ **62.** $x^2 - 9 = 0$ *5-7, 7-7, 7-10*

8-4 Solutions of Quadratic Equations

What You'll Learn

1. To determine the nature of the solutions of a quadratic equation with real coefficients
2. To find and use sums and products of solutions of quadratic equations
3. To find a quadratic equation given its solutions

. . . And Why

To solve problems about the nature of solutions to quadratic equations

The quadratic formula can be used when the coefficients are any complex numbers. Now we restrict our attention to equations with real-number coefficients.

PART 1 The Discriminant

Objective: Determine the nature of the solutions of a quadratic equation with real coefficients.

The expression $b^2 - 4ac$ in the quadratic formula is called the **discriminant.** From this number we can determine the nature of the solutions of a quadratic equation.

Theorem 8-3

An equation $ax^2 + bx + c = 0$, with $a \neq 0$, and all coefficients real numbers, has

A. exactly one real-number solution if $b^2 - 4ac = 0$.

B. two real-number solutions if $b^2 - 4ac > 0$.

C. two complex nonreal solutions that are conjugates of each other if $b^2 - 4ac < 0$.

EXAMPLE 1 Determine the nature of the solutions of $9x^2 - 12x + 4 = 0$.

$$a = 9, b = -12, \text{ and } c = 4$$

We compute the discriminant.

$$b^2 - 4ac = (-12)^2 - 4 \cdot 9 \cdot 4 = 144 - 144 = 0$$

By Theorem 8-3, there is just one solution and it is a real number.

EXAMPLE 2 Determine the nature of the solutions of $x^2 + 5x + 8 = 0$.

$$a = 1, b = 5, \text{ and } c = 8$$

We compute the discriminant.

$$b^2 - 4ac = 5^2 - 4 \cdot 1 \cdot 8 = 25 - 32 = -7$$

Since the discriminant is negative, there are two nonreal solutions that are complex conjugates of each other.

EXAMPLE 3 Determine the nature of the solutions of $x^2 + 5x + 6 = 0$.

$$a = 1, b = 5, \text{and } c = 6$$
$$b^2 - 4ac = 5^2 - 4 \cdot 1 \cdot 6 = 1$$

The discriminant is positive, so there are two real solutions.

Try This Determine the nature of the solutions of each equation.

a. $x^2 + 5x - 3 = 0$ **b.** $9x^2 - 6x + 1 = 0$ **c.** $3x^2 - 2x + 1 = 0$

PART 2 Sums and Products of Solutions

Objective: Find and use sums and products of solutions of quadratic equations.

Theorem 8-4

For the equation $ax^2 + bx + c = 0$, the sum of the solutions is $-\frac{b}{a}$, and the product of the solutions is $\frac{c}{a}$.

Note that if we express $ax^2 + bx + c = 0$ in the form $x^2 + \frac{b}{a}x + \frac{c}{a} = 0$, then the sum of the solutions is the additive inverse of the coefficient of the x-term, and the product of the solutions is the constant term.

We can find the sum and product of the solutions without solving the equation.

EXAMPLE 4 Find the sum and product of the solutions of $2x^2 = 6x + 5$.

Let x_1 and x_2 be the solutions to $2x^2 - 6x - 5 = 0$.

$$x_1 + x_2 = -\frac{b}{a} = -\left(\frac{-6}{2}\right) = 3 \qquad x_1 \cdot x_2 = \frac{c}{a} = \frac{-5}{2}$$

Try This Find the sum and product of the solutions.

d. $3x^2 + 4 = 12x$ **e.** $x^2 + \sqrt{2}x - 4 = 0$

EXAMPLE 5 Find a quadratic equation for which the sum of the solutions is $-\frac{4}{5}$, and the product of the solutions is $\frac{2}{3}$.

$$x^2 - \left(-\frac{b}{a}\right)x + \frac{c}{a} = 0$$
$$x^2 - \left(-\frac{4}{5}\right)x + \frac{2}{3} = 0$$
$$x^2 + \frac{4}{5}x + \frac{2}{3} = 0$$

We usually write the equation with integer coefficients.

$$15x^2 + 12x + 10 = 0 \quad \text{Multiplying by 15, the LCD}$$

Try This

f. Find a quadratic equation for which the sum of the solutions is 3 and the product is $-\frac{1}{4}$.

PART 3 Writing Equations from Solutions

Objective: Find a quadratic equation given its solutions.

We can use the principle of zero products to write a quadratic equation whose solutions are known.

EXAMPLE 6 Find a quadratic equation whose solutions are 3 and $-\frac{2}{5}$.

$$x = 3 \text{ or } x = -\frac{2}{5}$$

$$x - 3 = 0 \text{ or } x + \frac{2}{5} = 0$$

$$(x - 3)\left(x + \frac{2}{5}\right) = 0 \qquad \text{Multiplying}$$

$$x^2 - \frac{13}{5}x - \frac{6}{5} = 0$$

$$5x^2 - 13x - 6 = 0 \qquad \text{Multiplying by 5, the LCD}$$

When radicals are involved, it is sometimes easier to use the properties of the sum and product.

EXAMPLE 7 Find the quadratic equation whose solutions are $2 + \sqrt{5}$ and $2 - \sqrt{5}$.

Let the solutions be x_1 and x_2.

$$x_1 + x_2 = (2 + \sqrt{5}) + (2 - \sqrt{5}) \qquad \text{Finding the sum of the solutions; } -\frac{b}{a}$$
$$= 4$$

$$x_1 \cdot x_2 = (2 + \sqrt{5}) \cdot (2 - \sqrt{5}) \qquad \text{Finding the product of the solutions; } \frac{c}{a}$$
$$= 4 - 5 = -1$$

$$x^2 - \left(-\frac{b}{a}\right)x + \frac{c}{a} = 0 \qquad \text{Using Theorem 8-4}$$

$$x^2 - (4)x + (-1) = 0 \qquad \text{Substituting}$$

$$x^2 - 4x - 1 = 0 \qquad \text{Simplifying}$$

Try This Find a quadratic equation whose solutions are the following.

g. $-4, \frac{5}{3}$ **h.** $-7, 8$ **i.** m, n

j. $8, -9$ **k.** $3 + \sqrt{2}, 3 - \sqrt{2}$ **l.** $\frac{2 + \sqrt{5}}{2}, \frac{2 - \sqrt{5}}{2}$

8-4 Exercises

Extra Help On the Web

Look for worked-out examples at the Prentice Hall Web site.
www.phschool.com

A

Determine the nature of the solutions of each equation.

1. $x^2 - 6x + 9 = 0$
2. $x^2 + 10x + 25 = 0$
3. $x^2 + 7 = 0$
4. $x^2 + 2 = 0$
5. $x^2 - 2 = 0$
6. $x^2 - 5 = 0$
7. $4x^2 - 12x + 9 = 0$
8. $4x^2 + 8x - 5 = 0$
9. $x^2 - 2x + 4 = 0$
10. $x^2 + 3x + 4 = 0$
11. $9t^2 - 3t = 0$
12. $4m^2 + 7m = 0$
13. $y^2 = \frac{1}{2}y + \frac{3}{5}$
14. $y^2 + \frac{9}{4} = 4y$
15. $4x^2 - 4\sqrt{3}x + 3 = 0$

Find the sum and product of the solutions.

16. $x^2 + 7x + 8 = 0$
17. $x^2 - 2x + 10 = 0$
18. $x^2 - x + 1 = 0$
19. $x^2 + x - 1 = 0$
20. $8 - 2x^2 + 4x = 0$
21. $4 + x + 2x^2 = 0$
22. $m^2 = 25$
23. $t^2 = 49$
24. $(2 + 3x)^2 = 7x$
25. $2x - 1 = (1 - 5x)^2$
26. $5(t - 3)^2 = 4(t + 3)^2$
27. $3(y + 4)^2 = 2(y + 5)^2$

Find a quadratic equation for which the sum and product of the solutions are as given.

28. Sum $= -5$; product $= \frac{1}{2}$
29. Sum $= -\pi$; product $= \frac{1}{4}$
30. Sum $= \sqrt{3}$; product $= 8$
31. Sum $= 5$; product $= -\sqrt{2}$

Find a quadratic equation whose solution or solutions are the following.

32. $-11, 9$
33. $-4, 4$
34. 7 (only solution)
35. -5 (only solution)
36. $-\frac{2}{5}, \frac{6}{5}$
37. $-\frac{1}{4}, -\frac{1}{2}$
38. $\frac{c}{2}, \frac{d}{2}$
39. $\frac{k}{3}, \frac{m}{4}$
40. $\sqrt{2}, 3\sqrt{2}$
41. $-\sqrt{3}, 2\sqrt{3}$
42. $\pi, -2\pi$
43. $-3\pi, 4\pi$

Use the sum and product properties to write a quadratic equation whose solutions are the following.

44. $4, 3$
45. $5, 6$
46. $-2, \frac{5}{4}$
47. $-6, \frac{1}{4}$
48. $1 + \sqrt{2}, 1 - \sqrt{2}$
49. $2 + \sqrt{3}, 2 - \sqrt{3}$
50. $\frac{2 + \sqrt{3}}{2}, \frac{2 - \sqrt{3}}{2}$
51. $\frac{1 + \sqrt{13}}{2}, \frac{1 - \sqrt{13}}{2}$
52. $\frac{m}{n}, -\frac{n}{m}$
53. $\frac{g}{h}, -\frac{h}{g}$
54. $2 - 5i, 2 + 5i$
55. $4 + 3i, 4 - 3i$

B

Mathematical Reasoning Find the value of k for

a. two real-number solutions **b.** one real-number solution

c. two complex-conjugate solutions.

56. $x^2 + 3x + k = 0$ **57.** $x^2 + x + k = 0$ **58.** $kx^2 - 4x + 1 = 0$

59. $x^2 - x + 3x + k = 0$ **60.** $x^2 + x = 1 - k$ **61.** $3x^2 + 4x = k - 5$

For each equation, one solution is given. Find the other solution, and then find the value of k.

62. $kx^2 - 17x + 33 = 0; 3$ **63.** $kx^2 - 2x + k = 0; -3$

64. $x^2 - kx - 25 = 0; -5$

65. Find k if $kx^2 - 4x + (2k - 1) = 0$ and the product of the solution is 3.

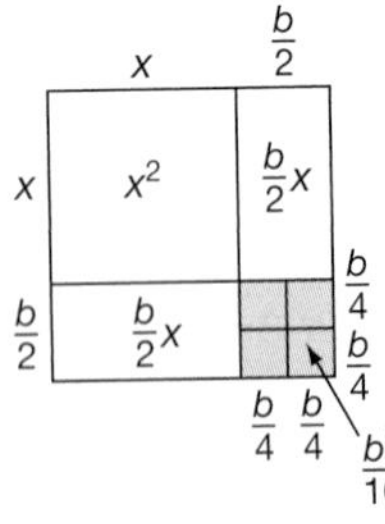

66. ***Critical Thinking*** Al-Khowarizmi, the Arabic mathematician (c. 825), used a "completing the square" method to solve quadratics of the form $x^2 + bx = c$. The unshaded portion represents $x^2 + bx$. To "complete the square" he added the area of the four small shaded squares, each with area $\frac{b^2}{16}$. This gives an area for the large square of $x^2 + bx + \frac{b^2}{4}$. Thus, $x^2 + bx + \frac{b^2}{4} = c + \frac{b^2}{4}$. Solve this equation for x. Then evaluate Al-Khowarizmi's solution.

Challenge

Suppose in a quadratic equation $ax^2 + bx + c = 0$, and a, b, and c are integers.

67. Prove that the quadratic equation has two rational-number solutions if the discriminant is positive and a perfect square.

68. Use the result of Exercise 67 to determine whether each equation has rational solutions.

a. $6x^2 + 5x + 1 = 0$ **b.** $x^2 + 4x - 2 = 0$

69. Prove that the solutions of $ax^2 + bx + c = 0$ and $ax^2 - bx + c = 0$ are additive inverses of each other.

70. Prove Theorem 8-3. (Hint: Use the quadratic formula.)

71. Find h and k if $3x^2 - hx + 4k = 0$, the sum of the solutions is -12, and the product of the solutions is 20.

72. Prove that if the coefficients of $ax^2 + bx + c = 0$ are real, and if a and c have opposite signs, then the solutions are real and unequal.

Self-Test On the Web

Check your progress. Look for a self-test at the Prentice Hall Web site. www.phschool.com

Mixed Review

Factor. **73.** $15x^2 + 11x + 2$ **74.** $2y^2 + y - 3$ **75.** $a^3 - a$ 5-4

Solve. **76.** $4y^2 - 1 = 7$ **77.** $9c^2 - 18c = 0$ **78.** $\frac{1}{2}x^3 - \frac{1}{18}x = 0$

79. $(a - 8)(a - 2) = -8$ **80.** $m(m - 5) = 2(m - 6)$ **81.** $3x^2 = 75$ 6-6

Equations Reducible to Quadratic Form

PART 1 Using Substitution for a Quadratic Form

Objective: Solve equations that are reducible to quadratic form.

What You'll Learn

1. To solve equations that are reducible to quadratic form

. . . And Why

To solve real-world problems using algebraic reasoning skills

This problem was found in the writings of the Hindu mathematician Mahavira (c. 850).

> One-fourth of a herd of camels was seen in the forest, twice the square root of the number of camels in the herd had gone to the mountain slope, and three times five camels were found to remain on the bank of a river. What is the numerical measure of that herd of camels?

The equation $\frac{1}{4}x + 2\sqrt{x} + 15 = x$, which models Mahavira's situation, is not quadratic. However, after a substitution for x, we get a quadratic equation. Such equations are said to be reducible to **quadratic form.** To solve such equations, we first make a substitution and solve for the new variable. Then we substitute back the original variable and solve again.

For centuries, camels carried traders and their goods from the shores of the Mediterranean Sea to central China. On page 361, you are asked to solve Mahavira's problem.

EXAMPLE 1 Solve $x^4 - 9x^2 + 8 = 0$.

Let $u = x^2$. Then we solve the equation found by substituting u for x^2.

$$u^2 - 9u + 8 = (u - 8)(u - 1) = 0$$
$$u - 8 = 0 \text{ or } u - 1 = 0$$
$$u = 8 \text{ or } u = 1$$

Now we substitute x^2 for u and solve these equations.

$$x^2 = 8 \text{ or } x^2 = 1$$
$$x = \pm\sqrt{8} \text{ or } x = \pm 1$$
$$x = \pm 2\sqrt{2} \text{ or } x = \pm 1$$

These four numbers check. The solutions are 1, −1, $2\sqrt{2}$, and $-2\sqrt{2}$.

EXAMPLE 2 Solve $x - 3\sqrt{x} - 4 = 0$.

Let $u = \sqrt{x}$. Then we solve the equation found by substituting u for $\sqrt{x}$.

$$u^2 - 3u - 4 = (u - 4)(u + 1) = 0$$
$$u = 4 \text{ or } u = -1$$
$$\sqrt{x} = 4 \text{ or } \sqrt{x} = -1 \quad \text{Substituting } \sqrt{x} \text{ for } u$$

Squaring the first equation we get $x = 16$. The second equation has no solution since principle square roots are never negative. The number 16 checks and is the only solution.

Try This Solve.

a. $x^4 - 10x^2 + 9 = 0$ **b.** $x^4 - 4 = 0$ **c.** $x + 3\sqrt{x} - 10 = 0$

EXAMPLE 3 Solve $(x^2 - 1)^2 - (x^2 - 1) - 2 = 0$.

Let $u = x^2 - 1$.

$$u^2 - u - 2 = 0 \qquad \text{Substituting } u \text{ for } x^2 - 1$$
$$(u - 2)(u + 1) = 0 \qquad \text{Factoring}$$
$$u = 2 \text{ or } u = -1 \qquad \text{Using the principle of zero products}$$

Now we substitute $x^2 - 1$ for u and solve these equations.

$$x^2 - 1 = 2 \text{ or } x^2 - 1 = -1$$
$$x^2 = 3 \text{ or } x^2 = 0$$
$$x = \pm\sqrt{3} \text{ or } x = 0$$

The numbers $\sqrt{3}$, $-\sqrt{3}$, and 0 check. They are the solutions.

Try This Solve.

d. $(x^2 - x)^2 - 14(x^2 - x) + 24 = 0$

EXAMPLE 4 Solve $t^{\frac{2}{5}} - t^{\frac{1}{5}} - 2 = 0$.

Let $u = t^{\frac{1}{5}}$. Then solve the equation found by substituting u for $t^{\frac{1}{5}}$.

$$u^2 - u - 2 = 0$$
$$(u - 2)(u + 1) = 0 \qquad \text{Factoring}$$
$$u = 2 \text{ or } u = -1$$

Now we substitute $t^{\frac{1}{5}}$ for u and solve these equations.

$$t^{\frac{1}{5}} = 2 \text{ or } t^{\frac{1}{5}} = -1$$
$$t = 32 \text{ or } t = -1 \qquad \text{Principle of powers; raising to the 5th power}$$

Check:

$t^{\frac{2}{5}} - t^{\frac{1}{5}} - 2$	$= 0$
$32^{\frac{2}{5}} - 32^{\frac{1}{5}} - 2$	0
$4 - 2 - 2$	0
0	0 ✓

$t^{\frac{2}{5}} - t^{\frac{1}{5}} - 2$	$= 0$
$(-1)^{\frac{2}{5}} - (-1)^{\frac{1}{5}} - 2$	0
$1 - (-1) - 2$	0
0	0 ✓

The numbers 32 and -1 check and are the solutions.

Try This Solve.

e. $t^{\frac{2}{3}} - 3t^{\frac{1}{3}} - 10 = 0$ **f.** $\sqrt[7]{y^2} + 4\sqrt[7]{y} + 4 = 0$

8-5 Exercises

Look for worked-out examples at the Prentice Hall Web site.
www.phschool.com

A

Solve.

1. $x - 10\sqrt{x} + 9 = 0$ **2.** $2x - 9\sqrt{x} + 4 = 0$

3. $x^4 - 10x^2 + 25 = 0$ **4.** $x^4 - 3x^2 + 2 = 0$

5. $(x^2 - 6x)^2 - 2(x^2 - 6x) - 35 = 0$ **6.** $(1 + \sqrt{x})^2 + (1 + \sqrt{x}) - 6 = 0$

7. $x^{-2} - x^{-1} - 6 = 0$ **8.** $4x^{-2} - x^{-1} - 5 = 0$

9. $t^{\frac{2}{3}} + t^{\frac{1}{3}} - 6 = 0$ **10.** $z^{\frac{1}{2}} - z^{\frac{1}{4}} - 2 = 0$

11. $\sqrt{x^2} + 5\sqrt{x} - 36 = 0$ **12.** $\sqrt[5]{t^2} + 5\sqrt[5]{t} + 6 = 0$

B

Solve.

13. $\left(\frac{x^2 - 1}{x}\right)^2 - \left(\frac{x^2 - 1}{x}\right) - 2 = 0$ **14.** $\left(\frac{x^2 - 2}{x}\right)^2 - 7\left(\frac{x^2 - 2}{x}\right) - 18 = 0$

15. $\left(\frac{x^2 + 1}{x}\right)^2 - 8\left(\frac{x^2 + 1}{x}\right) + 15 = 0$ **16.** $\frac{x}{x - 1} - 6\sqrt{\frac{x}{x - 1}} - 40 = 0$

17. $\left(\frac{x + 1}{x - 1}\right)^2 + \left(\frac{x + 1}{x - 1}\right) - 2 = 0$ **18.** $5\left(\frac{x + 2}{x - 2}\right)^2 - 3\left(\frac{x + 2}{x - 2}\right) - 2 = 0$

19. ***Critical Thinking*** Solve Mahavira's problem from the introduction, page 359. (How many camels were in the herd?)

Challenge

Solve.

20. $9x^{\frac{3}{2}} - 8 = x^3$ **21.** $\sqrt[3]{2x + 3} = \sqrt[6]{2x + 3}$ **22.** $\sqrt{x - 3} - \sqrt[4]{x - 3} = 2$

23. $a^3 - 26a^{\frac{3}{2}} - 27 = 0$ **24.** $x^8 - 20x^4 + 64 = 0$ **25.** $x^8 + 20x^4 + 64 = 0$

26. **TEST PREP** Solve $(x + 2)^2 + 2x + 4 = 1$ for x by completing the square. (Hint: Let $u = x + 2$.) Select the correct solution pair.

A. $x = -3 \pm \sqrt{2}$ **B.** $x = -2, -4$

C. $x = -3 \pm i\sqrt{7}$ **D.** $x = -3 \pm i\sqrt{2}$

Mixed Review

Rationalize the denominator. **27.** $\sqrt{\frac{15}{7}}$ **28.** $\frac{1}{\sqrt{ab}}$ **29.** $\frac{2\sqrt{5} - 3\sqrt{2}}{3\sqrt{2} - 2\sqrt{5}}$ *7-4*

Find an equation having the specified numbers as solutions.

30. $4i, -4i$ **31.** $7i, -7i$ **32.** $2 - 5i, 2 + 5i$ *7-10*

Solve. **33.** $x^2 - 5x - 6 = 0$ **34.** $2y^2 - y - 15 = 0$

35. $(a - 1)(a - 3) = 15$ **36.** $c(c - 2) = 3(c + 8)$ **37.** $4m^2 = 9$ *5-7*

8-6 Formulas and Problem Solving

What You'll Learn

1. To solve second-degree formulas for a given letter
2. To solve problems using quadratic equations

... And Why

To solve real-world problems using algebraic reasoning skills

The height of an object that has been fired upward with initial velocity v_0 at any given time t is given by the formula $h = v_0t - 16t^2$, where h is in feet, t is in seconds, and v_0 is in ft/s.

How long has an object been in the air, given it is at height h and was fired with initial velocity v_0? In other words, can we determine t if we know h and v_0?

PART 1 Solving Formulas

Objective: Solve second-degree formulas for a given letter.

EXAMPLE 1 Solve $h = v_0t - 16t^2$ for t, the time an object is in the air, given h, the height of the object, and v_0, the initial velocity.

$$16t^2 - v_0t + h = 0$$ Finding standard form

$$a = 16, b = -v_0, c = h$$

$$t = \frac{-b \pm \sqrt{b^2 - 4ac}}{2a}$$

$$t = \frac{v_0 \pm \sqrt{(-v_0)^2 - 4 \cdot 16 \cdot h}}{2 \cdot 16}$$ Substituting into the quadratic formula

$$t = \frac{v_0 \pm \sqrt{v_0^2 - 64h}}{32}$$

$$t = \frac{v_0 + \sqrt{x_0^2 - 64h}}{32} \text{ or } t = \frac{v_0 - \sqrt{v_0^2 - 64h}}{32}$$

Since h is nonnegative, both of these give nonnegative values for t.

Try This Solve for the indicated letter.

a. $V = \pi r^2h; r$

b. $2\pi r^2 + 2\pi rh = 1; r$

c. $S = 4\pi r^2; r$

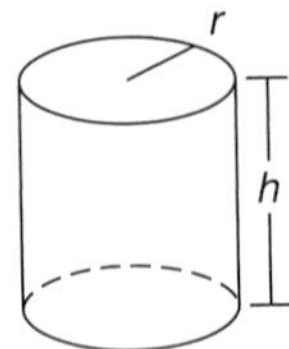

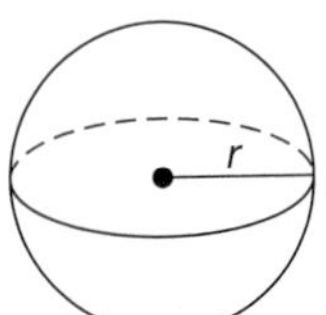

PART 2 Problem Solving: Quadratic Equations

Objective: Solve problems using quadratic equations.

When an object is dropped or thrown downward, the distance in meters that it falls in t seconds is given by $s = 4.9t^2 + v_0t$. In this formula v_0 is the initial velocity.

EXAMPLE 2

(a) An object is dropped from the top of the Gateway Arch in St. Louis, which is 195 meters high. How long does it take to reach the ground?
Since the object was dropped, its initial velocity was 0. Thus, we substitute 0 for v_0 and 195 for s, and then solve for t.

$$195 = 4.9t^2 + 0 \cdot t$$
$$195 = 4.9t^2$$
$$t^2 \approx 39.8$$
$$t \approx \sqrt{39.8}$$
$$t \approx 6.31$$

Finding the positive square root because t cannot be negative

Therefore, it takes about 6.31 seconds to reach the ground.

(b) An object is thrown downward from the top of the arch at an initial velocity of 16 meters per second (m/s). How long does it take to reach the ground?
We substitute 195 for s and 16 for v_0 and solve for t.

$$195 = 4.9t^2 + 16t$$
$$0 = 4.9t^2 + 16t - 195$$

By the quadratic formula we obtain $t \approx -8.15$ or $t \approx 4.88$. The negative answer is meaningless in this problem, so the answer is 4.88 seconds.

(c) How far will an object fall in 3 seconds if it is thrown downward from the top of the arch at an initial velocity of 16 m/s?

We substitute 16 for v_0 and 3 for t and solve for s.

$$s = 4.9t^2 + v_0t$$
$$= 4.9(3)^2 + 16 \cdot 3 = 92.1$$

Thus, the object falls 92.1 meters in 3 seconds.

Try This

d. An object is dropped from the top of a cliff, which is 92 meters high.
(1) How long does it take to reach the ground?
(2) An object is thrown downward from the top of the cliff at an initial velocity of 40 m/s. How long does it take to reach the ground?
(3) How far will an object fall in 1 second, thrown downward from the top of the cliff at an initial velocity of 40 m/s?

Extra Help On the Web

Look for worked-out examples at the Prentice Hall Web site.
www.phschool.com

8-6 Exercises

A

Solve for the indicated letter.

1. $P = 4s^2; s$

2. $A = \pi r^2; r$

3. $F = \frac{Gm_1m_2}{r^2}; r$

4. $K = \frac{Qab}{t^2}; t$

5. $x^2 + y^2 = r^2; r$

6. $a^2 + b^2 = h^2; h$

7. $h = v_0t - 4.9t^2; t$

8. $A = \pi rs + \pi r^2; r$

9. $S = \frac{1}{2}gt^2; t$

10. $h = \frac{V^2}{2g}; V$

11. $A = \pi r^2 + 2\pi rh; r$

12. $h = 2v_0 + 10t^2; t$

13. $t^2\sqrt{2} + 3k = \pi t; t$

14. $t^2\sqrt{3} - 4\pi = 0.2t; t$

Solve. Use the formula $s = 4.9t^2 + v_0t$.

15. An object is dropped from a balloon from a height of 75 m.

a. How long does it take to reach the ground?

b. If the object has an initial velocity of 30 m/s, how long does it take to reach the ground? How far will it fall in 2 seconds?

16. An object is dropped from a balloon from a height of 500 m.

a. How long does it take to reach the ground?

b. If the object has an initial velocity of 12 m/s, how long does it take to reach the ground? How far will it fall in 5 seconds?

17. An amount of money P is invested at interest rate r. In t years it will grow to the amount A given by $A = P(1 + r)^t$, where interest is compounded annually. For the following situations, find the interest rate if interest is compounded annually.

a. \$2560 grows to \$3610 in 2 years.

b. \$1000 grows to \$1210 in 2 years.

c. \$8000 grows to \$9856.80 in 2 years. (Use a calculator.)

d. \$1000 grows to \$1271.26 in 2 years. (Use a calculator.)

18. A ladder 10 ft long leans against a wall. The bottom of the ladder is 6 ft from the wall. How much would the lower end of the ladder have to be pulled away so that the top end would be pulled down by 3 ft?

19. A ladder 13 ft long leans against a wall. The bottom of the ladder is 5 ft from the wall. How much would the lower end of the ladder have to be pulled away so that the top end would be pulled down by 2 ft?

20. Trains A and B leave the same city at the same time, headed east and north respectively. Train B travels 5 mi/h faster than train A. After 2 hours they are 50 miles apart. Find the speed of each train.

21. Trains A and B leave the same city at the same time, headed west and south respectively. Train A travels 14 km/h faster than train B. After 5 hours they are 130 km apart. Find the speed of each train.

B

22. The diagonal of a square is 1.341 cm longer than a side. Use a calculator to find the length of the side.

23. The hypotenuse of a right triangle is 8.312 cm long. The sum of the lengths of the legs is 10.23 cm. Use a calculator to find the lengths of the legs.

Solve for the indicated letter.

24. $m = \dfrac{m_0}{\sqrt{1 - \frac{v^2}{c^2}}}$; v

25. $T = \sqrt{\dfrac{a^2 + b^2}{a^2}}$; a

For Exercises 26 and 27 use the formula $T = cN$, where T is the total cost, c is the cost per item or cost per person, and N is the number of items or number of persons.

26. A group of students shares equally in the $140 cost of a boat. At the last minute 3 students drop out, and this raises the share of each remaining student $15. How many students were in the group at the outset?

27. An investor had purchased a group of lots for $8400. All but 4 of them were later sold, also for a total of $8400. The selling price for each lot was $350 greater than the cost. How many lots were originally purchased?

28. *Critical Thinking* Solve the formula for a falling object, $s = 4.9t^2 + v_0t$, for time. Explain why there is only one solution.

Challenge

29. A rectangle of 12-cm² area is inscribed in the right triangle ABC as shown in the drawing. What are its dimensions?

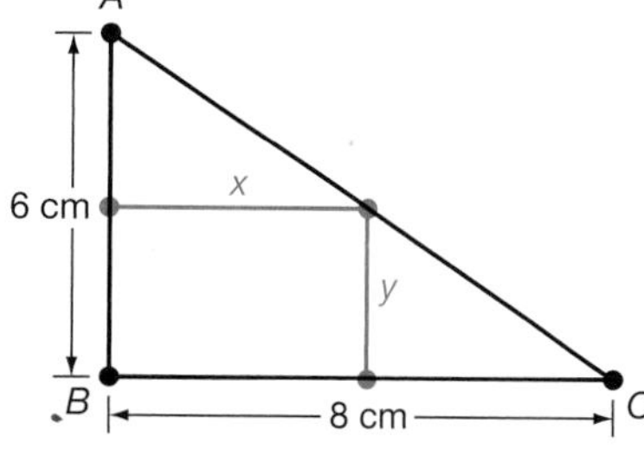

30. The world record for free fall to Earth without a parachute by a woman is 175 ft and is held by Kitty O'Neill. Approximately how long did the fall take?

Journal

Use a reference book to find a science formula that is quadratic. Write a description of the formula telling what each letter represents.

Mixed Review

Simplify. **31.** i^3 **32.** $(5i)^2$ **33.** $(-6i)^2$ **34.** $(1 + i)^2$ **35.** $(1 + i)^3$ *7-7*

Solve.

36. $8x^2 - 6x + 1 = 0$ **37.** $y(y - 7) = 12(y - 5)$ **38.** $5m^2 = 0$

39. $3a^2 + 12a = 0$ **40.** $2c^2 = 4$ **41.** $6x^2 = 25$

42. $x^2 - 4x + 7 = 0$ **43.** $y^2 + 4y + 8 = 0$ **44.** $6a^2 - a - 15 = 0$ *8-1*

Graph.

45. $y = |x - 1|$ **46.** $x - y = 3$ *3-9, 3-2*

8-7 Quadratic Variation and Applications

What You'll Learn

1. To find an equation of direct quadratic variation
2. To find equations of inverse and joint quadratic variation
3. To solve problems involving quadratic variation and proportion

... And Why

To solve real-world problems involving quadratic variation

The relationship between the usable height and girth of a tree and the volume of wood it produces can be modeled using a **quadratic variation** function.

Quantities of timber are bought and sold by the board foot. One board foot is a unit of measurement equal to one square foot by one inch thick. How many cubic feet are in 270 board feet?

PART 1 Direct Variation

Objective: Find an equation of direct quadratic variation.

Definition

Direct Quadratic Variation

y varies directly as the square of x if there is some nonzero number k such that $y = kx^2$.

Consider the equation for the area of a circle, $a = \pi r^2$. It shows that the area varies directly as the square of the radius and π is the constant of variation.

EXAMPLE 1 Find an equation of variation where y varies directly as the square of x, and $y = 12$ when $x = 2$.

We write an equation of variation and find k.

$$y = kx^2$$

$$12 = k \cdot 2^2 \quad \text{Substituting}$$

$$3 = k \quad \text{Solving for } k$$

Now we write an equation.

$$y = 3x^2 \quad \text{Substituting for } k \text{ in the original equation}$$

Try This

a. Find an equation of variation where y varies directly as the square of x, and $y = 175$ when $x = 5$.

PART 2 Inverse and Joint Variation

Objective: Find equations of inverse and joint quadratic variation.

Definition

Inverse Quadratic Variation

y varies inversely as the square of x if there is some nonzero number k such that $y = \frac{k}{x^2}$.

The law of gravity states that the weight (W) of an object varies inversely as the square of the distance (d) from the center of the Earth.

$$W = \frac{k}{d^2}$$

EXAMPLE 2 Find an equation of variation where W varies inversely as the square of d, and $W = 3$ when $d = 5$.

$W = \frac{k}{d^2}$ Definition of inverse quadratic variation

$3 = \frac{k}{5^2}$ Solving for k

$75 = k$

$W = \frac{75}{d^2}$ Substituting for k in the original equation

Try This

b. Find an equation of variation where y varies inversely as the square of x, and $y = \frac{1}{4}$ when $x = 6$.

Consider the equation for the area A of a triangle with height h and base b.

$$A = \frac{1}{2}bh$$

We say that the area varies jointly as the height and the base.

Definition

Joint Variation

y varies jointly as x and z if there is some nonzero number k such that $y = kxz$.

EXAMPLE 3 Find an equation of variation where y varies jointly as x and z, and $y = 42$ when $x = 2$ and $z = 3$.

$$y = kxz$$
$$42 = k \cdot 2 \cdot 3$$
$$7 = k \qquad \text{Solving for } k$$

Substituting for k in the original equation we have $y = 7xz$.

Try This

c. Find an equation of variation where y varies jointly as x and z, and $y = 65$ when $x = 10$ and $z = 13$.

The following equation asserts that y varies jointly as x and the cube of z, and inversely as w. Note that all these values are factors. There is no addition in the equation.

$$y = k \cdot \frac{xz^3}{w}$$

EXAMPLE 4 Find an equation of variation where y varies jointly as x and z and inversely as the square of w, and $y = 105$ when $x = 3$, $z = 20$, and $w = 2$.

$$y = k \cdot \frac{xz}{w^2}$$
$$105 = k \cdot \frac{3 \cdot 20}{2^2}$$
$$7 = k$$

Thus, $y = 7 \cdot \frac{xz}{w^2}$.

Try This

d. Find an equation of variation where y varies jointly as x and the square of z and inversely as w, and $y = 80$ when $x = 4$, $z = 10$, and $w = 25$.

Problem Solving: Variation and Proportion

Objective: Solve problems involving quadratic variation and proportion.

Many problem situations can be described with equations of variation.

EXAMPLE 5

Foresters measure the *girth*, or circumference, at $4\frac{1}{2}$ feet above the ground on the uphill side of a tree. The *usable height* of a tree extends from the girth to the point where the trunk narrows to 8 inches in diameter. The volume (V) of wood in a tree varies jointly as the usable height (h) and the square of the girth (g). The volume of a tree is 18.8 ft^3 for a usable height of 32 ft and a girth of 5 ft. What is the usable height of a tree whose volume is 46.06 ft^3 and girth is 7 ft?

First find k using the first set of data. Then solve for h using the second set of data.

$$V = khg^2$$
$$18.8 = k \cdot 32 \cdot 5^2$$
$$0.0235 = k \qquad \text{Solving for } k$$

Then

$$46.06 = 0.0235 \cdot h \cdot 7^2 \qquad \text{Using } k = 0.0235 \text{ to solve for } h$$
$$40 = h$$

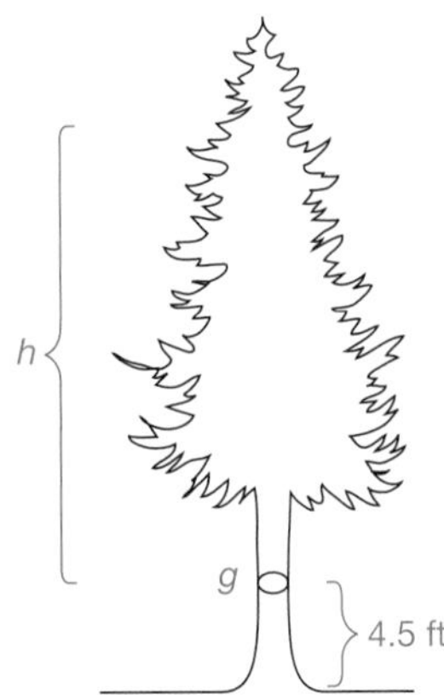

The usable height of the tree is 40 ft.

Proportions can be used to solve variation problems. In Example 5, the volumes of the two trees are proportional.

EXAMPLE 6 Use a proportion to solve the problem in Example 5.

Let h_1 represent the usable height of the first tree and h_2 the usable height of the second tree.

$$\frac{V_1}{V_2} = \frac{k \cdot h_1 \cdot g_1^2}{k \cdot h_2 \cdot g_2^2}$$

$$= \frac{h_1 g_1^2}{h_2 g_2^2} \qquad \frac{k}{k} = 1$$

Now we can solve directly for the unknown usable height (h_2) without first finding the constant of variation.

$$\frac{18.8}{46.06} = \frac{32 \cdot 5^2}{h_2 \cdot 7^2}$$

$$h_2 = \frac{46.06 \cdot 800}{18.8 \cdot 49}$$

$$h_2 = 40 \text{ ft}$$

EXAMPLE 7

The intensity (I) of a TV signal varies inversely as the square of the distance (d) from the transmitter. The intensity is 23 watts per square meter (W/m^2) at a distance of 2 km. What is the intensity at a distance of 6 km?

We use the proportion.

$$\frac{I_1}{I_2} = \frac{d_2^2}{d_1^2} \qquad I_1 = \frac{k}{d_1^2}, I_2 = \frac{k}{d_2^2}$$

$$\frac{I^2}{23} = \frac{2^2}{6^2}$$

$$I_2 = \frac{4 \cdot 23}{36}$$

$$I_2 = 2.56 \text{ W/m}^2 \qquad \text{Rounding to the nearest hundredth}$$

Try This

e. The distance (s) that an object falls when dropped from some point above the ground varies directly as the square of the time (t) it falls. If the object falls 19.6 m in 2 seconds, how far will the object fall in 10 seconds?

Extra Help On the Web

Look for worked-out examples at the Prentice Hall Web site.
www.phschool.com

8-7 Exercises

A

Find an equation of variation where

1. y varies inversely as the square of x, and $y = 6$ when $x = 3$.
2. y varies directly as the square of x, and $y = 0.6$ when $x = 0.4$.
3. y varies inversely as the square of x, and $y = 0.4$ when $x = 0.8$.
4. y varies directly as the square of x, and $y = 0.15$ when $x = 0.1$.
5. y varies directly as the square of x, and $y = 6$ when $x = 3$.
6. y varies inversely as the square of x, and $y = 0.15$ when $x = 0.1$.
7. y varies jointly as x and z, and $y = 56$ when $x = 7$ and $z = 8$.
8. y varies directly as x and inversely as z, and $y = 4$ when $x = 12$ and $z = 15$.
9. y varies directly as x and inversely as the square of z, and $y = 105$ when $x = 14$ and $z = 5$.
10. y varies jointly as x and z and inversely as w, and $y = \frac{3}{2}$ when $x = 2$, $z = 3$, and $w = 4$.
11. y varies jointly as x and z and inversely as the product of w and p, and $y = \frac{3}{28}$ when $x = 3$, $z = 10$, $w = 7$, and $p = 8$.
12. y varies jointly as x and z and inversely as the square of w, and $y = \frac{12}{5}$ when $x = 16$, $z = 3$, and $w = 5$.
13. The stopping distance (d) of a car after the brakes are applied varies directly as the square of the speed (r). A car traveling 60 km/h can stop in 80 m. How many meters will it take the same car to stop when it is traveling 90 km/h?
14. The area of a cube varies directly as the square of the length of a side. A cube has an area of 168.54 m^2 when the length of a side is 5.3 m. What will the area be when the length of a side is 10.2 m?
15. The weight (W) of an object varies inversely as the square of the distance (d) from the center of the Earth. At sea level (6400 km from the center of the Earth) an astronaut weighs 100 kg. Find the astronaut's weight in a spacecraft 200 km above the surface of the Earth. (Assume the spacecraft is not in motion.)
16. The intensity of light (I) from a light bulb varies inversely as the square of the distance (d) from the bulb. Suppose I is 90 W/m^2 when the distance is 5 m. Find the intensity at a distance of 10 m.

Obeying speed limits and maintaining an appropriate distance from the car ahead are critical to safety, especially while driving at high speeds. How many times more braking distance is required for a car speeding at 70 mi/h than for a car observing the 55-mi/h speed limit?

B

17. Show that if p varies directly as q, then q varies directly as p.

18. Show that if u varies inversely as v, then v varies inversely as u, and $\frac{1}{u}$ varies directly as v.

19. The area of a circle varies directly as the square of the length of its diameter. What is the variation constant?

20. *Mathematical Reasoning* P varies directly as the square of t. How does t vary in relationship to P?

21. *Write a Convincing Argument* In Example 7, explain why the equation is not appropriate when the distance is 0 km from a transmitter whose initial signal is 316,000 W/m^2.

22. *Critical Thinking*

a. Suppose y varies directly as the square of x. Predict what happens to y when x is doubled; when x is multiplied by n.

b. Suppose y varies inversely as the square of x. Predict what happens to y when x is tripled; when x is multiplied by n.

Challenge

23. It has been determined that the average number of daily phone calls (N) between two cities is directly proportional to the populations (P_1 and P_2) of the cities, and inversely proportional to the square of the distance (d) between the cities. That is, $N = \frac{kP_1P_2}{d^2}$. Use a calculator to find solutions to these problems.

a. The population of Indianapolis is about 740,000, and the population of Cincinnati is about 340,000. The distance between the cities is 174 km. The average number of daily phone calls between the two cities is 8205. Find the value (k) and write the equation of variation.

b. The population of Detroit is about 970,000, and it is 446 km from Indianapolis. Find the average number of daily phone calls between them.

c. The average number of daily phone calls between Indianapolis and New York City is 5034, and the population of New York City is about 7,400,000. Find the distance between Indianapolis and New York City.

d. Why is this model not appropriate for adjoining cities?

Mixed Review

Determine the nature of the solution of each equation.

24. $x^2 - 10x + 25 = 0$ **25.** $y^2 + y + 1 = 0$ **26.** $a^2 - 121 = 0$ *8-4*

Without solving, find the sum and product of the solutions.

27. $m^2 + 5m - 2 = 0$ **28.** $2x^2 + 6x = 0$ **29.** $2y^2 + 8y - 3 = 0$ *8-4*

Solve. **30.** $c^2 + 6c - 5 = 0$ **31.** $3m^2 - 10m + 3 = 0$ *8-1*

Find the conjugate of each number. **32.** $a - bi$ **33.** $-x + yi$ *7-9*

8-8 Reasoning Strategies

What You'll Learn

1 To solve problems using logical reasoning

. . . And Why

To draw conclusions and solve real-world problems by using the relationships among facts

PART 1 Use Logical Reasoning

Objective: Solve problems using *Logical Reasoning*.

Some problems must be solved by understanding the given relationships among the facts and using known facts and relationships to make conclusions.

PROBLEM-SOLVING GUIDELINES
■ UNDERSTAND the problem
■ Develop and carry out a PLAN
■ Find the ANSWER and CHECK

We can use a strategy called *Use Logical Reasoning* and the Problem-Solving Guidelines at left to help us solve problems.

EXAMPLE

A news service released facts about four officials in an election (president, vice-president, secretary-general, and chief of staff). The last names of those elected, not necessarily in order, are Ong, Vasquez, Martin, and Gray. Which person was elected to which office?

(a) Ong and the vice-president once shared the same office and were best friends.
(b) Gray and the chief of staff will continue to vacation together each year.
(c) Vasquez is the president's best source of information; the president does not consult with Gray, however.
(d) Martin will run for president for the first time in the next election.
(e) Ong and Gray have never been friends and never shared an office.
(f) Vasquez has always had an office of his own.

You can solve this problem by recording the given information in a *chart* and making conclusions based on it. The charts below show the reasoning you might go through.

	P	VP	S	C
O		n		
V	n			
M				
G	n			n

The first three statements allow us to write NO (n) in these cells.

	P	VP	S	C
O	(y)	n	n	n
V	n			
M	n			
G	n			n

(d) Martin is not president, so Ong must be. Ong can hold no other office.

	P	VP	S	C
O	(y)	n	n	n
V	n		n	
M	n		n	
G	n	n	(y)	n

(a) and (e) show that Gray is not vice-president. Gray must be secretary-general, since no one else can.

	P	VP	S	C
O	(y)	n	n	n
V	n	n	n	(y)
M	n	(y)	n	n
G	n	n	(y)	n

(a) and (f) show that Vasquez is not vice-president. Vasquez must be chief of staff. Martin must be vice-president.

The offices and those elected are president, Ong; vice-president, Martin; secretary-general, Gray; chief of staff, Vasquez.

Reasoning Strategies

Write an Equation	Draw a Diagram	Try, Test, Revise
Make an Organized List	Make a Table	Look for a Pattern
Use Logical Reasoning	Simplify the Problem	Work Backward

8-8 Problems

Extra Help On the Web

Look for worked-out examples at the Prentice Hall Web site.
www.phschool.com

Solve using one or more of the strategies.

1. An automobile factory needs to select other companies as suppliers for 3 different parts. The factory contacted a number of companies and found that some companies produce 1 needed item, others produce 2 needed items, and others produce 3 needed items. Thirty-five companies produce part A, 24 produce part B, and 27 produce part C. Of these companies, 12 produce both parts A and B, 19 produce parts B and C, and 13 produce parts A and C. Nine produce all 3 parts. What was the total number of companies contacted?
2. Adele accidentally hit the button on her clock radio that makes it go on and off repeatedly. The buzzer came on at exactly 7:00 A.M. Then it went on and off at regular intervals. At 7:09 A.M. the buzzer was off, at 7:17 A.M. it was on, and at 7:58 A.M. it was on. Was the buzzer on or off at 9:00 A.M.?
3. Six friends graduated from the same college with teaching degrees in mathematics. They all took jobs teaching in different states. The states were Indiana, Illinois, Florida, Hawaii, California, and New York. The friends' names, in no particular order, were Tracy, Sally, Juan, Herb, Rick, and Terry. Sally didn't get a job in Illinois, and Tracy didn't move to California. Herb got the job he wanted in New York, and Terry got the job she wanted in Florida. Juan hoped to get a job in Hawaii but did not. Sally turned down a job in Indiana just after Juan took a job in California, and Rick took a job in Indiana. In which state did each person get a job?
4. A rapidly expanding factory had to hire a large number of employees during the year. There were 220 employees at the beginning of the year. The plan was to hire 1 employee at the beginning of the first month. Then, at the beginning of each following month, 4 more employees would be hired than had been hired in the previous month, until the company expanded to 340 employees. Under this plan, how many months did it take to hire the needed number of employees?
5. It takes four regular triangles with sides of length 1, to make a regular triangle with sides of length 2. How many regular triangles with sides of length 1 does it take to make a regular triangle with sides of length 10?

8 Chapter Wrap Up

Key Terms

completing the square (p. 343)
direct quadratic variation (p. 366)
discriminant (p. 354)
inverse quadratic variation (p. 367)
joint variation (p. 367)
proportions (p. 369)
Pythagorean Theorem (p. 348)
quadratic equation (p. 342)
quadratic form (p. 359)
quadratic formula (p. 350)
quadratic variation (p. 366)
standard form (p. 342)

8-1

Some **quadratic equations** of the type $ax^2 + bx + c = 0$ can be solved easily by factoring.

Solve.

1. $7x^2 + 6x = 0$

2. $7x^2 - 21x = 0$

3. $3x^2 + 10x - 8 = 0$

4. $4x^2 - 27x + 18 = 0$

Equations of the type $ax^2 + c = 0$ can be changed to the form $x^2 = k$, where $x = \pm\sqrt{k}$.

Solve.

5. $4x^2 + 2 = 0$

6. $9x^2 - 4 = 0$

To **complete the square,** take half the coefficient of the x-term and square it.

Complete the square.

7. $x^2 + 16x$

8. $x^2 - 9x$

Solve by completing the square.

9. $x^2 + 4x - 6 = 0$

When the leading coefficient is not 1, we can use the multiplication property to make it 1.

Solve by completing the square.

10. $4x^2 - 4x - 15 = 0$

8-2

The Problem-Solving Guidelines and the methods of solving quadratic equations can be used to solve some problems.

11. One leg of a right triangle is 10 m less than the hypotenuse, and the other leg is 5 m less than the hypotenuse. Find the length of all three sides of the triangle.

8-3

The **quadratic formula** $x = \frac{-b \pm \sqrt{b^2 - 4ac}}{2a}$ can be used to find the solutions of any quadratic equation.

Solve.

12. $x^2 + 4x - 7 = 0$

13. $x^2 + 3x - 5 = 0$

14. $x^2 + 2x + 4 = 0$

15. $x^2 + x + 4 = 0$

A calculator or a square root table can be used to find rational number approximations to the exact solutions given by the formula.

16. Approximate solutions of $x^2 - 8x + 5 = 0$ to the nearest tenth.

8-4

An equation $ax^2 + bx + c = 0$, with $a \neq 0$ and all coefficients real numbers, has exactly one real-number solution if the **discriminant** $b^2 - 4ac = 0$, two real-number solutions if $b^2 - 4ac > 0$, and two complex nonreal solutions that are conjugates if $b^2 - 4ac < 0$.

Internet Activity On the Web

Look for extension problems for this chapter at the Prentice Hall Web site. www.phschool.com

17. Find the discriminant and the nature of the solutions of $4y^2 + 5y + 1 = 0$.

For $ax^2 + bx + c = 0$, the solutions have a sum of $-\frac{b}{a}$ and a product of $\frac{c}{a}$.

18. Find the sum and product of the solutions of $5y^2 - 4y + 2 = 0$.

19. Find a quadratic equation for which the sum of the solutions is $-\frac{1}{2}$ and the product of the solutions is $\frac{3}{5}$.

If the solutions of a quadratic equation are j and k, then $(x - j)(x - k) = 0$.

20. Write a quadratic equation in standard form with solutions -3 and $-\frac{1}{2}$.

8-5

Substitute for the variables to solve an equation that is **quadratic in form.**

21. Solve $y^4 - 2y^2 + 1 = 0$. **22.** Solve $(x^2 + 1)^2 - 15(x^2 + 1) + 50 = 0$.

8-6

A formula containing a second-degree term may require finding the square root of both sides when solving for a specified variable.

23. Solve $A^2 + a^2 = 1$ for A. **24.** Solve $S = at + \frac{1}{2}gt^2$ for t.

25. From a height of 200 m, an object is thrown downward at an initial velocity of 20 m/s. How long does it take to reach the ground? Use $s = 4.9t^2 + v_0t$.

8-7

y* varies directly as the square of *x if there is some positive number k such that $y = kx^2$. Find an equation of variation in which

26. y varies directly as the square of x, and $y = 2$ when $x = 3$.

27. y varies directly as the square of x, and $y = 0.1$ when $x = 0.2$.

y* varies inversely as the square of *x if there is some positive number k such that $y = \frac{k}{x^2}$. Find an equation of variation in which

28. y varies inversely as the square of x, and $y = 0.5$ when $x = 2$.

Many problem situations can be described with **equations of variation,** and can be solved by using **proportions.**

29. The surface area of a sphere varies directly as the square of its radius. If the surface area of a sphere is 1257 m^2 when the radius is 10 m, what is the area when the radius is 3 m?

8 Chapter Assessment

Solve.

1. $3x^2 - 15x = 0$ **2.** $5x^2 - 6x = 0$ **3.** $x^2 - 6x + 5 = 0$

4. $16x^2 - 9 = 0$ **5.** $5x^2 + 13x - 6 = 0$ **6.** $3x^2 + 15 = 0$

Complete the square.

7. $x^2 - \frac{1}{4}x$ **8.** $y^2 + 2.5y$

Solve by completing the square.

9. $x^2 + 4x - 11 = 0$ **10.** $2x^2 + 4x - 11 = 0$

11. Bicyclists Hilary and Eric leave the same point Q at the same time at right angles. Hilary travels four mi/h faster than Eric. After 4 hours they are 80 miles apart. Find the speed of each.

Solve.

12. $4x^2 + 8x + 1 = 0$ **13.** $2x^2 - 3x - 1 = 0$

14. $x^2 + x - 1 = 0$ **15.** $2x^2 + 2x + 9 = 0$

16. Approximate solutions of $2x^2 - 5x + 1 = 0$ to the nearest tenth.

17. Find the discriminant and determine the nature of the solutions of $2x^2 - 5x + 3 = 0$.

18. Without solving, find the sum and product of the solutions of $6y^2 + 8y - 7 = 0$.

19. Find a quadratic equation for which the sum of the solutions is $\frac{2}{3}$ and the product of the solutions is $\frac{5}{6}$.

20. Write an equation in standard form with solutions $3 + \sqrt{2}$ and $3 - \sqrt{2}$.

Solve.

21. $x^4 - 5x^2 + 4 = 0$ **22.** $y^4 - 13y^2 + 36 = 0$

23. $x^2 + x + 6 = 0$ **24.** $x - 2x^{\frac{1}{2}} + 1 = 0$

25. Solve $A^2 + a^2 = 4$, for A.

26. How far will an object fall in 4 seconds, thrown downward with an initial velocity of 20 m/s? Use $s = 4.9t^2 + v_0t$.

Find an equation of variation in which

27. y varies directly as the square of x, and $y = 7$ when $x = 2$.

28. y varies inversely as the square of x, and $y = \frac{1}{3}$ when $x = 3$.

29. y varies jointly as t and r and inversely as the square of w, and $y = 2$ when $t = 4$, $r = 9$, and $w = 6$.

Solve.

30. The distance (s) that an object falls when dropped from a point above the ground varies directly as the square of the time (t) it falls. If the object falls 44.1 m in 3 seconds, how far will it fall in 5 seconds?

1–8 Cumulative Review

1-4 Simplify.

1. $5x - 3 - (2 - 3x)$
2. $-3[y - 3(4y - 2) - (5 - y)]$

1-5 Solve.

3. $5x - 3 = 7 - x$
4. $3y - 20 - y = 6 - 3y - 6$

1-6 Solve.

5. A baby sitter charges $1.75 per hour. She also charges the parents another $1.00 per evening for each child. How much would she charge to baby-sit 4 children for 3 hours?

1-8 Write without negative exponents.

6. 9^{-2}
7. $\frac{-3x^{-2}y^{3}}{z^{-4}}$

1-9 Multiply. Write the answer in scientific notation.

8. $(3.6 \times 10^{5})(2.5 \times 10^{3})$
9. $(7.2 \times 10^{-8})(4.5 \times 10^{5})$

2-2 Solve.

10. The sum of three consecutive odd integers equals 240 more than the third integer. Find all three integers.

2-4 Solve, then graph.

11. $-3x \geq -15$
12. $3y - 9 < 6 + 6y$

2-5 Solve.

13. A car rents for $18.75 per day, plus 25¢ per mile. If you rent the car for one week, what is the greatest number of miles you can drive and still keep the cost of renting the car under $200 for the week?

2-7 Solve and graph.

14. $|x - 3| \leq 6$
15. $|2x - 5| \geq 7$

3-1 List the domain and range for the following relation.

16. $\{(3, 2), (3, -2), (0, 0)\}$

3-3 $g(x) = -2x^2 + 3x + 1$

17. Find $g(0)$.

18. Find $g(-2)$.

3-4 Graph.

19. $x = -2$

20. $3x - 2y = 12$

3-5

21. Find an equation of the line containing $(2, -5)$ and having slope $-\frac{5}{4}$.

3-6

22. Write the equation in slope-intercept form of the line containing $(-4, -5)$ and $(-2, -1)$.

23. Find the slope and y-intercept of $3x - 4y = 12$.

24. Write $y = \frac{2}{3}x + 3$ in standard form.

3-7 Find an equation in slope-intercept form of the line containing $(2, -5)$ and

25. parallel to the line $4x + 5y = 8$.

26. perpendicular to the line $4x + 5y = 8$.

3-8 The cost of a 8-oz can of tomato sauce is 30 cents, and the cost of a 15-oz can is 55 cents.

27. Fit a linear function to the data points.

28. Use the function to determine the cost of a 25-oz can.

3-9 $f(x) = 3x - 2$, $g(x) = 2x^2$, and $h(x) = -2x$.

29. Find $f(g(-3))$.

30. Find $h(f(g(x)))$.

4-2 Solve each system.

31. $-3x + 3y = -18$
$4x - y = 5$

32. $2x - 3y = 8$
$5x + 2y = 1$

4-3

33. The difference between two numbers is 10. When eight times the smaller number is added to 40, the result is ten less than three times the larger number. Find both numbers.

4-4 Solve.

34. $2x + y - z = 5$
$y - 2z = 7$
$2y + 3z = 0$

35. $5x + 3y + 2x = 1$
$2x - y + z = -1$
$-2x + 2y - z = 2$

4-7 Graph this system of inequalities.

36. $y \geq x$
$y > 2x - 1$

5-1 Collect like terms.

37. $3x - 2y - 5y - 3x$

38. $2x^2 - 3x - 4x + 5x^2 + x$

5-2 Add or subtract.

39. $(3x^2 + 5x - 2) + (-3x^2 - x)$

40. $(-2x^2 + x - 3) - (5x^2 - 3x - 3)$

5-3 Multiply.

41. $(x^2 - 3y)^2$

42. $(3x - 2y - 1)(3x + 2y + 1)$

5-4–5-6 Factor.

43. $24x^3 - 84x^2 + 72x$

44. $36y^2 - 100$

45. $x^2 - 2xy + y^2 - 36$

46. $z^3 - 27$

47. $-3y + 12y^3 - 12y^5$

48. $x^2 - 2xy + y^2 - r^2 + 8r - 16$

5-7 Solve.

49. $4x^2 + 11x + 6 = 0$

50. $3x^2 + 36x = 0$

5-8

51. Peter's pool table is 1 ft longer than twice its width. The area of the pool table is 15 ft^2. Find the dimensions of the pool table.

6-1–6-3 Simplify.

52. $\dfrac{3x^2 + xy - 2y^2}{x^2 - y^2}$

53. $\dfrac{8x^3 - 27}{64x^3 + 1} \div \dfrac{4x^2 - 12x + 9}{16x^2 + 8x + 1}$

54. $\dfrac{x - 1}{x - 2} - \dfrac{x + 1}{x + 2} + \dfrac{x - 6}{x^2 - 4}$

55. $\dfrac{\frac{1}{x} + \frac{1}{y}}{\frac{x^2 - y^2}{xy}}$

6-4 Divide.

56. $\dfrac{18xy^2 - 6x^2y + 9x^3y^3}{3x^2y}$

57. $(y^3 - y + 6) \div (y + 2)$

6-5 Use synthetic division to find the quotient and remainder.

58. $(x^3 - 2x^2 - 4x - 6) \div (x - 2)$

59. $(y^4 - 1) \div (y + 1)$

6-6 Solve.

60. $-\frac{1}{3} - \frac{5}{4x} = \frac{3}{4} - \frac{1}{6x}$

61. $\dfrac{x}{2x - 6} - \dfrac{3}{x^2 - 6x + 9} = \dfrac{x - 2}{3x - 9}$

6-7

62. Nigel can paint a room in 8 hours, while Phil can paint the same room in 6 hours. How long would it take them together to paint 4 rooms of that same size?

63. Train A travels 10 mi/h slower than train B. Train A travels 400 miles in the same time that train B travels 500 miles. Find the speed of each train.

6-8 Solve each equation for the given variable.

64. $\frac{x_1}{y_1} = \frac{x_2}{y_2}$ for y_2

65. $T = \frac{(k_1 + k_2)t}{3}$ for k_1

6-9

66. The number (N) of pizzas produced at a pizza parlor varies directly as the amount of time (t) the store is open. If the pizza parlor produces 350 pizzas in 15 hours, how many pizzas can it produce in 50 hours?

7-1–7-4 Simplify.

67. $\sqrt{(-25t)^2}$

68. $-\sqrt[5]{-32}$

69. $\sqrt[4]{16x^8y^4}$

70. $\sqrt[3]{12x^3}\sqrt[3]{2x^4}$

71. $\frac{\sqrt{60a^8}}{\sqrt{72a^5}}$

72. $\frac{\sqrt{y^3 + x^3}}{\sqrt{y + x}}$

73. $\sqrt[3]{108} - 2\sqrt{75} + \sqrt{147}$

74. $\sqrt[3]{x}(\sqrt[3]{3x^2} + \sqrt[3]{12x})$

7-5 Rewrite with positive exponents.

75. $\left(\frac{1}{8}\right)^{-\frac{2}{3}}$

76. $2x(y)^{-\frac{1}{4}}$

7-6 Solve.

77. $\sqrt{5x + 4} = 12$

78. $\sqrt{4x + 1} - \sqrt{x - 2} = 3$

7-7 Simplify.

79. $\sqrt{-3} \cdot 5i$

80. $(8 - 5i) - (-1 + 3i)$

7-8 Graph.

81. $2 + 3i, -2 - i, 2 - 2i$

Find the following absolute values.

82. $|3 - 2i|$

83. $|-3 + 4i|$

7-9 Multiply.

84. $(8 - 5i)(8 + 5i)$

85. $(2 - i\sqrt{3})(2 + i\sqrt{3})$

Divide.

86. $2 \div 4i$

87. $\frac{\sqrt{2} + i}{\sqrt{2} - i}$

7-10 Find an equation having the specified numbers as solutions.

88. $2i, -2i$

89. $3 + 4i, 3 - 4i$

Solve.

90. $x + 2ix - 1 = 2i + 3ix - 5i$

8-1 Solve.

91. $9x^2 - 15x + 4 = 0$

92. $4x^2 = 20$

Complete the square.

93. $x^2 + 14x$

94. $y^2 - \frac{1}{3}y$

Solve by completing the square.

95. $2x^2 - 7x = 15$

8-2

96. The length of a swimming pool is 10 m less than twice its width. The area of the swimming pool is 1000 m^2. Find the dimensions of the pool.

8-3 Solve.

97. $x^2 - 3x + 5 = 0$

98. $4x^2 - 2x + 5 = 0$

8-4 Find the discriminant and determine the number and nature of the solutions.

99. $x^2 + 3x + 5 = 0$

100. $10 - 2x^2 - 6x = 0$

101. Find an equation in which the sum of the solutions is -4 and the product of the solutions is $\frac{1}{4}$.

8-5 Solve.

102. $y - 5\sqrt{y} + 4 = 0$

103. $x^4 - 3x^2 - 18 = 0$

104. $x^{-2} - x^{-1} - 6 = 0$

8-6 Solve for the indicated variable.

105. $T = \frac{1}{3}gt^2$ for t

106. $\sqrt{\frac{x + 2}{y^2}} = k$ for y

Use the formula $s = 4.9t^2 + v_0t$

107. An object is thrown from an airplane at an initial velocity (v_0) of 30 m/s. If the object takes 5 seconds to hit the ground, what was the height (s) of the airplane?

8-7

108. Find an equation of variation when x varies jointly as y and inversely as the square of z, and $y = 50$ when $x = 20$ and $z = 60$.

109. The intensity of light (I) from a light bulb varies inversely as the square of the distance (d) from the bulb. Suppose I is 160 W/m^2 when the distance is 4 m. Find the intensity at a distance of 12 m.

CHAPTER 9

What You'll Learn in Chapter 9

- How to determine whether a function is even, odd, or neither
- How to sketch or graph quadratic functions
- How to find a standard form for a quadratic equation
- How to determine maximum or minimum values, and *x*-intercepts, of the graph of a quadratic function, if they exist
- How to fit a quadratic function to a graph or data points
- How to solve problems using quadratic functions

Skills & Concepts You Need for Chapter 9

3-2 Graph.

1. $2y = \frac{1}{3}x - 1$ **2.** $y = -2x + 3$

3-3 Tell whether each graph is the graph of a function.

3.

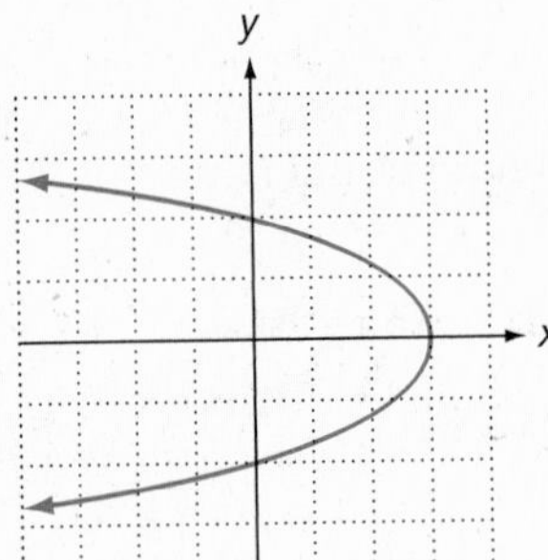

4.

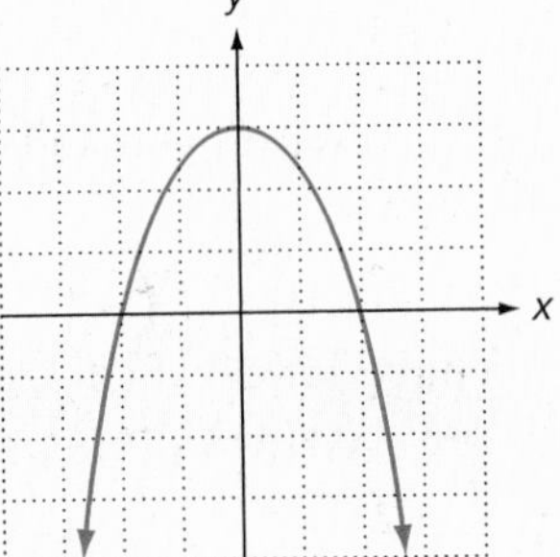

3-4 Find the *x*- and *y*-intercepts of each.

5. $2x - 5y = 10$ **6.** $3x + y = 6$

7. $-4x + 3y = 12$ **8.** $-x + 2y = 4$

9. $3x + 5y = 10$ **10.** $x - 7y = 4$

8-1 Solve by completing the square.

11. $x^2 - \frac{2}{3}x - \frac{1}{3} = 0$ **12.** $x^2 + 2x - 6 = 0$

Quadratic Functions and Transformations

This rare blue butterfly has nearly perfect symmetry with respect to a line drawn from anterior to posterior. Line symmetry is an underlying concept of certain transformations you will study in this chapter. Perhaps you notice that the fern leaf does *not* have line symmetry. Can you give a definition in your own words for the phrase "line symmetry"?

9-1 Symmetry

What You'll Learn

1. To test for symmetry with respect to an axis
2. To test for symmetry with respect to the origin
3. To determine whether a function is even or odd

. . . And Why

To graph any quadratic function

In this chapter we consider how changes in the equation $y = f(x)$ affect the graph of the function it defines. Then we use this information to graph quadratic functions $f(x) = ax^2 + bx + c$, where $a \neq 0$.

PART 1 Symmetry with Respect to the Axes

Objective: Test the equation of a relation for symmetry with respect to an axis.

Many examples of line symmetry can be found in nature. A butterfly, a bug, or a leaf all exhibit line symmetry. The idea of line symmetry can be described precisely in mathematical language.

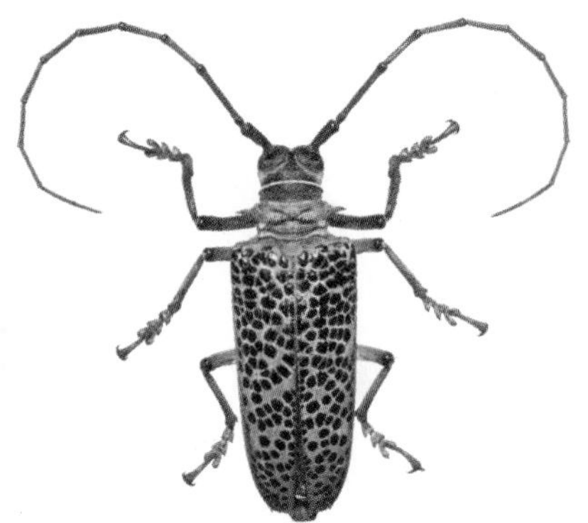

Symmetry in nature has fascinated humans for eons, from drawings in caves to beautiful color photos.

Definition

Two points, P and P_1, are **symmetric with respect to a line** l when they are the same distance from l, measured along a perpendicular to l. Line l is known as a **line** or **axis of symmetry.** P_1 is said to be the **image** of P. A figure, or set of points, is symmetric with respect to a line when the image of each point in the set is also in the set.

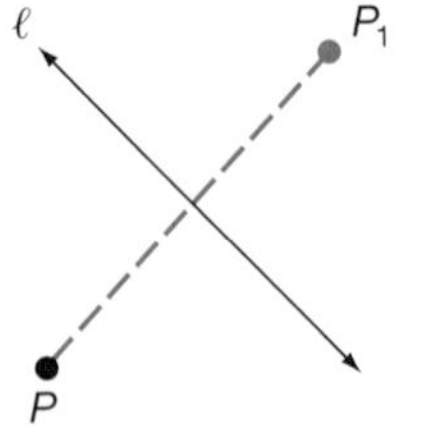

Two points symmetric with respect to a line are called **reflections** of each other across the line. The line is known as a line of symmetry.

The figure at the right is symmetric with respect to line l. Imagine picking this figure up and flipping it over line l. Points P and P_1 would be interchanged. Points Q and Q_1 would be interchanged. These are pairs of symmetric points. The entire figure would look exactly as it did before flipping.

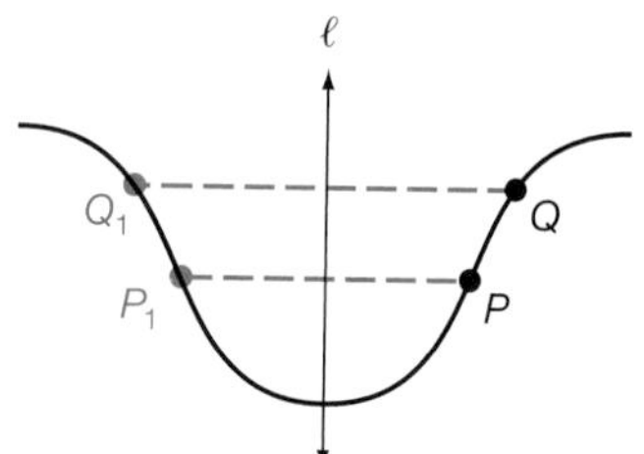

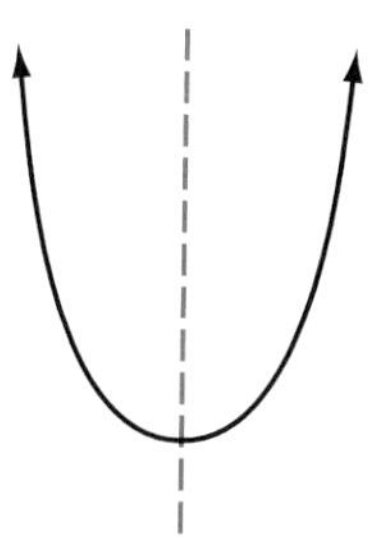

Symmetric with respect to the line

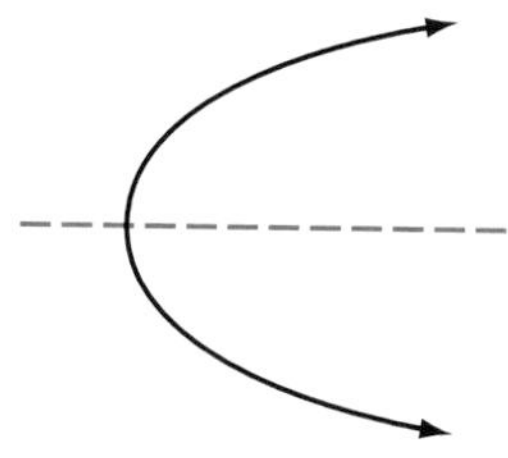

Symmetric with respect to the line

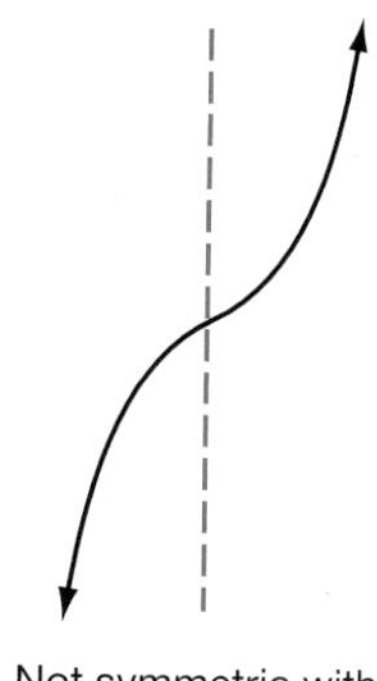

Not symmetric with respect to the line

Journal

Keep a learning log for this chapter. Write notes on new ideas, old ideas, and new techniques or skills that you have learned.

The figure at the right is not symmetric with respect to the vertical line shown, or with respect to a horizontal line. It is symmetric in other respects, as we will see later.

There are types of symmetry in which the x-axis or the y-axis is a line of symmetry.

Theorem 9-1

Two points are symmetric with respect to the x-axis if and only if their y-coordinates are additive inverses and they have the same x-coordinate.

Two points are symmetric with respect to the y-axis if and only if their x-coordinates are additive inverses and they have the same y-coordinate.

The relation defined by $y = x^2$ contains $(2, 4)$ and $(-2, 4)$. The first coordinates, 2 and -2, are additive inverses of each other. The second coordinates are the same. For every point (x, y) of the relation, there is another point $(-x, y)$. So the relation $y = x^2$ is symmetric with respect to the y-axis.

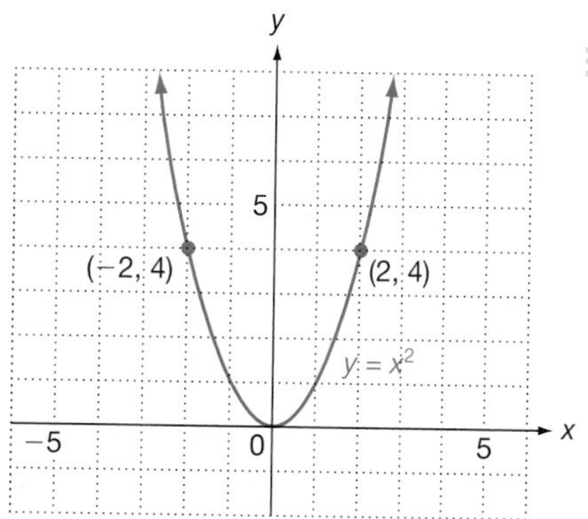

Quick Review

A relation is any set of ordered pairs.

We now have a means of testing a relation for symmetry with respect to the x- and y-axes when the relation is defined by an equation.

Theorem 9-2

When a relation is defined by an equation,

A. its graph is symmetric with respect to the y-axis if and only if replacing x by $-x$ produces an equivalent equation.

B. its graph is symmetric with respect to the x-axis if and only if replacing y by $-y$ produces an equivalent equation.

EXAMPLE 1 Test $y = x^2 + 2$ for symmetry with respect to the axes.

To test for symmetry with respect to the y-axis, we replace x by $-x$ and obtain $y = (-x)^2 + 2$. This is equivalent to $y = x^2 + 2$. Therefore, the graph is symmetric with respect to the y-axis.

To test for symmetry with respect to the x-axis, we replace y by $-y$ and obtain $-y = x^2 + 2$, or $y = -x^2 - 2$. This is not equivalent to $y = x^2 + 2$. Therefore, the graph is not symmetric with respect to the x-axis.

Try This Test for symmetry with respect to the axes.

a. $y = x^2 + 3$ **b.** $x^2 + y^2 = 2$

Symmetry with Respect to the Origin

Objective: Test the equation of a relation for symmetry with respect to the origin.

We can find examples of point symmetry in the real world. The bloom of a flower or a pinwheel exhibit point symmetry. The idea of point symmetry can also be defined precisely in mathematical language.

Definition

Two points, P and P_1, are **symmetric with respect to a point** Q when they are the same distance from Q, and all three points are on a line. P_1 is said to be the *image* of P. A figure or set of points is symmetric with respect to a point when the image of each point in the set is also in the set.

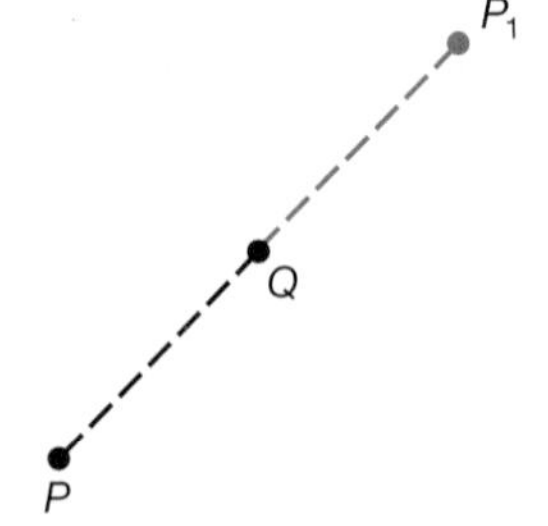

The figure below is symmetric with respect to the origin. Imagine sticking a pin in this figure at the origin and then rotating the figure 180°. Points P and P_1 would be interchanged. Points Q and Q_1 would be interchanged. These are pairs of symmetric points. The entire figure would look exactly as it did before rotating. This means that the image of each point of the figure is also on the figure.

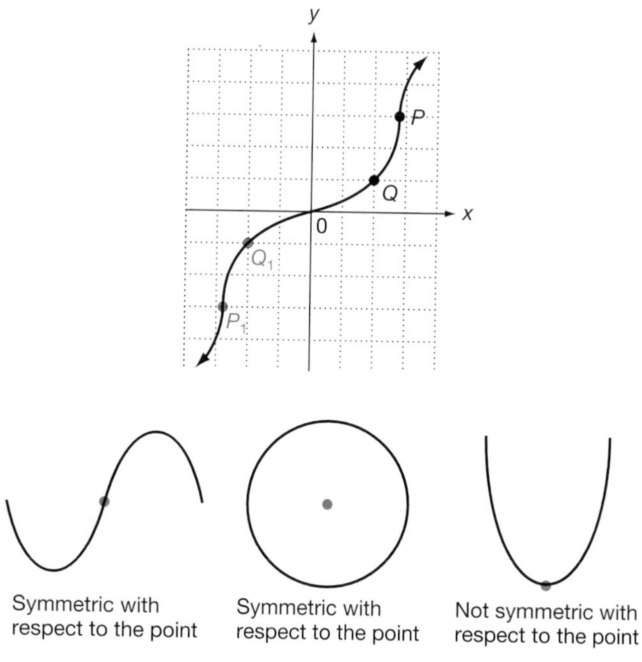

This four-leaf clover has point symmetry and line symmetry. Name a geometric figure that has both of these symmetries.

Symmetry with respect to the origin is a special kind of point symmetry.

Theorem 9-3

Two points are symmetric with respect to the origin if and only if both their x- and y-coordinates are additive inverses of each other.

The point symmetric to $(3, -5)$ with respect to the origin is $(-3, 5)$.

Theorem 9-4

A graph of a relation defined by an equation is symmetric with respect to the origin if and only if replacing x by $-x$ and replacing y by $-y$ produces an equivalent equation.

This gives us a means for testing a relation for symmetry with respect to the origin when it is defined by an equation.

EXAMPLE 2 Test $x^2 = y^2 + 2$ for symmetry with respect to the origin.

We replace x by $-x$ and y by $-y$. We obtain $(-x)^2 = (-y)^2 + 2$ which is equivalent to $x^2 = y^2 + 2$, the original equation. Therefore the graph is symmetric with respect to the origin.

Try This Test each relation for symmetry with respect to the origin.

c. $y^2 + x^2 = 16$ **d.** $y = x^3$

e. $y = x^2$ **f.** $\frac{1}{2}y^2 + x = \frac{3}{4}$

PART 3 Even and Odd Functions

Objective: Determine whether a function is even or odd.

Functions whose graphs are symmetric with respect to the y-axis are called **even functions.** If $y = f(x)$ defines an even function, then, by Theorem 9-1, $y = f(-x)$ will define the same function.

Writing Math

The ordered pair (x, y) of a function may be written as $(x, f(x))$. Since $y = x^2$ is a function, you can write $f(x) = x^2$.

Definition

A function is an **even function** when $f(-x) = f(x)$ for all x in the domain of f.

Functions whose graphs are symmetric with respect to the origin are called **odd functions.** If $y = f(x)$ defines an odd function, then, by Theorem 9-4, $-y = f(-x)$.

Definition

A function is an **odd function** when $f(-x) = -f(x)$ for all x in the domain of f.

EXAMPLE 3 Determine whether $f(x) = x^2 + 1$ is even, odd, or neither.

$$f(x) = x^2 + 1 \qquad \begin{aligned} f(-x) &= (-x)^2 + 1 \\ &= x^2 + 1 \end{aligned} \qquad \begin{aligned} -f(x) &= -(x^2 + 1) \\ &= -x^2 - 1 \end{aligned}$$

Compare $f(-x)$ and $f(x)$. They are the same for all x in the domain, so f is an even function.

Compare $f(-x)$ and $-f(x)$. They are *not* the same for all x in the domain. The function is not an odd function.

Try This Determine whether each function is even, odd, or neither.

g. $f(x) = x^4 - x^6$ **h.** $f(x) = 3x^2 + 3x^5$ **i.** $f(x) = x^3 + x$

9-1 Exercises

Extra Help On the Web

Look for worked-out examples at the Prentice Hall Web site. www.phschool.com

A

Test for symmetry with respect to the axes.

1. $3y = x^2 + 4$

2. $5y = 2x^2 - 3$

3. $2x^4 + 3 = y^2$

4. $3y^2 = 2x^4 - 5$

5. $2x - 5 = 3y$

6. $5y = 4x + 5$

7. $y^3 = 2x^2$

8. $3y^3 = 4x^2$

9. $2y^2 = 5x^2 + 12$

10. $3x^2 - 2y^2 = 7$

11. $3y^3 = 4x^3 + 2$

12. $x^3 - 4y^3 = 12$

Test for symmetry with respect to the origin.

13. $3x^2 - 2y^2 = 3$

14. $5y^2 = -7x^2 + 4$

15. $3x + 3y = 0$

16. $7x = -7y$

17. $3x = \frac{5}{y}$

18. $3y = \frac{7}{x}$

19. $3x^2 + 4x = 2y$

20. $5y = 7x^2 - 2x$

21. $3x = |y|$

22. ***Write a Convincing Argument*** Explain why y must be a nonnegative number in the relation $y = |2x|$.

Determine whether each function is even, odd, or neither.

23. $f(x) = 2x^2 + 4x$

24. $f(x) = -3x^3 + 2x$

25. $f(x) = 3x^4 - 4x^2$

26. $f(x) = 4x$

27. $f(x) = |3x|$

28. $f(x) = x^{24}$

29. $f(x) = x + \frac{1}{x}$

30. $f(x) = x - |x|$

31. $f(x) = \sqrt{x}$

32. $f(x) = \sqrt[3]{x}$

33. $f(x) = 7$

34. $f(x) = 0$

For each function, tell whether it is even, odd, or neither.

35.

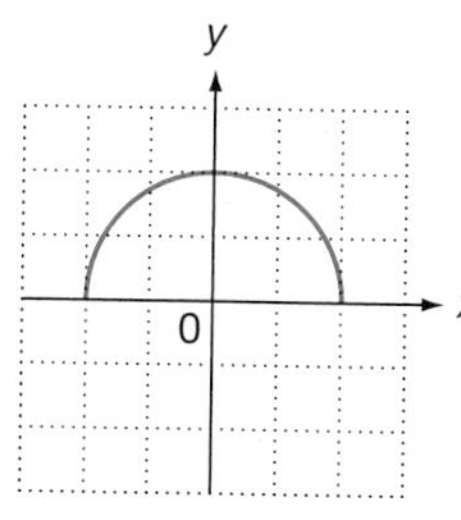

36.

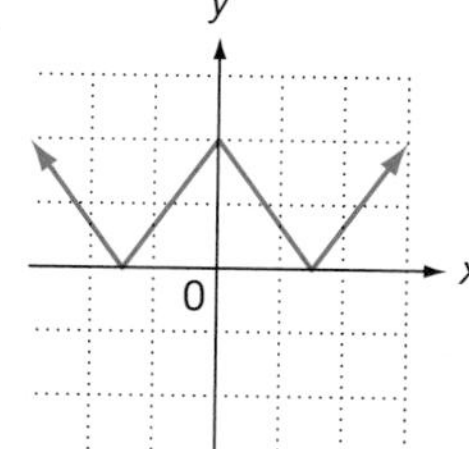

37.

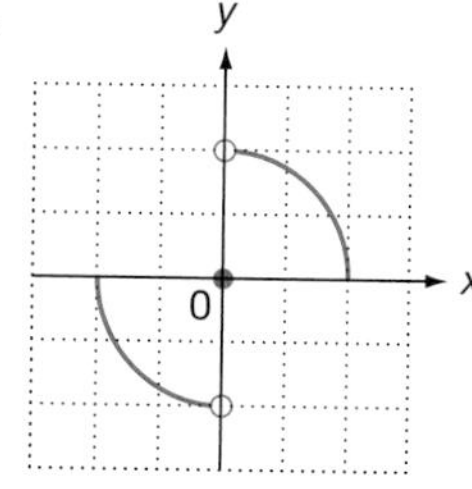

38.

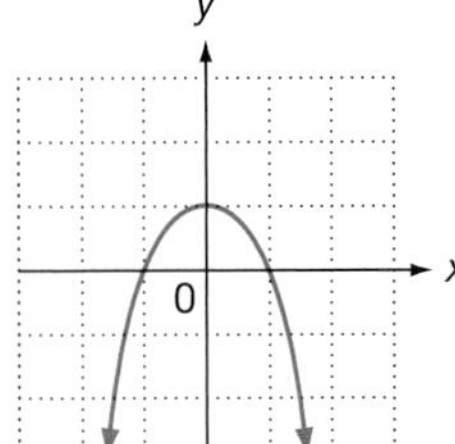

39.

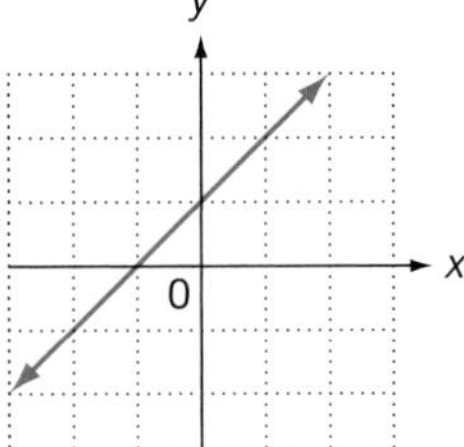

40.

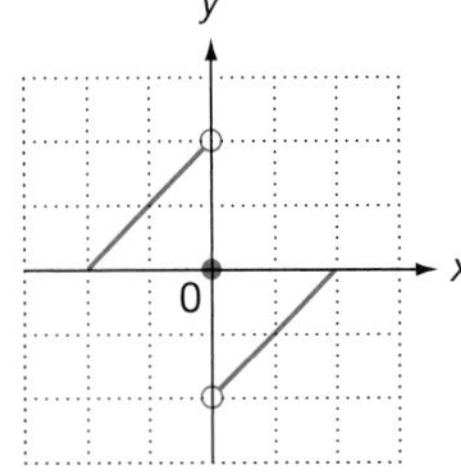

41.

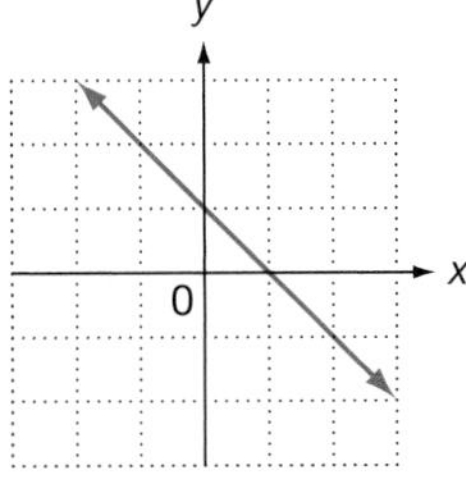

B

On a coordinate grid draw the quadrilateral with vertices (0, 4), (4, 4), (−2, −2), and (1, −2).

42. Graph the reflection across the x-axis.

43. Graph the reflection across the y-axis.

44. Graph the figure formed by reflecting each point through the origin.

45. ***Critical Thinking*** Find a function that is both odd and even. (Hint: There is only one.)

Challenge

Test for symmetry with respect to the axes.

46. $y = |x|$ **47.** $|x| = |y|$ **48.** $|y| = |x| + 1$

49. $y = |x| - 3$ **50.** $|x| + |y| = 3$ **51.** $|x| - |y| = 5$

Mixed Review

Simplify. **52.** $\sqrt{12}\sqrt{20}$ **53.** $\sqrt[3]{512}$ **54.** $\sqrt{80}$ **55.** $\sqrt{3}\sqrt{12}$ *7-2*

Find, without solving, the sum and product of the solutions.

56. $2x^2 + 8x - 3 = 0$ **57.** $3x^2 - 5x + 2 = 0$ **58.** $x^2 + 5x + 6 = 0$ *8-4*

Find a quadratic equation whose solutions are the following. **59.** 6, 4

60. 0, −4 **61.** $3 + \sqrt{3}, 3 - \sqrt{3}$ **62.** $3 + 2i, 3 - 2i$ *8-4*

Transformations

9-2

An alteration of a relation is called a **transformation.** If such an alteration results in moving the graph of the relation without changing its size or shape and without rotating it, the transformation is called a **translation.**

Vertical Translations

Objective: Sketch a graph that is a vertical translation of a given graph.

Consider the following relations and their graphs.

$y = x^2$

$y = x^2 + 1$

The graphs have the same shape except that $y = x^2 + 1$ is moved up a distance of 1 unit.

Consider any equation $y = f(x)$. Add a constant k to produce $y = f(x) + k$. This changes each function value by the same amount k but produces no change in the shape of the graph. If k is positive, the graph is moved, or translated, upward. If k is negative, the graph is translated downward.

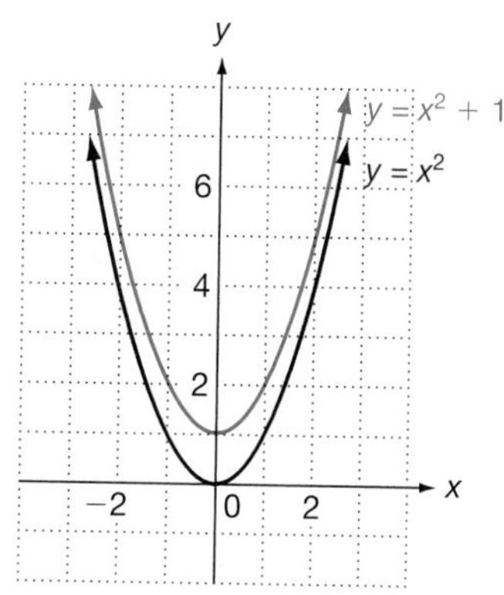

The equation $y = x^2 + 1$ can be rewritten as $y - 1 = x^2$.

Thus the transformation above is equivalent to replacing y by $y - 1$ in the original equation.

Theorem 9-5

In an equation of a relation, replacing y by $y - k$, where k is constant, translates the graph vertically a distance of $|k|$. If k is positive, the translation is upward. If k is negative, the translation is downward.

Replacing y by $(y + 3)$ in an equation is the same as replacing it by $y - (-3)$. In this case the constant k is -3, and the translation is downward. If we replace y by $y - 5$, the constant k is 5, and the translation is upward.

What You'll Learn

1. To sketch a graph showing vertical translation
2. To sketch a graph showing horizontal translation

. . . And Why

To graph any quadratic function

EXAMPLE 1

Consider the graph of $y = |x|$. Sketch the graph of $y = |x| - 2$ by translating.

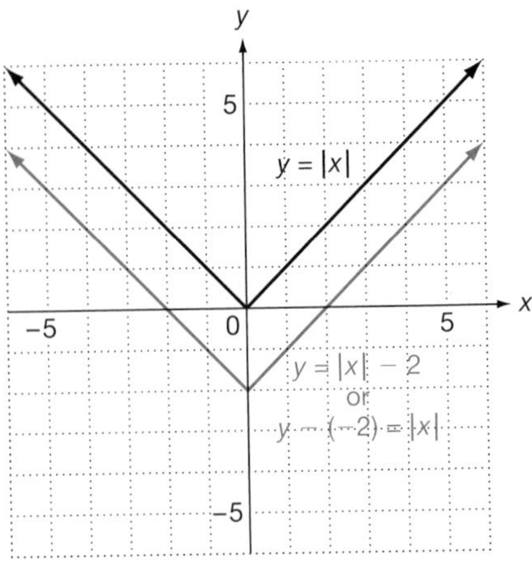

Note that $y = |x| - 2$ is equivalent to $y + 2 = |x|$ or $y - (-2) = |x|$. Thus the new equation can be obtained by replacing y by $y - (-2)$. Therefore, by Theorem 9-5, the translation is downward two units.

Try This

Consider the graph of $y = |x|$ as shown in Example 1. Sketch the graphs of the following by translating.

a. $y = -1 + |x|$

b. $y = 4 + |x|$

Horizontal Translations

Objective: Sketch a graph that is a horizontal translation of a given graph.

Translations can also be horizontal. If we replace x by $x - h$ everywhere it occurs in an equation, we translate the graph a distance of $|h|$ horizontally.

Theorem 9-6

In an equation of a relation, replacing x by $x - h$, where h is a constant, translates the graph horizontally a distance of $|h|$. If h is positive, the translation is to the right. If h is negative, the translation is to the left.

EXAMPLE 2

Consider the graph of $y = |x|$. Sketch the graph of $y = |x + 2|$ by translating.

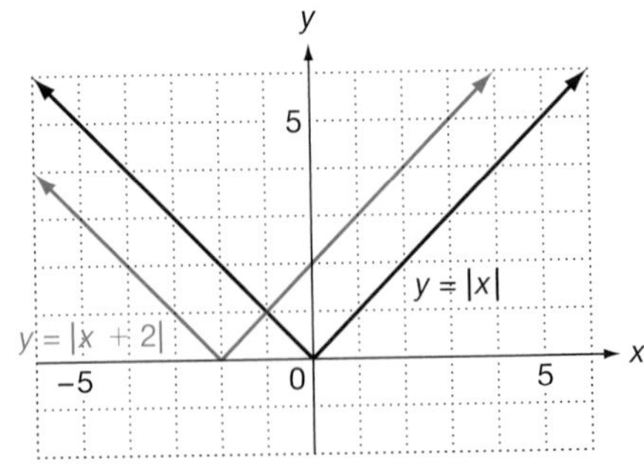

Here we note that x is replaced by $x + 2$, or $x - (-2)$. Thus $h = -2$, and by Theorem 9-6 the translated graph will be moved two units to the left.

Try This

Consider the graph of $y = |x|$ as shown in Example 2. Sketch the graphs of the following by translating.

c. $y = |x + 3|$ **d.** $y = |x - 1|$

9-2 Exercises

Look for worked-out examples at the Prentice Hall Web site.
www.phschool.com

A

Consider the graph of $y = |x|$ shown in Examples 1 and 2. Sketch graphs of the following by translating.

1. $y = |x| + 2$
2. $y = |x| - 3$
3. $y = |x| + 5$
4. $y = |x| + 6$
5. $y = |x| - 4$
6. $y = |x| - 5$
7. $y = |x| + \frac{1}{2}$
8. $y = |x| + \frac{3}{4}$
9. $y = |x - 3|$
10. $y = |x - 2|$
11. $y = |x + 4|$
12. $y = |x - 5|$
13. $y = |x + 5|$
14. $y = |x + 6|$

B

Sketch each graph.

15. $y = |x + 3| - 5$
16. $y = |x - 1| - 2$
17. $y = |x + 1| + 1$
18. $y = |x - 6| + 6$

A circle centered at the origin with radius of length 1 has an equation $x^2 + y^2 = 1$.

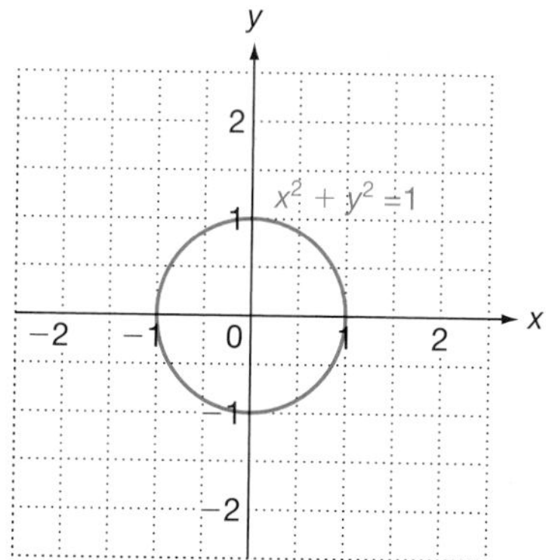

Sketch each circle by translating the center.

19. $(x - 1)^2 + y^2 = 1$
20. $x^2 + (y + 2)^2 = 1$
21. $(x + 2)^2 + (y - 1)^2 = 1$
22. $(x + 1)^2 + (y + 1)^2 = 1$

23. Consider the circle $x^2 + y^2 = 1$ centered at the origin. If we replace x by $x - 2$ and y by $y + 3$, what are the coordinates of the center of the translated circle?

24. Consider a circle centered at $(2, 4)$. What are the coordinates of the center of the translated circle if we replace x with $x - 3$ and y with $y + 5$ in the equation of the circle?

25. *Critical Thinking* In the equation of a relation, y is replaced by $y - 6$ and x is replaced by $x + 4$. Describe what happens to the graph of the relation.

Challenge

Consider the graph of $|x| + |y| = 1$.

26. Sketch the graph of $|x| + |y + 3| = 1$.

27. Sketch the graph of $|x - 4| + |y| = 1$.

28. Sketch the graph of $|x - 2| + |y + 4| = 1$.

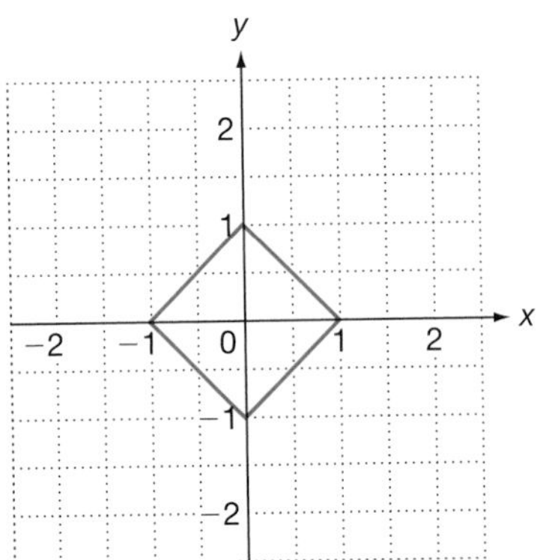

Mixed Review

Find a quadratic equation for which the sum and product of the solutions are the following.

29. Sum, $\frac{1}{3}$; product, 3 **30.** Sum, -3; product, 2 8-4

Multiply.

31. $(-7i)^2$ **32.** $(5 + i)(5 - i)$ **33.** $(\sqrt{5} + i)(\sqrt{5} - i)$ 7-9

Find the absolute value. **34.** $|m - ni|$ **35.** $|n + mi|$ **36.** $|3i|$ 7-8

Solve.

37. $x^4 - 20x^2 + 64 = 0$ **38.** $x^4 - 9x^2 = 0$ 8-5

39. Find an equation of variation where y varies directly as the square of x, and $y = 18$ when $x = 3$. 8-7

Stretching and Shrinking

9-3

PART 1 Vertical Stretchings and Shrinkings

Objective: Sketch a graph that is a vertical stretching or shrinking of a given graph.

Compare the graphs of $y = f(x)$, $y = 2f(x)$, and $y = \frac{1}{2}f(x)$. The graph of $y = 2f(x)$ looks like that of $y = f(x)$, but is stretched vertically. The graph of $y = \frac{1}{2}f(x)$ is flattened, or shrunk, vertically.

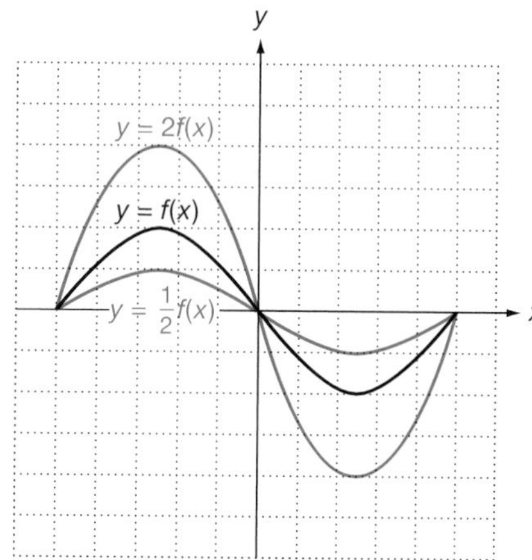

Consider any equation $y = f(x)$. If we multiply $f(x)$ by 2, then every function value is doubled. This has the effect of stretching the graph away from the horizontal axis. This is true for any constant greater than 1.

Multiplying $f(x)$ by $\frac{1}{2}$ will halve every function value, thus shrinking the graph toward the horizontal axis. This is true for any constant between 0 and 1.

Now compare the graphs of $y = f(x)$, $y = -2f(x)$, and $y = -\frac{1}{2}f(x)$.

When we multiply by a negative constant, the graph is reflected across the x-axis, and is also being stretched or shrunk. Note that multiplying $f(x)$ by -1 has the effect of replacing y by $-y$, and that we obtain a reflection without stretching or shrinking.

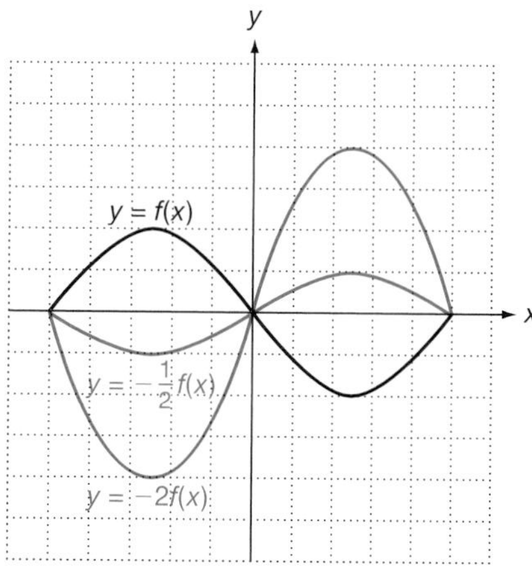

Consider $y = f(x)$. Multiply $f(x)$ by a constant c. We then have

$$y = c \cdot f(x). \quad \text{This is equivalent to } \frac{y}{c} = f(x).$$

Thus, in an equation of any relation, dividing y by 2 will stretch the graph in the y-direction. Similarly, dividing y by $\frac{1}{2}$ will shrink the graph in the y-direction.

What You'll Learn

1. To sketch a graph showing vertical stretching or shrinking
2. To sketch a graph showing horizontal stretching and shrinking

. . . And Why

To apply transformations to any relation

Theorem 9-7

In an equation of a relation, dividing y by a constant c does the following to the graph.

A. If $|c| > 1$, the graph is stretched vertically.
B. If $|c| < 1$, the graph is shrunk vertically.
C. If c is negative, the graph is also reflected across the x-axis.

Reading Math

A vertical stretch or shrink by constant c is sometimes called a vertical scale change of magnitude c.

EXAMPLE 1 Here is a graph of $y = f(x)$. Sketch a graph of $y = 2f(x)$.

$y = 2f(x)$ is equivalent to $\frac{y}{2} = f(x)$. By Theorem 9-7 the graph is stretched vertically. Every function value is doubled.

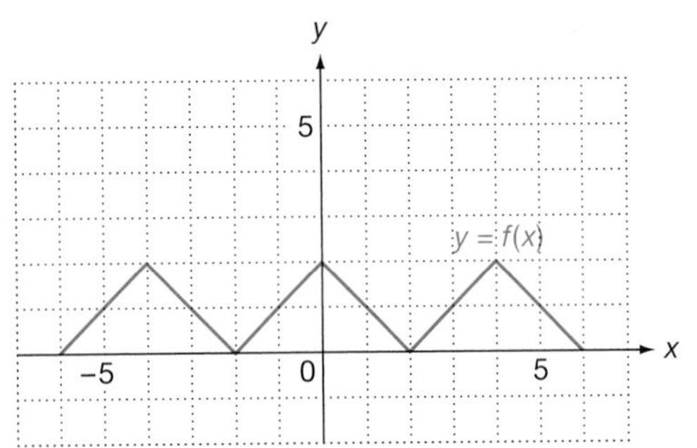

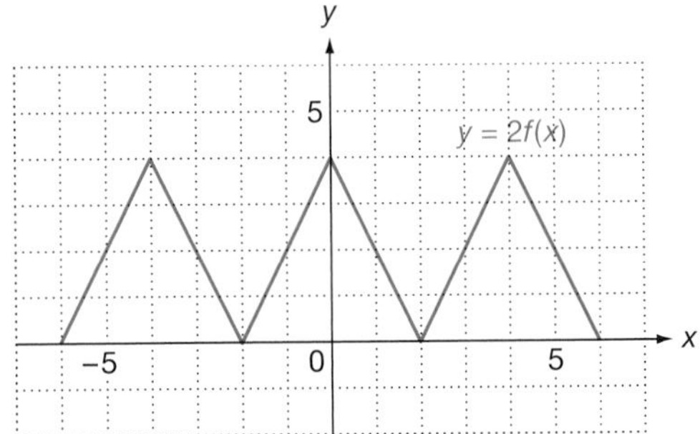

EXAMPLE 2 Here is a graph of $y = g(x)$. Sketch a graph of $y = -\frac{1}{2}g(x)$. $y = -\frac{1}{2}g(x)$ is equivalent to $\frac{y}{-\frac{1}{2}} = g(x)$. By Theorem 9-7 the graph is shrunk in the y-direction and also reflected across the x-axis. We halve each function value and change its sign.

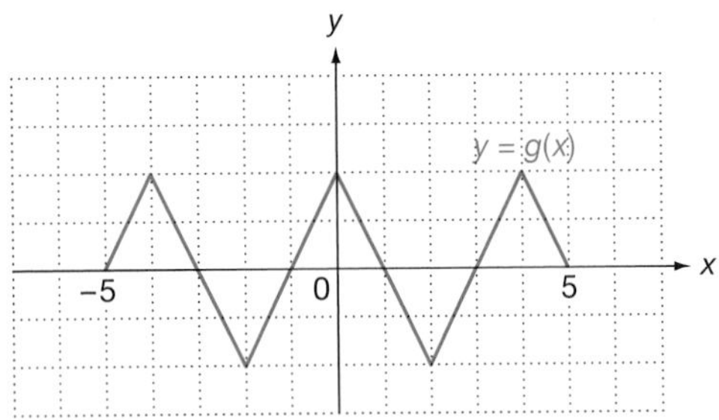

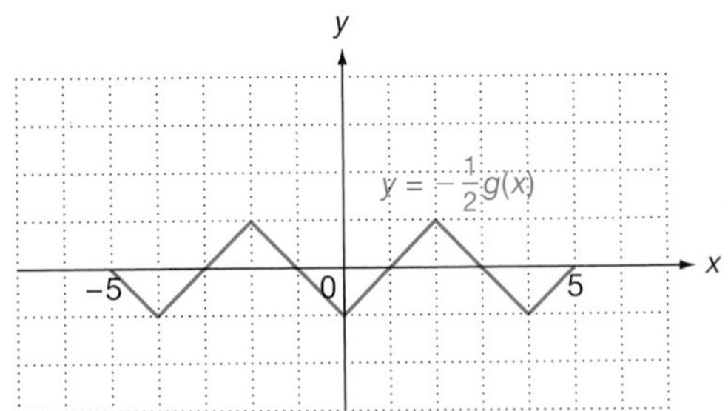

Try This

Here is a graph of $y = f(x)$. Sketch these graphs.

a. $y = 3f(x)$
b. $y = \frac{1}{2}f(x)$
c. $y = -\frac{1}{2}f(x)$

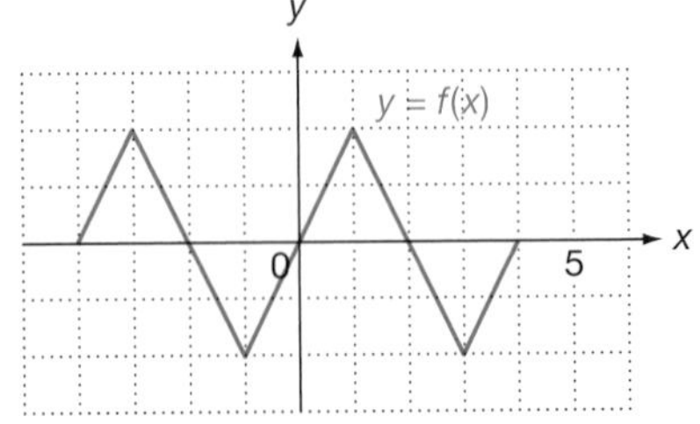

PART 2 Horizontal Stretchings and Shrinkings

Objective: Sketch a graph that is a horizontal stretching or shrinking of a given graph.

If we divide y by a constant, a graph is stretched or shrunk vertically. If we divide x by a constant, a graph is stretched or shrunk horizontally.

Theorem 9-8

In an equation of a relation, dividing x wherever it occurs by a constant d does the following to the graph.
A. If $|d| > 1$, the graph is stretched horizontally.
B. If $|d| < 1$, the graph is shrunk horizontally.
C. If d is negative, the graph is also reflected across the y-axis.

Note that if $d = -1$, this has the effect of replacing x by $-x$, and we obtain a reflection without stretching or shrinking.

EXAMPLE 3

Here is a graph of $y = f(x)$.

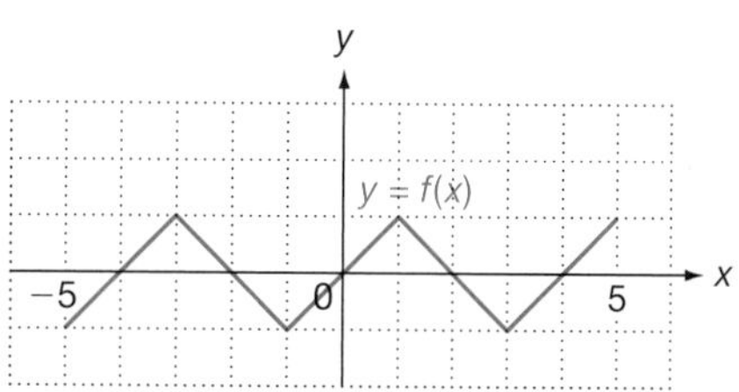

Reading Math

Notice that the graph of $f(x)$ in Example 3 does not have arrows at both ends. This means the domain is restricted to $-5 \le x \le 5$ for the function $y = f(x)$.

Sketch a graph of each of the following.

(a) $y = f(2x)$

$= f\left(\dfrac{x}{\frac{1}{2}}\right)$

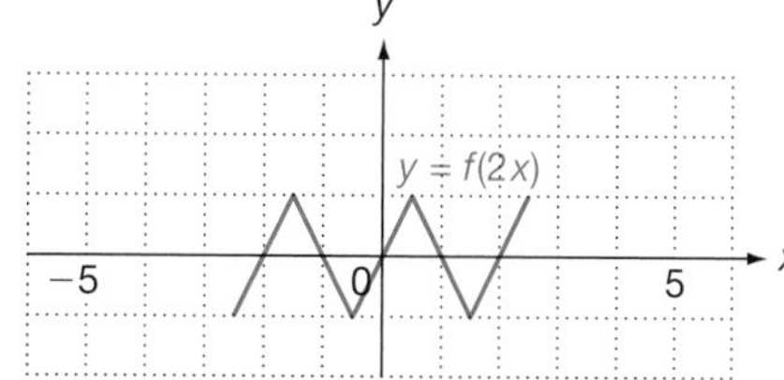

By Theorem 9-8 the graph will be shrunk. Each x-coordinate will be halved.

(b) $y = f\left(\frac{1}{2}x\right)$

$= f\left(\frac{x}{2}\right)$

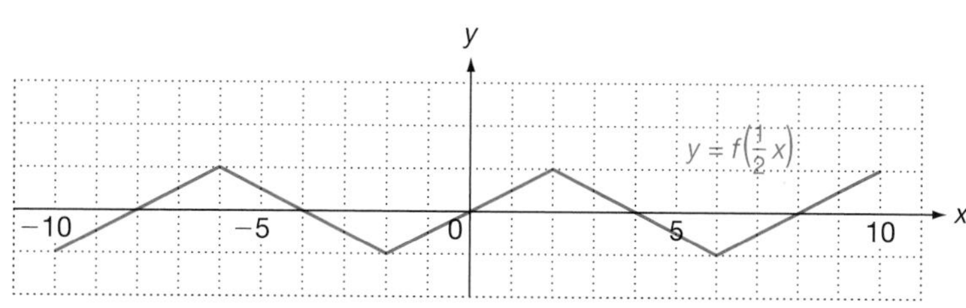

The graph will be stretched. Each x-coordinate will be doubled.

(c)

$$y = f\left(-\tfrac{1}{2}x\right) = f\left(\tfrac{x}{-2}\right)$$

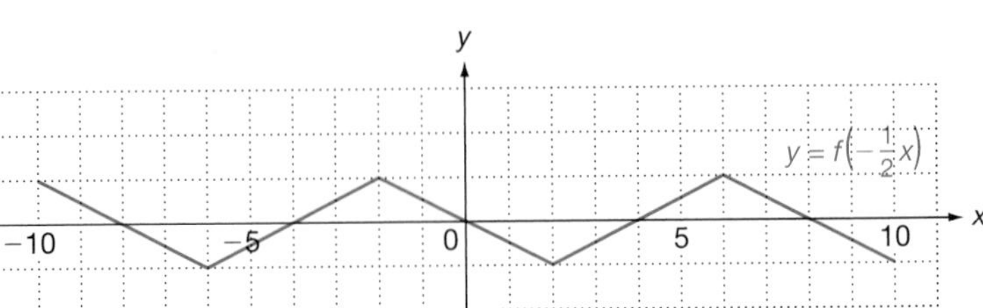

Try This Here is a graph of $y = f(x)$.

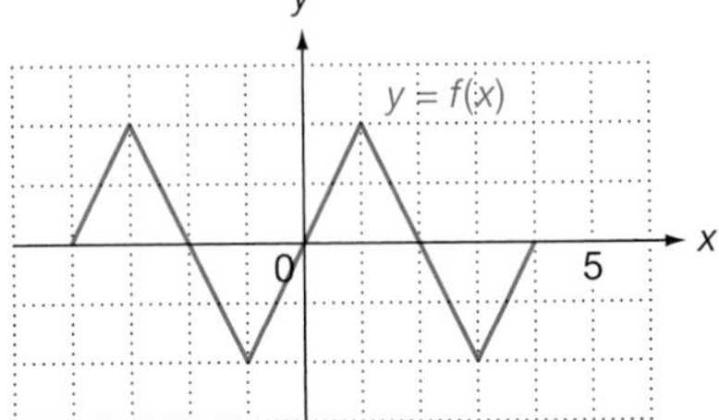

Sketch these graphs.

d. $y = -f(2x)$ **e.** $y = f\left(\frac{1}{2}x\right)$

f. $y = f\left(-\frac{1}{2}x\right)$

Extra Help On the Web

Look for worked-out examples at the Prentice Hall Web site.
www.phschool.com

9-3 Exercises

A

Here is a graph of $y = |x|$. Sketch these graphs.

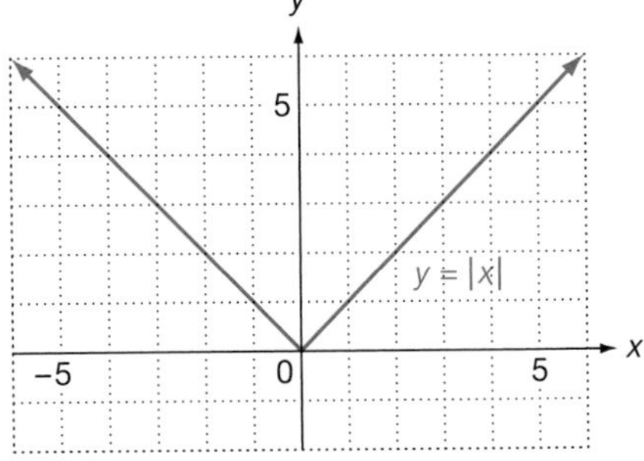

1. $y = 4|x|$ **2.** $y = 3|x|$

3. $y = 5|x|$ **4.** $y = 6|x|$

5. $y = \frac{1}{4}|x|$ **6.** $y = \frac{1}{3}|x|$

7. $y = -3|x|$ **8.** $y = -4|x|$

9. $y = -\frac{1}{4}|x|$

Here is a graph of $y = f(x)$. Sketch these graphs.

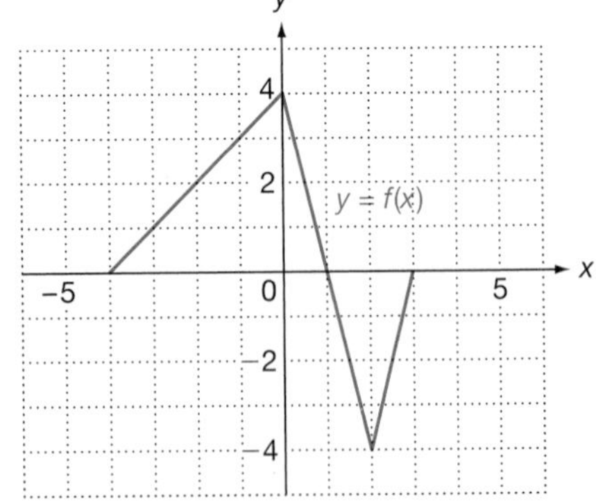

10. $y = 3f(x)$ **11.** $y = 2f(x)$

12. $y = -2f(x)$ **13.** $y = -3f(x)$

14. $y = 4f(x)$ **15.** $y = 5f(x)$

16. $y = \frac{1}{2}f(x)$ **17.** $y = \frac{1}{3}f(x)$

18. $y = -\frac{1}{2}f(x)$

Consider the graph of $y = |x|$ above. Sketch these graphs.

19. $y = |2x|$ **20.** $y = |3x|$ **21.** $y = \left|\frac{1}{2}x\right|$

Consider the graph of $y = f(x)$ from Exercises 10–18. Sketch these graphs.

22. $y = f(3x)$ **23.** $y = f(2x)$ **24.** $y = f(-2x)$ **25.** $y = f\left(\frac{1}{2}x\right)$

26. ***Error Analysis*** Gary graphed $y = f(-3x)$ by multiplying the x-coordinates of points of the graph of $y = f(x)$ by -3. This changed the graph by stretching and flipping it over the y-axis. Find the error(s) in Gary's work.

B

For Exercises 27–36, sketch graphs by transforming the graph of $y = f(x)$.

27. $y = 2 + f(x)$ **28.** $y + 1 = f(x)$

29. $y = f(x - 1)$ **30.** $y = f(x + 2)$

31. $\frac{y}{-2} = f(x)$ **32.** $y = \frac{1}{3}f(x)$

33. $y = 3f(x)$ **34.** $y = -\frac{1}{2}f(x)$

35. $y = f(x - 2) + 3$ **36.** $y = -3f(x - 2)$

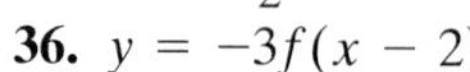

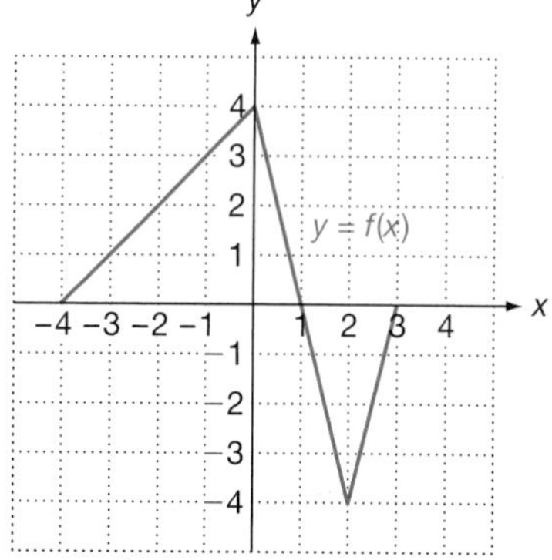

37. ***Critical Thinking*** In the equation of a relation, y is divided by $-\frac{1}{4}$ and x is divided by -5. Describe what happens to the graph of the relation.

Challenge

For Exercises 38–43, sketch graphs by transforming the graph of $y = f(x)$.

38. $y = 2f(x + 1) - 2$

39. $y = \frac{1}{2}f(x + 2) - 1$

40. $y = -2f(x + 1) - 1$

41. $y = 3f(x + 2) + 1$

42. $y = \frac{5}{2}f(x - 3) - 2$

43. $y = -\frac{1}{2}f(x + 2) - 3$

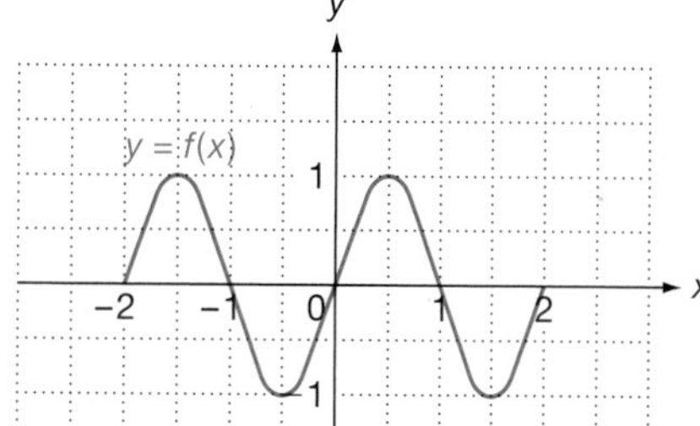

Mixed Review

Determine whether the given numbers are solutions of the equation.

44. $3i, -3i; x^2 + 9 = 0$ **45.** $i\sqrt{3}, -i\sqrt{5}; x^2 + 5 = 0$ *7-10*

Find a quadratic equation whose solutions are the following. **46.** $\frac{1}{3}, \frac{1}{2}$ **47.** $4, \frac{1}{3}$ *8-4*

Solve. **48.** $-4x - 10i = 2ix$ **49.** $x^4 - 10x^2 + 9 = 0$ **50.** $x - 2\sqrt{x} + 1 = 0$

51. $x^2 - 7x + 12 = 0$ **52.** $(x + 6)(x - 1) = 18$ **53.** $x^2 - 8x = 0$ *7-10, 8-1, 8-5*

9-4 Graphs of Quadratic Functions

What You'll Learn

1 To graph $f(x) = a(x - h)^2$ and determine its characteristics

. . . And Why

To solve problems using quadratic functions

Introducing the Concept: Transformations of the Graph of $y = x^2$

Graph the equations $y = x^2$, $y = 2x^2$, and $y = -2x^2$ on the same set of axes.

Study the graphs that you have drawn. In graphs of equations of the form $y = ax^2$, what effect does changing the value of a have on the graph?

Now graph the equation $y = (x - 3)^2$, $y = 2(x - 3)^2$, and $y = -2(x - 3)^2$. Use a new set of axes.

Again, study the graphs that you have drawn. In graphs of equations of the form $y = a(x - h)^2$, what effect does h have on the graph?

PART 1 Graphs of $f(x) = ax^2$ and $f(x) = a(x - h)^2$

Objective: Graph a function $f(x) = a(x - h)^2$, and determine its characteristics.

Definition

A **quadratic function** is a function that can be described as

$$f(x) = ax^2 + bx + c, \text{ where } a \neq 0.$$

Graphs of quadratic functions are called **parabolas.**

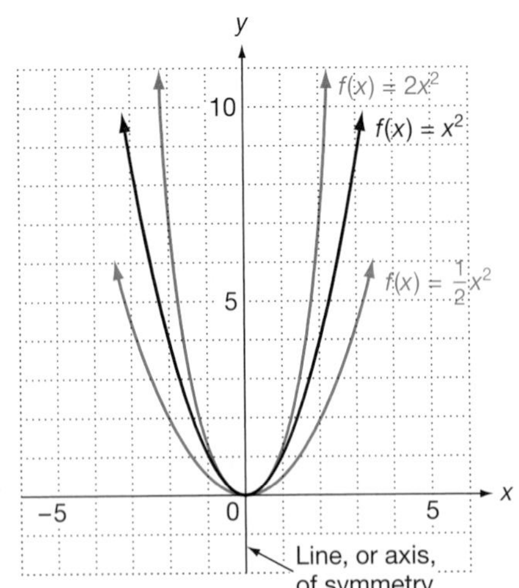

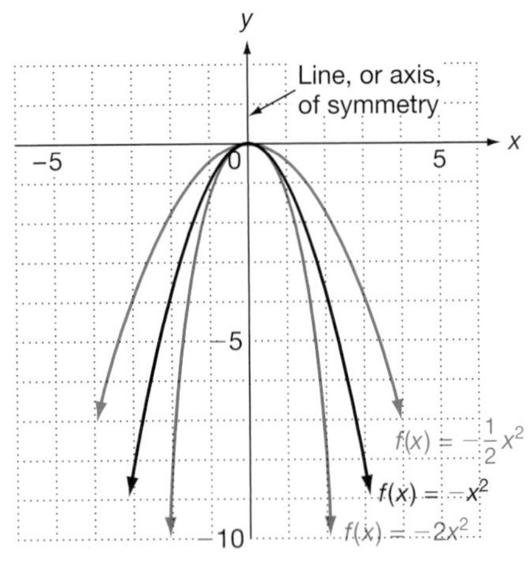

Consider the graph of $f(x) = x^2$ on page 400. The function is even because $f(x) = f(-x)$ for all x. Thus the y-axis is the line of symmetry. The point (0, 0), where the graph crosses the line of symmetry, is called the **vertex of the parabola.**

Next consider $f(x) = ax^2$. By Theorem 9-7 we know the following about its graph. Compared with the graph of $f(x) = x^2$,

1. if $|a| > 1$, the graph is stretched vertically.
2. if $|a| < 1$, the graph is shrunk vertically.
3. if $a < 0$, the graph is reflected across the x-axis.

EXAMPLE 1

(a) Graph $f(x) = 3x^2$.
(b) What is the line of symmetry?
(c) What is the vertex?

The line of symmetry is the y-axis.
The vertex is (0, 0).

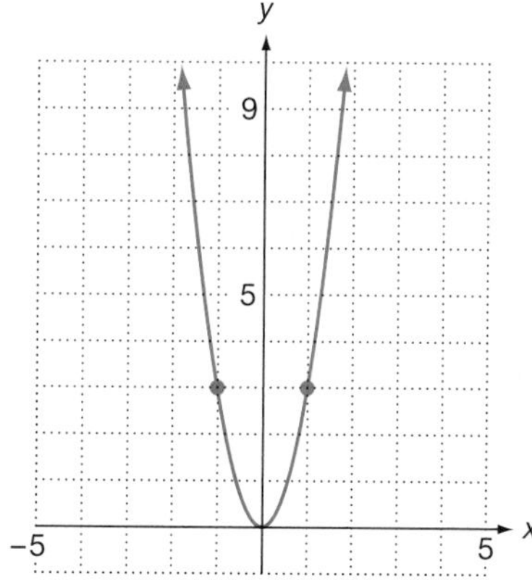

Quick Review

A short table of values will locate three points for $y = 3x^2$.

x	y
0	0
1	3
−1	3

Try This

a. (1) Graph $f(x) = -\frac{1}{4}x^2$.
(2) What is the line of symmetry?
(3) What is the vertex?

In $f(x) = ax^2$, let us replace x by $x - h$. By Theorem 9-6, if h is positive, the graph will be translated to the right. If h is negative, the translation will be to the left. The line, or axis, of symmetry and the vertex will also be translated the same way. Thus for $f(x) = a(x - h)^2$, the axis of symmetry is $x = h$ and the vertex is $(h, 0)$.

Reading Math

$f(x) = a(x - h)^2$ is read as "f of x equals a times the square of the quantity x minus h."

Compare the graph of $f(x) = 2(x + 3)^2$ to the graph of $f(x) = 2x^2$.

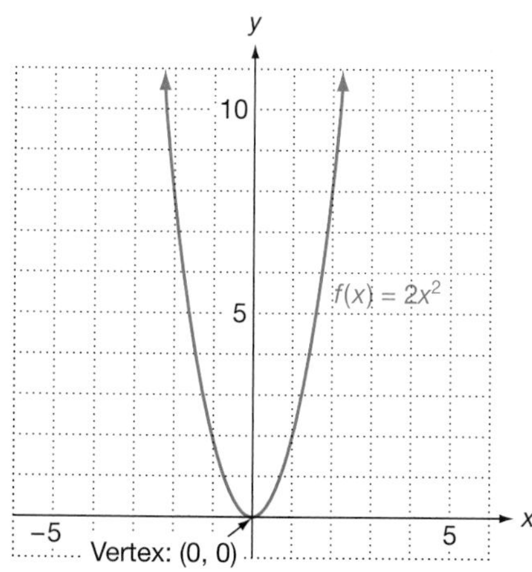

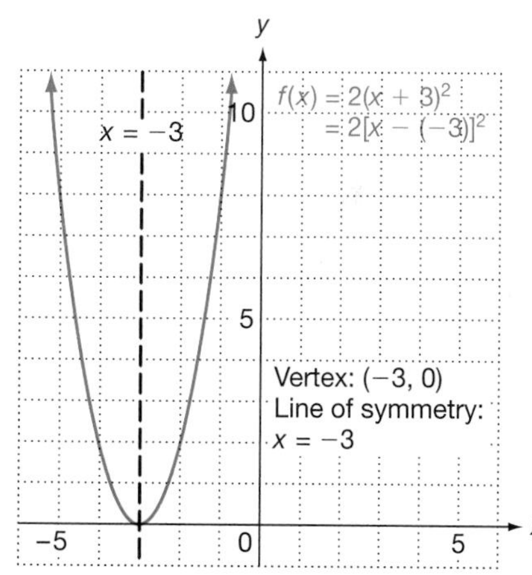

EXAMPLE 2

(a) Graph $f(x) = -2(x - 1)^2$.
(b) What is the line of symmetry?
(c) What is the vertex?

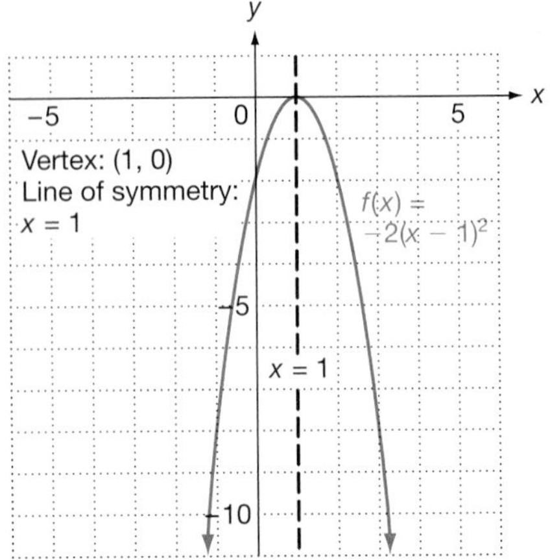

We obtain the line of symmetry from the equation $x - 1 = 0$; the line of symmetry is $x = 1$.

The vertex is $(1, 0)$.

Try This

b. (1) Graph $f(x) = 3(x - 2)^2$.
(2) What is the line of symmetry?
(3) What is the vertex?

Extra Help On the Web
Look for worked-out examples at the Prentice Hall Web site.
www.phschool.com

9-4 Exercises

A

Mental Math Without graphing, tell whether the graph is above or below the x-axis.

1. $f(x) = x^2$ **2.** $f(x) = -x^2$ **3.** $f(x) = -4x^2$ **4.** $f(x) = \frac{1}{2}x^2$

Graph the function, find the vertex, and find the line of symmetry.

5. $f(x) = 2x^2$ **6.** $f(x) = \frac{1}{4}x^2$ **7.** $f(x) = -\frac{1}{5}x^2$ **8.** $f(x) = \frac{1}{3}x^2$

9. $f(x) = (x - 7)^2$ **10.** $f(x) = -(x + 4)^2$ **11.** $f(x) = -(x - 2)^2$

12. $f(x) = 2(x - 3)^2$ **13.** $f(x) = -4(x - 7)^2$ **14.** $f(x) = -2(x + 9)^2$

15. $f(x) = 2(x + 7)^2$ **16.** $f(x) = 3(x - 1)^2$ **17.** $f(x) = \frac{1}{2}(x + 1)^2$

18. **TEST PREP** The line of symmetry for the graph of $f(x) = \frac{1}{3}(x - 2)^2$ has the equation

A. $x = -2$ **B.** $x = \frac{1}{3}$ **C.** $x = 2$ **D.** $x = -\frac{1}{3}$.

B

Graph these quadratic inequalities.

19. $y \leq x^2$ **20.** $y > 2x^2$ **21.** $y < -x^2$

22. $y \geq -x^2$ **23.** $y < -\frac{1}{3}x^2$ **24.** $y \leq 3(x + 4)^2$

25. *Critical Thinking* What does a quadratic function described by $y = ax^2$ have in common with a linear function described by $y = mx$?

Challenge

26. Describe the range of the quadratic function whose graph opens upward and whose vertex is (h, k).

27. ***Mathematical Reasoning*** Consider $y = mx^2$ and $y = nx^2$. Describe the relationship between m and n if

a. the graph of $y = mx^2$ is wider than the graph of $y = nx^2$.

b. the graphs of $y = mx^2$ and $y = nx^2$ open in opposite directions.

28. Consider the equation $f(x) = 2(x - 1)^4$.

a. Is there a vertex? If so, what is it?

b. Is there a line of symmetry? If so, what is it?

c. Is there a point of symmetry? If so, what is it?

29. Consider the equation $f(x) = 2(x - 1)^3$.

a. Is there a vertex? If so, what is it?

b. Is there a line of symmetry? If so, what is it?

c. Is there a point of symmetry? If so, what is it?

Self-Test On the Web

Check your progress. Look for a self-test at the Prentice Hall Web site.
www.phschool.com

Mixed Review

Determine the nature of the solutions of each equation. **30.** $x^2 + 6x + 9 = 0$

31. $x^2 - 3x + 9 = 0$ **32.** $x^2 - 81 = 0$ *8-4*

Solve. **33.** $x^2 + 6x + 4 = 0$ **34.** $x^4 - 25x^2 = 0$ **35.** $2x + 3\sqrt{x} - 2 = 0$ *8-3, 8-5*

Activity

1. Cut out a sheet of waxed paper about 5 inches by 5 inches.
2. Draw a line and a point on the waxed paper as shown.

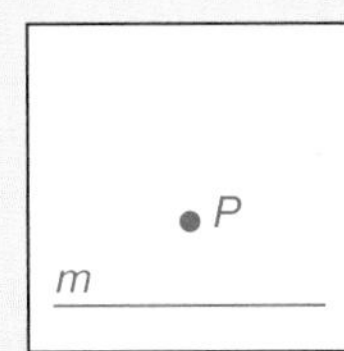

3. Fold and crease the paper so that point P is against line m. Repeat at least 50 times.

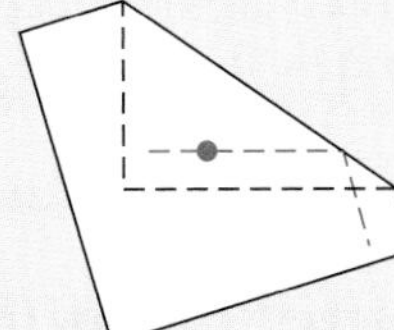

4. What figure seems to be formed by the creases?

9-5 Graphs of $f(x) = a(x - h)^2 + k$

What You'll Learn

1. To graph $f(x) = a(x - h)^2 + k$ and determine its characteristics
2. To analyze $f(x) = a(x - h)^2 + k$ without graphing

. . . And Why

To solve problems using quadratic functions

Introducing the Concept: Transformations of the Graph of $y = (x - h)^2$

Graph these equations.

$$y = (x - 2)^2$$
$$y = (x - 2)^2 + 4$$
$$y = (x - 2)^2 - 3$$

Study your graphs. What are the coordinates of the vertex of each graph? Predict the coordinates of the vertex of the function $y = (x - 20)^2 + 40$.

In graphs of equations of the form $y = (x - h)^2 + k$, what effect does k have on the graph?

PART 1 Graphs of $f(x) = a(x - h)^2 + k$

Objective: Graph a function $f(x) = a(x - h)^2 + k$, and determine its characteristics.

In $f(x) = a(x - h)^2$, let us replace $f(x)$ by $f(x) - k$.

$$f(x) - k = a(x - h)^2$$

Adding k on both sides gives $f(x) = a(x - h)^2 + k$.

By Theorem 9-5 we know that the graph will be translated upward if k is positive and downward if k is negative.

The vertex will be translated the same way. The line of symmetry will not be affected.

Guidelines for Graphing Quadratic Functions $f(x) = a(x - h)^2 + k$

When graphing quadratic functions in the form $f(x) = a(x - h)^2 + k$,

1. the line of symmetry is $x - h = 0$, or $x = h$.
2. the vertex is (h, k).
3. if $a > 0$, then (h, k) is the lowest point of the graph, and k is the **minimum value** of the function.
4. if $a < 0$, then (h, k) is the highest point of the graph, and k is the **maximum value** of the function.

EXAMPLE 1

(a) Graph $f(x) = 2(x + 3)^2 - 2$.
(b) What is the vertex?
(c) What is the line of symmetry?
(d) Is there a minimum or maximum value? If so, what is it?

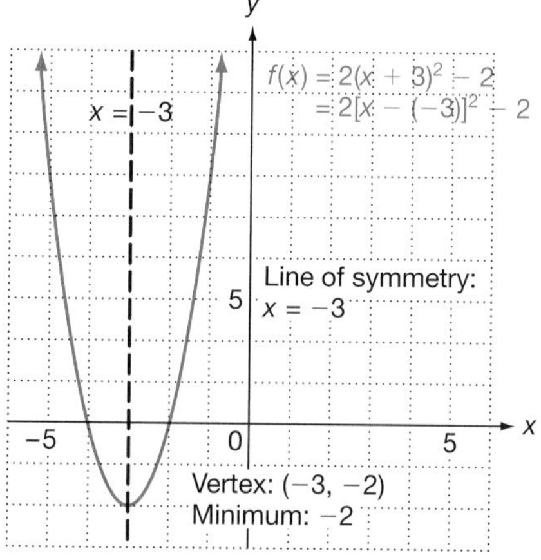

Try This For each of the following, graph the function, find the vertex, find the line of symmetry, and find the minimum or maximum value.

a. $f(x) = 3(x - 2)^2 + 4$ **b.** $f(x) = -3(x + 2)^2 - 1$

PART 2 Analyzing $f(x) = a(x - h)^2 + k$ Without Graphing

Objective: Determine the characteristics of a function $f(x) = a(x - h)^2 + k$.

EXAMPLES Without graphing, find the vertex, find the line of symmetry, and find the minimum or maximum value.

2 $f(x) = 3\left(x - \frac{1}{4}\right)^2 - 2$

It is best to break a complex question into its components. We make a chart.

(a) What is the vertex?	$\left(\frac{1}{4}, -2\right)$
(b) What is the line of symmetry?	$x - \frac{1}{4} = 0$ or $x = \frac{1}{4}$
(c) Is there a minimum or maximum value?	Minimum. The graph extends upward since $3 > 0$.
(d) What is the minimum or maximum value?	The minimum value is -2.

3 $g(x) = -4(x + 5)^2 + 7$
$= -4[x - (-5)]^2 + 7$

(a) What is the vertex?	$(-5, 7)$
(b) What is the line of symmetry?	$x = -5$
(c) Is there a minimum or a maximum value?	Maximum. The graph extends downward since $-4 < 0$.
(d) What is the minimum or maximum value?	The maximum value is 7.

Try This Without graphing, find the vertex, find the line of symmetry, and find the minimum or maximum value.

c. $f(x) = (x - 5)^2 + 40$

d. $f(x) = -3(x - 5)^2$

e. $f(x) = 2\left(x + \frac{3}{4}\right)^2 - 6$

f. $f(x) = -\frac{1}{4}(x + 9)^2 + 3$

Look for worked-out examples at the Prentice Hall Web site.
www.phschool.com

9-5 Exercises

A

For each of the following, graph the function, find the vertex, find the line of symmetry, and find the minimum or maximum value.

1. $f(x) = (x - 3)^2 + 1$

2. $f(x) = (x + 2)^2 - 3$

3. $f(x) = (x + 1)^2 - 2$

4. $f(x) = (x - 1)^2 + 2$

Mental Math Find the vertex and tell whether the graph has a minimum or a maximum value.

5. $f(x) = 2(x - 1)^2 - 3$

6. $f(x) = 2(x + 1)^2 + 4$

7. $f(x) = -3(x + 4)^2 + 1$

8. $f(x) = -2(x - 5)^2 - 3$

Without graphing, find the vertex, find the line of symmetry, and find the minimum or maximum value.

9. $f(x) = 8(x - 9)^2 + 5$

10. $f(x) = 10(x + 5)^2 - 8$

11. $f(x) = -7(x - 10)^2 - 20$

12. $f(x) = -9(x + 12)^2 + 23$

B

Write the equation of the parabola that is a transformation of $f(x) = 2x^2$ and has a minimum or maximum value at the given point.

13. Maximum $(0, 4)$ **14.** Minimum $(2, 0)$ **15.** Minimum $(6, 0)$

16. Maximum $(0, 3)$ **17.** Maximum $(3, 8)$ **18.** Minimum $(-2, 3)$

19. Minimum $(-3, 5)$ **20.** Maximum $(-4, -3)$ **21.** Minimum $(2, -3)$

22. *Critical Thinking* Suppose that y and x are interchanged in a quadratic function $y = a(x - h)^2 + k$. What happens to the graph?

Challenge

Write the equation of the parabola.

23. The parabola has a minimum value at the same point as $f(x) = 3(x - 4)^2$, but for all x in the domain of $f(x)$ the function values are doubled.

24. The parabola is a translation of $f(x) = -\frac{1}{2}(x - 2)^2 + 4$ and has a maximum value at the same point as $g(x) = -2(x - 1)^2 - 6$.

25. The parabola has a maximum value at $(2, 5)$ and contains $(1, 2)$.

26. The parabola has a minimum value at $(-2, -6)$ and contains $(1, 0)$.

27. The parabola is a reflection of $f(x) = 2(x - 5)^2 + 3$ across the line $y = -4$.

28. To graph on a certain computer's hi-res screen, it is necessary to translate to a coordinate system where the point $(0, 0)$ is in the upper left corner, and the point $(140, 80)$ is in the center of the screen. You want to graph using this screen, but you want $(0, 0)$ to graph in the center and $(-14, 16)$ in the upper left corner.

a. Write functions that will translate x and y values to this computer's coordinate system. (Hint: Fit linear functions to the data.)

b. Suppose you want to graph $y = x^2$. Find the computer's coordinates for the points $(-2, 4)$, $(0, 0)$, and $(2, 4)$.

Mixed Review

29. Find an equation of variation where y varies jointly as x and z, and $y = 24$ when $x = 4$ and $z = 3$. *8-7*

Solve for the indicated letter. **30.** $a^2 + b^2 = c^2$, for c

31. $A = \pi r^2$, for r **32.** $\frac{1}{R_1} + \frac{1}{R_2} = \frac{1}{t}$, for t **33.** $E = mc^2$, for c *8-6*

9-6 Standard Form for Quadratic Functions

What You'll Learn

1. To find the standard form for a quadratic function
2. To solve maximum- and minimum-value problems

. . . And Why

To solve problems using quadratic functions

PART 1 Standard Form for Quadratic Functions

Objective: Find standard form and characteristics for a quadratic function.

Consider a quadratic function described by $f(x) = ax^2 + bx + c, a \neq 0$. By completing the square we can rewrite it as $f(x) = a(x - h)^2 + k$. A quadratic function is in **standard form** when written as $f(x) = a(x - h)^2 + k$.

EXAMPLE 1 For $f(x) = x^2 - 6x + 4$,

(a) find standard form for the function.

$$\begin{aligned} f(x) &= x^2 - 6x + 4 \\ &= (x^2 - 6x) + 4 && \text{Writing with parentheses} \end{aligned}$$

We complete the square inside the parentheses. We take half of the x-coefficient and square it to get 9. Then we add $9 - 9$ inside the parentheses. Since $9 - 9 = 0$, we have not changed the value of the expression inside the parentheses.

$$\begin{aligned} f(x) &= (x^2 - 6x + 9 - 9) + 4 \\ &= (x^2 - 6x + 9) + (-9 + 4) && \text{Using the associative property for addition} \\ &= 1 \cdot (x - 3)^2 - 5 \end{aligned}$$

(b) find the vertex, line of symmetry, and the maximum or minimum value.

Using the standard form for the quadratic function, we find $a = 1,\ h = 3$, and $k = -5$. The vertex is $(3, -5)$. The line of symmetry is $x = 3$. Since the coefficient 1 is positive, there is a minimum function value. It is -5.

Try This

a. For $f(x) = x^2 - 4x + 7$,
(1) find standard form for the function.
(2) find the vertex, line of symmetry, and the maximum or minimum value.

EXAMPLE 2 For $f(x) = -2x^2 + 10x - 7$,

(a) find standard form for the function.

We first factor the expression $-2x^2 + 10x$. We factor -2 from the first two terms. This makes the coefficient of x^2 inside the parentheses 1.

$$f(x) = -2(x^2 - 5x) - 7$$

We take half of the x-coefficient and square it to get $\frac{25}{4}$. Then we add $\frac{25}{4} - \frac{25}{4}$ inside the parentheses.

$$\begin{aligned} f(x) &= -2\left(x^2 - 5x + \tfrac{25}{4} - \tfrac{25}{4}\right) - 7 \\ &= -2\left(x^2 - 5x + \tfrac{25}{4}\right) + 2\left(\tfrac{25}{4}\right) - 7 \quad \text{Multiplying by } -2\text{, using the distributive property, and rearranging terms} \\ &= -2\left(x - \tfrac{5}{2}\right)^2 + \tfrac{11}{2} \end{aligned}$$

(b) find the vertex, line of symmetry, and the maximum or minimum value. The vertex is $\left(\frac{5}{2}, \frac{11}{2}\right)$. The line of symmetry is $x = \frac{5}{2}$. The coefficient -2 is negative, so there is a maximum function value. It is $\frac{11}{2}$.

Try This

b. For $f(x) = -4x^2 + 12x - 5$,
(1) find standard form for the function.
(2) find the vertex, line of symmetry, and the maximum or minimum value.

Solving Problems: Maximum and Minimum Values

Objective: Solve maximum and minimum value problems that involve quadratic functions.

Maximum and minimum value problems are concerned with finding the largest or smallest value. Some maximum or minimum problems involve quadratic functions. To solve such a problem, we translate by finding the appropriate function. Then we find the maximum or minimum value of that function.

EXAMPLE 3

What are the dimensions of the largest rectangular pen that can be enclosed with 64 meters of fence?

We *draw a diagram* and label it. The perimeter must be 64 m, so we have

$$2w + 2l = 64.$$

We wish to find the maximum area.

$$A = lw$$

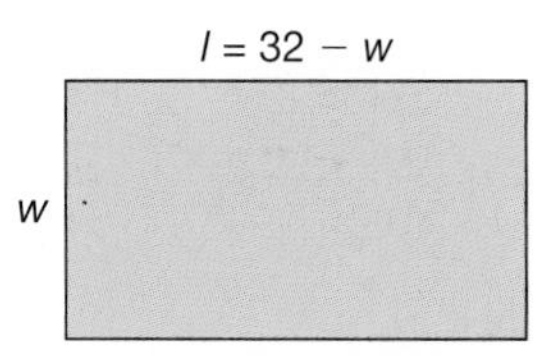

Solving $2w + 2l = 64$ for l, we get $l = 32 - w$.
We substitute for l in the area formula.

$$A = (32 - w)w = -w^2 + 32w$$

Then we complete the square.

$$A = -(w - 16)^2 + 256$$

The maximum function value is 256. It occurs when $w = 16$. Thus the dimensions are 16 m by 16 m.

Try This

c. What is the maximum product of two numbers whose sum is 30?

d. What are the dimensions of the largest rectangular pen that can be enclosed with 100 meters of fence?

Extra Help On the Web

Look for worked-out examples at the Prentice Hall Web site.
www.phschool.com

9-6 Exercises

A

For each function find standard form, the vertex, line of symmetry, and the maximum or minimum value.

1. $f(x) = x^2 - 2x - 3$

2. $f(x) = x^2 + 2x - 5$

3. $f(x) = -x^2 + 4x + 6$

4. $f(x) = -x^2 - 4x + 3$

5. $f(x) = x^2 + 3x - 10$

6. $f(x) = x^2 + 5x + 4$

7. $f(x) = x^2 - 9x$

8. $f(x) = x^2 + x$

9. $f(x) = 3x^2 - 24x + 50$

10. $f(x) = 4x^2 + 8x - 3$

11. *Error Analysis* In developing the standard form for $f(x) = \frac{3}{4}x^2 + 9x$, Emily wrote $f(x) = \frac{3}{4}(x^2 + 12x) + 0$ $= \frac{3}{4}(x^2 + 12x + 36) - 36 = \frac{3}{4}(x + 6)^2 - 36$. But the vertex should be $(-6, -27)$. Where is the error in Emily's work?

Solve.

12. A rancher is fencing off a rectangular area with a fixed perimeter of 76 m. What dimensions would yield the maximum area? Find the maximum area.

13. A carpenter is building a rectangular room with a fixed perimeter of 68 m. What dimensions would yield the maximum area? What is the maximum area?

14. What is the maximum product of two numbers whose sum is 22? What numbers yield this product?

15. What is the maximum product of two numbers whose sum is 45? What numbers yield this product?

16. What is the minimum product of two numbers whose difference is 4? What are the numbers?

17. What is the minimum product of two numbers whose difference is 5? What are the numbers?

B

18. Find an equation in standard form for $f(x) = 3x^2 + mx + m^2$.

Graph.

19. $f(x) = |x^2 - 1|$

20. $f(x) = |3 - 2x - x^2|$

Use a calculator to find the maximum or minimum value for each function.

21. $f(x) = 2.31x^2 - 3.135x - 5.89$ **22.** $f(x) = -18.8x^2 + 7.92x + 6.18$

23. You want to use 50 feet of fencing to surround a rectangular garden. Give a **counterexample** to show that a choice of making the garden 10 ft by 15 ft will not enclose the greatest possible area.

24. ***Mathematical Reasoning*** Find the vertex and line of symmetry for the function $f(x) = ax^2 + bx + c$.

25. ***Critical Thinking*** Apply the technique of completing the square to $f(x) = ax^2 + bx + c$. Find a formula for (h, k) in terms of a, b, and c.

Challenge

26. An orange grower finds that she gets an average yield of 40 bushels per tree when she plants 20 trees on an acre of ground. Each time she adds a tree to an acre, the yield per tree decreases by 1 bushel, due to congestion. How many trees per acre should she plant for maximum yield?

27. When a school play charges \$2 for admission, an average of 100 people attend. For each 10¢ increase in admission price, the average number decreases by 1. What charge would make the most money?

Determining the charge per ticket for an anticipated number of tickets for profit is an important concept in the business world.

28. Find the dimensions and area of the largest rectangle that can be inscribed as shown in a right triangle ABC, whose sides have lengths of 9 cm, 12 cm, and 15 cm.

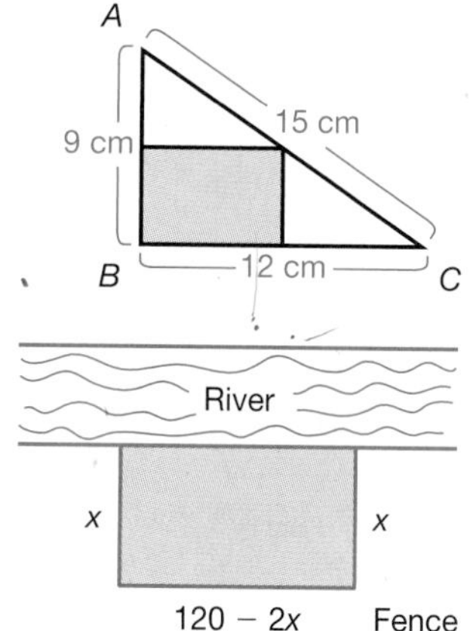

29. A farmer wants to build a rectangular fence near a river, and he will use 120 ft of fencing. The side next to the river will not be fenced. What is the area of the largest region that can be enclosed?

30. The sum of the base and the height of a triangle is 38 cm. Find the dimensions for which the area is a maximum, and find the maximum area.

31. The perimeter of a rectangle $RSTV$ is 44 ft. Find the least value of the diagonal RT.

Mixed Review

Test for symmetry with respect to the axes. **32.** $y = 2x^4 + 1$

33. $y^2 = 2x^4 + 1$ **34.** $y = 2x^3 + 1$ **35.** $y^2 = 2x^5 + 1$ *9-1*

Solve. **36.** $\sqrt{x + 2} = x$ **37.** $\sqrt{x^5} = 32$ **38.** $\sqrt[3]{r - 2} = 1$ *7-6*

Multiply. **39.** $-8i(-2)$ **40.** $\sqrt{-3}\sqrt{-7}$ **41.** $-\sqrt{-50}\sqrt{-2}$ *7-7*

Write using scientific notation. **42.** 0.07112 **43.** 34,095,600 *1-9*

9-7 Graphs and x-intercepts

What You'll Learn

1 To find the x-intercepts of the graph of a quadratic function

. . . And Why

To solve problems using quadratic functions

PART 1 Finding x-intercepts of a quadratic function

Objective: Find the x-intercepts of the graph of a quadratic function, if they exist.

The x-coordinates of the points where a graph crosses the x-axis are its **x-intercepts.** These are the points at which $y = 0$.

To find the x-intercepts of a quadratic function $f(x) = ax^2 + bx + c$, we solve the equation $0 = ax^2 + bx + c$.

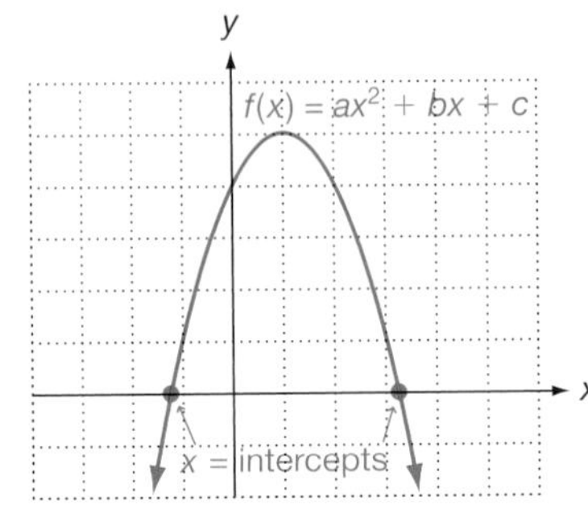

Recall that the discriminant $b^2 - 4ac$ tells us how many real-number solutions the equation $0 = ax^2 + bx + c$ has. Thus it also indicates how many x–intercepts there are. Compare.

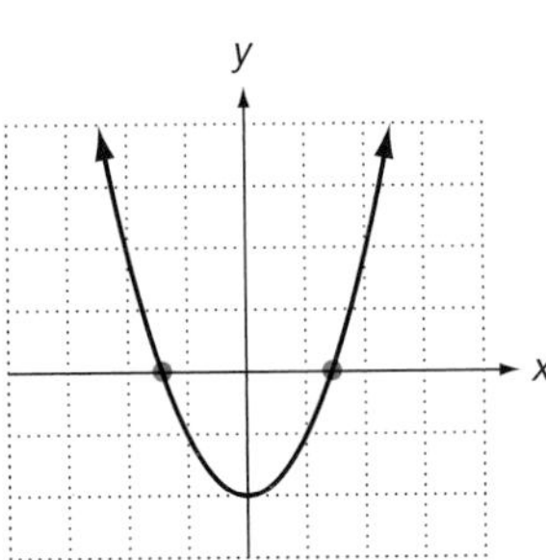

$y = ax^2 + bx + c$
$b^2 - 4ac > 0$
Two real solutions
Two x-intercepts

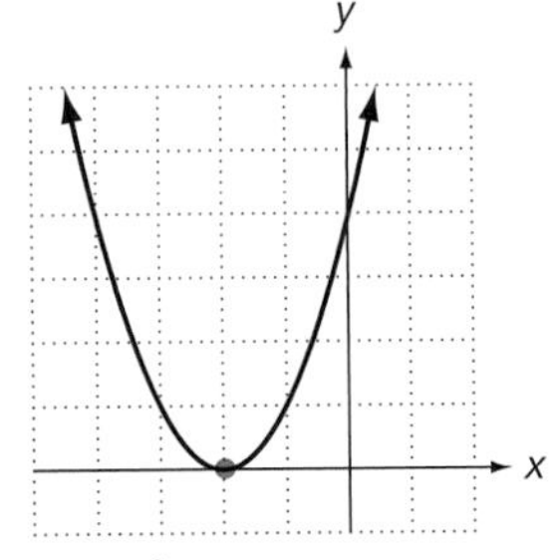

$y = ax^2 + bx + c$
$b^2 - 4ac = 0$
One real solution
One x-intercept

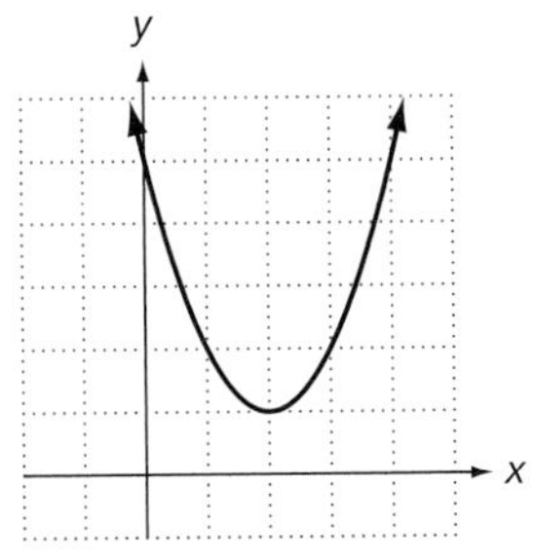

$y = ax^2 + bx + c$
$b^2 - 4ac < 0$
No real solutions
No x-intercepts

EXAMPLE

Find the x-intercepts of the graph of $f(x) = x^2 - 2x - 2$.

We solve the equation $0 = x^2 - 2x - 2$. We can use the quadratic formula

$x = \frac{2 \pm \sqrt{4 + 8}}{2} = \frac{2 \pm 2\sqrt{3}}{2} = 1 \pm \sqrt{3}$. Thus the x-intercepts are $1 + \sqrt{3}$ and $1 - \sqrt{3}$, and these occur at the points $(1 + \sqrt{3}, 0)$ and $(1 - \sqrt{3}, 0)$.

Try This Find the x-intercepts, if they exist. **a.** $f(x) = x^2 - 2x - 5$
b. $f(x) = x^2 + 8x + 16$ **c.** $f(x) = -2x^2 - 4x - 3$

9-7 Exercises

Extra Help On the Web

Look for worked-out examples at the Prentice Hall Web site.
www.phschool.com

A

Find the x-intercepts.

1. $f(x) = x^2 - 4x + 1$

2. $f(x) = x^2 + 6x + 10$

3. $f(x) = -x^2 + 2x + 3$

4. $f(x) = x^2 + 2x - 5$

5. $f(x) = x^2 - 3x - 4$

6. $f(x) = -x^2 + 3x + 4$

7. $f(x) = 2x^2 + 4x - 1$

8. $f(x) = x^2 - x + 2$

9. $f(x) = x^2 - x + 1$

10. $f(x) = 4x^2 + 12x + 9$

11. $f(x) = -x^2 - 3x - 3$

12. $f(x) = -5x^2 + 6x - 5$

13. $f(x) = 3x^2 - 6x + 1$

14. $f(x) = x^2 - 4x + 4$

15. If $f(x)$ equals a perfect square trinomial, then $f(x)$ (*sometimes*, *always*, *never*) has exactly one x-intercept.

B

16. *Estimation* Graph the function $f(x) = x^2 - x - 6$. Use your graph to sketch the graphs of the following equations. Then estimate the solutions from your sketches.

a. $x^2 - x - 6 = 2$ **b.** $x^2 - x - 6 = -3$

Quick Review

Recall the vertical translations of $y = f(x) + k$ in Lesson 9-2.

17. *Critical Thinking* Write an equation for a quadratic function that has x-intercepts of -3 and 5.

Challenge

Find the x-intercepts.

18. $f(x) = x^4 - 10$

19. $f(x) = x^4 - 3x^2 + 9$

Mixed Review

Test for symmetry with respect to the origin. **20.** $y + x = 1$

21. $y - x^2 = 4$ **22.** $4y = 3x - 7$ **23.** $x^2 + y^2 = 3$ *9-1*

For each function graph the function, find the vertex, and find the line of symmetry. **24.** $f(x) = x^2$ **25.** $f(x) = -2(x + 3)^2$ *9-4*

Graph the following relations. **26.** $y = |x|$ **27.** $y = |x + 4|$ *9-2*

28. *Multi-Step Problem* The distance s that an object falls when dropped from some point above the ground varies directly as the square of the time t it falls. The object falls 19.6 meters in 2 seconds.

a. Find the equation of variation.

b. How far will the object fall in 15 seconds?

c. How long will it take for the object to fall 122.5 meters? *8-7*

9-8 Mathematical Modeling: Using Quadratic Functions

What You'll Learn

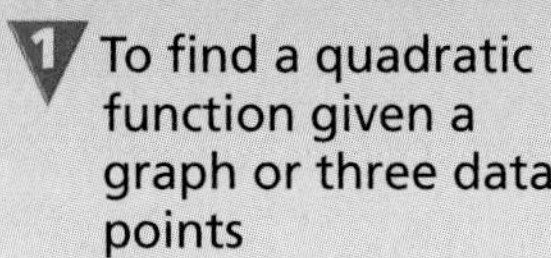

1. To find a quadratic function given a graph or three data points

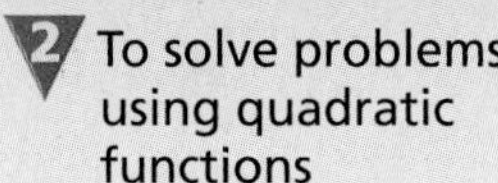

2. To solve problems using quadratic functions

. . . And Why

To solve real-world problems using quadratic functions

PART 1 Fitting Quadratic Functions

Objective: Find quadratic functions given a graph or three data points.

We can find a quadratic function that fits a curve if we know three **data points.**

EXAMPLE 1 Find the quadratic function that fits the curve.

Three data points on the graph are $(-2, 5)$, $(-1, 5)$, and $(0, 1)$. We substitute the three data points in $f(x) = ax^2 + bx + c$.

$$5 = a(-2)^2 + b(-2) + c$$
$$5 = a(-1)^2 + b(-1) + c$$
$$1 = a(0)^2 + b(0) + c$$

Simplifying, we have a system of three equations with three unknowns.

$$5 = 4a - 2b + c$$
$$5 = a - b + c$$
$$1 = c$$

Solving this system, we obtain $a = -2,\ b = -6$, and $c = 1$. These are the coefficients of the quadratic function $f(x) = ax^2 + bx + c$.

Thus the quadratic function is $f(x) = -2x^2 - 6x + 1$.

Reading Math

Data points that have integers as their coordinates are also called lattice points.

Try This

a. Find the quadratic equation that fits the curve at the right.

b. Find the quadratic function that fits the data points $(1, 6)$, $(-2, 3)$, and $(3, 18)$.

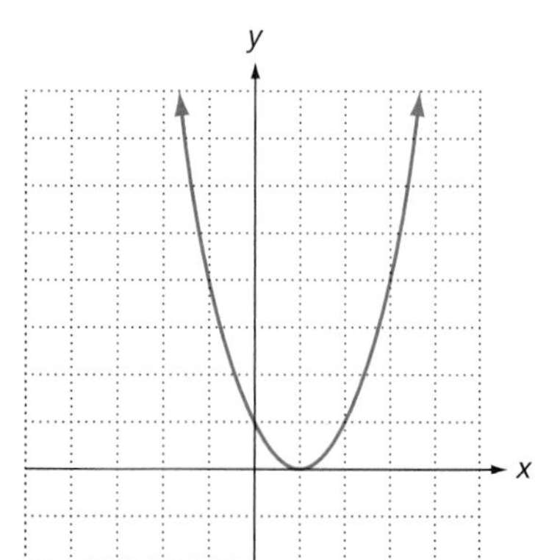

PART 2

Solving Problems: Quadratic Functions

Objective: Solve problems using quadratic functions.

Often, problems generate nonlinear data points that can be fit by quadratic functions. We can combine our knowledge of quadratic functions and problem-solving techniques to solve them.

EXAMPLE 2 A pizza shop lists the following prices for pizzas.

Diameter in cm	Price
20	\$ 6.00
30	\$ 8.50
40	\$11.50

What price should be given to a 35-cm pizza?

Is the 40-cm pizza twice the area of the 20-cm pizza? Is \$11.50 a reasonable price? Why or why not?

UNDERSTAND the problem

Question: What is the price of a 35-cm pizza?

Data: A 20-cm pizza costs \$6.00, a 30-cm pizza costs \$8.50, and a 40-cm pizza costs \$11.50.

Develop and carry out a PLAN

The area of a circular region is given by the formula $A = \pi r^2$, or $A = \frac{\pi d^2}{4}$. Thus the area of a pizza is a quadratic function of the diameter. Since the price should be related to the area, it should be a quadratic function of the diameter.

We can fit a quadratic function to the data points (20, 6), (30, 8.5) and (40, 11.5). Then we can use the function to find the price of a 35-cm pizza. Use the data points in $f(x) = ax^2 + bx + c$, where x is the diameter of a pizza and $f(x)$ represents the price.

$$\begin{aligned} 6 &= a \cdot 20^2 + b \cdot 20 + c \\ 8.5 &= a \cdot 30^2 + b \cdot 30 + c \\ 11.5 &= a \cdot 40^2 + b \cdot 40 + c \end{aligned}$$

Fitting a function to the data points

Simplifying, we get the following system.

$$\begin{aligned} 6 &= 400a + 20b + c \\ 8.5 &= 900a + 30b + c \\ 11.5 &= 1600a + 40b + c \end{aligned}$$

We solve this system, obtaining $a = 0.0025$, $b = 0.125$, and $c = 2.5$. Thus the function $f(x) = 0.0025x^2 + 0.125x + 2.5$ is the mathematical model of the situation. To find the price of a 35-cm pizza, we find $f(35)$.

$$f(35) = 0.0025(35)^2 + 0.125(35) + 2.5 = \$9.94$$

Find the ANSWER and CHECK

A 35-cm pizza should cost \$9.94. The answer is reasonable, since the price for the 35-cm pizza falls between the prices of a 30-cm and a 40-cm pizza.

Stating the answer clearly

Try This

c. The following table shows the accident records for a city. It has values that a quadratic function will fit.

Age of drivers	Number of accidents in a year
20	250
40	150
60	200

(1) Assuming that a quadratic function will describe the data, find the number of accidents as a function of age.

(2) Use the function to calculate the total number of accidents in which 30-year-olds might be involved.

A physics theory shows that when an object such as a ball is thrown upward with an initial velocity v_0, its approximate height is given by a quadratic function.

$$s = -4.9t^2 + v_0t + h$$

In the formula, h is the starting height in meters and s is the actual height in meters, t seconds after the object is thrown.

EXAMPLE 3 A model rocket is fired upward. At the end of the burn it has an upward velocity of 49 m/sec and is 155 m high.

(a) Find its maximum height and when it is attained.

We will start counting time at the end of the burn. Thus $v_0 = 49$ and $h = 155$. We will graph the appropriate function, and we begin by completing the square.

$$\begin{aligned}
s &= -4.9t^2 + 49t + 155 \\
&= -4.9\left(t^2 - \frac{49}{4.9}t\right) + 155 \\
&= -4.9(t^2 - 10t) + 155 \\
&= -4.9(t^2 - 10t + 25 - 25) + 155 && \text{Simplifying} \\
&= -4.9(t^2 - 10t + 25) + (-4.9)(-25) + 155 && \text{Completing the square} \\
&= -4.9(t - 5)^2 + 122.5 + 155 \\
&= -4.9(t - 5)^2 + 277.5
\end{aligned}$$

The vertex of the graph is the point $(5, 277.5)$. The graph is shown below. The maximum height reached is 277.5 m and it is attained 5 seconds after the end of the burn.

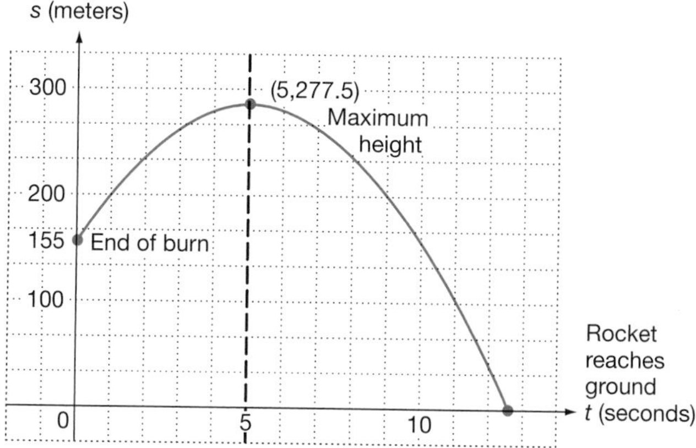

(b) Find when it reaches the ground.

To find when the rocket reaches the ground, we set $s = 0$ in our equation and solve for t.

$$\begin{aligned} -4.9(t-5)^2 + 277.5 &= 0 \\ 4.9(t-5)^2 &= 277.5 \\ (t-5)^2 &= \frac{277.5}{4.9} \\ t - 5 &= \pm\sqrt{\frac{277.5}{4.9}} \\ t - 5 &\approx \pm 7.525 \\ t &\approx 12.525 \qquad \text{t must be nonnegative.} \end{aligned}$$

We can use a calculator to check 12.525 seconds. Note that this is an approximation for time, so we will probably not find that the height s is *exactly* 0 meters for this value.

$$\begin{aligned} s &= -4.9t^2 + v_0t + h \\ &\approx -4.9(12.525)^2 + 49(12.525) + 155 \qquad \text{Substituting for t, v_0, and h} \\ &\approx -4.9(156.87563) + 613.725 + 155 \\ &\approx 0.034413 \end{aligned}$$

Our value for s is close to zero, so our approximation is reasonable. The rocket will reach the ground about 12.525 seconds after the end of the burn.

Try This

d. A ball is thrown upward from the top of a cliff 12 meters high, at a velocity of 2.8 m/sec. Find

(1) its maximum height and when it is attained.
(2) when it reaches the ground.

Extra Help On the Web

Look for worked-out examples at the Prentice Hall Web site.
www.phschool.com

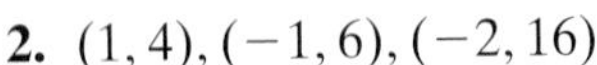

9-8 Exercises

A

Find the quadratic function that fits each set of data points.

1. $(1, 4), (-1, -2), (2, 13)$

2. $(1, 4), (-1, 6), (-2, 16)$

3.

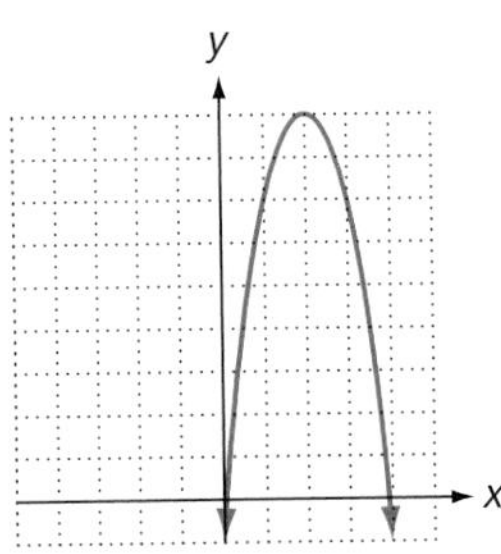

4.

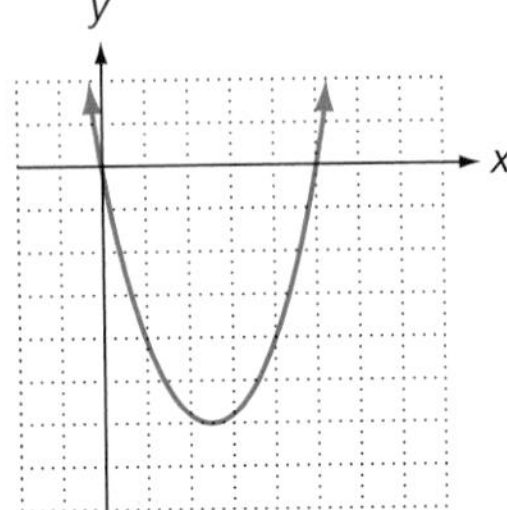

5. A business earns \$38 in the first day, \$66 in the second day, and \$86 in the third day. The manager plots the points $(1, 38)$, $(2, 66)$, and $(3, 86)$.

a. Find a quadratic function that fits the data.

b. Using the function, predict the earnings for the fourth day.

6. A business earns \$1000 in the first month, \$2000 in the second month, and \$8000 in the third month. The manager plots the points $(1, 1000)$, $(2, 2000)$, and $(3, 8000)$.

a. Find a quadratic function that fits the data.

b. Using the function, predict the earnings for the fourth month.

7. a. Find a quadratic function that fits the following data.

Travel speed in km/h	Number of daytime accidents
50	130
70	130
90	200

b. Use the function to calculate the number of accidents that occur at 60 km/h.

8. a. Find a quadratic function that fits the following data.

Travel speed in km/h	Number of nighttime accidents
40	250
60	265
80	430

b. Use the function to calculate the number of accidents that occur at 90 km/h.

9. A rocket is fired upward. At the end of the burn it has an upward velocity of 245 m/sec and is 14.7 m high. Find

a. its maximum height and when it is attained.

b. when it reaches the ground.

10. A rocket is fired upward. At the end of the burn it has an upward velocity of 147 m/sec and is 73.5 m high. Find

a. its maximum height and when it is attained.

b. when it reaches the ground.

B

11. Use the quadratic function you found in Exercise 7 to find the number of daytime accidents for 80 km/h. Then find another travel speed that has the same number of accidents.

12. Use the quadratic function you found in Exercise 8 to find the number of nighttime accidents for 70 km/h. Then find another travel speed that has the same number of accidents.

13. A rocket is fired upward from a mine shaft. At the end of the burn it has an upward velocity of 196 m/sec and is 29.4 m below ground level. Find
   a. its maximum height and when it is attained.
   b. when it first reaches ground level.
   c. when it falls to Earth.

14. *Write a Convincing Argument* Explain why there is no quadratic function that will fit the data points $(2, 5)$, $(-8, 5)$, and $(10, 5)$.

Challenge

15. *Mathematical Reasoning* Let $y = (x - p)^2 + (x - q)^2$ where p and q are constants. For what value of x is y a minimum?

16. A farmer wants to enclose two adjacent rectangular regions next to a river, one for sheep and one for cattle. No fencing will be used next to the river, but 60 m of fencing will be used. What is the area of the largest region that can be enclosed?

17. A city council is planning to use 200 yd of fencing to enclose a park for physically challenged citizens. The park will be adjacent to the community center and will have two rectangular areas connected by a bridge crossing a creek that is 10 yd from the building. The area next to the community center can have a length no greater than the length of the building, which is 75 yd, but the area across the creek may have any dimensions. No fencing will be used next to the creek. What is the total area of the largest park they may enclose? Be sure to use a drawing.

Wheelchair access to the community center in Exercise 17 is by means of a ramp that runs alongside the building for 20 ft, measured at the base. If the ramp is 20.5 ft in length, how many feet from the ground is the top of the ramp?

Mixed Review

Test for symmetry with respect to the x-axis and the y-axis.

18. $y^3 = 2x^5 + 1$ **19.** $y^2 = 2x^3 + 1$ **20.** $y = x^2$ **21.** $x^2 + y^2 = 1$ *9-1*

For each of the following functions graph the function, find the vertex, and find the line of symmetry.

22. $f(x) = 3x^2$ **23.** $f(x) = (x - 2)^2$ **24.** $f(x) = 3(x + 1)^2$ *9-5*

Solve. **25.** $x - 16\sqrt{x} + 64 = 0$ **26.** $x^4 - 5x^2 - 36 = 0$ *7-6, 8-5*

27. Find an equation of variation where y varies directly as x and inversely as z, and $y = 6$ when $x = 16$ and $z = 8$. *8-7*

Preparing for Standardized Tests

Odd and Even Problems

Another type of problem found on standardized tests is the "odd and even" problem. Here you are told that a given variable represents an odd or an even number, and you are asked to make a decision about one or more expressions involving that variable.

EXAMPLE 1

If n is odd, then which of the following could be even?

(A) $3n + 4$ **(B)** $5n + 2$ **(C)** $3n + 9$ **(D)** $6n + 3$ **(E)** $2n + 3$

A problem like this could be solved using the facts below.

odd + odd = even	odd × odd = odd
odd + even = odd	odd × even = even
even + odd = odd	even × odd = even
even + even = even	even × even = even

It is better, however, to develop specific shortcuts and strategies to arrive at answers quickly and easily.

Using the strategy *Look for a Pattern*, we discover that since the facts above are true for all integers, they are true for particular odds and evens. Therefore, a good beginning strategy is

if an unknown number is odd, use 1
if an unknown number is even, use 0 or 2

Applying the strategy to the example above, since n is odd, we will let $n = 1$. Then the problem could be solved as shown.

(A) $3n + 4 = 3(1) + 4 = 7$
(B) $5n + 2 = 5(1) + 2 = 7$
(C) $3n + 9 = 3(1) + 9 = 12$
(D) $6n + 3 = 6(1) + 3 = 9$
(E) $2n + 3 = 2(1) + 3 = 5$

The answer is **C** because the other four answers are odd and only 12 is even.

EXAMPLE 2

If x is a nonnegative integer, which of the following *must* be an odd integer?

(A) $x^3 + 2$ **(B)** $5x + 4$ **(C)** $4x + 2$ **(D)** $2x^2 + 1$ **(E)** $x^2 + x + 6$

Applying our strategy here means that since x can be either odd or even, we will check each answer for both cases. As soon as an answer becomes "even" we can go on to the next answer.

(A) $x^3 + 2 = (0)^3 + 2 = 2$
(B) $5x + 4 = 5(0) + 4 = 4$
(C) $4x + 2 = 4(0) + 2 = 2$
(D) $2x^2 + 1 = 2(0)^2 + 1 = 1$
$2x^2 + 1 = 2(1)^2 + 1 = 3$

At this point, we know **D** is correct because both answers are odd. To confirm our strategy, let's try **E.**

(E) $x^2 + x + 6 = (1)^2 + 1 + 6 = 8$

Problems

1. If a is an odd integer and b is an even integer, which of the following *could* be an odd integer?

(A) $2a + b$ **(B)** $4a - b$ **(C)** $a + 3b$ **(D)** $b \times b$ **(E)** $\frac{a}{2} + \frac{b}{2}$

2. If a and b are nonnegative odd integers, which of the following *must* be true?

I. $\frac{a + b}{2}$ is even.
II. $a + b$ is a multiple of 2.
III. $a - b$ is even.

(A) II only **(B)** II and III only **(C)** I and II only
(D) I and III only **(E)** I, II, and III

3. For any integer n, which of the following represents three consecutive odd integers?

(A) $n + 3, n + 5, n + 7$
(B) $n, n + 1, n + 2$
(C) $n, 3n, 5n$
(D) $2n, 2n + 2, 2n + 4$
(E) $2n + 1, 2n + 3, 2n + 5$

4. For what whole number w is the sum of w, $w + 1$, and $w + 2$ even?

(A) for all odd numbers w **(B)** for no w **(C)** for all w
(D) for all even numbers w **(E)** for some w, but for none of the sets above

5. If $3x + y = 18$ and x is an even positive integer, which of the following *must* be true?

I. y is an odd integer.
II. y is an even integer.
III. y is a multiple of 6.

(A) I only **(B)** II only **(C)** III only
(D) I and III only **(E)** II and III only

6. If $5x - 1$ is an even integer, which of the following represents the next consecutive even integer?

(A) $6x + 1$ **(B)** $5x$ **(C)** $6x - 1$ **(D)** $5x + 1$ **(E)** $6x$

Application

Merchandising

When merchandising experts set a selling price for a new product, their goal is to maximize profits. They begin by estimating the demand for the product at various selling prices. Generally, the demand for a given product will decrease as the selling price increases.

EXAMPLE

The following chart shows the estimated demand for a bicycle, given some possible selling prices.

Selling Price	Estimated Yearly Demand
100	5000
180	4000
260	3000
500	0

If a store wants to sell the \$500 mountain bike at a discount of 15%, what price should be marked on the retail price tag?

Determine the selling price that maximizes yearly profits, the demand at that price, and the maximum profit.

Suppose it costs \$100 to make one bicycle. This means the company cannot consider any selling price less than \$100. If we plot the data points given above, we will find that they lie on a straight line. The equation of the line is $d = -12.5s + 6250$, where d is the demand and s is the selling price. We find a selling price s that maximizes yearly profits.

Let P represent yearly profits. Then

$$\begin{aligned} P &= (\text{Gross receipts}) - (\text{Production costs}) \\ &= s \cdot d - 100d \\ &= d(s - 100) \\ &= (-12.5s + 6250)(s - 100) \quad \text{Substituting } -12.5s + 6250 \text{ for } d \\ &= -12.5s^2 + 7500s - 625{,}000 \end{aligned}$$

This is a quadratic function whose graph opens downward and thus has a maximum value.

We complete the square to find the maximum value.

$$\begin{aligned} P &= -12.5(s^2 - 600s) - 625{,}000 \\ &= -12.5[s^2 - 600s + (300)^2] - 625{,}000 + 12.5(300)^2 \\ &= -12.5(s - 300)^2 - 625{,}000 + 1{,}125{,}000 \\ &= -12.5(s - 300)^2 + 500{,}000 \end{aligned}$$

This means that profit P will be maximized for a selling price s of \$300. The maximum profit is thus \$500,000. The demand is $-12.5(300) + 6250$, or 2500 bicycles.

Checking,

$$\begin{aligned} P &= s \cdot d - 100d \\ &= 300(2500) - 100(2500) \\ &= 200(2500) \\ &= 500{,}000 \end{aligned}$$

Problems

1. For a new printer, the marketing experts have estimated the following:

Selling Price	Estimated Yearly Demand
\$100	7000
\$300	5000
\$600	2000
\$800	0

The production cost per item is \$40. Determine a selling price that maximizes the yearly profits, the demand at that price, and the maximum profit.

2. The production cost for the printer in problem 1 rises to \$60. What selling price will now maximize profits? What will the demand be, and what will the maximum profit be?

3. Sciact Corporation's marketing experts have estimated the demand for a new product as follows:

Selling Price	Estimated Yearly Demand
\$20	825
\$40	525
\$60	225

The production cost per item is \$75. Determine a selling price that maximizes the yearly profits, the demand at that price, and the maximum profit. What other decisions should be made about the profit?

9 Chapter Wrap Up

Key Terms

data points (p. 414)
even function (p. 388)
image of a point (p. 384)
line of symmetry (p. 384)
maximum value of a quadratic function (p. 404)
minimum value of a quadratic function (p. 404)
odd function (p. 388)
parabola (p. 400)
quadratic function (p. 400)
reflections (p. 384)
standard form (p. 408)
symmetry with respect to a line (p. 384)
symmetry with respect to a point (p. 386)
transformation (p. 391)
translation (p. 391)
vertex of a parabola (p. 401)
x-intercepts of a quadratic function (p. 412)

9-1

A graph is **symmetric with respect to the y-axis** if and only if replacing x with $-x$ produces an equivalent equation.

A graph is **symmetric with respect to the x-axis** if and only if replacing y with $-y$ produces an equivalent equation.

Test for symmetry with respect to the x-axis and the y-axis.

1. $x^2 + y^2 = 4$ **2.** $x = 3$ **3.** $x^3 = y^3 - y$

4. $x^2 = y + 3$ **5.** $x - y = 1$ **6.** $3 - x^2 = y$

A graph of a relation defined by an equation is **symmetric with respect to the origin** if and only if replacing x with $-x$ and replacing y with $-y$ produce an equivalent equation.

Test for symmetry with respect to the origin.

7. $x + y = 3$ **8.** $y = x^3$ **9.** $x = 2$

10. $y = -4$ **11.** $x^2 - y^2 = 1$ **12.** $1 - y^3 = x$

9-2

In an equation of a relation, replacing y with $y - k$, where k is a constant, **translates** the graph vertically a distance of $|k|$. If k is positive, the translation is upward. If k is negative, the translation is downward.

In an equation of a relation, replacing x with $x - h$, where h is a constant, translates the graph horizontally a distance of $|h|$. If h is positive, the translation is to the right. If h is negative, the translation is to the left.

Consider the graph of $y = |x|$.

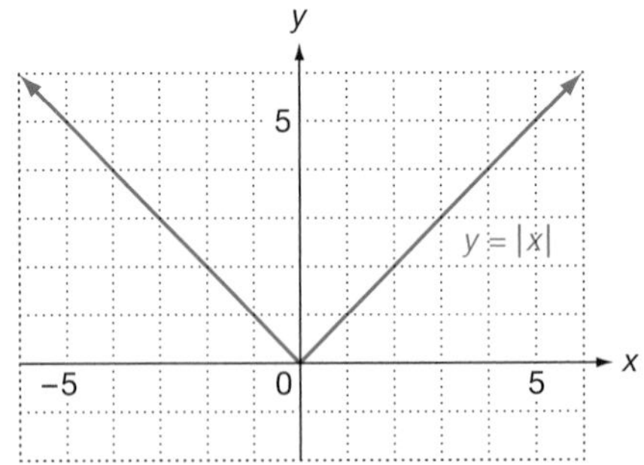

Sketch the graphs of the following by translating.

13. $y = |x| - 1$ **14.** $y = |x - 2|$ **15.** $y + 2 = |x - 1|$

9-3

In an equation of a relation, dividing y by a constant c changes the graph in these ways.

If $|c| > 1$, the graph is **stretched vertically.**
If $|c| < 1$, the graph is **shrunk vertically.**
If $c < 0$, the graph is **reflected across the x-axis.**

In an equation of a relation, dividing x by a constant d changes the graph in these ways.

If $|d| > 1$, the graph is **stretched horizontally.**
If $|d| < 1$, the graph is **shrunk horizontally.**
If $d < 0$, the graph is **reflected across the y-axis.**

Consider the graph of $y = |x|$ above. Sketch graphs of the following by stretching or shrinking.

16. $y = 2|x|$ **17.** $y = |2x|$ **18.** $y = -|x|$

19. Sketch $y - 2 = \frac{1}{3}|x + 1|$ by transforming $y = |x|$.

Internet Activity On the Web

Look for extension problems for this chapter at the Prentice Hall Web site. www.phschool.com

9-4

If a quadratic function is written in the form $f(x) = a(x - h)^2$, then the **axis of symmetry** is $x = h$ and the vertex is $(h, 0)$.

For each function graph the function, find the vertex, and find the line of symmetry.

20. $f(x) = -2x^2$ **21.** $f(x) = \frac{1}{4}x^2$

22. $f(x) = -2(x + 1)^2$ **23.** $f(x) = 3(x - 2)^2$

9-5

For the quadratic function $f(x) = a(x - h)^2 + k$, the line of symmetry is $x = h$, and the vertex is (h, k). If $a > 0$, there is a **minimum value** k. If $a < 0$, there is a **maximum value** k.

For each function graph the function, find the vertex, line of symmetry, and find the minimum or maximum value.

24. $f(x) = -2(x + 1)^2 - 2$ **25.** $f(x) = \frac{1}{2}(x - 1)^2 + 5$

26. $f(x) = -3(x + 2)^2 + 1$

9-6

Completing the square is useful in changing a quadratic function to **standard form** $f(x) = a(x - h)^2 + k$.

For each function find standard form.

27. $f(x) = x^2 - 8x + 5$

28. $f(x) = -\frac{1}{2}x^2 + 6x - 16$

29. $f(x) = -2x^2 - 4x + 3$

The vertex will be either the minimum or maximum value of the graph of a function.

30. What is the maximum product of two numbers whose sum is 32? What numbers yield this product?

31. What is the minimum product of two numbers whose difference is 8? What are the numbers?

9-7

To find the ***x*-intercepts** of a quadratic function $f(x) = ax^2 + bx + c$, solve the equation $0 = ax^2 + bx + c$.

Find the x-intercepts, if they exist.

32. $f(x) = -2x^2 - 4x + 3$

33. $f(x) = -x^2 - 2x + 4$

34. $f(x) = x^2 - 4x + 3$

9-8

A quadratic function that fits three **data points** can be found by substituting three times (using the three data points) into $f(x) = ax^2 + bx + c$, thereby creating a system of three equations with three unknowns.

Find the quadratic function that fits each set of data points.

35. $(1, -3), (-1, 5), (2, -13)$

36. $(1, 2), (0, 5), (-1, 14)$

37. $(3, 7), (4, 8), (5, 7)$

38. A baseball is released from a height of 7 feet, thrown towards the catcher. After it travels 20 ft, its height is 9 ft; after it travels 40 ft, its height is 7 ft.

a. Fit a quadratic function to the data.

b. Predict the height of the baseball after it travels 60 ft.

9 Chapter Assessment

Test for symmetry with respect to the x-axis and the y-axis.

1. $y = 4$

2. $y^2 = x^2 + 8$

3. $x^2 + y^2 = 9$

4. $x = 5$

5. $x^5 = y^5 - y$

6. $x^7 = y^4$

Test for symmetry with respect to the origin.

7. $x + y = 7$

8. $y = 2x^3$

9. $x = 4$

Consider the graph of $y = |x|$.

Sketch the graphs of the following by translating.

10. $y = |x| + 2$

11. $y = |x + 3|$

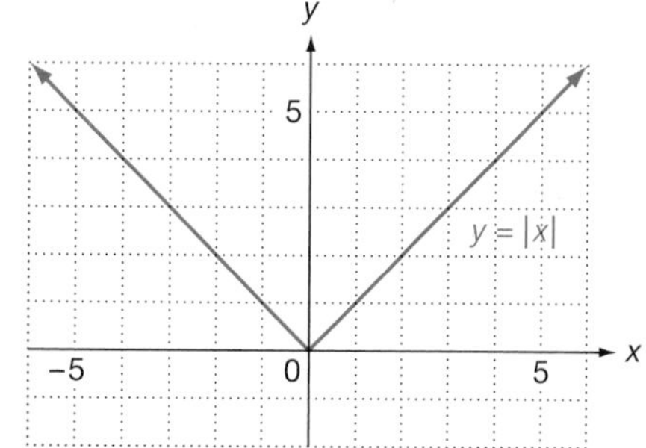

For each function, graph the function, find the vertex, and find the line of symmetry.

12. $f(x) = 2x^2$

13. $f(x) = 2(x - 5)^2$

For each of the following, graph the functions, find the vertex, find the line of symmetry, and find the maximum or minimum value.

14. $f(x) = 2(x - 5)^2 - 4$

15. $f(x) = -3(x + 1)^2 - 2$

For each function, find standard form and then find the vertex, line of symmetry, and the maximum or minimum value.

16. $f(x) = -x^2 - 6x + 7$

17. $f(x) = 2x^2 - 10x - 7$

18. What is the maximum product of two numbers whose sum is 40? What numbers yield this product?

Find the x-intercepts, if they exist.

19. $f(x) = 2x^2 - 5x + 8$

20. $f(x) = -x^2 - 2x + 2$

21. While Keisha made popcorn, she found 90 kernels popped during the third minute, 180 during the fifth minute, and 30 during the seventh minute.

a. Find a quadratic function that fits the data.

b. Using the function, calculate the number of kernels that popped during the fourth minute.

22. A ball is thrown upward from a rooftop 27 meters high at a velocity of 9.8 m/sec. Find

a. its maximum height and when it is attained.

b. when it reaches the ground.

Challenge

23. The sum of the lengths of the base and the height of a triangle is 24 cm. Find the dimensions for which the area is a maximum, and find the maximum area.

CHAPTER 10

What You'll Learn in Chapter 10

- How to find the length and midpoint of a segment
- How to find the equation of a conic section (a circle, an ellipse, a hyperbola, or a parabola) given certain characteristics
- How to find the coordinates of certain points or equations of certain lines related to a conic section, given its equation
- How to find the standard form of the equation of a conic section by completing the square
- How to graph a conic section
- How to identify conic sections from their equations or graphs
- How to solve systems of equations that involve equations of the second degree

Skills & Concepts You Need for Chapter 10

7-1, 7-2 Simplify.

1. $\sqrt{169}$

2. $\sqrt{48}$

8-1 Complete the square.

3. $x^2 - 4x$

4. $x^2 + 3x$

3-2, 9-4 Graph.

5. $y = 3x - 1$

6. $y = 3x^2$

4-2 Solve.

7. $6x + 3y = -12$
$2x - y = 6$

8. $3x - 5y = 44$
$y = 4x - 2$

5-7, 8-1, 8-3 Solve.

9. $x^2 - 9x + 14 = 0$

10. $x^2 = 5$

Equations of Second Degree

All planetary bodies travel in elliptical orbits. Jupiter, shown here with two moons visible, has sixteen moons, four of which (Europa, Ganymede, Callisto, and Io) are called Galilean satellites after their discoverer, Galileo Galilei, who first observed them in 1610. They are easily visible from Earth with a small telescope. Before accurate seagoing clocks were invented, the orbits of these four moons were used by mariners to determine their longitude. You will learn more about ellipses in Lesson 10-3.

10-1 Coordinate Geometry

What You'll Learn

1. To find the distance between two points in a plane
2. To find the coordinates of the midpoint of a segment, given the endpoints of the segment

. . . And Why

To establish the forms of the equations of the conic sections

PART 1 Finding Distances

Objective: Use the distance formula to find the distance between any two points in the plane.

The **distance formula** can be used to find the distance between two points when we know the coordinates of the points.

Theorem 10-1

The Distance Formula

The distance between any two points (x_1, y_1) and (x_2, y_2) is given by

$$d = \sqrt{(x_1 - x_2)^2 + (y_1 - y_2)^2}.$$

Proof of Theorem 10-1

We prove this theorem for the case where the points are not on a horizontal or vertical line.

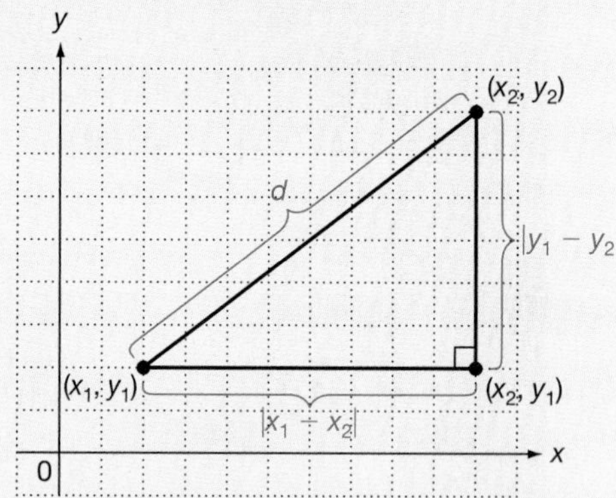

Consider any two points (x_1, y_1) and (x_2, y_2), where $x_1 \neq x_2$ and $y_1 \neq y_2$. These points are vertices of a right triangle as shown. The other vertex is (x_2, y_1). The legs of the triangle have lengths $|x_1 - x_2|$, and $|y_1 - y_2|$. By the Pythagorean theorem, $d^2 = |x_1 - x_2|^2 + |y_1 - y_2|^2$. Since squares of numbers are never negative, $d^2 = (x_1 - x_2)^2 + (y_1 - y_2)^2$. Finding the principal square root, we have $d = \sqrt{(x_1 - x_2)^2 + (y_1 - y_2)^2}$.

EXAMPLE 1 Find the distance between the points (8, 7) and (3, −5).

We substitute the coordinates into the distance formula.

$$d = \sqrt{(8 - 3)^2 + [7 - (-5)]^2}$$
$$= \sqrt{25 + 144} = \sqrt{169} = 13$$

Try This Find the distance between the points.

a. $(-5, 3)$ and $(2, -7)$ **b.** $(3, 3)$ and $(-3, -3)$

PART 2 Midpoints of Segments

Objective: Find the coordinates of the midpoint of a segment, given the coordinates of the endpoints.

The coordinates of the **midpoint of a segment** can be found by averaging the coordinates of the endpoints. We can use the distance formula to verify a formula for finding the coordinates of the midpoint of a segment when the coordinates of the endpoints are known.

Theorem 10-2

The Midpoint Formula

If the coordinates of the endpoints of a segment are (x_1, y_1) and (x_2, y_2), then the coordinates of the midpoint are $\left(\frac{x_1 + x_2}{2}, \frac{y_1 + y_2}{2}\right)$

Quick Review

Using subscripts is another way of distinguishing one variable from another.

EXAMPLE 2 Find the coordinates of the midpoint of the segment with endpoints $(-3, 5)$ and $(4, -7)$.

Using the midpoint formula, we get $\left(\frac{-3 + 4}{2}, \frac{5 + (-7)}{2}\right)$, or $\left(\frac{1}{2}, -1\right)$.

Try This Find the coordinates of the midpoints of the segments having the following endpoints.

c. $(-2, 1)$ and $(5, -6)$ **d.** $(9, -6)$ and $(9, -4)$

10-1 Exercises

Look for worked-out examples at the Prentice Hall Web site.
www.phschool.com

A

Find the distance between the points.

1. $(-3, -2)$ and $(1, 1)$ **2.** $(5, 9)$ and $(-1, 6)$ **3.** $(0, -7)$ and $(3, -4)$

4. $(\sqrt{2}, \sqrt{3})$ and $(0, 0)$ **5.** $(5, 2k)$ and $(-3, k)$ **6.** $(0, 0)$ and (a, b)

7. $(\sqrt{a}, \sqrt{b})$ and $(-\sqrt{a}, \sqrt{b})$ **8.** $(c - d, c + d)$ and $(c + d, d - c)$

Find the coordinates of the midpoint of the segments given the endpoints.

9. $(-4, 7)$ and $(3, -9)$ **10.** $(4, 5)$ and $(6, -7)$ **11.** $(2, -5)$ and $(-9, -10)$

12. $(8, -4)$ and $(-3, 9)$ **13.** $(2, 2)$ and $(6, 6)$ **14.** $(-2, 0)$ and $(3, 0)$

15. (a, b) and $(a, -b)$ **16.** $(-c, d)$ and (c, d)

B

Multi-Step Problem The converse of the Pythagorean theorem is true. That is, if the sides of a triangle have lengths a, b, and c, and $a^2 + b^2 = c^2$, then the triangle is a right triangle. Determine whether the points whose coordinates are given are vertices of a right triangle.

17. $(9, 6), (-1, 2), (1, -3)$ **18.** $(-8, -5), (6, 1), (-4, 5)$

19. *Mathematical Reasoning* Prove that Theorem 10-1 holds when two points are on either a vertical or a horizontal line.

20. *Mathematical Reasoning* Prove the midpoint formula, Theorem 10-2.

21. Prove that the diagonals of a rectangle bisect each other. (Hint: Locate the rectangle on the x- and y-axes of a graph as shown.)

22. Find the point on the x-axis that is equidistant from the points whose coordinates are $(1, 3)$ and $(8, 4)$.

23. Find the point on the y-axis that is equidistant from the points whose coordinates are $(-2, 0)$ and $(4, 6)$.

24. *Critical Thinking* A segment has an endpoint at (x_1, y_1) and a midpoint at (x_m, y_m).

a. What are the coordinates of the other endpoint?

b. Find the other endpoint for a segment with an endpoint $(3, -7)$ and midpoint $(-7, 3)$.

Challenge

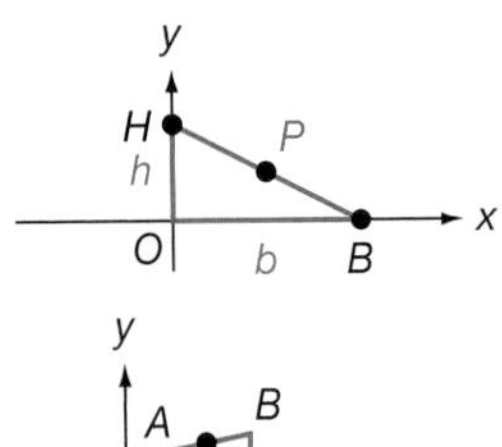

25. Consider any right triangle with base b and height h, situated as shown. Show that the midpoint P of the hypotenuse is equidistant from the three vertices of the triangle.

26. Consider any quadrilateral situated as shown. Show that the segments joining the midpoints of the sides, in order as shown, form a parallelogram.

27. *Write a Convincing Argument* Show that the distance between points with coordinates (a, b) and (c, d) is the same as the distance between points with the following coordinates, and write an argument to convince a classmate that this is true.

a. (a, d) and (c, b) **b.** (b, a) and (d, c) **c.** (b, c) and (d, a)

Mixed Review

Solve. **28.** $x(x + 7) = 4(x + 10)$ **29.** $m^2 + 5m = -6$ *8-1*

Test for symmetry with respect to the origin. **30.** $y = |x| + 1$

31. $5y^4 - 2x^2 = 1$ **32.** $x - y = 9$ **33.** $3n^2 - 4m = n$ *9-1*

Complete the square. **34.** $x^2 - 6x$ **35.** $m^2 + 7.4m$ **36.** $c^2 - c$ *8-1*

Conic Sections: Circles

10-2

Introducing the Concept: Conic Sections

Graph each equation.

$$x^2 + y^2 = 16 \qquad x^2 + 4y^2 = 16 \qquad x^2 - y^2 = 16 \qquad x^2 + y = 16$$

Study and contrast the graphs. For each successive graph, explain why it might differ from the first graph.

A **cone** is formed by rotating one of two distinct, non-perpendicular, intersecting lines about the other. The point of intersection is the **vertex** of the cone. Any position of the rotating line is an **element** of the cone.

The intersection of any plane with a cone is called a **conic section.** Some conic sections are shown below.

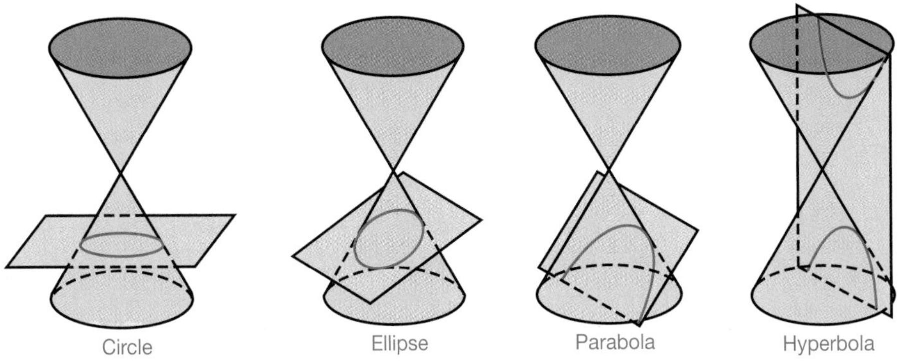

In this chapter we will study certain equations of second degree and their graphs. Graphs of most such equations are conic sections.

What You'll Learn

1. To find the equation of a circle given the radius and the coordinates of the center of the circle
2. To find the radius and the coordinates of the center of a circle, given the equation of the circle
3. To use the technique of completing the square to find the radius and coordinates of the center of a circle

. . . And Why

To solve problems involving circles

PART 1 Equations of Circles

Objective: Find the equation of a circle, given the coordinates of the center and the radius.

Some equations of second degree have graphs that are circles.

Definition

A **circle** is the set of all points in a plane that are at a constant distance, the **radius,** from a fixed point in that plane. The fixed point is the **center of the circle.**

We first consider an equation for a circle centered at the origin.

Theorem 10-3

The equation, in standard form, of the circle centered at the origin with **radius** r is $x^2 + y^2 = r^2$.

Depending on the angle a beam of light makes with a plane surface, the light pattern may be circular, ellipsoidal, parabolic, or hyperbolic.

Proof of Theorem 10-3

We must prove that a point (x, y) is on the circle centered at the origin with radius r if and only if $x^2 + y^2 = r^2$. To prove a sentence, *P if and only if Q*, we must prove *If P, then Q*, and *If Q, then P*. Thus, there are two parts to the proof.

1. Assume (x, y) is on the circle. Then it is a distance r from $(0, 0)$. By the distance formula, we get the following.

$$r = \sqrt{(x - 0)^2 + (y - 0)^2}$$
$$r^2 = x^2 + y^2$$

We have now shown that if (x, y) is on the circle, then $x^2 + y^2 = r^2$.

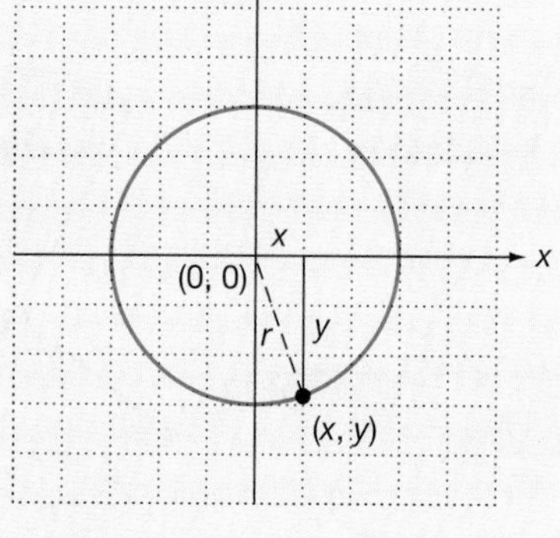

2. Now assume $x^2 + y^2 = r^2$ is true for a point (x, y). This can be expressed as

$$(x - 0)^2 + (y - 0)^2 = r^2.$$

Finding the principal square root, we have

$$\sqrt{(x - 0)^2 + (y - 0)^2} = r.$$

Thus, the distance from (x, y) to $(0, 0)$ is r, so (x, y) is on the circle. We have now shown that if $x^2 + y^2 = r^2$, then (x, y) is on the circle.

Thus, the two parts of the proof together show that the equation $x^2 + y^2 = r^2$ gives *all* the points of the circle, *and no others.*

EXAMPLE 1 Find an equation of a circle with center at $(0, 0)$ and radius $\sqrt{5}$.

$x^2 + y^2 = r^2$ — Standard form for a circle centered at the origin

$x^2 + y^2 = \left(\sqrt{5}\right)^2$ — Substituting $\sqrt{5}$ for r

$x^2 + y^2 = 5$

Consider an equation for a circle with its center anywhere in the coordinate plane.

Theorem 10-4

The equation, in standard form, of a circle with center (h, k) and radius r is $(x - h)^2 + (y - k)^2 = r^2$.

EXAMPLE 2 Find an equation of a circle with center at $(-1, 3)$ and radius $\sqrt{2}$.

$$[x - (-1)]^2 + (y - 3)^2 = (\sqrt{2})^2 \quad \text{Standard form}$$
$$(x + 1)^2 + (y - 3)^2 = 2 \quad \text{Simplifying}$$

Try This Find an equation of a circle with center and radius as given.

a. Center: $(0, 0)$; radius: $\sqrt{6}$ **b.** Center: $(-3, 7)$; radius: 5
c. Center: $(5, -2)$; radius: $\sqrt{3}$ **d.** Center: $(-2, -6)$; radius: $2\sqrt{7}$

PART 2 Finding the Center and Radius

Objective: Find the coordinates of the center and the radius of a circle, given its equation.

EXAMPLE 3 Find the center and radius of $(x - 2)^2 + (y + 3)^2 = 16$. Then graph the circle.

We first write standard form, $(x - 2)^2 + [y - (-3)]^2 = 4^2$. The center is $(2, -3)$ and the radius is 4. We then draw the graph using a compass.

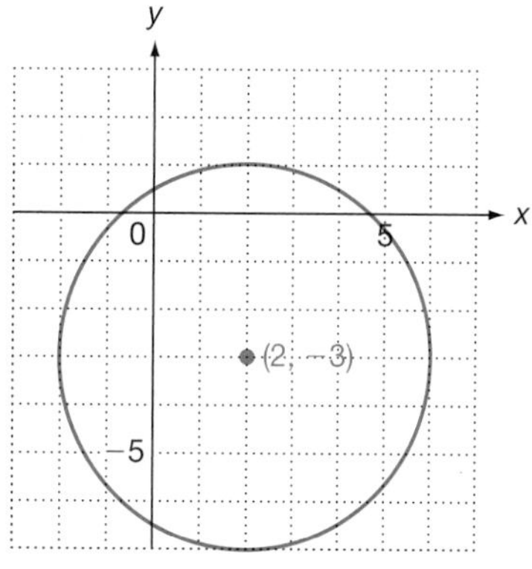

Writing Math

The equation of a circle is frequently referred to as *the circle,* rather than the more formal *the circle whose equation is....*

Try This

e. Find the center and radius of $(x + 1)^2 + (y - 3)^2 = 4$. Then graph the circle.

PART 3 Finding Standard Form by Completing the Square

Objective: Find the coordinates of the center and the radius of a circle by first completing the square.

Completing the square allows us to find the standard form for the equation of a circle.

EXAMPLE 4 Find the center and radius of $x^2 + y^2 + 8x - 2y + 15 = 0$.

We complete the squares to obtain standard form.

$$(x^2 + 8x \qquad) + (y^2 - 2y \qquad) = -15$$
$$(x^2 + 8x + 16) + (y^2 - 2y \qquad) = -15 + 16 \quad \text{Completing the square}$$
$$(x^2 + 8x + 16) + (y^2 - 2y + 1) = -15 + 16 + 1 \quad \text{Completing the square}$$
$$(x + 4)^2 + (y - 1)^2 = 2 \quad \text{Simplifying}$$

In standard form, the equation is $(x - (-4))^2 + (y - 1)^2 = (\sqrt{2})^2$. The center is $(-4, 1)$, the radius is $\sqrt{2}$.

Try This

f. Find the center and radius of the circle $x^2 + y^2 - 14x + 4y - 11 = 0$.
g. Find the center and radius of the circle $x^2 + y^2 - 12x - 8y + 27 = 0$.

Extra Help On the Web

Look for worked-out examples at the Prentice Hall Web site.
www.phschool.com

10-2 Exercises

A

Find an equation of a circle with center and radius as given.

1. Center: $(0, 0)$; radius: 7
2. Center: $(0, 0)$; radius: π
3. Center: $(-2, 7)$; radius: $\sqrt{5}$
4. Center: $(5, 6)$; radius: $2\sqrt{3}$

Mental Math Find the center and radius of each circle.

5. $(x + 1)^2 + (y + 3)^2 = 4$
6. $(x - 2)^2 + (y + 3)^2 = 1$
7. $(x - 8)^2 + (y + 3)^2 = 40$
8. $(x + 5)^2 + (y - 1)^2 = 75$
9. $x^2 + y^2 = 2$
10. $x^2 + y^2 = 3$
11. $(x - 5)^2 + y^2 = \frac{1}{4}$
12. $x^2 + (y - 1)^2 = \frac{1}{25}$

Find the center and radius of each circle. Then graph the circle.

13. $x^2 + y^2 - 8x + 2y + 13 = 0$
14. $x^2 + y^2 + 6x + 4y + 12 = 0$
15. $x^2 + y^2 - 4x = 0$
16. $x^2 + y^2 + 10y - 75 = 0$

B

Find an equation of a circle satisfying the given conditions.

17. Center $(0, 0)$, containing $(-3, 4)$
18. Center $(3, -2)$, containing $(11, -2)$
19. Center $(2, 4)$, tangent (touching at one point) to the x-axis
20. Center $(-3, -2)$, tangent to the y-axis
21. For the circle with center $(1, 2)$ and radius 9, find the x- and y-intercepts.
22. Find an equation of a circle such that the endpoints of a diameter are $(5, -3)$ and $(-3, 7)$.

23. For the circle with equation $(x - 2)^2 + (y + 3)^2 = 9$, find the x- and y-intercepts.

24. A **unit circle** is a circle with radius of 1. Determine whether each of the following points lies on the unit circle $x^2 + y^2 = 1$.

a. $(0, -1)$ **b.** $\left(\frac{\sqrt{3}}{2}, -\frac{1}{2}\right)$ **c.** $(\sqrt{2} + \sqrt{3}, 0)$ **d.** $\left(\frac{\pi}{4}, \frac{4}{\pi}\right)$

25. ***Mathematical Reasoning*** What is the graph of $x^2 + y^2 = r^2$ when $r = 0$?

26. ***Critical Thinking***

a. Graph $x^2 + y^2 = 4$. Is this relation a function?

b. Graph $y = \sqrt{4 - x^2}$. Find the domain and range. Is this relation a function?

c. Graph $y = -\sqrt{4 - x^2}$. Find the domain and range. Is this relation a function?

d. Solve $x^2 + y^2 = r^2$ for y. Is the result a function?

e. How can a computer program graph $x^2 + y^2 = r^2$ if it can only graph functions?

Challenge

27. Prove that in the diagram at the right, $\angle ABC$ is a right angle. Assume point B is on the circle whose radius is a and whose center is at the origin.

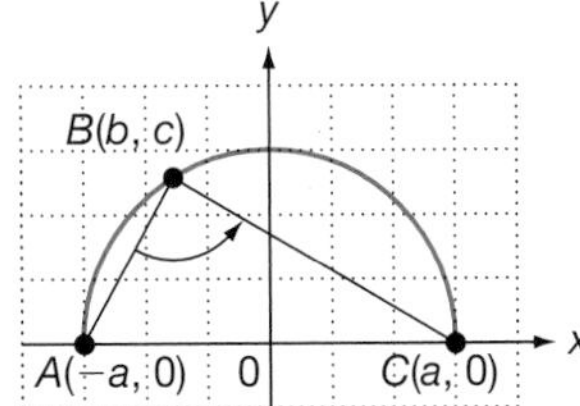

28. Write the equation for a circle that has area 25π and contains the points $(2, 2)$ and $(2, 10)$.

Graph these inequalities.

29. $x^2 + y^2 \leq 16$ **30.** $x^2 + y^2 > 25$ **31.** $(x + 1)^2 + (y - 3)^2 \leq 16$

32. ***Mathematical Reasoning*** Prove Theorem 10-4.

Mixed Review

Test for symmetry with respect to the axes. **33.** $3y^2 = 5x + 1$

34. $y^2 - x^2 = 1$ **35.** $y^3 = 5x^2 - 7$ *9-1*

Find the quadratic function that fits each set of data points.

36. $(1, -2), (-1, 8), (2, -1)$ **37.** $(1, -4), (2, -4), (-1, 8)$ *9-8*

Solve. **38.** $x(2x - 7) + 30 = (x + 9)(x - 2)$ **39.** $2 + \sqrt{x} = x$ *8-5*

40. A parking garage was 84% full. After 37 cars enter and 23 cars leave the garage, it is 91% full. How many cars does the garage hold? *2-9*

10-3 Ellipses

What You'll Learn

1. To find the vertices and foci, and draw a graph of an ellipse, given its equation
2. To use the technique of completing the square to find the center, vertices and foci, and draw a graph of an ellipse

. . . And Why

To solve problems involving ellipses

An interesting attraction found in museums is the whispering gallery. It is elliptical. Persons with their heads at the foci can whisper and hear each other clearly, while persons at other positions cannot hear them. This happens because sound waves emanating from one focus are all reflected to the other focus.

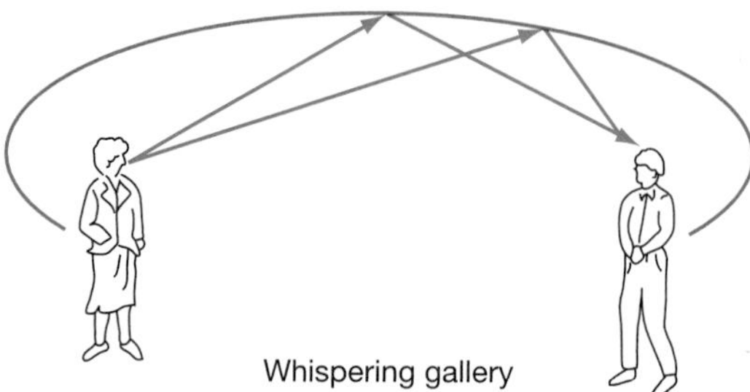

Whispering gallery

PART 1 Equations of Ellipses

Objective: Find the vertices and the foci, and draw a graph of an ellipse, given its equation.

Some equations of second degree have graphs that are ellipses.

Definition

An **ellipse** is the set of all points P in a plane such that the sum of the distances from P to two fixed points F_1 and F_2 is constant. Each fixed point is called a **focus** (plural: **foci**) of the ellipse. r_1 and r_2, shown in the diagram at the right, are called **focal radii.**

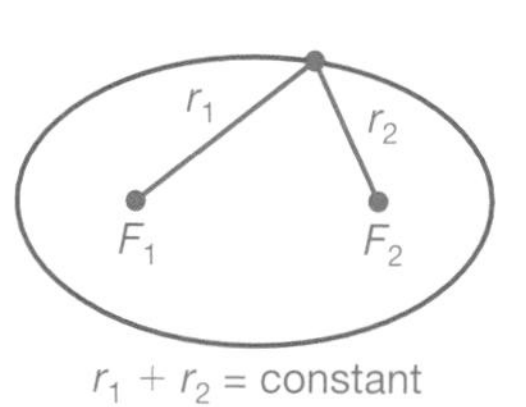

$r_1 + r_2 = \text{constant}$

Ellipses have many other applications. Earth satellites travel around Earth in elliptical orbits. The planets of the solar system travel around the sun in elliptical orbits with the sun located at one focus.

Jupiter, the fifth planet from the sun The orbits of Earth and Jupiter are nearly circular. In millions of kilometers, Earth's mean distance from the sun is 149.6, while Jupiter's is 778.3. About how much longer is Jupiter's orbit than Earth's?

An ellipse has two axes of symmetry. The longer axis is the **major axis,** and the shorter axis is the **minor axis.** The axes are perpendicular at their midpoints, the **center of the ellipse.** The foci lie on the major axis. The ellipse intersects the major and minor axes at the **vertices.**

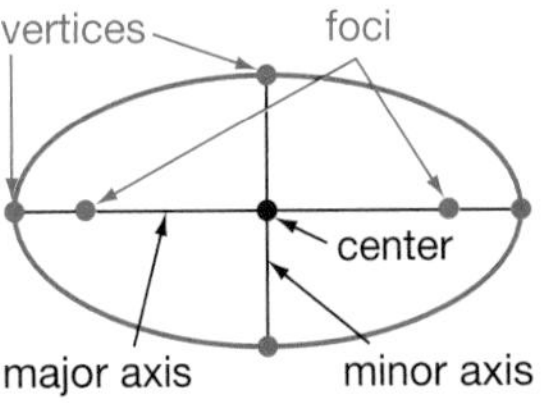

We first consider an equation of an ellipse whose center is at the origin with foci on either the x- or y-axes.

For foci on the x-axis, the ellipse is horizontal.

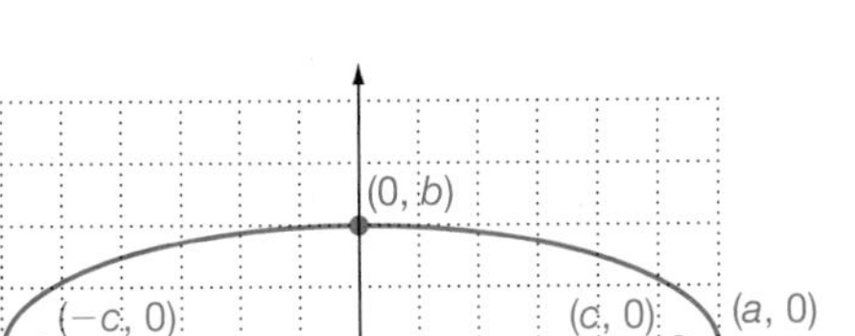

For foci on the y-axis, the ellipse is vertical.

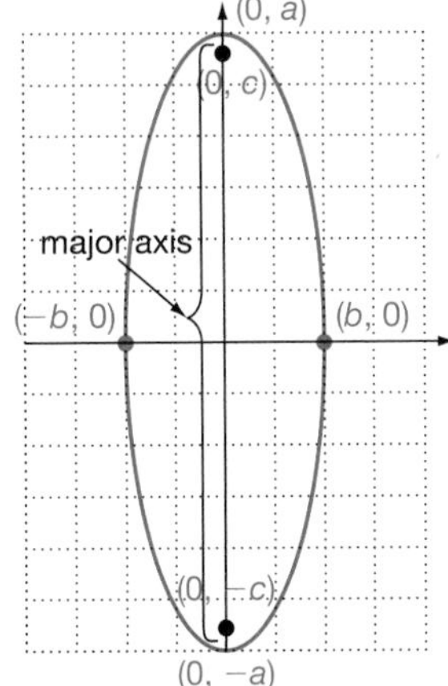

The sum of the focal radii is constant and is equal to the length of the major axis.

In the graph at the right, $r_1 + r_2 = 2a$.

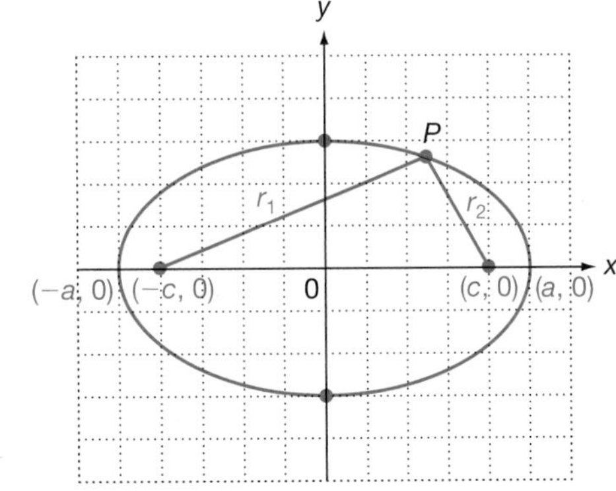

Theorem 10-5

The equation, in standard form, of an ellipse centered at the origin with foci on an axis and c units from the origin is

$$\frac{x^2}{a^2} + \frac{y^2}{b^2} = 1 \text{ (major axis horizontal), or } \frac{x^2}{b^2} + \frac{y^2}{a^2} = 1 \text{ (major axis vertical),}$$

where $c^2 = a^2 - b^2$.

EXAMPLE 1 For the ellipse $x^2 + 16y^2 = 16$, find the vertices and foci, and draw a graph.

We first multiply by $\frac{1}{16}$ to find standard form.

$$\frac{x^2}{16} + \frac{y^2}{1} = 1, \text{ or } \frac{x^2}{4^2} + \frac{y^2}{1^2} = 1$$

Since the denominator for x^2 is larger, the foci are on the x-axis, and the ellipse is horizontal. Thus, $a = 4$ and $b = 1$. The vertices on the major axis are $(-4, 0)$ and $(4, 0)$. The other vertices are $(0, -1)$ and $(0, 1)$.

$c^2 = a^2 - b^2$, so $c^2 = 16 - 1$, $c = \sqrt{15}$, and the foci are $(-\sqrt{15}, 0)$ and $(\sqrt{15}, 0)$.

To graph, we plot the vertices and draw a smooth curve.

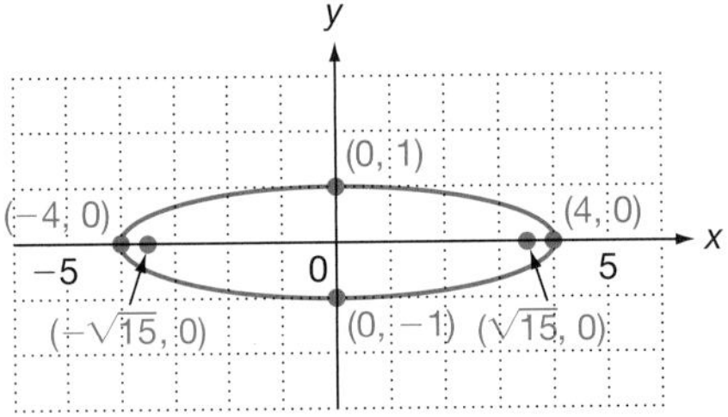

Journal

Graph $\frac{x^2}{4} + \frac{y^2}{9} = 1$ and $\frac{x^2}{9} + \frac{y^2}{4} = 1$ and write a comparison of the two graphs.

Try This For each ellipse find the vertices and foci, and draw a graph.

a. $x^2 + 9y^2 = 9$ **b.** $9x^2 + 25y^2 = 225$ **c.** $2x^2 + 4y^2 = 8$

EXAMPLE 2 For the ellipse $9x^2 + 2y^2 = 18$, find the vertices and foci, and draw a graph.

(a) We first multiply by $\frac{1}{18}$ to find standard form.

$$\frac{x^2}{2} + \frac{y^2}{9} = 1, \text{ or } \frac{x^2}{(\sqrt{2})^2} + \frac{y^2}{3^2} = 1$$

(b) Since the denominator for y^2 is larger, the foci are on the y-axis, and the ellipse is vertical. Thus, $a = 3$ and $b = \sqrt{2}$. The vertices on the major axis are $(0, -3)$ and $(0, 3)$. The other vertices are $(-\sqrt{2}, 0)$ and $(\sqrt{2}, 0)$. $c^2 = a^2 - b^2$, so $c^2 = 9 - 2$, $c = \sqrt{7}$, and the foci are $(0, -\sqrt{7})$ and $(0, \sqrt{7})$.

(c) The graph is at the left.

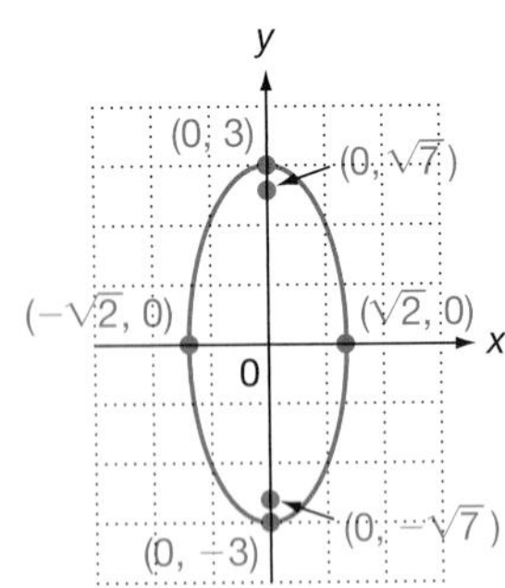

Try This For each ellipse find the center, vertices, and foci, and draw a graph.

d. $9x^2 + y^2 = 9$ **e.** $25x^2 + 9y^2 = 225$

f. $4x^2 + 2y^2 = 8$ **g.** $x^2 + 3y^2 = 48$

PART 2

Complete the Square to Find Standard Form

Objective: Find the center, vertices, and foci, and graph an ellipse by first completing the square.

If the center of an ellipse is not at the origin but at some point (h, k), then the standard form of the equation is as follows.

Theorem 10-6

The equation, in standard form, of an ellipse centered at (h, k) with foci c units from (h, k) is

$$\frac{(x-h)^2}{a^2} + \frac{(y-k)^2}{b^2} = 1, \text{ (major axis horizontal) or}$$

$$\frac{(x-h)^2}{b^2} + \frac{(y-k)^2}{a^2} = 1, \text{ (major axis vertical)}$$

where $c^2 = a^2 - b^2$.

EXAMPLE 3 For the ellipse $16x^2 + 4y^2 + 96x - 8y + 84 = 0$, find the center, vertices, and foci, and draw a graph.

(a) We first complete the square to get standard form.

$$16(x^2 + 6x \qquad) + 4(y^2 - 2y \qquad) = -84$$

$$16(x^2 + 6x + 9) + 4(y^2 - 2y + 1) = -84 + 16 \cdot 9 + 4 \cdot 1$$

Using the addition property

$$16(x^2 + 6x + 9) + 4(y^2 - 2y + 1) = -84 + 144 + 4$$

$$16(x+3)^2 + 4(y-1)^2 = 64$$

$$\frac{16(x+3)^2}{64} + \frac{4(y-1)^2}{64} = 1$$

Multiplying by $\frac{1}{64}$ to make the right side 1

$$\frac{(x+3)^2}{4} + \frac{(y-1)^2}{16} = 1$$

$$\frac{[x-(-3)]^2}{2^2} + \frac{(y-1)^2}{4^2} = 1$$

The center is $(-3, 1)$, $a = 4$, and $b = 2$. The major axis is vertical.

(b) The vertices of $\frac{x^2}{2^2} + \frac{y^2}{4^2} = 1$ are $(2, 0)$, $(-2, 0)$, $(0, 4)$, and $(0, -4)$. Since $c^2 = 16 - 4 = 12$, $c = 2\sqrt{3}$, and its foci are $(0, 2\sqrt{3})$ and $(0, -2\sqrt{3})$. This ellipse is centered at the origin. Thus, we need to translate the ellipse so that the center is at $(-3, 1)$.

(c) The vertices and foci of the translated ellipse are found by translation in the same way that the center has been translated. Thus, the vertices are $(-3 + 2, 1)$, $(-3 - 2, 1)$, $(-3, 1 + 4)$, and $(-3, 1 - 4)$, or, $(-1, 1)$, $(-5, 1)$, $(-3, 5)$, and $(-3, -3)$.
The foci are $\left(-3, 1 + 2\sqrt{3}\right)$ and $\left(-3, 1 - 2\sqrt{3}\right)$.

(d) The graph is at right.

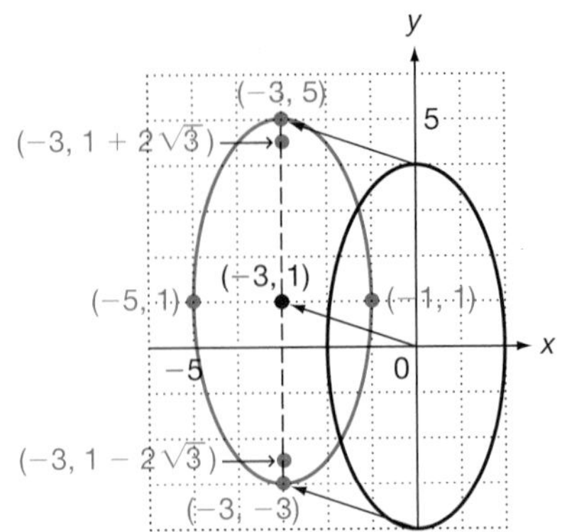

Try This For each ellipse find the center, vertices, and foci, and draw a graph.

h. $25x^2 + 9y^2 + 150x - 36y + 260 = 0$
i. $9x^2 + 25y^2 - 36x + 150y + 260 = 0$

Extra Help On the Web

Look for worked-out examples at the Prentice Hall Web site.
www.phschool.com

10-3 Exercises

A

For each ellipse find the vertices and foci, and draw a graph.

1. $\frac{x^2}{4} + \frac{y^2}{1} = 1$ **2.** $\frac{x^2}{1} + \frac{y^2}{4} = 1$ **3.** $16x^2 + 9y^2 = 144$

4. $9x^2 + 16y^2 = 144$ **5.** $2x^2 + 3y^2 = 6$ **6.** $5x^2 + 7y^2 = 35$

7. $4x^2 + 9y^2 = 1$ **8.** $25x^2 + 16y^2 = 1$

For each ellipse find the center, vertices, and foci, and draw a graph.

9. $\frac{(x-1)^2}{4} + \frac{(y-2)^2}{1} = 1$ **10.** $\frac{(x-1)^2}{1} + \frac{(y-2)^2}{4} = 1$

11. $\frac{(x+3)^2}{25} + \frac{(y-2)^2}{16} = 1$ **12.** $\frac{(x-2)^2}{25} + \frac{(y+3)^2}{16} = 1$

13. $3(x + 2^2) + 4(y - 1)^2 = 192$ **14.** $4(x - 5)^2 + 3(y - 5)^2 = 192$

15. $4x^2 + 9y^2 - 16x + 18y - 11 = 0$ **16.** $x^2 + 2y^2 - 10x + 8y + 29 = 0$

17. $4x^2 + y^2 - 8x - 2y + 1 = 0$ **18.** $9x^2 + 4y^2 + 54x - 8y + 49 = 0$

B

For each ellipse approximate the center and vertices. Use a calculator.

19. $\pi x^2 + \pi^2 y^2 - 5\pi x + 6\pi y - \pi^2 = 0$

20. $\pi^2 x^2 + \pi y^2 + \pi^3 x - \pi^2 y + \frac{5}{4}\pi = 0$

Find equations of the ellipses with the following vertices. (Hint: Graph the vertices.)

21. $(2, 0), (-2, 0), (0, 3), (0, -3)$ **22.** $(1, 0), (-1, 0), (0, 4), (0, -4)$

23. $(1, 1), (5, 1), (3, 6), (3, -4)$ **24.** $(-1, -1), (-1, 5), (-3, 2), (1, 2)$

Find equations of the ellipses satisfying the given conditions.

25. Center at $(-2, 3)$ with major axis of length 8 and parallel to the y-axis, minor axis of length 2

26. Vertices $(3, 0)$ and $(-3, 0)$, and containing the point $\left(2, \frac{22}{3}\right)$

27. **a.** Graph $9x^2 + y^2 = 9$. Is this relation a function?

 b. Solve $9x^2 + y^2 = 9$ for y.

 c. Graph $y = 3\sqrt{1 - x^2}$ and determine whether it is a graph of a function. Find the domain and range.

 d. Graph $y = -3\sqrt{1 - x^2}$ and determine whether it is a graph of a function. Find the domain and range.

28. Draw a large-scale precise graph of $\frac{x^2}{25} + \frac{y^2}{16} = 1$ by calculating and plotting a large number of points. Use a calculator to find the points.

29. The maximum distance from Earth to the sun is 9.3×10^7 miles. The minimum distance is 9.1×10^7 miles. The sun is at one focus of the elliptical orbit. Find the distance from the sun to the other focus.

30. Find F_1P, F_2P, a, and b for this figure.

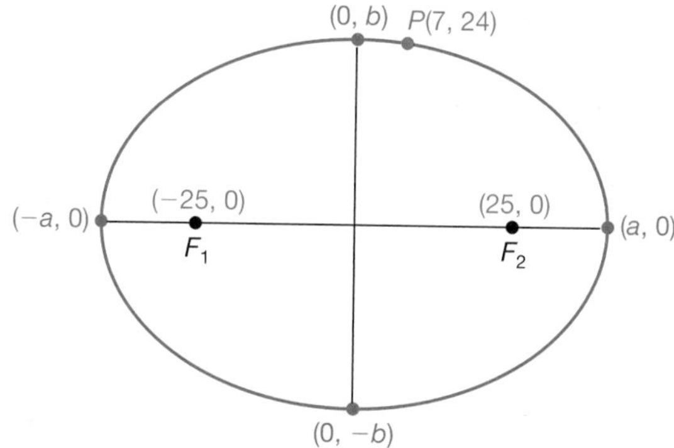

31. ***Critical Thinking*** Describe the graph of $\frac{x^2}{a^2} + \frac{y^2}{b^2} = 1$, where $a^2 = b^2$.

Challenge

32. An ellipse has foci $F_1(-c, 0)$ and $F_2(c, 0)$. $P(x, y)$ is a point on the ellipse and $F_1P + F_2P$ is the given constant distance. Let $F_1P + F_2P = 2a$. Use the distance formula to derive the standard form equation of the ellipse as given in Theorem 10-5. (Hint: $F_1P = \sqrt{(x + c)^2 + y^2}$.)

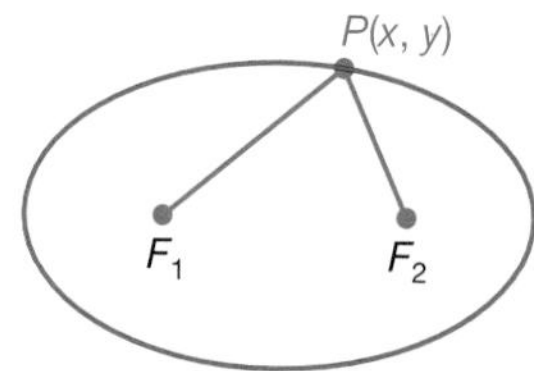

33. ***Mathematical Reasoning*** The **eccentricity, e,** of an ellipse is $\frac{c}{a}$. What is the range for the eccentricity of an ellipse?

34. ***Mathematical Reasoning*** What happens to the shape of an ellipse as the eccentricity gets closer to 1? What would be true if $e = 1$?

35. The unit square on the left is transformed to the rectangle on the right by a stretch or shrink in the x-direction and a stretch or shrink in the y-direction.

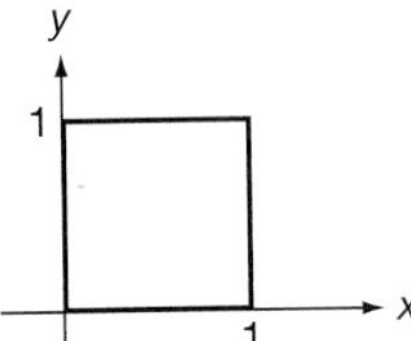

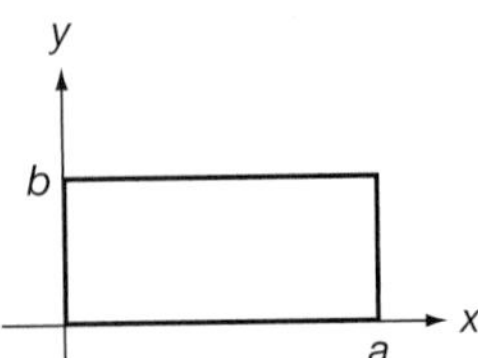

a. Use the above result to develop a formula for the area of the ellipse $\frac{x^2}{a^2} + \frac{y^2}{b^2} = 1$. (Hint: The area of the circle $x^2 + y^2 = r^2$ is $\pi \cdot r \cdot r$.)

b. Use the result of **a** to find the area of the ellipse $\frac{x^2}{16} + \frac{y^2}{25} = 1$.

c. Use the result of **a** to find the area of the ellipse $\frac{x^2}{4} + \frac{y^2}{3} = 1$.

36. Kidney stones can be treated using a lithotripter. An electrode at one focus of an elliptical reflector sends high-energy shock waves to crush the kidney stone at the other focus. How far must the electrode be placed from the kidney stone?

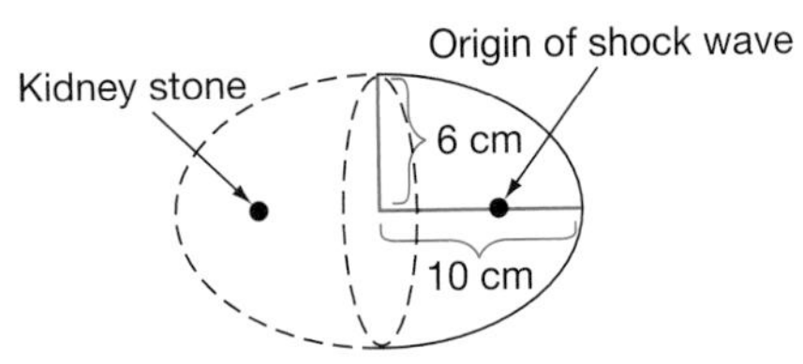

Graph these inequalities.

37. $\frac{x^2}{9} + \frac{y^2}{4} \leq 1$ **38.** $\frac{x^2}{9} + \frac{y^2}{25} > 1$ **39.** $\frac{(x-1)^2}{2} + \frac{(y-3)^2}{9} < 1$

Mixed Review

Find the standard form for each quadratic equation and then find the vertex, the line of symmetry, and the maximum or minimum value.

40. $f(x) = x^2 - 3x + 4$ **41.** $f(x) = x^2 + 5x - 1$ **42.** $f(x) = -x^2 + 2x - 5$ *9-6*

Find the x-intercepts. **43.** $f(x) = 2x^2 + 4x - 1$ **44.** $f(x) = 2x^2 - 2x - 24$ *9-9*

Find the distance between the points. **45.** (4, 5) and (7, 10)

46. (−5, −2) and (−2, 1) *10-1*

Find the quadratic function that fits each set of points.

47. (1, 1), (−1, −3), (2, 12) **48.** (1, −22), (−2, 14), (−1, −4) *9-8*

49. A computer programmer can be paid in two ways.

Plan A: \$315 plus \$28.00 per hour

Plan B: straight \$32.50 per hour

Suppose the job takes n hours. For what values of n is plan A better for the programmer than plan B? *3-8*

Hyperbolas

10-4

Hyperbolas have many applications. A jet breaking the sound barrier creates a sonic boom whose wave front has the shape of a cone. The cone intersects the ground in one branch of a hyperbola. Some comets travel in hyperbolic orbits.

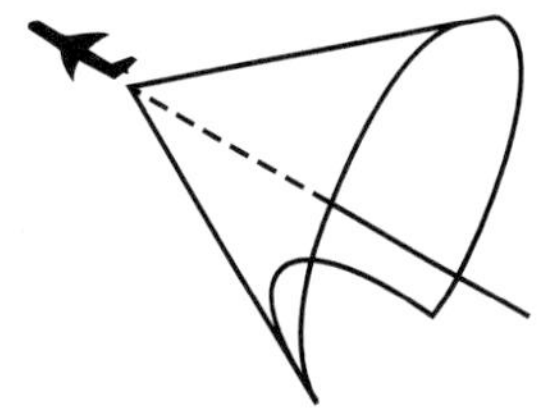

What You'll Learn

1. To find the vertices, foci, and asymptotes, and draw the graph of a hyperbola, given its equation
2. To use the technique of completing the square to find the standard form of a hyperbola and graph it
3. To graph a hyperbola that has an equation of the form $xy = c$

. . . And Why

To solve problems involving hyperbolas

PART 1 Equations of Hyperbolas

Objective: Find the vertices, foci, and asymptotes, and draw a graph of a hyperbola, given its equation.

Some equations of second degree have graphs that are hyperbolas.

Definition

A **hyperbola** is the set of all points P in a plane such that the absolute value of the difference of the distances from P to two fixed points, F_1 and F_2, is constant. The fixed points F_1 and F_2 are the foci. The midpoint of the segment F_1F_2 is the center. r_1 and r_2 are the **focal radii.**

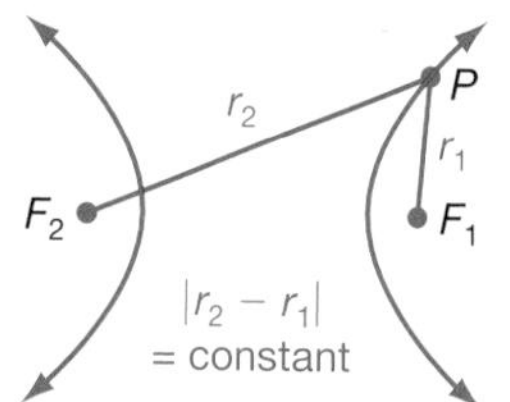

Theorem 10-7

The equation, in standard form, of a hyperbola centered at the origin, with foci on an axis and c units from the origin, is

$$\frac{x^2}{a^2} - \frac{y^2}{b^2} = 1, \text{ (foci on the } x\text{-axis)} \quad \text{or} \quad \frac{y^2}{a^2} - \frac{x^2}{b^2} = 1, \text{ (foci on the } y\text{-axis)}$$

where $c^2 = a^2 + b^2$.

The two parts of the hyperbola are **branches.** Points $(a, 0)$ and $(-a, 0)$ are the **vertices,** and the line segment joining them is the **transverse axis.** The line segment from $(0, b)$ to $(0, -b)$ is the **conjugate axis.** The intersection of the transverse and conjugate axes is the **center** of the hyperbola.

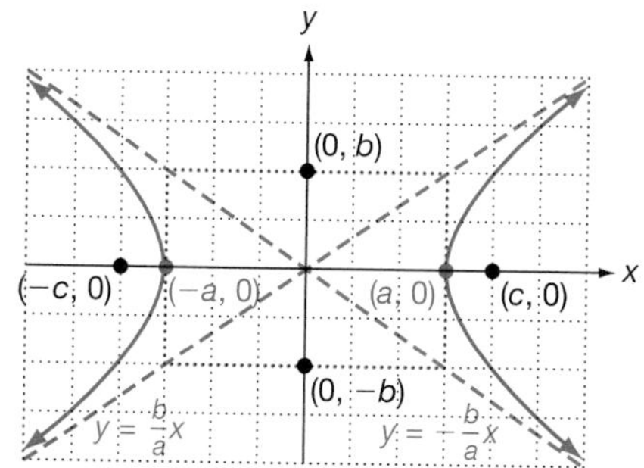

By looking at the equation, we can see that the hyperbola is symmetric with respect to the origin, and that the x-axis and y-axis are lines of symmetry.

The constant distance, $|r_2 - r_1|$, is $2a$.

Notice that the branches of the hyperbola approach the lines $y = \frac{b}{a}x$ and $y = -\frac{b}{a}x$ as $|x|$ increases. These lines are called **asymptotes.** A line is a nonvertical asymptote to a curve if the distance between the curve and the line approaches zero as x increases or decreases without limit.

EXAMPLE 1 For the hyperbola $9x^2 - 16y^2 = 144$, find the vertices, the foci, and the asymptotes. Then draw a graph.

(a) We first multiply by $\frac{1}{144}$ to find the standard form.

$$\frac{x^2}{16} - \frac{y^2}{9} = 1$$

Thus, $a = 4$ and $b = 3$. The vertices are $(4, 0)$ and $(-4, 0)$. Since $c^2 = a^2 + b^2$, $c = \sqrt{a^2 + b^2} = \sqrt{4^2 + 3^2} = 5$. Thus, the foci are $(5, 0)$ and $(-5, 0)$. The asymptotes are $y = \frac{3}{4}x$ and $y = -\frac{3}{4}x$.

(b) To graph the hyperbola it is helpful to first graph the asymptotes. An easy way to do this is to draw the rectangle formed by the lines $y = 3$, $y = -3$, $x = 4$, and $x = -4$. By extending the diagonals, we have the asymptotes. Then we draw the branches of the hyperbola outward from the vertices toward the asymptotes.

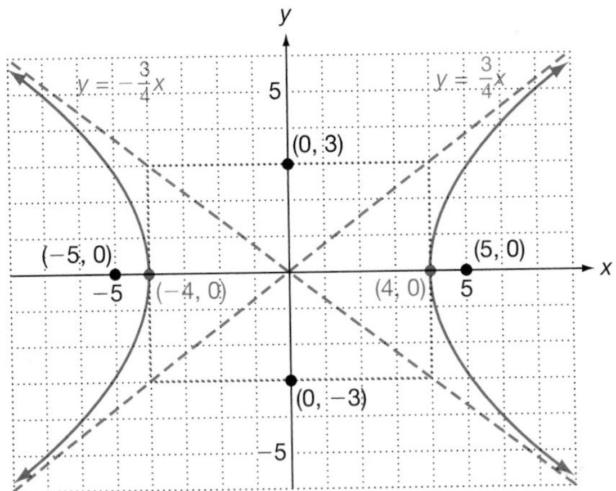

Try This For each hyperbola find the vertices, foci, and asymptotes. Then graph.

a. $4x^2 - 9y^2 = 36$ **b.** $x^2 - y^2 = 16$

The foci of a hyperbola can be on the y-axis.

The slopes of the asymptotes are $\pm \frac{a}{b}$.

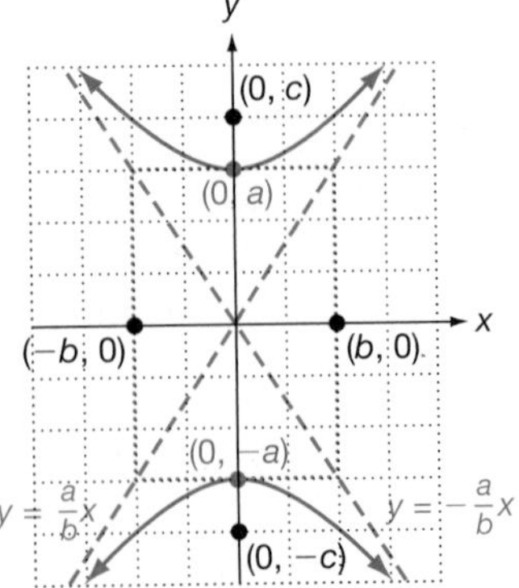

EXAMPLE 2 For the hyperbola $25y^2 - 16x^2 = 400$, find the vertices, foci, and asymptotes. Then draw a graph.

(a) We first multiply by $\frac{1}{400}$ to find the standard form.

$$\frac{y^2}{16} - \frac{x^2}{25} = 1$$

This is the equation of a hyperbola with foci and vertices on the y-axis.

From the equation, $a = 4$ and $b = 5$. The vertices are $(0, 4)$ and $(0, -4)$. Since $c = \sqrt{4^2 + 5^2} = \sqrt{41}$, the foci are $(0, \sqrt{41})$ and $(0, -\sqrt{41})$. The asymptotes are $y = \frac{4}{5}x$ and $y = -\frac{4}{5}x$.

(b) The graph is as shown.

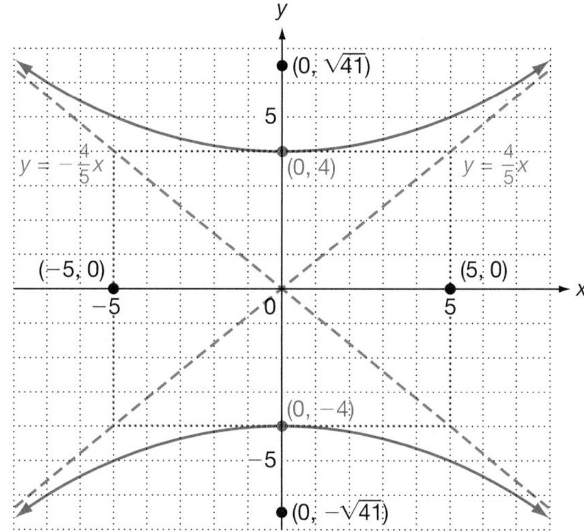

Try This For each hyperbola find the vertices, foci, and asymptotes. Then draw a graph.

c. $9y^2 - 25x^2 = 225$

d. $y^2 - x^2 = 25$

PART 2 Finding Standard Form by Completing the Square

Objective: Find standard form and graph a hyperbola by first completing the square.

If the center of a hyperbola is not at the origin but at some point (h, k), then the standard form for the equation is as follows.

The shape of the St. Louis Science Center Planetarium is called a hyperboloid of one sheet. A vertical cross section is a hyperbola.

Theorem 10-8

The equation, in standard form, of a hyperbola centered at (h, k) with foci c units from (h, k) is

$$\frac{(x-h)^2}{a^2} - \frac{(y-k)^2}{b^2} = 1, \text{ (foci horizontal) or}$$

$$\frac{(y-k)^2}{a^2} - \frac{(x-h)^2}{b^2} = 1, \text{ (foci vertical)}$$

where $c^2 = a^2 + b^2$.

EXAMPLE 3 For the hyperbola $4x^2 - y^2 + 24x + 4y + 28 = 0$, find the center, vertices, foci, and asymptotes, and draw a graph.

(a) First we complete the square to find standard form.

$$4(x^2 + 6x \qquad) - (y^2 - 4y \qquad) = -28$$

$$4(x^2 + 6x + 9) - (y^2 - 4y + 4) = -28 + 4 \cdot 9 - 1 \cdot 4$$

$$4(x+3)^2 - (y-2)^2 = 4$$

$$\frac{(x+3)^2}{1} - \frac{(y-2)^2}{4} = 1$$

The center is $(-3, 2)$.

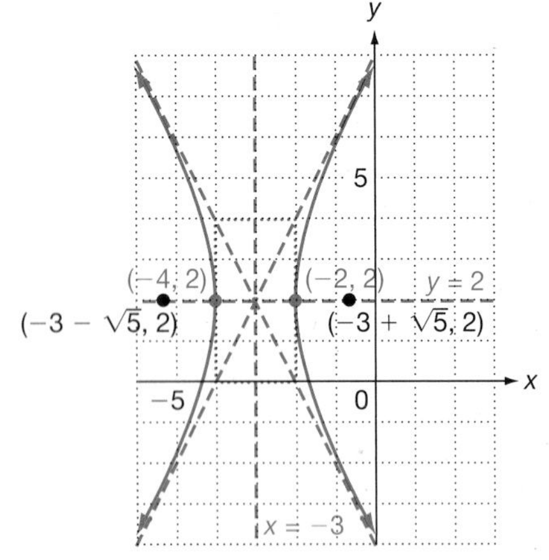

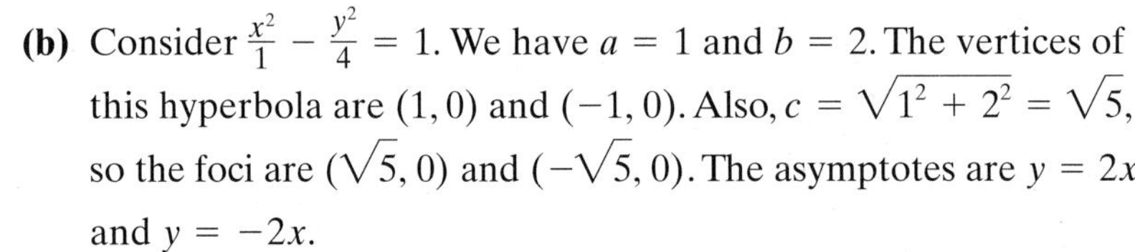

(b) Consider $\frac{x^2}{1} - \frac{y^2}{4} = 1$. We have $a = 1$ and $b = 2$. The vertices of this hyperbola are $(1, 0)$ and $(-1, 0)$. Also, $c = \sqrt{1^2 + 2^2} = \sqrt{5}$, so the foci are $(\sqrt{5}, 0)$ and $(-\sqrt{5}, 0)$. The asymptotes are $y = 2x$ and $y = -2x$.

(c) The vertices, foci, and asymptotes of the translated hyperbola are found in the same way by which the center has been translated. The vertices are $(-3 + 1, 2)$, $(-3 - 1, 2)$, or $(-2, 2)$, $(-4, 2)$. The foci are $(-3 + \sqrt{5}, 2)$ and $(-3 - \sqrt{5}, 2)$. The asymptotes are $y - 2 = 2(x + 3)$ and $y - 2 = -2(x + 3)$.

(d) The graph is at the left.

Try This For each hyperbola find the center, vertices, foci, and asymptotes. Then draw a graph.

e. $4x^2 - 25y^2 - 8x - 100y - 196 = 0$ **f.** $\frac{(y-2)^2}{9} - \frac{(x+1)^2}{16} = 1$

Asymptotes on the Coordinate Axes

Objective: Graph a hyperbola that has an equation of the form $xy = c$.

If a hyperbola has its center at the origin and its axes at 45° to the coordinate axes, it has a simple equation. The coordinate axes are its asymptotes. Such hyperbolas are known as equilateral or rectangular hyperbolas.

Theorem 10-9

The equation of a hyperbola with asymptotes on the axes is $xy = c$, where $c \neq 0$.

If c is positive, the branches of the hyperbola lie in the first and third quadrants. If c is negative, the branches lie in the second and fourth quadrants. In either case, the asymptotes are the x-axis and y-axis.

EXAMPLE 4 Graph $xy = 4$ and $xy = -4$.

x	y
1	4
−1	−4
4	1
−4	−1

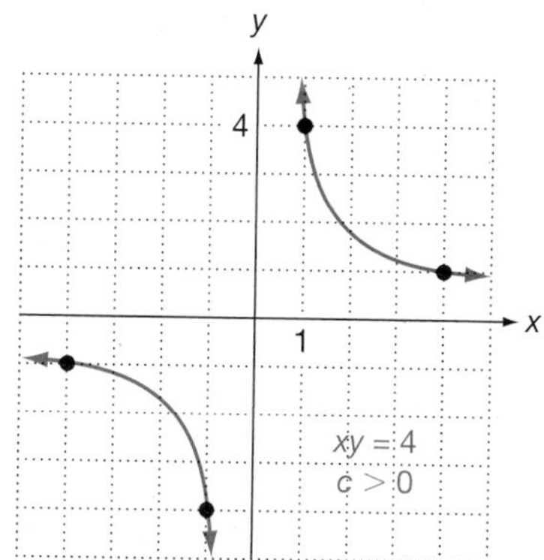

x	y
1	−4
−1	4
4	−1
−4	1

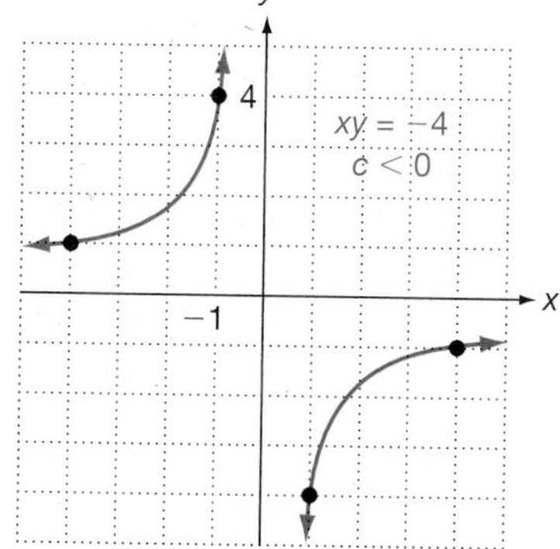

Try This

g. Graph $xy = 3$. **h.** Graph $xy = -12$.

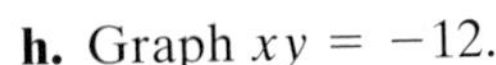

Extra Help On the Web

Look for worked-out examples at the Prentice Hall Web site.
www.phschool.com

10-4 Exercises

A

Mental Math For each of these hyperbolas centered at the origin find the vertices, foci, and asymptotes.

1. $\frac{x^2}{9} - \frac{y^2}{1} = 1$ **2.** $\frac{x^2}{1} - \frac{y^2}{9} = 1$ **3.** $\frac{y^2}{16} - \frac{x^2}{4} = 1$

4. $x^2 - 4y^2 = 4$ **5.** $4x^2 - y^2 = 4$ **6.** $4y^2 - x^2 = 4$

For each hyperbola find the center, vertices, foci, and asymptotes. Then draw a graph.

7. $y^2 - 4x^2 = 4$ **8.** $x^2 - y^2 = 2$ **9.** $x^2 - y^2 = 3$

10. $\frac{(x-2)^2}{1} - \frac{(y+5)^2}{9} = 1$ **11.** $\frac{(y+3)^2}{4} - \frac{(x+1)^2}{16} = 1$

12. $\frac{(x-2)^2}{9} - \frac{(y+5)^2}{1} = 1$ **13.** $\frac{(y+3)^2}{25} - \frac{(x+1)^2}{16} = 1$

14. $x^2 - y^2 - 2x - 4y - 4 = 0$ **15.** $4x^2 - y^2 + 8x - 4y - 4 = 0$

16. **TEST PREP** Find the vertex of the right branch of $36x^2 - y^2 - 24x + 6y - 41 = 0$.

A. $\left(\frac{1}{3}, 3\right)$ **B.** $\left(\frac{4}{3}, -3\right)$ **C.** $\left(\frac{4}{3}, 3\right)$ **D.** $\left(\frac{1}{3}, -3\right)$

Graph.

17. $xy = 1$ **18.** $xy = -1$ **19.** $xy = -8$ **20.** $xy = 3$

B

Find equations of the hyperbolas satisfying the given conditions.

21. vertices at $(1, 0)$ and $(-1, 0)$, and foci at $(2, 0)$ and $(-2, 0)$

22. asymptotes $y = \frac{3}{2}x$ and $y = -\frac{3}{2}x$, and one vertex $(2, 0)$

23. ***Critical Thinking*** Hyperbolas of the form $\frac{x^2}{a^2} - \frac{y^2}{b^2} = 1$ and $\frac{y^2}{a^2} - \frac{x^2}{b^2} = 1$ are **conjugate hyperbolas.** Graph a pair of conjugate hyperbolas on the same coordinate axes. What do you observe?

Challenge

24. A hyperbola has foci $F_1(c, 0)$ and $F_2(-c, 0)$ on the x-axis. Let $P(x, y)$ be any point in the first quadrant, and $PF_2 - PF_1 = 2a$. Use the distance formula to derive the standard form equation of the hyperbola as given in Theorem 10-8. (Hint: $PF_2 = \sqrt{(x+c)^2 + y^2}$.)

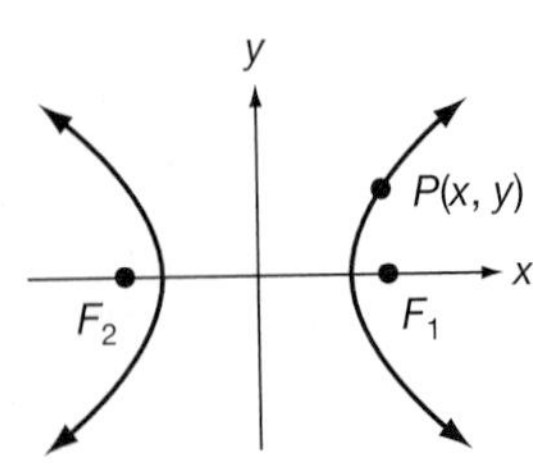

25. Solve the equation $\frac{x^2}{16} - \frac{y^2}{9} = 1$ for y^2. What happens to this equation as $|x|$ gets larger? What are the equations for the asymptotes of this graph?

26. The **eccentricity, e,** of a hyperbola is $\frac{c}{a}$. What is the range of e for any hyperbola?

27. What happens to the graph of $xy = k$ as $|k|$ gets smaller?

Graph these inequalities.

28. $\frac{x^2}{25} - \frac{y^2}{16} < 1$ 29. $\frac{y^2}{36} - \frac{x^2}{25} \geq 1$ 30. $\frac{(y + 4)^2}{1} - \frac{(x + 2)^2}{4} \geq 1$

Mixed Review

Find the coordinates of the midpoint of the segment having the following endpoints.

31. (2, 7), (4, 5) 32. (−1, 6), (4, −2) 33. (3, 0), (9, 0) *10-1*

Find the distance between the points. 34. (1, −2) and (13, −7)

35. (2, 6) and (−4, 14) 36. (−1, 6) and (−4, 10) 37. (−7, 2) and (−2, 2) *10-1*

Test for symmetry with respect to the axes.

38. $5y^4 = -4x^2 - 1$ 39. $y = x^3 + 2$ *9-1*

Determine whether the graphs are perpendicular.

40. $y = 2x - 3$ and $x = 2y - 3$

41. $y = \frac{1}{3}x + 2$ and $y = -3x + 2$ 42. $x = y - 10$ and $y - x = 5$ *3-7*

43. The surface area of a cube varies directly as the square of the length of one side. A cube has a surface area of 168.54 m² when the length of one side is 5.3 m. What will the surface area be when the length of one side is 4.8 m? *8-7*

Activity

1. Cut three sheets of waxed paper about 5″ × 5″.
2. Draw a circle and a point P on each as shown below.

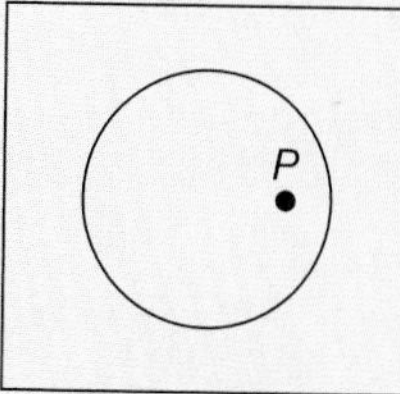

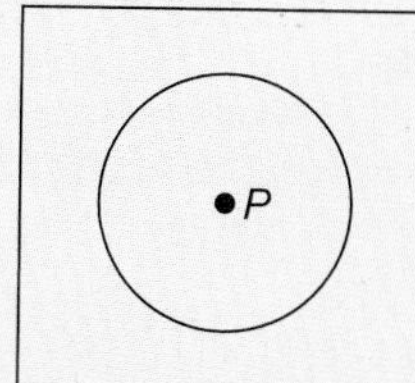

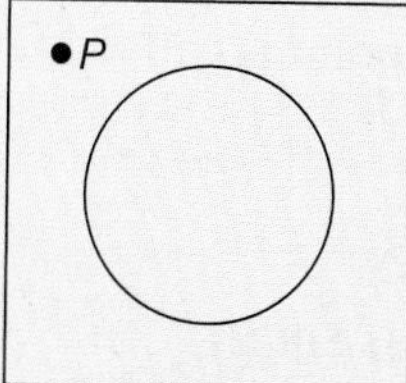

3. Fold and crease each piece of paper so that the point P touches the circle. Repeat at least 50 times from a variety of positions.
4. What types of figures seem to be formed by the creases?

10-5 Parabolas

What You'll Learn

1. To find the vertex, focus, and directrix, and draw a graph of a parabola, given its equation
2. To use the technique of completing the square to find the vertex, focus, and directrix of a parabola, and graph it
3. To find the equation of a parabola, given certain characteristics

. . . And Why

To solve problems involving parabolas

When a plane intersects a cone parallel to an element of the cone, a parabola is formed. Cross sections of some headlights are parabolas with the bulb located at the focus. All light from the focus is reflected outward, parallel to the axis of symmetry.

Radar and radio antennas may have cross sections that are parabolas. Incoming radio waves are reflected and concentrated at the focus. Some comets have parabolic orbits.

Some headlights are ellipsoidal; some are parabolic.

Cables hung from suspension bridges form parabolas. When a cable supports only its own weight, it does not form a parabola, but rather a curve called a **catenary.**

PART 1 Equations of Parabolas

Objective: Find the vertex, focus, and directrix, and draw a graph of a parabola, given its equation.

Some equations of second degree have graphs that are parabolas.

F d_1
P
d_2
directrix
$d_1 = d_2$

Definition

A **parabola** is a set of all points P in a plane equidistant from a fixed line and a fixed point F in the plane. The fixed line is called the **directrix** and the fixed point is called the **focus.**

Theorem 10-10

A parabola with focus at $(0, p)$ and vertex at $(0, 0)$ has directrix $y = -p$.

We first obtain an equation of a parabola with focus on the y-axis, directrix parallel to the x-axis with equation $y = -p$, and vertex at the origin.

Consider the point P with coordinates (x, y). We know from the definition of a parabola that $FP = PD$. Using the distance formula we have $FP = \sqrt{(x - 0)^2 + (y - p)^2}$. The distance $PD = y + p$. Thus, $\sqrt{(x - 0)^2 + (y - p)^2} = y + p$. Squaring both sides we have

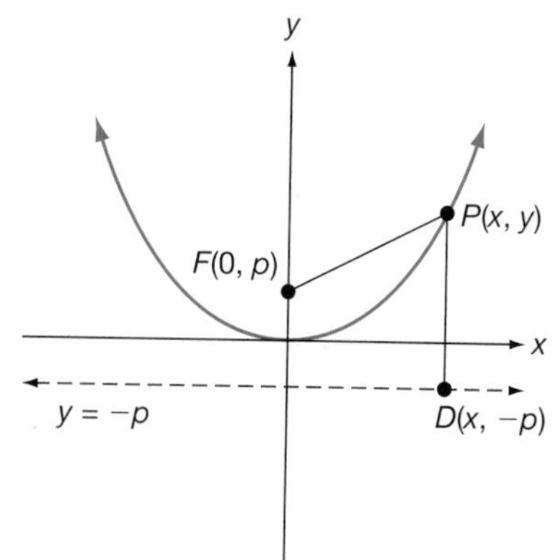

$$x^2 + (y - p)^2 = y^2 + 2py + p^2$$
$$x^2 + y^2 - 2py + p^2 = y^2 + 2py + p^2$$

This yields $x^2 = 4py$.

Theorem 10-11

The equation, in standard form, of a parabola with focus at $(0, p)$, directrix $y = -p$, vertex $(0, 0)$, and y-axis as the only line of symmetry is $x^2 = 4py$.

EXAMPLE 1 For the parabola $x^2 = y$, find the vertex, focus, and directrix. Then draw a graph.

The equation is in the form $x^2 = 4py$.

Since the coefficient of y is 1, $4p = 1$, so $p = \frac{1}{4}$.

Thus, the focus is $\left(0, \frac{1}{4}\right)$ and the directrix is $y = -\frac{1}{4}$. The vertex is $(0, 0)$.

If $p > 0$, the graph opens upward. If $p < 0$, the graph opens downward and the focus and directrix exchange sides of the x-axis.

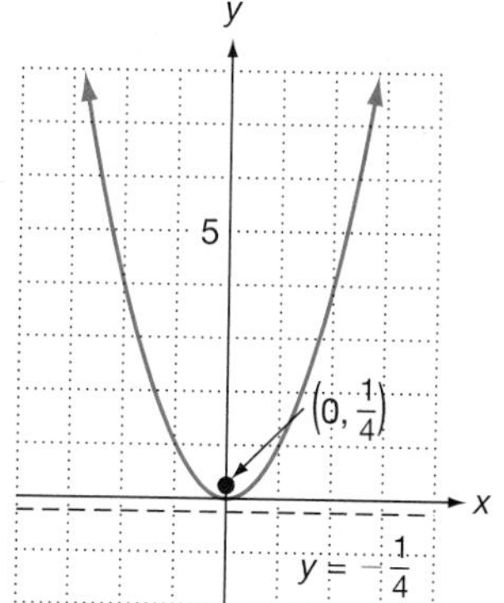

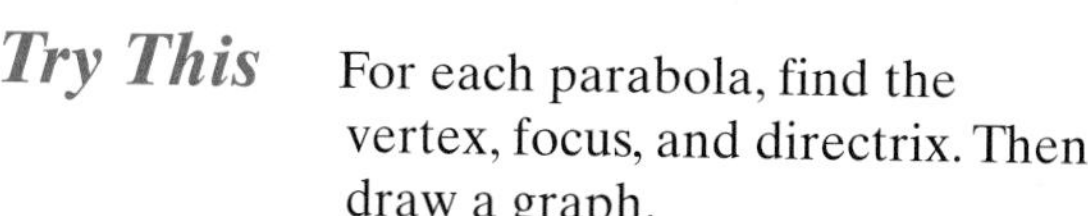

Try This For each parabola, find the vertex, focus, and directrix. Then draw a graph.

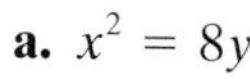

a. $x^2 = 8y$

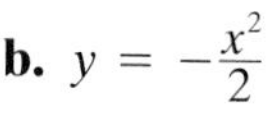

b. $y = -\frac{x^2}{2}$

Theorem 10-12

The equation, in standard form, of a parabola with focus $(p, 0)$, directrix $x = -p$, vertex $(0, 0)$, and x-axis as the line of symmetry is $y^2 = 4px$.

EXAMPLE 2 For the parabola $y^2 = -12x$, find the vertex, focus, and directrix. Then draw a graph.

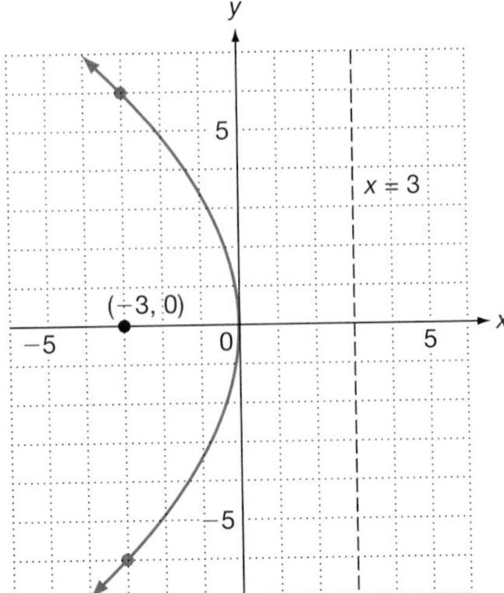

The equation is in the form $y^2 = 4px$.

Since the coefficient of x is -12, $4p = -12$, so $p = -3$.

Thus the focus is $(-3, 0)$ and the directrix is $x = -(-3) = 3$. The vertex is $(0, 0)$.

We find two other points on the graph by substituting -3 for x. Choosing -3 for x will give us a perfect square for y^2. This yields $(-3, 6)$ and $(-3, -6)$.

Try This For each parabola find the vertex, focus, and directrix. Then draw a graph.

c. $y^2 = 2x$

d. $x = -\frac{y^2}{4}$

PART 2 Finding Standard Form by Completing the Square

Objective: Find the vertex, focus, and directrix, and graph a parabola by first completing the square.

Theorem 10-13

If a parabola is translated so that its vertex is (h, k) and its axis of symmetry is parallel to the y-axis, it has an equation $\mathbf{(x - h)^2 = 4p(y - k)}$, where the focus is $(h, k + p)$ and the directrix is $y = k - p$.

If a parabola is translated so that its vertex is (h, k) and its axis of symmetry is parallel to the x-axis, it has an equation $\mathbf{(y - k)^2 = 4p(x - h)}$, where the focus is $(h + p, k)$, and the directrix is $x = h - p$.

EXAMPLE 3 For the parabola $x^2 + 6x + 4y + 5 = 0$, find the vertex, focus, and directrix. Then draw a graph.

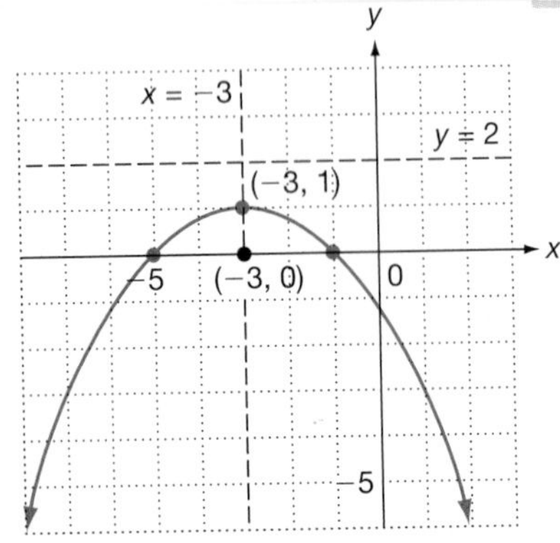

First, we complete the square.

$$\begin{aligned} x^2 + 6x &= -4y - 5 \\ x^2 + 6x + 9 &= -4y - 5 + 9 \\ x^2 + 6x + 9 &= -4y + 4 \\ (x + 3)^2 &= -4y + 4 \\ &= 4(-1)(y - 1) \end{aligned}$$

Vertex $(-3, 1)$; focus $(-3, 1 + (-1))$ or $(-3, 0)$; directrix $y = 2$

EXAMPLE 4 For the parabola $y^2 + 6y - 8x - 31 = 0$, find the vertex, focus, and directrix. Then draw a graph.

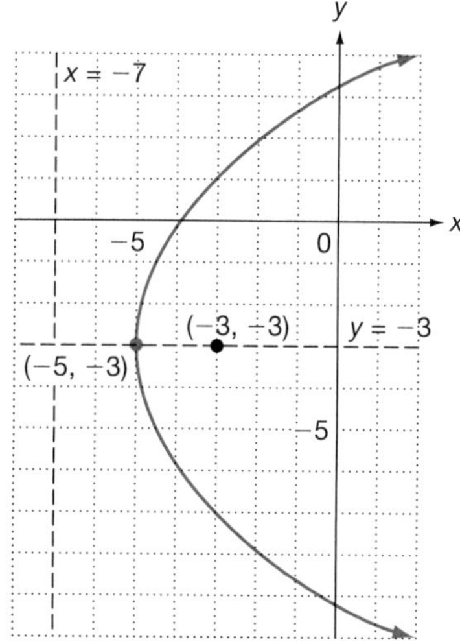

We complete the square.

$$\begin{aligned} y^2 + 6y &= 8x + 31 \\ y^2 + 6y + 9 &= 8x + 31 + 9 \\ y^2 + 6y + 9 &= 8x + 40 \\ (y + 3)^2 &= 8x + 40 \\ &= 8(x + 5) \\ &= 4(2)(x + 5) \end{aligned}$$

Vertex $(-5, -3)$; focus $(-5 + 2, -3)$ or $(-3, -3)$; directrix $x = -5 - 2 = -7$

Try This For each parabola find the vertex, focus, and directrix. Then graph.

e. $x^2 + 2x - 8y - 3 = 0$ **f.** $y^2 + 2y + 4x - 7 = 0$

PART 3 Finding Equations of Parabolas

Objective: Find the equation of a parabola, given certain characteristics.

EXAMPLE 5 Find the equation of a parabola with focus $(3, 9)$ and directrix $y = -1$.

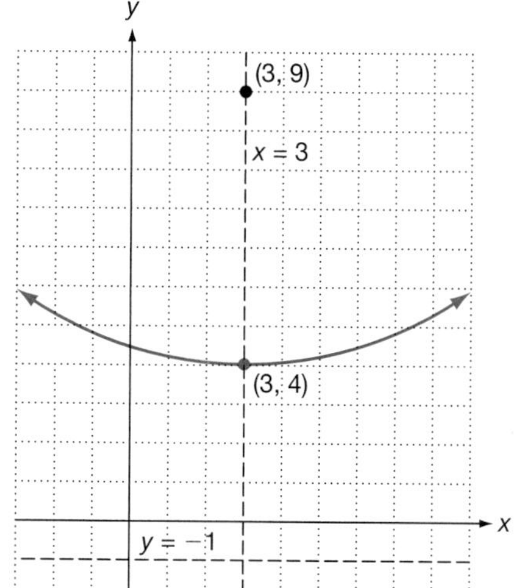

Since the directrix is a horizontal line below the focus, the parabola opens upward. The line of symmetry is $x = 3$. The vertex is the midpoint between $(3, -1)$ and $(3, 9)$, so the vertex is $(3, 4)$. The focus is 5 units in the positive direction (up) from the vertex, so $p = 5$.

Substituting in $(x - h)^2 = 4p(y - k)$, we have $(x - 3)^2 = 4(5)(y - 4)$, or $(x - 3)^2 = 20(y - 4)$.

EXAMPLE 6 Find the equation of a parabola with focus $(3, 9)$ and vertex $(5, 9)$.

Since the focus is to the left of the vertex, the parabola opens to the left. The line of symmetry is $y = 9$. The focus is 2 units in the negative direction (left) from the vertex, so $p = -2$. The directrix is thus 2 units in the positive direction (right) from the vertex, or $x = 7$.

Substituting in $(y - k)^2 = 4p(x - h)$, we have $(y - 9)^2 = 4(-2)(x - 5)$, or $(y - 9)^2 = -8(x - 5)$.

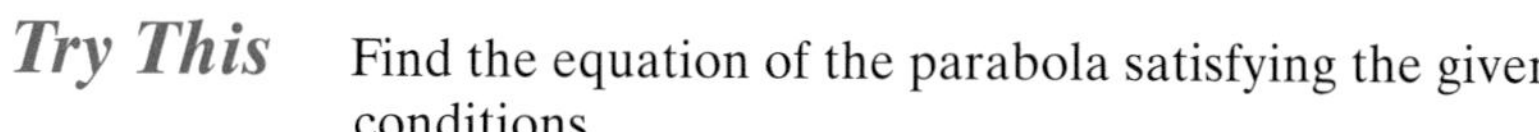

Try This Find the equation of the parabola satisfying the given conditions.

g. Focus $(0, 3)$, vertex $(0, 0)$

h. Focus $(-4, 2)$, directrix $x = -6$

i. Focus $(-4, 2)$, vertex $(-4, 5)$

Extra Help On the Web

Look for worked-out examples at the Prentice Hall Web site.
www.phschool.com

10-5 Exercises

A

Mental Math For each parabola with vertex at the origin find the focus and directrix.

1. $x^2 = 8y$

2. $x^2 = 16y$

3. $y^2 = -6x$

4. $y^2 = -2x$

5. $x^2 - 4y = 0$

6. $y^2 + 4x = 0$

7. $y = 2x^2$

8. $y = \frac{1}{2}x^2$

Find the vertex, focus, and directrix. Then draw a graph.

9. $(x + 2)^2 = -6(y - 1)$

10. $(y - 3)^2 = -20(x + 2)$

11. $x^2 + 2x + 2y + 7 = 0$

12. $y^2 + 6y - x + 16 = 0$

13. $x^2 - y - 2 = 0$

14. $x^2 - 4x - 2y = 0$

15. $y = x^2 + 4x + 3$

16. $y = x^2 + 6x + 10$

17. $4y^2 - 4y - 4x + 24 = 0$

18. $4y^2 + 4y - 4x - 16 = 0$

Find an equation of a parabola satisfying the given conditions.

19. Focus $(4, 0)$; directrix $x = -4$

20. Focus $(0, -\pi)$; directrix $y = \pi$

21. Focus $(-\sqrt{2}, 0)$; vertex $(0, 0)$

22. Focus $\left(0, \frac{1}{4}\right)$; vertex $(0, 0)$

23. Focus $(0, 3\sqrt{3})$; directrix $y = -3\sqrt{3}$

24. Focus $(\sqrt{2} - 2, 0)$; directrix $x = 0$

25. Focus $(3, 2)$; directrix $x = -4$

26. Focus $(-2, 3)$; directrix $y = -3$

27. Focus $(3, 4)$; vertex $(3, 7)$

28. Focus $(-2, -1)$; vertex $(0, -1)$

B

For each parabola find the vertex, focus, and directrix. Use a calculator.

29. $x^2 = 8056.25y$

30. $y^2 = -7645.88x$

Graph each of the following, using the same set of axes.

31. $x^2 - y^2 = 0,\ x^2 - y^2 = 1$
$x^2 + y^2 = 1,\ y = x^2$

32. $x^2 - 4y^2 = 0,\ x^2 - 4y^2 = 1$
$x^2 + 4y^2 = 1,\ x = 4y^2$

33. ***Error Analysis*** Connie says that any equation of the form $Ax^2 + By^2 + Cx + Dy + E = 0$ is a conic section. Suggest a counterexample Caroline can use to show Connie is mistaken.

34. Find equations of the following parabola: line of symmetry parallel to the y-axis, vertex $(-1, 2)$, and containing $(-3, 1)$.

35. **a.** Graph $(y - 3)^2 = -20(x + 1)$. Is this relation a function?

b. In general, is $(y - k)^2 = 4p(x - h)$ a function?

36. The cables of a suspension bridge are 50 ft above the roadbed near the towers of the bridge and 10 ft above it in the center of the bridge. The roadbed is 200 ft long and vertical cables are to be spaced every 20 ft along it. Calculate the lengths of these vertical cables.

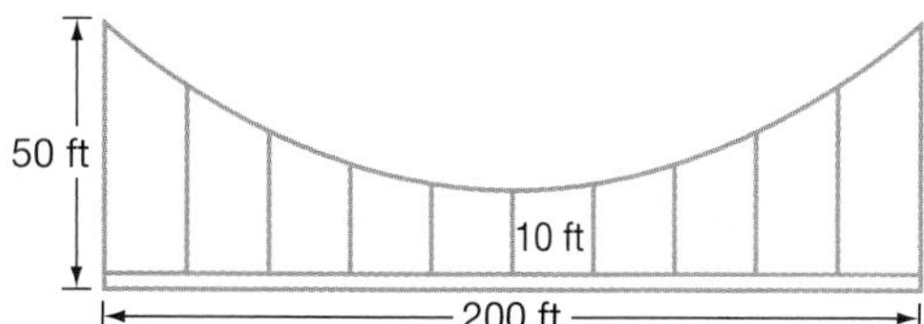

The George Washington Bridge connects New York City and New Jersey. When opened in 1931, its length of 4750 ft was over twice that of any existing bridge. The center span is 3500 ft long. The lengths of the vertical suspension cables could be determined as in Exercise 36.

37. *Critical Thinking* Write an equation in standard form for a parabola with vertex at $(-3, 1)$ that opens **a)** up, **b)** left, **c)** down, **d)** right.

Challenge

38. In the figure at right, the segment PP' is perpendicular to the axis of symmetry of the parabola and contains F, the focus. The lines OP and OP' are tangent to the parabola at P and P', and intersect at the same point that the axis of symmetry intersects the directrix.

a. Prove that $\angle POF$ has a measure of 45°. (Hint: Use the definition of a parabola.)

b. Suppose that the segment PP' is the hypotenuse of a right triangle. Explain how you can find the vertex of the parabola. Suppose that the vertex is three units from the segment. How long is the segment?

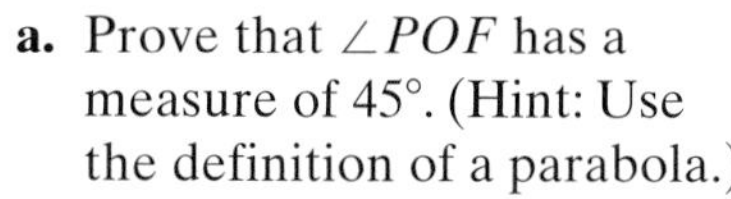

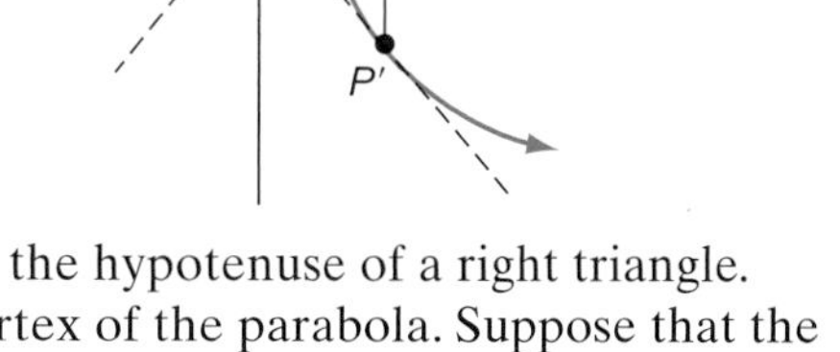

Graph these inequalities.

39. $y > 3x^2$ **40.** $x^2 \geq 25y$ **41.** $(x + 2)^2 > -6(y - 2)$

Mixed Review

Find the vertex, line of symmetry, and minimum or maximum value.

42. $f(x) = 5(x - 3)^2 + 11$ **43.** $f(x) = -2(x - 13.5)^2 + 1.6$ *9-6*

Complete the square. **44.** $y^2 - 8y$ **45.** $m^2 + 5m$ **46.** $a^2 - 0.2a$ *8-1*

Find the distance between the points. **47.** $(\sqrt{m}, \sqrt{n})$ and $(\sqrt{m}, -\sqrt{n})$ *10-1*

Solve. **48.** $3x^2 + 13x + 12 = 0$ **49.** $2x^2 - 3x - 9 = 0$

50. $10x^2 + x = 2$ **51.** $\frac{3}{5}x^2 + x + \frac{2}{5} = 0$ **52.** $\frac{6}{13}x^2 + x = \frac{5}{13}$ *8-3*

Self-Test On the Web

Check your progress. Look for a self-test at the Prentice Hall Web site. www.phschool.com

10-6  Second-Degree Equations and Systems

What You'll Learn

1. To recognize equations of circles, ellipses, hyperbolas, and parabolas
2. To determine a second-degree equation from its graph
3. To solve systems of second-degree equations graphically

. . . And Why

To solve problems involving conic sections

PART 1 Recognizing Conics

Objective: Recognize equations of circles, ellipses, hyperbolas, and parabolas.

It is important to be able to look at a second-degree equation and determine whether it is the equation of a circle, ellipse, hyperbola, or parabola. Following are some key points that will help in the recognition of conics.

Recognizing Conics

Consider the second-degree equation $Ax^2 + By^2 + Cx + Dy + E = 0$.

1. If $A = B$, the equation may define a circle.
2. If A and B have the same sign and $A \neq B$, the equation may define an ellipse.
3. If A and B have different signs, the equation may define a hyperbola.
4. If either A or B is 0, the equation may define a parabola.

Equations representing closed figures (circles or ellipses) must be checked to determine whether real solutions exist. For example, the equation $x^2 + y^2 = -1$ has no real solutions since x^2 and y^2 are nonnegative.

EXAMPLES Tell which conic is defined by each equation.

1 $3x^2 - 4y^2 + 2y - 5 = 0$

A and B have different signs. Thus, the equation defines a hyperbola.

2 $6x^2 + 17x - 9y - 7 = 0$

There is no y^2 term, so $B = 0$. The equation defines a parabola.

3 $2x^2 + 2y^2 - 3x + \frac{1}{2} = 0$

$A = B$. The equation may define a circle. We complete the square to check.

$$2x^2 - 3x + 2y^2 = -\frac{1}{2} \quad \text{Rearranging}$$

$$2\left(x^2 - \frac{3}{2}x + \frac{9}{16}\right) + 2y^2 = -\frac{1}{2} + \frac{9}{8}$$

$$2\left(x^2 - \frac{3}{2}x + \frac{9}{16}\right) + 2y^2 = \frac{5}{8}$$

After completing the square, the right side of the equation is positive, so real solutions exist. The equation defines a circle.

Try This Tell which conic is defined by each equation.

a. $4x^2 + 9y^2 + 16x - 54y - 61 = 0$ **b.** $-3x^2 - 3y^2 + 7y + 9 = 0$

c. $5y^2 - 3x + 9 = 0$ **d.** $2x^2 - 4y^2 - 5x + 8y + 19 = 0$

Finding Second-Degree Equations from Graphs

Objective: Determine a second-degree equation from its graph.

Geometric models can be represented algebraically to help solve some problems.

EXAMPLE 4 Determine the equation represented by the graph.

The graph shown is an ellipse. To solve this problem we can start by locating the vertices and the center.

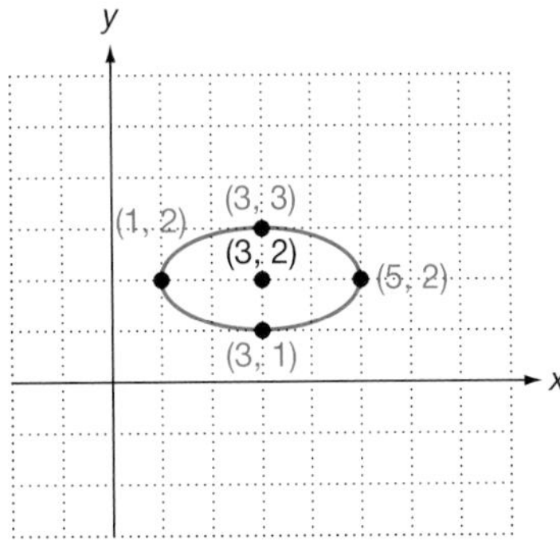

The vertices are at (1, 2), (5, 2), (3, 1), and (3, 3). Thus, the center is at the midpoint of the segment from (1, 2) to (5, 2), which is (3, 2).

The length of the major axis, $2a$, is 4. So $a = 2$. The length of the minor axis, $2b$, is 2. So $b = 1$.

Since the equation of an ellipse is $\frac{(x - h)^2}{a^2} + \frac{(y - k)^2}{b^2} = 1$, we substitute and have $\frac{(x - 3)^2}{4} + \frac{(y - 2)^2}{1} = 1$, as the equation of the ellipse shown.

EXAMPLE 5 Determine the equation represented by the graph.

The graph shown is a hyperbola. The vertices are (5, 1) and (−3, 1). So the center is (1, 1). The foci are (6, 1) and (−4, 1). This graph has been translated 1 unit to the right and 1 unit upward. For the untranslated graph, $c^2 = a^2 + b^2$. So we have

$$5^2 = 4^2 + b^2$$

$$25 = 16 + b^2$$

$$9 = b^2$$

Thus, the equation is

$$\frac{(x - 1)^2}{16} - \frac{(y - 1)^2}{9} = 1.$$

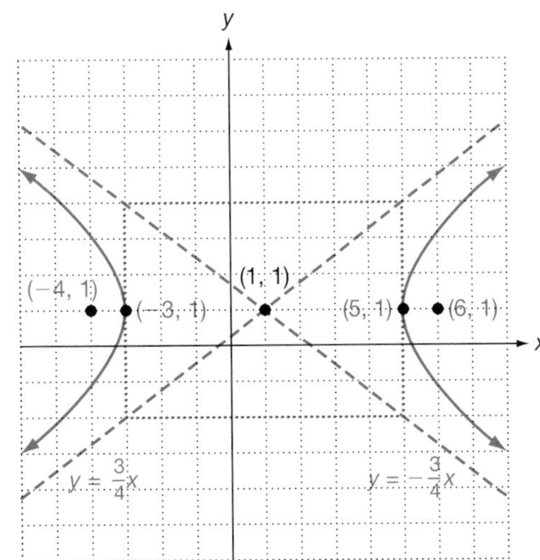

Try This Determine the equation represented by the graph.

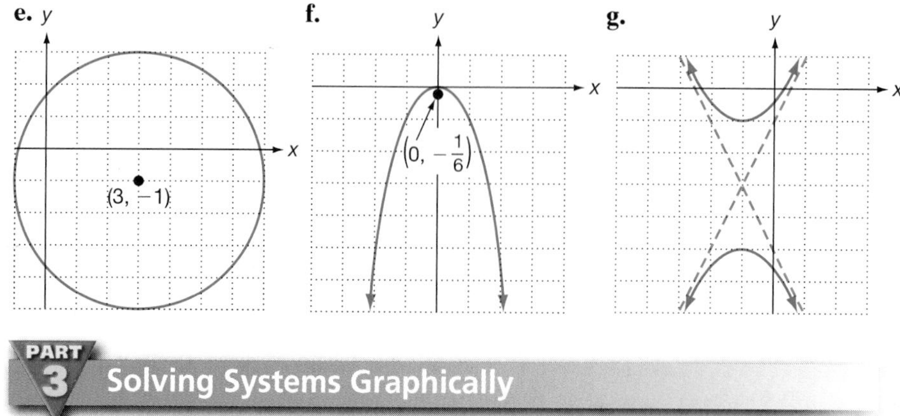

PART 3 Solving Systems Graphically

Objective: Solve second-degree systems graphically.

When we studied systems of linear equations, we solved them both graphically and algebraically. Here we study systems in which one equation is of first degree and one is of second degree. We will use graphical and then algebraic methods of solving. Recall that a solution is an ordered pair that satisfies all the equations in the system.

We consider a system of equations, an equation of a circle, and an equation of a line. Let us think about the possible ways in which a circle and a line can intersect. The three possibilities are shown in the figure at the right. For L_1 there is no point of intersection, hence the system of equations has no real solution. For L_2 there is one point of intersection, hence one real solution. For L_3 there are two points of intersection, hence two real solutions.

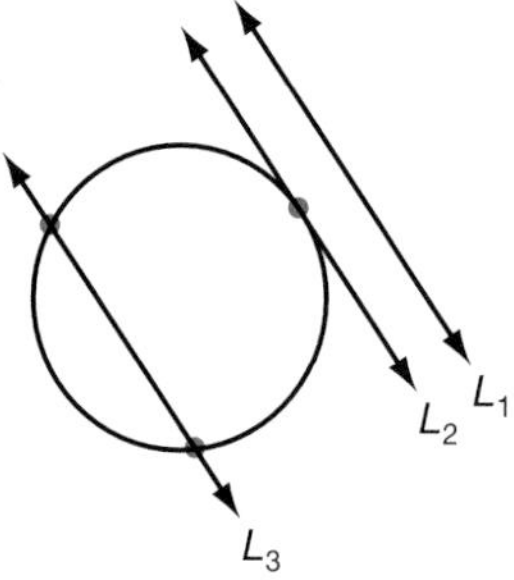

EXAMPLE 6 Solve graphically.

$$x^2 + y^2 = 25$$
$$3x - 4y = 0$$

We graph the two equations, using the same axes. The first is the graph of a circle. The points of intersection have coordinates that must satisfy both equations. The solutions appear to be (4, 3) and (−4, −3). These points each check in the system, so the solutions are (4, 3) and (−4, −3).

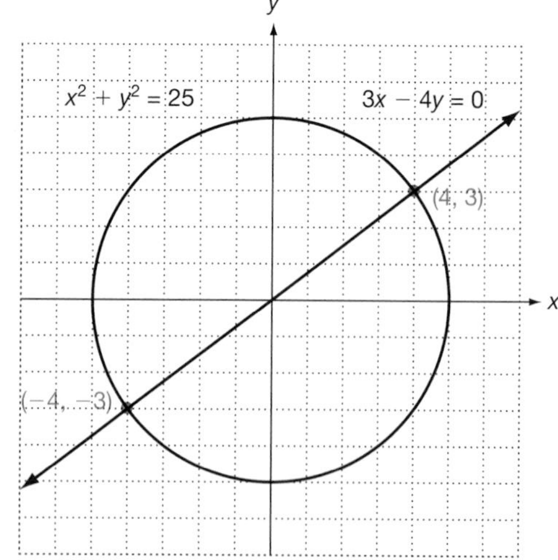

The following figures show ways in which a circle and a hyperbola can intersect.

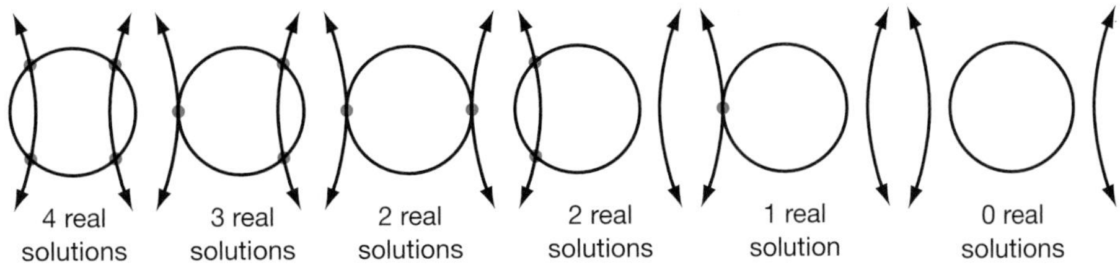

EXAMPLE 7 Solve this system graphically.

$$x^2 + y^2 = 25$$
$$\frac{x^2}{25} - \frac{y^2}{25} = 1$$

We graph the two equations using the same axes. The first equation is a circle and the second a hyperbola. The points of intersection have coordinates that must satisfy both equations; the solutions appear to be $(5, 0)$ and $(-5, 0)$.

Check: Since $(5)^2 = 25$ and $(-5)^2 = 25$, we can do both checks at once.

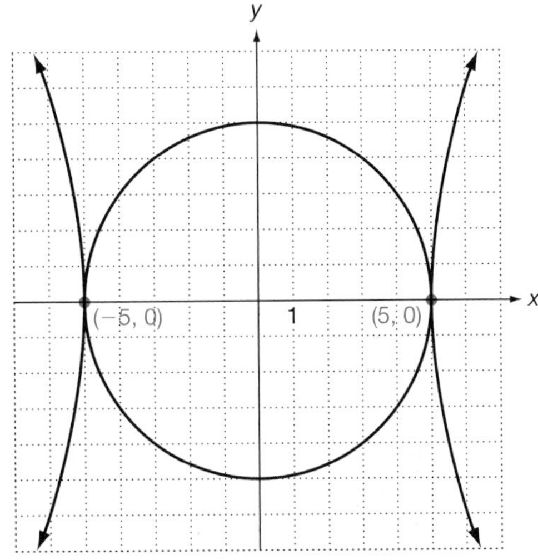

$x^2 + y^2 = 25$	
$(\pm 5)^2 + 0^2$	25
$25 + 0$	25
25	25 ✓

$\frac{x^2}{25} - \frac{y^2}{25} = 1$	
$\frac{(\pm 5)^2}{25} - \frac{0^2}{25}$	1
$1 - 0$	1
1	1 ✓

The solutions are $(5, 0)$ and $(-5, 0)$. This can be confirmed using computer graphing techniques.

Try This Solve these systems graphically.

h. $x^2 + y^2 = 25$
$y - x = -1$

i. $y = x^2 - 2x - 1$
$y = x + 3$

j. $x^2 + y^2 = 4$
$\frac{x^2}{4} - \frac{y^2}{4} = 1$

k. $x^2 + y^2 = 16$
$\frac{x^2}{16} + \frac{y^2}{9} = 1$

Look for worked-out examples at the Prentice Hall Web site.
www.phschool.com

10-6 Exercises

A

Tell which conic is defined by each equation.

1. $3x^2 - 2y^2 + 3y - 9 = 0$

2. $4x^2 + 4y^2 - 9y + 1 = 0$

3. $7x^2 + 8x - 3y + 7 = 0$

4. $-3x^2 - 4y^2 + 8y = 0$

5. $-4x^2 + 4y^2 + 6x - 2y + 3 = 0$

6. $-x^2 - y^2 - 3x + 2y + 4 = 0$

7. $\frac{x^2}{16} - \frac{y^2}{4} = 1$

8. $\frac{y^2}{25} + \frac{x^2}{16} = 1$

9. $20x^2 + y^2 + 10 = 0$

10. $\frac{x^2}{5} + \frac{y^2}{5} = 1$

Determine the equation represented by the graph.

11.

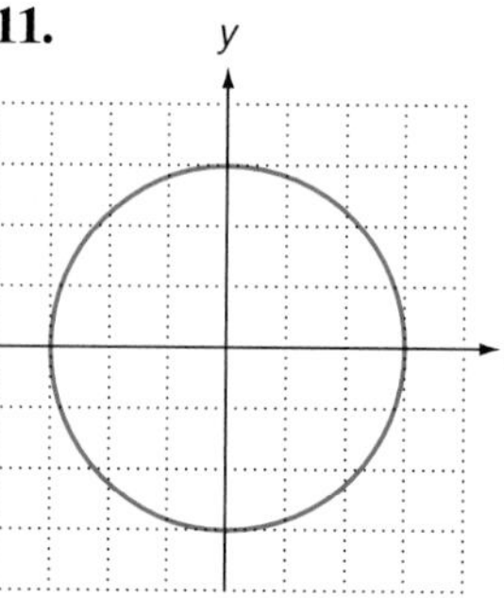

12.

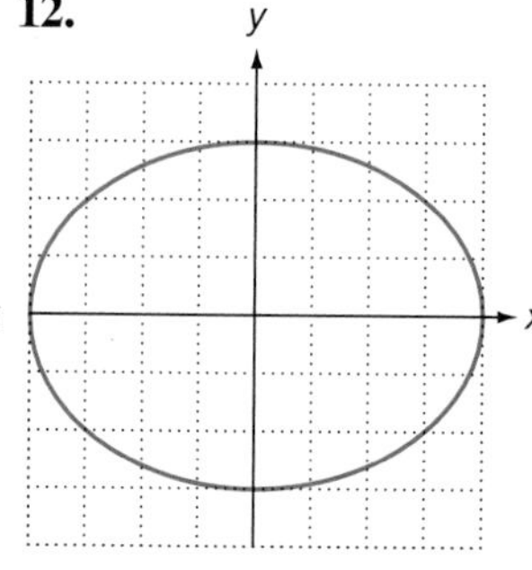

13.

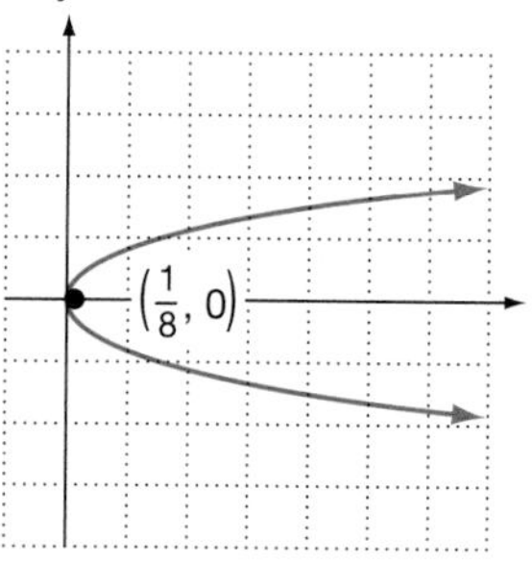

14.

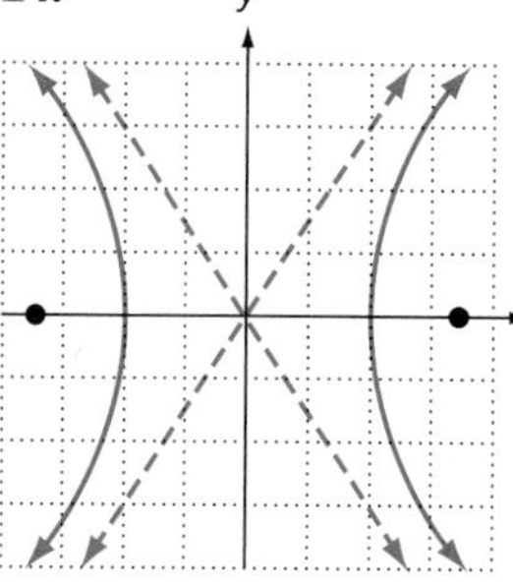

15.

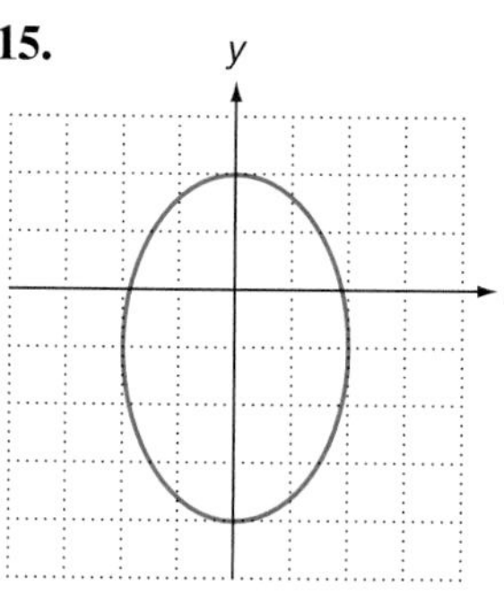

16.

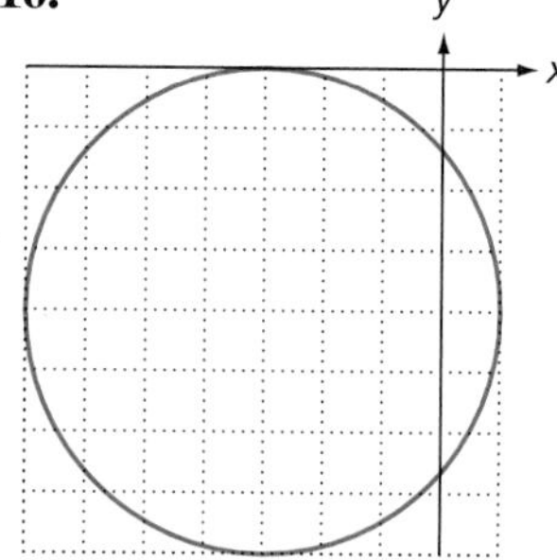

17.

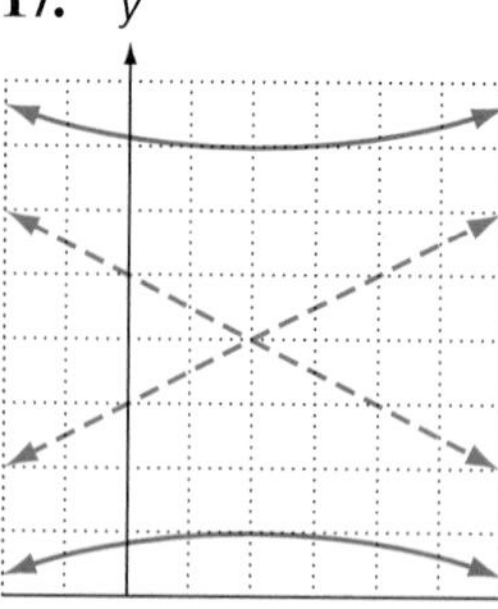

18.

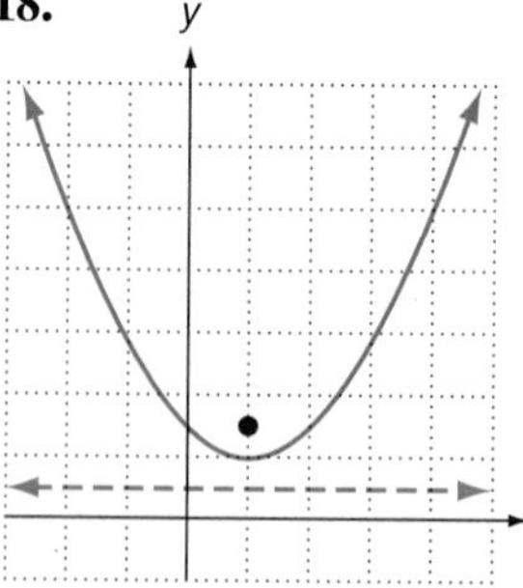

19.

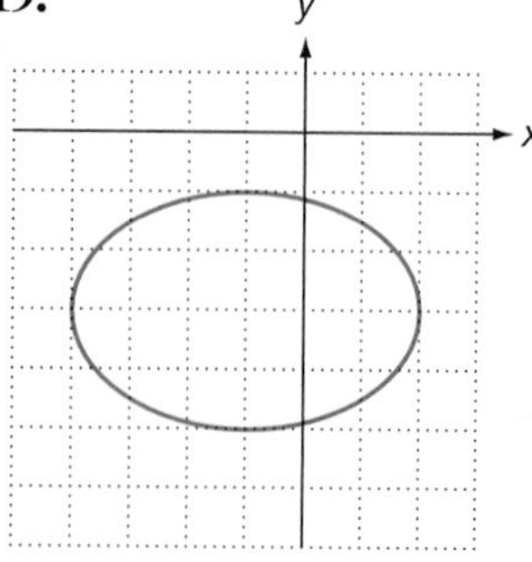

Solve each system graphically.

20. $x^2 + y^2 = 25$
$y - x = 1$

21. $x^2 + y^2 = 100$
$y - x = 2$

22. $y^2 - x^2 = 9$
$2x - 3 = y$

23. $x + y = -6$
$xy = -7$

24. $4x^2 + 9y^2 = 36$
$3y + 2x = 6$

25. $9x^2 + 4y^2 = 36$
$3x + 2y = 6$

26. $y^2 = x + 3$
$2y = x + 4$

27. $y = x^2$
$3x = y + 2$

28. $x^2 + y^2 = 25$
$y^2 = x + 5$

29. $y = x^2$
$x = y^2$

30. $x^2 + y^2 = 9$
$x^2 - y^2 = 9$

31. $y^2 - 4x^2 = 4$
$4x^2 + y^2 = 4$

32. $x^2 + y^2 = 25$
$xy = 12$

33. $x^2 - y^2 = 16$
$x + y^2 = 4$

34. $x^2 + y^2 = 4$
$16x^2 + 9y^2 = 144$

35. $x^2 + y^2 = 25$
$25x^2 + 16y^2 = 400$

B

Graph these systems of inequalities.

36. $x^2 + y^2 < 4$
$y < x + 2$

37. $x + 2 > y$
$y > x^2$

38. $x^2 + y^2 \leq 16$
$xy < 10$

39. $y \geq x^2 + 2$
$2x^2 + y^2 \leq 16$

40. $x^2 - y^2 \geq 10$
$x^2 + 4y^2 \geq 8$

41. ***Critical Thinking*** Begin with an equation of the form $Ax^2 + By^2 + Cx + Dy + E = 0$. Determine the conic section it defines. Then change *one* coefficient to obtain a different conic section. Do this two more times, obtaining all four conic sections.

Challenge

42. Graph $\frac{x^2}{4} + \frac{y^2}{12} = 1$. Then graph $x^2 + xy + y^2 = 6$ on a different set of axes. How do the graphs compare?

43. Consider the equation $x^2 + y^2 + 4x + 6y + 13 = 0$.

a. What figure is represented by the equation?
b. What, if any, ordered pairs are solutions of the equation?
c. Determine each coefficient for $Ax^2 + By^2 + Cx + Dy + E = 0$. Then find $C^2 + D^2 - 4AE$ for this equation. Generalize your results.

Mixed Review

Solve. **44.** $x^2 - 7x + 10 = 0$ **45.** $x^4 - 16x^2 = 0$ **46.** $x^4 - 16x^2 + 63 = 0$ *8-5*

Test for symmetry with respect to the origin. **47.** $|y| = 2x + 6$ *9-1*

Find the distance between the points. **48.** $(-4, -6)$ and $(1, 7)$

49. $(-1, 6)$ and $(-1, 3)$ **50.** $(2, -4)$ and $(-4, 4)$ **51.** $(0, 0)$ and $(\sqrt{m}, \sqrt{n})$ *10-1*

Find the coordinates of the midpoint of the segment having the following endpoints.

52. $(-2, 3)$ and $(-7, -1)$ **53.** $(3, 11)$ and $(2, 14)$ **54.** $(6, 0)$ and $(-11, 4)$ *10-1*

10-7 Solving Quadratic Systems Algebraically

What You'll Learn

1. To solve systems having a first-degree and a second-degree equation algebraically
2. To solve systems of second-degree equations algebraically

. . . And Why

To solve problems involving nonlinear systems of equations

PART 1 Solving Systems with One Second-Degree Equation

Objective: To solve systems with a first-degree and a second-degree equation algebraically.

Remember that we used linear combinations and the substitution method to solve systems of linear equations. In solving systems where one equation is of first degree and one is of second degree, it is preferable to use the substitution method.

EXAMPLE 1 Solve this system algebraically.

$$x^2 + y^2 = 25 \quad ①$$
$$3x - 4y = 0 \quad ②$$

We first solve the linear equation ② for x, finding $x = \frac{4}{3}y$. We then substitute $\frac{4}{3}y$ for x in the first equation and solve for y.

$$\left(\tfrac{4}{3}y\right)^2 + y^2 = 25$$
$$\tfrac{16}{9}y^2 + y^2 = 25$$
$$\tfrac{25}{9}y^2 = 25 \qquad \text{Combining like terms}$$
$$\tfrac{9}{25} \cdot \tfrac{25}{9}y^2 = \tfrac{9}{25} \cdot 25 \qquad \text{Multiplying both sides by } \tfrac{9}{25}$$
$$y^2 = 9$$
$$y = \pm 3$$

Now we substitute these numbers into the linear equation and solve for x.

$$3x - 4(3) = 0 \qquad 3x - 4(-3) = 0$$
$$3x = 12 \qquad 3x = -12$$
$$x = 4 \qquad x = -4$$

The pairs $(4, 3)$ and $(-4, -3)$ check and thus are the solutions.

Try This Solve these systems algebraically.

a. $x^2 + y^2 = 25$
$y - x = -1$

b. $y = x^2 - 2x - 1$
$y = x + 3$

c. $y = \frac{x^2}{4}$
$x + 2y = 4$

Sometimes an equation may not take on a familiar form like those studied previously in this chapter. We can still rely on the substitution method for the solution.

EXAMPLE 2 Solve this system.

$$y + 3 = 2x \quad ①$$
$$x^2 + 2xy = -1 \quad ②$$

We first solve the linear equation ① for y getting $y = 2x - 3$. We then substitute $2x - 3$ for y in equation ② and solve for x.

$$x^2 + 2x(2x - 3) = -1$$
$$x^2 + 4x^2 - 6x = -1$$
$$5x^2 - 6x + 1 = 0 \quad \text{Combining like terms}$$
$$(5x - 1)(x - 1) = 0 \quad \text{Factoring}$$
$$5x - 1 = 0 \text{ or } x - 1 = 0$$
$$x = \frac{1}{5} \text{ or } x = 1$$

Now we substitute these numbers into the linear equation and solve for y.

$$y + 3 = 2\left(\frac{1}{5}\right) \qquad y + 3 = 2(1)$$
$$y = \frac{2}{5} - 3 \qquad y = 2 - 3$$
$$y = -\frac{13}{5} \qquad y = -1$$

The pairs $\left(\frac{1}{5}, -\frac{13}{5}\right)$ and $(1, -1)$ check and thus are the solutions.

Try This Solve these systems.

d. $y - 3x = 1$
$xy = 10$

e. $xy = 18$
$y = 3x + 12$

f. $y^2 + 2xy + 5 = 2$
$2y + x = -4$

PART 2 Solving Systems of Second-Degree Equations

Objective: To solve systems of second-degree equations algebraically.

EXAMPLE 3 Solve this system of equations.

$$2x^2 + 5y^2 = 22 \quad ①$$
$$3x^2 - y^2 = -1 \quad ②$$

We recognize these as equations of an ellipse and a hyperbola. Here we use linear combinations.

$$2x^2 + 5y^2 = 22$$
$$15x^2 - 5y^2 = -5 \quad \text{Multiplying ② by 5}$$
$$17x^2 = 17 \quad \text{Adding}$$
$$x^2 = 1$$
$$x = \pm 1$$

If $x = 1$, $x^2 = 1$, and if $x = -1$, $x^2 = 1$, so we substitute 1 or -1 for x in equation ②.

$$3 \cdot 1^2 - y^2 = -1$$
$$y^2 = 4$$
$$y = \pm 2$$

Thus, if $x = 1$, $y = 2$ or $y = -2$. If $x = -1$, $y = 2$ or $y = -2$. The possible solutions are $(1, 2)$, $(1, -2)$, $(-1, 2)$, and $(-1, -2)$.

Each of these ordered pairs checks in the system, so the solutions are $(1, 2)$, $(1, -2)$, $(-1, 2)$, and $(-1, -2)$.

Try This Solve these systems.

g. $x^2 + y^2 = 4$
$\frac{x^2}{25} + \frac{y^2}{4} = 1$

h. $2y^2 - 3x^2 = 6$
$5y^2 + 2x^2 = 53$

i. $x^2 + y^2 = 25$
$y = x^2 - 13$

EXAMPLE 4 Solve this system of equations.

$$x^2 + 4y^2 = 20 \quad ①$$
$$xy = 4 \quad ②$$

Here we use the substitution method. First we solve equation ② for y.

$$y = \frac{4}{x}$$

Then we substitute $\frac{4}{x}$ for y in equation ① and solve for x.

$$x^2 + 4\left(\frac{4}{x}\right)^2 = 20$$
$$x^2 + \frac{64}{x^2} = 20$$
$$x^4 + 64 = 20x^2$$
$$x^4 - 20x^2 + 64 = 0$$
$$u^2 - 20u + 64 = 0 \quad \text{Letting } u = x^2$$
$$(u - 16)(u - 4) = 0$$
$$(x^2 - 16)(x^2 - 4) = 0 \quad \text{Substituting } x^2 \text{ for } u$$

Then $x = 4$ or $x = -4$ or $x = 2$ or $x = -2$. Since $y = \frac{4}{x}$, if $x = 4$, $y = 1$; if $x = -4$, $y = -1$; if $x = 2$, $y = 2$; if $x = -2$, $y = -2$. The solutions are $(4, 1)$, $(-4, -1)$, $(2, 2)$, and $(-2, -2)$.

Try This Solve these systems.

j. $x^2 + xy + y^2 = 19$
$xy = 6$

k. $xy = 8$
$8x^2 - y^2 = 16$

10-7 Exercises

Extra Help On the Web

Look for worked-out examples at the Prentice Hall Web site.
www.phschool.com

Solve.

1. $x^2 + 4y^2 = 25$
$x + 2y = 7$

2. $y^2 - x^2 = 16$
$2x - y = 1$

3. $x^2 - xy + 3y^2 = 5$
$x - y = 2$

4. $2y^2 + xy + x^2 = 7$
$x - 2y = 5$

5. $3x + y = 7$
$4x^2 + 5y = 24$

6. $2y^2 + xy = 5$
$4y + x = 7$

7. $x^2 + 3y^2 = 12$
$x + 3y = 6$

8. $2x + 3y = 2$
$2x^2 - 6xy + 3y^2 = -\frac{1}{6}$

9. $xy = -16$
$3x - 46 = 5y$

Solve.

10. $x^2 + y^2 = 16$
$y^2 - 2x^2 = 10$

11. $x^2 + y^2 = 14$
$x^2 - y^2 = 4$

12. $x^2 + y^2 = 5$
$xy = 2$

13. $x^2 + y^2 = 20$
$xy = 8$

14. $x^2 + y^2 = 13$
$xy = 6$

15. $x^2 + 4y^2 = 20$
$xy = 4$

16. $x^2 + y^2 = 7$
$xy = -12$

17. $2xy + 3y^2 = 7$
$3xy - 2y^2 = 4$

18. $y - x^2 = 0$
$x^2 = 20 - y^2$

19. $2x^2 + y^2 = 6$
$3x^2 - y^2 = 11$

Error Analysis **20.** Luc insists that since Exercise 19 is easily solved for x, it has a solution. What error is he making?

21. **TEST PREP** In how many points can a parabola and a circle intersect?

A. 0, 1, or 2
B. 0, 2, or 4
C. 0, 1, 2, 3, or 4
D. 0, 1, 2, or 4

B

Solve.

22. $x + y = 4$
$xy = 1$

23. $y = 3x^2$
$y = |x|$

24. $x^2 + y^2 + 6y + 5 = 0$
$x^2 + y^2 - 2x - 8 = 0$

25. *Critical Thinking* Write a system of equations whose graphs are **a)** a line and a circle, **b)** a hyperbola and an ellipse, **c)** a circle and a hyperbola, **d)** a parabola and an ellipse.

Challenge

26. Given the area (A) and the perimeter (P) of a rectangle, show that the length (L) and the width (W) are given by these formulas.

$$L = \frac{1}{4}(P + \sqrt{P^2 - 16A})$$
$$W = \frac{1}{4}(P - \sqrt{P^2 - 16A})$$

27. Show that a hyperbola does not intersect its asymptotes by solving the following system.

$$\frac{x^2}{a^2} - \frac{y^2}{b^2} = 1$$
$$y = \frac{b}{a}x \text{ or } y = -\frac{b}{a}x$$

28. Find an equation of a circle containing the points (2, 4) and (3, 3), and whose center is on the line $3x - y = 3$.

29. Find an equation of a circle containing the points (7, 3) and (5, 5), and whose center is on the line $y - 4x = 1$.

30. The area of a rectangle inscribed in a unit circle is 1. Find its length and width.

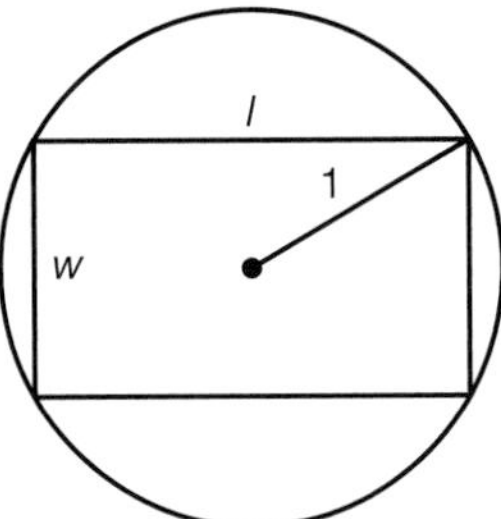

Mixed Review

Find the distance between points. **31.** (2, 5) and (2, 7) **32.** (1, −3) and (6, −8) *10-1*

33. Consider the circle $x^2 + y^2 = 49$. Find the center and radius. Draw a graph. *10-2*

34. The bottom of a hill is at an altitude of 273 feet above sea level. The top of the hill, which is 2640 feet horizontally from the bottom, is 603 feet above sea level.

a. Fit a linear function to the data, relating altitude to horizontal distance.

b. How far along the hill is a spot that is 500 feet above sea level? *3-8*

35. Calvin used to bicycle to school by traveling east for 3 km, then north for 4 km. A new road was constructed that allowed him to bicycle to school along a straight route. How much distance did the new route save him compared with the old route? *8-2*

Determine whether the graphs of each pair of equations are perpendicular.

36. $y = 3x - 6$ and $6y = 4 - 2x$

37. $y = 5x + 9$ and $2y = 11 - 10x$

38. $2x + 2y = 4$ and $y - x = 9$

39. $x - 5y = 4$ and $x + 5y = 9$

40. $y = 2$ and $y = -\frac{1}{2}$

41. $y = 2$ and $x = 2$ *3-7*

Using Systems of Second-Degree Equations

PART 1 Solving Problems Using Second-Degree Equations

Objective: Solve problems that translate to a system of second-degree equations.

What You'll Learn

1 To solve problems using systems of second-degree equations

. . . And Why

To solve problems involving nonlinear systems of equations

PROBLEM-SOLVING GUIDELINES
■ UNDERSTAND the problem
■ Develop and carry out a PLAN
■ Find the ANSWER and CHECK

Sometimes problem situations translate into a system of equations in which one equation is linear and the other is of second degree.

EXAMPLE 1 The perimeter of a rectangular field is 204 m and the area is 2565 m^2. Find the dimensions of the field.

■ **UNDERSTAND the problem**

Question: What are the dimensions of the field?
Data: The perimeter is 204 m. The area is 2565 m^2.

■ **Develop and carry out a PLAN**

We first translate the conditions of the problem to equations, using w for width and l for length. We also draw a diagram.

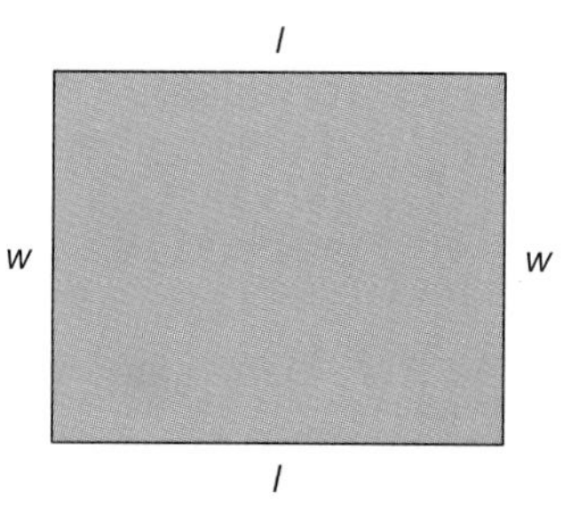

Perimeter: $2w + 2l = 204$ Linear equation
Area: $lw = 2565$ Equation of second degree

We next solve the system.

$$2w + 2l = 204$$
$$lw = 2565$$

The solution of the system is (45, 57).

■ **Find the ANSWER and CHECK**

The perimeter is $2 \cdot 45 + 2 \cdot 57$, or 204. Thus, the perimeter checks. The area is $45 \cdot 57$ or 2565. The area checks.

The dimensions of the field are 45 m by 57 m.

Try This

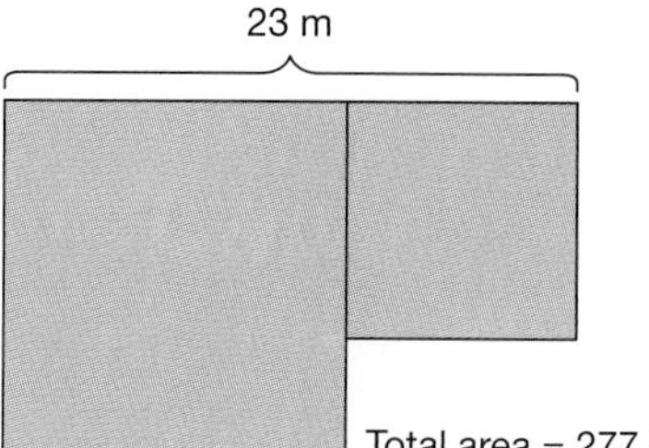

a. Find the length of a side of each square.
b. The perimeter of a rectangular field is 34 ft and the length of a diagonal is 13 ft. Find the dimensions of the field.

Some problem situations translate to a system of 2 second-degree equations.

EXAMPLE 2 The area of a rectangle is 300 yd^2 and the length of a diagonal is 25 yd. Find the dimensions.

First make a *drawing*.

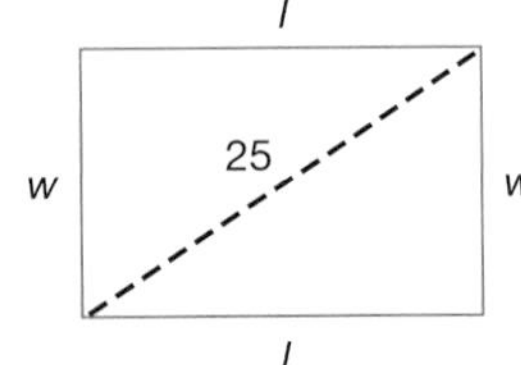

We use l for the length and w for the width and translate to equations.

$$l^2 + w^2 = 25^2 \quad \text{From the Pythagorean theorem}$$
$$lw = 300 \quad \text{Area}$$

Now we solve the system

$$l^2 + w^2 = 625$$
$$lw = 300$$

and get the solutions (15, 20) and (−15, −20). Now we check in the original problem, $20^2 + 15^2 = 25^2$ and $20 \cdot 15 = 300$, so (15, 20) is a solution of the problem. Lengths of sides cannot be negative, so (−15, −20) is not a solution. The answer is $l = 20$ yd and $w = 15$ yd.

Try This

c. The area of a rectangle is 2 ft^2 and the length of a diagonal is $\sqrt{5}$ ft. Find the dimensions of the rectangle.

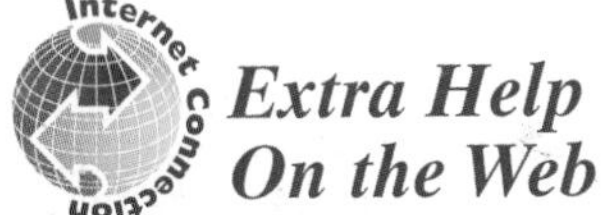

Extra Help On the Web

Look for worked-out examples at the Prentice Hall Web site.
www.phschool.com

10-8 Exercises

A

Solve.

1. A rectangle has perimeter 28 cm and the length of a diagonal is 10 cm. What are its dimensions?
2. A rectangle has perimeter 6 m and the length of a diagonal is $\sqrt{5}$ m. What are its dimensions?
3. A rectangle has area 20 $in.^2$ and perimeter 18 in. Find its dimensions.
4. A rectangle has area 2 yd^2 and perimeter 6 yd. Find its dimensions.
5. Find two numbers whose product is 156 if the sum of their squares is 313.
6. Find two numbers whose product is 60 if the sum of their squares is 136.
7. The area of a rectangle is $\sqrt{3}$ m^2 and the length of a diagonal is 2 m. Find its dimensions.
8. The area of a rectangle is $\sqrt{2}$ m^2 and the length of a diagonal is $\sqrt{3}$ m. Find its dimensions.
9. A garden contains two square beds of peanuts. The sum of their areas is 832 ft^2, and the difference of their areas is 320 ft^2. Find the length of each bed.

Peanuts are legumes, and grow underground at the ends of pegs sent into the ground from the plant's flowers. (See Exercise 9.)

10. A certain amount of money saved for 1 year at a certain interest rate yielded \$7.50. If the principal had been \$25 more and the interest rate 1% less, the interest would have been the same. Find the principal and the rate.

Find the length of the side of each square.

11. **12.**

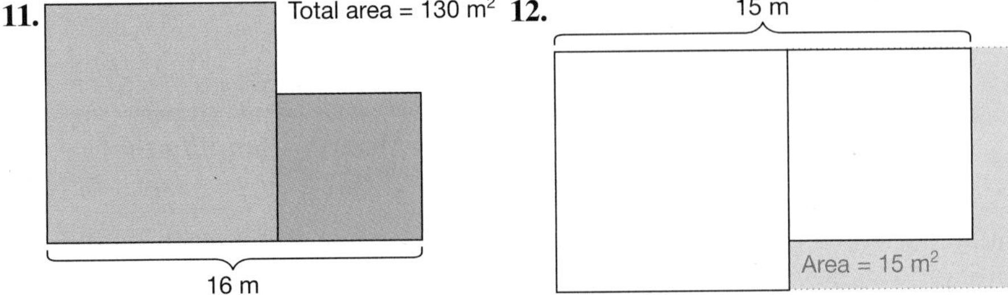

B

13. A right triangle has a hypotenuse of 50 cm and an area of 600 cm^2. Find the lengths of the legs of the triangle.

14. A rectangular lot has an area of 60 m^2. The length of a diagonal of the lot is 13 m. What are the length and the width of the lot?

15. *Critical Thinking* Suppose the green square in Exercise 11 is actually a rectangle that is half as high as the salmon square. What are the new dimensions of each figure?

Challenge

16. Starting from some point, Mark walks east and Erin walks north. After three hours, Erin has walked three miles farther than Mark and they are 15 miles apart. Find the rate of speed of each.

17. A carpenter worked alone on a job for two days and then hired a helper. The entire job was done in $5\frac{5}{7}$ days. Working alone, the carpenter could have done the job in four fewer days than the helper could have done the entire job alone. Find the time each would have needed to complete the job alone.

18. The graphs of two identical ellipses with foci on the x-axis are such that each ellipse passes through the center of the other. The equation of the first ellipse is $4x^2 + 9y^2 = 36$. The second ellipse is directly to the right of the first.

    a. Find the equation of the second ellipse in standard form.

    b. Find their points of intersection.

If the carpenter and helper of Exercise 17 had worked together to do the entire job, how long would it have taken?

Mixed Review

Find the midpoint coordinates of the segment having the following endpoints.

19. $(3, 11)$ and $(3, 9)$ **20.** $(6, -7)$ and $(11, 4)$ *10-1*

Find the quadratic function that fits the set of data points.

21. $(1, 5), (-1, -7), (-2, -7)$ **22.** $(1, 3), (2, 11), (-1, 5)$ *9-8*

10-9 Reasoning Strategies

What You'll Learn

1 To solve problems using the strategy *Simplify the Problem*

. . . And Why

To increase efficiency in solving problems by applying reasoning skills

PART 1 Simplify the Problem

Objective: Solve problems using the strategy *Simplify the Problem*, and other strategies.

Sometimes the numbers in a problem are so large that a direct solution is difficult. The problem-solving strategy called *Simplify the Problem* can often help. One way to simplify a problem is to find a solution using a small number. Then, using a larger number, find another solution. This process can then be repeated. When you have solutions to simpler problems, organizing the information in a *table* often helps you find a *pattern* and the solution to the original problem.

EXAMPLE How many squares are in the figure at the right?

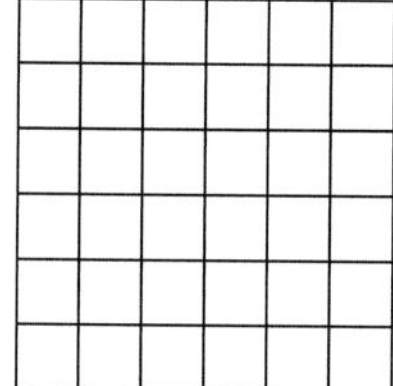

We can simplify the problem by asking how many squares are in a 1-by-1 square, then in a 2-by-2 square, a 3-by-3, and so on. *Drawing a diagram, making a table,* and *looking for a pattern* will help find the solution.

1 by 1

1 1×1 square
1 square in all

2 by 2

4 1×1 squares
1 2×2 square
5 squares in all

3 by 3

9 1×1 squares
4 2×2 squares
1 3×3 square
14 squares in all

4 by 4

16 1×1 squares
9 2×2 squares
4 3×3 squares
1 4×4 square
30 squares in all

Size of original square	Number of squares
1 by 1	1
2 by 2	$5 = 1 + 4$
3 by 3	$14 = 1 + 4 + 9$
4 by 4	$30 = 1 + 4 + 9 + 16$
5 by 5	$55 = 1 + 4 + 9 + 16 + 25$

Organizing the data in the *table* helps show the pattern in the number of squares. For an original square with n individual squares on a side, there are $1^2 + 2^2 + 3^2 + \cdots + n^2$ squares in the figure.

For the figure given in the Example, there are 6 individual squares on a side. So there are $1^2 + 2^2 + 3^2 + 4^2 + 5^2 + 6^2$ squares contained within the figure, or 91 squares.

Reasoning Strategies

Write an Equation	Draw a Diagram	Try, Test, Revise
Make an Organized List	Make a Table	Look for a Pattern
Use Logical Reasoning	Simplify the Problem	Work Backward

10-9 Problems

Look for worked-out examples at the Prentice Hall Web site.
www.phschool.com

Solve using one or more of the strategies.

1. A large circular park is to have six straight walking paths cut through it. The architect has been told to design the park so there will be a maximum number of flower and garden areas inside the park and around the paths. What is the greatest number of flower and garden areas possible with the six straight paths?
2. A tractor-trailer is to carry cartons and boxes. The cartons and boxes are different sizes, but all the cartons are the same size and all the boxes are the same size. When full, the trailer can carry 24 cartons and 20 boxes. When half full, the trailer can carry 6 cartons and 13 boxes. If the trailer is to carry only cartons or only boxes, how many of each can it carry?
3. In a holiday basketball tournament, there were a total of 64 teams. When a team lost, it was eliminated from the tournament and played no more games. To win the tournament, a team could not lose any games. How many games were needed to determine a champion?
4. What should be the dimensions of the bottom row of a pyramid that continues to build like the one at the right, if there are 100 blocks to work with and as many blocks as possible are to be used?
5. Some students were comparing the sizes of the bands in different schools. Roosevelt and Central Highs' bands have a combined total of 385 students. Roosevelt and Riverside Highs' bands have a combined total of 320 students. Central's band has 65 more members than Riverside's. Roosevelt's band has 70 more members than Riverside's. How many members are in each school's band?

In a tournament such as that described in Exercise 3, the number of teams is usually a power of 2. Explain why.

Application

Inferring Data

Often information is presented in journals, articles, papers, and other forms of communication. Problems then can be solved by gathering data and using them to make calculations. Read the following article and answer the questions below.

On January 24, 1986, the *Voyager II* spacecraft transmitted signals toward Earth. These transmissions were the first to contain explicit data about the planet Uranus. As these transmissions traveled at 186,000 miles per second (the speed of light), scientists on Earth waited for two hours and 25 minutes to receive them.

While this was certainly a long wait, scientists had waited much longer for *Voyager* to reach Uranus. Its trek began September 5, 1977, and its journey utilized the gravitational pull of Jupiter and Saturn to "fling" the spacecraft across the solar system.

Imagine swinging a piece of string with a weight attached, then letting go. This was the effect of the planets' gravitational pull on *Voyager*. In the same way, the gravitational pull of Uranus sent *Voyager* to Neptune for an August 24, 1989, rendezvous.

The planets must be in a specific position before this "gravity-powered" trip is possible. In fact, this configuration occurs only once every 177 years.

Because *Voyager* approached Uranus in a spiral path, its 1.8-billion-mile trip was considerably farther than the distance between Earth and Uranus. When describing distances of this magnitude, scientists often use more convenient units such as the astronomical unit (93,000,000 miles, the average distance between the Earth and the sun), or the light-year, the distance that light travels in one year.

Voyager II's journey has been a remarkable one. Consider that its scaled equivalent is tossing an atom several hundred yards in order to hit another atom. *Voyager II* is expected to continue sending information from beyond the solar system until around 2020.

Problems

1. **a.** How many miles did *Voyager* travel from Earth to Uranus?
   b. How long was its journey in astronomical units (AUs)?
   c. How far was its trip in light-years?
2. **a.** How many days did it take *Voyager* to travel from Earth to Uranus?
   b. How many hours did the trip take?
3. Calculate *Voyager*'s speed, in miles per hour, for the trip from Earth to Uranus.
4. What is the speed of light in miles per hour?
5. Express the ratio of the speed of light to the speed of *Voyager*.
6. Earth and the moon are 234,000 miles apart. How long did it take the words ". . . one small step for man, . . . " to reach Earth?
7. How many miles apart were Earth and Uranus on January 24, 1986?

10 Chapter Wrap Up

10-1 The **distance** between any two points (x_1, y_1) and (x_2, y_2) is given by $d = \sqrt{(x_1 - x_2)^2 + (y_1 - y_2)^2}$.

Find the distance between the points.

1. $(-3, 4)$ and $(7, 0)$ **2.** $(0, 3)$ and $(4, 0)$ **3.** $(2, -4)$ and $(-9, 6)$

If the coordinates of the endpoints of a segment are (x_1, y_1) and (x_2, y_2), then the coordinates of the **midpoint** are $\left(\frac{x_1 + x_2}{2}, \frac{y_1 + y_2}{2}\right)$.

Find the midpoint of the segments having the following endpoints.

4. $(-3, 4)$ and $(7, 0)$ **5.** $(-2, 4)$ and $(6, 8)$

6. $(-8, -1,)$ and $(4, 5)$ **7.** $(0, 3)$ and $(10, 7)$

10-2 The equation, in standard form, of a **circle** with center (h, k) and radius r is $(x - h)^2 + (y - k)^2 = r^2$.

Find an equation of the circle with center and radius as given.

8. $(-2, 6); \sqrt{13}$ **9.** $(3, -1); 2$

Completing the square can be used to produce the standard form of the equation of a circle.

Find the center and radius of the circle.

10. $(x - 4)^2 + (y + 3)^2 = 12$ **11.** $x^2 + y^2 = 36$

12. $x^2 + y^2 - 6x + 10y + 24 = 0$ **13.** $2x^2 + 2y^2 - 3x - 5y + 3 = 0$

10-3 The equation, in standard form, of an **ellipse** centered at (h, k) with foci c units from (h, k) and major axis of length $2a$, is $\frac{(x - h)^2}{a^2} + \frac{(y - k)^2}{b^2} = 1$ for a horizontal major axis, or $\frac{(x - h)^2}{b^2} + \frac{(y - k)^2}{a^2} = 1$ for a vertical major axis where $c^2 = a^2 - b^2$.

Remember that completing the square can be used to produce the standard form of the equation of an ellipse.

For each ellipse find the center, vertices, and foci. Then draw a graph.

14. $16x^2 + 25y^2 - 64x + 50y - 311 = 0$

15. $9x^2 + 16y^2 + 36x - 32y - 92 = 0$

10-4 The equation, in standard form, of a **hyperbola** centered at (h, k) with foci c units from (h, k) is $\frac{(x - h)^2}{a^2} - \frac{(y - k)^2}{b^2} = 1$ for horizontal foci, or $\frac{(y - k)^2}{a^2} - \frac{(x - h)^2}{b^2} = 1$ for vertical foci, where $c^2 = a^2 + b^2$.

Key Terms

asymptotes of a hyperbola (p. 446)
branches of a hyperbola (p. 445)
catenary (p. 452)
center of a circle (p. 433)
center of a hyperbola (p. 445)
center of an ellipse (p. 439)
circle (p. 433)
cone (p. 433)
conic section (p. 433)
conjugate axis (p. 445)
conjugate hyperbolas (p. 450)
directrix (p. 452)
distance formula (p. 430)
eccentricity of a hyperbola (p. 451)
eccentricity of an ellipse (p. 443)
element of a cone (p. 433)
ellipse (p. 438)
focal radii of a hyperbola (p. 445)
focal radii of an ellipse (p. 438)
foci (p. 438)
focus of a hyperbola (p. 445)
focus of a parabola (p. 452)
focus of an ellipse (p. 438)
hyperbola (p. 445)
major axis of an ellipse (p. 439)
midpoint of a segment (p. 431)
minor axis of an ellipse (p. 439)
parabola (p. 452)
radius of a circle (p. 433)
transverse axis (p. 445)
unit circle (p. 437)
vertex of a cone (p. 433)
vertices of a hyperbola (p. 445)
vertices of an ellipse (p. 439)

Look for extension problems for this chapter at the Prentice Hall Web site. www.phschool.com

For each hyperbola, find the center, vertices, foci, and asymptotes. Then draw a graph.

16. $x^2 - 2y^2 + 4x + y - \frac{1}{8} = 0$ **17.** $8x^2 - 3y^2 = 48$

10-5 A **parabola** with vertex (h, k) and axis of symmetry parallel to the y-axis has an equation $(x - h)^2 = 4p(y - k)$ with focus $(h, k + p)$ and directrix $y = k - p$. A parabola with vertex (h, k) and axis of symmetry parallel to the x-axis has an equation $(y - k)^2 = 4p(x - h)$ with focus $(h + p, k)$ and directrix $x = h - p$.

For each parabola find the vertex, focus, and directrix. Then draw a graph.

18. $y^2 = -12x$ **19.** $(x - 1)^2 - 2(y + 1) = 0$ **20.** $y^2 + 2y + 4x - 8 = 0$

10-6 Consider the second-degree equation $Ax^2 + By^2 + Cx + Dy + E = 0$.

1. If $A = B$, the equation may define a circle.
2. If A and B have the same sign and $A \neq B$, the equation may define an ellipse.
3. If A and B have different signs, the equation defines a hyperbola.
4. If either A or B is 0, the equation defines a parabola.

Tell which conic section is defined by the following equations.

21. $2x^2 - 2y^2 + 3x - 2 = 0$ **22.** $5y^2 + 10y + 2x + 2 = 0$

23. $2x - 2y^2 - 2x^2 - 3y + 16 = 0$

24. $\frac{x^2}{5^2} + \frac{y^2}{1} = 1$ **25.** $\frac{x^2}{3} + \frac{y^2}{3} + 2 = 1$

To solve a system of equations graphically, it is helpful to be able to recognize equations of the different conic sections.

Solve graphically.

26. $y^2 = 100 - x^2$
$y = x + 2$

27. $y = x^2 + 1$
$x + 2y = 5$

Solve graphically.

28. $x^2 + y^2 = 16$
$\frac{x^2}{16} + \frac{y^2}{9} = 1$

10-7 When one equation of a system is quadratic, the substitution method is preferable.

Solve.

29. $\frac{x^2}{16} + \frac{y^2}{9} = 1$
$3x + 4y = 12$

To solve systems of two second-degree equations algebraically, use either substitution or linear combinations.

Solve.

30. $x^2 + y^2 = 29$
$y^2 - 3x^2 = 13$

31. $4x^2 - 9y^2 = 108$
$xy = -12$

10-8 Some problems can be solved after translating to a system of second-degree equations.

32. The area of a rectangle is 240 cm^2 and the length of a diagonal is 26 cm. Find the dimensions of the rectangle.

33. Find two numbers whose product is -48 if the sum of their squares is 265.

10 Chapter Assessment

Find the distance between the points.

1. $(-3, 4)$ and $(7, 6)$

2. $(4, -1)$ and $(-2, 0)$

Find the midpoint of the segment having the following endpoints.

3. $(-3, 4)$ and $(7, 6)$

4. $(-2, -3)$ and $(0, 1)$

5. Find an equation of the circle with center $(4, -1)$ and radius 5.

6. Find the center and radius of the circle $x^2 + y^2 - 8x + 12y + 49 = 0$.

7. Find the center, vertices, and foci of the ellipse $x^2 + 4y^2 - 6x + 24y + 41 = 0$. Then graph the ellipse.

8. Find the center, vertices, foci, and asymptotes of the hyperbola $25x^2 - 9y^2 = 225$.

9. Find the vertex, focus, and directrix of the parabola $x^2 + 2x + 6y - 11 = 0$. Then graph the parabola.

10. Which conic section is defined by $2x^2 - 5y^2 + 2x - 3y - 6 = 0$?

11. Solve graphically.
$y = x^2 - 2$
$3x - 2y = 2$

12. Solve.
$x^2 + y^2 = 74$
$x - y = 2$

13. Solve graphically.
$x^2 + y^2 = 25$
$x + y = 5$

14. Solve.
$3x^2 - 8y^2 = 3$
$y^2 = x + 4$

15. Two squares whose sides differ in length by 9 m have areas that differ by 153 m^2. Find the length of a side of each.

Challenge

16. Find the equation of a circle containing the points $(0, -2)$ and $(6, 6)$ and whose center is on the line $x - y = 1$.

CHAPTER 11

What You'll Learn in Chapter 11

- How to find roots, zeros, and factors of polynomials, using the Factor Theorem, division, and synthetic division
- How to solve polynomial equations
- How to determine the nature and number of the roots of a polynomial equation
- How to use Descartes' rule of signs
- How to graph and find zeros of polynomial functions
- How to find polynomials with specific roots
- How to find rational and other roots of a polynomial given its degree and several roots

Skills & Concepts You Need for Chapter 11

5-4, 5-6 Factor.

1. $x^2 + x - 6$ **2.** $x^2 - 5x + 4$ **3.** $3x^2 + 2x - 1$

4. $2x^2 + 7x + 6$ **5.** $4x^2 + x - 5$ **6.** $x^2 - 11x + 24$

7-9 Find the conjugate of each.

7. $-3 + 8i$ **8.** $2 - 4i$

7-9 Multiply.

9. $(1 - 5i)(1 + 5i)$ **10.** $(3 - 2i)(3 + 2i)$

11. $(-6 - i)(-6 + i)$

7-10 Determine whether each of the following is a solution of $x^2 - 2x + 1 = 0$.

12. 1 **13.** $1 + i$ **14.** $1 - i$

15. Find an equation having -2, i, and $3i$ as solutions.

16. Show that $-1 - i$ is a square root of $2i$. Then find the other square root.

8-4 Find a quadratic equation having the given solutions.

17. $-5, \frac{2}{3}$ **18.** $\frac{1}{2}, -\frac{3}{2}$ **19.** $\sqrt{2}, -\sqrt{2}$

Polynomial Functions

Pallets in this picture hold cartons. If cartons are stacked on a pallet 3 long, 4 wide, and 4 high, how many cartons are on pallets stacked 5 high, 10 rows wide, and 20 rows long?

11-1 Polynomials and Polynomial Functions

What You'll Learn

1. To determine by division whether a number is a root or zero of a polynomial equation or function
2. To determine by division whether one polynomial is a factor of another

. . . And Why

To solve problems in which there is a remainder

Recall from Chapter 5 that a polynomial in x is any expression of the form

$$a_nx^n + a_{n-1}x^{n-1} + a_{n-2}x^{n-2} + \ldots + a_1x + a_0, \text{ with real coefficients.}$$

We usually assume the coefficients are complex numbers, but in some cases restrict them to be real or rational numbers, or integers. Recall that the coefficient of the term of highest degree, a_n, is the **leading coefficient.**

PART 1 Roots and Zeros

Objective: Determine whether a number is a root or zero of a given equation or function.

When a number is substituted for the variable in a polynomial, the result is some unique number. Thus every polynomial defines a function. We often refer to polynomials, therefore, using function notation $P(x)$.

When we set a polynomial equal to 0, we obtain a **polynomial equation** $P(x) = 0$.

Definition

If a number n is a solution of a **polynomial equation** $P(x) = 0$, then n is called a **root** of the equation.

If a number n, when substituted for x, makes a polynomial function $P(x)$ zero, then n is called a **zero** of the function.

EXAMPLE 1 Determine whether the given numbers are roots of the polynomial equation $P(x) = 0$, where $P(x) = x^3 - 5x^2 + x - 5$.

$$x^3 - 5x^2 + x - 5 = 0$$

(a) -5; $\quad (-5)^3 - 5(-5)^2 + (-5) - 5 = 0$ Substituting -5 for x

$$-125 - 125 - 5 - 5 = 0$$
$$-260 = 0$$

Substituting -5 for x yields a false equation, so -5 is not a root.

(b) $-i$; $\quad (-i)^3 - 5(-i)^2 + (-i) - 5 = 0$

$$i + 5 - i - 5 = 0 \qquad (-i)^3 = -i(-i)^2 = -i(-1) = i$$
$$0 = 0$$

Substituting $-i$ for x yields a true equation, thus $-i$ is a root of the equation $P(x) = 0$.

EXAMPLE 2 Determine whether the given numbers are zeros of the polynomial function $P(x)$, where $P(x)$ is given by $x^3 - 3x^2 + x - 3$.

$$
\begin{aligned}
& P(x) = x^3 - 3x^2 + x - 3 \\
\text{(a) } 3;\ & P(3) = 3^3 - 3(3)^2 + 3 - 3 \quad \text{Evaluating the function } P(x) \text{ for } x = 3 \\
& \qquad = 27 - 27 + 3 - 3 \\
& \qquad = 0
\end{aligned}
$$

$P(3) = 0$, so 3 is a zero of the function.

$$
\begin{aligned}
\text{(b) } 2i;\ & P(2i) = (2i)^3 - 3(2i)^2 + 2i - 3 \\
& \qquad = -8i + 12 + 2i - 3 \\
& \qquad = -6i + 9
\end{aligned}
$$

$P(2i) \neq 0$, so $2i$ is not a zero of the function.

Try This

a. Determine whether the given numbers are roots of the polynomial equation $P(x) = 0$, where $P(x) = x^3 + x^2 - 2x$.

(1) 0 (2) i

b. Determine whether the given numbers are zeros of the polynomial function $P(x)$, where $P(x)$ is given by $x^4 - 2x^3 + 4x^2 - 8x$.

(1) $2i$ (2) -2

PART 2 Factors and Division

Objective: Determine whether one polynomial is a factor of another by division.

When we divide one polynomial by another we obtain a quotient and a remainder. If the remainder is 0, then the divisor is a **factor** of the dividend.

EXAMPLE 3 Divide to determine whether $x^2 + 3$ is a factor of the polynomial $x^3 - x^2 + 5x - 4$.

We use polynomial long division here.

$$
\begin{array}{r|l}
 & x - 1 \\
\hline
x^2 + 3 & x^3 - x^2 + 5x - 4 \\
 & x^3 \qquad\quad + 3x \\
\hline
 & \quad - x^2 + 2x - 4 \\
 & \quad - x^2 \qquad\ - 3 \\
\hline
 & \qquad\quad 2x - 1
\end{array}
$$

Since the remainder is not 0, we know that $x^2 + 3$ is not a factor of the polynomial $x^3 - x^2 + 5x - 4$.

EXAMPLE 4 Divide to determine whether $x - 3$ is a factor of the polynomial $x^4 - 3x^3 - x + 3$.

We can use synthetic division here.

$$\begin{array}{r|rrrrr} 3 & 1 & -3 & 0 & -1 & 3 \\ & & 3 & 0 & 0 & -3 \\ \hline & 1 & 0 & 0 & -1 & \boxed{0} \end{array}$$

Since the remainder is 0, we know that $x - 3$ is a factor of the polynomial $x^4 - 3x^3 - x + 3$. That is, $x^4 - 3x^3 - x + 3 = (x - 3)(x^3 - 1)$.

Try This

c. Divide to determine whether the following polynomials are factors of the polynomial $x^3 + 2x^2 - 5x - 6$.

(1) $x - 3$ (2) $x + 1$

d. Divide to determine whether the following polynomials are factors of the polynomial $x^4 + 3x^3 - 3x - 1$.

(1) $x^2 + 3x + 1$ (2) $x^3 + 2x^2 - 2x + 1$

When we divide a polynomial $P(x)$ by a divisor $D(x)$ we obtain a polynomial $Q(x)$ for a quotient and a polynomial $R(x)$ for a remainder. The remainder must either be 0 or have degree less than that of $D(x)$.

Thus we can express every polynomial division as

$$\underbrace{P(x)}_{\text{dividend}} = \underbrace{D(x)}_{\text{divisor}} \cdot \underbrace{Q(x)}_{\text{quotient}} + \underbrace{R(x)}_{\text{remainder}}$$

Journal

Write a short paragraph in which you contrast a zero of a polynomial $P(x)$ and the solution of an equation $P(x) = 0$.

EXAMPLE 5 Let $P(x) = 5x^3 - 6x^2 + 18x - 4$ and $D(x) = x^2 - x + 3$. Find $P(x) \div D(x)$, then express the dividend as $P(x) = D(x) \cdot Q(x) + R(x)$.

We divide.

$$\begin{array}{r} 5x \quad - 1 \\ x^2 - x + 3 \overline{)5x^3 - 6x^2 + 18x - 4} \\ \underline{5x^3 - 5x^2 + 15x } \\ -x^2 + 3x - 4 \\ \underline{-x^2 + x - 3} \\ 2x - 1 \end{array}$$

The quotient is $5x - 1$ with a remainder of $2x - 1$. Now we express $P(x)$ as the product of a divisor and a quotient, plus a remainder.

$$\begin{array}{ccccc} P(x) & = & D(x) & \cdot\ Q(x) & + R(x) \\ 5x^3 - 6x^2 + 18x - 4 & = & (x^2 - x + 3) & \cdot\ (5x - 1) & + 2x - 1 \end{array}$$

Try This

e. Let $P(x) = x^3 + 2x^2 - 5x - 6$ and $D(x) = x - 3$. Find $P(x) \div D(x)$, then express the dividend as $P(x) = D(x) \cdot Q(x) + R(x)$.

11-1 Exercises

Look for worked-out examples at the Prentice Hall Web site.
www.phschool.com

A

Mental Math Determine whether the following numbers are roots of the polynomial equation $P(x) = 0$.

1. $P(x) = x^3 + 6x^2 - x - 30$; $2, 3, -1$

2. $P(x) = 2x^3 - 3x^2 + x - 1$; $2, 3, -1$

Determine whether the given numbers are zeros of the polynomial functions.

3. $P(x) = x^3 - 2x^2 + 8x$; $0, -1, 1 + i\sqrt{7}, 1 - i\sqrt{7}$

4. $P(x) = x^3 - 2x^2 + 2x$; $0, -2, 1 + i, 1 - i$

Divide to determine whether the following polynomials are factors of the polynomial $P(x)$.

5. $P(x) = x^3 + 6x^2 - x - 30$
  a. $x - 2$ **b.** $x - 3$ **c.** $x + 1$

6. $P(x) = 2x^3 - 3x^2 + x - 1$
  a. $x - 2$ **b.** $x - 3$ **c.** $x + 1$

7. $P(x) = x^4 - 81$
  a. $x - 3$ **b.** $x + 3$ **c.** $x + 9$

8. $P(x) = x^5 + 32$
  a. $x - 2$ **b.** $x + 2$ **c.** $x - 4$

9. $P(x) = x^6 - 1$
  a. $x - 1$ **b.** $x^2 + x + 1$ **c.** $x^2 - x + 1$

10. $P(x) = 2x^4 + 10x^3 - 3x^2 - 5x + 1$
  a. $2x^2 + 1$ **b.** $2x^2 - 1$ **c.** $x^2 + 5$

Divide each $P(x)$ by $D(x)$. Then express the dividend as $P(x) = D(x) \cdot Q(x) + R(x)$.

11. $P(x) = x^3 + 6x^2 - x - 30$
  a. $D(x) = x - 2$ **b.** $D(x) = x - 3$

12. $P(x) = 2x^3 - 3x^2 + x - 1$
  a. $D(x) = x - 2$ **b.** $D(x) = x - 3$

13. $P(x) = x^3 - 8$
  $D(x) = x + 2$

14. $P(x) = x^3 + 27$
  $D(x) = x + 1$

15. $P(x) = x^4 + 9x^2 + 20$
  $D(x) = x^2 + 4$

16. $P(x) = x^4 + x^2 + 2$
  $D(x) = x^2 + x + 1$

17. $P(x) = 5x^5 - 3x^4 + 2x^2 - 3$
  $D(x) = 2x^2 - x + 1$

18. $P(x) = 6x^5 + 4x^4 - 3x^2 + x - 2$
  $D(x) = 3x^2 + 2x - 1$

B

Given $P(x) = D(x) \cdot Q(x) + R(x)$, find $P(x)$ if

19. $D(x) = x + 3$; $Q(x) = 2x^2 + x - 3$; and $R(x) = 4$

20. $D(x) = 4x - 3$; $Q(x) = x^2 + x + 2$; and $R(x) = 2x + 1$

21. $D(x) = x^2 - x + 3$; $Q(x) = 6x - 2$; and $R(x) = 3x + 2$

22. *Critical Thinking* Suppose 2 is a zero of a polynomial function. After translating the graph left 3 units, 2 is a zero of the new function. What do you know about the original function?

23. **TEST PREP** Divide $x^3 - 4x^2 - 4x + 51$ by $x + 3$. Divide the resulting quotient by $x - 2$ to determine the remainder. Choose the correct answer.

A. -7 **B.** 7 **C.** 51 **D.** 43

Challenge

24. $P(x) = 2x^2 - ix + 1$

a. Find $P(-i)$.

b. Find the remainder when $P(x)$ is divided by $x + i$.

25. $P(x) = 2x^2 + ix - 1$

a. Find $P(i)$.

b. Find the remainder when $P(x)$ is divided by $x - i$.

26. Under what conditions is a polynomial function of real variables an even function, that is, $P(x) = P(-x)$ for all x? Does your answer hold for complex variables?

27. Under what conditions is a polynomial function of real variables an odd function, that is, $-P(x) = P(-x)$ for all x? Does your answer hold for complex variables?

Mixed Review

Determine whether each function is odd, even, or neither. **28.** $f(x) = |5x|$

29. $f(x) = \frac{2}{3}x$ **30.** $f(x) = |x| + x$ **31.** $f(x) = x^3 + x$ 9-1

Graph each equation. **32.** $y = |x|$ **33.** $y = -2|x|$ **34.** $y = |x + 1|$ 2-7

Solve by completing the square. **35.** $x^2 + \frac{1}{2}x = 0$ **36.** $y^2 - \frac{2}{3}y = 1$ 8-1

37. $a^2 - \frac{m}{n}a = 0$ (Solve for a.) 8-1

38. A contestant in a competition scores 4 points for working a math problem and 6 points for a chemistry problem. There are 12 of each type of problem. The contestant must work 7 math problems and 3 chemistry problems. A timer prevents the person from working more than 17 total problems.

a. How many of each type should the contestant work?

b. What is the maximum score? 4-8

The Remainder and Factor Theorems

11-2

Introducing the Concept: Comparing Evaluations and Remainders

Let $P(x) = x^5 - 64$.

Find $P(2)$.

Then find the remainder when $P(x)$ is divided by $x - 2$.
Compare your answers.

Find $P(-2)$. Then find the remainder when $P(x)$ is divided by $x + 2$.

Make a generalization about the results.

What You'll Learn

1. To use synthetic division and the Remainder Theorem
2. To determine whether a given number is a root of a polynomial
3. To determine whether $x - r$ is a factor of a polynomial function and to solve polynomial equations

. . . And Why

To find solutions of higher-degree equations

PART 1 Function Values of Polynomials

Objective: Use synthetic division and the remainder theorem to find *P*(*r*).

The introductory work suggests the following important theorem about function values.

Theorem 11-1

The Remainder Theorem

For a polynomial $P(x)$, the function value $P(r)$ is the remainder when $P(x)$ is divided by $x - r$.

We can now use synthetic division to find function values for polynomials.

EXAMPLE 1 Let $P(x) = 2x^5 - 3x^4 + x^3 - 2x^2 + x - 8$. Find $P(10)$.

By Theorem 11-1, $P(10)$ is the remainder when $P(x)$ is divided by $x - 10$. We use synthetic division to find that remainder.

10	2	−3	1	−2	1	−8
		20	170	1710	17,080	170,810
	2	17	171	1708	17,081	170,802

Thus $P(10) = 170{,}802$.

Try This Let $P(x) = x^5 - 2x^4 - 7x^3 + x^2 + 20$.

a. Use synthetic division to find $P(10)$ and $P(-8)$.

The following is a proof of the remainder theorem.

Proof of Theorem 11-1

The equation $P(x) = D(x) \cdot Q(x) + R(x)$ is the basis of this proof. If we divide $P(x)$ by $x - r$, we obtain a quotient $Q(x)$ and a remainder $R(x)$ related as follows.

$$P(x) = (x - r) \cdot Q(x) + R(x)$$

The remainder $R(x)$ must either be 0 or have degree less than the degree of $x - r$. Thus $R(x)$ must have a degree of 0, and thus must be a constant. Let us call this constant R. In the above expression we get a true sentence whenever we replace x by any number.

Let us replace x by r.

$$\begin{aligned} P(r) &= (r - r) \cdot Q(r) + R \\ P(r) &= \quad 0 \quad \cdot Q(r) + R \\ P(r) &= R \end{aligned}$$

This tells us that the function value $P(r)$ is the remainder obtained when we divide $P(x)$ by $x - r$.

Reading Math

Recall that a statement such as $P(x) = x^2$ is read as "P of x equals x-squared." To read expressions such as $P(2)$ and $P(-1)$, you would say "P of 2" and "P of negative 1." When you find "P of 2," you are finding the value of x^2 when x is 2.

PART 2 Roots

Objective: Determine whether a given number is a root of a polynomial *P(x)*.

Since the zeros of a polynomial function are the roots of the corresponding equation, we often refer to them as the roots of a polynomial.

Using the remainder theorem and synthetic division we can find $P(r)$.

If $P(r) = 0$, then r is a root of $P(x)$.

EXAMPLE 2 Determine whether -4 is a root of $P(x)$, where $P(x) = x^3 + 8x^2 + 8x - 32$.

We use synthetic division and Theorem 11-1 to find $P(-4)$.

$$\begin{array}{r|rrrr} -4 & 1 & 8 & 8 & -32 \\ & & -4 & -16 & 32 \\ \hline & 1 & 4 & -8 & 0 \end{array}$$

The remainder is zero.

Since $P(-4) = 0$, the number -4 is a root of $P(x)$.

Try This Let $P(x) = x^3 + 6x^2 - x - 30$. Using synthetic division, determine whether the given numbers are roots of $P(x)$.

b. 2 **c.** 5 **d.** -3

PART 3 Finding Factors of Polynomials

Objective: Determine whether $x - r$ is a factor of $P(x)$, and solve the equation $P(x) = 0$.

The next theorem follows from the remainder theorem.

Theorem 11-2

The Factor Theorem

For a polynomial $P(x)$, if $P(r) = 0$, then the polynomial $x - r$ is a factor of $P(x)$.

This theorem is very useful in factoring polynomials, and hence, in solving equations.

EXAMPLE 3 Determine whether $x + 6$ is a factor of $P(x)$, where $P(x) = x^4 + 2x^3 - 63x^2 - 288x - 324$.

We apply the factor theorem using synthetic division to divide $P(x)$ by $x + 6$.

$$\begin{array}{r|rrrr|r} -6 & 1 & 2 & -63 & -288 & -324 \\ & & -6 & 24 & 234 & 324 \\ \hline & 1 & -4 & -39 & -54 & 0 \end{array}$$

The remainder is 0.

Since $P(-6) = 0$, by Theorem 11-2, $x + 6$ is a factor of $x^4 + 2x^3 - 63x^2 - 288x - 324$.

Try This

e. Determine whether $x - \frac{1}{2}$ is a factor of $4x^4 + 2x^3 + 8x - 1$.

f. Determine whether $x + 5$ is a factor of $x^4 - 625$.

EXAMPLE 4 Let $P(x) = x^3 + 2x^2 - 5x - 6$. Factor the polynomial $P(x)$. Then solve the equation $P(x) = 0$.

We look for linear factors of the form $x - r$. Let us try $x - 1$. We use synthetic division to see whether $P(1) = 0$.

$$\begin{array}{r|rrr|r} 1 & 1 & 2 & -5 & -6 \\ & & 1 & 3 & -2 \\ \hline & 1 & 3 & -2 & -8 \end{array}$$

We know that $x - 1$ is not a factor of $P(x)$. We try $x + 1$.

$$\begin{array}{r|rrr|r} -1 & 1 & 2 & -5 & -6 \\ & & -1 & -1 & 6 \\ \hline & 1 & 1 & -6 & 0 \end{array}$$

We know that $x + 1$ is one factor and the quotient, $x^2 + x - 6$, is another.

$$P(x) = (x + 1)(x^2 + x - 6)$$

The trinomial is easily factored.

$$P(x) = (x + 1)(x + 3)(x - 2)$$

To solve the equation $P(x) = 0$, we use the principle of zero products.

$$x + 1 = 0 \quad \text{or} \quad x + 3 = 0 \quad \text{or} \quad x - 2 = 0$$
$$x = -1 \quad \text{or} \quad x = -3 \quad \text{or} \quad x = 2$$

The solutions are -1, -3, and 2.

Try This

g. Let $P(x) = x^3 + 6x^2 - x - 30$. Factor the polynomial $P(x)$. Then solve the equation $P(x) = 0$.

Extra Help On the Web

Look for worked-out examples at the Prentice Hall Web site.
www.phschool.com

11-2 Exercises

A

Mental Math Find the function values.

1. $P(x) = x^3 - 6x^2 + 11x - 6$. Find $P(1)$, $P(-2)$, $P(3)$.

2. $P(x) = x^3 + 7x^2 - 12x - 3$. Find $P(-3)$, $P(-2)$, $P(1)$.

Find the function values.

3. $P(x) = 2x^5 - 3x^4 + 2x^3 - x + 8$. Find $P(20)$ and $P(-3)$.

4. $P(x) = x^5 - 10x^4 + 20x^3 - 5x - 100$. Find $P(-10)$ and $P(5)$.

Determine whether the numbers are roots of the polynomials.

5. $-3, 2$; $P(x) = 3x^3 + 5x^2 - 6x + 18$

6. $-4, 2$; $P(x) = 3x^3 + 11x^2 - 2x + 8$

7. $-3, \frac{1}{2}$; $P(x) = x^3 - \frac{7}{2}x^2 + x - \frac{3}{2}$

8. $i, -i, -2$; $P(x) = x^3 + 2x^2 + x + 2$

Determine whether the expressions of the type $x - r$ are factors of the polynomial $P(x)$.

9. $P(x) = x^3 - 3x^2 - 4x - 12$; $x + 2$

10. $P(x) = x^3 - 4x^2 + 3x + 8$; $x + 1$

11. $P(x) = x^5 - 1$; $x - 1$

12. $P(x) = x^5 + 1$; $x + 1$

13. $P(x) = 2x^2 + 2x + 1$; $x - \left(-\frac{1}{2} - \frac{1}{2}i\right)$

14. $P(x) = 9x^2 + 6x + 2$; $x - \left(\frac{1}{3} - \frac{1}{3}i\right)$

15. Let $P(x) = x^3 + 2x^2 - x - 2$.

 a. Determine whether $x - 1$ is a factor of $P(x)$.

 b. Find another factor of $P(x)$.

 c. Find a complete factorization of $P(x)$.

 d. Solve the equation $P(x) = 0$.

16. Let $P(x) = x^3 + 4x^2 - x - 4$.

 a. Determine whether $x + 1$ is a factor of $P(x)$.

 b. Find another factor of $P(x)$.

 c. Find a complete factorization of $P(x)$.

 d. Solve the equation $P(x) = 0$.

Factor the polynomial $P(x)$. Then solve the equation $P(x) = 0$.

17. $P(x) = x^3 + 4x^2 + x - 6$

18. $P(x) = x^3 + 5x^2 - 2x - 24$

19. $P(x) = x^3 - 6x^2 + 3x + 10$

20. $P(x) = x^3 + 2x^2 - 13x + 10$

21. $P(x) = x^3 - x^2 - 14x + 24$

22. $P(x) = x^3 - 3x^2 - 10x + 24$

23. $P(x) = x^4 - x^3 - 19x^2 + 49x - 30$

24. $P(x) = x^4 + 11x^3 + 41x^2 + 61x + 30$

B

Solve.

25. $x^3 + 2x^2 - 13x + 10 > 0$

26. $x^4 - x^3 - 19x^2 + 49x - 30 < 0$

27. Find k so that $x + 2$ is a factor of $x^3 - kx^2 + 2x + 7k$.

28. Find k so that $x - 1$ is a factor of $x^3 - 3x^2 + kx - 1$.

29. ***Critical Thinking*** For what values of k will the remainder be the same when $x^2 + kx + 4$ is divided by $x - 1$ or $x + 1$?

30. When $x^2 - 3x + 2k$ is divided by $x + 2$ the remainder is 7. Find the value of k.

31. ***Write a Convincing Argument*** Write an argument to convince a classmate that "is a factor of" is transitive: that is, if $A(x)$ is a factor of $B(x)$ and $B(x)$ is a factor of $C(x)$, then $A(x)$ is a factor of $C(x)$.

Challenge

32. Use the factor theorem to prove that $x - a$ is a factor of $x^n - a^n$ for any natural number n.

33. Prove Theorem 11-2.

Mixed Review

For each function find standard form. Then find the vertex, line of symmetry, and the maximum or minimum value for each parabola.

34. $f(x) = x^2 - 4x$ 35. $f(x) = 2x^2 - 10x - 8$ 36. $f(x) = x^2 + c$ *9-6*

Find the center and radius of each circle. 37. $(x + 1)^2 + y^2 = 64$

38. $x^2 + y^2 - 6x - 2y - 15 = 0$ 39. $(x + 1)^2 + (y - 1)^2 = 45$ *10-2*

11-3 Theorems About Roots

What You'll Learn

1. To find the roots of a polynomial and to determine the multiplicity of each root
2. To find all the roots of a polynomial given its degree and several of its roots
3. To find polynomials with specific roots

. . . And Why

To determine more characteristics of the solutions for equations of degree greater than two

Carl Friedrich Gauss was one of the great mathematicians of all time. He contributed to many branches of mathematics and science, including non-Euclidean geometry and curvature of surfaces (later used in Einstein's theory of relativity). In 1798, at the age of 20, Gauss proved the fundamental theorem of algebra.

PART 1 Finding Roots by Factoring

Objective: Find the roots of a polynomial and determine the multiplicity of each root.

Theorem 11-3

The Fundamental Theorem of Algebra

Every polynomial of degree $n > 1$, with complex coefficients, has at least one linear factor.

Using this theorem, Gauss was able to prove another theorem.

Theorem 11-4

Every polynomial of degree $n > 1$, with complex coefficients, can be factored into exactly n linear factors.

In a polynomial equation, after a polynomial is factored into linear factors, its roots can be found using the principle of zero products.

EXAMPLE 1 Find the roots of the polynomial equation.

$$\begin{aligned} P(x) &= x^3 + x^2 - 25x - 25 \\ &= x^2(x + 1) - 25(x + 1) && \text{Factoring by grouping} \\ &= (x^2 - 25)(x + 1) \\ &= (x + 5)(x - 5)(x + 1) && \text{Factoring as a difference of two squares} \end{aligned}$$

Setting $P(x) = 0$ to find the roots,

$$\begin{aligned} 0 &= (x + 5)(x - 5)(x + 1) \\ x + 5 = 0 \text{ or } x - 5 &= 0 \text{ or } x + 1 = 0 && \text{Using the principle of zero products} \\ x = -5 \text{ or } x &= 5 \text{ or } x = -1 && \text{There are 3 linear factors. The roots are } -5, 5, \text{ and } -1. \end{aligned}$$

In Example 1, there are 3 linear factors and 3 roots. If a factor $(x - r)$ occurs k times, we say that r is a root of **multiplicity** k.

EXAMPLE 2 Find the roots of the polynomial equation and the multiplicity of each.

$$\begin{aligned} P(x) &= 3x^5 - 15x^4 + 18x^3 + 12x^2 - 24x \\ &= (3x)(x - 2)(x - 2)(x - 2)(x + 1) \quad \text{There are 5 linear factors.} \\ &= 3x(x - 2)^3(x + 1) \end{aligned}$$

Root	Multiplicity	
0	1	The monomial factor x occurs one time.
2	3	$x - 2$ occurs three times.
−1	1	$x + 1$ occurs one time.

The polynomial has 5 linear factors and 5 roots. The root 2 occurs 3 times, however, so we say that the root 2 has a multiplicity of 3.

Try This Find the roots of each polynomial equation and the multiplicity of each.

a. $P(x) = 4(x + 7)^2(x - 3)$ **b.** $P(x) = (x^2 - 7x + 12)^2$ **c.** $P(x) = 5x^2 - 5$

PART 2 Real and Rational Coefficients

Objective: Find all the roots of a polynomial given its degree and several roots.

Consider the quadratic equation $x^2 - 2x + 2 = 0$, with real coefficients. Its roots are $1 + i$ and $1 - i$. Note that the **complex roots** are conjugates.

Theorem 11-5

If a polynomial $P(x)$ of degree greater than or equal to 1 with real coefficients has a complex number $a + bi$ as a root, then its conjugate $a - bi$ is also a root. (Complex roots occur in conjugate pairs.)

When a polynomial has rational numbers for coefficients, certain **irrational roots** also occur in pairs, as described in the following theorem.

Theorem 11-6

Suppose $P(x)$ is a polynomial with rational coefficients and of degree greater than or equal to 1. Then if either of the following is a root, so is the other: $a + c\sqrt{b}$, $a - c\sqrt{b}$, where a, b, and c are rational numbers and $\sqrt{b}$ is irrational.

Writing Math

It is the definition

$$\sqrt{-1} = i$$

that distinguishes the set of complex numbers. We use a real component a and an imaginary component bi to make up a complex number of the form $a + bi$ or $a - bi$, for example, $5 + 3i$ or $7 - 2i$.

EXAMPLE 3 Suppose a polynomial of degree 3 with real coefficients has $3 - 4i$ and 9 as roots. Find all of the roots.

By Theorem 11-5, since $3 - 4i$ is a root, then $3 + 4i$ is also a root. Since the polynomial is of degree 3, by Theorem 11-4 there can be no more than 3 roots.

The roots are $3 - 4i$, $3 + 4i$, and 9.

EXAMPLE 4 Suppose a polynomial of degree 6 with rational coefficients has $-2 + 5i$, $-i$, and $1 - \sqrt{3}$ as roots. Find all of the roots.

By Theorem 11-5, the conjugates of $-2 + 5i$ and $-i$ are roots. They are $-2 - 5i$ and i. By Theorem 11-6, since $1 - \sqrt{3}$ is a root, $1 + \sqrt{3}$ is also a root. There are no other roots since the degree is 6.

Thus the six roots are $-2 + 5i$, $-2 - 5i$, i, $-i$, $1 + \sqrt{3}$, and $1 - \sqrt{3}$.

Try This

d. Suppose a polynomial of degree 5 with rational coefficients has -4, $7 - 2i$, and $3 + 7\sqrt{5}$ as roots. Find all roots of the polynomial.

EXAMPLE 5 Let $P(x) = x^4 - 5x^3 + 10x^2 - 20x + 24$. Find all roots of $P(x)$, given that $2i$ is a root.

Since $2i$ is a root, we know that $-2i$ is also a root.

$$P(x) = (x - 2i)(x + 2i) \cdot Q(x), \text{ for some } Q(x)$$

Since $(x - 2i)(x + 2i) = x^2 + 4$, we write $P(x)$ as follows.

$$P(x) = (x^2 + 4) \cdot Q(x)$$

We find, using division, that $Q(x) = x^2 - 5x + 6$. We factor $x^2 - 5x + 6$.

$$P(x) = (x^2 + 4)(x - 2)(x - 3)$$

Thus the roots are $2i$, $-2i$, 2, and 3.

Try This

e. Find all roots of $x^4 + x^3 - x^2 + x - 2$, given that i is a root.

PART 3 Finding Polynomials with Specific Roots

Objective: Find polynomials with specific roots.

Given several numbers, we can find a polynomial having them as its roots.

EXAMPLE 6 Find a polynomial of degree 3, having roots -2, 1, and $3i$.

By Theorem 11-2, such a polynomial has factors $x + 2$, $x - 1$, and $x - 3i$, so we have the polynomial $P(x) = a_n(x + 2)(x - 1)(x - 3i)$.

The number a_n can be any nonzero number. The simplest polynomial will be obtained if we let $a_n = 1$. If we then multiply the factors we obtain the following.

$$P(x) = x^3 + (1 - 3i)x^2 + (-2 - 3i)x + 6i$$

EXAMPLE 7 Find a polynomial of degree 5 with 0 as a root of multiplicity 1, -1 as a root of multiplicity 3, and 4 as a root of multiplicity 1.

We proceed as in Example 3, letting $a_n = 1$.

$$P(x) = x(x + 1)^3(x - 4)$$

$$P(x) = x^5 - x^4 - 9x^3 - 11x^2 - 4x \quad \text{Multiplying}$$

Try This

f. Find a polynomial of degree 3 that has -1, 2, and 5 as roots.

g. Find a polynomial of degree 5 with -2 as a root of multiplicity 3 and 0 as a root of multiplicity 2.

By Theorems 11-5 and 11-6, we know that complex roots occur in conjugate pairs, and certain irrational roots also occur in pairs. We can use these facts to find the polynomial of lowest degree with rational coefficients that has specific roots.

EXAMPLE 8 Find a polynomial of lowest degree with rational coefficients that has $1 - \sqrt{2}$ and $1 + 3i$ as roots.

By Theorem 11-5, $1 - 3i$ is a root. By Theorem 11-6, $1 + \sqrt{2}$ is a root. Thus, the polynomial is as follows.

$$P(x) = [x - (1 - \sqrt{2})][x - (1 + \sqrt{2})][x - (1 + 3i)][x - (1 - 3i)]$$

Using the principle of zero products

$$= [(x - 1) + \sqrt{2}][(x - 1) - \sqrt{2}][(x - 1) - 3i][(x - 1) + 3i]$$

Using the associative property

$$= [(x - 1)^2 - (\sqrt{2})^2][(x - 1)^2 - (3i)^2]$$

Multiplying the sum and difference of two expressions

$$= [x^2 - 2x + 1 - 2][x^2 - 2x + 1 + 9] \quad \text{Simplifying}$$

$$= [x^2 - 2x - 1][x^2 - 2x + 10]$$

$$= x^4 - 4x^3 + 13x^2 - 18x - 10$$

The polynomial is of degree 4.

Try This

h. Find a polynomial of lowest degree with rational coefficients that has $2 + \sqrt{3}$ and $1 - i$ as roots.

i. Find a polynomial of lowest degree with real coefficients that has $2i$ and 2 as roots.

Extra Help On the Web

Look for worked-out examples at the Prentice Hall Web site.
www.phschool.com

11-3 Exercises

A

Find the roots of each polynomial equation, and state the multiplicity of each root.

1. $P(x) = (x + 3)^2(x - 1)$

2. $P(x) = -4(x + 2)(x - \pi)^5$

3. $P(x) = -8(x - 3)^2(x + 4)^3x^4$

4. $P(x) = x^3(x - 1)^2(x + 4)$

5. $P(x) = (x^2 - 5x + 6)^2$

6. $P(x) = (x^2 - x - 2)^2$

Suppose a polynomial of degree 6 with real coefficients has the given roots. Find all roots of the polynomial.

7. $-5, 6, 5 + i, -2i$

8. $8, 6, -3 - 2i, 4i$

Suppose a polynomial of degree 5 with rational coefficients has the given roots. Find all roots of the polynomial.

9. $6, -3 + 4i, 4 - \sqrt{5}$

10. $8, 6 - 7i, \frac{1}{2} + \sqrt{11}$

11. $-2, 3, 4, 1 - i$

12. $3, 4, -5, 7 + i$

Given that the polynomial has the given root, find all roots of the polynomial.

13. $P(x) = x^4 - 5x^3 + 7x^2 - 5x + 6; -i$

14. $P(x) = x^3 - 4x^2 + x - 4; -i$

15. $P(x) = x^4 - 16; 2i$

16. $P(x) = x^4 - 1; i$

17. $P(x) = x^3 - x^2 - 7x + 15; -3$

18. $P(x) = x^3 - 6x^2 + 13x - 20; 4$

19. $P(x) = x^3 - 8; 2$

20. $P(x) = x^3 + 8; -2$

21. $P(x) = x^4 - 2x^3 + 7x^2 + 6x - 30; -\sqrt{3}$

22. $P(x) = x^4 + 4x^3 + 2x^2 - 28x - 63; \sqrt{7}$

Find a polynomial of degree 3 with the given numbers as roots.

23. $-2, 3, 5$

24. $3, 2, -1$

25. $2, i, -i$

26. $-3, 2i, -2i$

27. $2 + i, 2 - i, 3$

28. $1 + 4i, 1 - 4i, -1$

29. $\sqrt{2}, -\sqrt{2}, \sqrt{3}$ Are the coefficients rational?

30. $\sqrt{3}, -\sqrt{3}, \sqrt{2}$ Are the coefficients rational?

31. Find a polynomial of degree 4 with 0 as a root of multiplicity 2 and 5 as a root of multiplicity 2.

32. Find a polynomial of degree 4 with 0 as a root of multiplicity 4.

33. Find a polynomial of degree 4 with -2 as a root of multiplicity 1, 3 as a root of multiplicity 2, and -1 as a root of multiplicity 1.

34. Find a polynomial of degree 5 with 4 as a root of multiplicity 3 and -2 as a root of multiplicity 2.

Find a polynomial of lowest degree with rational coefficients that has the given numbers as some of its roots.

35. $1 + i, 2$

36. $2 - i, -1$

37. $3i, -2$

38. $-4i, 5$

39. $2 - \sqrt{3}, 1 + i$

40. $3 + \sqrt{2}, 2 - i$

41. $\sqrt{5}, -3i$

42. $-\sqrt{2}, 4i$

43. $-\sqrt{2}, 2 + i\sqrt{7}$

44. $3i, -3 - i\sqrt{5}$

B

Solve.

45. $ax^3 + bx^2 + ax + b = 0$

46. $ax^3 + ax^2 + bx + b = 0$

47. $x^4 - 2x^3 - 2x - 1 = 0$

48. The equation $x^2 + 2ax + b = 0$ has a root of multiplicity 2. Find it.

49. ***Critical Thinking*** Write a polynomial that has at least one, but no more than three, positive real roots.

Challenge

50. ***Mathematical Reasoning*** Prove that a polynomial with positive coefficients cannot have a positive root.

51. Prove that every polynomial of odd degree with real coefficients has at least one real root.

52. Prove Theorem 11-5.

53. Prove Theorem 11-6.

Mixed Review

For each of the following graph the function, and find the vertex, line of symmetry, and the maximum or minimum value.

54. $f(x) = (x - 2)^2 + 3$

55. $f(x) = -2(x + 1)^2 - 1$ *9-6*

For each parabola, find the vertex, the focus, and the directrix. **56.** $x^2 = 2y$

57. $x^2 - 8y + 8 = 0$

58. $y^2 - 4y - 12x + 28 = 0$ *10-5*

59. The Cup-a-Day coffeehouse has several blends of coffee. Its Mocha-Java blend contains 36% mocha beans. Its Manager's Blend contains 68% mocha beans. How many pounds of each blend should be mixed to make a 20-lb blend that contains 50% mocha beans? *4-3*

60. What is the minimum product of two numbers whose difference is 27? What are the numbers? *9-6*

61. The formula $p = \frac{h}{\sqrt[3]{w}}$, where h is a person's height in inches and w is weight in pounds, gives a value called the *ponderal index*.

a. Find the ponderal index for a 70-in.-tall person weighing 165 lb.

b. Solve the formula for w.

c. Find the weight of a person with height 62 in. and ponderal index of 12.5. *8-7*

11-4 Rational Roots

What You'll Learn

1 To find rational and other roots of a polynomial with integral coefficients

. . . And Why

To graph equations of degree greater than two

PART 1 Finding Roots

Objective: Find rational and other roots of a polynomial with integer coefficients.

If a polynomial has integer coefficients, there is a procedure for finding all of the rational roots.

Theorem 11-7

Rational Roots Theorem

Let $P(x) = a_nx^n + a_{n-1}x^{n-1} + \cdots + a_1x + a_0$ where all the coefficients are integers. Consider a rational number denoted by $\frac{c}{d}$, where c and d are relatively prime. For $\frac{c}{d}$ to be a root of $P(x)$, c must be a factor of a_0 (the constant) and d must be a factor of a_n (the leading coefficient).

EXAMPLE 1 Let $P(x) = 3x^4 - 11x^3 + 10x - 4$. Find the rational roots of $P(x)$, if they exist. Find the other roots, if possible.

By the rational roots theorem, if $\frac{c}{d}$ is a root of $P(x)$, then c must be a factor of -4, and d must be a factor of 3. Thus the possibilities for c and d are as follows.

c: 1, −1, 4, −4, 2, −2 — Listing all possible values for c and d

d: 1, −1, 3, −3

Then the resulting possibilities for $\frac{c}{d}$ are

$1, -1, 4, -4, 2, -2, \frac{1}{3}, -\frac{1}{3}, \frac{4}{3}, -\frac{4}{3}, \frac{2}{3}, -\frac{2}{3}$ — Listing all possible rational roots

Of these 12 possibilities, we know that at most 4 of them could be roots because $P(x)$ is of degree four. To find which are roots, we can use synthetic division.

We try 1.

$$\begin{array}{r|rrrrr} 1 & 3 & -11 & 0 & 10 & -4 \\ & & 3 & -8 & -8 & 2 \\ \hline & 3 & -8 & -8 & 2 & -2 \end{array}$$

Testing possible roots

$P(1) = -2$, so 1 is not a root.

We try -1.

$$\begin{array}{r|rrrrr} -1 & 3 & -11 & 0 & 10 & -4 \\ & & -3 & 14 & -14 & 4 \\ \hline & 3 & -14 & 14 & -4 & \vert\ 0 \end{array}$$

$P(-1) = 0$, so -1 is a root. Thus

$$P(x) = (x + 1)(3x^3 - 14x^2 + 14x - 4)$$

We now use $3x^3 - 14x^2 + 14x - 4$ and check the other possible roots.

We try $\frac{2}{3}$.

$$\begin{array}{r|rrrr} \frac{2}{3} & 3 & -14 & 14 & -4 \\ & & 2 & -8 & 4 \\ \hline & 3 & -12 & 6 & \vert\ 0 \end{array}$$

$P\left(\frac{2}{3}\right) = 0$, so $\frac{2}{3}$ is a root. We now know that

$$P(x) = (x + 1)\left(x - \frac{2}{3}\right)(3x^2 - 12x + 6)$$

Since the factor $3x^2 - 12x + 6$ is quadratic, we can use the quadratic formula to find the other roots. They are $2 + \sqrt{2}$ and $2 - \sqrt{2}$.

The rational roots of $P(x)$ are -1 and $\frac{2}{3}$. The irrational roots are $2 + \sqrt{2}$ and $2 - \sqrt{2}$.

Quick Review

Memorize the quadratic formula

$$x = \frac{-b \pm \sqrt{b^2 - 4ac}}{2a}.$$

It solves any quadratic equation.

Try This

a. Let $P(x) = 2x^4 + 3x^3 - 8x^2 - 9x + 6$. Find the rational roots of $P(x)$, if they exist. Find the other roots, if possible.

EXAMPLE 2 Let $P(x) = x^3 + 6x^2 + x + 6$. Find the rational roots of $P(x)$. Find the other roots, if possible.

By the rational roots theorem, if $\frac{c}{d}$ is a root of $P(x)$, then c must be a factor of 6 and d must be a factor of 1. Thus the possibilities for c and d are as follows.

c: 1, -1, 2, -2, 3, -3, 6, -6

d: 1, -1

Then the resulting possibilities for $\frac{c}{d}$ are

1, -1, 2, -2, 3, -3, 6, and -6

These are the same as the possibilities for c alone. Since the leading coefficient is 1, we need only check the factors of the constant term c.

There is another aid in eliminating possibilities for rational roots. Note that all coefficients of $P(x)$ are positive. Thus when any positive number is substituted in $P(x)$, we get a positive value (never 0). No positive number can be a root.

Thus we can eliminate 1, 2, 3, and 6 as possible roots. The only possibilities for roots are -1, -2, -3, and -6.

We try -6.

$$\begin{array}{r|rrrr} -6 & 1 & 6 & 1 & 6 \\ & & -6 & 0 & -6 \\ \hline & 1 & 0 & 1 & 0 \end{array}$$

$P(-6) = 0$, so -6 is a root. We now know that

$$P(x) = (x + 6)(x^2 + 1)$$

Since $x^2 + 1$ has no real roots, the only rational root of $P(x)$ is -6. The other roots are i and $-i$.

Try This

b. Let $P(x) = x^3 + 7x^2 + 4x + 28$, and let $\frac{c}{d}$ be a rational root of $P(x)$. Find the rational roots, if they exist, of $P(x)$. If possible, find the other roots.

EXAMPLE 3 Find only the rational roots of $x^4 + 2x^3 + 2x^2 - 4x - 8$.

Since the leading coefficient is 1, the only possibilities for rational roots are the factors of the last coefficient, -8.

$$1, -1, 2, -2, 4, -4, 8, -8$$

Using substitution or synthetic division, we find that none of the possibilities is a root. Thus there are no rational roots.

Try This

c. Find only the rational roots of $x^4 + x^2 + 2x + 6$.
d. Find only the rational roots of $x^5 - 2x^4 + 4x - 8$.

Here are some guidelines for finding rational roots.

Finding Rational Roots

To find possible rational roots of $P(x) = a_n x^n + a_{n-1}x^{n-1} + \cdots + a_0$,

1. find all factors of a_n and a_0.
2. find each rational number $\frac{c}{d}$ such that d is a factor of a_n and c is a factor of a_0.
3. if a_n is 1, test only the factors of a_0.
4. test each $\frac{c}{d}$ using synthetic division.

Once all of the rational roots are found, the polynomial can be simplified by factoring. It is then often possible to find the other roots.

Proof of Theorem 11-7

Since $\frac{c}{d}$ is a root of $P(x)$, we know that

$$a_n\left(\frac{c}{d}\right)^n + a_{n-1}\left(\frac{c}{d}\right)^{n-1} + \cdots + a_1\left(\frac{c}{d}\right) + a_0 = 0 \quad ①$$

We multiply by d^n and get the equation

$$a_nc^n + a_{n-1}c^{n-1}d + \cdots + a_1cd^{n-1} + a_0d^n = 0 \quad ②$$

Then we have

$$a_nc^n = (-a_{n-1}c^{n-1} - \cdots - a_1cd^{n-2} - a_0d^{n-1})d$$

Note that d is a factor of a_nc^n. Now d is not a factor of c because c and d are relatively prime. Thus d is not a factor of c^n. So d is a factor of a_n.

In a similar way we can show from equation ② that

$$a_0d^n = (-a_nc^{n-1} - a_{n-1}c^{n-2}d - \cdots - a_1d^{n-1})c$$

Thus c is a factor of a_0d^n. Again, c is not a factor of d^n, so it must be a factor of a_0.

11-4 Exercises

Look for worked-out examples at the Prentice Hall Web site.
www.phschool.com

A

Find the rational roots, if they exist, of each polynomial. Find the other roots, if possible.

1. $P(x) = x^3 + 3x^2 - 2x - 6$

2. $P(x) = x^3 - x^2 - 3x + 3$

3. $P(x) = 5x^4 - 4x^3 + 19x^2 - 16x - 4$

4. $P(x) = 3x^4 - 4x^3 + x^2 + 6x - 2$

5. $P(x) = x^4 - 3x^3 - 20x^2 - 24x - 8$

6. $P(x) = x^3 + 3x^2 - x - 3$

7. $P(x) = x^4 + 5x^3 - 27x^2 + 31x - 10$

8. $P(x) = x^3 + 5x^2 - x - 5$

9. $P(x) = x^3 + 8$

10. $P(x) = x^3 - 8$

11. $P(x) = 4x^3 - 3x^2 + 4x - 3$

12. $P(x) = 2x^3 - 3x^2 - x + 1$

Find only the rational roots.

13. $P(x) = x^5 - 5x^4 + 5x^3 + 15x^2 - 36x + 20$

14. $P(x) = x^5 - 3x^4 - 3x^3 + 9x^2 - 4x + 12$

15. $P(x) = x^4 + 32$

16. $P(x) = x^6 + 8$

17. $P(x) = x^3 - x^2 - 4x + 3$

18. $P(x) = 2x^3 + 3x^2 + 2x + 3$

19. $P(x) = x^4 + 2x^3 + 2x^2 - 4x - 8$

20. $P(x) = x^4 + 6x^3 + 17x^2 + 36x + 66$

Cardboard boxes and carriers can be opened to a flat piece to see how they are constructed. Candy boxes and shoe boxes are often more complicated than the t-shaped open packing carton. Bottle carriers are folded and glued to provide support for the contents.

Self-Test On the Web

Check your progress. Look for a self-test at the Prentice Hall Web site. www.phschool.com

B

21. Find the rational roots of each polynomial. (Hint: Use LCDs.)

a. $\frac{1}{12}x^3 - \frac{1}{12}x^2 - \frac{2}{3}x + 1$ **b.** $x^4 - \frac{1}{6}x^3 - \frac{4}{3}x^2 + \frac{1}{6}x + \frac{1}{3}$

c. $\frac{1}{3}x^3 - \frac{1}{2}x^2 - \frac{1}{6}x + \frac{1}{6}$ **d.** $\frac{2}{3}x^3 - \frac{1}{2}x^2 + \frac{2}{3}x - \frac{1}{2}$

22. A box manufacturer makes boxes of volume 48 ft^3 from pieces of cardboard 10 ft on a side by cutting squares from each corner and folding up the edges. Find the length of each side of a square.

23. A box manufacturer makes boxes of volume 500 cm^3 from pieces of tin 20 cm on a side by cutting squares from each corner and folding up the edges. Find the length of each side of a square.

24. ***Critical Thinking*** A polynomial $P(x)$ with all integral coefficients has $\frac{3}{5}$ as one root. The leading coefficient a_n of $P(x)$ is prime and the constant term a_0 is a multiple of 4 that is less than 20. What are a_n and a_0?

Challenge

25. Show that $\sqrt{5}$ is irrational by considering the equation $x^2 - 5 = 0$.

26. Show that $\sqrt[3]{3}$ is irrational by considering the equation $x^3 - 3 = 0$.

27. A box manufacturer makes boxes of volume 2160 in.^{2} from pieces of tin 38 in. by 32 in. by cutting squares from each corner and folding up the edges. Find the length of each side of a square.

Mixed Review

Find the distance between each pair of points. **28.** $(3, -2), (6, -6)$

29. $(4, 0), (0, 4)$ **30.** $(9, 1), (15, -7)$ **31.** $(5, 3), (5, -9)$ *10-1*

32. Find the center and radius of the circle $x^2 + y^2 + 14x + 2y + 1 = 0$. *10-2*

Solve each system graphically.

33. $y = x^2 - 4$
$y = x - 4$

34. $xy = 4$
$x + y = 4$ *10-7*

Determine whether the numbers are roots of the polynomial.

35. $P(x) = x^3 - 6x^2 + 3x + 10$; $5, -2, 2$ *11-1*

36. Callie bicycled in a bike-a-thon for charity. Twenty people pledged \$0.25 per kilometer toward her ride. She also had a separate pledge of \$35. The total amount pledged was \$350. How far did Callie ride? *1-11*

Descartes' Rule of Signs

11-5

René Descartes (1596–1650) was a French mathematician and philosopher whose work with algebra and geometry led to coordinate geometry. The Cartesian coordinate system is named for him. Descartes lived during the time made famous in *The Three Musketeers*, by Alexandre Dumas, and was reputed to be an excellent swordsman.

Because he developed the Cartesian plane, Descartes is also credited with inventing analytic geometry.

What You'll Learn

1. To use Descartes' rule of signs to find the number of positive roots of a polynomial
2. To use Descartes' rule of signs to find the number of negative roots of a polynomial

. . . And Why

To search more easily for solutions to equations of higher degree

PART 1 Positive Roots

Objective: Use Descartes' rule of signs to find the number of positive roots of a polynomial.

The number of **positive real roots** of a polynomial arranged in descending order can be found using **Descartes' rule of signs.** The rule uses the number of **variations of sign,** that is, the number of times successive coefficients have different signs. For $P(x) = 2x^6 - 3x^2 + x + 4$, there are 2 variations. For $P(x) = 3x^5 - 2x^3 + x^2 - x + 2$, there are 4 variations.

Theorem 11-8

Descartes' Rule of Signs

The number of positive real roots of a polynomial P(x) with real coefficients is

a. the same as the number of variations of sign of $P(x)$, or

b. less than the number of variations of sign of $P(x)$ by a positive even integer.

EXAMPLES Determine the number of positive real roots.

1 $P(x) = 2x^5 - 5x^2 + 3x + 6$

The number of variations of sign is two. Therefore, the number of positive real roots is 2 or is less than 2 by 2, 4, 6, etc. Thus the number of positive roots must either be 2 or 0 since a negative number of roots has no meaning. (If one positive root is known, you can be sure there is a second positive real root.)

2 $P(x) = 5x^4 - 3x^3 + 7x^2 - 12x + 4$

There are four variations of sign. Thus the number of positive real roots is 4, $4 - 2$, or $4 - 4$; there are 4, 2, or 0 roots.

3 $P(x) = 6x^5 - 2x - 5$

The number of variations of sign is one. Therefore, there is exactly one positive real root.

Try This Determine the number of positive real roots.

a. $P(x) = 5x^3 - 4x - 5$

b. $P(x) = 6p^6 - 5p^4 + 3p^3 - 7p^2 + p - 2$

c. $P(x) = 3x^2 - 2x + 4$

PART 2 Negative Roots

Objective: Use Descartes' rule of signs to find the number of negative roots of a polynomial.

Descartes' rule can also be used to help determine the number of **negative real roots** of a polynomial. Recall that the graph of $P(-x)$ is the reflection of the graph of $P(x)$ across the y-axis. The points at which the graph crosses the x-axis are the roots of the polynomial. Thus the positive roots of $P(-x)$ are the negative roots of $P(x)$.

Theorem 11-9

Corollary to Descartes' Rule of Signs

The number of negative real roots of a polynomial P(x) with real coefficients is

a. the number of variations of sign of $P(-x)$, or

b. less than the number of variations of sign $P(-x)$ by a positive even integer.

EXAMPLE 4 Determine the number of negative real roots.

$$P(x) = 5x^4 + 3x^3 + 7x^2 + 12x + 4$$

$$P(-x) = 5(-x)^4 + 3(-x)^3 + 7(-x)^2 + 12(-x) + 4 \quad \text{Substituting } -x \text{ for } x$$

$$= 5x^4 - 3x^3 + 7x^2 - 12x + 4 \quad \text{Simplifying}$$

There are four variations of sign, so the number of negative roots is 4, 2, or 0.

Note that, in all cases, a root of multiplicity m is counted m times.

Try This Determine the number of negative real roots.

d. $P(x) = 5x^3 - 4x - 5$

e. $P(x) = 6p^6 - 5p^4 + 3p^3 - 7p^2 + p - 2$

f. $P(x) = 3x^2 - 2x + 4$

11-5 Exercises

Look for worked-out examples at the Prentice Hall Web site.
www.phschool.com

A

Mental Math Determine the number of positive real roots.

1. $P(x) = 3x^5 - 2x^2 + x - 1$

2. $P(x) = 5x^6 - 3x^3 + x^2 - x$

3. $P(x) = 6x^7 + 2x^2 + 5x + 4$

4. $P(x) = -3x^5 - 7x^3 - 4x - 5$

5. $P(x) = 3x^{18} + 2x^4 - 5x^2 + x + 3$

6. $P(x) = 5x^{12} - 7x^4 + 3x^2 + x + 1$

7. $P(x) = 5x^9 - 3x^4 + 7x^3 + x - 2$

8. $P(x) = -9x^{20} + 5x^{14} - 6x + 2$

9. $P(x) = 4x^{13} + 4x^{12} - x^3 - 2x + 7$

10. $P(x) = -9x^{13} + x^5 - x^3 + 12x$

11–20. Determine the number of negative real roots for Exercises 1–10.

B

Without solving, determine the number of positive, negative, and complex roots of the following equations. Assume that n is a natural number.

21. $P(x) = x^4 - 2x^2 - 8$

22. $P(x) = x^3 - 7x^2 + 12$

23. $P(x) = x^4 + 5x^2 + 6$

24. $P(x) = 2x^3 - 2x^2 + 6x - 1$

25. $P(x) = x^{2n} - 1$

26. $P(x) = x^{2n+1} + 1$

27. ***Critical Thinking*** What can you determine about the real roots of $x^3 + bx + c = 0$, given $b > 0$ and $c \neq 0$?

Challenge

28. Prove that for a positive even integer n, $P(x) = x^n - 1$ has only two real roots.

29. Prove that any polynomial equation $P(x) = 0$ that contains only odd powers of x and positive coefficients has no real roots except 0.

Mixed Review

Solve each system of equations.

30. $y = x^2 - 4$
$y = -2x - 1$

31. $x^2 + y^2 = 25$
$y = x^2 - 13$ *10-7*

32. For $x^2 - 9y^2 = 9$, find the center, vertices, foci, and asymptotes. Then draw the graph. *10-4*

11-6 Graphs of Polynomial Functions

What You'll Learn

1. To graph polynomial functions
2. To use a graph to aid in approximating solutions to polynomial equations

. . . And Why

To increase efficiency in determining solutions to algebraic equations

Graphs of first-degree polynomial functions are lines; graphs of second-degree, or quadratic, polynomial functions are parabolas. We now consider polynomials of higher degree with real coefficients.

Graphs of Higher-Degree Polynomial Functions

1. Every polynomial function has as its domain the set of real numbers.
2. The graph of any function is a continuous unbroken curve that must pass the vertical line test.
3. Unless a polynomial function is linear, no part of its graph is straight.
4. A polynomial of degree n cannot have more than n real roots. This means that the graph cannot cross the x-axis more than n times.

Third-degree, or **cubic,** polynomial functions have graphs like the following.

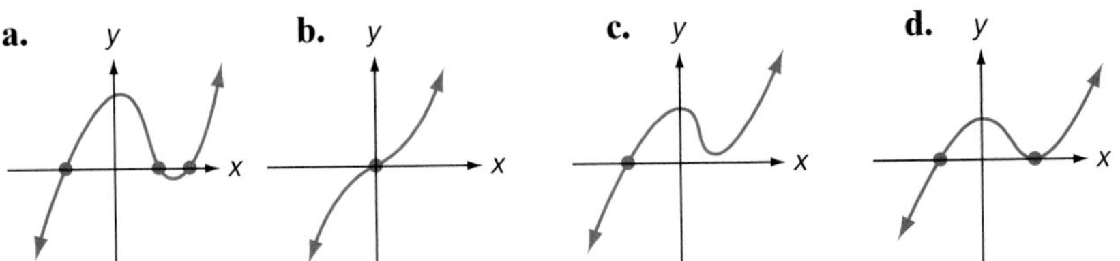

Graph **a.** crosses the x-axis three times, so there are three real roots. In graphs **b.** and **c.** there is only one x-intercept, so there is only one real root in each case. Graph **d.** crosses the x-axis once and touches it once, so there are two real roots.

The left and right ends of a graph of an odd-degree function go in opposite directions. In graph **c.,** the left arrow points downward, the right arrow points upward.

Graphs of fourth-degree, or **quartic,** polynomial functions look like these.

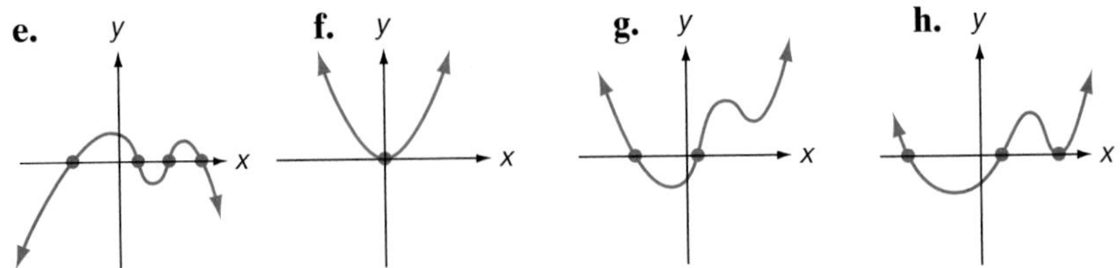

In graph **e.** there are four real roots, in graph **f.** there is one, in graph **g.** there are two, and in graph **h.** there are three.

The left and right ends of an even-degree function go in the same direction. In graph **e.,** both the left and right arrows point downward.

When multiple real roots occur, they occur at points like the following.

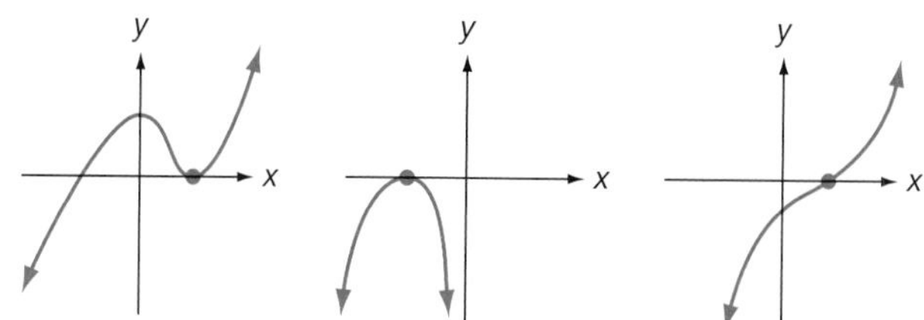

Graphing Polynomials

Objective: Graph polynomial functions.

To graph polynomials, keep in mind previously established results and proceed as follows.

Graphing Polynomials

1. Look at the degree of the polynomial and its leading coefficient. This gives a lot of information about the general shape of the graph.
2. Look for symmetries, as covered in Chapter 9. When symmetrical points occur, the rest of the graph can be plotted quickly.
3. Make a table of values using synthetic division.
4. Find the y-intercept and as many x-intercepts as possible (the latter are roots of the polynomial). In doing this, recall the theorems about roots, including Descartes' rule of signs.
5. Plot the points and connect them appropriately.

Quick Review

A function is even when $f(-x) = f(x)$. It is odd when $f(-x) = -f(x)$.

EXAMPLE 1 Graph $P(x) = 2x^3 - x + 2$.

1. This polynomial is of degree 3 with leading coefficient positive. The curve will have the general shape of the graph of a cubic function.
2. The function is not odd or even. However, $2x^3 - x$ is an odd function with the origin as a point of symmetry. $P(x)$ is a translation of this, upward 2 units. Hence, the point $(0, 2)$ is a point of symmetry.
3. We make a table of values.

x	$f(x)$
0	2
1	3
2	16
−1	1
−2	−12

The points $(1, 3)$, $(2, 16)$, $(-1, 1)$, and $(-2, -12)$ are on the graph.

4. Descartes' rule tells us that there are 2 or 0 positive roots and that there is just one negative root.
5. We plot this information and consider the three possibilities.

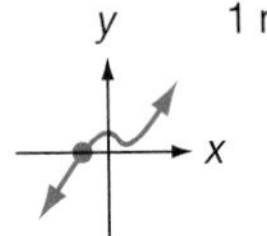

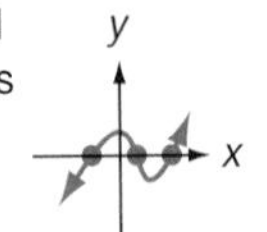

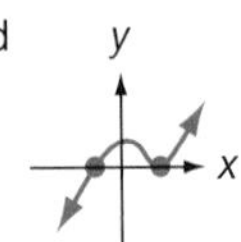

We do not know the shape of the curve between $(-1, 1)$ and $(0, 2)$ and between $(0, 2)$ and $(1, 3)$. We therefore need to plot some more points between -1 and 1. After we determine the points using a calculator, we sketch the complete graph. Computer graphing techniques may also be used to graph the function.

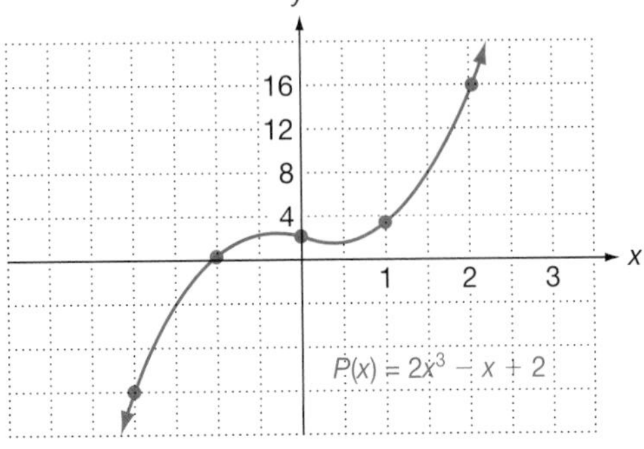

Try This Graph.

a. $P(x) = x^3 - 4x^2 - 3x + 12$

Solving Equations

Objective: Use a graph to aid in approximating solutions to polynomial equations.

Whenever we find the roots, or zeros, of a function $P(x)$, we have solved the equation $P(x) = 0$. One method of finding approximate solutions of polynomial equations is by graphing. We graph the function $y = P(x)$ and note where the graph crosses the x-axis. In Example 1, there is a real solution of the equation $2x^3 - x + 2 = 0$ at about -1.1.

We can approximate roots more precisely by further calculation or by graphing with a computer.

EXAMPLE 2 Use a calculator to find a closer approximation of the root of $P(x) = 2x^3 - x + 2$, which is near -1.1.

We know that $P(-1) = 1$ and $P(-2) = -12$, so there must be a root between -1 and -2. To find a better approximation we use synthetic division.

$P(-1.1) = 0.44$ and $P(-1.2) = -0.26$. Therefore, the graph crosses the x-axis between -1.1 and -1.2. Further calculation shows that $P(-1.16) = 0.04$ and $P(-1.17) = -0.03$, so we have a root between -1.16 and -1.17.

We now have an approximation to hundredths, -1.17.

Try This Graph each polynomial. Approximate roots to the nearest tenth.

b. $P(x) = x^3 - 3x^2 + 1$ **c.** $P(x) = x^4 + 3x^2 + 2$

Computer graphing programs and graphing calculators can be used to find approximations for both irrational and rational roots of higher-degree polynomial functions.

These programs and calculators allow you to change the viewing window so that the graph is enlarged. You can get increasingly better approximations of where a graph crosses the x-axis by "zooming" in.

EXAMPLE 3

Approximate the real roots of $P(x) = 2x^5 - 4x^4 + x^2 - 10$.

Descartes' rule of signs shows that there are 3 or 1 positive real roots, and 2 or 0 negative real roots.

Graphing using the computer shows that there are no negative roots, and there is one positive real root. The positive real root is approximately 2. Using the "zoom" function or changing the limits of x and y allows you to magnify the part of the graph around the intercept of the function.

We can zoom in on the root by changing the borders of the screen. First, we set the limits of x to show from 1.5 to 2.5. Then we set the limits of y to show from -0.5 to 0.5. We can see on the magnified screen that the graph crosses the x-axis at about 2.13.

Continuing to narrow down the x- and y-scales, we can find the root to seven or eight decimal places.

We find x is approximately 2.13200186.

Try This Approximate the real roots.

d. $2x^4 - 5x - 16 = 0$ **e.** $x^6 - 6 = 0$

11-6 Exercises

Extra Help On the Web

Look for worked-out examples at the Prentice Hall Web site.
www.phschool.com

A

Graph. A graphing calculator or graphing software may be used.

1. $P(x) = x^3 - 3x^2 - 2x - 6$
2. $P(x) = x^3 + 4x^2 - 3x - 12$
3. $P(x) = 2x^4 + x^3 - 7x^2 - x + 6$
4. $P(x) = 3x^4 + 5x^3 + 5x^2 - 5x - 6$
5. $P(x) = x^5 - 2x^4 - x^3 + 2x^2$
6. $P(x) = x^5 - 2x^4 + x^3 - 2x^2$

Graph each polynomial. Find approximate roots to the nearest tenth.

7. $P(x) = x^3 - 3x - 2$
8. $P(x) = x^3 - 3x^2 + 3$
9. $P(x) = x^3 - 3x - 4$
10. $P(x) = x^3 - 3x^2 + 5$

11. $P(x) = x^4 - 6x^2 + 8$ 12. $P(x) = x^4 - 4x^2 + 2$

13. $P(x) = x^5 + x^4 - x^3 - x^2 - 2x - 2$

14. $P(x) = x^5 - 2x^4 - 2x^3 + 4x^2 - 3x + 6$

15. $P(x) = x^4 + x^2 + 1$ 16. $P(x) = x^4 + 2x^2 + 2$

B

17. The equation $2x^5 + 2x^3 - x^2 - 1 = 0$ has a solution between 0 and 1. Use a calculator to approximate it to the nearest hundredth.

18. The equation $x^4 - 2x^3 - 3x^2 + 4x + 2 = 0$ has a solution between 1 and 2. Use a calculator to approximate it to the nearest hundredth.

Graph each polynomial. Find the irrational roots. (Use a calculator to approximate to the nearest hundredth.)

19. $P(x) = x^3 - 2x^2 - x + 4$

20. $P(x) = x^3 - 4x^2 + x + 3$

21. ***Critical Thinking*** Sketch the graph of a quartic polynomial that has two negative real roots and one nonnegative real root.

Challenge

22. Use a calculator to graph $P(x) = 5.8x^4 - 2.3x^2 - 6.1$.

23. ***Mathematical Reasoning*** A procedure for evaluating a polynomial, known as nested evaluation, is as follows. Given a polynomial, such as $3x^4 - 5x^3 + 4x^2 - 5$, successively factor out x.

$$x(x(x(3x - 5) + 4)) - 5$$

Given a value of x, substitute it in the innermost parentheses and work your way out, at each step multiplying, then adding or subtracting. Show that this process is identical to synthetic division.

Mixed Review

Write an equation for the line containing the given point and perpendicular to the given line. **24.** $(6, 4); -3x + 2y = 4$ **25.** $(4, 1); 2x - y = 7$ *3-7*

Solve. **26.** $|2x - 3| \leq 4$ **27.** $|3x + 2| \geq 5$ *2-7*

Solve. **28.** $\sqrt{y - 5} + \sqrt{y} = 5$ **29.** $\sqrt{x + 3} + \sqrt{x} = -3$

30. $P(x) = x^3 - 7x^2 + 5x - 4$; find $P(2), P(4), P(-1), P(-2)$. *11-1*

Factor the polynomial $P(x)$, then solve the equation $P(x) = 0$.

31. $P(x) = x^3 - 7x^2 + 4x + 12$ 32. $P(x) = x^3 + 2x^2 - 5x - 6$ *11-1*

Solve each system of equations.

33. $2x^2 - 3y = 0$
$4x - y - 6 = 0$

34. $y = 8x - x^2$
$y = 2x$ *10-7*

Reasoning Strategies

PART 1 Work Backward

Objective: Solve problems using the strategy *Work Backward* and other strategies.

What You'll Learn

1 To solve problems using the strategy *Work Backward*, and other strategies

. . . And Why

To solve algebraic problems using a variety of strategies

Sometimes a problem describes a sequence of actions involving numbers, gives the result, and asks for the number with which it started. A problem of this type can be solved by using a strategy called *Work Backward*.

EXAMPLE

A moving company put $\frac{1}{2}$ of the boxes from a house into a large truck and $\frac{1}{3}$ of the boxes into a smaller truck. Eight boxes were still in the garage of this house, and 6 were in the attic. These were to be moved the next day. How many boxes were in each truck?

To solve this problem, you can start with the number of boxes that were still in the garage and the attic, and then work backward.

DATA IN THE PROBLEM		WORK BACKWARD
↓		$\frac{1}{2}$ of the 84 boxes, or 42 boxes, were on the large truck; $\frac{1}{3}$ of the 84 boxes, or 28 boxes, were on the small truck.
		↑
$\frac{1}{2}$ of the boxes in one truck and $\frac{1}{3}$ of the boxes in another truck		The total number of boxes was $6 \cdot 14$, or 84.
		↑
↓		$\frac{1}{2} + \frac{1}{3} = \frac{5}{6}$, so 14 boxes were $\frac{1}{6}$ of the total boxes.
		↑
8 in the garage and 6 in the attic	→	8 + 6, or 14 boxes, had yet to be loaded.

There were 42 boxes on the large truck and 28 on the small truck.

Reasoning Strategies

Write an Equation	Draw a Diagram	Try, Test, Revise
Make an Organized List	Make a Table	Look for a Pattern
Use Logical Reasoning	Simplify the Problem	Work Backward

Extra Help On the Web

Look for worked-out examples at the Prentice Hall Web site.
www.phschool.com

Understanding the mathematics behind some games may improve your score. Computing the odds of an event such as drawing a card, rolling a certain number on a cube, or perhaps using a spinner to get directions are examples.

11-7 Problems

Solve using one or more of the strategies.

1. Three friends were playing a game. At one point they decided that they would play three more rounds. The loser of each round had to give each of the other two players as many points as each player had at the start of that round. Each player lost one of the last three rounds. They all ended with 40 points. How many points did each player have before starting the last three rounds?

2. A quadrilateral can be divided into 2 triangles as shown below. This shows that the sum of the interior angles of the quadrilateral is $2 \cdot 180 = 360°$. Use this idea to find the sum of the interior angles of an octagon (8 sides).

$$m\angle 1 + m\angle 2 + m\angle 3 = 180$$
$$m\angle 4 + m\angle 5 + m\angle 6 = 180$$
$$\text{so } m\angle 1 + m\angle 2 + m\angle 3 + m\angle 4 + m\angle 5 + m\angle 6 = 360$$

3. ***Multi-Step Problem*** In one family there have been 11 generations since the American Revolution. A man and woman were married in 1776 and subsequently had 2 children. Suppose both of these children married and had 2 children, and so on, for the succeeding generations. About how many people would there be in the 11 generations of this family born between 1776 and 1996?

4. What is the least number of toothpicks needed to build a regular hexagonal pattern with 10 hexagons?

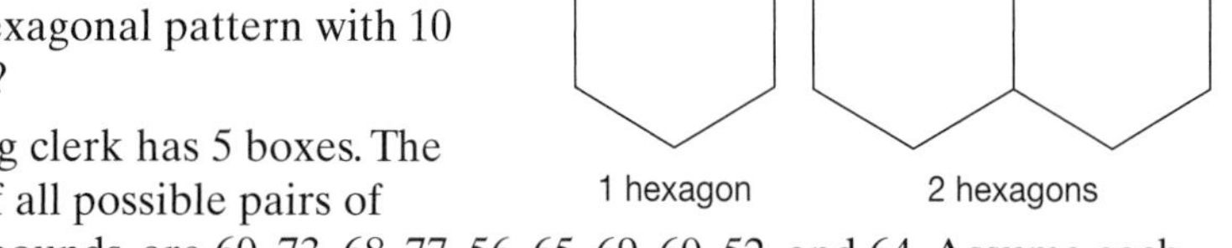

5. A shipping clerk has 5 boxes. The weights of all possible pairs of boxes, in pounds, are 60, 73, 68, 77, 56, 65, 69, 60, 52, and 64. Assume each box weighs a whole number of pounds. How much does each box weigh?

6. You have to cut a piece of wallboard out of a 4 ft by 8 ft sheet. The piece must fit around a 3 ft by 5 ft window located on part of a wall. The window is located 14 in. from the right end, 10 in. from the left end, 6 in. from the bottom, and 3 in. from the top. How much material would remain?

7. A company has 16 identical filing cabinets to be distributed to its 3 branches. Each branch must receive at least 1 cabinet. In how many ways can the cabinets be distributed?

8. A certain game had 2 possible scoring plays, a 3-point play and an 8-point play. How many different total scores for one player are impossible for this game?

11 Chapter Wrap Up

11-1

A **root** is a solution to the **polynomial equation** $P(x) = 0$. A **zero** is a value of x that makes the function $P(x)$ equal 0.

Determine whether the given numbers are **roots** of the polynomial equation $P(x) = 0$.

1. $P(x) = x^3 - x^2 + 25x - 25; -1, 5i$

2. $P(x) = x^4 + x^3 - x^2 - 2x - 2; \sqrt{2}, i$

Determine whether the given numbers are zeros of the polynomial function.

3. $P(x) = x^3 + 4x^2 - 4x - 16; -4, 4i$ **4.** $P(x) = x^4 - 2x^2 - 3; \sqrt{3}, i$

When one polynomial is divided by another, there will be a quotient and a remainder. When the remainder is zero, then the divisor and the quotient are **factors** of the dividend.

By division, determine whether the following polynomials are factors of the polynomial $P(x) = x^4 - 16$.

5. $x - 2$ **6.** $x^2 + 3x - 1$

Every polynomial division can be expressed as $P(x) = D(x) \cdot Q(x) + R(x)$, where $P(x)$ is the dividend, $D(x)$ is the divisor, $Q(x)$ is the quotient, and $R(x)$ is the remainder. Express each dividend as $P(x) = D(x) \cdot Q(x) + R(x)$.

7. Let $P(x) = x^3 - 2x^2 + 4$ and $D(x) = x - 1$. Find $P(x) \div D(x)$.

8. Let $P(x) = x^5 + 2x^4 + 2x^3 + 3x^2 + 3x + 3$ and $D(x) = x^2 + 2x + 1$. Find $P(x) \div D(x)$.

Key Terms

complex roots (p. 491)
cubic (p. 504)
Descartes' rule of signs (p. 501)
factor (p. 481)
Factor Theorem (p. 487)
Fundamental Theorem of Algebra (p. 490)
irrational roots (p. 491)
leading coefficient (p. 480)
multiplicity (p. 491)
negative real roots (p. 502)
polynomial equation (p. 480)
positive real roots (p. 501)
quartic (p. 504)
Remainder Theorem (p. 485)
root (p. 480)
variations of sign (p. 501)
zero (p. 480)

11-2

The **Remainder Theorem** states that for a polynomial $P(x)$, the function value $P(r)$ is the **remainder** when $P(x)$ is divided by $x - r$.

Find the function values.

9. Let $P(x) = -2x^4 - 8x^3 + 4x^2 - 2x + 1$. Find $P(0), P(1), P(-2)$, and $P(-4)$.

The **Factor Theorem** states that if $P(r) = 0$, then the polynomial $x - r$ is a factor of $P(x)$. Thus we can use synthetic division to find function values and to check factors.

Factor the polynomial $P(x)$, then solve the equation $P(x) = 0$.

10. $P(x) = x^3 - x^2 - 14x + 24$ **11.** $P(x) = x^3 - 18x^2 - x + 18$

11-3

If a polynomial is of degree n, then it can be factored into exactly n linear

Internet Activity On the Web

Look for extension problems for this chapter at the Prentice Hall Web site. www.phschool.com

factors. A factor may occur more than once. If a factor $x - r$ occurs k times, r is a root of **multiplicity** k.

Find the roots of the polynomial and the multiplicity of each root.

12. $P(x) = x^2(x - 2)^3(x + 1)$ **13.** $P(x) = (x^2 - 12x + 11)^2$

If r is a root of polynomial $P(x)$, then $x - r$ is a linear factor of $P(x)$.

Find a polynomial of degree 3 with the given numbers as roots.

14. $-1, -3, 4$

Complex roots occur in conjugate pairs in polynomials with real coefficients. **Irrational roots** occur in pairs in polynomials with rational coefficients.

Find a polynomial of lowest degree with rational coefficients that has the given numbers as some of its roots.

15. $1 - i, 2 + \sqrt{3}$ **16.** $2 + 3i, -\sqrt{2}$

11-4

To find possible **rational roots** of $a_nx^n + a_{n-1}x^{n-1} + \cdots + a_0$, find each rational number $\frac{c}{d}$ such that d is a factor of a_n and c is a factor of a_0, then test each $\frac{c}{d}$ using synthetic division.

Find the rational roots, if they exist, of each polynomial. If possible, find the other roots.

17. $P(x) = 20x^3 - 30x^2 + 12x - 1$ **18.** $P(x) = 2x^4 - x^3 - 3x - 18$

11-5

The number of **positive real roots** of a polynomial $P(x)$ with real coefficients is either the same as the number of the variations of sign of $P(x)$ or less than the number of variations by a positive even integer.

The number of **negative real roots** of a polynomial $P(x)$ with real coefficients is either the number of variations of sign of $P(-x)$ or less than the number of variations of sign by a positive even integer.

For each polynomial, determine the number of positive and the number of negative real roots.

19. $P(x) = 4x^5 - 3x^2 + x - 3$ **20.** $P(x) = 3x^7 - 2x^5 + 3x^2 + x - 1$

11-6

To graph polynomials:

1. look at the degree of the polynomial and its **leading coefficient.**
2. look for symmetries.
3. use synthetic division to make a table of values.
4. find the y-intercept and as many x-intercepts as possible.
5. plot the points and connect them appropriately.

After graphing, you can use the x-intercepts to aid in approximating roots.

Graph the polynomial functions and find solutions to the nearest tenth.

21. $P(x) = x^3 + 3x^2 - 2x - 6$ **22.** $P(x) = x^3 - 2x^2 - x$

11 Chapter Assessment

1. Is $x + 1$ a factor of $P(x) = x^3 + 6x^2 + x + 30$?
2. Is $x - 4$ a factor of $x^3 + 64$?
3. Let $P(x) = 4x^3 - 10x + 9$ and $D(x) = x + 2$. Find $P(x) \div D(x)$, then express the dividend as $P(x) = D(x) \cdot Q(x) + R(x)$.
4. If $P(x) = 2x^4 - 3x^3 + x^2 - 3x + 7$, find $P(-2)$, $P(3)$ and $P(-4)$.
5. Factor the polynomial $P(x)$, then solve the equation $P(x) = 0$ for $P(x) = x^4 - x^3 - 6x^2 + 4x + 8$.
6. Find a fourth-degree polynomial with rational coefficients that has roots $3 - 2i, 1 + \sqrt{5}$.
7. Suppose a polynomial of degree 5 with rational coefficients has $3 + \sqrt{3}, 1 + 2i, -1$ as roots. Find all the roots of the polynomial.
8. Given that the polynomial $x^4 - 2x^3 + 3x^2 - 2x + 2$ has the root i, find all the roots of the polynomial.
9. Find a polynomial of degree 5 with real coefficients and i as a root of multiplicity 2 and $\sqrt{5}$ as a root of multiplicity 1.
10. Find the rational roots, if they exist, of $x^3 - 7x^2 + 16x - 12$. If possible, find the other roots.
11. Find only the rational roots of $4x^5 + 16x^4 + 15x^3 + 8x^2 - 4x - 3$.
12. For $3x^9 + 2x^6 + 3x^3 + 2x^2 + x - 1$,
    a. find the possible number of positive real roots.
    b. find the possible number of negative real roots.
13. For $3x^5 - x^4 + 2x^3 - 5x^2 - 3x - 1$,
    a. find the possible number of positive real roots.
    b. find the possible number of negative real roots.
14. Graph $P(x) = x^3 - 2x^2 + x + 1$.
15. Find zeros of $P(x) = x^3 - 2x^2 + x + 1$. Approximate the zeros to the nearest tenth.

Challenge

16. Factor $x^6 + x^4 - 4x^2 - 4$. (Hint: Substitute z for x^2.)

CHAPTER 12

What You'll Learn in Chapter 12

- How to find an equation for the inverse of a relation or function
- How to graph exponential and logarithmic functions
- How to determine whether the graph of a relation is symmetric with respect to the line $y = x$
- How to simplify exponential and logarithmic expressions
- How to find natural and common logarithms and antilogarithms using a calculator, a table, or linear interpolation
- How to solve exponential and logarithmic equations

Skills & Concepts You Need for Chapter 12

1-7 Simplify.

1. 5^1 **2.** 8^0 **3.** 2^{-3}

1-8 Simplify.

4. $x^{-5} \cdot x^3$ **5.** $\frac{x^{-3}}{x^4}$ **6.** $(x^{-3})^4$

7. $\frac{24x^2y^2}{-16x^2y}$ **8.** $\frac{(2x^3y^{-2})^3}{3y^{-3}}$

1-9

9. Convert 0.0845 to scientific notation.

10. Convert 4.335×10^5 to decimal notation.

9-1 Test for symmetry with respect to the origin.

11. $4x + 4y = 6$ **12.** $y = 2x^2$

Exponential and Logarithmic Functions

An earthquake with a magnitude of 6.6 on the Richter scale collapsed this four-story parking garage in Northridge, California, in 1994. (See Lesson 12-7, Exercises 32–35.)

12-1 Inverse Relations and Functions

What You'll Learn

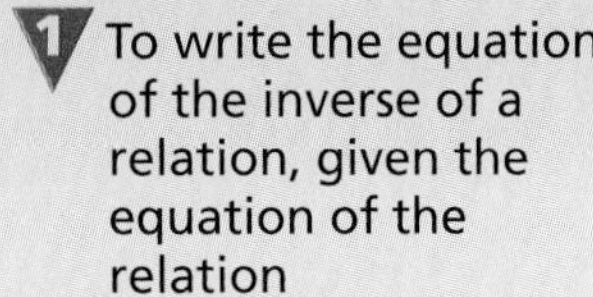

1. To write the equation of the inverse of a relation, given the equation of the relation

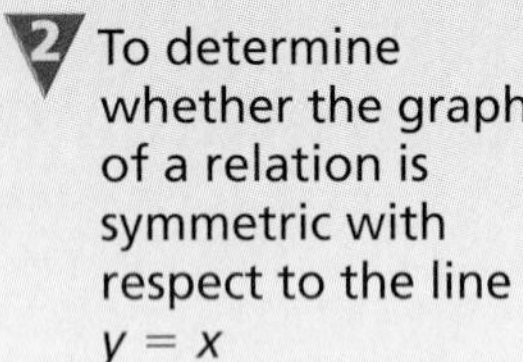

2. To determine whether the graph of a relation is symmetric with respect to the line $y = x$
3. To find an equation for the inverse function of a given function

. . . And Why

To find the inverses for exponential and logarithmic functions

PART 1 Inverses of Relations

Objective: Write the equation of the inverse of a relation, given the equation of the relation.

If in a relation we interchange the first and second coordinates of each ordered pair, we obtain a relation that is the **inverse** of the original relation. Thus the inverse of the relation $\{(2, 1), (3, 1), (4, 2)\}$ is $\{(1, 2), (1, 3), (2, 4)\}$.

Theorem 12-1

Interchanging x and y in the equation of a relation produces an equation of the **inverse relation.**

EXAMPLE 1 Write an equation of the inverse of $y = x^2 - 5$.

We interchange x and y, and obtain $x = y^2 - 5$. This is an equation of the inverse relation.

Try This

a. Write an equation of the inverse of $y = x^2 + 4$.

PART 2 Inverses and Symmetry

Objective: Determine whether the graph of a relation is symmetric with respect to the line $y = x$.

Quick Review

Symmetry with respect to a line was defined on page 384.

Interchanging first and second coordinates in each ordered pair of a relation has the effect of interchanging the x-axis and the y-axis.

Interchanging the x-axis and the y-axis has the effect of reflecting the graph of those points across the diagonal line whose equation is $y = x$, as shown. Thus the graphs of a relation and its inverse are always reflections of each other across the line $y = x$.

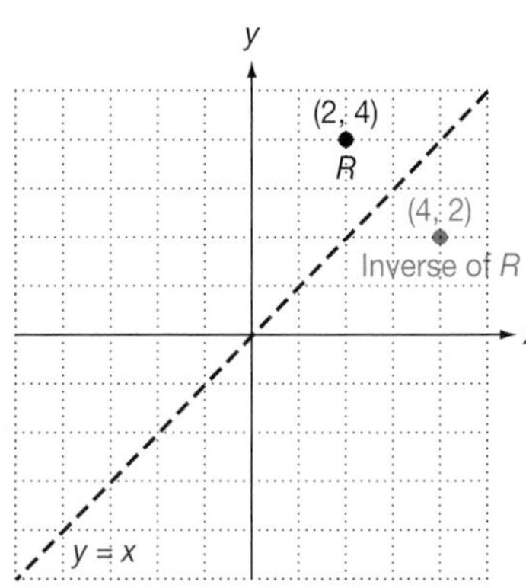

Here are some other graphs of relations and their inverses.

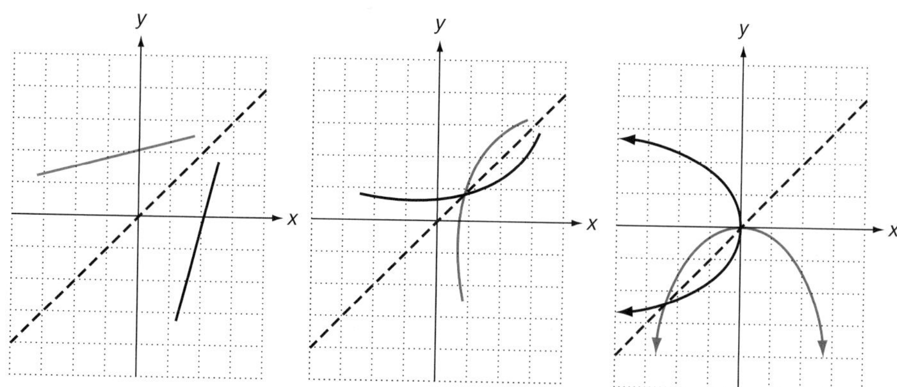

A relation may be its own inverse if, when the relation is reflected across the line $y = x$, the image is unchanged. Such a relation is symmetric with respect to the line $y = x$.

We can test the relation $3x + 3y = 5$ for symmetry with respect to the line $y = x$ by interchanging x and y in the equation. We obtain $3y + 3x = 5$. This is equivalent to the original equation, so the graph is symmetric with respect to the line $y = x$.

EXAMPLE 2 Test the relation $4x - 4y = 8$ for symmetry with respect to the line $y = x$.

We interchange x and y in the equation, obtaining $4y - 4x = 8$. This is not equivalent to the original equation, so the graph is not symmetric to $y = x$.

Try This Test for symmetry with respect to the line $y = x$.

b. $4x + 4y = 6$ **c.** $y = 2x^2$

PART 3 Inverses of Functions

Objective: Find an equation for the inverse function of a given function.

All functions have inverses, but the inverse is not necessarily a function. For instance, consider the function

$$G = \{(1, 3), (2, 4), (6, 3), (7, 7)\}$$

The inverse of G, $\{(3, 1), (4, 2), (3, 6), (7, 7)\}$, is not a function because the ordered pairs (3, 1) and (3, 6) have the same first coordinates but different second coordinates.

If the inverse of a function f is also a function, we denote it by f^{-1} (read "f inverse"). Recall that we obtain the inverse of a relation by interchanging the coordinates of each ordered pair. Thus the domain of a function f is the range of f^{-1} and the range of f is the domain of f^{-1}.

Writing Math

If $f(x)$ is a function and it has an inverse that is also a function, then we can write $f^{-1}(x)$ for the inverse.

Reading Math

Do not confuse the inverse of a function with the reciprocal (or multiplicative inverse) of a function. That is, in general $f^{-1} \neq \frac{1}{f}$, and $f^{-1}(x) \neq [f(x)]^{-1} = \frac{1}{f(x)}$.

When a function is defined by an equation, we can sometimes find an equation for its inverse by interchanging x and y.

EXAMPLE 3 Given $f(x) = 3x + 1$, find an equation for $f^{-1}(x)$.

(a) Let us think of this as $y = 3x + 1$.

(b) To find the inverse we interchange x and y: $x = 3y + 1$.

(c) Now we solve for y: $y = \frac{x - 1}{3}$.

(d) Thus $f^{-1}(x) = \frac{x - 1}{3}$.

In Example 3, f assigns $3x + 1$ to any number x. (This function multiplies each number of the domain by 3 and adds 1.) Its inverse, f^{-1}, assigns the number $\frac{x - 1}{3}$ to any number x. (This inverse function subtracts 1 from each member of its domain and divides by 3.) Thus the function and its inverse are inverse operations.

Try This

d. Given $g(x) = x + 2$, find an equation for $g^{-1}(x)$.

e. Given $g(x) = 5x + 2$, find an equation for $g^{-1}(x)$.

EXAMPLE 4 Let $S(x) = \sqrt{x}$. Find an equation for $S^{-1}(x)$.

(a) Let us think of this as $y = \sqrt{x}$. Note that the domain and range both consist of nonnegative real numbers only.

(b) To find the inverse we interchange x and y: $x = \sqrt{y}$.

(c) Now we solve for y, squaring both sides: $y = x^2$.

(d) Thus $S^{-1}(x) = x^2$, with the understanding that x cannot be negative.

In Example 4, the function S assigns $\sqrt{x}$ to any nonnegative number x. (This function takes the square root of any input.) Its inverse, S^{-1}, assigns x^2 to any nonnegative number x. (This function squares each input.) Thus the function and its inverse use inverse operations.

Try This

f. Let $f(x) = \sqrt{x + 1}$. Find an equation for $f^{-1}(x)$.

Quick Review

The composition of two functions was defined on page 149.

Suppose $f(x) = 2x + 3$. Then $f^{-1}(x) = \frac{x - 3}{2}$. Note that $f(5) = 13$, and $f^{-1}(13) = \frac{13 - 3}{2} = 5$. Also, $f(8) = 19$ and $f^{-1}(19) = 8$.

It appears that if we find $f(x)$ for some x and then find f^{-1} for this number, we will be back at x. In function notation the statement looks like the following equation.

$$f^{-1}(f(x)) = x$$

The notation $f^{-1}(f(x)) = x$ is read "f inverse of f of x equals x." It means, work from the inside out to take x, then find $f(x)$, and then find f^{-1} for that number. When we do, we will be back where we started, at x. For similar reasons, the following is true.

$$f(f^{-1}(x)) = x$$

For the statements above to be true, x must be in the domain of the function being considered. We summarize these ideas by stating the following theorem.

Theorem 12-2

For any function f whose inverse is a function, $f^{-1}(f(a)) = a$ for any a in the domain of f. Also $f(f^{-1}(a)) = a$ for any a in the domain of f^{-1}.

EXAMPLE 5 For the function $f(x) = 4x + 9$, find $f^{-1}(f(283))$ and $f(f^{-1}(-12{,}045))$.

We note that every real number is in the domain of both f and f^{-1}. Thus using Theorem 12-2, we may immediately write the answers, without calculating.

$$f^{-1}(f(283)) = 283$$
$$f(f^{-1}(-12{,}045)) = -12{,}045$$

Try This

g. For the function $f(x) = \frac{3x - 5}{4}$, find $f^{-1}(f(579))$ and $f(f^{-1}(-83{,}479))$.

12-1 Exercises

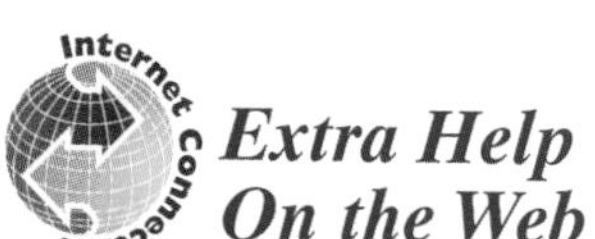

Extra Help On the Web

Look for worked-out examples at the Prentice Hall Web site.
www.phschool.com

A

Write an equation of the inverse relation of the following.

1. $y = 4x - 5$ **2.** $y = 3x + 5$ **3.** $y = 3x^2 + 2$

4. $y = 5x^2 - 4$ **5.** $x^2 - 3y^2 = 3$ **6.** $2x^2 + 5y^2 = 4$

7. $xy = 7$ **8.** $xy = -5$ **9.** $xy^2 = 1$

10. $\frac{x^2}{4} + \frac{y^2}{9} = 1$ **11.** $y = \frac{5}{x}$ **12.** $y = \sqrt{x + 1}$

Test for symmetry with respect to the line $y = x$.

13. $3x + 2y = 4$ **14.** $5x - 2y = 7$ **15.** $xy = 10$

16. $xy = 12$ **17.** $4x + 4y = 3$ **18.** $5x + 5y = -1$

19. $3x = \frac{4}{y}$ **20.** $4y = \frac{5}{x}$ **21.** $4x^2 + 4y^2 = 3$

22. $3x^2 + 3y^2 = 5$ **23.** $y = |2x|$ **24.** $3x = |2y|$

Find equations for $f^{-1}(x)$ for the following.

25. $f(x) = x - 1$
26. $f(x) = x - 2$
27. $f(x) = x + 4$
28. $f(x) = x + 3$
29. $f(x) = x + 8$
30. $f(x) = x + 7$
31. $f(x) = 2x + 5$
32. $f(x) = 3x + 2$
33. $f(x) = 3x - 1$
34. $f(x) = 4x - 3$
35. $f(x) = 0.5x + 2$
36. $f(x) = 0.7x + 4$
37. $f(x) = \sqrt{x - 1}$
38. $f(x) = \sqrt{x - 2}$
39. $f(x) = \sqrt{x + 2}$

40. $f(x) = 35x - 173$. Find $f^{-1}(f(3))$ and $f(f^{-1}(-125))$.

41. $g(x) = \frac{-173x + 15}{3}$. Find $g^{-1}(g(5))$ and $g(g^{-1}(-12))$.

42. $f(x) = x^3 + 2$. Find $f^{-1}(f(12{,}053))$ and $f(f^{-1}(-17{,}243))$.

43. $g(x) = x^3 - 486$. Find $g^{-1}(g(489))$ and $g(g^{-1}(-17{,}422))$.

B

44. Graph $y = x^2 + 1$. Then, by reflection across the line $y = x$, graph its inverse.

45. Graph $y = x^2 - 3$. Then, by reflection across the line $y = x$, graph its inverse.

46. Graph $y = |x|$. Then, by reflection across the line $y = x$, graph its inverse.

47. Graph $x = |y|$. Then, by reflection across the line $y = x$, graph its inverse.

Find the composition functions $f(g(x))$ and $g(f(x))$.

48. $f(x) = 3x + 1, g(x) = \frac{x - 1}{3}$
49. $f(x) = x^3 - 5, g(x) = \sqrt[3]{x + 5}$
50. $f(x) = 2x, g(x) = x^2 + 1$
51. $f(x) = x^2, g(x) = x + 3$
52. $f(x) = 2x + 3, g(x) = x - 4$
53. $f(x) = 3x^2 + 2, g(x) = 2x - 1$
54. $f(x) = 4x^2 - 1, g(x) = \frac{2}{x}$
55. $f(x) = x^2 - 1, g(x) = x^2 - 1$

56. ***Critical Thinking*** Suppose $f(x) = \frac{1}{x + 1} + 4$.

a. What is the domain of $f(x)$?

b. Find $f^{-1}(x)$. What is the domain of $f^{-1}(x)$?

c. For what values of x does $f^{-1}(f(x)) = x$?

Challenge

Graph each equation and its inverse. Then test for symmetry with respect to the x-axis, the y-axis, the origin, and the line $y = x$.

57. $y = \frac{1}{x^2}$
58. $|x| - |y| = 1$
59. $y = x^3$
60. $y = \frac{|x|}{x}$

Mixed Review

Multiply and simplify. **61.** $3^5 3^3$ **62.** $(2a)^2(2a)^4$ **63.** $(-3)^{-5}(-3)^7$
64. $(3x^4y^3)(7xy^5)$ **65.** $(m^5)^3$ **66.** $(2x^3y^2)^5$ **67.** $(4m^{-3}n^7)^{-2}$ *1-8*

68. Find the center and radius of the circle $x^2 + y^2 + 14x + 2y + 1 = 0$. *10-2*

Exponential and Logarithmic Functions

12-2

What You'll Learn

1. To graph exponential functions
2. To graph logarithmic functions

... And Why

To model real-world problems that involve exponential and logarithmic functions

We have defined exponential notation for rational exponents. We now consider irrational exponents. Let us consider 2^{π}. The number π has an unending decimal representation.

$$3.1415926535\ldots$$

Now consider this sequence of numbers.

$$3, \quad 3.1, \quad 3.14, \quad 3.141, \quad 3.1415, \quad 3.14159, \ldots$$

Each of these numbers is an approximation to π. The more decimal places, the better the approximation. Let us use these rational numbers to form a sequence as follows.

$$2^{3}, \quad 2^{3.1}, \quad 2^{3.14}, \quad 2^{3.141}, \quad 2^{3.1415}, \quad 2^{3.14159}, \ldots$$

Each of the numbers in this sequence is already defined, the exponent being rational. The numbers in this sequence get closer and closer to some real number. We define that number to be 2^{π}.

We can define exponential notation for any irrational exponent in a similar way. Thus any exponential expression a^x, $a > 0$, now has meaning, whether the exponent is rational or irrational.

PART 1 Exponential Functions

Objective: Graph exponential functions.

Exponential functions are defined using exponential notation.

Definition

The function $f(x) = a^x$, where a is some positive real-number constant different from 1, is called the **exponential function, base *a*.**

Here are some exponential functions.

$$f(x) = 2^x \qquad g(x) = \left(\frac{1}{2}\right)^x \qquad h(x) = (0.178)^x$$

Note that the variable is the exponent. The following are *not* exponential functions.

$$f(x) = x^2 \qquad g(x) = x^{\frac{1}{3}} \qquad h(x) = x^{0.178}$$

Note that the variable is not the exponent.

EXAMPLE 1 Graph $y = 2^x$. Use the graph to approximate $2^{\sqrt{2}}$.

We find some solutions, plot them, and then draw the graph.

x	y
0	1
1	2
2	4
3	8
-1	$\frac{1}{2}$
-2	$\frac{1}{4}$
-3	$\frac{1}{8}$

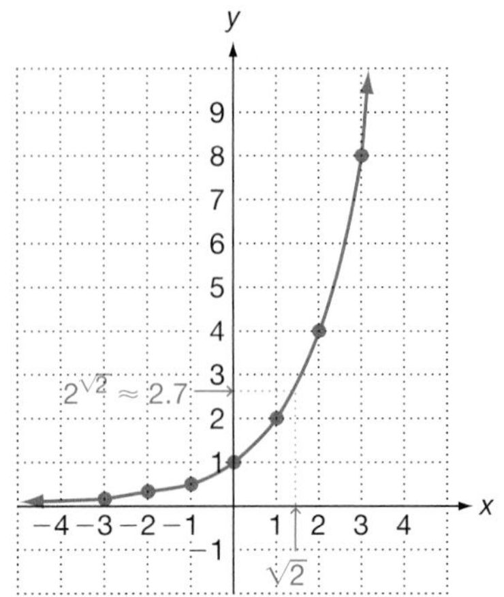

Note that as x increases, the function values increase. Check this on a calculator. As x decreases, the function values decrease toward 0.

To approximate $2^{\sqrt{2}}$ we locate $\sqrt{2}$ on the x-axis, at about 1.4. Then we find the corresponding function value. It is about 2.7. Approximations may be checked using computer graphing techniques.

Try This

a. Graph $y = 3^x$. Use the graph to approximate $3^{\frac{1}{2}}$.

We can make comparisons between functions using transformations.

EXAMPLE 2 Graph $y = 4^x$.

We could plot some points and connect them.

We note that $4^x = (2^2)^x = 2^{2x}$. Compare this with $y = 2^x$, graphed in Example 1. Notice that the graph of $y = 2^{2x}$ approaches the y-axis more rapidly than the graph of $y = 2^x$. The graph of $y = 2^{2x}$ is a shrinking of the graph of $y = 2^x$.

Knowing this allows us to graph $y = 2^{2x}$ at once. Each point on the graph of 2^x is moved half the distance to the y-axis.

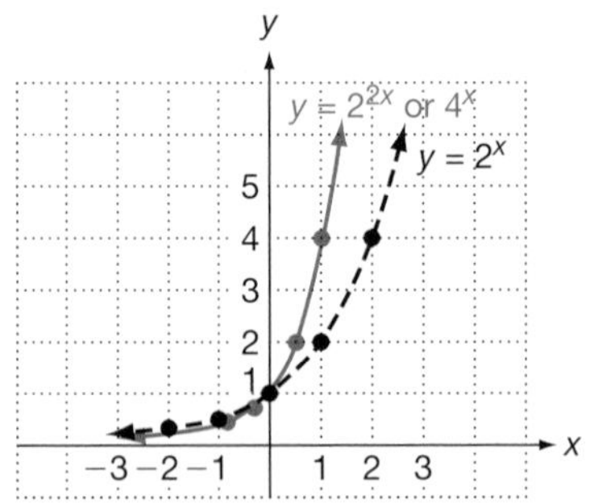

Try This

b. Graph $y = 8^x$. **c.** Graph $y = 9^x$.

EXAMPLE 3 Graph $y = \left(\frac{1}{2}\right)^x$.

We could plot some points and connect them, but again let us note that $\left(\frac{1}{2}\right)^x = \frac{1}{2^x} = 2^{-x}$. Compare this with the graph of $y = 2^x$ in Example 1. The graph of $y = 2^{-x}$ is a reflection, across the y-axis, of the graph of $y = 2^x$. Knowing this allows us to graph $y = 2^{-x}$ at once.

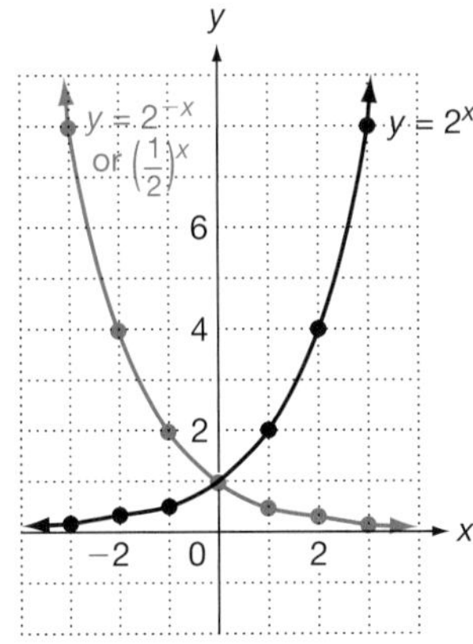

Try This

d. Graph $y = \left(\frac{1}{3}\right)^x$.

PART 2 Logarithmic Functions

Objective: Graph logarithmic functions.

Definition

A **logarithmic function** is the inverse of an exponential function.

One way to describe a logarithmic function is to interchange variables in the equation $y = a^x$. Thus the following equation is logarithmic.

$$x = a^y$$

For logarithmic functions we use the notation $\log_a (x)$ or $\mathbf{log_a x}$, which is read "log, base a, of x."

$$y = \log_a x \text{ means } x = a^y$$

Thus a logarithm is an exponent. That is, we use the symbol $\log_a x$ to denote the second coordinates of a function $x = a^y$.

The most useful and interesting logarithmic functions are those for which $a > 1$. The graph of such a function is a reflection of $y = a^x$ across the line $y = x$. The domain of a logarithmic function is the set of all positive real numbers.

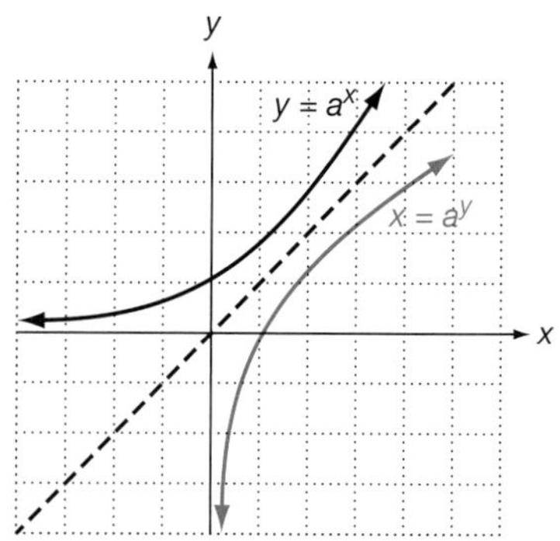

EXAMPLE 4 Graph $y = \log_3 x$.

The equation $y = \log_3 x$ is equivalent to $x = 3^y$. The graph of $x = 3^y$ is a reflection of $y = 3^x$ across the line $y = x$. We make a table of values for $y = 3^x$ and then interchange x and y.

For $y = 3^x$:

x	y
0	1
1	3
2	9
-1	$\frac{1}{3}$
-2	$\frac{1}{9}$

For $y = \log_3 x$ (or $x = 3^y$):

x	y
1	0
3	1
9	2
$\frac{1}{3}$	-1
$\frac{1}{9}$	-2

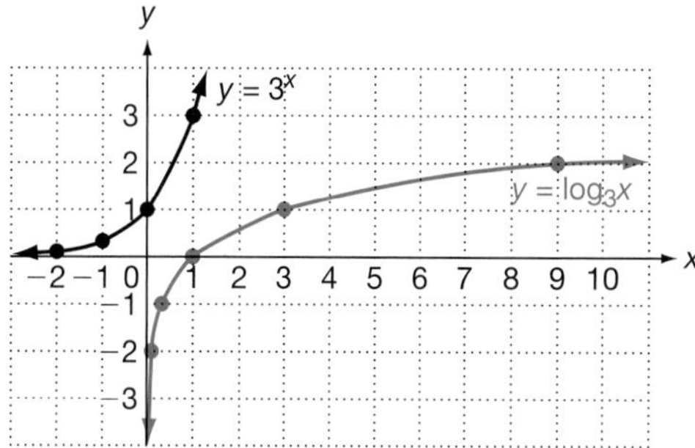

Since $a^0 = 1$ for any $a \neq 0$, the graph of $y = \log_a x$, for any a, has the x-intercept $(1, 0)$.

Try This

e. Graph $y = \log_2 x$.
What is the domain of this function? What is the range?

f. Graph $y = \log_4 x$.
What is the domain of this function? What is the range?

12-2 Exercises

Extra Help On the Web

Look for worked-out examples at the Prentice Hall Web site. www.phschool.com

A

Graph. Where possible, use transformations.

1. $y = 2^x$ **2.** $y = 3^x$ **3.** $y = 5^x$ **4.** $y = 6^x$

5. $y = \left(\frac{1}{2}\right)^x$ **6.** $y = \left(\frac{1}{6}\right)^x$ **7.** $y = \left(\frac{1}{4}\right)^x$ **8.** $y = \left(\frac{1}{5}\right)^x$

9. $y = (0.4)^x$ **10.** $y = (0.3)^x$ **11.** $y = (1.5)^x$ **12.** $y = (2.5)^x$

Graph. Where possible, use transformations.

13. $y = \log_2 x$ **14.** $y = \log_5 x$ **15.** $y = \log_3 x$ **16.** $y = \log_4 x$

17. $y = \log_7 x$ **18.** $y = \log_{10} x$ **19.** $y = \log_{1.5} x$ **20.** $y = \log_{3.5} x$

B

Consider the graph of $y = 4^x$ in Example 2.

21. What is the domain of $y = 4^x$? **22.** What is the y-intercept?

23. *Estimation* Use the graph to approximate $4^{0.7}$.

Graph.

24. $y = 2^{x-1}$ **25.** $y = 2^{x+1}$ **26.** $y = \log_2 (x + 1)$

27. $y = \log_3 (x - 2)$ **28.** $f(x) = 2^{|x-1|}$ **29.** $y = 2^x + 2^{-x}$

What is the domain of each function?

30. $f(x) = 3^x$ **31.** $f(x) = \log_{10} x$ **32.** $f(x) = \log_a x^2$

33. $f(x) = \log_4 x^3$ **34.** $f(x) = \log_{10}(3x - 4)$ **35.** $f(x) = \log_5 |x|$

36. Use a calculator to estimate each of the following to six decimal places.

a. 2^3 **b.** $2^{3.1}$ **c.** $2^{3.14}$ **d.** $2^{3.141}$ **e.** $2^{3.1415}$ **f.** $2^{3.14159}$

Mental Math Determine which of the two numbers is larger. Use a calculator to check your answer.

37. 5^π or π^5 **38.** $\sqrt{8^3}$ or $8^{\sqrt{3}}$

39. *Critical Thinking* Solve $3^{2x^2+5x-3} = 1$.

Challenge

Graph. **40.** $y = 2^{-x^2}$ **41.** $y = 3^{-(x+1)^2}$ **42.** $y = |2^{x^2} - 8|$

Mixed Review

Convert to scientific notation. **43.** 3,007,114 **44.** 0.002385 *1-9*

Convert to decimal notation. **45.** 5.709×10^{-5} **46.** 6.03791×10^8 *1-9*

47. Find an equation of a parabola with focus (6, 0) and vertex at the origin. *10-5*

48. Find a polynomial of degree 3 with 6, 2, and −1 as roots. *11-3*

12-3 Exponential and Logarithmic Relationships

What You'll Learn

1. To convert exponential equations to logarithmic equations and vice versa
2. To solve logarithmic equations
3. To simplify expressions of the form $a^{\log_a x}$ and $\log_a a^x$

. . . And Why

To solve real-world problems involving exponential and logarithmic equations

Part 1 Converting Exponential and Logarithmic Equations

Objective: Convert exponential equations to logarithmic equations and vice versa.

It is often helpful to be able to convert from an exponential equation to a logarithmic equation. Recall that the following are equivalent.

$x = a^y$ and $y = \log_a x$

EXAMPLES Convert to logarithmic equations.

1 $2^x = 8 \quad \rightarrow \quad x = \log_2 8$ The logarithm is the exponent.

2 $y^{-1} = 4 \quad \rightarrow \quad -1 = \log_y 4$

3 $10^3 = 1000 \quad \rightarrow \quad 3 = \log_{10} 1000$

In general, for an equation $a^b = c$ where $a > 0$, $b = \log_a c$.

Try This Convert to logarithmic equations.

a. $6^0 = 1$ **b.** $10^{-3} = 0.001$ **c.** $16^{\frac{1}{4}} = 2$ **d.** $\left(\frac{6}{5}\right)^{-2} = \frac{25}{36}$

It is also useful to be able to convert from a logarithmic equation to an exponential equation.

EXAMPLES Convert to exponential equations.

4 $y = \log_3 5 \quad \rightarrow \quad 3^y = 5$

5 $-2 = \log_a 7 \quad \rightarrow \quad a^{-2} = 7$

6 $a = \log_b d \quad \rightarrow \quad b^a = d$

Try This Convert to exponential equations.

e. $\log_2 32 = 5$ **f.** $\log_{10} 1000 = 3$ **g.** $\log_{10} 0.01 = -2$ **h.** $\log_{\sqrt{5}} 5 = 2$

Note that the domain of logarithmic functions is restricted to values greater than 0. Therefore, exponential equations with a negative base, such as $(-2)^y = 16$, cannot be converted to a logarithmic equation. This allows exponential functions and logarithmic functions to be inverses of each other. For this reason, many calculators will not calculate exponents with negative bases.

PART 2 Solving Logarithmic Equations

Objective: Solve logarithmic equations.

Certain equations containing logarithmic notation can be solved by first converting to exponential notation.

EXAMPLES

7 Solve $\log_2 x = -3$.
$\log_2 x = -3$ is equivalent to $2^{-3} = x$. So $x = \frac{1}{8}$.

8 Solve $\log_{27} 3 = x$.
$\log_{27} 3 = x$ is equivalent to $27^x = 3$. Since $27^{\frac{1}{3}} = 3$, we have $x = \frac{1}{3}$.

9 Solve $\log_x 4 = \frac{1}{2}$.
$\log_x 4 = \frac{1}{2}$ is equivalent to $x^{\frac{1}{2}} = 4$. Since $(x^{\frac{1}{2}})^2 = 4^2$, we have $x = 16$.

Try This Solve.

i. $\log_{10} x = 4$ **j.** $\log_x 81 = 4$ **k.** $\log_2 16 = x$ **l.** $\log_5 \frac{1}{25} = x$

PART 3 Simplifying the Expressions $a^{\log_a x}$ and $\log_a a^x$

Objective: Simplify expressions of the form $a^{\log_a x}$ and $\log_a a^x$.

From Theorem 12-2 we know that $f^{-1}(f(x)) = x$ and $f(f^{-1}(x)) = x$ with appropriate restrictions on the domains of the functions. Since exponential and logarithmic functions are inverses of each other, Theorem 12-2 applies to them. Thus if $f(x) = a^x$, then $f^{-1}(x) = \log_a x$.

Therefore, $f(f^{-1}(x)) = f(\log_a x) = a^{\log_a x} = x$.
Likewise, $f^{-1}(f(x)) = f^{-1}(a^x) = \log_a a^x = x$.

Theorem 12-3

For any positive number a, where $a \neq 1$,

$a^{\log_a x} = x$, for any positive number x and
$\log_a a^x = x$, for any number x.

EXAMPLES Simplify.

10 $2^{\log_2 5} = 5$ **11** $10^{\log_{10} t} = t$ **12** $\log_{10} 10^{5.6} = 5.6$

Try This Simplify.

m. $4^{\log_4 3}$ **n.** $b^{\log_b 42}$ **o.** $\log_5 5^{37}$ **p.** $\log_{10} 10^{3.2}$

Extra Help On the Web

Look for worked-out examples at the Prentice Hall Web site.
www.phschool.com

12-3 Exercises

A

Convert to logarithmic equations.

1. $10^5 = 100{,}000$ **2.** $10^2 = 100$ **3.** $8^{\frac{1}{3}} = 2$ **4.** $16^{\frac{1}{4}} = 2$

5. $5^{-3} = \frac{1}{125}$ **6.** $4^{-5} = \frac{1}{1024}$ **7.** $10^{0.3010} = 2$ **8.** $a^{-b} = c$

Convert to exponential equations.

9. $t = \log_3 8$ **10.** $h = \log_7 10$ **11.** $\log_5 25 = 2$

12. $\log_6 6 = 1$ **13.** $\log_{10} 0.1 = -1$ **14.** $\log_{10} 0.01 = -2$

15. $\log_{10} 7 = 0.845$ **16.** $\log_{10} 3 = 0.4771$ **17.** $\log_k A = c$

Solve.

18. $\log_3 x = 2$ **19.** $\log_4 x = 3$ **20.** $\log_x 16 = 2$

21. $\log_x 64 = 3$ **22.** $\log_2 x = -1$ **23.** $\log_3 x = -2$

24. $\log_8 x = \frac{1}{3}$ **25.** $\log_{32} x = \frac{1}{5}$ **26.** $\log_9 x = \frac{1}{2}$

Simplify.

27. $3^{\log_3 4}$ **28.** $7^{\log_7 10}$ **29.** $\log_t t^9$ **30.** $\log_p p^a$

Quick Review

A logarithm is an exponent in which $a^y = x$ implies that $\log_a x = y$.

B

Simplify.

31. $\log_2 64$ **32.** $\log_4 64$ **33.** $\log_{10} 10^2$ **34.** $\log_3 3^4$

35. $\log_{10} 0.1$ **36.** $\log_{10} 10{,}000$ **37.** $\log_{10} 1$ **38.** $\log_{10} 10$

Solve, using graphing.

39. $2^x > 1$ **40.** $3^x \leq 1$ **41.** $\log_2 x < 0$ **42.** $\log_2 x \geq 4$

43. *Critical Thinking* Find $\log_{\sqrt{2}} 16$.

Challenge

Solve.

44. $3^{(2^x)} = 6561$ **45.** $81^{(4^x)} = 9$ **46.** $3^{(3^x)} = 1$

Mixed Review

47. Find a polynomial of degree 5 with 1 as a root of multiplicity 3 and -1 as a root of multiplicity 2.

48. Find a polynomial of lowest degree with rational coefficients that has $\sqrt{3}$, 2 and $-5i$ as some of its roots. *11-3*

Find the quadratic function that fits the data points.

49. $(1, -8), (2, -5), (-1, 4)$ **50.** $(2, -4), (-3, 26), (5, 2)$ *9-8*

Properties of Logarithmic Functions

12-4

PART 1 Logarithms of Products, Quotients, and Powers

Objective: To apply the basic properties of logarithms.

What You'll Learn

1. To apply the basic properties of logarithms

. . . And Why

To simplify exponential and logarithmic expressions

Let us now establish some basic properties of logarithmic functions.

Theorem 12-4

For any positive numbers x and y, and $a > 0, a \neq 1$,

$$\log_a (x \cdot y) = \log_a x + \log_a y$$

Theorem 12-4 says that the logarithm of a product is the sum of the logarithms of the factors. Note that the base a must remain constant. The logarithm of a sum is *not* the sum of the logarithms of the addends.

Proof of Theorem 12-4

Since a is positive and different from 1, it can serve as a logarithm base. Since x and y are assumed positive, they are in the domain of $f(x) = \log_a x$. Now let $b = \log_a x$ and $c = \log_a y$. We write equivalent exponential equations and then find the product, xy.

$$x = a^b \text{ and } y = a^c$$
$$xy = a^b a^c$$
$$= a^{b+c}$$

Now writing an equivalent logarithmic equation, we obtain

$$\log_a (xy) = b + c.$$

Substituting for b and c, we obtain

$$\log_a (xy) = \log_a x + \log_a y.$$

EXAMPLE 1 Express as a sum of logarithms. Simplify, if possible.

$$\log_2 (4 \cdot 16) = \log_2 4 + \log_2 16$$
$$= 2 + 4 = 6$$

EXAMPLE 2 Express as a single logarithm.

$$\log_5 19 + \log_5 3 = \log_5 (19 \cdot 3)$$
$$= \log_5 57$$

Try This

a. Express as a sum of logarithms. Simplify, if possible.

(1) $\log_a MN$ (2) $\log_5 (25 \cdot 5)$

b. Express as a single logarithm.

(1) $\log_3 7 + \log_3 5$ (2) $\log_a C + \log_a A + \log_a B + \log_a I + \log_a N$

Theorem 12-5

For any positive number x, any number p, and $a > 0, a \neq 1$,

$$\log_a x^p = p \cdot \log_a x$$

Theorem 12-5 says that the logarithm of a power of a number is the exponent times the logarithm of the number.

Proof of Theorem 12-5

Let $b = \log_a x$. Then, writing an equivalent exponential equation, we have $x = a^b$. Next we raise both sides of the latter equation to the pth power.

$$x^p = (a^b)^p = a^{bp}, \text{ or } a^{pb}$$

Now we can write an equivalent logarithmic equation.

$$\log_a x^p = \log_a a^{pb}$$
$$= pb \quad \text{Using Theorem 12-3}$$

But $b = \log_a x$, so we have $\log_a x^p = p \cdot \log_a x$.

EXAMPLES Express as a product.

3 $\log_b 9^{-5} = -5 \cdot \log_b 9$

4 $\log_a \sqrt[4]{5} = \log_a 5^{\frac{1}{4}} = \frac{1}{4} \log_a 5$

Try This Express as a product.

c. $\log_7 4^5$ **d.** $\log_a \sqrt{5}$

Theorem 12-6

For any positive numbers x, y, and $a > 0, a \neq 1$,

$$\log_a \frac{x}{y} = \log_a x - \log_a y$$

Theorem 12-6 says that the logarithm of a quotient is the logarithm of the dividend minus the logarithm of the divisor.

Proof of Theorem 12-6

Since a is positive and different from 1, it can serve as a logarithm base. Since x and y are assumed positive, they are in the domain of $f(x) = \log_a x$. Now let $b = \log_a x$ and $c = \log_a y$. We write equivalent exponential equations.

$$x = a^b \text{ and } y = a^c$$

Next we divide.

$$\frac{x}{y} = \frac{a^b}{a^c}$$
$$= a^{b-c}$$

Now writing an equivalent logarithmic equation, we obtain

$$\log_a \left(\frac{x}{y}\right) = b - c, \text{ or}$$

substituting for b and c, we obtain

$$\log_a \frac{x}{y} = \log_a x - \log_a y$$

EXAMPLE 5 Express in terms of logarithms of x, y, and z.

$$\log_a \sqrt[4]{\frac{xy}{z^3}} = \log_a \left(\frac{xy}{z^3}\right)^{\frac{1}{4}}$$

$= \frac{1}{4} \cdot \log_a \frac{xy}{z^3}$ Using Theorem 12-5

$= \frac{1}{4}[\log_a xy - \log_a z^3]$ Using Theorem 12-6

$= \frac{1}{4}[\log_a x + \log_a y - 3 \log_a z]$ Using Theorems 12-4 and 12-6

$= \frac{1}{4}\log_a x + \frac{1}{4}\log_a y - \frac{3}{4}\log_a z$ Using the distributive property

Try This

e. Express as a difference.

(1) $\log_a \frac{M}{N}$ (2) $\log_c \frac{1}{4}$

f. Express as sums and differences of logarithms and without exponential notation or radicals.

$$\log_{10} \frac{4\pi}{\sqrt{23}}$$

g. Express in terms of logarithms of x, y, and z.

$$\log_a \sqrt{\frac{z^3}{xy}}$$

EXAMPLE 6 Express as a single logarithm.

$$\frac{1}{2}\log_a x - 7\log_a y + \log_a z = \log_a \sqrt{x} - \log_a y^7 + \log_a z$$
$$= \log_a \frac{\sqrt{x}}{y^7} + \log_a z = \log_a \frac{z\sqrt{x}}{y^7}$$

Try This

h. Express $5\log_a x - \log_a y + \frac{1}{4}\log_a z$ as a single logarithm.

EXAMPLE 7 Given that $\log_a 2 \approx 0.301$ and $\log_a 3 \approx 0.477$, find the following.

(a) $\log_a 6 = \log_a 2 \cdot 3 = \log_a 2 + \log_a 3 \approx 0.301 + 0.477 \approx 0.778$

(b) $\log_a \sqrt{3} = \log_a 3^{\frac{1}{2}} = \frac{1}{2} \cdot \log_a 3 \approx \frac{1}{2} \cdot 0.477 \approx 0.2385$

(c) $\log_a \frac{2}{3} = \log_a 2 - \log_a 3 \approx 0.301 - 0.477 \approx -0.176$

(d) $\log_a 5$ Using Theorems 12-4, 12-5, and 12-6, there is no way to find $\log_a 5$: $\log_a 5 \neq \log_a 2 + \log_a 3$.

(e) $\frac{\log_a 2}{\log_a 3} \approx \frac{0.301}{0.477} \approx 0.63$ Note that we could not use Theorems 12-4, 12-5, and 12-6; we simply divided.

Try This

i. Given that $\log_a 2 \approx 0.301$ and $\log_a 3 \approx 0.477$, find the following.

(1) $\log_a 9$ (2) $\log_a \sqrt{2}$ (3) $\log_a \sqrt[3]{2}$ (4) $\log_a \frac{3}{2}$ (5) $\frac{\log_a 3}{\log_a 2}$

Extra Help On the Web

Look for worked-out examples at the Prentice Hall Web site.
www.phschool.com

12-4 Exercises

A

Express as a sum of logarithms. Simplify, if possible.

1. $\log_2 (32 \cdot 8)$ **2.** $\log_3 (27 \cdot 81)$ **3.** $\log_4 (64 \cdot 16)$

4. $\log_5 (25 \cdot 125)$ **5.** $\log_c Bx$ **6.** $\log_t 5Y$

Express as a single logarithm.

7. $\log_a 6 + \log_a 70$ **8.** $\log_b 65 + \log_b 2$ **9.** $\log_c K + \log_c y$

Express as a product.

10. $\log_a x^3$ **11.** $\log_b t^5$ **12.** $\log_c y^6$

Express as a difference of logarithms.

13. $\log_a \frac{67}{5}$ **14.** $\log_t \frac{T}{7}$ **15.** $\log_b \frac{3}{4}$

Express in terms of logarithms of x, y, and z.

16. $\log_a x^2y^3z$ **17.** $\log_a 5xy^4z^3$ **18.** $\log_b \frac{xy^2}{z^3}$

Express as a single logarithm. Simplify, if possible.

19. $\frac{2}{3}\log_a x - \frac{1}{2}\log_a y$

20. $\frac{1}{2}\log_a x + 3\log_a y - 2\log_a x$

21. $\log_a 2x + 3(\log_a x - \log_a y)$

22. $\log_a x^2 - 2\log_a \sqrt{x}$

23. $\log_a \frac{a}{\sqrt{x}} - \log_a \sqrt{ax}$

24. $\log_a (x^2 - 4) - \log_a (x - 2)$

Given $\log_{10} 2 \approx 0.301$, $\log_{10} 3 \approx 0.477$, and $\log_{10} 10 = 1$, find the following.

25. $\log_{10} 5$

26. $\log_{10} 50$

27. $\log_{10} 12$

28. $\log_{10} \frac{1}{3}$

29. $\log_{10} \sqrt{\frac{2}{3}}$

30. $\log_{10} \sqrt[5]{12}$

31. $\log_{10} \frac{9}{8}$

32. $\log_{10} \frac{9}{10}$

B

Error Analysis Identify the following as true or false. If false, rewrite the left-hand side to make the statement an identity.

33. $\frac{\log_a M}{\log_a N} = \log_a M - \log_a N$

34. $\frac{\log_a M}{\log_a N} = \log_a \frac{M}{N}$

35. $\log_a 2x = 2\log_a x$

36. $\log_a 2x = \log_a 2 + \log_a x$

37. $\log_a (M + N) = \log_a M + \log_a N$

38. $\log_a x^3 = 3\log_a x$

Solve.

39. $\log_\pi \pi^{2x+3} = 4$

40. $\log_a 5x = \log_a 5 + \log_a x$

41. $4^{2\log_4 x} = 7$

42. $8^{2\log_8 x + \log_8 x} = 27$

43. $(x + 3) \cdot \log_a a^x = x$

44. $3^{\log_3 (8x-4)} = 5$

45. *Critical Thinking* If $\log x^2y^3 = a$ and $\log\left(\frac{x}{y}\right) = b$, what are the values of $\log x$ and $\log y$?

46. *Mathematical Reasoning* Use the properties of logarithms to evaluate:

$$\log_{10}\left(\frac{1}{2}\right) + \log_{10}\left(\frac{2}{3}\right) + \log_{10}\left(\frac{3}{4}\right) + \log_{10}\left(\frac{4}{5}\right) + \ldots + \log_{10}\left(\frac{9}{10}\right).$$

Challenge

47. If $\log_a x = 2$, what is $\log_a \left(\frac{1}{x}\right)$?

48. If $\log_a x = 2$, what is $\log_{\frac{1}{a}} x$?

Prove the following for any base a and any positive number x.

49. $\log_a \left(\frac{1}{x}\right) = -\log_a x$

50. $\log_a \left(\frac{1}{x}\right) = \log_{\frac{1}{a}} x$

51. Show that $\log_a \left(\frac{x + \sqrt{x^2 - 5}}{5}\right) = -\log_a \left(x - \sqrt{x^2 - 5}\right)$.

Check your progress. Look for a self-test at the Prentice Hall Web site. www.phschool.com

Mixed Review

Given that the polynomial has the given root, find all the roots of the polynomial.

52. $x^3 - 2x^2 + x - 2;\ i$

53. $x^4 - 3x^2 - 28;\ -2i$ *11-4*

Find the rational roots, if they exist, of each polynomial. Then find the other roots.

54. $x^4 - 6x^3 + 30x - 25$

55. $x^3 - 6x^2 + 3x + 10$ *11-4*

12-5 Logarithmic Function Values

What You'll Learn

1. To find common logarithms using a calculator
2. To find common logarithms using a table
3. To find antilogarithms using a calculator or a table

. . . And Why

To solve real-world problems involving exponential and logarithmic equations

Base 10 logarithms are called **common logarithms.** They are useful because they are of the same base as the decimal numeration system. Before calculators became so widely available, common logarithms were used extensively for calculations.

The abbreviation **log** is used for the logarithmic function base 10. Thus a symbol log 23 means $\log_{10} 23$.

PART 1 Finding Common Logarithms: Calculators

Objective: Find common logarithms using a calculator.

On scientific calculators the key for the common logarithm is marked LOG. To find the common logarithm of a number, we enter that number and then press the LOG key.

EXAMPLE 1 Find log 475,000.

We enter 475,000 and press LOG. We find that $\log 475{,}000 \approx 5.67669361$.

EXAMPLE 2 Find log 0.00372.

We enter 0.00372 and press LOG. We find that $\log 0.00372 \approx -2.42945706$.

Try This Use a calculator to find these logarithms.

a. log 210.78 **b.** log 658,629 **c.** log 2.90043 **d.** log 0.000043

PART 2 Finding Common Logarithms: Tables

Objective: Find common logarithms using a table.

If a scientific calculator is not available, logarithms can be found using the table in the appendix, part of which is shown below.

x	0	1	2	3	4	5	6	7	8	9
5.0	0.6990	0.6998	0.7007	0.7016	0.7024	0.7033	0.7042	0.7050	0.7059	0.7067
5.1	0.7076	0.7084	0.7093	0.7101	0.7110	0.7118	0.7126	0.7135	0.7143	0.7152
5.2	0.7160	0.7168	0.7177	0.7185	0.7193	0.7202	0.7210	0.7218	0.7226	0.7235
5.3	0.7243	0.7251	0.7259	0.7267	0.7275	0.7284	0.7292	0.7300	0.7308	0.7316

EXAMPLE 3 Find log 5.24.

At the left of the table we find the row headed 5.2. Then we move across the table to the column headed 4. At the intersection of this row and column we find log 5.24.

$$\log 5.24 \approx 0.7193$$

Try This Use Table 2 to find these logarithms.

e. log 7.09 **f.** log 4.00 **g.** log 9.99

Using Table 2 and scientific notation we can approximate logarithms of numbers that are not between 1 and 10. First recall the following.

$$\log_a a^k = k \text{ for any number } k. \qquad \text{Theorem 12-3}$$

Thus $\log_{10} 10^k = k$ for any number k.

EXAMPLES Use scientific notation and Table 2 to find each logarithm.

4
$$\begin{aligned} \log 52.4 &= \log(5.24 \times 10^1) && \text{Converting to scientific notation} \\ &= \log 5.24 + \log 10^1 && \text{Using Theorem 12-4} \\ &\approx 0.7193 + 1 \end{aligned}$$

5
$$\begin{aligned} \log 0.524 &= \log(5.24 \times 10^{-1}) \\ &= \log 5.24 + \log 10^{-1} \\ &\approx 0.7193 + (-1) \end{aligned}$$

6
$$\begin{aligned} \log 52{,}400 &= \log(5.24 \times 10^4) \\ &= \log 5.24 + \log 10^4 \\ &\approx 0.7193 + 4 \end{aligned}$$

7
$$\begin{aligned} \log 0.00524 &= \log(5.24 \times 10^{-3}) \\ &= \log 5.24 + \log 10^{-3} \\ &\approx 0.7193 + (-3) \end{aligned}$$

Try This Use scientific notation and Table 2 to find each logarithm.

h. log 289 **i.** log 0.000289

In Examples 4–7, the integer part of the logarithm is the exponent in the scientific notation. This integer is called the **characteristic** of the logarithm. The other part of the logarithm, a number between 0 and 1, is called the **mantissa** of the logarithm. Table 2 contains only mantissas.

EXAMPLE 8 Find log 0.0538, indicating the characteristic and mantissa.

We first write scientific notation for the number.

$$5.38 \times 10^{-2}$$

Then we find log 5.38. This is the mantissa.

$$\log 5.38 \approx 0.7308$$

The characteristic of the logarithm is the exponent -2. Now $\log 0.0538 \approx 0.7308 + (-2)$, or -1.2692. When negative characteristics occur, it is often best to name the logarithm so that the characteristic and mantissa are preserved.

$$\log 0.0538 \approx 0.7308 + (-2) = -1.2692$$

The latter notation displays neither the characteristic nor the mantissa. We can rename the characteristic, -2, as $8 - 10$, and then add the mantissa to preserve both the mantissa and characteristic.

$$8.7308 - 10$$

The characteristic and mantissa are useful when working with logarithm tables, but are not needed on a calculator. For example, on a calculator with a ten-digit readout, we find the following.

$$\log 0.0538 = -1.269217724$$

This shows neither the characteristic nor the mantissa. Check this on your calculator. How can you find the characteristic and mantissa?

EXAMPLE 9 Find log 0.00687.

We write scientific notation.

$$0.00687 = 6.87 \times 10^{-3}$$

The characteristic is

$$-3, \text{ or } 7 - 10.$$

The mantissa, from the table, is

$$0.8370.$$

Thus $\log 0.00687 = 7.8370 - 10$.

Try This Use Table 2 to find these logarithms.

j. log 0.0462 **k.** log 0.607 **l.** log 0.000639

PART 3 Finding Antilogarithms

Objective: Find antilogarithms using a calculator or a table.

When we find the common logarithm of a number M, we find an exponent x such that $10^x = M$. When we find the **antilogarithm,** we reverse this process. We start with the exponent x (logarithm) and find the number M such that $M = 10^x$.

On a calculator, there is generally no key marked "antilog." Instead, calculators have an "inverse" key INV, and pressing INV followed by LOG will give the antilog. Or, a key marked 10^x will find the antilog. If these keys are not on your calculator, use the y^x key to raise 10 to a power.

EXAMPLES Use a calculator to find these antilogarithms.

10 Find antilog 3.2546.

We enter 3.2546, then press INV and LOG, or we enter 10, press y^x, and enter 3.2546. We find antilog 3.2546 $\approx$ 1797.2149.

11 Find antilog -2.36589.

We enter -2.36589, then press INV and LOG, or we enter 10, press y^x, and enter -2.36589. We find antilog $-2.36589 \approx 0.0043064$.

Try This Use a calculator to find these antilogarithms.

m. antilog 4.3425
n. antilog 3.0098
o. antilog -3.0067
p. antilog -6.7628

To find antilogs using Table 2, we reverse the process for finding logarithms.

EXAMPLE 12 Find antilog 2.7251.

$$\text{antilog } 2.7251 = 10^{2.7251} = 10^{2+0.7251} = 10^2 \cdot 10^{0.7251}$$

From the table we find $10^{0.7251}$. We find 0.7251 inside the table and see that the antilog is approximately 5.31. Thus, antilog 2.7251 $\approx 10^2 \times 5.31$ or 531.

Note that in this example, we separated 2.7251 into an integer (2) and a number between 0 and 1.0 (0.7251). We use the latter number with Table 2, after which we have scientific notation for our answer.

EXAMPLE 13 Find antilog (7.7143 − 10).

The characteristic is -3 and the mantissa is 0.7143.

From the table we find that antilog 0.7143 $\approx$ 5.18.

$$\begin{aligned} \text{antilog } (7.7143 - 10) &\approx 5.18 \times 10^{-3} \\ &\approx 0.00518 \end{aligned}$$

EXAMPLE 14 Find antilog -2.2857.

We are to find the antilog of a number, but the number is given so that the mantissa is not apparent. To find the mantissa we add 10 − 10.

$$\begin{aligned} -2.2857 &= -2.2857 + (10 - 10) \\ &= (-2.2857 + 10) - 10 = 7.7143 - 10 \end{aligned}$$

Then we proceed as in Example 13. The answer is approximately 0.00518.

Try This Use Table 2 to find these antilogs.

q. antilog 4.8069
r. antilog (6.6284 − 10)
s. antilog -1.9788

Extra Help On the Web

Look for worked-out examples at the Prentice Hall Web site.
www.phschool.com

12-5 Exercises

A

Use a calculator or Table 2 to find these logarithms.

1. log 2.46 **2.** log 7.65 **3.** log 3.72 **4.** log 9.04
5. log 1.07 **6.** log 347 **7.** log 8720 **8.** log 52.5
9. log 20.6 **10.** log 834 **11.** log 3870 **12.** log 0.0702
13. log 0.64 **14.** log 0.173 **15.** log 0.00347 **16.** log 0.0000404

Use a calculator or Table 2 to find these antilogarithms.

17. antilog 0.8657 **18.** antilog 0.1399 **19.** antilog 0.9191
20. antilog 3.3674 **21.** antilog 4.9222 **22.** antilog 1.2553
23. antilog (9.7875 − 10) **24.** antilog (8.9881 − 10)
25. antilog (7.9881 − 10) **26.** antilog (8.5391 − 10)
27. antilog (6.7875 − 10) **28.** antilog (4.6294 − 10)

B

Find x.

29. $\log x = 0.8021$ **30.** $\log x = 4.1903$ **31.** $\log x = 9.7875 - 10$
32. $\log x = -1.0218$ **33.** $10^x = 345$ **34.** $10^x = 5670$

35. ***Critical Thinking***

a. How many digits are there in 8^{1000}?
b. What power of 8 has 1000 digits?
c. What number to the 1000th power has 500 digits?

Challenge

Use the properties of logarithms to do these calculations.

Example: Find $\sqrt[4]{16}$ using common logarithms.

$$\log_{10} \sqrt[4]{16} = \log_{10} 16^{\frac{1}{4}} = \frac{1}{4} \cdot \log_{10} 16 \approx \frac{1}{4} \cdot 1.2041 \approx 0.3010$$

$$\sqrt[4]{16} \approx \text{antilog}_{10}\, 0.3010 \approx 2$$

36. $\sqrt[3]{8}$ **37.** 2^3 **38.** $\frac{14}{2}$ **39.** 4×2

Mixed Review

Tell which conic is defined by the equation. **40.** $y^2 + 3x - 5y + 8 = 0$ *10-6*

Divide $P(x)$ by $D(x)$. Then express the dividend as $P(x) = D(x) \cdot Q(x) + R(x)$.

41. $P(x) = x^3 + 4x^2 + x - 6;\ D(x) = (x^2 + 5x + 6)$ *11-1*

Interpolation

12-6

Tables are often prepared giving function values for a continuous function. Suppose the table gives four-digit precision. By using a procedure called **interpolation,** we can estimate values between those listed in the table.

Interpolation can be done in various ways, the simplest and most common being **linear interpolation.** We describe it now in relation to Table 2 for common logarithms. Remember that this method applies to a table for *any* continuous function.

What You'll Learn

1. To use a table and linear interpolation to find logarithms
2. To find antilogarithms using a table and linear interpolation

. . . And Why

To solve real-world problems involving quadratic variation

Linear Interpolation

Objective: Use a table and linear interpolation to find logarithms.

Consider how a table of values for any function is made. We select members of the domain x_1, x_2, x_3, and so on. Then we compute the corresponding function values $f(x_1)$, $f(x_2)$, $f(x_3)$, and so on. Then we tabulate and graph the results.

x	x_1	x_2	x_3	x_4	...
$f(x)$	$f(x_1)$	$f(x_2)$	$f(x_3)$	$f(x_4)$	...

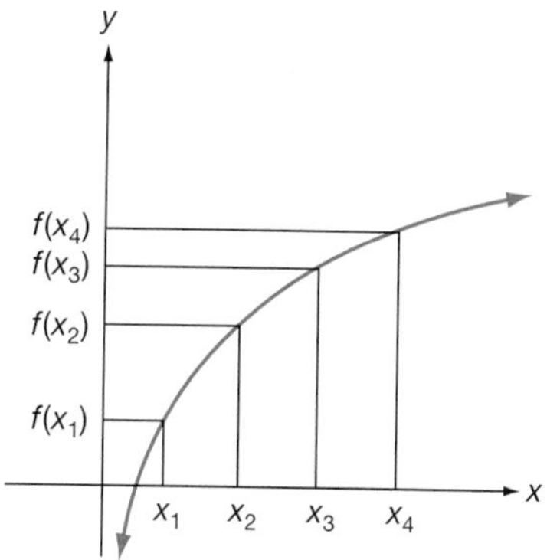

Suppose we want to find the function value $f(x)$ for an x not in the table. If x is halfway between x_1 and x_2, then we can take the number halfway between $f(x_1)$ and $f(x_2)$ as an approximation to $f(x)$. If x is one fifth of the way between x_1 and x_2, we take the number that is one fifth of the way between $f(x_1)$ and $f(x_2)$ as an approximation to $f(x)$. We divide the length from x_1 to x_2 in a certain ratio, and then divide the length from $f(x_1)$ to $f(x_2)$ in the same ratio. This is linear interpolation.

To interpolate, we fit a linear function to the two closest known data points. In the figure at the right, the approximation for $f(x)$ is obtained from the linear function, and not from the function itself. Let us apply linear interpolation to the logarithms in Table 2.

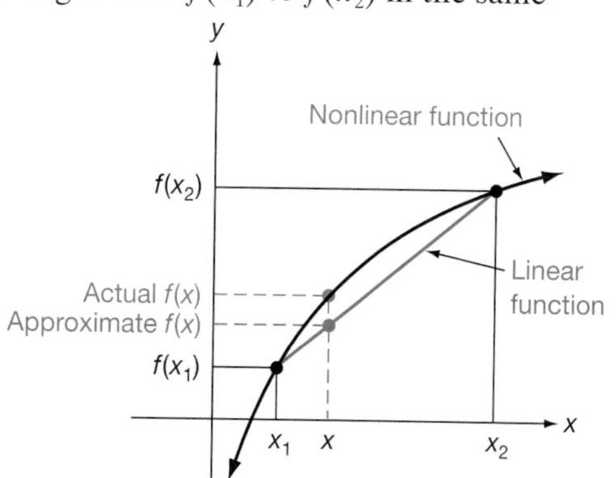

EXAMPLE 1 Find log 34,870.

(a) Since $34{,}870 = 3.487 \times 10^4$, the characteristic is 4.

(b) Find the mantissa. From Table 2 we have $\log 3.48 = 0.5416$ and $\log 3.49 = 0.5428$. We know that 3.487 is $\frac{7}{10}$ of the distance between 3.48 and 3.49. Thus to estimate log 3.487, we find the number $\frac{7}{10}$ of the way from 0.5416 to 0.5428.

0.5416	?	0.5428
(log 3.48)	(log 3.487)	(log 3.49)

The difference between log 3.48 and log 3.49 is 0.0012. Thus we take $\frac{7}{10}$ of 0.0012 and add it to 0.5416.

$$\begin{aligned} &0.5416 + 0.7(0.0012) \\ &= 0.5416 + 0.00084 \\ &= 0.54244 \end{aligned}$$

We round the result to 0.5424.

(c) Add the characteristic and mantissa.

$$\log 34{,}870 \approx 4.5424$$

EXAMPLE 2 Find log 0.01413.

(a) Since $0.01413 = 1.413 \times 10^{-2}$, the characteristic is -2, or $8 - 10$.

(b) Find the mantissa. From Table 2, we have

0.1492	?	0.1523
(log 1.41)	(log 1.413)	(log 1.42)

The difference between log 1.41 and log 1.42 is 0.0031. We know 1.413 is $\frac{3}{10}$ of the distance between 1.41 and 1.42, so we take $\frac{3}{10}$ of 0.0031 and add it to 0.1492.

$$\begin{aligned} &0.1492 + 0.3(0.0031) \\ &= 0.1492 + 0.00093 \\ &= 0.15013 \end{aligned}$$

We round the result to 0.1501.

(c) Add the characteristic and mantissa.

$$\log 0.01413 \approx 8.1501 - 10, \text{ or } -1.8499$$

Try This

a. Find log 4562.

b. Find log 0.02387.

PART 2 Finding Antilogarithms

Objective: Find antilogarithms using a table and linear interpolation.

EXAMPLE 3 Find antilog $(7.4122 - 10)$.

The characteristic is -3. The mantissa is 0.4122. From Table 2 we have

0.4116	0.4122	0.4133
(log 2.58)	(log ?)	(log 2.59)

The difference between 0.4116 and 0.4133 is 0.0017. We know that 0.4122 is $\frac{6}{17}$ of the distance between 0.4116 and 0.4133. So the antilog of 0.4122 is $\frac{6}{17}$ of the way from 2.58 to 2.59. We take $\frac{6}{17}$ of 0.01 and add it to 2.58.

$$2.58 + \frac{6}{17}(0.01)$$
$$\approx 2.58 + 0.0035$$
$$\approx 2.5835$$

We round the result to 2.584. Thus antilog $(7.4122 - 10) \approx 2.584 \times 10^{-3}$, or 0.002584.

Try This

c. Find antilog 3.4557.

d. Find antilog $(6.7749 - 10)$.

12-6 Exercises

Extra Help On the Web

Look for worked-out examples at the Prentice Hall Web site.
www.phschool.com

A

Find the following logarithms using interpolation and Table 2.

1. log 41.63
2. log 472.1
3. log 2.944
4. log 21.76
5. log 650.2
6. log 37.37
7. log 0.1425
8. log 0.09045
9. log 0.004257
10. log 4518
11. log 0.1776
12. log 0.08356
13. log 600.6
14. log 500.2
15. log 800.1

Find the following antilogarithms using interpolation and Table 2.

16. antilog 1.6350
17. antilog 2.3512
18. antilog 0.6478
19. antilog 1.1624
20. antilog 0.0342
21. antilog 4.8453
22. antilog $(9.8564 - 10)$
23. antilog $(8.9659 - 10)$
24. antilog $(7.4128 - 10)$
25. antilog $(9.7278 - 10)$
26. antilog $(8.2010 - 10)$
27. antilog $(7.8630 - 10)$

B

Find.

28. log (log 3) **29.** log (log 5) **30.** log (log 7)

31. *Critical Thinking* Compare estimates of logarithms as found by linear interpolation with those found using a table or calculator.

Challenge

Use logarithms and interpolation to do the following calculations. Use four-digit precision. Answers may be checked using a calculator.

32. $\dfrac{35.24 \times (16.77)^3}{12.93 \times \sqrt{276.2}}$ **33.** $\sqrt[5]{\dfrac{16.79 \times (4.234)^3}{18.81 \times 175.3}}$

Mixed Review

Use Descartes' rule of signs to determine the number of positive real roots.

34. $5x^4 + 2x^3 - 6x^2 + 11x + 6$ **35.** $-4x^3 + 5x^2 - 8x + 10$

Use Descartes' rule of signs to determine the number of negative real roots.

36. $5x^4 + 2x^3 - 6x^2 + 11x + 6$ **37.** $-4x^3 + 5x^2 - 8x + 10$ *11-5*

Test for symmetry with respect to the line $x = y$.

38. $2x + 3y = 5$ **39.** $xy = 2$ **40.** $7x - 7y = 1$ **41.** $3x^2 + 3y^2 = 7$

For each $f(x)$, find $f^{-1}(x)$. **42.** $f(x) = x + 2$ **43.** $f(x) = \sqrt{x + 3}$ *12-1*

44. A rectangular field is $53\frac{1}{3}$ yards wide and 100 yards long. How long is a diagonal of the rectangle? *8-2*

Log and Exponent Functions

1. Enter the largest number you can on a scientific calculator. Most calculators allow you to enter 9.9999×10^{99} (9.9999 EXP 99). Press LOG four times. What is the result?
   What happens if you press LOG again? Why?
2. Enter the smallest number you can on a scientific calculator. Most calculators allow you to enter 1×10^{-99} (1 EXP −99). Press 2nd LOG three times. What is the result?
   What happens if you press 2nd LOG again? Why?
3. Use function notation to explain these procedures.
4. Compare the results of taking successive logs of logs with taking successive powers of powers.

Exponential and Logarithmic Equations

12-7

Earthquake intensity, loudness of sound, and **compound interest** are all applications of exponential and logarithmic equations.

What You'll Learn

1. To solve exponential equations
2. To solve logarithmic equations
3. To solve problems involving exponential and logarithmic equations

. . . And Why

To solve real-world problems involving exponential and logarithmic relationships

PART 1 Exponential Equations

Objective: Solve exponential equations.

An equation with variables in exponents, such as $3^{2x-1} = 4$, is called an **exponential equation.** We can solve such equations by taking logarithms of both sides and then using Theorem 12-5.

EXAMPLE 1 Solve $3^x = 8$.

$\log 3^x = \log 8$ Taking the log of both sides (Remember $\log m = \log_{10} m$.)

$x \log 3 = \log 8$ Using Theorem 12-5

$x = \dfrac{\log 8}{\log 3}$ Solving for x

$x \approx \dfrac{0.9031}{0.4771} \approx 1.8929$ We look up the logs, or find them on a calculator, and divide.

EXAMPLE 2 Solve $2^{3x-5} = 16$.

$\log 2^{3x-5} = \log 16$ Taking the log of both sides

$(3x - 5) \log 2 = \log 16$ Using Theorem 12-5

$$3x - 5 = \frac{\log 16}{\log 2}$$

$$3x = \frac{\log 16}{\log 2} + 5$$

$$x = \frac{\frac{\log 16}{\log 2} + 5}{3}$$

$x \approx \dfrac{\frac{1.2041}{0.3010} + 5}{3}$ Solving for x and evaluating logarithms

$x \approx 3.0001$ Calculating

The answer is approximate because the logarithms are approximate. We can see that 3 is the solution since $2^{3(3)-5} = 2^4 = 16$.

The following is another method of solving exponential equations.

EXAMPLE 3 Solve $2^{3x-5} = 16$.

Note that $16 = 2^4$. Then we have $2^{3x-5} = 2^4$.

Since the base, 2, is the same on both sides, the exponents must be equal.

$$3x - 5 = 4, \text{ or } x = 3$$

Try This

a. Solve $2^x = 7$. **b.** Solve $4^x = 6$.
c. Solve $4^{2x-3} = 64$. Use the method in Example 3.

PART 2 Logarithmic Equations

Objective: Solve logarithmic equations.

Equations that contain logarithmic expressions are **logarithmic equations.** We solve them by converting to an equivalent exponential equation. For example, to solve $\log_2 x = -3$, we convert to $x = 2^{-3}$ and find that $x = \frac{1}{8}$.

To solve logarithmic equations we first try to obtain a single logarithmic expression on one side of the equation and then write an equivalent exponential equation.

EXAMPLE 4 Solve $\log_3 (5x + 7) = 2$.

We already have a single logarithmic expression, so we write an equivalent exponential equation.

$$5x + 7 = 3^2$$
$$5x + 7 = 9$$
$$x = \frac{2}{5}$$

Check:

$\log_3 (5x + 7)$	$= 2$
$\log_3 \left(5 \cdot \frac{2}{5} + 7\right)$	2
$\log_3 (2 + 7)$	2
$\log_3 9$	2
2	2 ✓

EXAMPLE 5 Solve $\log x + \log (x - 3) = 1$.

Here we must first obtain a single logarithmic equation.

$$\log x + \log (x - 3) = 1$$
$$\log x(x - 3) = 1$$ Using Theorem 12-4 to obtain a single logarithm
$$x(x - 3) = 10^1$$ Converting to an equivalent exponential equation
$$x^2 - 3x = 10$$
$$x^2 - 3x - 10 = 0$$
$$(x + 2)(x - 5) = 0$$ Factoring and using the principle of zero products
$$x = -2 \text{ or } x = 5$$

Possible solutions to logarithmic equations must be checked because domains of logarithmic functions consist only of positive numbers.

Check:

$\log x + \log (x - 3) = 1$	
$\log (-2) + \log (-2 - 3)$	1
$\log (-2) + \log (-5)$	1

$\log x + \log (x - 3) = 1$	
$\log 5 + \log (5 - 3)$	1
$\log 5 + \log 2$	1
$\log 10$	1
1	1 ✓

The number -2 is not a solution because negative numbers do not have logarithms. The solution is 5.

Try This Solve.

d. $\log_5 x = 3$ **e.** $\log_4 (8x - 6) = 3$ **f.** $\log x + \log (x + 3) = 1$

PART 3 Problem Solving: Logarithms

Objective: Solve problems involving exponential and logarithmic equations.

The amount A that principal P will be worth after t years at interest rate r, compounded annually, is given by the formula $A = P(1 + r)^t$.

EXAMPLE 6 Suppose \$4000 principal is invested at 6% interest and yields \$5353. For how many years was it invested?

We use the formula $A = P(1 + r)^t$.

$$5353 = 4000(1 + 0.06)^t, \text{ or } 5353 = 4000(1.06)^t$$

Then we solve for t.

$\log 5353 = \log (4000(1.06)^t)$ Taking the log of both sides

$\log 5353 = \log 4000 + t \log 1.06$ Using Theorems 12-4 and 12-5

$\dfrac{\log 5353 - \log 4000}{\log 1.06} = t$ Solving for t

$\dfrac{3.7286 - 3.6021}{0.0253} \approx t$ Evaluating logarithms

$5 \approx t$

The money was invested for approximately 5 years. We can use a calculator to check.

$4000(1.06)^5 \approx 5352.9023$ The solution checks.

Try This

g. Suppose \$5000 was invested at 14%, compounded annually, and it yielded \$18,540. For how long was it invested?

The sensation of loudness of sound is not proportional to the energy intensity, but rather is a logarithmic function.

Loudness is measured in bels (after Alexander Graham Bell) or in smaller units, *decibels*. Loudness in decibels of a sound of intensity (I) is defined to be

$$L = 10 \log \frac{I}{I_0}$$

where I_0 is the minimum intensity detectable by the human ear (such as the tick of a watch at 6 meters under quiet conditions). When a sound is 10 times as intense as another, its loudness is 10 decibels greater. If a sound is 100 times as intense as another, it is louder by 20 decibels, and so on.

EXAMPLE 7

(a) Find the loudness in decibels of the background noise in a radio studio, for which the intensity (I) is 199 times I_0.

We substitute into the formula and calculate, using a calculator.

$$\begin{aligned} L &= 10 \log \frac{199 \cdot I_0}{I_0} \\ &= 10 \log 199 \end{aligned}$$

10 [×] 199 [LOG] [=] 22.98853076

$$\approx 23 \text{ decibels}$$

Musicians can obtain special earplugs to avoid hearing loss when the loudness of a concert is in the range of 90–120 decibels. How many times more intense is the sound level at 120 decibels than it is at 80 decibels?

(b) Find the loudness of the sound of a rock concert, for which the intensity is 10^{11} times I_0.

$$\begin{aligned} L &= 10 \log \frac{10^{11} \cdot I_0}{I_0} \\ &= 10 \log 10^{11} \\ &= 10 \cdot 11 \\ &= 110 \text{ decibels} \end{aligned}$$

Try This

h. Find the loudness in decibels of the sound in a library, for which the intensity is 2510 times I_0.

i. Find the loudness in decibels of conversational speech, for which the intensity is 10^6 times I_0.

The magnitude R (on the Richter scale) of an earthquake of intensity I is defined as

$$R = \log \frac{I}{I_0}$$

where I_0 is a minimum intensity used for comparison.

EXAMPLE 8

An earthquake has an intensity 4×10^8 times I_0. What is its magnitude on the Richter scale?

We substitute into the formula.

$$R = \log \frac{4 \times 10^8 \cdot I_0}{I_0}$$
$$= \log \frac{4 \cdot I_0}{I_0} + \log \frac{10^8 I_0}{I_0}$$
$$= \log 4 + \log 10^8$$

4 LOG + 8 = 8.602059991 $\approx$ 8.6

The magnitude on the Richter scale is about 8.6.

Try This

j. The earthquake in Anchorage, Alaska, on March 27, 1964, had an intensity 2.5×10^8 times I_0. What was its magnitude on the Richter scale?

12-7 Exercises

Extra Help On the Web
Look for worked-out examples at the Prentice Hall Web site.
www.phschool.com

A

Solve.

1. $2^x = 8$ **2.** $2^x = 32$ **3.** $2^x = 10$

4. $2^x = 33$ **5.** $5^{4x-7} = 125$ **6.** $4^{3x+5} = 16$

7. $3^{x^2+4x} = \frac{1}{27}$ **8.** $3^{5x} \cdot 9^{x^2} = 27$ **9.** $4^x = 7$

10. $8^x = 10$ **11.** $2^x = 3^{x-1}$ **12.** $3^{x+2} = 5^{x-1}$

13. $(2.8)^x = 41$ **14.** $(3.4)^x = 80$ **15.** $(1.7)^x = 20$

Solve.

16. $\log x + \log (x - 9) = 1$ **17.** $\log x + \log (x + 9) = 1$

18. $\log x - \log (x + 3) = -1$ **19.** $\log (x + 9) - \log x = 1$

20. $\log_4 (x + 3) + \log_4 (x - 3) = 2$ **21.** $\log_5 (x + 4) + \log_5 (x - 4) = 2$

22. $\log \sqrt[3]{x} = \sqrt{\log x}$ **23.** $\log \sqrt[4]{x} = \sqrt{\log x}$

24. $\log_5 \sqrt{x^2 + 1} = 1$ **25.** $\log \sqrt[3]{x^2} + \log \sqrt[3]{x^4} = \log 2^{-3}$

Solve.

26. How many years will it take an investment of \$1000 to double itself when interest is compounded annually at 6%?

27. How many years will it take an investment of \$1000 to triple itself when interest is compounded annually at 5%?

28. Find the loudness in decibels of the sound of an automobile having an intensity 3,100,000 times I_0.

29. Find the loudness in decibels of the sound of a dishwasher having an intensity 2,500,000 times I_0.

30. Find the loudness in decibels of the threshold of sound pain, for which the intensity is 10^{14} times I_0.

31. Find the loudness in decibels of a jet aircraft having an intensity 10^{12} times I_0.

This parking garage was damaged by an earthquake with a magnitude of 6.6 on the Richter scale. What was its intensity? How many times as intense was the Los Angeles earthquake of 1971? (See Exercise 32.)

32. The Los Angeles earthquake of 1971 had an intensity 5×10^6 times I_0. What was its magnitude on the Richter scale?

33. The San Francisco earthquake of 1906 had an intensity 1.8×10^8 times I_0. What was its magnitude on the Richter scale?

34. An earthquake has a magnitude of 5 on the Richter scale. What is its intensity?

35. An earthquake has a magnitude of 7.8 on the Richter scale. What is its intensity?

In chemistry, pH is defined as

$$\text{pH} = -\log [\text{H}^+]$$

where $[\text{H}^+]$ is the hydrogen ion concentration in moles per liter. For example, the hydrogen ion concentration in milk is 4×10^{-7} moles per liter, so

$$\text{pH} = -\log (4 \times 10^{-7}) = -[\log 4 + (-7)] \approx 6.4$$

36. For tomatoes, $[\text{H}^+]$ is about 6.3×10^{-5}. Find the pH.

37. For eggs, $[\text{H}^+]$ is about 1.6×10^{-8}. Find the pH.

B

Solve.

38. $\log \sqrt{x} = \sqrt{\log x}$ 39. $\log_5 \sqrt{x^2 + 1} = 2$ 40. $|\log_5 x| = 2$

41. $(\log_a x)^{-1} = \log_a x^{-1}$ 42. $\log_3 |x| = 2$ 43. $\log x^{\log x} = 4$

44. $\dfrac{\sqrt{(a^{2x} \cdot a^{-5x})^{-4}}}{a^x \div a^{-x}} = a^7$ 45. $\dfrac{(a^{3x+1})^2}{a^4} = a^{10x}$

46. Solve $y = ax^n$, for n. Use $\log_x$. 47. Solve $y = kb^{at}$, for t. Use $\log_b$.

48. Solve $T = T_0 + (T_1 - T_0)\,10^{-kt}$, for t.

49. Solve $PV^n = c$, for n. Use $\log_V$.

50. Solve $\log_a Q = \frac{1}{3}\log_a y + b$, for Q.

51. Solve $\log_a y = 2x + \log_a x$, for y.

52. ***Critical Thinking*** Determine the relationship between (**a**), $\log_2 8$ and $\log_8 2$, (**b**) $\log_3 9$ and $\log_9 3$, and (**c**) $\log_4 16$ and $\log_{16} 4$. In general, how do $\log_a b$ and $\log_b a$ compare?

Challenge

Solve for x.

53. $x^{\log x} = \dfrac{x^3}{100}$ 54. $x^{\log x} = 100x$

55. $|\log_5 x| + 3\log_5 |x| = 4$ 56. $|\log_a x| = \log_a |x|$

57. $(0.5)^x < \frac{4}{5}$ **58.** $8x^{0.3} - 8x^{-0.3} = 63$

59. Find $x + y + z$, given that

$$\log_2 [\log_3 (\log_4 x)] = 0,$$
$$\log_3 [\log_2 (\log_4 y)] = 0,$$
$$\log_4 [\log_3 (\log_2 z)] = 0$$

60. Solve the system of equations.

$$5^{x+y} = 100$$
$$3^{2x-y} = 1000$$

61. If $2 \log_3 (x - 2y) = \log_3 x + \log_3 y$, find $\frac{x}{y}$.

62. Find the rational ordered pair (x, y) for which $4^{\log_{16} 27} = 2^x 3^y$.

Mixed Review

Given $f(x) = 2x + 5$, find the following. **63.** $f^{-1}(f(4))$ **64.** $f(f^{-1}(-7))$

Find an equation for $f^{-1}(x)$. **65.** $f(x) = 0.2x - 1$ **66.** $f(x) = \sqrt{x - 5}$ *12-1*

Convert to logarithmic equations.

67. $10^3 = 1000$ **68.** $2^{-4} = \frac{1}{16}$ **69.** $81^{\frac{1}{2}} = 9$ **70.** $r^s = t$

Convert to exponential equations.

71. $\log_8 8 = 1$ **72.** $\log_3 9 = 2$ **73.** $\log_2 64 = 6$ **74.** $\log_5 625 = 4$ *12-3*

Find only the rational roots.

75. $x^4 - 12x^2 + 35$ **76.** $x^4 - 28x^2 + 75$ **77.** $x^3 - x^2 - 4x + 4$ *11-3*

Historical Note: Logarithms

John Napier was responsible for the development of logarithms. In the late 1500s, he developed a method of making powers of numbers nearly continuous—that is, finding powers over small increments. By finding successive powers of numbers very close to 1, he was able to create tables of exponents using repeated multiplications. It was a tedious process, but with it he created a system that was, although inaccurate, the basis for logarithms as we know them today.

A geometry professor, Henry Briggs, was fascinated by Napier's work. Briggs and Napier began working together and decided to extend logarithms to base 10, beginning with $\log 1 = 0$ and $\log 10 = 1$. Napier, however, died within 3 years, and Briggs was left to develop a table of common logarithms on his own.

Briggs used successive roots to find accurate common logarithms of numbers from 1 to 20,000 and from 90,000 to 100,000. Many mathematicians of the time immediately began extending the use of logarithms to such topics as trigonometry and astronomy.

12-8 Natural Logarithms and the Number *e*

What You'll Learn

1. To graph functions related to the function $y = e^x$
2. To use a calculator or table to find natural logarithms
3. To solve problems involving natural logarithms
4. To change bases to find logarithms of any base in terms of common or natural logarithms

. . . And Why

To solve real-world problems that can be modeled by the function $y = ae^{kx}$, where $a, k \neq 0$

PART 1 Exponential Functions, Base *e*

Objective: Graph functions related to the function $y = e^x$.

One of the most important numbers, an irrational number called **e,** occurs in advanced mathematics, economics, statistics, probability, and in many situations involving growth.

$$e \approx 2.718281828459\ldots$$

The **exponential function, base e,** and its inverse, the logarithm function base e, are important in mathematical theory and in applications as well. Logarithms to the base e are called **natural logarithms.** Table 4 on page 876 gives function values for e^x and e^{-x}. Using a calculator or these tables we can construct graphs of $y = e^x$ and $y = \log_e x$.

EXAMPLE 1 Use Table 4 or a calculator to graph $y = e^x$.

x	y
0	1
1	2.7
1.5	4.5
2	7.4
−1	0.37
−2	0.13

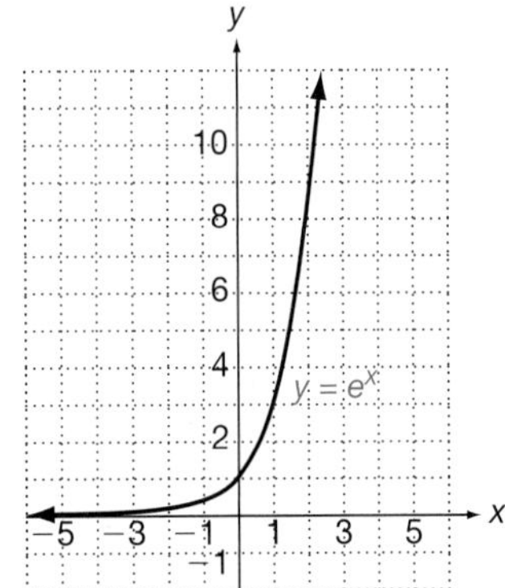

Finding e^x

You can use a scientific calculator to find base e exponential functions using the e^x key or the keys 2nd LN .

Find e^2.

2 e^x → 7.389056099

Try This Use Table 4 or a calculator to graph.

a. $y = e^{-x}$ **b.** $y = e^{\frac{1}{2}x}$

PART 2 Natural Logarithms

Objective: Use a calculator or table to find natural logarithms.

The number $\log_e x$ is abbreviated **ln x;** that is, $\ln x = \log_e x$. If you have an LN key on your calculator, you can find such logarithms directly. You can also use Table 3 on page 858.

EXAMPLES Use a calculator or Table 3 to find each logarithm.

2 $\ln 5.24 \approx 1.6563$ Using Table 3

3 $\ln 52.4 = \ln (5.24 \times 5 \times 2)$
$= \ln 5.24 + \ln 5 + \ln 2$
$\approx 1.6563 + 1.6094 + 0.6931 = 3.9588$ Using Table 3

4 $\ln 0.001277 \approx -6.663242$ Using a calculator

From ln 5.24 and ln 52.4 we note that natural logarithms do not have characteristics and mantissas. Common logarithms have characteristics and mantissas because our numeration system is based on 10. For any base other than 10, logarithms have neither characteristics nor mantissas.

Journal

Make a list of the new kinds of mathematical notation introduced in this chapter. For each entry in your list, give an example of how it may be used, and next to your example, write out how to read the notation.

Try This Use a calculator or Table 3 to find each logarithm.

c. ln 2 **d.** ln 100 **e.** ln 0.07432 **f.** ln 0.9999

PART 3 Solving Problems

Objective: Solve problems involving natural logarithms.

There are many applications of exponential functions, base e. We consider a few.

EXAMPLE 5 One example of **exponential growth** is a mathematical model for describing population growth. It has the formula

$$P = P_0 e^{kt}$$

where P_0 is the number of people at time 0, P is the number of people at time t, and k is a positive constant depending on the situation. The population of the United States in 1970 was about 203 million. In 1989 it was about 247 million. Use these data to find the value of k and then use the model to predict the population in 2020.

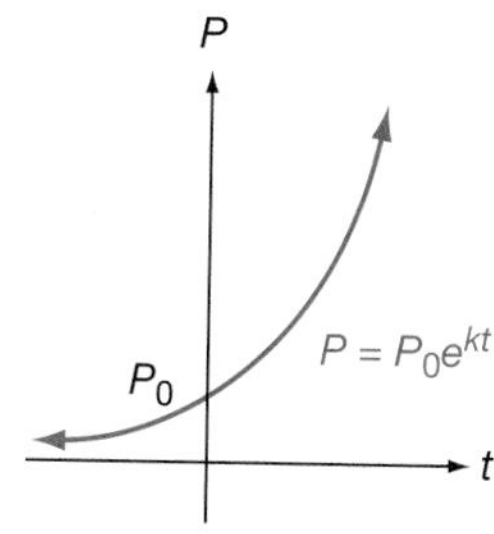

Time t begins with 1970. That is, $t = 0$ in 1970, $t = 19$ in 1989, and so on. Substituting the data into the formula, we get the equation $247 = 203e^{k \cdot 19}$.

We solve for k.

$$
\begin{aligned}
\ln 247 &= \ln 203e^{19k} && \text{Taking the natural logarithm on both sides} \\
\ln 247 &= \ln 203 + \ln e^{19k} && \text{Theorem 12-4} \\
\ln 247 &= \ln 203 + 19k && \text{Theorem 12-3} \\
k &= \frac{\ln 247 - \ln 203}{19} && \text{Solving for } k \\
k &\approx \frac{5.5094 - 5.3132}{19} && \text{Using a calculator} \\
k &\approx 0.0103 && \text{Calculating}
\end{aligned}
$$

To find the population in 2020, we will use $P_0 = 203$ (population in millions in 1970).

$$P \approx 203e^{0.0103t}$$

In 2020, t will be 50.

$$P \approx 203e^{(0.0103)(50)} \approx 203e^{0.515}$$

Using a calculator or Table 4, we find that $e^{0.515} \approx 1.6736$. Multiplying by 203 gives us about 340 million. This is our prediction for the population of the United States in the year 2020.

Try This

g. The population of Tempe, Arizona, was 64,000 in 1970. In 1980 it was 107,000.
(1) Use these data to determine k in the growth model.
(2) Use these data to predict the population of Tempe in 2010.

EXAMPLE 6

In a radioactive element some of the atoms are always transforming themselves into other elements. Thus the amount of a radioactive substance decreases. This is an example of **exponential decay** called *radioactive decay.* A model for radioactive decay is

$$N = N_0e^{-kt}$$

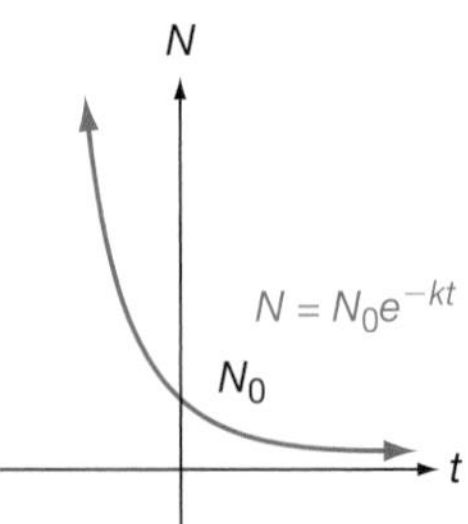

where N_0 is the amount of a radioactive substance at time 0, N is the amount at time t, and k is a positive constant depending on the rate at which a particular element decays. Strontium-90, a radioactive substance, has a **half-life** of 25 years. This means that half of a sample of the substance will remain as the original element in 25 years. Find k in the formula and then use the formula to find how much of a 36-gram sample will remain after 100 years.

When $t = 25$ (half-life), N will be half of N_0.

$$\tfrac{1}{2}N_0 = N_0e^{-25k} \text{ or } \tfrac{1}{2} = e^{-25k}$$

We take the natural log on both sides.

$$\ln \tfrac{1}{2} = \ln e^{-25k}$$

$$\ln \tfrac{1}{2} = -25k$$

Thus $k = -\frac{\ln 0.5}{25} \approx 0.0277$ 0.5 LN ÷ 25 = +/– → 0.027725887

Now to find the amount remaining after 100 years, we use the following formula.

$$N \approx 36e^{-0.0277 \cdot 100}$$

$$\approx 36e^{-2.77}$$ 2.77 +/– 2nd LN × 36 = 2.255832171

Using a calculator, we find that $N \approx 2.26$ grams.

Try This

h. Radioactive bismuth has a half-life of 5 days. A scientist buys 224 grams of it. How much of it will remain as the original bismuth in 30 days?

Logarithm Tables and Change of Base

Objective: Change bases to find logarithms of any base in terms of common or natural logarithms.

The following theorem shows how we can change logarithm bases. The theorem can be applied to find the logarithm of a number to any base, using a table of common or natural logarithms.

Theorem 12-7

For any bases a and b, and any positive number M,

$$\log_b M = \frac{\log_a M}{\log_a b}$$

Proof of Theorem 12-7

Let $x = \log_b M$.

$b^x = M$	Converting to exponential form
$\log_a b^x = \log_a M$	Taking the log of both sides
$x \log_a b = \log_a M$	Using Theorem 12-5
$x = \frac{\log_a M}{\log_a b}$	Solving for x
$\log_b M = \frac{\log_a M}{\log_a b}$	Substituting $\log_b M$ for x

EXAMPLE 7 Find $\log_5 346$.

$$\log_5 346 = \frac{\log_{10} 346}{\log_{10} 5}$$
$$\approx \frac{2.5391}{0.6990} \approx 3.6325$$

Try This

i. Find $\log_5 125$. **j.** Find $\log_6 4870$. **k.** Find $\log_{10} e$. Use 2.718 for e.

We can use Theorem 12-7 to convert between common logarithms and natural logarithms.

$$\log_e M = \frac{\log_{10} M}{\log_{10} e} \text{ and } \log_{10} M = \frac{\log_e M}{\log_e 10}$$

Abbreviating the notation, we can state these in a theorem.

Theorem 12-8

$$\ln M = \frac{\log M}{\log e} \text{ and } \log M = \frac{\ln M}{\ln 10}$$

Using approximations, $\log e \approx 0.4343$ and $\ln 10 \approx 2.3026$, so we have

$$\ln M \approx \frac{\log M}{0.4343} \text{ and } \log M \approx \frac{\ln M}{2.3026}$$

EXAMPLE 8 Use common (base 10) logarithms to find ln 257.

$$\ln 257 \approx \frac{\log 257}{\log e} \approx \frac{2.4099}{0.4343} \approx 5.5489$$

We can make use of this change-of-base procedure to solve certain exponential equations.

EXAMPLE 9 Solve $3^x = 8$.

$$\log_3 3^x = \log_3 8 \qquad \text{Taking logarithms, base 3, on both sides}$$
$$x = \log_3 8 \qquad \text{Theorem 12-3}$$
$$= \frac{\log 8}{\log 3} \approx \frac{0.9031}{0.4771} \approx 1.8929$$

Compare this with Example 1 in Section 12-7.

Try This Use common (base 10) logarithms.

l. Find ln 1030. **m.** Find ln 0.457. **n.** Solve $2^x = 7$.

12-8 Exercises

Extra Help On the Web

Look for worked-out examples at the Prentice Hall Web site.
www.phschool.com

A

Graph. A graphing calculator or software may be used.

1. $y = e^{2x}$ **2.** $y = e^{0.5x}$ **3.** $y = e^{-2x}$ **4.** $y = e^{-0.5x}$

5. $y = 1 - e^{-x}$, for $x \geq 0$ **6.** $y = 2\left(1 - e^{-x}\right)$, for $x \geq 0$

Find each natural logarithm. Use a calculator or Table 3.

7. ln 1.88 **8.** ln 18.8 **9.** ln 0.0188 **10.** ln 0.188

11. ln 2.13 **12.** ln 213 **13.** ln 0.213 **14.** ln 0.00213

15. ln 4500 **16.** ln 81,000 **17.** ln 0.00056 **18.** ln 0.999

19. ln 0.08 **20.** ln 0.0471 **21.** ln 980,000

22. The approximate population of Dallas was 680,000 in 1960. In 1980 it was 905,000. Find k in the growth formula and estimate the population in 2015.

23. The approximate population of San Jose was 460,000 in 1970. In 1980 it was 630,000. Find k in the growth formula and estimate the population in 2020.

24. The half-life of polonium-218 is 3 minutes. After 30 minutes, how much of a 410-gram sample will remain as the original polonium?

25. The half-life of a lead isotope is 22 years. After 66 years, how much of a 1000-gram sample will remain as the original isotope?

26. A certain radioactive substance decays from 66,560 grams to 6.5 grams in 16 days. What is its half-life?

27. Ten grams of uranium will decay to 2.5 grams in 496,000 years. What is its half-life?

28. When an organism dies, it takes in no more carbon. By determining the amount of carbon-14, it is possible to determine how long an organism has been dead, hence its age. Carbon-14 has a half-life of 5730 years.

a. How old is an animal bone that has lost 30% of its carbon-14?

b. A mummy discovered in a pyramid in the Valley of the Tombs of the Kings had lost 46% of its carbon-14. What is its age?

29. The Mesopotamian civilization was dated by using carbon-14 dating. A piece of wood discovered in an archaeological dig was found to have lost 62% of its carbon-14. Determine its age. (See Exercise 28.)

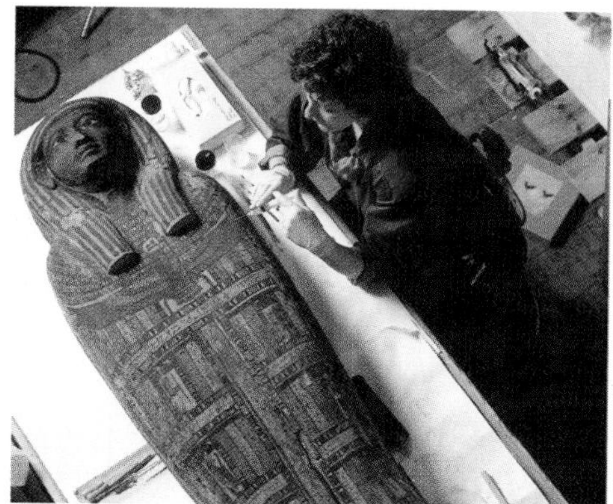

Archaeologists have recovered few mummies. Great care must be taken to preserve mummies that have been exposed to air and humidity after thousands of years. Carbon-14 dating can be used to determine the age of a mummy. (See Exercise 28.)

Use common (base 10) logarithms to find the following.

30. $\log_4 20$ **31.** $\log_8 0.99$ **32.** $\log_5 0.78$

33. $\log_{12} 15{,}000$ **34.** ln 12 **35.** ln 0.77

36. The *consumer price index* compares the costs of goods and services over various years. The base year is 1967. The same goods and services that cost \$100 in 1967 cost \$325 in 1986. Assuming the exponential model,

   a. find the value k and write the equation.

   b. estimate what the same goods and services would cost in 2020.

   c. find when the same goods and services cost five times that of 1967.

B

Solve for t.

37. $P = P_0e^{kt}$ **38.** $P = P_0e^{-kt}$

39. Banks use compound interest. The amount received after one year at an interest rate of 12% for each dollar deposited is given by $\left(1 + \frac{0.12}{n}\right)^n$, where n is the number of times interest is compounded. How much is received per dollar deposited for each?

   a. $n = 4$ (quarterly compounding) **b.** $n = 12$ (monthly compounding)

   c. $n = 365$ (daily compounding)

   d. Evaluate $e^{0.12}$. What can you conclude from this result?

40. Atmospheric pressure decreases exponentially with the height above sea level. The equation $P = 14.7e^{-kh}$, where k is a positive constant, relates the pressure, P, in pounds per square inch to the height, h, in feet above sea level.

   a. Find the value of k if the atmospheric pressure one mile above sea level is 11.9 pounds per square inch.

   b. The stratosphere is a layer of the Earth's atmosphere that extends outward beginning about 10 miles above the surface of the Earth at the equator. Use the value of k from **part a** to find the atmospheric pressure in the stratosphere.

41. *Critical Thinking* Graph $\sqrt[x]{x}$ from 1 to 10. For what value of x is $\sqrt[x]{x}$ a maximum? Use a graphing calculator to find the maximum value for the function.

Challenge

42. Find a general formula for radioactive decay involving H, the half-life.

Prove the following for any logarithm bases a and b.

43. $\log_a b = \frac{1}{\log_b a}$ **44.** $a^{(\log_b M) \div (\log_b a)} = M$

45. $a^{(\log_b M)(\log_b a)} = M^{(\log_b a)^2}$ **46.** $\log_a(\log_a x) = \log_a(\log_b x) - \log_a(\log_b a)$

Mixed Review

Determine whether the polynomials are factors of the polynomial $P(x)$.

47. $P(x) = x^3 - 3x^2 - 6x + 8$ **a.** $x - 1$ **b.** $x + 4$ **c.** $x - 3$

48. $P(x) = x^3 - 10x^2 + 11x + 70$ **a.** $x - 1$ **b.** $x + 2$ **c.** $x + 5$ *11-1*

Given $f(x) = x^2 + 7$, find **49.** $f^{-1}(f(26))$. **50.** $f(f^{-1}(-9))$. *12-1*

Preparing for Standardized Tests

Angle Problems

Many problems on college entrance exams involve work with angles and angle measures. The following facts are helpful in solving angle problems on college entrance exams.

Fact 1 The sum of the measures of the three angles of a triangle equals 180°.

$m\angle 1 + m\angle 2 + m\angle 3 = 180°$

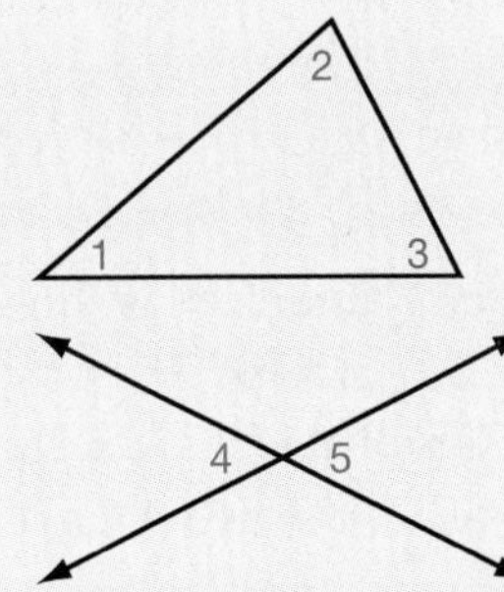

Fact 2 Vertical angles are congruent.

$m\angle 4 = m\angle 5$

Fact 3 The angles forming a straight line are supplementary.

$m\angle 6 + m\angle 7 = 180°$

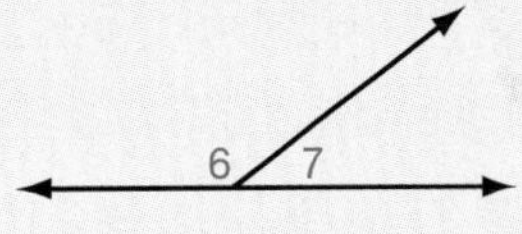

Fact 4 In a triangle, if two sides are congruent, then opposite angles are congruent.

$\overline{AC} = \overline{BC} \rightarrow m\angle 3 = m\angle 4$

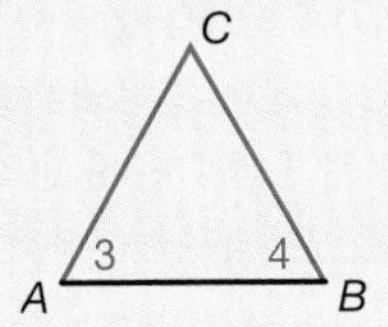

Fact 5 The sum of the measures of the four angles of a quadrilateral is 360°.

$m\angle 1 + m\angle 2 + m\angle 3 + m\angle 4 = 360°$

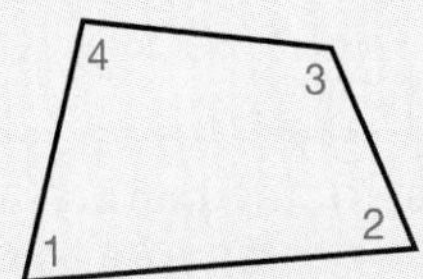

Fact 6 If a series of angles forms a complete "circle," then the sum of their measures is 360°.

$m\angle 1 + m\angle 2 + m\angle 3 + m\angle 4 + m\angle 5 = 360°$

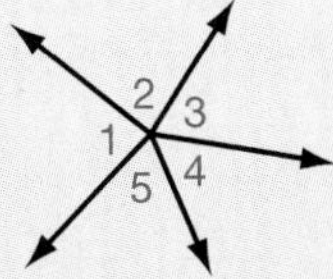

Fact 7 In a triangle, the largest angle is opposite the largest side.

$\overline{AB} > \overline{AC} \rightarrow m\angle 1 > m\angle 2$

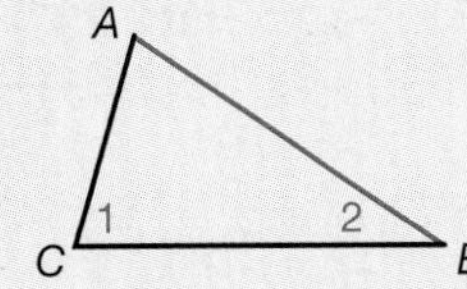

Fact 8 In a triangle, the measure of an exterior angle is the sum of the measures of the two remote interior angles.

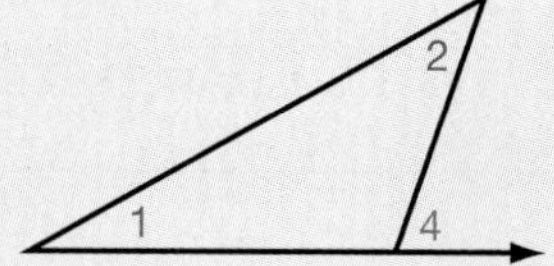

$m\angle 4 = m\angle 1 + m\angle 2$

Most items on college entrance exams involving angles require that several of the facts given above be applied to arrive at a solution.

EXAMPLE 1

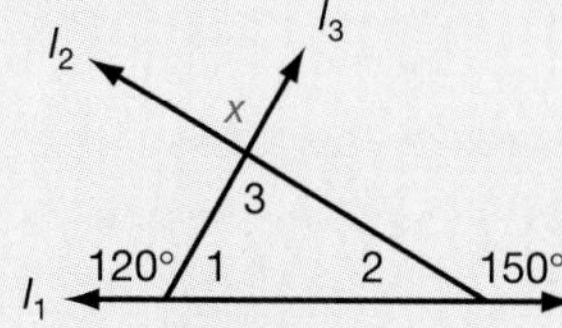

If l_1, l_2, and l_3 intersect as shown, then $x =$

(A) 60° **(B)** 70° **(C)** 80° **(D)** 90° **(E)** 100°

Solving this problem is a 3-step process.

First, we would use Fact 3 to conclude

$$m\angle 1 + 120° = 180° \quad \text{so } m\angle 1 = 60°$$
$$m\angle 2 + 150° = 180° \quad \text{so } m\angle 2 = 30°$$

Second, we would use Fact 1 to conclude

$$m\angle 1 + m\angle 2 + m\angle 3 = 180°$$
$$\text{so } m\angle 3 = 90°$$
$$60° + 30° + m\angle 3 = 180°$$

Finally, we would use Fact 2 to conclude

$$x = m\angle 3 \quad \text{so } x = 90°$$

So the correct answer is choice D.

EXAMPLE 2

Find the sum of the marked angles.

(A) 180° **(B)** 270° **(C)** 360° **(D)** 540° **(E)** 720°

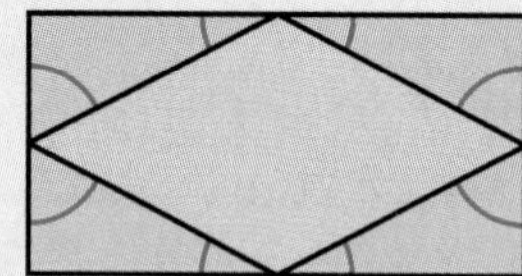

We can first find the sum of all blue and all red angles shown.

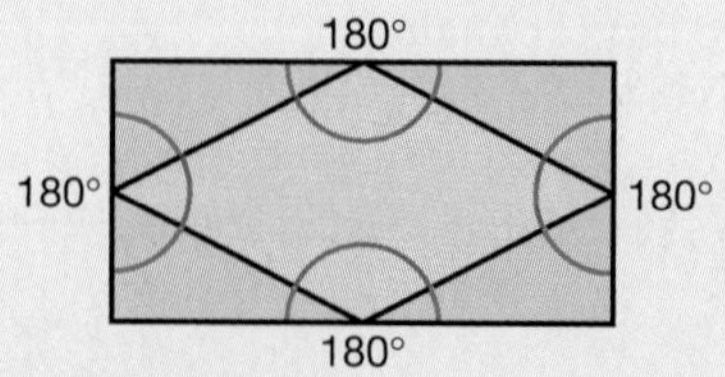

Next, we can find the sum of the red angles. Fact 5 tells us that the sum of the red angles will be 360°.

Finally, we can find the sum of the blue angles by subtracting the sum of the red angles from the sum of the blue and red angles.

$$\begin{aligned} \text{sum of blue angles} &= \text{sum (red and blue angles)} - \text{sum of red angles} \\ &= 720^\circ - 360^\circ \\ &= 360^\circ \end{aligned}$$

So the correct answer is choice C.

Problems

1.

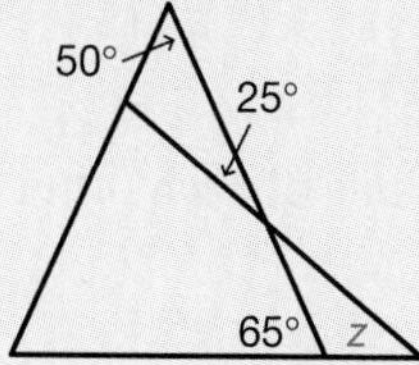

In the figure above, $z =$

(A) 55° **(B)** 50° **(C)** 45°
(D) 40° **(E)** 35°

2.

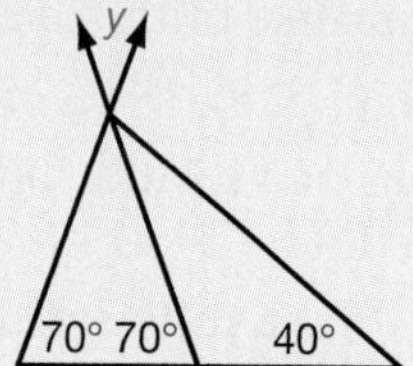

In the figure above, $y =$

(A) 70° **(B)** 65° **(C)** 60°
(D) 50° **(E)** 40°

3.

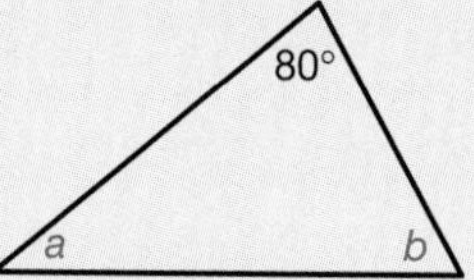

In the figure above, $\frac{1}{2}(a + b) =$

(A) 40° **(B)** 50° **(C)** 60°
(D) 70° **(E)** 80°

4.

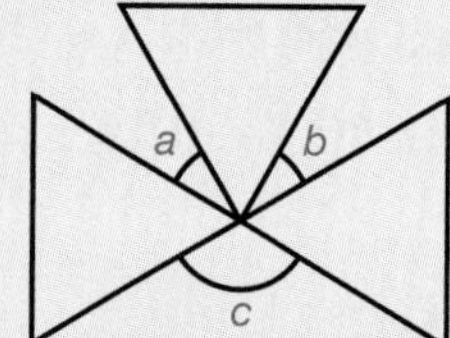

In the figure above, if the three equilateral triangles have a common vertex, then $a + b + c =$

(A) 120° **(B)** 150° **(C)** 180°
(D) 210° **(E)** 240°

5.

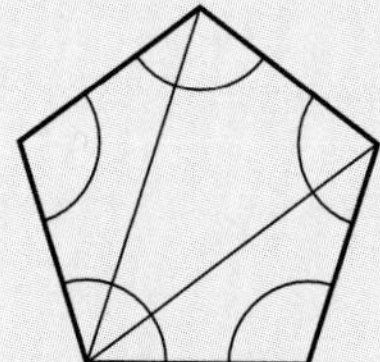

In the figure above, what is the average degree measure of the 5 marked angles?

(A) 75° **(B)** 108° **(C)** 90°
(D) 120° **(E)** 135°

6.

In ABC above, if $AB < BC < AC$, then which of the following is false?

(A) $x > z$ **(B)** $y > x$
(C) $y > z$ **(D)** $z > 60°$
(E) $y > 60°$

12 Chapter Wrap Up

Key Terms

antilogarithm (p. 536)
characteristic (p. 535)
common logarithm (p. 534)
compound interest (p. 543)
e (p. 550)
exponential decay (p. 552)
exponential equation (p. 543)
exponential function, base *a* (p. 521)
exponential function, base *e* (p. 550)
exponential growth (p. 551)
f^{-1} (p. 517)
half-life (p. 552)
interpolation (p. 539)
inverse (p. 516)
inverse relation (p. 516)
linear interpolation (p. 539)
log (p. 534)
$\log_a x$ (p. 523)
logarithmic equation (p. 544)
logarithmic function (p. 523)
ln *x* (p. 551)
mantissa (p. 535)
natural logarithm (p. 550)

12-1

Interchanging x and y in the equation of a relation produces an equation of **inverse relation.**

Write an equation of inverse relation.

1. $y = 3x - 1$ **2.** $y = 3x^2 + 2x - 1$

Find the inverse of the relation.

3. $(4, 1), (-3, 8), (-1, -5)$ **4.** $(2, 3), (5, 7), (6, -4)$

The graphs of a relation and its inverse are always reflections of each other across the line $y = x$.

Test each of the following for **symmetry** with respect to the line $y = x$.

5. $6x + 6y = 7$ **6.** $2x - y = 1$

Remember that $f^{-1}(x)$ is the inverse of $f(x)$.

Write an equation of the inverse relation.

7. Given $g(x) = \sqrt{x} + 2$, find an equation for $g^{-1}(x)$.

8. Given $h(x) = 0.5x - 1$, find an equation for $h^{-1}(x)$.

12-2

To graph **exponential** or **logarithmic functions,** find some solutions, then graph.

9. Graph $y = 5^x$. Give the domain, range, and y-intercept.

10. Graph $y = \log_5 x$.

The statements $x = a^y$ and $y = \log_a x$ are equivalent.

Write equivalent logarithmic equations.

11. $7^{2.3} = x$ **12.** $8^{\frac{1}{3}} = 2$

Write equivalent exponential equations.

13. $\log_3 81 = 4$ **14.** $\log_8 M = t$

12-3

Certain equations containing logarithmic notation can be solved by first converting to exponential notation.

15. Solve $\log_x 64 = 3$. **16.** Solve $\log_{16} 4 = x$.

For any number a suitable as a logarithm base, $a^{\log_a x} = x$ for $x > 0$ and $\log_a a^x = x$ for any x.

17. Simplify $\log_h h^3$. **18.** Simplify $3^{\log_3 t}$.

12-4

For any positive numbers x, y, and a, and $a \neq 1$,
$\log_a (x \cdot y) = \log_a x + \log_a y$, $\log_a x^p = p \cdot \log_a x$, and $\log_a \frac{x}{y} = \log_a x - \log_a y$.

19. Express $\frac{1}{2}\log_b a + \frac{3}{2}\log_b c - 4 \log_b d$ as a single logarithm.

20. Express $\log \sqrt[3]{\frac{M^2}{N}}$ in terms of logarithms of M and N.

Given that $\log_a 2 \approx 0.301$, $\log_a 3 \approx 0.477$, and $\log_a 7 \approx 0.845$, find the following.

21. $\log_a 18$ **22.** $\log_a \frac{7}{2}$ **23.** $\log_a \frac{1}{4}$ **24.** $\log_a \sqrt{3}$

Internet Activity On the Web

Look for extension problems for this chapter at the Prentice Hall Web site.
www.phschool.com

12-5

Finding $\log_{10} 1.23$, or finding x such that $10^x = 1.23$, are different ways of stating the same problem. Table 2 or a calculator will be helpful.

Use Table 2 or a calculator to find the following.

25. $\log 26.2$ **26.** $\log_{10} 0.00806$ **27.** $10^x = 5.82$

28. antilog 0.7686 **29.** antilog $(7.3617 - 10)$ **30.** antilog 2.3304

12-6

Interpolation can be used to estimate values between those listed in a table.

31. Find log 18.75 using interpolation and Table 2. Check using a calculator.

32. Find antilog 1.1629 using interpolation and Table 2. Check using a calculator.

12-7

Taking logarithms of both sides can be useful in solving **exponential equations.**

33. $3^{-1-x} = 9^{2x}$ **34.** $4^{2x} = 8^{x-1}$

Logarithmic equations can be solved by converting to exponential equations.

Solve.

35. $\log (x^2 - 1) - \log (x - 1) = 1$ **36.** $\log_4 \sqrt{x - 2} = 2$

Exponential and **logarithmic functions** and equations have many applications.

37. How many years will it take an investment of \$1000 to double itself if interest is compounded annually at 5%?

12-8

Logarithms to the base ***e*** are called **natural logarithms.**

Find each natural logarithm to four decimal places.

38. ln 1.6 **39.** ln 1600

For any bases a and b, and any positive number M, $\log_b M = \frac{\log_a M}{\log_a b}$.

40. Find $\log_4 80$.

12 Chapter Assessment

1. Write an equation of the inverse relation of $y = 2x^2 - 3x + 1$.

2. Test $x + y = 7$ for symmetry with respect to the line $y = x$.

3. Given $f(x) = \frac{\sqrt{x}}{3} + 1$, find an equation for $f^{-1}(x)$.

Graph.

4. $y = 4^x$

5. $y = \log_4 x$

Write the equivalent logarithmic expressions.

6. $3^x = 25$

7. $25^{\frac{1}{2}} = 5$

Write equivalent exponential equations.

8. $\log_3 9 = 2$

9. $\log_6 x = y$

Solve.

10. $\log_x 125 = 3$

11. $\log_{25} 5 = x$

Simplify.

12. $14^{\log_{14} 7t}$

Express as a single logarithm.

13. $\frac{2}{3}\log_2 8 + \frac{1}{3}\log_2 3 - 2\log_2 4$

Given that $\log_a 3 = 0.451$ and $\log_a 4 = 0.569$, find the following.

14. $\log_a 9$

15. $\log_a \frac{4}{3}$

Use Table 2 to find the following.

16. log 14.3

17. antilog (7.5340 − 10)

Solve.

18. $2^{x-1} = 32$

19. $\log 4x + \log x = 2$

20. Suppose $10,000 is invested at 10% interest compounded annually. The investment yields $19,487. For how many years was it invested?

21. Find ln 1.7 to four decimal places.

Solve.

22. The population of a colony of cells growing exponentially in a culture is 300 after 2 minutes and 1400 after 5 minutes. Find k in the growth formula and estimate the population of the colony after 20 minutes.

Use common logarithms to find the following.

23. $\log_9 100$

24. $\log_{16} 512$

Challenge

25. If $\log_a x = 1$, what is $\log_a \left(\frac{1}{x}\right)$?

1–12 Cumulative Review

1-3 Evaluate each expression for $a = 5$ and $c = -2$.

1. $-|a + c| + (3a + c)$
2. $ac + c^2 + |6c|$
3. $|a + c| - |a| - |c|$
4. $|a - c| + |c - a|$

2-4 Solve.

5. $4x - 3 \leq 5x + 2$
6. $-2x \leq 2(x + 3) - 1$
7. $-\frac{2}{5}x < -24$

3-6 Find an equation in standard form for the line containing

8. $(-1, 1)$ and $(-2, 1)$.
9. $(6, 3)$ and $(6, -3)$.

4-2 Solve.

10. $4x - 2y = 10$
$-x + 2y = -7$

11. $16x + 6y = -11$
$-7x + 9y = -1$

12. $19x + 18y = -12$
$14x + 9y = -6$

4-3

13. Solution A is 12% acid and Solution B is 60% acid. How many liters of each should be mixed together to get 24 liters of a solution that is 50% acid?

4-7 Graph.

14. $x < y$
15. $x - y > 0$
16. $y + x < 1$

5-3 Multiply.

17. $(2z + 4y)^2$
18. $(x - 5)^3$
19. $(a^2 + 2b)^3$

5-4–5-6 Factor.

20. $400x^2 - 441y^2$
21. $a^{16} - 1$
22. $x^4y^2 - x^2$
23. $y^3 + 125$
24. $y^3 + 2y^2 - 4y - 8$
25. $4x^3 - 16x^2 - 9x + 36$

5-7 Solve.

26. $2x^2 = 15 + x$
27. $3x^2 + 6 = 19x$
28. $20x^2 - 3 = -28x$

6-3
Simplify.

29. $\left(\frac{3x}{y} - x\right) \div \left(\frac{y}{x} - y\right)$
30. $\left(\frac{x - 1}{x} + \frac{x}{1 + x}\right) \div \left(\frac{x}{1 - x} + \frac{1 + x}{x}\right)$

6-4 Divide.

31. $(2x^4 + 7x^3 + 5x^2 - 17x - 9)$ by $(2x + 1)$

6-6 Solve.

32. $\frac{7}{5x - 2} = \frac{5}{4x}$

33. $\frac{1}{x} + \frac{2x + 3}{2} = 8x$

7-1–7-4 Simplify.

34. $\sqrt{36x^2}$

35. $\sqrt[3]{-125}$

36. $\sqrt[4]{16x^4y^8}$

37. $\sqrt{48y^3}$

38. $\frac{\sqrt{7} + \sqrt{5}}{\sqrt{7} - \sqrt{5}}$

39. $\frac{\sqrt{10}}{\sqrt{15}}$

40. $\frac{\sqrt{48a^5}}{\sqrt{36a^3}}$

41. $\frac{\sqrt[3]{96x^6}}{\sqrt{72x^2}}$

7-6 Solve.

42. $\sqrt{5x + 39} = x - 9$

43. $\sqrt[3]{4x + 7} + 2 = 5$

7-9 Simplify.

44. $(5 + 2i)^2$

45. $(1 + i) \div (2 - 3i)$

46. $-(-i^9)(i^4)$

8-1–8-3 Solve.

47. $4x^2 - 5x - 6 = 0$

48. $5x^2 - 4x = 0$

49. $2x^2 + 2x + 3 = 0$

8-4 Find a quadratic equation whose solutions are the following.

50. $\frac{3}{4}, -\frac{5}{3}$

51. $1 + \sqrt{3}, 1 - \sqrt{3}$

9-1 Test the following equations for symmetry with respect to the x-axis and the y-axis.

52. $4y = 3x^2 - 1$

53. $2x^2 - 3y^2 = 5$

54. $x^3 + 3y^3 = 10$

Determine whether each function is even, odd, or neither.

55. $f(x) = 5$

56. $f(x) = x^{23}$

57. $f(x) = \sqrt{x} + 1$

9-6

58. For $f(x) = -3x^2 + 12x - 5$,

a. find standard form for the quadratic function.

b. find the vertex, the line of symmetry, and the maximum or minimum value.

9-7

59. Find the x-intercepts, if they exist.

a. $f(x) = 4x^2 + 12x + 9$

b. $f(x) = 9x^2 - 12x - 1$

10-1

60. Find the distance between the points $(-2, 5)$ and $(3, -4)$.

10-4, 10-5

61. Find the vertices, foci, and asymptotes of the hyperbola $8x^2 - 3y^2 = 48$. Then graph the hyperbola.

62. Find the vertex, focus, and directrix of the parabola $x^2 + 2x + 6y - 11 = 0$. Then graph the parabola.

10-7 Solve the system.

63. $y^2 + x^2 = 13$
$x - 2y = 1$

64. $x^2 + y^2 = 20$
$xy = 8$

11-2–11-5 Solve.

65. Use synthetic division to find $P(-3)$ if $P(x) = -2x^3 + x^2 - 1$.

66. Find a polynomial of degree 3 with roots $3, i, -i$.

67. Find all roots of $2x^4 - 7x^3 + 5x^2 + 9x - 5$.

68. What does Descartes' rule of signs tell you about the number of positive real roots and negative real roots of $4x^5 + 3x^4 - 2x^3 + 2x^2 + 3x - 1$?

12-1

69. Find $f^{-1}(x)$ if $f(x) = 2x - 3$.

12-3

70. Solve $x = \log_4 16$.

71. Solve $\log_4 x = 3$.

12-4 Express as a single logarithm. Simplify if possible.

72. $\frac{1}{2}\log_5 x - 3\log_5 y$

73. $\log_a 3x + 2(\log_a 2x - \log_a x)$

12-5 Use Table 2 or a calculator to find the following.

74. $\log 0.00332$

75. antilog $(8.3215 - 10)$

12-7 Solve.

76. $3^{3x-2} = 27$

77. $\log(x + 19) - \log 2x = 1$

12-8

78. Find $\ln 73.2$.

79. Find $\log_3 45$.

CHAPTER 13

What You'll Learn in Chapter 13

- How to find the dimensions of a matrix
- How to add, subtract, and multiply certain kinds of matrices
- How to multiply a matrix by a scalar quantity
- How to evaluate determinants
- How to identify or find the inverse of a matrix
- How to write a matrix equation equivalent to a system of equations
- How to solve a system of equations using matrices, Cramer's rule, or the inverse of a matrix

Skills & Concepts You Need for Chapter 13

1-3 Evaluate for $x = -2$, $y = -3$, and $z = 8$.

1. $x(y + z)$

2. $xy(yz - xz)$

4-2, 4-4 Solve.

3. $5x + 3y = 7$
$3x - 5y = -23$

4. $2x - y + 4z = -3$
$x - 4z = 5$
$6x - y + 2z = 10$

5. $x + y - 2z = 9$
$2x + y - z = 4$
$x + 2y + z = 5$

Matrices and Determinants

To stay in business, bakeries must sell most of what is baked. Matrices can be used to keep track of sales and profits. See Exercise 1, Lesson 13-7.

13-1 Matrices and Systems of Equations

What You'll Learn

1. To find the dimensions of a matrix
2. To solve systems of equations using matrices

. . . And Why

To solve problems involving systems of equations

To solve systems of equations, we perform computations with the coefficients and constants. After the equations are in the form $Ax + By = C$, the variables play no important role in the process until we state the solution. We can simplify the process by omitting the variables. For example, the system

$$\begin{aligned} 3x + 4y &= 5 \\ x - 2y &= 1 \end{aligned} \quad \text{simplifies to} \quad \begin{matrix} 3 & 4 & 5 \\ 1 & -2 & 1 \end{matrix}$$

In the above example we have written a rectangular array of numbers. Such an array is called a **matrix** (plural: **matrices**). We ordinarily write brackets around matrices.

$$\begin{bmatrix} 3 & 4 & 5 \\ 1 & -2 & 1 \end{bmatrix}$$

Definition

An $m \times n$ **matrix,** for m and n positive integers, is an array of the form

$$\begin{bmatrix} a_{11} & a_{12} & a_{13} & \cdots & a_{1n} \\ a_{21} & a_{22} & a_{23} & \cdots & a_{2n} \\ a_{31} & a_{32} & a_{33} & \cdots & a_{3n} \\ \vdots & \vdots & \vdots & & \vdots \\ a_{m1} & a_{m2} & a_{m3} & \cdots & a_{mn} \end{bmatrix}$$

Each **element a_{ij}** of the matrix is a real number.

PART 1 Dimensions of a Matrix

Objective: State the dimensions of a matrix.

An $m \times n$ matrix (read "m by n") has m horizontal **rows** and n vertical **columns.** In the following 4×3 matrix, a_{12} (read "a sub one two") is the element in row 1, column 2, so a_{12} is -2. The element a_{21} is 9, the element a_{33} is -7, and so on.

	column 1	column 2	column 3
row 1	5	−2	2
row 2	9	0	4
row 3	0	1	−7
row 4	−3	6	8

Definition

A matrix of m rows and n columns is called a matrix with **dimensions** $m \times n$.

EXAMPLES Find the dimensions of each matrix.

1 $\begin{bmatrix} 2 & -3 & 4 \\ -1 & \frac{1}{2} & \pi \end{bmatrix}$

2×3 matrix

2 $\begin{bmatrix} -3 & 8 & 9 \\ \pi & -2 & 5 \\ -6 & 7 & 8 \end{bmatrix}$

3×3 matrix

3 $\begin{bmatrix} 10 \\ -7 \end{bmatrix}$

2×1 matrix

4 $[\,-3 \quad 4\,]$

1×2 matrix

Note that the row dimension is always listed first. A **row matrix** is any matrix with dimensions $1 \times n$. A **column matrix** is any matrix with dimensions $m \times 1$.

Try This Find the dimensions of each matrix.

a. $\begin{bmatrix} -3 & 5 \\ 4 & \frac{1}{4} \\ -\pi & 0 \end{bmatrix}$ **b.** $\begin{bmatrix} -3 & 0 \\ 0 & 3 \end{bmatrix}$ **c.** $\begin{bmatrix} 1 & 2 & 3 \\ 0 & 1 & 8 \\ 0 & 0 & 1 \end{bmatrix}$

d. $[\,\pi \quad \sqrt{2}\,]$ **e.** $\begin{bmatrix} -5 \\ \pi \end{bmatrix}$ **f.** $[\,-3\,]$

PART 2 Systems of Linear Equations

Objective: Solve systems of equations using matrices.

We can use matrices to solve systems of linear equations. All the operations used on the matrices correspond to operations with the equations. Since the operations produce equivalent matrices, we call them **row equivalent operations.** The matrices are said to be **row equivalent.**

Theorem 13-1

Each of the following row-equivalent operations produces equivalent matrices.

A. interchanging any two rows of a matrix
B. multiplying each element of a row by the same nonzero constant
C. multiplying each element of a row by a nonzero number and adding the result to another row

When solving a system of equations with matrices, our goal will be to get the matrix in the form where there are just 0s below the **main diagonal** formed by a, e, and h. Such a matrix is said to be in **triangular form.** Then we put the variables back and complete the solution.

$$\begin{bmatrix} a & b & c & d \\ 0 & e & f & g \\ 0 & 0 & h & k \end{bmatrix}$$

The dashed line indicates the main diagonal.

EXAMPLE 5 Solve using matrices.

$$\begin{aligned} 2x - y &= -1 \quad ① \\ 3x + 2y &= 16 \quad ② \end{aligned}$$

We write the matrix using only the coefficients and constants.

$$\begin{bmatrix} 2 & -1 & -1 \\ 3 & 2 & 16 \end{bmatrix}$$

We do the same calculations using the matrix that we would do with the system of equations. Our goal is to put the matrix in triangular form.

The first step is to multiply the first row by 3 and the second row by -2.

$$\begin{bmatrix} 6 & -3 & -3 \\ -6 & -4 & -32 \end{bmatrix}$$

This corresponds to multiplying equation ① by 3 and equation ② by -2.

Now we add the first row to the second row to make $a_{21} = 0$.

$$\begin{bmatrix} 6 & -3 & -3 \\ 0 & -7 & -35 \end{bmatrix}$$

This corresponds to adding equation ① to equation ②, thus eliminating the x-term of equation ②.

We now have the matrix in triangular form. If we put the variables back, we have the following.

$$\begin{aligned} 6x - 3y &= -3 \quad ① \\ -7y &= -35 \quad ② \end{aligned}$$

We solve ② for y and get $y = 5$. Substituting 5 for y in ① and solving for x, we get $x = 2$. The solution is (2, 5).

Writing Math

In writing the matrix of coefficients and constants for a system of linear equations, it is sometimes necessary to rewrite some of the equations. The variables must be in the same order on the left sides of the equal signs, and the constants must be on the right sides of the equal signs.

EXAMPLE 6 Solve using matrices.

$$\begin{aligned} 2x - y + 4z &= -3 \quad ① \\ x - 4z &= 5 \quad ② \\ 6x - y + 2z &= 10 \quad ③ \end{aligned}$$

We first write a matrix, using only the coefficients and constants. Note that where there are missing terms we must write 0s.

$$\begin{bmatrix} 2 & -1 & 4 & -3 \\ 1 & 0 & -4 & 5 \\ 6 & -1 & 2 & 10 \end{bmatrix}$$

We do exactly the same calculations using the matrix that we would do if we used the equations. The first step, if possible, is to interchange the rows so that $a_{11} = 1$. We do this by interchanging rows 1 and 2.

$$\begin{bmatrix} 1 & 0 & -4 & 5 \\ 2 & -1 & 4 & -3 \\ 6 & -1 & 2 & 10 \end{bmatrix}$$

This corresponds to interchanging equation ① and equation ②.

Next we multiply the first row by -2 and add it to the second row to make $a_{21} = 0$.

$$\begin{bmatrix} 1 & 0 & -4 & 5 \\ 0 & -1 & 12 & -13 \\ 6 & -1 & 2 & 10 \end{bmatrix}$$

This corresponds to multiplying equation ① by -2 and adding it to equation ②, thus eliminating the x-term in equation ②.

Now we multiply the first row by -6 and add it to the third row to make $a_{31} = 0$.

$$\begin{bmatrix} 1 & 0 & -4 & 5 \\ 0 & -1 & 12 & -13 \\ 0 & -1 & 26 & -20 \end{bmatrix}$$

This corresponds to multiplying equation ① by -6 and adding it to equation ③, thus eliminating the x-term in equation ③.

Next we multiply row 2 by -1 and add it to the third row to make $a_{32} = 0$.

$$\begin{bmatrix} 1 & 0 & -4 & 5 \\ 0 & -1 & 12 & -13 \\ 0 & 0 & 14 & -7 \end{bmatrix}$$

This corresponds to multiplying equation ② by -1 and adding it to equation ③, thus eliminating the y-term in equation ③.

Quick Review

Remember that subscripts are a convenient way to distinguish variables. In general, $a_{12} \neq a_{21}$.

We now have the matrix in triangular form.

If we put the variables back, we have the following.

$$x - 4z = 5$$
$$-y + 12z = -13$$
$$14z = -7$$

We solve ③ for z and get $z = -\frac{1}{2}$.

Next we substitute $-\frac{1}{2}$ for z in ② and solve for y.

$$-y + 12\left(-\tfrac{1}{2}\right) = -13, \text{ so } y = 7$$

Since there is no y-term in ①, we need only substitute $-\frac{1}{2}$ for z in ① and solve for x: $x - 4\left(-\frac{1}{2}\right) = 5$, so $x = 3$.

The solution is $\left(3, 7, -\frac{1}{2}\right)$.

Try This Solve using matrices.

g. $5x - 2y = -44$
$x + 5y = 2$

h. $x - 2y + 3z = 4$
$2x - y + z = -1$
$4x + y + z = 1$

Extra Help On the Web

Look for worked-out examples at the Prentice Hall Web site.
www.phschool.com

13-1 Exercises

A

Mental Math Find the dimensions of each matrix.

1. $\begin{bmatrix} 2 & -5 & 3 \\ 1 & 4 & -6 \end{bmatrix}$ **2.** $\begin{bmatrix} \pi & -8 & 3 & 5 \\ \frac{1}{2} & 0 & 0 & 7 \\ -8 & 0 & 0 & 0 \end{bmatrix}$ **3.** $\begin{bmatrix} 0 & 3 \\ 1 & -1 \\ 5 & -5 \\ 2 & 7 \\ 8 & 1.9 \end{bmatrix}$ **4.** $\begin{bmatrix} -3 \\ 4 \\ 12 \end{bmatrix}$

Solve using matrices.

5. $4x + 2y = 11$
$3x - y = 2$

6. $3x - 3y = -6$
$9x - 2y = 3$

7. $5x + 2 = 3y$
$4x + 2y - 5 = 0$

8. $x + 2y - 3z = 9$
$2x - y + 2z = -8$
$3x - y - 4z = 3$

9. $4x + y - 3z = 1$
$8x + y - z = 5$
$2x + y + 2z = 5$

10. $3x + 2y + 2z = 3$
$x + 2y - z = 5$
$2x - 4y + z = 0$

B

Solve using matrices.

11. $2w - 2x - 2y + 2z = 10$
$w + x + y + z = -5$
$3w + x - y + 4z = -2$
$w + 3x - 2y + 2z = -6$

12. $w - 2x + 3y - z = 8$
$w - x - y + z = 4$
$w + 2x + y + z = 26$
$w - x + y + z = 14$

13. *Critical Thinking* Show that subtracting a multiple of one row of a matrix from another row results in a row-equivalent matrix.

Challenge

Solve using matrices.

14. $x + y - 2z + 3w + 2n = 9$
$8x + 5y - 2z - w + 2n = 3$
$2x + 2y - z + w - 2n = 1$
$3x + 3y - z + w + n = 5$
$4x + 4y + z - 3n = 4$

15. $2x + 2y + 4z + 4w + 13n = 13$
$x - y + 2z + 2w + 6n = 6$
$y - z - w - 3n = -3$
$3x - 2y + 4z + 4w + 12n = 14$
$2x - 2y + 4z + 5w + 15n = 10$

Mixed Review

Subtract. **16.** $\frac{4x}{x+3} - \frac{3x}{x-3}$ **17.** $\frac{5a^2 + 4ab + 3b^2}{a^3 - b^3} - \frac{4}{a-b}$ *6-2*

Evaluate. **18.** log 0.497 **19.** antilog 0.497 **20.** log 9.04

21. $\log(9.04 \times 10^5)$ *12-5, 12-6*

22. Four more than the square of a number is 148. Find the number. *5-8*

Addition and Subtraction of Matrices

13-2

In 1857, Arthur Cayley, an English mathematician, developed the idea of matrix algebra. In this section we begin the study of operations with matrices.

What You'll Learn

1. To add matrices
2. To subtract matrices, and find the additive inverse of a matrix

. . . And Why

To manipulate matrices using some field properties

PART 1 Matrix Addition

Objective: Add matrices.

To *add* matrices, we add the corresponding elements. The matrices must have the same dimensions. Capital letters are used to denote matrices. Addition of matrices is both commutative and associative.

EXAMPLES Add.

1 $A = \begin{bmatrix} -5 & 0 \\ 4 & 1 \end{bmatrix}, B = \begin{bmatrix} 6 & -3 \\ 2 & 3 \end{bmatrix}; A + B = \begin{bmatrix} -5 + 6 & 0 - 3 \\ 4 + 2 & 1 + 3 \end{bmatrix} = \begin{bmatrix} 1 & -3 \\ 6 & 4 \end{bmatrix}$

A matrix having zeros for all of its members is called a **zero matrix** and is often denoted by O. When a zero matrix is added to another matrix of the same dimensions, that same matrix is obtained. Thus a zero matrix is an **additive identity.**

2 $\begin{bmatrix} 2 & -1 & 3 \\ 1 & 0 & -1 \end{bmatrix} + \begin{bmatrix} 0 & 0 & 0 \\ 0 & 0 & 0 \end{bmatrix} = \begin{bmatrix} 2 + 0 & -1 + 0 & 3 + 0 \\ 1 + 0 & 0 + 0 & -1 + 0 \end{bmatrix} = \begin{bmatrix} 2 & -1 & 3 \\ 1 & 0 & -1 \end{bmatrix}$

Try This Add.

a. Let $A = \begin{bmatrix} 4 & -1 \\ 6 & -3 \end{bmatrix}, B = \begin{bmatrix} -6 & -5 \\ 7 & 3 \end{bmatrix}, O = \begin{bmatrix} 0 & 0 \\ 0 & 0 \end{bmatrix}$

(1) $A + B$ **(2)** $B + A$ **(3)** $O + A$

PART 2 Additive Inverses and Subtraction

Objective: Subtract matrices and find the additive inverse of a matrix.

To subtract matrices, we subtract the corresponding elements. The matrices must have the same dimensions.

EXAMPLE 3 Subtract.

$$\begin{bmatrix} 1 & 2 \\ -2 & 0 \\ -3 & -1 \end{bmatrix} - \begin{bmatrix} 1 & -1 \\ 1 & 3 \\ 2 & 3 \end{bmatrix} = \begin{bmatrix} 1 - 1 & 2 - (-1) \\ -2 - 1 & 0 - 3 \\ -3 - 2 & -1 - 3 \end{bmatrix} = \begin{bmatrix} 0 & 3 \\ -3 & -3 \\ -5 & -4 \end{bmatrix}$$

Try This Subtract.

b. $\begin{bmatrix} 1 & 3 & -2 \\ 4 & 0 & 5 \end{bmatrix} - \begin{bmatrix} 2 & -1 & 5 \\ 6 & 4 & -3 \end{bmatrix}$ **c.** $\begin{bmatrix} 1 & 2 \\ 4 & 1 \\ -5 & 4 \end{bmatrix} - \begin{bmatrix} 7 & -4 \\ 3 & 5 \\ 2 & -1 \end{bmatrix}$

The **additive inverse of a matrix** can be obtained by replacing each element by its additive inverse. For a matrix A, the additive inverse is $\boldsymbol{-A}$. When two matrices that are additive inverses of each other are added, a zero matrix is obtained.

EXAMPLE 4 Find the additive inverse of $A = \begin{bmatrix} 1 & 0 & 2 \\ 3 & -1 & 5 \end{bmatrix}$.

$$-A = \begin{bmatrix} -1 & 0 & -2 \\ -3 & 1 & -5 \end{bmatrix}$$

Try This Find the additive inverse.

d. $\begin{bmatrix} 2 & -1 & 5 \\ 6 & 4 & -3 \end{bmatrix}$ **e.** $\begin{bmatrix} 1 & 3 & -5 \\ -2 & 0 & 0 \\ 6 & -10 & 7 \end{bmatrix}$

If we denote matrices by A and B and an additive inverse by $-B$, we can subtract by adding an inverse as we do with numbers.

Reading Math

Since we read from left to right and from top to bottom, many mathematicians read $\begin{bmatrix} a & b \\ c & d \end{bmatrix}$ *as the two by two matrix a, b, c, d.*

Theorem 13-2

For any matrices A and B, $A - B = A + (-B)$.

EXAMPLE 5 Subtract by adding an additive inverse.

$$\overset{A}{\begin{bmatrix} 3 & -1 \\ -2 & 4 \end{bmatrix}} - \overset{B}{\begin{bmatrix} 2 & 1 \\ 3 & -2 \end{bmatrix}} = \begin{bmatrix} 1 & -2 \\ -5 & 6 \end{bmatrix}$$

$$= \overset{A}{\begin{bmatrix} 3 & -1 \\ -2 & 4 \end{bmatrix}} + \overset{(-B)}{\begin{bmatrix} -2 & -1 \\ -3 & 2 \end{bmatrix}} = \begin{bmatrix} 1 & -2 \\ -5 & 6 \end{bmatrix}$$

Try This Subtract by adding an additive inverse.

f. $\begin{bmatrix} 1 & 3 & -2 \\ 4 & 0 & 5 \end{bmatrix} - \begin{bmatrix} -2 & 1 & -5 \\ -6 & -4 & 3 \end{bmatrix}$ **g.** $\begin{bmatrix} 9 & 3 & 7 \\ -1 & 5 & -3 \\ 0 & -4 & -6 \end{bmatrix} - \begin{bmatrix} -2 & 5 & 14 \\ 2 & -8 & 2 \\ -7 & -6 & 0 \end{bmatrix}$

13-2 Exercises

Extra Help On the Web

Look for worked-out examples at the Prentice Hall Web site. www.phschool.com

A

For Exercises 1–29, let

$$A = \begin{bmatrix} 1 & 2 \\ 4 & -3 \end{bmatrix} \quad B = \begin{bmatrix} -3 & -5 \\ 2 & -1 \end{bmatrix} \quad C = \begin{bmatrix} 1 & -1 \\ -1 & 1 \end{bmatrix} \quad D = \begin{bmatrix} 1 & 1 \\ 1 & 1 \end{bmatrix} \quad E = \begin{bmatrix} 1 & 3 \\ 2 & 6 \end{bmatrix}$$

$$F = \begin{bmatrix} 3 & 3 \\ -1 & -1 \\ 0 & 0 \end{bmatrix} \quad G = \begin{bmatrix} 1 & 0 & -2 \\ 0 & -1 & 3 \\ 3 & -2 & 4 \end{bmatrix} \quad H = \begin{bmatrix} -1 & -2 & 5 \\ 1 & 0 & -1 \\ -2 & -3 & 1 \end{bmatrix} \quad J = \begin{bmatrix} -2 & 3 & 4 \\ 8 & 0 & -1 \end{bmatrix}$$

$$M = \begin{bmatrix} -3 & 5 & -2 \\ 1 & 0 & -4 \\ -2 & -3 & -5 \end{bmatrix} \quad O = \begin{bmatrix} 0 & 0 \\ 0 & 0 \end{bmatrix} \quad Q = \begin{bmatrix} -3 & -3 & 7 \\ -5 & 2 & 1 \end{bmatrix} \quad R = \begin{bmatrix} -1 & 0 & 0 \\ 0 & 2 & 0 \end{bmatrix}$$

Mental Math Find the dimensions of each matrix.

1. A **2.** G **3.** Q **4.** O

Add or subtract if possible.

5. $A + B$ **6.** $B + C$ **7.** $J + Q$ **8.** $R + J$ **9.** $H + G$
10. $M + H$ **11.** $G + J$ **12.** $R + F$ **13.** $A - B$ **14.** $C - B$
15. $F - D$ **16.** $H - M$ **17.** $G - H$ **18.** $Q - J$ **19.** $M - R$

Find the additive inverse of each matrix.

20. D **21.** Q **22.** E **23.** M

Subtract by adding an additive inverse.

24. $D - C$ **25.** $M - H$ **26.** $J - Q$ **27.** $O - F$

B

Find the value of each sum.

28. $(A + B) + C$ and $A + (B + C)$ **29.** $(G + H) + M$ and $(M + H) + G$

30. ***Critical Thinking*** The **transpose** of A, $\mathbf{A^t}$, is formed by exchanging the rows and columns of A. (For $A = \begin{bmatrix} a & b \\ c & d \end{bmatrix}$, $A^t = \begin{bmatrix} a & c \\ b & d \end{bmatrix}$.) Show that $A^t + B^t = (A + B)^t$.

Challenge *Mathematical Reasoning*

31. Prove Theorem 13-2.

32. Prove that for any $m \times n$ matrices A and B, $A + B = B + A$.

Mixed Review

Solve. **33.** $7^x = 10$ **34.** $\log x + \log (x + 8) = 1$ **35.** $2x^2 = 5$
36. $2x^2 - 9x = 5$ **37.** $x^2 + 2x = 15$ *8-1, 8-3, 12-7*

38. Twenty-four less than the square of n is five times n. Find n. *5-8*

13-3  Determinants and Cramer's Rule

What You'll Learn

1. To evaluate a 2 × 2 determinant
2. To use Cramer's rule to solve a system of two equations in two variables
3. To evaluate a 3 × 3 determinant
4. To use Cramer's rule to solve a system of three equations in three variables

. . . And Why

To solve problems using systems of equations

PART 1 Determinants of 2 × 2 Matrices

Objective: Evaluate a 2 × 2 determinant.

A matrix with the same number of rows and columns is called a **square matrix.** With every square matrix is associated a number called its determinant. The determinant of a matrix A is denoted $|\mathbf{A}|$. The determinant of a 2 × 2 matrix is defined as follows.

Definition

The **determinant** of the matrix $\begin{bmatrix} a_1 & b_1 \\ a_2 & b_2 \end{bmatrix}$ is denoted $\begin{vmatrix} a_1 & b_1 \\ a_2 & b_2 \end{vmatrix}$ and is defined as

$$\begin{vmatrix} a_1 & b_1 \\ a_2 & b_2 \end{vmatrix} = a_1b_2 - a_2b_1$$

EXAMPLE 1 Evaluate $\begin{vmatrix} 7 & -3 \\ -4 & -8 \end{vmatrix}$.

$$\begin{vmatrix} 7 & -3 \\ -4 & -8 \end{vmatrix} = 7(-8) - (-4)(-3) = -68$$

The arrows indicate the products involved.

Try This Evaluate. **a.** $\begin{vmatrix} -4 & -5 \\ -2 & -6 \end{vmatrix}$ **b.** $\begin{vmatrix} 1 & 2 \\ 3 & 4 \end{vmatrix}$ **c.** $\begin{vmatrix} -2 & -3 \\ 4 & x \end{vmatrix}$

PART 2 Cramer's Rule for Two Equations

Objective: Solve a system of two equations in two variables using Cramer's rule.

Determinants have many uses. One is solving systems of linear equations in which the number of variables is the same as the number of equations. Let us consider a system of two equations, each in the form $ax + by = c$.

$$a_1x + b_1y = c_1$$
$$a_2x + b_2y = c_2$$

By eliminating variables, we obtain the following solution.

$$x = \frac{c_1b_2 - c_2b_1}{a_1b_2 - a_2b_1} \text{ and } y = \frac{a_1c_2 - a_2c_1}{a_1b_2 - a_2b_1}$$

We note that the numerators and denominators of the expressions for x and y are determinants. Thus we have the following theorem.

Theorem 13-3

Cramer's Rule (2 Equations)

The system of two equations in two variables

$$\begin{aligned} a_1x + b_1y &= c_1 \\ a_2x + b_2y &= c_2 \end{aligned}$$ has a solution given by

$$x = \frac{\begin{vmatrix} c_1 & b_1 \\ c_2 & b_2 \end{vmatrix}}{\begin{vmatrix} a_1 & b_1 \\ a_2 & b_2 \end{vmatrix}} \text{ and } y = \frac{\begin{vmatrix} a_1 & c_1 \\ a_2 & c_2 \end{vmatrix}}{\begin{vmatrix} a_1 & b_1 \\ a_2 & b_2 \end{vmatrix}}, \text{ where} \begin{vmatrix} a_1 & b_1 \\ a_2 & b_2 \end{vmatrix} \neq 0$$

Note that the denominator is the same for both variables, and it contains the coefficients of x and y in the same position as in the original equations. We refer to this determinant as $\boldsymbol{D}$.

For x, the numerator is obtained by replacing the x-coefficients (the a's) in D by the constants (the c's). For y, the numerator is obtained by replacing the y-coefficients (the b's) in D by the c's.

If $D = 0$, then one of these situations occurs:

1. If $D = 0$ and the determinants of the numerators are also 0, then the system of equations is dependent.
2. If $D = 0$ and at least one of the other determinants is nonzero, then the system is inconsistent.

EXAMPLE 2 Solve using Cramer's rule.

$$\begin{aligned} 2x + 5y &= 7 \\ 4x - 2y &= -3 \end{aligned}$$

$$D = \begin{vmatrix} 2 & 5 \\ 4 & -2 \end{vmatrix} = 2(-2) - 4(5) = -24.$$

$$x = \frac{\begin{vmatrix} 7 & 5 \\ -3 & -2 \end{vmatrix}}{-24} \qquad y = \frac{\begin{vmatrix} 2 & 7 \\ 4 & -3 \end{vmatrix}}{-24}$$

$$x = \frac{7(-2) - (-3)(5)}{-24} \qquad y = \frac{2(-3) - 4(7)}{-24}$$

$$x = \frac{-1}{24} \qquad y = \frac{17}{12}$$

The solution is $\left(-\frac{1}{24}, \frac{17}{12}\right)$.

Try This Solve using Cramer's rule.

d. $2x - y = 5$
$x - 2y = 1$

e. $3x + 4y = -2$
$5x - 7y = 1$

PART 3 Determinants of 3 × 3 Matrices

Objective: Evaluate a 3 × 3 determinant.

Definition

The **determinant** of a 3 × 3 matrix is defined as follows.

$$\begin{vmatrix} a_1 & b_1 & c_1 \\ a_2 & b_2 & c_2 \\ a_3 & b_3 & c_3 \end{vmatrix} = a_1 \cdot \begin{vmatrix} b_2 & c_2 \\ b_3 & c_3 \end{vmatrix} - a_2 \cdot \begin{vmatrix} b_1 & c_1 \\ b_3 & c_3 \end{vmatrix} + a_3 \cdot \begin{vmatrix} b_1 & c_1 \\ b_2 & c_2 \end{vmatrix}$$

$$= a_1b_2c_3 - a_1b_3c_2 - a_2b_1c_3 + a_2b_3c_1 + a_3b_1c_2 - a_3b_2c_1$$

Each 2 × 2 determinant may be obtained by crossing out the row and column in which the a-coefficient occurs.

$$a_1 \begin{vmatrix} a_1 & b_1 & c_1 \\ a_2 & b_2 & c_2 \\ a_3 & b_3 & c_3 \end{vmatrix} - a_2 \begin{vmatrix} a_1 & b_1 & c_1 \\ a_2 & b_2 & c_2 \\ a_3 & b_3 & c_3 \end{vmatrix} + a_3 \begin{vmatrix} a_1 & b_1 & c_1 \\ a_2 & b_2 & c_2 \\ a_3 & b_3 & c_3 \end{vmatrix}$$

EXAMPLE 3 Evaluate.

$$\begin{vmatrix} -1 & 0 & 1 \\ -5 & 1 & -1 \\ 4 & 8 & 1 \end{vmatrix} = -1 \cdot \begin{vmatrix} 1 & -1 \\ 8 & 1 \end{vmatrix} - (-5) \cdot \begin{vmatrix} 0 & 1 \\ 8 & 1 \end{vmatrix} + 4 \cdot \begin{vmatrix} 0 & 1 \\ 1 & -1 \end{vmatrix}$$

$$= -1(1 + 8) + 5(0 - 8) + 4(0 - 1) = -53$$

EXAMPLE 4 Evaluate.

$$\begin{vmatrix} -3 & 3 & 0 \\ 1 & -6 & 1 \\ -1 & 0 & -3 \end{vmatrix} = -3\begin{vmatrix} -6 & 1 \\ 0 & -3 \end{vmatrix} - 1\begin{vmatrix} 3 & 0 \\ 0 & -3 \end{vmatrix} + (-1)\begin{vmatrix} 3 & 0 \\ -6 & 1 \end{vmatrix}$$

$$a_1b_2c_3 - a_1b_3c_2 - a_2b_1c_3 + a_2b_3c_1 + a_3b_1c_2 - a_3b_2c_1$$

$$= -54 - 0 - (-9) + 0 + (-3) - 0 = -48$$

Try This Evaluate.

f. $\begin{vmatrix} 3 & 2 & 2 \\ -2 & 1 & 4 \\ 4 & -3 & 3 \end{vmatrix}$

g. $\begin{vmatrix} -5 & 0 & 0 \\ 4 & 2 & 0 \\ -3 & 5 & -6 \end{vmatrix}$

h. $\begin{vmatrix} 5 & 0 & 5 \\ 0 & 5 & 0 \\ 1 & 0 & 5 \end{vmatrix}$

Cramer's Rule for Three Equations

Objective: Solve a system of three equations in three variables using Cramer's rule.

Cramer's rule uses determinants to solve systems of three equations the same way we solved systems of two equations.

Theorem 13-4

Cramer's Rule (3 Equations)

The system of three equations in three variables

$$\begin{aligned} a_1x + b_1y + c_1z &= \mathbf{d_1} \\ a_2x + b_2y + c_2z &= \mathbf{d_2} \\ a_3x + b_3y + c_3z &= \mathbf{d_3} \end{aligned} \quad \text{has a solution given by}$$

$$x = \frac{D_x}{D},\ y = \frac{D_y}{D},\ z = \frac{D_z}{D},\ \text{where } D = \begin{vmatrix} a_1 & b_1 & c_1 \\ a_2 & b_2 & c_2 \\ a_3 & b_3 & c_3 \end{vmatrix},\ D \neq 0,$$

$$D_x = \begin{vmatrix} \mathbf{d_1} & b_1 & c_1 \\ \mathbf{d_2} & b_2 & c_2 \\ \mathbf{d_3} & b_3 & c_3 \end{vmatrix},\ D_y = \begin{vmatrix} a_1 & \mathbf{d_1} & c_1 \\ a_2 & \mathbf{d_2} & c_2 \\ a_3 & \mathbf{d_3} & c_3 \end{vmatrix},\ \text{and } D_z = \begin{vmatrix} a_1 & b_1 & \mathbf{d_1} \\ a_2 & b_2 & \mathbf{d_2} \\ a_3 & b_3 & \mathbf{d_3} \end{vmatrix}$$

Note that we obtain the determinant D_x, the numerator of x, by substituting the constants d_1, d_2, and d_3 for the x-coefficients. We obtain D_y and D_z similarly. We have thus extended Cramer's rule to solve systems of three equations in three variables.

EXAMPLE 5 Solve using Cramer's rule.

$$\begin{aligned} x - 3y + 7z &= 13 \\ x + y + z &= 1 \\ x - 2y + 3z &= 4 \end{aligned}$$

$$D = \begin{vmatrix} 1 & -3 & 7 \\ 1 & 1 & 1 \\ 1 & -2 & 3 \end{vmatrix} = -10 \quad D_x = \begin{vmatrix} 13 & -3 & 7 \\ 1 & 1 & 1 \\ 4 & -2 & 3 \end{vmatrix} = 20$$

$$D_y = \begin{vmatrix} 1 & 13 & 7 \\ 1 & 1 & 1 \\ 1 & 4 & 3 \end{vmatrix} = -6 \quad D_z = \begin{vmatrix} 1 & -3 & 13 \\ 1 & 1 & 1 \\ 1 & -2 & 4 \end{vmatrix} = -24$$

$$x = \frac{D_x}{D} = \frac{20}{-10} = -2,\ y = \frac{D_y}{D} = \frac{-6}{-10} = \frac{3}{5},\ z = \frac{D_z}{D} = \frac{-24}{-10} = \frac{12}{5}$$

The solution is $\left(-2, \frac{3}{5}, \frac{12}{5}\right)$. In practice, it is not necessary to evaluate D_z. When we find values for x and y we can substitute them into an equation to find z.

Try This Solve using Cramer's rule.

i. $x - 3y - 7z = 6$
$2x + 3y + z = 9$
$4x + y = 7$

j. $x + 2y - z = 2$
$2x - 2y + z = -1$
$6x + 4y + 3z = 5$

Extra Help On the Web

Look for worked-out examples at the Prentice Hall Web site.
www.phschool.com

13-3 Exercises

A

Evaluate.

1. $\begin{vmatrix} 2 & 7 \\ 1 & 5 \end{vmatrix}$ **2.** $\begin{vmatrix} 3 & 2 \\ 2 & -3 \end{vmatrix}$ **3.** $\begin{vmatrix} 6 & -9 \\ 2 & 3 \end{vmatrix}$ **4.** $\begin{vmatrix} 3 & 2 \\ -7 & 5 \end{vmatrix}$

5. $\begin{vmatrix} 1.3 & 2.7 \\ 4.2 & 0.8 \end{vmatrix}$ **6.** $\begin{vmatrix} 2.4 & 1.6 \\ 0.9 & 1.8 \end{vmatrix}$ **7.** $\begin{vmatrix} -7 & -7 \\ 3 & 3 \end{vmatrix}$ **8.** $\begin{vmatrix} 8 & -1 \\ 8 & -1 \end{vmatrix}$

Solve using Cramer's rule.

9. $3x - 4y = 6$
$5x + 9y = 10$

10. $5x + 8y = 1$
$3x + 7y = 5$

11. $2x - 2y = 2$
$6x - 5y = 1$

12. $5x - 6y = 8$
$2x - 5y = -2$

13. $4x - 4y = 4$
$7x + 2y = 1$

14. $-2x + 4y = 3$
$3x - 7y = 1$

Evaluate.

15. $\begin{vmatrix} 0 & 2 & 0 \\ 3 & -1 & 1 \\ 1 & -2 & 2 \end{vmatrix}$ **16.** $\begin{vmatrix} 3 & 0 & -2 \\ 5 & 1 & 2 \\ 2 & 0 & -1 \end{vmatrix}$ **17.** $\begin{vmatrix} -1 & -2 & -3 \\ 3 & 4 & 2 \\ 0 & 1 & 2 \end{vmatrix}$

18. $\begin{vmatrix} 1 & 2 & 2 \\ 2 & 1 & 0 \\ 3 & 3 & 1 \end{vmatrix}$ **19.** $\begin{vmatrix} 3 & -2 & -2 \\ -2 & 1 & -4 \\ 4 & -3 & 3 \end{vmatrix}$ **20.** $\begin{vmatrix} 2 & -1 & 1 \\ 1 & 2 & -1 \\ 3 & 4 & -3 \end{vmatrix}$

Solve using Cramer's rule.

21. $2x - 3y + 5z = 27$
$x + 2y - z = -4$
$5x - y + 4z = 27$

22. $x - y + 2z = -3$
$x + 2y + 3z = 4$
$2x + y + z = -3$

23. $r - 2s + 3t = 6$
$2r - s - t = -3$
$r + s + t = 6$

24. $a - 3c = 6$
$b + 2c = 2$
$7a - 3b - 5c = 14$

25. $3x + 2y - z = 4$
$3x - 2y + z = 5$
$4x - 5y - z = -1$

26. $3x - y + 2z = 1$
$x - y + 2z = 3$
$-2x + 3y + z = 1$

27. ***Write a Convincing Argument*** Write an argument to convince a classmate that Cramer's rule cannot be used to solve a system of equations where the number of variables does not equal the number of equations.

B

Evaluate.

28. $\begin{vmatrix} x & 4 \\ x & x^2 \end{vmatrix}$ **29.** $\begin{vmatrix} y^2 & -2 \\ y & 3 \end{vmatrix}$ **30.** $\begin{vmatrix} z & -3 \\ z^2 & 1 \end{vmatrix}$

Solve for x.

31. $\begin{vmatrix} 4 & 2 \\ 3 & x \end{vmatrix} = x$ **32.** $\begin{vmatrix} x & 5 \\ -4 & x \end{vmatrix} = 24$ **33.** $\begin{vmatrix} x+3 & 4 \\ x-3 & 5 \end{vmatrix} = -7$

34. **TEST PREP** What is the value of $\begin{vmatrix} 1 & x \\ -1 & x \end{vmatrix}$?

A. x^2 **B.** $-x$ **C.** $-2x$ **D.** $2x$

35. Solve using Cramer's rule. $\sqrt{3}\,x + \pi y = -5$
$\pi x - 3y = 4$

36. ***Error Analysis*** Jean wrote the determinant $D = \begin{vmatrix} 1 & -1 \\ -1 & 1 \end{vmatrix}$ for the system $\begin{matrix} x - y = 4 \\ 3 - x = y \end{matrix}$. What error(s) did he make?

37. ***Critical Thinking*** Is a determinant a *function* of an $n \times n$ matrix? Explain.

Challenge

38. Evaluate. $\begin{vmatrix} 1 & x & y \\ 1 & x & y \\ 1 & 1 & 1 \end{vmatrix}$ **39.** Verify. $\begin{vmatrix} 1 & x & x^2 \\ 1 & y & y^2 \\ 1 & z & z^2 \end{vmatrix} = (x - y)(y - z)(z - x)$

40. Use linear combinations to prove Cramer's rule for a system of two equations. That is, verify that the solution of the system

$\begin{matrix} a_1x + b_1y = c_1 \\ a_2x + b_2y = c_2 \end{matrix}$ is given by $x = \dfrac{c_1b_2 - c_2b_1}{a_1b_2 - a_2b_1}$ and $y = \dfrac{a_1c_2 - a_2c_1}{a_1b_2 - a_2b_1}$

when $a_1b_2 - a_2b_1 \neq 0$.

41. Rewrite each expression as a determinant two different ways.

a. $2l + w$ **b.** $a^2 + b^2$

42. Find the determinant of A^t for $A = \begin{bmatrix} a_1 & b_1 & c_1 \\ a_2 & b_2 & c_2 \\ a_3 & b_3 & c_3 \end{bmatrix}$. What is true of the determinant of a transposed matrix? (See Lesson 13-2, Exercise 30.)

Mixed Review

Solve. **43.** $v^{\frac{4}{3}} = 16$ **44.** $\frac{6}{y} + \frac{2y}{3} = 5$ **45.** $z^{\frac{2}{3}} - 2z^{\frac{1}{3}} - 48 = 0$

46. $3(x^2 - 2x + 5) - 2(3x - 5) = 4(x^2 - x - 5) - (x^2 + 3)$ *8-3, 8-5*

Divide. **47.** $(y^5 - 2y^4 - 2y^3 + 9y^2 - 10) \div (y^2 - 2)$ *11-1*

Check your progress. Look for a self-test at the Prentice Hall Web site.
www.phschool.com

13-4 Multiplying Matrices

What You'll Learn

1. To find the product of a scalar and a matrix, and the product of two matrices
2. To write a matrix equation equivalent to a system of equations

. . . And Why

To solve systems of equations using matrix multiplication and inverse matrices

PART 1 Multiplying Matrices

Objective: Find the product of a scalar and a matrix, and the product of two matrices.

There are two kinds of products involving matrices. First we define a product of a matrix and a number.

Definition

The **scalar product** of a real number k, called a scalar, and a matrix A is the matrix, denoted kA, obtained by multiplying each number in A by the number k.

EXAMPLES Multiply.

1 $3\begin{bmatrix} -3 & 0 \\ 4 & 5 \end{bmatrix} = \begin{bmatrix} -9 & 0 \\ 12 & 15 \end{bmatrix}$

2 $-\frac{1}{2}\begin{bmatrix} -3 & 0 \\ 4 & 5 \end{bmatrix} = \begin{bmatrix} \frac{3}{2} & 0 \\ -2 & -\frac{5}{2} \end{bmatrix}$

Try This Multiply.

a. $5\begin{bmatrix} 1 & -2 & x \\ 4 & y & 1 \\ 0 & -5 & x^2 \end{bmatrix}$

b. $-3t\begin{bmatrix} 1 & -1 & 4 & x \\ y & 3 & -2 & y \\ 1 & 4 & -5 & y \end{bmatrix}$

Now we consider the product of two matrices. We do not multiply two matrices by multiplying their corresponding members. The motivation for defining matrix products comes from systems of equations.

Let us begin by considering a system of equations.

$$\begin{aligned} 3x + 2y - 2z &= 4 \\ 2x - y + 5z &= 3 \\ -x + y + 4z &= 7 \end{aligned}$$

Consider the following equation involving the matrices A, X, and B.

$$\underset{A}{\begin{bmatrix} 3 & 2 & -2 \\ 2 & -1 & 5 \\ -1 & 1 & 4 \end{bmatrix}} \cdot \underset{X}{\begin{bmatrix} x \\ y \\ z \end{bmatrix}} = \underset{B}{\begin{bmatrix} 4 \\ 3 \\ 7 \end{bmatrix}}$$

The expression $3x + 2y - 2z$ is the sum of the pair-wise products of the first row of A and the column matrix X. Note that the first member of the first row of A (3) and the first member of X (x) are multiplied, the second members (2 and y) are multiplied, the third members (-2 and z) are multiplied, and the results are added to get a single expression with three terms.

If we multiply the second row of A by X in the same way, we get $2x - y + 5z$. If we then multiply the third row of A by X, we get $-x + y + 4z$.

We define the product AX to be the following 3×1 column matrix made up of these expressions.

$$\begin{bmatrix} 3x + 2y - 2z \\ 2x - y + 5z \\ -x + y + 4z \end{bmatrix}$$

Now consider this matrix equation.

$$\begin{bmatrix} 3x + 2y - 2z \\ 2x - y + 5z \\ -x + y + 4z \end{bmatrix} = \begin{bmatrix} 4 \\ 3 \\ 7 \end{bmatrix}$$

Two matrices are equal if their corresponding elements are equal. This means that $3x + 2y - 2z$ is 4, $2x - y + 5z$ is 3, and $-x + y + 4z$ is 7.

Thus the matrix equation $AX = B$ is equivalent to the original system of equations below.

$$\begin{aligned} 3x + 2y - 2z &= 4 \\ 2x - y + 5z &= 3, \\ -x + y + 4z &= 7 \end{aligned}$$

Quick Review

Remember that an algebraic expression is different from an algebraic equation.

EXAMPLE 3 Multiply.

$$\begin{bmatrix} 3 & 1 & -1 \\ 1 & 2 & 2 \\ -1 & 0 & 5 \\ 4 & 1 & 2 \end{bmatrix} \begin{bmatrix} 1 \\ 2 \\ 1 \end{bmatrix} = \begin{bmatrix} 3 \cdot 1 + 1 \cdot 2 - 1 \cdot 1 \\ 1 \cdot 1 + 2 \cdot 2 + 2 \cdot 1 \\ -1 \cdot 1 + 0 \cdot 2 + 5 \cdot 1 \\ 4 \cdot 1 + 1 \cdot 2 + 2 \cdot 1 \end{bmatrix} = \begin{bmatrix} 4 \\ 7 \\ 4 \\ 8 \end{bmatrix}$$

Try This Multiply.

c. $\begin{bmatrix} 1 & 4 & 2 \\ -1 & 6 & 3 \\ 3 & 2 & -1 \\ 5 & 0 & 2 \end{bmatrix} \begin{bmatrix} 2 \\ 1 \\ 3 \end{bmatrix}$

In the examples discussed so far, the second matrix had only one column. If it has more than one column, we multiply each row of the first matrix by each column of the second matrix separately. The product matrix will have as many columns as the second matrix.

EXAMPLE 4 Multiply. (Compare with Example 3.)

$$\begin{bmatrix} 3 & 1 & -1 \\ 1 & 2 & 2 \\ -1 & 0 & 5 \\ 4 & 1 & 2 \end{bmatrix} \begin{bmatrix} 1 & 0 \\ 2 & 1 \\ 1 & 3 \end{bmatrix} = \begin{bmatrix} 4 & 3\cdot 0 + 1\cdot 1 + (-1)\cdot 3 \\ 7 & 1\cdot 0 + 2\cdot 1 + 2\cdot 3 \\ 4 & -1\cdot 0 + 0\cdot 1 + 5\cdot 3 \\ 8 & 4\cdot 0 + 1\cdot 1 + 2\cdot 3 \end{bmatrix} = \begin{bmatrix} 4 & -2 \\ 7 & 8 \\ 4 & 15 \\ 8 & 7 \end{bmatrix}$$

A B

Same as in Example 3

The rows of A multiplied by the second column of B

EXAMPLE 5 Multiply.

$$\begin{bmatrix} 3 & 1 & -1 \\ 2 & 0 & 3 \end{bmatrix} \begin{bmatrix} 1 & 4 & 6 \\ 3 & -1 & 9 \\ 2 & 5 & 1 \end{bmatrix}$$

$$= \begin{bmatrix} 3\cdot 1 + 1\cdot 3 - 1\cdot 2 & 3\cdot 4 + 1(-1) - 1\cdot 5 & 3\cdot 6 + 1\cdot 9 - 1\cdot 1 \\ 2\cdot 1 + 0\cdot 3 + 3\cdot 2 & 2\cdot 4 + 0\cdot(-1) + 3\cdot 5 & 2\cdot 6 + 0\cdot 9 + 3\cdot 1 \end{bmatrix}$$

$$= \begin{bmatrix} 4 & 6 & 26 \\ 8 & 23 & 15 \end{bmatrix}$$

Try This Multiply.

d. $\begin{bmatrix} 4 & 1 & 2 \\ -3 & 2 & 3 \\ 2 & 0 & 5 \\ 3 & 1 & 4 \end{bmatrix} \begin{bmatrix} 1 & 4 \\ 2 & 0 \\ -3 & 5 \end{bmatrix}$

e. $\begin{bmatrix} 4 & 1 & 0 & 2 \end{bmatrix} \begin{bmatrix} 1 & 0 & 1 \\ 2 & -1 & 0 \\ 3 & 5 & 1 \\ 1 & 3 & 0 \end{bmatrix}$

If matrix A has n columns and matrix B has n rows, then we can compute the product AB, regardless of the other dimensions. The product will have as many rows as A and as many columns as B. The element in row i, column j, of the product AB is found by multiplying the elements in row i of A by the elements in column j of B, and adding.

Theorem 13-5

The product of an $m \times n$ matrix and an $n \times p$ matrix is an $m \times p$ matrix.

$$\begin{array}{ccccc} A & \times & B & = & AB \\ (m) \times n & & n \times (p) & & (m) \times (p) \end{array}$$

Consider the matrices $A = \begin{bmatrix} 3 & 1 & -1 \\ 2 & 0 & 3 \end{bmatrix}$ and $B = \begin{bmatrix} 1 & 4 & 6 \\ 3 & -1 & 9 \\ 2 & 5 & 1 \end{bmatrix}$.

$A + B$ and $A - B$ do not exist because the dimensions of A and B are not the same. AB does exist because the number of columns in A, 3, is the same as the number of rows in B, 3. But BA does not exist because the number of columns in B, 3, is not the same as the number of rows in A, 2. Since AB exists, and BA does not, matrix multiplication is not commutative.

EXAMPLES Find the product, if possible.

$$A = \begin{bmatrix} -2 & 3 & 1 \\ 1 & 0 & 4 \end{bmatrix} \qquad B = \begin{bmatrix} -2 & 0 & -1 \\ 1 & 5 & 6 \\ 0 & 2 & 3 \end{bmatrix}$$

6

$$AB = \begin{bmatrix} -2 & 3 & 1 \\ 1 & 0 & 4 \end{bmatrix}\begin{bmatrix} -2 & 0 & -1 \\ 1 & 5 & 6 \\ 0 & 2 & 3 \end{bmatrix}$$

$$= \begin{bmatrix} 7 & 17 & 23 \\ -2 & 8 & 11 \end{bmatrix}$$

7 BA We cannot find BA since B has 3 columns and A has only 2 rows.

Try This Find each product, if possible.

$$A = \begin{bmatrix} -2 & 4 & 0 \\ -3 & 0 & -8 \end{bmatrix} \qquad B = \begin{bmatrix} -1 & -2 & -3 \\ 0 & 1 & 0 \\ 4 & 5 & 2 \end{bmatrix} \qquad C = \begin{bmatrix} 1 & -1 \\ 2 & -1 \end{bmatrix}$$

f. AB **g.** AC **h.** CA

PART 2 Equivalent Matrix Equations

Objective: Write a matrix equation equivalent to a system of equations.

For later purposes it is important to be able to write a matrix equation equivalent to a system of equations.

EXAMPLE 8 Write a matrix equation equivalent to this system of equations.

$$4x + 2y - z = 3$$
$$9x + z = 5$$
$$4x + 5y - 2z = 1$$
$$x + y + z = 0$$

We write the coefficients on the left in a matrix. We write the product of that matrix by the column matrix containing the variables, and set the result equal to the column matrix containing the constants on the right.

$$\begin{bmatrix} 4 & 2 & -1 \\ 9 & 0 & 1 \\ 4 & 5 & -2 \\ 1 & 1 & 1 \end{bmatrix}\begin{bmatrix} x \\ y \\ z \end{bmatrix} = \begin{bmatrix} 3 \\ 5 \\ 1 \\ 0 \end{bmatrix}$$

Try This Write a matrix equation equivalent to each system of equations.

i. $3x + 4y - 2z = 5$
$2x - 2y + 5z = 3$
$6x + 7y - z = 0$

j. $5x + 7y = 19$
$3x - 2y + z = 1$
$-2x + 3y - z = -12$

k. $3v + 2x - 7y = 13$
$w - 2x = 0$
$5v + 5w - 3y = -5$
$10x - 3y = 15$
$v - x - y = 2$

l. $4w + 1 = 0$
$4w + x + 3 = 0$
$4w + 2x + y + 6 = 0$
$4w + 3x + 2y + z + 10 = 0$

The following theorem summarizes some of the properties of matrices whose elements are real numbers. The theorem supposes that the matrices have the appropriate dimensions so that all additions and multiplications are possible. Some of the proofs will be considered in the Challenge Exercises. Note that not all field properties hold.

Theorem 13-6

For any matrices A, B, and C of dimensions appropriate for them to be added or multiplied, the following properties hold.

Commutative Property of Addition

$$A + B = B + A$$

Associative Properties

$$A + (B + C) = (A + B) + C; \quad A(BC) = (AB)C$$

Additive Identity

There exists a unique matrix O, such that

$$A + O = O + A = A.$$

Additive Inverse

There exists a unique matrix $-A$, such that

$$A + (-A) = -A + A = O.$$

Distributive Property

$$A(B + C) = AB + AC$$

For any real numbers k and m,

$$k(A + B) = kA + kB$$
$$(k + m)A = kA + mA$$
$$(km)A = k(mA).$$

13-4 Exercises

Extra Help On the Web

Look for worked-out examples at the Prentice Hall Web site.
www.phschool.com

A

For Exercises 1–28, let

$A = \begin{bmatrix} 1 & 2 \\ 4 & 3 \end{bmatrix}$ $B = \begin{bmatrix} -3 & 5 \\ 2 & -1 \end{bmatrix}$ $C = \begin{bmatrix} 1 & -1 \\ -1 & 1 \end{bmatrix}$ $D = \begin{bmatrix} 1 & 1 \\ 1 & 1 \end{bmatrix}$

$E = \begin{bmatrix} 1 & 3 \\ 2 & 6 \end{bmatrix}$ $F = \begin{bmatrix} 3 & 3 \\ -1 & -1 \end{bmatrix}$ $I = \begin{bmatrix} 1 & 0 \\ 0 & 1 \end{bmatrix}$ $G = \begin{bmatrix} 1 & 0 & -2 \\ 0 & -1 & 3 \\ 3 & 2 & 4 \end{bmatrix}$

$H = \begin{bmatrix} -1 & -2 & 5 \\ 1 & 0 & -1 \\ 2 & -3 & 1 \end{bmatrix}$ $J = [-2 \quad 3 \quad -4]$ $K = [8 \quad -1]$ $L = [-1 \quad -2 \quad -3 \quad 4]$

$M = \begin{bmatrix} -2 \\ -4 \\ 7 \end{bmatrix}$ $N = \begin{bmatrix} 8 \\ -6 \\ \frac{1}{2} \end{bmatrix}$ $P = \begin{bmatrix} -3 \\ -2 \end{bmatrix}$ $Q = \begin{bmatrix} 10 \\ -4 \\ 5 \\ 2 \end{bmatrix}$ $Z = \begin{bmatrix} -2 & 9 & 6 \\ -3 & 3 & 4 \\ 2 & -2 & 1 \end{bmatrix}$

Mental Math Multiply.

1. $(-2)A$ **2.** $(-5)B$ **3.** $14C$ **4.** $12D$
5. tE **6.** pF **7.** $(-1)Z$ **8.** $(-1)H$

Find each product, if possible.

9. KP **10.** JM **11.** JN **12.** LQ
13. AB **14.** BC **15.** CD **16.** EF
17. JG **18.** KF **19.** JZ **20.** FP
21. FI **22.** IB **23.** GH **24.** HG
25. AP **26.** KC **27.** HA **28.** CG

Write a matrix equation equivalent to each of the following systems of equations.

29. $3x - 2y + 4z = 17$
$2x + y - 5z = 13$

30. $3x + 2y + 5z = 9$
$4x - 3y + 2z = 10$

31. $x - y + 2z - 4w = 12$
$2x - y - z + w = 0$
$x + 4y - 3z - w = 1$
$3x + 5y - 7z + 2w = 9$

32. $2x + 4y - 5z + 12w = 2$
$4x - y + 12z - w = 5$
$-x + 4y + 2w = 13$
$2x + 10y + z = 5$

B

33. For $A = \begin{bmatrix} 3 & 1 & 0 \\ 6 & 4 & 0 \\ 2 & 3 & 1 \end{bmatrix}$ and $B = \begin{bmatrix} 2 & 1 & 0 \\ 3 & 3 & 9 \\ 6 & 4 & 6 \end{bmatrix}$, find $3A + 2B$ and $B - 2A$.

34. ***Mathematical Reasoning*** For $A = \begin{bmatrix} 3 & 2 \\ -1 & 5 \end{bmatrix}$ and $I = \begin{bmatrix} 1 & 0 \\ 0 & 1 \end{bmatrix}$, find AI and IA. What can you conclude about matrix I?

35. Factor $\begin{bmatrix} \frac{1}{24} & -\frac{1}{6} & \frac{3}{8} \\ \frac{5}{12} & -\frac{1}{2} & \frac{7}{36} \end{bmatrix}$ so that all matrix elements are integers.

Do the following products exist? If they do, determine how many rows and columns are in the product matrix. Do not carry out the multiplication.

36. $\begin{bmatrix} 3 & 6 & 1 \\ 4 & 9 & 0 \\ 2 & 8 & 3 \end{bmatrix} \begin{bmatrix} 2 & 3 & 6 \\ 4 & 9 & 1 \end{bmatrix}$

37. $\begin{bmatrix} 4 & 3 & 2 & 1 & 5 \\ 6 & 9 & 3 & 25 & 6 \\ 4 & 18 & 2 & 18 & 2 \\ 3 & 6 & 1 & 1 & 2 \\ 2 & 4 & 8 & 25 & 23 \end{bmatrix} \begin{bmatrix} 6 & 3 & 7 & 9 & 11 & 24 \\ 4 & 7 & 59 & 8 & 2 & 12 \\ 3 & 2 & 6 & 0 & 1 & 7 \\ 2 & 19 & 4 & 2 & 4 & 1 \\ 1 & 23 & 3 & 9 & 0 & 1 \end{bmatrix}$

38. Is it *sometimes*, *always*, or *never* true that, if A and B both have dimensions $n \times n$, $AB = BA$?

39. ***Critical Thinking*** If for two matrices A and B, both AB and BA exist, what can you determine about A, B, and their products?

Challenge

40. ***Write a Convincing Argument*** $A = \begin{bmatrix} -1 & 0 \\ 2 & 1 \end{bmatrix}$ and $B = \begin{bmatrix} 1 & -1 \\ 0 & 2 \end{bmatrix}$

a. Show that $(A + B)(A - B) \neq A^2 - B^2$, where $A^2 = AA$ and $B^2 = BB$.

b. Show that $(A + B)(A + B) \neq A^2 + 2AB + B^2$.

c. Explain in writing why these formulas do not work for matrices.

For Exercises 41–46, let $A = \begin{bmatrix} a & c \\ b & d \end{bmatrix}$, $B = \begin{bmatrix} e & g \\ f & h \end{bmatrix}$, and $C = \begin{bmatrix} p & r \\ q & s \end{bmatrix}$. Prove.

41. $A + B = B + A$

42. $(A + B) + C = A + (B + C)$

43. $A - B = A + (-B)$

44. $(-1)A = -A$

45. $k(A + B) = kA + kB$

46. $(k + m)A = kA + mA$

Mixed Review

Simplify. **47.** $(x^2 - 3y)^2$ **48.** $x^2(-3y)^2x^{-3}(-y)^{-2}$ **49.** $\left(\frac{8m^3n^{-2}}{27n^4z^7}\right)^{\frac{2}{3}}$ *1-8*

Let $P(x) = 2x^4 + 3x^3 + 6x^2 + 12x - 8$.

50. List the possible rational roots of $P(x)$ and the number of positive and negative real roots. *11-3*

51. Solve $P(x) = 0$.

52. Find $P(3)$, $P(-1)$, $P(0)$, $P(0.5)$. *11-5*

53. The length of a rectangular swimming pool is 12 m longer than the width. The area is 325 m^2. Find the length and width. *8-6*

Inverses of Matrices

13-5

What You'll Learn

1. To determine whether two matrices are multiplicative inverses
2. To find the multiplicative inverse of a 2×2 matrix

... And Why

To solve systems of equations by using the multiplicative inverse of a matrix

Introducing the Concept: The Multiplicative Inverse of a Matrix

Let $A = \begin{bmatrix} 2 & 7 \\ 1 & 4 \end{bmatrix}$, $B = \begin{bmatrix} 1 & 0 \\ 0 & 1 \end{bmatrix}$, and $C = \begin{bmatrix} 4 & -7 \\ -1 & 2 \end{bmatrix}$.

Find AB, BA, AC, and CA. What relationships do you see?

PART 1 Inverses

Objective: Determine whether two matrices are inverses.

Square matrices with 1s from the upper left to the lower right along the main diagonal and zeros elsewhere are represented by the symbol I. A matrix I is an **identity matrix.**

Theorem 13-7

For any $n \times n$ matrices A and I, $AI = IA = A$
(I is a multiplicative identity).

Suppose a matrix A has a **multiplicative inverse** or simply an **inverse, A^{-1}.** Then A^{-1} is a matrix for which $A \cdot A^{-1} = A^{-1} \cdot A = I$.

EXAMPLE 1 Determine whether A and B are inverses.

$$A = \begin{bmatrix} 4 & 6 \\ 3 & 1 \end{bmatrix} \qquad B = \begin{bmatrix} -\frac{1}{14} & \frac{3}{7} \\ \frac{3}{14} & -\frac{2}{7} \end{bmatrix}$$

We can test whether $AB = BA = I$ by multiplying.

$$AB = \begin{bmatrix} 4 & 6 \\ 3 & 1 \end{bmatrix} \begin{bmatrix} -\frac{1}{14} & \frac{3}{7} \\ \frac{3}{14} & -\frac{2}{7} \end{bmatrix} = \begin{bmatrix} -\frac{1}{14} & \frac{3}{7} \\ \frac{3}{14} & -\frac{2}{7} \end{bmatrix} \begin{bmatrix} 4 & 6 \\ 3 & 1 \end{bmatrix} = \begin{bmatrix} 1 & 0 \\ 0 & 1 \end{bmatrix}$$

A and B are inverses. Thus $B = A^{-1}$, and $A = B^{-1}$.

Try This Determine whether A and B are inverses.

a. $A = \begin{bmatrix} 5 & -3 \\ -7 & 4 \end{bmatrix}$ $\quad B = \begin{bmatrix} -4 & 3 \\ -7 & 5 \end{bmatrix}$

b. $A = \begin{bmatrix} 3 & 1 & 0 \\ 1 & -1 & 2 \\ 1 & 1 & 1 \end{bmatrix}$ $\quad B = \begin{bmatrix} \frac{3}{8} & \frac{1}{8} & -\frac{2}{8} \\ -\frac{1}{8} & -\frac{3}{8} & \frac{6}{8} \\ -\frac{2}{8} & \frac{2}{8} & \frac{4}{8} \end{bmatrix}$

PART 2 Inverses of 2 × 2 Matrices

Objective: Find the inverse of a 2 × 2 matrix.

We can find the inverse of any 2 × 2 matrix, if it exists, using the following theorem.

Theorem 13-8

If $A = \begin{bmatrix} a & b \\ c & d \end{bmatrix}$ and $|A| \neq 0$, then $A^{-1} = \frac{1}{|A|}\begin{bmatrix} d & -b \\ -c & a \end{bmatrix}$

If the determinant of A is nonzero, then A^{-1} exists.

EXAMPLES Find A^{-1}, if it exists.

2 $A = \begin{bmatrix} 2 & 1 \\ 4 & 0 \end{bmatrix}$ $\quad a = 2 \quad b = 1$, $c = 4 \quad d = 0$

First find $|A|$.

$$|A| = 2 \cdot 0 - 4 \cdot 1 = -4$$

Since $|A| \neq 0$, we know A^{-1} exists.

Next, we interchange a and d and find the additive inverses of b and c.

$\begin{bmatrix} 0 & -1 \\ -4 & 2 \end{bmatrix}$ $\quad d = 0 \quad -b = -1$, $-c = -4 \quad a = 2$

We multiply by $\frac{1}{|A|}$ or $-\frac{1}{4}$.

Thus $A^{-1} = -\frac{1}{4}\begin{bmatrix} 0 & -1 \\ -4 & 2 \end{bmatrix} = \begin{bmatrix} 0 & \frac{1}{4} \\ 1 & -\frac{1}{2} \end{bmatrix}$.

We can verify this by finding $A \cdot A^{-1}$.

3 $A = \begin{bmatrix} 3 & 6 \\ -1 & -2 \end{bmatrix}$ We find $|A| = 0$. Thus A^{-1} does not exist.

Try This Find A^{-1}, if it exists.

c. $A = \begin{bmatrix} 5 & 10 \\ 2 & 4 \end{bmatrix}$ $\quad$ **d.** $A = \begin{bmatrix} 1 & 3 \\ -1 & 2 \end{bmatrix}$ $\quad$ **e.** $A = \begin{bmatrix} 3 & 5 \\ -3 & 5 \end{bmatrix}$

Proof of Theorem 13-8

Consider the 2×2 matrix $A = \begin{bmatrix} a & b \\ c & d \end{bmatrix}$. If A^{-1} exists, it is a matrix $\begin{bmatrix} x & y \\ w & z \end{bmatrix}$ such that $A \cdot A^{-1} = I$.

Thus $\begin{bmatrix} a & b \\ c & d \end{bmatrix}\begin{bmatrix} x & y \\ w & z \end{bmatrix} = \begin{bmatrix} ax + bw & ay + bz \\ cx + dw & cy + dz \end{bmatrix} = \begin{bmatrix} 1 & 0 \\ 0 & 1 \end{bmatrix}$

Since we are interested in the values x, y, z, and w, we consider these as two systems of equations.

$$\begin{aligned} ax + bw &= 1 \\ cx + dw &= 0 \end{aligned} \quad \text{and} \quad \begin{aligned} ay + bz &= 0 \\ cy + dz &= 1 \end{aligned}$$

We solve these systems and find the following:

$$x = \frac{d}{ad - bc} \qquad y = \frac{-b}{ad - bc} \qquad w = \frac{-c}{ad - bc} \qquad z = \frac{a}{ad - bc}$$

Thus $\begin{bmatrix} x & y \\ w & z \end{bmatrix} = \frac{1}{ad - bc}\begin{bmatrix} d & -b \\ -c & a \end{bmatrix} = \frac{1}{|A|}\begin{bmatrix} d & -b \\ -c & a \end{bmatrix}$

13-5 Exercises

Look for worked-out examples at the Prentice Hall Web site.
www.phschool.com

A

Determine whether A and B are inverses.

1. $A = \begin{bmatrix} 1 & 2 \\ 3 & 4 \end{bmatrix}$

$B = \begin{bmatrix} -2 & 1 \\ \frac{3}{2} & -\frac{1}{2} \end{bmatrix}$

2. $A = \begin{bmatrix} 3 & 4 \\ 2 & 6 \end{bmatrix}$

$B = \begin{bmatrix} \frac{3}{5} & -\frac{2}{5} \\ -\frac{1}{5} & -\frac{3}{10} \end{bmatrix}$

3. $A = \begin{bmatrix} 7 & 4 \\ 3 & 2 \end{bmatrix}$

$B = \begin{bmatrix} 1 & -2 \\ -\frac{3}{2} & \frac{11}{2} \end{bmatrix}$

4. $A = \begin{bmatrix} 2 & 3 \\ 3 & 6 \end{bmatrix}$

$B = \begin{bmatrix} 2 & -1 \\ -1 & \frac{2}{3} \end{bmatrix}$

5. **TEST PREP** Which of the following is the multiplicative inverse of $\begin{bmatrix} 2 & 3 \\ 5 & 7 \end{bmatrix}$?

A. $\begin{bmatrix} -7 & 3 \\ 5 & -2 \end{bmatrix}$ **B.** $\begin{bmatrix} \frac{1}{2} & \frac{1}{3} \\ \frac{1}{5} & \frac{1}{7} \end{bmatrix}$ **C.** $-\begin{bmatrix} 2 & 3 \\ 5 & 7 \end{bmatrix}$ **D.** $\begin{bmatrix} -7 & 5 \\ 3 & -2 \end{bmatrix}$

Find A^{-1}, if it exists. Check your answers by calculating AA^{-1} and $A^{-1}A$.

6. $A = \begin{bmatrix} 3 & 2 \\ 5 & 3 \end{bmatrix}$ **7.** $A = \begin{bmatrix} 3 & 5 \\ 1 & 2 \end{bmatrix}$ **8.** $A = \begin{bmatrix} 11 & 3 \\ 7 & 2 \end{bmatrix}$

9. $A = \begin{bmatrix} 8 & 5 \\ 5 & 3 \end{bmatrix}$ **10.** $A = \begin{bmatrix} 4 & -3 \\ 1 & 2 \end{bmatrix}$ **11.** $A = \begin{bmatrix} 0 & -1 \\ 1 & 0 \end{bmatrix}$

12. $A = \begin{bmatrix} 6 & 3 \\ 4 & 2 \end{bmatrix}$ **13.** $A = \begin{bmatrix} 4 & 0 \\ 0 & 1 \end{bmatrix}$ **14.** $A = \begin{bmatrix} 1 & 1 \\ -1 & -1 \end{bmatrix}$

B

Find A^{-1}, if it exists.

15. $A = \begin{bmatrix} \frac{1}{2} & 0 \\ 1 & \frac{1}{4} \end{bmatrix}$ **16.** $A = \begin{bmatrix} 0.5 & 0.1 \\ 1.5 & 0.2 \end{bmatrix}$ **17.** $A = \begin{bmatrix} x & 0 \\ 0 & y \end{bmatrix}$

18. $A = \begin{bmatrix} 0 & x \\ y & 0 \end{bmatrix}$ **19.** $A = \begin{bmatrix} x \end{bmatrix}$

20. ***Critical Thinking*** The inverse of a matrix A is $\begin{bmatrix} \frac{1}{11} & -\frac{2}{11} \\ \frac{3}{11} & \frac{5}{11} \end{bmatrix}$. Find A.

21. ***Multi-Step Problem*** Given $A = \begin{bmatrix} -4 & 4 \\ 3 & 5 \end{bmatrix}$ and $B = \begin{bmatrix} 2 & 10 \\ -3 & 11 \end{bmatrix}$, show that $(AB)^{-1} = B^{-1}A^{-1}$.

22. Find a counterexample to prove that $AB = I$ does not imply that $B = A^{-1}$.

Challenge

Mathematical Reasoning Prove that for any 2×2 matrix A, A^{-1} does not exist if

23. an entire row or column has elements that are 0.

24. either both rows or both columns have the same elements.

25. one row (or column) is a multiple of the other row (or column).

Mixed Review

Factor. **26.** $x^4 - 81y^8$ **27.** $a^2 + 10ab + 25b^2 - c^2$ **28.** $6m^2 - 13mn + 6n^2$ *5-4*

Simplify. **29.** $((((a^{-2}b)^{-1})^4)^{-\frac{1}{2}})^2$ **30.** $\sqrt[3]{54y^4z^9}$ **31.** $\left(\frac{16x^4y^{-3}}{y^5z^{-4}}\right)^{\frac{3}{4}}$

32. $\left(\frac{-4^{-2}m^3n^{-2}}{2^{-3}m^{-1}n^2}\right)^{-3}$ **33.** $\frac{3r^{-1} + 3s^{-1} - 6r^{-1}s^{-1}}{5r^{-1} + 5s^{-1} - 10r^{-1}s^{-1}}$ *1-8, 6-3*

Solve.

34. A farmer is fencing off a rectangular area with a fixed perimeter of 120 m. What dimensions would yield the maximum area? What is the maximum area? *9-6*

Inverses and Systems

13-6

PART 1 Calculating Matrix Inverses

Objective: Calculate the inverse of a square matrix.

What You'll Learn

1. To calculate the multiplicative inverse of a square matrix
2. To solve systems of equations using the multiplicative inverse of a matrix

. . . And Why

To solve systems of equations

In this lesson we consider a way of calculating the inverse of any square matrix, which, as with 2×2 matrices, exists only when the determinant of the matrix is nonzero.

Suppose we want to find the inverse of the following matrix.

$$A = \begin{bmatrix} 2 & -1 & 1 \\ 1 & -2 & 3 \\ 4 & 1 & 2 \end{bmatrix}$$

First we form a new matrix consisting, on the left, of the matrix A and, on the right, of the corresponding identity matrix I.

$$\left[\begin{array}{ccc|ccc} 2 & -1 & 1 & 1 & 0 & 0 \\ 1 & -2 & 3 & 0 & 1 & 0 \\ 4 & 1 & 2 & 0 & 0 & 1 \end{array}\right]$$

The matrix A The identity matrix I

We now proceed by applying Theorem 13-1. Using row-equivalent operations we attempt to transform A into the identity matrix. Whatever operations we perform, we do on the entire matrix. We will get a matrix like the following:

$$\left[\begin{array}{ccc|ccc} 1 & 0 & 0 & a & b & c \\ 0 & 1 & 0 & d & e & f \\ 0 & 0 & 1 & g & h & i \end{array}\right]$$

The identity matrix I The matrix A^{-1}

EXAMPLE 1 Find A^{-1}. $\quad A = \begin{bmatrix} 2 & -1 & 1 \\ 1 & -2 & 3 \\ 4 & 1 & 2 \end{bmatrix}$

(a) We begin with the matrix consisting of A and I.

$$\left[\begin{array}{ccc|ccc} 2 & -1 & 1 & 1 & 0 & 0 \\ 1 & -2 & 3 & 0 & 1 & 0 \\ 4 & 1 & 2 & 0 & 0 & 1 \end{array}\right]$$

(b) We interchange the first and second rows to begin with $a_{11} = 1$.

$$\left[\begin{array}{ccc|ccc} 1 & -2 & 3 & 0 & 1 & 0 \\ 2 & -1 & 1 & 1 & 0 & 0 \\ 4 & 1 & 2 & 0 & 0 & 1 \end{array}\right]$$

(c) Next we obtain 0s in the rest of the first column. We multiply the first row by -2 and add it to the second row. Then we multiply the first row by -4 and add it to the third row.

$$\left[\begin{array}{ccc|ccc} 1 & -2 & 3 & 0 & 1 & 0 \\ 0 & 3 & -5 & 1 & -2 & 0 \\ 0 & 9 & -10 & 0 & -4 & 1 \end{array}\right] \quad \begin{array}{l} \\ -2① + ② \\ -4① + ③ \end{array}$$

(d) Now we multiply row ② by 2 and add it to 3 times row ①. We also multiply row ② by -3 and add it to row ③. This creates 0s in the appropriate places in the second column.

$$\left[\begin{array}{ccc|ccc} 3 & 0 & -1 & 2 & -1 & 0 \\ 0 & 3 & -5 & 1 & -2 & 0 \\ 0 & 0 & 5 & -3 & 2 & 1 \end{array}\right] \quad \begin{array}{l} \\ 2② + 3① \\ -3② + ③ \end{array}$$

(e) We can now use the 5 in column 3 to get zeros above it in that column.

$$\left[\begin{array}{ccc|ccc} 15 & 0 & 0 & 7 & -3 & 1 \\ 0 & 3 & 0 & -2 & 0 & 1 \\ 0 & 0 & 5 & -3 & 2 & 1 \end{array}\right] \quad \begin{array}{l} \\ ③ + 5① \\ ③ + ② \end{array}$$

(f) Finally, we get all 1s on the main diagonal. We multiply the first row by $\frac{1}{15}$, the second by $\frac{1}{3}$, and the third by $\frac{1}{5}$.

$$\left[\begin{array}{ccc|ccc} 1 & 0 & 0 & \frac{7}{15} & -\frac{1}{5} & \frac{1}{15} \\ 0 & 1 & 0 & -\frac{2}{3} & 0 & \frac{1}{3} \\ 0 & 0 & 1 & -\frac{3}{5} & \frac{2}{5} & \frac{1}{5} \end{array}\right] \quad \begin{array}{l} \frac{1}{15}① \\ \frac{1}{3}② \\ \frac{1}{5}③ \end{array}$$

We now have the matrix I on the left and A^{-1} on the right.

$$A^{-1} = \begin{bmatrix} \frac{7}{15} & -\frac{1}{5} & \frac{1}{15} \\ -\frac{2}{3} & 0 & \frac{1}{3} \\ -\frac{3}{5} & \frac{2}{5} & \frac{1}{5} \end{bmatrix}$$

You can check by doing the multiplication $A^{-1}A$ or AA^{-1}. If we cannot obtain the identity matrix on the left, as would be the case when a system has no solution or infinitely many solutions, then A^{-1} does not exist.

Try This Find A^{-1}. **a.** $A = \begin{bmatrix} 1 & 0 & 1 \\ 2 & 1 & 0 \\ 1 & -1 & 1 \end{bmatrix}$ **b.** $A = \begin{bmatrix} 1 & 2 & 3 \\ 4 & 5 & 6 \\ 7 & 8 & 9 \end{bmatrix}$

Solving Systems Using Inverses

Objective: Solve systems of equations using the inverse of a matrix.

One application of inverses of square matrices is to solve systems of equations in which the number of variables equals the number of equations.

When we solve a system using matrices, we solve $AX = B$, where A is the coefficient matrix, X is the variable matrix, and B is the constant matrix. Solving,

$$AX = B$$
$$A^{-1}AX = A^{-1}B \qquad \text{Multiplying both sides by } A^{-1}$$
$$IX = A^{-1}B \qquad A^{-1} \cdot A = I$$
$$X = A^{-1}B \qquad \text{Since } I \text{ is an identity, } IX = X.$$

The solution of the matrix equation $AX = B$ can thus be found by multiplying the inverse matrix A^{-1} by the constant matrix B.

EXAMPLE 2 Solve this system using matrices.

$$3x + 5y = -1$$
$$x - 2y = 4$$

We write a matrix equation equivalent to this system.

$$\underset{A}{\begin{bmatrix} 3 & 5 \\ 1 & -2 \end{bmatrix}} \cdot \underset{X}{\begin{bmatrix} x \\ y \end{bmatrix}} = \underset{B}{\begin{bmatrix} -1 \\ 4 \end{bmatrix}}$$

Then we solve the following equation

$$AX = B$$

To solve this equation, we first find A^{-1}.

$$A^{-1} = \frac{1}{11}\begin{bmatrix} 2 & 5 \\ 1 & -3 \end{bmatrix}$$

Now we substitute.

$$X = A^{-1}B$$
$$\begin{bmatrix} x \\ y \end{bmatrix} = \frac{1}{11}\begin{bmatrix} 2 & 5 \\ 1 & -3 \end{bmatrix} \cdot \begin{bmatrix} -1 \\ 4 \end{bmatrix}$$
$$= \frac{1}{11}\begin{bmatrix} 18 \\ -13 \end{bmatrix}$$
$$= \begin{bmatrix} \frac{18}{11} \\ -\frac{13}{11} \end{bmatrix}$$

The solution of the system of equations is $x = \frac{18}{11}$ and $y = -\frac{13}{11}$.

EXAMPLE 3 Solve this system using matrices.

$$\begin{aligned} -x + 3y + 5z &= -15 \\ 2x + y &= 1 \\ -9x - 8y - 4z &= 12 \end{aligned}$$

The matrix equation equivalent to the system is

$$\underset{A}{\begin{bmatrix} -1 & 3 & 5 \\ 2 & 1 & 0 \\ -9 & -8 & -4 \end{bmatrix}} \underset{X}{\begin{bmatrix} x \\ y \\ z \end{bmatrix}} = \underset{B}{\begin{bmatrix} -15 \\ 1 \\ 12 \end{bmatrix}}$$

We know $X = A^{-1}B$. We find the inverse of A.

$$A^{-1} = \begin{bmatrix} \frac{4}{7} & 4 & \frac{5}{7} \\ -\frac{8}{7} & -7 & -\frac{10}{7} \\ 1 & 5 & 1 \end{bmatrix}$$

$$A^{-1}B = \begin{bmatrix} \frac{4}{7} & 4 & \frac{5}{7} \\ -\frac{8}{7} & -7 & -\frac{10}{7} \\ 1 & 5 & 1 \end{bmatrix} \begin{bmatrix} -15 \\ 1 \\ 12 \end{bmatrix} = \begin{bmatrix} 4 \\ -7 \\ 2 \end{bmatrix}$$

The solution of the system of equations is $(4, -7, 2)$.

Try This Solve using matrices.

c. $4x - 2y = -1$
$x + 5y = 1$

d. $x + 3y - 4z = -14$
$-2x + 2y - 5z = 0$
$y - 6z = 0$

Extra Help On the Web

Look for worked-out examples at the Prentice Hall Web site.
www.phschool.com

13-6 Exercises

A

Find A^{-1}, if it exists.

1. $A = \begin{bmatrix} 2 & 3 & 1 \\ 3 & 3 & 1 \\ 2 & 4 & 1 \end{bmatrix}$

2. $A = \begin{bmatrix} -1 & 1 & 0 \\ -1 & 0 & 1 \\ 6 & 2 & -3 \end{bmatrix}$

3. $A = \begin{bmatrix} -2 & 2 & 3 \\ 1 & -1 & 0 \\ 0 & 1 & 4 \end{bmatrix}$

4. $A = \begin{bmatrix} 3 & 1 & 0 \\ 1 & 1 & 1 \\ 1 & -1 & 2 \end{bmatrix}$

5. $A = \begin{bmatrix} 1 & 0 & 1 \\ 2 & 1 & 0 \\ 1 & -1 & 1 \end{bmatrix}$

6. $A = \begin{bmatrix} 1 & -1 & 2 \\ 0 & 0 & 0 \\ 2 & 1 & 2 \end{bmatrix}$

Solve using matrices.

7. $7x - 2y = 10$
$9x + 3y = 24$

8. $5x + 3y = 29$
$4x - y = 13$

9. $2x + 3y = 5$
$x + 4y = 10$

10. $2x + 4y = 2$
$x + 2y = 1$

11. $x + z = 1$
$2x + y = 3$
$x - y + z = 4$

12. $x + 2y + 3z = -1$
$2x - 3y + 4z = 2$
$-3x + 5y - 6z = 4$

B

Find A^{-1}, if it exists.

13. $A = \begin{bmatrix} x & 0 & 0 \\ 0 & y & 0 \\ 0 & 0 & z \end{bmatrix}$

14. $A = \begin{bmatrix} 1 & 2 & 3 & 4 \\ 2 & 3 & 4 & 1 \\ 3 & 4 & 1 & 2 \\ 4 & 1 & 2 & 3 \end{bmatrix}$

15. Find X such that $AX = B$ where $A = \begin{bmatrix} 3 & 2 \\ 7 & 5 \end{bmatrix}$ and $B = \begin{bmatrix} 3 & 2 \\ 11 & 8 \end{bmatrix}$.

16. ***Critical Thinking*** Write a 2×2 matrix. Apply the technique on p. 593 to find the inverse. Does this technique work for 2×2 matrices?

Challenge

17. Prove that $(A^{-1})^{-1} = A$.

18. Find A^{-1}.

$A = \begin{bmatrix} 0 & t & t \\ t & 0 & t \\ t & t & 0 \end{bmatrix}$

19. Find X such that $AX = B$.

$A = \begin{bmatrix} 2 & -2 & 4 \\ -3 & 1 & -4 \\ 1 & 0 & 3 \end{bmatrix}$ $B = \begin{bmatrix} 8 & 4 & 2 \\ -3 & 0 & 3 \\ 2 & -1 & -5 \end{bmatrix}$

Mixed Review

Solve. 20. $2y + 3x = 18$
$3y + x = 13$

21. $4y + 3x = 24$ *4-1, 4-2*
$5y - x = 49$

Simplify. 22. $\frac{\sqrt{u^3 + v^3}}{\sqrt{u + v}}$ 23. $\frac{5}{8 - \sqrt{6}}$ 24. $\frac{3}{4 - 3i}$ 25. $\frac{\sqrt[3]{2u^4}}{\sqrt[3]{6v^4}}$

26. $\sqrt[3]{108} - 2\sqrt{75} + \sqrt{98}$ *7-1, 7-3, 7-4, 7-5, 7-9*

Solve. 27. $2x - 6 < 5x - 9$ 28. $-1 < x + 2 \leq 6$ *2-4, 2-6*

29. Tao scored a total of 244 points on three tests. His first score exceeded his second score by 2 points; his third score exceeded his first by 6 points. Find the three scores. *2-9*

30. The cost of renting a car and driving it 250 miles is \$150. The cost of renting a car and driving it 380 miles is \$202.
   a. Fit a linear function to the data points.
   b. Use the function to find the cost of renting a car and driving it 300 miles. *3-8*

13-7  Using Matrices

What You'll Learn

1 To solve problems represented by matrices

. . . And Why

To more easily solve problems involving data related in the same ways

PART 1 Translating Problems to Matrices

Objective: Solve problems by translating to matrices.

PROBLEM-SOLVING GUIDELINES
■ UNDERSTAND the problem
■ Develop and carry out a PLAN
■ Find the ANSWER and CHECK

We know that some problems can be solved by translating to a system of equations. We can then use matrices to solve the system of equations. Other problems can be solved by translating directly to a matrix and then performing matrix operations.

EXAMPLE 1

An orchard grows McIntosh, Gravenstein, and Jonathan apples. The apples are sold in boxes to two different markets. The profit is \$5.75 on a box of McIntosh apples, \$3.25 on Gravensteins, and \$2.00 on Jonathans. The table shows the number of boxes sold.

Apples	Markets	
	Al's	Bell
McIntosh	200	180
Gravenstein	150	250
Jonathan	300	200

Find the amount of profit generated by sales to each market.

■ **UNDERSTAND the problem**

Question: What is the orchard's profit from each market? — Clarifying the question

Data: The quantities are given in the table. The profits on each box of the three types are \$5.75, \$3.25, and \$2.00. — Identifying the given data

■ **Develop and carry out a PLAN**

We can represent the market data in a 3×2 matrix as shown below.

$$M = \begin{bmatrix} 200 & 180 \\ 150 & 250 \\ 300 & 200 \end{bmatrix}$$

Likewise, we can write a 1×3 matrix to represent the respective profits.

$$P = \begin{bmatrix} 5.75 & 3.25 & 2.00 \end{bmatrix}$$

A Hudson River valley orchard

The product PM will then be a 1×2 matrix that will determine the profit from each market.

$$PM = \begin{bmatrix} 5.75 & 3.25 & 2.00 \end{bmatrix} \begin{bmatrix} 200 & 180 \\ 150 & 250 \\ 300 & 200 \end{bmatrix} = \begin{bmatrix} 2237.50 & 2247.50 \end{bmatrix}$$

■ **Find the ANSWER and CHECK**

The profit from Al's is \$2237.50, while the profit from Bell is \$2247.50. This is reasonable because 650 boxes were sent to Al's and 630 to Bell, and the average profit from each was between \$2.00 and \$5.75.

Writing Math

Clearly *PM* and not *MP* will solve Example 1. However, students may observe that M^tP^t will also solve the problem. (See Lesson 13-2, Exercise 30.)

EXAMPLE 2 Five students had the following currency. How much money did each student have?

	\$10 bills	\$5 bills	\$1 bills	Quarters	Dimes	Nickels	Cents
Teresa	2		3	5	1		3
Rick		1	8	2	3	1	1
Leah	1				2	2	
Chan	1	1	2	9		4	4
Sandi			2	3	3	3	16

We represent the data in matrices and multiply.

$$\begin{bmatrix} 2 & 0 & 3 & 5 & 1 & 0 & 3 \\ 0 & 1 & 8 & 2 & 3 & 1 & 1 \\ 1 & 0 & 0 & 0 & 2 & 2 & 0 \\ 1 & 1 & 2 & 9 & 0 & 4 & 4 \\ 0 & 0 & 2 & 3 & 3 & 3 & 16 \end{bmatrix} \begin{bmatrix} 10 \\ 5 \\ 1 \\ 0.25 \\ 0.10 \\ 0.05 \\ 0.01 \end{bmatrix} = \begin{bmatrix} 24.38 \\ 13.86 \\ 10.30 \\ 19.49 \\ 3.36 \end{bmatrix}$$

Teresa had \$24.38, Rick had \$13.86, Leah had \$10.30, Chan had \$19.49, and Sandi had \$3.36.

Try This

a. A farm raises two crops, which are shipped to three distributors. The table below shows the number of crates shipped to each distributor.

	Distributor A	B	C
Crop 1	400	250	600
Crop 2	180	300	250

The profit on crop 1 is \$2.25 per crate and the profit on crop 2 is \$3.15 per crate. Find the amount of profit from each distributor.

Extra Help On the Web

Look for worked-out examples at the Prentice Hall Web site.
www.phschool.com

13-7 Exercises

A

1. A nursery raises five kinds of trees: spruce, dogwood, pine, yew, and hemlock. The trees are shipped to three retail outlets. The number of trees shipped to each outlet is shown in the table at the right.

	Outlet		
	A	**B**	**C**
Spruce	25	50	100
Dogwood	15	75	25
Pine	50	25	50
Yew	25	100	75
Hemlock	50	50	125

Profit on each tree is as follows: spruce \$3.50, dogwood \$4.00, pine \$2.75, yew \$1.75, and hemlock \$2.00. Find the amount of profit from each outlet.

Some bakeries make more than two dozen kinds of breads and rolls. A matrix is a powerful tool that makes it easier to deal with large quantities of data.

2. A bread company has four different bakeries, each of which produces white, rye, and whole wheat bread. The number of these loaves produced daily at each bakery is shown in the table below.

	Bakery			
	A	**B**	**C**	**D**
White	180	200	250	100
Rye	50	75	100	50
Whole Wheat	200	250	300	175

Profit on each loaf is 70¢ for white, 45¢ for rye, and 50¢ for whole wheat. Find the amount of profit each bakery earns from these breads.

3. A tournament is to be organized with eight winning teams from different leagues. To determine pairings, points are awarded as follows: three points for a win, one point for a tie, and no points for a loss. The records of the eight teams are shown at the right. How many points did each team earn?

Team	Wins	Ties	Losses
Hawks	9	2	4
Eagles	10	2	3
Angels	9	4	2
Tornadoes	11	3	1
Cyclones	14	1	0
Zephyrs	12	2	1
Jays	13	1	1
Dynamos	12	1	2

B

4. Seventy high-school football coaches ranked county teams for a newspaper poll. The first matrix shows the number of first-place votes, second-place votes, and so on received by each school. The second matrix shows the value, in points, for each first-place vote, second-place vote, and so on. Determine the number of points received by each school and the ranking of the schools in the poll.

	1	2	3	4	5	6	7
Third Avenue	13	4	12	21	9	0	0
Northpoint	3	12	25	19	0	0	1
Don Ramos	10	10	8	4	9	11	0
St. Cecilia	0	0	5	15	21	11	2
Kennedy	26	17	7	2	3	1	1
Washington	0	0	0	0	1	19	33
Riverside	18	27	11	0	1	0	0

First	10
Second	8
Third	6
Fourth	4
Fifth	3
Sixth	2
Seventh	1

5. ***Critical Thinking*** Find the cost of each item, given the number purchased by each customer. Then find the total spent for each item by all the customers.

	Item 1	Item 2	Item 3	Total Paid
Customer A	2	3	5	\$82.50
Customer B	1	3	4	\$69.00
Customer C	4	2	1	\$48.50

Challenge

6. ***Multi-Step Problem*** A store sold the following amounts of three products over a three-week period. Find the wholesale and retail costs per item for each product.

	Silky Shampoo	Face It Scrub	Incandessence	Total Wholesale	Total Retail
Week 1	36	25	11	\$140.50	\$206.25
Week 2	29	16	27	\$157.25	\$228.75
Week 3	25	18	51	\$229.25	\$329.75

7. The matrix shows the number of direct flights between cities. Show that squaring the matrix gives the number of two-flight routes between cities.

	Peoria	Detroit	St. Louis	Denver
Peoria	0	1	3	2
Detroit	1	0	2	1
St. Louis	3	2	0	2
Denver	2	1	2	0

Mixed Review

Solve. **8.** $-10 \leq 3x - 5 \leq -1$ **9.** $|x| \leq 5$ **10.** $|3y - 4| > 8$ *2-6, 2-7*

11. Ricardo scores 82, 77, and 91 on three biology quizzes. He must have a total of 340 to get a B in the course. What score on the test will give him a B? *3-10*

Preparing for Standardized Tests

Quantitative Comparisons

One type of problem encountered on college entrance exams requires you to compare two expressions, one in column A and one in column B. The choices are often:

(A) if the quantity in column A is greater;
(B) if the quantity in column B is greater;
(C) if the two quantities are equal;
(D) if the relationship cannot be determined

A strategy that is often helpful for solving this type of problem is to simplify the expressions using the addition and multiplication principles. In the examples below, decide which of the choices above is correct.

EXAMPLE 1

	Column A	Column B
	$-x^2 + 1$	$-x^2 + 2$
We can subtract $-x^2$.		
	1	2

Since $1 < 2$, $-x^2 + 1 < -x^2 + 2$, the correct answer is B.

EXAMPLE 2

	Column A	Column B
Often, additional information is presented between the columns. →	$x > -2$	
	$(x + 2)(x + 3)$	$(x + 2)^2$
We first divide by $x + 2$ in each column.		
	$x + 3$	$x + 2$
Then we subtract x from each column.		
	3	2

Since $3 > 2$, the answer is A.

In the second example, dividing by $x + 2$ was an effective strategy, since $x + 2$ could not be negative. In inequality problems, when you multiply or divide by a negative number, you change the direction of the inequality symbol. In quantitative comparison problems, there is no inequality symbol, so we must be sure not to divide by numbers that could be negative.

EXAMPLE 3

	Column A	Column B
	$x < y < 0$	
	xy	x

We cannot divide by x, a negative number. Since xy is a product of negative numbers, xy is positive. We know x is negative, so the correct answer is A.

Problems

(A) if the quantity in column A is greater;
(B) if the quantity in column B is greater;
(C) if the two quantities are equal;
(D) if the relationship cannot be determined

Decide which of the above choices is correct.

	Column A		Column B
		$a > b > c$	
1.	ab		bc
		$n < m$	
2.	$m \times 8765$		$n \times 8765$
		$e > 1$ $f < 0$	
3.	$\frac{f}{e}$		ef
		$a > 0$	
4.	$(a - 3)(a + 6)$		$(a - 3)$
		$w > 1$	
5.	$w(x + y)$		$x + y$
6.	0.4×10^x		$40 \times 10^{x-2}$
		$m, n > 0$	
7.	$0.6m + 0.7n$		$0.6(m + n)$
		a and b are positive integers	
8.	$\frac{a}{b}$		$\frac{a+1}{b+1}$
9.	$6ab$		$(2a)(3b)$
		$mn > 0$	
10.	$m + n$		$m - n$

Application

Cryptography

Cryptography is the science of creating and deciphering codes. For centuries, codes have been used in diplomatic, intelligence, and military communications. Today, with so much secret data stored in computers, concealing computerized information with codes has become important to industry.

Matrices are often used to develop systems for creating codes. A first step in creating a code is to assign numbers to the letters of the alphabet.

A	01	G	07	L	12	Q	17	V	22
B	02	H	08	M	13	R	18	W	23
C	03	I	09	N	14	S	19	X	24
D	04	J	10	O	15	T	20	Y	25
E	05	K	11	P	16	U	21	Z	26
F	06								

Then, write any 2×2 matrix that has an inverse.

Consider the matrix $E = \begin{bmatrix} 1 & 2 \\ 3 & 4 \end{bmatrix}$.

It will be used as an *encoding matrix.*

Encode the message: STUDY MATH IT COUNTS

First, break it into pairs of letters.

ST UD YM AT HI TC OU NT SQ

The Q at the end is a "dummy" to complete the pairing. Using the numerical assignment of the alphabet shown above, these pairs can be written as the 2×1 matrices

$$\begin{bmatrix} 19 \\ 20 \end{bmatrix} \begin{bmatrix} 21 \\ 04 \end{bmatrix} \begin{bmatrix} 25 \\ 13 \end{bmatrix} \begin{bmatrix} 01 \\ 20 \end{bmatrix} \begin{bmatrix} 08 \\ 09 \end{bmatrix} \begin{bmatrix} 20 \\ 03 \end{bmatrix} \begin{bmatrix} 15 \\ 21 \end{bmatrix} \begin{bmatrix} 14 \\ 20 \end{bmatrix} \begin{bmatrix} 19 \\ 17 \end{bmatrix}$$

In World War II, neither the Japanese nor the Axis powers could crack one U.S. military radio "code." That was because it was not a code. [Navaho tribesmen, speaking their unique and very difficult language, were called "code talkers."]

Multiply each 2×1 matrix by the 2×2 encoding matrix $E = \begin{bmatrix} 1 & 2 \\ 3 & 4 \end{bmatrix}$.

This gives the following matrices.

$$\begin{bmatrix} 59 \\ 137 \end{bmatrix} \begin{bmatrix} 29 \\ 79 \end{bmatrix} \begin{bmatrix} 51 \\ 127 \end{bmatrix} \begin{bmatrix} 41 \\ 83 \end{bmatrix} \begin{bmatrix} 26 \\ 60 \end{bmatrix} \begin{bmatrix} 26 \\ 72 \end{bmatrix} \begin{bmatrix} 57 \\ 129 \end{bmatrix} \begin{bmatrix} 54 \\ 122 \end{bmatrix} \begin{bmatrix} 53 \\ 125 \end{bmatrix}$$

The encoded message could then be sent as

59 137 29 79 51 127 41 83 26 60 26 72 57 129 54 122 53 125

Having encoded a message, you should be able to decode it. To decode a message you need a *decoding matrix, D*, which is simply the inverse of the encoding matrix. That is, $D = E^{-1}$, where E is the encoding matrix. Therefore, if

$$E = \begin{bmatrix} 1 & 2 \\ 3 & 4 \end{bmatrix} \text{ then } D = \begin{bmatrix} -2 & 1 \\ \frac{3}{2} & -\frac{1}{2} \end{bmatrix}$$

Multiplying the coded matrices by D yields the original (uncoded) 2×1 matrices. For example,

$$D = \begin{bmatrix} 59 \\ 137 \end{bmatrix} = \begin{bmatrix} -2 & 1 \\ \frac{3}{2} & -\frac{1}{2} \end{bmatrix} \begin{bmatrix} 59 \\ 137 \end{bmatrix} = \begin{bmatrix} 19 \\ 20 \end{bmatrix}$$

The matrix $\begin{bmatrix} 19 \\ 20 \end{bmatrix}$ corresponds to the 19th and 20th letters of the alphabet, ST.

A message can be coded by breaking it into groups of three letters or more. In general, the greater the length of the units into which the message is broken, the more difficult it is for an unauthorized party to *break* the code. To encode a message broken into units of three letters, use a 3×3 encoding matrix that has an inverse and proceed as in the example above. For units of four letters use a 4×4 matrix, and so forth.

Problems

1. Decode the following messages based on the same coding used for STUDY MATH IT COUNTS.

a. 40 96 51 103 4 10 36 84
b. 29 77 22 58 43 99 24 62 73 171

2. Select a new 2×2 encoding matrix. Write a message and encode it. Find the decoding matrix.

3. Encode the message PEACE ASSURED, using the 3×3 encoding matrix below. Remember to group the letters into units of three letters.

$$\begin{bmatrix} 1 & -2 & 3 \\ -3 & 2 & 4 \\ 5 & -1 & -2 \end{bmatrix}$$

4. Decode the following message, which was encoded using $\begin{bmatrix} 4 & 3 \\ -1 & 12 \end{bmatrix}$.

51 0 126 147 36 93 31 56 51 0 115 35 55 152

5. Decode the following message, which was encoded using $\begin{bmatrix} 1 & -2 & 3 \\ -3 & 2 & 4 \\ 5 & -1 & -2 \end{bmatrix}$.

25 48 32 8 21 0 1 −2 15 26 −20 73 33 9 69 57
47 64

13 Chapter Wrap Up

Key Terms

$|A|$ (p. 576)
$-A$ (p. 574)
A^{-1} (p. 589)
additive identity of a matrix (p. 573)
additive inverse of a matrix (p. 574)
a_{ij} (p. 568)
A^t (p. 575)
column matrix (p. 569)
columns of a matrix (p. 568)
Cramer's Rule (pp. 577, 579)
determinant (pp. 576, 578)
dimensions of a matrix (p. 569)
element of a matrix (p. 568)
identity matrix (p. 589)
inverse of a matrix (p. 589)
$m \times n$ matrix (p. 568)
main diagonal (p. 570)
matrices (p. 568)
matrix (p. 568)
multiplicative inverse of a matrix (p. 589)
row equivalent matrices (p. 569)
row equivalent operations (p. 569)
row matrix (p. 569)
rows of a matrix (p. 568)
scalar product (p. 582)
square matrix (p. 576)
transpose of a matrix (p. 575)
triangular form (p. 570)
zero matrix (p. 573)

13-1

A matrix of m rows and n columns has **dimensions** $m \times n$.
Find the dimensions of each matrix.

1. $\begin{bmatrix} 3 & -1 & 4 \\ 2 & -3 & -1 \end{bmatrix}$

2. $\begin{bmatrix} 1 \\ 0 \\ -2 \end{bmatrix}$

To solve a system of equations using matrices, use **row-equivalent operations** to transform the matrix into a matrix that has only 0s below the main diagonal.

Solve using matrices.

3. $3x - 2y = 7$
$5x + 3y = -1$

4. $3x - y + z = 5$
$2x - y + 4z = -3$
$x + 2y - z = 1$

13-2

To add matrices, add the corresponding elements. To subtract matrices, subtract the corresponding elements. In either case, the matrices must have the same dimensions.

5. Find $\begin{bmatrix} -3 & 5 \\ 4 & -2 \end{bmatrix} + \begin{bmatrix} 1 & -5 \\ -3 & -2 \end{bmatrix}$

6. Find $\begin{bmatrix} -3 & 5 \\ 4 & -2 \end{bmatrix} - \begin{bmatrix} 1 & -5 \\ -3 & -2 \end{bmatrix}$

13-3

The **determinant** of $\begin{bmatrix} a_1 & a_2 \\ b_1 & b_2 \end{bmatrix}$ is written as $\begin{vmatrix} a_1 & a_2 \\ b_1 & b_2 \end{vmatrix}$ and is evaluated as $a_1b_2 - b_1a_2$.

Evaluate.

7. $\begin{vmatrix} 3 & -2 \\ 1 & 4 \end{vmatrix}$

8. $\begin{vmatrix} -2 & 3 \\ 0 & -3 \end{vmatrix}$

Cramer's rule for 2 equations in the form $a_1x + b_1y + c_1$
$a_2x + b_2y + c_2$

has a solution

$$x = \frac{\begin{vmatrix} c_1 & b_1 \\ c_2 & b_2 \end{vmatrix}}{\begin{vmatrix} a_1 & b_1 \\ a_2 & b_2 \end{vmatrix}} \text{ and } y = \frac{\begin{vmatrix} a_1 & c_1 \\ a_2 & c_2 \end{vmatrix}}{\begin{vmatrix} a_1 & b_1 \\ a_2 & b_2 \end{vmatrix}}.$$

Solve using Cramer's rule.

9. $3x - 5y = 9$
$-3x + y = -7$

10. $4x - y = 10$
$-3x + 5y = -4$

The determinant of a 3×3 matrix can be evaluated as follows.

$$\begin{vmatrix} a_1 & b_1 & c_1 \\ a_2 & b_2 & c_2 \\ a_3 & b_3 & c_3 \end{vmatrix} = a_1\begin{vmatrix} b_2 & c_2 \\ b_3 & c_3 \end{vmatrix} - a_2\begin{vmatrix} b_1 & c_1 \\ b_3 & c_3 \end{vmatrix} + a_3\begin{vmatrix} b_1 & c_1 \\ b_2 & c_2 \end{vmatrix}$$

Evaluate. **11.** $\begin{vmatrix} 3 & 2 & -3 \\ 1 & -1 & 1 \\ 0 & 1 & -1 \end{vmatrix}$ **12.** $\begin{vmatrix} -2 & 2 & -4 \\ -1 & 0 & 0 \\ 3 & -1 & 1 \end{vmatrix}$

Cramer's rule for 3 equations in the form

$$\begin{aligned} a_1x + b_1y + c_1z &= d_1 \\ a_2x + b_2y + c_2z &= d_2 \\ a_3x + b_3y + c_3z &= d_3 \end{aligned}$$

has a solution given by $x = \frac{D_x}{D}, y = \frac{D_y}{D}, z = \frac{D_z}{D}$, where $D \neq 0$,

$$D = \begin{vmatrix} a_1 & b_1 & c_1 \\ a_2 & b_2 & c_2 \\ a_3 & b_3 & c_3 \end{vmatrix}, D_x = \begin{vmatrix} d_1 & b_1 & c_1 \\ d_2 & b_2 & c_2 \\ d_3 & b_3 & c_3 \end{vmatrix}, D_y = \begin{vmatrix} a_1 & d_1 & c_1 \\ a_2 & d_2 & c_2 \\ a_3 & d_3 & c_3 \end{vmatrix}, \text{ and } D_z = \begin{vmatrix} a_1 & b_1 & d_1 \\ a_2 & b_2 & d_2 \\ a_3 & b_3 & d_3 \end{vmatrix}.$$

Solve using Cramer's rule.

13. $3x - 2y - z = -1$
$2x + y + z = 8$
$-x + 3y - 2z = 5$

14. $2x - 2y + z = 3$
$-4x + y - 3z = 1$
$-2x - 3y + z = 0$

13-4

The **scalar product** of a real number k, called a **scalar,** and a matrix A is the matrix, denoted kA, obtained by multiplying each number in A by the number k.

If $A = \begin{bmatrix} -3 & 0 \\ 2 & -1 \end{bmatrix}$, **15.** find $-3A$. **16.** find $4A$.

If matrix A has n columns and matrix B has n rows, then we can compute the product AB, which will have as many rows as A and as many columns as B. The element in row i, column j, of the product AB is found by multiplying the elements in row i of A by the elements in column j of B, and adding.

$$A = \begin{bmatrix} -3 & 0 \\ 2 & -1 \end{bmatrix} B = \begin{bmatrix} 2 & 1 & -1 \\ -1 & 0 & 2 \end{bmatrix} \quad C = \begin{bmatrix} -2 & 0 & 3 \\ -1 & 1 & 1 \\ 0 & 2 & 0 \end{bmatrix}$$

Find each product, if it exists.

17. AB **18.** BC **19.** AC

The system of equations $\begin{aligned} a_1x + b_1y + c_1z &= d_1 \\ a_2x + b_2y + c_1z &= d_2 \\ a_3x + b_3y + c_3z &= d_3 \end{aligned}$ has an equivalent matrix equation.

$$\begin{bmatrix} a_1 & b_1 & c_1 \\ a_2 & b_2 & c_2 \\ a_3 & b_3 & c_3 \end{bmatrix}\begin{bmatrix} x \\ y \\ z \end{bmatrix} = \begin{bmatrix} d_1 \\ d_2 \\ d_3 \end{bmatrix}$$

Internet Activity On the Web

Look for extension problems for this chapter at the Prentice Hall Web site. www.phschool.com

20. Write a matrix equation equivalent to the system of equations.

$$\begin{aligned} 5x + 2y - 4z &= 0 \\ -3x - 4y - 2z &= 6 \\ 6x + 7y + 5z &= 15 \end{aligned}$$

13-5

If $A = \begin{bmatrix} a & b \\ c & d \end{bmatrix}$, then to find the **inverse** of A, denoted A^{-1}, $A^{-1} = \frac{1}{|A|}\begin{bmatrix} d & -b \\ -c & a \end{bmatrix}$

Find A^{-1}, if it exists. Check by calculating AA^{-1}.

21. $A = \begin{bmatrix} 2 & 3 \\ 1 & 2 \end{bmatrix}$

22. $A = \begin{bmatrix} -3 & -1 \\ 6 & 2 \end{bmatrix}$

13-6

The inverse of any square matrix A exists only when the determinant of the matrix is nonzero. To find this inverse, form a new matrix consisting of matrix A on the left and the corresponding **identity matrix** I on the right. Use row-equivalent operations to transform the left half of the matrix into the identity matrix. Once this is done, the inverse, A^{-1}, will appear as the right half of the matrix.

Find A^{-1}, if it exists.

23. $\begin{bmatrix} 2 & 0 & 1 \\ 1 & -1 & 2 \\ 1 & 1 & 2 \end{bmatrix}$

24. $\begin{bmatrix} 3 & 1 & 2 \\ 1 & 0 & 1 \\ -2 & -1 & 1 \end{bmatrix}$

To solve $\begin{aligned} a_1x + b_1y &= c_1 \\ a_2x + b_2y &= c_2 \end{aligned}$, the variable matrix $\begin{bmatrix} x \\ y \end{bmatrix}$ equals the product of the inverse of the coefficient matrix $\begin{bmatrix} a_1 & b_1 \\ a_2 & b_2 \end{bmatrix}$ and the constant matrix $\begin{bmatrix} c_1 \\ c_2 \end{bmatrix}$.

Solve using matrices.

25. $\begin{aligned} 3x - 2y &= 7 \\ 5x + 3y &= -1 \end{aligned}$

26. $\begin{aligned} 2x + 3y &= 6 \\ x + 2y &= 2 \end{aligned}$

13-7

Some problems can be translated into a system of equations that can be solved by using matrices.

27. The Ticon Co. produces pens, pencils, and erasers. The items are sold by stores A, B, and C as indicated in this table.

	Stores		
	A	**B**	**C**
Pens	40	30	20
Pencils	50	30	60
Erasers	40	40	60

The profit on pencils is 5¢, on pens 8¢, and on erasers 20¢. Find the amount of profit each store made.

13 Chapter Assessment

1. Find the dimensions of $\begin{bmatrix} -2 & 3 \\ 1 & 2 \\ 0 & 5 \end{bmatrix}$.

2. Solve using matrices. $\begin{aligned} 2x - 5y &= 1 \\ 3x + 2y &= -2 \end{aligned}$

3. Add $\begin{bmatrix} 3 & -4 \\ 2 & 0 \\ 1 & -1 \end{bmatrix} + \begin{bmatrix} -2 & 4 \\ 3 & -3 \\ 1 & 1 \end{bmatrix}$.

4. Evaluate $\begin{vmatrix} 1 & -4 \\ -2 & 3 \end{vmatrix}$.

5. Solve $\begin{aligned} -4x - 2y &= 3 \\ 3x - 5y &= -4 \end{aligned}$ using Cramer's rule.

6. Evaluate $\begin{vmatrix} 3 & 0 & -2 \\ -2 & 1 & 0 \\ 1 & -1 & -3 \end{vmatrix}$.

7. Solve $\begin{aligned} 2x - 3y + z &= 2 \\ x - 2y + 3z &= 0 \\ 3x + y - z &= -1 \end{aligned}$ using Cramer's rule.

8. If $A = \begin{bmatrix} 2 & -1 & 0 \\ 0 & 1 & -4 \end{bmatrix}$, find $-2A$.

$$A = \begin{bmatrix} -3 & 2 & 0 \\ 1 & 1 & 1 \\ 0 & -1 & 0 \end{bmatrix} \text{ and } B = \begin{bmatrix} 2 & 3 & -1 \\ -1 & 0 & 1 \\ 1 & 1 & -2 \end{bmatrix}$$

9. find $A \cdot B$.

10. find $B \cdot A$.

11. Write a matrix equation equivalent to this system of equations.

$$\begin{aligned} 2x - y + 3z &= 5 \\ 3x + 2y - z &= 1 \\ x - 3y + 4z &= 0 \end{aligned}$$

12. If $A = \begin{bmatrix} 3 & 1 \\ -5 & 0 \end{bmatrix}$, find A^{-1}, if it exists.

13. If $B = \begin{bmatrix} 1 & 2 & 0 \\ 0 & -2 & 1 \\ -1 & 1 & -1 \end{bmatrix}$, find B^{-1}, if it exists.

14. This chart represents the standing at the end of a soccer season. If 2 points are awarded for a win, 1 point for a tie, and 0 points for a loss, how many points did each team earn?

Team	Wins	Losses	Ties
Fireballs	8	8	0
Blue Angels	5	8	3
Tigers	7	6	3
Dynamite	9	5	2
Rangers	4	6	6

What You'll Learn in Chapter 14

- How to define sequences, find specific terms and general terms of a sequence, and find partial sums
- How to use sigma notation
- How to find the first and *n*th terms and the common difference of an arithmetic sequence.
- How to find specific terms and find partial and infinite sums of a geometric series
- How to determine whether a geometric series has an infinite sum
- How to find the common ratio of a series
- How to use mathematical induction to prove statements about positive integers
- How to combine strategies to solve nonroutine problems

CHAPTER

Skills & Concepts You Need for Chapter 14

1-3 Evaluate each expression for $n = 5$.

1. $n(n - 1)$ **2.** $n(n - 1)(n - 2)$ **3.** $\dfrac{2n^2 - 3n - 5}{n - 3}$

1-7 Evaluate each expression for $n = 5$ and $r = 3$.

4. n^r **5.** $(r - 1)^n$ **6.** $\dfrac{(3r - 2n)^r}{2nr}$

3-3, 12-2 Given each function f, find $f(1), f(2), f(3)$.

7. $f(x) = 3x + 2$ **8.** $f(x) = 3x^2 - 1$

9. $f(x) = (-1)^x 3^x$ **10.** $f(x) = \left(\frac{1}{2}\right)^x$

Sequences, Series, and Mathematical Induction

Exercise 13 on page 636 searches for the link between dominoes and the Principle of Mathematical Induction.

14-1 Sequences and Series

What You'll Learn

1. To find specific terms of a sequence, given the nth term of the sequence
2. To find a general term for a sequence
3. To find partial sums for a sequence
4. To use the sigma notation

. . . And Why

To solve problems using arithmetic sequences

Leonardo Fibonacci, one of the best mathematicians of the Middle Ages, included the following problem in his famous work *Liber abaci.*

How many pairs of rabbits can be produced from a single pair in a year if every month each pair begets a new pair that, from the second month on, become productive?

This problem gave rise to the famous Fibonacci sequence.

See Exercise 42 on page 616.

PART 1 Sequences and General Terms

Objective: Find specific terms of a sequence, given the nth term of the sequence.

Definition

A **sequence** is an ordered set of numbers.

Here is an example of a sequence: $3, 5, 7, 9, \ldots$

The dots mean that there are more numbers in the sequence. A sequence that does not end is called an **infinite sequence.**

Each number is called a **term** of the sequence. The first term, a_1, is 3; the second term, a_2, is 5; the third term, a_3, is 7; and so on.

Some sequences have a rule which describes the ***n*th term** or **general term.** The above sequence could be described as $3, 5, 7, 9, \ldots, 2n + 1, \ldots$, where the nth term, a_n, is $2n + 1$. We also say $a_n = 2n + 1$.

We can find the terms of the sequence by consecutively substituting the natural numbers, $1, 2, 3, \ldots$, for n in the general term.

EXAMPLE 1 The general term of a sequence is given by $a_n = \frac{(-1)^n}{n + 1}$. Find the first three terms, the 10th term, and the 15th term.

$$a_1 = \frac{(-1)^1}{1 + 1} = -\frac{1}{2} \qquad a_2 = \frac{(-1)^2}{2 + 1} = \frac{1}{3} \qquad a_3 = \frac{(-1)^3}{3 + 1} = -\frac{1}{4}$$

$$a_{10} = \frac{(-1)^{10}}{10 + 1} = \frac{1}{11} \qquad a_{15} = \frac{(-1)^{15}}{15 + 1} = -\frac{1}{16}$$

Try This For each of the following, the general term of a sequence is given. Find the first three terms, the 10th term, and the 15th term.

a. $a_n = 2^n - 1$ **b.** $a_n = (-1)^n n^2$

Some sequences can be defined by **recursion.** We give a value of a_1 and then tell how each subsequent term is related to the term before it in the sequence.

EXAMPLE 2 Find the first five terms of this recursively defined sequence: $a_1 = 1$ and $a_{n+1} = 3a_n - 1$.

$a_1 = 1$, $a_2 = 3a_1 - 1 = 3 \cdot 1 - 1 = 2$, $a_3 = 3a_2 - 1 = 3 \cdot 2 - 1 = 5$, $a_4 = 3a_3 - 1 = 3 \cdot 5 - 1 = 14$, $a_5 = 3a_4 - 1 = 3 \cdot 14 - 1 = 41$

Try This Find the first five terms of these recursively defined sequences.

c. $a_1 = 0, \quad a_{n+1} = a_n + 4$ **d.** $a_1 = 4, \quad a_{n+1} = a_n - 2$

PART 2 Finding General Terms

Objective: Find a general term for a sequence.

We may know the first few terms of a sequence, but not the general term. In such a case, we look for a pattern.

EXAMPLES For each sequence, find a general term.

3 1, 4, 9, 16, 25, . . .

These are squares of numbers, so a rule for the nth term would be $a_n = n^2$.

4 −1, 2, −4, 8, −16, . . .

If we ignore the negative signs we have the powers of 2, which have a general term of $a_n = 2^{n-1}$. We can multiply each term by $(-1)^n$. This will multiply each odd term by −1 and each even term by 1. Thus a general term would be $a_n = (-1)^n 2^{n-1}$.

Try This For each sequence, find a general term.

e. 2, 4, 6, 8, 10, . . . **f.** −1, 2, −3, 4, −5, 6, . . .
g. 1, 8, 27, 64, 125, . . . **h.** 1, 2, 4, 8, 16, 32, . . .

PART 3 Series

Objective: Find partial sums for a sequence.

If we add the terms of a sequence we have a series. Given the sequence $1, 3, 5, 7, 9, \ldots, 2n - 1, \ldots$, we have the series $1 + 3 + 5 + 7 + 9 + \cdots + (2n - 1) + \cdots$.

Definition

An indicated sum, S_n, of the terms of a sequence, $a_1, a_2, a_3, \ldots, a_n$, is called a **series.**

$$S_n = a_1 + a_2 + a_3 + \cdots + a_n$$

Since many sequences are infinite, it is often convenient to consider the sum of only a finite number of terms of a sequence. We call this a **partial sum.** For the sequence $1, 3, 5, 7, 9, \ldots, 2n - 1, \ldots$, we construct some partial sums.

$S_1 = a_1 = 1$ Finding the first term of the given sequence

$S_2 = a_1 + a_2 = 1 + 3 = 4$ Finding the sum of the first two terms

$S_3 = a_1 + a_2 + a_3 = 1 + 3 + 5 = 9$

Finding the sum of the first three terms

EXAMPLE 5 Find S_5 for the sequence $-2, 4, -6, 8, -10, 12, -14, \ldots$.

$S_5 = -2 + 4 + (-6) + 8 + (-10)$ Finding the sum of the first five terms

$= -6$

Try This

i. Find S_1, S_2, S_3, and S_4 for the sequence $\frac{1}{2}, \frac{1}{4}, \frac{1}{8}, \frac{1}{16}, \frac{1}{32}, \ldots$.

PART 4 Sigma Notation

Objective: Use sigma notation.

The Greek letter **Σ (sigma)** can be used to simplify notation when a series has a formula for the general term.

The sum of the first four terms of the sequence $3, 5, 7, 9, \ldots, 2n + 1$, can be denoted

$\sum_{n=1}^{4} (2n + 1)$ Read "the sum as n goes from 1 to 4 of $(2n + 1)$"

EXAMPLES Rename and evaluate the following sums.

6 $\sum_{n=1}^{5} n^2 = 1^2 + 2^2 + 3^2 + 4^2 + 5^2$

$= 1 + 4 + 9 + 16 + 25 = 55$

7 $\sum_{n=1}^{3} (-1)^n(2n) = (-1)^1(2 \cdot 1) + (-1)^2(2 \cdot 2) + (-1)^3(2 \cdot 3)$

$= -2 + 4 - 6 = -4$

Try This Rename and evaluate the following sums.

j. $\sum_{n=1}^{3} \left(2 + \frac{1}{n}\right)$ **k.** $\sum_{n=1}^{4} (5^n - 1)$

EXAMPLES Write sigma notation for each sum.

8 $1 + 3 + 5 + 7$

This is the sum of the first four odd numbers. A general term for an odd number is $2n - 1$. So sigma notation is $\sum_{n=1}^{4} (2n - 1)$.

9 $1 - 3 + 5 - 7$

This is the sum of the first four odd numbers, but with alternating signs. The first is positive, the second negative, and so on. To cause this pattern we can multiply each term by $(-1)^{n+1}$. So sigma notation is $\sum_{n=1}^{4} (-1)^{n+1}(2n - 1)$.

10 $3 + 9 + 27 + 81 + \cdots$

This is a sum of powers of 3, and it is also an unending or **infinite series.** We use the symbol ∞ to represent **infinity:** $\sum_{n=1}^{\infty} 3^n$

Try This Write sigma notation for each sum.

l. $2 + 4 + 6 + 8 + 10$ **m.** $2 - 3 + 4 - 5 + \cdots$

Reading Math

$\sum_{3}^{7} (2n + 1)$ can be read as "the sum as n goes from 3 to 7 of the quantity $2n + 1$" or as "the sum of the quantity $2n + 1$ as n goes from 3 to 7." Use the one that sounds better to you.

14-1 Exercises

Extra Help On the Web

Look for worked-out examples at the Prentice Hall Web site.
www.phschool.com

A

Mental Math The general term of a sequence is given. In each case find the first four terms, the 10th term, and the 15th term.

1. $a_n = 3n + 1$ **2.** $a_n = 3n - 1$ **3.** $a_n = \frac{n}{n + 1}$ **4.** $a_n = n^2 + 1$

The general term of a sequence is given. In each case find the first four terms, the 10th term, and the 15th term.

5. $a_n = n^2 - 2n$ **6.** $a_n = \frac{n^2 - 1}{n^2 + 1}$ **7.** $a_n = n + \frac{1}{n}$ **8.** $a_n = \left(-\frac{1}{2}\right)^{n-1}$

Find the first five terms of these recursively defined sequences.

9. $a_1 = 2, a_{n+1} = 4a_n - 3$ **10.** $a_1 = -3, a_{n+1} = 2a_n - 5$

11. $a_1 = 8, a_{n+1} = \frac{1}{2}a_n + 2$ **12.** $a_1 = 3, a_2 = 3, a_{n+1} = a_n - a_{n-1}$

For each sequence, find a general term.

13. $1, 3, 5, 7, 9, \ldots$

14. $3, 9, 27, 81, 243, \ldots$

15. $\frac{2}{3}, \frac{3}{4}, \frac{4}{5}, \frac{5}{6}, \frac{6}{7}, \ldots$

16. $\sqrt{2}, \sqrt{4}, \sqrt{6}, \sqrt{8}, \sqrt{10}, \ldots$

17. $\sqrt{3}, 3, 3\sqrt{3}, 9, 9\sqrt{3}, \ldots$

18. $1 \cdot 2, 2 \cdot 3, 3 \cdot 4, 4 \cdot 5, \ldots$

19. $-1, -4, -7, -10, -13, \ldots$

20. $\log 1, \log 10, \log 100, \log 1000, \ldots$

Find S_1, S_2, S_3, and S_4 for each sequence.

21. $\frac{1}{3}, \frac{1}{6}, \frac{1}{12}, \frac{1}{24}, \frac{1}{48}, \ldots$

22. $-1, 3, -5, 7, -9, \ldots$

23. $4, 7, 10, 13, 16, \ldots$

24. $-3, 9, -27, 81, -243, \ldots$

Rename and evaluate each sum.

25. $\sum_{n=1}^{5} \frac{1}{2n}$

26. $\sum_{n=1}^{6} \frac{1}{2n+1}$

27. $\sum_{n=1}^{5} 2^n$

28. $\sum_{n=4}^{7} \sqrt{2n-1}$

29. $\sum_{n=7}^{10} \log n$

30. $\sum_{n=0}^{4} \pi n$

Write sigma notation for each sum.

31. $\frac{1}{2} + \frac{2}{3} + \frac{3}{4} + \frac{4}{5} + \frac{5}{6} + \frac{6}{7}$

32. $3 + 6 + 9 + 12 + 15$

33. $-2 + 4 - 8 + 16 - 32 + 64$

34. $\frac{1}{1^2} + \frac{1}{2^2} + \frac{1}{3^2} + \frac{1}{4^2} + \frac{1}{5^2}$

35. $4 - 9 + 16 - 25 + \cdots$

36. $9 - 16 + 25 - 36 + 49 - 64 + \cdots$

B

Find the first five terms of each sequence.

37. $a_n = \frac{1}{2n} \log 1000^n$

38. $a_n = i^n, i = \sqrt{-1}$

39. $a_n = \ln (1 \cdot 2 \cdot 3 \ldots n)$

Use a calculator to find S_6 rounded to six decimal places.

40. $a_n = \left(1 + \frac{1}{n}\right)^n$

41. $a_n = \sqrt{n+1} - \sqrt{n}$

42. ***Critical Thinking*** Determine the first twelve terms of the Fibonacci sequence and then give the answer to Fibonacci's problem. (Hint: In the first and second months there is only one pair of rabbits.)

Challenge

43. Find a formula for S_n, given that $a_n = \frac{1}{n} \cdot \frac{1}{n+1}$.

44. Write a recursive definition of the Fibonacci sequence.

Mixed Review

Let $A = \begin{bmatrix} 3 & -1 & 2 \\ -1 & 2 & 1 \\ 3 & 5 & 2 \end{bmatrix}$ $B = \begin{bmatrix} 6 \\ 5 \\ 4 \end{bmatrix}$ $C = \begin{bmatrix} 4 & 5 & 6 \\ 3 & 0 & 7 \\ 2 & 9 & 8 \end{bmatrix}$ Evaluate, if possible.

45. $A + 3C$ **46.** $tC + A$ **47.** AC **48.** AB **49.** BC **50.** CB *13-4*

Arithmetic Sequences and Series 14-2

At a temperature of 1°C, the speed of sound in air is about 332.1 meters per second. The speed increases about 0.6 m/s for each increase of 1°C. The number pattern this forms, 332.1, 332.7, 333.3, 333.9, 334.5, . . . , is an example of a **sequence.**

What You'll Learn

1. To find the first term and common difference of an arithmetic sequence
2. To solve problems involving the *n*th term of an arithmetic sequence
3. To construct an arithmetic sequence, given specific terms of the sequence
4. To find partial sums of arithmetic series

. . . And Why

To prove statements about integers using mathematical induction

PART 1 Arithmetic Sequences

Objective: Find the first term and common difference of an arithmetic sequence.

> **Definition**
>
> A sequence in which a constant d can be added to each term to get the next term is called an **arithmetic sequence.** The constant d is called the **common difference.**

In an arithmetic sequence with n terms, the terms are denoted $a_1, a_2, \ldots, a_n$.

To find the common difference, subtract any term from the one that follows it.

	a_1		a_2		a_3		a_4		a_5
Terms	2		5		8		11		14
Difference		3		3		3		3	

EXAMPLES Find the first term and the common difference of each arithmetic sequence.

	Sequence	First term	Common difference
1	4, 9, 14, 19, 24, . . .	4	5
2	34, 27, 20, 13, 6, −1 , −8 , . . .	34	−7
3	$2, 2\frac{1}{2}, 3, 3\frac{1}{2}, 4, 4\frac{1}{2}, \ldots$	2	$\frac{1}{2}$

Try This Find the first term and the common difference of each arithmetic sequence.

a. $2, 3, 4, 5, 6, \ldots$

b. $1, 4, 7, 10, 13, \ldots$

c. $19, 14, 9, 4, -1, -6, \ldots$

d. $10, 9\frac{1}{2}, 9, 8\frac{1}{2}, 8, 7\frac{1}{2}, \ldots$

PART 2 The *n*th Term

Objective: Solve problems involving the *n*th term of an arithmetic sequence.

The first term of an arithmetic sequence is a_1. We add d to get the next term, $a_1 + d$. We add d again to get the next term, $(a_1 + d) + d$, and so on. There is a pattern.

$$\begin{aligned} a_1 &= a_1 \\ a_2 &= a_1 + d \\ a_3 &= (a_1 + d) + d = a_1 + 2d \\ a_4 &= (a_1 + 2d) + d = a_1 + 3d \\ &\vdots \\ a_n &= a_1 + (n - 1)d \end{aligned}$$

Theorem 14-1

The nth term of an arithmetic sequence is given by

$$a_n = a_1 + (n - 1)d$$

EXAMPLE 4 Find the 14th term of the arithmetic sequence $4, 7, 10, 13, \ldots$.

First note that $a_1 = 4$, $d = 3$, and $n = 14$. Then, using the formula of Theorem 14-1, we have the following.

$$a_{14} = 4 + (14 - 1)3 = 4 + 39 = 43$$

Thus the 14th term, a_{14}, is 43.

EXAMPLE 5 In the arithmetic sequence $4, 7, 10, 13, \ldots$, which term has a value of 301?

$$\begin{aligned} a_n &= a_1 + (n - 1)d && \text{Theorem 14-1} \\ 301 &= 4 + (n - 1)3 && \text{Substituting} \\ 300 &= 3n \\ 100 &= n \end{aligned}$$

Thus the 100th term, a_{100}, is 301.

In a similar manner we can find a_1 if we know n, a_n, and d. Also, we can find d if we know a_1, n, and a_n.

Try This

e. Find the 13th term of the sequence 2, 6, 10, 14, ...
f. In the sequence 2, 6, 10, 14, . . . , which term has a value of 286?

PART 3 Constructing Sequences

Objective: Construct an arithmetic sequence, given specific terms of the sequence.

Given two terms in a sequence, we can find a_1 and d, and construct the sequence.

EXAMPLE 6 The 3rd term of an arithmetic sequence is 8 and the 16th term is 47. Find a_1 and d. Construct the sequence.

We use the formula $a_n = a_1 + (n - 1)d$, where $a_3 = 8$.

$$8 = a_1 + (3 - 1)d \text{ or } 8 = a_1 + 2d$$

We use the same formula, where $a_{16} = 47$.

$$47 = a_1 + (16 - 1)d \text{ or } 47 = a_1 + 15d$$

Now we solve the system of equations.

$$\begin{array}{lll} a_1 + 15d = 47 & \rightarrow & a_1 + 15d = 47 \\ a_1 + 2d = 8 & \rightarrow & -a_1 - 2d = -8 \quad \text{Multiplying by } -1 \\ & & 13d = 39 \quad \text{Adding} \\ & & d = 3 \quad \text{Solving for } d \\ & & a_1 + 2 \cdot 3 = 8 \quad \text{Substituting} \\ & & a_1 = 2 \quad \text{Solving for } a_1 \end{array}$$

Thus a_1 is 2, d is 3, and the sequence is 2, 5, 8, 11, 14, ... Sequence may be graphed by hand or with graphing technology. (See explanation on p. 633.)

Try This

g. The 7th term of an arithmetic sequence is 79 and the 13th term is 151. Find a_1 and d. Construct the sequence.

An **arithmetic mean** of two numbers, a and b, is simply their average, $\frac{a + b}{2}$. Notice that the numbers $a, \frac{a + b}{2}, b$ form an arithmetic sequence. Numbers $m_1, m_2, m_3, \ldots, m_n$ are called **arithmetic means** between a and b if $a, m_1, m_2, m_3, \ldots, m_n, b$ form an arithmetic sequence.

EXAMPLE 7 Insert three arithmetic means between 8 and 16.

Let 8 be the 1st term. Then 16 will be the 5th term. We use the formula $a_n = a_1 + (n - 1)d$.

$$16 = 8 + (5 - 1)d \text{ or } d = 2$$

So we have 8, 10, 12, 14, 16.

Try This

h. Insert two arithmetic means between 3 and 24.

PART 4 Arithmetic Series

Objective: Find partial sums of arithmetic series.

An **arithmetic series** is a series associated with an arithmetic sequence. Two theorems give useful formulas for finding the sum of the first n terms.

Theorem 14-2

The sum of the first n terms of an arithmetic series is given by

$$S_n = \frac{n}{2}(a_1 + a_n)$$

This formula is useful when we know the first and last terms, a_1 and a_n. If we do not know the last term of the series, we can substitute $a_1 + (n - 1)d$ for a_n in the above formula. This gives us our next theorem.

Theorem 14-3

The sum of the first n terms of an arithmetic series is given by

$$S_n = \frac{n}{2}[2a_1 + (n - 1)d]$$

EXAMPLE 8 Find the sum of the first 100 natural numbers.

The sum of the first 100 natural numbers is $1 + 2 + 3 + \cdots + 100$.

This is an arithmetic series.

$a = 1$, $a_n = 100$, and $n = 100$. We use Theorem 14-2.

$$S_n = \frac{n}{2}(a_1 + a_n)$$

Substituting, we get the following.

$$S_{100} = \frac{100}{2}(1 + 100)$$
$$= 50(101) = 5050$$

The sum of the first 100 natural numbers is 5050.

Try This

i. Find the sum of the first 200 natural numbers.
j. Find the sum of the first 473 natural numbers.

EXAMPLE 9 Find the sum of the first 14 terms of the arithmetic series $2 + 5 + 8 + 11 + 14 + 17 + \cdots$.

Note that $a_1 = 2$, $d = 3$, and $n = 14$. We use Theorem 14-3.

$$S_n = \frac{n}{2}[2a_1 + (n - 1)d]$$

$$S_{14} = \frac{14}{2} \cdot [2 \cdot 2 + (14 - 1)3]$$

$$= 7 \cdot [4 + 13 \cdot 3]$$

$$= 7 \cdot 43$$

$$S_{14} = 301$$

The sum of the first 14 terms of the series is 301.

Try This

k. Find the sum of the first 15 terms of the arithmetic series $1 + 3 + 5 + 7 + 9 + \cdots$.

EXAMPLE 10 Find the sum of the series $\sum_{n=1}^{13} (4n + 5)$.

First find a few terms.

$$9 + 13 + 17 + \cdots$$

We see that this is an arithmetic series with $a_1 = 9$, $d = 4$, and $n = 13$. We use Theorem 14-3.

$$S_n = \frac{n}{2}[2a_1 + (n - 1)d]$$

$$S_{13} = \frac{13}{2}[2 \cdot 9 + (13 - 1)4]$$

$$= \frac{13}{2}[18 + 12 \cdot 4] = \frac{13}{2} \cdot 66 = 429$$

The sum of the series is 429.

EXAMPLE 11 Find the sum of the series $\sum_{n=1}^{20} (-2n + 21)$.

The first 3 terms are 19, 17, 15, $a_1 = 19$, $d = -2$, and $n = 20$.

$$S_{20} = \frac{20}{2}[2 \cdot 19 + (20 - 1)(-2)]$$

$$= 10[38 + 19(-2)] = 10(0) = 0$$

The sum of the series is zero.

Try This

l. Find the sum of the series $\sum_{n=1}^{10} (9n - 4)$.

Extra Help On the Web

Look for worked-out examples at the Prentice Hall Web site.
www.phschool.com

Logs transported by truck are often stacked in a triangular array, similar to the arrangement of bowling pins. See Exercise 27.

14-2 Exercises

A

For the arithmetic sequences in Exercises 1–6, find the first term and the common difference.

1. $2, 7, 12, 17, \ldots$

2. $1.06, 1.12, 1.18, 1.24, \ldots$

3. $7, 3, -1, -5, \ldots$

4. $-9, -6, -3, 0, \ldots$

5. $\frac{3}{2}, \frac{9}{4}, 3, \frac{15}{4}, \ldots$

6. $\frac{3}{5}, \frac{1}{10}, -\frac{2}{5}, \ldots$

7. Find the 12th term of the arithmetic sequence $2, 6, 10, \ldots$.

8. Find the 11th term of the arithmetic sequence $0.07, 0.12, 0.17, \ldots$.

9. Find the 17th term of the arithmetic sequence $7, 4, 1, \ldots$.

10. Find the 14th term of the arithmetic sequence $3, \frac{7}{3}, \frac{5}{3}, \ldots$.

11. In the sequence $2, 6, 10, \ldots$, what term has a value of 106?

12. In the sequence $0.07, 0.12, 0.17, \ldots$, what term has a value of 1.67?

13. In the sequence $7, 4, 1, \ldots$, what term has a value of -296?

14. In the sequence $3, \frac{7}{3}, \frac{5}{3}, \ldots$, what term has a value of -27?

15. The 17th term of an arithmetic sequence is -40 and the 28th term is -73. Find a_1 and d. Construct the sequence.

16. The 17th term of an arithmetic sequence is $\frac{25}{3}$, and the 32nd term is $\frac{95}{6}$. Find a_1 and d. Construct the sequence.

17. Insert three arithmetic means between 2 and 22.

18. Insert four arithmetic means between 8 and 23.

19. Find the sum of the even numbers from 2 to 100, inclusive.

20. Find the sum of the odd numbers from 1 to 99, inclusive.

21. Find the sum of the first 20 terms of the series $5 + 8 + 11 + 14 + \cdots$.

22. Find the sum of the first 14 terms of the series $11 + 7 + 3 + \cdots$.

Find the sum of each series.

23. $\sum_{n=1}^{12} (6n - 3)$

24. $\sum_{n=1}^{16} (7n - 76)$

25. $\sum_{n=1}^{18} 5n$

26. $\sum_{n=1}^{20} 3n$

B

27. How many poles will be in a pile of telephone poles if there are 30 in the bottom layer, 29 in the second, and so on, until there is one in the top layer?

28. If 10¢ is saved on October 1, 20¢ on October 2, 30¢ on October 3, and so on, how much is saved during October? (October has 31 days.)

29. Find a formula for the sum of the first n odd natural numbers.

30. *Multi-Step Problem* Find three numbers in an arithmetic sequence such that the sum of the first and third is 10 and the product of the first and second is 15.

31. Insert enough arithmetic means between 1 and 50 so that the sum of the resulting arithmetic series will be 459.

32. Find the first term and the common difference for the arithmetic sequence $3x + 2y, 4x + y, 5x, 6x - y, \ldots$.

33. Find the first term and the common difference for the arithmetic sequence where $a_2 = 4p - 3q$ and $a_4 = 10p + q$.

34. Use a calculator to find the first 10 terms of the arithmetic sequence for which $a_1 = \$8760$ and $d = -\$798.23$.

35. Use a calculator to find the sum of the first 10 terms of the sequence given in Exercise 34.

36. *Critical Thinking* A **harmonic sequence** is a sequence whose reciprocals form an arithmetic sequence. Make up a harmonic sequence.

Challenge

37. Inserting a **harmonic mean** creates a sequence whose reciprocals form an arithmetic sequence. Insert four harmonic means between $\frac{1}{5}$ and $\frac{1}{20}$.

38. Prove that if p, m, and q form an arithmetic sequence, then $m = \frac{p + q}{2}$.

39. Prove Theorem 14-2.

40. Prove Theorem 14-3.

41. Prove that if x, y, and z are three consecutive terms of an arithmetic sequence, then $x + y + z = 3y$.

Mixed Review

Solve. **42.** $|x| \geq 5$ **43.** $|3y - 4| < 8$ *2-7*

$$\text{Let } A = \begin{bmatrix} -2 & 1 \\ 5 & 3 \end{bmatrix} \qquad B = \begin{bmatrix} 3 & -1 & 2 \\ -1 & 2 & 1 \\ 3 & 5 & 2 \end{bmatrix}$$

Find. **44.** $|A|$ **45.** $|B|$ **46.** A^{-1} **47.** B^{-1} *13-3, 13-5, 13-6*

Find $f^{-1}(x)$ for the given function. **48.** $f(x) = x^3 + 8$ **49.** $f(x) = \sqrt[3]{x + 1}$

50. $f(x) = x^3$ **51.** $f(x) = 3^x$ **52.** $f(x) = \log_3 x$ *12-1*

Convert to logarithmic equations. **53.** $7^x = 5$ **54.** $x^5 = 7$ **55.** $5^7 = x$

56. In triangle ABC, the measure of angle A is 10° more than the measure of angle B, and the measure of angle B is 10° more than the measure of angle C. Find the angle measures. *2-9*

14-3 Geometric Sequences and Series

What You'll Learn

1. To find the common ratio of a given geometric sequence
2. To solve problems involving the *n*th term of a geometric sequence
3. To find partial sums of a geometric series

. . . And Why

To find the sum of an infinite geometric series

The value of a car is reduced, or *depreciates,* a certain amount each year. Here is the value of a $30,000 car year by year.

$27,000 $24,300 $21,870 $19,683

This is not an *arithmetic* sequence because there is no common difference. However, multiplying any term by 0.9 gives us the next term. So the *ratio* of each term to the preceding one is 0.9 to 1.

PART 1 Geometric Sequences

Objective: Find the common ratio of a given geometric sequence.

Definition

A sequence in which a constant r can be multiplied by each term to get the next is called a **geometric sequence.**

The constant r is called the **common ratio.**

"Classic" automobiles can be worth more than their original purchase price. Cars depreciate at first, but if restored, they *appreciate.*

The notation for geometric sequences is the same as the notation for arithmetic sequences: a_1 is the first term, a_2 is the second term, a_3 is the third term, and so on.

To find the common ratio, divide any term by the one before it.

EXAMPLES Find the common ratio of each geometric sequence.

1 $3, 6, 12, 24, \ldots$

$6 \div 3 = 2,\ 12 \div 6 = 2, \ldots$
The common ratio is 2.

2 $3, -6, 12, -24, \ldots$

$-6 \div 3 = -2,\ 12 \div -6 = -2, \ldots$
The common ratio is -2.

3 $1, \frac{1}{2}, \frac{1}{4}, \frac{1}{8}, \ldots$

$\frac{1}{2} \div 1 = \frac{1}{2},\ \frac{1}{4} \div \frac{1}{2} = \frac{1}{2}, \ldots$
The common ratio is $\frac{1}{2}$.

Try This Find the common ratio of each geometric sequence.

a. $1, 5, 25, 125, \ldots$
b. $3, -9, 27, -81, \ldots$
c. $48, -12, 3, \ldots$
d. $54, 18, 6, \ldots$

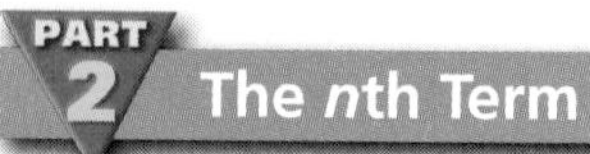

The *n*th Term

Objective: Solve problems involving the *n*th term of a geometric sequence.

We can think of the sequence 3, 6, 12, 24, . . . as

$$3 \cdot 2^0, \quad 3 \cdot 2^1, \quad 3 \cdot 2^2, \quad 3 \cdot 2^3, \quad \ldots$$

The pattern suggests that the *n*th term is $3 \cdot 2^{n-1}$. Likewise, in any geometric sequence, if we let a_1 be the first term and r be the common ratio, then a_1r is the second term, a_1r^2 is the third term, and so on. Generalizing, we have the following.

Theorem 14-4

In a geometric sequence, the *n*th term is given by $a_n = a_1r^{n-1}$.

Note that the exponent is one less than the number of the term.

EXAMPLE 4 Find the 11th term of the geometric sequence 64, −32, 16, −8, ...

Note that $a_1 = 64$, $n = 11$, and $r = \frac{-32}{64}$, or $-\frac{1}{2}$.

$$a_n = a_1r^{n-1}$$
$$a_{11} = 64 \cdot \left(-\frac{1}{2}\right)^{11-1}$$
$$= 64 \cdot \left(-\frac{1}{2}\right)^{10} = 2^6 \cdot \frac{1}{2^{10}} = 2^{-4}, \text{ or } \frac{1}{16}$$

This result can be verified by graphing the sequence (see p. 633).

Try This

e. Find the 6th term of the geometric sequence 3, −15, 75, ...

Numbers $m_1, m_2, m_3, \ldots, m_n$, are called **geometric means** of the numbers a and b if $a, m_1, m_2, m_3, \ldots, m_n, b$ form a geometric sequence. We can use Theorem 14-4 to insert geometric means between two numbers.

EXAMPLE 5 Insert two geometric means between 3 and 24.

3 is the 1st term and 24 is the 4th term.

$$24 = 3(r)^{4-1} \quad \text{Using Theorem 14-4; } a_n = a_1r^{n-1}$$
$$8 = r^3$$
$$2 = r$$

So we have 3, 6, 12, 24.

Try This

f. Insert one geometric mean between 5 and 20.

EXAMPLE 6 A student borrows \$600 at 12% interest compounded monthly. The student pays the loan in one payment at the end of 36 months. How much does the student pay?

For any principal (P), at 12% annual or 1% monthly interest, the student will owe $P + 0.01P$ at the end of 1 month, or $1.01P$. Then $1.01P$ is the principal for the second month. Thus at the end of the second month the student owes $1.01(1.01P)$. Then the principal at the beginning of the third month is $1.01(1.01P)$. It appears that the following sequence is being formed.

$$P, 1.01P, 1.01(1.01P), \ldots$$

This is a geometric sequence with $a_1 = 600$, $n = 37$, and $r = 1.01$.

$a_n = a_1 r^{n-1}$ Using Theorem 14-4

$a_{37} = 600 \cdot (1.01)^{37-1}$ Finding the 37th term (the principal at the *beginning* of the 37th month or *end* of the 36th month)

$= 600 \cdot 1.01^{36}$

$= 600 \cdot 1.430769 \approx 858.46$

The student pays \$858.46 (rounded to the nearest cent).

Try This

g. A college student borrows \$400 at 12% interest compounded monthly. The loan is repaid in one lump-sum payment at the end of 24 months. How much does the student pay?

Writing Math

By using subscripts we can write as many equations with as many variables as we need. For instance,

$$y_1 = a_{11}x_1 + a_{12}x_2 + \cdots + a_{1n}x_n$$
$$y_2 = a_{21}x_1 + a_{22}x_2 + \cdots + a_{2n}x_n$$
$$\vdots$$
$$y_n = a_{n1}x_1 + a_{n2}x_2 + \cdots + a_{nn}x_n$$

represents n equations with n variables and n constants.

PART 3 Geometric Series

Objective: Find partial sums of a geometric series.

A **geometric series** is a series associated with a geometric sequence. Suppose that we want to find the sum S_n of the first n terms of a geometric sequence.

$$S_n = a_1 + a_1 r + a_1 r^2 + \cdots + a_1 r^{n-1}$$

If we multiply both sides by r, we have

$$rS_n = a_1 r + a_1 r^2 + a_1 r^3 + \cdots + a_1 r^{n-1} + a_1 r^n$$

Subtracting the second equation from the first, we have

$S_n - rS_n = a_1 - a_1 r^n$

$S_n(1 - r) = a_1(1 - r^n)$ Factoring

$S_n = \dfrac{a_1(1 - r^n)}{1 - r}$ Dividing both sides by $1 - r$

This gives us a formula for the sum of the first n terms of a geometric series.

Theorem 14-5

The sum of the first n terms of a geometric series is given by

$$S_n = \frac{a_1(1 - r^n)}{1 - r}$$

EXAMPLE 7 Find the sum of the first 6 terms of the geometric series $3 + 6 + 12 + 24 + \cdots$.

$a_1 = 3, n = 6$, and $r = \frac{6}{3}$, or 2

$S_n = \frac{a_1(1 - r^n)}{1 - r}$ Using Theorem 14-5

$S_6 = \frac{3(1 - 2^6)}{1 - 2}$ Substituting

$= \frac{3(-63)}{-1} = 189$

Journal

Suppose you are an investigative reporter assigned to interview a sequence. Make a list of at least four questions that you would ask.

Try This

h. Find the sum of the first 6 terms of the geometric series $3 + 15 + 75 + 375 + \cdots$.

i. Find the sum of the first 10 terms of the geometric series $2 - 1 + \frac{1}{2} - \frac{1}{4} + \cdots$.

EXAMPLE 8 Find the sum of the geometric series $\sum_{n=1}^{5} \left(\frac{1}{2}\right)^{n+1}$.

First find a few terms.

$\left(\frac{1}{2}\right)^2 + \left(\frac{1}{2}\right)^3 + \left(\frac{1}{2}\right)^4 \ldots$

In this geometric series we have $a_1 = \frac{1}{4}$, $n = 5$, and $r = \frac{1}{2}$.

$S_n = \frac{a_1(1 - r^n)}{1 - r}$ Using Theorem 14-5

$S_5 = \frac{\frac{1}{4}\left(1 - \left(\frac{1}{2}\right)^5\right)}{1 - \frac{1}{2}} = \frac{\frac{1}{4}\left(\frac{31}{32}\right)}{\frac{1}{2}}$

$= \frac{31}{64}$

Try This Find the sum of each geometric series.

j. $\sum_{n=1}^{5} 3^n$

k. $\sum_{n=1}^{4} \left(\frac{2}{3}\right)^{n-1}$

Extra Help On the Web

Look for worked-out examples at the Prentice Hall Web site.
www.phschool.com

14-3 Exercises

A

Find the common ratio for each geometric sequence.

1. $12, -4, \frac{4}{3}, -\frac{4}{9}, \ldots$ **2.** $4, 8, 16, 32, \ldots$ **3.** $1, -1, 1, -1, 1, \ldots$

4. $-5, -0.5, -0.05, -0.005, \ldots$ **5.** $\frac{1}{x}, \frac{1}{x^2}, \frac{1}{x^3}, \ldots$ **6.** $5, \frac{5m}{2}, \frac{5m^2}{4}, \frac{5m^3}{8}, \ldots$

7. Find the 6th term of the geometric sequence $1, 3, 9, \ldots$.

8. Find the 10th term of the geometric sequence $\frac{8}{243}, \frac{4}{81}, \frac{2}{27}, \ldots$.

9. Find the 5th term of the geometric sequence $2, -10, 50, \ldots$.

10. Find the 9th term of the geometric sequence $2, 2\sqrt{3}, 6, \ldots$.

11. Insert one geometric mean between 3 and 48.

12. Insert two geometric means between 4 and 32.

13. Insert three geometric means between $\frac{1}{4}$ and $\frac{1}{64}$.

14. Insert four geometric means between $\frac{1}{9}$ and 27.

15. A college student borrowed $800 at 12% interest compounded monthly. The loan is paid in one lump sum at the end of 2 years. How much did the student pay?

16. A college student borrowed $1000 at 10% interest compounded monthly. The loan is paid in one lump sum at the end of 4 years. How much did the student pay?

17. Find the sum of the first 7 terms of the geometric series $6 + 12 + 24 + \cdots$.

18. Find the sum of the first 6 terms of the geometric series $16 - 8 + 4 - \cdots$.

19. Find the sum of the first 7 terms of the geometric series $\frac{1}{18} - \frac{1}{6} + \frac{1}{2} - \cdots$.

20. Find the sum of the first 5 terms of the geometric series $6 + 0.6 + 0.06 + \cdots$.

21. Find the sum of the first 8 terms of the series $1 + x + x^2 + x^3 + \cdots$.

22. Find the sum of the first 10 terms of the series $1 + x^2 + x^4 + x^6 + \cdots$.

Find the sum of each geometric series.

23. $\sum_{n=1}^{6} \left(\frac{1}{2}\right)^{n-1}$ **24.** $\sum_{n=1}^{8} 2^n$ **25.** $\sum_{n=1}^{7} 4^n$ **26.** $\sum_{n=1}^{5} \left(\frac{1}{3}\right)^{n-1}$

B

27. A Ping-Pong ball is dropped from a height of 16 ft and always rebounds $\frac{1}{4}$ of the distance of the previous fall.

a. What distance does it rebound the 6th time?

b. What is the total distance the ball has travelled after this time?

28. A town has a population of 100,000 now and the population is increasing 10% every year. What will be the population in 5 years?

29. Use a calculator to find the sum of the first 5 terms of each geometric sequence. Round to the nearest cent.

a. $\$1000, \$1000(1.08), \$1000(1.08)^2, \ldots$ **b.** $\$200, \$200(1.13), \$200(1.13)^2, \ldots$

30. Find the sum of the first n terms of $1 + x + x^2 + x^3 + \cdots$.

31. Find the geometric mean between each pair of numbers.

a. 4 and 9 **b.** 2 and 6

c. $\frac{1}{2}$ and $\frac{1}{3}$ **d.** $\sqrt{5} + \sqrt{2}$ and $\sqrt{5} - \sqrt{2}$

32. ***Critical Thinking*** The third term of a geometric sequence is 4. What is the product of the first five terms?

Challenge

33. If each term of a geometric sequence is multiplied by some number c, is the resulting sequence necessarily geometric?

34. If some number c is added to each term of a geometric sequence, is the resulting sequence necessarily geometric?

35. Show that each sequence is always a geometric sequence, given that $a_1, a_2, a_3, \ldots$ is a geometric sequence.

a. $a_1^{\,2}, a_2^{\,2}, a_3^{\,2}, \ldots$ **b.** $a_1^{\,-3}, a_2^{\,-3}, a_3^{\,-3}, \ldots$

36. A piece of paper is 0.01 in. thick. It is folded 20 times in such a way that its thickness is doubled each time. How thick is the result? (Use a calculator.)

37. A person decides to save money in a savings account for retirement. At the beginning of each year \$1000 is invested at 14% compounded annually. How much is in the retirement fund at the end of 40 years? (Hint: Remember that the end of year 40 is the beginning of year 41.)

38. ***Mathematical Reasoning*** Prove that if the corresponding terms of two geometric sequences are multiplied, then the products form a geometric sequence.

39. Suppose x, y, and z are three consecutive terms in a geometric sequence. Prove that $\frac{1}{y - x}$, $\frac{1}{2y}$, and $\frac{1}{y - z}$ are terms in an arithmetic sequence.

40. Explain why the number zero cannot be a term of a geometric sequence.

Mixed Review

Solve. **41.** $x^2 + y^2 - 25 = 0$, $y^2 + 8x - 40 = 0$ **42.** $xy - 25 = 0$, $y - x = 0$ *10-7*

43. The area of a triangle is 27 cm^2. The base is 3 cm shorter than the height. Find the height. *5-8*

14-4 Infinite Geometric Series

What You'll Learn

1. To determine whether a given geometric series has a sum
2. To find the sum of an infinite geometric series

. . . And Why

To solve problems using properties of a geometric series

PART 1 Convergent Geometric Series

Objective: Determine whether a given geometric series has a sum.

Let us consider an infinite geometric series.

$$2 + 4 + 8 + 16 + 32 + 64 + \cdots + 2^n + \cdots$$

As n becomes larger and larger, the sum of the first n terms gets larger without bound. The next example, however, is different.

$$\frac{1}{2} + \frac{1}{4} + \frac{1}{8} + \frac{1}{16} + \cdots + \frac{1}{2^n} + \cdots$$

Let us look at the sum of the first n terms for some values of n.

$$S_1 = \frac{1}{2}$$

$$S_2 = \frac{1}{2} + \frac{1}{4} = \frac{3}{4}$$

$$S_3 = \frac{1}{2} + \frac{1}{4} + \frac{1}{8} = \frac{7}{8}$$

$$S_4 = \frac{1}{2} + \frac{1}{4} + \frac{1}{8} + \frac{1}{16} = \frac{15}{16}$$

Each denominator is in the form 2^n. Each numerator appears to be one less than the denominator. There is a pattern, which can be described as $S_n = \frac{2^n - 1}{2^n}$. As n gets very large, S_n gets very close to 1. We say S_n approaches a **limit** of 1. We define the sum of this infinite series to be 1.

Definition

If, in an infinite series, S_n approaches some limit as n becomes very large, that **limit** is defined to be the sum of the series. If an infinite series has a sum, it is said to **converge** or to be **convergent.**

Some infinite series have sums (converge) and some do not.

Theorem 14-6

An infinite geometric series is convergent and thus has a sum if and only if $|r| < 1$ (the absolute value of the common ratio is less than 1).

EXAMPLES Determine which geometric series have sums.

1 $1 - \frac{1}{2} + \frac{1}{4} - \frac{1}{8} + \frac{1}{16} + \cdots \quad r = -\frac{1}{2}, |r| < 1$

The series has a sum, by Theorem 14-6.

2 $1 + 5 + 25 + 125 + \cdots \quad r = 5, |r| > 1$

The series does not have a sum.

3 $1 + (-1) + 1 + (-1) + \cdots \quad r = -1, |r| = 1$

The series does not have a sum.

Try This Determine which geometric series have sums.

a. $4 + 16 + 64 + \cdots$ **b.** $5 - 30 + 180 - \cdots$ **c.** $1 + \frac{1}{3} + \frac{1}{9} + \frac{1}{27} + \cdots$

PART 2 Finding Sums

Objective: Find the sum of an infinite geometric series.

Theorem 14-7

The sum of an infinite geometric series, with $|r| < 1$, is given by $S = \frac{a_1}{1 - r}$.

EXAMPLE 4 Find the sum of the infinite geometric series $5 + \frac{5}{2} + \frac{5}{4} + \frac{5}{8} + \cdots$.

Note that $a_1 = 5$ and $r = \frac{1}{2}$. We use Theorem 14-7.

$$S = \frac{5}{1 - \frac{1}{2}} = 10$$

Try This Find the sum of each infinite geometric series.

d. $1 + \frac{1}{3} + \frac{1}{9} + \frac{1}{27} + \cdots$ **e.** $4 - 1 + \frac{1}{4} - \frac{1}{16} + \cdots$

Proof of Theorem 14-7

The sum of the first n terms of an infinite geometric series is $S_n = \frac{a_1(1 - r^n)}{1 - r}$.

As n gets very large, we look at r^n and see that, since $|r| < 1$, r^n gets very small, approaching 0. Thus the numerator approaches a_1. The limit of S_n as n gets very large is, therefore, $\frac{a_1}{1 - r}$, and we have $S = \frac{a_1}{1 - r}$.

Extra Help On the Web

Look for worked-out examples at the Prentice Hall Web site.
www.phschool.com

14-4 Exercises

A

Determine which geometric series have sums.

1. $5 + 10 + 20 + 40 + \cdots$

2. $16 + 8 + 4 + 2 + \cdots$

3. $6 + 2 + \frac{2}{3} + \frac{2}{9} + \cdots$

4. $2 - 4 + 8 - 16 + 32 - \cdots$

5. $1 + 0.1 + 0.01 + 0.001 + \cdots$

6. $-\frac{5}{3} - \frac{10}{9} - \frac{20}{27} - \frac{40}{81} - \cdots$

7. $1 - \frac{1}{5} + \frac{1}{25} - \frac{1}{125} + \cdots$

8. $6 + \frac{42}{5} + \frac{294}{25} + \cdots$

Find the sum of each infinite geometric series.

9. $4 + 2 + 1 + \cdots$

10. $7 + 3 + \frac{9}{7} + \cdots$

11. $1 + \frac{1}{2} + \frac{1}{4} + \cdots$

12. $\frac{8}{3} + \frac{4}{3} + \frac{2}{3} + \cdots$

13. $16 + 1.6 + 0.16 + \cdots$

14. $4 + 2.4 + 1.44 + \cdots$

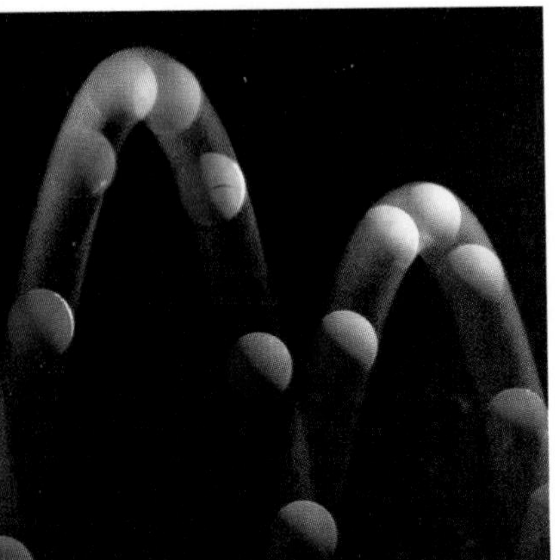

Slow motion photography can capture the movement of a bouncing ball. Graphing calculators can depict the graph of a bouncing ball using data collected by a motion detector.

B

Repeating decimals represent infinite geometric series. For example, $0.\overline{6}$ represents $0.6 + 0.06 + 0.006 + 0.0006 + \cdots$.

We can use Theorem 14-7 to find rational notation, using 0.6 for a_1 and 0.1 for r. Find rational notation for each number.

15. $0.\overline{7}$

16. $0.\overline{3}$

17. $0.\overline{21}$

18. $0.\overline{63}$

19. $5.\overline{15}$

20. $4.\overline{125}$

21. How far up and down will a ball travel before stopping if it is dropped from a height of 12 m, and each rebound is $\frac{1}{3}$ of the previous distance? (Hint: Use an infinite geometric series.)

22. ***Critical Thinking*** The number 2 is the first term of an infinite geometric series with a sum of 3. List the first 5 terms of the series.

Challenge

23. The sides of a square are each 16 cm long. A second square is inscribed by joining the midpoints of the sides, successively. In the second square we repeat the process, inscribing a third square. If this process is continued indefinitely, what is the sum of the areas of all the squares? (Hint: Use an infinite geometric series.)

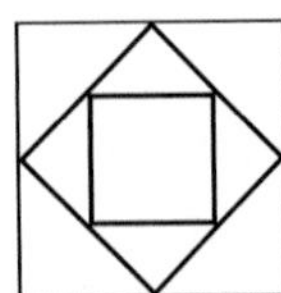

24. The infinite series

$$2 + \frac{1}{2} + \frac{1}{2 \cdot 3} + \frac{1}{2 \cdot 3 \cdot 4} + \frac{1}{2 \cdot 3 \cdot 4 \cdot 5} + \frac{1}{2 \cdot 3 \cdot 4 \cdot 5 \cdot 6} + \cdots$$

is not geometric, but does have a sum. Find values of S_1, S_2, S_3, S_4, S_5, and S_6. Make a conjecture about the value of S.

25. Find rational notation for 0.010101 . . . , which is in binary notation.

26. Consider the **harmonic series** $1 + \frac{1}{2} + \frac{1}{3} + \frac{1}{4} + \frac{1}{5} + \cdots$. Drop the first term and consider the remaining terms in the following way: Put $\frac{1}{2}$ in the first group, the next two terms in the second group, the next four terms in the third group, and the next eight terms in the fourth group. Compare the sum of each group with $\frac{1}{2}$ and use the result to argue whether the series converges.

27. **TEST PREP** What is the sum of the infinite geometric series $\sum_{-\infty}^{5} 2^n$?

A. 32 **B.** 64 **C.** -32 **D.** Cannot be done

Check your progress. Look for a self-test at the Prentice Hall Web site. www.phschool.com

Mixed Review

Let $P(x) = x^5 + 2x^4 - 15x^3 - 12x^2 - 76x - 80$.

28. List the possible rational roots of $P(x)$. *11-4*

29. Determine the number of possible positive and negative roots. *11-5*

30. Find $P(2)$, $P(5)$, $P(0)$, $P(-5)$. **31.** Solve $P(x) = 0$. *5-1, 11-1*

32. List the x-intercepts and roots of $P(x)$. **33.** Graph $P(x)$. *11-6*

Find the first three terms and the 12th term for each sequence.

34. $a_n = n^2 - 7$ **35.** $a_n = 10n + 17$ *14-1*

Graphing Sequences

Suppose we think of a sequence as a function. That is, to the number 1 is assigned the first term, to the number 2 is assigned the second term, and so on. We can graph a sequence by plotting a point for each term, or by using computer graphing techniques.

Graph.

a. $4, 2, 1, \frac{1}{2}, \ldots$ **b.** $a_n = 2n - 3$ **c.** $a_n = 10(0.8)^n$

14-5 Mathematical Induction

What You'll Learn

1 To prove statements about positive integers using the principle of mathematical induction

. . . And Why

To prove many algebraic formulas

PART 1 Proving Mathematical Statements

Objective: Prove statements about positive integers using mathematical induction.

Earlier we observed the sequence of odd numbers 1, 3, 5, 7, 9 . . . , $(2n - 1)$. The sequence of partial sums 1, 4, 9, 16, 25, . . . suggests that the sum of the first n odd integers is n^2. It is impossible to prove this by considering all possible cases. In order to deal with such problems we use the **principle of mathematical induction.**

The Principle of Mathematical Induction

If P_n is a statement concerning the positive integers n and

(a) P_1 is true, and
(b) assuming P_k is true implies that P_{k+1} is true,

then P_n must be true for all positive integers n.

The logic of the principle of mathematical induction is very reasonable. We first show **(a)** that the statement is true for $n = 1$. Then we show **(b)** that if the statement is true when n is some integer k, it must be true when n is the next integer $k + 1$. This means that if it is true for $n = 1$, it is true for $n = 2$. If it is true for $n = 2$, then it must be true for $n = 3$, and so on. To justify a statement using the principle of mathematical induction, both parts must be shown to be true.

EXAMPLE 1 Use the principle of mathematical induction to prove that the sum of n consecutive positive odd integers is n^2.

We are trying to prove that $1 + 3 + 5 + \cdots + (2n - 1) = n^2$.

First we must show **(a)** that the statement is true for $n = 1$.

$1 = n^2$
$1 = 1$ ✔

Now, suppose **(b)** that the statement is true when n is some integer k.

That is, $1 + 3 + 5 + \cdots + (2k - 1) = k^2$.

We must show that the statement is true when n is $k + 1$.

That is, we must show that if the sum of the first k odd positive integers is k^2, then the sum of the first $k + 1$ odd positive integers is $(k + 1)^2$.

$$1 + 3 + 5 + \cdots + (2k - 1) = k^2 \quad \text{Assumed true for } k$$

$$1 + 3 + 5 + \cdots + (2k - 1) + [2(k + 1) - 1] = k^2 + [2(k + 1) - 1]$$

Adding $2(k + 1) - 1$ to both sides

$$= k^2 + 2k + 2 - 1$$
$$= k^2 + 2k + 1$$
$$= (k + 1)^2 \ ✔$$

The principle of mathematical induction tells us that the statement is true for *all* odd positive integers n.

Now consider the sequence $1, 2, 4, 8, \ldots, 2^{n-1}$. Forming a series, we have $S_n = 1 + 2 + 4 + 8 + \cdots + 2^{n-1}$.

$$S_1 = 1;\ S_2 = 1 + 2 = 3;\ S_3 = 1 + 2 + 4 = 7;\ S_4 = 1 + 2 + 4 + 8 = 15$$

If we examine each partial sum, we see that in each case we have 1 less than a power of 2. This suggests that $S_n = 2^n - 1$.

EXAMPLE 2 Use the principle of mathematical induction to prove that $1 + 2 + 4 + 8 + \cdots + 2^{n-1} = 2^n - 1$.

First we must show **(a)** that this is true for $n = 1$.

$$2^{1-1} = 2^1 - 1; 2^0 = 2 - 1; 1 = 1 \ ✔$$

Now, suppose **(b)** that the statement is true when n is some integer k.
That is, $1 + 2 + 4 + 8 + \cdots + 2^{k-1} = 2^k - 1$.

We must show that the statement is true when $n = k + 1$.
That is, adding the $(k + 1)$st term should give us $2^{k-1} - 1$.

$$1 + 2 + 4 + 8 + \cdots + 2^{k-1} = 2^k - 1. \quad \text{Assumed true for } k$$

$$1 + 2 + 4 + 8 + \cdots + 2^{k-1} + [2^{(k+1)-1}] = 2^k - 1 + [2^{(k+1)-1}]$$

Adding $2^{(k+1)-1}$ to both sides

$$= 2^k - 1 + 2^k$$
$$= 2(2^k) - 1$$
$$= 2^{k+1} - 1 \ ✔$$

We have shown that if the statement $1 + 2 + 4 + 8 + \cdots + 2^{n-1} = 2^n - 1$ is true when n is some integer k, then it is true when n is $k + 1$. The principle of mathematical induction tells us that the statement is true for all positive integers.

Try This

a. Use the principle of mathematical induction to prove that $1 + 2 + 3 + 4 + \cdots + n = \frac{n(n + 1)}{2}$.

b. Use the principle of mathematical induction to prove that $1 + 3 + 7 + 15 + \cdots + (2^n - 1) = 2^{n+1} - n - 2$.

Extra Help On the Web

Look for worked-out examples at the Prentice Hall Web site. www.phschool.com

14-5 Exercises

A

Use the principle of mathematical induction to prove each of the following.

1. $3 + 4 + 5 + \cdots + (n + 2) = \frac{1}{2}n(n + 5)$

2. $3 + 5 + 7 + \cdots + (2n + 1) = n(n + 2)$

3. $-2 - 3 - 4 - 5 - \cdots - (n + 1) = -\frac{1}{2}n(n + 3)$

4. $4 + 4^2 + 4^3 + \cdots + 4^n = \frac{4}{3}(4^n - 1)$

5. $1^2 + 2^2 + 3^2 + 4^2 + \cdots + n^2 = \frac{n(n + 1)(2n + 1)}{6}$

6. $1^3 + 2^3 + 3^3 + 4^3 + \cdots + n^3 = \frac{n^2(n + 1)^2}{4}$

7. $\frac{1}{1 \cdot 2} + \frac{1}{2 \cdot 3} + \frac{1}{3 \cdot 4} + \frac{1}{4 \cdot 5} + \cdots + \frac{1}{n(n + 1)} = \frac{n}{n + 1}$

8. $2 + 5 + 8 + \cdots + (3n - 1) = \frac{n}{2}(3n + 1)$

9. $4 + 3 + 2 + \cdots + (5 - n) = \frac{1}{2}n(9 - n)$

10. $1 + \frac{1}{3} + \frac{1}{9} + \cdots + 3^{1-n} = \frac{3}{2}\left(1 - \left(\frac{1}{3}\right)^n\right)$

B

11. Prove that $\sum_{k=1}^{n} (2k + 3) = n(n + 4)$. **12.** Prove that $\sum_{k=1}^{n} 2^k = 2(2^n - 1)$.

13. ***Critical Thinking*** Explain how using the principle of mathematical induction is like knocking over an infinite arrangement of dominoes.

Challenge

14. Prove that $\left(1 + \frac{1}{1}\right)\left(1 + \frac{1}{2}\right)\left(1 + \frac{1}{3}\right)\cdots\left(1 + \frac{1}{n}\right) = n + 1$.

15. Prove that $\sum_{k=1}^{n} k^5 = \frac{n^2(n + 1)^2(2n^2 + 2n - 1)}{12}$.

16. Use Exercises 5 and 6 to find and prove a formula for $\sum_{k=1}^{n} (k^3 - k^2)$.

To fall sequentially as shown, dominoes must be set up so each will hit the next. Mathematical induction assumes each integer has a successor that it "touches."

Mixed Review

Let $P(x) = x^5 + x^4 - 16x - 16$. **17.** Solve $P(x) = 0$. *11-1*

18. For $D(x) = x - 3$, write $P(x) = Q(x) \cdot D(x) + R(x)$. *11-1*

Find the distance between **19.** $(5, -5)$ and $(-5, 5)$. **20.** $(\log 10, 3)$ and $(4, 7)$. *10-1*

Solve. **21.** $x^2 - 25 = 0$ **22.** $x^3 = 27$ **23.** $x^4 - 81 = 0$ *5-7, 8-5*

Reasoning Strategies

PART 1 Combine Strategies

Objective: Solve nonroutine problems using a combination of strategies.

What You'll Learn

1. To solve nonroutine problems using a combination of strategies

. . . And Why

To solve algebraic problems using a variety of strategies

The chart below shows the strategies that you have been introduced to in this book. We have seen that most problems are solved using a combination of strategies and that many problems can be solved in more than one way.

Reasoning Strategies

Write an Equation	Draw a Diagram	Try, Test, Revise
Make an Organized List	Make a Table	Look for a Pattern
Use Logical Reasoning	Simplify the Problem	Work Backward

EXAMPLE

How many rectangular arrays can be built using 36 blocks if all the blocks must be used?

UNDERSTAND the problem

The statement of the problem is simple. Understanding what the problem is asking us to find, however, may not be immediately clear. The strategies *Simplify the Problem* and *Draw a Diagram* can help us understand this problem. Suppose we had 6 blocks. By drawing diagrams we can find that there are 4 rectangular arrays that can be made using 6 blocks. This helps us understand what we must do, but we must use 36 blocks, not just 6.

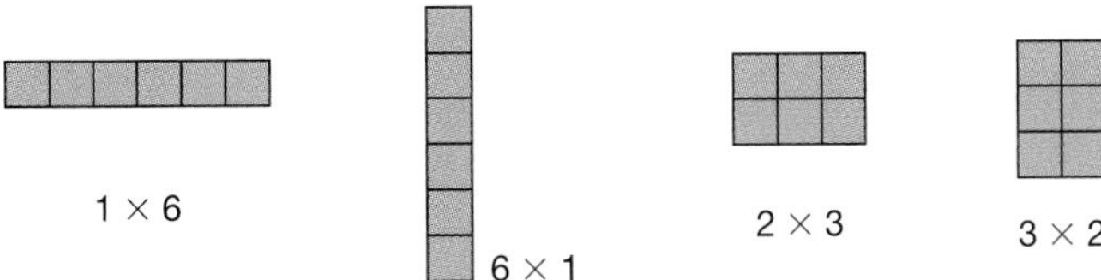

Develop and carry out a PLAN

We are asked to solve this problem for a large number of blocks, we might try to *Simplify the Problem* using arrays with 1 block, 2 blocks, 3 blocks, and so on. We will still *Draw a Diagram.*

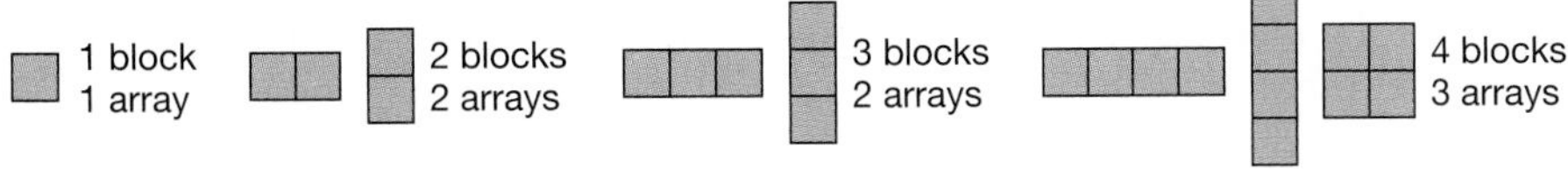

To organize our findings, we could *Make a Table* and *Look for a Pattern.* The table below has been completed through 10 blocks.

Number of blocks	1	2	3	4	5	6	7	8	9	10
Number of arrays	1	2	2	3	2	4	2	4	3	4

The pattern here is not like others you have seen before. The diagrams shown above, together with the table, help show the pattern. In the diagrams above for 6 blocks, we see arrays with these dimensions: $1 \times 6, 2 \times 3, 3 \times 2$, and 6×1. There are 4 arrays. Notice the first number in each array. They are 1, 2, 3, and 6. Notice that these are the factors of the number 6. There are 4 factors and 4 arrays. If we test this pattern with other numbers in the table, we find this always holds true. Thus if we find the factors of 36, we will know how many rectangular arrays can be made.

Find the ANSWER and CHECK

The factors of 36 are 1, 2, 3, 4, 6, 9, 12, 18, and 36. Thus there are 9 possible rectangular arrays using 36 blocks. The best way to check our work in this problem is to retrace our steps through the solution. Doing this shows that we have not made any errors, so the solution checks.

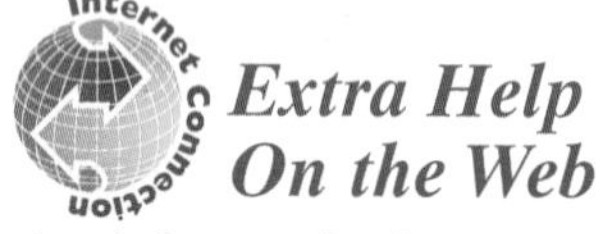

Extra Help On the Web

Look for worked-out examples at the Prentice Hall Web site.
www.phschool.com

14-6 Problems

Solve using one or more strategies.

1. All employees in a certain company agreed to take a 20% cut in wages for one year. What percent raise did they receive the following year in order to return to their original salaries?
2. Nancy has 16 identical doggy treats to be distributed among her 3 dogs. Each dog must receive at least 2 treats. In how many ways can she distribute the treats?
3. Find a, b, and c given the following conditions: $a(b + c) = 44$, $b(a + c) = 50$, and $c(a + b) = 54$.
4. A computer access-code number was designated in a special way. It was a 4-digit number. The number is the smallest integer that can be written as the sum of two positive cubes in two different ways, and the number is between 1000 and 2000. What is the code number?
5. A math test had 20 items. Students received 2 points for each correct answer and lost 1 point for each incorrect or missing answer. A student had a score of 16. How many items were answered correctly on the test?
6. Find the least positive integer with 8 different positive factors, including the number and 1. (Hint: Compare the number of factors of a number with the exponents in the prime factorization of the number.)

See Problem 2.

14 Chapter Wrap Up

14-1

You can find the terms of a **sequence** by substituting values for n.

The nth term of a sequence is given. Find the first four terms, the 10th term, and the 15th term.

1. $a_n = \frac{n-1}{n+1}$

2. $a_n = n - \frac{1}{n}$

Some sequences can be defined by **recursion.**

3. Find the first five terms of the sequence, when $a_1 = 2$ and $a_{n+1} = \frac{a_n}{1 - a_n}$.

Looking for a pattern in a sequence will help you find a **general term.** For each sequence, find a rule for the general term.

4. 0, 3, 8, 15, 24, . . .

5. $2, \frac{3}{2}, \frac{4}{3}, \frac{5}{4}, \frac{6}{5}, \ldots$

The Greek letter **Σ (sigma)** can be used to simplify notation when a series has a formula for the general term.

6. Rename $\sum_{n=1}^{3} 3^n$ without using sigma notation.

Write sigma notation for this sum.

7. $4 - 8 + 12 - 16 + 20 - 24$

14-2

a_n, the nth term of an **arithmetic sequence,** is found by using the formula $a_n = a_1 + (n - 1)d$, where a_1 is the first term and d is the **common difference.**

For the arithmetic sequence $3, 4\frac{1}{2}, 6, 7\frac{1}{2}, \ldots,$

8. Find a_1, d and find the 10th term.

9. What term has a value of 24?

Numbers $m_1, m_2, m_3, \ldots, m_n$ are called **arithmetic means** between a and b if $a, m_1, m_2, m_3, \ldots, m_n, b$ form an arithmetic sequence.

10. Insert three arithmetic means between 2 and 22.

There are two formulas for finding the sum of an **arithmetic series.**

$$S_n = \frac{n}{2}(a_1 + a_n) \qquad S_n = \frac{n}{2}(2a_1 + (n - 1)d)$$

11. Find the sum of the first 30 positive integers.

12. Find the sum of this series. $\sum_{k=1}^{20} (3k - 15)$

Key Terms

arithmetic means (p. 619)
arithmetic sequence (p. 617)
arithmetic series (p. 620)
common difference (p. 617)
common ratio (p. 624)
converge (p. 630)
convergent (p. 630)
general term (p. 612)
geometric means (p. 625)
geometric sequence (p. 624)
geometric series (p. 626)
harmonic mean (p. 623)
harmonic sequence (p. 623)
harmonic series (p. 633)
infinite sequence (p. 612)
infinite series (p. 615)
infinity, ∞ (p. 615)
limit (p. 630)
*n*th term (p. 612)
partial sums (p. 614)
principle of mathematical induction (p. 634)
recursion (p. 613)
sequence (p. 612)
series (p. 614)
sigma, Σ (p. 614)
term (p. 612)

Look for extension problems for this chapter at the Prentice Hall Web site. www.phschool.com

14-3

a_n, the nth term of a **geometric sequence,** is found by using the formula $a_n = a_1r^{n-1}$ where a_1 is the first term and r is the **common ratio.**

For the geometric sequence 4, −8, 16, −32, . . . ,

13. find the common ratio.

14. find the seventh term.

15. what term has a value of −512?

Numbers $m_1, m_2, \ldots, m_n$ are **geometric means** of a and b if $a, m_1, m_2, \ldots, m_n, b$ form a geometric sequence.

16. Insert two geometric means between 72 and 9.

The sum of the first n terms of a **geometric series** is given by $S_n = \frac{a_1(1 - r^n)}{1 - r}$.

17. Find the sum of the first six terms of the geometric series $2, 1, \frac{1}{2}, \frac{1}{4}, \ldots$.

18. Evaluate.

$$\sum_{n=1}^{7} (-3)^n$$

14-4

An **infinite geometric series** is **convergent** and has a sum if and only if $|r| < 1$. Determine which series have sums.

19. $1 - 2 + 4 - 8 + \cdots$

20. $3.2 + 1.6 + 0.8 + \cdots$

The sum, S, of an infinite geometric series with $|r| < 1$ is given by $S = \frac{a_1}{1 - r}$.

21. Find the sum of the geometric series 20, 10, 5, ...

22. Find the sum of the geometric series 10, −2, 0.4, −0.08, ...

14-5

We can use the **principle of mathematical induction** to prove statements. If P_n is a statement concerning the positive integers n and

(a) P_1 is true, and
(b) assuming P_k is true implies that P_{k+1} is true,

then P_n must be true for all positive integers.

Use mathematical induction to prove the following.

23. $1 + 4 + 7 + \cdots + (3n - 2) = \frac{n(3n - 1)}{2}$

14 ▷ Chapter Assessment

1. If $a_n = \frac{1}{2n + 1}$, find the first four terms, the 10th term, and the 15th term.
2. Find the first five terms of the sequence, where $a_1 = -3$ and $a_{n+1} = \frac{a_n}{1 + a_n}$.
3. Find a rule for a general term for this sequence.
   $-1, \frac{1}{2}, -\frac{1}{3}, \frac{1}{4}, -\frac{1}{5}, \ldots$
4. Rename without using sigma notation. $\sum_{n=1}^{4} 2^{n-1}$
5. Write using sigma notation. $-6 - 3 + 0 + 3 + 6 + 9 + 12$

For Exercises 6–9 use the following arithmetic sequence. $-4, -1\frac{1}{2}, 1, 3\frac{1}{2}, 6, \ldots,$

6. Find a_1, d, and find the 20th term.
7. What term has a value of 41?
8. Insert four arithmetic means between 2 and 8.
9. Find the sum of the first 84 positive integers.
10. Find the sum of this series.
    $\sum_{n=1}^{30} (7 - 2n)$

For Exercises 11–14 use the following geometric sequence. $24, 16, \frac{32}{3}, \ldots$

11. Find the common ratio.
12. Find the 6th term.
13. Find the sum of the first six terms.
14. What term is $\frac{1024}{729}$?
15. Insert five geometric means between $\frac{1}{16}$ and 4.
16. Find the sum of the first six terms of this geometric series.
    $\frac{2}{3} + \frac{1}{3} + \frac{1}{6} + \frac{1}{12} + \cdots$
17. Evaluate $\sum_{n=1}^{5} 4\left(-\frac{1}{2}\right)^n$.
18. Does this series have a sum?
    $\frac{1}{128} + \frac{1}{64} + \frac{1}{32} + \cdots$
19. Find the sum of the following geometric series. $81 - 27 + 9 - 3 + \cdots$
20. Use mathematical induction to prove
    $2 + 6 + 10 + 14 + \cdots + (4n - 2) = 2n^2$

CHAPTER 15

What You'll Learn in Chapter 15

- How to determine the number of ways a compound event may occur
- How to find the number of combinations or permutations of a set of *n* objects taken *r* at a time with and without replacement
- How to find circular permutations and permutations of a set of objects that are not all different
- How to use the binomial theorem to expand powers of binomials and how to find the *r*th term of the expansion
- How to compute the probability of a simple event
- How to find the probability of the intersection or union of sets
- How to design and use simulations to determine experimental probabilities

Skills & Concepts You Need for Chapter 15

1-2 Simplify.

1. $\frac{3}{8} \cdot \frac{4}{9} \cdot \frac{5}{10}$

2. $\frac{1}{9} \cdot \frac{2}{10} \cdot \frac{3}{11} \cdot \frac{4}{12}$

3. $\frac{13}{52} \cdot \frac{12}{51} \cdot \frac{11}{50}$

5-3 Multiply.

4. $(3x + 1)(3x + 1)$

5. $(2 - 3x)^2$

6. $(x - 1)^3$

7. $(x + 2)^4$

Counting and Probability

Satellites and space probes send messages to Earth in the form of electromagnetic impulses that are read as digits 0 or 1. Sometimes radiation, lightning, heat, or other factors interfere with a message and cause an error. Suppose that transmission errors are random and occur with probability p for each digit. What is the probability that more than one error occurs among 20 digits?

15-1 Counting Problems and Permutations

What You'll Learn

1. To determine the number of ways a compound event may occur
2. To find the total number of permutations of a set of *n* objects
3. To evaluate factorial notation
4. To find the number of permutations of *n* objects taken *r* at a time without replacement

. . . And Why

To use formulas to count the number of permutations of a set

PART 1 The Fundamental Counting Principle

Objective: Determine the number of ways a compound event may occur.

Many problems are concerned with the number of ways a set of objects can be arranged, combined, or chosen, or the number of ways a succession of events can occur. The study of such problems is called **combinatorics.**

EXAMPLE 1 A restaurant offers a dinner salad for \$3.75. There is a choice of a lettuce salad or a spinach salad. Then there is a choice of one topping from mushrooms, beans, or cheese. Finally, there is a choice of dressing from ranchstyle or oil and vinegar. How many different salad combinations are possible?

The possibilities are illustrated by this **tree diagram.**

Type	Topping	Dressing	Combination
lettuce	mushrooms	ranchstyle	1 lettuce, mushrooms, ranchstyle
		oil and vinegar	2 lettuce, mushrooms, oil and vinegar
	beans	ranchstyle	3 lettuce, beans, ranchstyle
		oil and vinegar	4 lettuce, beans, oil and vinegar
	cheese	ranchstyle	5 lettuce, cheese, ranchstyle
		oil and vinegar	6 lettuce, cheese, oil and vinegar
spinach	mushrooms	ranchstyle	7 spinach, mushrooms, ranchstyle
		oil and vinegar	8 spinach, mushrooms, oil and vinegar
	beans	ranchstyle	9 spinach, beans, ranchstyle
		oil and vinegar	10 spinach, beans, oil and vinegar
	cheese	ranchstyle	11 spinach, cheese, ranchstyle
		oil and vinegar	12 spinach, cheese, oil and vinegar

There are 12 possible salad combinations.

In situations where we consider combinations of items, or a succession of events such as flips of a coin or the drawing of cards, each result is called an **outcome.** An **event** is a subset of all possible outcomes. When an event is composed of two or more outcomes, such as choosing a card followed by choosing another card, we have a **compound event.**

Theorem 15-1

The Fundamental Counting Principle

In a compound event in which the first event may occur in n_1 different ways, the second event may occur in n_2 different ways and so on, and the kth event may occur in n_k different ways, the total number of ways the compound event may occur is

$$n_1 \cdot n_2 \cdot n_3 \cdot \cdots \cdot n_k.$$

For Example 1, there were $2 \cdot 3 \cdot 2 = 12$ salad combinations.

Try This

a. Jani can choose gray or blue jeans, a navy, white, green, or striped shirt, and running shoes, boots, or penny loafers. How many outfits can she form?

b. A restaurant offers four sizes of pizza, two types of crust, and eight toppings. How many combinations of pizza with one topping are there?

PART 2 Permutations

Objective: Find the total number of permutations of a set of *n* objects.

Consider a set of 3 objects, $\{A, B, C\}$. How many ways are there to arrange these objects? We can select any of the objects to be first, so there are 3 choices for the first object. Once the first object has been selected, there are 2 choices for the second object. The third object is then already determined, since it is the only one remaining. By the fundamental counting principle, there are $3 \cdot 2 \cdot 1$ possible arrangements. The set of all the arrangements is $\{ABC, ACB, BAC, BCA, CAB, CBA\}$.

We can generalize this to a set of n objects. We have n choices for the first selection, $n - 1$ for the second, $n - 2$ for the third, and so on. For the nth selection, there is only one choice.

Definition

A **permutation** of a set of n objects is an ordered arrangement of the objects.

The number of permutations of a set of n objects taken n at a time is denoted $\boldsymbol{{}_nP_n}$.

Theorem 15-2

The total number of permutations of a set of n objects is given by

$${}_nP_n = n(n - 1) \cdot (n - 2) \cdot \cdots \cdot 3 \cdot 2 \cdot 1.$$

EXAMPLES Find the following.

2 ${}_4P_4 = 4 \cdot 3 \cdot 2 \cdot 1 = 24$

3 ${}_7P_7 = 7 \cdot 6 \cdot 5 \cdot 4 \cdot 3 \cdot 2 \cdot 1 = 5040$

Try This Evaluate.

c. ${}_3P_3$ **d.** ${}_5P_5$ **e.** ${}_6P_6$

EXAMPLE 4 How many ways can 5 paintings be lined up on a wall?

Since this is an arrangement of objects, we use Theorem 15-2. There are ${}_5P_5$ ways.

$${}_5P_5 = 5 \cdot 4 \cdot 3 \cdot 2 \cdot 1 = 120$$

Try This

f. In how many ways can 6 people line up at a ticket window?

PART 3 Factorial Notation

Objective: Evaluate factorial notation.

For the product $5 \cdot 4 \cdot 3 \cdot 2 \cdot 1$, we write 5!, read "5 factorial."

Definition

n factorial or $\mathbf{n!}$ $= n(n-1)(n-2) \cdot \cdots \cdot 3 \cdot 2 \cdot 1$

EXAMPLES

5 $7! = 7 \cdot 6 \cdot 5 \cdot 4 \cdot 3 \cdot 2 \cdot 1 = 5040$

6 $3! = 3 \cdot 2 \cdot 1 = 6$

7 $1! = 1$

By Theorem 15-2 and the definition of $n!$, the total number of permutations of a set of n objects, ${}_nP_n$, is given by $n!$. We also define 0! to be 1 so that certain formulas and theorems can be stated concisely.

Try This

g. Evaluate 9!.
h. Using factorial notation only, represent the number of permutations of 18 objects.

Note the following.

$$\begin{aligned} 8! &= 8 \cdot 7 \cdot 6 \cdot 5 \cdot 4 \cdot 3 \cdot 2 \cdot 1 \\ &= 8 \cdot (7 \cdot 6 \cdot 5 \cdot 4 \cdot 3 \cdot 2 \cdot 1) \\ &= 8 \cdot 7! \end{aligned}$$

Theorem 15-3

For any natural number n,

$$n! = n(n - 1)!$$

By using Theorem 15-3 repeatedly, we can further manipulate factorial notation.

EXAMPLE 8 Rewrite 7! with a factor of 5!.

$$7! = 7 \cdot 6 \cdot 5!$$

Try This

i. Represent 10! in the form $n(n - 1)!$.
j. Rewrite 11! with the factor 8!.

PART 4 Permutations of n Objects Taken r at a Time

Objective: Find the number of permutations of n objects taken r at a time without replacement.

Consider a set of 7 objects. In how many ways can we construct an ordered subset having three members? We can select the first object in 7 ways. There are then 6 choices for the second and 5 choices for the third. By the fundamental counting principle, there are then $7 \cdot 6 \cdot 5$ ways to construct the subset. In other words, there are $7 \cdot 6 \cdot 5$ permutations of a set of 7 objects taken 3 at a time. Note that $7 \cdot 6 \cdot 5$ is equal to $\frac{7 \cdot 6 \cdot 5 \cdot 4!}{4!}$, or $\frac{7!}{4!}$. Generalizing gives us a theorem.

Theorem 15-4

The number of permutations of a set of n objects taken r at a time, denoted by ${}_nP_r$, is given by

$${}_nP_r = \frac{n!}{(n - r)!}$$

Each permutation is an ordered arrangement of r objects taken from the set of n objects.

EXAMPLE 9 Compute ${}_6P_4$.

$$\begin{aligned} {}_6P_4 &= \frac{6!}{(6-4)!} && \text{By Theorem 15-4} \\ &= \frac{6!}{2!} \\ &= \frac{6 \cdot 5 \cdot 4 \cdot 3 \cdot 2!}{2!} && \text{By Theorem 15-3} \\ &= 6 \cdot 5 \cdot 4 \cdot 3 = 360 \end{aligned}$$

Try This Compute.

k. ${}_7P_3$ **l.** ${}_{10}P_4$ **m.** ${}_8P_2$ **n.** ${}_{11}P_5$

EXAMPLE 10 In how many ways can letters of the set $\{R, S, T, U\}$ be arranged to form ordered codes of 2 letters? (No letters are repeated.)

$${}_4P_2 = \frac{4!}{(4-2)!} = \frac{4 \cdot 3 \cdot 2!}{2!} = 12 \text{ ways}$$

The 12 arrangements are *RS, RT, RU, ST, SU, TU, SR, TR, UR, TS, US, UT.*

EXAMPLE 11 In how many ways can the set $\{A, B, C, D, E, F, G\}$ be arranged to form ordered codes of (a) 7 letters? (b) 5 letters? (c) 2 letters?

(a) ${}_7P_7 = 7 \cdot 6 \cdot 5 \cdot 4 \cdot 3 \cdot 2 \cdot 1 = 5040$ ways

(b) ${}_7P_5 = 7 \cdot 6 \cdot 5 \cdot 4 \cdot 3 = 2520$ ways

(c) ${}_7P_2 = 7 \cdot 6 = 42$ ways

Try This

o. A teacher wants to write an ordered 6-question test from a pool of 10 questions. How many different forms of the test can the teacher write?

p. How many 7-digit numbers can be named, without repetition, using the digits 2, 3, 4, 5, 6, 7, and 8 if an even digit must come first?

Extra Help On the Web

Look for worked-out examples at the Prentice Hall Web site.
www.phschool.com

15-1 Exercises

A

Solve.

1. How many 4-letter code symbols can be formed with the letters *P, D, Q, X* without repetition?
2. How many 5-digit numbers can be formed using all the digits 0, 1, 2, 3, 4 without repetition?
3. In how many ways can 6 bicycles be parked in a row?
4. In how many ways can 7 different cards be laid out on a table in a row?

5. A woman is going out for the evening. She will put on one of 6 dresses, one pair out of 8 pairs of shoes, and go to one of 7 restaurants. In how many ways can this be done?

6. A man is going out for the evening. He will put on one of 7 suits, one pair out of 4 pairs of shoes, and go to one of 10 restaurants. In how many ways can this be done?

Mental Math Evaluate.

7. ${}_6P_6$ 8. ${}_5P_5$ 9. ${}_4P_4$ 10. ${}_2P_2$

Evaluate.

11. In how many ways can 7 people line up in a row?

12. In how many ways can 8 motorcycles be parked in a row?

13. How many permutations are there of the letters in the set $\{R, S, T, U, V, W\}$?

14. How many permutations are there of the letters in the set $\{M, N, O, P, Q, R, S\}$?

15. The owner of a business hires 8 secretaries, one for each of 8 department managers. How many different assignments of the secretaries are possible?

16. A fruit stand sells 9 different varieties of apples. How many different ways can the names of the apples be arranged on a sign?

Evaluate.

17. 5! 18. 6! 19. 1! 20. 0!

Represent each in the form $n(n - 1)!$.

21. 9! 22. 13! 23. $a!$ 24. $m!$

25. Rewrite 27! with a factor of 22!.

26. Rewrite 13! with a factor of 5!.

Compute.

27. ${}_4P_3$ 28. ${}_7P_5$ 29. ${}_{10}P_7$ 30. ${}_{10}P_3$

31. ${}_{20}P_2$ 32. ${}_{30}P_2$ 33. ${}_8P_3$ 34. ${}_7P_4$

35. In how many ways can the letters of the set $\{M, N, O, P, Q\}$ be arranged to form ordered codes of 4 letters? 3 letters?

36. In how many ways can the letters of the set $\{P, D, Q, W, T, Z\}$ be arranged to form ordered codes of 3 letters? 5 letters?

37. In how many ways can 4 people be assigned to 6 one-person offices?

38. In how many ways can 3 people be assigned to 5 one-person offices?

39. A special classroom has 8 sets of headphones for students who have difficulty hearing. How many possible combinations of students and headphones are there if 6 students in a class need to use headphones?

40. A special classroom has 10 sets of headphones for students who have difficulty hearing. How many possible combinations of students and headphones are there if 7 students in a class need to use headphones?

B

41. How many 7-digit telephone numbers can be formed, assuming that no digit is used more than once and the first digit is not 0?

42. **a.** In how many ways can a penny, nickel, dime, quarter, and half dollar be arranged in a straight line?

    b. Considering the coins and heads and tails, in how many ways can they be lined up?

43. **a.** What is the largest value of n for which a calculator will display $n!$ in standard notation?

    b. What is the largest value of n for which a calculator will find $n!$?

Solve for n.

44. ${}_nP_5 = 7 \cdot {}_nP_4$ **45.** ${}_nP_4 = 8 \cdot {}_{n-1}P_3$

46. ${}_nP_5 = 9 \cdot {}_{n-1}P_4$ **47.** ${}_nP_4 = 8 \cdot {}_nP_3$

48. ***Critical Thinking*** Give a convincing argument that $n! > 2^n$ for $n > 3$.

Challenge

49. ***Mathematical Reasoning*** Show that $2 \cdot 4 \cdot 6 \cdot \ldots \cdot (2n) = 2^n n!$.

50. ***Mathematical Reasoning*** Show that $n!$ is even for any $n > 1$.

51. ***Mathematical Reasoning*** Show that $n!$ ends in a zero for any $n > 4$.

Mixed Review

Solve. **52.** $x^3 + 20x^2 + 133x + 294 = 0$ *5-7* **53.** $x^4 + 27x^2 = 324$ *8-5*

For an arithmetic sequence find **54.** a_{50} when $a_{17} = 1$ and $d = 3$.

55. d when $a_3 = 0$ and $a_{13} = 33$. **56.** a_{17} when $a_{50} = 1$ and $d = 3$.

57. d when $a_{515} = 222$ and $a_{555} = 444$. *14-2*

Find the sum. **58.** $\sum_{n=3}^{33} (3n - 3)$ **59.** $\sum_{n=2}^{22} (2n - 22)$ **60.** $\sum_{n=4}^{44} (4n - 44)$

61. $\sum_{n=2}^{22} \left(\frac{1}{2}\right)^n$ **62.** $\sum_{n=3}^{33} 3^n$ **63.** $\sum_{n=4}^{44} \left(\frac{1}{4}\right)^{n-4}$ *14-3*

64. Three assemblers, A, B, and C, can produce 86 circuit boards per hour. A and B together can produce 59 circuit boards per hour, while A and C together can produce 58 circuit boards per hour. How many circuit boards can each assembler produce in an hour? *6-7*

65. Thanh Nguyen is a salesman who earns a salary plus commission. In a week when his gross sales are \$5000, he earns \$1300. In a week when his gross sales are \$7500, he earns \$1450.

a. Fit a linear function to the data points.

b. Use the function to find his earnings on gross sales of \$8500. *3-8*

Permutations for Special Counts

15-2

PART 1 Repeated Use of the Same Object

Objective: Find the number of permutations of *n* objects taken *r* at a time with replacement.

What You'll Learn

1. To find the number of permutations of *n* objects taken *r* at a time
2. To find permutations of a set of objects that are not all different
3. To find circular permutations

... And Why

To count the number of permutations for special circumstances

For an arrangement of objects to be a permutation, we cannot repeat any of the objects. In some situations, it is possible to use an object more than once.

Theorem 15-5

The number of orderings of n objects taken r at a time, with repetition, is n^r.

EXAMPLE 1 How many 5-letter ordered codes can be formed with the letters *A, B, C,* and *D* if we allow repeated use of the same letter?

We can select the first letter in 4 ways, the second in 4 ways, and so on. Thus there are 4^5, or 1024 orderings.

Try This

a. How many 5-letter ordered codes can be formed by repeated use of the letters of the alphabet? Find an expression. Do not evaluate.

EXAMPLE 2 A standard deck of cards has 52 different cards. How many 3-card ordered arrangements can be made by selecting the 3 cards (a) without replacement? (b) with replacement?

(a) The case 'without replacement' is the number of permutations of 52 objects taken 3 at a time.

$${}_{52}P_3 = 52 \cdot 51 \cdot 50 = 132{,}600 \qquad \text{By Theorem 15-4}$$

(b) The case 'with replacement' is the number of arrangements of 52 objects taken 3 at a time, with repetition.

$$52 \cdot 52 \cdot 52 = 52^3 = 140{,}608 \qquad \text{By Theorem 15-5}$$

Thus there are 132,600 possible ordered arrangements without replacement, and 140,608 with replacement.

To set up a game of solitaire, the first card is revealed by placing it face up. The next six cards are placed to the right of that card, face down. How many permutations are there for those six cards?

Try This

b. How many 2-card ordered arrangements can be made by selecting 2 cards from a deck of 52
(1) without replacement?
(2) with replacement?

PART 2 Permutations with Identical Objects

Objective: Find permutations of a set of objects that are not all different.

Consider the letters of the word HOOT. If the two Os were somehow different from each other, then the number of permutations of the four letters would be ${}_4P_4 = 4! = 24$. However, we cannot distinguish between the two Os.

There are only 12 permutations.
HOOT, HOTO, HTOO, TOOH, TOHO, THOO,
OTOH, OHOT, OHTO, OTHO, OOTH, OOHT

If the Os had been different, say Oo, there would have been 2! permutations of Oo (Oo and oO). If P is the number of permutations of the letters in HOOT, $P \cdot 2! = 4!$.

Hence, we have $P = \frac{4!}{2!} = 12$.

This method generalizes to the following theorem.

Theorem 15-6

The number of permutations, P, of n objects taken n at a time, with r objects alike, s of another kind alike, t of another kind alike, is

$$P = \frac{n!}{r!s!t!}$$

EXAMPLE 3 Find the number of permutations of the letters in DADDA.

There are five letters, including two As and three Ds. Thus, by Theorem 15-6 we have

$$P = \frac{5!}{3!2!} = \frac{5 \cdot 4 \cdot 3 \cdot 2 \cdot 1}{3 \cdot 2 \cdot 1 \cdot 2 \cdot 1} = 10$$

There are 10 permutations.

Review the explanation for finding the number of permutations for the letters of the word HOOT. Use the same reasoning to explain why dividing by 3!2! in Example 3 gives the correct number of permutations.

Try This

c. Find the number of permutations of the letters of the word BANANAS.
d. In how many ways can the product $a^2b^3c^2$ be written without using exponents?

Circular Permutations

Objective: Find circular permutations.

Consider the problem of seating four diplomats, X, Y, Z, and W, around a circular table. We cannot distinguish among these four arrangements.

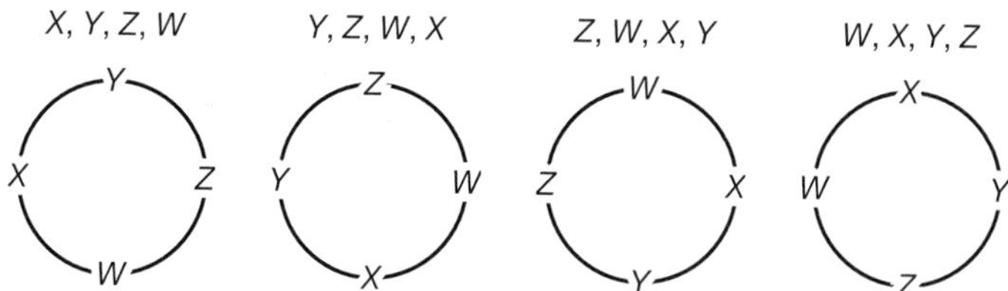

One way to think about the problem of circular permutations is to "fix" one of the objects and then consider how the other objects are arranged with respect to the "fixed" object. In the case of the four diplomats, suppose we fix diplomat X as shown. Then we arrange the three other diplomats.

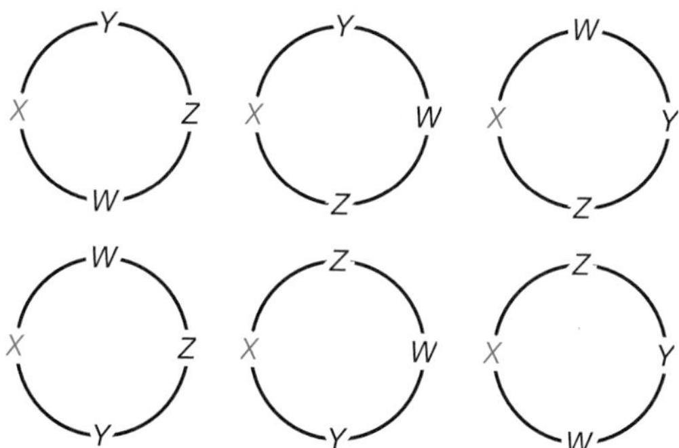

There are 6 circular permutations for the diplomats. Note that there were 4 permutations for the 4 diplomats that were indistinguishable (n permutations). This suggests the following theorem.

Theorem 15-7

The number of circular permutations of n objects is $\frac{n!}{n}$, or $(n - 1)!$.

EXAMPLE 4 Find the number of circular permutations of six people.

$$(n - 1)! = (6 - 1)! = 5! = 120$$

There are 120 circular permutations.

Try This

e. In how many ways can King Arthur arrange 8 knights around the Round Table?

Look for worked-out examples at the Prentice Hall Web site.
www.phschool.com

15-2 Exercises

A

1. How many 4-number license plates can be made using the digits 0, 1, 2, 3, 4, 5 if repetitions are allowed? not allowed?
2. How many 5-number license plates can be made using the digits 1, 2, 3, 4, 5, 6, 7 if repetitions are allowed? not allowed?
3. A teacher wants to write an ordered 4-question test from a pool of 12 questions. How many different forms of the test can the teacher write?
4. A teacher wants to write an ordered 5-question test from a pool of 8 questions. How many different forms of the test can the teacher write?
5. How many 4-number license plates can be made using the digits 0, 1, 2, 3, 4, 5 if an even digit must come first and repetitions are allowed? not allowed?
6. How many 5-number license plates can be made using the digits 1, 2, 3, 4, 5, 6, 7 if an odd digit must come first and repetitions are allowed? not allowed?
7. Suppose in Exercise 1 the license number must be even. Solve.
8. Suppose in Exercise 2 the license number must be odd. Solve.
9. A state forms its license plates by first listing a two-digit number that corresponds to the county in which the owner lives, then listing a letter of the alphabet, and finally a number from 1 to 9999. How many such plates are possible if there are 80 counties?

Find the number of permutations of the letters of these words.

10. DEED
11. ABBA
12. COMMITTEE
13. MISSISSIPPI
14. CINCINNATI
15. SUBSTITUTE
16. SATELLITE
17. ICICLE
18. MASSACHUSETTS
19. **TEST PREP** In how many ways can four blue flags, three red flags, and two green flags be arranged on a staff?
    A. 288 **B.** 1260 **C.** 15,120 **D.** 2520
20. **TEST PREP** A player in a word game has the letters E, E, B, D, G, G, G. In how many ways can these letters be arranged?
    A. 210 **B.** 1260 **C.** 840 **D.** 420
21. Find the number of permutations of five people around a circular table.
22. Find the number of permutations of six numbers on a spinner.
23. Find the number of circular permutations of eight cheerleaders.
24. In how many ways can the 10 swimmers on an aquatic ballet team be arranged in a circular pattern?

B

25. How many ordered codes can be formed using 4 of the letters of A, B, C, D, E if the letters
a. are not repeated? **b.** can be repeated?
c. are not repeated but must begin with D?
d. are not repeated but must end with DE?

26. How many different nine-digit numbers can be represented using the digits 1, 0, 0, 1, 5, 5, 6, 6, 6?

27. How many five-digit integers can be represented when 2, 6, and 7 may be used once and 0 may be used twice?

28. How many even five-digit integers can be represented when 1, 3, and 5 may be used once and 6 may be used twice?

29. ***Critical Thinking*** Provide an argument that the two following forms for the number of permutations for n objects taken r at a time are equivalent.

$$n \cdot (n-1) \cdot (n-2) \cdot \cdots \cdot (n-r+1) \quad \text{and} \quad \frac{n!}{(n-r)!}$$

Challenge

30. Find the number of permutations of five keys on a ring if two keys are identical.

31. In how many ways can King Arthur seat himself and eight knights, including Sir Lancelot, around the Round Table when Lancelot sits directly to the left of King Arthur?

32. In a sports tournament consisting of n teams, a team is eliminated when it loses one game. How many games are required to complete the tournament? Express your answer in terms of n.

33. In a softball tournament consisting of n teams, a team is eliminated when it loses two games. At most, how many games are required to complete the tournament? Express your answer in terms of n.

34. In how many ways can a 9-player baseball lineup be made if the pitcher always bats last, the shortstop always bats 6th or 7th, and the left fielder always bats 1st, 2nd, or 8th?

35. Show that ${}_nP_r = n(n-1)(n-2)\cdots(n-r+1)$.

The illustration above shows King Arthur encircled by 14 knights. How many circular permutations are there for 14 knights? (See Exercise 31.)

Mixed Review

Let $P(x) = x^4 + 2x^3 - 13x^2 - 14x + 24$.

36. Determine whether $-1, -2, -3$, and i are roots of $P(x)$.

37. Determine whether $(x+1)$, $(x+2)$, and $(x+4)$ are factors of $P(x)$.

38. Find $P(5), P(0), P(-4), P(-5)$.

39. Factor $P(x)$, solve $P(x) = 0$, and graph $P(x)$. *11-2, 11-6*

Sum the following series. **40.** $\frac{1}{2} + \frac{1}{4} + \frac{1}{8} + \cdots$ **41.** $8 + 4 + 2 + \cdots$

Insert three geometric means between **42.** 3 and 243. **43.** x^2 and x^4. *14-3*

15-3 Combinations

What You'll Learn

1 To find the number of combinations of a set of n objects taken r at a time

... And Why

To solve real-world problems involving combinations

PART 1 Selecting Elements of a Set

Objective: Find the number of combinations of a set of n objects taken r at a time.

Permutations of a set are arrangements of the elements of the set. Often we are concerned only with the number of ways we can select elements from a set. These are **combinations.**

EXAMPLE 1 How many combinations are there of the set $\{A, B, C, D\}$ taken 3 at a time?

The combinations are the following subsets.

$\{A, B, C\}$ $\{B, C, D\}$ $\{A, C, D\}$ $\{A, B, D\}$

Note that the set $\{A, B, C\}$ is the same as the set $\{B, A, C\}$, since they contain the same objects.

Try This

a. Consider the set $\{A, B, C, D\}$. How many combinations are there taken
(1) 4 at a time? (2) 3 at a time? (3) 2 at a time?
(4) 1 at a time? (5) 0 at a time?

Let us use the symbol $\binom{n}{r}$ to denote the number of ways we can select r elements from a set containing n elements. We read the symbol $\binom{n}{r}$ as "n choose r."

Consider the problem of finding the number of permutations of n objects taken r at a time, ${}_nP_r$. We can think of this process in two steps.

1. We *select* the r objects.
2. We *arrange* the r objects.

We can select the r objects from the n objects in $\binom{n}{r}$ ways. Then we can arrange the r objects in $r!$ ways. Thus by the fundamental counting principle we can select and then arrange in $\binom{n}{r} \cdot r!$ ways.

This means $\binom{n}{r} \cdot r! = {}_nP_r$. But we know ${}_nP_r = \frac{n!}{(n-r)!}$. Thus we now have $\binom{n}{r} \cdot r! = \frac{n!}{(n-r)!}$, which implies $\binom{n}{r} = \frac{n!}{r!(n-r)!}$.

Reading Math

$\binom{n}{r} = {}_nC_r$

Some books use the symbol ${}_nC_r$ to represent the number of combinations of a set of n objects taken r at a time

Theorem 15-8

The number of combinations of a set of n objects taken r at a time is

$$\binom{n}{r} = \frac{n!}{r!(n-r)!}$$

EXAMPLES Simplify.

2
$$\begin{aligned}\binom{5}{2} &= \frac{5!}{2!(5-2)!} && \text{By definition of } \binom{5}{2}\\ &= \frac{5!}{2!3!}\\ &= \frac{5 \cdot 4 \cdot 3!}{2!3!} && \text{By Theorem 15-3}\\ &= 10\end{aligned}$$

3
$$\binom{7}{4} = \frac{7!}{4!(7-4)!} = \frac{7!}{4!3!} = \frac{7 \cdot 6 \cdot 5 \cdot 4!}{3!4!} = \frac{7 \cdot 6 \cdot 5}{3 \cdot 2 \cdot 1} = 35$$

4
$$\binom{n}{3} = \frac{n!}{3!(n-3)!} = \frac{n(n-1)(n-2)(n-3)!}{3!(n-3)!} = \frac{n(n-1)(n-2)}{3!}$$

Try This Simplify.

b. $\binom{10}{8}$ **c.** $\binom{10}{2}$ **d.** $\binom{n}{1}$

EXAMPLE 5 For a sociological study 4 people are chosen at random from a group of 10 people. In how many ways can this be done?

No order is implied here, so the number of ways 4 people can be selected is $\binom{10}{4}$, by Theorem 15-8.

$$\binom{10}{4} = \frac{10!}{4!6!} = \frac{10 \cdot 9 \cdot 8 \cdot 7 \cdot 6!}{4!6!} = \frac{10 \cdot 9 \cdot 8 \cdot 7}{4 \cdot 3 \cdot 2 \cdot 1} = 210$$

EXAMPLE 6

How many ways can a congressional committee be formed from a set of 5 senators and 7 representatives if a committee contains 3 senators and 4 representatives?

The 3 senators can be selected in $\binom{5}{3}$ ways, the 4 senators in $\binom{7}{4}$ ways. Using the fundamental counting principle, $\binom{5}{3}\binom{7}{4} = 10 \cdot 35 = 350$.

Try This

e. In how many ways can a 5-player starting unit be selected from a 12-member basketball squad?

EXAMPLE 7 A hamburger restaurant advertises "We Fix Hamburgers 256 Ways!" This is accomplished using various combinations of catsup, onion, mustard, pickle, mayonnaise, relish, tomato, and lettuce. Of course, one can also have a plain hamburger. Use combination notation to show the number of possible hamburgers. Do not evaluate.

There are 8 basic seasonings. Each way of fixing a hamburger is a combination, or subset, of these toppings. There are $\binom{8}{0}$ subsets with 0 toppings, $\binom{8}{1}$ subsets with 1 topping, $\binom{8}{2}$ subsets with 2 toppings, and so on, up to $\binom{8}{8}$ subsets with 8 toppings. Thus the total number of combinations, or subsets, is given by the following expression.

$$\sum_{r=0}^{8}\binom{8}{r} = \binom{8}{0} + \binom{8}{1} + \binom{8}{2} + \cdots + \binom{8}{8}$$

Try This

f. Including cheese as a possibility, use combination notation to show the number of ways the restaurant could fix hamburgers. You do not need to evaluate your expression.

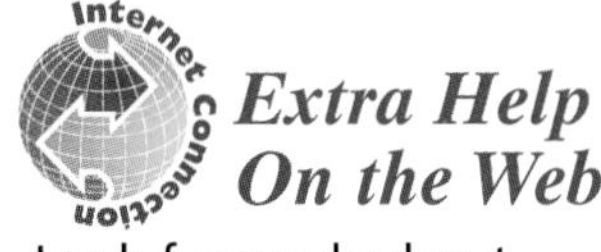

Extra Help On the Web

Look for worked-out examples at the Prentice Hall Web site.
www.phschool.com

15-3 Exercises

A

Simplify.

1. $\binom{9}{5}$ **2.** $\binom{14}{2}$ **3.** $\binom{50}{2}$ **4.** $\binom{40}{3}$

5. $\binom{12}{8}$ **6.** $\binom{14}{9}$ **7.** $\binom{n}{3}$ **8.** $\binom{n}{2}$

9. There are 23 students in a club. How many ways can 4 officers be selected?

10. On a test a student is to select 6 out of 10 questions, without regard to order. How many ways can this be done?

11. How many basketball games are played in a 9-team league if each team plays all other teams twice?

12. How many basketball games are played in a 10-team league if each team plays all other teams twice?

13. How many lines are determined by 8 points, no 3 of which are collinear? How many triangles are determined by the same points if no 4 are coplanar?

14. How many lines are determined by 7 points, no 3 of which are collinear? How many triangles are determined by the same points if no 4 are coplanar?

15. Of the first 10 questions on a test, a student must answer 7. Of the next 5 questions, 3 must be answered. In how many ways can this be done?

16. Of the first 8 questions on a test, a student must answer 6. Of the next 4 questions, 3 must be answered. In how many ways can this be done?

17. Suppose the Senate of the United States consisted of 58 Democrats and 42 Republicans. How many committees consisting of 6 Democrats and 4 Republicans could be formed? You do not need to simplify the expression.

18. Suppose the Senate of the United States consisted of 63 Republicans and 37 Democrats. How many committees consisting of 12 Republicans and 8 Democrats could be formed? You need not simplify the expression.

B

19. There are 8 points on a circle. How many triangles can be inscribed with these points as vertices?

Simplify.

20. $\binom{n}{n-1}$ **21.** $\binom{n}{n}$ **22.** $\binom{n+1}{n}$ **23.** $\binom{n+1}{n-1}$

Solve for n.

24. $\binom{n+1}{3} = 2 \cdot \binom{n}{2}$ **25.** $\binom{n}{n-2} = 6$

26. $\binom{n+2}{4} = 6 \cdot \binom{n}{2}$ **27.** $\binom{n}{3} = \binom{n-1}{1} \cdot \binom{n}{1}$

28. ***Critical Thinking*** Prove that for any natural numbers n and $r \leq n$, $\binom{n}{r} = \binom{n}{n-r}$. Explain what this means in terms of combinations.

Challenge

29. How many line segments are determined by the n vertices of an n-gon? Of these, how many are diagonals?

30. For a wrestling exhibition, 2 wrestlers per weight class were chosen from each of the following: 5 wrestlers at 106 lb, 3 at 115 lb, 2 at 126, 6 at 137, 5 at 150, 8 at 163, 7 at 181, 3 at 198, 2 at 220, and 4 over 220 lb. In how many ways could the wrestlers be chosen?

Mixed Review

Let $A = \begin{bmatrix} 2 & 1 & 4 \\ 3 & 0 & 7 \\ 4 & 5 & 6 \end{bmatrix}$ $B = \begin{bmatrix} 1 & 1 & 1 \\ 1 & 2 & 2 \\ 2 & 1 & 0 \end{bmatrix}$

Find. **31.** $3A + B$ **32.** $|A|$ **33.** $|B|$

34. B^{-1} **35.** BA **36.** AB^{-1} *13-2–13-5*

Find $f^{-1}(x)$. **37.** $f(x) = x^{\frac{2}{3}}$ **38.** $f(x) = 3^x$ **39.** $f(x) = 3x + \frac{3}{2}$ *12-1*

Evaluate. **40.** $|5 + 12i|$ **41.** $|6 + 8i|$ **42.** $|15 - 8i|$ *7-8*

Solve. **43.** $|3x + 4| \leq 10$ **44.** $|-8x + 9| < 1$ *2-7*

45. Find the dimensions of a rectangle with area 120 m^2 and perimeter 44 m. *5-8*

15-4 The Binomial Theorem

What You'll Learn

1. To find the rth term of the binomial expansion of $(a + b)^n$
2. To use the binomial theorem to expand powers of binomials
3. To determine the number of subsets of a finite set

. . . And Why

To compute binomial probabilities

Consider the following expanded powers of $(a + b)^n$ where $a + b$ is any binomial. Look for patterns.

$$\begin{aligned}
(a+b)^0 &= 1\\
(a+b)^1 &= a + b\\
(a+b)^2 &= a^2 + 2ab + b^2\\
(a+b)^3 &= a^3 + 3a^2b + 3ab^2 + b^3\\
(a+b)^4 &= a^4 + 4a^3b + 6a^2b^2 + 4ab^3 + b^4\\
(a+b)^5 &= a^5 + 5a^4b + 10a^3b^2 + 10a^2b^3 + 5ab^4 + b^5
\end{aligned}$$

$$\uparrow \quad \uparrow \quad \uparrow \quad \uparrow \quad \uparrow \quad \uparrow$$

$$\binom{5}{0}a^5b^0 + \binom{5}{1}a^4b^1 + \binom{5}{2}a^3b^2 + \binom{5}{3}a^2b^3 + \binom{5}{4}a^1b^4 + \binom{5}{5}a^0b^5$$

Note that each expansion is a polynomial. It is also a series, though not arithmetic or geometric. Notice these patterns.

1. In each term, the sum of the exponents is n.
2. The exponents of a start with n and decrease to 0. The exponents of b start with 0 and increase to n.
3. There is one more term than the degree of the polynomial. The expansion of $(a + b)^n$ has $n + 1$ terms.
4. The coefficients start with $\binom{n}{0}$ and go to $\binom{n}{n}$.

We generalize the expansion of a binomial raised to a whole number exponent as follows.

Theorem 15-9

The Binomial Theorem

For any binomial $(a + b)$ and any whole number n,

$$(a+b)^n = \binom{n}{0}a^n + \binom{n}{1}a^{n-1}b + \binom{n}{2}a^{n-2}b^2 + \cdots$$
$$+ \binom{n}{n-2}a^2b^{n-2} + \binom{n}{n-1}ab^{n-1} + \binom{n}{n}b^n.$$

The statement of Theorem 15-9 in sigma notation is as follows.

$$(a+b)^n = \sum_{r=0}^{n}\binom{n}{r}a^{n-r}b^r$$

Because of this theorem $\binom{n}{r}$ is called a **binomial coefficient.**

Finding the rth Term

Objective: Find the rth term of the binomial expansion of $(a + b)^n$.

Looking at the statement of the theorem we see that the $(r + 1)$th term is $\binom{n}{r}a^{n-r}b^r$.

That is, the 1st term is $\binom{n}{0}a^{n-0}b^0$, the 2nd term is $\binom{n}{1}a^{n-1}b^1$, the 3rd term is $\binom{n}{2}a^{n-2}b^2$, the 8th term is $\binom{n}{7}a^{n-7}b^7$, and so on.

EXAMPLE 1 Find the 7th term of $(4x - y^2)^9$.

We let $r = 6, n = 9, a = 4x$, and $b = -y^2$ in the formula $\binom{n}{r}a^{n-r}b^r$.

$$\begin{aligned}\binom{9}{6}(4x)^3(-y^2)^6 &= \frac{9!}{6!3!}(4x)^3(-y^2)^6\\ &= \frac{9 \cdot 8 \cdot 7}{3!}(64x^3y^{12})\\ &= 5376x^3y^{12}\end{aligned}$$

Try This

a. Find the 4th term of $(x - 3)^8$. **b.** Find the 6th term of $(y^2 + 2)^{10}$.

Binomial Expansion

Objective: Use the binomial theorem to expand powers of binomials.

EXAMPLE 2 Expand $(x^2 - 2y)^5$.

Note that $a = x^2, b = -2y$, and $n = 5$.

$$\begin{aligned}(x^2 - 2y)^5 &= \binom{5}{0}(x^2)^5 + \binom{5}{1}(x^2)^4(-2y) + \binom{5}{2}(x^2)^3(-2y)^2 +\\ &\quad \binom{5}{3}(x^2)^2(-2y)^3 + \binom{5}{4}x^2(-2y)^4 + \binom{5}{5}(-2y)^5 \quad \text{Using Theorem 15-9}\\ &= \frac{5!}{0!5!}x^{10} + \frac{5!}{1!4!}x^8(-2y) + \frac{5!}{2!3!}x^6(-2y)^2 +\\ &\quad \frac{5!}{3!2!}x^4(-2y)^3 + \frac{5!}{4!1!}x^2(-2y)^4 + \frac{5!}{5!0!}(-2y)^5\\ &= x^{10} - 10x^8y + 40x^6y^2 - 80x^4y^3 + 80x^2y^4 - 32y^5\end{aligned}$$

Try This Expand.

c. $(x^2 - 1)^5$

d. $\left(2x + \frac{1}{y}\right)^4$

662 Chapter

PART 3 Subsets

Objective: Determine the number of subsets of a finite set.

Suppose a set has n objects. The number of subsets containing r members is $\binom{n}{r}$, by Theorem 15-8. The total number of subsets of a set is the number with 0 elements, plus the number with 1 element, plus the number with two elements, and so on. The total number of subsets of a set with n members is $\binom{n}{0} + \binom{n}{1} + \binom{n}{2} + \cdots + \binom{n}{n}$. Now let us expand $(1 + 1)^n$, $(1 + 1)^n = \binom{n}{0} + \binom{n}{1} + \binom{n}{2} + \cdots + \binom{n}{n}$. Thus the total number of subsets is $(1 + 1)^n$ or 2^n.

Theorem 15-10

The total number of subsets of a set with n members is 2^n.

EXAMPLES

3 How many subsets are in the set $\{A, B, C, D, E\}$?
The set has 5 members, so the number of subsets is 2^5, or 32.

4 Show how a restaurant makes hamburgers 256 ways using 8 seasonings.

$$\binom{8}{0} + \binom{8}{1} + \cdots + \binom{8}{8} = 2^8 = 256$$

Try This

e. How many subsets are in the set of states of the United States?
f. In 10-pin bowling, how many possible pin combinations can remain after the first ball of a frame is thrown?

Extra Help On the Web
Look for worked-out examples at the Prentice Hall Web site.
www.phschool.com

15-4 Exercises

A

Find the indicated term of the binomial expression.

1. 3rd, $(a + b)^6$
2. 6th, $(x + y)^7$
3. 12th, $(a - 2)^{14}$
4. 11th, $(x - 3)^{12}$
5. Middle, $(2u - 3v^2)^{10}$
6. Middle two, $(\sqrt{x} + \sqrt{3})^5$

Expand.

7. $(m + n)^5$
8. $(a - b)^4$
9. $(x^2 - 3y)^5$
10. $(3c - d)^6$
11. $(1 - 1)^n$
12. $(1 + 3)^n$
13. $(\sqrt{2} + 1)^6$
14. $(1 - \sqrt{2})^4$

Determine the number of subsets of each of the following sets.

15. A set of 7 members

16. A set of 6 members

17. A set of 26 letters

18. A set of 24 letters

B

19. Expand and simplify $(\sqrt{2} - i)^4$.

20. Expand and simplify $(1 + i)^6$.

21. *Mathematical Reasoning* Find a formula for $(a - b)^n$. Use sigma notation.

22. *Mathematical Reasoning* Expand and simplify $\frac{(x + h)^n - x^n}{h}$. Use sigma notation.

23. *Critical Thinking* In the expansion of $(x + y)^3$, explain in terms of combinatorics why the coefficient for x^2y is the number of combinations of 3 things taken 1 at a time.

Challenge

Solve for x.

24. $\sum_{r=0}^{8} \binom{8}{r} x^{8-r} 3^r = 0$

25. $\sum_{r=0}^{4} \binom{4}{r} 5^{4-r} x^r = 64$

26. $\sum_{r=0}^{5} \binom{5}{r} (-1)^r x^{5-r} 3^r = 32$

27. Show that $\binom{n}{r} = \binom{n-1}{r-1} + \binom{n-1}{r}$.

28. Use Exercise 27 and the principle of mathematical induction to prove Theorem 15-9.

Quick Review

The principle of mathematical induction was introduced on page 634.

Mixed Review

Let $P(x) = x^4 - 8x^3 + 24x^2 - 32x + 16$.

29. List all the possible rational roots of $P(x)$. *11-4*

30. Solve $P(x) = 0$.

31. Find $P(-3), P(-1), P(0), P(2), P(30)$.

32. Graph $P(x)$. *11-6*

Simplify. **33.** $\frac{1}{2 + 2i}$ **34.** $(x - 2i)^{-1} - \frac{2i}{x^2 + 4}$ *7-9*

Evaluate. **35.** ${}_{10}P_{10}$ **36.** ${}_{69}P_{69}$ *15-1*

37. Atiba is planning to invest \$12,000, part at 15% and part at 9%. What is the most that he can invest at 9% in order to make at least \$1200 interest per year? *4-3*

Check your progress. Look for a self-test at the Prentice Hall Web site.
www.phschool.com

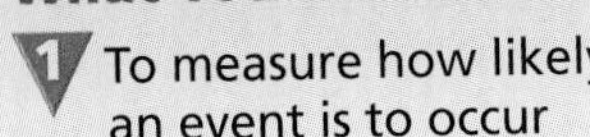

15-5 Probability

What You'll Learn

1 To measure how likely an event is to occur

. . . And Why

To solve real-world problems involving probability

PART 1 Computing Probability

Objective: Compute the probability of a simple event.

Suppose we perform an experiment such as flipping a coin, throwing a dart, drawing a card from a deck, or checking an item from an assembly line for quality. The result of an experiment is called an *outcome* or a **simple event.** The set of all possible outcomes is called a **sample space.** An *event* is a set of outcomes, that is, a subset of the sample space. For example, for the experiment "throwing a dart" at a three-colored dart board, the sample space has three outcomes, {red, yellow, blue}. One event may be to hit the yellow.

Definition

If an event E can occur m ways out of n possible equally likely outcomes of sample space S, the **probability** of that event is given by $P(E)$, where

$$P(E) = \frac{m}{n}$$

When the outcomes of an experiment all have the same probability of occurring, we say that they are *equally likely.* A number cube with six faces numbered from 1 to 6 is considered *fair* if each number is equally likely.

Reading Math

The notation $P(A)$ should be read as "the probability of event A" or simply "the probability of A."

EXAMPLES

1 What is the probability of rolling a 3 on a number cube?

On a fair number cube there are 6 equally likely outcomes and there is 1 way to get a 3. By the definition of probability, $P(3) = \frac{1}{6}$.

2 What is the probability of rolling an even number on a number cube?

The event $P(\text{even})$ can occur in 3 ways (getting a 2, 4, or 6). The number of possible outcomes is 6, so $P(\text{even}) = \frac{3}{6} = \frac{1}{2}$.

Try This

a. What is the probability of rolling a prime number on a number cube?

EXAMPLE 3 What is the probability of drawing an ace from a well-shuffled deck of 52 cards?

An ace can be drawn in 4 ways. There are 52 equally likely outcomes.

$$P\text{ (drawing an ace)} = \frac{4}{52}, \text{ or } \frac{1}{13}$$

Theorem 15-11

The probability of any event is a number from 0 to 1. If an event cannot occur its probability is 0. If an event is certain to occur its probability is 1.

EXAMPLE 4 Suppose 2 cards are drawn from a deck of 52 cards. What is the probability that both of them are spades?

13 of the 52 cards are spades, so the number m of ways of drawing 2 spades is $\binom{13}{2}$. The number of ways of drawing any two cards is $\binom{52}{2}$.

$$P(\text{getting 2 spades}) = \frac{m}{n} = \frac{\binom{13}{2}}{\binom{52}{2}} = \frac{78}{1326} = \frac{1}{17}$$

EXAMPLE 5 What is the probability of getting a total of 8 by rolling two number cubes?

On each number cube there are 6 possible outcomes. There are $6 \cdot 6$, or 36, possible outcomes for the pair. There are 5 ways of getting a total of 8, (2, 6), (3, 5), (4, 4), (5, 3), and (6, 2). Thus the probability of getting an 8 is $\frac{5}{36}$.

Try This

b. Suppose 3 cards are drawn from a deck of 52 cards. What is the probability that all three of them are diamonds?

c. What is the probability of getting a total of 7 by rolling two number cubes?

15-5 Exercises

Extra Help On the Web

Look for worked-out examples at the Prentice Hall Web site.
www.phschool.com

A

Suppose we draw a card from a deck of 52 cards. What is the probability of drawing

1. a heart? **2.** a queen? **3.** a 4? **4.** a club?

5. a black card? **6.** a red card? **7.** a 9 or a king? **8.** an ace or a two?

Suppose we select, without looking, one marble from a bag containing 4 red marbles and 10 green marbles. What is the probability of selecting

9. a red marble? **10.** a green marble? **11.** a purple marble?

Suppose 4 cards are drawn from a deck of 52 cards. What is the probability that

12. all 4 are spades? **13.** all 4 are hearts?

14. What is the probability of getting a total of 6 by rolling two number cubes?

15. What is the probability of getting a total of 3 by rolling two number cubes?

16. If 4 marbles are drawn at random all at once from a bag containing 8 white marbles and 6 black marbles, what is the probability that 2 will be white and 2 will be black?

17. From a bag containing 5 nickels, 8 dimes, and 7 quarters, 5 coins are drawn at random all at once. What is the probability of getting 2 nickels, 2 dimes, and 1 quarter?

18. From a bag containing 6 nickels, 10 dimes, and 4 quarters, 6 coins are drawn at random all at once. What is the probability of getting 3 nickels, 2 dimes, and 1 quarter?

B

Multi-Step Problem There are 52 marbles in a large tumbler: 13 red, 13 blue, 13 yellow, and 13 green. The marbles of each color are lettered A through M. Five marbles are chosen at random.

19. **a.** How many 5-marble choices are there?

b. How many 5-marble choices consist of exactly four marbles with the same letter?

c. What is the probability of choosing exactly four marbles with the same letter?

20. *Critical Thinking* Given that an event A either occurs (A) or does not occur (not A), give a convincing argument that $P(A) = 1 - P(\text{not } A)$.

Challenge

There are 52 marbles in a large tumbler: 13 red, 13 blue, 13 yellow, and 13 green. The marbles of each color are lettered A through M. Five marbles are chosen at random.

21. **a.** How many 5-marble choices have two of the same letter and three other, different letters?

b. What is the probability of choosing two of the same letter and three other, different letters?

22. **a.** How many 5-marble choices have two of the same letter, two of a second letter, and the fifth a different letter?

b. What is the probability of choosing two of the same letter, two of a second letter, and the fifth a different letter?

Mixed Review

Find the vertex, line of symmetry, focus, and directrix.

23. $4y = x^2 - 8x + 4$ **24.** $y^2 + 4y + 68 = 16x$ *10-5*

Compute. **25.** ${}_{15}P_5$ **26.** ${}_{8}P_4$ **27.** ${}_{9}P_3$ **28.** ${}_{22}P_2$ *15-1*

29. Mara has \$5000 to invest in two plans. Plan A earns 10%, and plan B earns 8%. What is the most she can invest at 8% in order to make at least \$450 per year? *4-3*

Compound Probability

15-6

Since the sample space of an experiment is the set of all possible outcomes, it will be helpful to consider some basic ideas about sets. Suppose $A = \{a, b, c, d\}$ and $B = \{b, c, e, f, g\}$. One important set of elements is the set containing those elements common to both A **and** B. This set is called the **intersection** of A and B, is symbolized by **$A \cap B$,** and is read "A intersect B."

Thus for sets A and B, we have $A \cap B = \{b, c\}$.

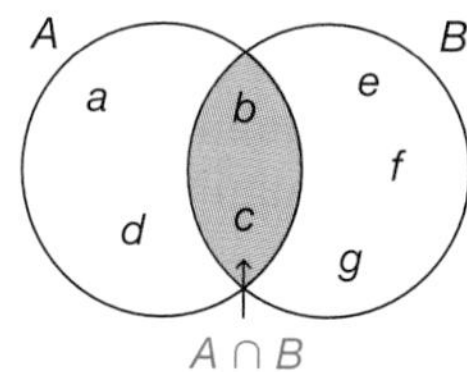

Another set that we can consider is the set of elements that belong to either A **or** B. This set is called the **union** of A and B and is symbolized by **$A \cup B$,** read "A union B."

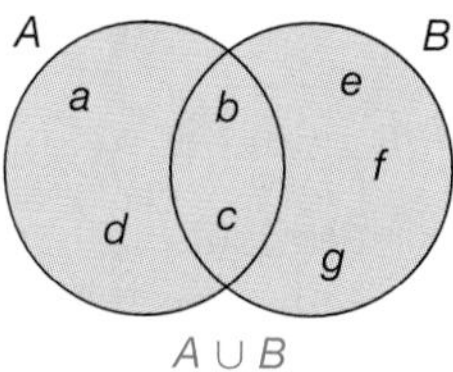

What You'll Learn

1. To find the probability that one event or another will occur
2. To find the probability that one event and another event will occur

. . . And Why

To solve real-world problems involving compound probability

Quick Review

Braces, { }, are used to show a collection of objects or a set. The intersection and union of sets was introduced on pages 82–84.

PART 1 Adding Probabilities

Objective: Find the probability that one event or another will occur.

Consider again the experiment of rolling a number cube. The sample space for this experiment is $S = \{1, 2, 3, 4, 5, 6\}$. What is the probability of rolling a prime number **or** an odd number? These two events can be represented by the sets $A = \{2, 3, 5\}$ and $B = \{1, 3, 5\}$. The diagram below shows the relationship between these two sets.

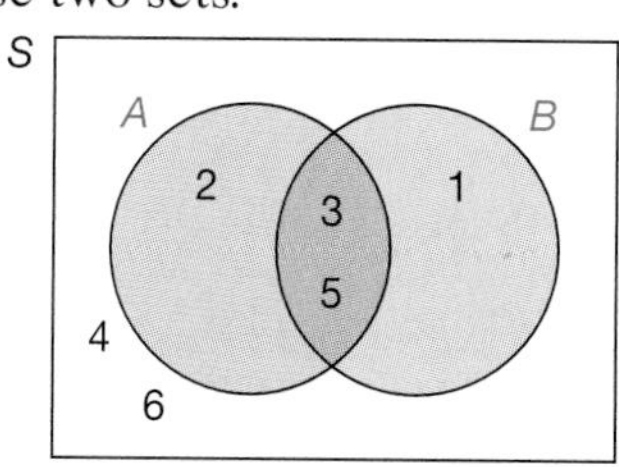

We know that $P(A) = \frac{3}{6}$ and $P(B) = \frac{3}{6}$. Thus it would seem reasonable to add the probabilities to find $P(A \cup B)$. However, the diagram shows that events A and B have something in common, namely, the outcomes 3 and 5. If we add the probabilities we would count the probabilities of these outcomes twice. To avoid this problem we can subtract $P(A \cap B)$. Thus $P(A \cup B) = P(A) + P(B) - P(A \cap B) = \frac{3}{6} + \frac{3}{6} - \frac{2}{6} = \frac{4}{6} = \frac{2}{3}$. Therefore, the probability of rolling a prime number **or** an odd number is $\frac{2}{3}$.

Theorem 15-12

If A and B are events from a sample space S, then

$$P(A \cup B) = P(A) + P(B) - P(A \cap B)$$

EXAMPLE 1 When rolling a number cube, what is the probability of rolling a prime number or an even number?

Let $A = \{2, 3, 5\}$ represent the event of rolling a prime number. Then $P(A) = \frac{3}{6}$.

Let $B = \{2, 4, 6\}$ represent the event of rolling an even number. Then $P(B) = \frac{3}{6}$.

$$A \cap B = \{2\}, \text{ so } P(A \cap B) = \frac{1}{6}$$

$$P(A \cup B) = P(A) + P(B) - P(A \cap B) = \frac{3}{6} + \frac{3}{6} - \frac{1}{6} = \frac{5}{6}$$

The probability of rolling a prime number or an even number is $\frac{5}{6}$.

Two events that have no common elements are said to be **mutually exclusive.** In the one die experiment, rolling an even number and rolling an odd number are mutually exclusive events. If A and B are mutually exclusive then $P(A \cup B) = P(A) + P(B)$.

EXAMPLE 2 When rolling a number cube, what is the probability of rolling a number less than 3 or a number greater than 3?

Let $A = \{1, 2\}$ be the set of numbers less than 3. Then $P(A) = \frac{2}{6}$.

Let $B = \{4, 5, 6\}$ be the set of numbers greater than 3. Then $P(B) = \frac{3}{6}$.

$$A \cap B = \emptyset, \text{ so } P(A \cap B) = 0$$

$$P(A \cup B) = P(A) + P(B) = \frac{2}{6} + \frac{3}{6} = \frac{5}{6}$$

The probability of rolling a number less than 3 or a number greater than 3 is $\frac{5}{6}$.

Try This

a. When rolling a number cube, what is the probability of rolling an even number or a divisor of 10?

b. What is the probability of drawing an ace or a red card from a deck of cards?

PART 2 Multiplying Probabilities

Objective: Find the probability that one event and another event will occur.

Suppose a number cube and a coin are tossed. The sample space for this experiment is $\{(1, H), (1, T), (2, H), (2, T), (3, H), (3, T), (4, H), (4, T), (5, H), (5, T), (6, H), (6, T)\}$. The probability of any of these compound events occurring is the **compound probability.**

If A is the event a number cube comes up 3, then $A = \{(3, H), (3, T)\}$. If B is the event that the coin lands heads, then $B = \{(1, H), (2, H), (3, H), (4, H), (5, H), (6, H)\}$. Notice the events are not mutually exclusive, since $A \cap B = \{(3, H)\}$. We also note that event A occurring has no effect on event B occurring and vice versa. Such events are said to be **independent.**

What is $P(A \cap B)$? This is the same as asking what the probability is of tossing a 3 *and* a head. This corresponds to outcome $(3, H)$. Since there are 12 possible outcomes we have $P(3, H) = \frac{1}{12}$. We can see that $P(A) = \frac{1}{2}$ and that $P(B) = \frac{1}{6}$. Notice also that $\left(\frac{1}{2}\right)\left(\frac{1}{6}\right) = \frac{1}{12}$. This suggests the following theorem.

Theorem 15-13

Two events A and B are independent if and only if

$$P(A \cap B) = P(A) \cdot P(B)$$

EXAMPLE 3 A bag contains three red marbles and five blue marbles. A marble is drawn and then replaced. A second marble is drawn. What is the probability that a blue marble will be drawn both times?

Let event A be that the first marble is blue and event B that the second marble is blue. Then we have $P(A) = \frac{5}{8}$ and $P(B) = \frac{5}{8}$. The events are independent, since replacing the marble means there is no effect on the second draw.

Thus we can apply Theorem 15-13.

$$P(A \cap B) = P(A) \cdot P(B) = \frac{5}{8} \cdot \frac{5}{8} = \frac{24}{64}$$

The probability of a blue marble being drawn both times is $\frac{25}{64}$.

Try This

c. A nickel and dime are tossed. What is the probability they both come up heads?

d. A number cube has A, B, C, D, E, and F on its faces. Another number cube has 1, 2, 3, 4, 5, and 6 on its faces. What is the probability that when both cubes are rolled a D and an odd number will come up? What is the probability that a vowel and a 6 will come up?

Extra Help
On the Web

Look for worked-out examples at the Prentice Hall Web site.
www.phschool.com

15-6 Exercises

A

A bag contains five red marbles, seven blue marbles, and ten green marbles. One marble is drawn at random.

1. What is the probability that it will be either red or green?
2. What is the probability that it will be either blue or green?
3. What is the probability that it will be either red or blue?

A number cube is rolled.

4. What is the probability of rolling an odd number or a power of two?
5. What is the probability of rolling an even number or a multiple of 6?
6. What is the probability of rolling a number less than 5 or a divisor of 12?
7. What is the probability of rolling a multiple of three or a prime number?

A cube with A, B, C, D, E, and F on its faces is rolled.

8. What is the probability of rolling a consonant or a letter in the word ALGEBRA?
9. What is the probability of rolling a vowel or a letter made with only straight lines?
10. What is the probability of rolling a letter in the word PROBABILITY or a letter in your name?

A card is drawn from an ordinary deck of 52 cards.

11. What is the probability that the card will be a spade or an ace?
12. What is the probability that the card will be a heart or a face card?
13. What is the probability that the card will be a red card or a card with a value less than six (ace being the lowest card in each suit)?

A number cube is rolled twice.

14. What is the probability of a 6 on the first roll and a 2 on the second roll?
15. What is the probability of a 3 on the first and second roll?
16. What is the probability of rolling an odd number on the first roll and a power of 5 on the second roll?

A number cube is rolled three times.

17. What is the probability of rolling an even number on all three rolls?
18. What is the probability of rolling an odd number on the first roll, an even number on the second roll, and a prime number on the third roll?
19. What is the probability of rolling a multiple of two on the first roll, an odd number on the second roll, and a divisor of 12 on the third roll?
20. One cube has A, B, C, D, E, and F on its faces. Another cube has 1, 2, 3, 4, 5, and 6 on its faces. When the two cubes are rolled, what is the probability that a consonant and a prime number come up?

B

21. A bag contains three red marbles and four green marbles. A marble is drawn from the bag and *not* put back before a second marble is drawn. What is the probability that the second marble is red?

22. Suppose S is a sample space and A is an event in S. The **complement** of A, which is symbolized $\overline{A}$, is the set of elements in S, which are not in A. What is $P(A \cup \overline{A})$? What is $P(A \cap \overline{A})$?

23. Multicolored balloons come in a package of 1000. There are 150 red and yellow balloons, 250 blue and red, 100 white and red, 300 yellow and white, and 200 yellow and blue.
    a. What is the probability of picking a balloon with yellow or white on it?
    b. What is the probability of picking a balloon without blue or red on it?

24. *Error Analysis* A kennel club has 400 dogs, of which 150 are poodles and 150 have shaggy hair. Fifty of the poodles have shaggy hair. Mao computes the probability of picking a poodle or a shaggy-haired dog to be 0.75. Is he correct? If not, find the correct probability and explain where he went wrong.

25. *Critical Thinking* Suppose S is a sample space with A and B events in S. Show that $\overline{A \cap B} = \overline{A} \cup \overline{B}$. (Hint: Draw a diagram. Also see Exercise 22.)

Challenge

26. Suppose two cards are drawn from an ordinary deck of 52 cards. What is the probability that at least one will not be a king or at least one will be red?

27. The letters of the word PROBABILITY are printed on file cards and the cards are shuffled. What is the probability that when the cards are dealt out, face up from left to right, they will spell PROBABILITY?

28. In Dave's drawer there are 4 pairs of different-colored socks, but they are all mixed up. Dave reaches into the drawer and pulls out 3 socks without looking. What is the probability that 2 of them match?

29. Sandra is one of 20 people entered in a drawing for a prize. Each person is given a sealed envelope which, when opened, will reveal whether they are winners. What is the probability that Sandra is a winner after 5 other people open their envelopes and are not winners?

Mixed Review

Find a parabola with **30.** focus $(-8, -2)$, vertex $(-4, -2)$.

31. focus $(-4, -2)$, vertex $(-4, -3)$.

32. vertex $(4, -2)$, containing the point $(5, 2)$.

33. vertex $(4, -3)$, containing the point $(2, -2)$. *10-5*

34. Find the variation constant and an equation of variation where y varies directly as x, and the following are true.
    a. $y = 3$ when $x = 6$ **b.** $y = -4$ when $x = -2$ **c.** $y = 4$ when $x = 7$ *6-9*

15-7 Simulating Events

What You'll Learn

1. To design and use simulations to determine experimental probability
2. To use a random number table to simulate an event and determine experimental probability

. . . And Why

To solve real-world problems that are difficult to analyze using theoretical probability

PART 1 Simulations and Probability

Objective: Design and use simulations to determine experimental probability.

It is not always possible to list the elements of the sample space for an event or calculate the actual or **theoretical probability.** In this case, we can design an **experiment** involving many **trials** and record the results of each trial to determine the **experimental probability.**

For example, if we flip a coin 1000 times and heads comes up 489 times, we would have an experimental probability of $\frac{489}{1000}$, or 0.489.

Often it is either impractical or impossible to perform an experiment directly. For example, suppose the probability that a computer chip is defective is 0.02. What is the probability that there are no more than 10 defective chips in a shipment of 1000? Testing every chip could take hundreds of hours and tie up all of a company's resources. We could simulate the situation quickly and easily, however, with a model.

To use a **simulation** to approximate the probability of an event, we first *define the problem,* then *select a model* and *define a trial.* Finally, we *collect data* by *running trials.* These steps are illustrated in the following example.

EXAMPLE 1

In a college playoff game, a player was fouled at the final buzzer with her team down by one point. The player has a 0.60 average from the free-throw line. What is the probability that she will make both shots to win the game?

■ **UNDERSTAND the problem**

Question: Find the probability that a player, who averages 0.60 from the free-throw line, will make two consecutive free throws.

■ **Develop and carry out a PLAN**

This can be modeled with two spinners that have $\frac{3}{5}$ of their areas labeled "made" and $\frac{2}{5}$ labeled "missed." One spinner can be marked "first shot" and the other "second shot." A *trial* would then consist of spinning each of the spinners once.

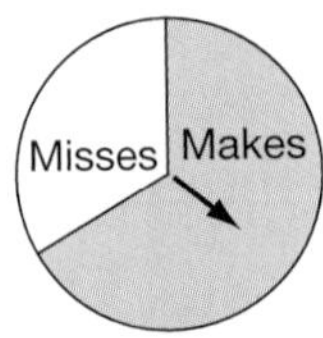

First Shot

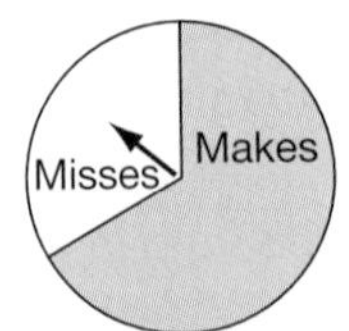

Second Shot

Using a chart to *record* the *data collected,* the results of 50 *trials* were as follows:

Makes both shots	~~||||~~ ~~||||~~ ~~||||~~ ||||
Does not make both shots	~~||||~~ ~~||||~~ ~~||||~~ ~~||||~~ ~~||||~~ ~~||||~~ |

Find the ANSWER and CHECK

There were 19 successes in 50 trials. This suggests that about 38% of the time, we would expect the player to make both shots and win the game.

In this case the theoretical probability is $0.6(0.6) = 0.36$. The difference between the theoretical probability of 0.36 and 0.38 from the simulation is that a simulation results in an approximation. The more trials that are run, the better the approximation.

Try This

a. Use a simulation to find the probability of making exactly one of two shots if the player averages 0.75 from the free-throw line.

EXAMPLE 2 What is the probability that a family with four children has three girls and one boy?

The problem can be modeled by flipping four coins, letting a head represent a girl and a tail represent a boy. Thus, a trial is represented by flipping the four coins, and a success is represented by 3 heads and 1 tail. We carry out 50 trials. Our results look like this:

HHTH	THTH	HHTH	HTTT	TTHH	HTHT	HHHT	HTHH	THTT	HHHH
HHHT	TTHT	HHTT	THHT	THHT	HHHT	HTHH	TTTT	TTTH	THTH
HTTT	HTHT	THTT	TTHT	THTH	THTH	TTHT	TTTT	TTTT	THTT
HHHT	HTHT	TTHH	TTTT	HTHT	THHT	TTHH	HHHT	HTHH	THHT
TTTT	HTHH	HHTT	THTH	TTTT	HTTH	HTHH	HHHH	HTHH	HHTT

After 50 trials, we had 13 successes. Thus, we conclude that the probability is about $\frac{13}{50} = 0.26$.

Try This

b. What is the probability that a four-child family has two boys and two girls?

Other problems require even more ingenuity in setting up the models. Sometimes they require the use of number cubes or other random devices.

EXAMPLE 3 A restaurant is giving away six different toy figures with children's meals. What is the probability of getting all six figures when purchasing ten meals?

The probability of getting any one figure is $\frac{1}{6}$. This can easily be modeled by the roll of a number cube. A trial for the problem could consist of rolling a number cube ten times and determining whether all six numbers turn up in the ten rolls. If they do, the trial is a success.

We carry out 25 trials and find that there are 7 successes. The experimental probability of getting all six of the figures in ten meals is $\frac{7}{25}$, or 0.28.

Try This

c. Suppose that a restaurant gives away one of three different figures with each child's meal. What is the probability you will get all three figures when purchasing five meals? (Hint: Use groups of digits from a number cube.)

PART 2 Using a Random Number Table

Objective: Use a random number table to simulate an event and determine experimental probability.

A table of random digits may also be used to simulate an event. Such a table contains the digits 0 through 9, generated so that each digit has the same probability of occurring. In the sample shown below, we see 4 rows of 50 digits, blocked in groups of five. The entire table is shown in the Appendix.

Row										
1	82350	90391	34806	35773	37006	34566	12787	35876	01956	45032
2	88640	70497	48430	23118	28843	63970	27630	48165	75403	56046
3	88866	78271	21214	37408	13072	74208	46567	72124	21437	58899
4	22024	15249	05312	06293	89938	86283	37555	47539	45303	79801

Of the 200 digits, there are approximately the same number of each of the digits 0 to 9.

Digit	**0**	**1**	**2**	**3**	**4**	**5**	**6**	**7**	**8**	**9**
Count	22	15	21	26	21	18	18	22	24	13

For a large number of rows, each count would approximate $\frac{1}{10}$ of the total number of digits.

EXAMPLE 4

The manager of a river canoeing company estimates that one tenth of the individuals who purchase tickets for a 9-person trip will not show up. Therefore, 10 tickets are sold for each trip. What is the probability that more than 9 people will show up for a trip?

We model the situation using the random number table, letting the digit 0 represent an individual who does not show up for a given trip. Because 10 tickets are sold for each trip, a trial will consist of examining 10 random numbers drawn from the table. If one or more zeros appear in a list of 10 digits, the manager's policy works. If not, the trip is overbooked.

We can start with row 1 of the table, which is given on page 866. We run 50 trials.

82350 90391
34806 35773
37006 34566 and so on.

We find that in 18 of the 50 trials, all 10 ticketholders show up. Thus, the probability that more than 9 people show up is $\frac{18}{50}$, or 0.36.

Try This

d. What is the probability that more than 8 individuals holding tickets show up, if 10 tickets are sold for each trip? (Begin with row 12 of the random number table.)

15-7 Exercises

Look for worked-out examples at the Prentice Hall Web site.
www.phschool.com

A

Use simulations to answer the following questions.

1. If a basketball player has a free-throw average of 0.80, what is the probability that the player will make two free throws in a row?
2. If a basketball player has a free-throw average of 0.50, what is the probability that the player will make two free throws in a row?
3. If a basketball player has a free-throw average of 0.25, what is the probability that the player will miss two free throws in a row?
4. If a basketball player has a free-throw average of 0.75, what is the probability that the player will miss two free throws in a row?
5. What is the probability that a family with 5 children has 3 boys and 2 girls?
6. What is the probability that a family with 5 children has 1 boy and 4 girls?
7. What is the probability that a family with 5 children has either all boys or all girls?
8. If a baseball club is giving out 5 different baseball posters to people attending games, what is the probability that a fan will get all 5 posters in 10 trips to the park?
9. If a baseball club is giving out 10 different team pictures, what is the probability that a fan will get one of each in 20 trips to the park?

10. Suppose the junior class made a mistake in ordering and selling tickets for its play. The class accidentally sold 25 tickets for each row of 24 seats. If there is a 10% chance that a ticketholder will not show up, at what proportion of the showings will there be enough seats in a given row?
11. A commuter airline normally books seats on its flights by selling 15 tickets for each flight capable of carrying 13 passengers. What proportion of the flights have more ticketholders present than seats for passengers if, on average, 10% of the ticketholders do not show up?

Driving from home to school, a mathematics teacher passes through 4 traffic signals, A, B, C, and D. The probability that any one light is green is 0.4 and the probability that it is not green is 0.6. Use this information and a simulation to answer the following.

12. What is the probability that the teacher will hit each light on green?
13. What is the probability that the teacher will hit each light on red?
14. What is the probability that the teacher will find at least one light red?
15. What is the probability that the teacher will find the first light green and the last two lights red?
16. What is the probability that the teacher will find the last light green?
17. Suppose that a racing car tire manufacturer claims that only one tire in twenty is defective (will not run 100 miles). Find the probability that in a set of 10 tires, exactly 2 tires are defective.
18. A doctor knows that, on average, a given medicine is effective in $\frac{4}{5}$ of the cases for which it is prescribed. What is the probability that it is effective in five straight cases?
19. There was a major defect in 10% of the cars produced by Lemon Motors. What is the probability of a business getting two or more such cars if it buys five company cars from Lemon?
20. Police estimate that the probability of a driver not wearing a seatbelt is about 30 percent. If they stop 20 cars, what is the probability that they will find at least 10 such drivers?

B

21. Make your own table of 100 random digits. Count the frequency of each of the digits. Compare your frequencies with the results of a table made from the first 100 digits in the random number table on page 865.
22. A student takes a ten-question, multiple-choice test with four choices per item. If the student guesses, what is the expected score for the examination?
23. What is the probability that in a group of four people, at least two were born in the same month?
24. What is the probability that any two people were born in the same month?
25. The probability that an event does not happen is known as the *complement* of the event. Using the fact that the probability of an event plus the probability of the complement of the event is 1, find the solution to Exercise 24 using theoretical probability.

26. *Critical Thinking* Explain why the following digits probably are not random. (Hint: make a table of digits and study row 3 of table 6.)

27439 16058 35641 79082 03864 57219 38502 71694 60591 82437

Challenge

27. If a car attendant at a theater gets the keys to six cars mixed up, what is the probability that randomly putting the keys back on the six pegs will result in at least one of the keys being correctly assigned to the car to which it belongs?
28. What is the probability that exactly 5 keys in Exercise 27 are placed on the correct pegs?

Mixed Review

29. Divide $\frac{x^2 - 9}{x^2 + 6x + 9}$ by $\frac{x^2 + 4x - 21}{x^2 - 4x - 21}$. *6-1*

Convert to exponential notation. **30.** $\log_a 7 = 4$ **31.** $\ln u = 8$

Convert to logarithmic notation. **32.** $14^2 = 196$ **33.** $e^{t+1} = t$ *12-3*

Extension: Binomial Probabilities

Given that an event can either occur or not occur, the probability of r successes in a sample of size n is given by $\binom{n}{r}p^r(1 - p)^{n-r}$.

EXAMPLE 1 What is the probability that a family with 9 children has 7 girls?

This is the binomial probability of 7 successes in a sample of size 9, where $p = 0.5$. The probability is $\binom{9}{7}(0.5)^7(0.5)^{9-7} = 36(0.5)^9 \approx 0.07$.

EXAMPLE 2 A baseball player is a .300 hitter (hits safely 30% of the time). What is the probability that the player will get at least 4 hits in 5 times at bat?

This is the probability of 4 hits + the probability of 5 hits.

$$\binom{5}{4}(0.3)^4(0.7)^1 + \binom{5}{5}(0.3)^5(0.7)^0 = 5(0.0081)(0.7) + 0.00243 = 0.03078$$

Find the following using binomial probabilities.

1. What is the probability that a family with 7 children has at least 5 boys?
2. The probability that a medicine is effective is 0.9. What is the probability that it will be effective in at least 9 of 10 cases?
3. Use the binomial theorem to expand $(p + (1 - p))^n$. What is the sum of the terms? (Hint: Simplify $(p + (1 - p)^n)$. How can you relate this to what you know about probability?

15-8  Advanced Simulations

What You'll Learn

1. To use a computer to simulate events and find experimental probability

. . . And Why

To determine an experimental probability for a given real-world simulation

Mathematicians John von Neumann (1903–1957), shown above, and Stanislaw Ulam (1907–1984) developed Monte Carlo methods to assist them in their work in nuclear physics.

PART 1 Using Monte Carlo Methods

Objective: Use a computer to simulate events and find experimental probability.

Simulating events by hand or by using a random number table can be quite time-consuming. Using computer software makes the process much easier. In this lesson we use a computer to list the trials, check the output for successful trials, and compute the approximate probabilities.

Another advantage of using a computer to run trials is that many more trials can be conducted in the time available. This allows for better approximations since the difference between an approximation and the true answer narrows as the number of trials increases.

Methods that use simulations to determine the probability of a certain event occurring are known as **Monte Carlo** methods.

EXAMPLE 1 If 25% of the qualified workers for a certain job have Ph.D.s, what is the probability that there would be more than 3 Ph.D.s on a 12-person staff?

We need to find the probability that a 12-person staff would contain 4 or more Ph.D.s. Here is a way to use one type of spreadsheet to do this.

We will generate groups of 12 numbers, each number randomly chosen from the set {0, 1, 2, 3}. A worker with a Ph.D. is represented by a 0 (25% of the numbers in the set). The numbers 1, 2, and 3 represent workers without Ph.D.s.

For one type of spreadsheet, the function RAND() generates random numbers greater than or equal to zero and less than 1. The function INT(*variable*) gives the greatest integer less than or equal to *variable*. Therefore INT(RAND()*4) generates random integers greater than or equal to zero and less than 4. (The symbol "*" is the computer's symbol for multiplication.) The rows in the spreadsheet are represented by numbers and the columns by letters. A cell is identified by its column and row: B3 represents the cell in row 3 column 2.

Type =INT(RAND( )*4) in A1 and press ENTER. Then select the cell A1 and with the fill handle, drag to L1, filling 11 more cells to the right. Each of the 12 cells will contain a 0, 1, 2, or 3. A sample first row is shown here.

	A	B	C	D	E	F	G	H	I	J	K	L
1	2	2	2	0	0	2	3	3	1	3	2	2

On selecting any cell, the formula bar will read "=INT(RAND()*4)."

To count the number of 0s, or Ph.D.s, we will test each entry and generate a 2nd group of 12 numbers consisting of 1s for the Ph.D.s and 0s for the other workers.

The function *IF(logical test, value if TRUE, value if FALSE)* is used to enter the 0 or 1 as appropriate. In cell M1 type =IF(A1<1,1,0) and press ENTER. Then select M1 and, with the fill handle, drag to X1. This enters "=IF(B1<1,1,0)" as the function for N1, "=IF(C1<1,1,0)" as the function for O1, and so on. In each cell a 1 or a 0 appears, depending on whether the worker had a Ph.D. or not. A1 $= 2$, and it is FALSE that $2 < 1$, so a 0 appears in M1. Similarly, E1 $= 0$, and it is TRUE that $0 < 1$ so a 1 appears in P1. Our first row now looks like this:

	A	**B**	**C**	**D**	**E**	**F**	**G**	**H**	**I**	**J**	**K**	**L**	**M**	**N**	**O**	**P**	**Q**	**R**	**S**	**T**	**U**	**V**	**W**	**X**
1	2	2	2	0	0	2	3	3	1	3	2	2	0	0	0	1	1	0	0	0	0	0	0	0

The sum of the entries in this 2nd group of numbers tells us how many of the 12 workers have Ph.D.s. In cell Y1, type =SUM(M1:X1) to add the entries in cells M1 through X1, and press ENTER. A 2 will appear in Y1 to represent the 0s in columns D and E.

Finally, we are interested in whether each group of 12 random numbers has 4 or more 0s (Ph.D.s). We again use the IF function to test the Y entries, entering a 1 in column Z if there are more than three 0s (Y value is greater than 3), or entering a 0 otherwise. In Z1 type =IF(Y1>3,1,0) and press ENTER. Since $2 < 3$ in this example, Z1 $= 0$. Our first row now looks like this:

	A	**B**	**C**	**D**	**E**	**F**	**G**	**H**	**I**	**J**	**K**	**L**	**M**	**N**	**O**	**P**	**Q**	**R**	**S**	**T**	**U**	**V**	**W**	**X**	**Y**	**Z**
1	2	2	2	0	0	2	3	3	1	3	2	2	0	0	0	1	1	0	0	0	0	0	0	0	2	0

Decide how many trials you wish to run, select cells A1 through Z1 and, with the fill handle, drag down until that many rows are filled. In each row, columns A through L represent groups of 12 workers; columns M through X use a 1 to indicate which workers have Ph.D.s; column Y indicates how many of each group have Ph.D.s; and column Z uses a 1 to indicate whether there are more than 3 Ph.D.s in the group of 12 workers.

To find the probability that a 12-person staff would contain 4 or more Ph.D.s, add column Z. If you chose 200 trials, select Z201, click on Σ on the tool bar, and press ENTER. The sum represents the number of groups of 12 workers with more than 3 Ph.D.s. If Z201 $= 78$, the experimental probability is $\frac{78}{200} \approx 0.39$ that a 12-person staff would have more than 3 Ph.D.s.

Try This

a. If fifty percent of the qualified workers for a certain job in a geographical area are male, what is the probability that a company would have 3 or fewer males on a staff of 10? (Hint: Adapt the process of Example 1.)

EXAMPLE 2 For every 1000 balloons manufactured by PoP! Corporation, there are 200 red, 200 white, 100 yellow, 100 green, and 400 blue. A machine packs 4 balloons randomly in a package. What is the probability that a package contains balloons that are all different colors?

In this case, the computer is asked to generate 200 lists of four digits selected from the digits 0 through 9. The digits 0 and 1 represent a red balloon, 2 and 3 represent white, 4 yellow, 5 green, and 6, 7, 8, and 9 represent a blue balloon.

Enter =INT(RAND()*10) in A1 through D1 to generate a group of 4 random numbers, each an integer from 0 to 9.

To test 4 of 5 possibilities, we will construct nested IF functions. The IF *value if FALSE* is replaced by the next IF function until the final *value if FALSE* is reached. In E1, type =IF(A1<2,1,IF(AND(A1>1,A1<4),2,IF(A1=4,3,IF (A1=5,4,5)))). Press ENTER, and then select E1 and drag it with the fill handle to H1. In E1, this function evaluates the random number in A1 and enters 1 for red, 2 for white, 3 for yellow, 4 for green, or 5 for blue. Similarly, in F1, it evaluates the random number in B1, and so on, entering the appropriate number for the color represented in each cell.

To test whether columns E through H have four distinct entries, we will use the function *OR(logical test, logical test, . . .)* as the *logical test* for the IF function. OR is TRUE if any of the logical tests is true, and FALSE if all of the logical tests are false. In cell I1, type =IF(OR(E1=F1,E1=G1,E1=H1, F1=G1,F1=H1,G1=H1),0,1) and then press ENTER. If the 4 balloons are different colors, a 1 is entered in column I.

Choose the number of trials to run; select cells A1 through I1 and drag down with the fill handle to generate the appropriate number of rows. In each row, columns A through D represent 4 balloons, columns E through H represent their colors, and column I uses a 1 to indicate if all 4 are different colors. Summing column I gives the number of trials in which all 4 balloons have different colors. If 24 of 200 trials show 4 different colored balloons, the experimental probability is 0.12.

Try This

b. What is the probability that a three-balloon package contains balloons that are all the same color?

EXAMPLE 3 Any of four different safety systems can shut down a machine in case of a problem. Any one of the systems can shut the machine off. Each has a 0.5 probability of shutting down the machine. What is the probability that the machine will be shut down if a problem occurs?

In this case, each trial consists of a list of 4 digits. Because the probability of a machine shutdown for each system is 0.5, we let the digits from 0 to 4 stand for the system being shut down and 5 to 9 stand for no intervention by the safety system. Hence, any trial with a digit less than 5 in it will indicate that the machine was shut down.

As in Example 2, type INT(RAND()*10) to generate random numbers in cells A1 through D1. In cell E1, type =IF(OR(A1<5,B1<5,C1<5,D1<5),1, 0) and then press ENTER. Select these 5 cells and drag down with the fill handle to generate a row for each desired trial. Summing column E gives the number of trials in which at least one of the digits was less than 5. If there are 186 out of 200, the experimental probability that the machine will be shut down by a safety system when a problem occurs is 0.93.

Try This

c. The systems are improved so that the probability that a particular system will shut down the machine if there is a problem is 0.60. System 4 is then removed. What is the probability that at least one safety system will shut down the machine if there is a problem?

15-8 Exercises

Look for worked-out examples at the Prentice Hall Web site.
www.phschool.com

A

Use a simulation to solve each problem.

1. A basketball player has a free-throw average of 0.80. What is the probability that the player will make two free throws in a row?
2. A basketball player has a free-throw average of 0.60. What is the probability that the player will make four free throws in a row?
3. Assume that 30% of the qualified individuals for a certain job are male. What is the probability that a company would have at most 2 males out of the 10 individuals assigned to that job?
4. Assume that 60% of the qualified individuals for a certain job are male. What is the probability that a company would have at most 3 males out of the 11 individuals assigned to that job?
5. If a local movie theater is giving away posters of 5 movie stars, what is the probability that you will get one of each of the posters in 10 trips to the theater?
6. If a cereal box contains one of 4 different Loco Men, what is the probability that you will get one of each after buying 10 boxes of cereal?
7. If 10 people are in a room, what is the probability that at least 3 were born in the same month? (Assume an equal probability for each month.)
8. If 8 people are in a room, what is the probability that each was born in a different month? (Assume an equal probability for each month.)

9. A successful launch of a three-stage rocket requires that all three motors fire on time. The probability that the first engine will ignite properly is 0.9. The probability that the second and third engines will fire properly is 0.8 and 0.7, respectively. What is the probability that on a given launch all three engines will fire correctly?

10.–14. Reconsider problems 12–16 from Exercise Set 15-7, this time using a greater number of trials. Compare your results with the answers you found in your previous work.

B

A mixture of a large number of balloons in a sack consists of about $\frac{1}{3}$ red balloons, $\frac{1}{2}$ blue balloons, and $\frac{1}{6}$ yellow balloons. Assuming that picking a balloon has no effect on these probabilities, answer the following questions.

15. What is the probability that the first five balloons drawn at random from the sack will be only red or blue?

16. What is the probability that 4 out of the first 5 balloons drawn from the sack will be only blue or yellow?

17. Find the probability that in a World Series between two equally matched teams that one team will win the first 3 games but lose the 7-game series.

18. *Critical Thinking* Find the exact probability, using theoretical methods, for the problem in Exercise 19 and compare your answers.

Challenge

19. A deck of cards is composed of 10 red cards and 20 blue cards. We pick 5 cards. What is the probability that there are more red cards than blue cards chosen?

20. On average, how many people would you need to ask before you found someone who has the same birthday as you do? (If you were born February 29, consider that your birthday occurs every 1461 days.)

21. A football team plays a 16-game season. If the team has a 0.5 probability of winning each game, what is the probability that the team will have no winning or losing streaks of 4 or more games?

22. Suppose the home team has a 70% chance of winning a basketball game. In a 7-game playoff, where the series ends when one team wins 4 games, team A plays at home for games 1, 2, 6, and 7. If the teams are evenly matched, what is the probability that team A wins the series?

Mixed Review

Simplify. 23. $\frac{a + 2}{a^2 + 3a} \cdot \frac{a^2 - 5a + 6}{4 - a^2}$

24. $\frac{8x^3 + 19x^2 - 15x}{x^2 + 7x + 12} \div \frac{8x^2 + 35x - 25}{x^2 + 9x + 20}$ *6-1*

25. $\sqrt[6]{6^{12}}$ *7-5*

Application

Space Message Error Codes

What is the probability of two or more errors in a message where the probability of error is $p = 0.05$?

Satellites and space probes send messages to Earth in the form of electromagnetic impulses that are read as either 0 or 1. A 12-digit message might be read 001001101010. Sometimes radiation, lightning, heat, or other factors interfere with a message and cause an error. To determine whether a single error exists in a message, the following procedure is used.

The message is grouped into three rows with four columns each. The message above would be grouped like this:

0010
0110
1010

If a row or column has an even number of 1s, a 0 is added to the row or column as a **check digit.** If a row or a column has an odd number of 1s, a 1 is added to the row or column as a check digit. So after the 0s and 1s have been added, every row or column will have an even number of 1s. The message to be sent would now look like this:

00101
01100
10100
11101

Now, suppose that radiation caused a single error in the message, and when it was received it looked like this:

00111
01100
10100
11101

By examining the rows and columns you can see an odd number of 1s in the first row and in the fourth column. This means that the digit at the intersection of this row and column must be incorrect.

The "error correcting code" described above is called a **rectangular code** because the information is arranged in a row-column format. The check digit added to each row and column can be used to detect and correct a *single* error.

However, an even number of errors could remain undetected. Also, an odd number of errors greater than or equal to 3 could give the appearance of a single error. Although the rectangular code has these limitations, it can be used in applications for which the probability of more than one error in 20 digits (4 rows, 5 columns) is extremely low.

Suppose that transmission errors are random and occur with probability p for each digit. The probability that more than one error occurs among the 20 digits is

$$1 - (\text{probability of no error } \textbf{or} \text{ one error})$$

Finding the probability of no errors:

The probability of no errors for a single digit is $1 - p$. So, using the fundamental counting principle, the probability of no errors among the 20 digits is

$$(1 - p)(1 - p)(1 - p) \ldots (1 - p) \quad \text{or} \quad (1 - p)^{20}$$

Finding the probability of one error:

If exactly one error is to occur, it could occur on the first digit *or* the second digit *or* the third digit, and so on. If a given digit is to be the single error, then all the other 19 digits cannot be the error. So the probability that a given digit is the only error is $p(1 - p)^{19}$. Since there are 20 such cases we have the probability of one error as $20p(1 - p)^{19}$.

Finding the probability of no errors or *one error:*

The probability of no errors or one error is the sum of their probabilities.

$$(1 - p)^{20} + 20p(1 - p)^{19}$$

Thus, the probability T of two or more errors among the 20 digits is

$$T = 1 - [P(\text{no errors}) + P(\text{one error})]$$
$$T = 1 - [(1 - p)^{20} + 20p(1 - p)^{19}]$$

For $p = 0.05$, for example,

$$\begin{aligned} T &= 1 - [(0.95)^{20} + 20(0.05)(0.95)^{19}] \\ &\approx 1 - [0.358 + 0.377] \\ &\approx 1 - 0.735 \\ &\approx 0.265 \end{aligned}$$

Problems

Examine each message. Determine whether a single error exists in each message, and correct the errors.

1.	**2.**	**3.**	**4.**	**5.**
00011	11000	00100	00000	10001
10010	00011	11011	11000	01001
11001	01101	11011	00011	10100
01100	10010	01100	11010	01100

Find the probability of two or more errors, T, in a 4×5 matrix given p.

6. $p = 0.1$ **7.** $p = 0.01$ **8.** $p = 0.001$ **9.** $p = 0.0001$

Suppose a 90-digit message is sent in a 10×11 matrix (a 9×10 matrix with a row and column of check digits added).

10. Find T for $p = 0.01$.

11. Find the probability of two or more errors for $p = 0.05$.

15 Chapter Wrap Up

15-1

In a **compound event** in which the first event may occur in n_1 different ways, the second event in n_2 different ways, and so on, and the kth event may occur in n_k ways, the total number of ways the compound event may occur is $n_1 \cdot n_2 \cdot n_3 \cdot \cdots \cdot n_k$.

1. When Carla made her yogurt sundae, she had a choice of vanilla, strawberry, or chocolate yogurt. On top of her yogurt, she had a choice of granola, fruit, carob bits, or no topping. She also had a choice of a large or a small sundae. From how many different combinations did Carla have to choose?

A **permutation** of a set of n objects is an ordered arrangement of the objects, and the total number of these permutations is given by

${}_nP_n = n \cdot (n-1) \cdot (n-2) \cdot \cdots \cdot 3 \cdot 2 \cdot 1.$

Find the following.

2. ${}_4P_4$ **3.** ${}_6P_6$

***n* factorial** or $\boldsymbol{n!} = n \cdot (n-1) \cdot (n-2) \cdot \cdots \cdot 3 \cdot 2 \cdot 1$

Find the following.

4. 8! **5.** 1! **6.** 0!

For any natural number n, $n! = n(n-1)!$.

7. Represent 14! in the form $n(n-1)!$.

The number of permutations of a set of n objects taken r at a time is given by ${}_nP_r = \frac{n!}{(n-r)!}$ where each permutation is an **ordered arrangement.**

Compute.

8. ${}_7P_3$ **9.** ${}_{10}P_8$

15-2

The number of orderings of n objects taken r at a time, with repetition, is n^r.

10. How many different 4-digit numbers can be formed using the digits 3, 4, 5, 6, 7, and 8 if you are allowed to repeat digits?

If P represents the number of permutations of n things taken n at a time, and if there are r things all alike, s other things all alike, t things all alike, then $P = \frac{n!}{r!s!t!}$.

11. Find the number of permutations of the letters of the word TOMORROW.

The number of circular permutations of n objects is $(n-1)!$.

12. Find the number of permutations of 8 numbers on a spinner.

Key Terms

$A \cap B$ (p. 667)
$A \cup B$ (p. 667)
and (p. 667)
binomial coefficient (p. 660)
check digit (p. 683)
combinations (p. 656)
combinatorics (p. 644)
compound event (p. 644)
compound probability (p. 669)
complement (pp. 671, 676)
event (p. 644)
experiment (p. 672)
experimental probability (p. 672)
independent events (p. 669)
intersection of sets (p. 667)
Monte Carlo methods (p. 678)
mutually exclusive events (p. 668)
$\binom{n}{r}$ (p. 656)
$n!$ (p. 646)
n factorial (p. 646)
${}_nP_n$, ${}_nP_r$ (pp. 645, 647)
or (p. 667)
outcome (p. 644)
permutations (p. 645)
probability (p. 664)
rectangular code (p. 683)
sample space (p. 664)
simple event (p. 664)
simulation (p. 672)
theoretical probability (p. 672)
tree diagram (p. 644)
trial (p. 672)
union of sets (p. 667)

15-3

Combinations concern the number of ways we can select r elements from n elements and are symbolized by $\binom{n}{r} = \frac{n!}{r!(n-r)!}$.

13. From a class of 15 students, 5 are chosen to represent the class in a contest. In how many ways could the five students be chosen?

Evaluate.

14. $\binom{5}{2}$

15. $\binom{10}{7}$

15-4

For any binomial $(a + b)$ and any natural number n,

$$(a + b)^n = \binom{n}{0}a^n + \binom{n}{1}a^{n-1}b + \binom{n}{2}a^{n-2}b^2 + \cdots + \binom{n}{n}b^n.$$

16. Find the 4th term of $(2x - 3)^8$.

17. Expand $(2x - 4)^5$.

The total number of subsets of a set with n members is 2^n.

18. How many subsets does a set with 8 members have?

15-5

If an event E can occur m ways out of n possible equally likely outcomes of **sample space** S, the **probability** of that event is given by $P(E) = \frac{m}{n}$.

19. Suppose 2 cards are drawn from a deck of 52 cards. What is the probability that both cards are black?

20. Roll two number cubes. What is the probability the sum is 5?

15-6

If A and B are events from a sample space S then
$P(A \text{ or } B) = P(A \cup B) = P(A) + P(B) - P(A \cap B)$.

21. What is the probability of drawing a king or a heart from a well-shuffled deck of cards in one draw?

Two events, A and B, are **independent** if and only if $P(A \cap B) = P(A) \cdot P(B)$.

22. A bag contains 4 red marbles and 6 green marbles. A marble is drawn and then replaced. A second drawing is made. What is the probability that a green marble is drawn both times?

15-7

A **simulation** requires that one define a problem, select a model, define a trial, and collect data through running a large number of trials.

23. A grocer gives out game cards with each purchase. Fifty percent have a W, 40% have an N, and 10% have an I. What is the probability of getting at least one of each with 10 purchases?

Accurate approximations of events are found by **Monte Carlo** methods where the simulation's trials are run by a computer, giving a large number of trials.

24. A two-player game consists of player 1 rolling two number cubes and player 2 rolling one. The player who rolls the largest of the numbers showing is the winner. What is the probability that player 1 wins?

15 Chapter Assessment

1. Joe has 4 different colored pairs of jeans, 4 different colored shirts, and 2 belts. How many different outfits can he make?

2. Find ${}_5P_5$. **3.** Find 7!. **4.** Find 0!.

5. Represent 11! in the form $n(n - 1)!$.

6. Compute ${}_9P_4$.

7. In how many ways can a sedan, a coupe, a sports car, a station wagon, and a van be parked in a row?

8. Find the number of permutations of the letters of the word MEMENTO.

9. Find the number of permutations of five people sitting at a round table.

10. In how many ways can 9 players be chosen from a team with 14 players?

11. Evaluate $\binom{8}{3}$.

12. Find the 5th term of $(x^2 - 2)^6$.

13. Expand $(3x - 2)^4$.

14. How many subsets does a set with 6 members have?

15. Suppose 3 cards are drawn from a well-shuffled deck of 52 cards. What is the probability that all three cards are clubs?

16. Roll two number cubes. What is the probability the sum is 7?

17. What is the probability of drawing a queen or a diamond from a well-shuffled deck of 52 cards in one draw?

18. A bag contains 3 red marbles and 6 green marbles. A marble is drawn and then replaced. A second marble is drawn and replaced, and then a third marble is drawn. What is the probability that a red marble is drawn all 3 times?

19. The probability of a defect in a manufacturing process is 0.2. Use the random numbers below to find the probability of 2 or more defects in 5 randomly sampled items.

38321	22226	40307	74347	79972	67851	32300	76354	87500	49716
87073	68858	90416	01915	36139	26589	35492	19669	36504	28157
95751	41919	30546	03902	40274	26484	03784	02472	08932	52209
22716	42951	14478	28692	58257	82510	69084	68465	09410	73160

What You'll Learn in Chapter 16

- How to construct stem-and-leaf diagrams, frequency distributions, and box-and-whisker plots for sets of data
- How to find the range, mean, mean deviation, median, mode, variance, and standard deviation of a set of data
- How to determine the proportion of data falling within a range of standard deviations
- How to find and use *z*-scores to determine probabilities
- How to solve problems using normal distributions
- How to evaluate and select sampling methods and take a stratified random sample
- How to calculate chi-square values, and use them to test a hypothesis

CHAPTER

Skills & Concepts You Need for Chapter 16

12-5 Use Table 2 to find these logarithms.

1. log 9.14
2. log 5.27
3. log 0.000124
4. log 67100

12-8 Use Table 3 to find these natural logarithms.

5. ln 1.85
6. ln 0.0376
7. ln 12.9

14-1 Rename and evaluate each sum.

8. $\sum_{n=1}^{8} \frac{n}{2}$
9. $\sum_{n=1}^{5} 3^n$
10. $\sum_{n=1}^{4} \left(\frac{2^n - 5}{4}\right)$

Statistics and Data Analysis

Most running tracks are oval and have 6 or 8 lanes. A staggered start of a race is necessary when the length of a race requires using curved parts of the track. This equalizes the chance of winning when starting in any lane. (See Lesson 16-6, Example 3.)

16-1 Statistics: Organizing Data

What You'll Learn

1. To construct a stem-and-leaf diagram for a set of data
2. To construct a frequency distribution for a set of data

. . . And Why

To gain information about a set of data and use it to solve problems

Statistics is the branch of mathematics that is concerned with the collection, organization, display, and interpretation of data. Many problems are solved and important decisions made using statistical methods.

PART 1 Stem-and-Leaf Diagrams

Objective: Construct a stem-and-leaf diagram for a set of data.

We can organize data by placing them in charts and tables or ordering them in some way. Another useful way to organize data is to construct a **stem-and-leaf diagram.**

EXAMPLE 1 Here is a set of systolic blood pressures of 40 patients.

Construct a stem-and-leaf diagram.

122, 143, 156, 162, 134, 122, 119, 136, 148, 160, 146, 154, 132, 116, 153, 143, 129, 121, 143, 154, 127, 118, 128, 120, 163, 156, 117, 128, 149, 135, 143, 167, 139, 121, 115, 163, 157, 138, 129, 143

As we look at this set of data we see that there are some numbers in the 110s, some in the 120s, some in the 130s, and so on. We use this idea to construct a stem-and-leaf diagram. We split each numeral into two parts: a stem, such as 11 or 15, and a leaf, such as 2 or 5. The first value, 122, is split into 12 and 2. We write the leaf, 2, in the row opposite the stem, 12.

Stem	Leaf
11	9, 6, 8, 7, 5
12	2, 2, 9, 1, 7, 8, 0, 8, 1, 9
13	4, 6, 2, 5, 9, 8
14	3, 8, 6, 3, 3, 9, 3, 3
15	6, 4, 3, 4, 6, 7
16	2, 0, 3, 7, 3

We can see that the stem-and-leaf diagram has organized the data for us. It is easy to find the lowest blood pressure, 115, and the highest, 167. Also, it is obvious that in this set of patients, most had a systolic blood pressure in the 120s.

Try This

a. Here is a set of cholesterol readings for 35 male patients in the 40-year age bracket. Construct a stem-and-leaf diagram.

132, 122, 143, 126, 154, 164, 126, 121, 148, 132, 135, 125, 137, 120, 129, 127, 132, 145, 164, 154, 143, 153, 123, 128, 132, 148, 144, 153, 132, 126, 143, 125, 131, 173, 123

EXAMPLE 2 Here is the set of gasoline octane ratings from 21 producers. Construct a stem-and-leaf diagram.

87.6, 84.8, 84.9, 86.2, 88.6, 89.5, 84.6, 85.4, 84.8, 86.3, 87.6, 86.7, 85.2, 86.5, 87.3, 88.8, 85.3, 86.2, 85.3, 87.3, 91.2

When reading from the diagram we must remember to include a decimal point after the stem.

Stem	Leaf
84	8, 9, 6, 8
85	4, 2, 3, 3
86	2, 3, 7, 5, 2
87	6, 6, 3, 3
88	6, 8
89	5
90	
91	2

Sometimes the leaves in a stem-and-leaf diagram are arranged in order from least to greatest. This is called a **ranked stem-and-leaf diagram.**

Try This

b. Here is a set of earned-run averages for former big-league pitcher Red Ruffing. Construct a stem-and-leaf diagram.

6.65, 5.01, 4.39, 4.66, 3.89, 4.86, 4.38, 4.41, 3.09, 3.91, 3.93, 3.12, 3.85, 2.98, 3.31, 2.93, 3.38, 3.54, 3.21, 2.89, 1.77, 6.11

Frequency Distributions

Objective: Construct a frequency distribution for a set of data.

A stem-and-leaf diagram records every value. We can also organize data by constructing a **frequency distribution.** In a frequency distribution we may group data into intervals. Then we indicate how frequently values fall within that interval. A general rule is to form 10 to 15 intervals. We can also show the **relative frequency** by dividing the frequency by the total number of values.

EXAMPLE 3 Here is the height, in feet, of 20 of the world's waterfalls. Construct a frequency distribution. Show the relative frequency.

2415, 2154, 3212, 1304, 1500, 1612, 1841, 1259, 2625, 1904, 2000, 1325, 3110, 1650, 2120, 1280, 1600, 1476, 1400, 2540

We see that the highest waterfall is 3212 ft and the lowest is 1259 ft. The difference between 3212 and 1259 is 1953. Suppose we decide to have about ten intervals. We divide 1953 by 10. This gives us 195.3, which suggests that the interval be 200. Thus the intervals can be 1201–1400, 1401–1600, and so on.

Writing Math

The list of values for the stems in a stem-and-leaf diagram must be an arithmetic sequence. It is important to see the spaces.

Interval	Tally	f Frequency	f/n Relative Frequency
1201–1400	𝍸	5	0.25
1401–1600	|||	3	0.15
1601–1800	||	2	0.10
1801–2000	|||	3	0.15
2001–2200	||	2	0.10
2201–2400		0	0.00
2401–2600	||	2	0.10
2601–2800	|	1	0.05
2801–3000		0	0.00
3001–3200	|	1	0.05
3201–3400	|	1	0.05

Try This

c. Here is a set of raw scores on a standardized algebra test. Construct a frequency distribution. Show the relative frequency.

32, 21, 40, 22, 15, 14, 23, 34, 19, 22, 26, 34, 36, 21, 29, 23, 38, 15, 27, 26, 38, 31, 20, 25, 33, 24, 21, 17, 16, 25, 35, 37, 23, 32, 19, 27, 28, 32

Extra Help On the Web

Look for worked-out examples at the Prentice Hall Web site.
www.phschool.com

16-1 Exercises

A

1. ***Error Analysis*** Identify the error made in constructing this stem-and-leaf diagram from the given data.

7.3, 6.5, 9.3, 7.2, 7.3, 7.1, 6.9, 7.0, 9.2

Stem	Leaf
6	5, 9
7	0, 1, 2, 3, 3
9	2, 3

Here are four sets of data. Construct a stem-and-leaf diagram for

2. the number of home runs hit by Babe Ruth each year of his career.

0, 4, 3, 2, 11, 29, 54, 59, 35, 41, 46, 25, 47, 60, 54, 46, 49, 46, 41, 34, 22, 6

3. the radar-recorded speeds, in miles per hour, of cars traveling on an interstate highway.

56, 63, 49, 56, 55, 49, 61, 60, 63, 58, 59, 60, 49, 57, 68, 56, 55, 46, 65, 67, 54, 53, 58, 63, 61, 64, 56, 64, 48

4. the number of ounces dispensed per drink from a sample of vending machines that are supposed to serve seven ounces.

5.5, 6.5, 7.0, 6.7, 3.9, 5.6, 6.7, 7.1, 4.5, 6.7, 6.8, 6.9, 7.0, 5.9, 6.8, 4.6, 3.8, 4.8, 6.5, 4.9, 4.0, 6.8, 7.2, 5.6, 7.0, 6.9, 6.5, 6.7, 4.8, 4.9, 4.9, 5.9

5. the height, in inches, of a sample of a variety of wheat.

13.6, 16.4, 14.8, 16.9, 17.2, 13.6, 17.4, 18.3, 16.4, 15.8, 13.9, 21.5, 16.5, 14.7, 23.9, 15.2, 13.8, 20.6, 12.5, 16.8, 15.4, 18.9, 25.4, 23.8, 17.9, 13.6, 22.4, 18.5, 17.4, 19.0, 20.7, 22.5, 21.2, 14.6, 18.9, 17.6, 14.2, 21.3, 15.6, 17.4, 12.5, 21.5, 19.6, 14.8, 19.2

Construct a frequency distribution showing the relative frequency for

6. the numbers of hours it took for a sample of 40 light bulbs to burn out.

990, 987, 1065, 1203, 996, 1206, 1332, 1502, 1563, 1290, 1339, 1432, 898, 1356, 1465, 1604, 1365, 989, 1546, 1453, 1676, 1221, 1546, 1453, 987, 1205, 1546, 1332, 1435, 1543, 1632, 1365, 1229, 1548, 1453, 1332, 1602, 1544, 1475, 1322

7. the time, in seconds, of 28 runners to run the 200-yard dash.

25.4, 27.6, 24.9, 25.7, 25.6, 24.8, 27.8, 25.6, 26.7, 27.8, 26.9, 25.8, 28.8, 26.8, 25.7, 26.9, 27.2, 26.5, 25.9, 26.6, 27.8, 25.9, 25.2, 27.4, 27.4, 28.1, 27.3, 26.4

8. the height, in feet, of some of the principal active volcanoes of the world.

19,882, 19,652, 19,347, 19,167, 18,504, 17,887, 17,159, 16,197, 15,913, 15,604, 13,812, 13,680, 13,350, 13,333, 12,582, 12,450, 12,224, 12,198, 12,080, 12,060, 11,385, 11,339, 11,268, 11,253, 11,247, 11,070, 10,705, 10,453, 9351

9. the diastolic blood pressure of 42 patients.

89, 99, 72, 87, 69, 78, 74, 69, 90, 88, 76, 65, 99, 78, 89, 87, 69, 90, 102, 86, 76, 84, 100, 89, 73, 78, 89, 76, 70, 64, 87, 79, 97, 90, 76, 69, 78, 89, 69, 70, 74, 73

B

10. Study the stem-and-leaf diagrams made in Exercise 1-4. How can you draw a simple bar graph of the data?

11. *Mathematical Reasoning* List some advantages and disadvantages of using a stem-and-leaf diagram for a set of data. Do the same for a frequency distribution.

12. *Critical Thinking* Devise a method of estimating the average height of the 20 waterfalls, given only the frequency distribution from Example 3.

Challenge

13. Use your frequency distribution from Exercise 5. What is the probability that a light bulb will burn at least 1500 hours?

Mixed Review

For each hyperbola find the center, vertices, foci, and asymptotes, and then graph the hyperbola.

14. $x^2 - 4x - y^2 - 10y = 30$ 15. $16y^2 + 96y - 25x^2 - 50x = 281$ *10-4*

Find the number of permutations of the letters of these words.

16. MULTIDIMENSIONAL 17. NANOSECOND 18. TERRITORIALISM *15-2*

19. Find the variation constant and an equation of variation where y varies inversely as x and the following are true.

a. $y = 3$ when $x = 6$ **b.** $y = -4$ when $x = -2$ **c.** $y = 4$ when $x = 7$ *6-9*

16-2 Using Measures of Central Tendency

What You'll Learn

1. To find the mean, median, and mode of a set of data
2. To construct a box-and-whisker plot of a set of data

. . . And Why

To gain information about a set of data and use it to solve problems

PART 1 Central Tendency

Objective: Find the mean, median, and mode of a set of data.

When considering a set of data, it is reasonable to look for a single number that is representative of the entire set. Numbers at the middle or center of the set of data serve this purpose well. There are a variety of ways of thinking of the center of a set of data. One way that is often used is the **mean** or **average.** To find the mean of a set of data, we add all the values and divide by the number of values. The mean is usually denoted by $\bar{x}$, and the formula for finding the mean when the data are $\{x_1, x_2, x_3, \ldots, x_n\}$ is

$$\bar{x} = \frac{\sum_{i=1}^{n} x_i}{n}$$

Reading Math

$\bar{x}$ is read "x bar."

EXAMPLE 1 Here is a set of golf scores for a club tournament. Find the mean score.

81, 78, 79, 80, 76, 88, 83, 90, 87, 76, 79, 83, 74, 82, 76

There are 15 scores, so $n = 15$.

First we find the sum, then we divide by 15.

$$\bar{x} = \frac{\sum_{i=1}^{15} x_i}{15} = \frac{1212}{15} = 80.8$$

The mean score is 80.8.

When we look at the scores in Example 1 we can see that they tend to fall around 80. Thus the mean 80.8 is a representative score.

Try This

a. Here is a set of weights, in pounds, of players on a high-school football team. Find the mean weight.

178, 192, 201, 217, 195, 176, 202, 183, 179, 221, 203, 188, 192, 178, 187, 203, 221, 234, 196, 184, 173, 183, 180, 191, 179, 173, 182, 187, 191, 178, 172, 184, 179, 177, 185, 183, 179

Another value that can be used to represent a set of data is the **mode.** The mode is the value that occurs most often.

EXAMPLE 2 Here is a stem-and-leaf diagram of a set of pulse rates. Find the mode

Stem	Leaf
6	8, 8, 3, 7, 9
7	1, 2, 3, 2, 1, 0, 0, 5, 2, 3, 1, 1, 4, 8, 1, 1
8	0, 1, 1, 0, 3, 2, 2, 0

By inspecting the stem-and-leaf diagram, we see that the mode is 71.

Try This

b. Here is a set of diastolic blood pressures. Find the mode.

Stem	Leaf
6	7, 9, 4, 7, 9
7	8, 8, 9, 0, 3, 2, 5, 8, 6, 8, 0, 2, 2, 6, 8, 4, 8, 4
8	2, 6, 4, 7, 9, 0, 0, 3, 1
9	1, 8, 7, 2, 0, 4
10	0, 9, 7, 4, 0, 2, 3, 7

A third central value that can be used to represent a set of data is the **median.** The median is the middle value when all the values are arranged in order. For instance, the median of the five numbers 11, 16, 27, 34, and 51 is the third number, 27.

EXAMPLE 3

Here is a stem-and-leaf diagram showing the number of home runs hit each year from 1954 to 1976 by Henry (Hank) Aaron. Find the median number of home runs.

Stem	Leaf
1	3, 2, 0
2	7, 6, 4, 9, 0
3	0, 9, 4, 2, 9, 8, 4
4	4, 0, 5, 4, 4, 4, 7, 0

The stem-and-leaf diagram makes it easy to arrange the numbers from least to greatest.

10, 12, 13, 20, 24, 26, 27, 29, 30, 32, 34, 34, 38, 39, 39, 40, 40, 44, 44, 44, 44, 45, 47

There are 23 numbers. Thus the median is the 12th number, 34. The median number of home runs hit by Hank Aaron is 34.

There will always be exactly one middle value if there is an odd number of values. If the number of values is even, then we use the average of the two middle values as the median. For instance, the median of 17, 20, 24, 33, 41, and 52 is $\frac{24 + 33}{2}$ or 28.5.

Henry Aaron is shown here on April 8, 1974, in the act of hitting his 715th home run, breaking Babe Ruth's record. By the end of his 23-year career, Aaron had hit 755 homers.

Try This

c. Here is a stem-and-leaf diagram of the number of home runs hit by Willie Mays from 1951 to 1973. Find the median.

Stem	Leaf
0	4, 8, 6
1	3, 8
2	0, 9, 9, 2, 3, 8
3	6, 5, 4, 8, 7
4	1, 0, 9, 7
5	1, 2

Box-and-Whisker Plots

Objective: Construct a box-and-whisker plot of a set of data.

Data can be displayed in charts, graphs, and tables. Another method of displaying a set of data is a **box-and-whisker plot.** To make a box-and-whisker plot we first find the median. This divides the set of data in half. We then find the **upper hinge,** or the median of the upper half of the data. Next we find the **lower hinge,** or the median of the lower half of the data. A box is then drawn that encloses the middle half of the data. A thin whisker is drawn from the box to the highest value and lowest value. Here is a box-and-whisker plot of the number of home runs hit by Hank Aaron.

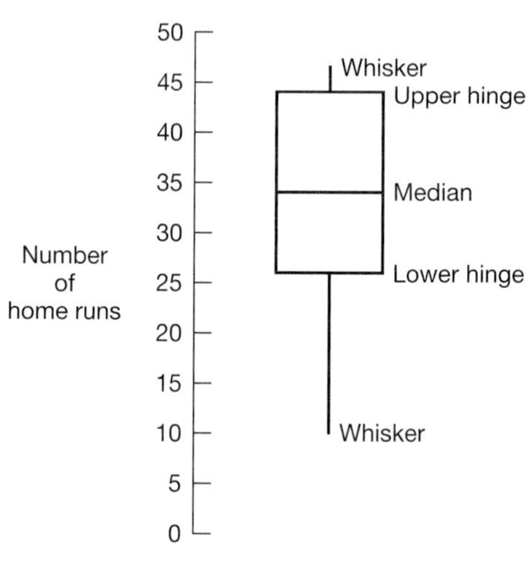

The box-and-whisker plot gives us a picture of the set of data. We can easily see that in most years Hank Aaron hit over 25 home runs.

EXAMPLE 4 Here is a stem-and-leaf diagram of the number of stories in 29 buildings. Construct a box-and-whisker plot of the data.

Stem	Leaf
2	8
3	3
4	8, 6
5	4, 2, 7, 2, 7, 9
6	0, 0, 4, 0, 4, 0, 2, 7
7	0, 4, 1, 1, 2, 7
8	0
9	
10	0, 2
11	0, 0

We find that the median is the 15th value, or 62. There are 14 values above and below the median. The lower hinge is the median of the 14 lower values. Thus the lower hinge is midway between the seventh and eighth values of 54 and 57. It is 55.5. The upper hinge is the median of the 14 upper values. Thus it is between the seventh and eighth values above the median, or between the 22nd and 23rd values of 72 and 74. It is 73. We use these numbers to construct the box-and-whisker plot.

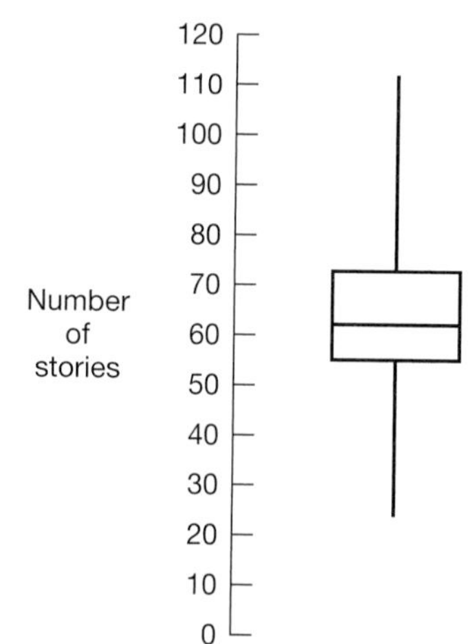

EXAMPLE 5 The Dow Jones Industrial Average is a measure of stock market performance that uses data from 30 well-known stocks. Construct a box-and-whisker plot of the gains and losses listed in the table at the right.

Alcoa	−1/2
AmerExp	−5/8
AT&T	−1/4
Boeing	−1 3/8
Caterpillar	−1/4
Citigroup	−1/8
Coca Cola	−3/8
Disney	+3/8
DuPont	−1 3/4
EastKod	−5/8
Exxon Mobil Corp.	—
GenElec	−1/8
GenMotors	−1 1/2
HewPackard	+1 1/4
Home Depot	−3/4

Honeywell	−3/8
IBM	−3/8
Intel Corp.	−3/8
IntPaper	−3/8
J.P. Morgan & Co.	+1/8
Johnson&Johnson	−3/4
McDonalds	−1 1/4
Merck	−5/8
Microsoft	+1/8
MinnM&M	−1 3/8
PhilMorr	−3/4
Proct&Gm	−7/8
SBC Communications	−1/8
UnitedTch	+1/2
Wal-Mart	−1

The range is from $-1\frac{3}{4}$ to $1\frac{1}{4}$.

Here are the values, written in order.

$-1\frac{3}{4}, -1\frac{1}{2}, -1\frac{3}{8}, -1\frac{3}{8}, -1\frac{1}{4}, -1, -\frac{7}{8}, -\frac{3}{4}, -\frac{3}{4}, -\frac{3}{4}, -\frac{5}{8}, -\frac{5}{8}, -\frac{5}{8}, -\frac{1}{2}, -\frac{3}{8}, -\frac{3}{8}, -\frac{3}{8}, -\frac{3}{8}, -\frac{3}{8}, -\frac{1}{4}, -\frac{1}{4}, -\frac{1}{8}, -\frac{1}{8}, -\frac{1}{8}, 0, \frac{1}{8}, \frac{1}{8}, \frac{3}{8}, \frac{1}{2}, 1\frac{1}{4}$

This photo is of traders on the floor of the New York Stock Exchange. Sometime in the early 21st century, the Exchange will begin to quote all data in decimal form.

Pick 20 NASDAQ stocks and record their net gain or loss for one day. Find the range for this set of data, and draw a box-and-whisker plot.

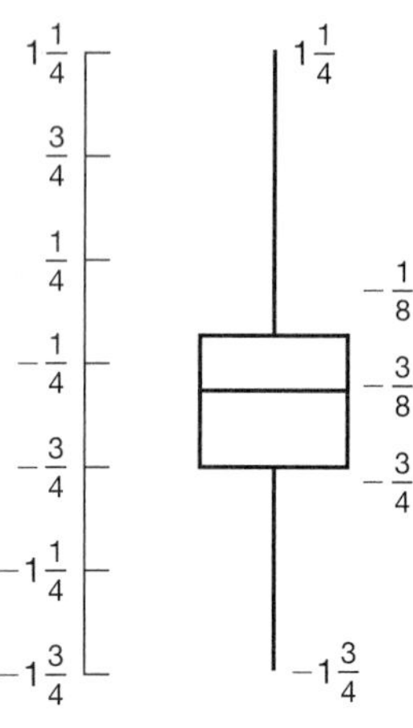

The median change is the average of the 15th and 16th values. These are both $-\frac{3}{8}$, so the median is $-\frac{3}{8}$.

There are 15 values below the median, so the lower hinge is the 8th value, $-\frac{3}{4}$. There are 15 values above the median, so the upper hinge is the 8th value from the end, $-\frac{1}{8}$.

Try This

d. Here is a stem-and-leaf diagram of the heights, in feet, of 29 of the world's tallest buildings. Construct a box-and-whisker plot.

Stem	Leaf
7	50, 50, 56, 64, 78, 84, 87, 90, 92
8	00, 08, 13, 41, 50, 50, 53, 58, 59
9	00, 14, 27, 35, 50
10	46
11	27, 36
12	50
13	50
14	54

Extra Help On the Web

Look for worked-out examples at the Prentice Hall Web site.
www.phschool.com

16-2 Exercises

A

Mental Math Find the mean, median, and mode of

1. the heights, in feet, of some of the world's highest dams.

Stem	Leaf
7	61, 64, 70, 77, 78, 94, 94
8	58, 92
9	32
10	17

2. the pulse rate for a set of 30 patients.

Stem	Leaf
6	0, 3, 5, 6, 6, 7, 8, 9
7	1, 2, 2, 3, 3, 4, 4, 4, 4, 4, 4, 5, 6, 7, 7, 8
8	0, 1, 2, 2, 5, 7

Here are two sets of data. Find the mean, median, and mode of

3. the temperatures, in degrees Fahrenheit, for a set of 40 patients.

97.8, 96.7, 98.6, 100.3, 102.1, 97.8, 98.8, 98.6, 98.5, 102.4, 103.2, 104.1, 98.6, 98.5, 97.3, 98.7, 103.6, 102.4, 98.6, 98.6, 97.9, 99.9, 97.4, 98.6, 98.6, 99.7, 101.7, 104.8, 103.6. 98.7, 99.0, 98.6, 105.2, 98.6, 99.3, 97.9, 98.5, 102.7, 103.8, 98.9

4. the lengths, in miles, of ten of the world's longest canals.

53, 62.2, 28, 39.7, 141, 60.9, 50.7, 19.8, 100.6, 56.7

5–8. Construct a box-and-whisker plot for each set of data in Exercises 1–4.

B

9. Is it *sometimes*, *always* or *never* true that if the mean of a set of data is greater than the mode, the mean is also greater than the median?

10. *Error Analysis* Maria asserts that if the mean of a set of data is equal to the mode, it must also be equal to the median. Find a counterexample and explain why she is mistaken.

11. *Write a Convincing Argument* The numbers 1.3, 4.2, 5.7, 8.1, and 4.9 are the maximum, minimum, hinge, and median values of a data set. They determine a box-and-whisker plot for the data. Draw the plot and write an argument to convince a classmate that the median of the data is 4.9.

12. Collect a set of data that is of interest to you. Find the mean, median, and mode for the set of data, and construct a box-and-whisker plot.

13. A **bimodal** set of data has two modes. Are any of the data sets in Exercises 1–4 bimodal?

14. *Critical Thinking* Make up small sets of data with the following properties.

a. mean $<$ median $<$ mode

b. mode $<$ mean $<$ median

c. median $<$ mean $<$ mode

Challenge

15. The mean is sensitive to extremely high or low values. A **trimmed** mean is found by ordering the values from least to greatest, deleting an equal number from each end, and finding the mean of the remaining values. The **trimming percentage** is the percentage of values that were deleted. Find a trimmed mean for the heights of the buildings in Try This **d** by deleting two values from each end, and find the trimming percentage.

16. Suppose an element is added to a set of data that has a greater value than any element already present in the set. Of the mean, median, and mode, which will be affected the least by the new element? Why?

Mixed Review

Find the center, vertices, and foci of each ellipse.

17. $x^2 - 2x + 4y^2 - 16y = -13$ **18.** $16x^2 - 64x + 25y^2 + 150y = 111$ *10-3*

19. Find a polynomial of lowest degree with rational coefficients and $(3 - 2i)$, $\sqrt{6}$ as some of its roots. *11-3*

16-3 Measures of Variation

What You'll Learn

1. To find the range and mean deviation of a set of data
2. To find the variance of a set of data
3. To find the standard deviation of a set of data

. . . And Why

To answer statistical questions about sets of data

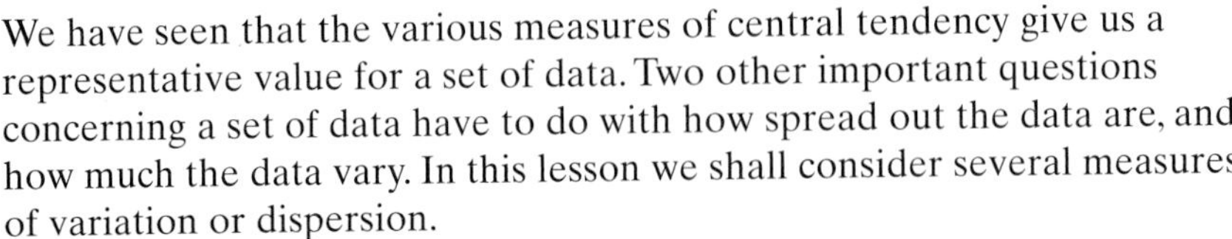

We have seen that the various measures of central tendency give us a representative value for a set of data. Two other important questions concerning a set of data have to do with how spread out the data are, and how much the data vary. In this lesson we shall consider several measures of variation or dispersion.

PART 1 Range and Mean Deviation

Objective: Find the range and mean deviation of a set of data.

One way to get a feeling for the variation, or spread, of a set of data is to find the difference between the greatest value and the least value. This difference is called the **range.**

For instance, here is a set of scores on a chemistry test.

98, 78, 60, 87, 83, 56, 99, 76, 73, 81, 75, 89, 71, 70, 68, 93, 67, 85

The highest score is 99 and the lowest score is 56.

$$99 - 56 = 43$$

Thus the range of the set of scores is 43.

Another possibility for measuring the variability of a set of data is to find the difference between each value x_i and the mean $\overline{x}$, and then find the sum of these differences. It turns out, however, that this sum is always 0, since the positive and negative differences offset each other. To avoid the problem of positive and negative differences we can find the absolute value of each difference.

This measure of spread, or variation, is called the **mean deviation,** or the average amount that a set of data deviates from the mean. To find the mean deviation we first find the deviation of each value from the mean. We do this by finding the absolute value of the difference between each value and the mean. Then we find the mean of these deviations.

The mean and mean deviation of a data set can be affected by any extreme value. Compute the mean deviation in Example 1 after eliminating 88 and the two 59s. Which mean deviation seems to represent the data better?

EXAMPLE 1 Consider this set of high-school basketball scores.

59, 73, 68, 81, 65, 78, 88, 72, 69, 59, 76, 81

Find the range and the mean deviation.

The highest score is 88, the lowest is 59, so the range is 29.

The sum of the scores is 869.

$$869 \div 12 \approx 72.4$$

The mean of the set of data is 72.4.

We now find the absolute value of the difference between each value and the mean.

The mean deviation is $\dfrac{\sum_{i=1}^{n} |\overline{x} - x_i|}{n}$.

$|72.4 - 59| = 13.4,\ |72.4 - 73| = 0.6,\ |72.4 - 68| = 4.4, \ldots, |72.4 - 81| = 8.6$

Next we find the mean of these deviations. The sum of the deviations is 85.

$85 \div 12 \approx 7.08$

The mean deviation is 7.08. This tells us that, typically, each score was about 7 greater or less than the mean of 72.4

Try This

a. Here is a set of temperatures, in degrees Celsius, for a winter week in Richmond, Virginia. Find the range and the mean deviation.
10, 12, 9, 10, 8, 9, 13

Variance

Objective: Find the variance of a set of data.

The spread of a set of data can be measured using a statistic called the **variance.** To find the variance we square the deviation of each value from the mean and then find the mean of these squares. Note that since we square each deviation, avoiding the problem of positive and negative differences, it is not necessary to find absolute values. We denote the variance by $\boldsymbol{\sigma^2}$ (sigma squared).

$$\sigma^2 = \frac{\sum_{i=1}^{n} (\overline{x} - x_i)^2}{n}$$

EXAMPLE 2 Find the variance for this set of temperatures.

10, 12, 9, 10, 8, 9, 13

The mean is 10.1. The deviations from the mean are 0.1, −1.9, 1.1, 0.1, 2.1, 1.1, and −2.9. Squaring each of these values we have 0.01, 3.61, 1.21, 0.01, 4.41, 1.21, and 8.41. We next find the mean of these squares.

The sum of the squares is 18.87. Dividing by n, $\frac{18.87}{7} \approx 2.7$.

The variance of the set of temperatures is 2.7.

When using measures of spread such as the range, the mean deviation, and the variance, we note that the larger the number found, the greater the spread of the set of data.

Try This

b. Find the variance of the set of scores in Example 1.

PART 3 Standard Deviation

Objective: Find the standard deviation of a set of data.

When we find the variance, we square the deviations. This tends to magnify the measure of variation. Thus we can use another measure of the variation called the **standard deviation.** To find the standard deviation of a set of data we find the square root of the variance. The standard deviation is denoted by $\boldsymbol{\sigma}$.

$$\sigma = \sqrt{\frac{\sum_{i=1}^{n} (\bar{x} - x_i)^2}{n}}$$

The standard deviation is the most frequently used measure of the spread of a set of data.

EXAMPLE 3 Find the standard deviation of the set of temperatures in Example 2.

In Example 2 we found that the variance was 2.7. We find $\sqrt{2.7} \approx 1.64$. The standard deviation of the set of temperatures is 1.64.

Try This

c. Find the standard deviation of the set of scores in Example 1.

Extra Help On the Web

Look for worked-out examples at the Prentice Hall Web site.
www.phschool.com

16-3 Exercises

A

Find the range, mean deviation, variance, and standard deviation for

1. passenger capacities of the ten largest cruise ships.
   1499, 1022, 2400, 1970, 821, 2400, 2217, 1146, 758, 1636
2. the lengths, in miles, of the 12 longest highway tunnels.
   2.0, 2.1, 1.8, 2.8, 1.73, 1.7, 7.2, 8.7, 10.01, 3.6, 1.6, 3.1
3. the percentages of fat in 10 samples of ground beef at a grocery store.
   23.5, 22.4, 25.6, 26.8, 28.1, 22.3, 25.6, 24.5, 25.7, 28.2
4. the production costs, in millions of dollars, of 12 recent movies.
   1.4, 4.5, 2.0, 7.0, 4.8, 7.0, 5.0, 7.0, 2.9, 10.5, 1.4, 4.8
5. the distances, in feet, of the left-field foul line in American League baseball parks.
   309, 315, 333, 341, 320, 340, 330, 315, 343, 312, 330, 316, 330, 330
6. the scores of ten girls on the balance beam in a girls' gymnastics meet.
   8.5, 7.9, 8.2, 9.0, 8.3, 7.8, 9.1, 9.2, 8.4, 9.2

B

7. Consider these two sets of data: {20, 22, 30, 36} and {20, 22, 30, 1000}. Find the mean deviation and the standard deviation for each set of data. Which measure of variation is less affected by an extreme value?

8. *Critical Thinking* Set A has a mean of 42 and a standard deviation of 2.5. Set B has a mean of 50 and a standard deviation of 27.
   - **a.** Which set is more likely to contain a value of 34?
   - **b.** Which set is more likely to have a range of 11?
   - **c.** Which set is likely to have more elements?
   - **d.** For which set would the standard deviation decrease if a value of 46 were added to the set?

Challenge

9. Here is a formula for the variance, which can be used with a large set of data to simplify calculations.

$$\sigma^2 = \frac{\sum_{i=1}^{n} x_i^2 - \frac{\left(\sum_{i=1}^{n} x_i\right)^2}{n}}{n}$$

Use this formula to calculate the variance of any of the sets of data in Exercises 1–6. Compare this to the variance already calculated.

10. Statisticians also use the following formula to compute standard deviation.

$$s = \sqrt{\frac{\sum_{i=1}^{n} (\overline{x} - x_i)^2}{n - 1}} \quad \text{where } \overline{x} \text{ is the mean of the set of data}$$

Use this formula to calculate the standard deviation of any of the sets of data in Exercises 1–6. Compare this to the standard deviation already calculated.

Self-Test On the Web

Check your progress. Look for a self-test at the Prentice Hall Web site. www.phschool.com

Mixed Review

Given two points $A(-2, -6)$ and $B(4, 2)$ find **11.** the slope of $\overline{AB}$. *3-5*
12. the distance between A and B. **13.** the midpoint of $\overline{AB}$. *10-1*

Computing the Mean and Standard Deviation

The Σ+ key on some calculators can be used to collect data so that the mean and standard deviation of the data can be found. MODE STAT may not be required. Find the mean and standard deviation of 7, 13, 25, and 4.

mean **standard deviation**

MODE STAT 7 Σ+ 13 Σ+ 25 Σ+ 4 Σ+ $\overline{x}$ 12.25 σ_n 8.0428540

16-4 The Normal Distribution

What You'll Learn

1. To find the proportion of data falling within a range of standard deviations
2. To find and use *z*-scores to determine probability
3. To solve problems involving normal distributions

. . . And Why

To derive statistical information from data sets

The heights of 16-year-old girls are not distributed uniformly, or evenly. Many more girls are average height than are very short or very tall. The values are distributed so that they are frequent near the mean, and become more rare and infrequent the farther they are from the mean. The most common distribution with this characteristic is a **normal distribution.**

When data are distributed in a bell-shaped or **normal curve** about 68% of the data lie within one standard deviation on either side of the mean, and about 95% lie within two standard deviations of the mean.

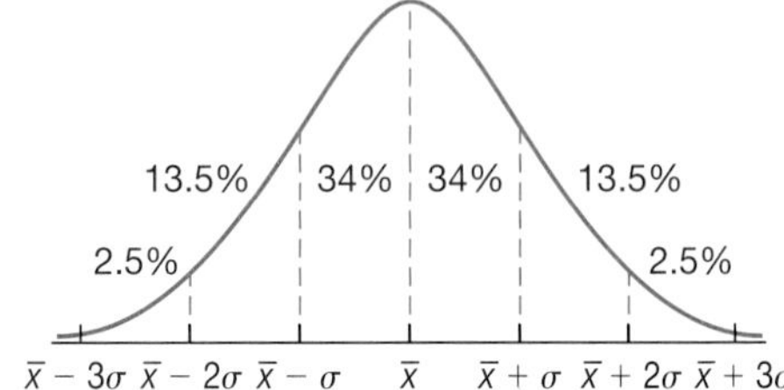

Normal curves are symmetric with respect to the vertical line at the mean. The spread of each curve is defined by its standard deviation. For a large standard deviation, the height of the curve at the mean decreases, and the range increases.

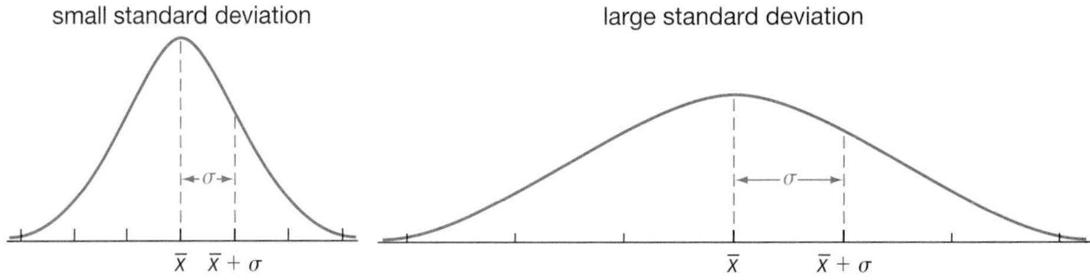

PART 1 Proportion

Objective: Determine the proportion of data falling within a range of standard deviations.

EXAMPLE 1 Consider the bell-shaped distribution of IQ scores for students in a school. The mean is 100 and the standard deviation is 15. What percent of students in the school would we expect to have IQs between 85 and 115?

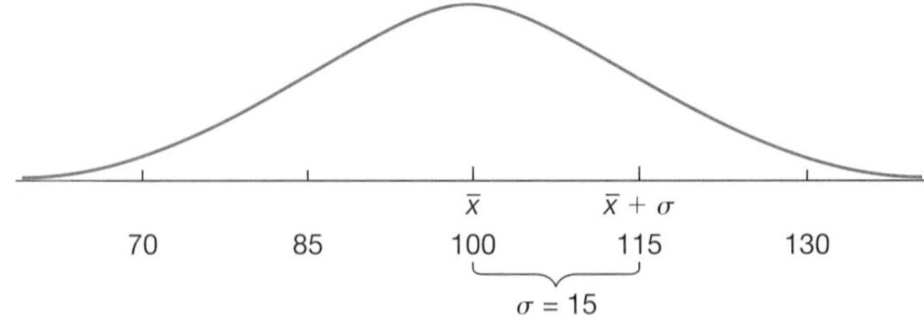

Since 115 and 85 mark positions in the distribution that are one standard deviation above and below the mean, we would expect 34% of the scores to fall between 85 and 100, and another 34% to fall between 100 and 115.

We can expect 68% of the students' scores to fall between 85 and 115.

EXAMPLE 2 What percent of the students can we expect to have IQs between 70 and 115?

Since 70 is two standard deviations below the mean of 100, $13.5 + 34 = 47.5\%$ of the distribution lies between 70 and 100. Also, 115 is one standard deviation above the mean and 34% of the distribution is between the mean and this point.

Thus, we can expect $47.5 + 34 = 81.5\%$ of the students' IQs to fall in the range from 70 to 115.

Try This

a. What percent of the students in the school can we expect to have IQs above 115?

b. What percent of the students in the school can we expect to have IQs in the range from 85 to 145?

PART 2 z-scores and Probability

Objective: Find and use z-scores to determine probability.

A **z-score** for a value is the number of standard deviations the value is from the mean. The sign of the z-score is its direction from the mean. For example, if a value has a z-score of -2, it is two standard deviations below the mean.

The z-score for x is found by dividing the difference between x and the mean by the standard deviation.

$$z = \frac{x - \overline{x}}{\sigma}$$

z-scores translate any normal distribution to a **standard normal distribution** with a mean of 0 and a standard deviation of 1.

Quick Review

Recall that substituting $(x - h)$ for x translates a graph a horizontal distance of h. Multiplying by $\frac{1}{\sigma}$ changes the vertical scale of the graph.

EXAMPLE 3 What is the z-score for 46 in a normal distribution whose mean is 44 and whose standard deviation is 2?

For this distribution, $\overline{x} = 44$ and $\sigma = 2$.

Using the formula, we have $z = \frac{46 - 44}{2} = 1$.

The z-score for 46 is 1. Thus, 46 is one standard deviation above the mean.

Try This What are the z-scores for the following?

c. 45, where $\overline{x} = 50$ and $\sigma = 4$ **d.** 90, where $\overline{x} = 70$ and $\sigma = 8$
e. 56, where $\overline{x} = 60$ and $\sigma = 10$ **f.** 120, where $\overline{x} = 120$ and $\sigma = 17$

The area between the graph of the standard normal distribution and the x-axis is equal to 1. Therefore, any part of the area can be interpreted as the probability that a z-score falls within a given interval.

Table 7 on page 883 gives the probability that a value in the distribution has a z-score that is less than a given value.

EXAMPLE 4 A value is selected randomly from a normal distribution. What is the probability that its z-score is less than -1.46?

The probability that a value has a z-score less than -1.46 is equal to the area of the shaded region under the curve. This value is given in Table 7, a portion of which is shown below.

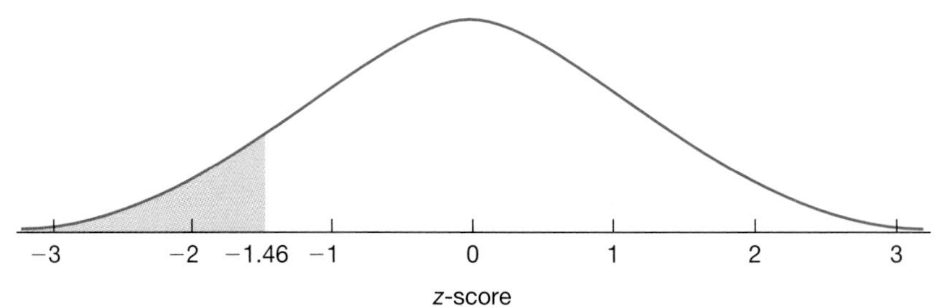

We find -1.4 in the column headed z on the left side of the table and go across the row to the column headed 6.

z	**0**	**1**	**2**	**3**	**4**	**5**	**6**	**7**	**8**	**9**
−1.5	.0668	.0655	.0643	.0630	.0618	.0606	.0594	.0582	.0571	.0559
−1.4	.0808	.0793	.0778	.0764	.0749	.0735	.0721	.0708	.0694	.0681
−1.3	.0968	.0951	.0934	.0918	.0901	.0885	.0869	.0853	.0838	.0823

The probability that a z-score is less than -1.46 is 0.0721 (7.21% of the area under the curve is shaded). We write $P(z < -1.46) = 0.0721$.

EXAMPLE 5 A value is selected randomly from a normal distribution. Find $P(z > -1.46)$.

In Example 4 we found the probability of a z-score *less* than -1.46 is 0.0721. Since the area under the entire curve is 1, the probability of a greater z-score is $1 - 0.0721$, or 0.9279.

Thus $P(z > -1.46) = 0.9279$.

Try This

g. A value is selected randomly from a normal distribution. What is the probability that its z-score is less than 1.65?

h. A value is selected randomly from a normal distribution. Find $P(z > -0.7)$.

PART 3 Solving Problems

Objective: Solve problems involving normal distributions.

Journal

Write a paragraph describing three other data sets that are usually considered to have a normal distribution.

EXAMPLE 6 A student received a score of 56 on a normally distributed standardized test. The test had a mean of 50 and a standard deviation of 5. What is the probability that a randomly selected student achieved a higher score?

We need to find the probability that a value greater than 56 is selected from a normal distribution with a mean of 50 and a standard deviation of 5.

$$z = \frac{x - \bar{x}}{\sigma} = \frac{56 - 50}{5} = 1.2$$

The value 56 has a z-score of 1.2 (56 is 1.2 standard deviations above the mean), so we look up 1.2 in Table 7. The probability that a value is less than 56 is 0.8849. Thus, the probability of a greater value is $1 - 0.8849 = 0.1151$.

The probability that a randomly selected student has a higher score is about 0.12.

EXAMPLE 7 How often would we expect to find an IQ greater than 142 in a sample of students whose mean IQ was 110 where the standard deviation was 16?

A value of 142 would have a z-score of $\frac{142 - 110}{16}$, or 2.0 in this distribution. Thus, we want to find $P(z > 2.0)$.

Using the table, we find $P(z < 2.0) = 0.9772$. Thus, the probability of a greater value is $1 - 0.9772$, or 0.0228.

We can expect to find such a score in a similar distribution about 2 times out of 100.

Try This

Mountain Mineral Water bottles have a mean volume of 12 oz with a standard deviation of 0.4 oz.

i. What is the probability that a bottle contains less than 11 oz of water?

j. How often can we expect to find a bottle containing more than 12.5 oz of water?

Many mineral waters come from springs such as this one. What percent of bottles of Mountain Mineral Water will contain between 11.5 and 12.5 oz of water? (See Try This **j.**)

Extra Help On the Web

Look for worked-out examples at the Prentice Hall Web site.
www.phschool.com

16-4 Exercises

A

A set of test scores is normally distributed with mean 50 and standard deviation 10.

1. What percent of the scores can you expect to fall between 40 and 50?
2. What percent of the scores can you expect to be less than 30?
3. What percent of the scores can you expect to find above 70?

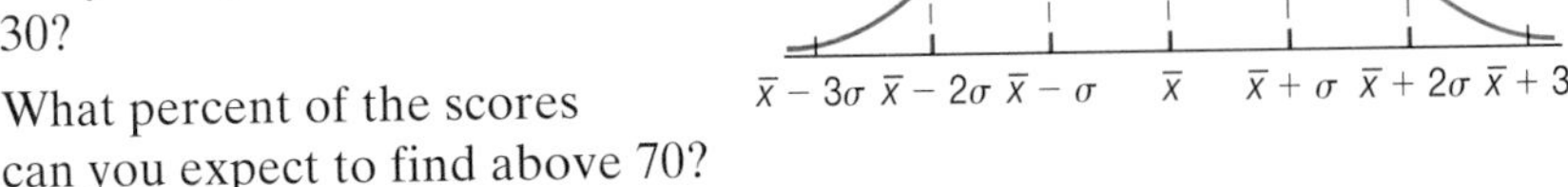

4. What percent can you expect to find between 0 and 40?

Find the z-score associated with each of the following test scores.

5. 67, where $\overline{x} = 50$ and $\sigma = 10$
6. 74, where $\overline{x} = 40$ and $\sigma = 17$
7. 137, where $\overline{x} = 170$ and $\sigma = 44$
8. 108, where $\overline{x} = 112$ and $\sigma = 40$

Use Table 7 to determine the probability of observing z-scores in each range.

9. $P(z < -1.79)$
10. $P(z > 2.4)$
11. $P(z > 1.92)$
12. $P(z < -2.43)$
13. $P(z > -2.88)$
14. $P(z < 0.43)$

For Exercises 15–18, assume a normal distribution.

15. A battery is found to have a mean life of 219 hours with a standard deviation of 70 hours. What is the probability that a battery will not last 100 hours?
16. Students in one grade have an average height of 66 in. with a standard deviation of 3 in. What is the probability that a student is less than 68 in. tall?
17. A bolt manufacturer makes bolts that have a mean diameter of 1 cm with a standard deviation of 0.05 cm. What is the probability that the diameter of a bolt will exceed 1.03 cm?
18. Of popcorn kernels that pop successfully, the mean popping time for one batch is 4 minutes with a standard deviation of 1 minute. What is the probability that a specific kernel will pop after $5\frac{1}{2}$ minutes?

B

Use Table 7 to find x.

19. $P(z < x) = 0.9066$
20. $P(z > x) = 0.9783$
21. $P(z < x) = 0.1056$
22. $P(z < x) = 0.0244$
23. $P(z > x) = 0.3622$
24. $P(z > x) = 0.4404$

Use Table 7 to find the probability of observing z-scores in the following ranges.

25. $P(0 < z < 0.6)$
26. $P(-0.2 < z < 0)$
27. $P(-0.5 < z < 0.15)$
28. $P(0.43 < z < 1.96)$
29. $P(-2.12 < z < 3.0)$
30. $P(0.48 < z < 2.37)$
31. $P(|z| > 1.65)$
32. $P(|z| < 0.84)$

The College Entrance Examination Board scores are developed to approximate a normal distribution with mean 500 and standard deviation 100. What proportion of test takers can we expect to score in the following ranges?

33. Between 350 and 600 **34.** Between 450 and 700 **35.** Below 550

36. Above 620 **37.** Above 750 **38.** Below 450 or above 550

39. **TEST PREP** Given a standard normal distribution with standard deviation σ, approximately what is the value of $P(z < 2)$?

A. 48% **B.** 68% **C.** 95% **D.** 98%

40. ***Critical Thinking*** Suppose ten coins were flipped and the number of heads was recorded. This was done 1000 times and the following data were recorded.

Number of heads	0	1	2	3	4	5	6	7	8	9	10
Frequency	1	10	44	117	205	246	205	117	44	10	1

If the mean of the data is 5 and the standard deviation is 1.58, does the proportion of the scores between the mean and the standard z-scores suggest that the sums observed are normally distributed?

Challenge

41. Half of normal data lie within x standard deviations of the mean. Find x.

42. A company manufactures cover plates for boxes with lengths of 4 inches. Due to variation in the process, the lengths of the plates are normally distributed about a mean of 4 inches with a standard deviation of 0.01 inch. A plate is considered a "reject" if its length is less than 3.98 inches or greater than 4.02 inches. What percent of the production are considered "rejects"?

43. Suppose a coin is flipped n times. If n is a large number, and p is the probability of a head on any given toss, the mean number of heads is given by np, and the standard deviation by $\sqrt{np(1 - p)}$. A coin is tossed 10,000 times.

a. Find $\bar{x}$ and σ.

b. What is the probability of throwing between 4900 and 5100 heads?

Mixed Review

Expand. **44.** $(x + 2y)^5$ **45.** $\left(y - \frac{1}{2}x\right)^4$ **46.** $(x - 1)^3$ *15-4*

Find the 3rd and 7th terms of the expression. **47.** $(p + q)^6$ **48.** $(x - 3)^7$ *15-4*

49. The stopping distance d of a car after brakes are applied varies directly as the square of the speed r. A car traveling 60 km/h can stop in 80 m. How many meters will it take the same car to stop when it is traveling 75 km/h? *6-9*

Find a polynomial of lowest degree with

50. roots 3, 4, and with root -3 having multiplicity 2.

51. root -2 of multiplicity 4. *11-3*

16-5 Collecting Data: Randomness and Bias

What You'll Learn

1. To evaluate and choose a sampling method
2. To describe taking a stratified random sample

. . . And Why

To evaluate the usefulness of statistical information

To prevent over- or underrepresentation of some population group that the data are to represent, statisticians use methods of **sampling,** or effectively drawing and examining samples from a **population** to make accurate statements about the population's characteristics. Samples are used because obtaining information about each member of a population may be expensive, difficult, time-consuming, or even impossible.

PART 1 Random Sampling

Objective: Evaluate and select sampling methods.

Definition

A **random sample** is a sample selected such that

1. each object (person) in the population has an equal chance of being selected for the sample.
2. each object (person) in the sample is chosen independently of any other objects in the sample.

EXAMPLE 1 A scientist is studying the weight gain or loss of mice that are given a certain treatment. When choosing mice for the experiment, the scientist reaches into a cage with 30 mice and selects the 5 largest mice in the cage. Is the sample random?

No. The scientist did not choose randomly. Each mouse did not have an equal chance of being chosen.

EXAMPLE 2 Describe how a random sample of 10 individuals might be chosen from a high school graduating class of 202 to receive a gift certificate.

A random sample of 10 individuals from the graduating class might be selected by placing each class member's name on a slip of paper, placing the slips in a large bowl, and mixing them thoroughly. Ten names could then be drawn from the bowl to determine the winners.

This process has allowed each class member an equal chance to be selected when each name is drawn. In addition, there were no connections between the names drawn, that is, a name being drawn or not drawn did not affect the probability of another name being drawn or not drawn.

Try This

a. Is a survey of students in this algebra class a random sample of the students in your grade?
b. Describe how to select a random sample of 10 individuals attending a movie.

Journal

Find and compare several ways in which random numbers can be generated.

A table of random numbers or a random number generator on a computer is a helpful tool to select objects for a random sample. In Example 1, each class member could have been assigned a number from 1 to 202. Then, the table or computer program could have selected 10 random numbers from 1 to 202.

EXAMPLE 3 Describe how to use a random number table or generator to select a random sample of 15 watchbands for a quality control inspection from a line of 400 watchbands.

This process might be handled by developing a list of 15 random numbers between 1 and 400, ordering the list from smallest to largest, such as 10, 32, 55, and so on, then selecting the tenth band, the thirty-second band, the fifty-fifth band, and so on.

Try This

c. A news magazine has asked for a random sampling of community members to be interviewed. Describe how you might use a table of random numbers to select 20 people from your community for this purpose.

Although the processes involved in the development of a random sample guarantee that requirements of equal probability and independence are satisfied, they do not guarantee that the sample drawn will be **representative.**

EXAMPLE 4 A town newsletter is doing an article on high school students. A questionnaire is sent to a random sample of school-aged students. Are the data representative?

No. A sample of students from kindergarten through grade 12 would not give results representative of high school students.

Even when the sample is restricted to high school students, the data may not be representative. Data might have been collected largely from members of the high school chorus. In this case, the data would most likely be **biased.** That is, it is likely that the data would be overly influenced by factors that are related to musical interests.

Try This

d. A polling organization wants to know how a community feels about irradiation of produce. Discuss the representativeness of each sampling method.
1. Taking a random sample of customers outside a health food store.
2. Calling random numbers from a telephone book.
3. Questioning owners of large farms.

PART 2 Stratified Random Sampling

Objective: Describe how to take a stratified random sample.

To draw a representative sample, we may need to divide the population into distinct subgroups, called **strata.** Then we can use **stratified random sampling** to assure that the sample has the same characteristics as the population.

Each member of the population must be placed in one and only one stratum. A random sample is drawn so that the sample has the same distribution among the strata as the population. For example, if $\frac{2}{3}$ of the voters in an area are Democrats, we would want a sample of voters to contain $\frac{2}{3}$ Democrats.

EXAMPLE 5 A college has 1260 freshmen, 1176 sophomores, 840 juniors, and 924 seniors. Describe how to take a stratified random sample of 200 students.

There are a total of 4200 students. 30% are freshmen, 28% are sophomores, 20% are juniors, and 22% are seniors. We want 30% of the sample of 200 to be freshmen, so we sample 60 freshmen, and so on for sophomores, juniors, and seniors.

	Freshmen	Sophomores	Juniors	Seniors	Total
Population	1260 30%	1176 28%	840 20%	924 22%	4200
Sample	60 30%	56 28%	40 20%	44 22%	200

We would randomly sample 60 freshmen, 56 sophomores, 40 juniors, and 44 seniors.

Try This

e. In a given community, 40% of the voters are under 35 years old, 20% are 35–44 years old, 20% are age 45–54, 15% are age 55–64, and the remaining 5% are age 65 or older. If there are 10,000 registered voters, describe how to take a stratified random sample to predict the election outcome.

The work of Suffragettes such as (from left) Hildegarde Hawthorne, Edith Ellis Furness, Rose Young, Katherine Licily, and Sally Splint almost doubled the number of registered voters by providing women the right to vote. (See Try This **e.**)

16-5 Exercises

Extra Help On the Web

Look for worked-out examples at the Prentice Hall Web site.
www.phschool.com

Which of the following methods of drawing a sample will result in random samples? Explain why or why not.

1. Selecting six friends you meet at a basketball game to participate in a survey about clothing styles at your high school.
2. Surveying five people leaving a hardware store on their views about new construction in the community.
3. Forty students are assigned random numbers from 1 to 40. Two ten-sided number cubes are rolled and the first ten two-digit numbers selected are used to determine the sample members.
4. A survey is conducted to get a sample of 5000 individuals from a state by selecting 50 cities in the state and interviewing 100 individuals in each city.
5. Each individual in a population of 300 is assigned a random number from 1 to 300. First a number less than 100 is selected, then a number from 100 to 199, and finally a number from 200 to 300.
6. Describe how a random sample of 15 sophomores might be chosen from a class of 431.
7. Describe how the 5 mice in Example 1 could have been chosen randomly.

Discuss the representativeness of the samples. Mention possible sources of bias.

8. The results of readers' survey responses to an advice columnist's poll in the newspaper
9. The results of a poll taken on a street corner outside the county court building
10. The results of a sample survey conducted via a computer telecommunications network for personal computer users
11. The results of a survey about the use of preferred brands of hair curling irons at a wrestling meet
12. The results of a survey about knowledge of the warning signs of heart problems at a hospital cardiac care ward
13. The results of a poll about a state governor's election race taken outside of the largest polling place in each county
14. Describe how you might select a random sample of 20% of the students from your school to collect data to determine students' wishes concerning the school lunch program.
15. Delaware has a population of about 666,000; 111,000 people live in Kent County, 442,000 live in New Castle County, and 113,000 live in Sussex County. Describe how you might take a random sample of 200 Delaware residents.

B

16. Describe how to set up a stratified sampling design for a situation having four strata representing 24, 33, 23, and 20 percent of the population, respectively. Suppose that the population is the citizens of a town and the four strata represent political wards in the town. The only information you have are the individuals' names, the locations of their homes, and their ages.
17. Describe how 12 people might be randomly selected from 20,000 names in a 480-page telephone book.
18. *Critical Thinking* In 1969, the Selective Service System began a draft lottery. Each 19-year-old male was eligible to be drafted. Capsules containing slips of paper with each of the 366 days of the year were mixed, drawn randomly, and the order of selection was determined by the order of the draw. September 14 was chosen first, and so on. Was the selection process representative, random, biased? Discuss.

Challenge

19. In 1936, near the end of the Great Depression, the *Literary Digest* took a poll of 10 million people regarding the upcoming presidential election. Names were chosen from telephone books and club membership lists. Almost 2.5 million people responded to the poll by mail. The magazine used the results to predict that Alf Landon would defeat Franklin D. Roosevelt by a landslide. What was the actual result? Interpret the relationship between the poll and the actual result.

Mixed Review

Factor **20.** $x^3 + 216$ **21.** $y^3 + 3y^2 + 3y + 1$ *5-4, 5-5*

22. Divide $x^4 + 5x^3 + 7x^2 - 7x - 18$ by $x + 2$. *11-1*
23. Happy Trail Mix is 70% peanuts; Mountain Top Trail Mix is 55% peanuts. How many ounces of each should be mixed together to get 12 ounces of trail mix that is 60% peanuts? *4-3*
24. Find the equation of variation where y varies inversely as the square of x, and $y = 12$ when $x = 3$. *8-7*

Activity

Design a sample survey questionnaire with your classmates. Decide on a topic of current interest to members of your school. Then have each member of the class collect data from 20 randomly chosen students. Compare the results from the individual surveys; then pool all of the data and consider the overall picture. To what extent do the individual results mirror the overall class results?

Testing Hypotheses

16-6

Introducing the Concept: Hypothesis Testing

A coin is tossed 30 times and lands tails 23 times. Did this result occur by chance or was it due to some other circumstances? Can you repeat this experiment and get 23 tails in 30 tosses?

PART 1 Calculating Chi-Square

Objective: Calculate chi-square values.

Statisticians are often asked to test whether a given set of observational data represents what one would expect to observe by chance or whether it differs greatly from what one might expect.

To determine what constitutes a **significant difference,** statisticians establish a level of error they are willing to tolerate. For example, if we throw a coin 30 times and the coin shows tails 23 times, we may decide either that

1. the results occurred by chance.
   The coin is fair and randomly showed 23 tails, although the likelihood that a coin lands tails 23 times is remote.
2. the results did *not* occur by chance.
   The coin is unevenly weighted or was tossed so that tails had a higher probability of being thrown.

Before stating that the results were biased or influenced by other circumstances, we want to be sure there is a 5% or less probability that the results occurred by chance. Then we can state that the coin is fair at the 5% **level of significance.**

In fact, the probability of throwing tails 23 times in 30 throws is 0.0026, or less than 0.1%. Since the probability is less than 5%, we may state that at the 5% level of significance, the results did *not* occur by chance.

One of the most common ways to test whether a given set of data differs from what one would expect by chance is to use the **chi-square (χ^2) test.** This test is used to compare observed data with expected data, using the following formula.

$$\chi^2 = \sum \frac{(\text{observed} - \text{expected})^2}{\text{expected}}$$

If there is a large difference between observed and expected data, we get a large value for χ^2. If there is no difference, $\chi^2 = 0$.

What You'll Learn

1. To calculate chi-square values
2. To test a hypothesis by using chi-square

. . . And Why

To judge the validity of statistical information

EXAMPLE 1 Calculate chi-square for the coin experiment given in the Introduction.

Since the coin was tossed 30 times, we must account for all 30 events when computing chi-square. There are 2 possible outcomes—heads and tails. Each contributes one term to the value of χ^2.

	Heads	Tails	
We observe	23	7	There are 30 events observed.
We expect	15	15	There are also 30 events expected.
$\frac{\textbf{(observed − expected)}^2}{\textbf{expected}}$	$\frac{(23-15)^2}{15}$	$\frac{(7-15)^2}{15}$	

$$\chi^2 = \frac{(23-15)^2}{15} + \frac{(7-15)^2}{15} = \frac{128}{15} = 8.5\overline{3}$$

Thus, the value of chi-square associated with the coin toss is $8.5\overline{3}$.

Try This

a. A number cube, rolled 90 times, showed a six 19 times. Calculate chi-square.

PART 2 Testing Hypotheses Using Chi-Square

Objective: Test a hypothesis by using chi-square.

The chi-square test is typically used to *accept* or *reject* a hypothesis about a set of data and to generalize about a population. The hypothesis usually tested is the **null hypothesis.** The null hypothesis most often tested is: *There is no statistical difference between the expected and the observed data. Thus, the observed results occurred by chance.* The larger the value of χ^2, the higher the probability the null hypothesis is false.

How large must χ^2 be for us to *reject* the above hypothesis? For a specific level of significance, we reject the hypothesis if the calculated value of chi-square exceeds the table value for the number of possible outcomes.

Possible Outcomes	Level of significance 10%	5%	2.5%	1%	0.1%
2	2.71	3.84	5.02	6.63	7.88
3	4.61	5.99	7.38	9.21	10.6
4	6.25	7.81	9.35	11.3	12.8
5	7.78	9.59	11.1	13.3	14.9
6	9.24	11.1	12.8	15.1	16.7
7	10.6	12.6	14.4	16.8	18.5
8	12.0	14.1	16.0	18.5	20.3
9	13.4	15.5	17.5	20.1	22.0
10	14.7	16.9	19.0	21.7	23.6

We can see for Example 1, the χ^2 value of $8.5\overline{3}$ was greater than the 7.88 table value for a 0.1% level of significance. We can *reject* the null hypothesis that the results occurred by chance.

EXAMPLE 2 Suppose we rolled a number cube 72 times and found that we had 13 ones, 18 threes, and 12 sixes. Determine whether these results occurred by chance. Use a 5% level of significance. The null hypothesis is that the results occurred by chance.

The expected outcome for each of the three possible outcomes is $\frac{1}{6}$ of the total number of rolls, so we expected one, three, and six to have occurred 12 times each. We also expected the other three numbers to have occurred 12 times each, or a total of 36 times. To compute the value of chi-square we make the following table.

Outcome	Observed	Expected	Difference	(Difference)^2	$\frac{(\text{Difference})^2}{\text{Expected}}$
One	13	12	1	1	$\frac{1}{12}$
Three	18	12	6	36	$\frac{36}{12}$
Six	12	12	0	0	$\frac{0}{12}$
Other	29	36	−7	49	$\frac{49}{36}$
Total	72	72			$\frac{160}{36}$

Thus, $\chi^2 = \frac{160}{36} \approx 4.44.$

There are 4 possible outcomes. The chi-square value for a 5% significance level for 4 possible outcomes is 7.81. Since 4.44 does not exceed this value, we can state that our results occurred by chance. Thus, we can *accept* the null hypothesis.

Try This

b. One hundred students are asked, "On a multiple-choice question, if you were to guess, would you choose a, b, c, or d?" Thirty-nine students chose c, 16 chose a. Determine whether this result occurred by chance. Use a 1% level of significance.

Given the data of Example 3, which lane would be the best lane in which to start?

EXAMPLE 3 For two years, the winners in eighty-eight 100-meter dashes held at Central High School's new track were distributed as follows:

Lane of track	1	2	3	4	5	6	7	8
Number of winners	15	12	19	13	11	6	7	5

Test the hypothesis that there is no difference between the respective lanes in terms of the number of race winners associated with each lane

a. at the 5% level of significance.
b. at the 2.5% level of significance.

There were a total of 88 races, so we would expect 11 winners from each lane if runners were assigned randomly to the lanes.

Using the formula for chi-square we calculate the value associated with the data.

$$\chi^2 = \frac{(15-11)^2}{11} + \frac{(12-11)^2}{11} + \frac{(19-11)^2}{11} + \frac{(13-11)^2}{11} + \frac{(11-11)^2}{11} + \frac{(6-11)^2}{11} + \frac{(7-11)^2}{11} + \frac{(5-11)^2}{11}$$
$$= \frac{16}{11} + \frac{1}{11} + \frac{64}{11} + \frac{4}{11} + 0 + \frac{25}{11} + \frac{16}{11} + \frac{36}{11} + \frac{162}{11} \approx 14.73$$

There are 8 possible outcomes. The chi-square value 14.73 exceeds the table value of 14.1 for a 5% level of significance. We would *reject* the null hypothesis that there is no difference between the lanes at the 5% level of significance.

A chi-square of 14.73 does *not* exceed the table value of 16.0 for a 2.5% level of significance. We would *accept* the null hypothesis that there is no difference between the lanes at the 2.5% level of significance.

Try This

c. Group the data in Example 3 so that there are 4 possible outcomes—lanes 1 and 2, lanes 3 and 4, lanes 5 and 6, lanes 7 and 8. Test the hypothesis that there is no difference between each pair of lanes in terms of the number of race winners
1. at the 5% level of significance. **2.** at the 1% level of significance.

Extra Help On the Web
Look for worked-out examples at the Prentice Hall Web site.
www.phschool.com

16-6 Exercises

Calculate the value of chi-square.

1. A coin is tossed 55 times and lands heads 24 times.
2. A number cube is tossed 30 times and shows a one 7 times.
3. One hundred students are asked to pick a number from 1 to 10; 35 pick 7, 28 pick 3, and the rest pick another number.

4. In a class of 260, 65 have last names beginning with J, 56 have last names beginning with T, and the others have last names beginning with a different letter.

Complete the table and determine chi-square.

5.

Outcome	Observed	Expected	Difference	$(\text{Difference})^2$	$\frac{(\text{Difference})^2}{\text{Expected}}$
1	20	12			
2	19	15			
3	18	18			
4	24	21			
5	17	21			
6	10	18			
7	14	15			
8	10	12			

6.

Outcome	Observed	Expected	Difference	$(\text{Difference})^2$	$\frac{(\text{Difference})^2}{\text{Expected}}$
1	2	5			
2	12	8			
3	23	11			
4	16	14			
5	14	17			
6	8	20			

7. **TEST PREP** Two number cubes, each with faces numbered 4 through 9, are rolled 10 times, and the sum is computed and recorded as even or odd. How many outcomes are there for a χ^2 test of the null hypothesis that the cubes are fair?

A. 2 **B.** 5 **C.** 11 **D.** 12

8. ***Multi-Step Problem*** Two swim meets of 72 races each were held in a six-lane pool. The numbers of winners in lanes 1 through 6 respectively in the first meet were

14, 14, 8, 6, 9, and 21;

in the second meet they were

13, 11, 14, 16, 8, and 10.

a. Test the null hypothesis at the 5% level for each meet.

b. Combine the data for each lane. Can the null hypothesis be rejected at the 2.5% level?

9. In testing metal bars for breaks under a series of laboratory tests, technicians obtained the following data relating the distributions of theoretical and observed breaks. Test the null hypothesis at the 1% level.

Number of Breaks	**0**	**1**	**2**	**3**	**4**	**5 or more**
Observed breaks	157	125	35	17	1	1
Expected breaks	131	107	54	27	11	6

10. The expected frequency of students passing through the school computer center was calculated and a survey taken to see how closely the predictions matched the theoretical solution. Test the null hypothesis at the 0.1% level of significance.

Period of Observation	1	2	3	4	5	6	7	8
Observed number	43	27	28	67	43	31	25	46
Expected number	30	40	40	60	50	30	30	30

B

11. ***Mathematical Reasoning*** Are chi-square values for the *proportion* of observed values equal to the chi-square values for the data? Give an example.

12. ***Critical Thinking***
   a. Write a 51-digit string of "random" digits.
   b. Count the number of times you have the same digit following itself. Count the number of times that a number one less or one greater follows a digit (± 1 number).
   c. Fill in the table and test the data at a 5% level of significance.
   d. ***Write a Convincing Argument*** Compare your work with that of several classmates. Explain why most people do not get enough of the same followers and ± 1 numbers in their strings of "random" numbers in the experiment described in **parts a** and **b**.

	Number observed	Number expected
Same follower		
± 1 number		
Other		

Challenge

13. ***Write a Convincing Argument***
   a. Chi-square tests are not recommended when expected values are 5 or less. Write an argument to convince a classmate that such results would not be reliable.
   b. Explain how grouping the following data to test for significance at the 5% level will give a more useful result.

Observed	0	3	7	15	18	11	10
Expected	1	6	15	20	15	6	1

Mixed Review

Simplify. **14.** $\frac{\sqrt{729}}{\sqrt{64}}$ **15.** $\frac{\sqrt[3]{729}}{\sqrt[3]{64}}$ **16.** $\frac{\sqrt[6]{729}}{\sqrt[6]{64}}$ *7-3, 7-5*

Application

Statistical Studies

You have been asked by the principal of a school to do a statistical study of the previous year's grades. She needs to know the following:

a. The grade-point average, or mean grade, for each subject and for the total of all subjects.
b. The distribution of grades for different subjects and for the total.
c. How the distribution of grades for a subject and for the total compares with the expected distribution of grades—20% As, 25% Bs, 30% Cs, 20% Ds, and 5% Fs.

After asking the appropriate teachers and school records office for the number of As, Bs, Cs, Ds, and Fs for each class, you find the following grade distributions.

	A	B	C	D	F	
Mathematics	67	112	84	43	32	338
Science	51	70	86	53	21	281
History	111	103	75	40	11	340
English	101	110	73	46	29	359
Social Studies	49	84	89	37	19	278
Languages	38	57	41	22	6	164
Total	417	536	448	241	118	1760

The grades are assigned the numerical values 4 for A, 3 for B, 2 for C, 1 for D, and 0 for F. To find the grade-point average, or mean grade, for English,

$\overline{x} = \dfrac{\sum_{i=1}^{5} f_i w_i}{n}$, where w_i is the value of each grade and f_i is the frequency of grade i.

$\overline{x} = \dfrac{101(4) + 110(3) + 73(2) + 46(1) + 29(0)}{359} = \dfrac{926}{359} \approx 2.58$, which is just over halfway from C to B.

Problems

1. What is the grade-point average for each subject? for the total?
2. Choose an appropriate level of significance. Use chi-square to test whether the grades were as expected for each subject; for the total.
3. Are the grades normally distributed for each subject? for the total?
4. What is the expected grade-point average for any or all subjects?
5. What other statistical information could you present?
6. To find the variance, $\sigma^2 = \dfrac{\sum_{i=1}^{5} f_i(w_i - \overline{x})^2}{n}$. Find the standard deviation of grades for the total.

16 Chapter Wrap Up

Key Terms

σ (p. 702)
σ^2 (p. 701)
χ^2 (p. 715)
average (p. 694)
biased (p. 711)
bimodal (p. 699)
box-and-whisker plot (p. 696)
chi-square test (p. 715)
frequency distribution (p. 691)
level of significance (p. 715)
lower hinge (p. 696)
mean (p. 694)
mean deviation (p. 700)
median (p. 695)
mode (p. 694)
normal curve (p. 704)
normal distribution (p. 704)
null hypothesis (p. 716)
population (p. 710)
random sample (p. 710)
range (p. 700)
ranked stem-and-leaf diagram (p. 691)
relative frequency (p. 691)
representative (p. 711)
sampling (p. 710)
significant difference (p. 715)
standard deviation (p. 702)
standard normal distribution (p. 705)
stem-and-leaf diagram (p. 690)
strata (p. 712)
stratified random sampling (p. 712)
trimmed (p. 699)
trimming percentage (p. 699)
upper hinge (p. 696)
variance (p. 701)
$\overline{x}$ (p. 694)
z-score (p. 705)

16-1

Stem-and-leaf diagrams and **frequency distributions** are helpful in organizing data.

1. Construct a stem-and-leaf diagram for these math test scores.

   92, 73, 82, 53, 67, 77, 78, 63, 93, 96, 80, 71, 63, 90, 81, 74, 76, 72, 73, 80, 91, 65, 49, 50, 74, 80, 77, 80, 83, 70, 72.

2. Construct a frequency distribution showing the **relative frequency** for the following latitudes, in degrees, of some North American cities.

   32, 41, 42, 35, 40, 82, 40, 35, 38, 62, 33, 39, 33, 44, 30, 64, 35, 39, 44, 30, 32, 42, 51, 43, 30, 44, 64, 48, 37, 40, 45, 40

16-2

The following are three important **measures of central tendency.**

The **mean** or average is $\overline{x} = \dfrac{\sum_{i=1}^{n} x_i}{n}$.

The **mode** is the value that occurs most often.
The **median** is the middle value when all the values are arranged in order. If there is no middle value, then the median is the average of the two middle values.

3. Find the mean, mode, and median for the length, in miles, of some major United States rivers.

   3710, 1243, 1306, 1900, 135, 2533, 900, 1270, 680, 780, 1038, 1459, 280, 620, 300, 444, 270, 735, 720, 530, 490, 525, 720, 310, 470

A **box-and-whisker plot** is a valuable method of displaying data.

4. Construct a box-and-whisker plot of the average speed of winds, in mi/h, in some North American cities.

   9.1, 6.8, 9.1, 10.3, 12.4, 12.1, 11.4, 6.2, 10.3, 10.7, 8.9, 10.2

16-3

The **range** is the difference between the greatest and least values.

5. The Rams scored 14, 15, 22, 20, 27, 24, and 18 points in 7 games. What is the range?

The **mean deviation** is the average amount that a set of data differs from the mean. To find the mean deviation, first we find the deviation of each value from the mean. We do this by finding the absolute value of the difference between each value and the mean. Then we find the mean of these deviations.

6. Find the mean deviation for these basketball scores.

   80, 99, 89, 125, 113, 117, 142, 131, 103, 111, 123, 135, 97, 109, 86, 117, 107, 125, 94, 121

To find the **variance**, square the deviation of each value from the mean and then find the mean of these squares.

7. Find the variance for the following running speeds, in mi/h, of various animals.

   50, 40, 45, 35, 30, 70, 25, 30, 39, 47, 61, 11, 28, 35, 45, 50, 32, 20

To find the **standard deviation, σ,** take the square root of the variance.

8. Find the standard deviation for the height, in meters, of the world's highest dams.

   243, 237, 261, 272, 237, 226, 300, 285, 267, 233, 335, 262, 253, 230, 237, 242, 245

Internet Activity On the Web

Look for extension problems for this chapter at the Prentice Hall Web site.
www.phschool.com

16-4

When data are distributed in a bell-shaped curve, or **normal curve,** about 68% of the data lie within one standard deviation on either side of the mean, and about 95% lie within two standard deviations of the mean.

9. A test has a mean score of 23 with a standard deviation of 4. What percent of the students would we expect to have a score below 19?

The ***z*-score** for x is found by dividing the difference between x and the mean by the standard deviation. The probability of a lower z-score is given in Table 7.

10. Find the z-score for 90, where $\overline{x} = 120$ and $\sigma = 37.5$.
11. Rolling Wheels tires have a mean lifetime of 40,000 miles with a standard deviation of 8000 miles. What is the probability that a specific tire will go more than 50,000 miles? Assume a normal distribution.

16-5

A **random sample** is a sample selected such that each object (person) in the population has an equal chance of being selected for the sample, and each object (person) in the sample is chosen independently of any other objects in the sample.

12. If we are surveying students' ice cream flavor preferences and the first student picks chocolate, are we taking a random sample if we make sure the second student picks a flavor other than chocolate?
13. Describe how to select a random sample of 5 physicians from a telephone listing of 200 for a health survey.

To draw a representative sample, we may need to divide the population into distinct subgroups, called **strata.** Then we can use **stratified random sampling** to assure that the sample has the same characteristics as the population.

14. A college has 1400 freshmen, 1800 sophomores, 1200 juniors, and 600 seniors. Describe how to take a stratified random sample of 200 students.

16-6

The **chi-square**(χ^2) test is used to compare observed data with expected data, using the formula

$$\chi^2 = \sum \frac{(\text{observed} - \text{expected})^2}{\text{expected}}$$

15. A rub-off game card has 5 scratch-off spots. There is one winning spot and 4 losing spots. The player scratches off exactly one spot. Out of 1000 game cards, there were 223 winners. Calculate chi-square.

The hypothesis usually tested is the **null hypothesis,** which states

> There is no statistical difference between the expected and the observed data. Thus, the observed results occurred by chance.

To reject the null hypothesis at a specific level of significance, the calculated value of chi-square must exceed the value given for the number of possible outcomes reported.

Possible Outcomes	**Level of significance** 10%	5%	2.5%	1%	0.1%
2	2.71	3.84	5.02	6.63	7.88
3	4.61	5.99	7.38	9.21	10.6
4	6.25	7.81	9.35	11.3	12.8
5	7.78	9.59	11.1	13.3	14.9
6	9.24	11.1	12.8	15.1	16.7
7	10.6	12.6	14.4	16.8	18.5
8	12.0	14.1	16.0	18.5	20.3
9	13.4	15.5	17.5	20.1	22.0
10	14.7	16.9	19.0	21.7	23.6

16. Test the null hypothesis for Exercise 15 at the 5% level of significance.

17. The manager of a fast-food restaurant noticed the following numbers of customers served by the different cashiers during one day.

Cashiers	**Customers**
1	85
2	68
3	41
4	78
5	96
6	72
7	50

Test the null hypothesis at the 5% level of significance.

16 Chapter Assessment

Use the data for Problems 1–8.

The temperatures in several western cities on a certain date were as follows.

40, 43, 44, 44, 47, 51, 70, 68, 56, 56, 52 67, 53, 63, 56

1. Construct a stem-and-leaf diagram for these data.
2. Construct a frequency distribution showing the relative frequency for these data.
3. Find the mean, mode, and median for these data.
4. Construct a box-and-whisker plot for these data.
5. What is the range for these data?
6. Find the mean deviation for these data.
7. Find the variance for these data.
8. Find the standard deviation for these data.
9. A test has a mean score of 73 with a standard deviation of 12. Students with scores of 85 and up receive an A. What percent of the students would we expect to get an A? Assume a normal distribution.
10. Find the z-score for 29, where $\overline{x} = 31$ and $\sigma = 1.25$.
11. A tool withstands an average pressure of 38 lb, with a standard deviation of 1.6 lb. The manufacturer must throw out tools that cannot withstand pressures of at least 40 lb. What is the probability that a certain tool must be thrown out? Assume a normal distribution.
12. If we are studying customer satisfaction for Leopard XX cars, are we taking a random sample if we select every third customer from a list of customers who have purchased two Leopard XX cars?
13. Describe how to select a random sample of 25 athletes for a sports trivia contest.
14. There are three high schools in a town. There are 1350 students at Martin Luther King High, 925 at Wayne High, and 1475 at Jordan School. Describe how to take a stratified random sample of 150 students.
15. A game show asks the contestants to choose door 1, 2, or 3. The big prize is behind one of the doors. Of 60 contestants, 29 chose the door with the big prize. Calculate chi-square.
16. Test the null hypothesis for Problem 15 at the 5% level of significance.
17. A toll collector noticed that the following numbers of cars came through four different toll booths during one day.

Toll booth	1	2	3	4
Customers	131	185	172	112

Test the null hypothesis at the 1% level of significance.

CHAPTER 17

What You'll Learn in Chapter 17

- How to find the six trigonometric function values for an angle
- How to find the reference angle of a rotation and use it to find trigonometric function values
- How to convert from degrees to radian measure and vice versa
- How to find arc length and angular speed
- How to use a table for values of trigonometric functions
- How to graph trigonometric functions using the periodicity and amplitude
- How to derive and use trigonometric identities
- How to solve equations involving trigonometric expressions

Skills & Concepts You Need for Chapter 17

3-3

1. Given $f(x) = 2x^2 + 1$, find $f(3)$ and $f(-2)$.

5-3 Simplify.

2. $(3t + 2)(t - 4)$

5-4, 5-5, 5-6 Factor completely.

3. $24a^2 - 96b^2$

4. $3x^3y - 15x^2y^2 + 18xy^3$

6-1 Simplify.

5. $\dfrac{(a^2 - 4)}{-2a - 6} \cdot \dfrac{a + 3}{a - 2}$

6-2 Simplify.

6. $\dfrac{4}{-x} + \dfrac{6}{x}$

7. $\dfrac{5cd}{4c^2 - 1} - \dfrac{c - d}{2c + 1}$

8-1, 8-3, 8-5 Solve.

8. $a^2 + a - 12 = 0$

9. $6y^2 + 20y = 16$

10. $1 + \dfrac{3}{x^2} = \dfrac{1}{x}$

11. $2x + x(x - 1) = 1$

9-1

12. Show that $f(x) = x^3 - x$ is odd.

13. Show that $g(x) = 2x^2 - x^4$ is even.

Trigonometric Functions

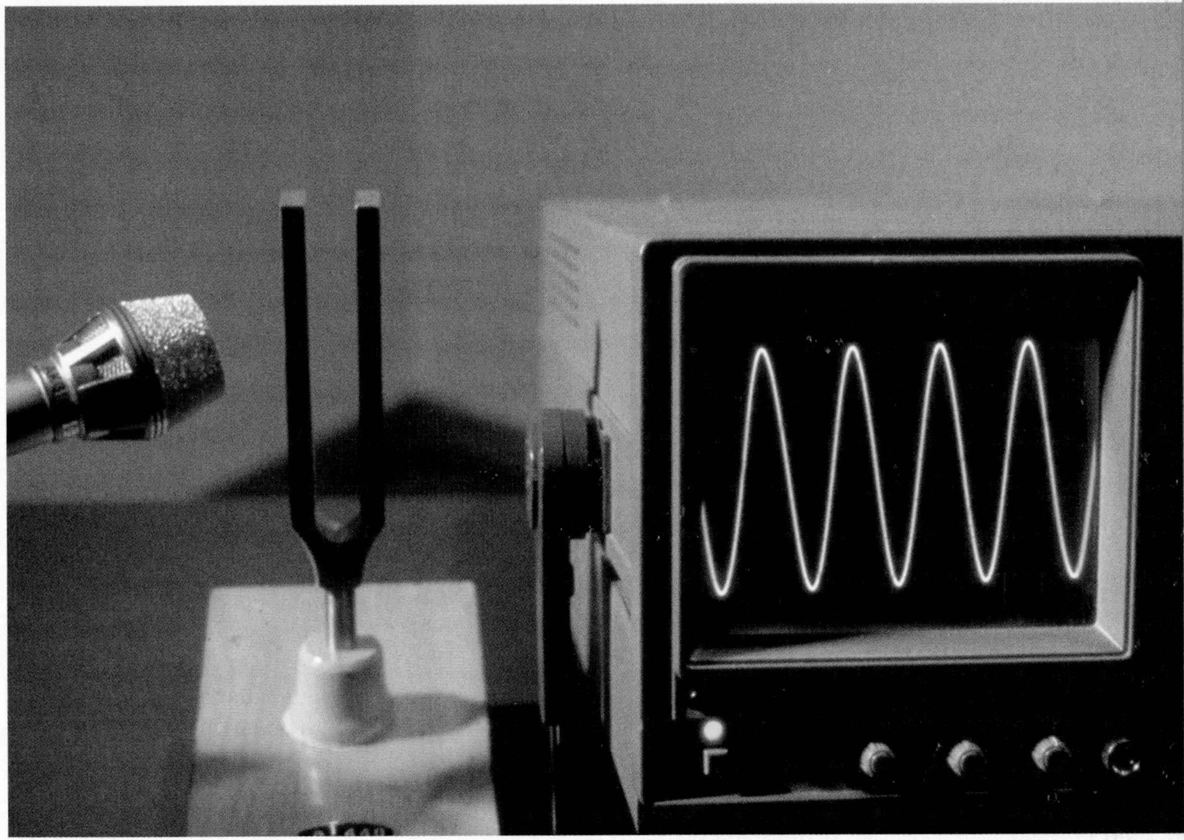

In this chapter you will learn about sine curves, cosine curves, and their graphs. The graphs look like the sound waves pictured on the oscilloscope, an instrument that shows various forms of energy—like sound—as waves.

17-1 Trigonometric Functions in Triangles

What You'll Learn

1. To find the sine, cosine, and tangent for an angle of a right triangle
2. To find the lengths of sides in special triangles
3. To find the six trigonometric function values for an angle given one of the function values

. . . And Why

To graph the trigonometric functions

We now consider an important class of functions, known as **trigonometric functions.** The word **trigonometry** means "triangle measurement." The Greeks and Hindus saw trigonometry mainly as a tool for use in astronomy. The early Arabian mathematicians are credited as the first to use all six trigonometric functions.

PART 1 Trigonometric Ratios

Objective: Find the sine, cosine, and tangent for an angle of a right triangle.

In a right triangle, the side opposite the right angle is the **hypotenuse.** In the triangle shown, the hypotenuse has length c, the side **opposite** the **angle θ (theta)** has length a, and the side **adjacent** to θ has length b.

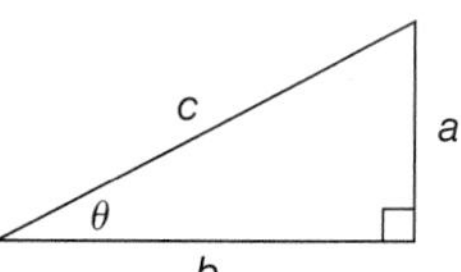

The ratio $\frac{a}{b}$ depends on θ, and thus is a function of θ. This function is the **sine** function. There are six such functions, three of which are defined as follows.

Definition

sine function: $\sin\theta = \dfrac{\text{length of the side opposite } \theta}{\text{length of the hypotenuse}}$

cosine function: $\cos\theta = \dfrac{\text{length of the side adjacent to } \theta}{\text{length of the hypotenuse}}$

tangent function: $\tan\theta = \dfrac{\text{length of the side opposite } \theta}{\text{length of the side adjacent to } \theta}$

Because all right triangles with an angle of measure θ are similar, function values depend only on the size of the angle, not the size of the triangle.

EXAMPLE 1 In this triangle, find $\sin\theta$, $\cos\theta$, and $\tan\theta$.

$$\sin\theta = \frac{\text{side opposite } \theta}{\text{hypotenuse}} = \frac{3}{5}$$

$$\cos\theta = \frac{\text{side adjacent to } \theta}{\text{hypotenuse}} = \frac{4}{5}$$

$$\tan\theta = \frac{\text{side opposite } \theta}{\text{side adjacent to } \theta} = \frac{3}{4}$$

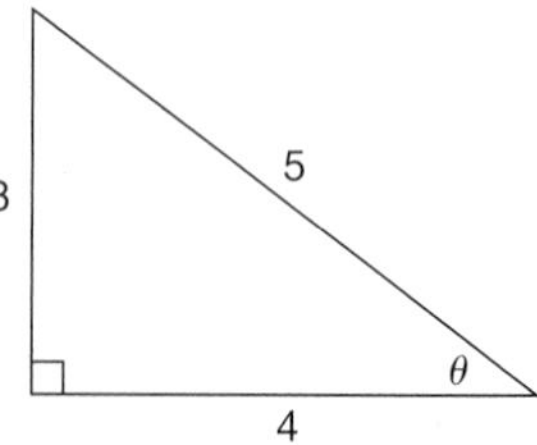

Try This

a. In this triangle, find $\sin \theta$, $\cos \theta$, and $\tan \theta$.

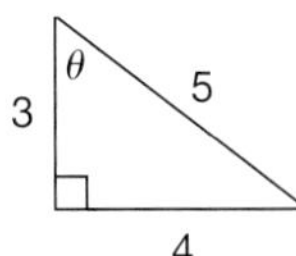

PART 2 Special Angles

Objective: Find the lengths of sides in special triangles.

Quick Review

Frequently used Pythagorean triples to remember include (3, 4, 5), (5, 12, 13), (8, 15, 17), and (7, 24, 25). The 30-60-90 triangle ratios are $1{:}\sqrt{3}{:}2$ while the 45-45-90 triangle ratios are $1{:}1{:}\sqrt{2}$.

Our knowledge of triangles enables us to determine trigonometric function values for certain angles. First recall the Pythagorean theorem. It says that in any right triangle $a^2 + b^2 = c^2$, where c is the length of the hypotenuse.

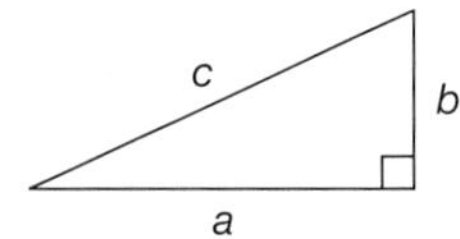

In a 45° right triangle the legs are the same length. Let us consider such a triangle whose legs have length 1. Then its hypotenuse has length c.

$$1^2 + 1^2 = c^2, \text{ or } c^2 = 2, \text{ or } c = \sqrt{2}$$

Such a triangle is shown below. From this diagram we can easily determine the trigonometric function values for 45°.

$$\sin 45° = \frac{1}{\sqrt{2}} = \frac{\sqrt{2}}{2}$$

$$\cos 45° = \frac{1}{\sqrt{2}} = \frac{\sqrt{2}}{2}$$

$$\tan 45° = \frac{1}{1} = 1$$

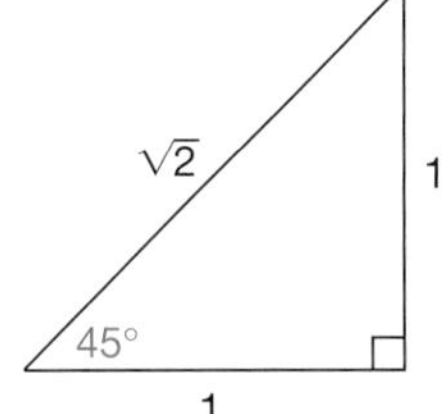

Next we consider an equilateral triangle with sides of length 2. If we bisect one angle, we obtain a right triangle that has a hypotenuse of length 2 and a leg of length 1. The other leg has length a, given by the Pythagorean theorem as follows.

$$a^2 + 1^2 = 2^2, \text{ or } a^2 = 3, \text{ or } a = \sqrt{3}$$

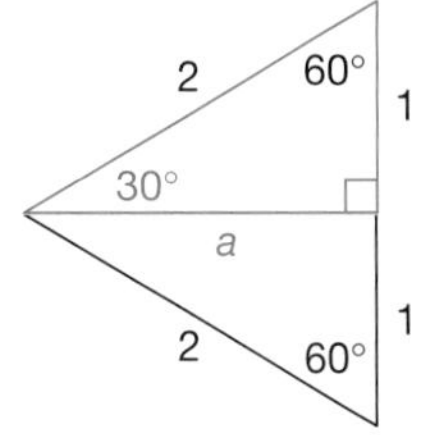

The acute angles of this triangle have measures of 30° and 60°. We can now determine function values for 30° and 60°.

$$\sin 30° = \frac{1}{2} \qquad \sin 60° = \frac{\sqrt{3}}{2}$$

$$\cos 30° = \frac{\sqrt{3}}{2} \qquad \cos 60° = \frac{1}{2}$$

$$\tan 30° = \frac{1}{\sqrt{3}} = \frac{\sqrt{3}}{3} \qquad \tan 60° = \sqrt{3}$$

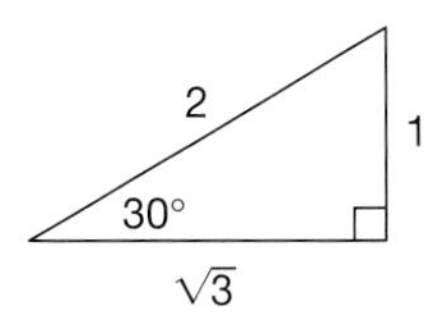

We can use what we have learned about trigonometry to solve problems.

EXAMPLE 2 In $\triangle ABC$, $b = 40$ cm and $m\angle A = 60°$. What is the length of side c?

$$\cos A = \frac{b}{c}$$

$$\cos 60° = \frac{40}{c} \quad \text{Substituting}$$

$$\frac{1}{2} = \frac{40}{c} \quad \text{Using } \cos 60° = \tfrac{1}{2}$$

$$c = 80 \text{ cm}$$

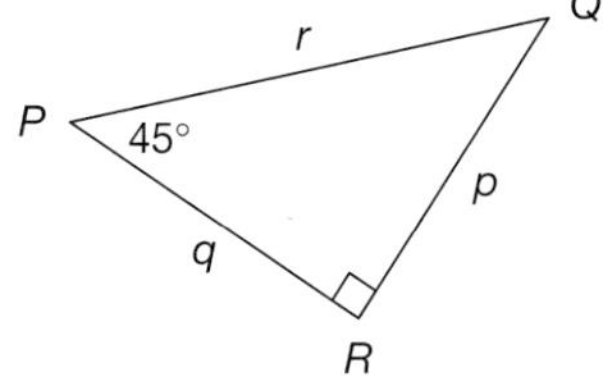

Try This

b. In $\triangle PQR$, $q = 12$ ft. Use the cosine function to find the length of side r.

PART 3 Reciprocal Functions

Objective: Find the six trigonometric function values for an angle given one of the function values.

We define the three other trigonometric functions by finding the reciprocals of the sine, cosine, and tangent functions.

Definition

The **cotangent, secant,** and **cosecant functions** are the respective reciprocals of the tangent, cosine, and sine functions.

$$\textbf{cot}\ \boldsymbol{\theta} = \frac{1}{\tan\theta} = \frac{\text{length of the side } \textbf{adjacent} \text{ to } \theta}{\text{length of the side } \textbf{opposite}\ \theta}$$

$$\textbf{sec}\ \boldsymbol{\theta} = \frac{1}{\cos\theta} = \frac{\text{length of the } \textbf{hypotenuse}}{\text{length of the side } \textbf{adjacent} \text{ to } \theta}$$

$$\textbf{csc}\ \boldsymbol{\theta} = \frac{1}{\sin\theta} = \frac{\text{length of the } \textbf{hypotenuse}}{\text{length of the side } \textbf{opposite}\ \theta}$$

EXAMPLE 3 Find the cotangent, secant, and cosecant of the angle shown. Approximate to two decimal places.

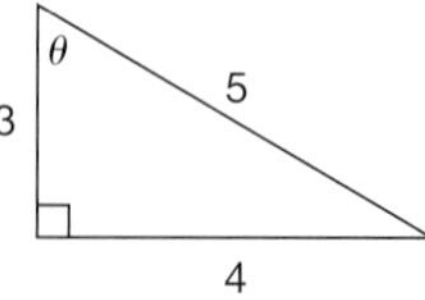

$$\cot\theta = \frac{\text{side adjacent to } \theta}{\text{side opposite } \theta} = \frac{3}{4} = 0.75$$

$$\sec\theta = \frac{\text{hypotenuse}}{\text{side adjacent to } \theta} = \frac{5}{3} \approx 1.67$$

$$\csc\theta = \frac{\text{hypotenuse}}{\text{side opposite } \theta} = \frac{5}{4} = 1.25$$

Try This

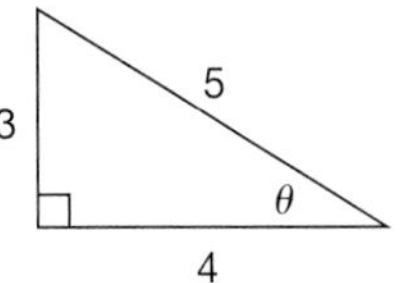

c. Approximate $\cot \theta$, $\sec \theta$, and $\csc \theta$ to two decimal places.

By using the Pythagorean theorem we can find all six trigonometric function values of θ when one of the ratios is known.

EXAMPLE 4 If $\sin \theta = \frac{12}{13}$, find the other five trigonometric function values for θ.

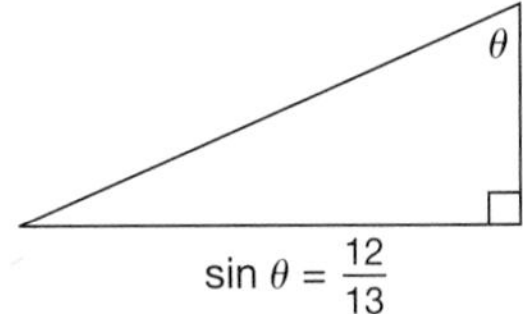

We know from the definition of the sine function that the ratio

$$\frac{\text{side opposite } \theta}{\text{hypotenuse}} \text{ is } \frac{12}{13}.$$

Let us consider a similar right triangle in which the hypotenuse has length 13 and the side opposite θ has length 12.

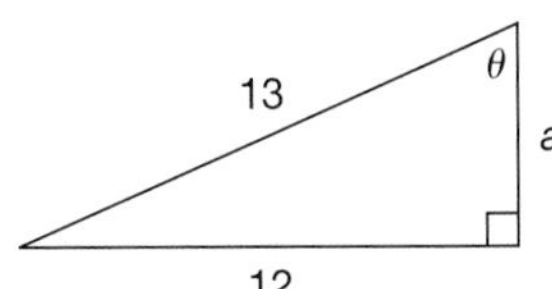

To find the length of the side adjacent to θ, we use the Pythagorean theorem.

$$a^2 + 12^2 = 13^2$$
$$a^2 = 169 - 144 = 25$$
$$a = 5 \quad \text{Choosing the positive square root, since we are finding length}$$

We can use $a = 5$, $b = 12$, and $c = 13$ to find all of the ratios in our original triangle.

$$\sin \theta = \frac{12}{13} \qquad \csc \theta = \frac{13}{12}$$
$$\cos \theta = \frac{5}{13} \qquad \sec \theta = \frac{13}{5}$$
$$\tan \theta = \frac{12}{5} \qquad \cot \theta = \frac{5}{12}$$

Try This

d. If $\cos \theta = \frac{8}{17}$, find the other five trigonometric function values for θ.

Extra Help On the Web

Look for worked-out examples at the Prentice Hall Web site. www.phschool.com

17-1 Exercises

A

Find the indicated trigonometric function values for θ in each of the following triangles. Use rational notation.

1. Find $\sin\theta$, $\cos\theta$, and $\tan\theta$.

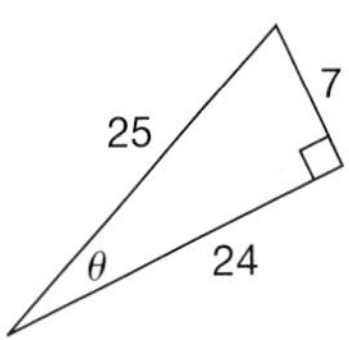

2. Find $\sin\theta$, $\cos\theta$, and $\tan\theta$.

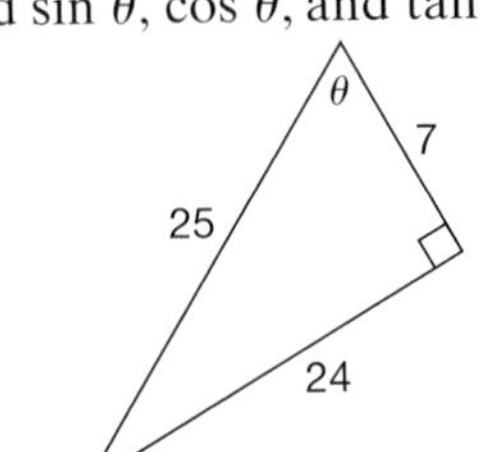

3. Find $\sin\theta$, $\cos\theta$, and $\tan\theta$.

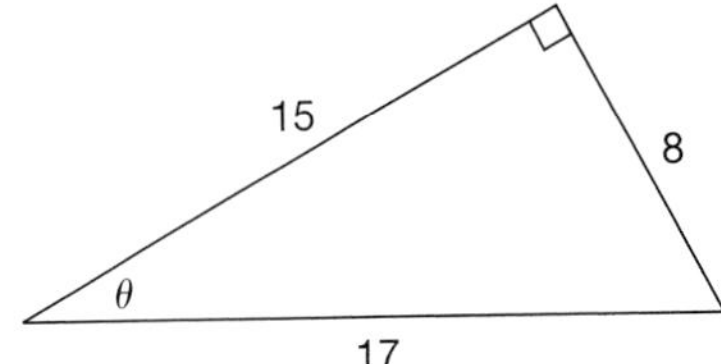

4. Find $\sin\theta$, $\cos\theta$, and $\tan\theta$.

Find the length of each labeled side.

5.

6.

7.

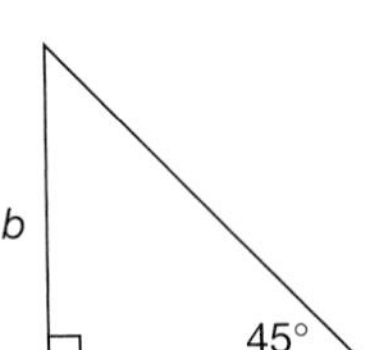

8.

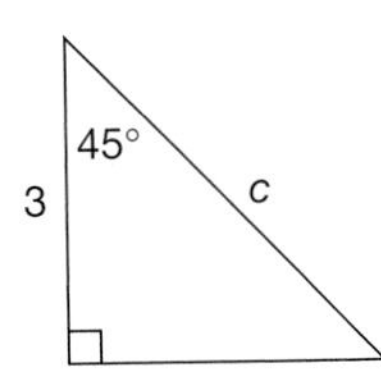

Find the cotangent, secant, and cosecant of the angles shown. Approximate to two decimal places.

9.

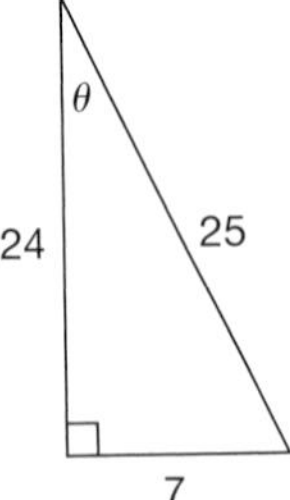

10.

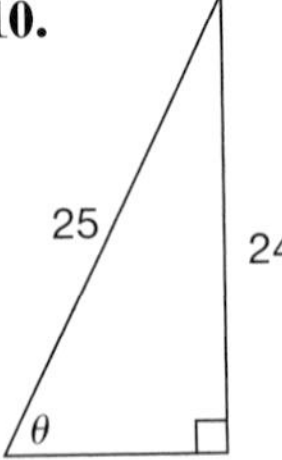

11.

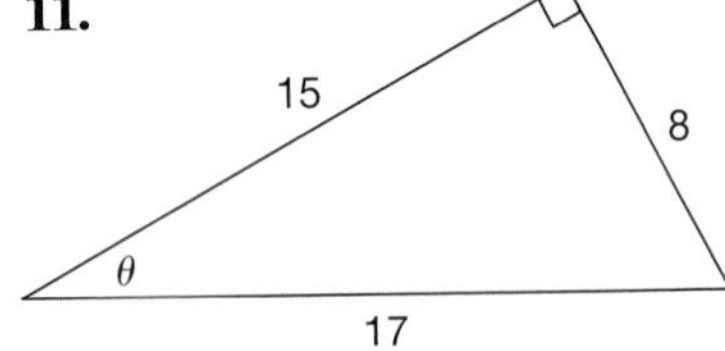

12.

For Exercises 13–16, assume all angles are in the first quadrant.

13. If $\tan \theta = \frac{\sqrt{3}}{1}$, find the other five trigonometric function values for θ.

14. If $\cos \theta = \frac{\sqrt{2}}{2}$, find the other five trigonometric function values for θ.

15. If $\sin \theta = \frac{1}{2}$, find the other five trigonometric function values for θ.

16. If $\sec \theta = 2$, find the other five trigonometric function values for θ.

B

Find the six trigonometric function values for each of the following angles. Do not convert the values to decimal notation.

17. $30°$ **18.** $60°$ **19.** $45°$

20. ***Write a Convincing Argument*** Write an argument to convince a classmate that $\tan \theta = \frac{\sin \theta}{\cos \theta}$.

21. ***Critical Thinking*** An observer stands 120 m from a tree and finds that the line of sight to the top of the tree is 30° above the horizontal. Find the height of the tree above eye level. Then explain how to find the actual height of the tree.

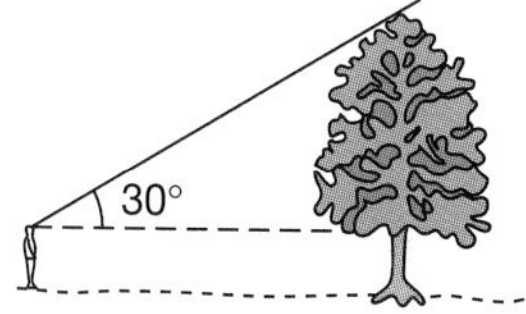

Challenge

22. A guy wire is attached to a 28-ft pole and makes an angle of 60° with the ground. Find

a. the distance b from A to the pole.

b. the length of the wire.

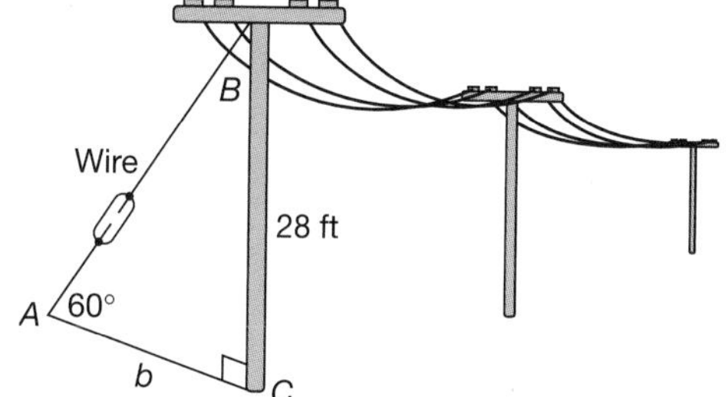

23. Find a. (Hint: Recall from geometry that the altitude of an isosceles triangle from the vertex angle bisects the base and the vertex angle.)

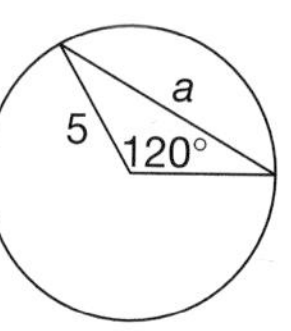

Mixed Review

Simplify. **24.** $\sqrt[3]{16x^4}\sqrt[3]{256x^6y^6}$ **25.** $5\sqrt{13} - 18\sqrt[4]{7} + 8\sqrt{13} + 11\sqrt[4]{7}$

26. $\frac{\sqrt{b}}{\sqrt{b} + \sqrt{a}}\left(\frac{1}{b + \sqrt{ab}}\right)^{-1}$ *7-2, 7-3, 7-4*

Write without rational exponents. **27.** $a^{\frac{2}{5}}b^{\frac{3}{4}}$ **28.** $b^{-\frac{3}{4}}c$ **29.** $(4096)^{\frac{1}{3}}(4096)^{\frac{1}{4}}$

Evaluate. **30.** $\log_{10} 10^4$ **31.** $3^{\log_3 \pi}$ *7-5*

32. Two pipes carry water to the same tank. Pipe A can fill the tank in 6 hours. Pipe B can fill the tank in 4 hours. If both pipes are used simultaneously, how long will it take to fill the tank? *6-7*

17-2 More on Trigonometric Functions

What You'll Learn

1. To find the quadrant in which the terminal side of an angle lies
2. To find the trigonometric function values of an angle, or of a rotation
3. To find trigonometric function values for angles whose terminal sides lie on an axis
4. To find the reference angle of a rotation and use it to find trigonometric function values

... And Why

To work with different units in relation to the unit circle

Consider a rotating ray with its endpoint at the origin. The ray starts in position along the positive half of the x-axis. Counterclockwise rotations will be called positive. Clockwise rotations will be called negative.

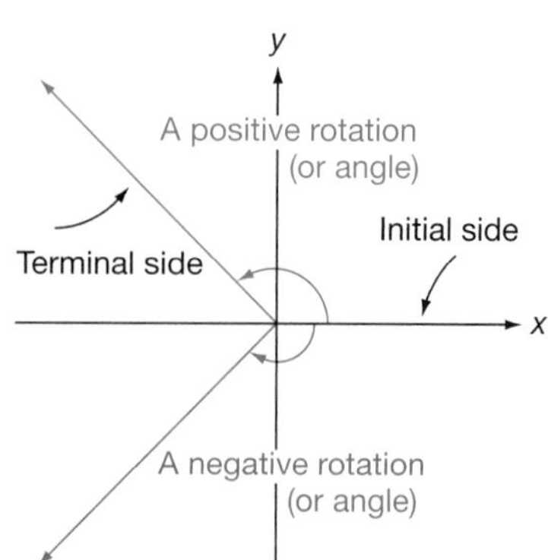

Note that the rotating ray and the positive half of the x-axis form an angle. Thus we often speak of "rotations" and "angles" interchangeably. The rotating ray is often called the **terminal side** of the angle, and the positive half of the x-axis is called the **initial side.**

PART 1 Measures of Rotations of Angles

Objective: Find the quadrant in which the terminal side of an angle lies.

The measure of an angle, or rotation, may be given in degrees. For example, a complete revolution has a measure of 360°, half a revolution has a measure of 180°, a triple revolution has a measure of 360° · 3 or 1080°, and so on. We also speak of angles of 90° or 720° or −240°.

An angle between 0° and 90° has its terminal side in the first quadrant. An angle between 90° and 180° has its terminal side in the second quadrant. An angle between 0° and −90° has its terminal side in the fourth quadrant, and so on.

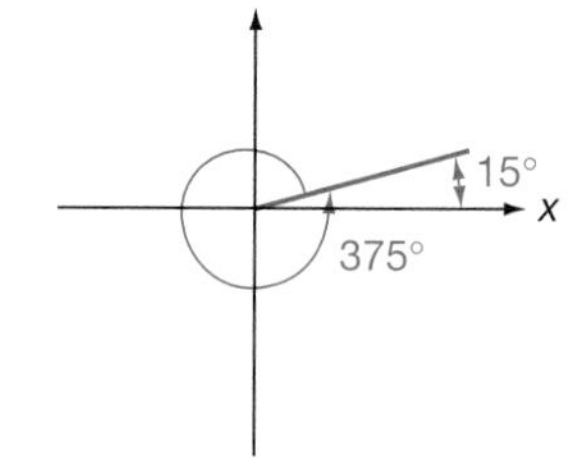

When the measure of an angle is greater than 360°, the rotating ray has gone through at least one complete revolution. For example, an angle of 375° will have the same terminal side as an angle of 15°. Thus the terminal side will be in the first quadrant.

EXAMPLES In which quadrant does the terminal side of each angle lie?

1 53° First quadrant

2 253° Third quadrant

3 −126° Third quadrant

4 −373° Fourth quadrant

5 460° Second quadrant

Try This In which quadrant does the terminal side of each angle lie?

a. $47°$ **b.** $212°$ **c.** $-43°$ **d.** $-135°$ **e.** $365°$ **f.** $740°$

PART 2 Trigonometric Functions of Rotations

Objective: Find the trigonometric function values of an angle or rotation.

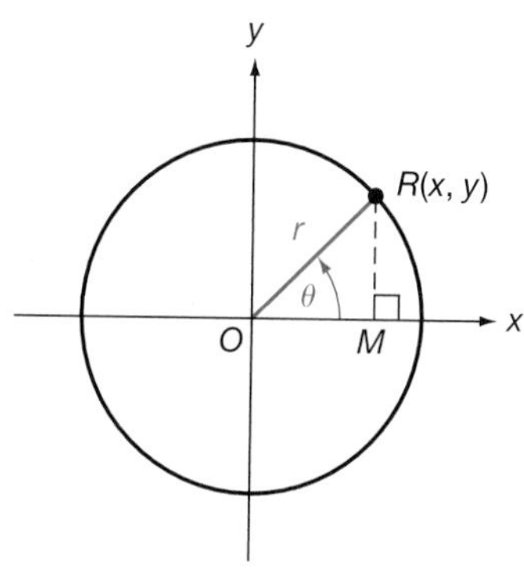

In the preceding discussion of trigonometric functions we worked with right triangles, so the angle θ was always less than $90°$. We can use rotations to apply trigonometric functions to angles of any measure.

Consider a right triangle with one vertex at the origin of a coordinate system and one vertex on the positive x-axis. The other vertex is at R, a point of the circle whose center is at the origin and whose radius (r) is the length of the hypotenuse of the triangle.

Note that three of the trigonometric functions of θ are defined as follows.

$$\sin\theta = \frac{\text{side opposite } \theta}{\text{hypotenuse}} = \frac{y}{r} \qquad \cos\theta = \frac{\text{side adjacent to } \theta}{\text{hypotenuse}} = \frac{x}{r}$$

$$\tan\theta = \frac{\text{side opposite } \theta}{\text{side adjacent to } \theta} = \frac{y}{x}$$

Since x and y are coordinates of the point R, we could also define these functions as follows.

$$\sin\theta = \frac{y\text{-coordinate}}{\text{radius}} \qquad \cos\theta = \frac{x\text{-coordinate}}{\text{radius}} \qquad \tan\theta = \frac{y\text{-coordinate}}{x\text{-coordinate}}$$

We will use these definitions for functions of angles of any measure. Note that while x and y may be either positive, negative, or 0, r is always positive.

EXAMPLES Find $\sin\theta$, $\cos\theta$, and $\tan\theta$ for the angle θ.

6

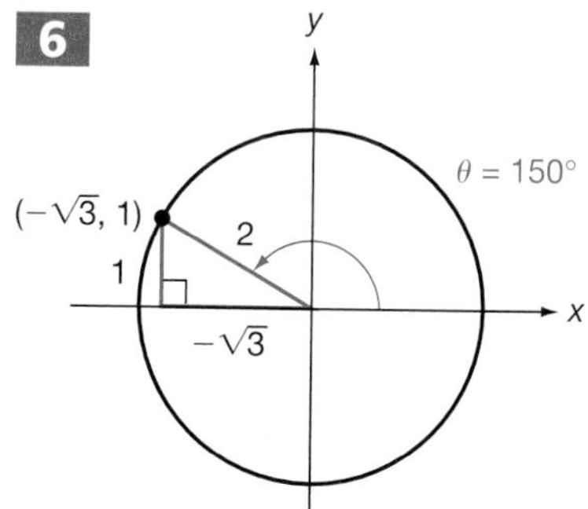

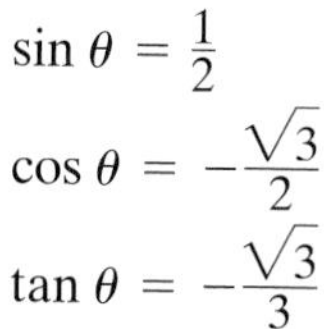

$$\sin\theta = \frac{1}{2}$$

$$\cos\theta = -\frac{\sqrt{3}}{2}$$

$$\tan\theta = -\frac{\sqrt{3}}{3}$$

7

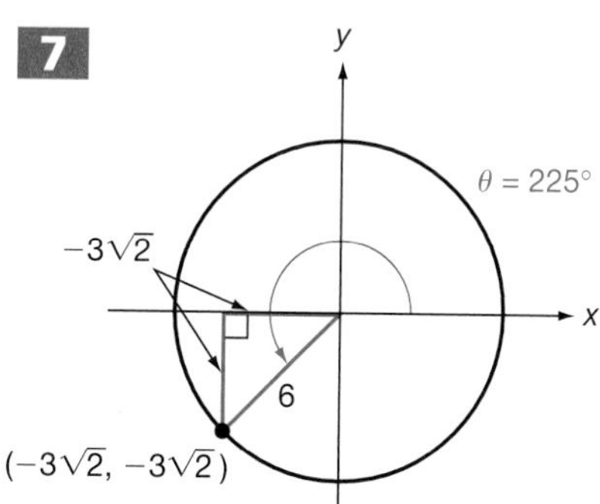

$$\sin\theta = \frac{-3\sqrt{2}}{6} = -\frac{\sqrt{2}}{2}$$

$$\cos\theta = \frac{-3\sqrt{2}}{6} = -\frac{\sqrt{2}}{2}$$

$$\tan\theta = \frac{-3\sqrt{2}}{-3\sqrt{2}} = 1$$

Try This

g. Find $\sin \theta$, $\cos \theta$, and $\tan \theta$ for the angle θ shown.

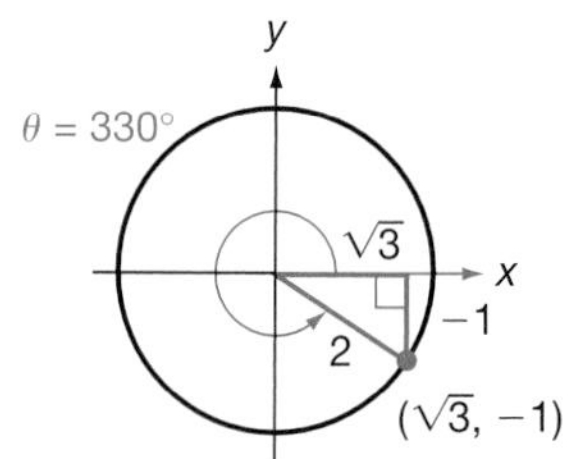

The cosecant, secant, and cotangent functions can also be defined in terms of x, y, and r. We find the reciprocals of the sine, cosine, and tangent, respectively.

$$\csc \theta = \frac{r}{y} \qquad \sec \theta = \frac{r}{x} \qquad \cot \theta = \frac{x}{y}$$

The values of the trigonometric functions can be positive, negative, or zero, depending on where the terminal side of the angle lies. The figure at the right shows which of the trigonometric function values are positive in each of the quadrants.

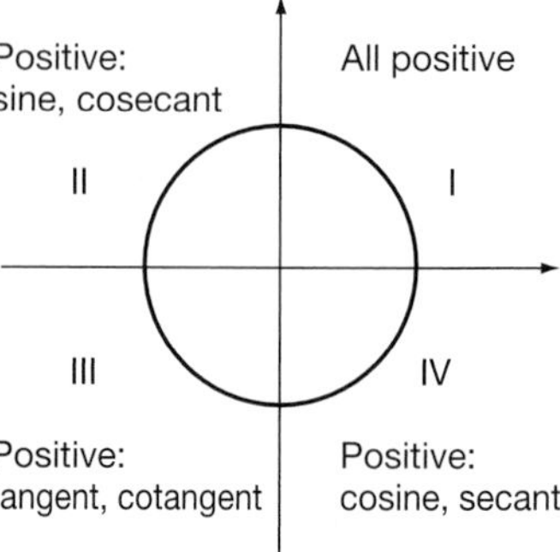

EXAMPLE 8 Give the signs of the six trigonometric function values for a rotation of 225°.

$180 < 225 < 270$, so $R(x, y)$ is in the third quadrant.

The tangent and cotangent are positive, and the other four function values are negative.

Try This

h. Give the signs of the six trigonometric function values for a rotation of −30°.

Terminal Side on an Axis

Objective: Find trigonometric function values for angles whose terminal sides lie on an axis.

If the terminal side of an angle falls on one of the axes, the definitions of the functions still apply, but in some cases functions will not be defined because a denominator will be 0. Notice the coordinates of the points for angles of 0°, 90°, 180°, and 270°. For example, the coordinates for an angle of 90° are $x = 0$ and $y = r$.

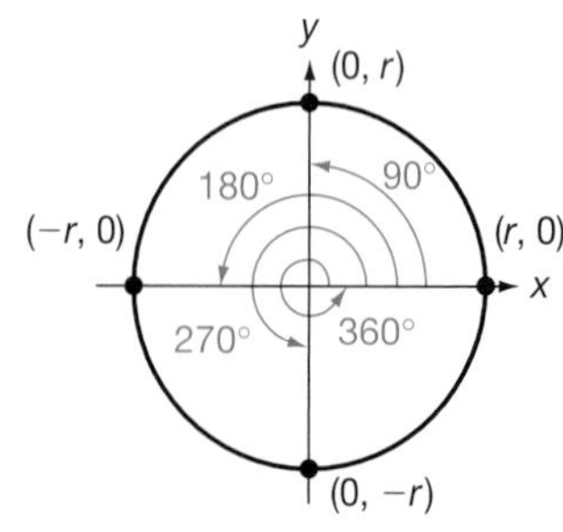

EXAMPLE 9 Find the sine, cosine, and tangent function values for 0° and 90°.

$$\sin 0^\circ = \frac{y}{r} = \frac{0}{r} = 0 \qquad \sin 90^\circ = \frac{y}{r} = \frac{r}{r} = 1$$

$$\cos 0^\circ = \frac{x}{r} = \frac{r}{r} = 1 \qquad \cos 90^\circ = \frac{x}{r} = \frac{0}{r} = 0$$

$$\tan 0^\circ = \frac{y}{x} = \frac{0}{r} = 0 \qquad \tan 90^\circ = \frac{y}{x} = \frac{r}{0}$$

Undefined

Try This

i. Find the sine, cosine, and tangent function values for 180° and 270°.

Reference Angles

Objective: Find the reference angle of a rotation and use it to find trigonometric function values.

We can now determine the trigonometric function values for angles in other quadrants by using the values of the functions for angles between 0° and 90°. We do so by using a reference angle.

Definition

The **reference angle** for a rotation is the acute angle formed by the terminal side and the x-axis.

EXAMPLES Find the reference angle for θ.

10

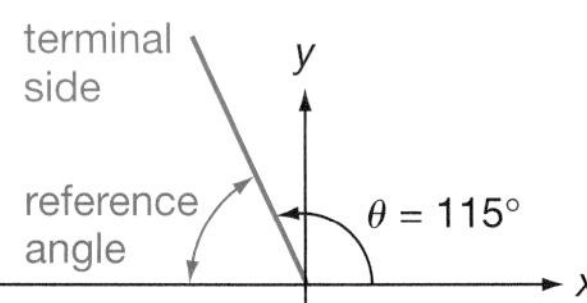

To find the measure of the acute angle formed by the terminal side and the x-axis, we subtract the measure of θ from 180°.

$$180 - 115 = 65$$

The reference angle is 65°.

11

We are looking for the acute angle formed by the terminal side and the x-axis. We subtract 180° from 225° to get the reference angle.

$$225 - 180 = 45$$

The reference angle is 45°.

Try This Find the reference angle for θ.

j.

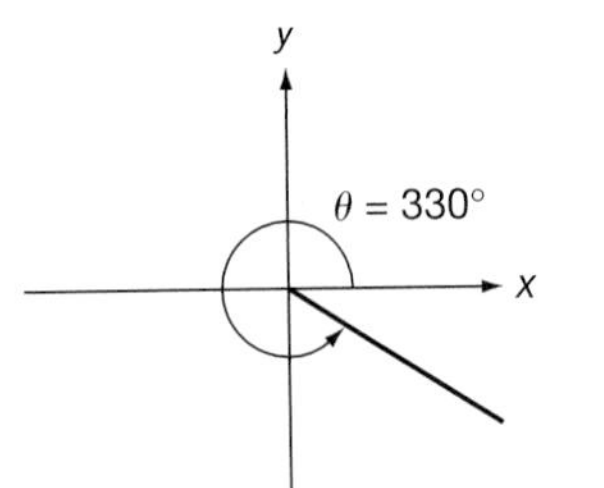

k.

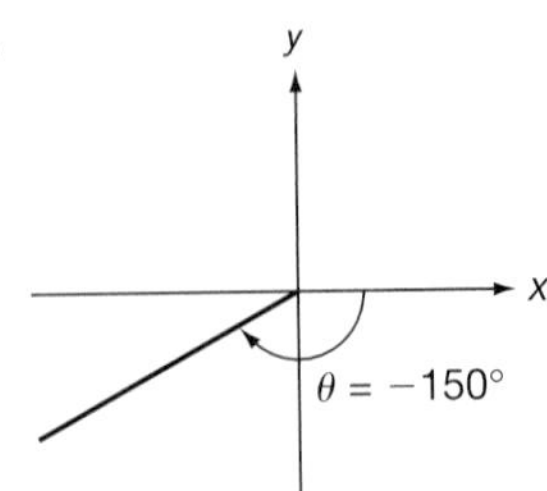

We now use the reference angle to determine trigonometric function values. Consider, for example, an angle of 150°. The terminal side makes a 30° angle with the x-axis, since $180 - 150 = 30$. As the diagram shows, triangle ONR is congruent to triangle $ON'R'$. Hence the ratios of the lengths of the sides of the two triangles are the same.

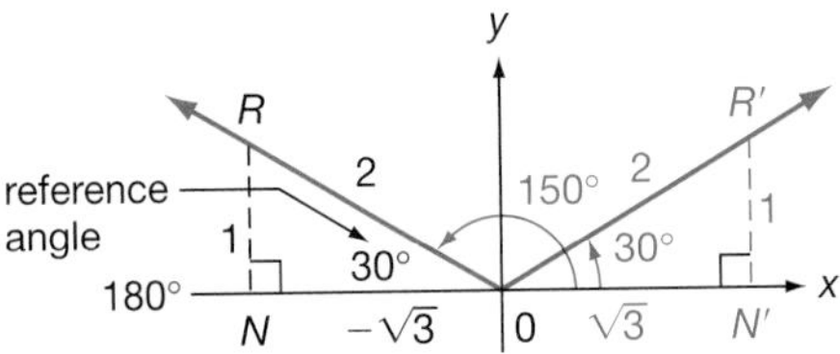

We could determine the function values directly from triangle ONR, but this is not necessary. If we remember that the sine is positive in quadrant II and that the cosine and tangent are negative, we can simply use the values for 30°, prefixing the appropriate sign.

EXAMPLE 12 Find the sine, cosine, and tangent of 1320°.

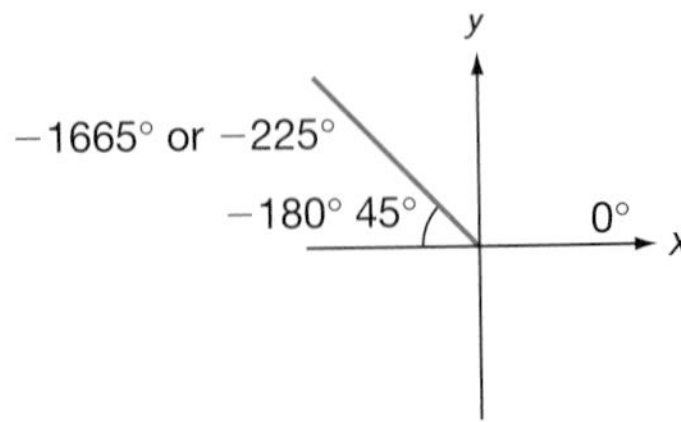

We can subtract multiples of 360°. We do this by dividing 1320 by 360 and taking the integer part. Thus we subtract three multiples of 360.

$$1320 - 3(360) = 240$$

The angle with the same terminal side is 240°. This gives us a reference angle of 60°. Since 1320° is in the third quadrant, $\sin 1320° = -\frac{\sqrt{3}}{2}$, $\cos 1320° = -\frac{1}{2}$, and $\tan 1320° = \sqrt{3}$.

EXAMPLE 13 Find the sine, cosine, and tangent of −1665°.

We can add multiples of 360°. We divide 1665 by 360 and take the integer part. Thus we add four multiples of 360.

$$-1665 + 4(360) = -225$$

The angle with the same terminal side is $-225°$. This gives us a reference angle of 45°. Since $-1665°$ is in the second quadrant,
$\sin -1665° = \frac{\sqrt{2}}{2}$, $\cos -1665° = -\frac{\sqrt{2}}{2}$, and $\tan -1665° = -1$.

In general, to find the function values of an angle, we find them for the reference angle and then prefix the appropriate sign.

Try This Find the sine, cosine, and tangent of each angle.

l. 2370° **m.** $-765°$ **n.** $-2340°$

Extra Help On the Web

Look for worked-out examples at the Prentice Hall Web site.
www.phschool.com

17-2 Exercises

A

In which quadrant does the terminal side of each angle lie?

1. 34° **2.** 320° **3.** $-120°$ **4.** $-175°$
5. 60° **6.** $-135°$ **7.** 495° **8.** 855°
9. 160° **10.** 230° **11.** $-400°$ **12.** $-555°$

Find $\sin \theta$, $\cos \theta$, and $\tan \theta$ for the angle θ shown.

13.

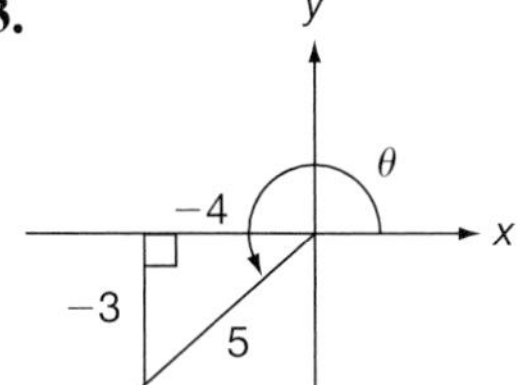

14.

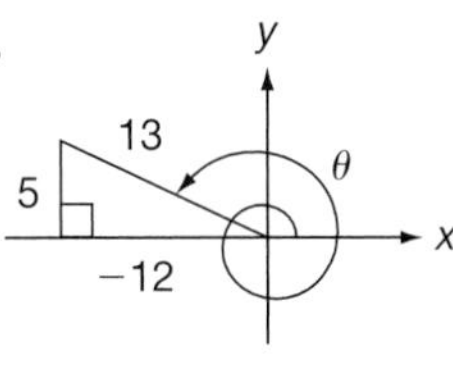

15.

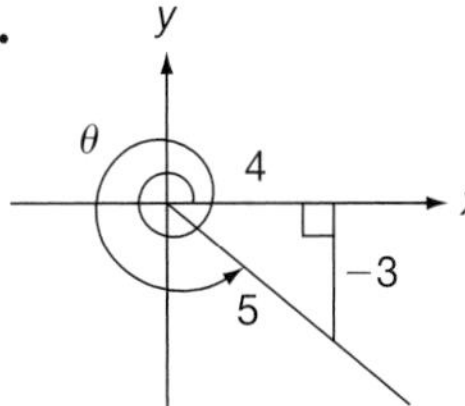

16.

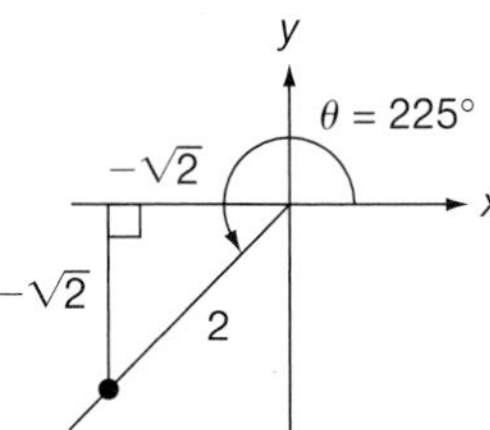

17.

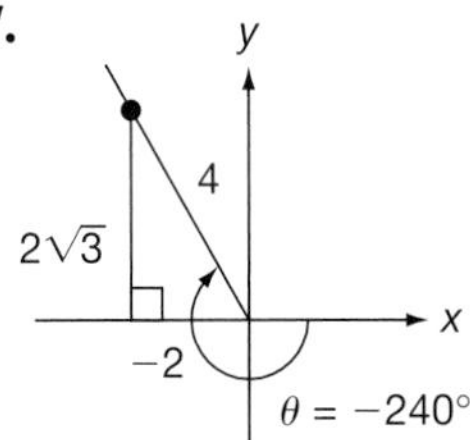

18.

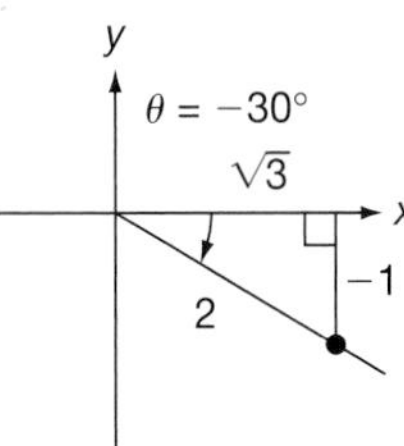

Mental Math Give the signs of the six trigonometric function values for the following angles of rotation.

19. 57° **20.** $-57°$ **21.** 315° **22.** $-100°$ **23.** 760° **24.** 460°

25. Find the cotangent, secant, and cosecant function values for 0°, 90°, 180°, and 270°.

Find the reference angle for the following angles of rotation.

26. 405° **27.** 210° **28.** $-300°$ **29.** 315° **30.** 240° **31.** $-225°$

Find each of the following, or indicate those that are undefined.

32. cos 180° **33.** sin 360° **34.** tan 90° **35.** cot 180°

36. sec 720° **37.** csc 720° **38.** sin (−135°) **39.** cos 135°

40. sin 150° **41.** cos 150° **42.** tan 240° **43.** cot 240°

44. sec 315° **45.** csc 315° **46.** tan (−315°) **47.** cot (−315°)

Find the sine, cosine, and tangent of each angle.

48. 1590° **49.** −3000° **50.** −4095° **51.** 2700° **52.** −4680°

B

Find decimal notation to three places for the six trigonometric functions of each of the following angles. Use the fact that $\sqrt{2} \approx 1.414$ and $\sqrt{3} \approx 1.732$.

53. 30° **54.** 60° **55.** 120° **56.** 225° **57.** −1020° **58.** 2295°

Find the six trigonometric function values for the angle θ shown.

59.

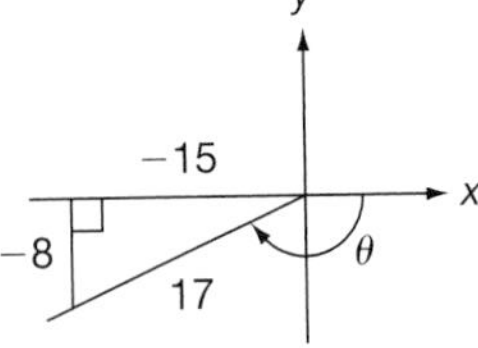

60.

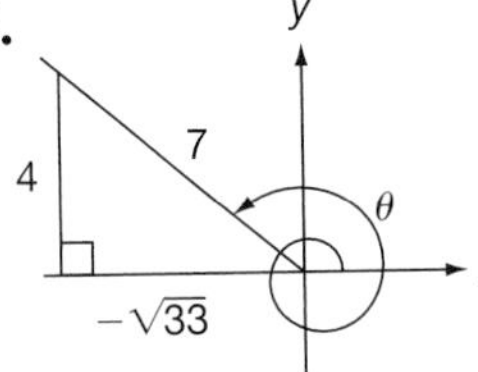

61.

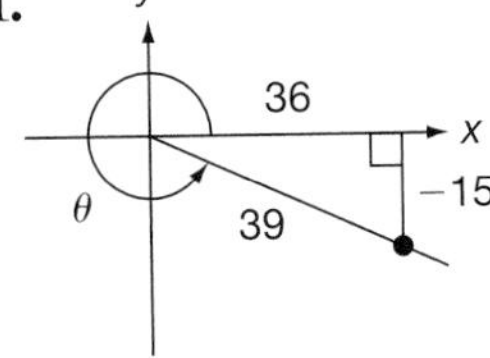

62. ***Critical Thinking*** Given that $\tan \theta = \frac{2\sqrt{5}}{5}$ and the terminal side is in quadrant III, what are the values of the other five trigonometric functions?

Challenge

63. The valve cap on a bicycle wheel is 11.5 in. from the center of the wheel. From the position shown, the wheel starts rolling. After the wheel has turned 480°, how far above the ground is the valve cap? Assume that the outer diameter of the tire is 26 in.

See Exercise 63.

Mixed Review

Test for symmetry about the x-axis. **64.** $x^2 + y^2 = 36$ **65.** $xy = 25$ *9-1*

Solve. **66.** $\log_9 x = \frac{3}{2}$ **67.** $x^2 = \frac{1}{25}$ **68.** $x^4 = 625$ *12-3, 5-7, 8-5*

Suppose a card is drawn from an ordinary deck. Find the probability of drawing a

69. red card or king. **70.** spade or ace. **71.** club or face card. *15-5*

72. A barge travels 90 mi downstream in the same time that it travels 60 mi upstream. The speed of the current is 3 mi/h. Find the speed of the barge in still water. *6-7*

Radians, Cofunctions, and Problem Solving

17-3

Radian Measure

Objective: Convert from degree to radian measure and vice versa.

What You'll Learn

1. To convert from degree to radian measure and vice versa
2. To find arc length given the radian measure of an angle and vice versa
3. To use cofunction identities to find trigonometric function values
4. To solve problems concerning angular speed

. . . And Why

To find values for all angle measures using tables and interpolation

So far we have measured angles using degrees. Another useful angle measure is a **radian.** Consider a circle of radius 1, a **unit circle.** Since the circumference of a circle is $2\pi r$, the unit circle has a circumference of 2π. A rotation of 360° (1 revolution) has a measure of 2π radians. Half of a revolution is a rotation of 180°, or π radians. A quarter of a revolution is a rotation of 90°, or $\frac{\pi}{2}$ radians, and so on.

Radians

When the distance around the circle from the initial side to the terminal side equals 1, the measure of θ is called 1 radian. One radian is about 57°. To convert between degrees and radians we can use the notion of "multiplying by one."

$$\frac{1 \text{ revolution}}{1 \text{ revolution}} = 1 = \frac{2\pi \text{ radians}}{360 \text{ degrees}} = \frac{\pi \text{ radians}}{180 \text{ degrees}}$$

The following equation is also true.

$$\frac{180 \text{ degrees}}{\pi \text{ radians}} = 1$$

When a rotation is given in radians, the word "radians" is optional and often omitted. Thus if no unit is given for a rotation, it is understood to be in radians.

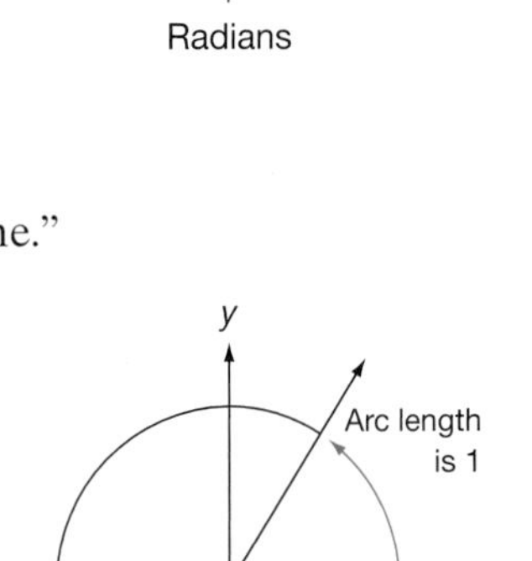

1 Radian

EXAMPLE 1 Convert 60° to radians.

$$60° = 60° \cdot \frac{\pi \text{ radians}}{180°} \quad \text{Multiplying by 1}$$

$$= \frac{60°}{180°}\pi \text{ radians}$$

$$= \frac{\pi}{3} \text{ radians, or } \frac{\pi}{3}$$

Try This Convert to radian measure. Give answers in terms of π.

a. 225° **b.** 300° **c.** $-315°$

EXAMPLE 2 Convert $\frac{3\pi}{4}$ to degrees.

$$\begin{aligned} \frac{3\pi}{4} \text{ radians} &= \frac{3\pi}{4} \text{ radians} \cdot \frac{180^\circ}{\pi \text{ radians}} \qquad \text{Multiplying by 1} \\ &= \frac{3\pi}{4\pi} \cdot 180^\circ \\ &= 135^\circ \end{aligned}$$

The diagram below shows a unit circle marked in both radians and degrees.

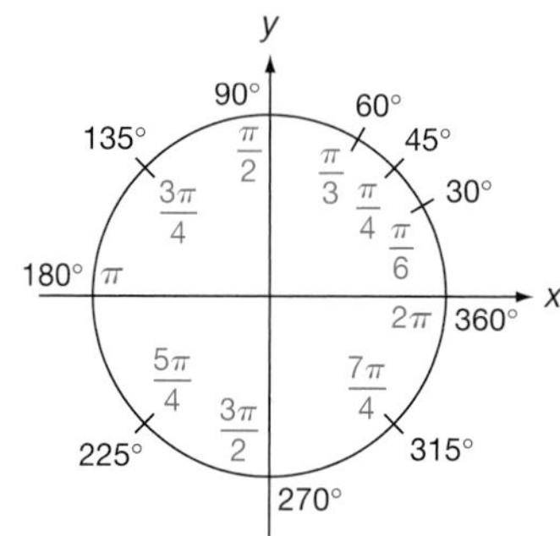

Try This Convert to degree measure.

d. $\frac{4\pi}{3}$ radians **e.** $\frac{5\pi}{2}$ radians **f.** $-\frac{4\pi}{5}$ radians

Arc Length and Central Angles

Objective: Find arc length given the radian measure of an angle and vice versa.

Radian measure can be determined using a circle other than a unit circle. In the following drawing a unit circle is shown along with another circle. The angle shown is a central angle of both circles. Hence the lengths of the intercepted arcs are proportional to the radii of the circles. The radii of the circles are r and 1.

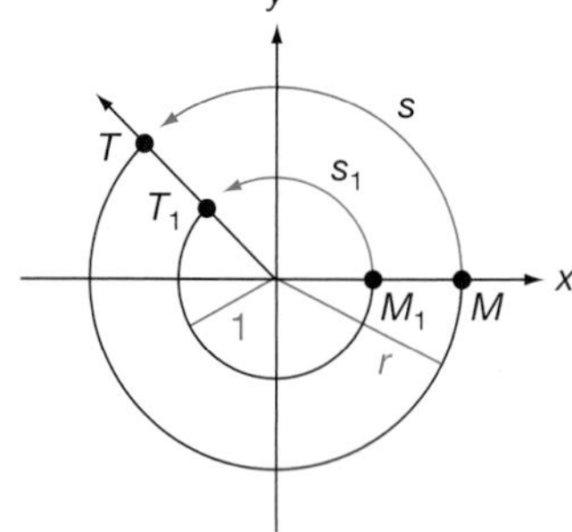

The corresponding arc lengths are MT and M_1, T_1, or more simply, s and s_1. We therefore have the proportion

$$\frac{s}{r} = \frac{s_1}{1}$$

Now s_1 is the radian measure of the rotation in question. It is more common to use a Greek letter, such as θ, for the measure of an angle or rotation. We commonly use the letter s for arc length. Adopting this convention, the above proportion becomes $\theta = \frac{s}{r}$. In any circle, arc length, central angle, and length of the radius are related in this fashion. Or, in general, the following is true.

Theorem 17-1

The radian measure θ of a rotation is the ratio of the distance s traveled by a point at a radius r from the center of rotation to the length of the radius.

$$\theta = \frac{s}{r}$$

EXAMPLE 3 Find the length of an arc of a circle of 5 cm radius associated with a central angle of $\frac{\pi}{3}$ radians.

$$\theta = \frac{s}{r}, \text{ or } s = r\theta$$

Therefore, $s = 5 \cdot \frac{\pi}{3}$ cm, or using 3.14 for π, about 5.23 cm.

EXAMPLE 4 Find the measure of a rotation in radians where a point 2 m from the center of rotation travels 4 m.

$$\theta = \frac{s}{r} = \frac{4\text{ m}}{2\text{ m}} = 2$$ The unit is understood to be radians.

In using the formula $\theta = \frac{s}{r}$, we must be sure that θ is measured in radians and that s and r are measured using the same unit.

Try This

g. Find the length of an arc of a circle with 10-cm radius, associated with a central angle of measure $\frac{11\pi}{6}$. (Use 3.14 for π.)

h. Find the radian measure of a rotation where a point 2.5 cm from the center of rotation travels 15 cm.

Cofunctions and Complements

Objective: Use cofunction identities to find trigonometric function values.

Since the sum of all three angle measures of a triangle is 180°, and the right angle accounts for 90° of this total, the acute angles are complementary. Thus if one acute angle of a right triangle is θ, the other is $90° - \theta$, $\left(\text{or } \frac{\pi}{2} - \theta\right)$.

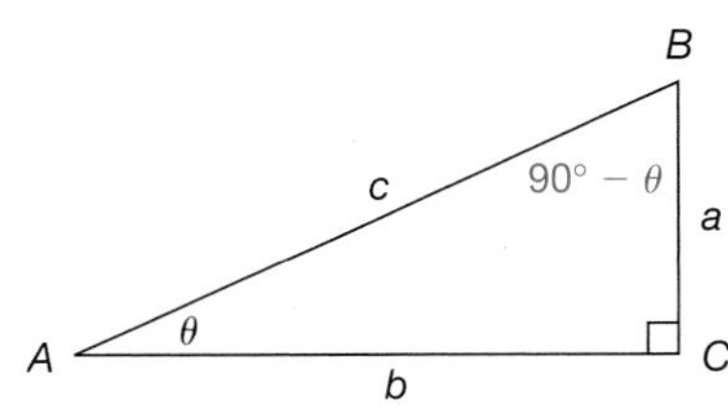

Note that the sine of $\angle A$ is also the cosine of $\angle B$, its complement.

$$\sin \theta = \frac{a}{c} \qquad \cos (90° - \theta) = \frac{a}{c}$$

Similarly, the tangent of $\angle A$ is the cotangent of its complement and the secant of $\angle A$ is the cosecant of its complement.

These pairs of functions are called **cofunctions.** The name *cosine* originally meant the sine of the complement. The name *cotangent* meant the tangent of the complement, and *cosecant* meant the secant of the complement. A complete list of the cofunction relations follows. Equations that hold for all acceptable replacements for the variables are known as **identities.** We use the **identity symbol** $\equiv$ when stating identities.

Cofunction Identities

$\sin\theta \equiv \cos(90° - \theta)$	$\cos\theta \equiv \sin(90° - \theta)$	$\tan\theta \equiv \cot(90° - \theta)$
$\cot\theta \equiv \tan(90° - \theta)$	$\sec\theta \equiv \csc(90° - \theta)$	$\csc\theta \equiv \sec(90° - \theta)$

EXAMPLES Find the function values.

5 $\cot 60° = \tan(90° - 60°) = \tan 30° = \frac{\sqrt{3}}{3}$

6 $\csc 30° = \sec(90° - 30°) = \sec 60° = \frac{1}{\cos 60°} = \frac{1}{\frac{1}{2}} = 2$

Try This Find the function values.

i. $\sec 60°$ **j.** $\cot 30°$ **k.** $\csc 45°$

Problem Solving: Angular Speed

Objective: Solve problems concerning angular speed.

Speed is defined as the distance traveled per unit of time. Similarly, **angular speed** is defined as the amount of rotation per unit of time. For example, we might speak of the angular speed of a wheel as 150 revolutions per minute or the angular speed of the Earth as 2π radians per day. The Greek letter **ω (omega)** is usually used for angular speed.

$$\omega = \frac{\theta}{t} \quad \theta \text{ is the angle of rotation.}$$

For many applications it is important to know a relationship between angular speed and linear speed. For example, we might wish to find the linear speed of a point on the Earth, knowing its angular speed. Or, we might wish to know the linear speed of an Earth satellite, knowing its angular speed. To develop the relationship we seek, we recall the relation between angle and distance from the preceding section, $\theta = \frac{s}{r}$. This is equivalent to $s = r\theta$.

We divide by the time (t) to obtain $\frac{s}{t} = r\frac{\theta}{t}$.

Now $\frac{s}{t}$ is linear speed v, and $\frac{\theta}{t}$ is angular speed ω. We thus have the relation we seek.

Definition

The **linear speed** v of a point a distance of r from the center of rotation is given by

$$v = r\omega$$

where ω is the angular speed in radians per unit of time.

In deriving this formula we used the equation $s = r\theta$, in which the units for s and r must be the same and θ must be in radians. Thus for our new formula $v = r\omega$, the units of distance for v and r must be the same, ω must be in radians per unit of time, and the units of time must be the same for v and ω.

EXAMPLE 7

An Earth satellite in a circular orbit 1200 km high makes one complete revolution every 90 min. What is its linear speed? Use 6400 km for the length of a radius of the Earth.

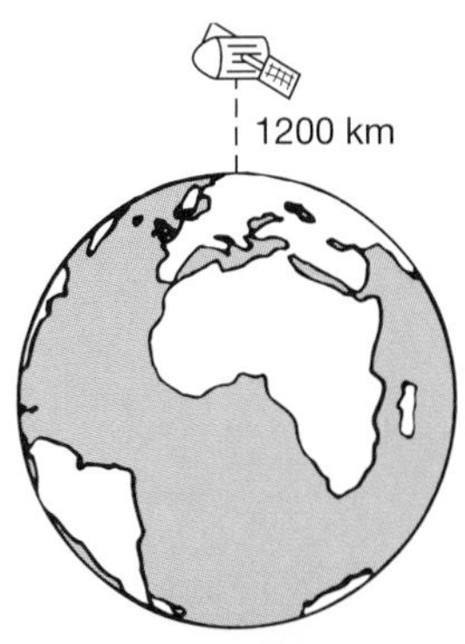

Use the formula $v = r\omega$.

$$\begin{aligned} r &= \text{radius of the earth} + \text{height of satellite} \\ &= 6400 \text{ km} + 1200 \text{ km} \\ &= 7600 \text{ km} \end{aligned}$$

$$\omega = \frac{2\pi \text{ radians}}{90 \text{ min}} = \frac{\pi}{45 \text{ min}}$$ Finding the angular speed

$$v = r\omega$$

$$v = 7600 \text{ km} \cdot \frac{\pi}{45 \text{ min}}$$ Substituting

$$\begin{aligned} &= 7600 \cdot \frac{\pi}{45} \cdot \frac{\text{km}}{\text{min}} \\ &\approx 7600 \cdot \frac{3.14}{45} \cdot \frac{\text{km}}{\text{min}} \\ &\approx 530 \frac{\text{km}}{\text{min}} \end{aligned}$$

The linear speed of the satellite is about 530 km/min.

If the orbit were 1201 km high, how much farther would the satellite be traveling in one revolution than it does in Example 7?

Try This

1. A wheel with 12-cm diameter is rotating at 10 revolutions per second. What is the velocity of a point on the rim?

EXAMPLE 8

An anchor is being hoisted at 2 ft/sec, winding the chain around a capstan with a 1.8-yd diameter. What is the angular speed of the capstan?

Capstan

Chain

We will use the formula $\omega = \frac{v}{r}$, taking care to use the proper units. Since v is in ft/sec, we need r in ft. Then ω will be in radians/sec.

$$r = \frac{1.8}{2}\text{ yd} \cdot \frac{3\text{ ft}}{\text{yd}} = 2.7\text{ ft}$$

$$\omega = \frac{v}{r} = \frac{2}{2.7} \approx 0.741\text{ radian/sec}$$

In applying the formula $v = r\omega$, we must be sure that the units for v and r are the same and that ω is in radians per unit of time. The units of time must be the same for v and ω.

Try This

m. A bucket is being raised at 3 ft/sec. The radius of the drum is 10 in. What is the angular speed of the handle?

See *Try This* **m.**

Extra Help On the Web

Look for worked-out examples at the Prentice Hall Web site.
www.phschool.com

17-3 Exercises

A

Mental Math Convert to radian measure. Give answers in terms of π.

1. $30°$ **2.** $15°$ **3.** $100°$ **4.** $200°$

5. $75°$ **6.** $105°$ **7.** $120°$ **8.** $240°$

9. $-320°$ **10.** $-250°$ **11.** $-85°$ **12.** $-175°$

Convert to degree measure.

13. 1 radian **14.** 2 radians **15.** 8π

16. -12π **17.** $\frac{3\pi}{4}$ **18.** $\frac{5\pi}{4}$

19. Find the length of an arc of a circle with a 10-cm radius associated with a central angle of $\frac{2\pi}{3}$ radians.

20. Find the length of an arc of a circle with a 5-m radius associated with a central angle of 2.1 radians.

21. Find the radian measure of rotation where a point 3.5 cm from the center of rotation travels 20 cm.

22. Find the radian measure of rotation where a point 5 m from the center of rotation travels 30 m.

For each of the following, find the function value using cofunctions.

23. tan 60°	**24.** csc 60°	**25.** sec 30°
26. csc 30°	**27.** cot 45°	**28.** sec 45°
29. cot 60°	**30.** sec 60°	**31.** cos 90°

32. A flywheel is rotating at 7 radians/sec. It has a 15-cm diameter. What is the speed of a point on its rim, in cm/min?

33. A wheel is rotating at 3 radians/sec. The wheel has a 30-cm radius. What is the speed of a point on its rim, in m/min?

34. If a compact disc (CD) has a radius of 6 cm and spins at 500 rpm, what is the linear velocity of a point on the rim, in cm/sec?

35. A microwave oven's 6-rpm turntable has a radius of 15 cm. What is the linear velocity of a point on the rim, in cm/sec?

36. Earth has a 4000-mi radius and rotates one revolution every 24 hours. What is the linear speed of a point on the equator, in mi/h?

37. Earth is 93,000,000 miles from the sun and traverses its orbit, which is nearly circular, every 365.25 days. What is the linear velocity of Earth in its orbit, in mi/h?

38. A wheel has a 32-cm diameter. The speed of a point on its rim is 11 m/s. What is its angular speed?

39. A horse on a merry-go-round is 7 m from the center and travels at 10 km/h. What is its angular speed?

40. A water wheel has a 20-ft radius. The wheel revolves 7 times per minute. What is the speed of the river, in mi/h?

41. A water wheel has a 10-ft radius. The wheel revolves 16 times per minute. What is the speed of the river, in mi/h?

42. Through how many radians does the minute hand of a clock rotate in 50 min?

The river is flowing about 7.71 mi/h. How many revolutions per minute will a water wheel turn if it has a 9-ft radius?

43. ***Multi-Step Problems*** The *grad* is a unit of angle measure similar to a degree. A right angle has a measure of 100 grads. Convert the following to grads.

a. 48° **b.** 153° **c.** $\frac{\pi}{8}$ radians **d.** $\frac{5\pi}{7}$ radians

44. The *mil* is a unit of angle measure. A right angle has a measure of 1600 mils. Convert the following to degrees.

a. 100 mils **b.** 350 mils

45. On Earth, one degree of latitude is how many kilometers? How many miles? Use 3.14 for π. (Assume that the radius of Earth is $\approx$ 6400 km, or 4000 mi.)

46. One degree of latitude on Earth is equivalent to 60 *nautical miles.* Find the circumference and radius of Earth in nautical miles. Use 3.14 for π.

47. ***Critical Thinking*** For any acute angle θ, $\cos(90 - \theta) = \sin \theta$. Consider angles other than acute angles. Does this relation still hold, and if so, to what extent?

Challenge

48. An astronaut on the moon observes Earth, about 240,000 miles away. The diameter of Earth is about 8000 miles. Find the angle α.

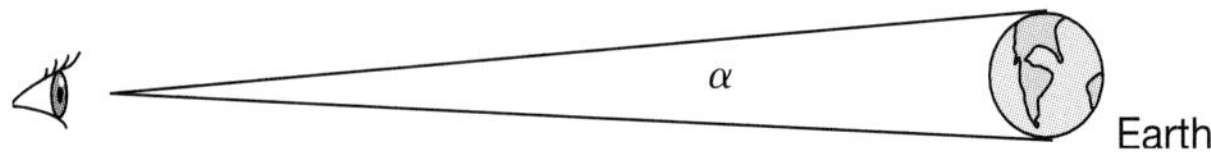

49. The circumference of Earth was computed by Eratosthenes (276–195 B.C.). He knew the distance from Aswan to Alexandria to be about 500 miles. From each town he observed the sun at noon, finding the angular difference to be 7.2°. Do Eratosthenes' calculation.

Mixed Review

Test for symmetry with respect to the y-axis.

50. $x^2 + y^2 = 36$ **51.** $xy = 25$ **52.** $y = x^4 + 3x^2 - 2$ *9-1*

In each of the following, find equations for $f^{-1}(x)$.

53. $f(x) = x^3$ **54.** $f(x) = 3^x$ **55.** $f(x) = \sqrt{x^4 - 1}$ *12-1*

Evaluate. **56.** $\log_7 343$ **57.** $7^{\log_7 e}$ *12-3*

Find the sum. **58.** $1 - \frac{1}{5} + \frac{1}{25} - \cdots$ **59.** $1 + 0.1 + 0.01 + \cdots$ *14-3*

60. Find the mean, median, and mode for $\{5, 4, 0, 1, 3, 0, 4, 7, 3, 4, 1, 7\}$. *16-2*

Finding Function Values: Tables and Calculators

17-4

What You'll Learn

1. To find trigonometric function values using a table
2. To convert between degree and minute notation and decimal degree notation
3. To use a table and linear interpolation to find trigonometric function values

. . . And Why

To graph trigonometric functions based on their characteristics such as period and amplitude

The early Greeks, Hindus, and Arabians created tables of some trigonometric function values. George Rheticus (1514–1574), an associate of Copernicus, spent 12 years developing what we now know as the tables of sines and cosines. He eventually made tables for all six functions.

PART 1 Finding Function Values

Objective: Find trigonometric function values using a table.

Table 5, in the back of the book, is a table of trigonometric functions with four-digit accuracy. A portion of Table 5 is shown below.

The headings on the left of Table 5 range only from 0° to 45°. For angles from 45° to 90° the headings on the right are used, together with the headings at the bottom, because these values are the same as the cofunction values of their complements. For example, sin 43° is found to be 0.6820 using the top and left headings; cos 47° (the complement of 43°) is found also to be 0.6820 using the bottom and right headings.

Degrees	Radians	Sin	Cos	Tan	Cot	Sec	Csc		
43°00′	0.7505	0.6820	0.7314	0.9325	1.072	1.367	1.466	0.8203	47°00′
10	534	841	294	380	066	371	462	174	50
20	563	862	274	435	060	375	457	145	40
30	0.7592	0.6884	0.7254	0.9490	1.054	1.379	1.453	0.8116	30
40	621	905	234	545	048	382	448	087	20
50	650	926	214	601	042	386	444	058	10
44°00′	0.7679	0.6947	0.7193	0.9657	1.036	1.390	1.440	0.8029	46°00′
10	709	967	173	713	030	394	435	999	50
		Cos	**Sin**	**Cot**	**Tan**	**Csc**	**Sec**	**Radians**	**Degrees**

Scientific calculators give approximations of the sine, cosine, and tangent. The cosecant, secant, and cotangent can be found by taking reciprocals. Some calculators require angles to be entered in degrees. For most, degrees or radians may be used. To find sin 28°, enter 28 and press [SIN]. We find $\sin 28° \approx 0.4694716$. To find the cosine of π radians, press [π], press [DRG] to use radians, then press [COS]. We find $\cos \pi = -1$.

A sub-unit of a degree is a minute, which is designated by an apostrophe. There are 60 minutes in a degree. The table gives trigonometric function values for intervals of 10′.

EXAMPLE 1 Find cos 37°20′.

We find 37°20′ in the left column of Table 5 and then Cos at the top. At the intersection of this row and column we find the entry we seek.

$$\cos 37°20' = 0.7951$$

Try This Use Table 5 to find the following.

a. sin 15°20′ **b.** cot 64°50′

Table 5 gives function values for angles from 0° to 90°. To find the function value for any other angle, we first find the reference angle, which is the angle the terminal side makes with the x-axis. We then look up the function values for the reference angle in the table and use the appropriate sign, depending on the quadrant in which the terminal side lies.

EXAMPLE 2 Find sin 285°40′.

To find sin 285°40′, we determine that the terminal side of the angle is in the fourth quadrant.

$$\begin{aligned} 360° &= 359°60' \\ &- \underline{285°40'} \\ &\quad 74°20' \end{aligned}$$

The reference angle is 74°20′.

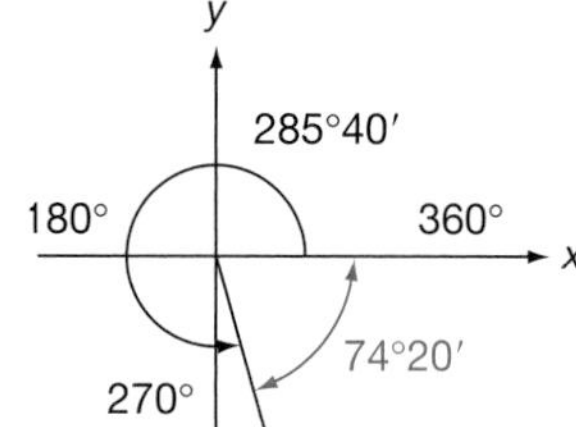

We find sin 74°20′ = 0.9628. In quadrant IV the sine is negative, so sin 285°40′ = −0.9628.

Try This

c. Find cos 410°20′. **d.** Find sin 260°40′.

There are many occasions when we will have to use the table in reverse. That is, we will have a trigonometric function value and will want to find the measure of the angle.

EXAMPLE 3 Given tan B = 0.9545, find B (between 0° and 90°).

In the column headed Tan, we find 0.9545. That value is in the row headed 43°40′. Thus B = 43°40′.

Try This

e. Given sec B = 1.655, find B (between 0° and 90°).

PART 2 Decimal Notation for Degrees and Minutes

Objective: Convert between degree and minute notation and decimal degree notation.

If we use a scientific calculator to find an angle when given a trigonometric function value, we find the angle expressed in tenths and hundredths of a degree. For instance, suppose we know that $\cos B = 0.7030$ and we use a calculator to find B. We enter 0.7030 and press [INV] [COS], or [COS^{-1}]. The display shows 45.33180728. Thus $B \approx 45.33°$.

EXAMPLE 4 Convert 16.35° to degrees and minutes.

$$\begin{aligned} 16.35° &= 16° + (0.35 \times 1°) && 1° = 60' \\ &= 16° + (0.35 \times 60') && \text{Substituting } 60' \text{ for } 1° \\ &= 16° + 21' && \text{Multiplying} \\ 16.35° &= 16°21' \end{aligned}$$

EXAMPLE 5 Convert 34°39′ to degrees and decimal parts of degrees.

$$\begin{aligned} 34°39' &= 34° + 39' \\ &= 34° + \left(\frac{39}{60}\right)° && 1' = \left(\frac{1}{60}\right)° \\ &= 34° + 0.65° && \text{Dividing} \\ 34°39' &= 34.65° \end{aligned}$$

Try This

f. Convert 37.45° to degrees and minutes.
g. Convert 43°55′ to degrees and decimal parts of degrees.

PART 3 Interpolation

Objective: Use a table and linear interpolation to find trigonometric function values.

The process of linear **interpolation** used with logarithmic functions can be applied to tables of any function. We can use it with tables of the trigonometric functions.

EXAMPLE 6 Find tan 27°43′.

0.5243	?	0.5280
(tan 27°40′)	(tan 27°43′)	(tan 27°50′)

The difference between tan 27°40′ and tan 27°50′ is 0.0037. Because 43′ is $\frac{3}{10}$ of the distance from 40′ to 50′, we take $\frac{3}{10}$ of 0.0037 and add it to 0.5243.

$$0.5243 + 0.3(0.0037) = 0.5243 + 0.00111 = 0.52541$$
$$\tan 27°43' \approx 0.5254$$

EXAMPLE 7 Find cot 6°18′.

9.255	?	9.010
(cot 6°10′)	(cot 6°18′)	(cot 6°20′)

The difference between cot 6°10′ and cot 6°20′ is 0.245. We know 18′ is $\frac{8}{10}$ of the distance from 10′ to 20′. We take $\frac{8}{10}$ of 0.245 and subtract it from 9.255, since the cotangent function decreases over this interval.

$$\begin{aligned}&9.255 - 0.8(0.245)\\&= 9.255 - 0.196\\&= 9.059\end{aligned}$$

$\cot 6°18' \approx 9.059$

Try This Use Table 5 and interpolation to find the following.

h. sin 38°47′ **i.** cot 27°45′

Once the process of interpolation is understood, it will not be necessary to write as much as we did in the examples above. After a bit of practice you will find that interpolation is rather easy, and you can accomplish some of the steps without writing them.

Let us look at an example of using the tables in reverse, that is, given a function value, to find the measure of an angle.

EXAMPLE 8 Given $\tan B = 0.6193$, find $m\angle B$ (between 0° and 90°).

0.6168	0.6193	0.6208
(tan 31°40′)	(tan ?)	(tan 31°50′)

The difference between 0.6168 and 0.6208 is 0.0040. We know that 0.6193 is $\frac{25}{40}$ of the distance between 0.6168 and 0.6208. The tabular difference is 10′. We take $\frac{25}{40}$ of 10′ and add it to 31°40′.

$$\begin{aligned}&31°40' + \tfrac{25}{40}(10')\\&= 31°40' + 6.25'\\&= 31°46.25'\end{aligned}$$

Thus $m\angle B \approx 31°46'$.

Try This

j. Given $\sin \theta = 0.3624$, find θ. **k.** Given $\cot \theta = 1.614$, find θ.

17-4 Exercises

Extra Help On the Web

Look for worked-out examples at the Prentice Hall Web site. www.phschool.com

A

Use Table 5 to find the following.

1. sin 13°20′ **2.** sin 41°40′ **3.** cos 56°30′ **4.** cos 71°50′

5. tan 28°40′ **6.** tan 57°10′ **7.** csc 62°30′ **8.** csc 70°10′

Use Table 5 to find the following.

9. sin 307°10′ **10.** sin 336°30′ **11.** cos 410°20′ **12.** cos 456°40′

13. tan 208°20′ **14.** csc 324°40′ **15.** cot 375°10′ **16.** sec 520°10′

Given the following function values, find B (between 0° and 90°).

17. $\sin B = 0.9881$ **18.** $\cos B = 0.9983$ **19.** $\sec B = 1.435$

20. $\csc B = 1.111$ **21.** $\tan B = 0.2432$ **22.** $\cot B = 1.199$

Convert to degrees and minutes.

23. 46.65° **24.** 85.2° **25.** 67.05° **26.** 38.45°

27. −48.95° **28.** −94.8° **29.** 412.55° **30.** 714.1°

Convert to degrees and decimal parts of degrees.

31. 45°25′ **32.** 36°17′ **33.** 76°53′ **34.** 12°23′

35. −68°47′ **36.** −113°22′ **37.** 225°33′ **38.** 414°07′

Use Table 5 and interpolation to find the following.

39. sin 28°31′ **40.** sin 36°42′ **41.** cos 53°55′

42. cos 80°33′ **43.** tan 24°12′ **44.** cot 54°18′

Given the following function values, use interpolation to find θ (between 0° and 90°).

45. $\sin \theta = 0.6391$ **46.** $\cot \theta = 1.655$ **47.** $\tan \theta = 1.026$

48. $\cos \theta = 0.5771$ **49.** $\sec \theta = 3.835$ **50.** $\csc \theta = 2.916$

B

Use a calculator to convert to radian measure. Leave answers in terms of π.

51. 37.71° **52.** 12.73° **53.** 214.6° **54.** 73.87°

Use a calculator to convert these radian measures to degree measure.

55. 1.303 **56.** 2.347 **57.** 37.89 **58.** 7.005

59. 8.206π **60.** -14.13π **61.** 0.7532π **62.** -1.205π

Use a calculator to find the following function values.

63. tan 29°43′ **64.** cot 73°21′ **65.** sin 213.56°

66. tan −545°29′ **67.** cot −2.556° **68.** cos 4.223°

For each function value, use a calculator to find the angle in radians.

69. $\cot A = 11.546$ **70.** $\tan A = 15.234$

71. $\sin A = -0.0089$ **72.** $\tan A = -43.467$

73. ***Critical Thinking*** How would you use a calculator to find θ given $\sec\theta = 1.706$?

Challenge

74. How would you use a calculator to find $\csc 27°32'$?
75. Use a calculator. Find $\sin\theta$ for some very small values of θ in radians. What can you conclude?
76. Use a calculator. Find $\tan\theta$ for some very small values of θ in radians. What can you conclude?
77. Use a calculator. Convert $61°38'22''$ to degrees and decimal parts of degrees. (Hint: $22''$ means 22 seconds. $60'' = 1'$)
78. Find $\log \sin 57°$ (the logarithm of the sine of 57°). What is the domain of the log sin function?
79. ***Estimation*** Calculate the diameter of the sun. The sun is 93 million miles away from Earth, and the angle it forms at Earth's surface is about $0°32'$.

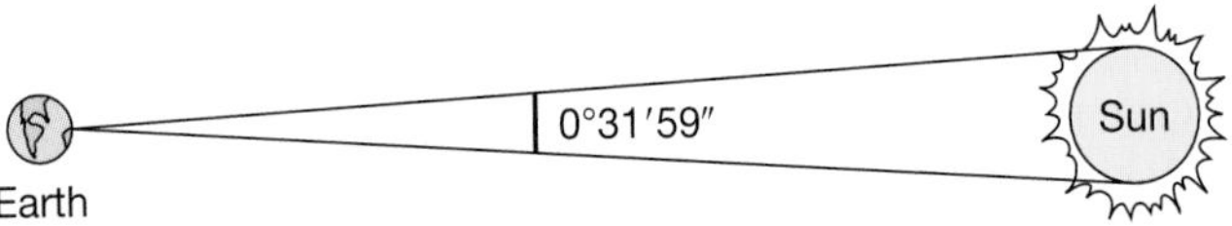

Self-Test On the Web

Check your progress. Look for a self-test at the Prentice Hall Web site. www.phschool.com

Mixed Review

Test for symmetry about the origin and the line $x = y$.

80. $x^2 + y^2 = 36$
81. $xy = 25$
82. $4(x - 3)^2 + (y - 3)^2 = 25$
83. $f(x) = x^3 - x$ *9-1, 12-1*

Solve each system using Cramer's rule.

84. $4x + 2y = 9$
    $7x + 4y = 16$
85. $x + y + z = 0$
    $2x + y + 2z = 2$
    $x + 2y = -5$ *13-3*

Solve.

86. $|5 - 2x| > 7$
87. $|3 + 7x| \geq -11$ *2-7*

Find the sum.

88. $\sum_{n=1}^{10} (6n + 4)$
89. $\sum_{n=5}^{15} (2n + 2)$
90. $\sum_{n=1}^{13} 3^n$
91. $\sum_{n=3}^{13} \left(\frac{1}{3}\right)^n$ *14-2, 14-3*

92. A typist can be paid in two ways.
    Plan A: \$50 plus \$0.15 per page
    Plan B: straight \$0.55 per page

Graphs of Trigonometric Functions

17-5

PART 1 Periodic Functions

Objective: Identify periodic functions from their graphs.

Certain functions with a repeating pattern are called **periodic.** The function whose graph is shown is periodic. The function values repeat every two units as we move from left to right. In other words, for any x, we have $f(x) = f(x + 2)$. To see this another way, think of the part of the graph between 0 and 2 on the x-axis, and note that the rest of the graph consists of copies of it. If we translate the graph two units to the left or right, the original graph will be obtained. We say f has a **period** of 2.

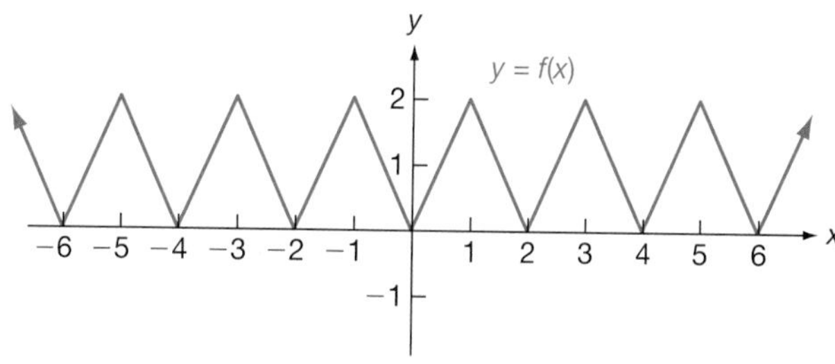

EXAMPLE 1 What is the period of this function?

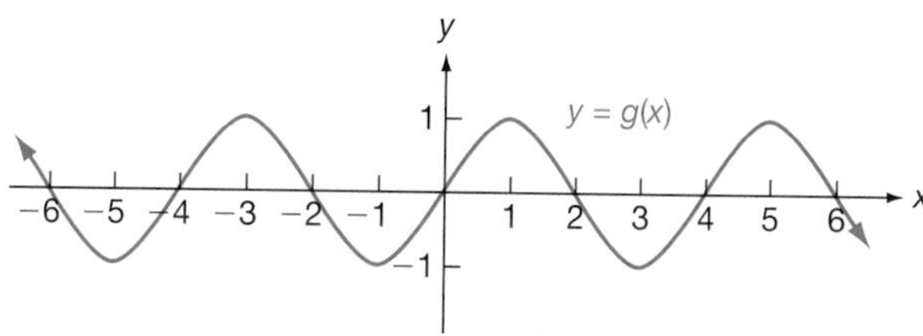

In the function g, the function values repeat every four units. Hence $g(x) = g(x + 4)$ for any x, and if the graph is translated four units to the left or right, it will coincide with itself. The period of g is 4.

Definition

If a function f has the property that $f(x + p) = f(x)$ for all x in the domain where p is a constant, then f is said to be a **periodic function.** The smallest positive number p, if there is one, for which $f(x + p) = f(x)$ for all x, is the **period** of the function.

What You'll Learn

1. To identify periodic functions from their graphs
2. To graph the sine and cosine functions and interpret their graphs
3. To graph the other trigonometric functions and interpret their graphs

. . . And Why

To prove trigonometric identities

Try This

a. What is the period of this function?

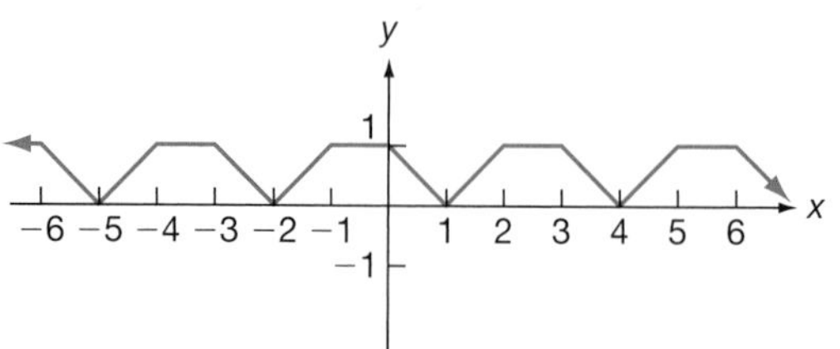

PART 2 The Sine and Cosine Functions

Objective: Graph the sine and cosine functions and interpret their graphs.

To graph the sine function we look at special angles in the first two quadrants. We will use radian measure for the angles.

θ	0	$\frac{\pi}{6}$	$\frac{\pi}{4}$	$\frac{\pi}{3}$	$\frac{\pi}{2}$	$\frac{2\pi}{3}$	$\frac{3\pi}{4}$	$\frac{5\pi}{6}$	π
sin θ (exact)	0	$\frac{1}{2}$	$\frac{\sqrt{2}}{2}$	$\frac{\sqrt{3}}{2}$	1	$\frac{\sqrt{3}}{2}$	$\frac{\sqrt{2}}{2}$	$\frac{1}{2}$	0
sin θ (approximate)	0	0.5	0.7	0.9	1	0.9	0.7	0.5	0

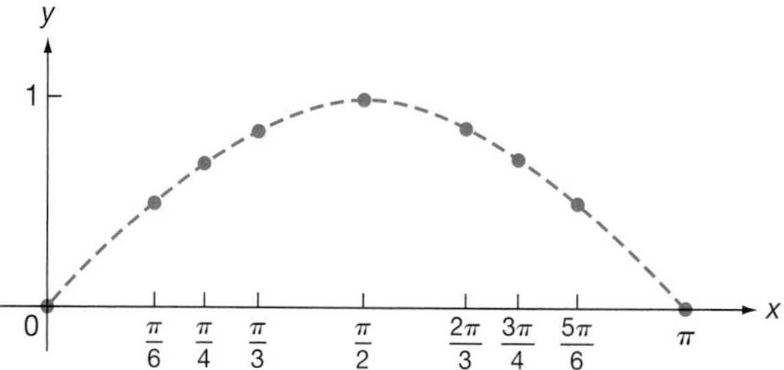

In Section 17-4 we used tables that gave us the values for angles between 0 and $\frac{\pi}{2}$. Thus it seems reasonable that we join the above points with a smooth curve. If we choose negative values for θ, we will be choosing rotations from the third and fourth quadrants.

θ	$-\pi$	$-\frac{5\pi}{6}$	$-\frac{3\pi}{4}$	$-\frac{2\pi}{3}$	$-\frac{\pi}{2}$	$-\frac{\pi}{3}$	$-\frac{\pi}{4}$	$-\frac{\pi}{6}$	0
sin θ (exact)	0	$-\frac{1}{2}$	$-\frac{\sqrt{2}}{2}$	$-\frac{\sqrt{3}}{2}$	-1	$-\frac{\sqrt{3}}{2}$	$-\frac{\sqrt{2}}{2}$	$-\frac{1}{2}$	0
sin θ (approximate)	0	−0.5	−0.7	−0.9	−1	−0.9	−0.7	−0.5	0

Here is a graph of the sine function. Function values increase to a maximum of 1 at $\frac{\pi}{2}$, then decrease to 0 at π, decrease further to a minimum of -1 at $\frac{3}{2}\pi$, then increase to 0 at 2π, and so on. The **amplitude** of a periodic function is half the difference between its maximum and minimum function values. The amplitude of the sine function is 1. It is always positive.

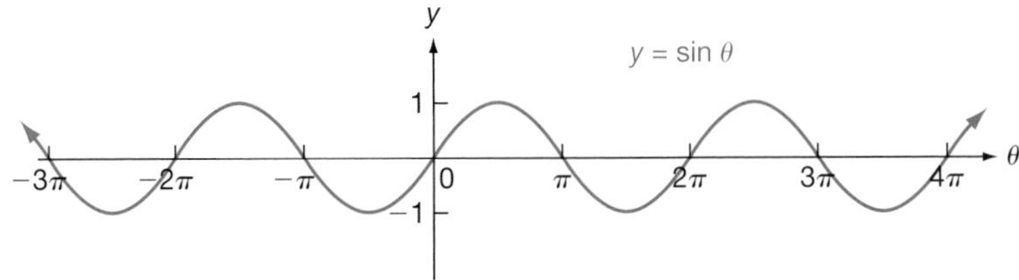

EXAMPLE 2

(a) Is the sine function periodic? If so, what is its period?
(b) Is the sine function even? odd?

From the graph of the sine function, certain properties are apparent.

(a) The sine function is periodic, with period 2π.
(b) The sine function is an odd function because it is symmetric with respect to the origin. Thus we know that $\sin(-\theta) = -\sin\theta$ for all real numbers θ.

Try This

b. What are the domain and range of the sine function?

Here is the graph of the cosine function.

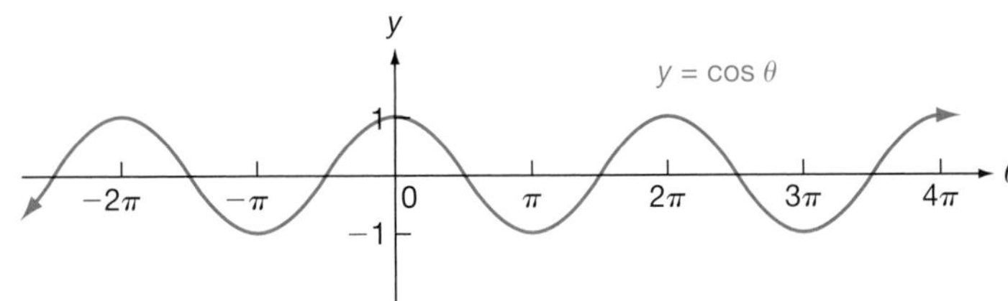

EXAMPLE 3

(a) What is the amplitude of the cosine function?
(b) Is the cosine function even? odd?
(c) What is the domain? What is the range?

From the graph of the cosine function, we notice certain properties.

(a) The range is the set of all real numbers from -1 to 1 inclusive. Thus the amplitude is 1.
(b) The cosine function is an even function, by symmetry with respect to the y-axis. Thus we know that $\cos(-\theta) = \cos\theta$ for all real numbers θ.
(c) The domain is the set of all real numbers. The range is -1 to 1 inclusive.

Try This

c. Is the cosine function periodic? If so, what is its period?

The following summarizes some properties of the sine and cosine functions.

Theorem 17-2

The sine function is periodic, with period 2π.

$\sin\theta = \sin(\theta + 2\pi) = \sin(\theta - 2\pi) = \sin(\theta + 4\pi)$, and so on, or
$\sin\theta = \sin(\theta \pm 2\pi k)$ where k is an integer

The cosine function is periodic, with period 2π.

$\cos\theta = \cos(\theta + 2\pi) = \cos(\theta - 2\pi) = \cos(\theta + 4\pi)$, and so on, or
$\cos\theta = \cos(\theta \pm 2\pi k)$ where k is an integer

Graphs of Other Trigonometric Functions

Objective: Graph the other trigonometric functions and interpret their graphs.

Not every angle has a tangent. For example, using the relationship $\tan\theta = \frac{\sin\theta}{\cos\theta}$, the tangent ratio for $\frac{\pi}{2}$ would be $\frac{1}{0}$, since $\cos\frac{\pi}{2} = 0$. Since division by 0 is undefined, $\tan\frac{\pi}{2}$ is meaningless. In this graph of the tangent function we use x instead of θ. The variable x represents any real number. Note that the function value is 0 when $x = 0$, and the values increase as x increases toward $\frac{\pi}{2}$, becoming very large. In fact, they increase without bound. The dashed vertical lines are not part of the graph. They are **asymptotes.** The graph approaches each asymptote, but never reaches it because there are no values of the function for $\frac{\pi}{2}, \frac{3\pi}{2}$, and so on.

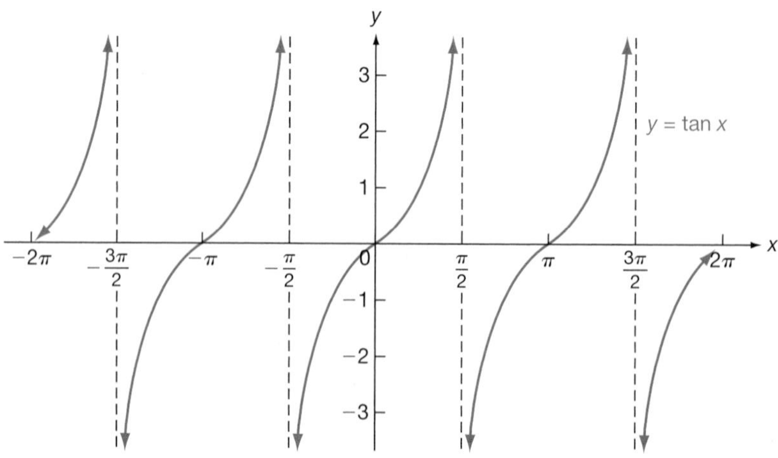

EXAMPLE 4 Is the tangent function periodic? If so, what is its period? What is its domain? What is its range?

We see that the graph from $-\frac{\pi}{2}$ to $\frac{\pi}{2}$ repeats in the interval from $\frac{\pi}{2}$ to $\frac{3\pi}{2}$. Consequently, the tangent function is periodic, with a period of π.

Its domain is $\{x \mid x \neq \frac{\pi}{2} + k\pi, k \text{ an integer}\}$.

Its range is the set of all real numbers.

Try This

d. Is the tangent function even or odd?

Quick Review

Regarding *Try This* **d.**, remember that an even function is symmetric to the *y*-axis; an odd function is symmetric to the origin. Remember also that some functions are neither even nor odd.

The secant and cosine functions are reciprocals. The secant function is undefined for those numbers for which $\cos x = 0$.

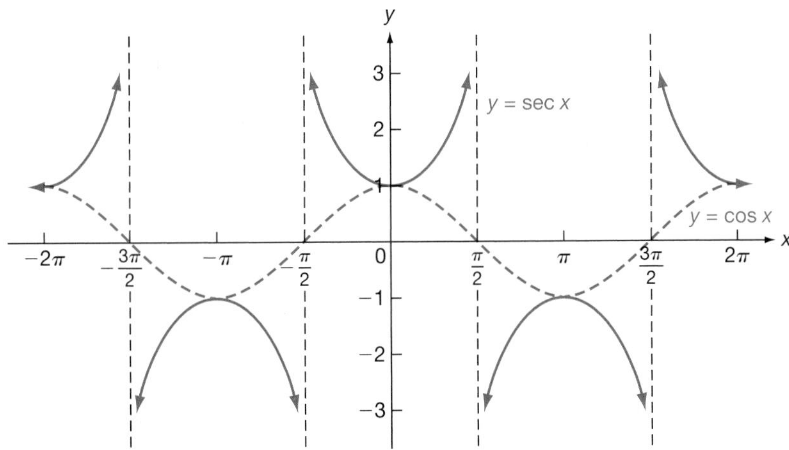

Journal

Write a description of the graph of any of the trigonometric functions. If you read your description to your classmates, would they be able to identify the function from that description?

EXAMPLE 5 What is the domain of the secant function?

The domain of the secant function is the set of all real numbers except $\frac{\pi}{2} + k\pi$, k an integer; that is

$$\{x \mid x \neq \frac{\pi}{2} + k\pi, k \text{ an integer}\}$$

Try This

e. What is the period of the secant function?

f. What is the range of the secant function?

g. Graph the cotangent function.

h. What is the period of the cotangent function?

i. What is the domain of the cotangent function? What is the range?

j. Is the cotangent function even or odd?

Look for worked-out examples at the Prentice Hall Web site.
www.phschool.com

17-5 Exercises

A

Mental Math Which of the following functions are periodic?

1.

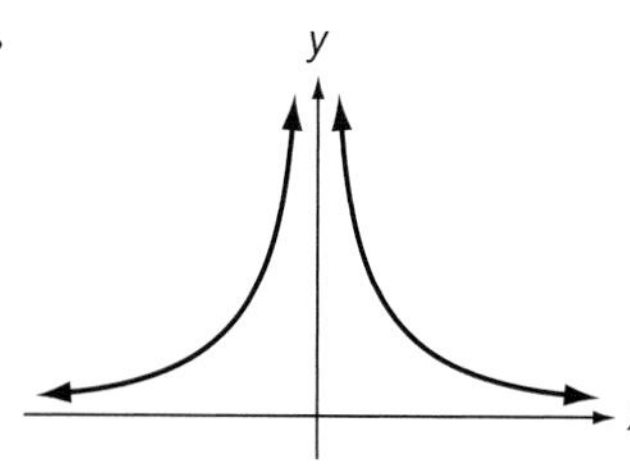

2.

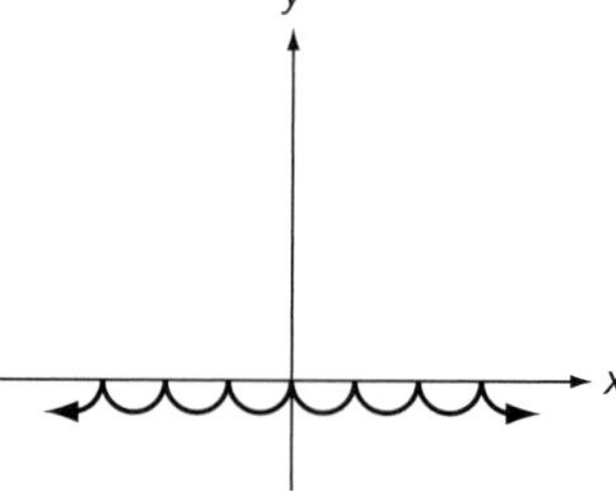

3.

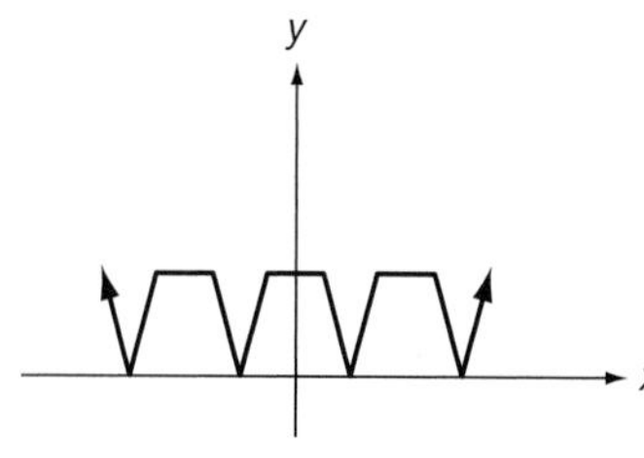

4.

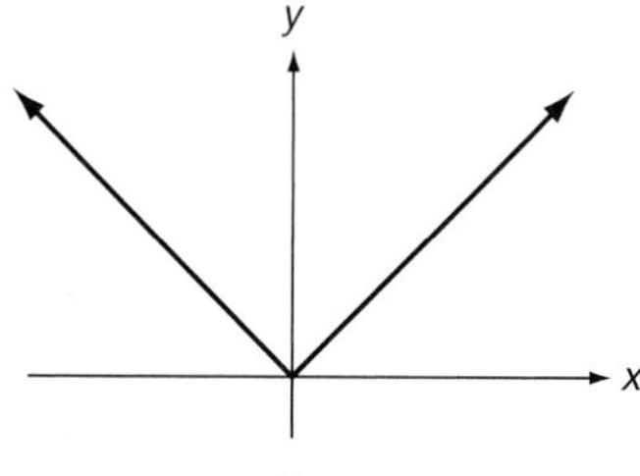

5.

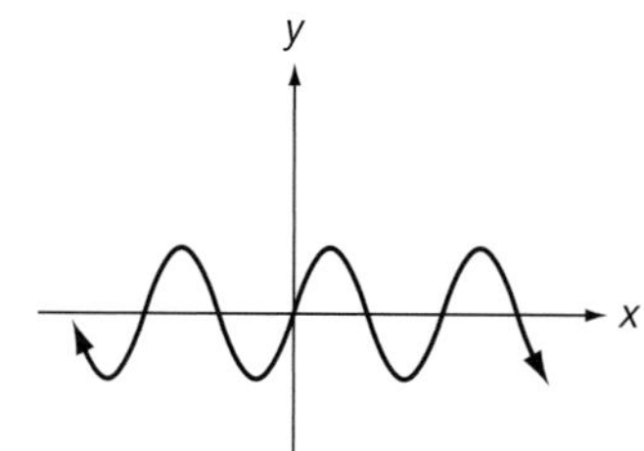

6.

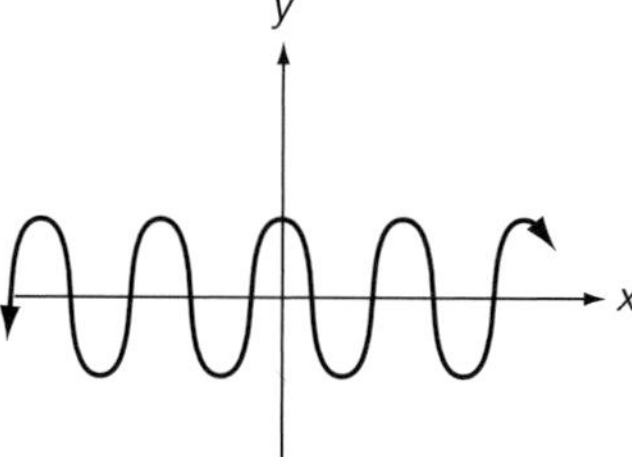

7. What is the period of this function?

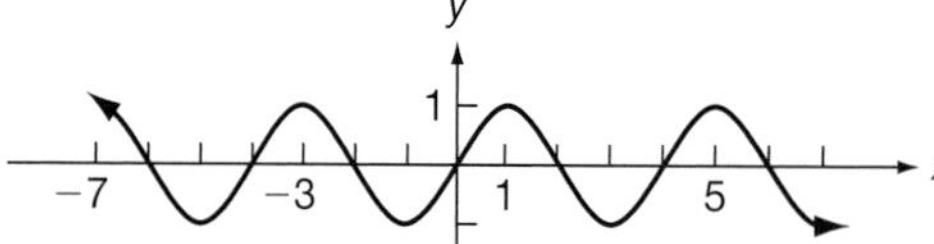

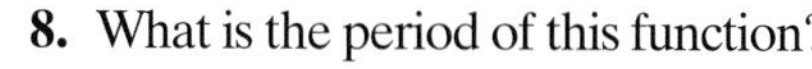

8. What is the period of this function?

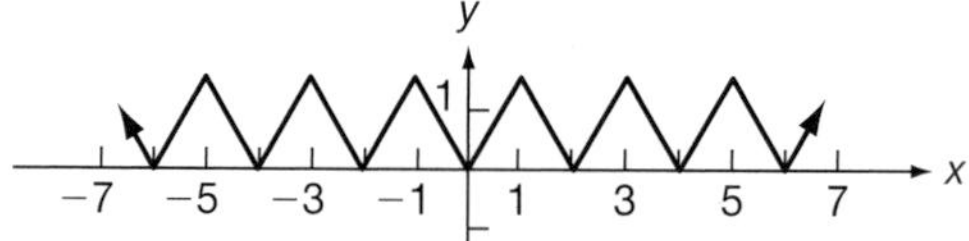

9. Use Table 5 in the back of the book to plot the points and sketch the sine curve.

10. Copy and complete this table of values for the cosine function in the first and second quadrants.

θ	0	$\frac{\pi}{6}$	$\frac{\pi}{4}$	$\frac{\pi}{3}$	$\frac{\pi}{2}$	$\frac{2\pi}{3}$	$\frac{3\pi}{4}$	$\frac{5\pi}{6}$	π
cos θ (exact)									
cos θ (approximate)									

11. Copy and complete this table of values for the cosine function in the third and fourth quadrants.

θ	$-\pi$	$-\frac{5\pi}{6}$	$-\frac{3\pi}{4}$	$-\frac{2\pi}{3}$	$-\frac{\pi}{2}$	$-\frac{\pi}{3}$	$-\frac{\pi}{4}$	$-\frac{\pi}{6}$	0
cos θ (exact)									
cos θ (approximate)									

Here is a table of approximate values of functions. Use this table, plus your knowledge of the properties of the functions, to make graphs.

	$\frac{\pi}{16}$	$\frac{\pi}{8}$	$\frac{\pi}{6}$	$\frac{\pi}{4}$	$\frac{\pi}{3}$	$\frac{3\pi}{8}$	$\frac{7\pi}{16}$	$-\frac{\pi}{16}$	$-\frac{\pi}{8}$	$-\frac{\pi}{6}$	$-\frac{\pi}{4}$
tan	0.2	0.4	0.6	1.0	1.7	2.4	4.9	−0.2	−0.4	−0.6	−1.0
cot	4.9	2.4	1.7	1.0	0.6	0.4	0.2	−4.9	−2.4	−1.7	−1.0
sec	1.02	1.1	1.2	1.4	2.0	2.6	5.0	1.02	1.1	1.2	1.4
csc	5.0	2.6	2.0	1.4	1.2	1.08	1.02	−5.0	−2.6	−2.0	−1.4

12. Graph the tangent function between -2π and 2π.

13. Graph the cotangent function between -2π and 2π.

14. Graph the secant function between -2π and 2π.

15. Graph the cosecant function between -2π and 2π.

B

16. a. Sketch a graph of $y = \sin x$.
b. By reflecting the graph in **a.**, sketch a graph of $y = \sin(-x)$.
c. By reflecting the graph in **a.**, sketch a graph of $y = -\sin x$.
d. How do the graphs in **b.** and **c.** compare?

17. a. Sketch a graph of $y = \cos x$.
b. By reflecting the graph in **a.**, sketch a graph of $y = \cos(-x)$.
c. By reflecting the graph in **a.**, sketch a graph of $y = -\cos x$.
d. How do the graphs in **a.** and **b.** compare?

18. a. Sketch a graph of $y = \sin x$.
b. By translating, sketch a graph of $y = \sin(x + \pi)$.
c. By reflecting the graph in **a.**, sketch a graph of $y = -\sin x$.
d. How do the graphs in **b.** and **c.** compare?

19. a. Sketch a graph of $y = \sin x$.
b. By translating, sketch a graph of $y = \sin(x - \pi)$.
c. By reflecting the graph in **a.**, sketch a graph of $y = -\sin x$.
d. How do the graphs in **b.** and **c.** compare?

20. **a.** Sketch a graph of $y = \cos x$.

b. By translating, sketch a graph of $y = \cos(x + \pi)$.

c. By reflecting the graph in **a.**, sketch a graph of $y = -\cos x$.

d. How do the graphs in **b.** and **c.** compare?

21. ***Mathematical Reasoning*** Which pairs of circular functions have the same zeros?

22. Graph $f(x) = |\tan x|$.

23. ***Critical Thinking***

a. Describe how the graphs of the tangent and cotangent functions are related.

b. Describe how the graphs of the secant and cosecant functions are related.

24. **TEST PREP** In right triangle ABC, $\angle C$ is a right angle. The measure of $\angle B$ is 60°. What is the value of $\tan \angle A$?

A. 2 **B.** $\frac{\sqrt{3}}{2}$ **C.** $\frac{\sqrt{3}}{3}$ **D.** $\frac{1}{2}$

Challenge

25. Solve $\cos x \leq \sec x$.

26. Solve $\sin x > \csc x$.

27. Construct a graph of the sine function by copying the coordinate axes on other paper. Then, from the unit circle shown here, transfer vertical distances with a compass.

28. Construct a graph of the cosine function. Follow the instructions for Exercise 27, but transfer *horizontal* distances from the unit circle with a compass.

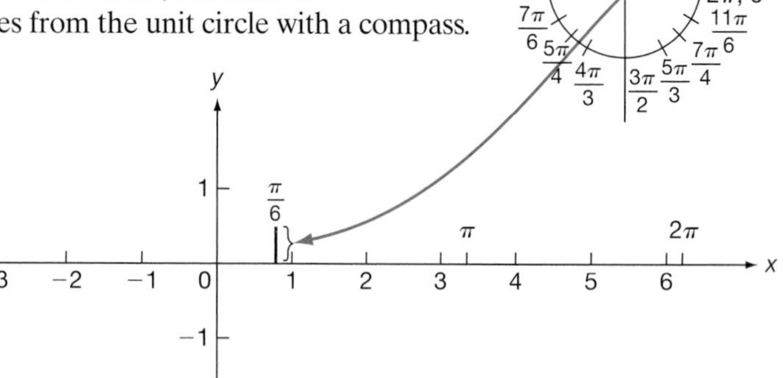

Mixed Review

Tell whether the function is odd, even, or neither.

29. $f(x) = \sin x$

30. $f(x) = x^3 - x$

31. $f(x) = \cos x$

32. $f(x) = x^4 - x^2 + x$ *9-1*

33. For an arithmetic sequence, find d when $a_{25} = 10$ and $a_{50} = 260$. *14-2*

Trigonometric Function Relationships

17-6

We have already seen some of the important relationships that exist among the six trigonometric functions. There are certain other relationships called identities. Recall that an identity is an equation that is true for all acceptable replacements for the variables.

What You'll Learn

1. To derive identities from the quotient and Pythagorean identities
2. To derive identities from the cofunction identities

. . . And Why

To expand the use of algebraic concepts with trigonometry to sketch graphs of the functions

PART 1 Quotient and Pythagorean Identities

Objective: Derive identities from the quotient and Pythagorean identities.

The tangent and cotangent functions can be expressed in terms of the sine and cosine functions.

Theorem 17-3

Quotient Identities

$$\tan\theta \equiv \frac{\sin\theta}{\cos\theta},\ \cos\theta \neq 0 \qquad \cot\theta \equiv \frac{\cos\theta}{\sin\theta},\ \sin\theta \neq 0$$

EXAMPLE 1 Derive an identity that gives $\sin\theta$ in terms of $\tan\theta$ and $\cos\theta$.

By Theorem 17-3 we have $\tan\theta \equiv \frac{\sin\theta}{\cos\theta}$. Solving for $\sin\theta$ we have

$$\sin\theta \equiv \tan\theta \cdot \cos\theta$$

Try This

a. Derive an identity that gives $\cos\theta$ in terms of $\sin\theta$ and $\cot\theta$.

Suppose θ determines a point T on the unit circle, with coordinates (x, y). By the Pythagorean theorem, $x^2 + y^2 = 1$. Since $x = \cos\theta$ and $y = \sin\theta$, we obtain the following identity.

$$\sin^2\theta + \cos^2\theta \equiv 1$$

When exponents are used with the trigonometric functions, we write $\sin^2\theta$ instead of $(\sin\theta)^2$.

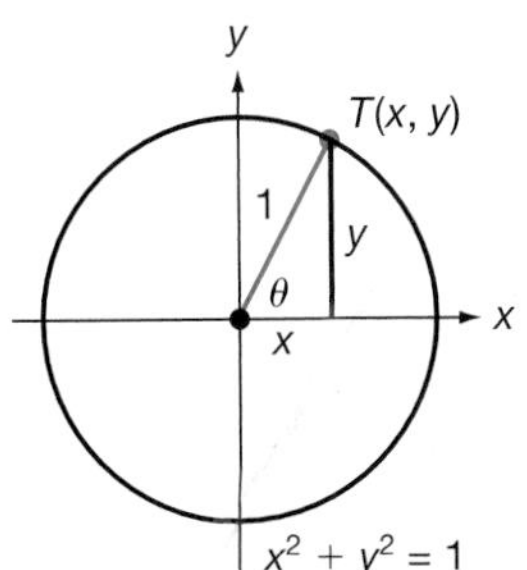

This identity relates the sine and cosine of any angle. It is known as one of the Pythagorean identities. Now we will divide the above identity by $\sin^2\theta$.

$$\frac{\sin^2\theta}{\sin^2\theta} + \frac{\cos^2\theta}{\sin^2\theta} \equiv \frac{1}{\sin^2\theta}$$

Since the cosecant is the reciprocal of the sine, this can be further simplified.

$$1 + \cot^2 \theta \equiv \csc^2 \theta$$

This identity is valid for any rotation θ for which $\sin^2 \theta \neq 0$, since we divided by $\sin^2 \theta$.

The third Pythagorean identity is obtained by dividing the first by $\cos^2 \theta$.

$$1 + \tan^2 \theta \equiv \sec^2 \theta$$

Theorem 17-4

Pythagorean Identities

$$\sin^2 \theta + \cos^2 \theta \equiv 1 \qquad 1 + \cot^2 \theta \equiv \csc^2 \theta \qquad 1 + \tan^2 \theta \equiv \sec^2 \theta$$

EXAMPLE 2 Derive identities that give $\cos^2 \theta$ and $\cos \theta$ in terms of $\sin \theta$.

$\sin^2 \theta + \cos^2 \theta \equiv 1$ — Pythagorean identity

$\cos^2 \theta \equiv 1 - \sin^2 \theta$ — Solving for $\cos^2 \theta$

$|\cos \theta| \equiv \sqrt{1 - \sin^2 \theta}$ — Finding the principal square root

$\cos \theta \equiv \pm\sqrt{1 - \sin^2 \theta}$

The sign of $\cos \theta$ is positive if the terminal side of θ is in the first or fourth quadrant. Otherwise, it is negative.

Try This

b. Derive an identity for $\sin^2 \theta$ in terms of $\cos \theta$.
c. Derive an identity for $\sin \theta$ in terms of $\cos \theta$.

EXAMPLE 3 Derive two other identities from $1 + \cot^2 \theta \equiv \csc^2 \theta$.

We obtain $\csc^2 \theta - \cot^2 \theta \equiv 1$ and $\cot^2 \theta \equiv \csc^2 \theta - 1$.

EXAMPLE 4 Derive an identity for $\cot \theta$ in terms of $\sin \theta$.

$\cot^2 \theta \equiv \csc^2 \theta - 1$ — From the identity derived in Example 3

$\cot^2 \theta \equiv \frac{1}{\sin^2 \theta} - 1$

$\cot \theta \equiv \pm\sqrt{\frac{1}{\sin^2 \theta} - 1}$

Try This

d. From the identity $1 + \tan^2 \theta \equiv \sec^2 \theta$, derive two other identities.
e. Derive an identity for $\sec \theta$ in terms of $\sin \theta$ and $\cos \theta$.

Other Identities

Objective: Derive identities from the graphs of cofunctions.

We know that the sine and cosine are called cofunctions of each other. Another class of identities gives functions in terms of their cofunctions.

Consider this graph. The graph of $y = \sin\theta$ has been translated to the left a distance of $\frac{\pi}{2}$. Thus we obtain the graph of $y = \sin\left(\theta + \frac{\pi}{2}\right)$. The latter is also a graph of the cosine function. Thus we obtain the identity $\sin\left(\theta + \frac{\pi}{2}\right) \equiv \cos\theta$.

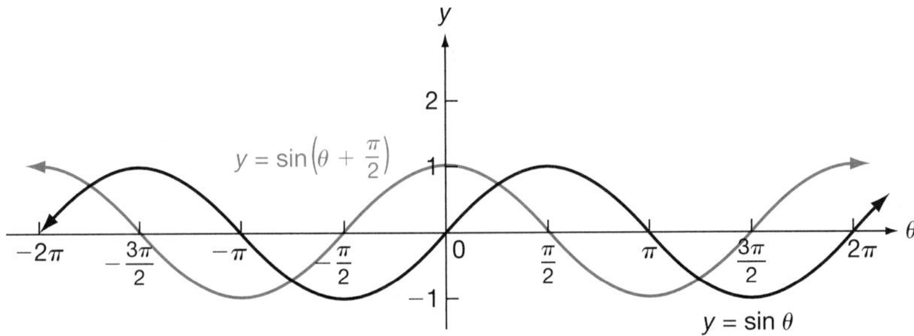

EXAMPLE 5 Check the identity $\sin\left(\theta + \frac{\pi}{2}\right) \equiv \cos\theta$ by using $\theta = \frac{\pi}{6}$.

$$\sin\left(\theta + \frac{\pi}{2}\right) = \sin\left(\frac{\pi}{6} + \frac{\pi}{2}\right) = \sin\left(\frac{2\pi}{3}\right) = \frac{\sqrt{3}}{2} = \cos\frac{\pi}{6}$$

By translating the graph of $y = \cos\theta$ to the right a distance of $\frac{\pi}{2}$, we obtain the following identity.

$$\cos\left(\theta - \frac{\pi}{2}\right) \equiv \sin\theta$$

Try This

f. Check the identity $\cos\left(\theta - \frac{\pi}{2}\right) \equiv \sin\theta$ by using $\theta = 0$ radians.

If the graph of $y = \sin\theta$ is translated to the right a distance of $\frac{\pi}{2}$, we obtain the graph of $y = \sin\left(\theta - \frac{\pi}{2}\right)$. The latter is a reflection of the cosine function across the x-axis. In other words, it is a graph of $y = -\cos\theta$. We thus obtain the following identity.

$$\sin\left(\theta - \frac{\pi}{2}\right) \equiv -\cos\theta$$

By means similar to those above, we obtain this identity.

$$\cos\left(\theta + \frac{\pi}{2}\right) \equiv -\sin\theta$$

We now consider function values at $\frac{\pi}{2} - \theta$. Since the sine function is odd, we know the following.

$$\sin\left(\frac{\pi}{2} - \theta\right) \equiv \sin\left[-\left(\theta - \frac{\pi}{2}\right)\right] \equiv -\sin\left(\theta - \frac{\pi}{2}\right)$$

Now consider the identity already established.

$$\sin\left(\theta - \frac{\pi}{2}\right) \equiv -\cos\theta$$

This is equivalent to the following.

$$-\sin\left(\theta - \frac{\pi}{2}\right) \equiv \cos\theta \qquad \text{Multiplying by } -1$$

Since the sine function is odd, we now have the following identity.

$$\sin\left(\frac{\pi}{2} - \theta\right) \equiv \cos\theta$$

Similarly, we can establish the identity $\cos\left(\frac{\pi}{2} - \theta\right) \equiv \sin\theta$.

The following theorem summarizes these identities derived by analyzing graphs of cofunctions. The identities should be memorized.

Theorem 17-5

$$\sin\left(\theta + \frac{\pi}{2}\right) \equiv \cos\theta \qquad \cos\left(\theta + \frac{\pi}{2}\right) \equiv -\sin\theta$$

$$\sin\left(\theta - \frac{\pi}{2}\right) \equiv -\cos\theta \qquad \cos\left(\theta - \frac{\pi}{2}\right) \equiv \sin\theta$$

$$\sin\left(\frac{\pi}{2} - \theta\right) \equiv \cos\theta \qquad \cos\left(\frac{\pi}{2} - \theta\right) \equiv \sin\theta$$

EXAMPLE 6 Find an identity for $\tan\left(\theta + \frac{\pi}{2}\right)$.

$$\tan\left(\theta + \frac{\pi}{2}\right) \equiv \frac{\sin\left(\theta + \frac{\pi}{2}\right)}{\cos\left(\theta + \frac{\pi}{2}\right)} \qquad \text{Theorem 17-3 (quotient identity)}$$

$$\equiv \frac{\cos\theta}{-\sin\theta} \qquad \text{Theorem 17-5}$$

$$\equiv -\cot\theta \qquad \text{Theorem 17-3 (quotient identity)}$$

Try This

g. Find an identity for $\cot\left(\theta + \frac{\pi}{2}\right)$.

17-6 Exercises

Extra Help On the Web

Look for worked-out examples at the Prentice Hall Web site.
www.phschool.com

A

1. Derive an identity for $\cos \theta$ in terms of $\sin \theta$ and $\tan \theta$.
2. Derive an identity for $\sin \theta$ in terms of $\cot \theta$ and $\cos \theta$.

Use the Pythagorean identities to derive an identity for

3. $\csc \theta$ in terms of $\cot \theta$.
4. $\tan \theta$ in terms of $\sec \theta$.
5. $\cot \theta$ in terms of $\csc \theta$.
6. $\sec \theta$ in terms of $\tan \theta$.
7. $\tan \theta$ in terms of $\cos \theta$.
8. $\csc \theta$ in terms of $\cos \theta$.
9. Check the identity $\sin\left(\theta - \frac{\pi}{2}\right) \equiv -\cos \theta$ by using $\theta = \frac{\pi}{4}$.
10. Check the identity $\cos\left(\theta - \frac{\pi}{2}\right) \equiv \sin \theta$ by using $\theta = 0$.
11. Check the identity $\sin\left(\frac{\pi}{2} - \theta\right) \equiv \cos \theta$ by using $\theta = \frac{5\pi}{4}$.
12. Check the identity $\cos\left(\frac{\pi}{2} - \theta\right) \equiv \sin \theta$ by using $\theta = \frac{\pi}{3}$.

Derive an identity for the following, using a cofunction of each.

13. $\tan\left(\theta - \frac{\pi}{2}\right)$
14. $\cot\left(\theta - \frac{\pi}{2}\right)$
15. $\sec\left(\frac{\pi}{2} - \theta\right)$
16. $\csc\left(\frac{\pi}{2} - \theta\right)$

B

Use the given function values to find the six function values of the complement angle.

17. $\sin 65° = 0.9063$ $\cos 65° = 0.4226$
 $\tan 65° = 2.145$ $\cot 65° = 0.4663$
 $\sec 65° = 2.366$ $\csc 65° = 1.103$

18. $\sin 32° = 0.5299$ $\cos 32° = 0.8480$
 $\tan 32° = 0.6249$ $\cot 32° = 1.600$
 $\sec 32° = 1.179$ $\csc 32° = 1.887$

Write an equivalent expression for each of the following.

19. $\sin(\theta + \pi)$
20. $\sin(\theta - \pi)$
21. $\cos(\pi - \theta)$
22. $\sin(\pi - \theta)$
23. $\cos(\theta + 2k\pi)$
24. $\sin(\theta + 2k\pi)$
25. $\cos(\theta - \pi)$
26. $\cos(\theta + \pi)$

Given that $\sin \frac{\pi}{8} = 0.38268$, use identities to find the following.

27. $\cos \frac{\pi}{8}$

28. $\cos \frac{5\pi}{8}$

29. $\sin \frac{5\pi}{8}$

30. $\sin -\frac{3\pi}{8}$

31. $\cos -\frac{3\pi}{8}$

32. $\cos -\frac{\pi}{8}$

33. ***Critical Thinking***

a. For the six trigonometric functions, state the cofunction identities for $\frac{\pi}{2} - \theta$.

b. Describe the pattern you see in part **a.**

Challenge

Choose values for θ or x. Then check these identities.

34. $\frac{1 - \sin \theta}{\cos \theta} \equiv \frac{\cos \theta}{1 + \sin \theta}$

35. $\frac{1 - \cos \theta}{\sin \theta} \equiv \frac{\sin \theta}{1 + \cos \theta}$

36. $\csc x - \cos x \cot x \equiv \sin x$

37. $\sec x - \sin x \tan x \equiv \cos x$

Mixed Review

Factor. **38.** $6x^2 - 13x + 6$ **39.** $x^4 - 625$ **40.** $24x^3y^2 - 54xy^4$

41. $x^3 + 15x^2 + 74x + 120$ *5-4, 5-5, 5-6*

Divide. **42.** $(x^3 - 4x^2 + 5x - 2) \div (x - 1)$

43. $(3x^4 + x^3 - x^2 + x - 4) \div (3x + 4)$ *6-4*

Simplify. **44.** $\left(\frac{-32a^{12}b^{-3}c^7d^4}{a^2b^2c^2d^2}\right)^{\frac{3}{5}}$ **45.** $\left(\frac{-125n^7m^{-7}l^7}{343n^3m^2l}\right)^{\frac{5}{3}}$ *1-8, 7-5*

46. Use rational exponents to simplify. $\sqrt{\frac{\sqrt{2}}{2}}$ *7-5*

47. Find the six trigonometric function values for θ and α. Leave answers as fractions.

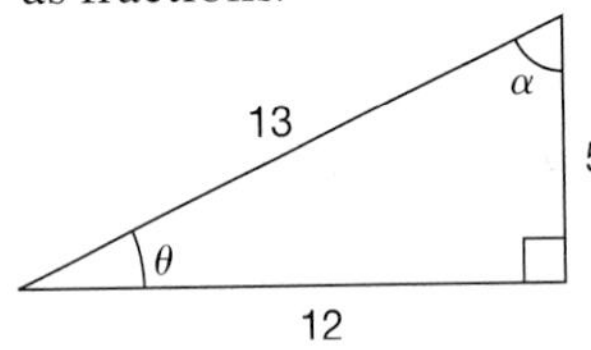

Find the lengths of a and b.

48.

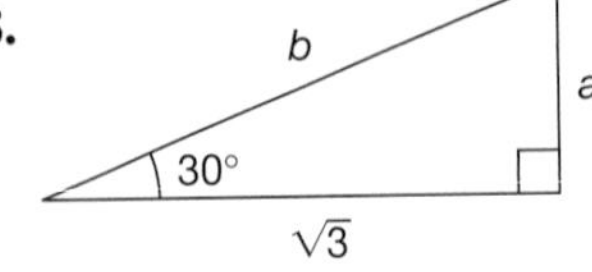

49.

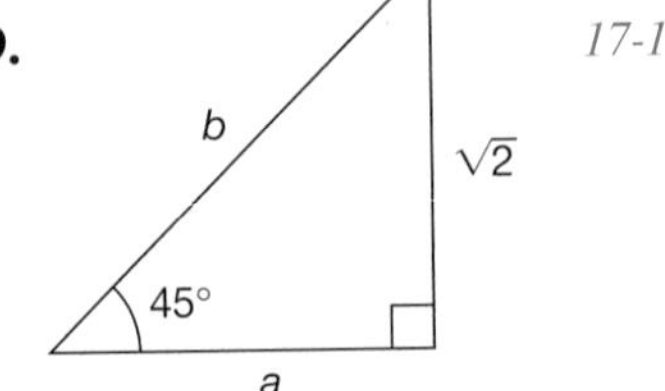

17-1

More Trigonometric Graphs

17-7

We will consider graphs of some variations of the sine and cosine functions. In particular, we are interested in $y = A \sin B\theta$ and $y = A \cos B\theta$ where A and B are constants.

What You'll Learn

1. To sketch graphs in which the amplitude or period is changed
2. To sketch graphs in which the amplitude and period are changed

. . . And Why

To solve trigonometric equations and draw graphs to picture the results

PART 1 Change of Amplitude or Period

Objective: Sketch graphs in which the amplitude or period is changed.

Changing the constant A in $y = A \sin \theta$ causes a vertical stretching or shrinking of the graph and thus a change in the amplitude.

EXAMPLE 1 Sketch a graph of $y = 2 \sin \theta$. What is the amplitude?

The function $y = 2 \sin \theta$ is equivalent to $\frac{y}{2} = \sin \theta$. Thus the graph is a vertical stretching of the graph of $y = \sin \theta$. The amplitude of this function is 2. That is, $A = 2$.

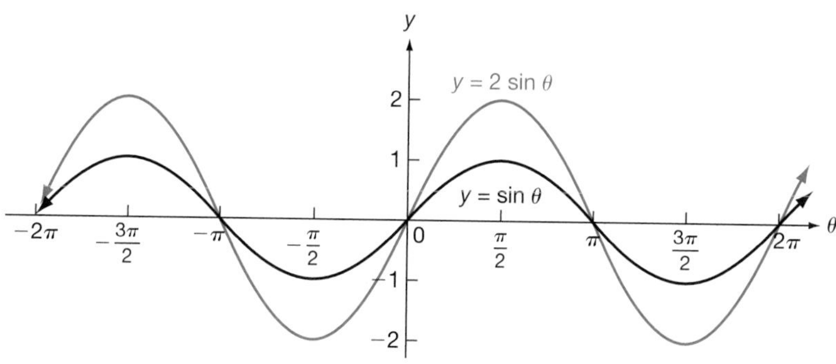

If the constant A in $y = A \sin x$ is negative, there will also be a reflection across the x-axis. If the absolute value of A is less than 1, then there will be a vertical shrinking. The amplitude will be $|A|$. Thus the graph of $y = -\frac{1}{2} \sin \theta$ is a reflection of $y = \sin \theta$ and has an amplitude of $\left|-\frac{1}{2}\right|$ or $\frac{1}{2}$.

Try This

a. Sketch a graph of $y = 2 \cos \theta$. What is the amplitude?

Changing the constant B in $y = \sin B\theta$ causes a horizontal stretching or shrinking of the graph and thus a change in the period.

EXAMPLE 2 Sketch a graph of $y = \sin 2\theta$. What is the period?

The function $y = \sin 2\theta$ is equivalent to $y = \sin \frac{\theta}{\frac{1}{2}}$. Thus the graph is a horizontal shrinking of the graph of $y = \sin \theta$. The period is π.

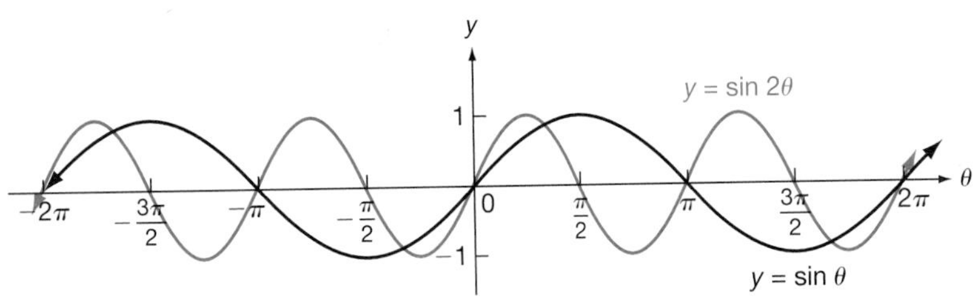

If $|B| > 1$, there will be a horizontal shrink. If $|B| < 1$, there will be a horizontal stretch. If B is negative, there will also be a reflection across the y-axis. The period will be $\frac{2\pi}{|B|}$.

Thus the graph of $y = \sin\left(-\frac{1}{2}\theta\right)$ is a reflection of $y = \sin \theta$, and has a period of $\frac{2\pi}{\left|-\frac{1}{2}\right|}$ or 4π.

Try This

b. Sketch a graph of $y = \cos 2\theta$. What is the period?

PART 2 Change of Amplitude and Period

Objective: Sketch graphs in which the amplitude and period are changed.

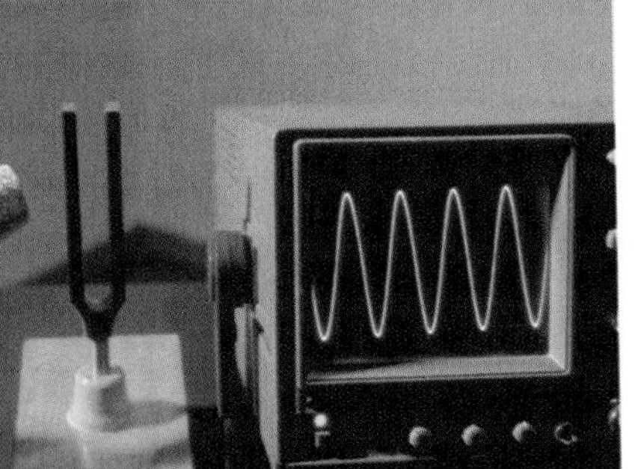

Piano tuners compare the wave produced by a tuning fork to the wave produced by striking a piano key. If they coincide, the string is in tune; if not, the piano string is adjusted.

Changing the constants A and B in $y = A \sin B\theta$ causes both a vertical and a horizontal stretching or shrinking of the graph.

EXAMPLE 3 Sketch a graph of $y = 3 \sin 2\theta$. What are the amplitude and period?

The graph is a vertical stretching and a horizontal shrinking of the graph of $y = \sin \theta$. The function $y = 3 \sin 2\theta$ is equivalent to

$$\frac{y}{3} = \sin \frac{\theta}{\frac{1}{2}}$$

The amplitude is 3.
The period is π.

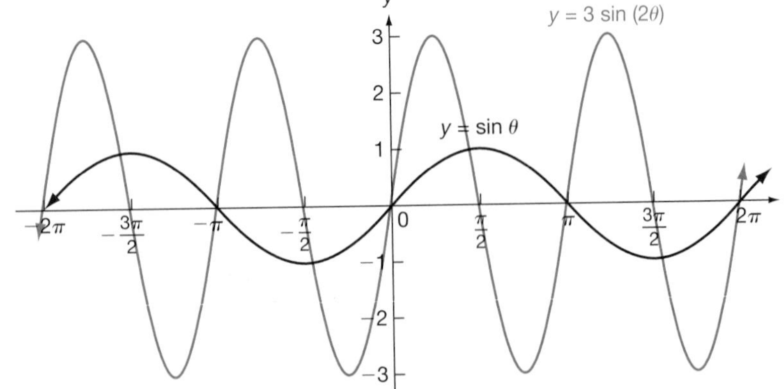

Try This

c. Sketch a graph of $y = 3 \cos 2\theta$. What are the amplitude and the period?

17-7 Exercises

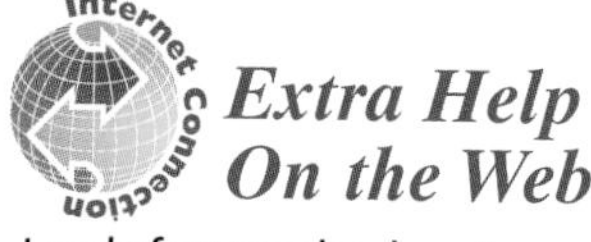

Extra Help On the Web

Look for worked-out examples at the Prentice Hall Web site.
www.phschool.com

A

Sketch graphs of these functions. Determine the amplitude.

1. $y = \frac{1}{2} \sin \theta$ **2.** $y = \frac{1}{2} \cos \theta$ **3.** $y = 3 \sin \theta$

4. $y = 3 \cos \theta$ **5.** $y = -\frac{1}{3} \sin \theta$ **6.** $y = -\frac{1}{3} \cos \theta$

7. $y = 4 \sin \theta$ **8.** $y = 4 \cos \theta$ **9.** $y = -2 \sin \theta$

Sketch graphs of these functions. Determine the period.

10. $y = \sin 3\theta$ **11.** $y = \cos 3\theta$ **12.** $y = \sin \frac{1}{2}\theta$

13. $y = \cos \frac{1}{2}\theta$ **14.** $y = \sin \left(-\frac{1}{3}\theta\right)$ **15.** $y = \cos \left(-\frac{1}{3}\theta\right)$

16. $y = \sin (-2\theta)$ **17.** $y = \cos (-2\theta)$ **18.** $y = \sin (-3\theta)$

Sketch graphs of these functions. Determine the amplitude and the period.

19. $y = 2 \sin 2\theta$ **20.** $y = 2 \cos 2\theta$ **21.** $y = \frac{1}{2} \sin 2\theta$

22. $y = \frac{1}{2} \cos 2\theta$ **23.** $y = -2 \sin \frac{1}{2}\theta$ **24.** $y = -2 \cos \frac{1}{2}\theta$

25. $y = \frac{1}{2} \sin (-2\theta)$ **26.** $y = \frac{1}{2} \cos (-2\theta)$ **27.** $y = -\frac{1}{2} \sin (-2\theta)$

B

Sketch graphs of these functions.

28. $y = \cos (2\theta - \pi)$ **29.** $y = \sin (2\theta + \pi)$ **30.** $y = 2 + \sin \theta$

31. ***Critical Thinking*** Write a function to quadruple the amplitude of $\sin \theta$, stretch its graph horizontally by a factor of 3, and reflect the graph across the x-axis.

Challenge

Sketch graphs of these functions. Determine the amplitude and period.

32. $y = 2 + 2 \sin (2\theta + \pi)$ **33.** $y = -3 + \frac{1}{2} \sin \left(\frac{1}{2}\theta - \pi\right)$

Mixed Review

Let $P(x) = x^3 + 6x^2 + 11x + 6$.

34. Determine the number of positive and negative real roots of $P(x)$. *11-5*

35. Determine whether the following are factors of $P(x)$: $(x - 1)$, $(x + 1)$, $(x - 2)$, $(x + 2)$, $(x - 3)$. *11-1, 11-2*

36. Factor $P(x)$, list the x-intercepts, and then graph $P(x)$. *11-6*

17-8 Algebraic Manipulations

What You'll Learn

1. To compute and simplify trigonometric expressions
2. To solve equations involving trigonometric expressions

. . . And Why

To solve algebraic problems using a variety of concepts and strategies

Algebraic expressions represent numbers; so do trigonometric expressions such as $\sin 2\theta$ or $\tan(x - \pi)$. We can work with trigonometric expressions much the same way we work with purely algebraic expressions.

PART 1 Computing and Simplifying

Objective: Compute and simplify trigonometric expressions.

EXAMPLE 1 Multiply and simplify $\cos y(\tan y - \sec y)$.

$$\begin{aligned} \cos y(\tan y - \sec y) &= \cos y \tan y - \cos y \sec y && \text{Multiplying} \\ &= \cos y \frac{\sin y}{\cos y} - \cos y \frac{1}{\cos y} && \text{Simplifying} \\ &= \sin y - 1 \end{aligned}$$

In Example 1, we used certain identities to accomplish simplification. There is no general rule for doing this, but it is often helpful to put everything in terms of sines and cosines, as we did here.

Reading Math

In Example 1, $\cos y(\tan y - \sec y)$ is **not** read as "cosine of y times the quantity tangent y − secant y." It **is** read as "cosine y times the quantity tangent y − secant y." The little word "of" can make a big difference!

EXAMPLE 2 Factor and simplify $\sin^2 x \cos^2 x + \cos^4 x$.

$$\begin{aligned} \sin^2 x \cos^2 x + \cos^4 x &= \cos^2 x(\sin^2 x + \cos^2 x) && \text{Factoring} \\ &= \cos^2 x(1) && \text{Pythagorean identity} \\ &= \cos^2 x \end{aligned}$$

EXAMPLE 3 Simplify $\sin\left(\frac{\pi}{2} - x\right)(\sec x - \cos x)$.

$$\begin{aligned} \sin\left(\frac{\pi}{2} - x\right)(\sec x - \cos x) &= \cos x(\sec x - \cos x) && \sin\left(\tfrac{\pi}{2} - x\right) \text{ is } \cos x \\ &= \cos x\left(\frac{1}{\cos x} - \cos x\right) && \sec x \text{ is } \tfrac{1}{\cos x} \\ &= \frac{\cos x}{\cos x} - \cos^2 x && \text{Multiplying} \\ &= 1 - \cos^2 x && \text{Dividing} \\ &= \sin^2 x && \text{Pythagorean identity} \end{aligned}$$

Try This

a. Multiply and simplify $\sin x(\cot x + \csc x)$.

b. Factor $\sin^3 \theta + \sin \theta \cos^2 \theta$.

c. Simplify $\dfrac{1 - \cos^2 x}{\cos\left(\frac{\pi}{2} - x\right)}$.

PART 2 Solving Equations

Objective: Solve equations involving trigonometric expressions.

EXAMPLE 4 Solve for $\tan x$: $\tan^2 x + \tan x = 56$.

$\tan^2 x + \tan x - 56 = 0$ Rewriting as a quadratic equation
$(\tan x + 8)(\tan x - 7) = 0$ Factoring
$\tan x + 8 = 0$ or $\tan x - 7 = 0$
$\tan x = -8$ or $\tan x = 7$

EXAMPLE 5 Solve for $\sec x$: $\sec^2 x - \frac{3}{4}\sec x = \frac{1}{2}$.

$\sec^2 x - \frac{3}{4}\sec x - \frac{1}{2} = 0$

We now use the quadratic formula and obtain

$$\sec x = \frac{\frac{3}{4} \pm \sqrt{\frac{9}{16} - 4 \cdot 1 \cdot \left(-\frac{1}{2}\right)}}{2} = \frac{\frac{3}{4} \pm \sqrt{\frac{41}{16}}}{2} = \frac{\frac{3}{4} \pm \frac{\sqrt{41}}{4}}{2} = \frac{3 \pm \sqrt{41}}{8}$$

Since $\frac{3 - \sqrt{41}}{8} \approx -0.43$, which is not within the range of the secant function, the solution is $\frac{3 + \sqrt{41}}{8}$.

Try This

d. Solve for $\cot x$ in $\cot^2 x + \cot x = 12$.

Writing Math

In Example 1 on page 772, the problem may seem to need more parentheses. However, by tradition we do not use them unless absolutely necessary. Thus, the problem does not need to be written as $(\cos y)\,(\tan y - \sec y)$. It is understood that parentheses are not needed around $\cos y$ to keep the expression from being interpreted as $\cos\,(y(\tan y - \sec y))$.

17-8 Exercises

Extra Help On the Web

Look for worked-out examples at the Prentice Hall Web site.
www.phschool.com

A

Multiply and simplify.

1. $(\sin x - \cos x)(\sin x + \cos x)$
2. $(\tan \theta - \cot \theta)(\tan \theta + \cot \theta)$
3. $\tan x\,(\cos x - \csc x)$
4. $\cot x\,(\sin x + \sec x)$
5. $\cos \theta \sin \theta(\sec \theta + \csc \theta)$
6. $\tan y \sin y\,(\cot y - \csc y)$
7. $(\sin x + \cos x)(\csc x - \sec x)$
8. $(\sin x + \cos x)(\sec x + \csc x)$
9. $(\sin y - \cos y)^2$
10. $(\sin \theta + \cos \theta)^2$
11. $(1 + \tan \theta)^2$
12. $(1 + \cot x)^2$

Factor and simplify.

13. $\sin x \cos x + \cos^2 x$
14. $\sec x \csc x - \csc^2 x$
15. $\sin^2 y - \cos^2 y$
16. $\tan^2 y - \cot^2 y$

17. $\sin^2\left(\frac{\pi}{2} - x\right)(\sec^2 x - \tan^2 x)$

18. $\cot\theta - \cos(\pi - \theta)$

19. $\sin^4\theta - \cos^4\theta$

20. $\tan^4 x - \sec^4 x$

21. $3\cot^2 y + 6\cot y + 3$

22. $4\sin^2 y + 8\sin y + 4$

23. $\csc^4\theta + 4\csc^2\theta - 5$

24. $\tan^4 x - 2\tan^2 x - 3$

25. $\dfrac{\sin^2 x\cos x}{\cos^2 x\sin x}$

26. $\dfrac{\cos^2 x\sin x}{\sin^2 x\cos x}$

27. $\dfrac{4\sin\theta\cos^3\theta}{18\sin^2\theta\cos\theta}$

28. $\dfrac{30\sin^3 x\cos x}{6\cos^2 x\sin x}$

29. $\dfrac{\cos^2 x - 2\cos x + 1}{\cos x - 1}$

30. $\dfrac{\sin^2 x + 2\sin x + 1}{\sin x + 1}$

31. $\dfrac{\cos^2 x - 1}{\cos x - 1}$

32. $\dfrac{\sin^2\theta - 1}{\sin\theta + 1}$

Solve for the indicated trigonometric expression.

33. $\tan^2 x + 4\tan x = 21$, for $\tan x$

34. $\sec^2\theta - 7\sec\theta = -10$, for $\sec\theta$

35. $8\sin^2\theta - 2\sin\theta = 3$, for $\sin\theta$

36. $6\cos^2 x + 17\cos x = -5$, for $\cos x$

37. $\tan^2\theta - 6\tan\theta = 4$, for $\tan\theta$

38. $\csc^2\theta + 3\csc\theta - 10 = 0$, for $\csc\theta$

39. $\sin^2\theta + \cos\left(\theta + \frac{\pi}{2}\right) = 6$, for $\sin\theta$

40. $\cot^2 x + 9\cot x - 10 = 0$, for $\cot x$

41. $2\csc^2 x - 3\csc x - 4 = 0$, for $\csc x$

42. $2\cos^2\left(x - \frac{\pi}{2}\right) - 3\cos\left(x - \frac{\pi}{2}\right) - 2 = 0$, for $\sin x$

B

Show that the following identities are true.

43. $\csc\theta - \cos\theta\cot\theta \equiv \sin\theta$

44. $\sec\theta - \sin\theta\tan\theta \equiv \cos\theta$

45. $\dfrac{1 - \sin\theta}{\cos\theta} \equiv \dfrac{\cos\theta}{1 + \sin\theta}$

46. $\dfrac{1 - \cos\theta}{\sin\theta} \equiv \dfrac{\sin\theta}{1 + \cos\theta}$

47. ***Critical Thinking*** Does $\sin(A + B) = \sin A + \sin B$? If not, give a counterexample.

Challenge

Simplify.

48. $\sqrt{\sin^2 x\cos x} \cdot \sqrt{\cos x}$

49. $(2 - \sqrt{\tan y})(\sqrt{\tan y} + 2)$

50. $\sqrt{\dfrac{\sin x}{\cos x}}$

51. $\sqrt{\dfrac{1 + \sin x}{1 - \sin x}}$

Mixed Review

Factor. 52. $x^3 + 12x^2 + 47x + 60$ 53. $x^4 + 8x^3 + 24x^2 + 32x + 16$ *11-2*

Convert to radian measure. 54. 45° 55. 72° 56. −270° 57. 210° *17-3*

Convert to degree measure. 58. $\frac{2\pi}{3}$ 59. $\frac{7\pi}{4}$ 60. $-\frac{5\pi}{6}$ 61. $\frac{\pi}{6}$ *17-3*

62. The area of a circle varies directly as the square of the radius. A circle with radius 6.4 cm has area 128.6 cm^2. What is the area of a circle with radius 9.2 cm? *8-7*

Application

Making a Business Plan

In the problems presented so far, the data have been given and the questions have been easily identified. In real-world situations you need to clarify the assumptions and what you are being asked to do, and collect the data from a variety of sources. You may need to solve many subproblems before arriving at the answer. These are *situational problems.*

To be competitive, a video store owner needs to develop a good "business plan." See the situational problem.

Situational Problem

You have been asked to develop a rental plan for a new video store. The new store owner has invested $90,000 to lease a store and buy videotapes and furniture for the store. The store owner wants to spend an additional $300 per month for new and replacement videotapes and wants $2000 per month for personal expenses. Determine a rental plan that will allow the store owner to meet the necessary costs, be competitive, and have a return on the initial investment in about 2 years.

Possible Assumptions

1. The utilities and miscellaneous expenses for the store will cost about $600 per month after an initial $1000 fee.
2. The store owner can purchase videotapes for $15 each.
3. Additional furniture and equipment can be purchased for $3500.
4. No one else will be hired to work in the store.
5. A nearby video store, which charges $3.50 per day to rent a videotape, rents about 500 videos each weekend and 125 videos each weekday.
6. Another store, with a $40-per-year membership club, rents tapes for $2.50 to members and $4.00 to nonmembers. About 40% of the customers join the club. They rent about 525 videos each weekend and 110 videos each weekday.

Possible Subproblems

1. What will the total expenses be for the first year?
2. What will the total expenses be for subsequent years?
3. How many tapes can the store owner expect to rent each month?
4. Would it be advisable to have a special video club with reduced prices for members?

17 Chapter Wrap Up

Key Terms

adjacent (p. 728)
amplitude (p. 757)
angle θ (theta) (p. 728)
angular speed: ω (omega) (p. 744)
asymptote (p. 758)
cofunctions (p. 744)
cosecant (csc) function (p. 730)
cosine (cos) function (p. 728)
cotangent (cot) function (p. 730)
hypotenuse (p. 728)
identities (pp. 744, 763–766)
identity symbol: $\equiv$ (p. 744)
initial side (p. 734)
interpolation (p. 751)
linear speed (p. 745)
opposite (p. 728)
period (p. 755)
periodic function (p. 755)
Pythagorean identities (p. 764)
quotient identities (p. 763)
radian (p. 741)
reference angle (p. 737)
secant (sec) function (p. 730)
sine (sin) function (p. 728)
tangent (tan) function (p. 728)
terminal side (p. 734)
trigonometric functions (p. 728)
trigonometry (p. 728)
unit circle (p. 741)

17-1

$$\sin\theta = \frac{\text{length of the side opposite }\theta}{\text{length of the hypotenuse}} = \frac{1}{\csc\theta}$$

$$\cos\theta = \frac{\text{length of the side adjacent }\theta}{\text{length of the hypotenuse}} = \frac{1}{\sec\theta}$$

$$\tan\theta = \frac{\text{length of the side opposite }\theta}{\text{length of the side adjacent }\theta} = \frac{1}{\cot\theta}$$

1. In triangle ABC, $\angle C$ is a right angle, $b = 10$ cm, and $m\angle A = 60°$. If sides a, b, and c are opposite angles A, B, and C respectively, what is the length of side c?

2. If $\tan\theta = \frac{\sqrt{3}}{3}$, find the other five trigonometric function values.

17-2

An angle between 0° and 90° has its **terminal side** in the first quadrant. An angle between 90° and 180° has its terminal side in the second quadrant. An angle between 0° and −90° has its terminal side in the fourth quadrant, and so on.

In which quadrant does the terminal side of each angle lie?

3. 14° **4.** 201° **5.** 116° **6.** −131°

A right triangle has two of its vertices at the origin and on the positive x-axis. If the third point $R\ (x, y)$, is in the first quadrant and on a circle with radius r and center at the origin, then we can define these functions.

$$\sin\theta = \tfrac{y}{r} \qquad \cos\theta = \tfrac{x}{r} \qquad \tan\theta = \tfrac{y}{x}$$

For angles in the second, third, and fourth quadrants use a **reference angle,** the acute angle formed by the terminal side and the x-axis.

7. Find the six trigonometric function values for the angle θ shown at the right.

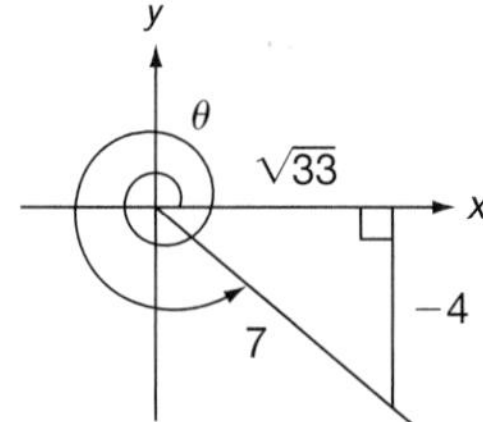

Find the reference angles for the following angles of rotation.

8. 330° **9.** −510° **10.** 220°

If the terminal side of an angle falls on one of the axes, then in some cases trigonometric functions will not be defined because a denominator is 0. Pay special attention to angles that are multiples of 90.

Find each of the following function values, or indicate if it is undefined.

11. tan 270° **12.** tan −315° **13.** sin 495°

17-3

To convert between degrees and **radians** we can use the notion of multiplying by one and the equation $\frac{180 \text{ degrees}}{\pi \text{ radians}} = 1$.

Convert to radian measure. Give answers in terms of π.

14. 45° **15.** 150° **16.** 270° **17.** −60°

Convert to degree measure.

18. $\frac{7\pi}{6}$ **19.** $-\frac{\pi}{3}$ **20.** 4π

The **cofunction identities** are

$$\sin\theta \equiv \cos(90 - \theta) \qquad \cos\theta \equiv \sin(90 - \theta)$$
$$\tan\theta \equiv \cot(90 - \theta) \qquad \cot\theta \equiv \tan(90 - \theta)$$
$$\sec\theta \equiv \csc(90 - \theta) \qquad \csc\theta \equiv \sec(90 - \theta)$$

Find the function value using cofunctions.

21. csc 45° **22.** cot 30° **23.** sin 90°

The following equations can be helpful in problem solving.

$\theta = \frac{s}{r}$ where θ is the **radian measure of a rotation** and s is the distance traveled by a point at a radius r from the center of rotation

$\omega = \frac{\theta}{t}$ where ω is **angular speed,** θ is radian measure of a rotation, and t is time

$v = r\omega$ where v is **linear speed,** r is the distance from the center of rotation, and ω is the angular speed in radians per unit of time

24. A wheel has a 60-cm radius. The speed of a point on its rim is 30 cm/s. What is its angular speed?

Internet Activity
On the Web

Look for extension problems for this chapter at the Prentice Hall Web site.
www.phschool.com

17-4

Table 5 or a calculator may be used to find trigonometric function values.

Find the following. Interpolate, if necessary.

25. sin 8°20′ **26.** cos 391°30′ **27.** tan 27°14′ **28.** sin 42°18′

Occasionally you will have to use a table or calculator to find the measure of an angle.

Express θ in degrees and minutes, between 0° and 90°.

29. $\cos\theta = 0.9094$ **30.** $\tan\theta = 1.103$

17-5

To sketch a graph of a trigonometric function, look at special angles in the first two quadrants, using radian measure for the angles.

31. Sketch a graph of the secant function.

17-6

It is useful to learn certain **identities.**

Quotient Identities

$$\tan\theta \equiv \frac{\sin\theta}{\cos\theta}, \ \cos\theta \neq 0$$

$$\cot\theta \equiv \frac{\cos\theta}{\sin\theta}, \ \sin\theta \neq 0$$

Pythagorean Identities

$$\sin^2\theta + \cos^2\theta \equiv 1$$
$$1 + \cot^2\theta \equiv \csc^2\theta$$
$$1 + \tan^2\theta \equiv \sec^2\theta$$

Cofunction Identities

$$\sin\left(\theta + \frac{\pi}{2}\right) \equiv \cos\theta \qquad \cos\left(\theta + \frac{\pi}{2}\right) \equiv -\sin\theta$$

$$\sin\left(\theta - \frac{\pi}{2}\right) \equiv -\cos\theta \qquad \cos\left(\theta - \frac{\pi}{2}\right) \equiv \sin\theta$$

$$\sin\left(\frac{\pi}{2} - \theta\right) \equiv \cos\theta \qquad \cos\left(\frac{\pi}{2} - \theta\right) \equiv \sin\theta$$

Check each identity by using $\theta = \frac{\pi}{4}$.

32. $\tan\theta \equiv \frac{\sin\theta}{\cos\theta}$

33. $\sin\left(\frac{\pi}{2} - \theta\right) \equiv \cos\theta$

The quotient identities, Pythagorean identities, and cofunction identities given above can be used to derive other identities.

Use the Pythagorean identities to derive an identity for

34. $\cot\theta$ in terms of $\csc\theta$.

35. $\csc\theta$ in terms of $\cos\theta$.

36. Use the cofunction identities to derive an identity for $\cot\left(\theta - \frac{\pi}{2}\right)$.

Use the values given in Exercises 37–42 to find the six trigonometric function values of the **complement** of 75°.

37. $\sin 75° = 0.9659$

38. $\cos 75° = 0.2588$

39. $\tan 75° = 3.732$

40. $\cot 75° = 0.2679$

41. $\sec 75° = 3.864$

42. $\csc 75° = 1.035$

17-7

Changing the constant A in $y = A\sin\theta$ causes a vertical stretching or shrinking of the graph and thus a change in the amplitude. Changing the constant B in $y = \sin B\theta$ causes a horizontal stretching or shrinking of the graph and thus a change in the period.

43. Sketch a graph of $y = 3\cos\theta$. What is the amplitude of the function?

44. Sketch a graph of $y = \sin 2\theta$. What is the period of the function?

17-8

Trigonometric expressions can be changed or simplified by using **algebraic manipulations** and trigonometric identities.

45. Simplify $\cos\theta\,(\tan\theta + \cot\theta)$.

46. Solve $3\tan^2\theta - 2\tan\theta - 2 = 0$ for $\tan\theta$.

17 Chapter Assessment

1. In triangle ABC, $\angle C$ is a right angle, $b = 10$ cm, and $m\angle A = 45$. What is the length of side c?

2. If $\sin\theta = \frac{\sqrt{5}}{5}$, find the other five trigonometric function values.

3. Find the six trigonometric function values for the angle θ shown.

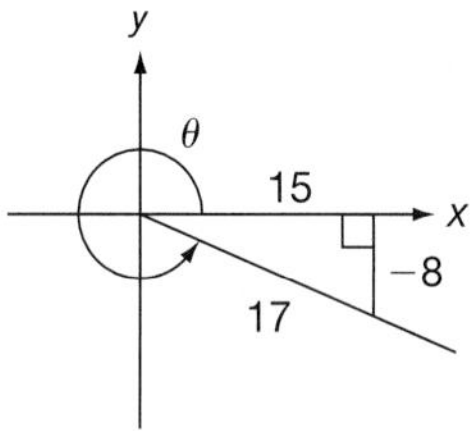

y
θ
15
x
−8
17

Find each of the following function values or indicate if it is undefined.

4. $\sin(-135°)$

5. $\tan 540°$

6. Convert $-225°$ to radian measure, in terms of π.

7. Convert $-\frac{3\pi}{2}$ to degree measure.

8. A wheel with a 150-cm diameter is rotating at a rate of 15 radians/sec. Find the speed of a point on its rim in cm/sec.

Use Table 5 and interpolation to find the following.

9. $\cos 32°24'$

10. $\tan 54°18'$

Find θ in degrees and minutes between 0° and 90°.

11. $\sin\theta = 0.6259$

12. $\tan\theta = 1.331$

13. Use the given function values to find the six function values of the complement of 54°.

$\sin 54° = 0.8090$, $\cos 54° = 0.5878$, $\tan 54° = 1.376$

14. Sketch a graph of $y = 4\sin\theta$. What is the amplitude of the function?

15. Sketch a graph of $y = \sin\frac{1}{2}\theta$. What is the period of the function?

16. Simplify $\dfrac{\csc\theta(\sin^2\theta + \cos^2\theta\tan\theta)}{\sin\theta + \cos\theta}$.

17. Solve $6\sec^2\theta - 5\sec\theta - 2 = 0$ for $\sec\theta$.

18. Use the Pythagorean identities to derive an identity for $\sec\theta$ in terms of $\sin\theta$.

19. Use the cofunction identities to derive an identity for $\cot\left(\frac{\pi}{2} - \theta\right)$.

Challenge

20. Solve for θ between 0° and 360°.

$2\sin^2\theta - 3\sin\theta + 1 = 0$

What You'll Learn in Chapter 18

- How to use cosine, sine, and tangent identities to simplify trigonometric expressions
- How to use the double-angle and half-angle identities to find function values
- How to prove trigonometric identities
- How to find values and principal values of the inverses of sine, cosine, and tangent
- How to use trigonometry to solve problems involving triangles
- How to express a complex number in either rectangular or trigonometric notation
- How to multiply and divide complex numbers, and find powers and roots of complex numbers
- How to solve problems by applying trigonometric equations

CHAPTER

Skills & Concepts You Need for Chapter 18

7-1 Simplify.

1. $\sqrt{(-81)^2}$

2. $\sqrt{(9c)^2}$

7-4 Simplify by rationalizing the denominators.

3. $\dfrac{\sqrt[3]{4m}}{\sqrt[3]{5n}}$

4. $\dfrac{5\sqrt{5} - 2\sqrt{3}}{2\sqrt{3} - 3\sqrt{5}}$

7-8 Find the absolute value of each complex number.

5. $|-a + bi|$

6. $|5 - 12i|$

12-1 Find $f^{-1}(x)$.

7. $f(x) = 3x - 2$

8. $f(x) = 2 + \sqrt{x + 3}$

17-6 Find an identity for $\tan \theta$ in terms of each function.

9. $\sin \theta$

10. $\cos \theta$

11. $\csc \theta$

12. $\cot \theta$

13. $\sec \theta$

Trigonometric Identities and Equations

This lighthouse on the rocky shore of Portsmouth Harbor, Newcastle, New Hampshire, was built in 1877. Many lighthouses such as this are historic landmarks, and some are powered by an automatic light system. In Lesson 18-6 you will learn how to calculate distances across the water from a lighthouse.

 18-1 Sum and Difference Identities

What You'll Learn

1. To simplify trigonometric expressions by using sum and difference identities for cosine
2. To simplify trigonometric expressions by using sum and difference identities for sine and tangent

. . . And Why

To solve trigonometric equations

PART 1 Cosines of Sums or Differences

Objective: Use the sum and difference identities for cosine to simplify trigonometric expressions.

We will now consider identities involving sums or differences of angles or rotations.

A basic identity shows that the cosine of the difference of two angles is related to the cosines and sines of the angles themselves. This identity can be used to simplify expressions.

$$\cos(\alpha - \beta) \equiv \cos\alpha\cos\beta + \sin\alpha\sin\beta$$

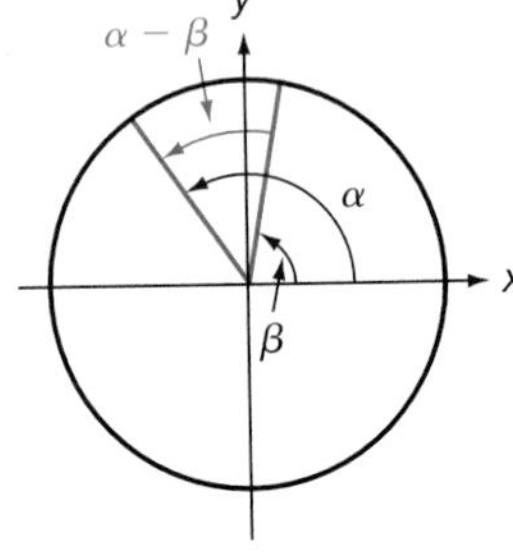

EXAMPLE 1 Simplify $\cos\left(\frac{3\pi}{4} - \frac{\pi}{3}\right)$.

$$\cos\left(\frac{3\pi}{4} - \frac{\pi}{3}\right) = \cos\frac{3\pi}{4} \cdot \cos\frac{\pi}{3} + \sin\frac{3\pi}{4} \cdot \sin\frac{\pi}{3}$$ Applying the cosine identity

$$= -\frac{\sqrt{2}}{2} \cdot \frac{1}{2} + \frac{\sqrt{2}}{2} \cdot \frac{\sqrt{3}}{2}$$ Evaluating each factor

$$= \frac{\sqrt{2}}{4}(-1 + \sqrt{3}), \text{ or } \frac{\sqrt{2}}{4}(\sqrt{3} - 1), \text{ or } \frac{\sqrt{6} - \sqrt{2}}{4}$$

Reading Math

The variables in $\cos(\alpha - \beta)$ are the lowercase Greek letters *alpha* and *beta*. Here, α and β represent measures in radians or degrees.

Try This

a. Simplify $\cos\left(\frac{\pi}{2} - \frac{\pi}{6}\right)$.

We can use known values of the functions to find other values.

EXAMPLE 2 Find $\cos 15°$.

$$\cos 15° = \cos(45° - 30°)$$ Writing 15° in terms of angles with known function values

$$= \cos 45° \cos 30° + \sin 45° \sin 30°$$

$$= \frac{\sqrt{2}}{2} \cdot \frac{\sqrt{3}}{2} + \frac{\sqrt{2}}{2} \cdot \frac{1}{2}$$

$$= \frac{\sqrt{2}}{4}(\sqrt{3} + 1), \text{ or } \frac{\sqrt{6} + \sqrt{2}}{4}$$

Try This

b. Find $\cos 105°$ by evaluating $\cos(150° - 45°)$.

Proof of the Difference Identity for Cosine

We have applied the identity $\cos(\alpha - \beta) \equiv \cos\alpha\cos\beta + \sin\alpha\sin\beta$. Let us see how this identity is developed.

Consider the unit circle where angles α and β have coordinates as shown.

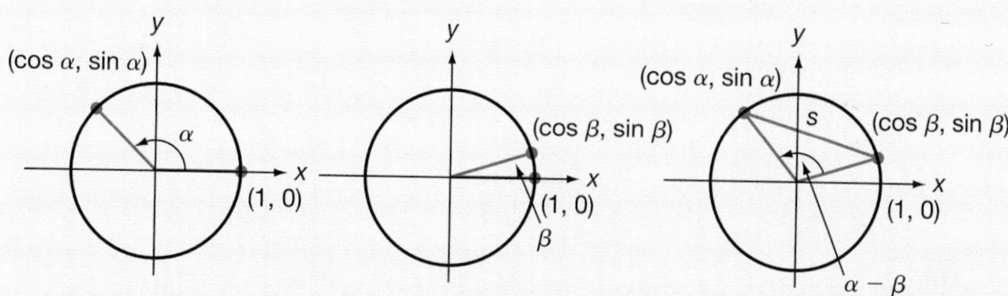

The figure on the right shows these angles on the same coordinate axes. Notice that the size of the angle between them is $\alpha - \beta$. We use the distance formula to write an expression for s, the length of the segment between $(\cos\alpha, \sin\alpha)$ and $(\cos\beta, \sin\beta)$.

$$
\begin{aligned}
s^2 &= (\cos\alpha - \cos\beta)^2 + (\sin\alpha - \sin\beta)^2 \\
&= (\cos^2\alpha - 2\cos\alpha\cos\beta + \cos^2\beta) + (\sin^2\alpha - 2\sin\alpha\sin\beta + \sin^2\beta) \\
&= (\cos^2\alpha + \sin^2\alpha) + (\cos^2\beta + \sin^2\beta) - 2\cos\alpha\cos\beta - 2\sin\alpha\cos\beta \\
&= 1 + 1 - 2\cos\alpha\cos\beta - 2\sin\alpha\sin\beta \\
&= 2 - 2(\cos\alpha\cos\beta + \sin\alpha\sin\beta)
\end{aligned}
$$

Now imagine that the unit circle above is rotated so that $(\cos\beta, \sin\beta)$ is at $(1, 0)$. The length s has not changed.

$$
\begin{aligned}
s^2 &= [\cos(\alpha - \beta) - 1]^2 + [\sin(\alpha - \beta) - 0]^2 \\
&= [\cos^2(\alpha - \beta) - 2\cos(\alpha - \beta) + 1] + \sin^2(\alpha - \beta) \\
&= [\cos^2(\alpha - \beta) + \sin^2(\alpha - \beta)] + 1 - 2\cos(\alpha - B) \\
&= 2 - 2\cos(\alpha - \beta)
\end{aligned}
$$

Equating our two expressions for s^2, we obtain

$$2 - 2\cos(\alpha - \beta) = 2 - 2(\cos\alpha\cos\beta + \sin\alpha\sin\beta).$$

This simplifies to the identity

$$\cos(\alpha - \beta) \equiv \cos\alpha\cos\beta + \sin\alpha\sin\beta.$$

Next let us consider $\cos(\alpha + \beta)$. This is equal to $\cos[\alpha - (-\beta)]$, and by the cosine of a difference identity, we have the following.

$$\cos(\alpha + \beta) \equiv \cos\alpha\cos(-\beta) + \sin\alpha\sin(-\beta)$$

But $\cos(-\beta) \equiv \cos\beta$ and $\sin(-\beta) \equiv -\sin\beta$, so the identity becomes

$$\boldsymbol{\cos(\alpha + \beta) \equiv \cos\alpha\cos\beta - \sin\alpha\sin\beta.}$$

EXAMPLE 3 Find cos 105°.

$$\begin{aligned}\cos 105° &= \cos(60° + 45°)\\ &= \cos 60° \cos 45° - \sin 60° \sin 45°\\ &= \frac{1}{2} \cdot \frac{\sqrt{2}}{2} - \frac{\sqrt{3}}{2} \cdot \frac{\sqrt{2}}{2}\\ &= \frac{\sqrt{2} - \sqrt{6}}{4}\end{aligned}$$

Writing 105° in terms of angles with known function values

Try This

c. Find cos 75° by evaluating cos (30° + 45°).

PART 2 Other Identities

Objective: Use sum and difference identities for sin and tan to simplify trigonometric expressions.

To develop an identity for the sine of a sum $\alpha + \beta$, we recall the following.

$$\sin\theta \equiv \cos\left(\frac{\pi}{2} - \theta\right)$$

In this identity we shall substitute $\alpha + \beta$ for θ.

$$\sin(\alpha + \beta) \equiv \cos\left[\frac{\pi}{2} - (\alpha + \beta)\right]$$

We can now use the identity for the cosine of a difference.

$$\begin{aligned}\sin(\alpha + \beta) &\equiv \cos\left[\frac{\pi}{2} - (\alpha + \beta)\right]\\ &\equiv \cos\left[\left(\frac{\pi}{2} - \alpha\right) - \beta\right]\\ &\equiv \cos\left(\frac{\pi}{2} - \alpha\right)\cos\beta + \sin\left(\frac{\pi}{2} - \alpha\right)\sin\beta\\ &\equiv \sin\alpha\cos\beta + \cos\alpha\sin\beta\end{aligned}$$

Thus, $\boldsymbol{\sin(\alpha + \beta) \equiv \sin\alpha\cos\beta + \cos\alpha\sin\beta}$.

Quick Review

$\frac{\pi}{4} = 45°$

$\frac{\pi}{3} = 60°$

EXAMPLE 4 Simplify $\sin\left(\frac{5\pi}{4} + \frac{\pi}{3}\right)$.

$$\begin{aligned}\sin\left(\frac{5\pi}{4} + \frac{\pi}{3}\right) &= \sin\frac{5\pi}{4}\cos\frac{\pi}{3} + \cos\frac{5\pi}{4}\sin\frac{\pi}{3}\\ &= -\frac{\sqrt{2}}{2} \cdot \frac{1}{2} + \left(-\frac{\sqrt{2}}{2}\right)\frac{\sqrt{3}}{2}\\ &= \frac{-\sqrt{2}}{4} - \frac{\sqrt{6}}{4}\\ &= \frac{-\sqrt{2} - \sqrt{6}}{4}\end{aligned}$$

Try This

d. Simplify $\sin\left(\frac{\pi}{4} + \frac{\pi}{3}\right)$.

To find an identity for the sine of a difference, we can use the identity just derived, substituting $-\beta$ for β.

$$\mathbf{\sin(\alpha - \beta) \equiv \sin\alpha\cos\beta - \cos\alpha\sin\beta}$$

An identity for the tangent of a sum can be derived as follows, using identities already established.

$$\tan(\alpha + \beta) \equiv \frac{\sin(\alpha + \beta)}{\cos(\alpha + \beta)}$$

$$\equiv \frac{\sin\alpha\cos\beta + \cos\alpha\sin\beta}{\cos\alpha\cos\beta - \sin\alpha\sin\beta} \cdot \frac{\frac{1}{\cos\alpha\cos\beta}}{\frac{1}{\cos\alpha\cos\beta}}$$

$$\equiv \frac{\frac{\sin\alpha\cos\beta}{\cos\alpha\cos\beta} + \frac{\cos\alpha\sin\beta}{\cos\alpha\cos\beta}}{\frac{\cos\alpha\cos\beta}{\cos\alpha\cos\beta} - \frac{\sin\alpha\sin\beta}{\cos\alpha\cos\beta}}$$

$$\equiv \frac{\frac{\sin\alpha}{\cos\alpha} + \frac{\sin\beta}{\cos\beta}}{1 - \frac{\sin\alpha\sin\beta}{\cos\alpha\cos\beta}}$$

$$\mathbf{\tan(\alpha + \beta) \equiv \frac{\tan\alpha + \tan\beta}{1 - \tan\alpha\tan\beta}}$$

Similarly, an identity for the tangent of a difference can be established. The following theorem summarizes the sum and difference formulas. These should be memorized.

Theorem 18-1

$$\cos(\alpha - \beta) \equiv \cos\alpha\cos\beta + \sin\alpha\sin\beta$$
$$\cos(\alpha + \beta) \equiv \cos\alpha\cos\beta - \sin\alpha\sin\beta$$
$$\sin(\alpha - \beta) \equiv \sin\alpha\cos\beta - \cos\alpha\sin\beta$$
$$\sin(\alpha + \beta) \equiv \sin\alpha\cos\beta + \cos\alpha\sin\beta$$
$$\tan(\alpha - \beta) \equiv \frac{\tan\alpha - \tan\beta}{1 + \tan\alpha\tan\beta}$$
$$\tan(\alpha + \beta) \equiv \frac{\tan\alpha + \tan\beta}{1 - \tan\alpha\tan\beta}$$

The identities involving sines and tangents can be used in the same way as those involving cosines in the earlier examples. Simply write the angle as a sum or difference of angles with known function values.

Writing Math

When the values of a function are expressed in simplest radical form, that value is called an exact number. To check if an equation is true, use a calculator or a table.

EXAMPLE 5 Find tan 15°.

$$\tan 15^\circ = \tan(45^\circ - 30^\circ)$$
$$= \frac{\tan 45^\circ - \tan 30^\circ}{1 + \tan 45^\circ \tan 30^\circ}$$
$$= \frac{1 - \frac{\sqrt{3}}{3}}{1 + \frac{\sqrt{3}}{3}} = \frac{3 - \sqrt{3}}{3 + \sqrt{3}} = 2 - \sqrt{3}$$

Try This

e. Find tan 105° by evaluating $\tan(45^\circ + 60^\circ)$.

Extra Help On the Web

Look for worked-out examples at the Prentice Hall Web site.
www.phschool.com

18-1 Exercises

A

Use the cosine sum and difference identities to simplify the following.

1. $\cos(A - B)$ **2.** $\cos(A + B)$
3. $\cos(45^\circ - 30^\circ)$ **4.** $\cos(45^\circ + 30^\circ)$
5. $\cos(60^\circ + 45^\circ)$ **6.** $\cos(60^\circ - 45^\circ)$
7. $\cos\left(\frac{\pi}{2} + \frac{\pi}{3}\right)$ **8.** $\cos\left(\frac{3\pi}{2} - \frac{\pi}{3}\right)$

Use the cosine sum and difference identities to find the following.

9. $\cos 165^\circ$ **10.** $\cos 195^\circ$ **11.** $\cos 225^\circ$ **12.** $\cos 135^\circ$

Use sine and tangent sum and difference identities to simplify the following.

13. $\sin(P + Q)$ **14.** $\sin(P - Q)$ **15.** $\tan(P - Q)$
16. $\tan(P + Q)$ **17.** $\sin(60^\circ + 45^\circ)$ **18.** $\sin(60^\circ - 45^\circ)$
19. $\tan(60^\circ - 45^\circ)$ **20.** $\tan(60^\circ + 45^\circ)$ **21.** $\sin\left(\frac{\pi}{4} - \frac{\pi}{6}\right)$
22. $\sin\left(\frac{\pi}{4} + \frac{\pi}{6}\right)$ **23.** $\tan\left(\frac{\pi}{4} + \frac{\pi}{6}\right)$ **24.** $\tan\left(\frac{\pi}{4} - \frac{\pi}{6}\right)$

Use sum and difference formulas to find the following.

25. $\sin 15^\circ$ **26.** $\sin 105^\circ$ **27.** $\sin 135^\circ$ **28.** $\sin 150^\circ$
29. $\tan 75^\circ$ **30.** $\tan 105^\circ$ **31.** $\tan 15^\circ$ **32.** $\tan 135^\circ$

B

Use the cosine, sine, and tangent sum and difference identities to simplify each of the following.

33. $\sin\left(-\frac{5\pi}{2}\right) \cdot \sin\frac{\pi}{2} + \cos\frac{\pi}{2} \cdot \cos\left(-\frac{5\pi}{2}\right)$

34. $\sin\frac{\pi}{3} \cdot \sin\left(-\frac{\pi}{4}\right) + \cos\left(-\frac{\pi}{4}\right) \cdot \cos\frac{\pi}{3}$

35. $\cos A \cos B + \sin A \sin B$ **36.** $\cos A \cos B - \sin A \sin B$

37. $\cos(\alpha + \beta) + \cos(\alpha - \beta)$

38. $\cos(\alpha + \beta) - \cos(\alpha - \beta)$

39. $\dfrac{\tan A - \tan B}{1 + \tan A \tan B}$

40. $\dfrac{\tan A + \tan B}{1 - \tan A \tan B}$

41. $\dfrac{\tan 20^\circ + \tan 32^\circ}{1 - \tan 20^\circ \tan 32^\circ}$

42. $\dfrac{\tan 35^\circ - \tan 12^\circ}{1 + \tan 35^\circ \tan 12^\circ}$

43. $\sin(\alpha + \beta) + \sin(\alpha - \beta)$

44. $\sin(\alpha + \beta) - \sin(\alpha - \beta)$

45. $\sin\frac{\pi}{3} \cdot \cos\pi + \sin\pi \cdot \cos\frac{\pi}{3}$

46. $\sin\frac{\pi}{2} \cdot \cos\frac{\pi}{3} - \sin\frac{\pi}{3} \cdot \cos\frac{\pi}{2}$

47. Derive an identity for $\cot(\alpha + \beta)$ in terms of $\cot\alpha$ and $\cot\beta$.

48. Derive an identity for $\cot(\alpha - \beta)$ in terms of $\cot\alpha$ and $\cot\beta$.

The cofunction identities can be derived from the sum and difference formulas. Derive the following cofunction identities.

49. $\sin\left(\frac{\pi}{2} - x\right)$ **50.** $\sin\left(x - \frac{\pi}{2}\right)$ **51.** $\cos\left(\frac{\pi}{2} - x\right)$ **52.** $\cos\left(x + \frac{\pi}{2}\right)$

53. Find $\sin 45^\circ + \sin 30^\circ$ and compare with $\sin 75^\circ$. (Use Table 3.)

54. Find $\cos 45^\circ - \cos 30^\circ$ and compare with $\cos 15^\circ$. (Use Table 3.)

55. ***Critical Thinking*** Find identities for $\sin 2\theta$, $\cos 2\theta$, and $\tan 2\theta$. (Hint: Think of 2θ as a sum.)

Challenge

Given that $\sin\theta = 0.6249$ and $\cos\phi = 0.1102$, and that θ and ϕ are both first-quadrant angles, use a calculator to find the following.

56. $\sin(\theta + \phi)$ **57.** $\cos(\theta + \phi)$ **58.** $\tan(\theta + \phi)$

Reading Math

θ (theta)

ϕ (phi)

Use the idea of *composition of functions* to find a formula for each of the following. You may use the following substitutions.

$$u = \sin x \text{ and } v = \sin y$$

59. $\sin(\sin x + \sin y)$ **60.** $\cos(\cos x + \cos y)$ **61.** $\sin(x + y + z)$

Mixed Review

Simplify. **62.** $\dfrac{2}{q^2 - 1} - \dfrac{1}{q^2 - q}$ **63.** $\dfrac{1 - m}{1 - m^{-1}}$

64. $\dfrac{\frac{4}{x - 5} + \frac{2}{x + 2}}{\frac{-3x}{x^2 - 3x - 10} + \frac{3}{x - 5}}$ **65.** $\sqrt{\frac{2}{3}} + \sqrt{\frac{3}{2}}$ **66.** $\sqrt[3]{9}\sqrt[6]{9}$ *6-2, 6-3, 7-4, 7-5*

Evaluate. **67.** $\sin 20.4167^\circ$ **68.** $\cos 36.8699^\circ$ **69.** $\log 6.95$ **70.** $\tan 80.5^\circ$ *17-4, 12-5*

Solve. **71.** $v^{\frac{2}{5}} = 9$ **72.** $x^{\frac{2}{3}} - x^{\frac{1}{3}} - 12 = 0$ *8-5*

73. The distance s that an object falls when dropped from some point above the ground varies directly as the square of the time t it falls. If the object falls 19.6 meters in 2 seconds, how far will the object fall in 15 seconds? *8-7*

18-2 Double-Angle and Half-Angle Identities

What You'll Learn

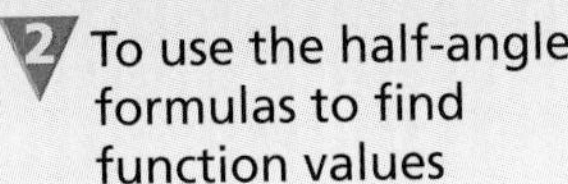

1. To use the double-angle identities to find function values
2. To use the half-angle formulas to find function values

... And Why

To solve trigonometric equations

Two important classes of trigonometric identities are known as the double-angle identities and the half-angle identities.

PART 1 Double-Angle Identities

Objective: Use the double-angle identities to find function values.

Identities involving $\sin 2\theta$ or $\cos 2\theta$ are called **double-angle identities.** To develop these identities we shall use the sum identities from the preceding lesson.

We first develop an identity for $\sin 2\theta$. We shall consider an angle θ and substitute it for both α and β in the identity for $\sin(\alpha + \beta)$.

$$\begin{aligned}\sin 2\theta &\equiv \sin(\theta + \theta)\\ &\equiv \sin\theta\cos\theta + \cos\theta\sin\theta\\ &\equiv \sin\theta\cos\theta + \sin\theta\cos\theta \quad \text{Using the commutative property}\\ &\equiv 2\sin\theta\cos\theta\end{aligned}$$

Thus we have the following identity.

$$\boldsymbol{\sin 2\theta \equiv 2\sin\theta\cos\theta}$$

EXAMPLE 1 If $\sin\theta = \frac{3}{8}$ and θ is in the first quadrant, what is $\sin 2\theta$?

From the diagram, we see that $\cos\theta = \frac{\sqrt{55}}{8}$.

$$\begin{aligned}\sin 2\theta &\equiv 2\sin\theta\cos\theta\\ &= 2\cdot\frac{3}{8}\cdot\frac{\sqrt{55}}{8}\\ &= \frac{3\sqrt{55}}{32}\end{aligned}$$

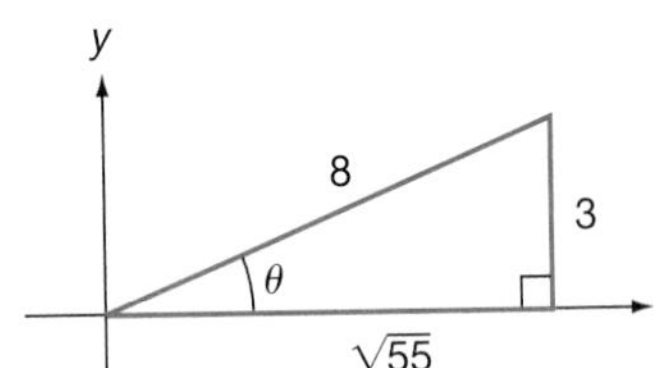

Try This

a. If $\sin\theta = \frac{3}{5}$ and θ is in the first quadrant, what is $\sin 2\theta$?

Double-angle identities for the cosine and tangent functions can be derived in much the same way as the identity above.

$$\begin{aligned}\cos 2\theta &\equiv \cos(\theta + \theta)\\ &\equiv \cos\theta\cos\theta - \sin\theta\sin\theta\\ &\equiv \cos^2\theta - \sin^2\theta\end{aligned}$$

Thus we have the following identity.

$$\cos 2\theta \equiv \cos^2 \theta - \sin^2 \theta$$

By using the same kind of substitution, we can derive the double-angle identity for the tangent function.

$$\tan 2\theta \equiv \frac{2 \tan \theta}{1 - \tan^2 \theta}$$

EXAMPLE 2 Given that $\tan \theta = -\frac{3}{4}$ and θ is in the second quadrant, find $\sin 2\theta$, $\cos 2\theta$, $\tan 2\theta$, and the quadrant in which 2θ lies.

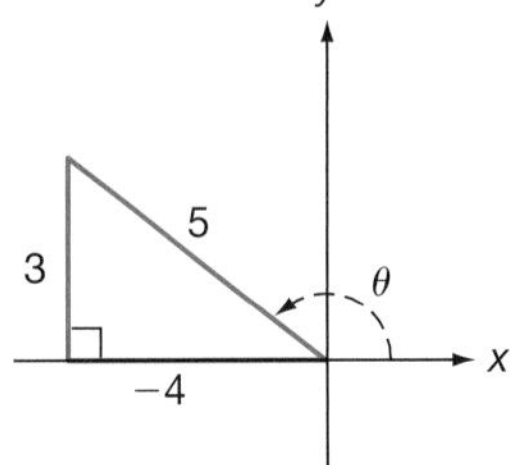

By drawing a diagram as shown, we find that $\sin \theta = \frac{3}{5}$ and $\cos \theta = -\frac{4}{5}$.

$$\sin 2\theta = 2 \sin \theta \cos \theta = 2 \cdot \frac{3}{5} \cdot \left(-\frac{4}{5}\right) = -\frac{24}{25}$$

$$\cos 2\theta = \cos^2 \theta - \sin^2 \theta = \left(-\frac{4}{5}\right)^2 - \left(\frac{3}{5}\right)^2 = \frac{16}{25} - \frac{9}{25} = \frac{7}{25}$$

$$\tan 2\theta = \frac{2 \tan \theta}{1 - \tan^2 \theta} = \frac{2 \cdot \left(-\frac{3}{4}\right)}{1 - \left(-\frac{3}{4}\right)^2} = \frac{-\frac{3}{2}}{1 - \frac{9}{16}} = \frac{-\frac{24}{16}}{\frac{7}{16}} = -\frac{24}{7}$$

Since $\sin 2\theta$ is negative and $\cos 2\theta$ is positive, we know that 2θ is in quadrant IV. Note that $\tan 2\theta$ could have been found more easily in this case by dividing the values of $\sin 2\theta$ and $\cos 2\theta$; that is, $-\frac{24}{25} \div \frac{7}{25} = -\frac{24}{7}$.

Try This

b. Given that $\cos \theta = -\frac{5}{13}$ with θ in the third quadrant, find $\sin 2\theta$, $\cos 2\theta$, and $\tan 2\theta$. Also, determine the quadrant in which 2θ lies.

Two other useful identities for $\cos 2\theta$ can easily be derived as follows.

$$\begin{aligned} \cos 2\theta &\equiv \cos^2 \theta - \sin^2 \theta \\ &\equiv (1 - \sin^2 \theta) - \sin^2 \theta && \text{Using } \cos^2 \theta = 1 - \sin^2 \theta \\ &\equiv 1 - 2 \sin^2 \theta \\ \cos 2\theta &\equiv \cos^2 \theta - \sin^2 \theta \\ &\equiv \cos^2 \theta - (1 - \cos^2 \theta) && \text{Using } \sin^2 \theta = 1 - \cos^2 \theta \\ &\equiv 2 \cos^2 \theta - 1 \end{aligned}$$

Solving these two identities for $\sin^2 \theta$ and $\cos^2 \theta$, respectively, we obtain two more identities, which are often useful. The following theorem summarizes the double-angle identities and three important derivations. They should be memorized.

Theorem 18-2

$$\sin 2\theta \equiv 2 \sin \theta \cos \theta \qquad \sin^2 \theta \equiv \frac{1 - \cos 2\theta}{2}$$

$$\cos 2\theta \equiv \cos^2 \theta - \sin^2 \theta$$

$$\cos 2\theta \equiv 1 - 2 \sin^2 \theta \qquad \cos^2 \theta \equiv \frac{1 + \cos 2\theta}{2}$$

$$\cos 2\theta \equiv 2 \cos^2 \theta - 1$$

$$\tan 2\theta \equiv \frac{2 \tan \theta}{1 - \tan^2 \theta} \qquad \tan^2 \theta \equiv \frac{1 - \cos 2\theta}{1 + \cos 2\theta}$$

From the basic identities listed in Theorems 18-1 and 18-2, others can be obtained.

EXAMPLE 3 Find a formula for $\sin 3\theta$ in terms of function values of θ.

$$\begin{aligned} \sin 3\theta &\equiv \sin (2\theta + \theta) \\ &\equiv \sin 2\theta \cos \theta + \cos 2\theta \sin \theta \\ &\equiv (2 \sin \theta \cos \theta) \cos \theta + (2 \cos^2 \theta - 1) \sin \theta \\ &\equiv 2 \sin \theta \cos^2 \theta + 2 \sin \theta \cos^2 \theta - \sin \theta \\ &\equiv 4 \sin \theta \cos^2 \theta - \sin \theta \end{aligned}$$

Try This

c. Find a formula for $\cos 3\theta$ in terms of function values of θ.

PART 2 Half-Angle Identities

Objective: Use the half-angle identities to find function values.

To develop these identities, we use previously developed ones. Consider the following identity.

$$\sin^2 \theta \equiv \frac{1 - \cos 2\theta}{2}$$

Note that the right side of this identity is in terms of 2θ. Letting $2\theta = \phi$ we have $\theta = \frac{\phi}{2}$. Taking the square roots gives the following.

$$\left| \sin \frac{\phi}{2} \right| \equiv \sqrt{\frac{1 - \cos \phi}{2}}$$

Similarly for cosine and tangent, by taking square roots and replacing θ by $\frac{\phi}{2}$ we derive the following.

$$\left| \cos \frac{\phi}{2} \right| \equiv \sqrt{\frac{1 + \cos \phi}{2}} \qquad \left| \tan \frac{\phi}{2} \right| \equiv \sqrt{\frac{1 - \cos \phi}{1 + \cos \phi}}$$

We can eliminate the absolute value signs by introducing $\pm$ signs with the understanding that we use $+$ or $-$ depending on the quadrant in which the angle $\frac{\phi}{2}$ lies. We thus obtain the formulas summarized in the following theorem.

Theorem 18-3

$$\sin\frac{\phi}{2} \equiv \pm\sqrt{\frac{1-\cos\phi}{2}} \quad \cos\frac{\phi}{2} \equiv \pm\sqrt{\frac{1+\cos\phi}{2}} \quad \tan\frac{\phi}{2} \equiv \pm\sqrt{\frac{1-\cos\phi}{1+\cos\phi}}$$

EXAMPLE 4 Use Theorem 18-3 to find sin 15°.

$$\begin{aligned}\sin 15^\circ &= \sin\frac{30^\circ}{2}\\ &= \pm\sqrt{\frac{1-\cos 30^\circ}{2}}\\ &= \pm\sqrt{\frac{1-\left(\frac{\sqrt{3}}{2}\right)}{2}}\\ &= \pm\sqrt{\frac{2-\sqrt{3}}{4}} = \frac{\sqrt{2-\sqrt{3}}}{2}\end{aligned}$$

The expression is positive, because 15° is in the first quadrant.

Two other formulas for $\tan\frac{\phi}{2}$ can be obtained. These formulas give the correct sign of $\tan\left(\frac{\phi}{2}\right)$ directly.

Theorem 18-4

$$\tan\frac{\phi}{2} \equiv \frac{\sin\phi}{1+\cos\phi} \qquad \tan\frac{\phi}{2} \equiv \frac{1-\cos\phi}{\sin\phi}$$

EXAMPLE 5 Use Theorem 18-4 to find tan 15°.

$$\begin{aligned}\tan 15^\circ &= \tan\frac{30^\circ}{2}\\ &= \frac{1-\cos 30^\circ}{\sin 30^\circ}\\ &= \frac{1-\left(\frac{\sqrt{3}}{2}\right)}{\frac{1}{2}}\\ &= \frac{\frac{2}{2}-\frac{\sqrt{3}}{2}}{\frac{1}{2}} = 2-\sqrt{3}\end{aligned}$$

Try This

d. Use Theorem 18-3 to find cos 15°.
e. Use Theorem 18-4 to find tan 45°.

Extra Help On the Web

Look for worked-out examples at the Prentice Hall Web site.
www.phschool.com

18-2 Exercises

A

Find $\sin 2\theta$, $\cos 2\theta$, $\tan 2\theta$, and the quadrant in which 2θ lies.

1. $\sin \theta = \frac{4}{5}$ (θ in quadrant I)
2. $\sin \theta = \frac{5}{13}$ (θ in quadrant I)
3. $\cos \theta = -\frac{4}{5}$ (θ in quadrant III)
4. $\cos \theta = -\frac{3}{5}$ (θ in quadrant III)
5. $\tan \theta = \frac{4}{3}$ (θ in quadrant III)
6. $\tan \theta = \frac{3}{4}$ (θ in quadrant III)

Use Theorem 18-3 and Theorem 18-4 to find the following.

7. $\sin 75^\circ$
8. $\cos 75^\circ$
9. $\tan 75^\circ$
10. $\tan 67.5^\circ$
11. $\sin \frac{5\pi}{8}$
12. $\cos \frac{5\pi}{8}$
13. $\sin \frac{3\pi}{8}$
14. $\cos \frac{3\pi}{8}$
15. $\tan \frac{\pi}{8}$

B

Simplify.

16. $1 - 2\sin^2 \frac{x}{2}$
17. $2\cos^2 \frac{x}{2} - 1$
18. $2\sin \frac{x}{2} \cos \frac{x}{2}$
19. $2\sin 2x \cos 2x$
20. $\cos^2 \frac{x}{2} - \sin^2 \frac{x}{2}$
21. $2\sin^2 \frac{x}{2} + \cos x$
22. $\cos^4 x - \sin^4 x$
23. $(\sin x + \cos x)^2 - \sin 2x$
24. $(\sin x - \cos x)^2 + \sin 2x$
25. $2\sin x \cos^3 x + 2\sin^3 x \cos x$
26. $2\sin x \cos^3 x - 2\sin^3 x \cos x$
27. ***Critical Thinking*** Find formulas for $\sin 4\theta$ and $\cos 4\theta$ in terms of function values of θ.

Challenge

Find a formula for

28. $\sin^4 \theta$ in terms of function values of θ or 2θ or 4θ, raised only to the first power.
29. $\cos^4 \theta$ in terms of function values of θ or 2θ or 4θ, raised only to the first power.
30. Derive the formula for $\tan 2\theta$ given in Theorem 18-2.

Mixed Review

Find an equation for $f^{-1}(x)$. **31.** $f(x) = \sqrt[3]{x^2 + 1}$ **32.** $f(x) = \log_4 x$
33. $f(x) = e^x$
34. $f(x) = 2x - 6$ *12-1, 12-2, 12-3*
35. Graph the equation $f(x) = 3^x$. *12-2*
36. The hypotenuse of a right triangle is 10 cm long. One leg is 2 cm less than the other. Find the lengths of the legs. *8-2*

Proving Identities

18-3

Proving Trigonometric Identities

Objective: Prove trigonometric identities.

Following is a minimal list of identities that should be memorized.

Basic Identities

$$\sin(-x) \equiv -\sin x$$
$$\cos(-x) \equiv \cos x$$
$$\tan(-x) \equiv -\tan x$$

Pythagorean Identities

$$\sin^2 x + \cos^2 x \equiv 1$$
$$1 + \tan^2 x \equiv \sec^2 x$$
$$1 + \cot^2 x \equiv \csc^2 x$$

Cofunction Identities

$$\sin\left(\frac{\pi}{2} - x\right) \equiv \cos x$$
$$\cos\left(\frac{\pi}{2} - x\right) \equiv \sin x$$
$$\tan\left(\frac{\pi}{2} - x\right) \equiv \cot x$$

Sum and Difference Identities

$$\sin(\alpha \pm \beta) \equiv \sin\alpha\cos\beta \pm \cos\alpha\sin\beta$$
$$\cos(\alpha \pm \beta) \equiv \cos\alpha\cos\beta \mp \sin\alpha\sin\beta$$
$$\tan(\alpha \pm \beta) \equiv \frac{\tan\alpha \pm \tan\beta}{1 \mp \tan\alpha\tan\beta}$$

Double-angle Identities

$$\sin 2x \equiv 2\sin x\cos x$$
$$\cos 2x \equiv \cos^2 x - \sin^2 x \equiv 1 - 2\sin^2 x \equiv 2\cos^2 x - 1$$
$$\tan 2x \equiv \frac{2\tan x}{1 - \tan^2 x}$$
$$\sin^2 x \equiv \frac{1 - \cos 2x}{2}$$
$$\cos^2 x \equiv \frac{1 + \cos 2x}{2}$$

Half-angle Identities

$$\sin\frac{x}{2} \equiv \pm\sqrt{\frac{1 - \cos x}{2}}$$
$$\cos\frac{x}{2} \equiv \pm\sqrt{\frac{1 + \cos x}{2}}$$
$$\tan\frac{x}{2} \equiv \pm\sqrt{\frac{1 - \cos x}{1 + \cos x}} \equiv \frac{\sin x}{1 + \cos x} \equiv \frac{1 - \cos x}{\sin x}$$

EXAMPLE 1 Prove the following identity.

$$\tan^2 x - \sin^2 x \equiv \sin^2 x \tan^2 x$$

$\tan^2 x - \sin^2 x$	$\sin^2 x \tan^2 x$	
$\frac{\sin^2 x}{\cos^2 x} - \sin^2 x$	$\sin^2 x \frac{\sin^2 x}{\cos^2 x}$	Writing each side in terms of sin *x* and cos *x*
$\frac{\sin^2 x - \sin^2 x\cos^2 x}{\cos^2 x}$		Finding common denominators and subtracting
$\frac{\sin^2 x(1 - \cos^2 x)}{\cos^2 x}$		
$\frac{\sin^2 x(\sin^2 x)}{\cos^2 x}$		
$\sin^2 x \frac{\sin^2 x}{\cos^2 x}$		

Therefore, $\tan^2 x - \sin^2 x \equiv \sin^2 x \tan^2 x$.

What You'll Learn

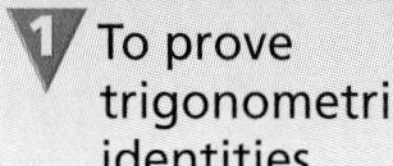

To prove trigonometric identities

. . . And Why

To solve trigonometric equations

Write a short paragraph in which you describe a general strategy for proving a trigonometric identity.

Most formulas involving secants, cosecants, and cotangents can be easily derived because these functions are reciprocals of the sine, cosine, and tangent.

Try This Prove the following identity.

a. $\cot^2 x - \cos^2 x \equiv \cos^2 x \cot^2 x$

The next identity shows the use of double-angle formulas.

EXAMPLE 2 Prove the following identity.

$$\frac{\sin 2\theta}{\sin \theta} - \frac{\cos 2\theta}{\cos \theta} \equiv \sec \theta$$

$\frac{2 \sin \theta \cos \theta}{\sin \theta} - \frac{\cos^2 \theta - \sin^2 \theta}{\cos \theta}$	$\frac{1}{\cos \theta}$
$\frac{2 \cos^2 \theta - \cos^2 \theta + \sin^2 \theta}{\cos \theta}$	
$\frac{\cos^2 \theta + \sin^2 \theta}{\cos \theta}$	
$\frac{1}{\cos \theta}$	

Therefore, $\frac{\sin 2\theta}{\sin \theta} - \frac{\cos 2\theta}{\cos \theta} \equiv \sec \theta$.

Try This Prove the following identity.

b. $\frac{\sin 2\theta + \sin \theta}{\cos 2\theta + \cos \theta + 1} \equiv \tan \theta$

Look for worked-out examples at the Prentice Hall Web site.
www.phschool.com

18-3 Exercises

A

Prove these identities.

1. $\csc x - \cos x \cot x \equiv \sin x$

2. $\sec x - \sin x \tan x \equiv \cos x$

3. $\frac{1 + \cos \theta}{\sin \theta} + \frac{\sin \theta}{\cos \theta} \equiv \frac{\cos \theta + 1}{\sin \theta \cos \theta}$

4. $\frac{1}{\sin \theta \cos \theta} - \frac{\cos \theta}{\sin \theta} \equiv \frac{\sin \theta \cos \theta}{1 - \sin^2 \theta}$

5. $\frac{1 - \sin x}{\cos x} \equiv \frac{\cos x}{1 + \sin x}$

6. $\frac{1 - \cos x}{\sin x} \equiv \frac{\sin x}{1 + \cos x}$

7. $\frac{1 + \tan \theta}{1 + \cot \theta} \equiv \frac{\sec \theta}{\csc \theta}$

8. $\frac{\cot \theta - 1}{1 - \tan \theta} \equiv \frac{\csc \theta}{\sec \theta}$

9. $\frac{\sin x + \cos x}{\sec x + \csc x} \equiv \frac{\sin x}{\sec x}$

10. $\frac{\sin x - \cos x}{\sec x - \csc x} \equiv \frac{\cos x}{\csc x}$

11. $\frac{1 + \tan \theta}{1 - \tan \theta} + \frac{1 + \cot \theta}{1 - \cot \theta} \equiv 0$

12. $\frac{\cos^2 \theta + \cot \theta}{\cos^2 \theta - \cot \theta} \equiv \frac{\cos^2 \theta \tan \theta + 1}{\cos^2 \theta \tan \theta - 1}$

13. $\frac{1 + \cos 2\theta}{\sin 2\theta} \equiv \cot \theta$

14. $\frac{2 \tan \theta}{1 + \tan^2 \theta} \equiv \sin 2\theta$

15. $\sec 2\theta \equiv \frac{\sec^2 \theta}{2 - \sec^2 \theta}$

16. $\cot 2\theta \equiv \frac{\cot^2 \theta - 1}{2 \cot \theta}$

B

17. $\frac{\sin(\alpha+\beta)}{\cos\alpha\cos\beta} \equiv \tan\alpha + \tan\beta$

18. $\frac{\cos(\alpha-\beta)}{\cos\alpha\sin\beta} \equiv \tan\alpha + \cot\beta$

19. $\frac{\tan\theta + \sin\theta}{2\tan\theta} \equiv \cos^2\frac{\theta}{2}$

20. $\frac{\tan\theta - \sin\theta}{2\tan\theta} \equiv \sin^2\frac{\theta}{2}$

21. $\cos^4 x - \sin^4 x \equiv \cos 2x$

22. $\frac{\cos^4 x - \sin^4 x}{1 - \tan^4 x} \equiv \cos^4 x$

23. $\frac{\tan 3\theta - \tan\theta}{1 + \tan 3\theta\tan\theta} \equiv \frac{2\tan\theta}{1 - \tan^2\theta}$

24. $\left(\frac{1+\tan\theta}{1-\tan\theta}\right)^2 \equiv \frac{1+\sin 2\theta}{1-\sin 2\theta}$

25. $\sin(\alpha+\beta)\sin(\alpha-\beta) \equiv \sin^2\alpha - \sin^2\beta$

26. $\cos(\alpha+\beta)\cos(\alpha-\beta) \equiv \cos^2\alpha - \sin^2\beta$

27. $\cos(\alpha+\beta) + \cos(\alpha-\beta) \equiv 2\cos\alpha\cos\beta$

28. $\sin(\alpha+\beta) + \sin(\alpha-\beta) \equiv 2\sin\alpha\cos\beta$

29. ***Critical Thinking*** Create a trigonometric identity. (Hint: Start with a simple trigonometric expression and work backward.)

Challenge

30. Show that $\log(\cos x - \sin x) + \log(\cos x + \sin x) \equiv \log(\cos 2x)$.

31. The following equation occurs in the study of mechanics.

$$\sin\theta = \frac{I_1\cos\phi}{\sqrt{(I_1\cos\phi)^2 + (I_2\sin\phi)^2}}$$

If $I_1 = I_2$, simplify the equation.

32. The following equations occur in the theory of alternating current.

$$R = \frac{1}{\omega C(\tan\theta + \tan\phi)} \quad \text{and} \quad R = \frac{\cos\theta\cos\phi}{\omega C\sin(\theta+\phi)}$$

Show that these equations are equivalent.

33. In electrical theory the following equations occur.

$$E_1 = \sqrt{2}\,E_t\cos\left(\theta + \frac{\pi}{\rho}\right), \qquad E_2 = \sqrt{2}\,E_t\cos\left(\theta - \frac{\pi}{\rho}\right)$$

Show that $\frac{E_1 + E_2}{2} = \sqrt{2}\,E_t\cos\theta\cos\frac{\pi}{\rho}$ and $\frac{E_1 - E_2}{2} = -\sqrt{2}\,E_t\sin\theta\sin\frac{\pi}{\rho}$.

Reading Math

ω (omega)

ρ (rho)

Mixed Review

Sketch the graph of each equation. 34. $y = 2\sin(-2x)$

35. $y = -4\cos\left(\frac{1}{2}x\right)$

36. $y = -6\sin\left(\frac{1}{3}x\right)$ *17-7*

Solve. 37. $\log_8 x = \frac{2}{3}$

38. $x^4 = 1$ *12-3, 8-5*

39. A ladder 25 ft long leans against a wall. The bottom of the ladder is 15 ft from the wall. How much would the lower end of the ladder have to be pulled away so that the top of the ladder would be pulled down the same distance? *8-6*

18-4 Inverses of the Trigonometric Functions

What You'll Learn

1. To find the inverse values of the sine, cosine, and tangent functions
2. To find the principal values of the inverses of the trigonometric functions

... And Why

To solve trigonometric equations

PART 1 Finding Inverse Values

Objective: Find values of arcsin, arccos, and arctan.

To obtain the inverse of any relation, we interchange the first and second members of each ordered pair in the relation. If a relation is defined by an equation, say in x and y, interchanging x and y produces an equation of the inverse relation. The graphs of a relation and its inverse are reflections of each other across the line $y = x$.

Consider the function $y = \sin x$. The inverse of this function may be denoted in several ways as follows.

$x = \sin y \qquad y = \sin^{-1} x \qquad y = \arcsin x$

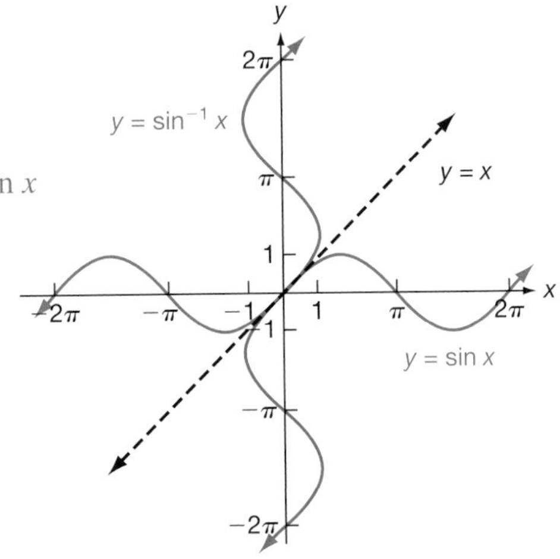

Thus $\sin^{-1} x$ is a number whose sine is x. The notation $\sin^{-1} x$ is not exponential notation. It does *not* mean $\frac{1}{\sin x}$. Either of the latter two kinds of notation above can be read "the inverse sine of x" or "the arc sine of x" or "the number (or angle) whose sine is x." Notation is chosen similarly for the inverses of the other trigonometric functions: $\cos^{-1} x$ or $\arccos x$, $\tan^{-1} x$ or $\arctan x$, and so on.

EXAMPLE 1 Sketch a graph of $y = \cos^{-1} x$. Is this relation a function?

First sketch a graph of $y = \cos x$.

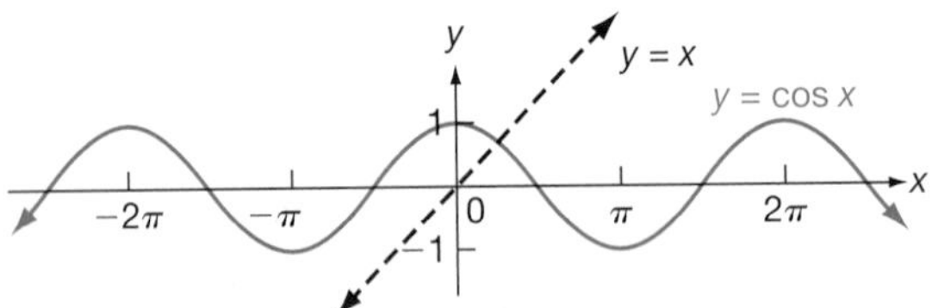

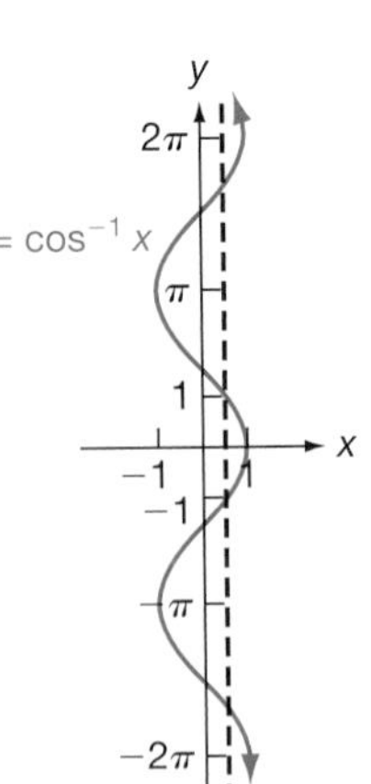

Reflect this graph over the line $y = x$. There is more than one value of y for each x, so the graph is not a function.

Try This

a. Sketch a graph of $y = \cot^{-1} x$. Is this relation a function?

We can find inverse values using either a graph or a unit circle. In practice the unit circle is easier to use.

EXAMPLE 2 Find all values of $\arcsin \frac{1}{2}$.

We can use the unit circle to find inverse values. On the unit circle there are two points at which the sine is $\frac{1}{2}$. The rotation for the point in the first quadrant is $\frac{\pi}{6}$ plus any multiple of 2π. The rotation for the point in the second quadrant is $\frac{5\pi}{6}$ plus any multiple of 2π.

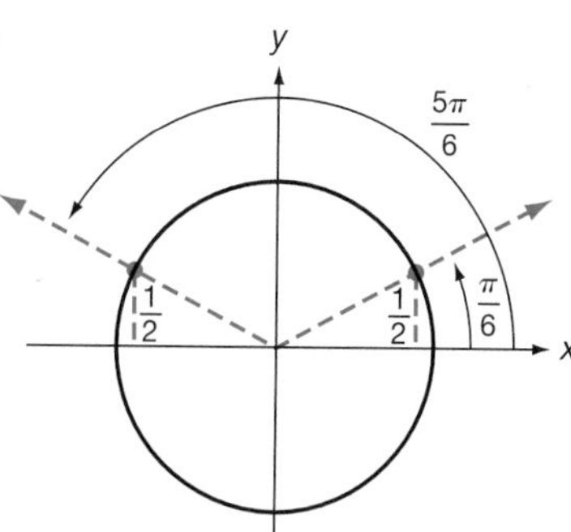

Hence we obtain all values of $\arcsin \frac{1}{2}$ as follows.

$$\frac{\pi}{6} + 2k\pi \text{ and } \frac{5\pi}{6} + 2k\pi, k \text{ an integer}$$

In degree notation, we write $30° + k \cdot 360°$ and $150° + k \cdot 360°$.

Try This Find all values of the following.

b. $\arccos \frac{\sqrt{2}}{2}$ **c.** $\sin^{-1} \frac{\sqrt{3}}{2}$

We can also use a graph to find inverse values.

On the graph of $y = \arcsin x$, we draw a vertical line at $x = \frac{1}{2}$ as shown. It intersects the graph at points whose y-value is $\arcsin \frac{1}{2}$. Some of the numbers whose sine is $\frac{1}{2}$ are seen to be $\frac{\pi}{6}, \frac{5\pi}{6}, -\frac{7\pi}{6}$, and so on. From the graph we can see that $\frac{\pi}{6}$ plus any multiple of 2π is such a number. Also, $\frac{5\pi}{6}$ plus any multiple of 2π is such a number.
Thus the complete set of values is given by $\frac{\pi}{6} + 2k\pi$ and $\frac{5\pi}{6} + 2k\pi$, k an integer.

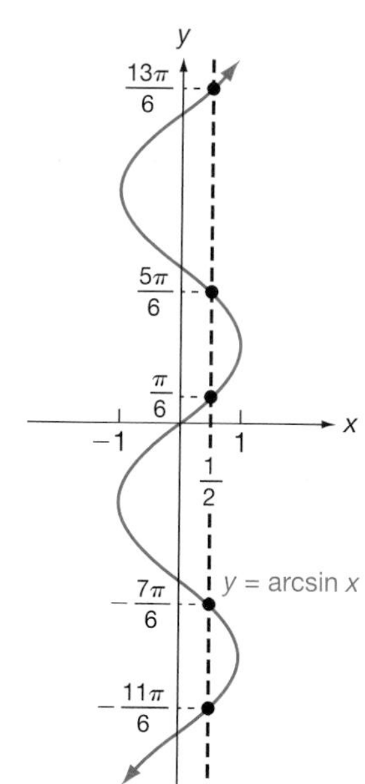

EXAMPLE 3 Find all values of $\cos^{-1}(-0.9397)$ in degrees.

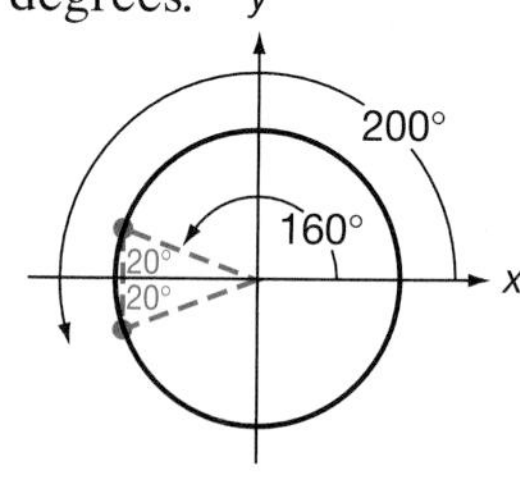

From Table 5 or a calculator, we find that the angle whose cosine is 0.9397 is 20°. This is the reference angle. We sketch this on a unit circle to find the two points where the cosine is -0.9397. The angles are 160° and 200°, plus any multiple of 360°. Thus the values of $\cos^{-1}(-0.9397)$ are

$$160^\circ + k \cdot 360^\circ \quad \text{or} \quad 200^\circ + k \cdot 360^\circ, \text{ where } k \text{ is any integer.}$$

EXAMPLE 4 Find all values of arctan 1. (See the figure at right.)

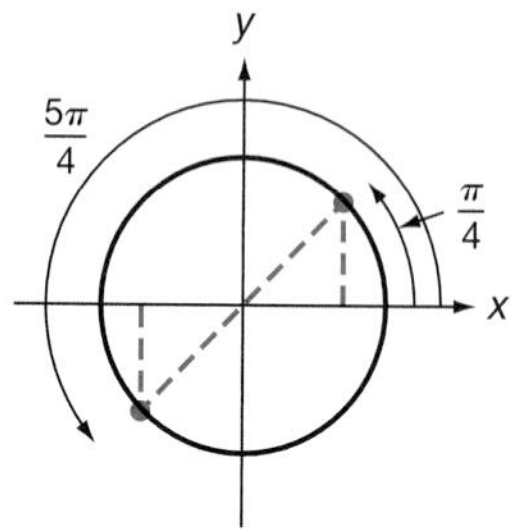

We find the two points on the unit circle at which the tangent is 1. These points are opposite ends of a diameter. Hence, the arc lengths differ by π. Thus we have for all values of arctan 1

$$\frac{\pi}{4} + k\pi, \ k \text{ an integer.}$$

Try This Find all values of the following.

d. $\sin^{-1} 0.4226$ in degrees **e.** $\arctan(-1)$

PART 2 Principal Values

Objective: Find principal values of the inverses of the trigonometric functions.

The inverses of the trigonometric functions are not themselves functions. However, if we restrict the ranges of these relations, we can obtain functions. The following graphs show how this restriction is made.

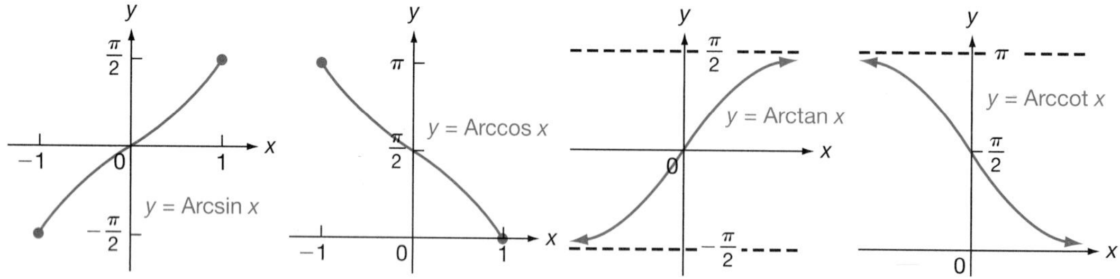

These relations with their ranges so restricted are functions, and the values in these restricted ranges are called **principal values.** To denote principal values we shall capitalize as follows: Arcsin x, $\text{Sin}^{-1} x$, Arccos x, $\text{Cos}^{-1} x$, and so on. Thus whereas arcsin $\frac{1}{2}$ represents an infinite set of numbers, Arcsin $\frac{1}{2}$ represents the single number $\frac{\pi}{6}$.

Note that for the function $y = \text{Arcsin}\, x$ the range is $\left\{y \mid -\frac{\pi}{2} \le y \le \frac{\pi}{2}\right\}$.

For the function $y = \text{Arctan}\, x$ the range is $\left\{y \mid -\frac{\pi}{2} < y < \frac{\pi}{2}\right\}$.

For the function $y = \text{Arccos}\, x$ the range is $\{y \mid 0 \le y \le \pi\}$.

For the function $y = \text{Arccot}\, x$ the range is $\{y \mid 0 < y < \pi\}$.

EXAMPLE 5 Find $\text{Arcsin}\, \frac{\sqrt{2}}{2}$ and $\text{Cos}^{-1}\left(-\frac{1}{2}\right)$.

In the restricted range as shown in the figure, the only number whose sine is $\frac{\sqrt{2}}{2}$ is $\frac{\pi}{4}$. Hence $\text{Arcsin}\, \frac{\sqrt{2}}{2} = \frac{\pi}{4}$. The only number whose cosine is $-\frac{1}{2}$ in the restricted range is $\frac{2\pi}{3}$. Hence $\text{Cos}^{-1}\left(-\frac{1}{2}\right) = \frac{2\pi}{3}$.

Try This Find each of the following.

f. $\text{Arcsin}\, \frac{\sqrt{3}}{2}$ **g.** $\text{Cos}^{-1} -\frac{\sqrt{2}}{2}$ **h.** $\text{Arccot}\,(-1)$ **i.** $\text{Tan}^{-1}\,(-1)$

18-4 Exercises

Look for worked-out examples at the Prentice Hall Web site. www.phschool.com

A

Find all values of the following.

1. $\arcsin \frac{\sqrt{2}}{2}$ **2.** $\arcsin \frac{\sqrt{3}}{2}$ **3.** $\cos^{-1} \frac{\sqrt{2}}{2}$ **4.** $\cos^{-1} \frac{\sqrt{3}}{2}$

5. $\sin^{-1}\left(-\frac{\sqrt{2}}{2}\right)$ **6.** $\sin^{-1}\left(-\frac{\sqrt{3}}{2}\right)$ **7.** $\arccos\left(-\frac{\sqrt{2}}{2}\right)$ **8.** $\arccos\left(-\frac{\sqrt{3}}{2}\right)$

9. $\arctan \sqrt{3}$ **10.** $\arctan \frac{\sqrt{3}}{3}$ **11.** $\cot^{-1} 1$ **12.** $\cot^{-1} \sqrt{3}$

13. $\arctan\left(-\frac{\sqrt{3}}{3}\right)$ **14.** $\arctan\,(-\sqrt{3})$ **15.** $\text{arccot}\,(-1)$ **16.** $\text{arccot}\,(-\sqrt{3})$

17. $\text{arcsec}\, 1$ **18.** $\text{arcsec}\, 2$ **19.** $\csc^{-1} 1$ **20.** $\csc^{-1} 2$

Use a table or calculator to find, in degrees, all values of the following.

21. $\arcsin 0.3907$ **22.** $\arcsin 0.9613$ **23.** $\sin^{-1} 0.6293$ **24.** $\sin^{-1} 0.8746$

25. $\arccos 0.7990$ **26.** $\arccos 0.9265$ **27.** $\cos^{-1} 0.9310$ **28.** $\cos^{-1} 0.2735$

29. $\tan^{-1} 0.3673$ **30.** $\tan^{-1} 1.091$ **31.** $\cot^{-1} 1.265$ **32.** $\cot^{-1} 0.4770$

33. $\sec^{-1} 1.167$ **34.** $\sec^{-1} 1.440$ **35.** $\text{arccsc}\, 6.277$ **36.** $\text{arccsc}\, 1.111$

Find the following without using a table or a calculator.

37. $\text{Arcsin}\, \frac{\sqrt{2}}{2}$ **38.** $\text{Arcsin}\, \frac{1}{2}$ **39.** $\text{Cos}^{-1} \frac{1}{2}$

40. $\text{Cos}^{-1} \frac{\sqrt{2}}{2}$ **41.** $\text{Sin}^{-1}\left(-\frac{\sqrt{3}}{2}\right)$ **42.** $\text{Sin}^{-1}\left(-\frac{1}{2}\right)$

43. ***Error Analysis*** Dion found the value of Arccos $\left(\frac{\sqrt{2}}{2}\right)$ to be $-\frac{\pi}{4}$. Explain why this is an error in terms of the range of the inverse cosine function.

44. Arccos $\left(-\frac{\sqrt{3}}{2}\right)$ 45. $\text{Tan}^{-1}(-\sqrt{3})$ 46. Arccot $(-\sqrt{3})$

B

Find all values of the following by sketching the graph.

47. arccot (-1) 48. arccot $(-\sqrt{3})$ 49. arcsec 1

50. arcsec 2 51. $\csc^{-1} 1$ 52. $\csc^{-1} 2$

For each of the following, indicate on separate graphs of the unit circle where principal values are found.

53. Arcsin 54. Arccos 55. Arctan 56. Arccot

Find the following, in radians, using a calculator.

57. Arcsin 0.2334 58. Arcsin 0.4514

59. Arccos (-0.8897) 60. Arccos (-0.2924)

61. $\text{Tan}^{-1}(-0.4074)$ 62. $\text{Tan}^{-1}(-0.2401)$

63. ***Critical Thinking*** The angle to minimize friction in the flow of blood where two arteries meet is found using $\text{Cos}^{-1}\left(\frac{r^4}{R^4}\right)$, where r is the radius of the smaller artery and R is the radius of the larger artery.

a. A heart surgeon must join arteries with radii of 4 mm and 5 mm. What angle should be formed?

b. Under what condition will the formula not work? Why?

Each member of a surgical team has specific responsibilities in any surgery. See Exercise 63.

Challenge

Evaluate or simplify.

64. $\text{Cos}^{-1}\left(\cos \frac{\pi}{7}\right)$ 65. $\text{Tan}^{-1}\left(\tan \frac{2\pi}{3}\right)$

66. $\tan(\text{Tan}^{-1} -4.2)$ 67. $\sin(\text{Arctan}\sqrt{3})$

68. $\sin(\text{Arccot}\ x)$ 69. $\text{Sin}^{-1}\left(\tan -\frac{\pi}{4}\right)$

Self-Test On the Web

Check your progress. Look for a self-test at the Prentice Hall Web site. www.phschool.com

Mixed Review

70. Find the equation of the line containing (100, 2500) with slope -12.5. *3-5*

Solve. 71. $4^x = 10$ 72. $x^4 + x^3 - x - 1 = 0$ 73. $x^6 = 10$ *12-7, 11-3, 11-6*

74. Bob and Phil ride their bikes, headed west and north respectively, from the same point (P), starting at the same time. Bob rides 7 km/h faster than Phil. After two hours, they are 26 km apart. Find the speed of each. *8-2*

Trigonometric Equations

PART 1 Solving Trigonometric Equations

Objective: Solve simple trigonometric equations.

What You'll Learn

1. To solve simple trigonometric equations

. . . And Why

To solve problems using trigonometric equations

When an equation contains a trigonometric expression with a variable such as $\sin x$, it is called a **trigonometric equation.** To solve such an equation, we find all replacements for the variable that make the equation true.

EXAMPLE 1 Solve $2 \sin x = 1$.

We first solve for $\sin x$.

$$\sin x = \frac{1}{2}$$

Now we note that the solutions are those angles having a sine of $\frac{1}{2}$. We look for them. The unit circle is helpful. There are just two points on it for which the sine is $\frac{1}{2}$, as shown. They are points for $\frac{\pi}{6}$ and $\frac{5\pi}{6}$. These angles, plus any multiple of 2π, are the solutions.

$$\frac{\pi}{6} + 2k\pi \text{ and } \frac{5\pi}{6} + 2k\pi \text{ where } k \text{ is any integer}$$

In degrees, the solutions are $30° + k \cdot 360°$ and $150° + k \cdot 360°$ where k is any integer.

EXAMPLE 2 Solve $4 \cos^2 x = 1$.

$$\cos^2 x = \frac{1}{4}$$

$$|\cos x| = \frac{1}{2} \quad \text{Taking principal square roots}$$

$$\cos x = \pm\frac{1}{2}$$

Now we use the unit circle to find those numbers having a cosine of $\pm\frac{1}{2}$. The solutions are $\frac{\pi}{3}, \frac{2\pi}{3}, \frac{4\pi}{3}, \frac{5\pi}{3}$, plus any multiple of 2π.

In solving trigonometric equations, it is usually sufficient to find just the solutions from 0 to 2π. Any multiple of 2π may be added to obtain all the solutions.

Try This Solve.

a. $4 \sin^2 x = 1$

The following example illustrates that when we look for solutions to equations involving a double angle, we must be cautious.

EXAMPLE 3 Find the solutions of $2 \sin 2x = 1$ from 0 to 2π.

We first solve for $\sin 2x$: $\sin 2x = \frac{1}{2}$. Points on the unit circle for which $\sin 2x = \frac{1}{2}$ are points where $2x = \frac{\pi}{6}$ and $2x = \frac{5\pi}{6}$. So $\frac{\pi}{12}$ and $\frac{5\pi}{12}$ are solutions. However, since x values must be in the interval from 0 to 2π, $2x$ must be in the interval from 0 to 4π. Thus other values of $2x$ are $\frac{13\pi}{6}$ and $\frac{17\pi}{6}$. Therefore, $\frac{13\pi}{12}$ and $\frac{17\pi}{12}$ are also solutions.

$$x = \frac{\pi}{12}, \frac{5\pi}{12}, \frac{13\pi}{12}, \frac{17\pi}{12}$$

Try This Find all solutions (in terms of π) from 0 to 2π.

b. $2 \cos 2x = 1$

In solving trigonometric equations, we often apply algebraic manipulations before working with the trigonometric part. In the next example, we recognize that the equation is reducible to a quadratic, with $\cos \theta$ as the variable. We begin by putting the equation in standard form.

EXAMPLE 4 Solve $8 \cos^2 \theta - 2 \cos \theta = 1$, finding all solutions from 0° to 360°.

$8 \cos^2 \theta - 2 \cos \theta - 1 = 0$ Getting 0 on one side

$(4 \cos \theta + 1)(2 \cos \theta - 1) = 0$ Factoring

$4 \cos \theta + 1 = 0$ or $2 \cos \theta - 1 = 0$ Principle of zero products

$\cos \theta = -\frac{1}{4}$ or $\cos \theta = \frac{1}{2}$

$= -0.25$

From Table 5 we find that for $\cos \theta = -0.25$, $\theta = 104°30'$ or $255°30'$. For $\cos \theta = \frac{1}{2}$, $\theta = 60°$ or $300°$. The solutions from 0 to 360° are $104°30'$, $255°30'$, 60°, and 300°.

Try This Solve. Find all solutions from 0° to 360°.

c. $8 \cos^2 \theta + 2 \cos \theta = 1$ **d.** $2 \cos^2 \phi + \cos \phi = 0$

Extra Help On the Web

Look for worked-out examples at the Prentice Hall Web site.
www.phschool.com

18-5 Exercises

A

Solve. Find all solutions from 0 to 2π or 0° to 360°.

1. $2 \sin x + \sqrt{3} = 0$

2. $\sqrt{3} \tan x + 1 = 0$

3. $4 \sin^2 x - 1 = 0$

4. $2 \cos^2 x = 1$

5. $2 \sin^2 x + \sin x = 1$

6. $2 \cos^2 x + 3 \cos x = -1$

7. $\cos^2 x + 2 \cos x = 3$

8. $2 \sin^2 x - \sin x = 3$

9. $2 \sin^2 \theta + 7 \sin \theta = 4$

10. $2 \sin^2 \theta - 5 \sin \theta + 2 = 0$

11. **TEST PREP** Choose the correct set of solutions from 0° to 360° for $2 \sin x^2 + \sin x - 1 = 0$.

A. 30°, 90° **B.** 30°, 150°, 270° **C.** 90°, 210°, 330° **D.** 0°, 90°, 180°

Find all solutions of the following equations from 0 to 2π.

12. $\cos 2x \sin x + \sin x = 0$

13. $\sin 2x \cos x - \cos x = 0$

14. $\tan x \sin x - \tan x = 0$

15. $2 \sin x \cos x + \sin x = 0$

16. $2 \sec x \tan x + 2 \sec x + \tan x + 1 = 0$

17. $2 \csc x \cos x - 4 \cos x - \csc x + 2 = 0$

18. $\sin 2x + 2 \sin x \cos x = 0$

19. $\cos 2x \sin x + \sin x = 0$

20. $\cos 2x \cos x + \sin 2x \sin x = 1$

21. $\sin 2x \sin x - \cos 2x \cos x = -\cos x$

22. $\sin 2x + 2 \sin x - \cos x - 1 = 0$

23. $\sin 2x + \sin x + 2 \cos x + 1 = 0$

24. $\sec^2 x = 4 \tan^2 x$

25. $\sec^2 x - 2 \tan^2 x = 0$

B

26. $\cos(\pi - x) + \sin\left(x - \frac{\pi}{2}\right) = 1$

27. $\sin(\pi - x) + \cos\left(\frac{\pi}{2} - x\right) = 1$

28. $2 \cos x + 2 \sin x = \sqrt{6}$

29. $2 \cos x + 2 \sin x = \sqrt{2}$

30. $\sqrt{3} \cos x - \sin x = 1$

31. $\sqrt{2} \cos x - \sqrt{2} \sin x = 2$

32. ***Critical Thinking*** Make up a trigonometric equation with solutions of $\frac{\pi}{12}, \frac{5\pi}{12}$, and $\frac{3\pi}{4}$ in the domain $\{0, 2\pi\}$.

Challenge

Find solutions to the following equations from 0 to 360°.

33. $|\sin x| = \frac{\sqrt{3}}{2}$

34. $|\cos x| = \frac{1}{2}$

35. $\sqrt{\tan x} = \sqrt[4]{3}$

36. $12 \sin x - 7\sqrt{\sin x} + 1 = 0$

37. $16 \cos^4 x - 16 \cos^2 x + 3 = 0$

38. Find the solution to $\operatorname{Arccos} x = \operatorname{Arccos} \frac{3}{5} - \operatorname{Arcsin} \frac{4}{5}$ from 0 to 1.

Mixed Review

Let $P(x) = x^4 + x^3 + 7x^2 + 9x - 18$. **39.** Find the zeros and x-intercepts.

40. Find $P(-5), P(-3), P(0), P(2), P(4)$.

41. Factor $P(x)$, then graph $P(x)$. *11-1, 11-2, 11-6*

Solve. **42.** $\sqrt{x + 2} = x + 2$ **43.** $z^4 + 7z^2 = 144$ *7-6, 8-5*

Evaluate. **44.** ${}_6P_6$ **45.** ${}_{10}P_5$ **46.** ${}_9P_4$ **47.** $\binom{9}{4}$ **48.** $\binom{10}{5}$ *15-1, 15-3*

18-6 Right Triangles and Problem Solving

What You'll Learn

1. To find missing parts of right triangles
2. To solve problems using right triangles

... And Why

To know when to use right-triangle applications to solve problems

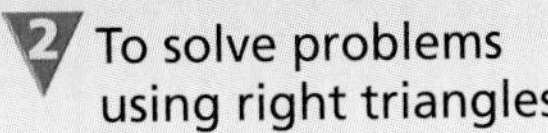

PART 1 Solving Triangles

Objective: Solve right triangles.

In Chapter 17 the trigonometric functions were defined, solving of right triangles was introduced, and tables were considered. We continue consideration of solving right triangles, a topic important in many applications of trigonometry.

EXAMPLE 1 Find the length b in this triangle. Use four-digit precision.

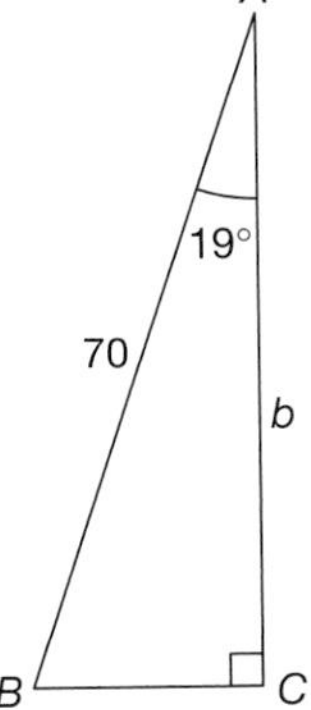

The known side is the hypotenuse. The side we seek is adjacent to the known angle. Thus we shall use the cosine function $\cos A = \frac{b}{70}$. We solve for b.

$$\text{cosine} = \frac{\text{adjacent}}{\text{hypotenuse}}$$

$$\cos 19° = \frac{b}{70}$$

$$b = 70 \cdot \cos 19°$$

$$b \approx 70 \cdot 0.9455$$

$$b \approx 66.19$$

When we solve a triangle, we find the *measures* of its sides and angles not already known. We sometimes shorten this by saying that we "find the angles" or "find the sides."

Try This

a. Find the lengths a and b in this triangle. Angle A is given to the nearest minute, and length AB to four-digit precision.

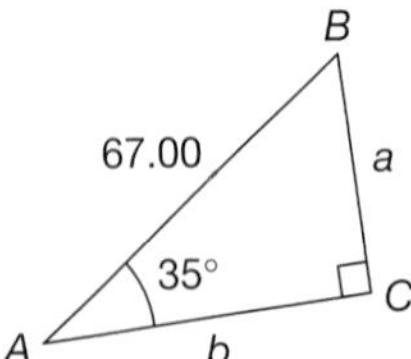

b. Solve this triangle. Use four-digit precision.

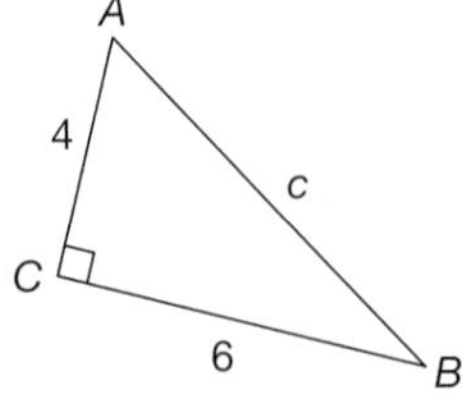

PART 2 Using Right Triangles

Objective: Solve problems using right triangles.

Right triangles have many applications. To solve a problem, we locate a right triangle and then solve that triangle to find a solution to the problem. There are many real-world applications or situations that involve right triangles.

EXAMPLE 2

A device for measuring cloud height at night consists of a vertical beam of light that makes a spot on the clouds. The spot is viewed from a point 135 m away. The angle of elevation is 67°40′. (The angle between the horizontal and a line of sight is called an **angle of elevation** or an **angle of depression,** the latter if the line of sight is below the horizontal.) Find the height of the clouds.

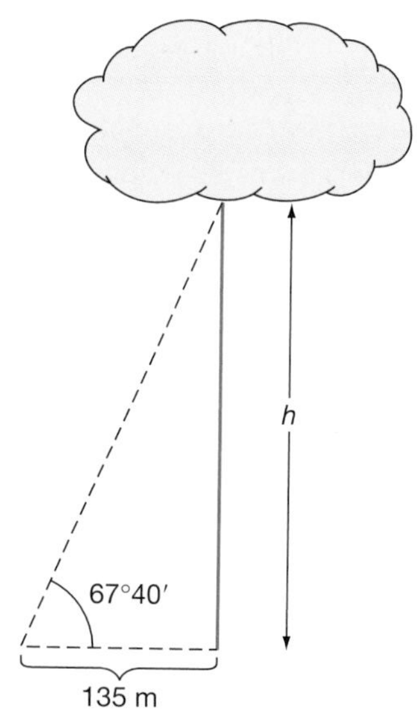

From the drawing we have

$$\text{tangent} = \frac{\text{opposite}}{\text{adjacent}}$$

$$\tan 67°40' = \frac{h}{135}$$

$$135 \cdot \tan 67°40' = h$$

$$135 \cdot 2.434 \approx h$$

$$329 \approx h$$

The cloud is approximately 329 m high.

EXAMPLE 3

An observer stands on level ground, 200 m from the base of a TV tower, and looks up at an angle of 26.5° to see the top of the tower. How high is the tower above the observer's eye level?

We draw a diagram and see that a right triangle is formed. We use one of the trigonometric functions. The tangent function is most convenient. From the definition of the tangent function, we have

$$\text{tangent} = \frac{\text{opposite}}{\text{adjacent}}$$

$$\tan 26.5° = \frac{h}{200}$$

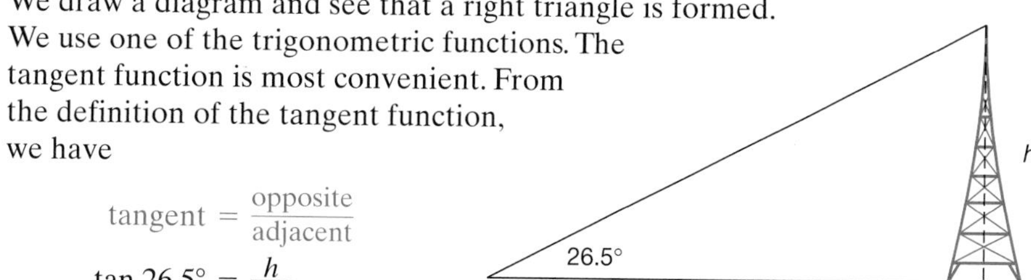

Then $h = 200 \tan 26.5°$. We find, from a table or calculator, that $\tan 26.5° \approx 0.4986$. Thus $h \approx 200 \cdot 0.4986 \approx 99.7$. The height of the tower is about 99.7 meters.

Try This

c. An observer stands 120 m from a tree, and finds that the line of sight to the top of the tree is 32.3° above the horizontal. The tangent of 32.3° is 0.632. Find the height of the tree above eye level.

d. A guy wire is 13.6 m long, and is fastened from the ground to a pole at a point 6.5 m above the ground. What angle does the wire make with the ground?

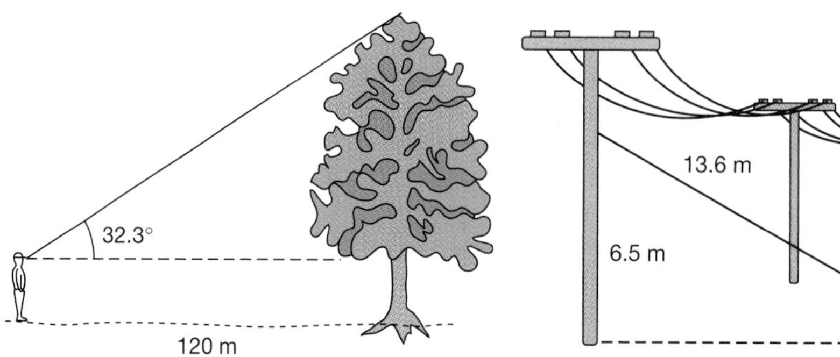

EXAMPLE 4

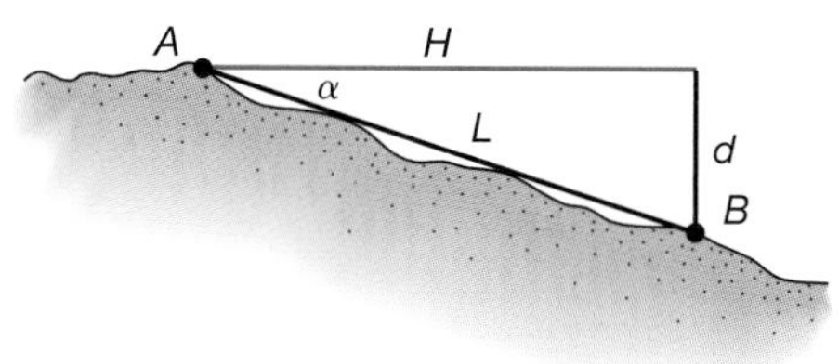

In surveying, horizontal distances must often be measured, even where terrain is not level. One way of doing it is as follows. Distance down a slope is measured with a surveyor's tape, and the distance d is measured by making a level sighting from A to a pole held vertically at B, or the angle α is measured by an instrument placed at A. Suppose that a slope distance L is measured to be 121.3 ft and the angle α is measured to be 3°25′. Find the horizontal distance H.

From the drawing we see that $\frac{H}{L} = \cos \alpha$. Thus $H = L \cos \alpha$, and in this case,

$$\begin{aligned} H &= 121.3 \times 0.9982 \\ &= 121.1 \text{ ft} \end{aligned}$$

EXAMPLE 5

In aerial navigation, directions are given in degrees, clockwise from north. Thus east is 90°, south is 180°, and so on. An airplane leaves an airport and travels for 100 miles in a direction 300°. How far north and how far west of the airport is the plane?

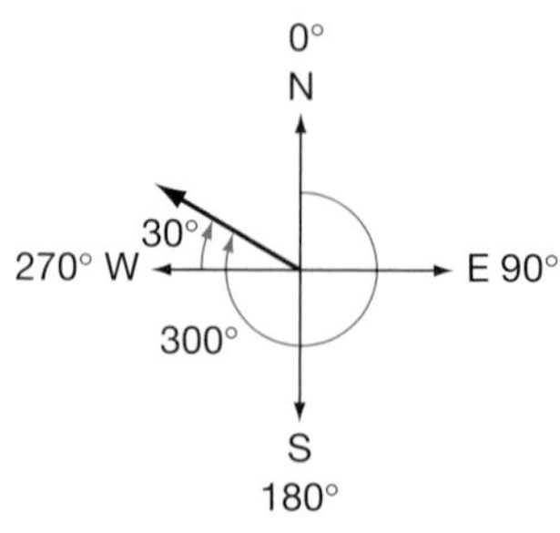

The direction of flight is as shown.

In the triangle, d_1 is the northerly distance and d_2 is the westerly distance. Then

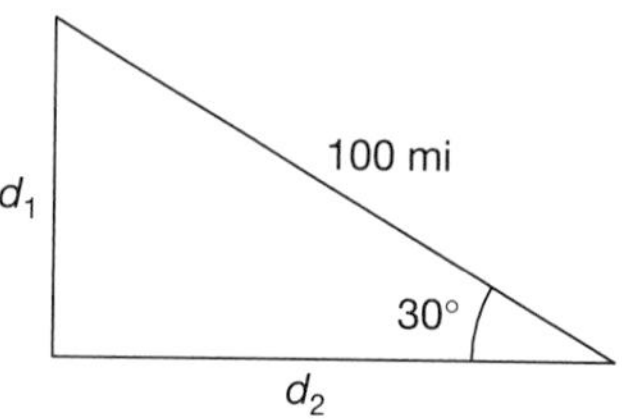

$$\frac{d_1}{100} = \sin 30^\circ \quad \text{and} \quad \frac{d_2}{100} = \cos 30^\circ$$

$$d_1 = 100 \sin 30^\circ = 100 \times 0.5$$
$$= 50 \text{ mi}$$
$$d_2 = 100 \cos 30^\circ = 100 \times 0.866$$
$$= 87 \text{ mi (to the nearest mile)}$$

The plane is about 50 miles north and 87 miles west of the airport.

Guidelines for Solving a Triangle Problem

1. Draw a sketch of the problem situation.
2. Look for triangles and sketch them in.
3. Mark the known and unknown sides and angles.
4. Express the desired side or angle in terms of known trigonometric ratios. Then solve.

Try This

e. A downslope distance is measured to be 241.3 ft and the angle of depression α is measured to be 5°15′. Find the horizontal distance.

f. An airplane flies 150 km from an airport in a direction of 115°. It is then how far east of the airport? how far south?

18-6 Exercises

Extra Help On the Web

Look for worked-out examples at the Prentice Hall Web site. www.phschool.com

A

In Exercises 1–15, standard lettering for a right triangle will be used. A, B, and C are the angles, C being the right angle. The sides opposite A, B, and C are a, b, and c, respectively. Solve the triangles using three-digit precision.

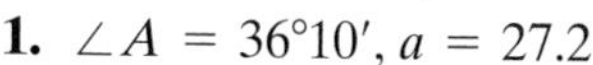

1. $\angle A = 36°10', a = 27.2$

2. $\angle A = 87°40', a = 9.73$

3. $\angle B = 12°40', b = 98.1$

4. $\angle B = 69°50', b = 127$

5. $\angle A = 17°20', b = 13.6$

6. $\angle A = 78°40', b = 1340$

7. $\angle B = 69°20', a = 0.0049$

8. $\angle A = 88°50', c = 3950$

9. $\angle B = 56°30', c = 0.0447$

10. $\angle B = 82°20', c = 0.982$

11. $b = 1.80, c = 4.00$

12. $b = 100, c = 450$

13. $a = 12.0, b = 18.0$

14. $a = 10.0, b = 20.0$

15. ***Write a Convincing Argument*** If $a = 16.0$ and $c = 20.0$, explain how the length of side b can be found without using a trigonometric ratio. Find b. Then find $\angle A$ and $\angle B$.

16. A guy wire attached to a pole makes an angle of 73°10′ with the level ground, and is 14.5 ft from the pole at the ground. How far above the ground is the wire attached to the pole?

17. A guy wire attached to a pole makes an angle of 74°20′ with the level ground and is attached to the pole 34.2 ft above the ground. How far from the base of the pole is the wire attached to the ground?

18. A kite string makes an angle of 31°40′ with the level ground, and 455 ft of string is out. How high is the kite?

19. A kite string makes an angle of 41°40′ with the level ground when the kite is 114 ft high. How long is the string?

20. A road rises 3 m per 100 horizontal m. What angle does it make with the horizontal?

21. A kite is 120 ft high when 670 ft of kite string is out. What angle does the kite make with the ground?

22. What is the angle of elevation of the sun when a 6-ft man casts a 10.3-ft shadow?

23. What is the angle of elevation of the sun when a 35-ft mast casts a 20-ft shadow?

24. From a balloon 2500 ft high, a command post is seen with an angle of depression of 7°40′. How far is it from a point on the ground below the balloon to the command post?

In Exercise 25, what is the angle of elevation of the top of the lighthouse from the small boat?

25. From a lighthouse 55 ft above sea level, the angle of depression to a small boat is 11°20′. How far from the foot of the lighthouse is the boat?

26. An observer sights the top of a building 173 ft higher than the eye at an angle of elevation of 27°50′. How far is the observer from the building?

27. An observer sights the top of a building 212 ft higher than the eye at an angle of elevation of 19°10′. How far is the observer from the building?

28. An airplane travels at 120 km/h for 2 hr in a direction of 243° from Chicago. At the end of this time, how far south of Chicago is the plane?

29. An airplane travels at 150 km/h for 2 hr in a direction of 138° from Omaha. At the end of this time, how far east of Omaha is the plane?

30. A regular pentagon has sides 30.5 cm long. Find the radius of the circumscribed circle.

31. A regular pentagon has sides 42.8 cm long. Find the radius of the inscribed circle.

32. A regular hexagon has a perimeter of 50 cm and is inscribed in a circle. Find the radius of the circle.

33. A regular octagon is inscribed in a circle of radius 15.8 cm. Find the perimeter of the octagon.

34. ***Multi-Step Problem*** An observer on a ladder looks at a building 100 ft away, noting that the angle of elevation of the top of the building is 18°40′ and the angle of depression of the bottom of the building is 6°20′. How tall is the building?

35. From a balloon 2 km high, the angles of depression to two towns in line with the balloon are 81°20′ and 13°40′. How far apart are the towns?

36. From a balloon 1000 km high, the angles of depression to two artillery posts in line with the balloon are 11°50′ and 84°10′. How far apart are the artillery posts?

Pilot Bertrand Piccard of Switzerland and co-pilot Brian Jones of Great Britain flew this Breitling Orbiter 3 above the Swiss Alps after liftoff from Chateau d'Oex, March 1, 1999. See Exercise 35.

37. A weather balloon is directly west of two observing stations 10 km apart. The angles of elevation of the balloon from the two stations are 17°50′ and 78°10′. How high is the balloon?

38. From two points south of a hill on level ground and 1000 ft apart, the angles of elevation of the hill are 12°20′ and 82°40′. How high is the hill?

B

39. ***Mathematical Reasoning***

Show that the area of a right triangle is $\frac{1}{2}bc \sin A$.

40. ***Critical Thinking*** Use the information given in the diagram at the right to find y without using a table or calculator. (Hint: Use a double-angle identity.)

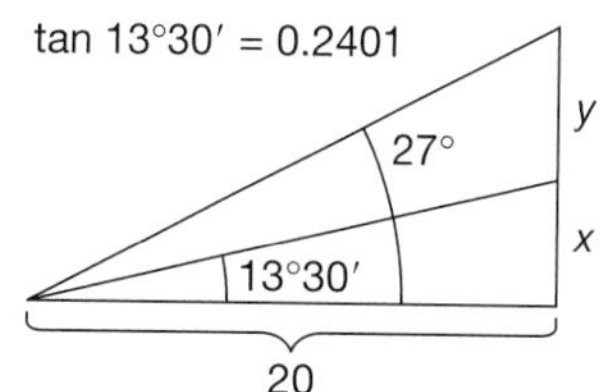

Challenge

41. Find a formula for the distance to the horizon as a function of the height of the observer above Earth. Calculate the distance to the horizon from an airplane at an altitude of 1000 ft. (You will need to look up the radius of Earth.)

Mixed Review

Solve. **42.** $x^3 + 24x^2 + 191x + 504 = 0$ **43.** $25x^2 + 49 = 0$

44. $\sqrt[3]{4y + 7} - 3 = 0$ *11-3, 8-1, 7-6*

18-7 The Law of Sines

What You'll Learn

1. To solve triangles given two angles and a side
2. To solve triangles given two sides and an angle opposite one of them
3. To use the Law of Sines to find the area of a triangle

. . . And Why

To solve problems involving data about triangles

The trigonometric functions can be used to solve triangles that are not right triangles (oblique triangles). In order to solve oblique triangles we need to derive some properties, one of which is called the **Law of Sines.** We shall consider any oblique triangle. It may or may not have an obtuse angle. We will consider both cases, but the derivations are essentially the same.

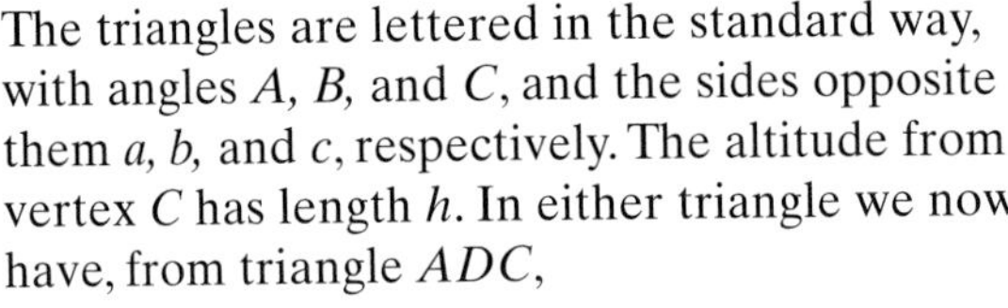

The triangles are lettered in the standard way, with angles A, B, and C, and the sides opposite them a, b, and c, respectively. The altitude from vertex C has length h. In either triangle we now have, from triangle ADC,

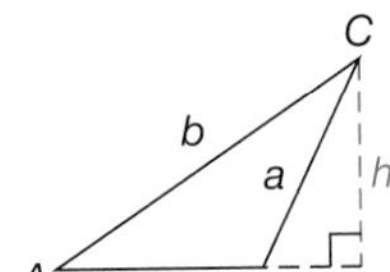

$$\frac{h}{b} = \sin A, \text{ or } h = b \sin A$$

From triangle DBC we have $\frac{h}{a} = \sin B$, or $h = a \sin B$.

Thus we have $\frac{h}{a} = \sin \angle CBD = \sin (180^\circ - B) = \sin B$. So in either kind of triangle we now have

$$h = a \sin B \text{ and } h = b \sin A$$

Thus it follows that $a \sin B = b \sin A$.

$$\frac{a}{\sin A} = \frac{b}{\sin B}$$

If we were to consider an altitude from vertex A in the triangles shown, the same argument would give us the following.

$$\frac{b}{\sin B} = \frac{c}{\sin C}$$

We combine these results to obtain the Law of Sines, which holds for right triangles as well as oblique triangles.

Theorem 18-5

The Law of Sines

In any triangle ABC, $\frac{a}{\sin A} = \frac{b}{\sin B} = \frac{c}{\sin C}$.

(The sides are proportional to the sines of the opposite angles.)

PART 1 Solving Triangles (AAS)

Objective: Use the Law of Sines to solve triangles, given two angles and a side opposite one of them.

When two angles and a side of any triangle are known, the Law of Sines can be used to solve the triangle.

EXAMPLE 1

In triangle ABC, $a = 4.56$, $m\angle A = 43$, and $m\angle C = 57$. Solve the triangle.

We first draw a sketch. We find $m\angle B$, as follows.

$$m\angle B = 180^\circ - (43^\circ + 57^\circ)$$
$$= 80^\circ$$

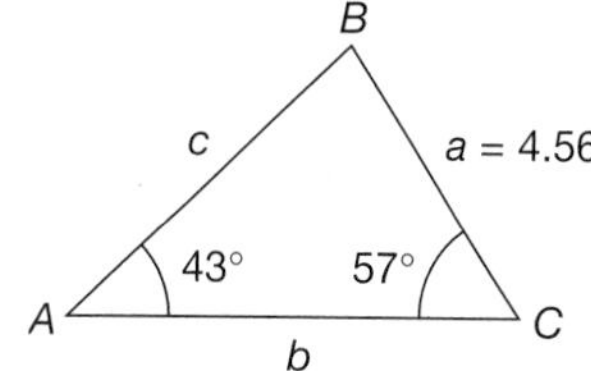

We can now find the other two sides, using the Law of Sines.

$$\frac{c}{\sin C} = \frac{a}{\sin A}$$

$$c = \frac{a \sin C}{\sin A}$$

$$= \frac{4.56 \sin 57^\circ}{\sin 43^\circ}$$

$$\approx \frac{4.56 \times 0.8387}{0.6820}$$

$$\approx 5.61$$

$$\frac{b}{\sin B} = \frac{a}{\sin A}$$

$$b = \frac{a \sin B}{\sin A}$$

$$= \frac{4.56 \sin 80^\circ}{0.6820}$$

$$\approx \frac{4.56 \times 0.9848}{0.6820}$$

$$\approx 6.58$$

We have now found the unknown parts of the triangle, $B = 80^\circ$, $c \approx 5.61$, and $b \approx 6.58$. A calculator is of great help in doing calculations like these.

Try This

a. In triangle ABC, $m\angle A = 41$, $m\angle C = 52$, and $a = 6.53$. Solve the triangle.

b. In triangle ABC, $m\angle B = 2$, $m\angle C = 119$, and $b = 9$. Solve the triangle.

PART 2 The Ambiguous Case (SSA)

Objective: Use the Law of Sines to solve triangles, given two sides and an angle opposite one of them.

When two sides of a triangle and an angle opposite one of them are known, the Law of Sines can be used to solve the triangle. However, there may be more than one solution. This is known as the ambiguous case. Suppose a, b, and $m\angle A$ are given. The various possibilities are shown in the four cases below.

Case I

C
a
b
A

No solution

Case II

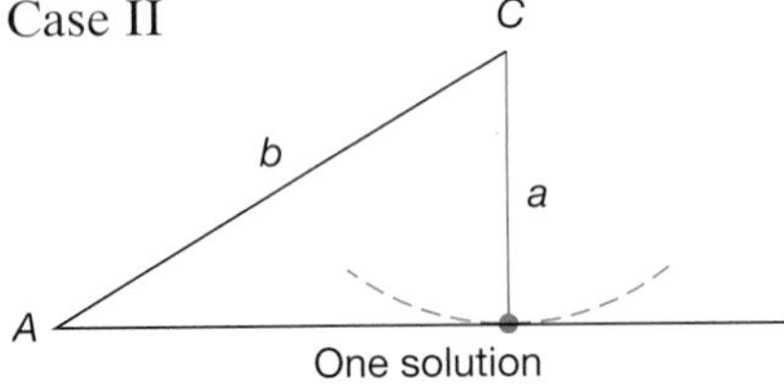

One solution

Case III

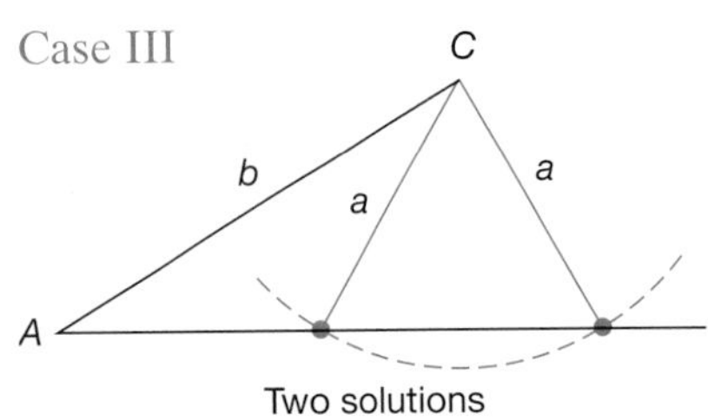

Two solutions

Case IV

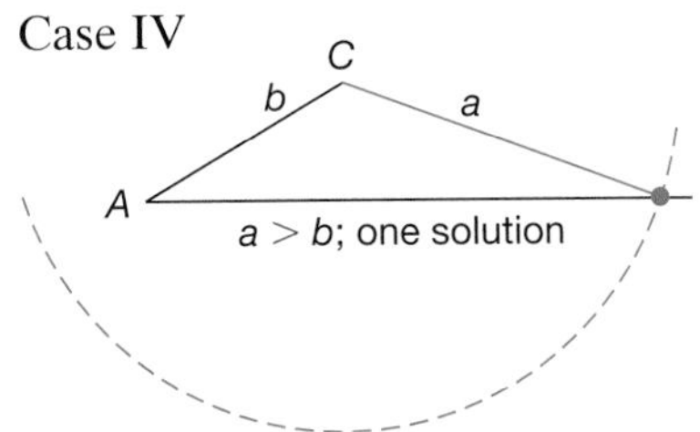

$a > b$; one solution

EXAMPLE 2 In triangle ABC, $a = 15$, $b = 25$, and $m\angle A = 47$. Solve the triangle.

This is Case I. We look for $m\angle B$.

$$\frac{a}{\sin A} = \frac{b}{\sin B}$$

Then $\sin B = \dfrac{b \sin A}{a} = \dfrac{25 \sin 47^\circ}{15} \approx \dfrac{25 \times 0.7314}{15} \approx 1.219.$

Since there is no angle having a sine greater than 1, there is no solution.

EXAMPLE 3 In triangle ABC, $a = 12$, $b = 5$, and $\angle B = 24°38'$. Solve the triangle.

This is Case II. We look for $m\angle A$.

$$\frac{a}{\sin A} = \frac{b}{\sin B}$$

Then $\sin A = \dfrac{a \sin B}{b} = \dfrac{12 \sin 24°38'}{5} \approx \dfrac{12 \times 0.4168}{5} \approx 1.000.$

$$m\angle A \approx 90$$

Thus $\angle C \approx 90° - 24°38' \approx 65°22'$.

Since $\frac{c}{a} = \cos B$, $c = a \cos B \approx 12 \times 0.9090 \approx 10.9$.

Try This Solve triangle ABC.

c. $a = 40, b = 12, m\angle B = 57$
d. $a = 4, b = 3, \angle A = 53°08'$

EXAMPLE 4 In triangle ABC, $a = 20$, $b = 15$, and $m\angle B = 30$. Solve the triangle.

This is Case III. We look for $m\angle A$.

$$\frac{a}{\sin A} = \frac{b}{\sin B}$$
$$\sin A = \frac{a \sin B}{b} = \frac{20 \sin 30°}{15} = \frac{20 \times 0.5}{15} \approx 0.667$$

There are two angles less than 180° having a sine of approximately 0.667. They are 42° and 138°. This gives us two possible solutions.

Possible solution 1

We know that $m\angle A = 42$.
Then $\angle C = 180° - (30° + 42°) = 108°$.

We now find c.

$$\frac{c}{\sin C} = \frac{b}{\sin B}$$
$$c = \frac{b \sin C}{\sin B} = \frac{15 \sin 108°}{\sin 30°} \approx \frac{15 \times 0.9511}{0.5} \approx 28.5$$

These parts make a triangle, as shown. Hence we have a solution.

Possible solution 2

$$m\angle A = 138$$
$$m\angle C = 180 - (30 + 138) = 12$$

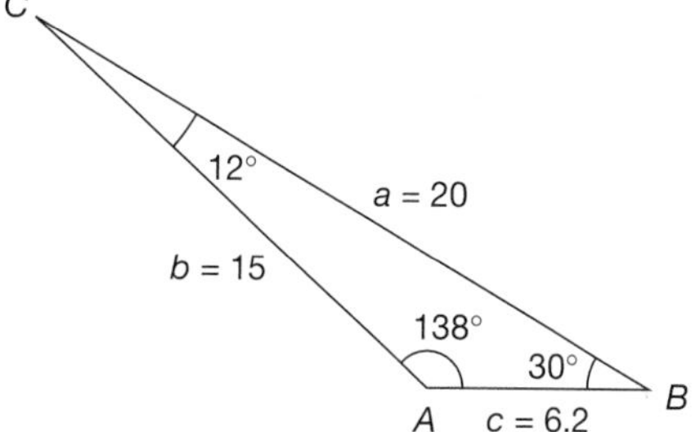

We now find c.

$$c = \frac{b \sin C}{\sin B} = \frac{15 \sin 12°}{\sin 30°}$$
$$\approx \frac{15 \times 0.2079}{0.5} \approx 6.2$$

These parts make a triangle. Hence we have a second solution.

EXAMPLE 5 In triangle ABC, $a = 25$, $b = 10$, and $m\angle A = 42$. Solve the triangle.

This is Case IV. We look for $m\angle B$.

$$\frac{b}{\sin B} = \frac{a}{\sin A}$$
$$\sin B = \frac{b \sin A}{a} = \frac{10 \sin 42°}{25}$$
$$\approx \frac{10 \times 0.6691}{25} \approx 0.2676$$

Quick Review

In any triangle, if two angles have unequal measures, the lengths of the sides opposite the angles are unequal in the same order.

Then $\angle B = 15°30'$ or $\angle B = 164°30'$. Since $a > b$, we know there is only one solution. An angle of $164°30'$ cannot be an angle of this triangle because it already has an angle of $42°$, and these two would total more than $180°$.

$$\angle C = 180° - (42° + 15°30') = 122°30'$$

$$\frac{c}{\sin C} = \frac{a}{\sin A}$$

$$c = \frac{a \sin C}{\sin A} \approx \frac{25 \sin 122°30'}{\sin 42°} \quad \text{Solving for } c$$

$$c \approx \frac{25 \times 0.8434}{0.6691} \approx 31.5$$

Try This Solve triangle ABC.

e. $a = 25, b = 20, m\angle B = 33$ **f.** $b = 20, c = 10, m\angle B = 38$

PART 3 Area of a Triangle

Objective: Use the Law of Sines to find the area of a triangle.

We can use the Law of Sines in finding areas of triangles. Look again at the triangles at the beginning of this lesson. Each triangle has area $\frac{1}{2}hc$. Remember that $h = b \sin A$. Thus area $= \frac{1}{2}(b \sin A)c$.

$$\text{area} = \frac{1}{2}bc \sin A$$

EXAMPLE 6 In triangle ABC, $b = 9$, $c = 12$, and $m\angle A = 40$. Find the area.

Using area $= \frac{1}{2}bc \sin A$, we have the following.

$$\text{area} \approx \frac{1}{2} \times 9 \times 12 \times 0.6428 \approx 34.7 \text{ square units}$$

EXAMPLE 7 Find the area of the triangle drawn below.

We assign $\angle A$ to the known angle. The side lengths b and c can be assigned arbitrarily to 7 m and 10 m.

$$m\angle A = 35, \quad b = 7 \text{ m}, \quad c = 10 \text{ m}$$

$$\text{area} = \frac{1}{2}bc \sin A$$

$$= \frac{1}{2}(7)(10) \sin 35$$

$$\approx 35 \cdot 0.5736 \approx 20.1 \text{ m}^2$$

Try This

g. In triangle ABC, $b = 5$, $c = 8$, and $m\angle A = 25$. Find the area.

18-7 Exercises

Extra Help On the Web

Look for worked-out examples at the Prentice Hall Web site.
www.phschool.com

A

Solve triangle ABC.

1. $m\angle A = 60, m\angle B = 70, b = 20$
2. $m\angle A = 48, m\angle B = 62, b = 35$
3. $m\angle A = 36, m\angle B = 48, a = 12$
4. $m\angle A = 40, m\angle B = 60, b = 100$
5. $m\angle A = 133, m\angle B = 30, b = 18$
6. $m\angle B = 120, m\angle C = 30, a = 16$
7. $m\angle B = 38, m\angle C = 21, b = 24$
8. $m\angle A = 131, m\angle C = 23, b = 10$
9. $m\angle A = 68°30', m\angle C = 42°40', c = 23.5$
10. $m\angle B = 118°20', m\angle C = 45°40', b = 42.1$
11. $m\angle B = 150, a = 3, b = 7$
12. $m\angle A = 30, a = 6, c = 9$
13. $m\angle C = 60, a = 12, c = 30$
14. $m\angle B = 45, a = 15, b = 17$
15. $m\angle A = 36, a = 24, b = 34$
16. $m\angle C = 43, c = 28, b = 27$
17. $\angle A = 116°20', a = 17.2, c = 13.5$
18. $\angle A = 47°50', a = 28.3, b = 18.2$
19. $\angle C = 61°10', c = 30.3, b = 24.2$
20. $\angle B = 58°40', a = 25.1, b = 32.6$

Find the area of triangle ABC.

21. $b = 8, c = 15, m\angle A = 30$
22. $b = 7, c = 18, m\angle A = 54$
23. $b = 1, c = 1, m\angle A = 10$
24. $b = 100, c = 75, m\angle A = 170$

Find the area of each triangle.

25.

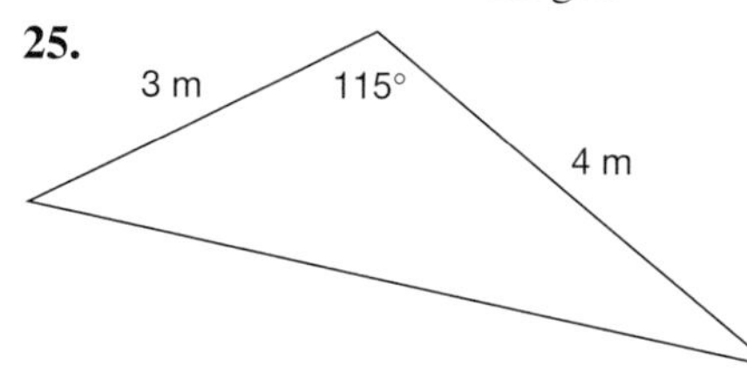

26.

9 m
27°
25 m

B

Solve.

27. Points A and B are on opposite sides of a lunar crater. Point C is 50 m from A. The measure of $\angle BAC$ is determined to be 112° and the measure of $\angle ACB$ is determined to be 42°. What is the width of the crater?
28. A guy wire to the top of a pole makes a 71° angle with level ground. At a point 25 ft farther from the pole than the guy wire, the angle of elevation to the top of the pole is 37°. How long is the guy wire?
29. A pole leans away from the sun at an angle of 7° to the vertical. When the angle of elevation of the sun is 51°, the pole casts a shadow 47 ft long on level ground. How long is the pole?
30. A vertical pole stands by a road that is inclined 10° to the horizontal. When the angle of elevation of the sun is 23°, the pole casts a shadow 38 ft long directly downhill along the road. How long is the pole?

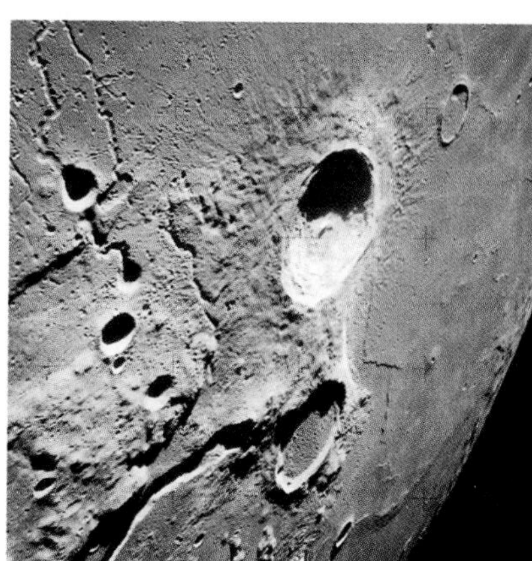

The Copernicus crater of the moon measures 93 km in diameter. How much smaller is the crater in Exercise 27?

Taking the bearings from at least two ranger lookout stations is important in providing data to determine the location of a forest fire. See Exercise 32.

31. A reconnaissance airplane leaves its airport on the east coast of the United States and flies in a direction of 85°. Because of bad weather it returns to another airport 230 km to the north of its home base. For the return it flies in a direction of 283°. What is the total distance flown?

32. Ranger Station B in a state forest is 10.2 km east of station A. The bearing of a fire from A is S 10°40′W. The bearing of the fire from B is S 31°20′W. How far is the fire from A? from B?

33. A boat leaves lighthouse A and sails 5.1 km. At this time it is sighted from lighthouse B, 7.2 km west of A. The bearing of the boat from B is N 65°10′E. How far is the boat from B?

34. ***Critical Thinking*** Find a formula for the area of a parallelogram in terms of two sides, a and b, and an included angle θ.

Challenge

35. ***Mathematical Reasoning*** Prove that the area of a quadrilateral is half the product of the lengths of its diagonals and the sine of an angle between the diagonals.

36. Consider two objects, such as ships, airplanes, or runners, moving in straight-line paths. If the distance between them is decreasing, and if the bearing from one of them to the other is constant, they will collide. ("Constant bearing means collision," as mariners put it.) Prove that this statement is true.

Mixed Review

Simplify. **37.** $\left(\frac{216a^{-2}b^5c^4d^2}{a^4b^2c^{10}d^{-2}}\right)^{\frac{2}{3}}$ **38.** $(2 - i)^4$

39. $\left|\frac{1}{2} - \frac{\sqrt{3}}{2}i\right|$ **40.** $\frac{i}{1 + i}$ *7-5, 7-8, 7-9*

Find the sum. **41.** $\sum_{n=-4}^{4} (4n + 6)$ **42.** $\sum_{n=-3}^{3} \left(\frac{1}{2}\right)^n$

43. $\sum_{n=1}^{10} (-4)^{n-1}$ **44.** $0.7 + 0.07 + 0.007 + \cdots$. *14-2, 14-3, 14-4*

Find the function of lowest degree with rational coefficients.

45. with roots $4i, -\sqrt{6}$ **46.** with roots $1, 2, 1 + 2i$ *11-3*

Connections: Geometry

Draw a circle with a diameter of 3 in. Mark the center of the circle as point M. Then choose 3 points, A, B, and C, on the circle so that when you draw a triangle with these points as vertices, M is inside the triangle. Measure the angles and side lengths. Then find $\frac{a}{\sin A}$, $\frac{b}{\sin B}$, and $\frac{c}{\sin C}$. Compare these ratios to the diameter of the circle.

The Law of Cosines

18-8

A second property used for solving oblique triangles is the **Law of Cosines.** This law can be thought of as a generalization of the Pythagorean theorem.

Consider any triangle ABC placed on a coordinate system. We will place the origin at one of the vertices, say C, and the positive half of the x-axis along one of the sides, say CB. Then the coordinates of B are $(a, 0)$, and the coordinates of A are $(b \cos C, b \sin C)$. We use the distance formula to determine c^2.

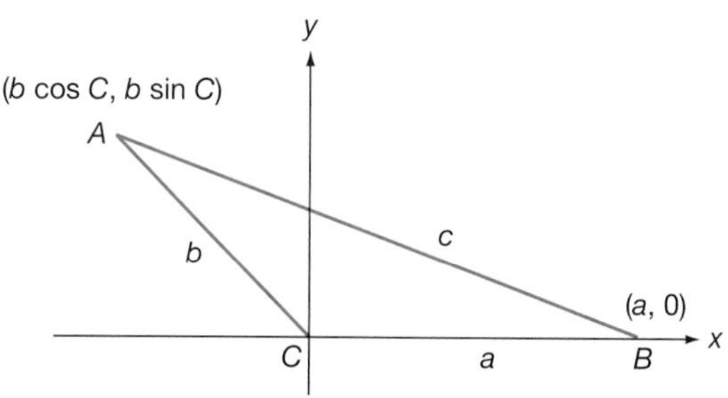

$$c^2 = (b \cos C - a)^2 + (b \sin C - 0)^2$$
$$c^2 = b^2 \cos^2 C - 2ab \cos C + a^2 + b^2 \sin^2 C \quad \text{Multiplying and simplifying}$$
$$c^2 = a^2 + b^2(\sin^2 C + \cos^2 C) - 2ab \cos C$$
$$c^2 = a^2 + b^2 - 2ab \cos C$$

Had we placed the origin at one of the other vertices, we would have obtained $a^2 = b^2 + c^2 - 2bc \cos A$, or $b^2 = a^2 + c^2 - 2ac \cos B$.

This result can be summarized as follows.

Theorem 18-6

The Law of Cosines

In any triangle ABC,

$$a^2 = b^2 + c^2 - 2bc \cos A$$
$$b^2 = a^2 + c^2 - 2ac \cos B$$
$$c^2 = a^2 + b^2 - 2ab \cos C$$

(In any triangle, the square of a side is the sum of the squares of the other two sides, minus twice the product of those sides and the cosine of the included angle.)

Only one of the above formulas needs to be memorized. The other two can be obtained by a change of letters.

What You'll Learn

1. To solve a triangle given two sides and an included angle
2. To solve a triangle given three sides

. . . And Why

To solve real-world problems that involve applying trigonometry

PART 1 Solving Triangles (SAS)

Objective: Solve a triangle given two sides and an included angle.

When two sides of a triangle and the included angle are known, we can use the Law of Cosines to find the third side. The Law of Sines can then be used to solve the triangle.

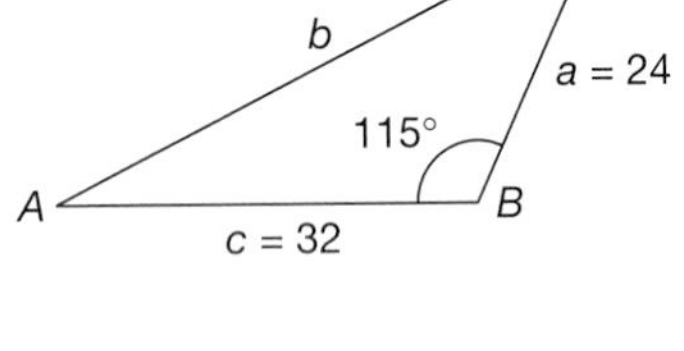

EXAMPLE 1 In triangle ABC, $a = 24$, $c = 32$, and $m\angle B = 115$. Solve the triangle.

We first find the third side. Apply the Law of Cosines.

$$b^2 = a^2 + c^2 - 2ac\cos B$$
$$\approx 24^2 + 32^2 - 2 \cdot 24 \cdot 32(-0.4226) \approx 2249$$
$$b \approx \sqrt{2249} \approx 47.4$$

Next we use the Law of Sines to find a second angle.

$$\frac{a}{\sin A} = \frac{b}{\sin B}, \sin A = \frac{a \sin B}{b} = \frac{24 \sin 115°}{47.4} \approx \frac{24 \times 0.9063}{47.4} \approx 0.4589$$
$$\angle A = 27°20'$$
$$\angle C = 180° - (115° + 27°20') = 37°40'$$

Try This Solve the triangle using the Law of Cosines.

a. In triangle ABC, $b = 18$, $c = 28$, and $m\angle A = 122$.

Write a short paragraph in which you contrast the Law of Sines and the Law of Cosines.

PART 2 Solving Triangles (SSS)

Objective: Solve a triangle given three sides.

When all three sides are known, the Law of Cosines can be used to solve the triangle.

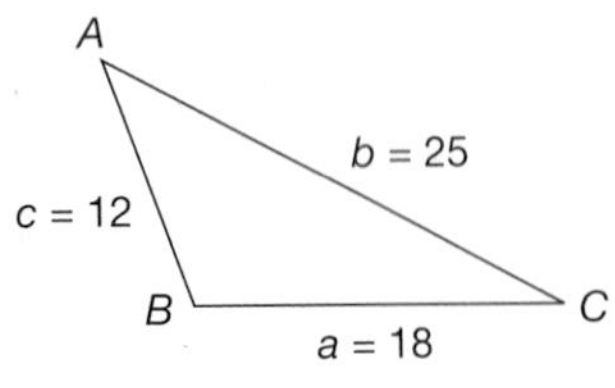

EXAMPLE 2 In triangle ABC, $a = 18$, $b = 25$, and $c = 12$. Solve the triangle.

Let us first find $m\angle B$. We select the formula from the Law of Cosines that contains $\cos B$; in other words, $b^2 = a^2 + c^2 - 2ac\cos B$. We solve this for $\cos B$ and substitute.

$$\cos B = \frac{a^2 + c^2 - b^2}{2ac} = \frac{18^2 + 12^2 - 25^2}{2 \cdot 18 \cdot 12} = -0.3634$$
$$\angle B = 111°20'$$

Using the formula that contains $\cos A$, we find that $\cos A = 0.7417$. So $\angle A = 42°10'$. Then $\angle C = 180° - (111°20' + 42°10') = 26°30'$.

Try This Solve the triangle using the Law of Cosines.

b. In triangle ABC, $a = 25$, $b = 10$, and $c = 20$.

18-8 Exercises

Extra Help On the Web

Look for worked-out examples at the Prentice Hall Web site.
www.phschool.com

A

Solve the triangles.

1. $m\angle C = 135$, $a = 6$, $b = 7$

2. $m\angle A = 116$, $b = 31$, $c = 25$

3. $m\angle A = 30$, $b = 12$, $c = 24$

4. $m\angle C = 120$, $a = 5$, $b = 8$

5. $m\angle A = 133$, $b = 12$, $c = 15$

6. $m\angle C = 60$, $a = 15$, $b = 12$

7. $\angle B = 72°40'$, $c = 16$, $a = 78$

8. $\angle A = 24°30'$, $b = 68$, $c = 109.8$

9. Using the Law of Cosines to solve a triangle ABC, if $\cos A$ is a nonnegative number less than 1, $\angle A$ is (*sometimes, always, never*) an acute angle.

Solve the triangles.

10. $a = 2$, $b = 3$, $c = 4$

11. $a = 7$, $b = 9$, $c = 10$

12. $a = 4$, $b = 6$, $c = 7$

13. $a = 7$, $b = 8$, $c = 10$

14. $a = 12$, $b = 14$, $c = 20$

15. $a = 22$, $b = 22$, $c = 35$

16. $a = 3.3$, $b = 2.7$, $c = 2.8$

17. $a = 16$, $b = 20$, $c = 32$

B

18. Two ships leave harbor at the same time. The first sails N 15°W at 25 knots (a knot is one nautical mile per hour). The second sails N 32°E at 20 knots. After 2 hours, how far apart are the ships?

19. Two airplanes leave an airport at the same time. The first flies 150 km/h in a direction of 320°. The second flies 200 km/h in a direction of 200°. After 3 hours, how far apart are the planes?

20. A hill is inclined 5° to the horizontal. A 45-ft pole stands at the top of the hill. How long a rope will it take to reach from the top of the pole to a point 35 ft downhill from the base of the pole?

21. A hill is inclined 15° to the horizontal. A 40-ft pole stands at the top of the hill. How long a rope will it take to reach from the top of the pole to a point 68 ft downhill from the base of the pole?

22. A piece of wire 5.5 m long is bent into a triangular shape. One side is 1.5 m long and another is 2 m long. Find the angles of the triangle.

23. A triangular lot has sides 120 ft long, 150 ft long, and 100 ft long. Find the angles of the lot.

24. A baseball diamond is a square 90 ft on a side. The pitcher's mound is 60.5 ft from home. How far does the pitcher have to run to cover first?

25. *Multi-Step Problem* The longer base of an isosceles trapezoid measures 14 ft. The nonparallel sides measure 10 ft, and the base angles measure 80°.

  a. Find the length of a diagonal. **b.** Find the area.

26. After flying 75 miles of a 180-mile trip, an aircraft is 10 miles off course. How much should the heading be corrected to then fly straight to the destination, assuming no wind correction?

27. *Critical Thinking* Find a formula for $a^2 + b^2 + c^2$ in any triangle.

Challenge

28. A bridge has been built across the canyon shown below. The length of the bridge is 5042 ft. From the deepest point in the canyon, the angles of elevation of the ends of the bridge are 78° and 72°. How deep is the canyon?

In order to design a bridge over a canyon such as the one in Exercise 28, a structural engineer needs to know a great deal of mathematics, including basic trigonometry.

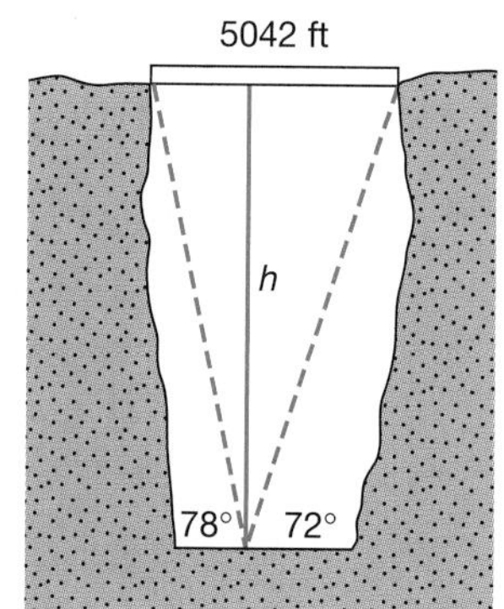

29. *Mathematical Reasoning* Find a formula for the area of an isosceles triangle in terms of the congruent sides and their included angle. Under what conditions will the area of a triangle with fixed congruent sides be a maximum?

30. Show that in any triangle ABC the following is true.
$$\frac{\cos A}{a} + \frac{\cos B}{b} + \frac{\cos C}{c} = \frac{a^2 + b^2 + c^2}{2abc}$$

Mixed Review

Solve. **31.** $\frac{1}{4}x + \frac{1}{6}x + \frac{1}{8}x = \frac{13}{12}$ **32.** $0.3x + 0.02x - 0.004x = -1.264$

33. $2^x \cdot 2^{2x} = 2^6$ **34.** $16^x = 1$ **35.** $x^3 = 1000$ *2-1, 12-7*

Divide. **36.** $(3x^4 - 2x^2 + 12x) \div 6x$ **37.** $(4x^4 - 2x^2 + 3x - 4) \div (x - 1)$

38. $(x^5 + 2x^3 - x^2) \div (x^2 - 3)$ *6-4, 6-5*

Factor. **39.** $x^8 - 16y^4$ **40.** $x^4 - 13x^2 + 36$ **41.** $2c^2 - 28c - 30$ *5-6*

Trigonometric Notation for Complex Numbers

18-9

In Chapter 7, we studied complex numbers. We now use our knowledge of trigonometry to develop trigonometric notation for complex numbers.

Consider any complex number $a + bi$. Recall that the length r of the segment from the origin to $a + bi$ is $\sqrt{a^2 + b^2}$. This distance r is called the **absolute value of a complex number.** Thus $r = |a + bi|$.

Suppose that the segment makes an angle θ with the real axis. As the diagram shows,

$$a = r \cos \theta \text{ and } b = r \sin \theta$$

Thus $a + bi = r \cos \theta + ir \sin \theta$
$= r(\cos \theta + i \sin \theta)$

This is trigonometric notation for $a + bi$. The angle θ is called the **argument.**

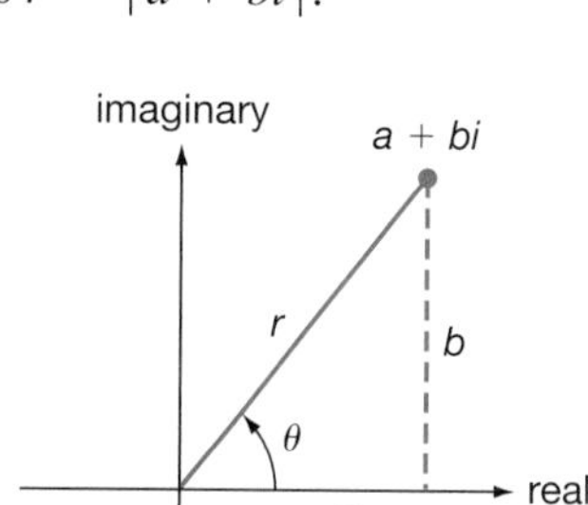
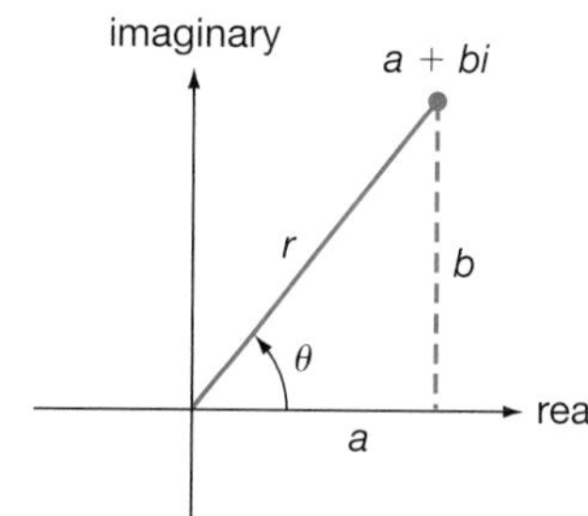

What You'll Learn

1. To change from rectangular notation for a complex number to trigonometric notation, and vice versa
2. To use trigonometric notation to multiply and divide complex numbers
3. To use De Moivre's Theorem to find powers and roots of complex numbers

. . . And Why

To solve problems using either rectangular or trigonometric notation

Definition

Trigonometric, or **polar, notation** for the complex number $a + bi$ is $r(\cos \theta + i \sin \theta)$ where $r = |a + bi|$ and θ is the argument. This is often shortened to $\boldsymbol{r \text{ cis } \theta}$.

PART 1 Change of Notation

Objective: Change from rectangular to trigonometric notation for a complex number and vice versa.

To change from trigonometric notation to **rectangular notation** $a + bi$, we use the formulas $a = r \cos \theta$ and $b = r \sin \theta$.

EXAMPLE 1 Write rectangular notation for $2(\cos 120° + i \sin 120°)$.

$a = 2 \cos 120° = -1$ Identifying and evaluating a and b
$b = 2 \sin 120° = \sqrt{3}$

Thus $2(\cos 120° + i \sin 120°) = -1 + i\sqrt{3}$.

To change from rectangular notation to trigonometric notation, we remember that $r = \sqrt{a^2 + b^2}$ and θ is an angle for which $\sin \theta = \frac{b}{r}$ and $\cos \theta = \frac{a}{r}$.

EXAMPLE 2 Find trigonometric, or polar, notation for $1 + i$.

We note that $a = 1$ and $b = 1$.

$$r = \sqrt{1^2 + 1^2} = \sqrt{2}$$

$$\sin \theta = \frac{1}{\sqrt{2}} \text{ and } \cos \theta = \frac{1}{\sqrt{2}} \qquad \sin \theta = \frac{b}{r},\ \cos \theta = \frac{a}{r}$$

Thus $\theta = \frac{\pi}{4}$, or 45°, and we have the following.

$$1 + i = \sqrt{2} \operatorname{cis} \frac{\pi}{4} \text{ or } 1 + i = \sqrt{2} \operatorname{cis} 45°$$

In changing to trigonometric, or polar, notation, note that there are many angles satisfying the given conditions. We ordinarily choose the smallest positive angle between 0° and 360°.

Try This

a. Write rectangular notation for $\sqrt{2}(\cos 315° + i \sin 315°)$.

b. Write trigonometric, or polar, notation for $1 + i\sqrt{3}$.

Multiplication and Trigonometric Notation

Objective: Use trigonometric notation to multiply and divide complex numbers.

Multiplication of complex numbers is somewhat easier to do with trigonometric notation than with rectangular notation. We simply multiply the absolute values and add the arguments. To divide, we divide absolute values and subtract the arguments.

Theorem 18-7

For any complex numbers $r_1 \operatorname{cis} \theta_1$ and $r_2 \operatorname{cis} \theta_2$,

$$(r_1 \operatorname{cis} \theta_1)(r_2 \operatorname{cis} \theta_2) = r_1 \cdot r_2 \operatorname{cis} (\theta_1 + \theta_2)$$

Theorem 18-8

For any complex numbers $r_1 \operatorname{cis} \theta_1$ and $r_2 \operatorname{cis} \theta_2$, $(r_2 \neq 0)$,

$$\frac{r_1 \operatorname{cis} \theta_1}{r_2 \operatorname{cis} \theta_2} = \frac{r_1}{r_2} \operatorname{cis} (\theta_1 - \theta_2)$$

EXAMPLE 3 Find the product of 3 cis 40° and 7 cis 20°.

$$3 \operatorname{cis} 40° \cdot 7 \operatorname{cis} 20° = 3 \cdot 7 \operatorname{cis} (40° + 20°) = 21 \operatorname{cis} 60°$$

EXAMPLE 4 Divide $2 \text{ cis } \pi$ by $4 \text{ cis } \frac{\pi}{2}$.

$$\frac{2 \text{ cis } \pi}{4 \text{ cis } \frac{\pi}{2}} = \frac{2}{4} \text{ cis } \left(\pi - \frac{\pi}{2}\right) = \frac{1}{2} \text{ cis } \frac{\pi}{2}$$

Try This

c. Multiply $5 \text{ cis } 25°$ by $4 \text{ cis } 30°$.
d. Divide $10 \text{ cis } \frac{\pi}{2}$ by $5 \text{ cis } \frac{\pi}{4}$.

PART 3 De Moivre's Theorem

Objective: Use De Moivre's theorem to find powers and roots of complex numbers.

An important theorem about powers and roots of complex numbers is named for French mathematician Abraham De Moivre (1667–1754). Let us consider a number $r \text{ cis } \theta$ and its square.

$$\begin{aligned}(r \text{ cis } \theta)^2 &= (r \text{ cis } \theta)(r \text{ cis } \theta)\\ &= r \cdot r \text{ cis } (\theta + \theta)\\ &= r^2 \text{ cis } 2\theta\end{aligned}$$

Similarly, we see that $(r \text{ cis } \theta)^3 = r \cdot r \cdot r \text{ cis } (\theta + \theta + \theta) = r^3 \text{ cis } 3\theta$. The generalization of this is **De Moivre's Theorem.**

Theorem 18-9

De Moivre's Theorem

For any complex number $r \text{ cis } \theta$ and any natural number n, $(r \text{ cis } \theta)^n = r^n \text{ cis } n\theta$.

EXAMPLE 5 Find $(1 + i)^9$.

We first find polar notation.

$$1 + i = \sqrt{2} \text{ cis } 45°$$

Then
$$\begin{aligned}(1 + i)^9 &= (\sqrt{2} \text{ cis } 45°)^9\\ &= (\sqrt{2})^9 \text{ cis } 9 \cdot 45° && \text{Applying De Moivre's Theorem}\\ &= 2^{\frac{9}{2}} \text{ cis } 405°\\ &= 16\sqrt{2} \text{ cis } 45° && \text{405° has the same terminal side as 45°.}\end{aligned}$$

Try This

e. Find $(1 - i)^{10}$.

f. Find $(\sqrt{3} + i)^4$.

As we shall see, every nonzero complex number has two square roots, three cube roots, four fourth roots, and so on. In general, a nonzero complex number has n different nth roots. These can be found by the formula, which we now state and prove.

Theorem 18-10

The nth roots of a complex number $r \text{ cis } \theta$ are given by

$$r^{\frac{1}{n}} \text{ cis } \left(\frac{\theta}{n} + k \cdot \frac{360^\circ}{n}\right), \text{ where } k = 0, 1, 2, \ldots, n - 1$$

Proof of Theorem 18-10

We show that this formula gives us n different roots by using De Moivre's theorem. We take the expression for the nth roots and raise it to the nth power to show that we get $r \text{ cis } \theta$.

$$\left[r^{\frac{1}{n}} \text{ cis } \left(\frac{\theta}{n} + k \cdot \frac{360^\circ}{n}\right)\right]^n = \left(r^{\frac{1}{n}}\right)^n \text{ cis } \left(\frac{\theta}{n} \cdot n + k \cdot n \cdot \frac{360^\circ}{n}\right)$$

$$= r \text{ cis } (\theta + k \cdot 360^\circ) = r \text{ cis } \theta$$

Thus we know that the formula gives us nth roots for any natural number k. Next we show that there are at least n different roots. To see this, consider substituting 0, 1, 2, and so on, for k. From 0 to $n - 1$ the angles obtained and their sines and cosines are all different. But when $k = n$ the cycle begins to repeat. There cannot be more than n different nth roots. This fact follows from the **Fundamental Theorem of Algebra**, considered in Chapter 11.

EXAMPLE 6 Find the square roots of $2 + 2\sqrt{3}i$.

We first find trigonometric notation.

$$2 + 2\sqrt{3}i = 4 \text{ cis } 60^\circ$$

Then

$$(4 \text{ cis } 60^\circ)^{\frac{1}{2}} = 4^{\frac{1}{2}} \text{ cis } \left(\frac{60^\circ}{2} + k \cdot \frac{360^\circ}{2}\right), k = 0, 1 \qquad \text{Using Theorem 18-10}$$

$$= 2 \text{ cis } \left(30^\circ + k \cdot \frac{360^\circ}{2}\right), k = 0, 1$$

Thus the roots are $2 \text{ cis } 30^\circ$ and $2 \text{ cis } 210^\circ$, or $\sqrt{3} + i$ and $-\sqrt{3} - i$.

Try This

g. Find the square roots of $2i$.

h. Find the cube roots of $8i$.

18-9 Exercises

Look for worked-out examples at the Prentice Hall Web site.
www.phschool.com

A

Find rectangular notation.

1. $3(\cos 30° + i \sin 30°)$

2. $5(\cos 60° + i \sin 60°)$

3. $4(\cos 135° + i \sin 135°)$

4. $6(\cos 150° + i \sin 150°)$

5. $10 \text{ cis } 270°$

6. $12 \text{ cis } 90°$

7. $5 \text{ cis } (-45°)$

8. $5 \text{ cis } (-60°)$

9. $\sqrt{8}\left(\cos \frac{\pi}{4} + i \sin \frac{\pi}{4}\right)$

10. $\sqrt{8}\left(\cos \frac{3\pi}{4} + i \sin \frac{3\pi}{4}\right)$

11. $4\left(\cos \frac{\pi}{6} + i \sin \frac{\pi}{6}\right)$

12. $5\left(\cos \frac{\pi}{3} + i \sin \frac{\pi}{3}\right)$

13. $\sqrt{8} \text{ cis } \frac{5\pi}{4}$

14. $\sqrt{8} \text{ cis } \left(-\frac{\pi}{4}\right)$

Find trigonometric notation.

15. $-1 + i$

16. $-1 - i$

17. $\sqrt{3} + i$

18. $-\sqrt{3} + i$

19. $10\sqrt{3} - 10i$

20. $-10\sqrt{3} + 10i$

21. $2i$

22. $3i$

23. -5

24. -10

25. $-4i$

26. $-5i$

Convert to trigonometric notation and then multiply or divide.

27. $(1 - i)(2 + 2i)$

28. $(\sqrt{3} + i)(1 + i)$

29. $(10\sqrt{3} + 10i)(\sqrt{3} - i)$

30. $(1 + i\sqrt{3})(1 + i)$

31. $(2\sqrt{3} + 2i)(2i)$

32. $(3\sqrt{3} - 3i)(2i)$

33. $\frac{1 + i}{1 - i}$

34. $\frac{1 - i}{1 + i}$

35. $\frac{-1 + i}{\sqrt{3} + i}$

36. $\frac{1 - i}{\sqrt{3} - i}$

37. $\frac{2\sqrt{3} - 2i}{1 + i\sqrt{3}}$

38. $\frac{3 - 3i\sqrt{3}}{\sqrt{3} - i}$

Raise the number to the power. Give your answer in polar notation.

39. $\left(2 \text{ cis } \frac{\pi}{3}\right)^3$

40. $\left(3 \text{ cis } \frac{\pi}{2}\right)^4$

41. $\left(2 \text{ cis } \frac{\pi}{6}\right)^6$

42. $\left(2 \text{ cis } \frac{\pi}{5}\right)^5$

43. $(1 + i)^6$

44. $(1 - i)^6$

Raise the number to the power. Give your answer in rectangular notation.

45. $(2 \text{ cis } 240°)^4$

46. $(2 \text{ cis } 120°)^4$

47. $(1 + \sqrt{3}i)^4$

48. $(-\sqrt{3} + i)^6$

49. $\left(\frac{1}{\sqrt{2}} + \frac{1}{\sqrt{2}}i\right)^{10}$

50. $\left(\frac{1}{\sqrt{2}} - \frac{1}{\sqrt{2}}i\right)^{12}$

51. $\left(\frac{\sqrt{3}}{2} + \frac{1}{2}i\right)^{12}$

52. $\left(\frac{\sqrt{3}}{2} - \frac{1}{2}i\right)^{14}$

Find the following.

53. the square roots of $-1 + \sqrt{3}i$

54. the square roots of $-\sqrt{3} - i$

55. the cube roots of i

56. the cube roots of $-i$

57. the fourth roots of 16

58. the fourth roots of -16

B

59. Every complex number, including 1, has three different cube roots. Show that the three cube roots of 1 are 1, $-\frac{1}{2} + \frac{\sqrt{3}}{2}i$, and $-\frac{1}{2} - \frac{\sqrt{3}}{2}i$, by raising each to the third power. Locate them on a graph.

60. Write -1 as 1 cis 180° to find the three cube roots of -1. Graph the roots.

61. Find the fourth roots of 1.

62. Show that for any complex numbers z, w, $|z \cdot w| = |z| \cdot |w|$. (Hint: Let $z = r_1 \text{ cis } \theta_1$ and $w = r_2 \text{ cis } \theta_2$.)

63. Show that for any complex number z and any nonzero complex number w, $\left|\frac{z}{w}\right| = \frac{|z|}{|w|}$.

64. Find the cube roots of 68.4321.

65. ***Critical Thinking*** Find the number whose fourth roots are cis 0°, cis 90°, cis 180°, and cis 270°.

Challenge

66. Find polar notation for $(\cos\theta + i\sin\theta)^{-1}$.

67. Compute $\begin{bmatrix} i & 0 \\ 0 & -i \end{bmatrix}^3$.

Mixed Review

Change radian measure to degrees. **68.** π **69.** 4π **70.** $-\frac{\pi}{3}$ **71.** $\frac{7\pi}{12}$ *17-3*

Change degree measure to radians. **72.** 165° **73.** 75° **74.** 22.5° **75.** $-90°$

For each polynomial find all rational roots. Find the other roots, if possible.

76. $x^4 - 1$ **77.** $x^4 + x^3 - 8x^2 - 2x + 12$ **78.** $2x^3 - 3x^2 - 11x + 6$ *11-4*

79. Radioactive Radon-222 is found in certain building materials. It has a half-life of 3.8 days. How much of a 50-mg sample will remain after

a. 1 day? **b.** 7 days? **c.** 14 days? *12-8*

Application

Predicting Records

Past events can be used as models for making predictions for such events as athletic competitions. You can use the Problem-Solving Guidelines to help you solve a situational problem about predicting times for the mile run.

Situational Problem

The track record in 1875 for the mile run was set by Walter Slade of Great Britain. He ran a mile in 4 minutes, 24.5 seconds. Since that time, the record for the mile race has declined steadily. Use the data below to "predict" the time for 1999 (compare your results with the actual time for 1999), then make predictions for 2020 and 2100.

1875	Walter Slade, Britain	4:24.5	1954	Roger Bannister, Britain	3:59.4
1880	Walter George, Britain	4:23.2	1954	John Landry, Australia	3:58
1882	George	4:21.4	1957	Derek Ibbotson, Britain	3:57.2
1884	George	4:18.4	1958	Herb Elliott, Australia	3:54.5
1894	Fred Bacon, Scotland	4:18.2	1962	Peter Snell, New Zealand	3:54.4
1895	Bacon	4:17	1964	Snell	3:54.1
1911	John Paul Jones, U.S.	4:15.4	1965	Michel Jazy, France	3:53.6
1913	Jones	4:14.6	1966	Jim Ryun, U.S.	3:51.3
1915	Norman Taber, U.S.	4:12.6	1967	Ryun	3:51.1
1923	Paavo Nurmi, Finland	4:10.4	1975	Filbert Bayi, Tanzania	3:51.0
1931	Jules Ladoumegue, France	4:09.2	1975	John Walker, New Zealand	3:49.4
1933	Jack Lovelock, New Zealand	4:07.6	1979	Sebastian Coe, Britain	3:49
1934	Glenn Cunningham, U.S.	4:06.8	1980	Steve Ovett, Britain	3:48.8
1937	Sydney Wooderson, Britain	4:06.4	1981	Coe	3:48.5
1942	Arne Andersson, Sweden	4:06.2	1981	Ovett	3:48.4
1942	Gunder Haegg, Sweden	4:04.6	1981	Coe	3:47.3
1943	Andersson	4:02.6	1985	Steve Cram, Britain	3:46.3
1944	Andersson	4:01.6	1993	Noureddine Morceli, Algeria	3:44.4
1945	Haegg	4:01.4	1999	Hicham El Guerrouj, Morocco	3:43.1

Possible Assumption

Data in subsequent years follow this trend.

Possible Subproblems

1. Convert the track records to a workable unit of measure (minutes, seconds, and so on).
2. Graph the data. What curve best fits the data?
3. Can you determine an equation for the curve?
4. Use the equation to predict the times for subsequent years. What do you predict the record will be in the year 2020? 2100?

Hicham El Guerrouj set the world outdoor 1-mile record on July 7, 1999, in Rome, Italy.

Application

Satellite Tracking

Suppose a satellite is to be put in orbit over the equator 300 miles above Earth. Tracking stations are to be located along the equator. Each tracking station has a scanning screen that covers 180°, as illustrated below.

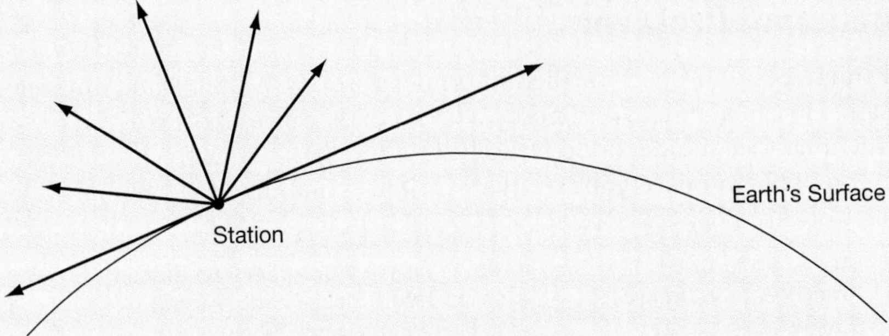

Tracking stations must be located close enough to each other so that there are no "blind spots" or regions where the satellite is not being observed by at least one scanner. The illustration below shows a satellite in a blind spot.

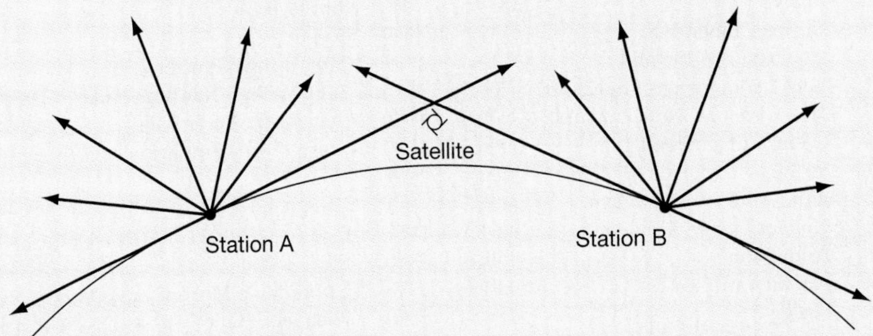

The illustration below shows the farthest distance apart that Stations A and B can be if they are to track the satellite.

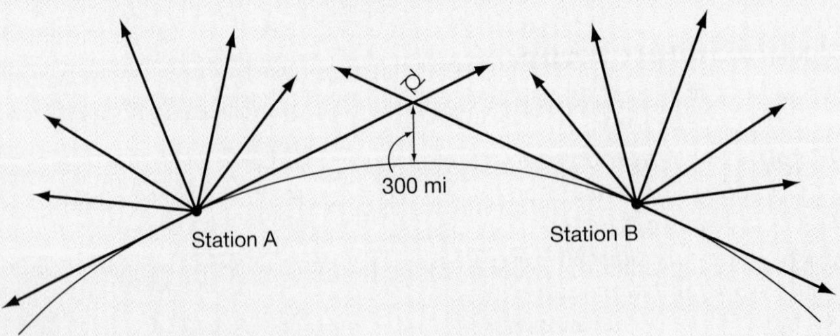

EXAMPLE

Find the maximum possible distance between two tracking stations if they are to scan a satellite in orbit 300 miles above Earth's surface. Use 4000 miles as the radius of Earth.

To solve the problem, first find the distance d, the ground distance from the satellite to one tracking station, and then double it.

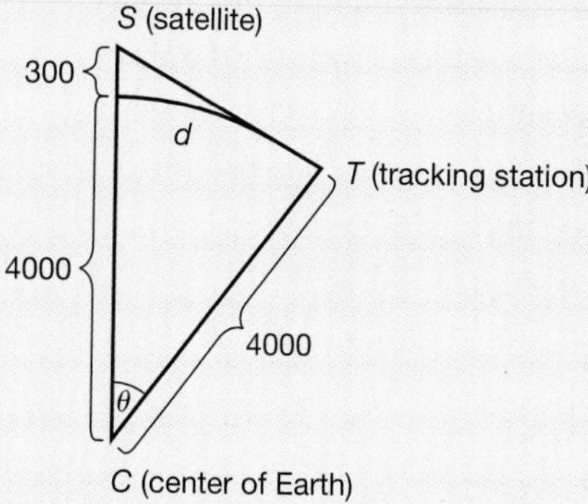

Since $\overline{ST}$ is tangent to Earth's surface, we know that $\angle CTS$ is a right angle and thus

$$\cos\theta = \frac{4000}{4300}$$
$$\approx 0.9302$$

Thus, $\theta \approx 0.3758$ radians.

It follows that $\frac{d}{4000} \approx 0.3758$ or $d \approx 1503$ miles. Applying Theorem 17-1

Hence, the maximum distance between the two tracking stations is about 3006 miles.

Problems

1. A satellite is to be placed in an equatorial orbit 558 miles above Earth's surface. Find the maximum possible distance between two tracking stations that are to scan the satellite.
2. A satellite is to be placed in an equatorial orbit 70 miles above the moon's surface. The moon has a diameter of 2160 miles. How far apart could tracking stations be placed on the moon's surface to track the satellite?
3. Given that Earth's circumference is approximately 25,000 miles, what is the fewest number of stations needed along the equator to track a satellite in orbit 300 miles above Earth?
4. Suppose only 7 stations could be built along the equator for the satellite in Problem 3. What would need to be done so that the satellite could be tracked through its orbit?
5. What is the lowest orbit possible for the given number of equally spaced stations located along the equator?
   a. 10 **b.** 6

18 Chapter Wrap Up

Key Terms

absolute value of a complex number (p. 821)
angle of depression (p. 805)
angle of elevation (p. 805)
argument in trigonometric notation (p. 821)
basic identities (p. 793)
cofunction identities (p. 793)
De Moivre's Theorem (p. 823)
double-angle identities (p. 788)
half-angle identities (p. 790)
law of cosines (p. 817)
law of sines (p. 810)
polar notation (see trigonometric notation)
principal values of inverses (p. 798)
Pythagorean identities (p. 793)
rectangular notation (p. 821)
sum and difference identities (p. 785)
trigonometric equations (p. 801)
trigonometric notation for complex number (p. 821)

18-1

These **sum and difference identities** can be used to change or simplify expressions.

$$\cos(\alpha - \beta) \equiv \cos\alpha\cos\beta + \sin\alpha\sin\beta$$
$$\cos(\alpha + \beta) \equiv \cos\alpha\cos\beta - \sin\alpha\sin\beta$$
$$\sin(\alpha - \beta) \equiv \sin\alpha\cos\beta - \cos\alpha\sin\beta$$
$$\sin(\alpha + \beta) \equiv \sin\alpha\cos\beta + \cos\alpha\sin\beta$$
$$\tan(\alpha - \beta) \equiv \frac{\tan\alpha - \tan\beta}{1 + \tan\alpha\tan\beta}$$
$$\tan(\alpha + \beta) \equiv \frac{\tan\alpha + \tan\beta}{1 - \tan\alpha\tan\beta}$$

Use sum and difference identities to simplify the following.

1. $\cos(x + y)$ **2.** $\tan(45° - 30°)$ **3.** $\sin 75°$

4. $\cos\frac{7\pi}{12}$ **5.** $\tan\frac{\pi}{12}$

18-2

These **double-angle identities** can be used to change or simplify expressions.

$$\sin 2\theta \equiv 2\sin\theta\cos\theta \qquad \cos 2\theta \equiv \cos^2\theta - \sin^2\theta$$
$$\cos 2\theta \equiv 1 - 2\sin^2\theta \qquad \cos 2\theta \equiv 2\cos^2\theta - 1$$
$$\tan 2\theta \equiv \frac{2\tan\theta}{1 - \tan^2\theta} \qquad \sin^2\theta \equiv \frac{1 - \cos 2\theta}{2}$$
$$\cos^2\theta \equiv \frac{1 + \cos 2\theta}{2}$$

Find $\sin 2\theta$, $\cos 2\theta$, $\tan 2\theta$, and the quadrant in which 2θ lies.

6. $\sin\theta = \frac{3}{5}(\theta \text{ is in quadrant I})$ **7.** $\tan\theta = \frac{4}{3}(\theta \text{ is in quadrant III})$

These **half-angle identities** can be used to change or simplify expressions.

$$\sin\frac{\phi}{2} \equiv \pm\sqrt{\frac{1 - \cos\phi}{2}} \qquad \cos\frac{\phi}{2} \equiv \pm\sqrt{\frac{1 + \cos\phi}{2}}$$
$$\tan\frac{\phi}{2} \equiv \pm\sqrt{\frac{1 - \cos\phi}{1 + \cos\phi}} \qquad \tan\frac{\phi}{2} \equiv \frac{\sin\phi}{1 + \cos\phi}$$
$$\tan\frac{\phi}{2} \equiv \frac{1 - \cos\phi}{\sin\phi}$$

Find the following without using a table or calculator.

8. $\cos 15°$ **9.** $\sin\frac{\pi}{8}$

18-3

Internet Activity On the Web

Look for extension problems for this chapter at the Prentice Hall Web site. www.phschool.com

Memorizing certain trigonometric identities can help you prove other identities.

Prove the identity.

10. $\tan 2\theta = \dfrac{2\tan\theta}{1 - \tan^2\theta}$

18-4

There are several ways of denoting the **inverse** of the sine function $y = \sin x$. They are $x = \sin y$, $y = \sin^{-1} x$, and $y = \arcsin x$. Unit circles are useful in finding inverse values for trigonometric functions.

Find all values of the following.

11. $\sin^{-1}\frac{1}{2}$

12. $\arccos -\frac{\sqrt{2}}{2}$

Find the following.

13. $\text{Arcsin} -\frac{\sqrt{2}}{2}$

14. $\text{Cos}^{-1}\frac{\sqrt{3}}{2}$

18-5

In solving **trigonometric equations,** find all solutions from 0 to 2π that make the equation true. You may add any multiple of 2π to obtain other solutions.

Solve, finding all solutions from 0 to 2π.

15. $\sin^2 x - 7\sin x = 0$

16. $\sin 2x - \cos x = 0$

18-6

The guidelines for solving a right-triangle problem are as follows.

1. Draw a sketch of the problem situation.
2. Look for right triangles and sketch them.
3. Mark the known and unknown sides and angles.
4. Express the desired side or angle in terms of known trigonometric ratios, and then solve.

Solve the triangles. Use three-digit precision.

17.

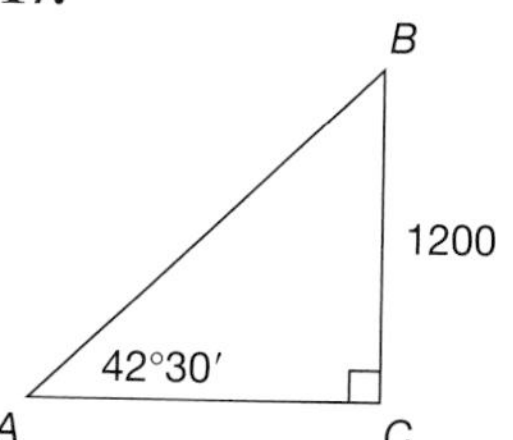

18.

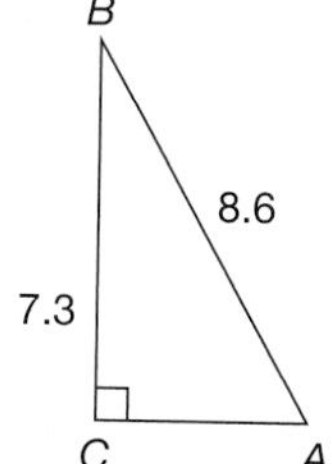

19.

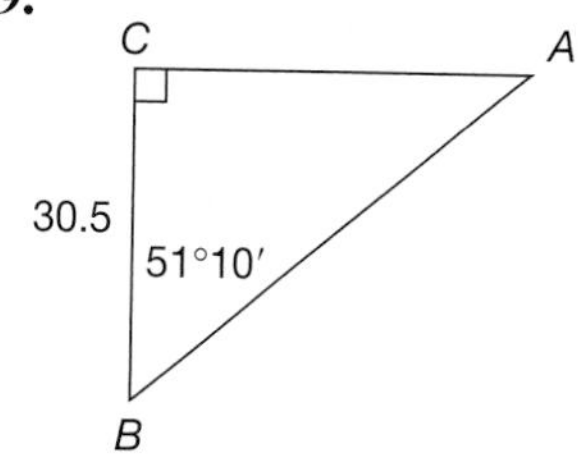

20. A student was asked to estimate the height of a cliff. She stood at the bottom of the cliff and walked to a spot 100 ft away. From this distance, she used a protractor to estimate the angle to the top of the cliff as 41°. What did she calculate as the height of the cliff?

21. A supersonic plane flew from New York to Paris at a speed of 1000 mi/h in a direction of 8°30′ for $3\frac{3}{4}$ hrs. How far north did the aircraft travel?

18-7, 18-8

To solve for missing parts in triangles that are not right triangles, use either or both of the following.
The **Law of Sines:** In any triangle ABC, $\frac{a}{\sin A} = \frac{b}{\sin B} = \frac{c}{\sin C}$;

or the **Law of Cosines:**

In any triangle ABC,
$$a^2 = b^2 + c^2 - 2bc \cos A$$
$$b^2 = a^2 + c^2 - 2ac \cos B$$
$$c^2 = a^2 + b^2 - 2ab \cos C$$

Solve triangle ABC.

22. $m\angle A = 40, m\angle B = 80, b = 25$

23. $\angle B = 118°20', \angle C = 27°40', b = 0.974$

24. $m\angle A = 72, a = 5, b = 4$

25. 26.

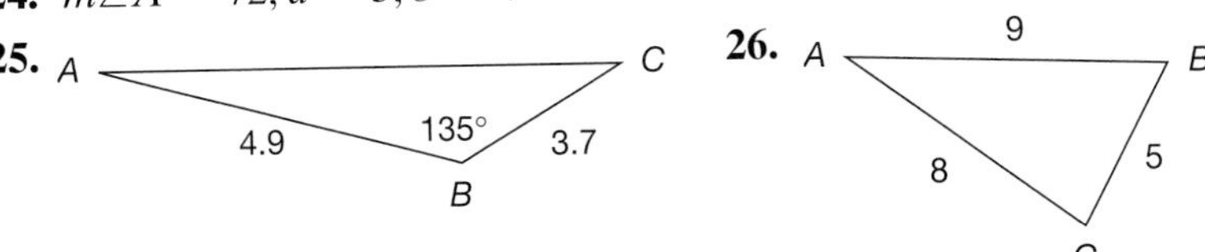

Use the formula area $= \frac{1}{2}bc \sin A$ to find the area of a triangle ABC.

27. $b = 5, c = 9, m\angle A = 65$

18-9

Trigonometric, or **polar, notation** for the complex number $a + bi$ is $r(\cos\theta + i\sin\theta)$, where r is the absolute value and θ is the argument. This is sometimes shortened to $r \text{ cis } \theta$ and is derived by using the formulas $a = r\cos\theta$ and $b = r\sin\theta$.

28. Find rectangular notation for $2(\cos 135° + i \sin 135°)$.

29. Find trigonometric notation for $1 + i$.

30. Find 2 cis 120°. Write your answer in rectangular notation.

Recall that the nth roots of a complex number $r \text{ cis } \theta$ are given by

$$r^{\frac{1}{n}} \text{cis}\left(\frac{\theta}{n} + k \cdot \frac{360°}{n}\right) \text{ where } k = 0, 1, 2, \ldots, n - 1$$

31. Find the cube roots of $1 + i$.

18 Chapter Assessment

Use sum and difference identities to simplify the following.

1. $\sin(x - y)$
2. $\cos\left(\frac{\pi}{2} + \frac{\pi}{3}\right)$
3. $\tan 105°$
4. $\sin 15°$

Find $\sin 2\theta$, $\cos 2\theta$, $\tan 2\theta$, and the quadrant in which 2θ lies.

5. $\cos\theta = \frac{4}{5}(\theta \text{ in Quadrant I})$
6. $\tan\theta = -\frac{3}{4}(\theta \text{ in Quadrant II})$

Find the following without using tables.

7. $\sin\frac{\pi}{12}$
8. $\sin\frac{7\pi}{8}$
9. Prove the identity $\tan\theta \equiv \frac{\sin 2\theta}{1 + \cos 2\theta}$.

Find the following.

10. $\arccos\frac{1}{2}$
11. $\text{Arccos}\frac{\sqrt{3}}{2}$

Solve, finding all solutions from 0 to 2π.

12. $2\cos^2 x + 1 = -3\cos x$
13. $\cos^2 x = 1 + \sin^2 x$

Solve the triangles. Angle C is a right triangle. Use three-digit precision.

14. $a = 9.2, c = 10.1$
15. $a = 28.5, \angle B = 49°10'$
16. While walking through Chicago, Jenna estimated that the angle of elevation to the top of the 1454-ft-tall Sears Tower was 15°. How far was she from the building?

Solve triangle ABC.

17. $\angle B = 117°10', \angle C = 26°50', b = 0.9763$
18. $m\angle A = 50, a = 9, b = 10$
19. $a = 3.8, c = 4.6, m\angle B = 132$
20. 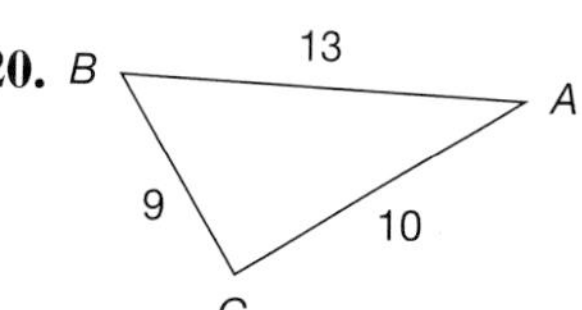

21. Find rectangular notation for $3(\cos 120° + i\sin 120°)$.
22. Find trigonometric notation for $1 - i$.
23. Find $(2 \text{ cis } 150°)^3$. Give your answer in rectangular notation.

Challenge

24. Solve $\sqrt{\sin x} = \frac{1}{2}\sqrt{2\sqrt{2}}$.

1–18 Cumulative Review

1-3 Evaluate each expression for $a = -2$ and $c = 7$.

1. $|a - 2c| - |2a - c| - ac$

2. $-5|a^2 + ac| - 3|2ac - 1|$

2-1 Solve.

3. $4x - 3[4(x + 6) + 1] = 2x - 5$

4. $\frac{2}{3}x + \frac{3}{4} = 2(x - 11) + \frac{7}{4}$

2-4, 2-6 Solve.

5. $4a + 3 < 9a - 7$

6. $6.1x - 1.1 < 0.8x + 4.2$

7. $-14 < 3x + 1 < 40$

8. $|4 - y| \leq 10$

3-8

9. The cost of driving one new car 20,000 miles in a year is $4380. The cost of driving 15,000 miles in a year is $3690. Fit a linear function to the data, and predict the cost of driving the car 1000 miles in a year.

4-1, 4-4 Solve these systems.

10. $5a - b = -11$
$4a + 12b = 4$

11. $a + b - 4c = -22$
$-a - 2b + 3c = 13$
$-2a + b + c = 11$

5-1–5-3 Simplify.

12. $(8x^3 - 6x + 5) - (10x^4 + 4x^2 + 2x)$

13. $(4xy + 5y)(x^2 - 2)$

14. $(2x - 1)^3$

5-4, 5-5 Factor.

15. $12x^2 - 132xy + 363y^2$

16. $\frac{1}{9}x^6 - 49y^2$

17. $2x^3 + 6x^2 - 8x - 24$

5-7 Solve.

18. $6x - x^2 = 0$

19. $x^2 - 9x = -8$

6-1, 6-2 Simplify.

20. $\dfrac{x^2 + 4x - 12}{3x^2 - 12x + 12}$

21. $\dfrac{5a - 2}{a + 3} \div \dfrac{25a^2 - 4}{a^2 - 9}$

6-6 Solve.

22. $\dfrac{a - 3}{a + 2} = \dfrac{1}{5}$

23. $\dfrac{15}{m} - \dfrac{15}{m + 2} = 2$

7-1–7-9 Simplify.

24. $\sqrt[4]{32}$ 25. $\sqrt{90x^3}$ 26. $\sqrt{24}\sqrt{75}$ 27. $\sqrt{x^2 + 6x + 9}$

28. $5\sqrt[3]{32} - 2\sqrt[3]{108} - 5\sqrt[3]{4}$ 29. $(2\sqrt{7} - 3\sqrt{5})(\sqrt{7} + \sqrt{5})$

30. $(5 - 3i) - (6 - 4i)$ 31. $(8 + 4i)(-5 - 3i)$ 32. $\frac{2 + i}{3 - 2i}$

8-1, 8-3 Solve.

33. $9x^2 - 2 = 0$ 34. $x^2 - 3x - 9 = 0$ 35. $2x^{\frac{2}{3}} - x^{\frac{1}{3}} - 28 = 0$

8-7

36. The surface area of a sphere varies directly with the square of its radius. A sphere with radius $\frac{10}{\sqrt{\pi}}$ cm has a surface area of 400 cm^2. What is the surface area of a sphere with radius 2 cm?

9-1 Test for symmetry with respect to the x-axis and the y-axis.

37. $4y^2 = 2x - 1$ 38. $5x^2 - 2y^2 = 6$ 39. $y^3 - x^3 = -7$

9-6 For each of the following functions, graph the function and find the vertex, the line of symmetry, and the maximum or minimum value.

40. $f(x) = (x + 2)^2 - 4$ 41. $f(x) = -2(x - 1)^2 + 3$

10-1–10-4 Solve.

42. Find the midpoint of the segment with endpoints (4, 5) and (6, −7).

43. Find the center and radius of the circle $(x + 1)^2 + (y + 3)^2 = 4$.

44. Find the center, vertices, foci, and asymptotes for the hyperbola $\frac{(y + 3)^2}{25} - \frac{(x + 1)^2}{16} = 1$. Graph the hyperbola.

11-2–11-4 Solve.

45. Use synthetic division to find the quotient and remainder $(x^3 - 27) \div (x - 3)$.

46. Suppose a polynomial of degree 5 with rational coefficients has roots $8, 6 - 7i, \frac{1}{2} + \sqrt{11}$. Find the other roots.

47. Find the rational roots of $2x^3 - 3x^2 - x + 1$, if they exist. If possible, find the other roots.

12-1 Write an equation of the inverse relation.

48. $2x + 3y - 7 = 0$ 49. $y = 2x^2 + 3$ 50. $f(x) = 2x$

12-3 Convert to logarithmic equations.

51. $10^{0.4771} = 3$ 52. $y = 3^x$ 53. $x^y = z$

12-7 Solve.

54. $4^{3x+5} = 16$ **55.** $\log(x+9) - \log x = 1$ **56.** $9^{y^2} \cdot 3^{5y} = 27$

13-1–13-6

$$\text{Let } A = \begin{bmatrix} -1 & 2 & 10 \\ 3 & -4 & 8 \\ 0 & 5 & -1 \end{bmatrix} \text{ and } B = \begin{bmatrix} 2 & 1 \\ -5 & -3 \\ 4 & 0 \end{bmatrix}$$

57. Find $3A$. **58.** Find AB. **59.** Find A^{-1}. **60.** Evaluate $|A|$.

61. Solve using Cramer's rule. $7x - 2y = 10$
$9x + y = 20$

14-1–14-4

62. State a rule for finding the nth term of $-2, 3, -4, 5, \ldots$.

63. Find the 17th term of the arithmetic sequence, $7, 4, 1, \ldots$.

64. Evaluate $\sum_{k=1}^{6} \left(\frac{1}{3}\right)^{k-3}$.

65. Find the sum of the infinite geometric series $9 - 3 + 1 - \ldots$.

15-1–15-4 Evaluate.

66. ${}_9P_5$ **67.** $5!$ **68.** $\binom{8}{4}$

69. Expand $(2a + 3y)^4$.

15-6

70. If one card is drawn from a deck of 52 cards, what is the probability of that card being black or a king?

15-7

71. If a die is rolled, what is the probability of rolling an even number or a multiple of 3?

16-1–16-3

For Problems 72–79, the scores on an English quiz are
16, 23, 24, 31, 33, 29, 28, 27, 23, 17, 13, 23, 31, 34, 29, 27, 22, 23, 22.

72. Construct a stem-and-leaf diagram.

73. Construct a frequency distribution showing the relative frequency.

74. Find the mean, mode, and median.

75. Construct a box and whisker plot.

76. What is the range? **77.** Find the mean deviation.

78. Find the variance. **79.** Find the standard deviation.

17-2 In which quadrant does the terminal side of each angle lie?

80. $-45°$ **81.** $240°$ **82.** $-120°$ **83.** $460°$

84. Give the signs of the six trigonometric function values for a rotation of $-420°$.

17-3 Convert each of the following.

85. $100°$ to radian measure **86.** $\frac{2\pi}{3}$ radians to degree measure

17-4–17-8

87. Graph the sine function between -2π and 2π.

88. Check the identity $\cos\left(\frac{\pi}{2} - \theta\right) \equiv \sin\theta$.

89. Sketch the graph of $y = \frac{1}{2}\cos(2\theta)$. Determine the amplitude and the period.

90. Simplify $\tan y \sin y(\cot y - \csc y)$.

18-1,18-2 Simplify.

91. $\cos(\alpha + \beta) + \cos(\alpha - \beta)$ **92.** $\cos^2\frac{x}{2} - \sin^2\frac{x}{2}$

18-3

93. Prove $\frac{1 - \cos x}{\sin x} \equiv \frac{\sin x}{1 + \cos x}$.

18-4

94. Find all values of $\arcsin\frac{1}{2}$.

18-5 Solve. Find all solutions from 0 to 2π.

95. $\cos^2 x - 1 = 2\sin x$ **96.** $2\tan x = 1 - \tan^2 x$

18-6 Solve triangle ABC. Angle C is the right angle.

97. $a = 9.2, c = 10.1$ **98.** $\angle A = 67°40', b = 135$

18-7 Solve triangle ABC.

99. $m\angle B = 150, a = 3, b = 7$

18-8 Solve triangle ABC.

100. $a = 6, b = 7, c = 10$

18-9 Write in trigonometric, or polar, notation.

101. $-\sqrt{3} - i$ **102.** $\frac{1}{2} + \frac{\sqrt{3}}{2}i$

Write in rectangular notation.

103. $10 \text{ cis } 270°$ **104.** $4(\cos 135° + i\sin 135°)$

Table 1: Squares and Square Roots

N	N^2	$\sqrt{N}$	N	N^2	$\sqrt{N}$
1	1	1	51	2,601	7.141
2	4	1.414	52	2,704	7.211
3	9	1.732	53	2,809	7.280
4	16	2	54	2,916	7.348
5	25	2.236	55	3,025	7.416
6	36	2.449	56	3,136	7.483
7	49	2.646	57	3,249	7.550
8	64	2.828	58	3,364	7.616
9	81	3	59	3,481	7.681
10	100	3.162	60	3,600	7.746
11	121	3.317	61	3,721	7.810
12	144	3.464	62	3,844	7.874
13	169	3.606	63	3,969	7.937
14	196	3.742	64	4,096	8
15	225	3.873	65	4,225	8.062
16	256	4	66	4,356	8.124
17	289	4.123	67	4,489	8.185
18	324	4.243	68	4,624	8.246
19	361	4.359	69	4,761	8.307
20	400	4.472	70	4,900	8.367
21	441	4.583	71	5,041	8.426
22	484	4.690	72	5,184	8.485
23	529	4.796	73	5,329	8.544
24	576	4.899	74	5,476	8.602
25	625	5	75	5,625	8.660
26	676	5.099	76	5,776	8.718
27	729	5.196	77	5,929	8.775
28	784	5.292	78	6,084	8.832
29	841	5.385	79	6,241	8.888
30	900	5.477	80	6,400	8.944
31	961	5.568	81	6,561	9
32	1,024	5.657	82	6,724	9.055
33	1,089	5.745	83	6,889	9.110
34	1,156	5.831	84	7,056	9.165
35	1,225	5.916	85	7,225	9.220
36	1,296	6	86	7,396	9.274
37	1,369	6.083	87	7,569	9.327
38	1,444	6.164	88	7,744	9.381
39	1,521	6.245	89	7,921	9.434
40	1,600	6.325	90	8,100	9.487
41	1,681	6.403	91	8,281	9.539
42	1,764	6.481	92	8,464	9.592
43	1,849	6.557	93	8,649	9.644
44	1,936	6.633	94	8,836	9.695
45	2,025	6.708	95	9,025	9.747
46	2,116	6.782	96	9,216	9.798
47	2,209	6.856	97	9,409	9.849
48	2,304	6.928	98	9,604	9.899
49	2,401	7	99	9,801	9.950
50	2,500	7.071	100	10,000	10

x	0	1	2	3	4	5	6	7	8	9
1.0	.0000	.0043	.0086	.0128	.0170	.0212	.0253	.0294	.0334	.0374
1.1	.0414	.0453	.0492	.0531	.0569	.0607	.0645	.0682	.0719	.0755
1.2	.0792	.0828	.0864	.0899	.0934	.0969	.1004	.1038	.1072	.1106
1.3	.1139	.1173	.1206	.1239	.1271	.1303	.1335	.1367	.1399	.1430
1.4	.1461	.1492	.1523	.1553	.1584	.1614	.1644	.1673	.1703	.1732
1.5	.1761	.1790	.1818	.1847	.1875	.1903	.1931	.1959	.1987	.2014
1.6	.2041	.2068	.2095	.2122	.2148	.2175	.2201	.2227	.2253	.2279
1.7	.2304	.2330	.2355	.2380	.2405	.2430	.2455	.2480	.2504	.2529
1.8	.2553	.2577	.2601	.2625	.2648	.2672	.2695	.2718	.2742	.2765
1.9	.2788	.2810	.2833	.2856	.2878	.2900	.2923	.2945	.2967	.2989
2.0	.3010	.3032	.3054	.3075	.3096	.3118	.3139	.3160	.3181	.3201
2.1	.3222	.3243	.3263	.3284	.3304	.3324	.3345	.3365	.3385	.3404
2.2	.3424	.3444	.3464	.3483	.3502	.3522	.3541	.3560	.3579	.3598
2.3	.3617	.3636	.3655	.3674	.3692	.3711	.3729	.3747	.3766	.3784
2.4	.3802	.3820	.3838	.3856	.3874	.3892	.3909	.3927	.3945	.3962
2.5	.3979	.3997	.4014	.4031	.4048	.4065	.4082	.4099	.4116	.4133
2.6	.4150	.4166	.4183	.4200	.4216	.4232	.4249	.4265	.4281	.4298
2.7	.4314	.4330	.4346	.4362	.4378	.4393	.4409	.4425	.4440	.4456
2.8	.4472	.4487	.4502	.4518	.4533	.4548	.4564	.4579	.4594	.4609
2.9	.4624	.4639	.4654	.4669	.4683	.4698	.4713	.4728	.4742	.4757
3.0	.4771	.4786	.4800	.4814	.4829	.4843	.4857	.4871	.4886	.4900
3.1	.4914	.4928	.4942	.4955	.4969	.4983	.4997	.5011	.5024	.5038
3.2	.5051	.5065	.5079	.5092	.5105	.5119	.5132	.5145	.5159	.5172
3.3	.5185	.5198	.5211	.5224	.5237	.5250	.5263	.5276	.5289	.5307
3.4	.5315	.5328	.5340	.5353	.5366	.5378	.5391	.5403	.5416	.5428
3.5	.5441	.5453	.5465	.5478	.5490	.5502	.5514	.5527	.5539	.5551
3.6	.5563	.5575	.5587	.5599	.5611	.5623	.5635	.5647	.5658	.5670
3.7	.5682	.5694	.5705	.5717	.5729	.5740	.5752	.5763	.5775	.5786
3.8	.5798	.5809	.5821	.5832	.5843	.5855	.5866	.5877	.5888	.5899
3.9	.5911	.5922	.5933	.5944	.5955	.5966	.5977	.5988	.5999	.6010
4.0	.6021	.6031	.6042	.6053	.6064	.6075	.6085	.6096	.6107	.6117
4.1	.6128	.6138	.6149	.6160	.6170	.6180	.6191	.6201	.6212	.6222
4.2	.6232	.6243	.6253	.6263	.6274	.6284	.6294	.6304	.6314	.6325
4.3	.6335	.6345	.6355	.6365	.6375	.6385	.6395	.6405	.6415	.6425
4.4	.6435	.6444	.6454	.6464	.6474	.6484	.6493	.6503	.6513	.6522
4.5	.6532	.6542	.6551	.6561	.6571	.6580	.6590	.6599	.6609	.6618
4.6	.6628	.6637	.6646	.6656	.6665	.6675	.6684	.6693	.6702	.6712
4.7	.6721	.6730	.6739	.6749	.6758	.6767	.6776	.6785	.6794	.6803
4.8	.6812	.6821	.6830	.6839	.6848	.6857	.6866	.6875	.6884	.6893
4.9	.6902	.6911	.6920	.6928	.6937	.6946	.6955	.6964	.6972	.6981
5.0	.6990	.6998	.7007	.7016	.7024	.7033	.7042	.7050	.7059	.7067
5.1	.7076	.7084	.7093	.7101	.7110	.7118	.7126	.7135	.7143	.7152
5.2	.7160	.7168	.7177	.7185	.7193	.7202	.7210	.7218	.7226	.7235
5.3	.7243	.7251	.7259	.7267	.7275	.7284	.7292	.7300	.7308	.7316
5.4	.7324	.7332	.7340	.7348	.7356	.7364	.7372	.7380	.7388	.7396

Table 2: Common Logarithms

x	0	1	2	3	4	5	6	7	8	9
5.5	.7404	.7412	.7419	.7427	.7435	.7443	.7451	.7459	.7466	.7474
5.6	.7482	.7490	.7497	.7505	.7513	.7520	.7528	.7536	.7543	.7551
5.7	.7559	.7566	.7574	.7582	.7589	.7597	.7604	.7612	.7619	.7627
5.8	.7634	.7642	.7649	.7657	.7664	.7672	.7679	.7686	.7694	.7701
5.9	.7709	.7716	.7723	.7731	.7738	.7745	.7752	.7760	.7767	.7774
6.0	.7782	.7789	.7796	.7803	.7810	.7818	.7825	.7832	.7839	.7846
6.1	.7853	.7860	.7868	.7875	.7882	.7889	.7896	.7903	.7910	.7917
6.2	.7924	.7931	.7938	.7945	.7952	.7959	.7966	.7973	.7980	.7987
6.3	.7993	.8000	.8007	.8014	.8021	.8028	.8035	.8041	.8048	.8055
6.4	.8062	.8069	.8075	.8082	.8089	.8096	.8102	.8109	.8116	.8122
6.5	.8129	.8136	.8142	.8149	.8156	.8162	.8169	.8176	.8182	.8189
6.6	.8195	.8202	.8209	.8215	.8222	.8228	.8235	.8241	.8248	.8254
6.7	.8261	.8267	.8274	.8280	.8287	.8293	.8299	.8306	.8312	.8319
6.8	.8325	.8331	.8338	.8344	.8351	.8357	.8363	.8370	.8376	.8382
6.9	.8388	.8395	.8401	.8407	.8414	.8420	.8426	.8432	.8439	.8445
7.0	.8451	.8457	.8463	.8470	.8476	.8482	.8488	.8494	.8500	.8506
7.1	.8513	.8519	.8525	.8531	.8537	.8543	.8549	.8555	.8561	.8567
7.2	.8573	.8579	.8585	.8591	.8597	.8603	.8609	.8615	.8621	.8627
7.3	.8633	.8639	.8645	.8651	.8657	.8663	.8669	.8675	.8681	.8686
7.4	.8692	.8698	.8704	.8710	.8716	.8722	.8727	.8733	.8739	.8745
7.5	.8751	.8756	.8762	.8768	.8774	.8779	.8785	.8791	.8797	.8802
7.6	.8808	.8814	.8820	.8825	.8831	.8837	.8842	.8848	.8854	.8859
7.7	.8865	.8871	.8876	.8882	.8887	.8893	.8899	.8904	.8910	.8915
7.8	.8921	.8927	.8932	.8938	.8943	.8949	.8954	.8960	.8965	.8971
7.9	.8976	.8982	.8987	.8993	.8998	.9004	.9009	.9015	.9020	.9025
8.0	.9031	.9036	.9042	.9047	.9053	.9058	.9063	.9069	.9074	.9079
8.1	.9085	.9090	.9096	.9101	.9106	.9112	.9117	.9122	.9128	.9133
8.2	.9138	.9143	.9149	.9154	.9159	.9165	.9170	.9175	.9180	.9186
8.3	.9191	.9196	.9201	.9206	.9212	.9217	.9222	.9227	.9232	.9238
8.4	.9243	.9248	.9253	.9258	.9263	.9269	.9274	.9279	.9284	.9289
8.5	.9294	.9299	.9304	.9309	.9315	.9320	.9325	.9330	.9335	.9340
8.6	.9345	.9350	.9355	.9360	.9365	.9370	.9375	.9380	.9385	.9390
8.7	.9395	.9400	.9405	.9410	.9415	.9420	.9425	.9430	.9435	.9440
8.8	.9445	.9450	.9455	.9460	.9465	.9469	.9474	.9479	.9484	.9489
8.9	.9494	.9499	.9504	.9509	.9513	.9518	.9523	.9528	.9533	.9538
9.0	.9542	.9547	.9552	.9557	.9562	.9566	.9571	.9576	.9581	.9586
9.1	.9590	.9595	.9600	.9605	.9609	.9614	.9619	.9624	.9628	.9633
9.2	.9638	.9643	.9647	.9652	.9657	.9661	.9666	.9671	.9675	.9680
9.3	.9685	.9689	.9694	.9699	.9703	.9708	.9713	.9717	.9722	.9727
9.4	.9731	.9736	.9741	.9745	.9750	.9754	.9759	.9763	.9768	.9773
9.5	.9777	.9782	.9786	.9791	.9795	.9800	.9805	.9809	.9814	.9818
9.6	.9823	.9827	.9832	.9836	.9841	.9845	.9850	.9854	.9859	.9863
9.7	.9868	.9872	.9877	.9881	.9886	.9890	.9894	.9899	.9903	.9908
9.8	.9912	.9917	.9921	.9926	.9930	.9934	.9939	.9943	.9948	.9952
9.9	.9956	.9961	.9965	.9969	.9974	.9978	.9983	.9987	.9991	.9996

Table 3: Natural Logarithms (ln x)

x	0.00	0.01	0.02	0.03	0.04	0.05	0.06	0.07	0.08	0.09
1.0	0.0000	0.0100	0.0198	0.0296	0.0392	0.0488	0.0583	0.0677	0.0770	0.0862
1.1	0.0953	0.1044	0.1133	0.1222	0.1310	0.1398	0.1484	0.1570	0.1655	0.1740
1.2	0.1823	0.1906	0.1989	0.2070	0.2151	0.2231	0.2311	0.2390	0.2469	0.2546
1.3	0.2624	0.2700	0.2776	0.2852	0.2927	0.3001	0.3075	0.3148	0.3221	0.3293
1.4	0.3365	0.3436	0.3507	0.3577	0.3646	0.3716	0.3784	0.3853	0.3920	0.3988
1.5	0.4055	0.4121	0.4187	0.4253	0.4318	0.4383	0.4447	0.4511	0.4574	0.4637
1.6	0.4700	0.4762	0.4824	0.4886	0.4947	0.5008	0.5068	0.5128	0.5188	0.5247
1.7	0.5306	0.5365	0.5423	0.5481	0.5539	0.5596	0.5653	0.5710	0.5766	0.5822
1.8	0.5878	0.5933	0.5988	0.6043	0.6098	0.6152	0.6206	0.6259	0.6313	0.6366
1.9	0.6419	0.6471	0.6523	0.6575	0.6627	0.6678	0.6729	0.6780	0.6831	0.6881
2.0	0.6931	0.6981	0.7031	0.7080	0.7130	0.7178	0.7227	0.7275	0.7324	0.7372
2.1	0.7419	0.7467	0.7514	0.7561	0.7608	0.7655	0.7701	0.7747	0.7793	0.7839
2.2	0.7885	0.7930	0.7975	0.8020	0.8065	0.8109	0.8154	0.8198	0.8242	0.8286
2.3	0.8329	0.8372	0.8416	0.8459	0.8502	0.8544	0.8587	0.8629	0.8671	0.8713
2.4	0.8755	0.8796	0.8838	0.8879	0.8920	0.8961	0.9002	0.9042	0.9083	0.9123
2.5	0.9163	0.9203	0.9243	0.9282	0.9322	0.9361	0.9400	0.9439	0.9478	0.9517
2.6	0.9555	0.9594	0.9632	0.9670	0.9708	0.9746	0.9783	0.9821	0.9858	0.9895
2.7	0.9933	0.9969	1.0006	1.0043	1.0080	1.0116	1.0152	1.0188	1.0225	1.0260
2.8	1.0296	1.0332	1.0367	1.0403	1.0438	1.0473	1.0508	1.0543	1.0578	1.0613
2.9	1.0647	1.0682	1.0716	1.0750	1.0784	1.0818	1.0852	1.0886	1.0919	1.0953
3.0	1.0986	1.1019	1.1053	1.1086	1.1119	1.1151	1.1184	1.1217	1.1249	1.1282
3.1	1.1314	1.1346	1.1378	1.1410	1.1442	1.1474	1.1506	1.1537	1.1569	1.1600
3.2	1.1632	1.1663	1.1694	1.1725	1.1756	1.1787	1.1817	1.1848	1.1878	1.1909
3.3	1.1939	1.1970	1.2000	1.2030	1.2060	1.2090	1.2119	1.2149	1.2179	1.2208
3.4	1.2238	1.2267	1.2296	1.2326	1.2355	1.2384	1.2413	1.2442	1.2470	1.2499
3.5	1.2528	1.2556	1.2585	1.2613	1.2641	1.2669	1.2698	1.2726	1.2754	1.2782
3.6	1.2809	1.2837	1.2865	1.2892	1.2920	1.2947	1.2975	1.3002	1.3029	1.3056
3.7	1.3083	1.3110	1.3137	1.3164	1.3191	1.3218	1.3244	1.3271	1.3297	1.3324
3.8	1.3350	1.3376	1.3403	1.3429	1.3455	1.3481	1.3507	1.3533	1.3558	1.3584
3.9	1.3610	1.3635	1.3661	1.3686	1.3712	1.3737	1.3762	1.3788	1.3813	1.3838
4.0	1.3863	1.3888	1.3913	1.3938	1.3962	1.3987	1.4012	1.4036	1.4061	1.4085
4.1	1.4110	1.4134	1.4159	1.4183	1.4207	1.4231	1.4255	1.4279	1.4303	1.4327
4.2	1.4351	1.4375	1.4398	1.4422	1.4446	1.4469	1.4493	1.4516	1.4540	1.4563
4.3	1.4586	1.4609	1.4633	1.4656	1.4679	1.4702	1.4725	1.4748	1.4770	1.4793
4.4	1.4816	1.4839	1.4861	1.4884	1.4907	1.4929	1.4952	1.4974	1.4996	1.5019
4.5	1.5041	1.5063	1.5085	1.5107	1.5129	1.5151	1.5173	1.5195	1.5217	1.5239
4.6	1.5261	1.5282	1.5304	1.5326	1.5347	1.5369	1.5390	1.5412	1.5433	1.5454
4.7	1.5476	1.5497	1.5518	1.5539	1.5560	1.5581	1.5602	1.5623	1.5644	1.5665
4.8	1.5686	1.5707	1.5728	1.5748	1.5769	1.5790	1.5810	1.5831	1.5851	1.5872
4.9	1.5892	1.5913	1.5933	1.5953	1.5974	1.5994	1.6014	1.6034	1.6054	1.6074
5.0	1.6094	1.6114	1.6134	1.6154	1.6174	1.6194	1.6214	1.6233	1.6253	1.6273
5.1	1.6292	1.6312	1.6332	1.6351	1.6371	1.6390	1.6409	1.6429	1.6448	1.6467
5.2	1.6487	1.6506	1.6525	1.6544	1.6563	1.6582	1.6601	1.6620	1.6639	1.6658
5.3	1.6677	1.6696	1.6715	1.6734	1.6752	1.6771	1.6790	1.6808	1.6827	1.6845
5.4	1.6864	1.6882	1.6901	1.6919	1.6938	1.6956	1.6974	1.6993	1.7011	1.7029

Table 3: Natural Logarithms (ln *x*)

x	0.00	0.01	0.02	0.03	0.04	0.05	0.06	0.07	0.08	0.09
5.5	1.7047	1.7066	1.7084	1.7102	1.7120	1.7138	1.7156	1.7174	1.7192	1.7210
5.6	1.7228	1.7246	1.7263	1.7281	1.7299	1.7317	1.7334	1.7352	1.7370	1.7387
5.7	1.7405	1.7422	1.7440	1.7457	1.7475	1.7492	1.7509	1.7527	1.7544	1.7561
5.8	1.7579	1.7596	1.7613	1.7630	1.7647	1.7664	1.7682	1.7699	1.7716	1.7733
5.9	1.7750	1.7766	1.7783	1.7800	1.7817	1.7834	1.7851	1.7867	1.7884	1.7901
6.0	1.7918	1.7934	1.7951	1.7967	1.7984	1.8001	1.8017	1.8034	1.8050	1.8066
6.1	1.8083	1.8099	1.8116	1.8132	1.8148	1.8165	1.8181	1.8197	1.8213	1.8229
6.2	1.8245	1.8262	1.8278	1.8294	1.8310	1.8326	1.8342	1.8358	1.8374	1.8390
6.3	1.8406	1.8421	1.8437	1.8453	1.8469	1.8485	1.8500	1.8516	1.8532	1.8547
6.4	1.8563	1.8579	1.8594	1.8610	1.8625	1.8641	1.8656	1.8672	1.8687	1.8703
6.5	1.8718	1.8733	1.8749	1.8764	1.8779	1.8795	1.8810	1.8825	1.8840	1.8856
6.6	1.8871	1.8886	1.8901	1.8916	1.8931	1.8946	1.8961	1.8976	1.8991	1.9006
6.7	1.9021	1.9036	1.9051	1.9066	1.9081	1.9095	1.9110	1.9125	1.9140	1.9155
6.8	1.9169	1.9184	1.9199	1.9213	1.9228	1.9242	1.9257	1.9272	1.9286	1.9301
6.9	1.9315	1.9330	1.9344	1.9359	1.9373	1.9387	1.9402	1.9416	1.9430	1.9445
7.0	1.9459	1.9473	1.9488	1.9502	1.9516	1.9530	1.9544	1.9559	1.9573	1.9587
7.1	1.9601	1.9615	1.9629	1.9643	1.9657	1.9671	1.9685	1.9699	1.9713	1.9727
7.2	1.9741	1.9755	1.9769	1.9782	1.9796	1.9810	1.9824	1.9838	1.9851	1.9865
7.3	1.9879	1.9892	1.9906	1.9920	1.9933	1.9947	1.9961	1.9974	1.9988	2.0001
7.4	2.0015	2.0028	2.0042	2.0055	2.0069	2.0082	2.0096	2.0109	2.0122	2.0136
7.5	2.0149	2.0162	2.0176	2.0189	2.0202	2.0215	2.0229	2.0242	2.0255	2.0268
7.6	2.0282	2.0295	2.0308	2.0321	2.0334	2.0347	2.0360	2.0373	2.0386	2.0399
7.7	2.0412	2.0425	2.0438	2.0451	2.0464	2.0477	2.0490	2.0503	2.0516	2.0528
7.8	2.0541	2.0554	2.0567	2.0580	2.0592	2.0605	2.0618	2.0631	2.0643	2.0656
7.9	2.0669	2.0681	2.0694	2.0707	2.0719	2.0732	2.0744	2.0757	2.0769	2.0782
8.0	2.0794	2.0807	2.0819	2.0832	2.0844	2.0857	2.0869	2.0882	2.0894	2.0906
8.1	2.0919	2.0931	2.0943	2.0956	2.0968	2.0980	2.0992	2.1005	2.1017	2.1029
8.2	2.1041	2.1054	2.1066	2.1078	2.1090	2.1102	2.1114	2.1126	2.1138	2.1150
8.3	2.1163	2.1175	2.1187	2.1199	2.1211	2.1223	2.1235	2.1247	2.1258	2.1270
8.4	2.1282	2.1294	2.1306	2.1318	2.1330	2.1342	2.1353	2.1365	2.1377	2.1389
8.5	2.1401	2.1412	2.1424	2.1436	2.1448	2.1459	2.1471	2.1483	2.1494	2.1506
8.6	2.1518	2.1529	2.1541	2.1552	2.1564	2.1576	2.1587	2.1599	2.1610	2.1622
8.7	2.1633	2.1645	2.1656	2.1668	2.1679	2.1691	2.1702	2.1713	2.1725	2.1736
8.8	2.1748	2.1759	2.1770	2.1782	2.1793	2.1804	2.1815	2.1827	2.1838	2.1849
8.9	2.1861	2.1872	2.1883	2.1894	2.1905	2.1917	2.1928	2.1939	2.1950	2.1961
9.0	2.1972	2.1983	2.1994	2.2006	2.2017	2.2028	2.2039	2.2050	2.2061	2.2072
9.1	2.2083	2.2094	2.2105	2.2116	2.2127	2.2138	2.2148	2.2159	2.2170	2.2181
9.2	2.2192	2.2203	2.2214	2.2225	2.2235	2.2246	2.2257	2.2268	2.2279	2.2289
9.3	2.2300	2.2311	2.2322	2.2332	2.2343	2.2354	2.2364	2.2375	2.2386	2.2396
9.4	2.2407	2.2418	2.2428	2.2439	2.2450	2.2460	2.2471	2.2481	2.2492	2.2502
9.5	2.2513	2.2523	2.2534	2.2544	2.2555	2.2565	2.2576	2.2586	2.2597	2.2607
9.6	2.2618	2.2628	2.2638	2.2649	2.2659	2.2670	2.2680	2.2690	2.2701	2.2711
9.7	2.2721	2.2732	2.2742	2.2752	2.2762	2.2773	2.2783	2.2793	2.2803	2.2814
9.8	2.2824	2.2834	2.2844	2.2854	2.2865	2.2875	2.2885	2.2895	2.2905	2.2915
9.9	2.2925	2.2935	2.2946	2.2956	2.2966	2.2976	2.2986	2.2996	2.3006	2.3016

x	e^x	e^{-x}	x	e^x	e^{-x}	x	e^x	e^{-x}
0.00	1.0000	1.0000	0.55	1.7333	0.5769	3.6	36.598	0.0273
0.01	1.0101	0.9900	0.60	1.8221	0.5488	3.7	40.447	0.0247
0.02	1.0202	0.9802	0.65	1.9155	0.5220	3.8	44.701	0.0224
0.03	1.0305	0.9704	0.70	2.0138	0.4966	3.9	49.402	0.0202
0.04	1.0408	0.9608	0.75	2.1170	0.4724	4.0	54.598	0.0183
0.05	1.0513	0.9512	0.80	2.2255	0.4493	4.1	60.340	0.0166
0.06	1.0618	0.9418	0.85	2.3396	0.4274	4.2	66.686	0.0150
0.07	1.0725	0.9324	0.90	2.4596	0.4066	4.3	73.700	0.0136
0.08	1.0833	0.9231	0.95	2.5857	0.3867	4.4	81.451	0.0123
0.09	1.0942	0.9139	1.0	2.7183	0.3679	4.5	90.017	0.0111
0.10	1.1052	0.9048	1.1	3.0042	0.3329	4.6	99.484	0.0101
0.11	1.1163	0.8958	1.2	3.3201	0.3012	4.7	109.95	0.0091
0.12	1.1275	0.8869	1.3	3.6693	0.2725	4.8	121.51	0.0082
0.13	1.1388	0.8781	1.4	4.0552	0.2466	4.9	134.29	0.0074
0.14	1.1503	0.8694	1.5	4.4817	0.2231	5	148.41	0.0067
0.15	1.1618	0.8607	1.6	4.9530	0.2019	6	403.43	0.0025
0.16	1.1735	0.8521	1.7	5.4739	0.1827	7	1,096.6	0.0009
0.17	1.1853	0.8437	1.8	6.0496	0.1653	8	2,981.0	0.0003
0.18	1.1972	0.8353	1.9	6.6859	0.1496	9	8,103.1	0.0001
0.19	1.2092	0.8270	2.0	7.3891	0.1353	10	22,026	0.00005
0.20	1.2214	0.8187	2.1	8.1662	0.1225	11	59,874	0.00002
0.21	1.2337	0.8106	2.2	9.0250	0.1108	12	162,754	0.000006
0.22	1.2461	0.8025	2.3	9.9742	0.1003	13	442,413	0.000002
0.23	1.2586	0.7945	2.4	11.023	0.0907	14	1,202,604	0.0000008
0.24	1.2712	0.7866	2.5	12.182	0.0821	15	3,269,017	0.0000003
0.25	1.2840	0.7788	2.6	13.464	0.0743			
0.26	1.2969	0.7711	2.7	14.880	0.0672			
0.27	1.3100	0.7634	2.8	16.445	0.0608			
0.28	1.3231	0.7558	2.9	18.174	0.0550			
0.29	1.3364	0.7483	3.0	20.086	0.0498			
0.30	1.3499	0.7408	3.1	22.198	0.0450			
0.35	1.4191	0.7047	3.2	24.533	0.0408			
0.40	1.4918	0.6703	3.3	27.113	0.0369			
0.45	1.5683	0.6376	3.4	29.964	0.0334			
0.50	1.6487	0.6065	3.5	33.115	0.0302			

Degrees	Radians	Sin	Cos	Tan	Cot	Sec	Csc		
0° 00′	0.0000	0.0000	1.0000	0.0000	—	1.000	—	1.5708	90° 00′
10	029	029	000	029	343.8	000	343.8	679	50
20	058	058	000	058	171.9	000	171.9	650	40
30	0.0087	0.0087	1.0000	0.0087	114.6	1.000	114.6	1.5621	30
40	116	116	0.9999	116	85.94	000	85.95	592	20
50	145	145	999	145	68.75	000	68.76	563	10
1° 00′	0.0175	0.0175	0.9998	0.0175	57.29	1.000	57.30	1.5533	89° 00′
10	204	204	998	204	49.10	000	49.11	504	50
20	233	233	997	233	42.96	000	42.98	475	40
30	0.0262	0.0262	0.9997	0.0262	38.19	1.000	38.20	1.5446	30
40	291	291	996	291	34.37	000	34.38	417	20
50	320	320	995	320	31.24	001	31.26	388	10
2° 00′	0.0349	0.0349	0.9994	0.0349	28.64	1.001	28.65	1.5359	88° 00′
10	378	378	993	378	26.43	001	26.45	330	50
20	407	407	992	407	24.54	001	24.56	301	40
30	0.0436	0.0436	0.9990	0.0437	22.90	1.001	22.93	1.5272	30
40	465	465	989	466	21.47	001	21.49	243	20
50	495	494	988	495	20.21	001	20.23	213	10
3° 00′	0.0524	0.0523	0.9986	0.0524	19.08	1.001	19.11	1.5184	87° 00′
10	553	552	985	553	18.07	002	18.10	155	50
20	582	581	983	582	17.17	002	17.20	126	40
30	0.0611	0.0610	0.9981	0.0612	16.35	1.002	16.38	1.5097	30
40	640	640	980	641	15.60	002	15.64	068	20
50	669	669	978	670	14.92	002	14.96	039	10
4° 00′	0.0698	0.0698	0.9976	0.0699	14.30	1.002	14.34	1.5010	86° 00′
10	727	727	974	729	13.73	003	13.76	1.4981	50
20	756	756	971	758	13.20	003	13.23	952	40
30	0.0785	0.0785	0.9969	0.0787	12.71	1.003	12.75	1.4923	30
40	814	814	967	816	12.25	003	12.29	893	20
50	844	843	964	846	11.83	004	11.87	864	10
5° 00′	0.0873	0.0872	0.9962	0.0875	11.43	1.004	11.47	1.4835	85° 00′
10	902	901	959	904	11.06	004	11.10	806	50
20	931	929	957	934	10.71	004	10.76	777	40
30	0.0960	0.0958	0.9954	0.0963	10.39	1.005	10.43	1.4748	30
40	989	987	951	992	10.08	005	10.13	719	20
50	0.1018	0.1016	948	0.1022	9.788	005	9.839	690	10
6° 00′	0.1047	0.1045	0.9945	0.1051	9.514	1.006	9.567	1.4661	84° 00′
10	076	074	942	080	9.255	006	9.309	632	50
20	105	103	939	110	9.010	006	9.065	603	40
30	0.1134	0.1132	0.9936	0.1139	8.777	1.006	8.834	1.4573	30
40	164	161	932	169	8.556	007	8.614	544	20
50	193	190	929	198	8.345	007	8.405	515	10
7° 00′	0.1222	0.1219	0.9925	0.1228	8.144	1.008	8.206	1.4486	83° 00′
10	251	248	922	257	7.953	008	8.016	457	50
20	280	276	918	287	7.770	008	7.834	428	40
30	0.1309	0.1305	0.9914	0.1317	7.596	1.009	7.661	1.4399	30
40	338	334	911	346	7.429	009	7.496	370	20
50	367	363	907	376	7.269	009	7.337	341	10
8° 00′	0.1396	0.1392	0.9903	0.1405	7.115	1.010	7.185	1.4312	82° 00′
10	425	421	899	435	6.968	010	7.040	283	50
20	454	449	894	465	6.827	011	6.900	254	40
30	0.1484	0.1478	0.9890	0.1495	6.691	1.011	6.765	1.4224	30
40	513	507	886	524	6.561	012	6.636	195	20
50	542	536	881	554	6.435	012	6.512	166	10
9° 00′	0.1571	0.1564	0.9877	0.1584	6.314	1.012	6.392	1.4137	81° 00′
		Cos	Sin	Cot	Tan	Csc	Sec	Radians	Degrees

Degrees	Radians	Sin	Cos	Tan	Cot	Sec	Csc		
9° 00′	0.1571	0.1564	0.9877	0.1584	6.314	1.012	6.392	1.4137	81° 00′
10	600	593	872	614	197	013	277	108	50
20	629	622	868	644	084	013	166	079	40
30	0.1658	0.1650	0.9863	0.1673	5.976	1.014	6.059	1.4050	30
40	687	679	858	703	871	014	5.955	021	20
50	716	708	853	733	769	015	855	1.3992	10
10° 00′	0.1745	0.1736	0.9848	0.1763	5.671	1.015	5.759	1.3963	80° 00′
10	774	765	843	793	576	016	665	934	50
20	804	794	838	823	485	016	575	904	40
30	0.1833	0.1822	0.9833	0.1853	5.396	1.017	5.487	1.3875	30
40	862	851	827	883	309	018	403	846	20
50	891	880	822	914	226	018	320	817	10
11° 00′	0.1920	0.1908	0.9816	0.1944	5.145	1.019	5.241	1.3788	79° 00′
10	949	937	811	974	066	019	164	759	50
20	978	965	805	0.2004	4.989	020	089	730	40
30	0.2007	0.1994	0.9799	0.2035	4.915	1.020	5.016	1.3701	30
40	036	0.2022	793	065	843	021	4.945	672	20
50	065	051	787	095	773	022	876	643	10
12° 00′	0.2094	0.2079	0.9781	0.2126	4.705	1.022	4.810	1.3614	78° 00′
10	123	108	775	156	638	023	745	584	50
20	153	136	769	186	574	024	682	555	40
30	0.2182	0.2164	0.9763	0.2217	4.511	1.024	4.620	1.3526	30
40	211	193	757	247	449	025	560	497	20
50	240	221	750	278	390	026	502	468	10
13° 00′	0.2269	0.2250	0.9744	0.2309	4.331	1.026	4.445	1.3439	77° 00′
10	298	278	737	339	275	027	390	410	50
20	327	306	730	370	219	028	336	381	40
30	0.2356	0.2334	0.9724	0.2401	4.165	1.028	4.284	1.3352	30
40	385	363	717	432	113	029	232	323	20
50	414	391	710	462	061	030	182	294	10
14° 00′	0.2443	0.2419	0.9703	0.2493	4.011	1.031	4.134	1.3265	76° 00′
10	473	447	696	524	3.962	031	086	235	50
20	502	476	689	555	914	032	039	206	40
30	0.2531	0.2504	0.9681	0.2586	3.867	1.033	3.994	1.3177	30
40	560	532	674	617	821	034	950	148	20
50	589	560	667	648	776	034	906	119	10
15° 00′	0.2618	0.2588	0.9659	0.2679	3.732	1.035	3.864	1.3090	75° 00′
10	647	616	652	711	689	036	822	061	50
20	676	644	644	742	647	037	782	032	40
30	0.2705	0.2672	0.9636	0.2773	3.606	1.038	3.742	1.3003	30
40	734	700	628	805	566	039	703	1.2974	20
50	763	728	621	836	526	039	665	945	10
16° 00′	0.2793	0.2756	0.9613	0.2867	3.487	1.040	3.628	1.2915	74° 00′
10	822	784	605	899	450	041	592	886	50
20	851	812	596	931	412	042	556	857	40
30	0.2880	0.2840	0.9588	0.2962	3.376	1.043	3.521	1.2828	30
40	909	868	580	994	340	044	487	799	20
50	938	896	572	0.3026	305	045	453	770	10
17° 00′	0.2967	0.2924	0.9563	0.3057	3.271	1.046	3.420	1.2741	73° 00′
10	996	952	555	089	237	047	388	712	50
20	0.3025	979	546	121	204	048	356	683	40
30	0.3054	0.3007	0.9537	0.3153	3.172	1.049	3.326	1.2654	30
40	083	035	528	185	140	049	295	625	20
50	113	062	520	217	108	050	265	595	10
18° 00′	0.3142	0.3090	0.9511	0.3249	3.078	1.051	3.236	1.2566	72° 00′
		Cos	Sin	Cot	Tan	Csc	Sec	Radians	Degrees

Degrees	Radians	Sin	Cos	Tan	Cot	Sec	Csc		
18° 00′	0.3142	0.3090	0.9511	0.3249	3.078	1.051	3.236	1.2566	72° 00′
10	171	118	502	281	047	052	207	537	50
20	200	145	492	314	018	053	179	508	40
30	0.3229	0.3173	0.9483	0.3346	2.989	1.054	3.152	1.2479	30
40	258	201	474	378	960	056	124	450	20
50	287	228	465	411	932	057	098	421	10
19° 00′	0.3316	0.3256	0.9455	0.3443	2.904	1.058	3.072	1.2392	71° 00′
10	345	283	446	476	877	059	046	363	50
20	374	311	436	508	850	060	021	334	40
30	0.3403	0.3338	0.9426	0.3541	2.824	1.061	2.996	1.2305	30
40	432	365	417	574	798	062	971	275	20
50	462	393	407	607	773	063	947	246	10
20° 00′	0.3491	0.3420	0.9397	0.3640	2.747	1.064	2.924	1.2217	70° 00′
10	520	448	387	673	723	065	901	188	50
20	549	475	377	706	699	066	878	159	40
30	0.3578	0.3502	0.9367	0.3739	2.675	1.068	2.855	1.2130	30
40	607	529	356	772	651	069	833	101	20
50	636	557	346	805	628	070	812	072	10
21° 00′	0.3665	0.3584	0.9336	0.3839	2.605	1.071	2.790	1.2043	69° 00′
10	694	611	325	872	583	072	769	014	50
20	723	638	315	906	560	074	749	1.1985	40
30	0.3752	0.3665	0.9304	0.3939	2.539	1.075	2.729	1.1956	30
40	782	692	293	973	517	076	709	926	20
50	811	719	283	0.4006	496	077	689	897	10
22° 00′	0.3840	0.3746	0.9272	0.4040	2.475	1.079	2.669	1.1868	68° 00′
10	869	773	261	074	455	080	650	839	50
20	898	800	250	108	434	081	632	810	40
30	0.3927	0.3827	0.9239	0.4142	2.414	1.082	2.613	1.1781	30
40	956	854	228	176	394	084	595	752	20
50	985	881	216	210	375	085	577	723	10
23° 00′	0.4014	0.3907	0.9205	0.4245	2.356	1.086	2.559	1.1694	67° 00′
10	043	934	194	279	337	088	542	665	50
20	072	961	182	314	318	089	525	636	40
30	0.4102	0.3987	0.9171	0.4348	2.300	1.090	2.508	1.1606	30
40	131	0.4014	159	383	282	092	491	577	20
50	160	041	147	417	264	093	475	548	10
24° 00′	0.4189	0.4067	0.9135	0.4452	2.246	1.095	2.459	1.1519	66° 00′
10	218	094	124	487	229	096	443	490	50
20	247	120	112	552	211	097	427	461	40
30	0.4276	0.4147	0.9100	0.4557	2.194	1.099	2.411	1.1432	30
40	305	173	088	592	177	100	396	403	20
50	334	200	075	628	161	102	381	374	10
25° 00′	0.4363	0.4226	0.9063	0.4663	2.145	1.103	2.366	1.1345	65° 00′
10	392	253	051	699	128	105	352	316	50
20	422	279	038	734	112	106	337	286	40
30	0.4451	0.4305	0.9026	0.4770	2.097	1.108	2.323	1.1257	30
40	480	331	013	806	081	109	309	228	20
50	509	358	001	841	066	111	295	199	10
26° 00′	0.4538	0.4384	0.8988	0.4877	2.050	1.113	2.281	1.1170	64° 00′
10	567	410	975	913	035	114	268	141	50
20	596	436	962	950	020	116	254	112	40
30	0.4625	0.4462	0.8949	0.4986	2.006	1.117	2.241	1.1083	30
40	654	488	936	0.5022	1.991	119	228	054	20
50	683	514	923	059	977	121	215	1.1025	10
27° 00′	0.4712	0.4540	0.8910	0.5095	1.963	1.122	2.203	1.0996	63° 00′
		Cos	Sin	Cot	Tan	Csc	Sec	Radians	Degrees

Degrees	Radians	Sin	Cos	Tan	Cot	Sec	Csc		
27° 00′	0.4712	0.4540	0.8910	0.5095	1.963	1.122	2.203	1.0996	63° 00′
10	741	566	897	132	949	124	190	966	50
20	771	592	884	169	935	126	178	937	40
30	0.4800	0.4617	0.8870	0.5206	1.921	1.127	2.166	1.0908	30
40	829	643	857	243	907	129	154	879	20
50	858	669	843	280	894	131	142	850	10
28° 00′	0.4887	0.4695	0.8829	0.5317	1.881	1.133	2.130	1.0821	62° 00′
10	916	720	816	354	868	134	118	792	50
20	945	746	802	392	855	136	107	763	40
30	0.4974	0.4772	0.8788	0.5430	1.842	1.138	2.096	1.0734	30
40	0.5003	797	774	467	829	140	085	705	20
50	032	823	760	505	816	142	074	676	10
29° 00′	0.5061	0.4848	0.8746	0.5543	1.804	1.143	2.063	1.0647	61° 00′
10	091	874	732	581	792	145	052	617	50
20	120	899	718	619	780	147	041	588	40
30	0.5149	0.4924	0.8704	0.5658	1.767	1.149	2.031	1.0559	30
40	178	950	689	696	756	151	020	530	20
50	207	975	675	735	744	153	010	501	10
30° 00′	0.5236	0.5000	0.8660	0.5774	1.732	1.155	2.000	1.0472	60° 00′
10	265	025	646	812	720	157	1.990	443	50
20	294	050	631	851	709	159	980	414	40
30	0.5323	0.5075	0.8616	0.5890	1.698	1.161	1.970	1.0385	30
40	352	100	601	930	686	163	961	356	20
50	381	125	587	969	675	165	951	327	10
31° 00′	0.5411	0.5150	0.8572	0.6009	1.664	1.167	1.942	1.0297	59° 00′
10	440	175	557	048	653	169	932	268	50
20	469	200	542	088	643	171	923	239	40
30	0.5498	0.5225	0.8526	0.6128	1.632	1.173	1.914	1.0210	30
40	527	250	511	168	621	175	905	181	20
50	556	275	496	208	611	177	896	152	10
32° 00′	0.5585	0.5299	0.8480	0.6249	1.600	1.179	1.887	1.0123	58° 00′
10	614	324	465	289	590	181	878	094	50
20	643	348	450	330	580	184	870	065	40
30	0.5672	0.5373	0.8434	0.6371	1.570	1.186	1.861	1.0036	30
40	701	398	418	412	560	188	853	007	20
50	730	422	403	453	550	190	844	0.9977	10
33° 00′	0.5760	0.5446	0.8387	0.6494	1.540	1.192	1.836	0.9948	57° 00′
10	789	471	371	536	530	195	828	919	50
20	818	495	355	577	520	197	820	890	40
30	0.5847	0.5519	0.8339	0.6619	1.511	1.199	1.812	0.9861	30
40	876	544	323	661	501	202	804	832	20
50	905	568	307	703	492	204	796	803	10
34° 00′	0.5934	0.5592	0.8290	0.6745	1.483	1.206	1.788	0.9774	56° 00′
10	963	616	274	787	473	209	781	745	50
20	992	640	258	830	464	211	773	716	40
30	0.6021	0.5664	0.8241	0.6873	1.455	1.213	1.766	0.9687	30
40	050	688	225	916	446	216	758	657	20
50	080	712	208	959	437	218	751	628	10
35° 00′	0.6109	0.5736	0.8192	0.7002	1.428	1.221	1.743	0.9599	55° 10′
10	138	760	175	046	419	223	736	570	50
20	167	783	158	089	411	226	729	541	40
30	0.6196	0.5807	0.8141	0.7133	1.402	1.228	1.722	0.9512	30
40	225	831	124	177	393	231	715	483	20
50	254	854	107	221	385	233	708	454	10
36° 00′	0.6283	0.5878	0.8090	0.7265	1.376	1.236	1.701	0.9425	54° 00′
		Cos	Sin	Cot	Tan	Csc	Sec	Radians	Degrees

Table 5: Trigonometric Function Values

Degrees	Radians	Sin	Cos	Tan	Cot	Sec	Csc		
36° 00′	0.6283	0.5878	0.8090	0.7265	1.376	1.236	1.701	0.9425	54° 00′
10	312	901	073	310	368	239	695	396	50
20	341	925	056	355	360	241	688	367	40
30	0.6370	0.5948	0.8039	0.7400	1.351	1.244	1.681	0.9338	30
40	400	972	021	445	343	247	675	308	20
50	429	995	004	490	335	249	668	279	10
37° 00′	0.6458	0.6018	0.7986	0.7536	1.327	1.252	1.662	0.9250	53° 00′
10	487	041	969	581	319	255	655	221	50
20	516	065	951	627	311	258	649	192	40
30	0.6545	0.6088	0.7934	0.7673	1.303	1.260	1.643	0.9163	30
40	574	111	916	720	295	263	636	134	20
50	603	134	898	766	288	266	630	105	10
38° 00′	0.6632	0.6157	0.7880	0.7813	1.280	1.269	1.624	0.9076	52° 00′
10	661	180	862	860	272	272	618	047	50
20	690	202	844	907	265	275	612	0.9018	40
30	0.6720	0.6225	0.7826	0.7954	1.257	1.278	1.606	0.8988	30
40	749	248	808	0.8002	250	281	601	959	20
50	778	271	790	050	242	284	595	930	10
39° 00′	0.6807	0.6293	0.7771	0.8098	1.235	1.287	1.589	0.8901	51° 00′
10	836	316	753	146	228	290	583	872	50
20	865	338	735	195	220	293	578	843	40
30	0.6894	0.6361	0.7716	0.8243	1.213	1.296	1.572	0.8814	30
40	923	383	698	292	206	299	567	785	20
50	952	406	679	342	199	302	561	756	10
40° 00′	0.6981	0.6428	0.7660	0.8391	1.192	1.305	1.556	0.8727	50° 00′
10	0.7010	450	642	441	185	309	550	698	50
20	039	472	623	491	178	312	545	668	40
30	0.7069	0.6494	0.7604	0.8541	1.171	1.315	1.540	0.8639	30
40	098	517	585	591	164	318	535	610	20
50	127	539	566	642	157	322	529	581	10
41° 00′	0.7156	0.6561	0.7547	0.8693	1.150	1.325	1.524	0.8552	49° 00′
10	185	583	528	744	144	328	519	523	50
20	214	604	509	796	137	332	514	494	40
30	0.7243	0.6626	0.7490	0.8847	1.130	1.335	1.509	0.8465	30
40	272	648	470	899	124	339	504	436	20
50	301	670	451	952	117	342	499	407	10
42° 00′	0.7330	0.6691	0.7431	0.9004	1.111	1.346	1.494	0.8378	48° 00′
10	359	713	412	057	104	349	490	348	50
20	389	734	392	110	098	353	485	319	40
30	0.7418	0.6756	0.7373	0.9163	1.091	1.356	1.480	0.8290	30
40	447	777	353	217	085	360	476	261	20
50	476	799	333	271	079	364	471	232	10
43° 00′	0.7505	0.6820	0.7314	0.9325	1.072	1.367	1.466	0.8203	47° 00′
10	534	841	294	380	066	371	462	174	50
20	563	862	274	435	060	375	457	145	40
30	0.7592	0.6884	0.7254	0.9490	1.054	1.379	1.453	0.8116	30
40	621	905	234	545	048	382	448	087	20
50	650	926	214	601	042	386	444	058	10
44° 00′	0.7679	0.6947	0.7193	0.9657	1.036	1.390	1.440	0.8029	46° 00′
10	709	967	173	713	030	394	435	999	50
20	738	988	153	770	024	398	431	970	40
30	0.7767	0.7009	0.7133	0.9827	1.018	1.402	1.427	0.7941	30
40	796	030	112	884	012	406	423	912	20
50	825	050	092	942	006	410	418	883	10
45° 00′	0.7854	0.7071	0.7071	1.000	1.000	1.414	1.414	0.7854	45° 00′
		Cos	Sin	Cot	Tan	Csc	Sec	Radians	Degrees

Table 6: Random Numbers

ROW 1	82350	90391	34806	35773	37006	34566	12787	35876	01956	45032
ROW 2	88640	70497	48430	23118	28843	63970	27630	48165	75403	56046
ROW 3	88866	78271	21214	37408	13072	74208	46567	72124	21437	58899
ROW 4	22024	15249	05312	06293	89938	86283	37555	47539	45303	79801
ROW 5	78557	94906	43513	91811	65765	57999	04300	42085	14656	63862
ROW 6	00614	15626	32753	52056	40241	38191	38697	95113	87484	07445
ROW 7	60592	31356	78993	71554	67376	89165	83024	04971	33173	10565
ROW 8	99577	72094	87220	93468	12634	73241	90887	81145	44514	74872
ROW 9	41315	42978	08197	63928	39692	54237	62467	68393	50329	08419
ROW 10	24822	55560	78253	28041	15083	23942	02291	35719	81950	15762
ROW 11	06944	49907	61851	15463	39526	69032	07495	59166	50508	45936
ROW 12	80275	62418	44439	46123	10849	85380	08856	99522	69693	85205
ROW 13	85627	88368	81809	37340	77503	38405	78698	48913	10950	89533
ROW 14	51362	50793	29447	27773	30305	39479	40929	07584	86797	33690
ROW 15	78651	52923	63819	65496	52373	63226	97608	62619	11184	59319
ROW 16	43661	42921	70123	33169	37210	93951	37789	62622	36278	90576
ROW 17	83917	70635	53187	85377	09437	67836	00119	52705	09146	40761
ROW 18	08353	94629	74422	38676	11789	14744	37819	18874	43442	83293
ROW 19	10175	66887	35564	02091	83380	49556	89774	80413	67593	88292
ROW 20	62685	25884	93733	82093	77453	56403	31764	89720	18365	17074
ROW 21	90744	10792	94318	09771	30806	06889	57351	65908	73715	52729
ROW 22	10970	86189	75787	23891	91605	27770	22993	14397	93809	99067
ROW 23	89348	98603	04061	24420	29620	12504	35604	33671	14026	79021
ROW 24	97567	08941	18747	28969	53541	62222	57756	27990	04849	95722
ROW 25	93364	93512	86803	45856	97968	32641	24790	14548	79975	93491
ROW 26	95184	87663	74975	32858	02713	03348	91694	15908	78438	17265
ROW 27	21634	20106	93095	63081	04331	86360	48376	35879	90502	04342
ROW 28	35119	47963	25706	70328	90299	59639	96541	14381	71896	63691
ROW 29	10645	91688	35173	49893	18670	61188	53479	49512	19594	89066
ROW 30	20301	52310	28855	98311	75943	61868	66021	26565	37821	95791
ROW 31	70882	53420	46615	24653	91161	95603	89257	58094	44898	39646
ROW 32	71622	29832	57867	76963	52298	53556	42094	70948	20460	41980
ROW 33	32564	94559	90961	40398	50486	78439	12035	03923	27190	29849
ROW 34	19517	22450	62071	42815	64508	57543	00781	19440	21033	51421
ROW 35	91023	99839	93150	85480	09602	18857	36956	26273	97932	59352
ROW 36	74723	30908	83036	79236	46616	19522	30264	07118	61968	34319
ROW 37	04075	39146	98046	27426	27975	42670	48233	81370	93529	14139
ROW 38	60422	91391	96638	21680	31257	52601	64065	22417	32568	17772
ROW 39	20803	27478	44995	57419	58728	91408	86083	90531	62338	07438
ROW 40	20891	51357	73166	42323	42263	58243	77894	94763	49214	54829
ROW 41	36866	24285	45072	92763	69855	81929	33035	49712	34754	55166
ROW 42	75062	79115	89308	57338	01250	18914	10440	28981	67780	16264
ROW 43	09254	46288	72174	68439	05838	49878	56368	29642	16889	65994
ROW 44	69812	85750	77334	23167	63327	60612	58371	49078	35413	67035
ROW 45	88377	33535	02459	88695	88054	23776	54180	41184	59714	08985
ROW 46	49407	69576	87952	72323	94393	27844	79365	37197	35972	35367
ROW 47	94187	44459	93685	12069	32502	55403	08306	35970	96564	23604
ROW 48	23735	49509	49844	54546	68312	89793	38860	45076	82780	52100
ROW 49	51275	75658	61962	11966	49096	06965	48613	58890	59220	07371
ROW 50	09569	28121	93532	97064	03536	49673	35029	59577	63577	08083

Table 7: Normal Curve

AREAS UNDER THE STANDARD NORMAL CURVE (AREAS TO THE LEFT OF z)

z

z	0	1	2	3	4	5	6	7	8	9
−3.0	.0013	.0013	.0013	.0012	.0012	.0011	.0011	.0011	.0010	.0010
−2.9	.0019	.0018	.0017	.0017	.0016	.0016	.0015	.0015	.0014	.0014
−2.8	.0026	.0025	.0024	.0023	.0023	.0022	.0021	.0021	.0020	.0019
−2.7	.0035	.0034	.0033	.0032	.0031	.0030	.0029	.0028	.0027	.0026
−2.6	.0047	.0045	.0044	.0043	.0041	.0040	.0039	.0038	.0037	.0036
−2.5	.0062	.0060	.0059	.0057	.0055	.0054	.0052	.0051	.0049	.0048
−2.4	.0082	.0080	.0078	.0075	.0073	.0071	.0069	.0068	.0066	.0064
−2.3	.0107	.0104	.0102	.0099	.0096	.0094	.0091	.0089	.0087	.0084
−2.2	.0139	.0136	.0132	.0129	.0125	.0122	.0119	.0116	.0113	.0110
−2.1	.0179	.0174	.0170	.0166	.0162	.0158	.0154	.0150	.0146	.0143
−2.0	.0227	.0222	.0217	.0212	.0207	.0202	.0197	.0192	.0188	.0183
−1.9	.0287	.0281	.0274	.0268	.0262	.0256	.0250	.0244	.0239	.0233
−1.8	.0359	.0351	.0344	.0336	.0329	.0322	.0314	.0307	.0301	.0294
−1.7	.0446	.0436	.0427	.0418	.0409	.0401	.0392	.0384	.0375	.0367
−1.6	.0548	.0537	.0526	.0516	.0505	.0495	.0485	.0475	.0465	.0455
−1.5	.0668	.0655	.0643	.0630	.0618	.0606	.0594	.0582	.0571	.0559
−1.4	.0808	.0793	.0778	.0764	.0749	.0735	.0721	.0708	.0694	.0681
−1.3	.0968	.0951	.0934	.0918	.0901	.0885	.0869	.0853	.0838	.0823
−1.2	.1151	.1131	.1112	.1093	.1075	.1056	.1038	.1020	.1003	.0985
−1.1	.1357	.1335	.1314	.1292	.1271	.1251	.1230	.1210	.1190	.1170
−1.0	.1587	.1562	.1539	.1515	.1492	.1469	.1446	.1423	.1401	.1379
−0.9	.1841	.1814	.1788	.1762	.1736	.1711	.1685	.1660	.1635	.1611
−0.8	.2119	.2090	.2061	.2033	.2005	.1977	.1949	.1921	.1894	.1867
−0.7	.2420	.2389	.2358	.2327	.2296	.2266	.2236	.2206	.2177	.2148
−0.6	.2743	.2709	.2676	.2643	.2611	.2578	.2546	.2514	.2483	.2451
−0.5	.3085	.3050	.3015	.2981	.2946	.2912	.2877	.2843	.2810	.2776
−0.4	.3446	.3409	.3372	.3336	.3300	.3264	.3228	.3192	.3156	.3121
−0.3	.3821	.3783	.3745	.3707	.3669	.3632	.3594	.3557	.3520	.3483
−0.2	.4207	.4168	.4129	.4090	.4052	.4013	.3974	.3936	.3897	.3859
−0.1	.4602	.4562	.4522	.4483	.4443	.4404	.4364	.4325	.4286	.4247
−0.0	.5000	.4960	.4920	.4880	.4840	.4801	.4761	.4721	.4681	.4641
0.0	.5000	.5040	.5080	.5120	.5160	.5199	.5239	.5279	.5319	.5359
0.1	.5398	.5438	.5478	.5517	.5557	.5596	.5636	.5675	.5714	.5753
0.2	.5793	.5832	.5871	.5910	.5948	.5987	.6026	.6064	.6103	.6141
0.3	.6179	.6217	.6255	.6293	.6331	.6368	.6406	.6443	.6480	.6517
0.4	.6554	.6591	.6628	.6664	.6700	.6736	.6772	.6808	.6844	.6879
0.5	.6915	.6950	.6985	.7019	.7054	.7088	.7123	.7157	.7190	.7224
0.6	.7257	.7291	.7324	.7357	.7389	.7422	.7454	.7486	.7517	.7549
0.7	.7580	.7611	.7642	.7673	.7704	.7734	.7764	.7794	.7823	.7852
0.8	.7881	.7910	.7939	.7967	.7995	.8023	.8051	.8079	.8106	.8133
0.9	.8159	.8186	.8212	.8238	.8264	.8289	.8315	.8340	.8365	.8389
1.0	.8413	.8438	.8461	.8485	.8508	.8531	.8554	.8577	.8599	.8621

z	0	1	2	3	4	5	6	7	8	9
1.1	.8643	.8665	.8686	.8708	.8729	.8749	.8770	.8790	.8810	.8830
1.2	.8849	.8869	.8888	.8907	.8925	.8944	.8962	.8980	.8997	.9015
1.3	.9032	.9049	.9066	.9082	.9099	.9115	.9131	.9147	.9162	.9177
1.4	.9192	.9207	.9222	.9236	.9251	.9265	.9279	.9292	.9306	.9319
1.5	.9332	.9345	.9357	.9370	.9382	.9394	.9406	.9418	.9429	.9441
1.6	.9452	.9463	.9474	.9484	.9495	.9505	.9515	.9525	.9535	.9545
1.7	.9554	.9564	.9573	.9582	.9591	.9599	.9608	.9616	.9625	.9633
1.8	.9641	.9649	.9656	.9664	.9671	.9678	.9686	.9693	.9699	.9706
1.9	.9713	.9719	.9726	.9732	.9738	.9744	.9750	.9756	.9761	.9767
2.0	.9773	.9778	.9783	.9788	.9793	.9798	.9803	.9808	.9812	.9817
2.1	.9821	.9826	.9830	.9834	.9838	.9842	.9846	.9850	.9854	.9857
2.2	.9861	.9864	.9868	.9871	.9875	.9878	.9881	.9884	.9887	.9890
2.3	.9893	.9896	.9898	.9901	.9904	.9906	.9909	.9911	.9913	.9916
2.4	.9918	.9920	.9922	.9925	.9927	.9929	.9931	.9932	.9934	.9936
2.5	.9938	.9940	.9941	.9943	.9945	.9946	.9948	.9949	.9951	.9952
2.6	.9953	.9955	.9956	.9957	.9959	.9960	.9961	.9962	.9963	.9964
2.7	.9965	.9966	.9967	.9968	.9969	.9970	.9971	.9972	.9973	.9974
2.8	.9974	.9975	.9976	.9977	.9977	.9978	.9979	.9979	.9980	.9981
2.9	.9981	.9982	.9983	.9983	.9984	.9984	.9985	.9985	.9986	.9986
3.0	.9987	.9987	.9987	.9988	.9988	.9989	.9989	.9989	.9990	.9990

Table 8: Symbols

Symbol	Meaning
$\cdot, \times$	times
$\pm$	positive or negative
$\approx$	is approximately equal to
$\lvert n \rvert$	absolute value of n
π	pi, ≈ 3.14159
{ }	braces
[ ]	brackets
$\cap$	the intersection of
$\cup$	the union of
$\emptyset$	the empty set
$\{x \mid x > 1\}$	the set of all numbers x such that $x > 1$
i	imaginary unit, $\sqrt{-1}$
$^\circ$	degree
$\triangle$	triangle
$\angle$	angle
$m\angle$	measure of an angle
$\sim$	is similar to
$\overline{AB}$	segment AB
AB	the length of $\overline{AB}$
$\log_a x$	log, base a, of x
e	base of natural logarithms, ≈ 2.7183
$\lvert A \rvert$	determinant of matrix A
a_{ij}	matrix element in row i, column j
$A \times B$	Cartesian product of sets A and B
A^t	transpose of matrix A
∞	infinity
${}_nP_r$	number of arrangements of r of n things
$\binom{n}{r}$	number of choices of r of n things
$\overline{x}$	mean of a data set
σ	sigma, standard deviation
σ^2	variance
χ^2	chi-square (test)
α	alpha
β	beta
θ	theta
ω	omega
ϕ	phi
ρ	rho

Table 9: Geometric Formulas

Rectangle
Area: $A = lw$
Perimeter: $P = 2l + 2w$

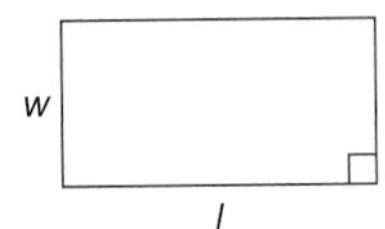

Parallelogram
Area: $A = bh$

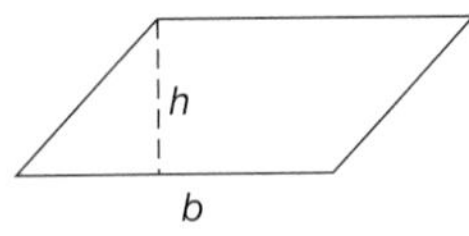

Square
Area: $A = s^2$
Perimeter: $P = 4s$

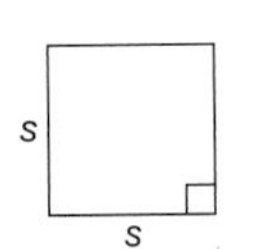

Trapezoid
Area: $A = \frac{1}{2}h(a + b)$

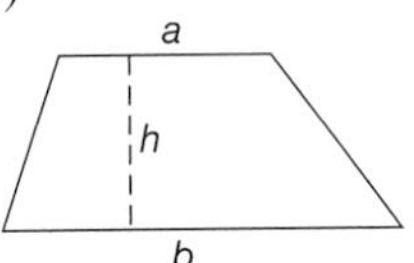

Triangle
Area: $A = \frac{1}{2}bh$
Sum of Angle Measures:
$A + B + C = 180°$

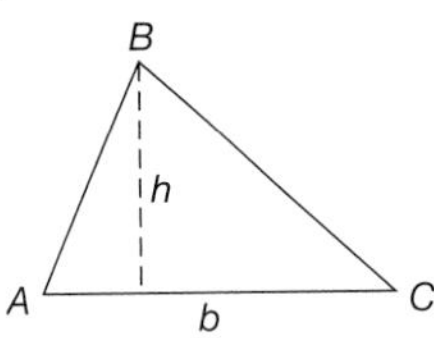

Circle
Area: $A = \pi r^2$
Circumference:
$C = \pi d = 2\pi r$

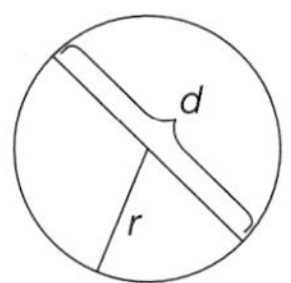

Right Triangle
Pythagorean Property:
$a^2 + b^2 = c^2$

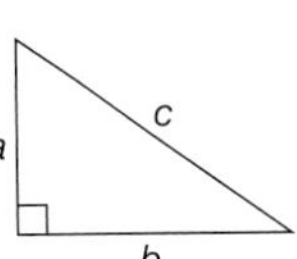

Rectangular Solid
Volume: $V = lwh$

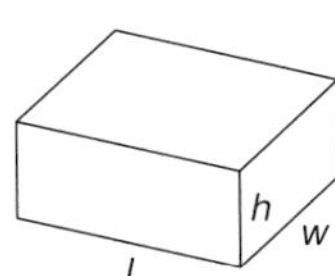

Polygon
Sum of Angle Measures:
$S = 180(n - 2)$

Number of Diagonals:

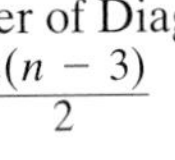
$N = \frac{n(n - 3)}{2}$

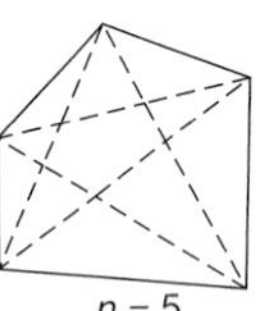

Cylinder
Volume: $V = \pi r^2 h$

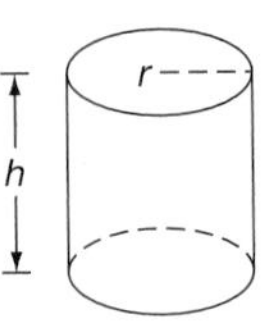

Prism
Volume: $V = Bh$
B = base area

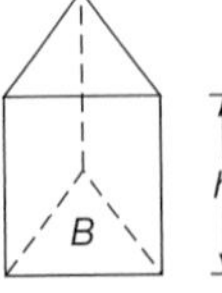

Cone
Volume: $V = \frac{1}{3}\pi r^2 h$

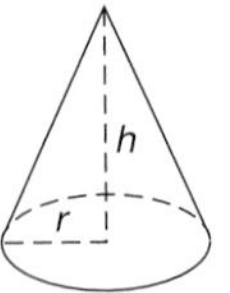

Abscissa (p. 110) The first number in an ordered pair; the x-coordinate.

Absolute value (pp. 5, 87, 324) The absolute value of x, represented as $|x|$, is its distance from zero on a number line. For any real number x, $|x| = x$ if $x \geq 0$, and $|x| = -x$ if $x < 0$. The absolute value of a complex number $a + bi$ is denoted $|a + bi|$ and is defined to be $\sqrt{a^2 + b^2}$.

Addition property of equality (p. 26) For all numbers a, b, and c, if $a = b$, then $a + c = b + c$.

Addition property of inequality (p. 74) For all numbers a, b, and c, if $a < b$, then $a + c < b + c$. If $a > b$, then $a + c > b + c$. Similar statements hold for $\leq$ and $\geq$.

Additive identity (p. 17) The number 0 is the additive identity. For any real number a, $a + 0 = a$.

Additive inverse (p. 6) If the sum of two numbers is 0, each is the *additive inverse* of the other.

Algorithm (p. 263) A systematic procedure for performing a computation.

Amplitude (p. 757) The amplitude of a periodic function is half the difference between its maximum and minimum function values. It is always positive.

Angle of depression or elevation (p. 805) The angle from the horizontal downward or upward to a line of sight.

Antecedent (p. 92) See *If-then statement*.

Antilogarithm (p. 536) Given $\log_a x = m$, the antilogarithm of m is the number x such that $x = a^m$.

Arcsine (p. 796) The inverse of the sine function. While arcsin 0.5 represents all angles whose sine is 0.5 $\left(\arcsin 0.5 = \left\{\frac{\pi}{6} + 2k\pi, \frac{5\pi}{6} + 2k\pi\right\}\right)$, $\text{Arcsin } 0.5 = \frac{\pi}{6}$.

Arithmetic means (p. 619) Numbers $m_1, m_2, m_3, \ldots, m_n$ are arithmetic means between a and b if $a, m_1, m_2, m_3, \ldots m_n, b$ form an arithmetic sequence.

Arithmetic sequence (p. 617) A sequence in which a constant d can be added to each term to get the next term. The constant d is called the common difference.

Arithmetic series (p. 620) A series associated with an arithmetic sequence.

Associative properties (p. 16) For any numbers a, b, and c: Addition: $a + (b + c) = (a + b) + c$.
Multiplication: $(a \cdot b) \cdot c = a \cdot (b \cdot c)$.

Asymptote (p. 446) A line is an asymptote to a curve if the distance between the curve and the line approaches zero as x or y increases or decreases without limit.

Augmented matrix (p. 593) A matrix consisting of the coefficients of a system of linear equations and an identity matrix.

Axes (p. 110) Two (perpendicular) number lines dividing a plane into four regions.

Axiom (p. 49) A property assumed or accepted without proof.

Base (pp. 35, 523) In exponential notation, n^x, n is the base. In logarithmic notation, $\log_a x$, a is the base.

Binomial (p. 206) A polynomial with exactly two terms.

Binomial coefficient (p. 660) The binomial coefficient $\binom{n}{a}$ means $\frac{n!}{a!(n-a)!}$. It is the coefficient of $x^{n-a}y^a$ in the expansion of $(x + y)^n$.

Binomial expansion (p. 661) The sum of terms that results from expanding a power of a binomial.

Binomial theorem (p. 660) A theorem that tells how to expand a power of a binomial.

Box-and-whisker plot (p. 696) A method of presenting data that shows maximum, minimum, and median values, and the boundaries (*hinges*) of the middle 50% of the data.

Boundary (p. 188) The edge of a half-plane.

Cartesian coordinate system (p. 110) The identification of each point in a plane with a unique ordered pair of numbers determined by intersecting axes.

Cartesian product (p. 106) The Cartesian product of two sets A and B, symbolized $A \times B$, is the set of all ordered pairs with the first member from A and the second member from B.

Glossary

Characteristic (of logarithm) (p. 535) The integer part of a base 10 logarithm.
Chi-square test (p. 715) A hypothesis test used to determine whether a given set of data differs from data one would expect by chance.
Circle (p. 433) The set of all points in a plane that are at a constant distance (the *radius*) from a fixed point in that plane. The fixed point is the *center* of the circle.
Closure (p. 49) A set is closed under an operation if performing that operation on any elements within the set results in another element in the set.
Coefficient (p. 21) In any term, the coefficient is the numeric factor of the term or the number that is multiplied by the variable. In $-3x$, the coefficient is -3; in x^4, the coefficient is 1.
Combination (p. 656) A selection of a group of objects from a set without regard to order.
Combinatorics (p. 644) The study of problems concerned with the number of ways a set of objects can be arranged, combined, or chosen, or the number of ways a succession of events can occur.
Common logarithm (p. 534) A base 10 logarithm.
Commutative properties (p. 15) For any numbers a and b,
Addition: $a + b = b + a$.
Multiplication: $a \cdot b = b \cdot a$.
Complement (p. 676) Suppose S is a sample space and A is an event in S. The *complement* of A is the set of elements in S that are not in A.
Completing the square (p. 343) Adding a term to a quadratic expression to make it the square of a binomial.
Complex number (p. 322) The complex numbers consist of all sums $a + bi$, where a and b are real numbers and i is the imaginary unit. The real part is a; the imaginary part is bi.
Complex rational expression (p. 256) An expression that has a rational expression in its numerator, its denominator, or both.
Composition of functions (p. 149) If f and g are functions, the composition of f and g is $f \circ g(x) = f(g(x))$.
Conditional statement (p. 92) A statement in the form *If a, then b*. See *If-then statement*.
Cone (p. 433) The set of points determined by the rotation of one line around another intersecting line not perpendicular to it. The point of intersection is called the *vertex*. Any position of the rotating line is called an *element* of the cone.
Conic section (p. 433) The (nonempty) intersection of any plane with a cone.
Conjugates (Rational, Complex) (pp. 307, 327) The sum and difference of pairs of numbers, one of which is rational, such as $7 + \sqrt{2}$ and $7 - \sqrt{2}$, or imaginary, such as $1 + 2i$ and $1 - 2i$.
Conjugate axis (p. 445) A line segment perpendicular to the transverse axis of a *hyperbola* (connecting points $(0, b)$ and $(0, -b)$ or points $(b, 0)$ and $(-b, 0)$, if the hyperbola is given in standard form).
Conjunction (p. 82) A sentence such as "$x > 5$ *and* $x < 12$." A conjunction of two statements is formed by connecting them with "and" and is true when *both* statements are true.
Consequent (p. 92) See *If-then statement.*
Consistent system (p. 183) A system of equations or inequalities having at least one solution.
Constant of variation (p. 279) The coefficient k in equations of the form $y = kx$ and $y = \frac{k}{x}$.
Constant term (p. 14) A term with no variable.
Converge (p. 630) If, in an infinite series, S_n approaches some limit as n becomes very large, that limit is defined to be the sum of the series. If an infinite series has a sum, it is said to *converge* or *be convergent.*
Converse (p. 93) The converse of a sentence "if a, then b" is "if b, then a."
Coordinate(s) (pp. 88, 110) The number(s) used to locate a point in space.
Cosecant (p. 730) The reciprocal of the sine function; $\csc \theta = \frac{1}{\sin \theta}$.
Cosine (pp. 728, 735) In a right triangle, the cosine of acute angle A is the ratio of the length of the side adjacent to angle A to the length of the hypotenuse. In the Cartesian plane, if $R(x, y)$ is a point on the terminal side of angle θ and $r = \sqrt{x^2 + y^2}$, $\cos \theta = \frac{x}{r}$.
Cotangent (p. 730) The reciprocal of the tangent function; $\cot \theta = \frac{1}{\tan \theta}$.
Counterexample (p. 8) One example that demonstrates a given assumption is false.
Cramer's rule (pp. 166, 577) An algorithm for solving systems of equations by using *determinants.*

Degree of a monomial (p. 206) The sum of the exponents of the variables in the monomial.
Degree of a polynomial (p. 206) The greatest of the degrees of the terms after like terms are combined.
Dependent system (p. 184) A consistent system of n equations and n variables is dependent if it has infinitely many solutions.
Determinant (pp. 576, 578) A number assigned to a matrix, determined by summing certain products of its elements.
Dimensions of a matrix (p. 568) A matrix of m rows and n columns is called a matrix with dimensions $m \times n$.
Direct variation (p. 279) A functional relationship that can be described by an equation $y = kx$ where k is a nonzero constant.

Direct quadratic variation (p. 366) y varies directly as the square of x if there is some positive number k such that $y = kx^2$.
Discriminant (p. 354) For a quadratic equation $ax^2 + bx + c = 0$, the expression $b^2 - 4ac$ is called the discriminant.
Disjunction (p. 84) A sentence such as "$x < -3$ *or* $x > 6$." A disjunction of two statements is formed by connecting them with "or." It is true when *one or both* statements are true.
Distance formula (p. 430) The distance between any two points (x_1, y_1) and (x_2, y_2) is given by $d = \sqrt{(x_1 - x_2)^2 + (y_1 - y_2)^2}$.
Distributive property (p. 20) The distributive property of multiplication over addition: For any real numbers a, b, and c, $a \cdot (b + c) = a \cdot b + a \cdot c$.
Domain (p. 107) See *Function*.

e (p. 550) An irrational number approximately equal to 2.718281828459; the base of natural logarithms.
Element (of a set) (p. 106) Any member of a set. Also see *Cone*.
Ellipse (p. 438) In a plane, the set of all points P such that the sum of the distances from P to two fixed points, F_1 and F_2, is constant. Each fixed point is called a *focus*.
Empty set (p. 82) The set with no elements.
Equation (p. 26) A statement of equality between two expressions.
Equivalent equations (p. 95) If equations are equivalent, they have the same solution set.
Equivalent expressions (p. 15) Expressions that are equal for all acceptable replacement values of their variables.
Equivalent inequalities (p. 95) If inequalities are equivalent, they have the same solution set.
Even function (p. 388) If $f(-x) = f(x)$ for all x in the domain of a function f, then that function is even.
Event (p. 644) A set of outcomes that is a subset of the sample space of an experiment. An event made up of several events is a *compound event*.
Exponent (p. 35) In exponential notation n^x, x is the exponent. The exponent tells how many times the base is used as a factor.
Exponential function (p. 521) The function $f(x) = a^x$, where a is some positive real-number constant different from 1, is called the exponential function, base a.
Extraneous root (p. 318) A solution, found in the process of solving an equation, that is not a solution to the original equation.

Factorial ($n!$) (p. 646) For any natural number n, the product of the first n natural numbers. 0! is defined to be 1.
Factor theorem (p. 487) For a polynomial $P(x)$, if $P(r) = 0$, then $x - r$ is a factor of $P(x)$.
Field (p. 50) Any number system, with two operations defined, in which certain axioms hold. The axioms are known as the *field axioms*.
Finite sequence (p. 620) A sequence with a last term.
Focus, Foci See *Ellipse*, *Hyperbola*, or *Parabola*.
Formula (p. 71) An equation or mathematical rule for calculating a quantity.
Frequency distribution (p. 691) A table showing the frequencies with which data fall into intervals.
Function (p. 116) A relation or rule that assigns to each member of one set (called the *domain*) exactly one member of some set (called the *range*).
Fundamental counting principle (p. 645) In a compound event in which the first event may occur in n_1 different ways, the second event may occur in n_2 different ways, and the kth event may occur in n_k different ways, the total number of ways the compound event may occur is $n_1 \cdot n_2 \cdot n_3 \ldots \cdot n_k$.
Fundamental theorem of algebra (p. 490) Every polynomial with complex coefficients and of degree n (where $n > 1$) can be factored into n linear factors.

General term (p. 612) The nth term of a sequence.
Geometric means (p. 625) The numbers $m_1, m_2, m_3, \ldots, m_k$ are geometric means of a and b if $a, m_1, m_2, m_3, \ldots, m_k, b$ form a geometric sequence.
Geometric sequence (p. 624) A sequence in which each term can be multiplied by a constant r to get the next term. The constant r is called the *common ratio*.
Geometric series (p. 626) A series associated with a geometric sequence.
Graph (p. 110) The graph of an equation (or inequality) is the set of all points whose coordinates satisfy the equation (or inequality).
Greatest common factor (pp. 21, 219) The greatest integer that is a factor of two or more integers. The product of all factors common to given expressions.
Greatest integer function (p. 148) $f(x) = [x]$; $[x]$ is the greatest integer that is less than or equal to x.

Half-plane (p. 188) One of the two regions into which a line separates a plane. The line itself is called a *boundary* and is not included in the half-plane.
Harmonic sequence (p. 623) A sequence whose reciprocals form an arithmetic sequence.

Glossary

Hinge (Upper, Lower) (p. 696) Median of the upper/lower half of a set of data (excluding the median if necessary).

Hyperbola (p. 445) In a plane, the set of all points P such that the absolute value of the difference of the distances from P to two fixed points, F_1 and F_2, is constant. The fixed points F_1 and F_2 are the *foci.*

Identity matrix (p. 589) A square matrix with all elements equal to 0 except for 1s along the main diagonal.

Identity properties (p. 16) For any real number a,
Addition: $a + 0 = 0 + a = a$.
Multiplication: $a \cdot 1 = 1 \cdot a = a$.

If-then statement (p. 92) A conditional statement made up of two statements: "If . . . , then. . . ." The first statement, following *if*, is called the *antecedent*. The second statement, following *then*, is called the *consequent*.

Image (p. 384) Under a *transformation*, the point corresponding to a given point.

Imaginary number (p. 321) The square root of a negative number; expressed as $a + bi$, where $b \neq 0$ and $i = \sqrt{-1}$.

Inconsistent system (p. 183) A system of equations or inequalities having no solution.

Index (p. 294) The number k in $\sqrt[k]{\ }$, the kth root, is called the index of the radical.

Inequality (p. 73) A mathematical sentence containing $>$, $<$, $\geq$, or $\leq$ between two expressions.

Infinite sequence/series (pp. 612, 615) A sequence/series with no last term.

Integers (p. 4) The numbers in the set $\{\ldots\ -3, -2, -1, 0, 1, 2, 3 \ldots\}$.

Intercept (p. 123) In the graph of an equation in two variables, the x-intercept is the x-coordinate, and the y-intercept is the y-coordinate of the point where the graph intersects an axis.

Interpolation (p. 539) A process by which approximate function values can be determined between other values in a table.

Intersection (p. 82) The intersection of two sets is the set of all members that are common to both. The intersection of sets A and B is represented by the notation $A \cap B$. See *Conjunction*.

Inverse of a sum (p. 22) The inverse of a sum is equal to the sum of the inverses.

Inverse variation (p. 280) A functional relationship that can be described by an equation $y = \frac{k}{x}$, where k is a nonzero constant.

Irrational number (p. 4) A number that cannot be expressed using rational notation $\frac{a}{b}$ where $b \neq 0$ and a and b are integers.

Joint variation (p. 367) An equation of the form $z = kxy$ where k is a nonzero constant.

***k*th root** (p. 294) The kth root of a number a is a number c such that $c^k = a$.

Least common denominator (pp. 62, 251) The least common multiple of a set of denominators.

Least common multiple (p. 251) The smallest nonzero number that is a multiple of two or more given numbers. A nonzero expression that is a multiple of each of a set of expressions and contains the fewest possible factors.

Like terms (p. 21) Terms whose variable factors are exactly the same.

Line of symmetry (p. 384) In any figure, a line that divides the figure so that if it is folded on the line the two halves will match.

Linear equation (p. 122) An equation is linear if the variables occur to the first power only. The graph of a linear equation in two variables is a line.

Linear function (p. 143) A function defined by an equation equivalent to $y = mx + b$ where m and b are real numbers and $m \neq 0$.

Linear inequality (p. 188) An inequality in which the variables occur to the first power only.

Linear programming (p. 193) The mathematical theory of the minimization or maximization of a linear function subject to linear constraints.

Linear speed (p. 745) The linear speed v of a point that lies a distance of r from the center of rotation is given by $v = r\omega$ where ω is the angular speed in radians per unit of time.

Logarithm (p. 523) If $a > 0$ and $x > 0$, $y = \log_a x$ if and only if $x = a^y$.

Logarithmic function (p. 523) The inverse of an *exponential function.*

Mantissa (p. 535) The portion of a base 10 logarithm less than 1.

Matrix (p. 568) A rectangular array of numbers or expressions.

Mean (p. 694) The average of a set of values.

Mean deviation (p. 700) The average amount that a set of data deviates from the mean.

Median (p. 695) The middle value in a set of data when all the values are arranged in order.

Mode (p. 695) In a set of data, the value that occurs most often. Some sets of data have more than one mode and some have no mode.

Monomial (p. 206) An expression made up of a single term that is a product of numbers and variables.
Multiplication property of equality (p. 26) If an equation $a = b$ is true, then $a \cdot c = b \cdot c$ is true for any number c.
Multiplication property of inequality (p. 75) For all real numbers a, b, and c, if $a > b$ and $c > 0$, then $ac > bc$. If $a > b$ and $c < 0$, then $ab < bc$.
Multiplicative identity (p. 17) The number 1 is the multiplicative identity. For any number n, $n \cdot 1 = n$.
Multiplicative inverse (p. 9) Two expressions are *multiplicative inverses* if their product equals one. See *Reciprocal.*
Mutually exclusive (p. 668) Two events that cannot happen at the same time are mutually exclusive.

Natural logarithm (p. 551) Logarithm to the base e.
Natural numbers (p. 4) The numbers we use for counting. They are 1, 2, 3, 4, and so on.
Normal curve (p. 704) A symmetric bell-shaped curve describing the normal distribution.
Normal distribution (p. 704) Describes the relative arrangement of a set of elements such that they fit the normal curve.

Odd function (p. 388) If $f(-x) = -f(x)$ for all x in the domain of a function f, then that function is odd.
Ordered pair (p. 106) A pair of numbers in a particular order; the coordinates of a point in a plane.
Ordinate (p. 110) The y-coordinate or the second number of an ordered pair.
Origin (p. 110) The point at which the axes of a coordinate system cross; the point (0, 0) in the Cartesian coordinate system.
Outcome (p. 644) In situations in which we consider combinations of items or a succession of events such as flips of a coin or the drawing of cards, each result is called an *outcome.*

Parabola (p. 452) In a plane, the set of all points equidistant from a fixed point (the *focus*) and a fixed line (the *directrix*). The graph of the quadratic function $y = ax^2 + bx + c, a \neq 0$, is a parabola.
Partial sum (p. 614) The sum of a specified number of terms of a sequence.
Period (p. 304) The smallest horizontal interval in which a graph completes a cycle.
Periodic function (p. 755) Functions with a repeating graph pattern are periodic.
Permutation (p. 645) A permutation of a set is an ordered arrangement of that set, without repetition.
Polar notation (p. 821) See *Trigonometric notation.*
Polynomial (p. 206) A sum of monomials.
Polynomial function (p. 207) A function that can be defined by a polynomial.
Power (p. 35) A number that can be named with exponential notation as n^x.
Prime polynomial (p. 224) A polynomial that cannot be factored.
Principal square root (p. 293) The nonnegative square root of a number.
Principle of powers (p. 317) For any natural number n, if $a = b$ is true, then $a^n = b^n$.
Principle of zero products (p. 63) For any numbers a and b, if $ab = 0$, then $a = 0$ or $b = 0$, and if $a = 0$ or $b = 0$, then $ab = 0$.
Probability (p. 664) If an event E can occur m ways out of n equally likely ways, the probability of that event is $P(E) = \frac{m}{n}$.
Proof (p. 49) A series of logical steps that leads from a hypothesis to a conclusion.

Quadrant (p. 110) Any one of the four regions into which coordinate axes divide a plane.
Quadratic equation (p. 342) An equation that can be written in the form $ax^2 + bx + c = 0$ where a, b, and c are real numbers and $a \neq 0$.
Quadratic formula (p. 350) A formula for finding the solutions of a quadratic equation $ax^2 + bx + c = 0$. The formula is

$$x = \frac{-b \pm \sqrt{b^2 - 4ac}}{2a}.$$

Quadratic function (p. 400) A function defined by an equation of the form $y = ax^2 + bx + c$ where a, b, and c are real numbers and $a \neq 0$.
Quotient (p. 10) The quotient $\frac{a}{b}$ is the number (if it exists) which when multiplied by b gives a.

Radian (p. 741) A measure of angles. There are 2π radians in a circle.
Radical (p. 293) The symbol $\sqrt{}$ is called the radical symbol. Any expression that contains a radical is called a *radical expression.*
Radicand (p. 293) The expression under a radical.
Random sample (p. 710) A sample that is selected in such a fashion that each object in the population of interest has an equal chance of being selected and each object is chosen independently of any other objects in the sample.
Range (p. 116) See *Function.*
Rational expression (p. 244) The quotient of two polynomials.
Rational number (p. 4) Any number that can be expressed as the ratio of two integers in the form $\frac{a}{b}$ where $b \neq 0$.

Glossary

Real number (p. 4) The real numbers consist of the *rational numbers* and the *irrational numbers*. There is a real number for each point on the number line.
Reciprocal (p. 9) Two expressions are reciprocals if their product is 1. A reciprocal is also called a *multiplicative inverse*.
Rectangular notation (p. 821) To change from trigonometric notation to rectangular notation $a + bi$, we use the formulas $a = r \cos \theta$ and $b = r \sin \theta$.
Recursion (p. 613) In a recursively defined *sequence*, each term is related to the previous term or terms by a rule or formula.
Reference angle (p. 737) The acute angle that the terminal side of an angle makes with the x-axis.
Reflection (p. 384) A transformation in which points are reflected across a line.
Reflexive property of equality (p. 49) For every real number a, $a = a$.
Relation (p. 107) Any set of *ordered pairs*.
Replacement set (p. 26) The set of all values that may replace the variables in a sentence.
Root of a polynomial (p. 480) Any solution of a polynomial equation.

Sample space (p. 664) The set of all possible outcomes of an experiment.
Scalar (p. 582) A constant k that is used as a multiplier for a matrix.
Scientific notation (p. 44) A number expressed as the product of a power of 10 and a numeral greater than or equal to 1 but less than 10. The numbers 4.25×10^3 and 2.3×10^{-2} are expressed in scientific notation.
Secant (p. 730) The reciprocal of the cosine function; $\sec \theta = \frac{1}{\cos \theta}$.
Sequence (p. 612) An ordered set of numbers.
Series (p. 614) An indicated sum of the terms of a sequence.
Simple event (p. 664) A single outcome of an experiment.
Sine (pp. 728, 735) In a right triangle, the sine of acute angle A is the ratio of the length of the side opposite angle A to the length of the hypotenuse. In the Cartesian plane, if $R(x, y)$ is a point on the terminal side of angle θ and $r = \sqrt{x^2 + y^2}$, $\sin \theta = \frac{y}{r}$.
Sigma notation (p. 614) The Greek letter Σ (sigma) is the symbol for summation.
Slope of a line (p. 127) A number that tells how steeply the line slants; the ratio of rise to run.
Solution (p. 111) A replacement for a variable that makes an equation or inequality true.
Solution set (p. 26) The set of all replacements that makes a sentence true.
Square root (p. 293) The number c is a square root of the number a if $c^2 = a$.
Standard deviation (p. 702) The square root of the *variance*.
Standard form (pp. 135, 342, 408) Standard form of a linear equation is $ax + by + c = 0$. Standard form of a quadratic equation is $ax^2 + bx + c = 0$. Standard form of a quadratic function is $f(x) = a(x - h)^2 + k$.
Statement (p. 92) A sentence that is either true or false.
Stem-and-leaf diagram (p. 690) A method of ordering data which preserves the value of each entry.
Step function (p. 148) A function whose graph is a series of discontinuous (usually equally spaced) horizontal segments.
Subset (p. 662) Set A is a subset of set B if every element of set A is an element of set B.
Subtrahend (p. 7) In subtraction, the number to be subtracted.
Synthetic division (p. 263) An algorithm for dividing a polynomial by a binomial, $x - a$, in which the variables are not written.
Symmetric property of equality (p. 49) For all numbers a and b, if $a = b$, then $b = a$.
System of equations (p. 160) A set of equations for which a common solution is sought.

Tangent (pp. 728, 735) In a right triangle, the tangent of acute angle A is the ratio of the length of the side opposite angle A to the length of the side adjacent to angle A. In the Cartesian plane, if $R(x, y)$ is a point on the terminal side of angle θ and $r = \sqrt{x^2 + y^2}$, $\tan \theta = \frac{y}{x}$.
Terms (p. 21) The parts of an algebraic expression that are separated by an addition or subtraction sign.
Theorem (p. 7) A property that can be proved.
Transformation (p. 391) An alteration to a relation.
Transitive property of equality (p. 49) If $a = b$ and $b = c$, then $a = c$.
Translation (p. 391) A geometric transformation in which all points are moved the same distance in the same direction.
Trichotomy (p. 97) For any real number a, one and only one of the following is true: $a > 0$, $a = 0$, $a < 0$.
Trigonometric function (pp. 728, 735) A function that uses one of the six trigonometric ratios to associate a value with an acute angle of a right triangle. A function whose domain is the real numbers—the measure of an angle (in standard position in the Cartesian plane)—and whose values are defined in terms of the coordinates of a point on the terminal side of the angle. See also *Sine*, *Cosine*, and *Tangent*.

Trigonometric notation (p. 821) Trigonometric or *polar notation* for the complex number $a + bi$ is $r(\cos\theta + i\sin\theta)$, where $r = |a + bi|$ and θ is the argument such that $\cos\theta = \frac{a}{r}$ and $\sin\theta = \frac{b}{r}$. This is often shortened to $r \text{ cis } \theta$.

Trinomial (p. 206) A polynomial with three terms.

Trinomial square (p. 219) The square of a binomial; contains three terms.

Union (p. 84) The union of two sets is the set of all members that are in either or both sets. The union of sets A and B is represented by the notation $A \cup B$. See *Disjunction*.

Variable (p. 14) A letter (or other symbol) used to represent one or several numbers.

Variance (p. 701) A measure of the amount of variation in a set of data. It is found by taking the mean of all the squared distances of the values from the mean.

x-coordinate (p. 110) The first member of an ordered pair.

x-intercept (p. 123) The x-coordinate of the point where a graph intersects the x-axis.

y-coordinate (p. 110) The second member of an ordered pair.

y-intercept (p. 123) The y-coordinate of the point where a graph intersects the y-axis.

z-score (p. 705) Used to define the number of standard deviations a point on the horizontal axis of the normal curve is from the mean.

Zero of a polynomial (p. 480) A number that when substituted into a polynomial function makes the function equal to zero.

Chapter 1

Skills & Concepts You Need for Chapter 1

1. $\frac{16}{5}$ **2.** $\frac{103}{20}$ **3.** $\frac{1}{25}$ **4.** $\frac{1001}{1000}$ **5.** 0.55 **6.** 0.72 **7.** 3.6 **8.** $4.\overline{142857}$ **9.** 37.37 **10.** 10.19 **11.** 1.47 **12.** 0.166 **13.** 12.8 **14.** 3.978 **15.** 2.5 **16.** 0.375 **17.** $\frac{14}{15}$ **18.** $4\frac{11}{12}$ **19.** $\frac{1}{14}$ **20.** $\frac{11}{12}$ **21.** $\frac{5}{48}$ **22.** $2\frac{1}{4}$ **23.** $\frac{16}{15}$ **24.** $2\frac{1}{2}$ **25.** 33.12 **26.** 6.25 **27.** 83.2 **28.** 2 **29.** $>$ **30.** $<$ **31.** $>$ **32.** $=$ **33.** 7:1 **34.** 13:3 **35.** 23:2 **36.** 4:11

LESSON 1-1

Try This **a.** Rational **b.** Rational **c.** Rational **d.** Irrational **e.** Rational **f.** Irrational **g.** −17 **h.** −18.6 **i.** $-\frac{7}{2}$ **j.** −14 **k.** 3.3 **l.** $-\frac{11}{24}$ **m.** 17 **n.** 17.8 **o.** $\frac{59}{48}$

Exercises **1.** Rational **3.** Rational **5.** Rational **7.** Rational **9.** Rational **11.** −28 **13.** −15 **15.** 1.2 **17.** $\frac{1}{7}$ **19.** $-\frac{4}{3}$ **21.** −11.6 **23.** 5 **25.** −29.25 **27.** $-\frac{13}{5}$ **29.** Sample: For the first term, Pac probably got −4 and Tom probably got −2.

For Exercises 31 and 33, answers may vary.

31. X, $\sqrt{100}$, $(\sqrt{10})^2$, $\sqrt[3]{1000}$, $\frac{20}{2}$ **33.** $-\sqrt{9}$, $-(\sqrt{3})^2$, $-(\sqrt[3]{27})$, $-\frac{18}{6}$, $\left(-\frac{1}{3}\right)^{-1}$ **35. a.** $\frac{2}{3}$ **b.** $\frac{7}{9}$ **c.** $\frac{37}{45}$ **37. a.** No **b.** No **c.** No **d.** No **e.** Densely ordered **f.** Densely ordered

Mixed Review **39.** $\frac{7}{24}$ **41.** $\frac{43}{40}$ **43.** 259.08 **45.** $\frac{1}{4}$ **47.** 2 **49.** 1 **51.** 60 **53.** 396

LESSON 1-2

Try This **a.** −24 **b.** 28.35 **c.** −42.77 **d.** $\frac{5}{8}$ **e.** −3 **f.** −2 **g.** $\frac{1}{4} = 0.25$ **h.** $-\frac{6}{7}$ **i.** $\frac{36}{7}$ **j.** Possible **k.** Not possible **l.** Not possible **m.** Not possible

Exercises **1.** −21 **3.** −8 **5.** 16 **7.** 126 **9.** −34.2 **11.** 26.46 **13.** 2 **15.** 60 **17.** 24 **19.** $-\frac{12}{35}$ **21.** 1 **23.** $-\frac{8}{27}$ **25.** $\frac{1}{5}$ **27.** −8 **29.** −4 **31.** 0.7 **33.** −3 **35.** 110 **37.** $-\frac{1}{10}$ **39.** $\frac{5}{4}$ **41.** $-\frac{4}{3}$ **43.** Possible **45.** Not possible **47.** $-\frac{1}{2}$ **49.** −2 **51.** Yes **53.** never **55.** Rational; the reciprocal of a rational number $\frac{p}{q}$, where p and q are integers, and $p \neq 0$ and $q \neq 0$, is $\frac{q}{p}$. **57.** $-\frac{1}{4}$

Mixed Review **59.** 5.0625 **61.** Irrational **63.** Rational **65.** −9.4 **67.** 7 **69.** 0 **71.** $\frac{1}{2}$ **73.** $-\frac{1}{6}$ **75.** $-\frac{13}{60}$ **77.** 81

LESSON 1-3

Try This **a.** 45 **b.** −8 **c.** 8 **d.** $-5x + (-3y)$ **e.** $17m + (-45)$ **f.** $-6p - (-5t)$ **g.** $8m + (5n + 6p)$ **h.** $(-9t)(17x)$ **i.** $16r(4q \cdot 9p)$ **j.** $\frac{171t}{27x}$ **k.** $2y$ **l.** $8a + x - b - x$

Exercises **1.** 54 **3.** 11 **5.** 103 7
13. −15 **15.** 6 **17.** 115 **19.** 30 21
25. $9x - (-7)$ **27.** $-18m - (-n)$
31. $(12x + 9y) + 89z$ **33.** $(6x + 9$
37. $\frac{714}{35xy}$ **39.** $\frac{y}{x}$ **41.** $\frac{5}{-2x}$ **43.** 5 +
47. $|p| + |q|$ **49.** $3|p| = 8$ **51.** A
are $x - 3y$, $4x - 2y$, $7x - y$ **53.** Y

Mixed Review **55.** −54 **57.** −4
65. $-\frac{2}{5}$ **67.** $\frac{91}{10}$ **69.** $\frac{-4}{1}$ **71.** Irrational **73.** Rational

Connections: Limits of $\frac{1}{x}$

a. The value of $\frac{1}{x}$ increases.

LESSON 1-4

Try This **a.** $5x + 45$ **b.** $8y - 80$ **c.** $ax + ay - az$ **d.** $2(l + w)$ **e.** $a(c - y)$ **f.** $6(x - 2)$ **g.** $5(-5y + 3w + 1)$ **h.** $20x$ **i.** $-7x$ **j.** $23.4x + 3.9$ **k.** $-7x$ **l.** $-y - 10$ **m.** $3x + 2y - 1$ **n.** $2x + 5z - 24$ **o.** $-\frac{1}{4}t - 41w + rd - 23$ **p.** $3x + 8$ **q.** $-x - 2y$ **r.** $23x - 10y$ **s.** $23x + 52$ **t.** $12a + 12$

Exercises **1.** $3a + 3$ **3.** $-10a - 15b$ **5.** $2\pi rh + 2\pi r$ **7.** $8(x + y)$ **9.** $7(x - 3)$ **11.** $2(x - y + z)$ **13.** $3(x + 2y - 1)$ **15.** $a(b + c - d)$ **17.** $\pi r(r + s)$ **19.** $9a$ **21.** $15y$ **23.** $14x$ **25.** $-5x$ **27.** $-6x$ **29.** $2c + 10d$ **31.** $22x + 18$ **33.** $5a - 21b$ **35.** $5x - x = (5 - 1)x \neq 5$ **37.** $2[(-3)(-6)] \neq 2(-3) \cdot 2(-6)$ **39.** $5x$ **41.** $-b - 9$ **43.** $-x + 8$ **45.** $-r + s$ **47.** $-x - y - z$ **49.** $-9a + 7b - 24$ **51.** $4x - 8y + 5w - 9z$ **53.** $-4x - 9$ **55.** $a + 3$ **57.** $13x - 16$ **59.** $-15y - 45$ **61.** $-12y + 24$ **63.** $47b - 51$ **65.** −1449 **67.** $-42x - 360y - 276$ **69.** 9 **71.** 8 **73.** Sometimes **75.** \$535.00 **77.** $-31a$ **79.** The answer is positive for an even number of negative signs, and negative for an odd number of negative signs.

Mixed Review **81.** 64 **83.** $(9y \cdot 8x)17z$ **85.** 0.5 **87.** $1.\overline{428571}$ **89.** $\frac{9}{20}$ **91.** $\frac{5}{4}$

LESSON 1-5

Try This **a.** $y = 38$ **b.** $x = -16$ **c.** $x = \frac{4}{3}$ **d.** $y = 4$ **e.** $y = -\frac{4}{9}$ **f.** $x = -\frac{5}{2}$

Exercises **1.** −3 **3.** 40 **5.** −15 **7.** −14 **9.** 39 **11.** 7 **13.** −9 **15.** −9 **17.** 36 **19.** 18 **21.** 5 **23.** 24 **25.** 7 **27.** 8 **29.** 21 **31.** 2 **33.** 2 **35.** $\frac{18}{5}$ **37.** 0 **39.** $\frac{4}{5}$ **41.** All real numbers **43.** No solution **45.** $w = 0$ **47.** All real numbers **49.** $\frac{45}{2}$ **51.** $\frac{5}{2}$ **53.** True; suppose $a + c = b + c$. Add $-c$ to both sides. Then $a = b$. This is false, so $a + c \neq b + c$. **55.** No **57.** Yes

Mixed Review **59.** $-86a + 74$ **61.** $8(n - m)$ **63.** $6(n + 2)$ **65.** 5 **67.** Answers may vary. Ex: $\left(2x + \frac{1}{2}x\right) + \left(5y + \frac{1}{5}y\right)$

-6

a. \$7.42 **b.** ≈ 1.54 min **c.** 150% **d.** $\approx 11.1\%$

ercises **1.** $C = 8.50 + 7 \cdot 6.75$; \$55.75 **3.** $C = 3 \cdot 32 + 320 \cdot 0.23$; \$169.60 **5.** $0.005D = 240{,}000$; $\approx 48{,}000{,}000$ mi **7.** $93 = 0.27h$; ≈ 340 m **9.** $1.96m = 1220$; 622.45°F **11.** $t = 44.0 - 0.1(2010 - 1924)$; 35.4 s **13.** $t = 52 - 0.09(2010 - 1930)$; 44.8 s **15.** $p \cdot 26\frac{3}{8} = 22\frac{1}{2}$; $\approx 85.3\%$ **17.** $p = \frac{25{,}968 - 6689}{6689}$; $\approx 288.2\%$ **19.** $5p + 22 = 10(p - 1.5)$; \$7.40 **21.** $p = \frac{\frac{1}{3}}{1 - \frac{2}{5}}$; $\approx 55.6\%$ **23.** $80 + 40t = 55t$; $t = 5\frac{1}{3}$ hrs; 1:20 P.M.

Mixed Review **25.** $15t$ **27.** $-8x$ **29.** $-\frac{1}{2}$ **31.** 14 **33.** -3 **35.** -3 **37.** 1

LESSON 1-7

Try This **a.** $512x^3$ **b.** $81m^4$ **c.** 81 **d.** $243y^3$ **e.** $\frac{1}{10{,}000}$ **f.** $-\frac{1}{64}$ **g.** $\frac{1}{125y^3}$ **h.** $\frac{1}{625}$ **i.** 4^{-3} **j.** $(-5)^{-4}$ **k.** $(2x)^{-6}$ **l.** $(-8x)^{-5}$

Exercises **1.** $27y^3$ **3.** 1 **5.** $6m$ **7.** -125 **9.** $\frac{1}{9^5}$ **11.** $\frac{1}{11^1}$ **13.** $\frac{1}{(6x)^3}$ **15.** $\frac{1}{(3m)^4}$ **17.** $\frac{2a^2}{b^5}$ **19.** x^2y^2 **21.** 3^{-4} **23.** $(-16)^{-2}$ **25.** $(5y)^{-3}$ **27.** $\frac{y^{-4}}{3}$ **29.** x^2yz^{-7} **31.** $b^{-10}x^{-10}y^{-10}$ **33.** $\frac{1}{16}$ **35.** $-26\frac{15}{16}$ **37.** $25\frac{1}{4}$ **39.** 7 **41. a.** 16,807; Sample argument: A tree diagram shows that the computation should be 7^5. **b.** Answers will vary.

Mixed Review **43.** $17(1 - 3y^2)$ **45.** $\frac{2c}{3x}\left(\frac{ab}{d} - \frac{4bd}{5a} + \frac{2ad}{3b}\right)$ **47.** 2 **49.** -6.5

LESSON 1-8

Try This **a.** 4096 **b.** $-75x^{-14}$ **c.** $-10x^{-12}y^2$ **d.** $30x^{m+7}y^{n+4}$ **e.** 5^6 **f.** 10^6 **g.** $-2y^{10}x^{-4}$, or $-\frac{2y^{10}}{x^4}$ **h.** $\frac{3}{2}a^{-2}b^2$, or $\frac{3b^2}{2a^2}$ **i.** -8 **j.** 3^{42} **k.** x^{-14}, or $\frac{1}{x^{14}}$ **l.** t^6 **m.** $8x^3y^3$ **n.** $-32x^{20}y^{10}$ **o.** $1000x^{-12}y^{21}z^{-6}$, or $\frac{1000y^{21}}{x^{12}z^6}$ **p.** x^9y^{12} **q.** $\frac{9x^4}{4y^4}$, or $\frac{9}{4}x^4y^{-4}$ **r.** 16 **s.** 24 **t.** 27

Exercises **1.** 5^9 **3.** 8^{-4} or $\frac{1}{8^4}$ **5.** 8^{-6} or $\frac{1}{8^6}$ **7.** b^{-3} or $\frac{1}{b^3}$ **9.** a^3 **11.** $6x^5$ **13.** $-28m^5n^5$ **15.** $-14x^{-11}$ or $-\frac{14}{x^{11}}$ **17.** $-30(x^{a+5})(y^{b+9})$ **19.** 6^5 **21.** $\frac{1}{10^9}$ **23.** a^5 **25.** 1 **27.** $\frac{-4x^9}{3y^2}$ **29.** $\frac{3x^3}{2y^2}$ **31.** $-10x^{5a}$ **33.** $-3x^{a-2}y^{b-5}$ **35.** 4^6 **37.** 6^{12} **39.** $(-2)^{-2}x^{-6}y^8$ or $\frac{y^8}{4x^6}$ **41.** $(-6)^{-2}a^4b^{-6}c^{-2}$ or $\frac{a^4}{36b^6c^2}$ **43.** $\frac{1}{4^9 \cdot 3^{12}}$ **45.** $\frac{8x^9y^3}{27}$ **47.** 10 **49.** 24 **51.** Answers will vary. It is true when $x = 1$. **53.** $\frac{2^4x^4}{3^6y^{62}}$ **55.** $64x^{18}y^4$ **57.** Suppose we substitute $-n$ for n in Theorem 1-11, which states $(a^mb^n)^p = a^{mp}b^{np}$. Then $(a^mb^{-n})^p = a^{mp}b^{-np}$. Since $b^{-n} = \frac{1}{b^n}$ and $b^{-np} = \frac{1}{b^{np}}$, we have $\left(a^m \cdot \frac{1}{b^n}\right)^p = a^{mp} \cdot \frac{1}{b^{np}}$, or $\left(\frac{a^m}{b^n}\right)^p = \frac{a^{mp}}{b^{np}}$. **59.** 1 **61.** m^{bp} **63.** $m^{x^2}n^{x^2}$ **65.** $\frac{x^{4r}}{y^{8s}}$

Mixed Review **67.** 2 **69.** 0 **71.** x

LESSON 1-9

Try This **a.** 4.6×10^{11} **b.** 1.235×10^{-9} **c.** 1.7×10^{-24}g **d.** 1.5×10^8 km **e.** 789,300,000,000 **f.** 0.0000567 **g.** 7.462×10^{-13} **h.** 2.0×10^3 **i.** 5.5×10^2 **j.** 3×10^{-4}

Exercises **1.** 4.7×10^{10} **3.** 8.63×10^{17} **5.** 1.6×10^{-8} **7.** 7×10^{-11} **9.** 9.11×10^{-28} g **11.** 4.8×10^{-10} eu **13.** 1×10^{-9} **15.** 3.0699×10^5 pounds **17.** 0.0004 **19.** 673,000,000 **21.** 0.0000000008923 **23.** 9.66×10^{-5} **25.** 1.3338×10^{-11} **27.** 8.32×10^{10} **29.** 2.5×10^3 **31.** 5×10^{-4} **33.** 3×10^{11} **35.** 4.5×10^2 **37.** 1.1×10^{11} **39.** 6.5×10^1 **41.** 3.8715403×10^3 **43.** 2.0000000029×10^7 **45.** $\approx 1.4 \times 10^{12}$ mi **47.** 500,000,000 **49.** $\approx 6.82 \times 10^{-1}$ mi/h **51.** $\approx 2.37 \times 10^1$ ft/sec **53.** $\approx 28.4\%$ **55.** 3.05×10^{-7} sec

Mixed Review **57.** $35y + 98$ **59.** -132 **61.** t^2 **63.** $-2(a + b)$ **65.** $(w - y)\left(\frac{x}{2}\right)$

LESSON 1-10

Try This **a.** Associative property of addition **b.** Distributive property **c.** Identity property of addition **d.** Identity property of multiplication and property of multiplicative inverses **e.** No; no additive or multiplicative inverses **f.** Yes **g.** Distributive property

Exercises **1.** Property of additive inverses **3.** None; division theorem **5.** Symmetric property of equality **7.** Commutative property of addition **9.** None; subtraction theorem **11.** D **13.** No; there is no multiplicative inverse. **15.** No; there is no additive inverse. **17.** No; $-(x + 2) = -x - 2$ and $-2x + 4x = 2x$

19.

$-(a - b) = -(a + (-b))$	Subtrac. Th.
$= -1 \cdot (a + (-b))$	Mult. prop. of -1
$= (-1)(a) + (-1)(-b)$	Dist. prop.
$= -a + b$	Mult. prop. of -1
$= b + (-a)$	Commut. prop. of addition
$= b - a$	Subtrac. Th.
So $-(a - b) = b - a$	Trans. prop.

21. By the definition of division, $\frac{a}{b}$ is *that number* which when multiplied by b gives a. We can show that $a \cdot \frac{1}{b}$ is *that number* by multiplying it by b to get a.

$\left(a \cdot \frac{1}{b}\right)b = a\left(b \cdot \frac{1}{b}\right)$	Assoc. and commut. prop. of mult.
$= a \cdot 1$	Prop. of mult. inv.
$= a$	Iden. prop. of mult.

Since $\left(a \cdot \frac{1}{b}\right)b = a$, $a \cdot \frac{1}{b} = \frac{a}{b}$.

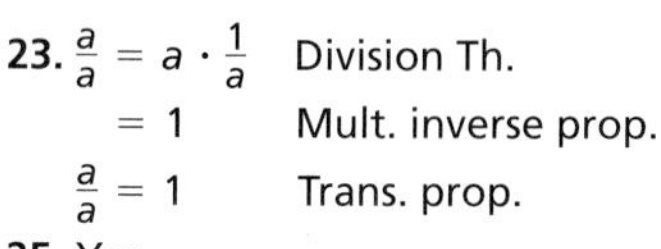

23. $\frac{a}{a} = a \cdot \frac{1}{a}$ Division Th.
$= 1$ Mult. inverse prop.
$\frac{a}{a} = 1$ Trans. prop.

25. Yes

Mixed Review **27.** $6ab - 9ac$ **29.** 6^6 **31.** y^{-2} **33.** 50 **35.** 16 **37.** \$840 **39.** 2×10^{-3} **41.** 1.25×10^{-1}

LESSON 1-11

Problems **1.** There are 16 spokes for a wheel with 16 spaces. **3.** Train A goes 600 miles in the same time train B goes 400 miles, so train A goes 900 miles in the time train B goes 600 miles. Thus, train B needs a 300-mile head start. **5.** There will be 10 liters at 5 hours, so there would be less than 10 liters after 5 hours.

CHAPTER 1 WRAP UP

1. No, no, yes, yes **3.** Rational **5.** $-\frac{27}{10}$ **7.** $-\frac{1}{24}$ **9.** -19.7 **11.** -8.4 **13.** 6010 **15.** $\frac{7}{6}$ **17.** $7y \cdot 4x$ **19.** $\frac{5}{12}$ **21.** -4 **23.** $6x - 6y + 6z$ **25.** $6a - 4b + 3c$ **27.** $-5(4x - y + 2z)$ **29.** $-10y - 5z$ **31.** $-r + t$ **33.** $-a + 4$ **35.** $6x + 2$ **37.** 6 **39.** 0 **41.** 8^{-3} **43.** $\frac{y^{-5}}{3}$ **45.** $\frac{1}{(-4)^3}$, or $-\frac{1}{64}$ **47.** $\frac{3a^3}{c^5}$ **49.** $-\frac{14}{x}$ **51.** $-\frac{3y^5}{x^8}$ **53.** $-\frac{1}{8x^9}$ **55.** 8.0×10^7 **57.** 3.78×10^9

Chapter 2

Skills & Concepts You Need for Chapter 2

1. $>$ **2.** $=$ **3.** $<$ **4.** 0 **5.** -3.6 **6.** $-\frac{13}{24}$ **7.** 13 **8.** -22.9 **9.** $-\frac{2}{21}$ **10.** -24 **11.** -47 **12.** 6 **13.** $3(x - 6)$ **14.** $5(x - 2y + 3)$ **15.** $2(2x - 4 + 3y)$ **16.** $4a(3b + c - 4d)$ **17.** $5y - 20$ **18.** $2a - ab$ **19.** $cx + cy - cz$ **20.** $-3x + 3y - 3$ **21.** $-x$ **22.** $7y + 2$

LESSON 2-1

Try This **a.** $y = \frac{2}{5}$ **b.** $x = 2$ **c.** $y = -\frac{19}{8}$ **d.** $\{19, -5\}$ **e.** $\left\{0, \frac{17}{3}\right\}$ **f.** $\left\{-\frac{2}{9}, \frac{1}{2}\right\}$

Exercises **1.** $\frac{4}{3}$ **3.** $\frac{37}{5}$ **5.** 13 **7.** 2 **9.** 2 **11.** 7 **13.** 5 **15.** $-\frac{51}{31}$ **17.** 5 **19.** 2 **21.** $\{-2, 5\}$ **23.** $\{8, 9\}$ **25.** $\left\{\frac{3}{2}, \frac{2}{3}\right\}$ **27.** $\{0, 8\}$ **29.** $\{0, 1, -2\}$ **31.** $\left\{3, -\frac{4}{7}\right\}$ **33.** $-\frac{10}{31}$ **35.** $\frac{f + 4}{16}$ **37.** $\frac{3 + 5b}{7 - a}$ **39.** $\frac{19}{5 + a}$ **41.** Answers may vary. Sample: $x^2 + x - 56 = 0$ **43.** $\{1, 0\}$ **45.** $\{0\}$

Mixed Review **47.** 4^5 **49.** x^{-2} **51.** 3.9004×10^5 **53.** 2.4072×10^1 **55.** $-8,220,000$

LESSON 2-2

Try This **a.** $5\frac{3}{4}$ ft; $17\frac{1}{4}$ ft **b.** $\frac{1}{2}$ **c.** $3x + 30 = 5x$; \$15 **d.** \$124 **e.** \$725 **f.** 17, 19 **g.** (1) Harold 22, Gunther 24 (2) Harold 11, Gunther 12

Exercises **1.** 8 cm; 4 cm **3.** $-\frac{1}{22}$ **5.** \$176.58 **7.** \$650 **9.** 32°, 96°, 52° **11.** Length is 31 m; width is 17 m **13.** \$15,000 **15.** C **17.** \$3644 **19.** 98% **21.** 84 **23.** 143 gallons **25.** 20 cm, 32 cm **27.** 84 years

Mixed Review **29.** $3x^4 + 3x^2y - xy^2$ **31.** -1 **33.** $2x(x + 1)$ **35.** $6xy(5x + y - 2x^2)$

LESSON 2-3

Try This **a.** $b = \frac{2A}{h}$ **b.** $c = \frac{5}{3}P - 10$ **c.** $m = \frac{H - 2r}{3}$ **d.** $p = \frac{Q - 3r}{5}$ **e.** $Q = \frac{T}{1 + iy}$ **f.** $G = \frac{x}{1 - r^2p}$

Exercises **1.** $l = \frac{A}{w}$ **3.** $l = \frac{W}{E}$ **5.** $m = \frac{F}{a}$ **7.** $t = \frac{I}{Pr}$ **9.** $m = \frac{E}{c^2}$ **11.** $l = \frac{P - 2w}{2}$ **13.** $a^2 = c^2 - b^2$ **15.** $r^2 = \frac{A}{\pi}$ **17.** $F = \frac{9}{5}C + 32$ **19.** $r^3 = \frac{3V}{4\pi}$ **21.** $h = \frac{2A}{(a + b)}$ **23.** $m = \frac{rF}{v^2}$ **25.** $a = \frac{2s - 2v_it}{t^2}$ **27.** 0.4 yr **29.** Answers may vary. **31.** $T_2 = \frac{P_2V_2T_1}{P_1V_1}$

Mixed Review **33.** 6^{-6} **35.** 8^6 **37.** $\frac{13}{10}$ **39.** 2 **41.** 4 or -5

LESSON 2-4

Try This **a.** Solution **b.** Not a solution **c.** Solution

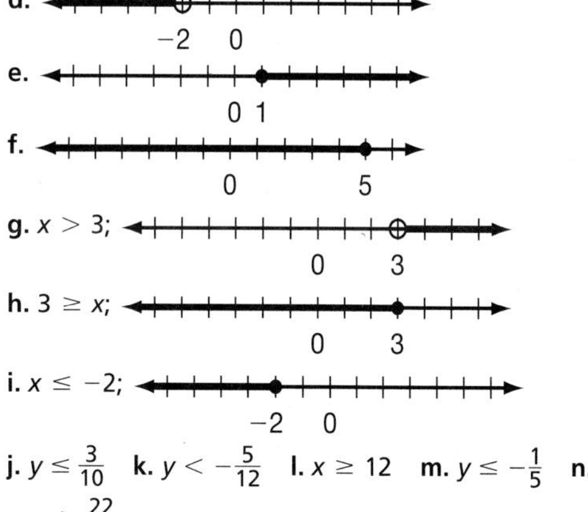

j. $y \le \frac{3}{10}$ **k.** $y < -\frac{5}{12}$ **l.** $x \ge 12$ **m.** $y \le -\frac{1}{5}$ **n.** $x < \frac{1}{2}$ **o.** $y \ge \frac{22}{13}$

Exercises **1.** Yes **3.** No (You may wish to have students write answers in set notation. For example, the answer to Exercise 9 would be $\{x \mid x > -3\}$.)

5.
−1 0

Selected Answers

7. 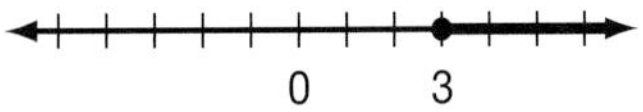 0 3 **9.** $x > -3$ **11.** $t \geq -5$
13. $y > -6$ **15.** $x < 50$ **17.** $y \geq -0.4$ **19.** $y \geq \frac{9}{10}$ **21.** $y > 3$
23. $x \leq 4$ **25.** $x < -\frac{2}{5}$ **27.** $y < 5$ **29.** No solution
31. $y \leq -\frac{53}{6}$ **33.** Answers may vary. Ex: $x < -5$, $3x + 2 < -13$
35. $y > 0$ or $y < -5$ **37.** $-1 < x < 2$
Mixed Review **39.** a^4 **41.** $4m^{10}$ **43.** $\frac{x^6}{y^6}$

LESSON 2-5

Try This **a.** Score ≥ 71 **b.** $n < 50$ hours
Exercises **1.** Less than 520.5 miles **3.** \$20,000
5. Less than \$2 (\$1.99) **7.** Less than 100 hours **9.** 10%
11. 92 **13.** $w \leq 4.5$ cm and cannot be negative **15.** Never; maximum height is 3136 ft **17.** Greater than $\frac{f}{3.75}$ hours
Mixed Review **19.** $a = \frac{c - b}{2}$ **21.** $c = \frac{g - ab - ef}{d}$

LESSON 2-6

Try This **a.**  −1 0 4
b. 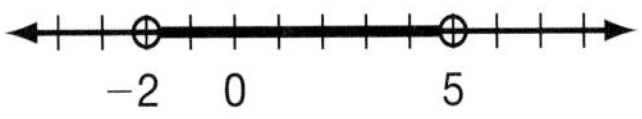 −2 0 5 **c.** $\{x \mid -2 \leq x \leq 1\}$
d. $\{x \mid -1 \leq x < 9\}$ **e.** −2 0 4
f. 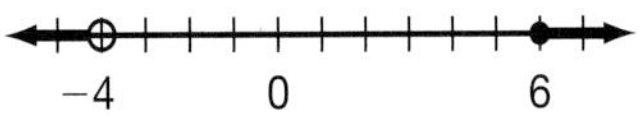 −4 0 6 **g.** $\{x \mid x < 1 \text{ or } x \geq 7\}$
h. $\left\{x \mid x < -2 \text{ or } x \geq \frac{7}{2}\right\}$
Exercises **1.**  0 1 6
3. 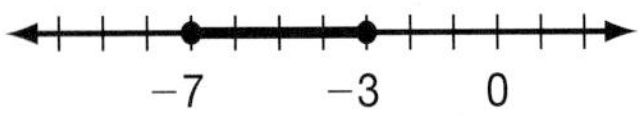 −7 −3 0 **5.** $-4 < x < 6$
7. $-\frac{5}{3} \leq x \leq \frac{4}{3}$ **9.** $0 < x < 14$
11. 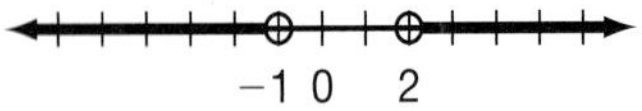 −1 0 2
13. 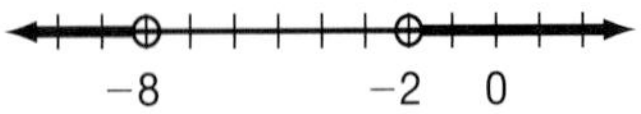 −8 −2 0 **15.** B
17. $x < -13$ or $x > -5$ **19.** $x \leq 5$ or $x \geq 3$ (any real number)
21. $x < -1$ or $x > 16$ **23.** No solution **25.** All real numbers
27. $-\frac{3}{2} \leq a \leq 1$ **29.** $\frac{2}{5} \leq x < \frac{4}{5}$ **31.** $-\frac{1}{8} < x < \frac{1}{2}$ **33.** Always
35. Sometimes **37.** Sometimes **39.** Answers may vary. Sample: ($x < 0$ or $x > 2$) and ($x > 1$ or $x < -1$)
41. $-\frac{5}{4} \leq m < 1$ **43.** $x \leq -\frac{1}{5}$ or $x \geq 0$ **45. a.** q **b.** 1
Mixed Review **47.** 24 **49.** 54 **51.** $-96c^2$ **53.** 2048

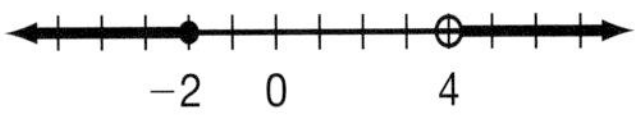

LESSON 2-7

Try This **a.** $7|x|$ **b.** x^8 **c.** $5a^2|b|$ **d.** $\frac{7|a|}{b^2}$ **e.** $9|x|$
f. 29 **g.** 5 **h.** 20
i. $\{6, -6\}$; 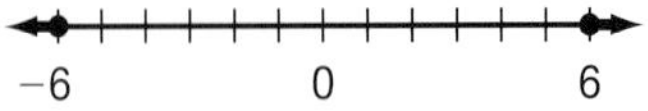 −6 0 6
j. $\left\{\frac{1}{2}, -\frac{1}{2}\right\}$; $-\frac{1}{2}$ 0 $\frac{1}{2}$ 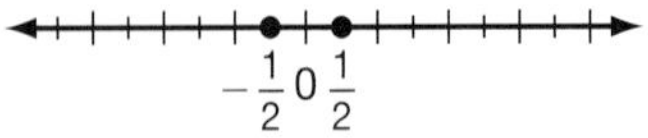
k. $\{x \mid -5 < x < 5\}$; −5 0 5
l. $\{x \mid -6.5 \leq x \leq 6.5\}$; −6.5 0 6.5 
m. $\{y \mid y \leq -8 \text{ or } y \geq 8\}$; 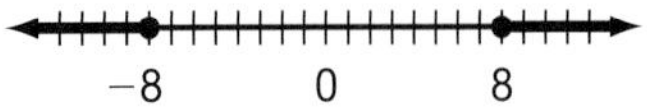 −8 0 8
n. $\left\{x \mid x < -\frac{1}{2} \text{ or } x > \frac{1}{2}\right\}$; $-\frac{1}{2}$ 0 $\frac{1}{2}$ 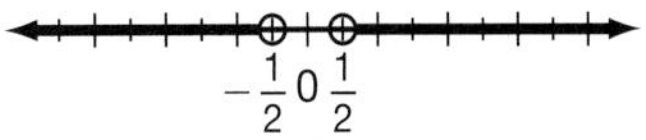
o. $\left\{x \mid x = -\frac{13}{3} \text{ or } x = \frac{5}{3}\right\}$; $-\frac{13}{3}$ 0 $\frac{5}{3}$
p. $\{x \mid -2 \leq x \leq 5\}$; −2 0 5 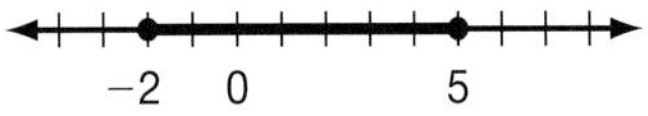
q. $\left\{x \mid x < -\frac{3}{2} \text{ or } x > \frac{11}{2}\right\}$; $-\frac{3}{2}$ 0 $\frac{11}{2}$ 
Exercises **1.** $3|x|$ **3.** y^8 **5.** $9x^2y^2|y|$ **7.** $\frac{a^2}{|b|}$ **9.** $16|m|$
11. $t^2|t|$ **13.** 34 **15.** 11 **17.** 33 **19.** 5 **21.** −3, 3
23. $-3 < x < 3$ **25.** $x \leq -2$ or $x \geq 2$ **27.** $t \leq -5.5$ or $t \geq 5.5$
29. −9, 15 **31.** $-\frac{1}{2} \leq x \leq \frac{7}{2}$ **33.** $y < -\frac{3}{2}$ or $y > \frac{17}{2}$
35. $x \leq -\frac{5}{4}$ or $x \geq \frac{23}{4}$ **37.** $x > -\frac{3}{5}$ or $x < -1$
39. $t \leq 6$ or $t \geq 8$ **41.** 0, 7 **43.** All real numbers
45. $-\frac{13}{54} < x < -\frac{7}{54}$ **47.** All real numbers **49.** $-\frac{1}{4}$, 1 **51.** $x \leq 1$
Mixed Review **53.** m^{-2} **55.** $-8w^8n^{-6}$ **57.** $c = -2$
59. Answers may vary. $ab + (d + c)$; $(c + d) + ab$; $ba + (c + d)$

LESSON 2-8

Try This
a.
1. $3x + 5 = 20$ — Hypothesis (assumed true)
2. $3x = 15$ — Add. property
3. $x = 5$ — Mult. property
4. If $3x + 5 = 20$, then $x = 5$. — Statements 1–3

b.
1. $-3x + 8 > 23$ — Hypothesis (assumed true)
2. $-3x > 15$ — Add. prop. for inequalities
3. $x < -5$ — Mult. prop. for inequalities
4. If $-3x + 8 > 23$, then $x < -5$ — Statements 1–3

c. If $x = 10$, then $3x + 7 = 37$. **d.** If $x > 12$, then $x > 15$.

e.

Statement	Reason
1. $x = 5$	Hypothesis
2. $3x = 15$	Mult. property
3. $3x + 5 = 20$	Add. property
4. If $x = 5$, then $3x + 5 = 20$	Statements 1–3

f. (1)

Statement	Reason
1. $x < -5$	Hypothesis
2. $-3x > 15$	Multiply both sides by -3
3. $-3x + 8 > 23$	Add 8 to both sides
4. If $x < -5$, then $-3x + 8 > 23$	Statements 1–3

(2) Solution set of antecedent and consequent: $\{x \mid x < -5\}$ since the consequent is the solution set of the antecedent.

g. Statement $7x - 1 > 34$

$7x > 35$	Add. property
$x > 5$	Mult. property
Converse $x > 5$	
$7x > 35$	Mult. property
$7x - 1 > 34$	Add. property

h. (1) Statement $9x - 5 = 103$

$9x = 108$	Add. property
$x = 12$	Mult. property
Converse $x = 12$	
$9x = 108$	Mult. property
$9x - 5 = 103$	Add. property

(2) $9x - 5 = 103$

$9x = 108$	Add. property
$x = 12$	Mult. property
$9(12) - 5 = 103$	Substituting
$108 - 5 = 103$	
$103 = 103$	

i. Yes **j.** No **k.** Yes **l.** Yes **m.** No **n.** No

Exercises **1.** $7x - 12 = 37$

$7x = 49$	Add. Property
$x = 7$	Mult. Property

3. $15x - 5 \geq 11 - 2x$

$17x \geq 16$	Add. Property
$x \geq \frac{16}{17}$	Mult. Property

5. If $6y = 10$, then $3y = 5$. **7.** If $x < 20$, then $x < 12$.

9. If $x = 7$, then $7x - 12 = 37$.

$x = 7$	Hypothesis
$7x = 49$	Mult. Property
$7x - 12 = 37$	Add. Property

11. If $x \geq \frac{16}{17}$, then $15x - 5 \geq 11 - 2x$.

$x \geq \frac{16}{17}$	Hypothesis
$17x \geq 16$	Mult. Property
$17x - 5 \geq 11$	Add. Property
$15x - 5 \geq 11 - 2x$	Add. Property

13. $\left\{x \middle| -\frac{9}{2} < x\right\}$ **15.** $-\frac{4}{7}$ **17.** $-\frac{17}{2}$ **19.** No **21.** No

23.

Statement	Reason
1. $a = b$	Hypothesis
2. $a - a = 0$	Prop. of additive inverses
3. $a - b = 0$	Statements 1 and 2 (substitution)
4. $a - b + 0 = 0$	Additive identity property
5. $a - b + c - c = 0$	Prop. of additive inverses
6. $a + c - b - c = 0$	Commutative property
7. $a + c - (b + c) = 0$	Inverse of a sum property
8. $a + c = b + c$	Prop. of additive inverses

25. Part 1. If $a = 0$ or $b = 0$ then $ab = 0$

Statement	Reason
1. $a = 0$	Hypothesis
2. $ab = 0(b)$	Mult. property
3. $ab = 0$	Mult. prop. of zero
4. If $a = 0$ then $ab = 0$	Statements 1–3
5. $b = 0$	Hypothesis
6. $ab = a(0)$	Mult. property
7. $ab = 0$	Mult. prop. of zero
8. If $b = 0$ then $ab = 0$	Statements 5–7
9. If $a = 0$ or $b = 0$ then $ab = 0$	Statements 4 and 8

Part 2. If $ab = 0$ then $a = 0$ or $b = 0$

Statement	Reason
1. $ab = 0$ $(a \neq 0)$	Hypothesis
2. $\frac{1}{a} \cdot ab = \frac{1}{a} \cdot 0$	Mult. property
3. $1(b) = 0$	Prop. of reciprocals
4. $b = 0$	Mult. identity prop.
5. If $ab = 0$ and $a \neq 0$ then $b = 0$	Statements 1–4
6. $ab = 0$ $(b \neq 0)$	Hypothesis
7. $ab \cdot \frac{1}{b} = 0 \cdot \frac{1}{b}$	Mult. property
8. $a(1) = 0$	Prop. of reciprocals
9. $a = 0$	Mult. identity prop.
10. If $ab = 0$ and $b \neq 0$ then $a = 0$	Statements 6–9
11. If $ab = 0$ then $a = 0$ or $b = 0$	Statements 5 and 10

27.

Statement	Reason
1. $a < b$	Hypothesis
2. $a - a < b - a$	Addn. prop. for ineq.
3. $0 < b - a$	Additive inv. prop.
4. $b < c$	Hypothesis
5. $b - b < c - b$	Addn. prop. for ineq.
6. $0 < c - b$	Additive inv. prop.
7. $0 < (b - a) + (c - b)$	Add. of pos. #'s is pos.
8. $0 < c - a + b - b$	Comm. prop.
9. $0 < c - a$	Additive inverse prop.
10. $0 + a < c - a + a$	Addn. prop. for ineq.
11. $a < c$	Add. ident., add. inv. prop.
12. If $a < b$ and $b < c$ then $a < c$	Statements 1, 4, 11

Selected Answers

29. Part 1. ($c > 0$)

1. $a < b$	Hypothesis
2. $0 < b - a$	Defn. of <
3. $0 < c(b - a)$	Prod. of pos. #'s is pos.
4. $0 < cb - ca$	Dist. prop.
5. $ca < cb$	Defn. of <
6. If $a < b$ and $c > 0$ then $ac < bc$	Statements 1–5

Part 2. ($c < 0$)

1. $a < b$	Hypothesis
2. $0 < b - a$	Defn. of <
3. $0 > c(b - a)$	Prod. of neg. and pos. # is neg.
4. $0 > cb - ca$	Dist. prop.
5. $ca > cb$	Defn. of >
6. If $a < b$ and $c < 0$ then $ac > bc$	Statements 1–5

31. If x is a quitter, then x never wins. If x never wins, then x is a quitter.

Mixed Review **33.** $\frac{1}{8}$ **35.** $\frac{1}{6}$ **37.** 13 **39.** −43

LESSON 2-9

Problems **1.** They would use 905 kWh. **3.** There might be about 364 customers in 4 years. **5.** Some possible solutions: 20 km, 40 km, 60 km; 30 km, 60 km, 70 km

Application **1.** Internal loading **3.** Internal loading **5.** Internal loading

CHAPTER 2 WRAP UP

1. 2 **2.** $13\frac{1}{4}$ **3.** 1 **4.** 2 **5.** $-5\frac{5}{6}$ **6.** 8 **7.** −4, 3 **8.** $2\frac{1}{2}, -\frac{4}{3}$

9. 26°, 130°, 24° **10.** $150 **11.** $\frac{2A}{h}$ **12.** $\frac{V}{b + t}$

13. $y \geq 1$; 0 1

14. $x > -16$; −16 −15

15. $x \geq -27$; −27 −26

16. $y \leq 5$; 0 5

17. $x \leq 30$; 29 30

18. $x \geq -\frac{13}{4}$; $-\frac{13}{4}$ −2 −1 0

19. 3, 5, 7 **20.** $-3 < x < 5$; −3 0 5

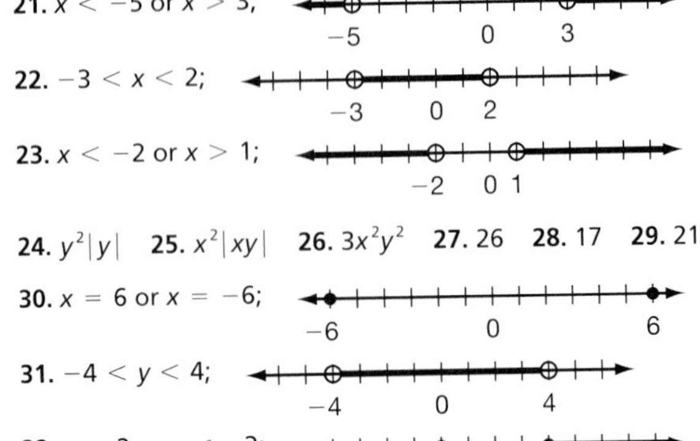

21. $x < -5$ or $x > 3$; −5 0 3

22. $-3 < x < 2$; −3 0 2

23. $x < -2$ or $x > 1$; −2 0 1

24. $y^2|y|$ **25.** $x^2|xy|$ **26.** $3x^2y^2$ **27.** 26 **28.** 17 **29.** 21

30. $x = 6$ or $x = -6$; −6 0 6

31. $-4 < y < 4$; −4 0 4

32. $x \geq 2$ or $x \leq -2$; −2 0 2

33. $x \geq 8$ or $x \leq -2$; −2 0 8

34. $-4 < x < \frac{2}{3}$; −4 0 $\frac{2}{3}$

Chapter 3

Skills & Concepts You Need for Chapter 3 **1.** −4 **2.** −9 **3.** −6.2 **4.** 7 **5.** −5.7 **6.** $\frac{1}{15}$ **7.** −5 **8.** 4 **9.** −20 **10.** 7 **11.** 4 **12.** 3 **13.** $\frac{1}{6}$ **14.** $-\frac{13}{12}$ **15.** $-\frac{12}{5}$ **16.** 24 **17.** −4 **18.** $\frac{11}{3}$ **19.** 3 **20.** $x < 4$ **21.** $y \geq 8$ **22.** $y \leq -2$ **23.** $x < -2$ **24.** $x > 3$ **25.** $y \leq \frac{1}{7}$ **26.** $y < 1$ **27.** $x \leq 2$

LESSON 3-1

Try This **a.** {(*d*, 1), (*d*, 2), (*e*, 1), (*e*, 2)} **b.** {(*x*, *x*), (*x*, *y*), (*x*, *z*), (*y*, *x*), (*y*, *y*), (*y*, *z*), (*z*, *x*), (*z*, *y*), (*z*, *z*)} **c.** {(1, 1), (2, 2)} **d.** Domain {*a*, *b*, *c*, *e*}; Range {1, 2, 3} **e.** Domain {1, 2}; Range {1, 2, 3} **f.** {6} **g.** {(3, 4), (3, 5), (4, 4), (4, 5), (5, 4), (5, 5)}

Exercises **1.** {(chili, cheese), (chili, onions), (chili, peppers), (pizza, cheese), (pizza, onions), (pizza, peppers), (salad, cheese), (salad, onions), (salad, peppers)} **3.** {(*x*, 1), (*x*, 2), (*y*, 1), (*y*, 2), (*z*, 1), (*z*, 2)} **5.** {(5, 5), (5, 6), (5, 7), (5, 8), (6, 5), (6, 6), (6, 7), (6, 8), (7, 5), (7, 6), (7, 7), (7, 8), (8, 5), (8, 6), (8, 7), (8, 8)} **7.** {(−7, −3), (−7, 1), (−7, 2), (−7, 5), (−3, 1), (−3, 2), (−3, 5), (1, 2), (1, 5), (2, 5)} **9.** {(−7, −7), (−7, −3), (−7, 1), (−7, 2), (−7, 5), (−3, −3), (−3, 1), (−3, 2), (−3, 5), (1, 1), (1, 2), (1, 5), (2, 2), (2, 5), (5, 5)} **11.** {(−7, −7), (−3, −3), (1, 1), (2, 2), (5, 5)} **13.** Domain {5}; Range {6} **15.** Domain {7, 8, 9}; Range {1, 2, 5} **17.** Domain {6, 7, 8}; Range {0, 5} **19.** Domain {8, 5}; Range {1} **21.** {8, 10, 12} **23.** {2, 8, 10, 12} **25.** {(5, 2), (5, 3)} **27.** {(2, 4), (2, 5), (3, 4), (3, 5)} **29.** {(3, 3), (3, 4)} **31. a.** {(−1, −1), (−1, 1), (−1, 3), (−1, 5), (1, −1), (1, 1), (1, 3), (1, 5), (3, −1), (3, 1), (3, 3), (3, 5), (5, −1), (5, 1), (5, 3), (5, 5)} **b.** {(−1, −1), (−1, 1), (−1, 3), (−1, 5), (1, 1), (1, 3), (1, 5), (3, 3), (3, 5), (5, 5)}

c. Domain $\{-1, 1, 3, 5\}$; Range $\{-1, 1, 3, 5\}$ **d.** $\{(-1, 3), (-1, 5), (1, 3), (1, 5), (3, 5)\}$ **33.** Possible anwers: (3, 1, 1), (3, 2, 4), (3, 3, 9), (3, 4, 16), (3, 5, 25)

Mixed Review **35.** 4 **37.** 1 **39.** c^6

41. $y < 12$

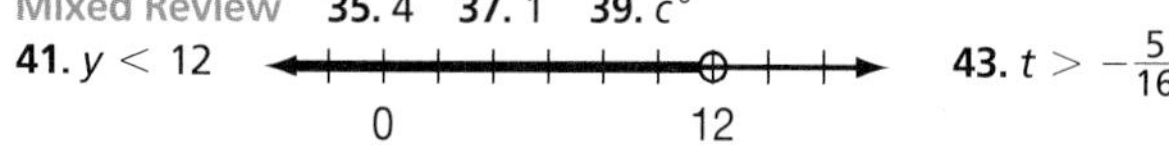

43. $t > -\frac{5}{16}$

LESSON 3-2

Try This

a.

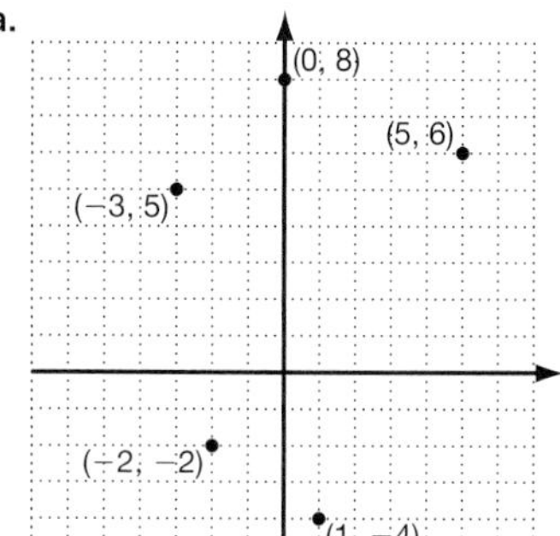

b.

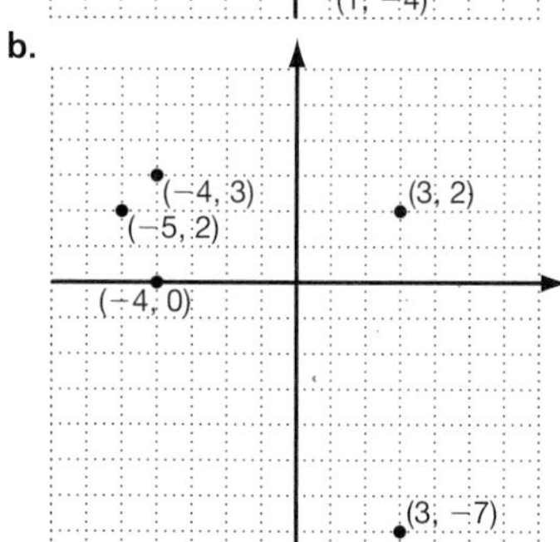

c. Yes; yes **d.** No; no **e.** No; yes

f.

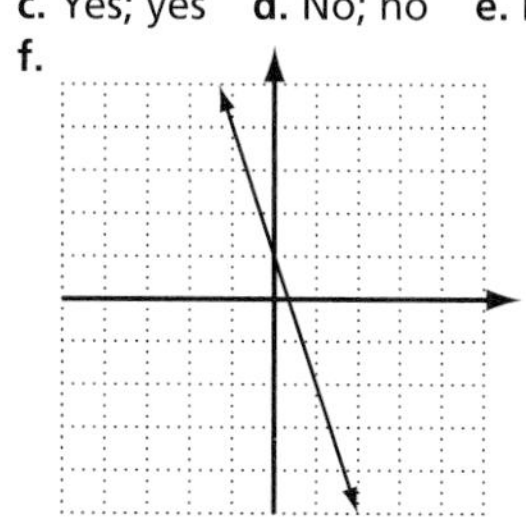

g.

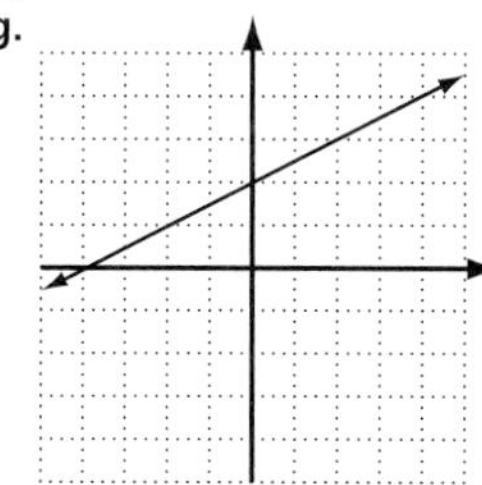

h.

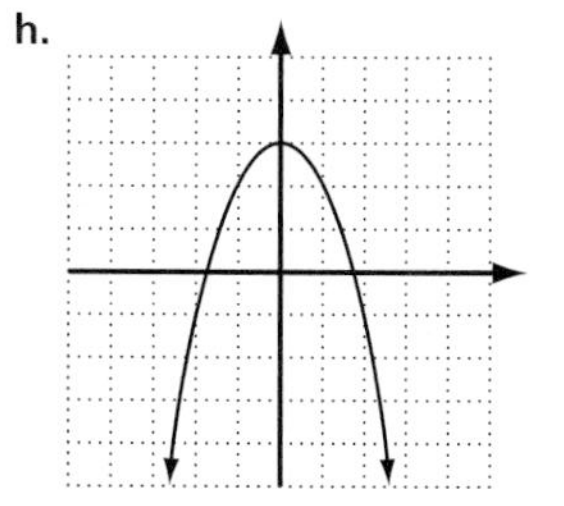

i.

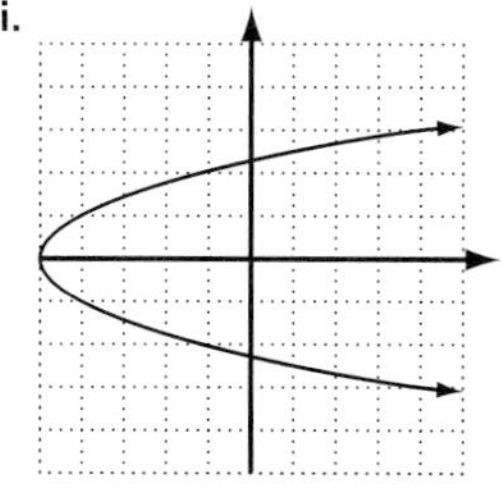

Exercises

1. **3.**

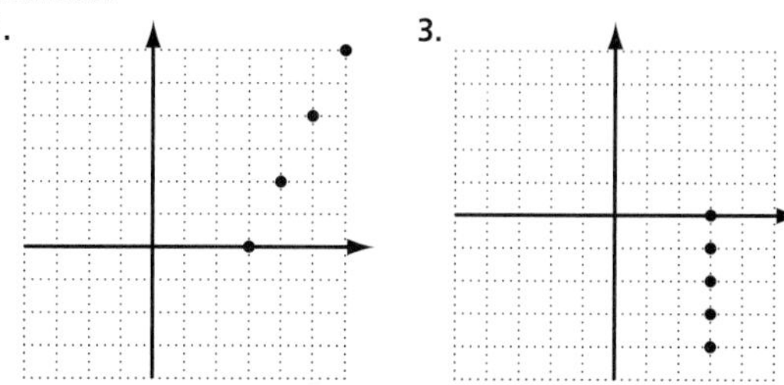

7. Answers may vary. Sample: Always look for repeating x-coordinates. **9.** Yes; no **11.** No; no **13.** Yes; yes **15.** Yes; no **17.** Yes; no **19.** No; yes

25.

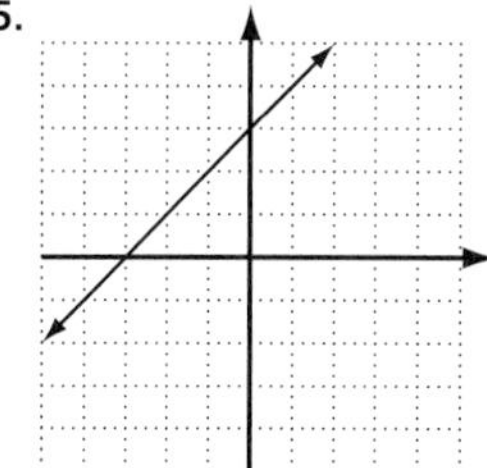

27.

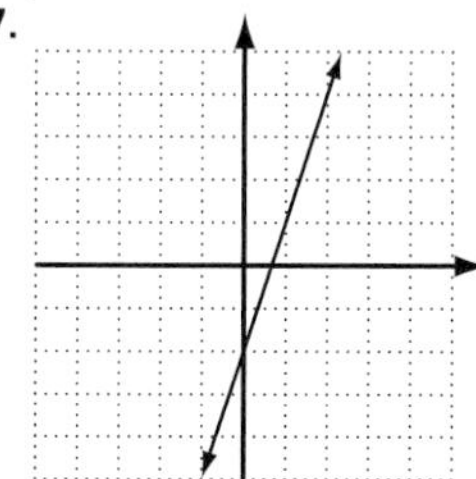

37. Domain R; Range $\{y \mid y \leq 0\}$ **39.** Domain R; Range $\{y \mid y \geq -2\}$ **41.** Domain $\{x \mid x \geq -2\}$; Range R **43. a.** $\{x \mid 2 \leq x \leq 6\}$ **b.** $\{y \mid 1 \leq y \leq 5\}$

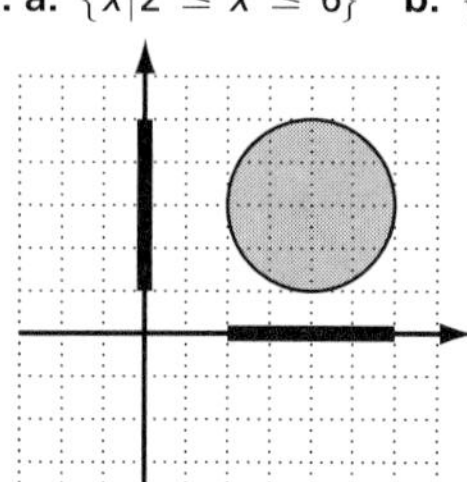

45.

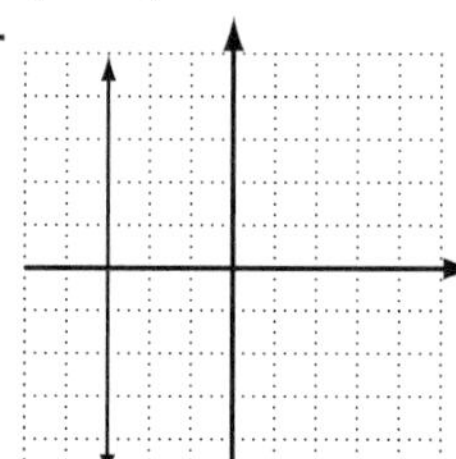

47.

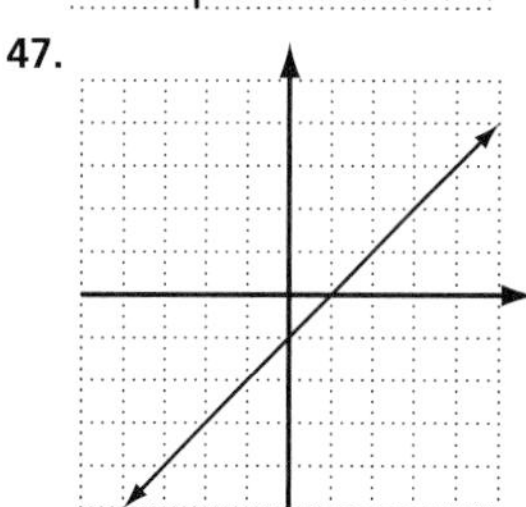

49.

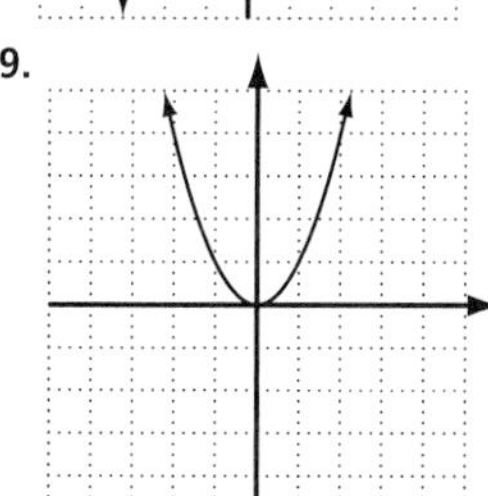

51.

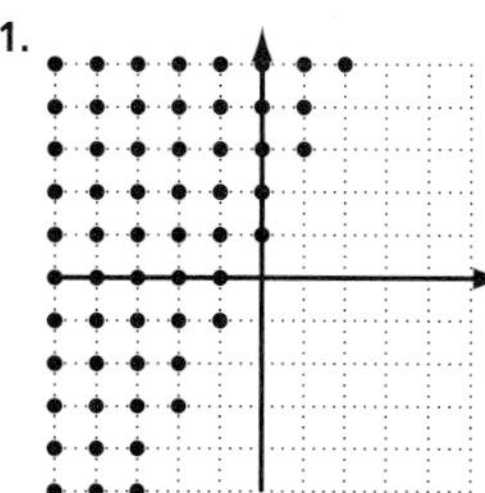

53.

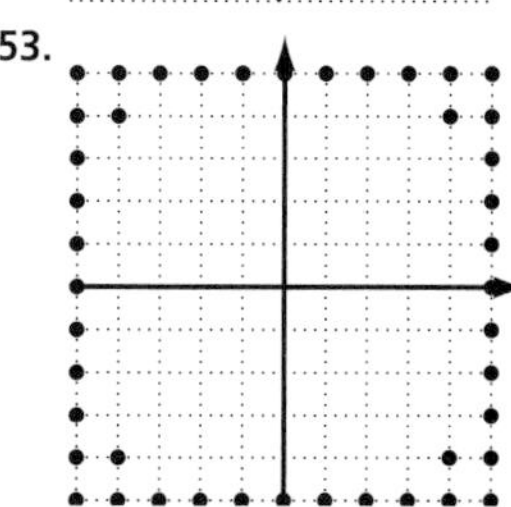

Selected Answers

55. Answers may vary. Samples:
a) $y = x + 3$, b) $y = x^2 - 3$ c) $y = 2x + 5$

57.

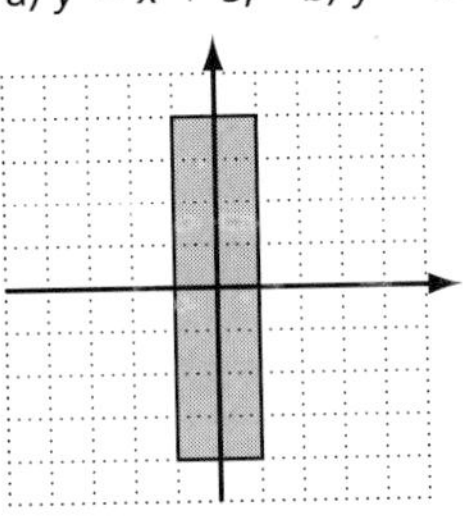

59.

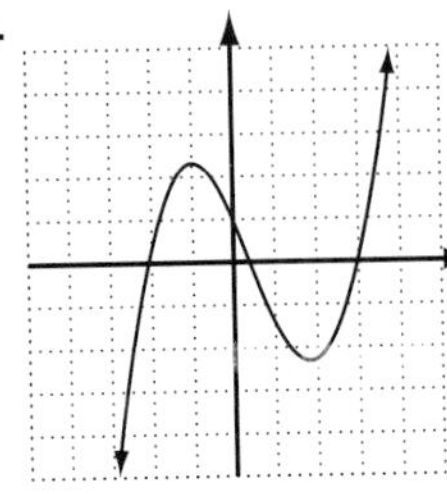

Mixed Review **61.** $y = -\frac{5}{2}$ **63.** 6 in., 24 in.

LESSON 3-3

Try This **a.** A is not a function. B–E are functions. **b.** (1) Yes (2) Yes (3) Yes (4) No **c.** $h(9) = 1$; $h(6) = 6$; $h(0) = -2$ **d.** 1 **e.** 4 **f.** 4 **g.** $12a^2 + 1$ **h.** $\{x|x \neq 1 \text{ and } x \neq -3\}$ **i.** $\{x|x \text{ is a real number}\}$ **j.** $\{x|x \neq 0\}$

Exercises **1.** Yes **3.** No **5.** Yes **7.** Yes **9.** No **11.** Yes **13. a.** 1 **b.** -3 **c.** -6 **d.** 9 **15. a.** 0 **b.** 1 **c.** 57 **d.** $5t^2 + 4t$ **17. a.** 15 **b.** 32 **c.** 20 **d.** 4 **19. a.** $\frac{2}{3}$ **b.** $\frac{10}{9}$ **c.** 0 **d.** Not possible **21.** R **23.** $\{x|x \neq 0\}$ **25.** $\left\{x|x \neq -\frac{8}{5}\right\}$ **27.** $\{x|x \neq 0, x \neq -2, \text{ and } x \neq 1\}$ **29. a.** $\frac{1}{2}$ **b.** $\frac{1}{3}$ **c.** $-\frac{1}{2}$ **d.** 0 is not an acceptable element of the domain. **31.** 0, 1 **33.** No. For example, if A = {rational numbers} and B = {rational numbers}, the function $y = \frac{1}{x - 3}$ is a function from A to B, but is not defined when $x = 3$. **35. a.** 0 **b.** Not possible **c.** Not possible **d.** $\{x|x \neq 0 \text{ and } \neq 2\}$

Mixed Review **37.** 8 **39.** 47.5
41. $x > 3$ or $x < 2$;
43. $11 > x > 6$;

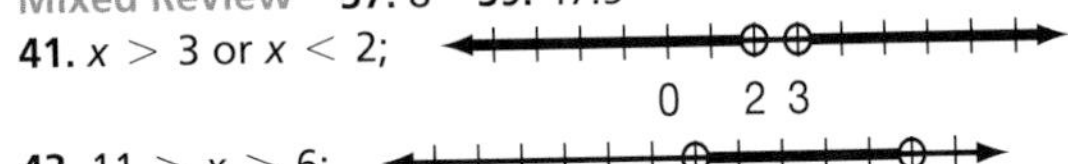

45. None

LESSON 3-4

Try This **a.** Yes **b.** Yes **c.** No, has a variable to a power **d.** No, has a variable in a denominator **e.** No, has a product of variables **f.** Yes

g.

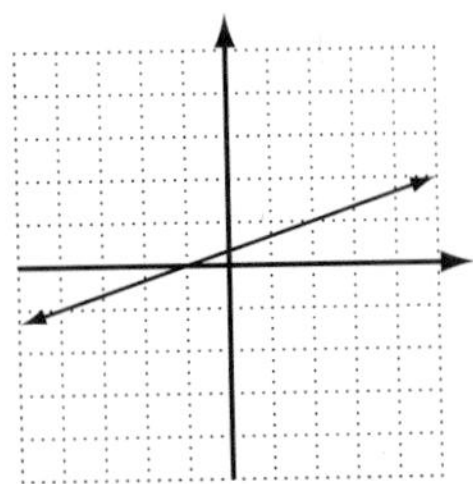

h.

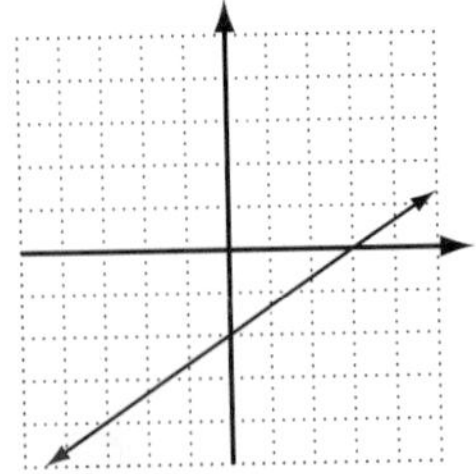

i.

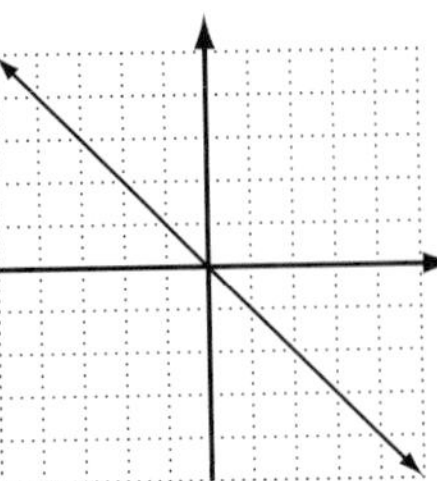

j.

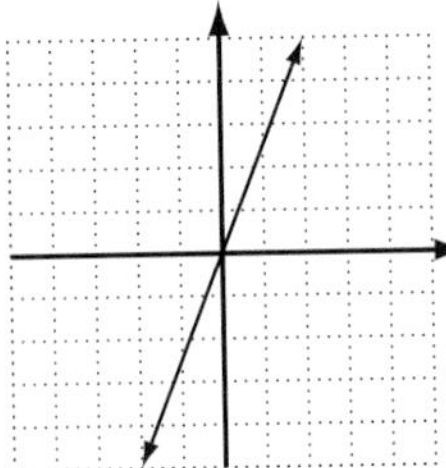

k. The graph of $y = 2x + 1$ is a line moved up 1 unit from the graph of $y = 2x$. **l.** The graph of $y = 2x - 4$ is a line moved down 4 units from the graph of $y = 2x$.

k, l.

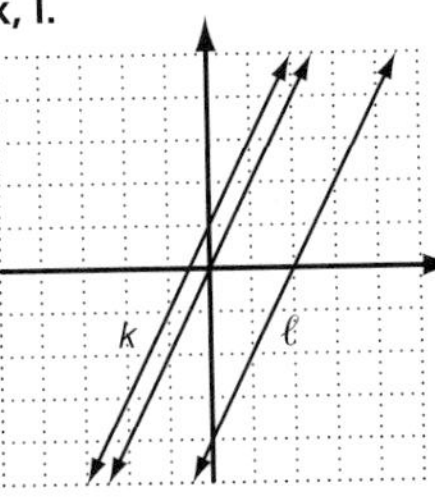

m–o.

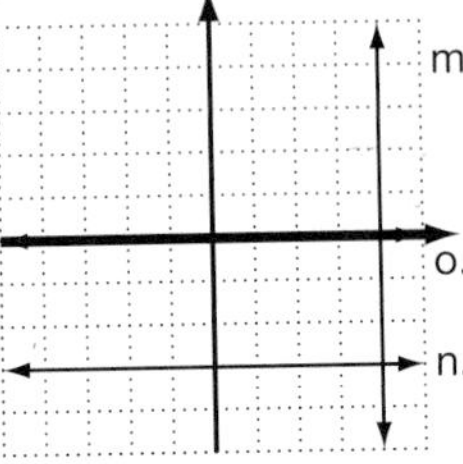

Exercises **1.** Yes **3.** No; 2nd degree **5.** Yes **7.** Yes **9.** Yes

23.

2.8
2.4
2
1.6
1.2
.8
.4
−.1 .1 .2 .3 .4 .5 .6 .7 .8 .9
−.4

$y \approx 1.7$

25.

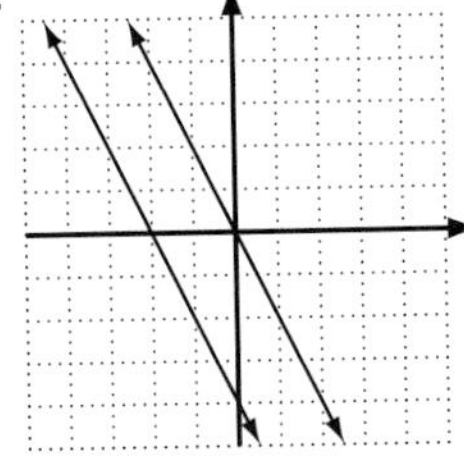

27.

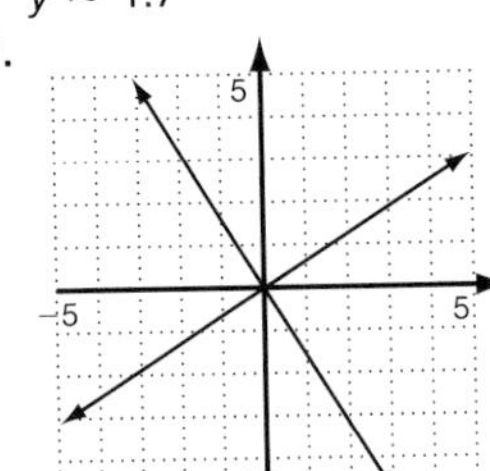

29.

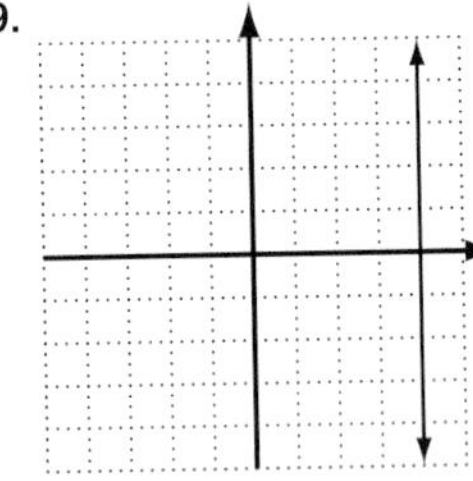

31.

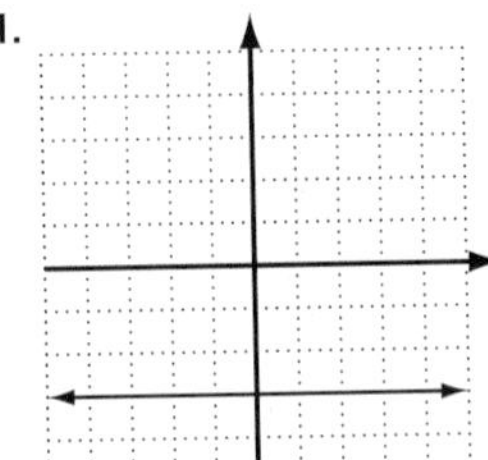

33.

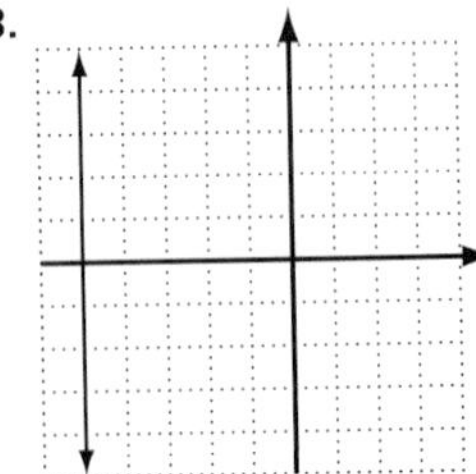

37. $\left(0, -\frac{7}{2}\right), \left(-\frac{7}{16}, 0\right)$ **39.** $\left(0, -\frac{6}{77}\right), \left(-\frac{2}{11}, 0\right)$
41. Answers may vary.

Mixed Review **43.** $4x^{14}y^{10}$ **45.** 1
47. $\{(0, a), (0, b), (0, c), (1, a), (1, b), (1, c)\}$

LESSON 3-5

Try This **a.** $\frac{13}{11}$ **b.** 1 **c.** $\frac{11}{5}$ **d.** -1 **e.** 0 **f.** No slope
g. $y = -3x - 2$ **h.** $y = \frac{1}{4}x - 9$ **i.** $y = -\frac{1}{2}x + \frac{5}{2}$

Exercises **1.** 8 **3.** -1 **5.** $-\frac{1}{2}$ **7.** 2 **9.** $\frac{3}{7}$ **11.** $\frac{1}{2}$ **13.** $\frac{2}{5}$
15. No slope **17.** No slope **19.** 0 **21.** No slope **23.** 0
25. No slope **27.** 0 **29.** 0 **31.** No slope **33.** $y = 4x - 10$
35. $y = -x - 7$ **37.** $y = \frac{1}{2}x + 7$ **39.** $y = -7$ **41.** 1.7441860
43. $y = 3.516x - 13.1602$ **45.** Yes **47.** $\frac{5}{8}$ **49.** Answers may vary. Sample: $(-25, 1), (-50, 2), (-75, 3), (25, -1)$
51. $m = -\frac{3}{5}$ **53.** Figure $ABCD$ is a parallelogram and its opposite sides are parallel. $\overline{AB}$ and $\overline{CD}$ have equal slopes. $\overline{BC}$ and $\overline{DA}$ have equal slopes. **55. a.** Grade = 4%; $y = 0.04x$
b. Grade = 6.7%; $y = 0.067x$

Mixed Review **57.** R **59.** 15 **61.** $-\frac{1}{6}$ **63.** $-\frac{36}{5}$

LESSON 3-6

Try This **a.** $y = -3x + 7$ **b.** $y = -\frac{10}{3}x + 4$ **c.** $m = -5; b = \frac{1}{3}$
d. $m = \frac{2}{3}; b = 2$ **e.** $m = 0; b = 3$

f.

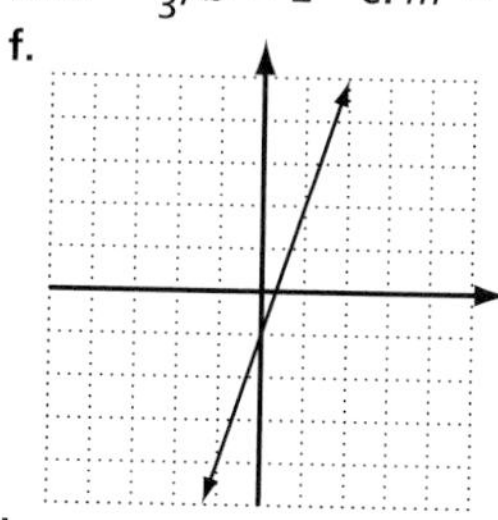

g.

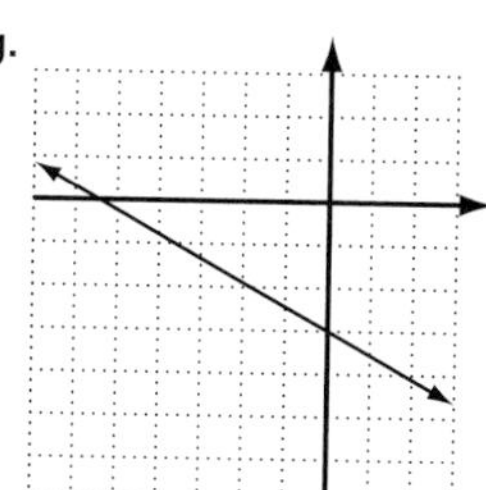

h.

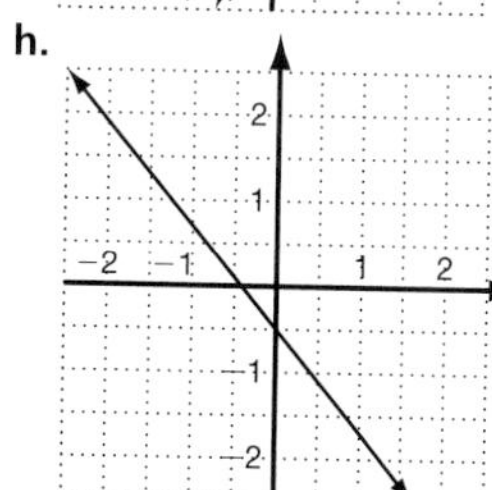

i. $5x - 5y + \frac{1}{2} = 0; m = 1$ **j.** $8x - 5y - 10 = 0; m = \frac{8}{5}$

Exercises **1.** $y = \frac{1}{2}x + \frac{7}{2}$ **3.** $y = x$ **5.** $y = \frac{5}{2}x + 5$
7. $y = \frac{1}{4}x + \frac{17}{4}$ **9.** $y = \frac{2}{5}x$ **11.** $y = 3x + 5$ **13.** $m = 2; b = 3$
15. $m = -4; b = 9$ **17.** $m = -1; b = 6$ **19.** $m = -3; b = 5$
21. $m = \frac{3}{4}; b = -3$ **23.** $m = -3; b = 4$ **25.** $m = -\frac{7}{3}; b = -3$
27. $m = 0; b = 7$ **29.** $m = 0; b = -\frac{10}{3}$

37. $4x - y - 8 = 0; m = 4$ **39.** $2x - y + 3 = 0; m = 2$
41. $x - 6 = 0$; no slope **43.** $x + y - 2 = 0; m = -1$
45. $2x - 6 = 0$; no slope **47.** Not a linear equation
49. $y = \frac{2}{5}x - 4$ **51.** $y = -0.36x + 10$ **53.** $y = \frac{5}{2}x + \frac{3}{11}$
55. $y = -2x + 2; a = -3; b = -8$ **57.** Equation (b) does not belong because it has a negative slope.
59. $a = \frac{7}{5}, b = -\frac{7}{4}, m = \frac{5}{4}$ **61.** $a = -5, b = -14.4, m = -2.88$

Mixed Review **63.** Function **65.** Function **67.** Not a function
69. Domain $\{1\}$; Range $\{2, 6\}$ **71.** Domain R; Range $\{3\}$
73. 9.80 or more

LESSON 3-7

Try This **a.** Yes **b.** No **c.** No **d.** $y = -4x - 12$ **e.** Yes
f. No **g.** $y = -\frac{8}{7}x + \frac{6}{7}$ **h.** $y = \frac{1}{2}x + \frac{5}{2}$

Exercises **1.** Yes **3.** No **5.** Yes **7.** $y = -\frac{1}{2}x + \frac{17}{2}$
9. $y = \frac{5}{7}x - \frac{17}{7}$ **11.** $y = \frac{1}{3}x + 4$ **13.** Yes **15.** No
17. $y = \frac{1}{2}x + 4$ **19.** $y = \frac{4}{3}x - 6$ **21.** $y = \frac{5}{2}x + 9$
23. $y = -\frac{7}{3}x + \frac{22}{3}$ **25.** The side that contains (3, 4) and (6, 9) has slope $\frac{5}{3}$. The side that contains $(-2, 7)$ and (3, 4) has slope $-\frac{3}{5}$. Since $\frac{5}{3} \cdot \left(-\frac{3}{5}\right) = -1$, these two sides are perpendicular.
27. $y = -0.5x - 0.6$ **29.** Yes. If a slope is multiplied by its reciprocal, the product is -1. **31.** 2

Mixed Review **33.** No **35.** No **37.** No **39.** 22 **41.** 7
43. 102

LESSON 3-8

Try This **a. 1.** $R = -0.0079t + 10.43$ **2.** ≈ 9.76 s, ≈ 9.40 s
3. ≈ 2101 **b.** Answers may vary. $T = 5t + 50$; 90°; 2 min

Exercises **1. a.** $E = \frac{3}{20}t + 72$ **b.** 79.95 yr in 2003; 82.2 yr in 2018 **3. a.** $D = \frac{1}{5}t + 20$ **b.** 30.8 quadrillion joules in 2004; 33 quadrillion joules in 2015 **5. a.** $R = -0.075t + 46.8$
b. 40.65 sec in 2012, 41.325 in 2003 **c.** 2021
7. a. $C = 0.16m + 24$ **b.** \$56.00 **9.** Answers may vary. Samples: $P = 0.3663o + 1.56$; \$10.35; 45 oz **11.** 21.1°C
13. a. $f(x) = \frac{1}{3}x + 3\frac{1}{3}$ **b.** $4\frac{1}{3}$ **c.** 290 **15. a.** Plan A: $E = 600 + 0.04x$; Plan B: $E = 100 + 0.06x$ **b.** $x > 25{,}000$

Mixed Review **17.** 0 **19.** $y = x - 3$ **21.** $y = 2$ **23.** $5m$
25. $3t$ **27.** $33y$

Selected Answers

LESSON 3-9

Try This a. & b.

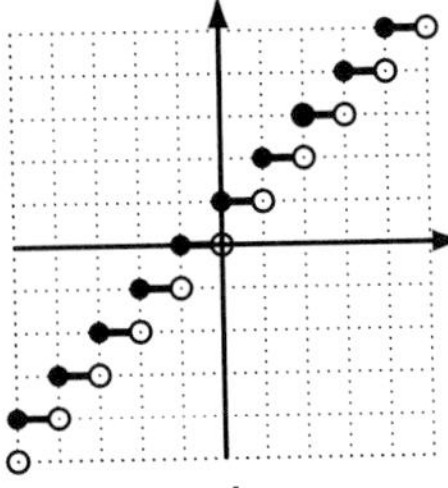

c.

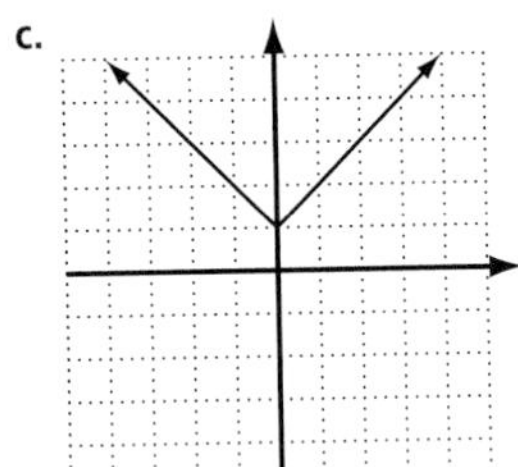

d.

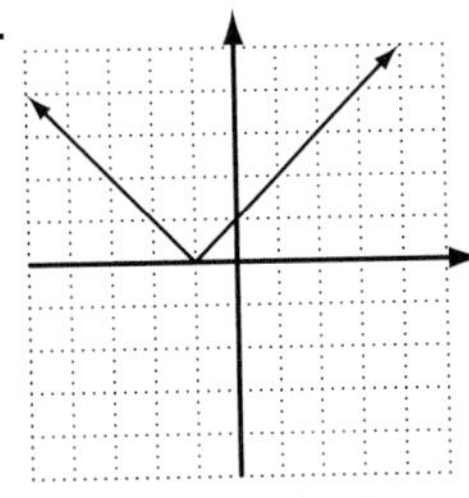

e. −10 **f.** −3 **g.** −7 **h.** −24 **i.** $-3x + 12$ **j.** $-3x - 4$ **k.** $9x$ **l.** $x - 8$

Exercises **1.**

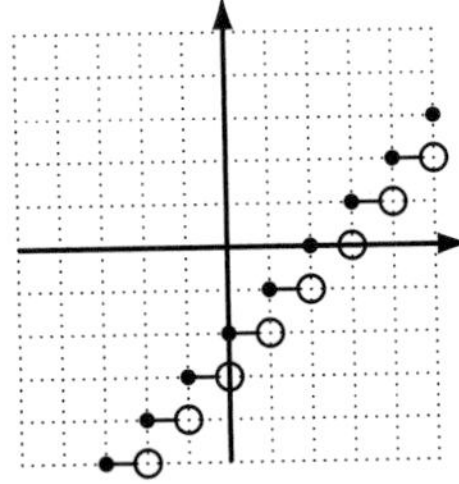

3.

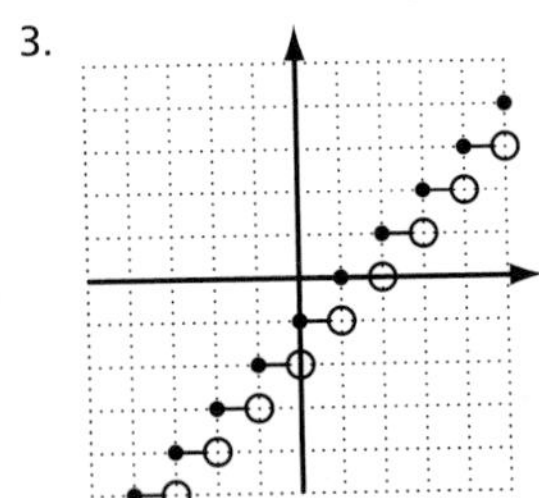

5.

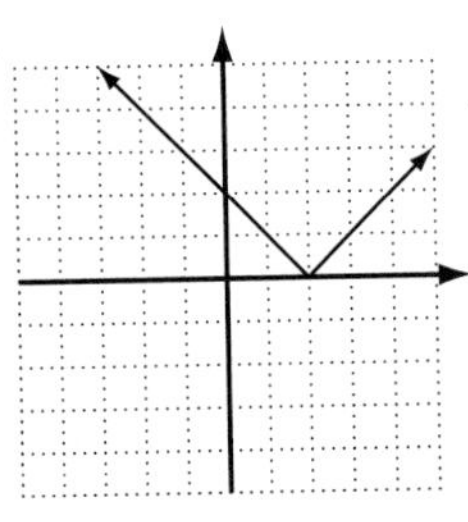

11. 0 **13.** 64 **15.** 35 **17.** −52 **19.** $4x - 1$ **21.** $x^2 - 1$ **23.** x^4 **25.** $16x$ **27.**

Domain: $\{x \mid x > 0\}$ Range: $\{y \mid y = 33 + 22n,\ n$ is a whole number$\}$ **29.** 10 **31.** 36 **33.** −49 **35.** −25 **37.** 38

39. $10x + 45$ **41.** $10x + 4$ **43.** a. $K(F) = \frac{5}{9}F + 255\frac{2}{9}$ b. 248 K **45.** *C*

47.

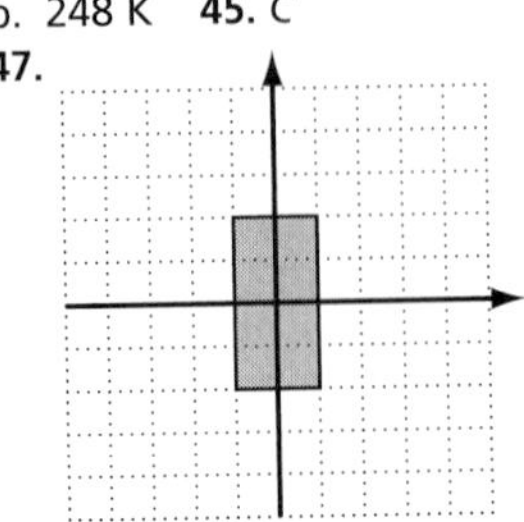

49.

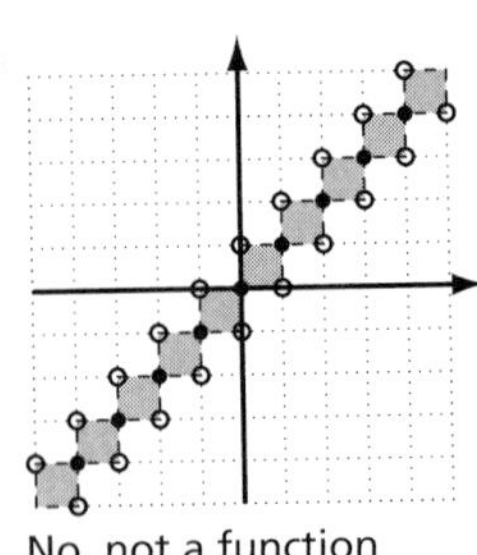

No, not a function

51. $a^2x + ab + b$

Mixed Review **53.** $y = x$ **55.** $\frac{1}{5^4}$ **57.** $\frac{m^2}{n^9}$ **59.** −1.87 **61.** $181.25

LESSON 3-10

Problems **1.**

$6 tapes	$4 tapes
8	0
6	3
4	6
2	9
0	12

The announcer could spend all of the money in 5 ways. **3.** There can be 11 rows of letters on the poster. **5.** There could be 60 people at the party. (Note: You can show that there could also be 59 people at the party. Since 2, 3, and 4 divide evenly into 60, each bowl of each type would be used with no extra dishes. For 59 people, 65 dishes would still be needed, but there would be extra dishes.) **7.** $1.19 (3 quarters, 4 dimes, 4 pennies, or 1 quarter, 9 dimes, 4 pennies) **9.** 27

Application

1. Rent a Roadster **3.** Rent a Roadster **5.** No situation

CHAPTER 3 WRAP UP

1. $\{(a, 1), (a, 2), (b, 1), (b, 2), (c, 1), (c, 2)\}$
2. $\{(1, 0), (1, -1), (1, -2), (0, -1), (0, -2), (-1, -2)\}$
3. Domain $\{-6, -1, 0, 1, 2\}$; range $\{-4, 1, 2, 4, 5\}$ **4.** (0, 3)

5.

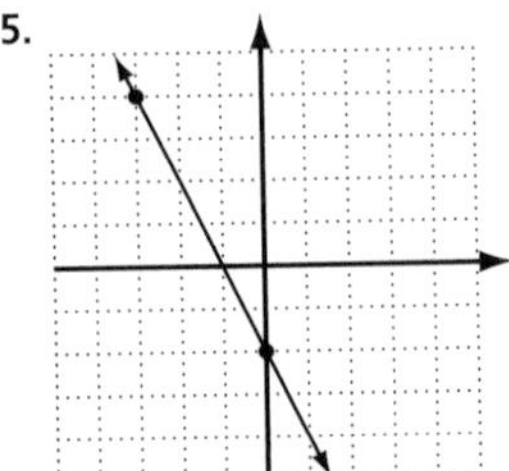

6.

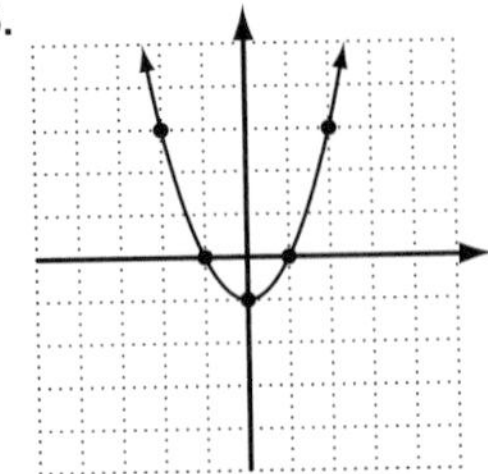

7. No **8.** Yes **9.** Yes **10.** No **11.** Yes **12.** No

13. 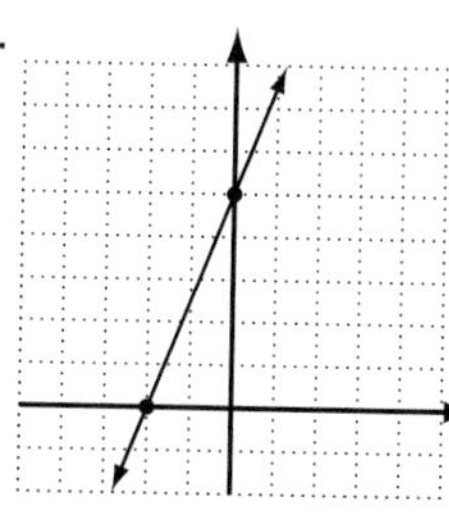

14. 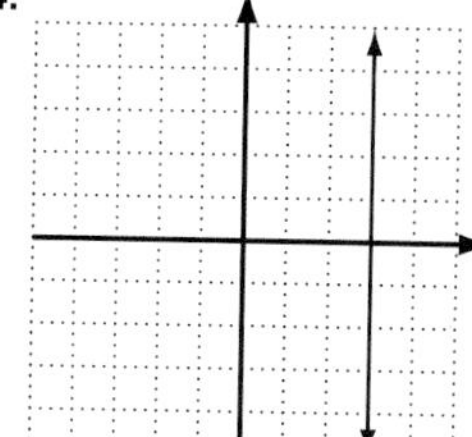

15. 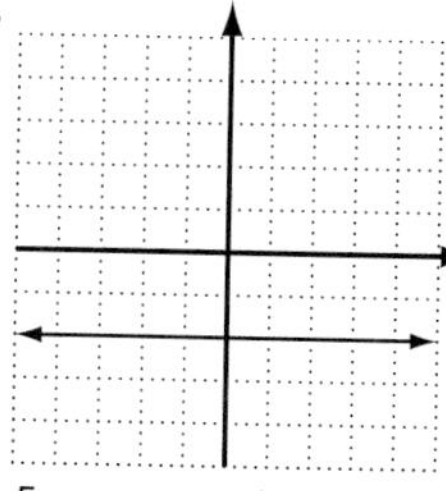

16. $\frac{5}{12}$ **17.** $y = \frac{1}{2}x + 4$ **18.** $y = \frac{5}{12}x - \frac{4}{3}$ **19.** $m = \frac{5}{2}$; $b = -2$ **20.** $5x - 3y + 4 = 0$; $m = \frac{5}{3}$ **21.** a. $y = -\frac{5}{3}x + 2$ b. $y = \frac{3}{5}x + \frac{44}{5}$ **22.** $R = -\frac{7}{250} \cdot t + 20.8$ **23.** 18.448 s **24.** 2002

25. 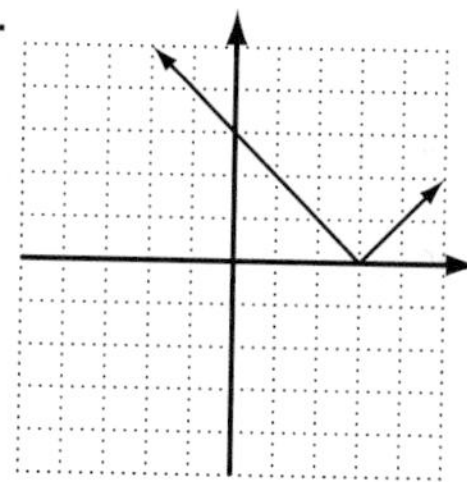

26. 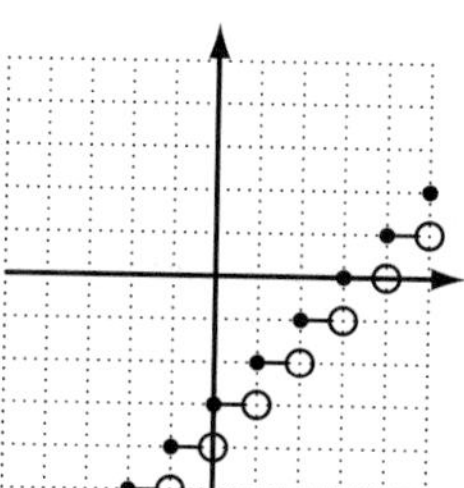

27. 16 **28.** 16 **29.** $2x^2 + 4x$

Chapter 4

Skills & Concepts You Need for Chapter 4

1. 8 **2.** -7 **3.** $-\frac{3}{4}$ **4.** 0 **5.** $-\frac{7}{12}$ **6.** 0 **7.** -12 **8.** 10 **9.** $-\frac{22}{15}$ **10.** 4.9

13. 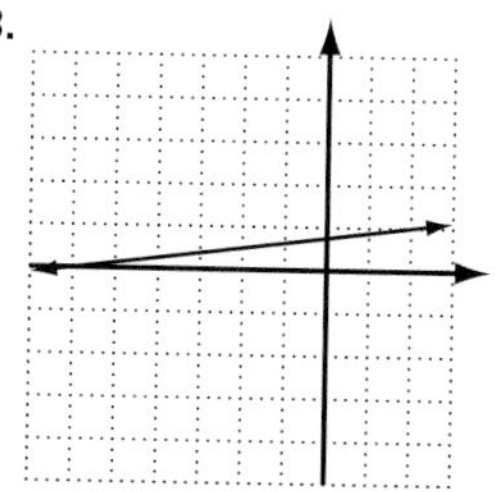

14. 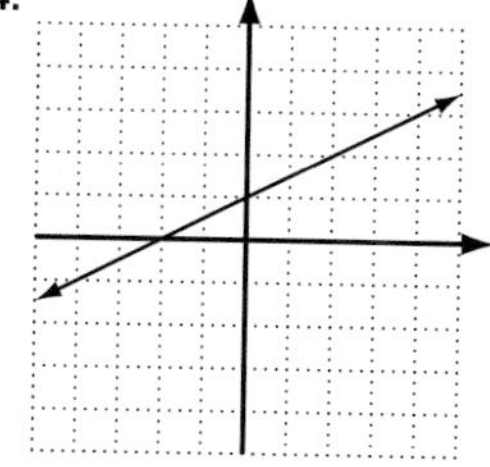

17. $y > -1$ **18.** $x > 4$ **19.** $x \leq 4$ and $x \geq -8$ **20.** $0 \leq x$ and $x < 7$ **21.** No

LESSON 4-1

Try This **a.** (4, 7) **b.** (3, −1)

Exercises

1. (3, 1) 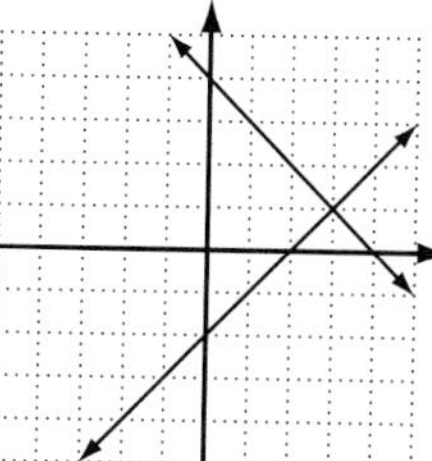

3. (3, 2) 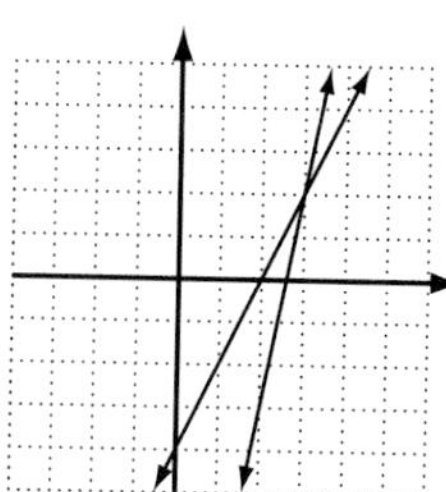

5. (1, −5) **7.** (2, 1) **9.** $\left(\frac{5}{2}, -2\right)$ **11.** (3, −2) **13.** No solution **15.** Answers may vary. **a.** $x + y = 6, x - y = 4$ **b.** $x + 2y = -1, x + 3y = 2$ **c.** $x + y = 3, x + y = 1$ **d.** $x + y = 3, 2x + 2y = 6$ **17.** $\{(x, y) | x = y \text{ and } x \geq 0\}$

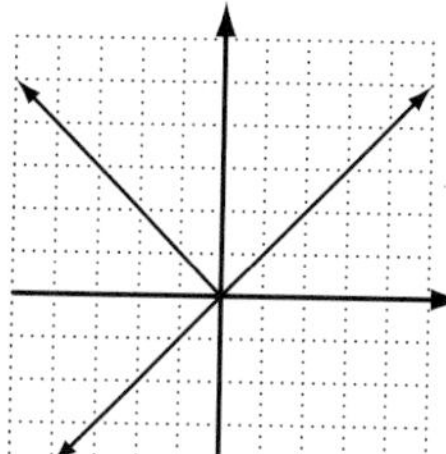

Mixed Review **19.** 15 **21.** 3 **23.** 21 **25.** $m = -2, b = 4$ **27.** $\left\{a \mid a > 2 \text{ or } a < -\frac{8}{5}\right\}$

LESSON 4-2

Try This **a.** (−3, 2) **b.** $\left(\frac{3}{8}, \frac{11}{8}\right)$ **c.** (1, 4) **d.** (−3, 1) **e.** (5, 3) **f.** (2, −1) **g.** (20, 3)

Cramer's Rule for Two Equations

a. (3.5, 2) **c.** (2.2, 4)

Exercises **1.** (2, −2) **3.** (−2, 1) **5.** (1, 2) **7.** (3, 0) **9.** (−1, 2) **11.** (−3, 2) **13.** (6, 2) **15.** (3, −3) **17.** $\left(\frac{1}{2}, -\frac{1}{2}\right)$ **19.** $\left(-\frac{4}{3}, -\frac{19}{3}\right)$ **21.** $\left(90\frac{10}{11}, -90\frac{10}{11}\right)$ **23.** $\left(-\frac{1}{4}, -\frac{1}{2}\right)$ **25.** {(5, 3), (5, −3), (−5, −3), (−5, 3)} **27.** $x = -\frac{4}{7}$ **29.** 0, 3

Mixed Review **31.** $0x + y + 7 = 0$ **33.** Not linear **35.** Linear

LESSON 4-3

Try This a. 35, 140 b. 30 L of 5%, 70 L of 15% c. 280 km

Selected Answers

Exercises **1.** 5, −47 **3.** 24, 8 **5.** 150 lb soybean meal, 200 lb corn meal **7.** 5 L of each **9.** \$4100 at 14%, \$4700 at 16% **11.** \$725 at 12%, \$425 at 11% **13.** 375 km **15.** $1\frac{3}{4}$ **17.** 8 white, 22 yellow **19.** 13 at \$9.75, 32 at \$8.50 **21.** Maria 20, Carlos 28 **23.** $l = 160$ m, $w = 154$ m **25.** $l = 31$ cm, $w = 12$ cm **27.** Irwin, 32 years; Lippi, 14 years **29.** 82 **31.** 137° **33.** $4\frac{4}{7}$ L

Mixed Review **35.** m^4 **37.** $w^6|w|$ **39.** $75a^2|a|$ **41.** −1 **43.** $y = -x + 3$ **45.** $x + 1$ **47.** $x + \frac{1}{2}$

LESSON 4-4

Try This **a.** $\left(2, \frac{1}{2}, -2\right)$ **b.** (1, −2, 3) **c.** (5, −1, 2)

Exercises **1.** (1, 2, 3) **3.** (−1, 5, −2) **5.** (3, 1, 2) **7.** (−3, −4, 2) **9.** (2, 4, 1) **11.** (−3, 0, 4) **13.** (2, 2, 4) **15.** $\left(\frac{1}{2}, 4, -6\right)$ **17.** $\left(\frac{1}{2}, \frac{1}{3}, \frac{1}{6}\right)$ **19.** $\left(\frac{1}{2}, \frac{2}{3}, -\frac{5}{6}\right)$ **21.** (1, −1, 2) **23.** (1, −2, 4, −1) **25.** $\left(-1, \frac{1}{5}, -\frac{1}{2}\right)$ **27.** False. Counter examples may vary. Sample: If $(x, y, z) = (1, 2, 3)$,

$x + y + z = 6$ $\quad 2x + 2y + z = 9$
$2x + y + z = 7$ $\quad 3x + 2y + z = 10$
$3x + y + z = 8$ $\quad 3x + y + 2z = 11$

29. $3x + 4y + 2z = 12$

Mixed Review **31.** $y = -\frac{1}{3}x + \frac{8}{3}$ **33.** $\{x \mid x \neq 0\}$ **35.** $-2x + 4y + 8 = 0$; $y = \frac{1}{2}x - 2$ **37. a.** $c = 4.5d + 15$ **b.** \$132

LESSON 4-5

Try This **a.** A: 112, B: 90, C: 85

Exercises **1.** 17, 9, 79 **3.** 4, 2, −1 **5.** A = 34°, B = 104°, C = 42° **7.** T = 25°, U = 50°, V = 105° **9.** \$21 on Thur., \$18 on Fri., \$27 on Sat. **11.** First score: 74.5, second score: 68.5, third score: 82 **13.** A: 2200, B: 2500, C: 2700 **15.** 20 **17.** 35 **19.** 8 mi/h, 15 mi/h, and 20 mi/h

Mixed Review **21.** 11 **23.** 6 **25.** Not parallel

LESSON 4-6

Try This **a.** Inconsistent **b.** Consistent **c.** Inconsistent **d.** Consistent **e.** Dependent **f.** Not dependent **g.** Dependent **h.** Not dependent

Exercises **1.** Inconsistent **3.** Consistent **5.** Consistent **7.** Inconsistent **9.** Consistent **11.** Dependent **13.** Not dependent **15.** Dependent **17.** Not dependent **19.** Dependent **21.** No solution **23.** No solution **25.** 21: Consistent and dependent 23: Inconsistent 24: Inconsistent **27.** There is no solution. Each vertex satisfies two equations, but not the third. The system is inconsistent. It is not dependent. **29.** 25 **31.** $\left(\frac{2y - 5}{3}, y\right)$

Mixed Review **33.** $\{x \mid x \neq 1 \text{ and } x \neq 0\}$ **35.** $m = -\frac{2}{3}, b = \frac{5}{3}$ **37.** 2

LESSON 4-7

Try This

a.

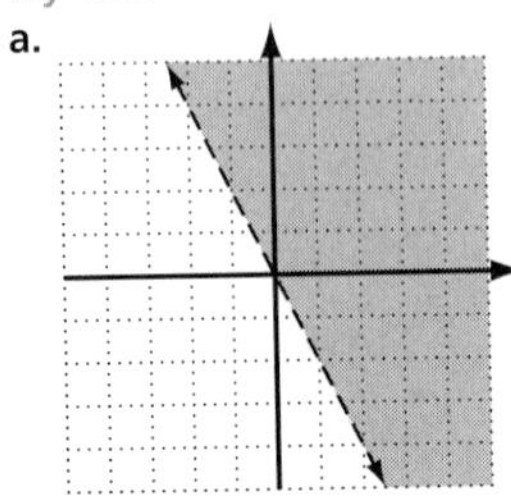

b.

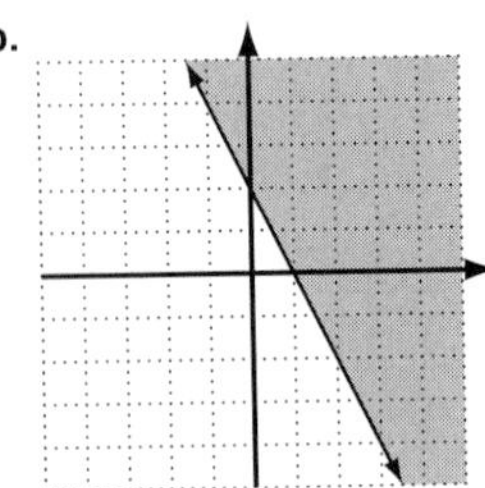

c.

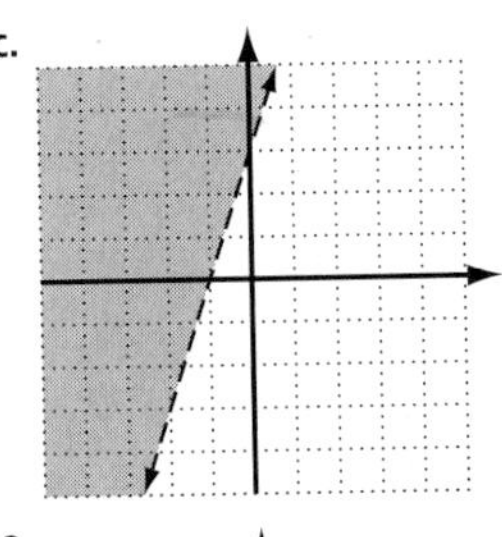

d.

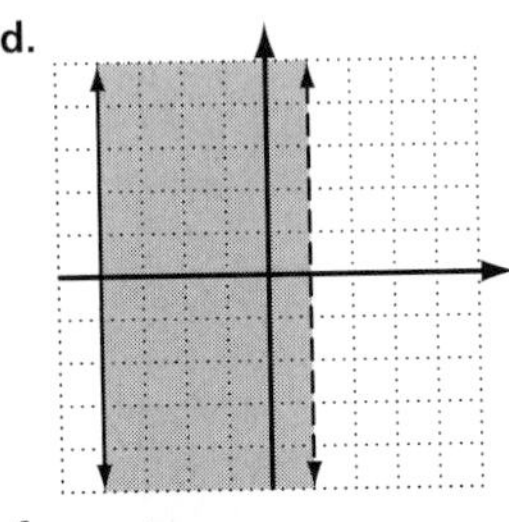

e.

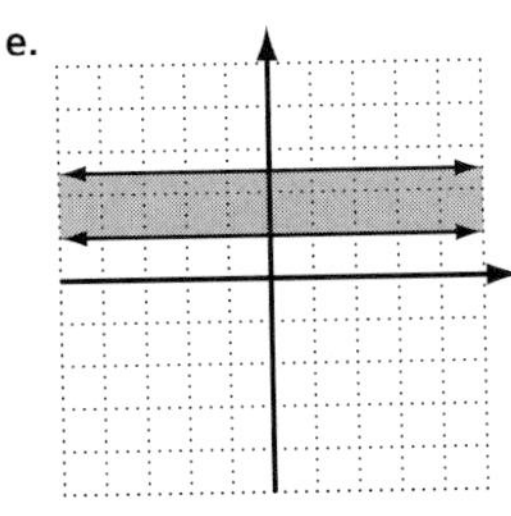

f.

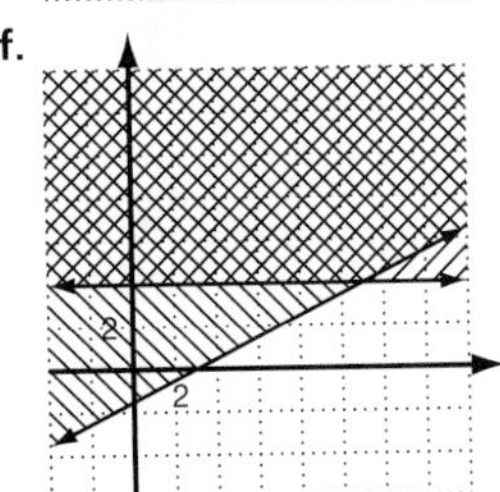

g.

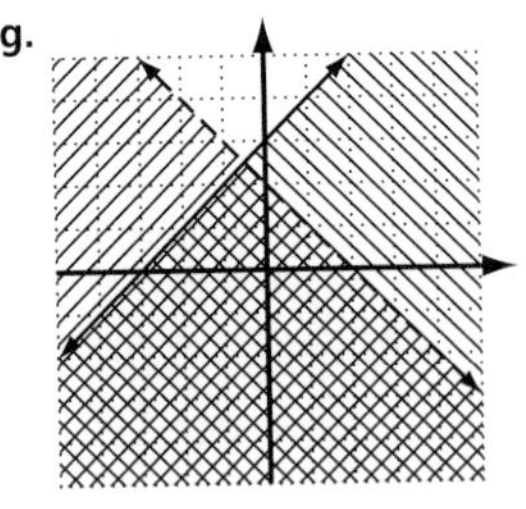

h.

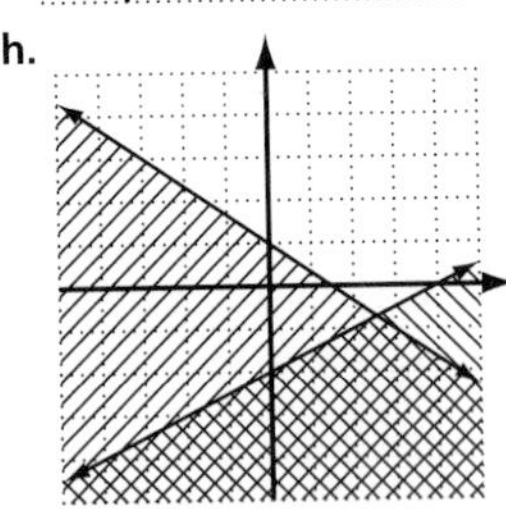

i. $\left(-\frac{1}{2}, \frac{3}{2}\right)$

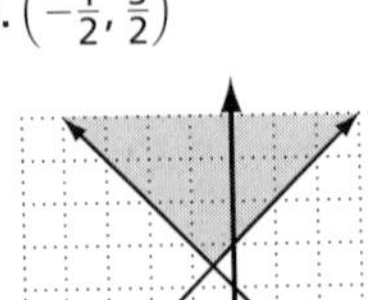

j. (0, 0), (0, 3), (4, 0), $\left(\frac{12}{5}, 3\right)$, $\left(4, \frac{5}{3}\right)$

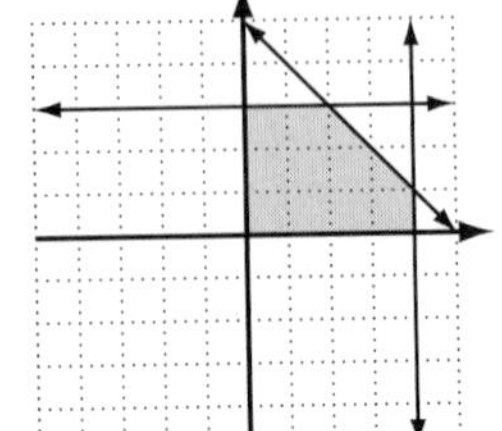

Exercises 1.

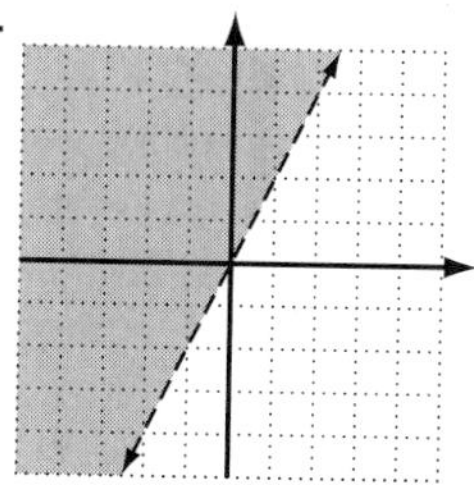

3.

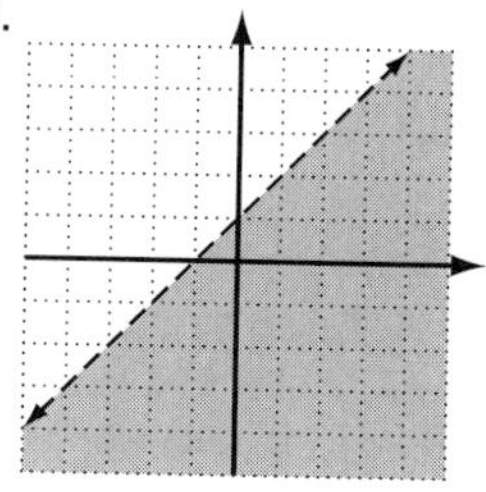

5.

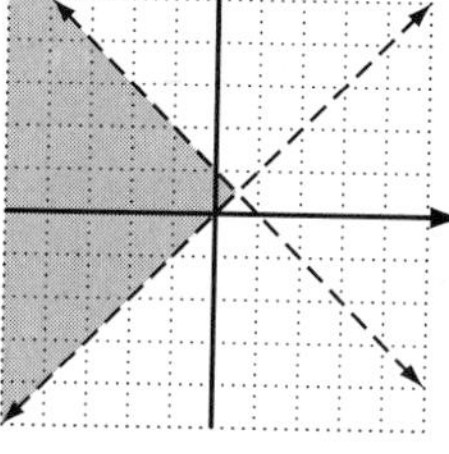

15.

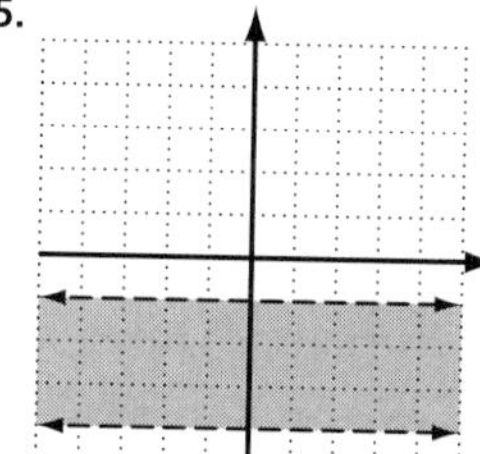

17.

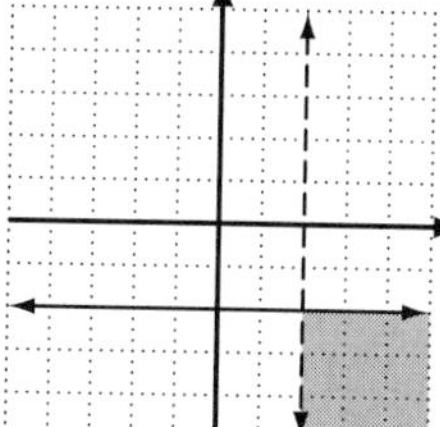

19.

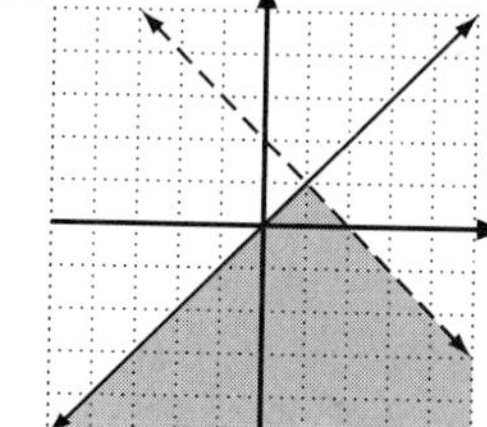

21.

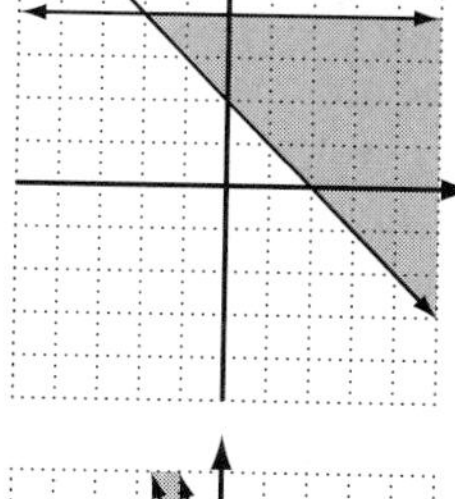

23.

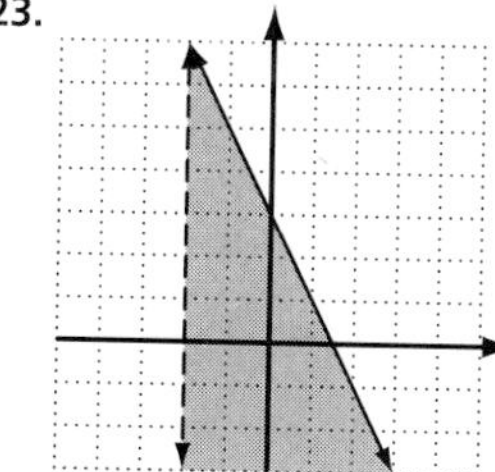

25.

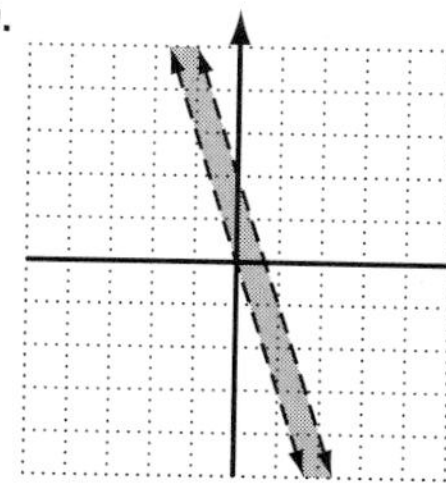

27.

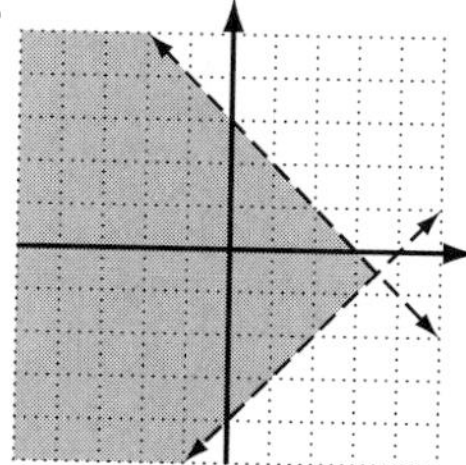

29.

31. (0, 0), (0, −3), (−4, −6), (−12, 0)

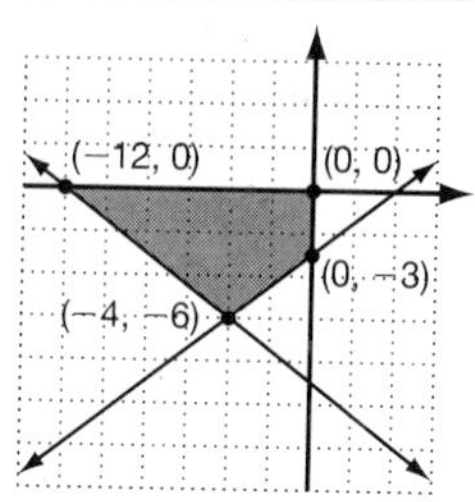

33. $\left(1, \frac{9}{4}\right), \left(1, \frac{25}{6}\right), \left(3, \frac{3}{4}\right), \left(3, \frac{5}{2}\right)$

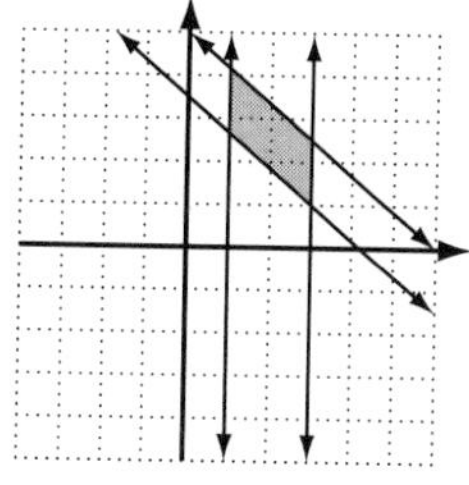

35.

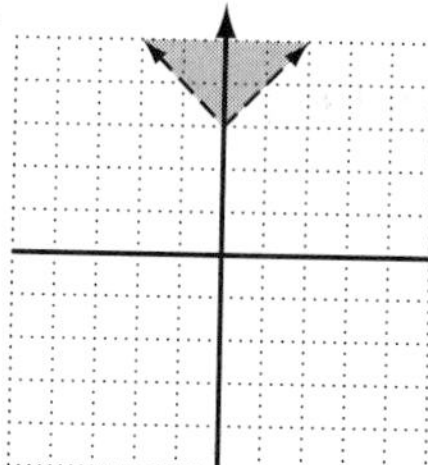

37.

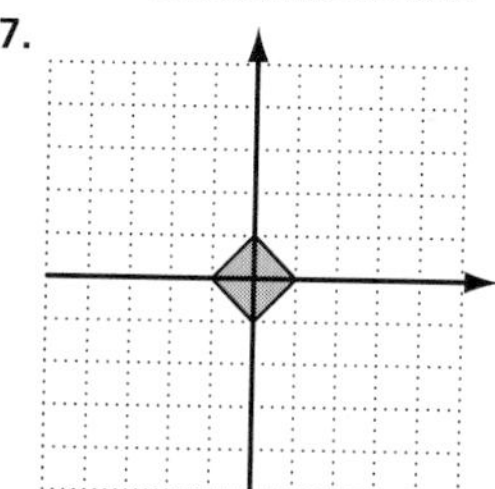

39.

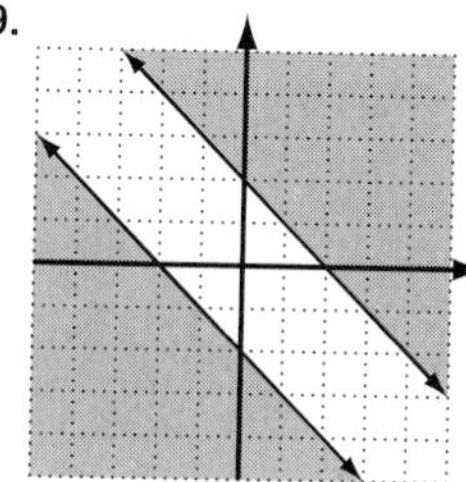

41. Yes, for example: $y > 2x + 1$ and $y < 2x + 1$.

Mixed Review **43.** $y = -2x + 4$ **45.** $y = \frac{4}{5}x - \frac{22}{5}$ **47.** −6

LESSON 4-8

Try This **a.** 40 hamburgers, 50 hot dogs

Exercises **1.** You must correctly answer 8 questions of type A and 10 of type B to maximize your score. The maximum score is 102. **3.** \$7000 should be invested at bank X and \$15,000 at bank Y to maximize his income at \$1395. **5.** The profit for (40, 120) or (60, 100) is \$16,000. Since the number produced must be an integer, the number of mopeds can be any integer from 40 to 60; the number of bicycles is 160 minus the number of mopeds.

Mixed Review **7.** 1 **9.** $c < 9$

Preparing for Standardized Tests

1. (A) **3.** (B) **5.** (A) **7.** (E) **9.** (E)

CHAPTER 4 WRAP UP

1. (0, 1) **2.** (3, 3) **3.** (−5, −1) **4.** (2, 4) **5.** (5, 2) **6.** (−6, 2) **7.** $\left(\frac{7}{5}, \frac{10}{3}\right)$ **8.** $\left(\frac{1}{3}, \frac{1}{2}\right)$ **9.** Carol's speed = 51 km/h; Ellie's speed = 68 km/h **10.** (1, −2, 3) **11.** $\left(2, -2, \frac{1}{2}\right)$

12. A = 31, B = 28, C = 27 **13.** Inconsistent **14.** Dependent

15.

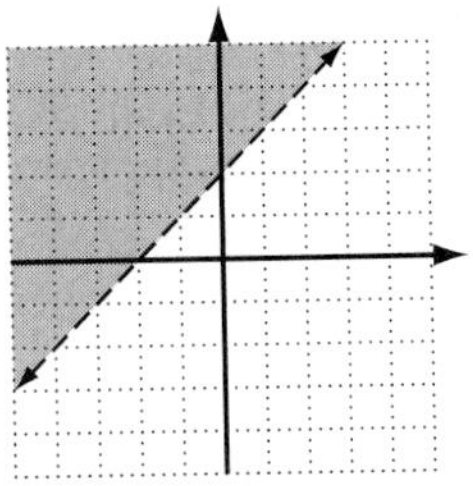

16.

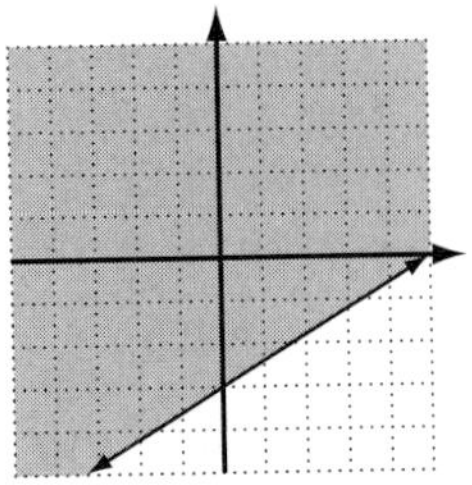

17.

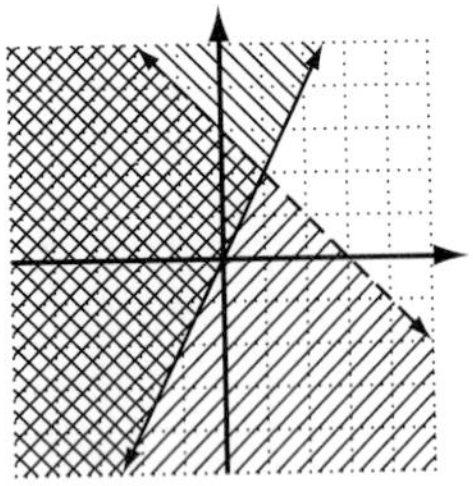

18.

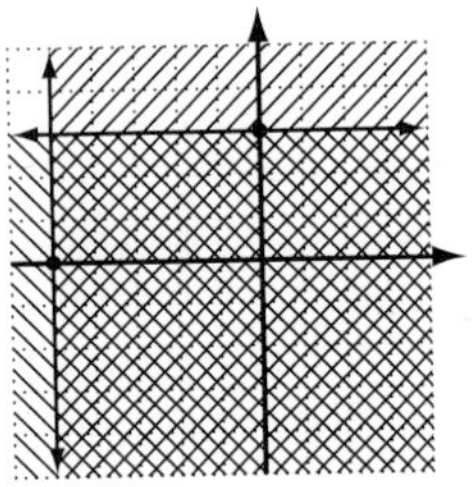

19. \$40,000 in municipal bonds, \$20,000 in mutual funds; \$6800 maximum income

CHAPTERS 1–4 CUMULATIVE REVIEW

1. $-\frac{107}{65}$ **3.** $17\frac{4}{31}$ **5.** 12.65 **7.** 12 **9.** -9 **11.** $11y - 7$ **13.** 5 **15.** \$260 **17.** $81x^4$ **19.** $-10x^{-3}y^7$ **21.** $\frac{1}{64}x^{-6}$ **23.** 1.5×10^{-3} **25.** -1 **27.** $7, -\frac{1}{2}$ **29.** $\frac{e}{c^2}$ **31.** $x > 7$ **33.** $x < \frac{12}{5}$ **35.** $-1 < x < \frac{5}{4}$;

37. $-\frac{1}{2} < x < \frac{1}{2}$ **39.** $x \leq 4$ or $x \geq 10$ **41.** {(−1, −1), (−1, 0), (−1, 1), (−1, 2), (−1, 3), (0, 0), (0, 1), (0, 2), (0, 3), (1, 1), (1, 2), (1, 3), (2, 2), (2, 3), (3, 3)}

43.

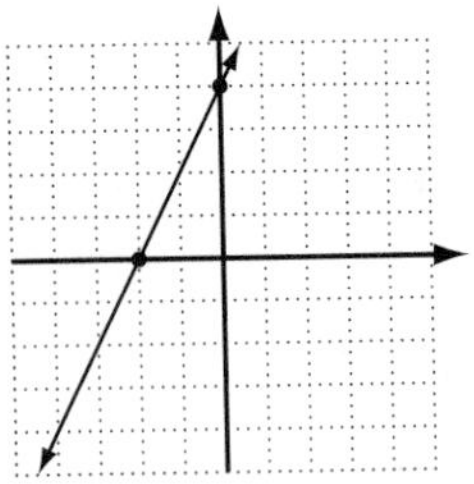

45. *R*

47.

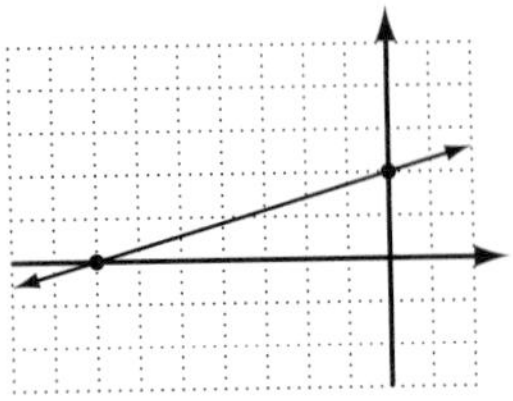

49. $8x + Y + 17 = 0$ **51.** Slope = $\frac{3}{5}$, *y*-intercept = $-\frac{8}{5}$ **53.** $2x - y = 7$ **55.** -20 **57.** $(-2, -3)$ **59.** Rice \$0.28/lb, seeds \$0.98/lb **61.** $(-2, 5, -1)$ **63.** Inconsistent

65.

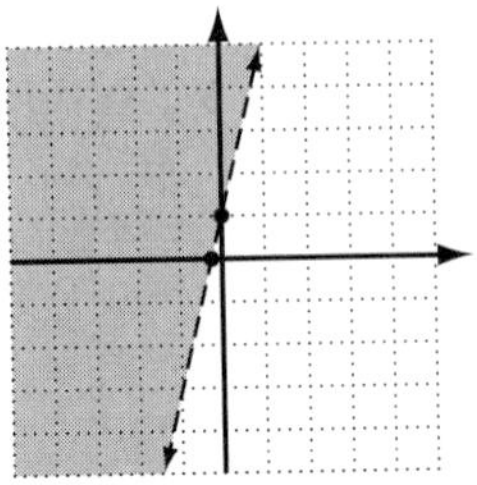

67. 0 windows, 6 doors

Chapter 5

Skills & Concepts You Need for Chapter 5

1. -2 **2.** $5(x + y)$ **3.** $5(2x + 3y - 1)$ **4.** $3y - 6$ **5.** $4x + 48$ **6.** $ct + cs - cf$ **7.** $5y$ **8.** $5a$ **9.** 0 **10.** $x - 4$ **11.** $-y + 2$ **12.** 3^3 **13.** $8a^9b$ **14.** $24x^{-12}y^2$ **15.** $9a^2$ **16.** $-8y^3$ **17.** 2^{-12} **18.** x^8 **19.** 3, -5 **20.** 0, -5

LESSON 5-1

Try This **a.** (1) 5 (2) 85 (3) -23 **b.** $3x^2 + 2x^4$ **c.** $9x^3y^2 - 2x^2y^3$ **d.** $7xy^2 + 3x^2 - y^2$

Exercises **1.** 54, 2 **3.** $-45, -\frac{235}{27}$ **5.** $2x^2$ **7.** $3x + y$ **9.** $a + 6$ **11.** $-6a^2b - 2b^2$ **13.** $9x^2 + 2xy + 15y^2$ **15.** $-4a^3 + 2a^2 - 7a + 5$ **17.** $8a^3 - 16a^2 + 6a - 7$ **19.** $55x^5 - 59x^4 + 14x^3 + 12x^2 + 18x + 175$ **21.** $29x^5 - 15x^4 + 86x^3 - 68x^2 + 50x + 25$ **23.** 160 **25.** 18,562.2 in.^{3} or 10.7 ft^3 **27.** 7.36% **29.** Answers may vary. **31.** 2 **33.** $\frac{n-5}{2}$ **35.** $x^2 + 4hx$ square units

Mixed Review **37.** $3m(2m + 1)$ **39.** $2a(b + 2c)$ **41.** $y = \frac{1}{2}x$ **43.** -0.5

LESSON 5-2

Try This **a.** $-4x^3 + 2x^2 - 4x - \frac{3}{2}$ **b.** $5p^2q^4 + p^2q^2 - 6pq^2 - 3q + 5$ **c.** $-5x^2t^2 + 4xy^2t + 3xt - 6x + 5$ **d.** $3x^2y - 5xy + 7x - 4y - 2$ **e.** $8xy^4 - 9xy^2 + 4x^2 + 2y - 7$ **f.** $7x^2y - 9x^3y^2 + 5x^2y^3 - x^2y^2 + 9y$

Exercises **1.** $3x^3 - x^2 + 7x$ **3.** $3x^2y - 5xy^2 + 7xy + 2$ **5.** $3x + 2y - 2z - 3$ **7.** $9.46y^4 + 2.5y^3 - 11.8y - 3.1$ **9.** $\frac{3}{4}x^3 + \frac{1}{4}x^2 + \frac{1}{16}x + \frac{23}{24}$ **11.** $4y^4 - 7y^2 + 2y + 1$ **13.** $-20x^4y^4 + 12x^3y^3 - 5x^2y^2 + 3xy - 19$ **15.** $-2x^3 - 6x^2 - x + 11$ **17.** $-4x^2 - 5y^2 + 3$ **19.** $6x^4 - 8x^2 + 9x - 4$ **21.** $0.06y^4 + 0.032y^3 - 0.94y^2 + 0.93$ **23.** $-\frac{4}{9}y^3 + \frac{4}{9}y^2 + \frac{26}{27}y + \frac{4}{9}$ **25.** $47x^{4a} + 40x^{3a} + 30x^{2a} + x^a + 4$

27. $x^{5b} + 4x^{4b} + x^{3b} - 6x^{2b} - 9x^b$
29. $5x^3y^2z - 4x^2y^2z^2 + 2xyz - 12x^3yz + 4x^2y^2z - xyz^2 - 9$
31. $17 - 30pq^2 + 8p^2qr + 3pqr$
33. $f(2) = 19, g(2) = -5, f(2) + g(2) = 14;$
$h(x) = 8x^2 - 6x - 6, h(2) = 14 = f(2) + g(2)$
35. $-2a^4 + 12a^3 + 3a^2$

Mixed Review **37.** $\frac{1}{64}$ **39.** $-2x - 4y + 6 = 0$ or $2x + 4y - 6 = 0$
41. -2 **43.** 10 **45.** 47

LESSON 5-3

Try This **a.** $3x^3y^2 + 4x^2y^2 - xy^2 + 6y^2$
b. $2p^4q^2 + 3p^3q^2 + 3p^2q^2 + 2q^2$ **c.** $2x^3y - 4xy + 3x^3 - 6x$
d. $15x^2 - xy - 6y^2$ **e.** $6xy - 40x + 60y - 400$
f. $16x^2 - 40xy + 25y^2$ **g.** $4y^4 + 24x^2y^3 + 36x^4y^2$ **h.** $16x^2 - 49$
i. $25x^4y^2 - 4y^2$ **j.** $4x^2 + 12x + 9 - 25y^2$ **k.** $25t^2 - 4x^6y^4$
l. $x^3 + 3x^2 + 3x + 1$ **m.** $x^3 - 3x^2 + 3x - 1$
n. $t^6 + 9t^4b + 27t^2b^2 + 27b^3$
o. $8a^9 - 60a^6b^2 + 150a^3b^4 - 125b^6$

Exercises **1.** $6x^3 + 4x^2 + 32x - 64$
3. $4a^3b^2 - 10a^2b^2 + 3ab^3 + 4ab^2 - 6b^3 + 4a^2b - 2ab + 3b^2$
5. $a^3 - b^3$ **7.** $4x^2 + 8xy + 3y^2$ **9.** $12x^3 + x^2y - \frac{3}{2}xy - \frac{1}{8}y^2$
11. $4x^3 - 4x^2y - 2xy^2 + 2y^3$ **13.** $4x^2 + 12xy + 9y^2$
15. $4x^4 - 12x^2y + 9y^2$ **17.** $4x^6 + 12x^3y^2 + 9y^4$ **19.** $9x^2 - 4y^2$
21. $x^4 - y^2z^2$ **23.** $9x^4 - 4$ **25.** $y^3 + 15y^2 + 75y + 125$
27. $m^6 - 6m^4n + 12m^2n^2 - 8n^3$ **29.** $\frac{1}{4}x^4 - \frac{3}{5}x^2y + \frac{9}{25}y^2$
31. $0.25x^2 + 0.70xy^2 + 0.49y^4$ **33.** $4x^2 + 12xy + 9y^2 - 16$
35. $16x^4 - y^4$ **37.** $16x^4 - 32x^3 + 16x^2$ **39.** $x^{4a} - y^{4b}$
41. a. \$1368.90 **b.** \$1367.63 **c.** \$1360.49
d. $b = 2, A(r) = 1000(r^2 + 2r + 1);$
$b = 3, A(r) = 1000(r^3 + 3r^2 + 3r + 1);$
$b = 4, A(r) = 1000(r^4 + 4r^3 + 6r^2 + 4r + 1)$
43. $16x^4 - 32x^3 + 16x^2$ **45.** $x^3 + y^3 + 3y^2 + 3y + 1$
47. $a^2 + 2ac + c^2 - b^2 - 2bd - d^2$ **49.** $y^{3+3n}z^{n+3} - 4y^4z^{3n}$

Mixed Review **51.** $(2c)^{-3}$ **53.** m^{-1} **55.** $-8x^{3+a}y^8$
57. $-3(c + 1)$

LESSON 5-4

Try This **a.** $3x(x - 2)$ **b.** $3y^2(3y^2 - 5y + 1)$
c. $3x^2y(2 - 7xy + y^2)$ **d.** $(x + 7)^2$ **e.** $(3y - 5)^2$ **f.** $(9y + 4x)^2$
g. Not a trinomial square **h.** $(4x^2 - 5y^3)^2$ **i.** $-3y^2(2x^2 - 5y^3)^2$
j. $(y + 2)(y - 2)$ **k.** $(7x^2 + 5y^5)(7x^2 - 5y^5)$
l. $(6x^2 + 4y^3)(6x^2 - 4y^3)$ **m.** $(x + 1 + p)(x + 1 - p)$
n. $(12 + x)(4 - x)$ **o.** $(x + 4)(x + 5)$ **p.** $(5y + 2)(y + 2)$
q. $(p - q)(x + y)$

Exercises **1.** y **3.** $3y$ **5.** x^2 **7.** 5 **9.** $4y^2$ **11.** $2x$ **13.** $5x^2y^2$
15. y **17.** $5a$ **19.** $(x - 4)^2$ **21.** $(x + 8)^2$ **23.** Not a trinomial square **25.** $(a - 2)^2$ **27.** $(y + 6)^2$ **29.** $a(a + 12)^2$
31. $5(2y + 5)^2$ **33.** $2(4x + 3)^2$ **35.** $(5y - 8)^2$
37. $(y + 3)(y - 3)$ **39.** $(2a + 7)(2a - 7)$ **41.** $(10y + 9)(10y - 9)$
43. $8(x + y)(x - y)$ **45.** $5(x^2 + y^2)(x + y)(x - y)$
47. $a^2(3a + b)(3a - b)$ **49.** $(x - y - 5)(x - y + 5)$
51. $3(2x + 1 - y)(2x + 1 + y)$ **53.** $(4 - x + y)(4 + x - y)$
55. $(x + w)(y + z)$ **57.** $(y - 1)(y - 8)$ **59.** $(2y^2 + 5)(y^2 + 3)$
61. $\frac{1}{7}x(4x^5 - 6x^3 + x - 3)$ **63.** $(0.5 + y)(0.5 - y)$
65. $\left(\frac{1}{5} + x\right)\left(\frac{1}{5} - x\right)$ **67.** Answers may vary.
69. $(x^a - y)(x^a + y)$ **71.** $(x + a)(x + b)$ **73.** $(bx + a)(dx + c)$
75. $x^{a-b}(4x^{2b} + 7)$

Mixed Review **77.** 1 **79.** -8 **81.** -11 **83.** $m = 3, b = -1$
85. $m = \frac{1}{2}, b = 0$ **87.** 2

LESSON 5-5

Try This **a.** $(10x + 1)(100x^2 - 10x + 1)$
b. $(y + 4x)(y^2 - 4xy + 16x^2)$ **c.** $(x - 2)(x^2 + 2x + 4)$
d. $(3y - 2x)(9y^2 + 6xy - 4x^2)$ **e.** $(x + 7)(x - 2)$
f. $(x - 7)(x - 3)$ **g.** $(y - 2)(y + 1)$ **h.** $(y + 16)(y + 2)$
i. $(3x + 2)(x + 1)$ **j.** $(2x + 3)(2x - 1)$ **k.** $2(4y - 1)(3y - 5)$
l. $(2x^2y^3 + 5)(x^2y^3 - 4)$

Exercises **1.** $(x + 2)(x^2 - 2x + 4)$ **3.** $(y - 4)(y^2 + 4y + 16)$
5. $(w + 1)(w^2 - w + 1)$ **7.** $(2a + 1)(4a^2 - 2a + 1)$
9. $(y - 2)(y^2 + 2y + 4)$ **11.** $(2 - 3b)(4 + 6b + 9b^2)$
13. $(4y + 1)(16y^2 - 4y + 1)$ **15.** $(7x + 3)(49x^2 - 21x + 9)$
17. $(a - b)(a^2 + ab + b^2)$ **19.** $\left(a + \frac{1}{2}b\right)\left(a^2 - \frac{1}{2}ab + \frac{1}{4}b^2\right)$
21. $(2x - 3y)(4x^2 + 6xy + 9y^2)$ **23.** $(y + 5)(y + 3)$
25. $(a - 5)^2$ **27.** $(t - 5)(t + 3)$ **29.** $(x - 4)(x + 2)$
31. $(y + 8)(y + 4)$ **33.** $(x + 8)(x - 5)$ **35.** $(y - 5)(y - 9)$
37. $(x + 3)(x - 2)$ **39.** $(y + 7)(y + 1)$ **41.** $(8 - x)(7 + x)$
43. $(3b + 2)(b + 2)$ **45.** $(3y - 2)(2y + 1)$ **47.** $(6a + 5)(a - 2)$
49. $(3a + 4)(3a - 2)$ **51.** $(3x + 2)(x - 6)$ **53.** $(3x - 5)(2x + 3)$
55. $(3a - 4)(a - 2)$ **57.** $(5t - 3)(t + 1)$ **59.** $4(2x + 1)(x - 4)$
61. $x(3x + 1)(x - 2)$ **63.** $(24x + 1)(x - 2)$ **65.** $(5y + 4)(2y + 3)$
67. $(6y + 5)(4y - 3)$ **69.** $(4a - 3)(5a - 2)$
71. $(y^2 + 12)(y^2 - 7)$ **73.** $\left(y + \frac{4}{7}\right)\left(y - \frac{2}{7}\right)$ **75.** $(t + 0.9)(t - 0.3)$
77. $(2t + s)(t - 4s)$ **79.** $(9xy - 4)(xy + 1)$
81. $a(b + 5)(b^2 - 5b + 25)$ **83.** $2(y - 3z)(y^2 + 3yz + 9z^2)$
85. $(y + 0.5)(y^2 - 0.5y + 0.25)$
87. $(5c^2 - 2d^2)(25c^4 + 10c^2d^2 + 4d^4)$ **89.** $3(x - 11)(x + 15)$
91. $4y(y - 12)^2$ **93.** $(ax - by)(a^2x^2 + abxy + b^2y^2)$
95. $15t(t - 7)(t + 3)$ **97.** $(x^a + 8)(x^a - 3)$
99. $\left(\frac{2}{3}x + \frac{1}{4}y\right)\left(\frac{4}{9}x^2 - \frac{1}{6}xy + \frac{1}{16}y^2\right)$ **101.** $(4x + 1)(2x - 3)$; if we include negative factors $(-4x - 1)(-2x + 3) = -1(4x + 1)(-2x + 3) = (-1)^2(4x + 1)(2x - 3) = (4x + 1)(2x - 3)$. The negative factorization is equivalent.

Mixed Review 103. $(1, -3, 5)$ 105. $y = -x + 1$
107. 2×10^{-1}

LESSON 5-6

Try This **a.** $2(1 + 4x^2)(1 + 2x)(1 - 2x)$

Selected Answers

b. $7(a-1)(a-1)(a^2-a+1)(a^2+a+1)$
c. $(3+x)(4+x)$ **d.** $(c-d+t+4)(c-d-t-4)$
e. $5(y^4+4x^6)$ **f.** $3(2x+3)(x-2)$ **g.** $(a+b)(a-b)^2$
h. $3(x+3a)^2$ **i.** $(a+b-c)(a+b+c)$

Exercises **1.** $(x+12)(x-12)$ **3.** $3(x^2+2)(x^2-2)$
5. $(a+5)^2$ **7.** $2(x-11)(x+6)$ **9.** $(2c-d)^2$
11. $(x^2+2)(2x-7)$ **13.** $(4x-15)(x-3)$
15. $(m^3+10)(m^3-2)$ **17.** $(c-b)(a+d)$
19. $(m+1)(m^2-m+1)(m-1)(m^2+m+1)$
21. $(x+y+3)(x-y+3)$
23. $(a^4+b^4)(a^2+b^2)(a+b)(a-b)$
25. $(2p+3q)(4p^2-6pq+9q^2)$
27. $(4p-1)(16p^2+4p+1)$ **29.** $ab(a+4b)(a-4b)$
31. $(4xy-3)(5xy-2)$ **33.** $2(x+2)(x-2)(x+3)$
35. $2(5x-4y)(25x^2+20xy+16y^2)$ **37.** sometimes
39. $(5y^2-12x)(6y^2-5x)$ **41.** $3(a+b+c+d)(a+b-c-d)$
43. $(y^2+11)(2-y)(2+y)$ **45.** $y(y-1)^2(y-2)$
47. $c(c^W+1)^2$

Mixed Review **49.** $y=-2x-3$ **51.** 0 **53.** -1

LESSON 5-7

Try This **a.** 2, 4 **b.** 1, $-\frac{3}{4}$ **c.** -5 **d.** 0, 2 **e.** 0, -3 **f.** 3, 1, -1

Exercises **1.** -7, 4 **3.** 6 **5.** -5, -4 **7.** 0, -8 **9.** -3, 3
11. -6, 6 **13.** -9, 7 **15.** 7, 4 **17.** 8, -4 **19.** $\frac{3}{4}, \frac{1}{2}$ **21.** $-\frac{3}{4}, \frac{2}{3}$
23. -2, 2 **25.** $\frac{1}{2}$, 7 **27.** $-\frac{5}{7}, \frac{2}{3}$ **29.** 0, $\frac{1}{5}$ **31.** He did not use the principle of zero products. **33.** $-\frac{1}{8}, \frac{1}{8}$ **35.** 0, $\frac{1}{3}$, $-\frac{1}{3}$
37. -5, 4 **39.** -3, 15 **41.** 1 **43.** $-2a$, 3 **45.** a, $-a$

Mixed Review **47.** $(-1, 1)$ **49.** $(1, 2)$

LESSON 5-8

Try This **a.** 8 or -6 **b.** Length is 8 cm; width is 3 cm.

Exercises **1.** $\frac{7}{2}$ or $-\frac{3}{2}$ **3.** -12 or 11 **5.** Length is 12 ft; width is 7 ft **7.** Length is 100 m; width is 75 m **9.** 9 and 11
11. Height is 7 cm; base is 16 cm. **13.** (C) **15.** 9, 10, and 11; 3, 4, and 5 **17.** 15 m by 12 m **19.** 12 m

Mixed Review **21.** $9x^2y+2xy^2-xy-15$ **23.** $(x+2)(x-2)$
25. $2y(2y-1)$ **27.** -6

Preparing for Standardized Tests

1. (D) **2.** (E) **3.** (B) **4.** (C) **5.** (C) **6.** (A) **7.** (B) **8.** (B) **9.** (C)

CHAPTER 5 WRAP UP

1. -9 **2.** -102 **3.** $4a+7$
4. $-3x^2y+3xy+7xy^2$ **5.** $-4x^3+10x^2+2x+7$
6. $8a^4+6a^3+a^2-5$ **7.** $5p^3+pq+4pq^2+3pq^3-5q^2$
8. $-x^5+x^3+2x^2-18x+1$ **9.** $4y^4+16x^3y^3-13xy^2$
10. $13y^2-y+9$ **11.** $6p-10q+11r$ **12.** $4x^2+3xy+y^2$
13. $10a-4b-9c$ **14.** $-32x^3y^3$ **15.** $3x^3y+4x^2y+6xy-8y$
16. $-9x^2+6xy-3xz-8yz+20z^2$
17. $30y^6-2y^4-y^3+12y^2+45y-42$ **18.** a^3-b^3
19. $-9x^4y^6+4t^2$ **20.** $49x^2-70xy+25y^2$
21. $8x^3+12x^2+6x+1$ **22.** $8y(3x^2-5y)$
23. $7t^2(4t^2-5t+2)$ **24.** $(7y-9)(7y+9)$ **25.** $(3y-8)(3y+8)$
26. $xy(4x-y)$ **27.** $9(x+y)(x-y)$ **28.** $(x-y-3)(x-y+3)$
29. $(y-2-2x)(y-2+2x)$ **30.** $(2a-1)(4a^2+2a+1)$
31. $(5x-2y)^2$ **32.** $(x+y^2)(x^2-xy^2+y^4)$ **33.** $(a-4)(a-6)$
34. $(ab+3)(ab+4)$ **35.** $(9+x)(8-x)$ **36.** $(2y+1)(y-2)$
37. $(4x-3)(2x-3)$ **38.** $(x+9)(x-9)$ **39.** $3(x+3)(x-3)$
40. $2(2x+5)^2$ **41.** $4(y+7)(y-2)$ **42.** $y(x+4y)(x-4y)$
43. $(2x-3y)(4x^2+6xy+9y^2)$ **44.** $5(x+2)(x+3)(x-3)$
45. $(w+y)(k-t)$ **46.** 0, 8 **47.** $-\frac{1}{2}$, -4 **48.** -3, -4
49. 9 cm by 6 cm

Chapter 6

Skills & Concepts You Need for Chapter 6

1. $-\frac{31}{63}$ **2.** $\frac{34}{15}$ **3.** $-\frac{14}{3}$ **4.** $\frac{3}{14}$ **5.** $\frac{8}{9}$ **6.** $-\frac{14}{3}$ **7.** -3 **8.** -18
9. $4(x+y)$ **10.** $3(y+2)$ **11.** $c(x-r+w)$ **12.** $14xy^2$
13. $\frac{5x^4}{y^2}$ **14.** $16x^8y^{-16}z^{12}$ **15.** 3 **16.** $m=\frac{E}{c^2}$

LESSON 6-1

Try This **a.** $\frac{3x^2+2xy}{5x^2+4xy}$ **b.** $\frac{6x^3+4x^2-3xy-2y}{9x^2+18x+8}$ **c.** $\frac{5-2a}{b-a}$
d. $7x$ **e.** $2a+3$ **f.** $5y+8$ **g.** $\frac{3x+2}{x+2}$ **h.** $\frac{y+2}{y-1}$ **i.** $\frac{5(2x-3y)}{7(x+2y)}$
j. $\frac{3(x-y)}{x+y}$ **k.** $a-b$ **l.** $\frac{x-5}{x+3}$ **m.** $\frac{1}{x+7}$ **n.** y^3-9
o. $\frac{(x+5)}{2(x-5)}$ **p.** $\frac{2ab(a+b)}{(a-b)}$

Exercises **1.** $\frac{3x^2+3x}{3x^2+9x}$ **3.** $\frac{t^2-9}{t^2+5t+6}$ **5.** $a-2$ **7.** $\frac{x+2}{x-2}$
9. $\frac{p-5}{p+5}$ **11.** $\frac{y+6}{3(y-2)}$ **13.** $\frac{a^2+ab+b^2}{a+b}$ **15.** $\frac{(x+4)(x-4)}{x(x+3)}$
17. $\frac{y+4}{2}$ **19.** $\frac{(x+5)(2x+3)}{7x}$ **21.** $\frac{1}{x+y}$ **23.** 3
25. $\frac{(y-3)(y+2)}{y}$ **27.** $\frac{2a+1}{a+2}$ **29.** $\frac{(x+4)(x+2)}{3(x-5)}$
31. $\frac{x^2+4x+16}{(x+4)^2}$ **33.** $\frac{x-3}{(x+1)(x+3)}$ **35.** $\frac{m-t}{m+t+1}$
37. $\frac{x^2+xy+y^2+x+y}{x-y}$ **39.** Answers may vary.
41. By the definition of division, $\frac{ac}{bd}$ is that number which when multiplied by bd gives ac. We can show that $\frac{a}{b}\cdot\frac{c}{d}$ is that number by multiplying it by bd to get ac.

$\left(\frac{a}{b}\cdot\frac{c}{d}\right)(bd)=\left(a\cdot\frac{1}{b}\right)\left(c\cdot\frac{1}{d}\right)(bd)$	Division Theorem 1-2
$=\left\{\left[\left(ac\cdot\frac{1}{b}\right)\frac{1}{d}\right]d\right\}b$	Asso. and Com. prop. of mult.
$=\left(ac\cdot\frac{1}{b}\right)b$	Prop. of mult. inverses
$=ac$	Prop. of mult. inverses

Since $\left(\frac{a}{b} \cdot \frac{c}{d}\right)(bd) = ac, \frac{a}{b} \cdot \frac{c}{d} = \frac{ac}{bd}$. **43.** $\frac{a}{b} \div \frac{c}{d}$ is that number which when multiplied by $\frac{c}{d}$ gives $\frac{a}{b}$. We assert that $\frac{a}{b} \cdot \frac{d}{c}$ is that number by multiplying it by $\frac{c}{d}$.
$\left(\frac{a}{b} \cdot \frac{d}{c}\right) \cdot \frac{c}{d} = \frac{a}{b} \cdot \left(\frac{d}{c} \cdot \frac{c}{d}\right) = \frac{a}{b} \cdot 1 = \frac{a}{b}$

Mixed Review **45.** $-x^7 + x^4 + 4x^3y^3 + 2xy^2 - \frac{1}{2}$ **47.** $(x - 2 + y)(x - 2 - y)$

Connections: Calculus **a.** $f'(x) = 3x^2$ **c.** $f'(x) = 5x^4$

LESSON 6-2

Try This **a.** $\frac{12 + y}{y}$ **b.** $3x + 1$ **c.** $\frac{a - b}{b + 2}$ **d.** $\frac{y + 12}{x^2 + y^2}$ **e.** $\frac{2x^2 + 11}{x - 5}$ **f.** $\frac{11x^2}{2x - y}$ **g.** $\frac{9x^2 + 28y}{21x}$ **h.** $\frac{3y^2 + 12y + 3}{(y - 4)(y - 3)(y + 5)}$ **i.** $\frac{a + 12}{a(a + 3)}$ **j.** $\frac{2}{x - 1}$ **k.** $\frac{4y^2 - y + 18}{(y - 1)(2 - y)(y + 2)}$

Exercises **1.** $\frac{8y}{x}$ **3.** $\frac{7y}{x + y}$ **5.** $\frac{9xy}{x^2 + y^2}$ **7.** 2 **9.** $a + b$ **11.** $\frac{11}{x}$ **13.** $\frac{1}{x + 5}$ **15.** $\frac{x + y}{x - y}$ **17.** $\frac{3x - 4}{(x - 2)(x - 1)}$ **19.** $\frac{8x + 1}{x^2 - 1}$ **21.** $\frac{2x - 14}{15x + 75}$ **23.** $\frac{-a^2 + 7ab - b^2}{a^2 - b^2}$ **25.** $\frac{3y^2 - 3y - 29}{(y - 3)(y + 8)(y - 4)}$ **27.** $\frac{2x^2 - 13x + 7}{(x + 3)(x - 1)(x - 3)}$ **29.** 0 **31.** A **33.** $\frac{2y^2 + 3 - 7x^3y}{x^2y^2}$ **35.** $\frac{5y + 23}{5 - 2y}$ **37.** $\frac{x - y + x^2 + xy}{x + y - x^2 + xy}$ **39.** $\frac{a}{c} - \frac{b}{c} = ac^{-1} - bc^{-1} = (a - b)c^{-1} = \frac{a - b}{c}$ **41.** $\frac{x - 4}{x - 5}$ **43.** $\frac{x^2 - 30}{x^2 - 11}$
45. $8a^4, 8a^4b, 8a^4b^2, 8a^4b^3, 8a^4b^4, 8a^4b^5, 8a^4b^6, 8a^4b^7$

Mixed Review **47.** Dependent; $25x + 125y = 84$ **49.** 1, 11 **51.** 0, −1, 4

Graphing Rational Functions **1.** As x approaches 2 from the positive side, $f(x)$ becomes larger. As x approaches 2 from the negative side, $f(x)$ becomes smaller.

3. a.

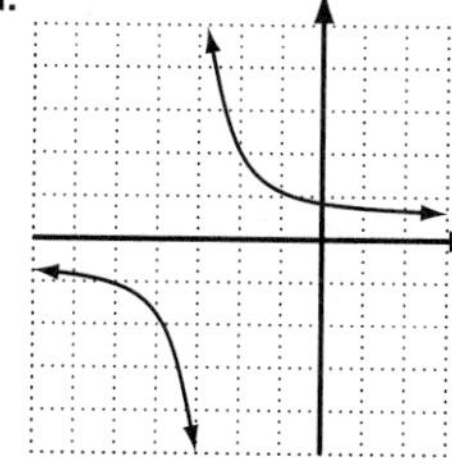

b.

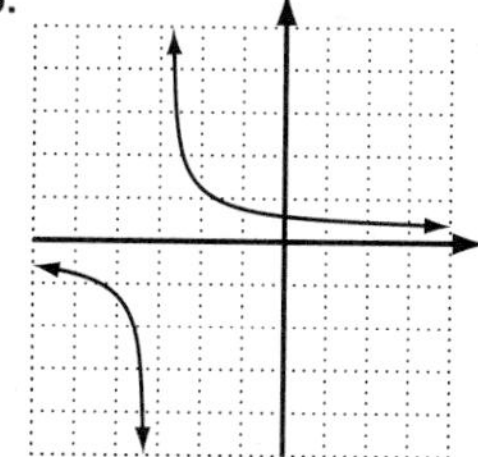

LESSON 6-3

Try This **a.** $\frac{14y + 7}{14y - 2}$ **b.** $\frac{x}{x + 1}$ **c.** $\frac{c + 1}{4}$ **d.** $a - b$ **e.** $\frac{y + x}{y + 3x}$ **f.** $\frac{x + 2}{(x - 2)(x - 1)}$

Exercises **1.** $\frac{1 + 4x}{1 - 3x}$ **3.** $\frac{(x + 1)(x - 1)}{x^2 + 1}$ **5.** $\frac{3y + 4x}{4y - 3x}$ **7.** $\frac{x + y}{x}$ **9.** $\frac{a^2(b - 3)}{b^2(a - 1)}$ **11.** $\frac{1}{a - b}$ **13.** $\frac{1 + x^2}{x}$ **15.** $\frac{y - 3}{y + 5}$ **17.** $\frac{1 + x}{1 - x}$ **19.** $\frac{5(y - x + 2)}{6(x + 2)}$ **21.** $\frac{x}{x + 1}$ **23.** a **25.** Answers may vary. **27.** $\frac{x - 1}{x}, x$

Mixed Review **29.** −6 or 7

LESSON 6-4

Try This **a.** $\frac{x^2}{2} + 8x + 3$ **b.** $4x^2 + x + 2$ **c.** $2x^6 + \frac{3}{2}x^5 + 3x^4 + 6x^3 + x^2 + \frac{1}{2}x + 1$ **d.** $5y^3 - 2y^2 + 6y$ **e.** $\frac{x^2}{2} + 5x + 8$ **f.** $4y^3 + y^2 + \frac{1}{2}y$ **g.** $x + 5$ **h.** $3y^3 - 2y^2 + 6y - 4$ **i.** $y^2 - 8y - 24$, R: −66 **j.** $y - 11 + \frac{3y - 27}{y^2 - 3}$

Exercises **1.** $6x^4 - 3x^2 + 8$ **3.** $y^3 - 2y^2 + 3y$ **5.** $1 - ab^2 - a^3b$ **7.** $x + 7$ **9.** No remainder **11.** Yes, R: 32 **13.** No remainder **15.** $y - 5$, R: −50 **17.** $y^2 - 2y - 1$, R: −8 **19.** $a^2 + 4a + 15$, R: 72 **21.** $16y^2 + 8y + 4$ **23.** $4x^2 - 1$, R: $-2x + 1$ **25.** $2y^2 + 2y - 1 + \frac{8}{5y - 2}$ **27.** $a^2 + ab$ **29.** $a^6 - a^5b + a^4b^2 - a^3b^3 + a^2b^4 - ab^5 + b^6$ **31.** $\frac{14}{3}$

Mixed Review **33.** $4n^8m^{-13}$ **35.** $\frac{9m^2n^4}{16}$ **37.** 1040 **39.** $(y + 6)^2$ **41.** $x(x - 7)$

LESSON 6-5

Try This **a.** Q: $x^2 + 8x + 15$, R: 0 **b.** Q: $8x + 12$, R: 40 **c.** Q: $x^2 - 4x + 13$, R: −30 **d.** Q: $y^2 - y + 1$, R: 0

Exercises **1.** Q: $x^2 - x + 1$, R: 6 **3.** Q: $a + 7$, R: −47 **5.** Q: $y^2 + 2y + 1$, R: 12 **7.** Q: $9x^2 + 12x + 40$, R: 120 **9.** Q: $x^2 + 3x + 9$, R: 0 **11.** Q: $5x + 8$, R: 24 **13.** No; it is not correct to subtract the 16 in column 2.

4	4	−4	4	−9
		16	48	208
	4	12	52	199

15. Q: $3x^3 + 7.23x^2 - 6.58x - 15.85$ R: −51.19 **17. a.** 218; −8992 **b.** 218; −8992 **c.** The answers are equal; the algorithms are equivalent. **19.** Q: $7x^6 + 6x^3 + 15$, R: 55

Mixed Review **21.** $\{x \mid x \neq -3\}$ **23.** $\{x \mid x \neq 0, x \neq -3\}$ **25.** $2(2x - y)^2$ **27.** $(3x - 1)(9x^2 + 3x + 1)$

LESSON 6-6

Try This **a.** $\frac{2}{3}$ **b.** $-\frac{120}{11}$ **c.** $y = 57$ **d.** No solution **e.** 3 **f.** −3, 4 **g.** $1, -\frac{1}{2}$ **h.** $1, -\frac{1}{2}$ **i.** $x = 7$ **j.** $x = -13$

Selected Answers

Exercises **1.** $\frac{51}{2}$ **3.** $\frac{40}{9}$ **5.** $-5, -1$ **7.** -1 **9.** $\frac{17}{4}$ **11.** No solution **13.** 2 **15.** $\frac{3}{5}$ **17.** 6 **19.** -145 **21.** $-\frac{10}{3}$ **23.** -3 **25.** $-6, 5$ **27.** No solution **29.** Yes **31.** All real numbers except -2 **33.** $-\frac{7}{2}$

Mixed Review **35.** $2.5y$ **37.** $\frac{x+3}{x-3}$ **39.** -1 **41.** -2.75

LESSON 6-7

Try This **a.** $2\frac{2}{5}$ h **b.** A, 32 h; B, 96 h **c.** 35.5 mi/h

Exercises **1.** $3\frac{3}{14}$ h **3.** $2\frac{2}{9}$ h **5.** C **7.** 22 h **9.** 2.475 h **11.** 12 km/h **13.** Train X, 80 km/h; Train Y, 66 km/h **15.** $1\frac{1}{5}$ km/h **17.** 3 km **19.** 90 km/h and 120 km/h **21.** 2 **23.** $-3, -7$ **25.** $\frac{13}{21}$ **27.** 48 mi/h **29.** $\frac{2}{3}$ h or 40 min **31.** $10{:}38\frac{2}{11}$ **33. a.** $1044\frac{5}{16}$ mi from San Francisco **b.** Return to San Francisco

Mixed Review **35.** $\frac{y^2-2}{y^2+2}$ **37.** $4(x+2)(2x-1)$ **39.** $(x+3)(x^2-3x+9)$ **41.** -6

LESSON 6-8

Try This **a.** $T = \frac{PV}{k}$ **b.** 6 cm

Exercises **1.** $d_1 = \frac{d_2W_1}{W_2}$ **3.** $t = \frac{2S}{V_1 + V_2}$ **5.** $r_2 = \frac{Rr_1}{r_1 - R}$ **7.** $s = \frac{Rg}{g-R}$ **9.** $r = \frac{2V - IR}{2I}$ **11.** $r = \frac{nE - IR}{In}$ **13.** $H = m(t_1 - t_2)S$ **15.** $e = \frac{Er}{R+r}$ **17.** $a = \frac{S - Sr}{1 - r^n}$ **19.** $\frac{120}{23}$ ohms **21.** 12 cm **23.** a. $t = \frac{ab}{b+a}$ b. $a = \frac{tb}{b-t}$ c. $b = \frac{ta}{a-t}$ **25.** $F = \frac{mv^2}{r}$; $r = \frac{mv^2}{F}$; $r = 2$ m

Mixed Review **27.** $42ab$ **29.** $-7, -3$

LESSON 6-9

Try This **a.** $k = 0.4, y = 0.4x$ **b.** $k = 0.6, y = \frac{0.6}{x}$ **c.** 50 volts **d.** $7\frac{1}{2}$ hours

Exercises **1.** $k = 8, y = 8x$ **3.** $k = 16, y = 16x$ **5.** $k = 5, y = 5x$ **7.** $k = 1, y = x$ **9.** $k = 60, y = \frac{60}{x}$ **11.** $k = 36, y = \frac{36}{x}$ **13.** $k = 9, y = \frac{9}{x}$ **15.** 6 amperes **17.** $\frac{2}{9}$ ampere **19.** 125,000 straws **21.** 160 cm^3 **23.** 532,500 tons **25.** 204,000,000 **27.** 50 kg **29.** 100 oz **31.** Always; $P = kQ$, so $Q = \frac{1}{k}P$, and $\frac{1}{k}$ becomes the constant of variation.

Mixed Review **33.** $7a^3b$ **35.** 2×10^{-2} **37.** $-8x^5y^{-1}$ **39.** $(x-3)(x^2+3x+9)$ **41.** $3x^2(2x^2 - x + 6)$

LESSON 6-10

Problems **1.** Observing the pattern in B_1 through B_4, the number of rows equals the number of the term, and there is one more column than row. So there are $10(10 + 1) = 10 \times 11 = 110$ dots in B_{10}. **3.** One can buy one 3-lb and nine 5-lb bags, or six of each, or eleven 3-lb bags and three 5-lb bags, or sixteen 3-lb bags. **5.** One worked 10 days and the other worked 15 days. **7.** They could have scored 34 points 7 different ways.

CHAPTER 6 WRAP UP

1. $\frac{4y^2 - 3y}{2y^2 + 5y}$ **2.** $\frac{4x^3 - 3x^2 - 4x + 3}{x^3 + 5x^2 - x - 5}$ **3.** $\frac{3(a-b)}{4(a+b)}$ **4.** $\frac{3x+2}{4x+5}$ **5.** $\frac{(x-4)(2x-1)}{4x^2 - 2x + 1}$ **6.** $\frac{2(2y+1)}{y-3}$ **7.** $\frac{-4a+21}{a+3}$ **8.** $\frac{2}{y-3}$ **9.** $\frac{-x^2 + 16x + 50}{(x+9)(x-9)(3x+2)}$ **10.** $\frac{34y^2 + 21y - 1}{3y(y-1)(y+1)}$ **11.** $\frac{b+a}{b-a}$ **12.** $\frac{x+4}{x-3}$ **13.** $\frac{ab}{b+a}$ **14.** $5y^2 - 4y + 6$ **15.** $2x^3 + 3x^2 + 2x + 4 + \frac{2}{2x-3}$ **16.** Q: $x^3 - x^2 - 2x - 6$, R: -8 **17.** Q: $3x^2 + 2x - 2$, R: -1 **18.** 3 **19.** $5, -3$ **20.** 3 **21.** 30 km/h and 20 km/h **22.** $13\frac{7}{11}$ h **23.** 84 mi/h **24.** $p = \frac{mn}{T - Rn}$ **25.** $q = \frac{fp}{p-f}$ **26.** $y = 4.5x$ **27.** 168.75 kg **28.** $y = \frac{288}{x}$ **29.** 40 days

Chapter 7

Skills & Concepts You Need for Chapter 7 **1.** 8 **2.** 0 **3.** $\sqrt{3}$ **4.** y^{10} **5.** 8 **6.** $12x^5y^{-2}$ **7.** 4^6 **8.** 3^2 **9.** $8x^{-1}y^6$ **10.** 4^8 **11.** a^{12} **12.** $64x^3y^{-9}$ **13.** $100x^6y^{-4}z^{-8}$ **14.** 8 **15.** $-\frac{14}{11}$ **16.** $5, -3$ **17.** $-5, 7$ **18.** $2 + 5y - 12y^2$ **19.** $9x^2 + 48x + 64$ **20.** $4x^2 - 9$ **21.** $(x+1)(x-1)$ **22.** $(4x^2 - 5y^4)^2$ **23.** $-3(3x-2)^2$ **24.** $(x-4)(x-9)$

LESSON 7-1

Try This **a.** $3, -3$ **b.** $6, -6$ **c.** $11, -11$ **d.** 1 **e.** -6 **f.** $\frac{9}{10}$ **g.** -0.08 **h.** 24 **i.** $5|y|$ **j.** $4|y|$ **k.** $|x+7|$ **l.** -4 **m.** $3y$ **n.** $-\frac{7}{4}$ **o.** $b^5 = a$ **p.** $c^{12} = 63$ **q.** $n^9 = 16a$ **r.** -3 **s.** -3 **t.** $-2x$ **u.** $3x + 2$ **v.** 3 **w.** -3 **x.** No real root **y.** $2|x-2|$ **z.** $|x+3|$

Exercises **1.** $4, -4$ **3.** $3, -3$ **5.** $\frac{7}{6}, -\frac{7}{6}$ **7.** 15 **9.** $-\frac{19}{3}$ **11.** 0.3 **13.** $4|x|$ **15.** $5|t|$ **17.** $|a+1|$ **19.** $|x-2|$ **21.** $-4x$ **23.** 10 **25.** $0.7(x+1)$ **27.** $p^4 = 10$ **29.** $r^{28} = 500h$ **31.** 5 **33.** -1 **35.** $-\frac{2}{3}$ **37.** $|x|$ **39.** $5|a|$ **41.** $x - 2$ **43. a.** 13 spaces **b.** 15 spaces **c.** 18 spaces **d.** 20 spaces **45.** All real numbers **47.** $\{x \mid x \leq \frac{4}{3}\}$ **49.** All real numbers **51.** $\{x \mid x \geq 0 \text{ and } x \neq \frac{5}{2}\}$ **53.** $\{x \mid x > 0\}$

Mixed Review **55.** 4, −1 **57.** 3 or −2

LESSON 7-2

Try This **a.** $\sqrt{133}$ **b.** $\sqrt{x^2 - 4y^2}$ **c.** $\sqrt[4]{2821}$ **d.** $\sqrt[3]{8x^5 + 40x}$ **e.** $4\sqrt{2}$ **f.** $2\sqrt[3]{10}$ **g.** $10\sqrt{3}$ **h.** $|x + 2|\sqrt{3}$ **i.** $2|bc|\sqrt{3ab}$ **j.** $2\sqrt[3]{2}$ **k.** $3|x|y^2$ **l.** $(a + b)\sqrt[3]{a + b}$ **m.** $3\sqrt{2}$ **n.** $6|y|\sqrt{7}$ **o.** $3\sqrt[3]{4x^2y^2}$ **p.** $7\sqrt{3ab}$

Exercises **1.** $\sqrt{6}$ **3.** $\sqrt[3]{10}$ **5.** $\sqrt[4]{72}$ **7.** $\sqrt{\frac{6y}{5x}}$ **9.** $\sqrt[5]{18t^3}$ **11.** $\sqrt{x^2 - a^2}$ **13.** $\sqrt[3]{0.06x^2}$ **15.** $2\sqrt{6}$ **17.** $6x^2\sqrt{5}$ **19.** $3x^2\sqrt[3]{2x^2}$ **21.** $2\sqrt[4]{2}$ **23.** $3|cd|\sqrt[4]{2d^2}$ **25.** $(x + y)\sqrt[3]{x + y}$ **27.** $3\sqrt{2}$ **29.** 8 **31.** $2x^2|y|\sqrt{6}$ **33.** $25t^3\sqrt[3]{t}$ **35.** $(x + y)^2\sqrt[3]{(x + y)^2}$ **37.** 37.4 mi/h **39.** Answers may vary. Examples are $\sqrt{125} \cdot \sqrt{2}$, $\sqrt{25} \cdot \sqrt{10}$, and $\sqrt{50} \cdot \sqrt{5}$. **41.** −16.6°C

Mixed Review **43.** $2(2x + 1)(x + 1)$ **45.** $3a(3a - 1)$ **47.** $3y + 2$, *R*: −2

LESSON 7-3

Try This **a.** $\frac{5}{6}$ **b.** $\frac{10}{3}$ **c.** $\frac{|x|}{10}$ **d.** $\frac{2|a|\sqrt{a}}{b^2}$ **e.** 5 **f.** $56\sqrt{xy}$ **g.** $\frac{20}{7}$ **h.** $\frac{2ab}{3}$ **i.** $13\sqrt{2}$ **j.** $10\sqrt[4]{5x} - \sqrt{7}$ **k.** $19\sqrt{5}$ **l.** $(3y + 4)\sqrt[3]{y^2} + 2y^2$ **m.** $2\sqrt{x - 1}$ **n.** $3\left(\sqrt[3]{2} - \sqrt{6}\right)$

Exercises **1.** $\frac{4}{5}$ **3.** $\frac{4}{3}$ **5.** $\frac{11}{|x|}$ **7.** $\frac{5|y|\sqrt{y}}{x^2}$ **9.** $\frac{2x\sqrt[3]{x^2}}{3y}$ **11.** $\sqrt{7}$ **13.** 3 **15.** $|y|\sqrt{5y}$ **17.** $2\sqrt[3]{a^2b}$ **19.** $3\sqrt{xy}$ **21.** $\sqrt{x^2 + xy + y^2}$ **23.** $8\sqrt{3}$ **25.** $3\sqrt[3]{5}$ **27.** $13\sqrt[3]{y}$ **29.** $7\sqrt{2}$ **31.** $6\sqrt[3]{5}$ **33.** $23\sqrt{2}$ **35.** $21\sqrt{3}$ **37.** $38\sqrt{5}$ **39.** $122\sqrt{2}$ **41.** $9\sqrt[3]{2}$ **43.** $4\sqrt[3]{4}$ **45.** $29\sqrt{2}$ **47.** $10(a - 1)\sqrt[3]{a}$ **49.** $3\sqrt{2y} - 2$ **51.** $(|x| + 3)\sqrt{x - 1}$ **53.** 1.62 s **55.** 2.20 s **57.** $a = -b$, $a = 0$, or $b = 0$ **59.** D **61.** 0

Mixed Review **63.** $y = \frac{1}{2}x$ **65.** $y = \frac{4}{7}x$ **67.** 1.4×10^{-1} **69.** 4, −2 **71.** $\frac{5}{2}$, $-\frac{5}{2}$ **73.** 4 L of A, 8 L of B

LESSON 7-4

Try This **a.** $5\sqrt{6} + 3\sqrt{14}$ **b.** $3\sqrt{ab} - 4\sqrt{3a} + 6\sqrt{3b} - 24$ **c.** $20 - 4y\sqrt{5} + y^2$ **d.** $64 - 25|x|$ **e.** $\frac{\sqrt{6}}{3}$ **f.** $\frac{\sqrt{70}}{7}$ **g.** $\frac{\sqrt[3]{4}}{2}$ **h.** $\frac{2\sqrt{3ab}}{3|b|}$ **i.** $\frac{2x^2\sqrt{3xy}}{3y^2}$ **j.** $\frac{\sqrt[3]{28}}{2}$ **k.** $\frac{\sqrt[7]{192y^6x^5}}{2y}$ **l.** $-5(1 + \sqrt{2})$ **m.** $-\sqrt{2} + \sqrt{3}$ **n.** $\frac{\sqrt{15} + \sqrt{3} + \sqrt{5} + 1}{2}$ **o.** $\frac{3 - \sqrt{3}}{6}$

Exercises **1.** $2\sqrt{6} - 18$ **3.** $\sqrt{6} - \sqrt{10}$ **5.** $2\sqrt{15} - 6\sqrt{3}$ **7.** −6 **9.** $3a\sqrt[3]{2}$ **11.** 1 **13.** $|a| - |b|$ **15.** $1 + \sqrt{5}$ **17.** $7 + 3\sqrt{3}$ **19.** −6 **21.** $|a| + \sqrt{3a} + \sqrt{2a} + \sqrt{6}$ **23.** $2\sqrt[3]{9} - 3\sqrt[3]{6} - 2\sqrt[3]{4}$ **25.** $7 + 4\sqrt{3}$ **27.** $21 - 6\sqrt{6}$ **29.** C **31.** $\frac{\sqrt{66}}{6}$ **33.** $\frac{\sqrt{66}}{3}$ **35.** $\frac{\sqrt{6}}{5}$ **37.** $\frac{\sqrt[3]{9}}{3}$ **39.** $\frac{\sqrt[3]{63xy^2}}{3y}$ **41.** $\frac{a\sqrt[3]{147ab}}{7b}$ **43.** $\frac{\sqrt[3]{a^2b^2}}{ab}$ **45.** $\frac{7(9 - \sqrt{10})}{71}$ **47.** $\frac{3\sqrt{2}(\sqrt{3} + \sqrt{5})}{2}$ **49.** $-\frac{3\sqrt{2} + 2\sqrt{42} - 3\sqrt{15} - 6\sqrt{35}}{25}$ **51.** $\frac{|a| + 2\sqrt{ab} + |b|}{|a| - |b|}$ **53.** $\frac{4\sqrt{6} + 9}{3}$ **55.** $\frac{2}{\sqrt{6}}$ **57.** $\frac{7}{\sqrt[3]{98}}$ **59.** $\frac{5y^2}{x\sqrt[3]{150x^2y^2}}$ **61.** $\frac{-22}{\sqrt{6} + 5\sqrt{2} + 5\sqrt{3} + 25}$ **63.** $|x + 3| - 9$ **65.** Answers may vary. Samples: $(\sqrt{15} + \sqrt{7})(\sqrt{15} - \sqrt{7})$; $(\sqrt{10} + \sqrt{2})(\sqrt{10} - \sqrt{2})$ **67.** $\frac{x}{|x|}$ **69.** $\frac{\sqrt{p^2 - 16q^2}}{|p + 4q|}$

Mixed Review **71.** $y = \frac{28}{x}$ **73.** $(3y - x - 1)(3y + x + 1)$ **75.** 5 **77.** $\frac{1}{4}x^2 - 3x + 10$ **79.** 4, 6, and −6, −4 **81.** $50,000

LESSON 7-5

Try This **a.** $\sqrt[3]{8^2} = 4$ $(\sqrt[3]{8})^2 = 4$ **b.** $(\sqrt{6y})^3 = 6|y|\sqrt{6y}$ $\sqrt{(6y)^3} = 6|y|\sqrt{6y}$ **c.** $\sqrt[4]{y}$ **d.** $\sqrt{3a}$ **e.** $\sqrt[4]{16}$, or 2 **f.** $(a^3b^2c)^{\frac{1}{4}}$ **g.** $\left(\frac{x^2y}{16}\right)^{\frac{1}{5}}$ **h.** $|x|\sqrt{x}$ **i.** 4 **j.** $(7abc)^{\frac{4}{3}}$ **k.** $6^{\frac{7}{5}}$ **l.** $(x^2y^3)^{\frac{1}{4}}$, or $x^{\frac{1}{2}}y^{\frac{3}{4}}$ **m.** $\frac{1}{5^{\frac{1}{4}}}$ **n.** $\frac{1}{(3xy)^{\frac{7}{8}}}$ **o.** $7^{\frac{14}{15}}$ **p.** $5^{\frac{1}{3}}$ **q.** $9^{\frac{2}{5}}$ **r.** $\sqrt{a}$ **s.** x **t.** $\sqrt{2}$ **u.** xy^3 **v.** $\sqrt[4]{xy^2}$ **w.** $\sqrt[4]{63}$ **x.** $\sqrt[4]{a - b}$ **y.** $\sqrt[6]{x^{-4}y^3z^5}$ **z.** $\sqrt[4]{ab}$

Exercises **1.** $6a\sqrt{6a}$ **3.** $4b\sqrt[3]{4b}$ **5.** $54a^3b\sqrt{2b}$ **7.** $2c\sqrt[3]{18cd^2}$ **9.** $\sqrt[4]{x}$ **11.** 2 **13.** $\sqrt[5]{a^2b^2}$ **15.** $\sqrt[3]{a^2}$ **17.** 8 **19.** $\sqrt{a^5t^3}$ **21.** $\sqrt{y^7}$ **23.** $\sqrt[4]{m^3n^5}$ **25.** $19^{\frac{1}{3}}$ **27.** $6^{\frac{1}{2}}$ **29.** $(xy)^{\frac{1}{5}}$ **31.** $(x^3y^2z^2)^{\frac{1}{7}}$ **33.** $(7xy)^{\frac{4}{3}}$ **35.** $(2a^5b)^{\frac{7}{6}}$ **37.** $(12ab)^{\frac{1}{2}}$ or $2(3ab)^{\frac{1}{2}}$ **39.** $(3a^4b^3)^{\frac{4}{7}}$ **41.** $\frac{1}{y^{1/4}}$ **43.** $\frac{1}{(5xy)^{5/6}}$ **45.** $8^{\frac{3}{4}}$ **47.** $x^{\frac{5}{6}}$ **49.** $11^{\frac{7}{6}}$ **51.** $9^{\frac{2}{11}}$ **53.** $3.9^{\frac{7}{20}}$ **55.** $5^{\frac{15}{28}}$ **57.** $\sqrt[3]{y}$ **59.** x^2y^3 **61.** $2x^3y^4$ **63.** $\frac{x^3y^4}{2}$ **65.** $\sqrt[4]{3xy^2 + 24xy + 48x}$ **67.** $\sqrt[12]{(x + y)^{-1}}$ **69.** $\sqrt[12]{x^4y^3z^2}$ **71.** $\sqrt[5]{xy^5}$ **73.** $\sqrt{(a^2 - b^2)}$ **75.** $\sqrt{x^2 - y^2}$ **77.** $\frac{\sqrt{a - b}}{(a - b)^2}$ **79.** $(x + 6)^{\frac{1}{2}}$ **81.** Answers may vary. Should include the idea that $a^{\frac{m}{n}} \cdot a^{-\frac{m}{n}} = 1$ **83.** 45.9 m

Mixed Review **85.** No **87.** $4x^3 + 3x^2$

LESSON 7-6

Try This **a.** 100 **b.** No solution **c.** 9 **d.** 5 **e.** $h = \frac{1}{\pi r}\sqrt{S^2 - \pi^2r^4}$; $h = 4$

Exercises **1.** 2 **3.** 168 **5.** 3 **7.** 19 **9.** $\frac{80}{3}$ **11.** 4 **13.** −27 **15.** 397 **17.** No solution **19.** $\frac{1}{64}$ **21.** −6 **23.** 5 **25.** $-\frac{1}{4}$ **27.** 3 **29.** 9 **31.** 7 **33.** $\frac{80}{9}$ **35.** −1 **37.** 6, 2 **39.** No solution

41. $s = \frac{v^2}{2g}$; $512g$ **43.** 8 **45.** $5 + 2\sqrt{2}$ **47.** 2 **49.** $\frac{5}{4}$

51. Let $a = b$.
$a^n = a \cdot a^{n-1}$ Substituting b for a, $a^n = b \cdot a^{n-1}$.
Continuing to factor an a out of the right side and substituting b, $a^n = b \cdot a^{n-1} = b^2 \cdot a^{n-2} = \ldots b^{n-1} \cdot a = b^n$.
So if $a = b$, $a^n = b^n$. **53.** No solution

Mixed Review **55.** $2|y|\sqrt{3}$ **57.** 4

LESSON 7-7

Try This **a.** $i\sqrt{7}$ **b.** $-6i$ **c.** $4i\sqrt{10}$ **d.** -18 **e.** $-3\sqrt{3}$ **f.** $-3\sqrt{2}$ **g.** 0 **h.** $-i$ **i.** $-2 + 7i$

Exercises **1.** $i\sqrt{2}$ **3.** $6i$ **5.** $-3i$ **7.** $8i\sqrt{2}$ **9.** $\frac{3}{4}i$ **11.** $-4i\sqrt{5}$ **13.** $92i$ **15.** $-4\sqrt{3}$ **17.** $-\sqrt{6}$ **19.** 6 **21.** $-3\sqrt{5}$ **23.** -10 **25.** $3i$ **27.** $8 + i$ **29.** $9 - 5i$ **31.** $-5 + 5i$ **33.** $-9 + 5i$ **35.** 1 **37.** $-i$ **39.** $-2i$ **41.** $i^{4k} = 1$ and $i^{4k-2} = -1$ for $k = 1, 2, 3, \ldots$ **43.** -1 **45.** 1 **47.** i **49.** -1 **51.** 1 **53.** -1

Mixed Review **55.** $\sqrt[3]{35}$ **57.** $2|m|\sqrt[4]{7mn^2}$ **59.** $y - 1$ **61.** 4, 2 **63.** 1, $-\frac{2}{3}$

LESSON 7-8

Try This a–e.

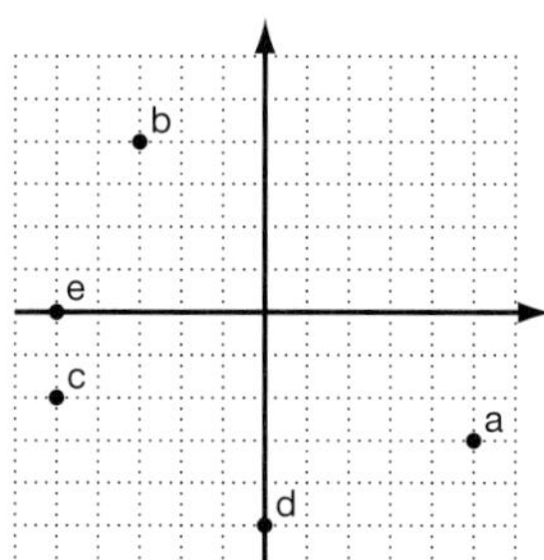

f. 5 **g.** 13 **h.** $\sqrt{2}$

Exercises

1.

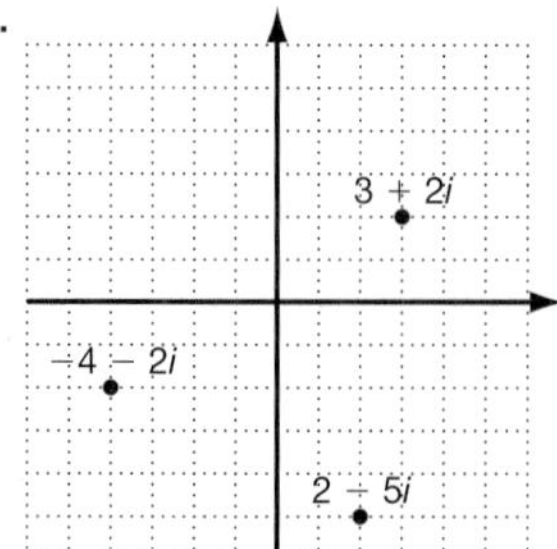

3.

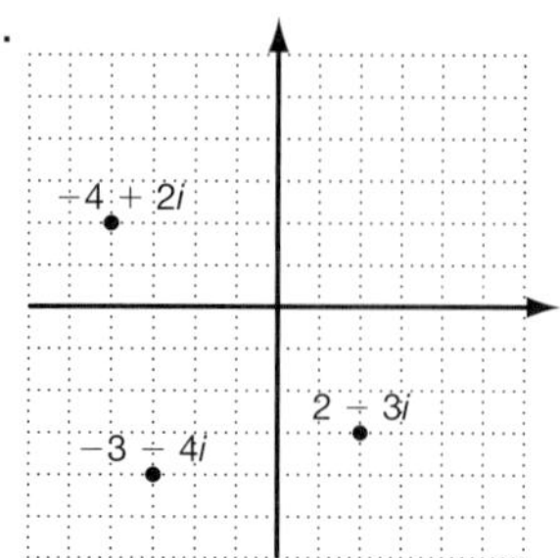

5. 5 **7.** 17 **9.** 3 **11.** $\sqrt{c^2 + d^2}$

13. a.

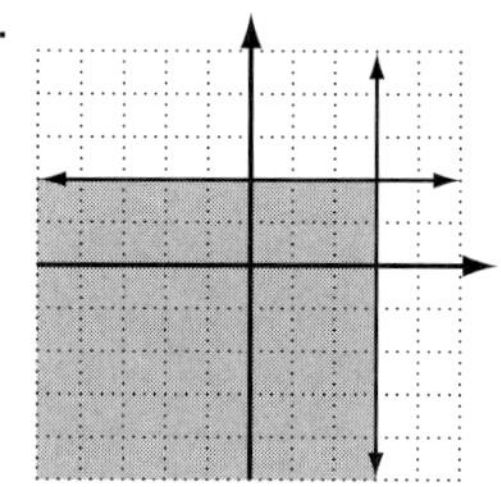

b.

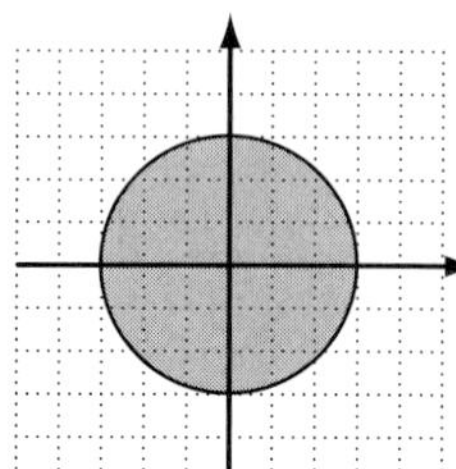

c.

15. The absolute value does not change. The coordinates of the graph change from (a, b) to $(-b, a)$. (The point is rotated 90°.)

Mixed Review **17.** $3\sqrt{3}$ **19.** $2a\sqrt[3]{2}$ **21.** $(a + 3)(a^2 - 3a + 9)$ **23.** $(x - 4)^3$

LESSON 7-9

Try This **a.** $x = -1, y = 2$ **b.** -30 **c.** -100 **d.** $3 - 28i$ **e.** $6 - 3i$ **f.** $-9 + 5i$ **g.** $7i$ **h.** -8 **i.** 53 **j.** 10 **k.** $9p^2 + 4q^2$ **l.** $2i$ **m.** $\frac{10}{17} - \frac{11}{17}i$ **n.** $\frac{3}{25} - \frac{4}{25}i$

Exercises **1.** $x = -\frac{3}{2}, y = 7$ **3.** $x = -2, y = -8$ **5.** -3 **7.** -25 **9.** $5 + 10i$ **11.** $-8i$ **13.** $7 + i$ **15.** $-m - ni$ **17.** 45 **19.** $\frac{8}{5} + \frac{1}{5}i$ **21.** $-\frac{11}{5} + \frac{2}{5}i$ **23.** $-i$ **25.** $\frac{1}{10} + \frac{1}{5}i$ **27.** $-\frac{4}{65} - \frac{7}{65}i$ **29.** i **31.** $-\frac{1}{2} - \frac{1}{2}i$ **33.** $\frac{a}{a^2 + b^2} - \frac{b}{a^2 + b^2}i$ **35.** $\frac{5}{61} - \frac{6}{61}i$ **37.** $-26 - 8\sqrt{3}$

Mixed Review **39.** $\frac{3\sqrt{2}}{2}$ **41.** $\frac{|m| + |n| - 2\sqrt{mn}}{|m| - |n|}$

LESSON 7-10

Try This a. No;
$(1 - i)^2 + 2(1 - i) + 1 = 1 - 2i + i^2 + 2 - 2i + 1 = 3 - 4i$;
Therefore, $(1 - i)$ is not a solution of $x^2 + 2x + 1 = 0$.
b. $x^2 - 2x + 2 = 0$ **c.** $x^2 - 4x + 13 = 0$ **d.** $2 + 5i$
e. $(x + 2i)(x - 2i) = x^2 + 2ix - 2ix - 4i^2 = x^2 + 4$
f. $(-1 + i)^2 = 1 - 2i + i^2 = 1 - 2i - 1 = -2i$;
The other square root is $1 - i$.

Exercises **1.** Yes, yes **3.** No, yes **5.** Yes, yes **7.** $x^2 + 25 = 0$ **9.** $x^2 - 4x + 13 = 0$ **11.** $x^2 + 3 = 0$ **13.** $x^2 - 12x + 42 = 0$ **15.** $x^2 - 6x + 26 = 0$ **17.** $\frac{12}{5} - \frac{1}{5}i$ **19.** $\frac{8}{29} + \frac{9}{29}i$ **21.** $\frac{11}{25} + \frac{2}{25}i$
23. $(2x + i)(2x - i) = 4x^2 - 2ix + 2ix - i^2 = 4x^2 + 1$
25. $(2 + i)^2 = 4 + 4i + i^2 = 3 + 4i$. The other squre root is $-2 - i$. **27.** $x^3 - x^2 + 9x - 9 = 0$
29. $x^3 - 2ix^2 + x - 2i = 0$
31. $(a + bi)^2 = a^2 + 2abi - b^2 = (a^2 - b^2) + 2abi = (a + b)(a - b) + 2abi$

Mixed Review **33.** 0.00005023 **35.** $\frac{2 + 3x}{2 - 5x}$ **37.** $\frac{2y + 5x}{5y - 2x}$

Preparing for Standardized Tests

1. (B) **3.** (A) **5.** (A) **7.** (B) **9.** (E) **11.** (D)

CHAPTER 7 WRAP UP

1. 36 **2.** $4|x|$ **3.** $-\frac{2x}{3}$ **4.** -3 **5.** $2|x|$
6. $6|x|\sqrt{6}$ **7.** $a^2b^2\sqrt[3]{b}$ **8.** $2cd^2\sqrt[3]{6cd}$ **9.** $2\sqrt[3]{2}$
10. $\frac{2|a|}{b^4}\sqrt{3ab}$ **11.** $\frac{x^2\sqrt{5}}{2}$ **12.** $12\sqrt{2}$ **13.** $-\sqrt[3]{3}$
14. $(5|y| - 2)\sqrt{3y}$ **15.** 1 **16.** $58 + 12\sqrt{6}$
17. $2\sqrt[3]{4} + 7\sqrt[3]{6} + 3\sqrt[3]{9}$ **18.** $\frac{2\sqrt{6}}{3}$ **19.** $\frac{9 + 3\sqrt{17}}{-4}$
20. $\frac{\sqrt{3} + 16}{23}$ **21.** $4\sqrt[3]{4}$ **22.** $3|x|\sqrt{3x}$ **23.** $|a^3|b^2$ **24.** $\frac{3}{a^2}$
25. $\sqrt[3]{x^2}$ **26.** 3 **27.** 4 **28.** $128x^2\sqrt{2x}$ **29.** $15^{\frac{1}{3}}$ **30.** $2^{\frac{5}{3}}$
31. $x^1y^{\frac{4}{3}}z^{\frac{5}{3}}$ **32.** $2^{\frac{3}{4}}x^{\frac{3}{4}}y^{\frac{1}{2}}$ **33.** $\frac{1}{x^{\frac{1}{2}}}$ **34.** x^4 **35.** 4 **36.** 4 **37.** $\sqrt{x}$
38. $2y^2\sqrt[3]{2}$ **39.** $\frac{|y^3|}{2x^2}$ **40.** $\sqrt[5]{\frac{8x^3z^2}{y^4}}$ or $\frac{\sqrt[5]{8x^3z^2y}}{y}$ **41.** $-\frac{31}{3}$
42. $-\frac{1}{2}, \frac{3}{2}$ **43.** $L = \frac{gT^2}{16\pi^2}$ **44.** $E = mc^2$ **45.** $w_2 = \frac{w_1}{A^2}$
46. $7i$ **47.** $-5i$ **48.** $-6\sqrt{6}$ **49.** $2 - i$ **50.** $1 - 4i$
53. $\sqrt{34}$ **54.** 5 **55.** $14 + 2i$ **56.** $12 - 5i$ **57.** 13 **58.** 40
59. $\frac{8}{5} - \frac{1}{5}i$ **60.** $\frac{3}{5} - \frac{4}{5}i$ **61.** $\frac{1}{10} - \frac{1}{5}i$ **62.** $\frac{1}{2} + \frac{1}{2}i$ **63.** $-\frac{16}{13} - \frac{11}{13}i$

Chapter 8

Skills & Concepts You Need for Chapter 8

1. 7, −2 **2.** 0, 2 **3.** −5 **4.** 3, −3 **5.** $\frac{2}{5}$; $y = \frac{2}{5}x$ **6.** 160; $y = \frac{160}{x}$
7. $\frac{2\sqrt{14}}{7}$ **8.** $\frac{\sqrt{2}}{4}$ **9.** $\frac{3 + \sqrt{3}}{6}$ **10.** $i\sqrt{7}$ **11.** $2i\sqrt{5}$

LESSON 8-1

Try This **a.** $0, -\frac{8}{5}$ **b.** $\frac{2}{7}, \frac{1}{2}$ **c.** $-3, 2$ **d.** $\pm\frac{\sqrt{35}}{7}$ **e.** $\pm\frac{\sqrt{2}}{2}i$ **f.** $\pm\frac{2}{7}i$ **g.** $x^2 + 14x + 49$ **h.** $y^2 - 11y + \frac{121}{4}$
i. $x^2 - \frac{2}{5}x + \frac{1}{25}$ **j.** $x^2 + 2ax + a^2$ **k.** $\frac{-1 \pm \sqrt{5}}{2}$ **l.** $-\frac{1}{2}, 1$
m. $\frac{1 \pm \sqrt{33}}{16}$ **n.** $\frac{2}{3}, -\frac{5}{3}$

Exercises **1.** $0, \frac{3}{7}$ **3.** $0, -\frac{8}{19}$ **5.** $-7, -2$ **7.** $-\frac{3}{2}, -5$ **9.** $\frac{2}{3}, -4$ **11.** $\frac{5}{3}, -4$ **13.** $-\frac{7}{2}, -1$ **15.** 4 **17.** 10, 5 **19.** $\pm\sqrt{7}$
21. $\pm\frac{\sqrt{21}}{3}$ **23.** $\pm\frac{\sqrt{2}}{2}$ **25.** $\pm\frac{i\sqrt{5}}{5}$ **27.** $\pm i\sqrt{5}$ **29.** $\pm\frac{5}{4}$
31. $4x\sqrt{2}$ **33.** $x^2 + 8x + 16$ **35.** $a^2 - 7a + \frac{49}{4}$
37. $x^2 + \frac{1}{2}x + \frac{1}{16}$ **39.** 1, 2 **41.** $\frac{-1 \pm i\sqrt{3}}{2}$ or $-\frac{1}{2} \pm \frac{i\sqrt{3}}{2}$
43. $-3 \pm 2\sqrt{3}$ **45.** $1, -\frac{9}{2}$ **47.** $-\frac{1}{2} \pm \frac{\sqrt{7}}{2}i$ **49.** $-8, -\frac{10}{3}, 0, \frac{7}{2}$
51. $\pm\frac{\sqrt{ab}}{a}$ **53.** $0, \frac{3}{2}$ **55.** 0, 10 **57.** $-10 \pm \sqrt{101}$
59. $\left(x + \frac{a}{2}\right)^2$

x ? $\frac{a}{2}$
x x^2 ? $\frac{ax}{2}$
$\frac{a}{2}$? ? $\frac{ax}{2}$? $\frac{a^2}{4}$

61. $\sqrt[n]{-\frac{b}{a}}$

Mixed Review **63.** $(m + 4)^2$ **65.** $4m^2n^4\sqrt{3m}$ **67.** $m - n$
69.

2 + 5i
−1 + 5i
1 + 2i
−5 + i
−3 − 2i
3 − 4i

71. 5 **73.** $412.09

LESSON 8-2

Try This **a.** 2 cm **b.** *A*: 16 km/h; *B*: 12 km/h

Exercises **1.** 2 cm **3.** Length 6 m; width 2 m **5.** 24 m and 10 m **7.** A: 15 km/h; B: 8 km/h **9.** 35 km/h **11.** Answers may vary. **13.** Not possible. The length of a side must be 0 or 12. If $s = 0$, no box can be made. If $s = 12$, all side lengths would be negative.

Mixed Review **15.** 5 **17.** 100 **19.** 20

Selected Answers

LESSON 8-3

Try This **a.** $\frac{-1 \pm \sqrt{22}}{3}$ **b.** $\frac{-3 \pm 3\sqrt{21}}{10}$ **c.** $\frac{1 \pm i\sqrt{7}}{2}$ **d.** $\frac{-1 \pm i\sqrt{5}}{3}$ **e.** 1.23, −1.90

Exercises **1.** $-3 \pm \sqrt{5}$ **3.** 1, −5 **5.** 3, −10 **7.** 2, $-\frac{1}{2}$ **9.** −1, $-\frac{5}{3}$ **11.** $\frac{1 \pm i\sqrt{3}}{2}$ **13.** $-1 \pm 2i$ **15.** $1 \pm 2i$ **17.** $2 \pm 3i$ **19.** $\pm i\sqrt{3}$ **21.** 0, −1 **23.** $\frac{-1 \pm 2i}{5}$ **25.** $\frac{3}{4}$, −2 **27.** $\frac{1 \pm 3i}{2}$ **29.** $\frac{3}{2}, \frac{2}{3}$ **31.** The solution is not correct. The error occurred when the 1 was not subtracted from both sides of the equation before applying the quadratic formula. **33.** 5.24, 0.76 **35.** 2.77, −1.27 **37.** $\frac{-1 \pm \sqrt{1 + 4\sqrt{2}}}{2}$ **39.** $\frac{-5\sqrt{2} \pm \sqrt{34}}{4}$ **41.** $\frac{-3 \pm \sqrt{9 - 4i}}{2}$ **43.** −1, 2 **45.** $x^2 + 3x - 28 = 0$; 4 **47.** Answers may vary. **49.** $c > 1$ **51.** $\frac{1}{2}$

Mixed Review **53.** $\sqrt{5}$ **55.** $|y|\sqrt{6x}$ **57.** $\frac{1}{10} + \frac{3}{10}i$ **59.** $\frac{3}{25} + \frac{4}{25}i$ **61.** $3i, -3i$

LESSON 8-4

Try This **a.** Two real **b.** One real **c.** Two nonreal **d.** Sum = 4; product = $\frac{4}{3}$ **e.** Sum = $-\sqrt{2}$; product = −4 **f.** $4x^2 - 12x - 1 = 0$ **g.** $3x^2 + 7x - 20 = 0$ **h.** $x^2 - x - 56 = 0$ **i.** $x^2 - (m + n)x + mn = 0$ **j.** $x^2 + x - 72 = 0$ **k.** $x^2 - 6x + 7 = 0$ **l.** $4x^2 - 8x - 1 = 0$

Exercises **1.** One real **3.** Two nonreal **5.** Two real **7.** One real **9.** Two nonreal **11.** Two real **13.** Two real **15.** One real **17.** Sum = 2; product = 10 **19.** Sum = −1; product = −1 **21.** Sum = $-\frac{1}{2}$; product = 2 **23.** Sum = 0; product = −49 **25.** Sum = $\frac{12}{25}$; product = $\frac{2}{25}$ **27.** Sum = −4; product = −2 **29.** $4x^2 + 4\pi x + 1 = 0$ **31.** $x^2 - 5x - \sqrt{2} = 0$ **33.** $x^2 - 16 = 0$ **35.** $x^2 + 10x + 25 = 0$ **37.** $8x^2 + 6x + 1 = 0$ **39.** $12x^2 - (4k + 3m)x + km = 0$ **41.** $x^2 - \sqrt{3}x - 6 = 0$ **43.** $x^2 - \pi x - 12\pi^2 = 0$ **45.** $x^2 - 11x + 30 = 0$ **47.** $4x^2 + 23x - 6 = 0$ **49.** $x^2 - 4x + 1 = 0$ **51.** $x^2 - x - 3 = 0$ **53.** $ghx^2 - (g^2 - h^2)x - gh = 0$ **55.** $x^2 - 8x + 25 = 0$ **57. a.** $k < \frac{1}{4}$ **b.** $k = \frac{1}{4}$ **c.** $k > \frac{1}{4}$ **59. a.** $k < 1$ **b.** $k = 1$ **c.** $k > 1$ **61. a.** $k > \frac{11}{3}$ **b.** $k = \frac{11}{3}$ **c.** $k < \frac{11}{3}$ **63.** $-\frac{1}{3}$, $k = -\frac{3}{5}$ **65.** −1 **67.** Given $a^2x + bx + c = 0$, $a \neq 0$, a, b, c rational numbers, $b^2 - 4ac > 0$ and $b^2 - 4ac = d^2$ where d is rational, $x = \frac{-b \pm \sqrt{b^2 - 4ac}}{2a} = \frac{-b \pm d}{2a}$. By the closure property of rationals both $\frac{-b + d}{2a}$ and $\frac{-b - d}{2a}$ are rational. **69.** The solutions of $ax^2 + bx + c = 0$ can be written as $-\frac{b}{2a} + \frac{\sqrt{b^2 - 4ac}}{2a}$ or $-\frac{b}{2a} - \frac{\sqrt{b^2 - 4ac}}{2a}$. The solutions of $ax^2 - bx + c = 0$ are $\frac{b \pm \sqrt{(-b)^2 - 4ac}}{2a}$, or $\frac{b}{2a} \pm \frac{\sqrt{b^2 - 4ac}}{2a}$.

$$\left(\frac{b}{2a} - \frac{\sqrt{b^2 - 4ac}}{2a}\right) + \left(-\frac{b}{2a} + \frac{\sqrt{b^2 - 4ac}}{2a}\right) = 0$$

$$\left(\frac{b}{2a} + \frac{\sqrt{b^2 - 4ac}}{2a}\right) + \left(-\frac{b}{2a} - \frac{\sqrt{b^2 - 4ac}}{2a}\right) = 0$$

Thus the solutions are additive inverses. **71.** $h = -36$, $k = 15$

Mixed Review **73.** $(5x + 2)(3x + 1)$ **75.** $a(a + 1)(a - 1)$ **77.** 2, 0 **79.** 4, 6 **81.** 5, −5

LESSON 8-5

Try This **a.** ±3, ±1 **b.** $\pm\sqrt{2}, \pm\sqrt{2}i$ **c.** 4 **d.** 4, 2, −1, −3 **e.** 125, −8 **f.** −128

Exercises **1.** 81, 1 **3.** $\pm\sqrt{5}$ **5.** 7, −1, 5, 1 **7.** $\frac{1}{3}, -\frac{1}{2}$ **9.** −27, 8 **11.** 16 **13.** $1 \pm \sqrt{2}, \frac{-1 \pm \sqrt{5}}{2}$ **15.** $\frac{5 \pm \sqrt{21}}{2}, \frac{3 \pm \sqrt{5}}{2}$ **17.** $\frac{1}{3}$ **19.** 36 camels **21.** $-\frac{3}{2}$, −1 **23.** 9 **25.** $1 \pm i, -1 \pm i, \sqrt{2} \pm i\sqrt{2}, -\sqrt{2} \pm i\sqrt{2}$

Mixed Review **27.** $\frac{\sqrt{105}}{7}$ **29.** −1 **31.** $x^2 + 49 = 0$ **33.** 6, −1 **35.** −2, 6 **37.** $\pm\frac{3}{2}$

LESSON 8-6

Try This **a.** $r = \sqrt{\frac{V}{\pi h}}$ **b.** $r = \frac{-\pi h + \sqrt{\pi^2h^2 + 2\pi}}{2\pi}$ **c.** $r = \sqrt{\frac{3S}{4\pi}}$ **d.** (1) 4.33 sec (2) 1.87 sec (3) 44.9 m

Exercises **1.** $s = \frac{\sqrt{P}}{2}$ **3.** $r = \sqrt{\frac{Gm_1m_2}{F}}$ **5.** $r = \sqrt{x^2 + y^2}$ **7.** $t = \frac{v_0 \pm \sqrt{v_0^2 - 19.6h}}{9.8}$ **9.** $t = \sqrt{\frac{2S}{g}}$ **11.** $r = \frac{-\pi h \pm \sqrt{\pi^2h^2 + \pi A}}{\pi}$ **13.** $t = \frac{\pi \pm \sqrt{\pi^2 - 12k\sqrt{2}}}{2\sqrt{2}}$ **15. a.** 3.91 s **b.** 1.91 s, 75 m **17. a.** 18.75% **b.** 10% **c.** 11% **d.** 12.75% **19.** 7 ft **21.** A: 24 km/h; B: 10 km/h **23.** 2.2199 cm; 8.0101 cm **25.** $a = \frac{b}{\sqrt{T^2 - 1}}$ **27.** 12 **29.** 3 cm × 4 cm

Mixed Review **31.** $-i$ **33.** −36 **35.** $-2 + 2i$ **37.** 4, 15 **39.** 0, −4 **41.** $\frac{5\sqrt{6}}{6}, \frac{-5\sqrt{6}}{6}$ **43.** $-2 \pm 2i$

LESSON 8-7

Try This **a.** $y = 7x^2$ **b.** $y = \frac{9}{x^2}$ **c.** $y = \frac{1}{2}xz$ **d.** $y = \frac{5xz^2}{w}$ **e.** 490 m

Exercises **1.** $y = \frac{54}{x^2}$ **3.** $y = \frac{0.256}{x^2}$ **5.** $y = \frac{2}{3}x^2$ **7.** $y = xz$ **9.** $y = 187.5\frac{x}{z^2}$ **11.** $y = \frac{xz}{5wp}$ **13.** 180 m **15.** 94.03 kg **17.** If p varies directly as q, then $p = kq$. Thus $q = \frac{1}{k}p$, so q varies directly as p. **19.** $\frac{\pi}{4}$ **21.** Division by zero is undefined.

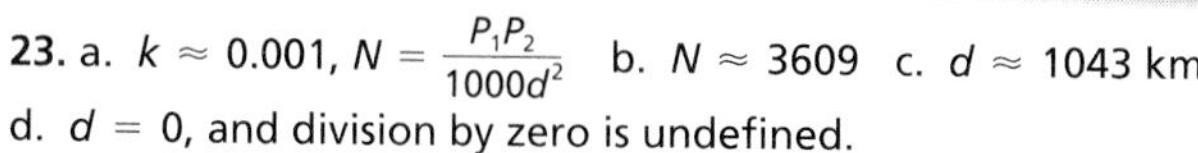

23. a. $k \approx 0.001$, $N = \frac{P_1P_2}{1000d^2}$ b. $N \approx 3609$ c. $d \approx 1043$ km d. $d = 0$, and division by zero is undefined.

Mixed Review **25.** 2 nonreal **27.** Sum $= -5$; product $= -2$ **29.** Sum $= -4$; product $= -\frac{3}{2}$ **31.** $3, \frac{1}{3}$ **33.** $-x - yi$

LESSON 8-8

Problems **1.** There were 51 companies contacted. **3.** Tracy: Illinois; Sally: Hawaii; Juan: California; Herb: New York; Rick: Indiana; Terry: Florida **5.** $10^2 = 100$

CHAPTER 8 WRAP UP

1. $0, -\frac{6}{7}$ **2.** 0, 3 **3.** $\frac{2}{3}, -4$ **4.** $\frac{3}{4}, 6$ **5.** $\pm\frac{i\sqrt{2}}{2}$ **6.** $\pm\frac{2}{3}$ **7.** $x^2 + 16x + 64$ **8.** $x^2 - 9x + \frac{81}{4}$ **9.** $-2 \pm \sqrt{10}$ **10.** $-\frac{3}{2}, \frac{5}{2}$ **11.** 25 m, 20 m, 15 m **12.** $-2 \pm \sqrt{11}$ **13.** $\frac{-3 \pm \sqrt{29}}{2}$ **14.** $-1 \pm i\sqrt{3}$ **15.** $\frac{-1 \pm i\sqrt{15}}{2}$ **16.** 7.3, 0.7 **17.** Discriminant $= 9$. There are two real roots. **18.** Sum $= \frac{4}{5}$; product $= \frac{2}{5}$ **19.** $10x^2 + 5x + 6 = 0$ **20.** $2x^2 + 7x + 3 = 0$ **21.** ± 1 **22.** $\pm 3, \pm 2$ **23.** $A = \sqrt{1 - a^2}$ **24.** $t = \frac{-a \pm \sqrt{a^2 + 2gS}}{g}$ **25.** 4.67 s **26.** $y = \frac{2}{9}x^2$ **27.** $y = \frac{5}{2}x^2$ **28.** $y = \frac{2}{x^2}$ **29.** 113.13 m^2

CHAPTERS 1–8 CUMULATIVE REVIEW

1. $8x - 5$ **3.** $\frac{5}{3}$ **5.** \$9.25 **7.** $-\frac{3y^3z^4}{x^2}$ **9.** 3.24×10^{-2} **11.** $x \leq 5$;

0 5

13. Less than 275 mi **15.** $x \geq 6$ or $x \leq -1$;

−1 0 6

17. 1 **19.**

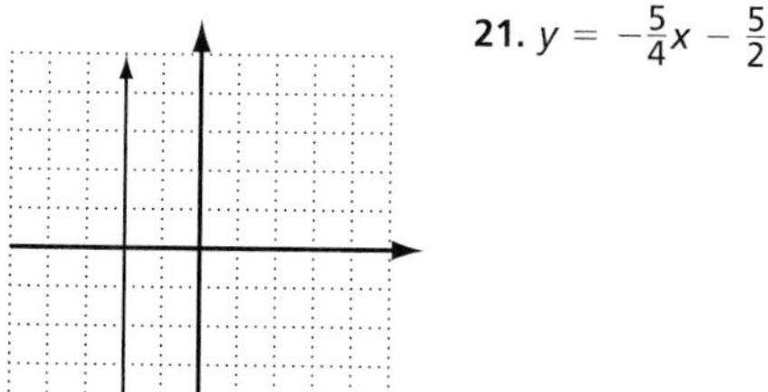

21. $y = -\frac{5}{4}x - \frac{5}{2}$ **23.** $m = \frac{3}{4}, b = -3$ **25.** $y = -\frac{4}{5}x - \frac{17}{5}$ **27.** $y = \frac{25}{7}x + \frac{10}{7}$ **29.** 52 **31.** $\left(-\frac{1}{3}, -\frac{19}{3}\right)$ **33.** 6, −4 **35.** (−2, 1, 4) **37.** $-7y$ **39.** $4x - 2$ **41.** $x^4 - 6x^2y + 9y^2$ **43.** $12x(2x - 3)(x - 2)$ **45.** $(x - y + 6)(x - y - 6)$ **47.** $-3y(2y^2 - 1)(2y^2 - 1)$ **49.** $-2, -\frac{3}{4}$ **51.** $2\frac{1}{2}$ ft by 6 ft **53.** $\frac{(4x + 1)(4x^2 + 6x + 9)}{(2x - 3)(16x^2 - 4x + 1)}$

55. $\frac{1}{x - y}$ **57.** $y^2 - 2y + 3$ **59.** Q: $y^3 - y^2 + y - 1$, R: 0 **61.** −6, 5 **63.** Train A travels 40 mi/h; train B travels 50 mi/h. **65.** $k_1 = \frac{3T}{t} - k_2$ **67.** $25|t|$ **69.** $2x^2|y|$ **71.** $\frac{|a|}{6}\sqrt{30a}$ **73.** $3\sqrt[3]{4} - 3\sqrt{3}$ **75.** 4 **77.** 28 **79.** $-5\sqrt{3}$ **81.**

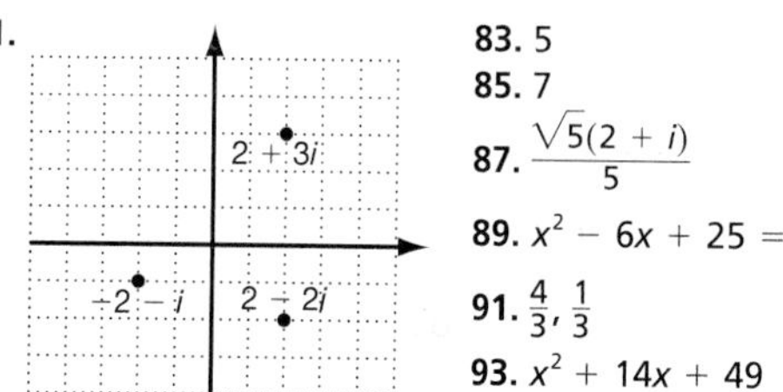

83. 5 **85.** 7 **87.** $\frac{\sqrt{5}(2 + i)}{5}$ **89.** $x^2 - 6x + 25 = 0$ **91.** $\frac{4}{3}, \frac{1}{3}$ **93.** $x^2 + 14x + 49$ **95.** $-\frac{3}{2}, 5$ **97.** $\frac{3 \pm i\sqrt{11}}{2}$ **99.** Discriminant $= -11$. There are two complex roots. **101.** $4x^2 + 16x + 1 = 0$ **103.** $\pm\sqrt{6}, \pm i\sqrt{3}$ **105.** $t = \pm\sqrt{\frac{3T}{g}}$ **107.** 272.5 m **109.** $\frac{160}{9}$ W/m^2

Chapter 9

Skills & Concepts You Need for Chapter 9

1. Line containing (3, 0) and (−3, −1) **2.** Line containing (0, 3) and (1, 1) **3.** No **4.** Yes **5.** 5, −2 **6.** 2, 6 **7.** −3, 4 **8.** −4, 2 **9.** $\frac{10}{3}, 2$ **10.** $4, -\frac{4}{7}$ **11.** $-\frac{1}{3}, 1$ **12.** $-1 \pm \sqrt{7}$

LESSON 9-1

Try This **a.** Symmetric with respect to the y-axis **b.** Symmetric with respect to both axes **c.** Yes **d.** Yes **e.** No **f.** No **g.** Even **h.** Neither **i.** Odd

Exercises **1.** y-axis **3.** Both axes **5.** Neither axis **7.** y-axis **9.** Both axes **11.** Neither axis **13.** Yes **15.** Yes **17.** Yes **19.** No **21.** No **23.** Neither **25.** Even **27.** Even **29.** Odd **31.** Neither **33.** Even **35.** Even **37.** Odd **39.** Neither **41.** Neither **43.**

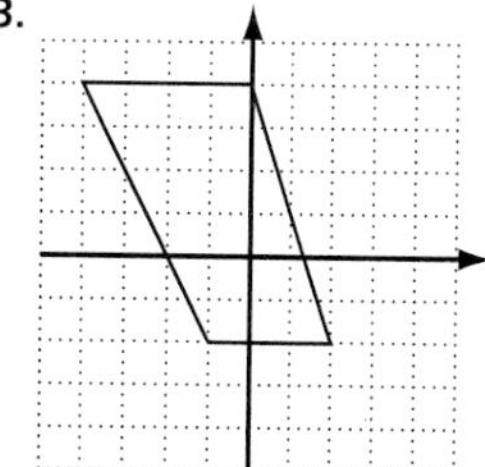

45. $f(x) = 0$ **47.** Both axes **49.** y-axis **51.** Both axes

Mixed Review **53.** 8 **55.** 6 **57.** $\frac{5}{3}, \frac{2}{3}$ **59.** $x^2 - 10x + 24 = 0$ **61.** $x^2 - 6x + 6 = 0$

Selected Answers

LESSON 9-2

Try This

a.

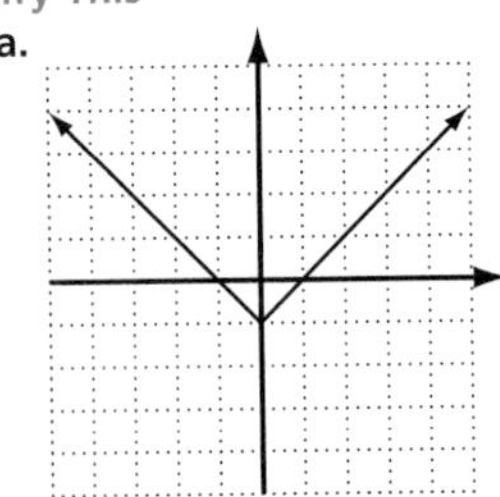

b.

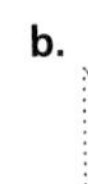

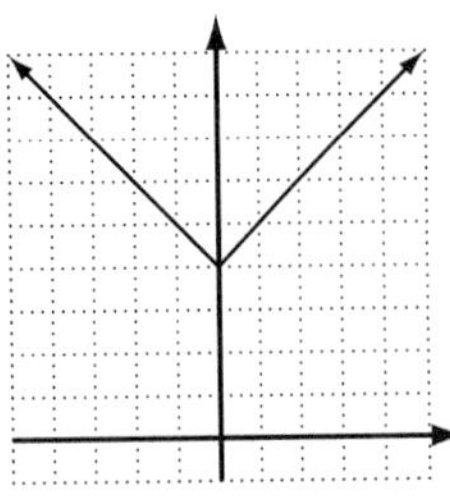

c.

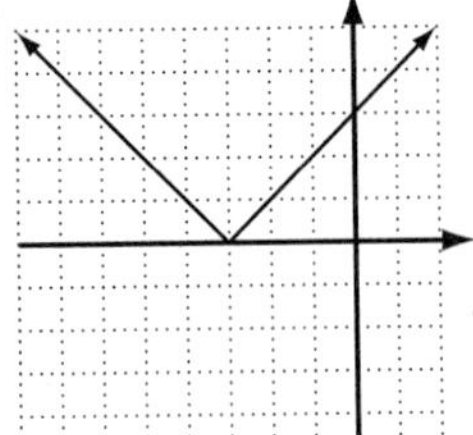

d.

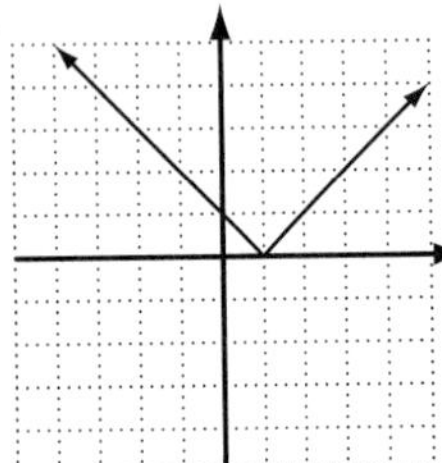

Exercises

1.

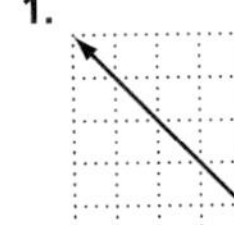

3.

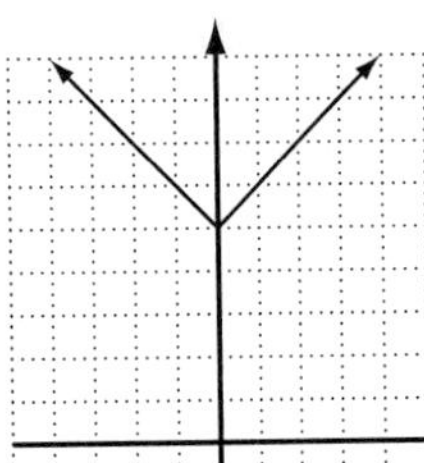

21.

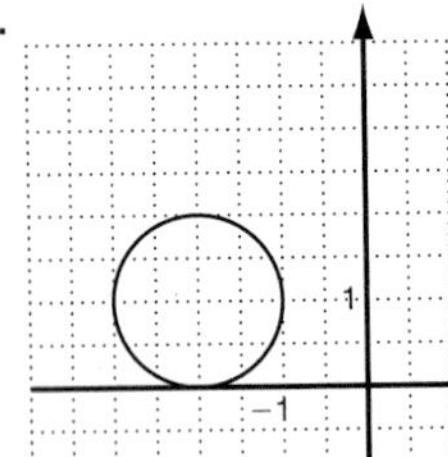

23. (2, −3)

25. The graph of the relation is translated upward 6 units and 4 units to the left.

27.

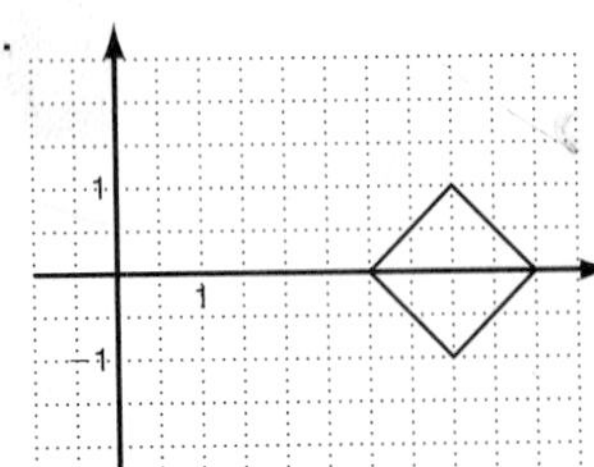

Mixed Review **29.** $3x^2 - x + 9 = 0$ **31.** -49 **33.** 6 **35.** $\sqrt{n^2 + m^2}$ **37.** $\pm 4, \pm 2$ **39.** $y = 2x^2$

LESSON 9-3

Try This

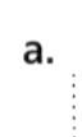

a.

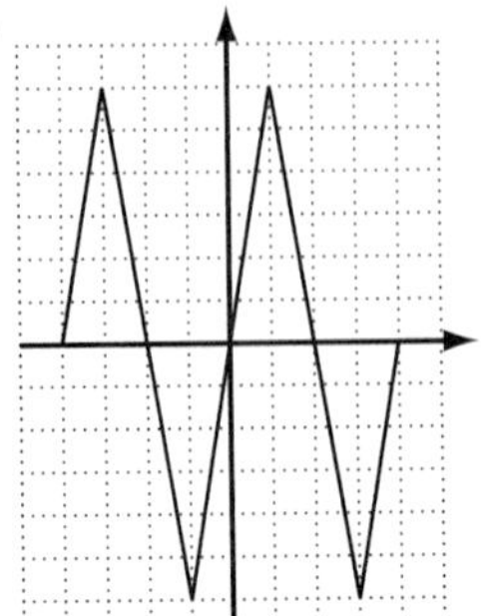

b.

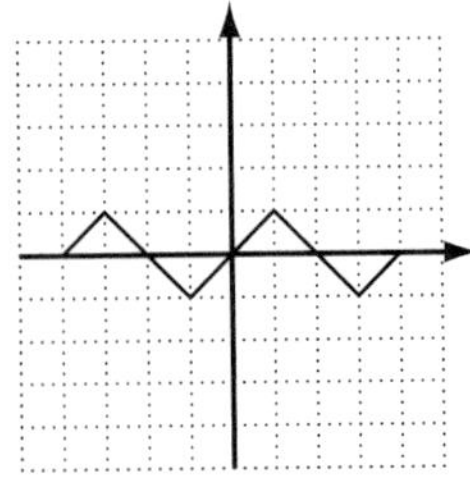

c.

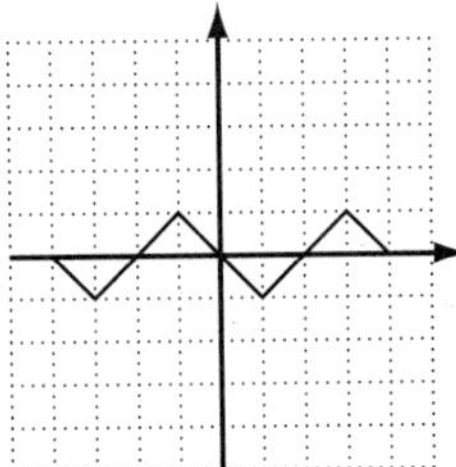

d.

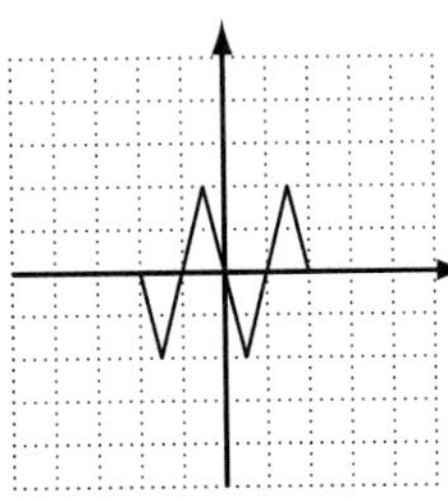

e.

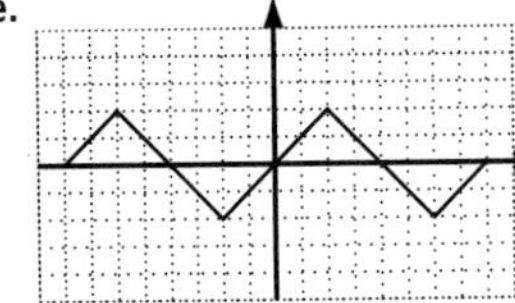

f.

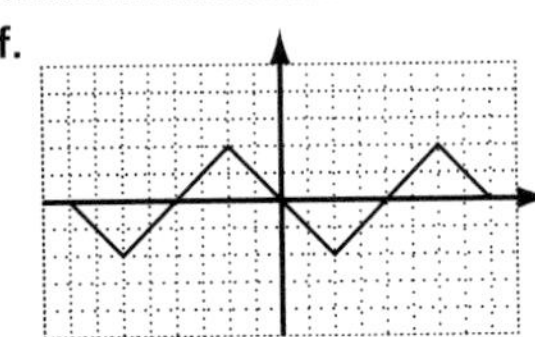

Exercises

1.

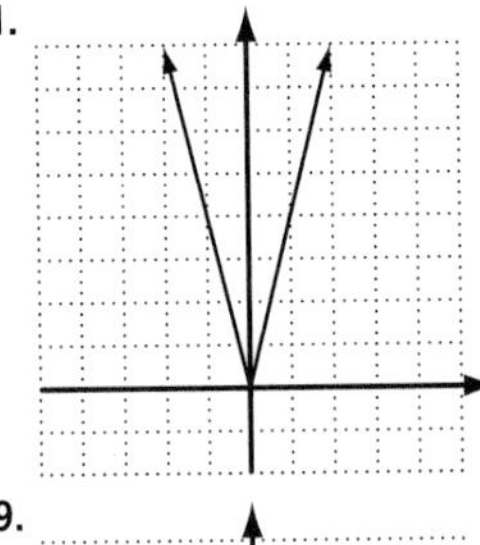

7.

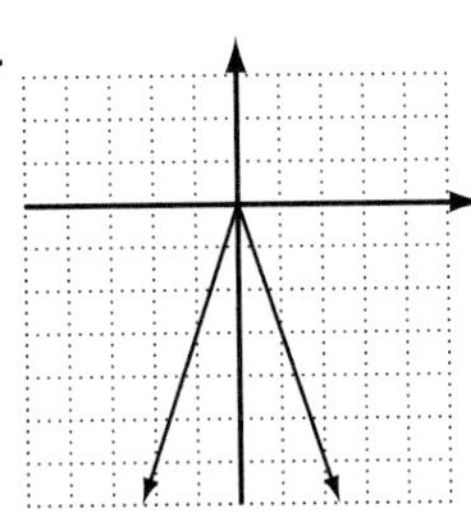

9.

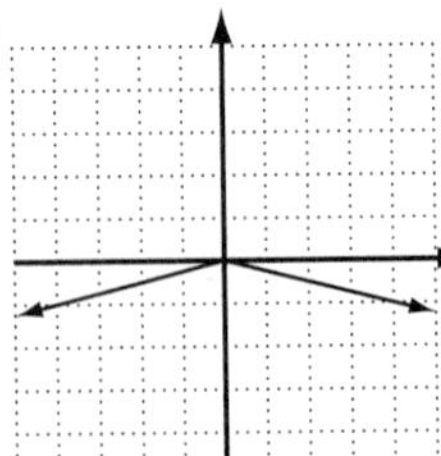

13.

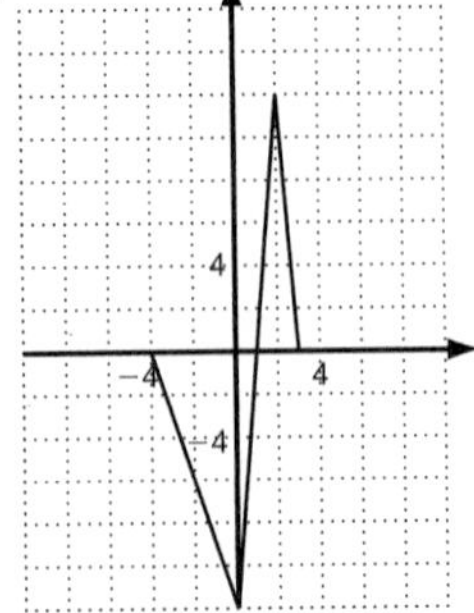

37. The graph is stretched horizontally, shrunk vertically and reflected across both the x-axis and the y-axis.

39.

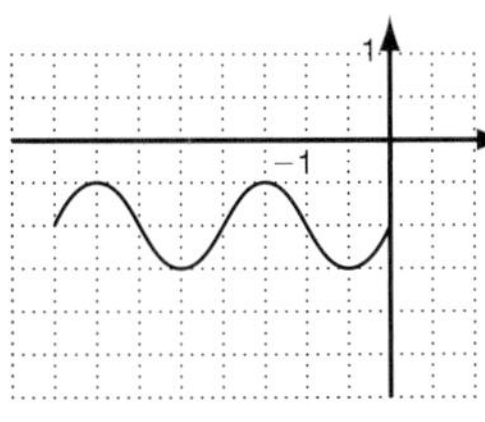

41.

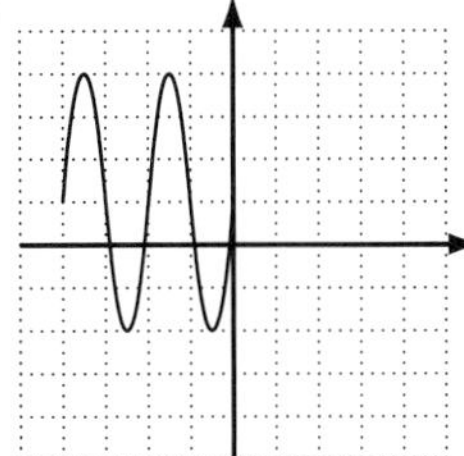

43.

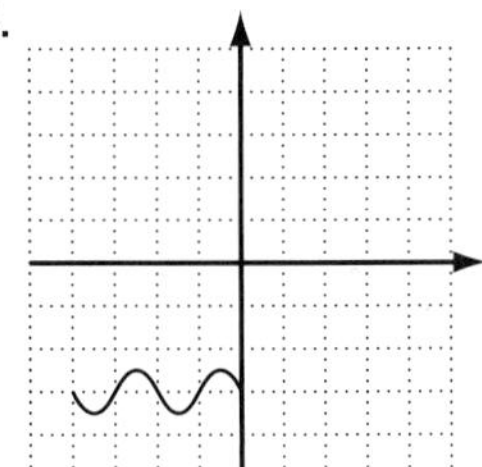

Mixed Review

45. No, yes

47. $3x^2 - 13x + 4 = 0$

49. $\pm 3, \pm 1$

51. 3, 4

53. 0, 8

LESSON 9-4

Try This **a.** (1)

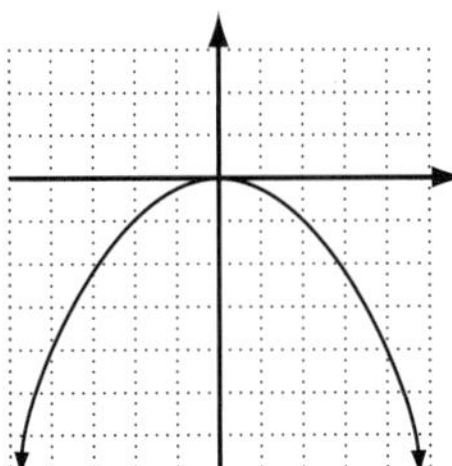

(2) y-axis ($x = 0$)
(3) (0, 0)

b. (1)

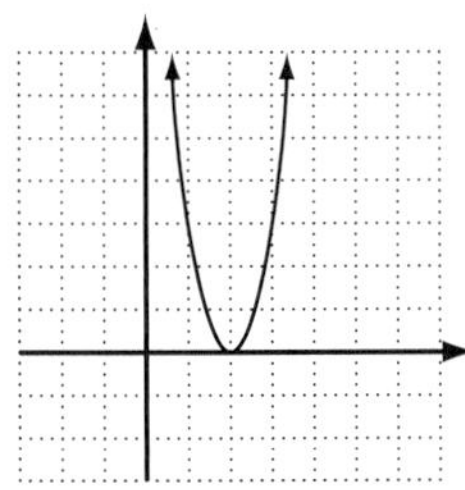

(2) $x = 2$ (3) (2, 0)

Exercises **1.** Above **3.** Below

5. Vertex: (0, 0)
Line of sym: $x = 0$

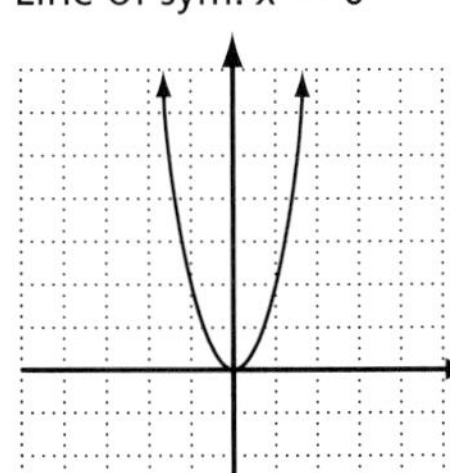

7. Vertex: (0, 0)
Line of sym: $x = 0$

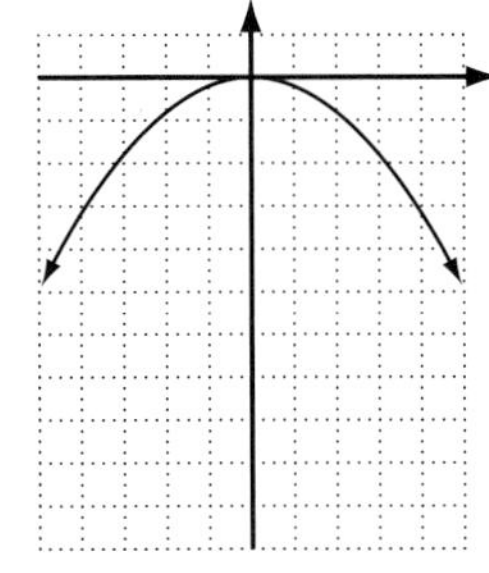

9. Vertex: (7, 0) Line of sym: $x = 7$
11. Vertex: (2, 0) Line of sym: $x = 2$
13. Vertex: (7, 0) Line of sym: $x = 7$
15. Vertex: $(-7, 0)$ Line of sym: $x = -7$
17. Vertex: $(-1, 0)$ Line of sym: $x = -1$

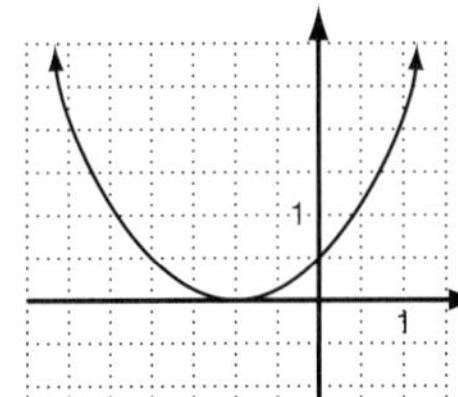

19.

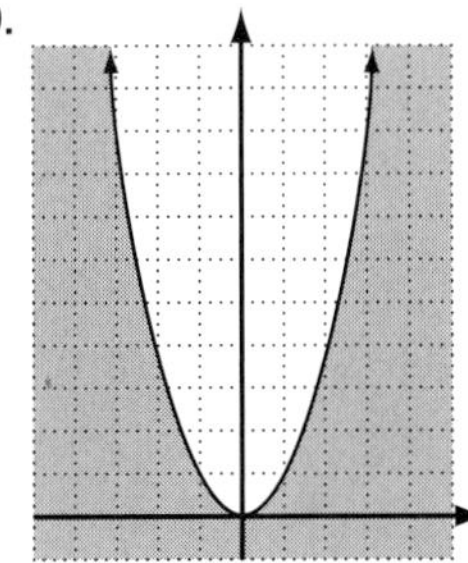

21.

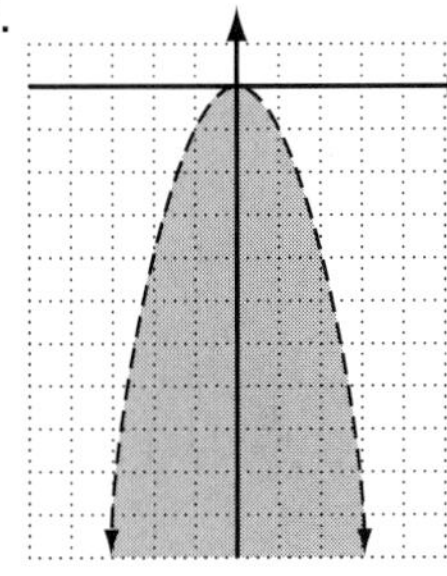

25. Both go through the origin. **27. a.** $|n| > |m|$ **b.** m is negative and n is positive, or n is negative and m is positive.
29. a. No **b.** No **c.** Yes, (1, 0)

Mixed Review **31.** 2 nonreal **33.** $-3 \pm \sqrt{5}$ **35.** $\frac{1}{4}$

LESSON 9-5

Try This **a.** Vertex: (2, 4);
Line of symmetry: $x = 2$;
Minimum: 4

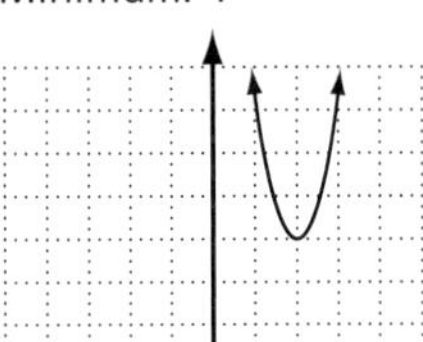

b. Vertex: $(-2, -1)$;
Line of symmetry: $x = -2$;
Maximum: -1

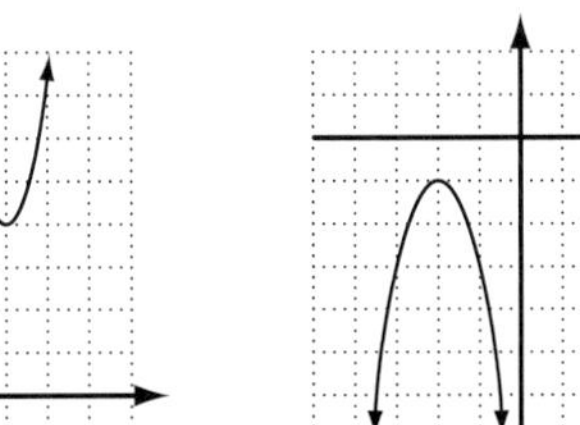

c. Vertex: (5, 40); Line of symmetry: $x = 5$; Minimum: 40
d. Vertex: (5, 0); Line of symmetry: $x = 5$; Maximum: 0
e. Vertex: $\left(-\frac{3}{4}, -6\right)$; Line of symmetry: $x = -\frac{3}{4}$; Minimum: -6
f. Vertex: $(-9, 3)$; Line of symmetry: $x = -9$; Maximum: 3

Selected Answers

Exercises **1.** Vertex: (3, 1); Line of symmetry: $x = 3$; Minimum: 1

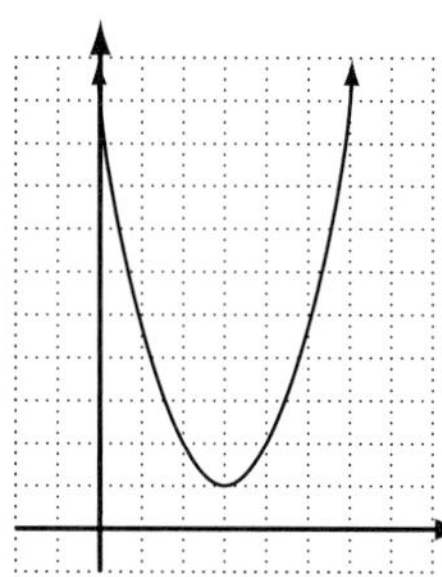

3. Vertex: $(-1, -2)$; Line of symmetry: $x = -1$; Minimum: -2

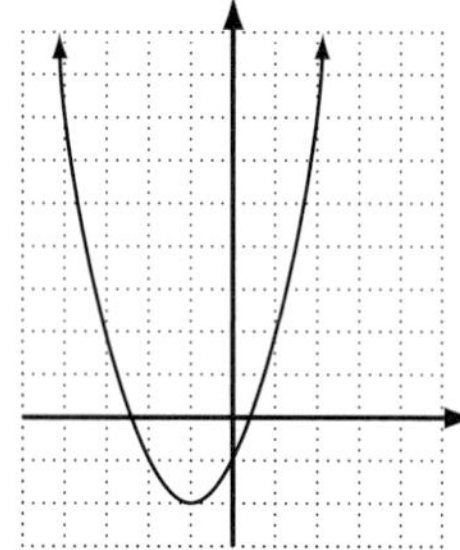

5. Vertex: $(1, -3)$; Minimum **7.** Vertex: $(-4, 1)$; Maximum
9. $(9, 5)$; $x = 9$; min. $= 5$ **11.** $(10, -20)$; $x = 10$; max. $= -20$
13. $f(x) = -2x^2 + 4$ **15.** $f(x) = 2(x - 6)^2$
17. $f(x) = -2(x - 3)^2 + 8$ **19.** $f(x) = 2(x + 3)^2 + 5$
21. $f(x) = 2(x - 2)^2 - 3$ **23.** $g(x) = 6(x - 4)^2$
25. $f(x) = -3(x - 2)^2 + 5$ **27.** $g(x) = -2(x - 5)^2 - 11$

Mixed Review **29.** $y = 2xz$ **31.** $r = \pm\frac{\sqrt{A\pi}}{\pi}$ **33.** $c = \pm\frac{\sqrt{Em}}{m}$

LESSON 9-6

Try This **a.** (1) $f(x) = (x - 2)^2 + 3$
(2) $(2, 3)$, $x = 2$, minimum $= 3$

b. (1) $f(x) = -4\left(x - \frac{3}{2}\right)^2 + 4$ (2) $\left(\frac{3}{2}, 4\right)$, $x = \frac{3}{2}$, maximum $= 4$ **c.** 225 **d.** 25 m by 25 m

Exercises **1.** $f(x) = (x - 1)^2 - 4$; Vertex: $(1, -4)$; Line of symmetry: $x = 1$; Minimum: -4

3. $f(x) = -(x - 2)^2 + 10$; Vertex: $(2, 10)$; Line of symmetry: $x = 2$; Maximum: 10

5. $f(x) = \left(x + \frac{3}{2}\right)^2 - \frac{49}{4}$; Vertex: $\left(-\frac{3}{2}, -\frac{49}{4}\right)$; Line of symmetry: $x = -\frac{3}{2}$; Minimum: $-\frac{49}{4}$

7. $f(x) = \left(x - \frac{9}{2}\right)^2 - \frac{81}{4}$; Vertex: $\left(\frac{9}{2}, -\frac{81}{4}\right)$; Line of symmetry: $x = \frac{9}{2}$; Minimum: $-\frac{81}{4}$

9. $f(x) = 3(x - 4)^2 + 2$; Vertex: $(4, 2)$; Line of symmetry: $x = 4$; Minimum: 2

11. The error is in her second step. Emily did not multiply $+36$ by $\frac{3}{4}$ when taking it out of the parentheses. The equation should be $\frac{3}{4}(x + 6)^2 - 27$.
13. 17 m by 17 m; 289 m^2 **15.** 506.25; 22.5 and 22.5
17. $-\frac{25}{4}$; $\frac{5}{2}$ and $-\frac{5}{2}$ **19.**

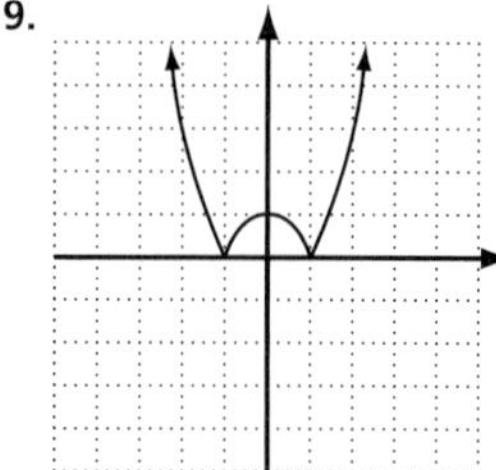

21. Minimum: -6.95 **23.** Answers may vary. Sample: A garden 10 ft by 15 ft has area 150 ft^2, but a 12.5 ft by 12.5 ft garden will have an area of 156.25 ft^2. **25.** $h = -\frac{b}{2a}$
$k = \frac{4ac - b^2}{4a}$ **27.** \$6 **29.** 1800 ft^2 **31.** $11\sqrt{2}$ ft

Mixed Review **33.** Both **35.** x-axis **37.** 4 **39.** $16i$ **41.** 10
43. 3.40956×10^7

LESSON 9-7

Try This **a.** $1 + \sqrt{6}$, $1 - \sqrt{6}$ **b.** -4 **c.** None

Exercises **1.** $2 + \sqrt{3}$, $2 - \sqrt{3}$ **3.** 3, -1 **5.** 4, -1
7. $\frac{-2 \pm \sqrt{6}}{2}$ **9.** None **11.** None **13.** $\frac{3 \pm \sqrt{6}}{3}$ **15.** Always
17. $f(x) = x^2 - 2x - 15$ **19.** None

Mixed Review **21.** No **23.** Yes
25. Vertex: $(-3, 0)$; Line of symmetry: $x = -3$

LESSON 9-8

Try This **a.** $f(x) = x^2 - 2x + 1$ **b.** $f(x) = x^2 + 2x + 3$
c. (1) $f(x) = 0.1875x^2 - 16.25x + 500$ (2) About 181
d. (1) Maximum height $= 12.4$ m in 0.286 s (2) 1.876 s

Exercises **1.** $f(x) = 2x^2 + 3x - 1$ **3.** $f(x) = -3x^2 + 13x - 5$
5. a. $f(x) = -4x^2 + 40x + 2$ **b.** \$98
7. a. $f(x) = 0.0875x^2 - 10.5x + 436.25$ **b.** about 121.25
9. a. 3077 m at 25 s **b.** 50.1 s **11.** 156.25, 40 km/h
13. a. 1931 m at 20 s **b.** 0.15 s **c.** 39.9 s **15.** $\frac{p + q}{2}$
17. 4800 yd^2

Mixed Review **19.** x-axis **21.** Both
23. Vertex: (2, 0); Line of symmetry: $x = 2$

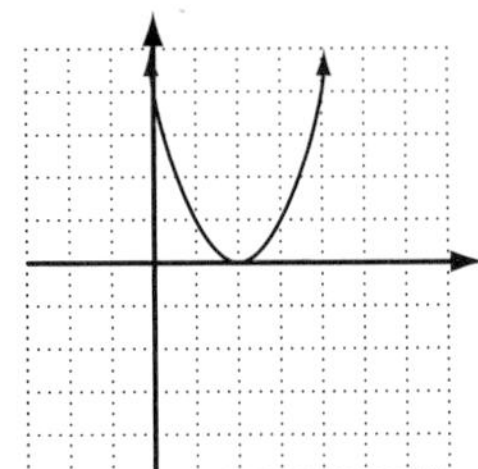

25. 64 **27.** $y = \frac{3x}{z}$

Preparing for Standardized Tests

1. (C) **3.** (E) **5.** (E)

Application

1. $d = -10s + 8000$;

$$P = d(s - 40)$$
$$= (-10s + 8000)(s - 40)$$
$$= -10s^2 + 8000s + 400s - 320{,}000$$
$$= -10s^2 + 8400s - 320{,}000$$
$$= -10(s^2 - 840s + 32{,}000)$$

$s = 420$, $d = 3800$, $P = 1{,}444{,}000$ **3.** The selling price is \$75. At this price, demand is 0, so the expected profit is 0. The product should not be marketed unless demand rises or costs are reduced.

CHAPTER 9 WRAP UP

1. Both **2.** x-axis **3.** Neither **4.** y-axis **5.** Neither **6.** y-axis **7.** No **8.** Yes **9.** No **10.** No **11.** Yes **12.** No

13.

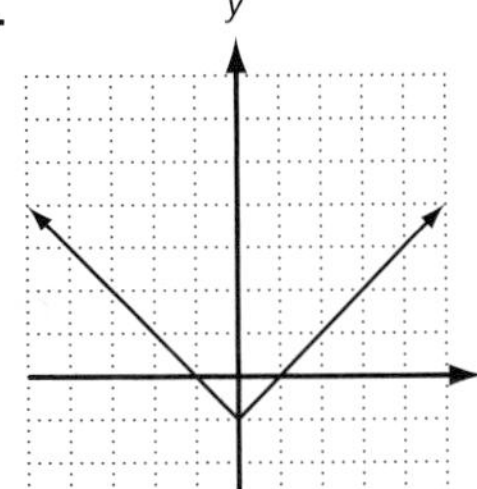

14.

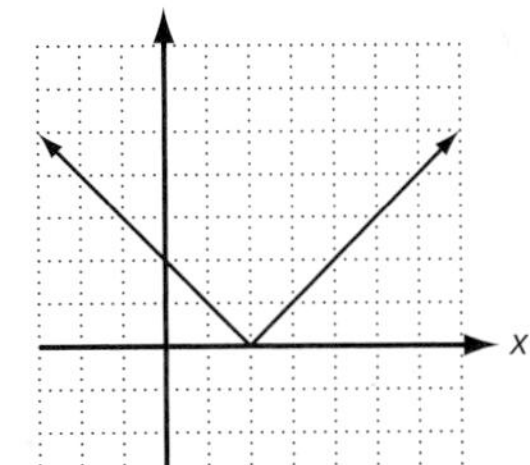

15.

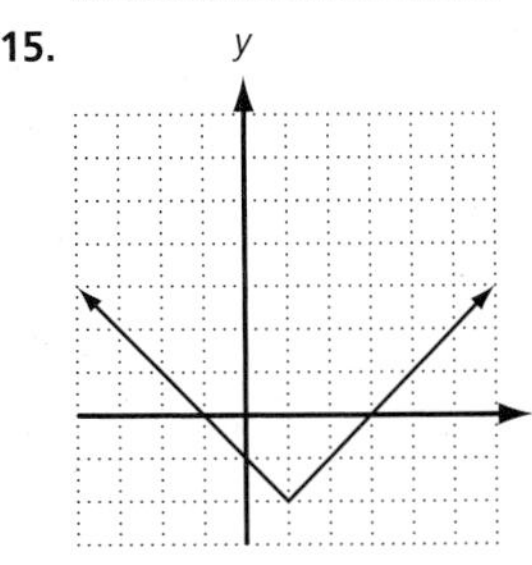

16.

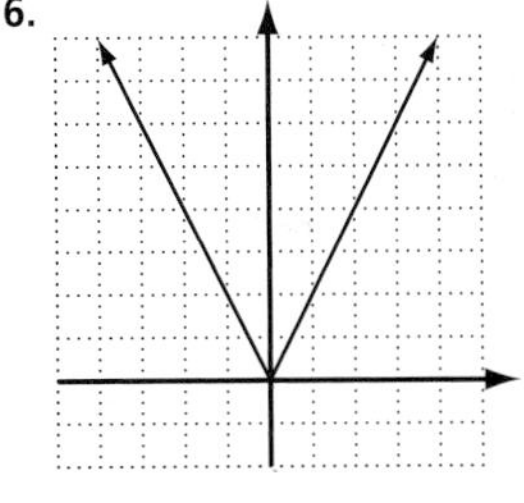

17. Graph same as 16.

18.

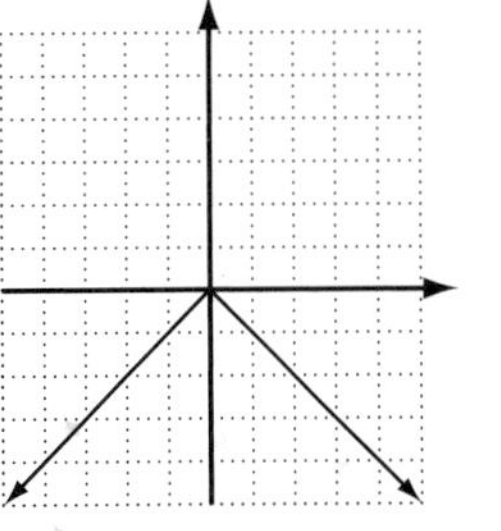

19.

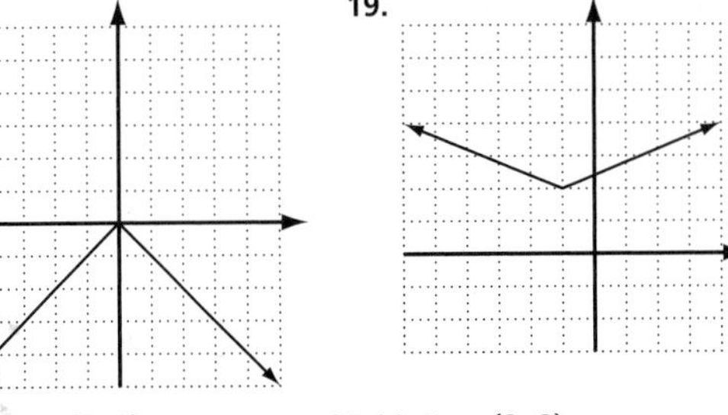

20. Vertex: (0, 0);
Line of symmetry: $x = 0$

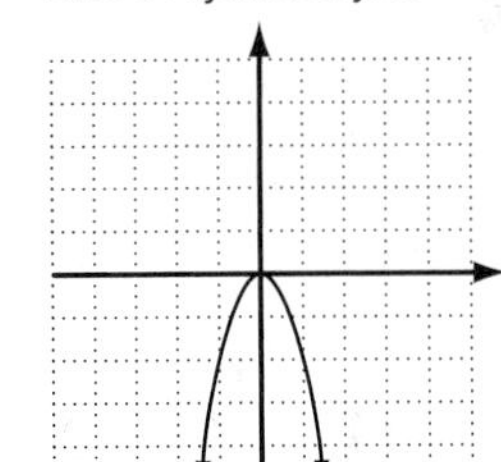

21. Vertex: (0, 0);
Line of symmetry: $x = 0$

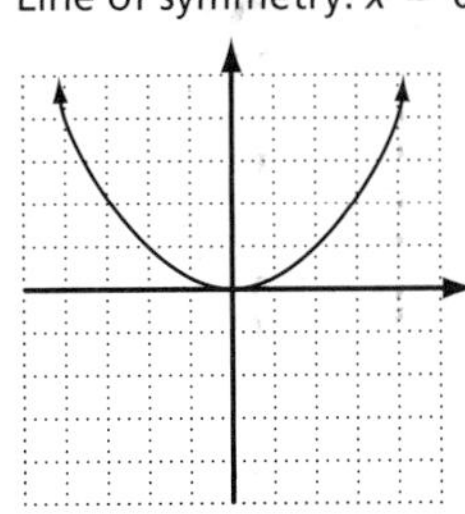

22. Vertex: $(-1, 0)$;
Line of symmetry: $x = -1$

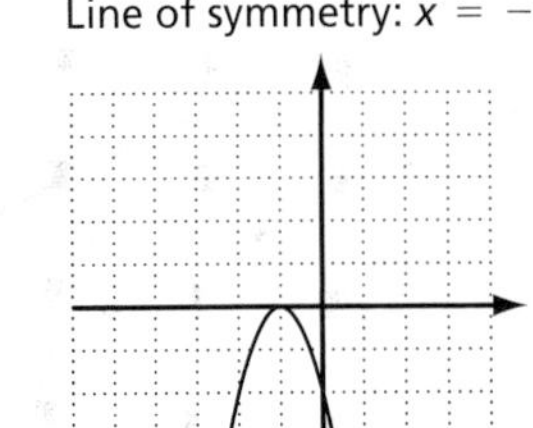

23. Vertex: (2, 0);
Line of symmetry: $x = 2$

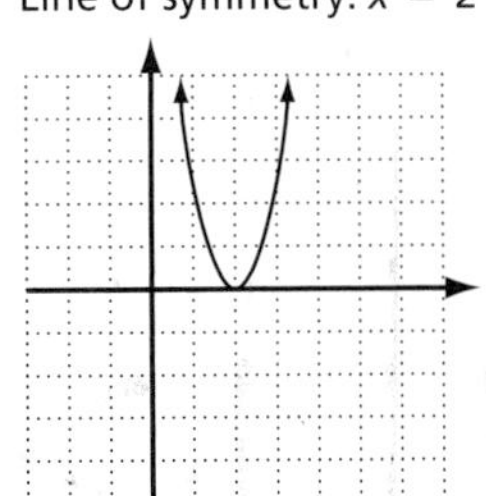

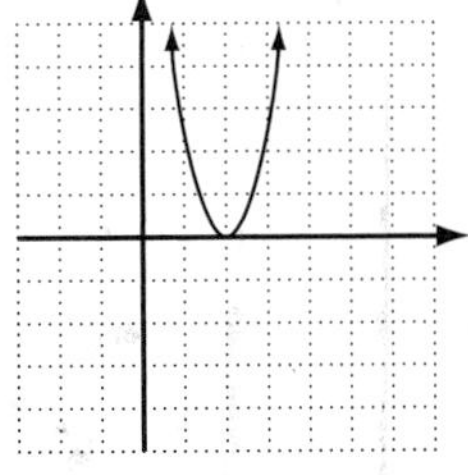

24. Vertex: $(-1, -2)$;
Line of symmetry: $x = -1$;
Maximum: -2

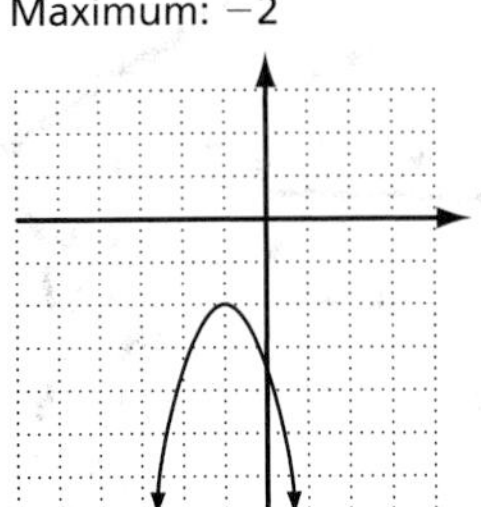

25. Vertex: (1, 5);
Line of symmetry:
$x = 1$; Minimum: 5

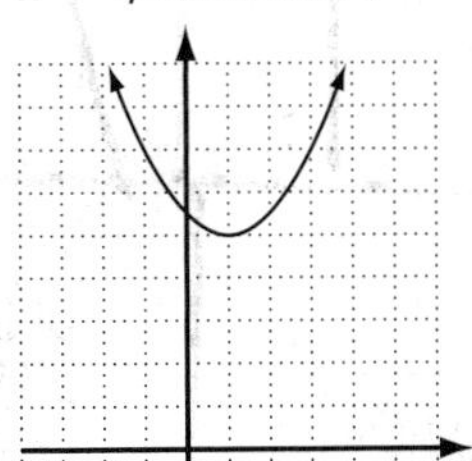

26. Vertex: $(-2, 1)$;
Line of symmetry: $x = -2$;
Maximum: 1

27. $f(x) = (x - 4)^2 - 11$ **28.** $f(x) = -\frac{1}{2}(x - 6)^2 + 2$ **29.** $f(x) = -2(x + 1)^2 + 5$ **30.** 256; 16 and 16 **31.** -16; 4 and -4 **32.** $\frac{-2 \pm \sqrt{10}}{2}$ **33.** $-1 \pm \sqrt{5}$ **34.** 3, 1 **35.** $f(x) = -2x^2 - 4x + 3$ **36.** $f(x) = 3x^2 - 6x + 5$ **37.** $f(x) = -x^2 + 8x - 8$ **38. a.** $f(x) = -0.005x^2 + 0.2x + 7$ **b.** 1 ft

Chapter 10

Skills & Concepts You Need for Chapter 10

1. 13 **2.** $4\sqrt{3}$ **3.** $x^2 - 4x + 4$ **4.** $x^2 + 3x + \frac{9}{4}$

5.

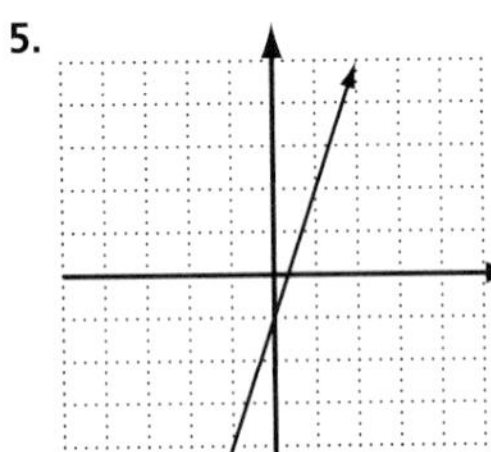

6.

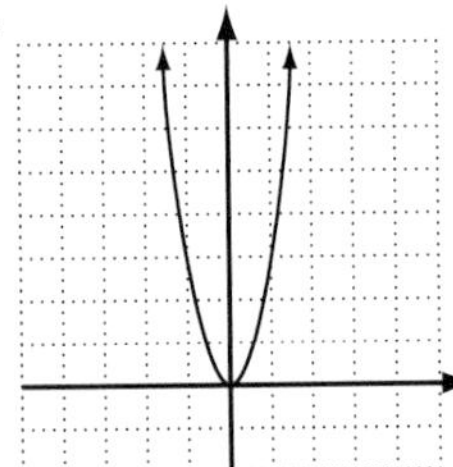

7. $\left(\frac{1}{2}, -5\right)$ **8.** $(-2, -10)$ **9.** 2, 7 **10.** $\sqrt{5}, -\sqrt{5}$

LESSON 10-1

Try This **a.** $\sqrt{149}$ **b.** $6\sqrt{2}$ **c.** $\left(\frac{3}{2}, -\frac{5}{2}\right)$ **d.** $(9, -5)$

Exercises **1.** 5 **3.** $3\sqrt{2}$ **5.** $\sqrt{64 + k^2}$ **7.** $2\sqrt{a}$ **9.** $\left(-\frac{1}{2}, -1\right)$ **11.** $\left(-\frac{7}{2}, -\frac{15}{2}\right)$ **13.** $(4, 4)$ **15.** $(a, 0)$ **17.** Yes **19.** If two points are on a vertical line, they have coordinates (a, y_1) and (a, y_2). Thus, the distance from one to the other is $|y_2 - y_1|$. Now $\sqrt{(a - a)^2 + (y_2 - y_1)^2} = \sqrt{0 + (y_2 - y_1)^2}$ $= \sqrt{(y_2 - y_1)^2} = |y_2 - y_1|$. The proof for a horizontal line is similar. **21.** The midpoint of $\overline{DB}$ has coordinates $\left(\frac{a}{2}, \frac{b}{2}\right)$, which is the same as the midpoint of $\overline{AC}$. **23.** $(0, 4)$ **25.** The vertices are $O(0, 0)$, $H(0, h)$, and $B(b, 0)$. Then $P = \left(\frac{b}{2}, \frac{h}{2}\right)$. Use the distance formula to find the distances between P and H, P and B, and P and O. **27.** The distance between (a, b) and (c, d) is $\sqrt{(a - c)^2 + (b - d)^2}$. **a.** The distance between (a, d) and (c, b) is $\sqrt{(a - c)^2 + (d - b)^2}$. **b.** The distance between (b, a) and (d, c) is $\sqrt{(b - d)^2 + (a - c)^2}$. **c.** The distance between (b, c) and (d, a) is $\sqrt{(b - d)^2 + (c - a)^2}$. Since $(a - c)^2 = (c - a)^2$ and $(b - d)^2 = (d - b)^2$, the distances are all the same.

Mixed Review **29.** $-3, -2$ **31.** Yes **33.** No **35.** $m^2 + 7.4m + 13.69$

LESSON 10-2

Try This **a.** $x^2 + y^2 = 6$ **b.** $(x + 3)^2 + (y - 7)^2 = 25$ **c.** $(x - 5)^2 + (y + 2)^2 = 3$ **d.** $(x + 2)^2 + (y + 6)^2 = 28$ **e.** $(-1, 3)$, 2

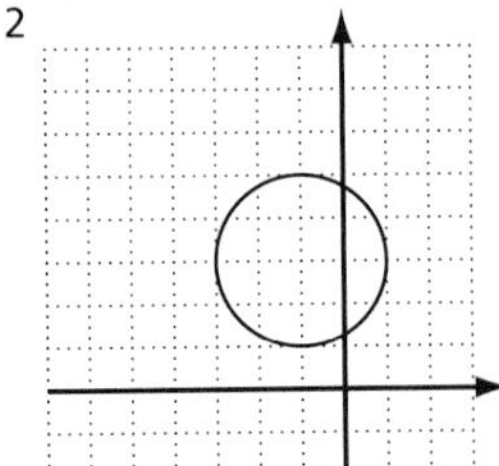

f. $(7, -2)$, 8 **g.** $(6, 4)$, 5

Exercises **1.** $x^2 + y^2 = 49$ **3.** $(x + 2)^2 + (y - 7)^2 = 5$ **5.** $(-1, -3)$, 2 **7.** $(8, -3)$, $2\sqrt{10}$ **9.** $(0, 0)$, $\sqrt{2}$ **11.** $(5, 0)$, $\frac{1}{2}$ **13.** $(4, -1)$, 2 **15.** $(2, 0)$, 2 **17.** $x^2 + y^2 = 25$ **19.** $(x - 2)^2 + (y - 4)^2 = 16$ **21.** $1 \pm \sqrt{77}$, $2 \pm 4\sqrt{5}$ **23.** 2, $-3 \pm \sqrt{5}$ **25.** The origin **27.** From the equation of a circle we have $b^2 + c^2 = a^2$; $c^2 = a^2 - b^2$; the slope of $\overline{AB}$ is $\frac{c}{b + a}$ and the slope of $\overline{BC}$ is $\frac{c}{b - a}$; since $\frac{c}{b + a} \cdot \frac{c}{b - a} = \frac{c^2}{b^2 - a^2} = \frac{a^2 - b^2}{b^2 - a^2} = -1$, $\overline{AB}$ and $\overline{BC}$ are perpendicular and angle ABC is a right angle.

29.

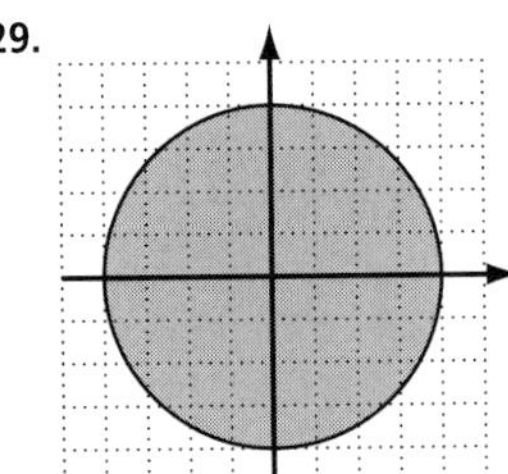

31.

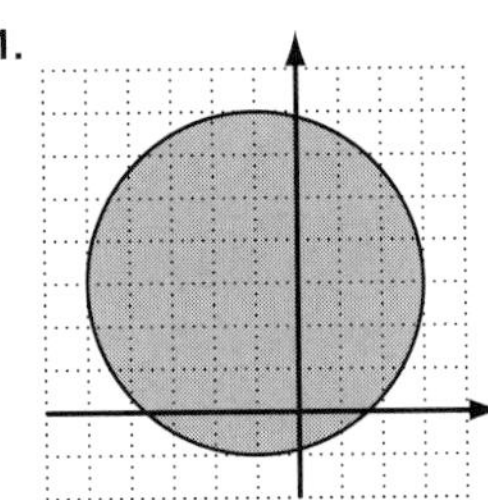

Mixed Review **33.** x-axis **35.** y-axis **37.** $f(x) = 2x^2 - 6x$ **39.** 4

LESSON 10-3

Try This **a.** Vertices: $(\pm 3, 0)$, $(0, \pm 1)$; foci: $(\pm 2\sqrt{2}, 0)$

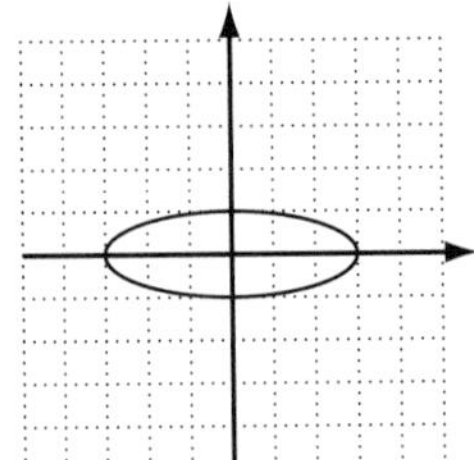

b. Vertices: $(\pm 5, 0)$, $(0, \pm 3)$; foci: $(\pm 4, 0)$

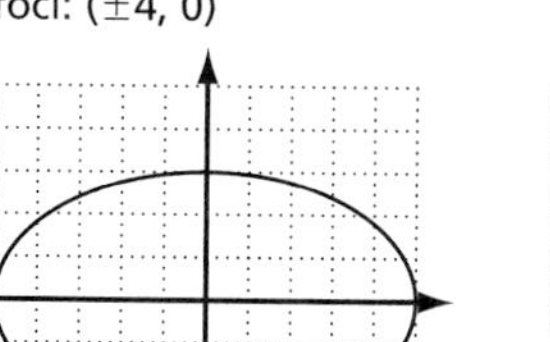

c. Vertices: $(\pm 2, 0)$, $(0, \pm\sqrt{2})$; foci: $(\pm\sqrt{2}, 0)$

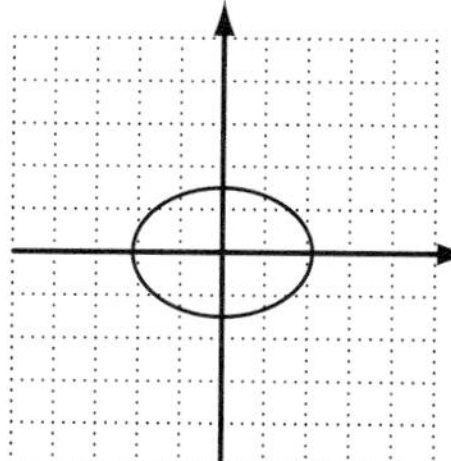

d. Center: $(0, 0)$; vertices: $(\pm 1, 0)$, $(0, \pm 3)$; foci: $(0, \pm 2\sqrt{2})$

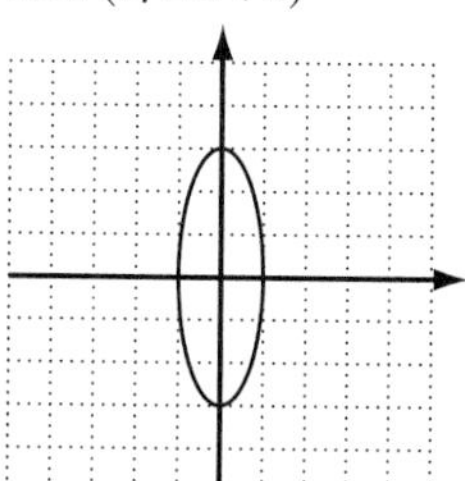

e. Center: $(0, 0)$; vertices: $(\pm 3, 0)$, $(0, \pm 5)$; foci: $(0, \pm 4)$

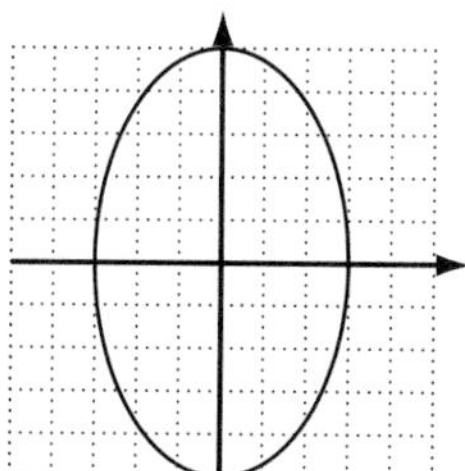

f. Center: $(0, 0)$; vertices: $(\pm\sqrt{2}, 0)$, $(0, \pm 2)$; foci: $(0, \pm\sqrt{2})$

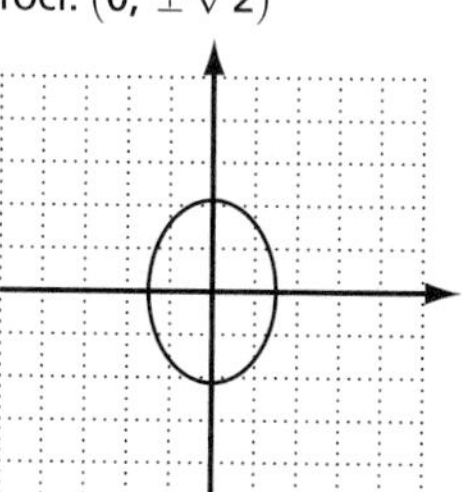

g. Center: $(0, 0)$; vertices: $(\pm 4\sqrt{3}, 0)$, $(0, \pm 4)$;
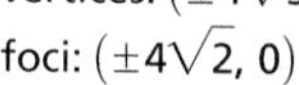
foci: $(\pm 4\sqrt{2}, 0)$

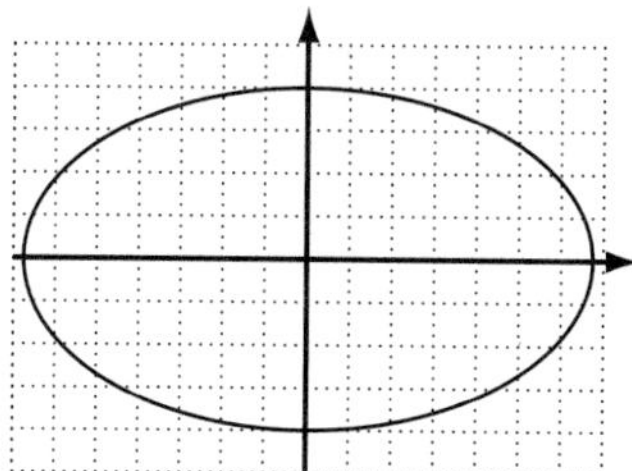

h. Center: $(-3, 2)$; vertices: $\left(-3\frac{1}{5}, 2\right)$, $\left(-3, 2\frac{1}{3}\right)$, $\left(-3, 1\frac{2}{3}\right)$, $\left(-2\frac{4}{5}, 2\right)$;
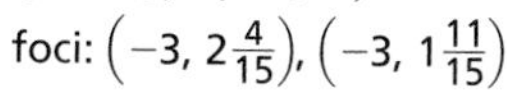
foci: $\left(-3, 2\frac{4}{15}\right)$, $\left(-3, 1\frac{11}{15}\right)$

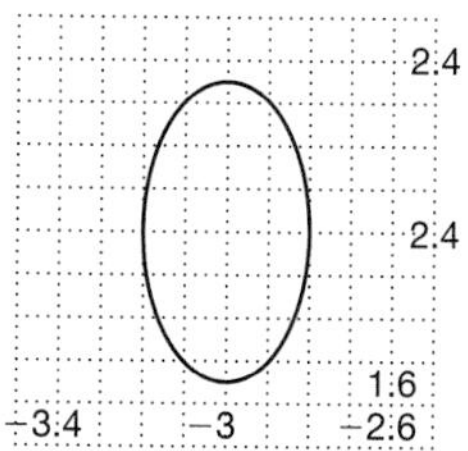

i. Center: $(2, -3)$; vertices: $\left(2\frac{1}{3}, -3\right)$, $\left(2, -3\frac{1}{5}\right)$, $\left(2, -2\frac{4}{5}\right)$, $\left(1\frac{2}{3}, -3\right)$; foci: $\left(2\frac{4}{15}, -3\right)$, $\left(1\frac{11}{15}, -3\right)$

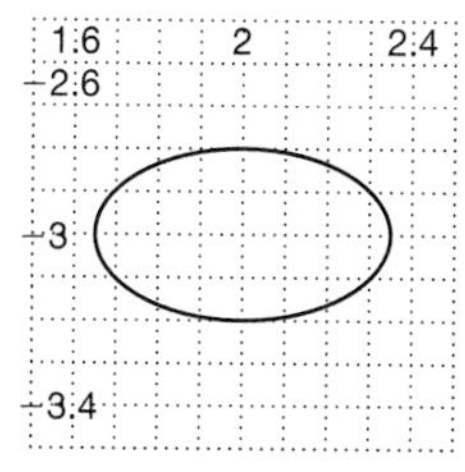

Exercises **1.** Vertices: $(\pm 2, 0)$, $(0, \pm 1)$; foci: $(\pm\sqrt{3}, 0)$

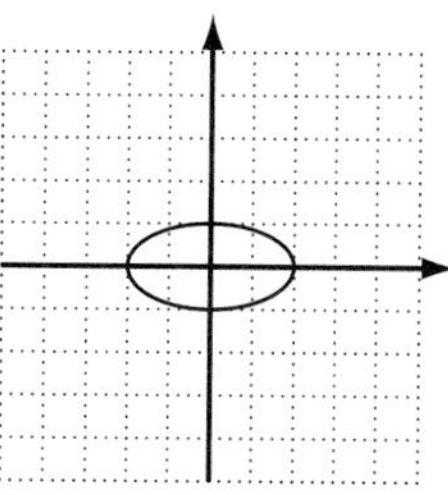

3. Vertices: $(\pm 3, 0)$, $(0, \pm 4)$; foci: $(0, \pm\sqrt{7})$

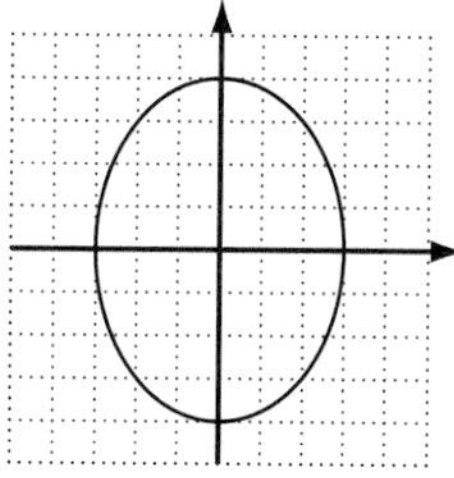

5. Vertices: $(\pm\sqrt{3}, 0)$, $(0, \pm\sqrt{2})$; foci: $(\pm 1, 0)$
7. Vertices: $\left(\pm\frac{1}{2}, 0\right)$, $\left(0, \pm\frac{1}{3}\right)$; foci: $\left(\pm\frac{\sqrt{5}}{6}, 0\right)$
9. Center: $(1, 2)$; vertices: $(-1, 2)$, $(3, 2)$, $(1, 1)$, $(1, 3)$; foci: $(1 \pm \sqrt{3}, 2)$
11. Center: $(-3, 2)$; vertices: $(-8, 2)$, $(2, 2)$, $(-3, -2)$, $(-3, 6)$; foci: $(-6, 2)$, $(0, 2)$
13. Center: $(-2, 1)$; vertices: $(-10, 1)$, $(6, 1)$, $(-2, 1 \pm 4\sqrt{3})$; foci: $(-6, 1)$, $(2, 1)$
15. Center: $(2, -1)$; vertices: $(-1, -1)$, $(5, -1)$, $(2, -3)$, $(2, 1)$; foci: $(2 \pm \sqrt{5}, -1)$
17. Center: $(1, 1)$; vertices: $(0, 1)$, $(2, 1)$, $(1, -1)$, $(1, 3)$; foci: $(1, 1 \pm \sqrt{3})$
19. Center: $(2.5, -0.95)$; vertices: $(6, -0.95)$, $(-1, 0.95)$, $(2.5, 1.02)$, $(2.5, -2.93)$ **21.** $\frac{x^2}{4} + \frac{y^2}{9} = 1$
23. $\frac{(x-3)^2}{4} + \frac{(y-1)^2}{25} = 1$ **25.** $(x+2)^2 + \frac{(y-3)^2}{16} = 1$
27. a. No **b.** $y = \pm 3\sqrt{1 - x^2}$ **c.** Yes; domain $\{x \mid -1 \le x \le 1\}$; range $\{y \mid 0 \le y \le 3\}$

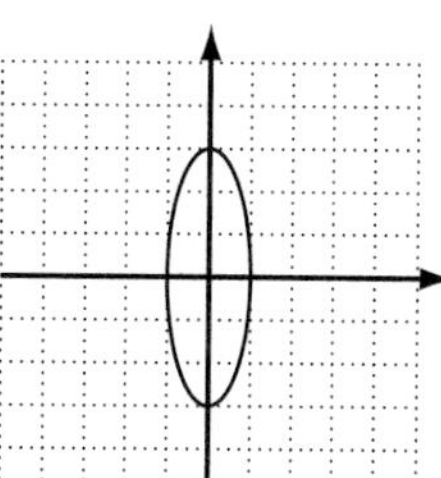

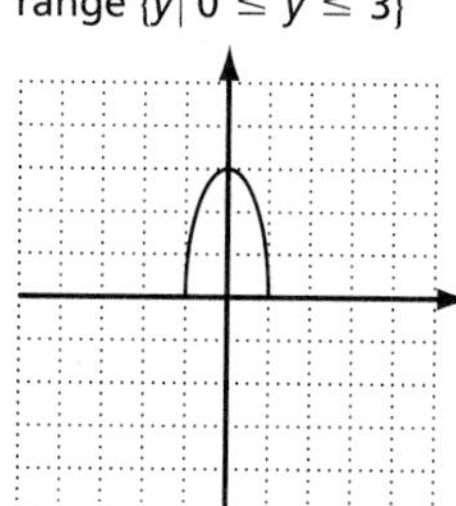

d. Yes; domain $\{x \mid -1 \leq x \leq 1\}$; range $\{y \mid -3 \leq y \leq 0\}$

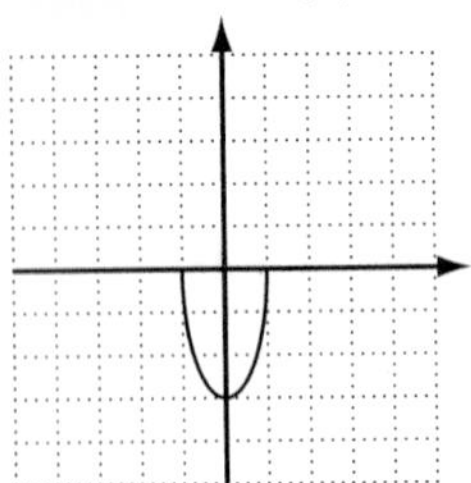

29. 2.0×10^6 miles **31.** A circle with radius a centered at the origin **33.** $0 < e < 1$ **35. a.** $A = \pi ab$ **b.** 20π **c.** $2\pi\sqrt{3}$

37.

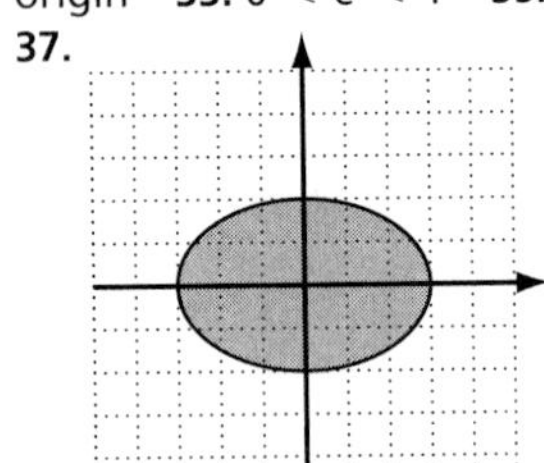

39.

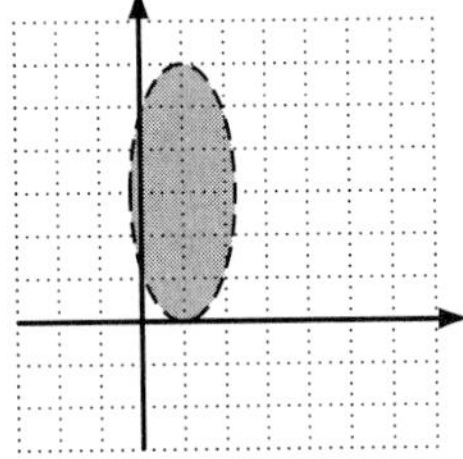

Mixed Review **41.** $f(x) = (x + 2.5)^2 - 7.25$; vertex: $(-2.5, -7.25)$; line of symmetry: $x = -2.5$; minimum: -7.25 **43.** $\left(-1 + \frac{\sqrt{6}}{2}, 0\right), \left(-1 - \frac{\sqrt{6}}{2}, 0\right)$ **45.** $\sqrt{34}$ **47.** $f(x) = 3x^2 + 2x - 4$ **49.** $n < 70$

LESSON 10-4

Try This **a.** Vertices: $(-3, 0)$, $(3, 0)$; foci: $(-\sqrt{13}, 0)$, $(\sqrt{13}, 0)$; asymptotes: $y = -\frac{2}{3}x$, $y = \frac{2}{3}x$

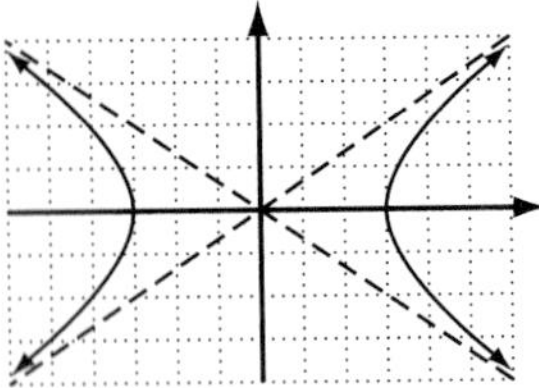

b. Vertices: $(-4, 0)$, $(4, 0)$; foci: $(-4\sqrt{2}, 0)$, $(4\sqrt{2}, 0)$; asymptotes: $y = x$, $y = -x$

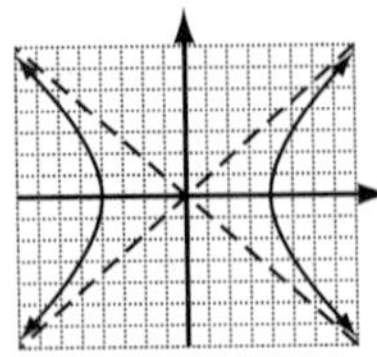

c. Vertices: $(0, -5)$, $(0, 5)$; foci: $(0, -\sqrt{34})$, $(0, \sqrt{34})$; asymptotes: $y = -\frac{5}{3}x$, $y = \frac{5}{3}x$

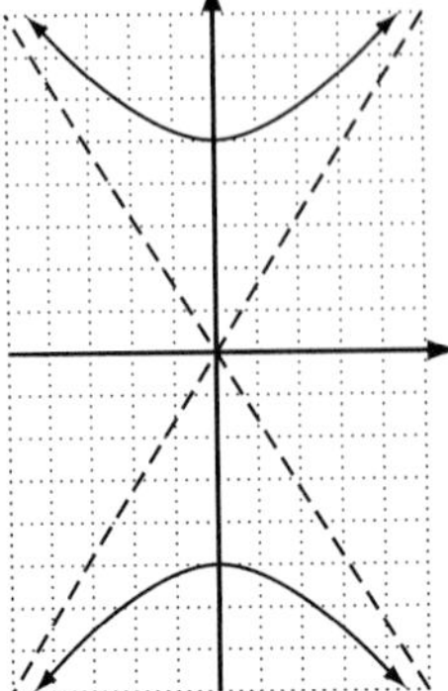

d. Vertices: $(0, 5)$, $(0, -5)$; foci: $(0, -5\sqrt{2})$, $(0, 5\sqrt{2})$; asymptotes: $y = x$, $y = -x$

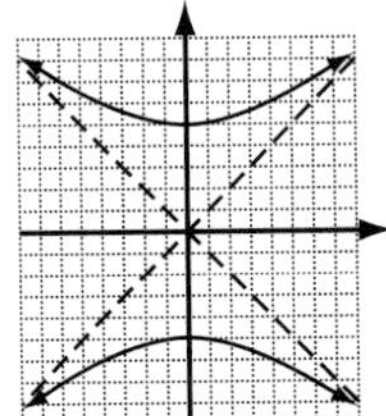

e. Center: $(1, -2)$; vertices: $(-4, -2)$, $(6, -2)$; foci: $(1 \pm \sqrt{29}, -2)$; asymptotes: $y + 2 = \pm\frac{2}{5}(x - 1)$

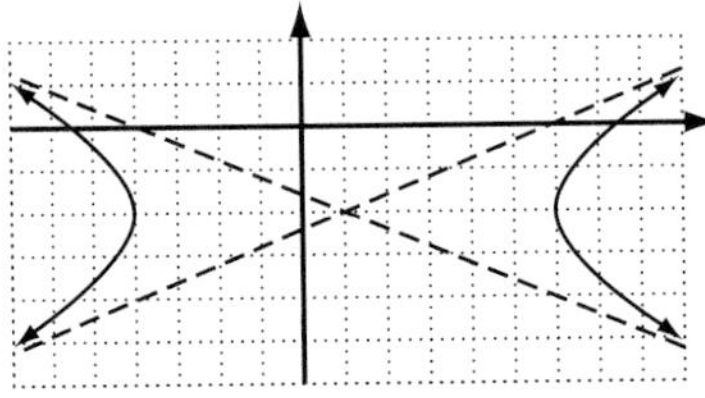

f. Center: $(-1, 2)$; vertices: $(-1, -1)$, $(-1, 5)$; foci: $(-1, -3)$, $(-1, 7)$; asymptotes: $y - 2 = \pm\frac{3}{4}(x + 1)$

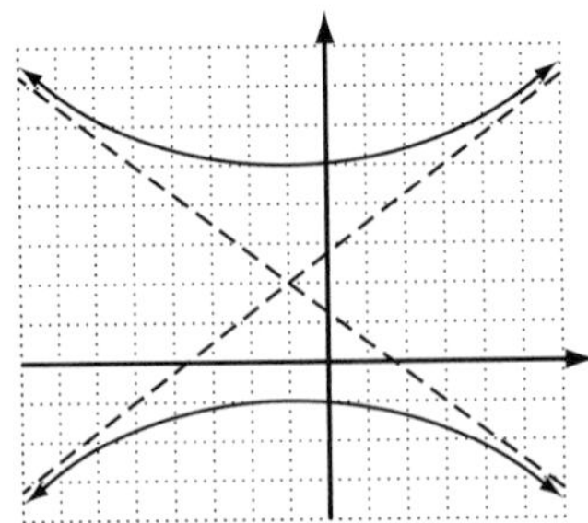

g.

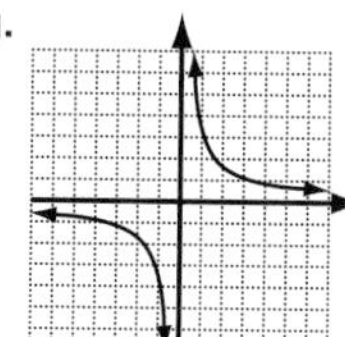

h.

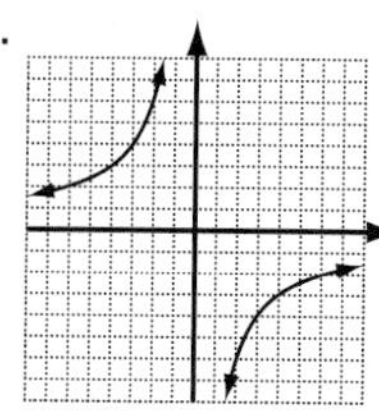

Exercises **1.** Foci: $(\pm\sqrt{10}, 0)$; vertices: $(\pm 3, 0)$; asym: $y = \pm\frac{1}{3}x$
3. Foci: $(0, \pm 2\sqrt{5})$; vertices: $(0, \pm 4)$; asym: $y = \pm 2x$
5. Foci: $(\pm\sqrt{5}, 0)$; vertices: $(\pm 1, 0)$; asym: $y = \pm 2x$
7. Center: (0, 0); foci: $(0, \pm\sqrt{5})$; vertices: $(0, \pm 2)$; asym: $y = \pm 2x$

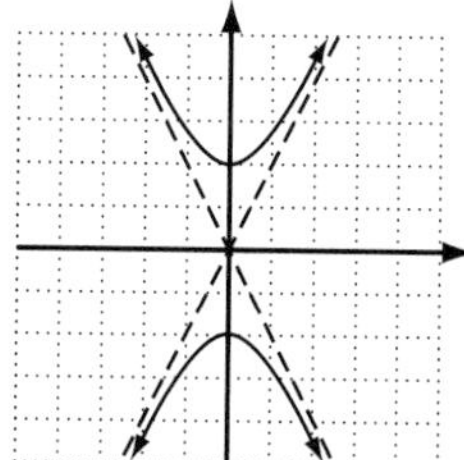

9. Center: (0, 0); foci: $(\pm\sqrt{6}, 0)$; vertices: $(\pm\sqrt{3}, 0)$; asym: $y = \pm x$

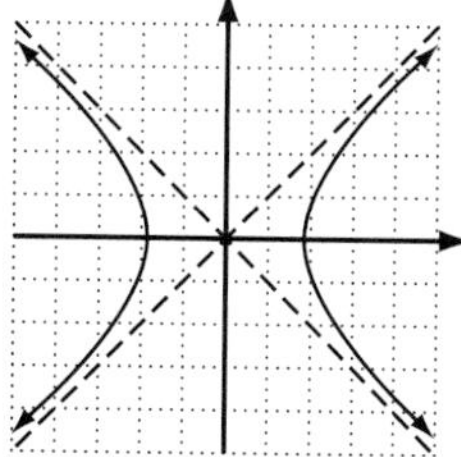

11. Center: $(-1, -3)$; foci: $(-1, -3 \pm 2\sqrt{5})$; vertices: $(-1, -1)$ and $(-1, -5)$; asym: $y = \frac{1}{2}x - \frac{5}{2}$ and $y = -\frac{1}{2}x - \frac{7}{2}$

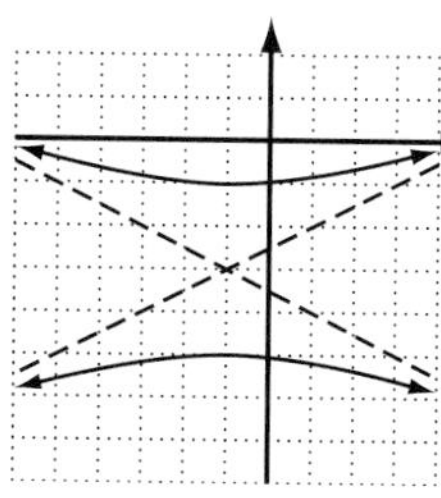

13. Center: $(-1, -3)$; foci: $(-1, -3 \pm \sqrt{41})$; vertices: $(-1, -8)$ and $(-1, 2)$; asym: $y = \frac{5}{4}x - \frac{7}{4}$ and $y = -\frac{5}{4}x - \frac{17}{4}$

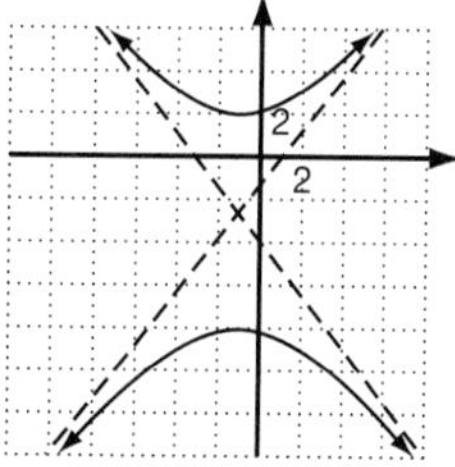

15. Center: $(-1, -2)$; foci: $(-1 \pm \sqrt{5}, -2)$; vertices: $(-2, -2)$ and $(0, -2)$; asym: $y = 2x$ and $y = -2x - 4$

21. $\frac{x^2}{1} - \frac{y^2}{3} = 1$ **23.** They have the same asymptotes.

25. $y^2 = 9\left(\frac{x^2}{16} - 1\right)$; y^2 gets large as $|x|$ gets large. Asymptotes: $y = \pm\frac{3}{4}x$

27. The graph gets closer to the coordinate axes.

29.

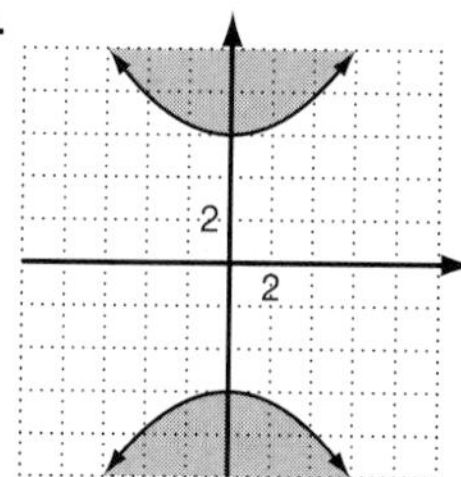

Mixed Review **31.** (3, 6) **33.** (6, 0) **35.** 10 **37.** 5 **39.** Neither **41.** Yes **43.** 138.24 m^2

LESSON 10-5

Try This **a.** Vertex (0, 0); focus (0, 2); directrix $y = -2$

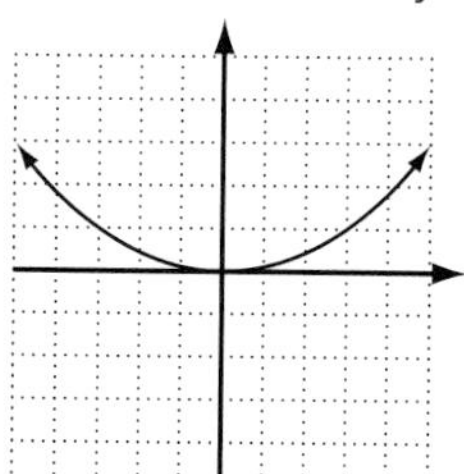

b. Vertex (0, 0); focus $\left(0, -\frac{1}{2}\right)$; directrix $y = \frac{1}{2}$

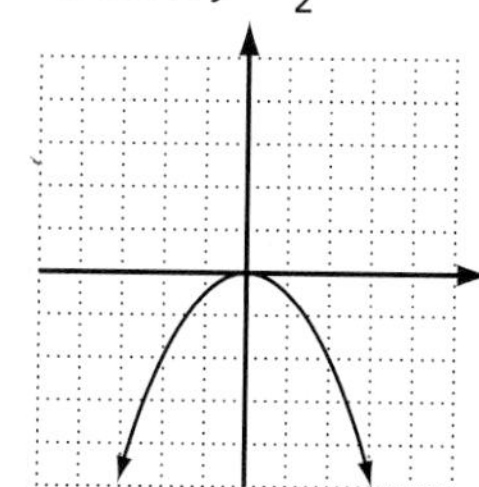

Selected Answers

c. Vertex (0, 0); focus $\left(\frac{1}{2}, 0\right)$; directrix $x = -\frac{1}{2}$

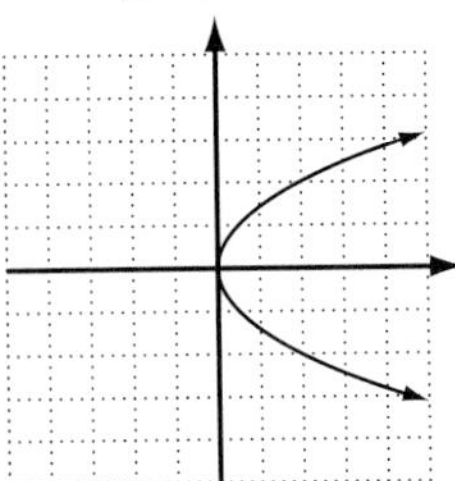

d. Vertex (0, 0); focus (−1, 0); directrix $x = 1$

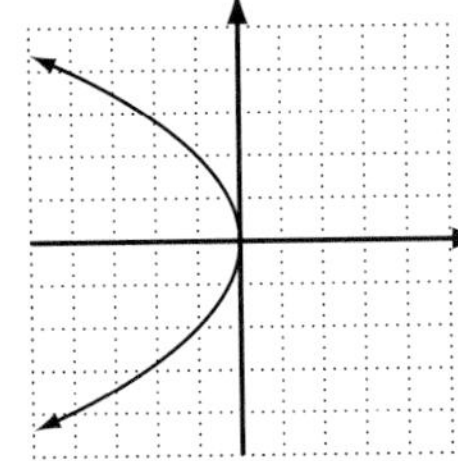

e. Vertex: $\left(-1, -\frac{1}{2}\right)$; focus: $\left(-1, \frac{3}{2}\right)$; directrix: $y = -\frac{5}{2}$

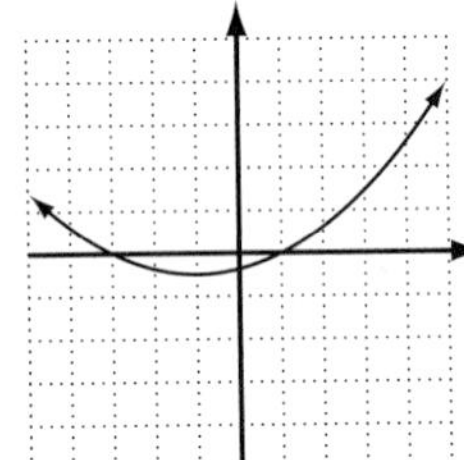

f. Vertex: (2, −1); focus: (1, −1); directrix: $x = 3$

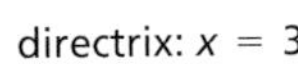

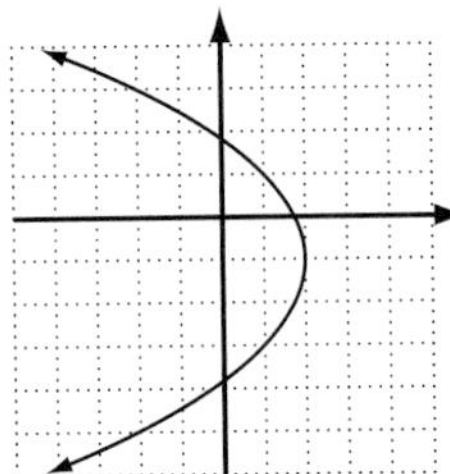

g. $x^2 = 12y$ **h.** $(y - 2)^2 = 4(x + 5)$
i. $(x + 4)^2 = -12(y - 5)$

Exercises **1.** $F(0, 2)$; $y = -2$ **3.** $F\left(-\frac{3}{2}, 0\right)$; $x = \frac{3}{2}$
5. $F(0, 1)$; $y = -1$ **7.** $F\left(0, \frac{1}{8}\right)$; $y = -\frac{1}{8}$
9. $V(-2, 1)$; $F\left(-2, -\frac{1}{2}\right)$; $y = \frac{5}{2}$

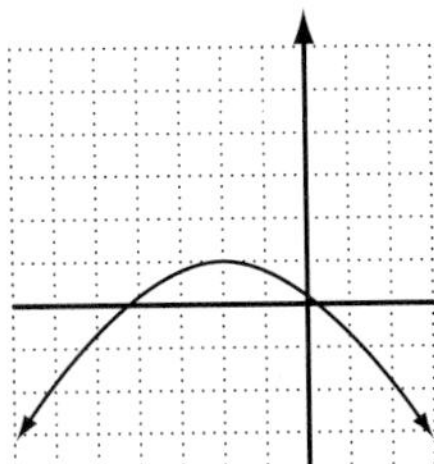

11. $V(-1, -3)$; $F\left(-1, -\frac{7}{2}\right)$; $y = -\frac{5}{2}$

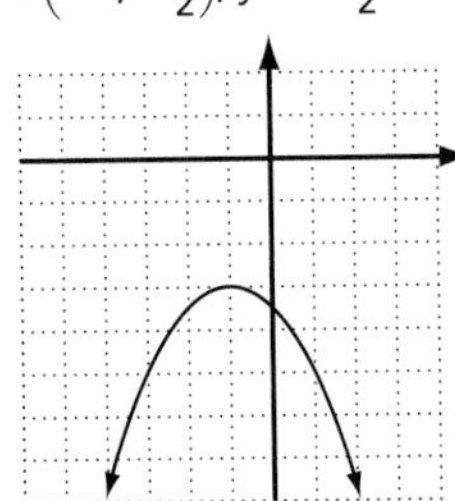

13. $V(0, -2)$; $F\left(0, -\frac{7}{4}\right)$; $y = -\frac{9}{4}$
15. $V(-2, -1)$; $F\left(-2, -\frac{3}{4}\right)$; $y = -\frac{5}{4}$
17. $V\left(\frac{23}{4}, \frac{1}{2}\right)$; $F\left(6, \frac{1}{2}\right)$; $x = \frac{11}{2}$
19. $y^2 = 16x$ **21.** $y^2 = -4\sqrt{2}x$ **23.** $x^2 = 12\sqrt{3}y$
25. $(y - 2)^2 = 14\left(x + \frac{1}{2}\right)$ **27.** $(x - 3)^2 = -12(y - 7)$
29. Vertex: (0, 0);
Focus: (0, 2014.0625);
Directrix: $y = -2014.0625$

31.

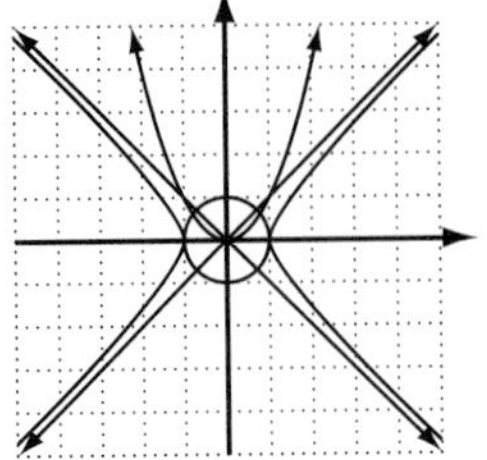

33. Sample: $4x^2 + 3y^2 + 1 = 0$
35. a. No **b.** No, unless $p = 0$

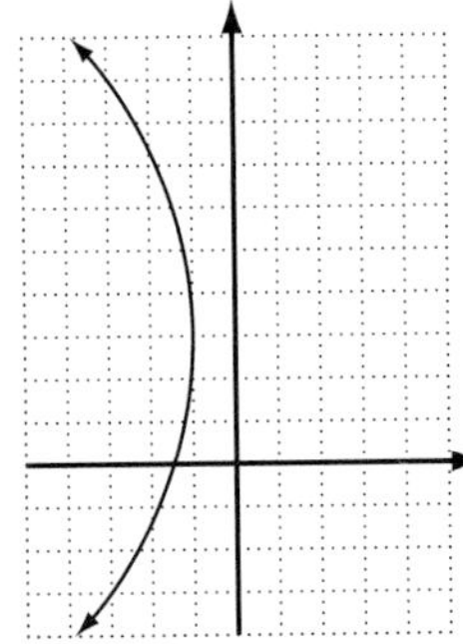

37. Answers may vary. Examples: **a.** $(x + 3)^2 = 4(y - 1)$
b. $(y - 1)^2 = -4(x + 3)$ **c.** $(x + 3)^2 = -4(y - 1)$
d. $(y - 1)^2 = 4(x + 3)$

39.

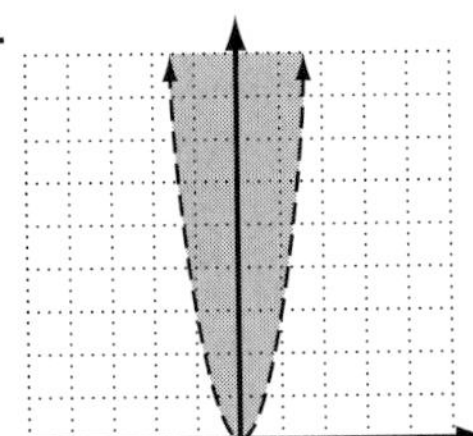

41.

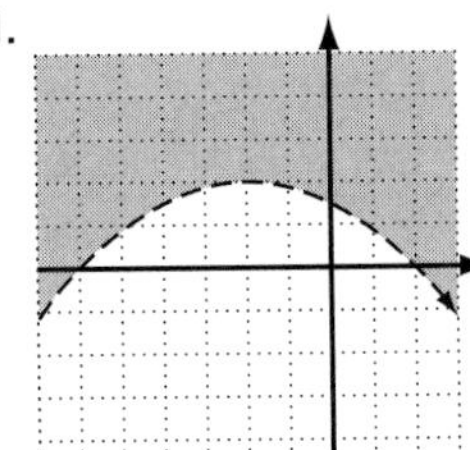

Mixed Review **43.** Vertex: (13.5, 1.6); max: 1.6; line of symmetry: $x = 13.5$ **45.** $m^2 + 5m + \frac{25}{4}$ **47.** $2\sqrt{n}$
49. $-\frac{3}{2}, 3$ **51.** $-\frac{2}{3}, -1$

LESSON 10-6

Try This **a.** Ellipse **b.** Circle **c.** Parabola **d.** Hyperbola
e. $(x - 3)^2 + (y + 1)^2 = 16$ **f.** $x^2 = -\frac{2}{3}y$
g. $\frac{(y + 3)^2}{4} - \frac{(x + 1)^2}{1} = 1$

h. (4, 3), (−3, −4)

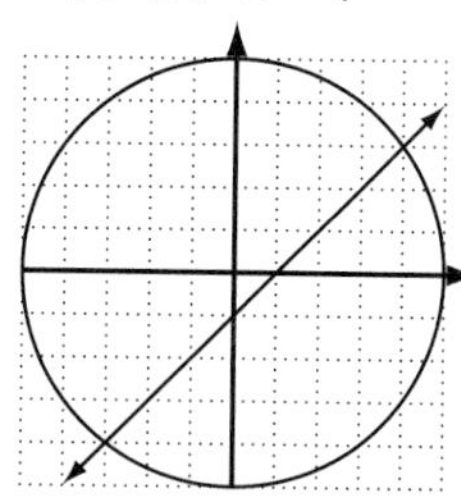

i. (4, 7), (−1, 2)

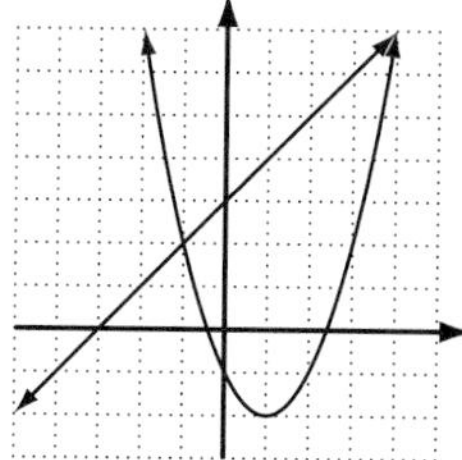

j. (±2, 0)

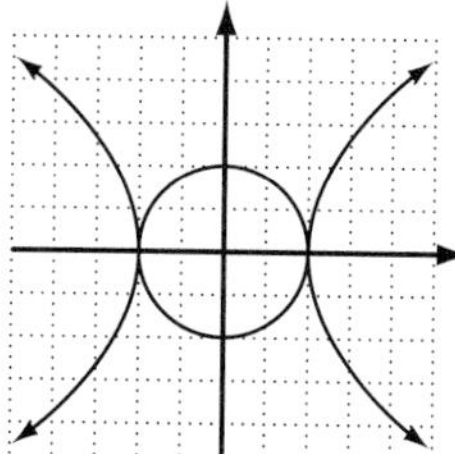

k. (±4, 0)

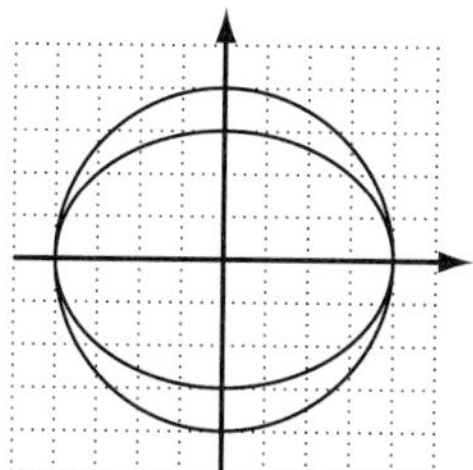

Exercises **1.** Hyperbola **3.** Parabola **5.** Hyperbola **7.** Hyperbola **9.** Does not exist **11.** $x^2 + y^2 = 9$ **13.** $x = 2y^2$
15. $\frac{x^2}{9} + \frac{(y+1)^2}{4} = 1$ **17.** $\frac{(y-4)^2}{9} - \frac{(x-2)^2}{36} = 1$
19. $\frac{(x+1)^2}{4} + \frac{(y+3)^2}{9} = 1$

21. (−8, −6), (6, 8)

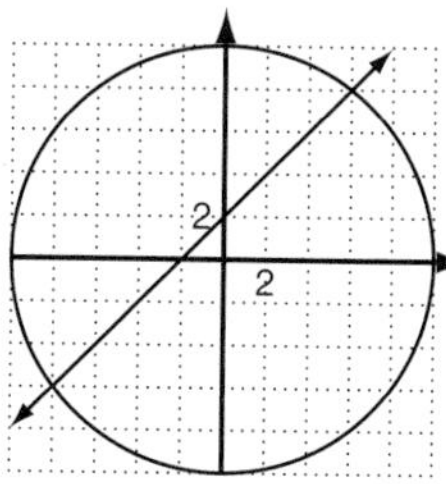

23. (−7, 1), (1, −7)

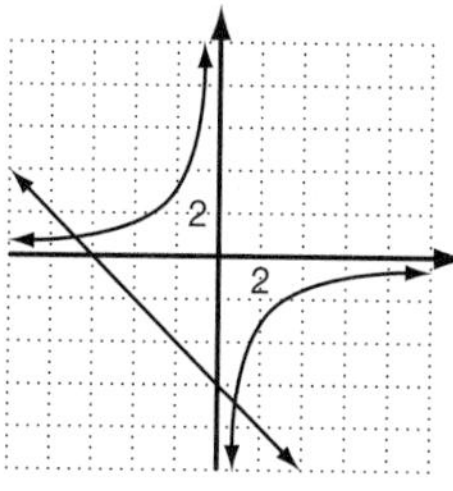

25. (0, 3), (2, 0)

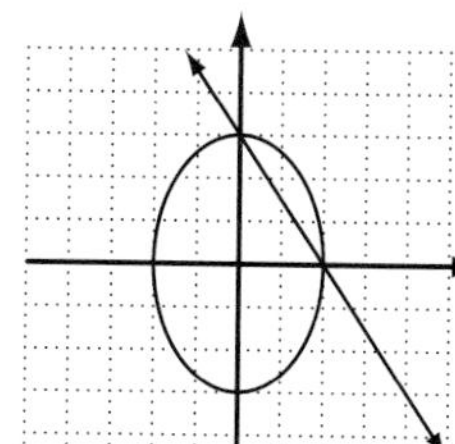

27. (1, 1), (2, 4)

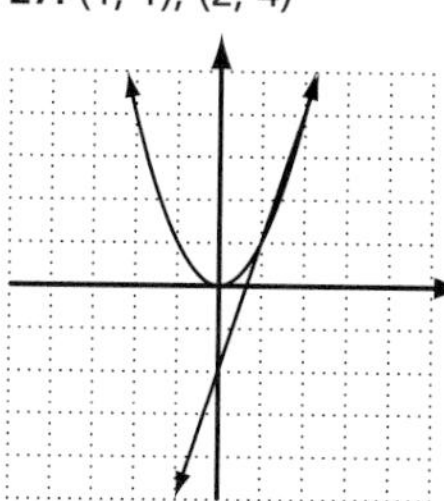

29. (1, 1), (0, 0)

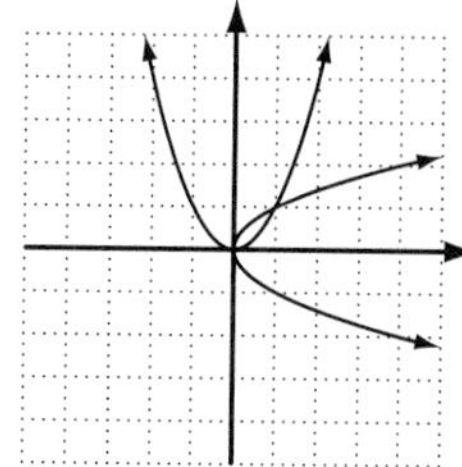

31. (0, −2), (0, 2)

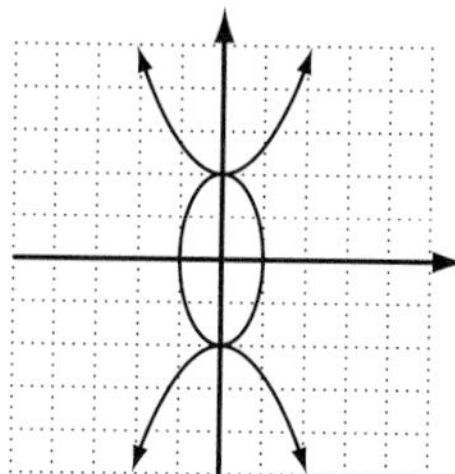
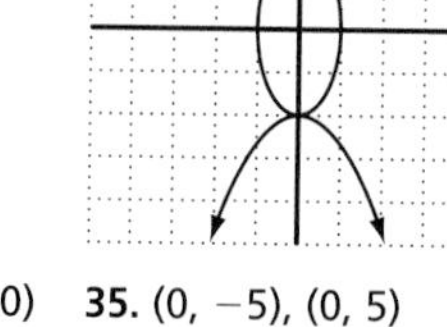

33. (−5, −3), (−5, 3), (4, 0)

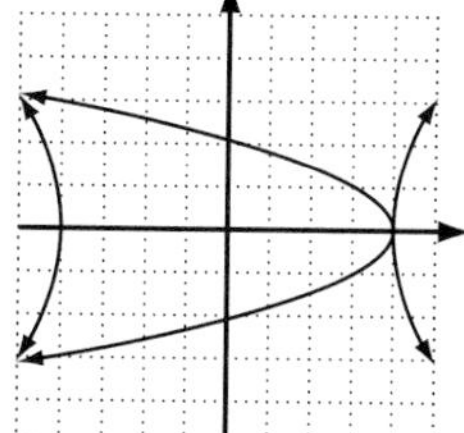

35. (0, −5), (0, 5)

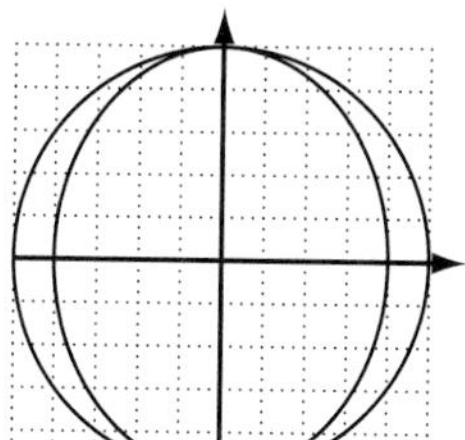

37.

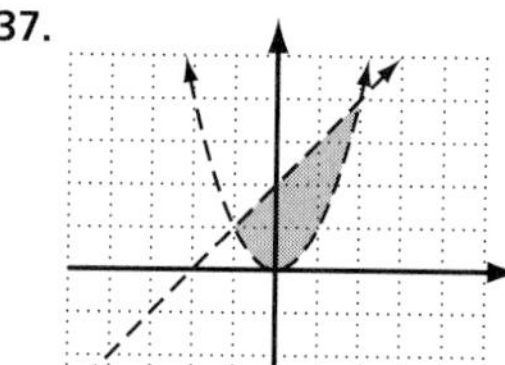

39.

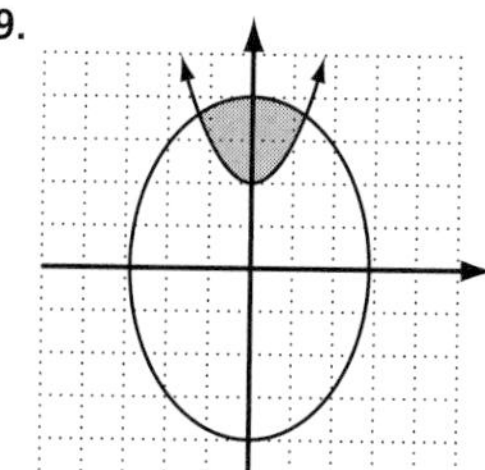

41. Answers may vary. Example:
Circle: $x^2 + y^2 + 2x + 2y - 9 = 0$
Ellipse: $x^2 + 2y^2 + 2x + 2y - 9 = 0$
Hyperbola: $x^2 - 2y^2 + 2x + 2y - 9 = 0$
Parabola: $x^2 + 0y^2 + 2x + 2y - 9 = 0$

43. a. A circle **b.** The point (−2, −3) **c.** $A = 1, B = 1, C = 4, D = 6, E = 13$. $C^2 + D^2 - 4AE = 0$. If $C^2 + D^2 - 4AE = 0$, the equation represents a single point.

Mixed Review **45.** 4, 0, −4 **47.** No **49.** 3 **51.** $\sqrt{m+n}$
53. $\left(\frac{5}{2}, \frac{25}{2}\right)$

LESSON 10-7

Try This **a.** (−3, −4), (4, 3) **b.** (4, 7), (−1, 2)
c. (2, 1), (−4, 4) **d.** (−2, −5), $\left(\frac{5}{3}, 6\right)$
e. $\left(-2 + \sqrt{10}, 6 + 3\sqrt{10}\right)$ and $\left(-2 - \sqrt{10}, 6 - 3\sqrt{10}\right)$
f. (2, −3), $\left(-\frac{14}{3}, \frac{1}{3}\right)$ **g.** (0, −2), (0, 2) **h.** (−2, −3), (−2, 3), (2, −3), (2, 3) **i.** (3, −4), (−3, −4), (4, 3), (−4, 3) **j.** (−3, −2), (−2, −3), (3, 2), (2, 3) **k.** (2, 4), (−2, −4)

Exercises **1.** (3, 2), $\left(4, \frac{3}{2}\right)$ **3.** $\left(\frac{7}{3}, \frac{1}{3}\right)$, (1, −1) **5.** (1, 4), $\left(\frac{11}{4}, -\frac{5}{4}\right)$ **7.** (0, 2), (3, 1) **9.** (2, −8), $\left(\frac{40}{3}, -\frac{6}{5}\right)$ **11.** $(-3, -\sqrt{5})$, $(-3, \sqrt{5})$, $(3, -\sqrt{5})$, $(3, \sqrt{5})$ **13.** (−4, −2), (−2, −4), (2, 4), (4, 2) **15.** (−2, −2), (2, 2), (4, 1), (−4, −1) **17.** (−2, −1), (2, 1) **19.** No solution **21.** C **23.** $\left(\frac{1}{3}, \frac{1}{3}\right)$, $\left(-\frac{1}{3}, \frac{1}{3}\right)$, (0, 0) **25.** Answers may vary. Examples: **a.** $y = x$; $x^2 + y^2 = 4$ **b.** $x^2 - 2y^2 = 4$; $x^2 + 2y^2 = 9$ **c.** $x^2 + y^2 = 9$; $x^2 - y^2 = 9$ **d.** $y = x^2 + 2x + 3$; $3x^2 + y^2 = 16$ **27.** There is no number x such that $\frac{x^2}{a^2} - \frac{\left(\frac{b}{a}x\right)^2}{b^2} = 1$, because the left side simplifies to $\frac{x^2}{a^2} - \frac{x^2}{a^2}$, which is 0. **29.** $(x + 1)^2 + (y + 3)^2 = 100$

Mixed Review **31.** 2 **33.** (0, 0); 7

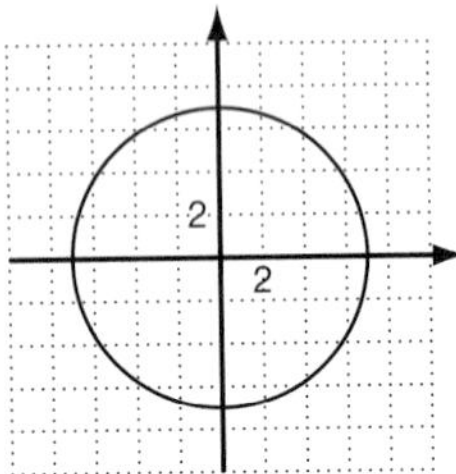

35. 2 km **37.** No **39.** No **41.** Yes

LESSON 10-8

Try This **a.** 14 m, 9 m **b.** $l = 12$, $w = 5$ **c.** $w = 1$ ft, $l = 2$ ft

Exercises **1.** 6 cm, 8 cm **3.** 4 in., 5 in. **5.** 12, 13 and −12, −13 **7.** $l = \sqrt{3}$ m, $w = 1$ m **9.** 16 ft, 24 ft **11.** 9, 7 **13.** 30 cm, 40 cm **15.** 10 by 10 and 5 by 6 **17.** Carpenter: 8.21 days, helper: 12.21 days

Mixed Review **19.** (3, 10) **21.** $f(x) = 2x^2 + 6x - 3$

LESSON 10-9

Problems **1.** There would be 22 sections with 6 paths. **3.** A total of 63 games (1 less game than the number of teams) were needed to determine the championship. **5.** Roosevelt 195, Riverside 125, Central 190

Application **1. a.** 1.8×10^9 mi **b.** ≈ 19 AU **c.** ≈ 3×10^{-4} light years **3.** approximately 24,000 mi/h **5.** ≈ 30,400:1 **7.** ≈ 1.62×10^9 mi

CHAPTER 10 WRAP UP

1. $2\sqrt{29}$ **2.** 5 **3.** $\sqrt{221}$ **4.** (2, 2) **5.** (2, 6) **6.** (−2, 2) **7.** (5, 5) **8.** $(x + 2)^2 + (y - 6)^2 = 13$ **9.** $(x - 3)^2 + (y + 1)^2 = 4$ **10.** Center (4, −3); radius $2\sqrt{3}$ **11.** Center (0, 0); radius 6 **12.** Center (3, −5); radius $\sqrt{10}$ **13.** Center $\left(\frac{3}{4}, \frac{5}{4}\right)$; radius $\frac{\sqrt{10}}{4}$

14. Center: (2, −1); vertices: (7, −1), (−3, −1), (2, 3), (2, −5); foci: (5, −1), (−1, −1)

15. Center: (−2, 1); vertices: (−6, 1), (2, 1), (−2, 4), (−2, −2); foci: $(-2 + \sqrt{7}, 1)$, $(-2 - \sqrt{7}, 1)$

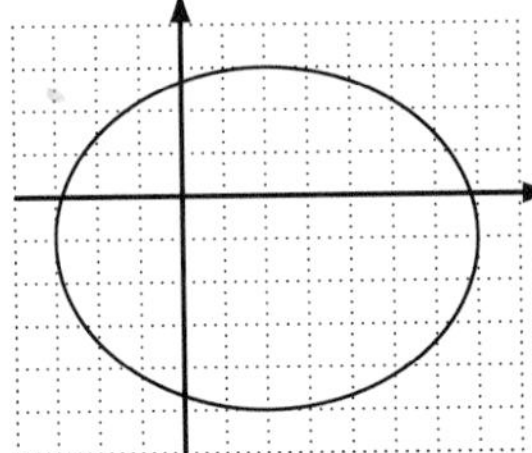

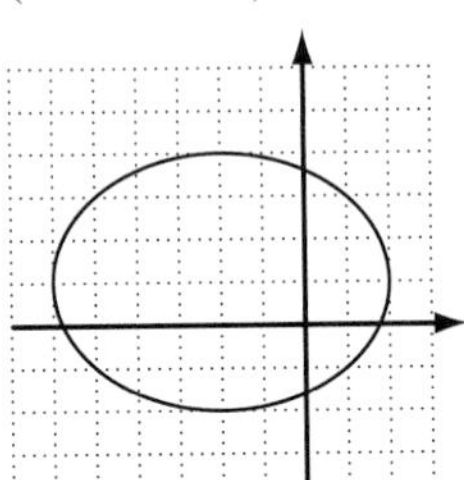

16. Center: $\left(-2, \frac{1}{4}\right)$; vertices: $\left(0, \frac{1}{4}\right)$, $\left(-4, \frac{1}{4}\right)$; foci: $\left(-2 + \sqrt{6}, \frac{1}{4}\right)$, $\left(-2 - \sqrt{6}, \frac{1}{4}\right)$; asymptotes: $y - \frac{1}{4} = \pm\frac{\sqrt{2}}{2}(x + 2)$ **17.** Center: (0, 0); vertices: $(\sqrt{6}, 0)$, $(-\sqrt{6}, 0)$; foci: $(\sqrt{22}, 0)$, $(-\sqrt{22}, 0)$; asymptotes: $y = \pm\frac{2\sqrt{6}}{3}x$ **18.** Vertex: (0, 0); focus: (−3, 0); directrix: $x = 3$ **19.** Vertex: (1, −1); focus: $\left(1, -\frac{1}{2}\right)$; directrix: $y = -\frac{3}{2}$ **20.** Vertex: $\left(\frac{9}{4}, -1\right)$; focus: $\left(\frac{5}{4}, -1\right)$; directrix: $x = \frac{13}{4}$ **21.** Hyperbola **22.** Parabola **23.** Circle **24.** Ellipse **25.** No conic **26.** (6, 8), (−8, −6) **27.** (1, 2), $\left(-\frac{3}{2}, \frac{13}{4}\right)$ **28.** (4, 0), (−4, 0) **29.** (4, 0), (0, 3) **30.** (2, 5), (2, −5), (−2, 5), (−2, −5) **31.** (6, −2), (−6, 2) **32.** 10 cm by 24 cm **33.** 3 and −16, or −3 and 16

Chapter 11

Skills & Concepts You Need for Chapter 11

1. $(x + 3)(x - 2)$ **2.** $(x - 4)(x - 1)$ **3.** $(3x - 1)(x + 1)$ **4.** $(x + 2)(2x + 3)$ **5.** $(x - 1)(4x + 5)$ **6.** $(x - 3)(x - 8)$ **7.** $-3 - 8i$ **8.** $2 + 4i$ **9.** 26 **10.** 13 **11.** 37 **12.** Yes **13.** No **14.** No **15.** $x^3 - 4ix^2 + 2x^2 - 8ix - 3x - 6 = 0$ **16.** $(-1 - i)^2 = 1 + 2i + i^2 = 1 + 2i - 1 = 2i$, $1 + i$ **17.** $3x^2 + 13x - 10 = 0$ **18.** $4x^2 + 4x - 3 = 0$ **19.** $x^2 - 2 = 0$

LESSON 11-1

Try This **a.** (1) Yes (2) No **b.** (1) Yes (2) No **c.** (1) No (2) Yes **d.** (1) Yes (2) No
e. $x^3 + 2x^2 - 5x - 6 = (x - 3)(x^2 + 5x + 10) + 24$

Exercises **1.** Yes, no, no **3.** Yes, no, yes, yes **5. a.** Yes **b.** No **c.** No **7. a.** Yes **b.** Yes **c.** No **9. a.** Yes **b.** Yes **c.** Yes
11. a. $x^3 + 6x^2 - x - 30 = (x - 2)(x^2 + 8x + 15) + 0$
b. $x^3 + 6x^2 - x - 30 = (x - 3)(x^2 + 9x + 26) + 48$
13. $x^3 - 8 = (x + 2)(x^2 - 2x + 4) + (-16)$
15. $x^4 + 9x^2 + 20 = (x^2 + 4)(x^2 + 5) + 0$
17. $5x^5 - 3x^4 + 2x^2 - 3 = (2x^2 - x + 1) \cdot \left(\frac{5}{2}x^3 - \frac{1}{4}x^2 - \frac{11}{8}x + \frac{7}{16}\right) + \frac{29x - 55}{16}$ **19.** $2x^3 + 7x^2 - 5$
21. $6x^3 - 8x^2 + 23x - 4$ **23.** B **25. a.** -4 **b.** -4
27. All exponents odd; yes

Mixed Review **29.** Odd **31.** Odd **35.** 0 or $-\frac{1}{2}$ **37.** 0 or $\frac{m}{n}$

LESSON 11-2

Try This **a.** 73,120; −37,292 **b.** Yes **c.** No **d.** Yes **e.** No **f.** Yes **g.** $P(x) = (x - 2)(x + 3)(x + 5)$; 2, −3, −5

Exercises **1.** $P(1) = 0$; $P(-2) = -60$; $P(3) = 0$
3. $P(20) = 5{,}935{,}988$; $P(-3) = -772$ **5.** Yes, no **7.** No, no
9. No **11.** Yes **13.** Yes **15. a.** Yes **b.** $x^2 + 3x + 2$
c. $(x - 1)(x + 2)(x + 1)$ **d.** 1, −2, −1
17. $P(x) = (x - 1)(x + 2)(x + 3)$; 1, −2, −3
19. $P(x) = (x - 2)(x - 5)(x + 1)$; 2, 5, −1
21. $P(x) = (x - 2)(x - 3)(x + 4)$; 2, 3, −4
23. $P(x) = (x - 1)(x - 2)(x - 3)(x + 5)$; 1, 2, 3, −5
25. $-5 < x < 1$ or $x > 2$ **27.** 4 **29.** 0 **31.** Answers may vary. If $A(x)$ is a factor of $B(x)$, then $A(x) \cdot P(x) = B(x)$ for some $P(x)$. If $B(x)$ is a factor of $C(x)$, then $B(x) \cdot Q(x) = C(x)$ for some $Q(x)$. Thus, $A(x) \cdot P(x) \cdot Q(x) = C(x)$. Therefore $A(x)$ is a factor of $C(x)$. **33.** $P(r)$ is the remainder of $P(x) \div (x - r)$ by the remainder theorem. If $P(r) = 0$, then $P(x) \div (x - r)$ has a remainder of 0. Thus, $(x - r)$ must be a factor of $P(x)$.

Mixed Review **35.** $f(x) = 2\left(x - \frac{5}{2}\right)^2 - \frac{41}{2}$; vertex: $\left(\frac{5}{2}, -\frac{41}{2}\right)$; line of symmetry: $x = \frac{5}{2}$; minimum: $\frac{-41}{2}$ **37.** Center $(-1, 0)$; radius 8 **39.** Center $(-1, 1)$; radius $3\sqrt{5}$

LESSON 11-3

Try This **a.** −7 (multiplicity 2), 3 (multiplicity 1)
b. 4 (multiplicity 2), 3 (multiplicity 2) **c.** 1 (multiplicity 1), −1 (multiplicity 1) **d.** $7 + 2i$ and $-7\sqrt{5}$ are the other roots.
e. $i, -i, -2, 1$ **f.** $P(x) = x^3 - 6x^2 + 3x + 10$
g. $P(x) = x^5 + 6x^4 + 12x^3 + 8x^2$
h. $x^4 - 6x^3 + 11x^2 - 10x + 2$ **i.** $x^3 - 2x^2 + 4x - 8$

Exercises **1.** −3 (multiplicity 2), 1 (multiplicity 1)
3. 3 (multiplicity 2), −4 (multiplicity 3), 0 (multiplicity 4)
5. 2 (multiplicity 2), 3 (multiplicity 2) **7.** $5 - i$, $2i$ are the other roots. **9.** $-3 - 4i$, $4 + \sqrt{5}$ **11.** $1 + i$ **13.** i, 3, 2
15. $-2i$, 2, −2 **17.** $2 + i$, $2 - i$ **19.** $-1 + i\sqrt{3}$, $-1 - i\sqrt{3}$
21. $\sqrt{3}$, $1 + 3i$, $1 - 3i$ **23.** $P(x) = x^3 - 6x^2 - x + 30$
25. $P(x) = x^3 - 2x^2 + x - 2$ **27.** $P(x) = x^3 - 7x^2 + 17x - 15$
29. $P(x) = x^3 - \sqrt{3}x^2 - 2x + 2\sqrt{3}$; no
31. $P(x) = x^4 - 10x^3 + 25x^2$
33. $P(x) = x^4 - 3x^3 - 7x^2 + 15x + 18$
35. $P(x) = x^3 - 4x^2 + 6x - 4$ **37.** $P(x) = x^3 + 2x^2 + 9x + 18$
39. $P(x) = x^4 - 6x^3 + 11x^2 - 10x + 2$
41. $P(x) = x^4 + 4x^2 - 45$
43. $P(x) = x^4 - 4x^3 + 9x^2 + 8x - 22$ **45.** $i, -i, -\frac{b}{a}$
47. $i, -i, 1 + \sqrt{2}, 1 - \sqrt{2}$ **49.** Answers may vary. Ex: $P(x) = x - 2$ **51.** By Theorem 11-3, $P(x)$ can be factored into n linear factors, where n is the degree of $P(x)$. Since by Theorem 11-5 the nonreal roots occur in conjugate pairs, there is at least one factor $(x - a)$ with a real.
53. Let $P(x) = s_n x^n + s_{n-1}x^{n-1} + \cdots + s_1 x + s_0$, where the coefficients are rational numbers. Suppose $a + c\sqrt{b}$ is a root of $P(x)$. Then $P(a + c\sqrt{b}) = 0$, or $s_n(a + c\sqrt{b})^n + s_{n-1}(a + c\sqrt{b})^{n-1} + \cdots + s_1(a + c\sqrt{b}) + s_0 = 0$. The conjugate of a power is the power of the conjugate of the base. Take the conjugate of each side:

$$\begin{aligned}0 = \overline{0} &= \overline{s_n(a + c\sqrt{b})^n + s_{n-1}(a + c\sqrt{b})^{n-1} + \cdots + s_1(a + c\sqrt{b}) + s_0} \\ &= \overline{s_n(a + c\sqrt{b})^n} + \overline{s_{n-1}(a + c\sqrt{b})^{n-1}} + \cdots + \overline{s_1(a + c\sqrt{b})} + \overline{s_0} \\ &= \overline{s_n} \cdot \overline{(a + c\sqrt{b})^n} + \overline{s_{n-1}} \cdot \overline{(a + c\sqrt{b})^{n-1}} + \cdots + \overline{s_1} \cdot \overline{(a + c\sqrt{b})} + \overline{s_0} \\ &= s_n\overline{(a + c\sqrt{b})^n} + s_{n-1}\overline{(a + c\sqrt{b})^{n-1}} + \cdots + s_1\overline{(a + c\sqrt{b})^n} + s_0 \\ &= s_n(a - c\sqrt{b})^n + s_{n-1}(a - c\sqrt{b})^{n-1} + \cdots + s_1(a - c\sqrt{b}) + s_0\end{aligned}$$

Thus $P(a + c\sqrt{b}) = 0$ implies $P(a - c\sqrt{b}) = 0$. The converse is proved in the same fashion.

Mixed Review **55.** Vertex: $(-1, -1)$; line of symmetry: $x = -1$; maximum: −1

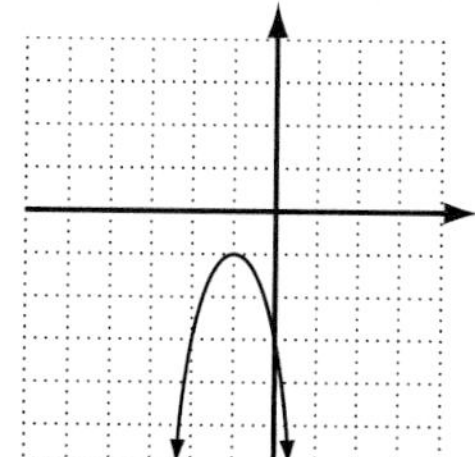

Selected Answers

57. Vertex: (0, 1); focus: (0, 3); directrix: $y = -1$ **59.** $11\frac{1}{4}$ lb of Mocha-Java, $8\frac{3}{4}$ lb of Manager's Blend **61. a.** 12.76 **b.** $w = \left(\frac{h}{p}\right)^3$ **c.** 122 lb

LESSON 11-4

Try This **a.** $\frac{1}{2}, -2, \sqrt{3}, -\sqrt{3}$ **b.** $-7, 2i, -2i$ **c.** None **d.** 2

Exercises **1.** $-3; \sqrt{2}, -\sqrt{2}$ **3.** $1, -\frac{1}{5}; 2i, -2i$ **5.** $-1, -2; 3 + \sqrt{13}, 3 - \sqrt{13}$ **7.** $1, 2; -4 + \sqrt{21}, -4 - \sqrt{21}$ **9.** $-2; 1 + i\sqrt{3}, 1 - i\sqrt{3}$ **11.** $\frac{3}{4}; i, -i$ **13.** 1, 2, −2 **15.** No rational **17.** No rational **19.** No rational **21. a.** 2 (multiplicity 2), −3 (multiplicity 1) **b.** $1, -1, \frac{2}{3}, -\frac{1}{2}$ **c.** $\frac{1}{2}$ **d.** $\frac{3}{4}$ **23.** 5 cm, $\frac{15 - 5\sqrt{5}}{2}$ cm ($\approx$ 1.9098 cm) **25.** The possible rational roots of $x^2 - 5 = 0$ are $\pm1, \pm5$. None of these are roots. **27.** 10 in., $\frac{25 - \sqrt{409}}{2}$ in. ($\approx$ 2.3881 in.)

Mixed Review **29.** $4\sqrt{2}$ **31.** 12 **33.** (0, −4), (1, −3) **35.** Yes, no, yes

LESSON 11-5

Try This **a.** 1 **b.** 5, 3, or 1 **c.** 2 or 0 **d.** 2 or 0 **e.** 1 **f.** 0

Exercises **1.** 3 or 1 **3.** 0 **5.** 2 or 0 **7.** 3 or 1 **9.** 2 or 0 **11.** 0 **13.** 3 or 1 **15.** 2 or 0 **17.** 0 **19.** 1 **21.** 1 positive, 1 negative, 2 complex **23.** No positive, no negative, 4 complex **25.** 1 positive, 1 negative, $2n - 2$ complex **27.** If $c > 0$, the only real root is negative. If $c < 0$, the only real root is positive. **29.** Let $P(x) = a_nx^n + a_{n-2}x^{n-2} + a_{n-4}x^{n-4} + \cdots + a_3x^3 + a_1x^1$ where n is odd. By Theorem 11-7 there are no positive roots. If we replace x with $(-x)$, every term changes sign. Therefore, by Theorem 11-8, there are no negative roots. We can, however, factor an x from every term; thus, $x = 0$ is a root.

Mixed Review **31.** (3, −4), (−3, −4), (4, 3), (−4, 3)

LESSON 11-6

Try This

a.

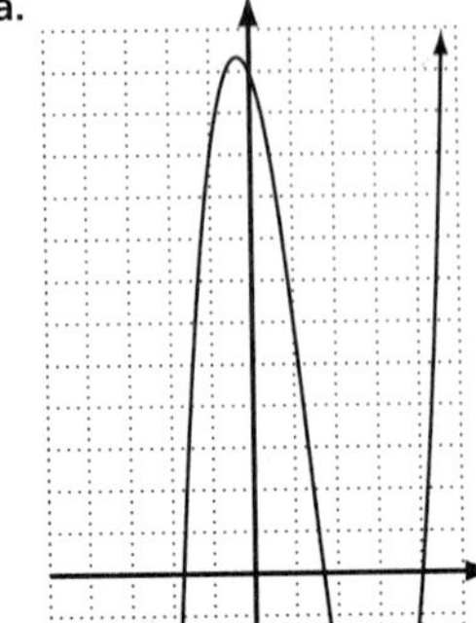

b. 0.7, −0.5, 2.9

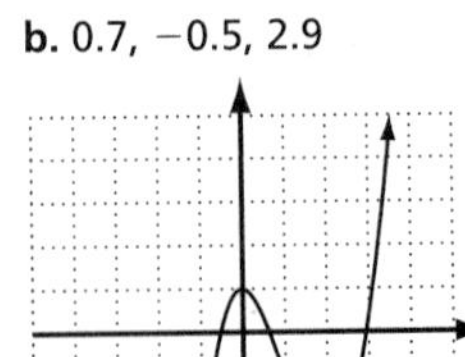

c. No real solution

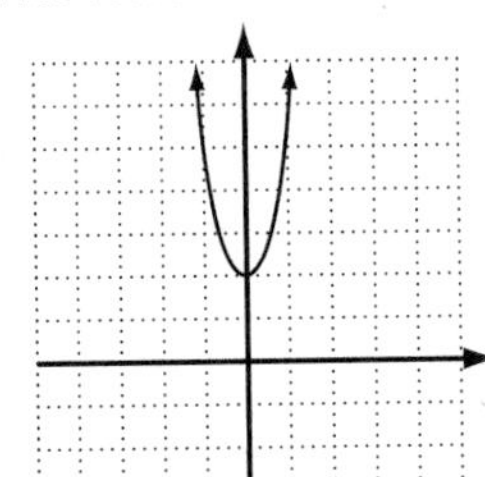

d. −1.44689491, 1.88857409
e. 1.3480062

Exercises

1.

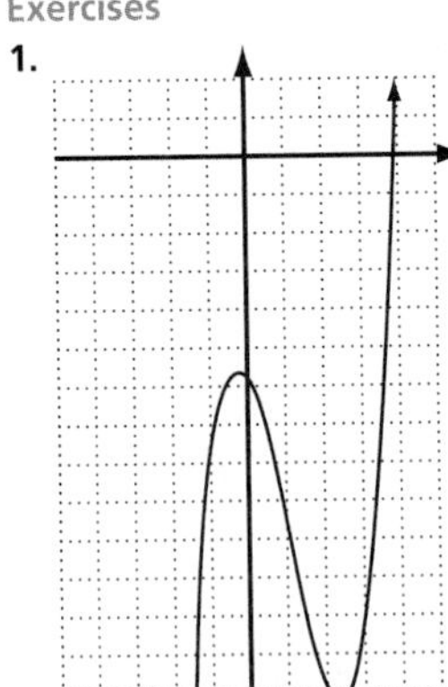

3.

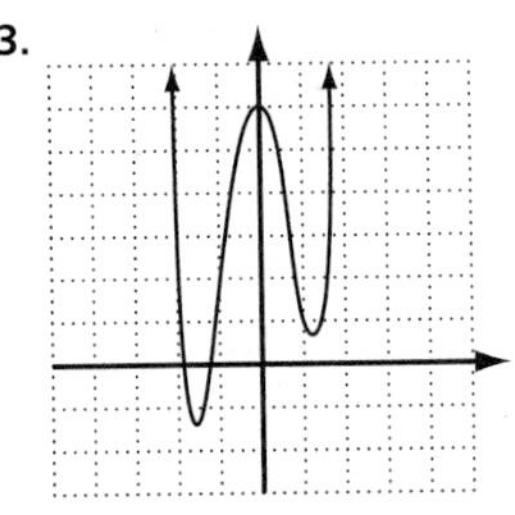

7. −1, 2
9. 2.2

11. ±1.4, ±2

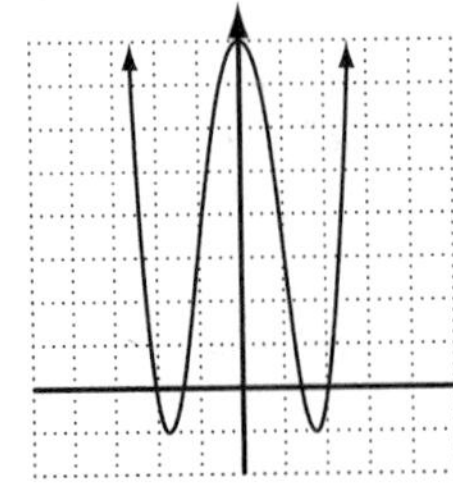

13. −1, ±1.4
15. No real solution
17. 0.79
19. −1.27

21. Answers may vary. See p. 504 for examples of graphs of quartic equations. **23.** $P(x) = 3x^4 - 5x^3 + 4x^2 - 5$. Perform synthetic division using a as the divisor and 3, -5, 4, 0, and -5 as the coefficients to find $P(a) = a[a(a(3a - 5) + 4)] - 5$. This expression is the same expression obtained by factoring to find nested form.

Mixed Review **25.** $y = -\frac{1}{2}x + 3$ **27.** $x \leq -\frac{7}{3}$ or $x \geq 1$ **29.** No solution **31.** 6, 2, -1 **33.** (3, 6)

LESSON 11-7

Problems **1.** They started with 65, 35, and 20 points. **3.** There would be a total of 4094 people in the 11 generations. **5.** The boxes weigh 24, 28, 32, 36, and 41 pounds. **7.** There are 105 ways to divide the 16 filing cabinets among the three stores.

CHAPTER 11 WRAP UP

1. No, yes **2.** Yes, no **3.** Yes, no
4. Yes, yes **5.** Yes **6.** No
7. $x^3 - 2x^2 + 4 = (x - 1)(x^2 - x - 1) + 3$
8. $x^5 + 2x^4 + 3x^3 + 3x^2 + 3 = (x^2 + 2x + 1) \cdot (x^3 + x + 1) + 2$
9. 1, -7, 53, 73 **10.** 2, 3, -4 **11.** -1, 1, 18
12. 0 (multiplicity 2), 2 (multiplicity 3), -1 (multiplicity 1)
13. 1 (multiplicity 2), 11 (multiplicity 2)
14. $P(x) = x^3 - 13x - 12$
15. $P(x) = x^4 - 6x^3 + 11x^2 - 10x + 2$
16. $P(x) = x^4 - 4x^3 + 11x^2 + 8x - 26$
17. $\frac{1}{2}, \frac{5 + \sqrt{15}}{10}, \frac{5 - \sqrt{15}}{10}$ **18.** $2, -\frac{3}{2}, i\sqrt{3}, -i\sqrt{3}$
19. 3 or 1 positive roots, 0 negative roots
20. 3 or 1 Positive roots, 2 or 0 negative roots
21. -3, -1.4, 1.4 **22.** -0.4, 0, 2.4

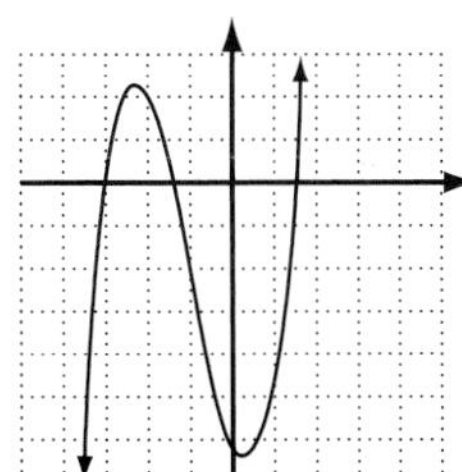

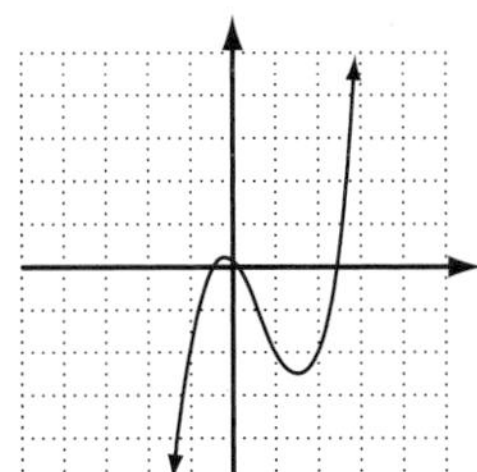

Chapter 12

Skills & Concepts You Need for Chapter 12

1. 5 **2.** 1 **3.** $\frac{1}{8}$ **4.** x^{-2} or $\frac{1}{x^2}$ **5.** x^{-7} or $\frac{1}{x^7}$ **6.** x^{-12} or $\frac{1}{x^{12}}$ **7.** $-\frac{3y}{2}$ **8.** $\frac{8x^9}{3y^3}$ **9.** 8.45×10^{-2} **10.** 433,500 **11.** No **12.** No

LESSON 12-1

Try This **a.** $x = y^2 + 4$ **b.** Yes **c.** No **d.** $g^{-1}(x) = x - 2$ **e.** $g^{-1}(x) = \frac{1}{5}(x - 2)$ **f.** $f^{-1}(x) = x^2 - 1, x \geq 0$ **g.** $f^{-1}(f(579)) = 579$, $f(f^{-1}(-83{,}479)) = -83{,}479$

Exercises **1.** $x = 4y - 5$ **3.** $x = 3y^2 + 2$ **5.** $y^2 - 3x^2 = 3$ **7.** $y \cdot x = 7$ **9.** $yx^2 = 1$ **11.** $x = \frac{5}{y}$ **13.** No **15.** Yes **17.** Yes **19.** Yes **21.** Yes **23.** No **25.** $f^{-1}(x) = x + 1$ **27.** $f^{-1}(x) = x - 4$ **29.** $f^{-1}(x) = x - 8$ **31.** $f^{-1}(x) = \frac{x - 5}{2}$ **33.** $f^{-1}(x) = \frac{x + 1}{3}$ **35.** $f^{-1}(x) = 2(x - 2)$ **37.** $f^{-1}(x) = x^2 + 1; x \geq 0$ **39.** $f^{-1}(x) = x^2 - 2; x \geq 0$ **41.** 5, -12 **43.** 489, $-17{,}422$

45.

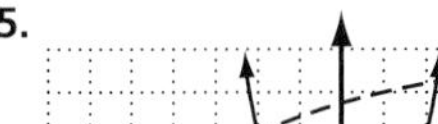

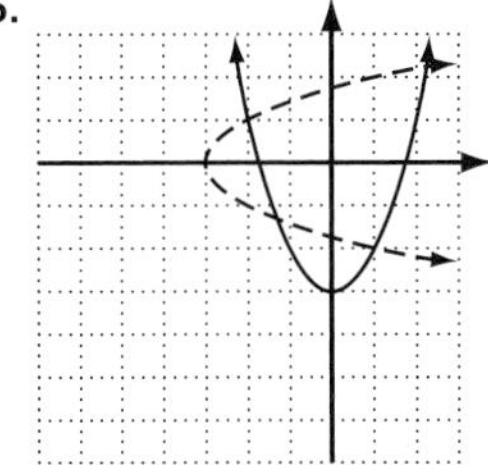

47.

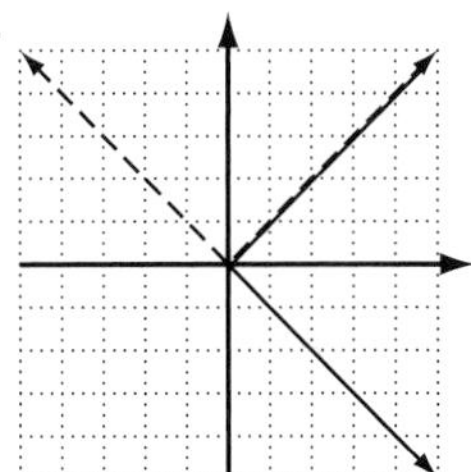

49. x, x **51.** $x^2 + 6x + 9; x^2 + 3$ **53.** $12x^2 - 12x + 5; 6x^2 + 3$ **55.** $x^4 - 2x^2; x^4 - 2x^2$

57. x-axis: no; y-axis: yes; origin: no; $y = x$: no

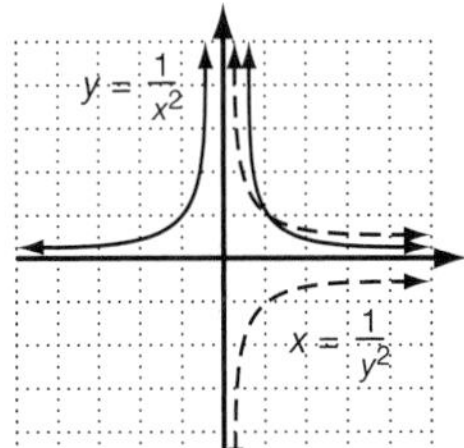

59. x-axis: no; y-axis: no; origin: yes; $y = x$: no

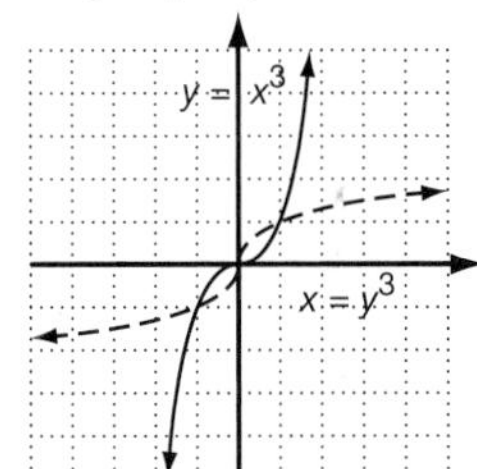

Mixed Review **61.** 3^8 **63.** 9 **65.** m^{15} **67.** $\frac{m^6}{16n^{14}}$

LESSON 12-2

Try This

a.

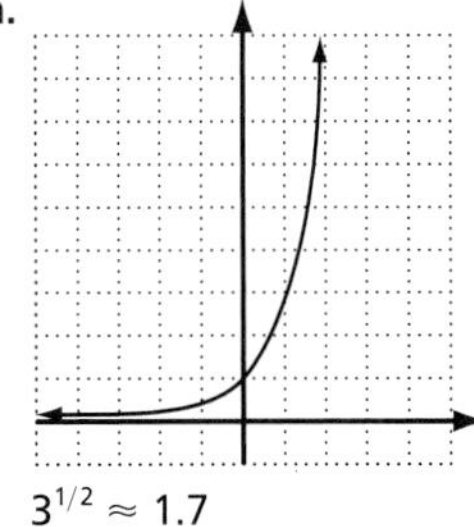

$3^{1/2} \approx 1.7$

b.

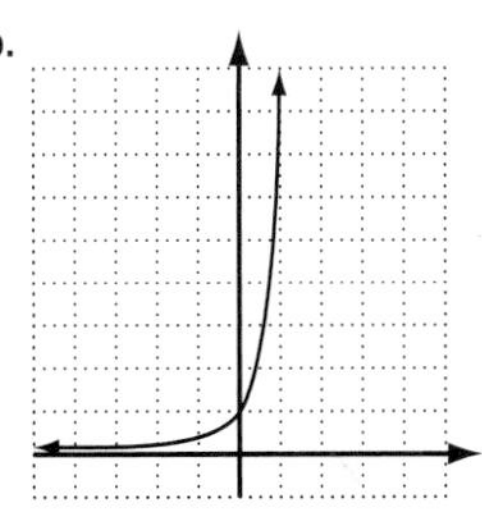

c.

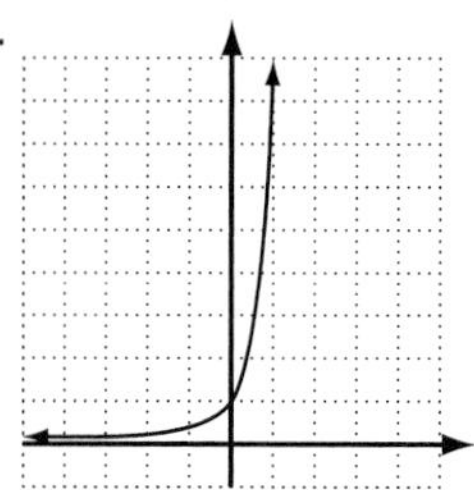

d.

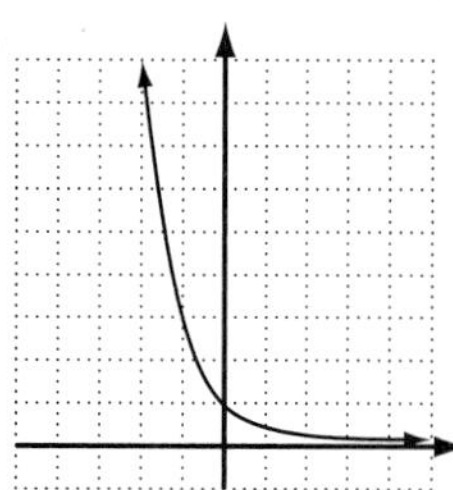

e. Domain: positive real numbers; range: all real numbers

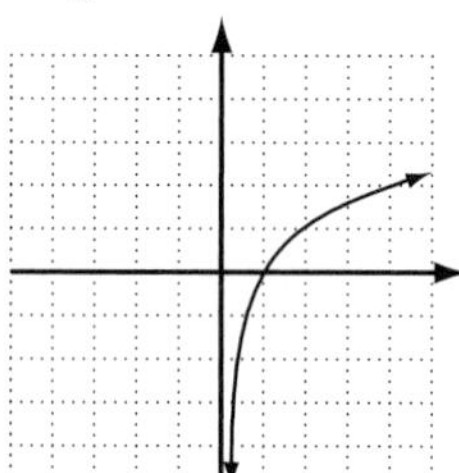

f. Domain: positive real numbers; range: all real numbers

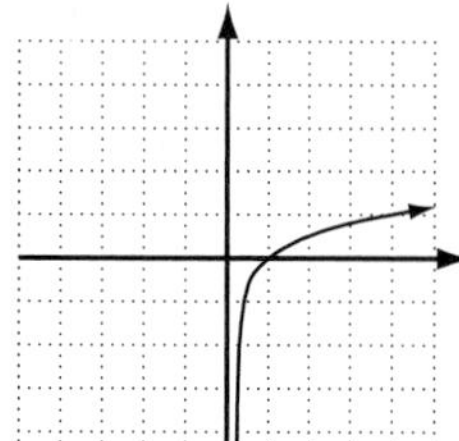

Exercises

1.

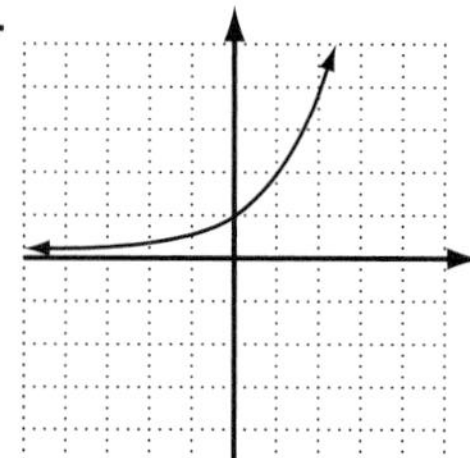

5.

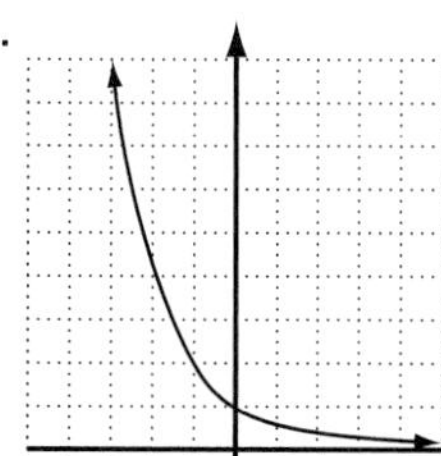

9.

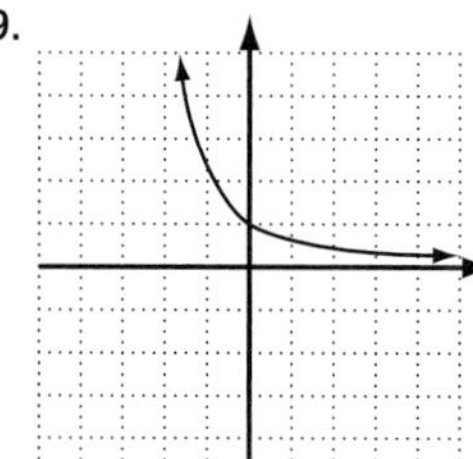

13.

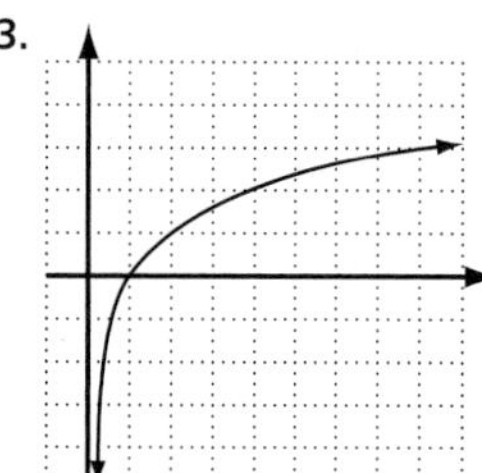

21. Set of all real numbers **23.** 2.6

31. $\{x|x > 0\}$ **33.** $\{x|x > 0\}$ **35.** $\{x|x \neq 0\}$ **37.** π^5

39. $\frac{1}{2}$, -3

41.

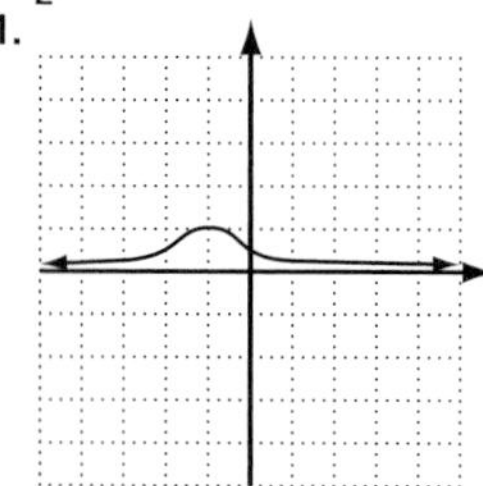

Mixed Review **43.** 3.007114×10^6 **45.** 0.00005709 **47.** $y^2 = 24x$

LESSON 12-3

Try This **a.** $\log_6 1 = 0$ **b.** $\log_{10} 0.001 = -3$ **c.** $\log_{16} 2 = \frac{1}{4}$ **d.** $\log_{6/5} \frac{25}{36} = -2$ **e.** $2^5 = 32$ **f.** $10^3 = 1000$ **g.** $10^{-2} = 0.01$ **h.** $(\sqrt{5})^2 = 5$ **i.** 10,000 **j.** 3 **k.** 4 **l.** -2 **m.** 3 **n.** 42 **o.** 37 **p.** 3.2

Exercises **1.** $5 = \log_{10} 100{,}000$ **3.** $\frac{1}{3} = \log_8 2$ **5.** $-3 = \log_5 \frac{1}{125}$ **7.** $0.3010 = \log_{10} 2$ **9.** $3^t = 8$ **11.** $5^2 = 25$ **13.** $10^{-1} = 0.1$ **15.** $10^{0.845} = 7$ **17.** $k^C = A$ **19.** 64 **21.** 4 **23.** $\frac{1}{9}$ **25.** 2 **27.** 4 **29.** 9 **31.** 6 **33.** 2 **35.** -1 **37.** 0 **39.** $\{x|x > 0\}$ **41.** $\{x|0 < x < 1\}$ **43.** 8 **45.** $-\frac{1}{2}$

Mixed Review **47.** $x^5 - x^4 - 2x^3 + 2x^2 + x - 1$ **49.** $f(x) = 3x^2 - 6x - 5$

LESSON 12-4

Try This **a.** (1) $\log_a M + \log_a N$ (2) $\log_5 25 + \log_5 5 = 3$ **b.** (1) $\log_3 35$ (2) $\log_a CABIN$ **c.** $5 \log_7 4$ **d.** $\frac{1}{2}\log_a 5$ **e.** (1) $\log_a M - \log_a N$ (2) $\log_c 1 - \log_c 4$ **f.** $\log_{10} 4 + \log_{10} \pi - \frac{1}{2} \log_{10} 23$ **g.** $\frac{3}{2} \log_a z - \frac{1}{2} \log_a x - \frac{1}{2} \log_a y$ **h.** $\log_a \frac{x^5 \sqrt[4]{z}}{y}$ **i.** (1) 0.954 (2) 0.1505 (3) 0.1003 (4) 0.176 (5) 1.585

Exercises **1.** $\log_2 32 + \log_2 8 = 5 + 3 = 8$ **3.** $\log_4 64 + \log_4 16 = 3 + 2 = 5$ **5.** $\log_c B + \log_c x$ **7.** $\log_a (6 \cdot 70)$ **9.** $\log_c (K \cdot y)$ **11.** $5\log_b t$ **13.** $\log_a 67 - \log_a 5$ **15.** $\log_b 3 - \log_b 4$ **17.** $\log_a 5 + \log_a x + 4 \log_a y + 3 \log_a z$ **19.** $\log_a \frac{\sqrt[3]{x^2}\sqrt{y}}{y}$ **21.** $\log_a \frac{2x^4}{y^3}$ **23.** $\log_a \frac{\sqrt{a}}{x}$ **25.** 0.699 **27.** 1.079 **29.** -0.088 **31.** 0.051 **33.** False **35.** False **37.** False **39.** $\frac{1}{2}$ **41.** $\sqrt{7}$ **43.** $-2, 0$ **45.** $\log x = \frac{a + 3b}{5}$, $\log y = \frac{a - 2b}{5}$ **47.** -2

49. $\log_a \left(\frac{1}{x}\right) = \log_a 1 - \log_a x = 0 - \log_a x = -\log_a x$

51. $\log_a \left(\frac{x + \sqrt{x^2 - 5}}{5} \cdot \frac{x - \sqrt{x^2 - 5}}{x - \sqrt{x^2 - 5}}\right) = \log_a \left(\frac{x^2 - (x^2 - 5)}{5(x - \sqrt{x^2 - 5})}\right)$

$= \log_a \left(\frac{1}{x - \sqrt{x^2 - 5}}\right) = -\log_a \left(x - \sqrt{x^2 - 5}\right)$

Mixed Review **53.** $\sqrt{7}, -\sqrt{7}, 2i, -2i$ **55.** 5, 2, -1

LESSON 12-5

Try This **a.** 2.3238 **b.** 5.8186 **c.** 0.4625 **d.** -4.3665

e. 0.8506 **f.** 0.6021 **g.** 0.9996 **h.** 0.4609 + 2 **i.** 0.4609 + (−4) **j.** 8.6646 − 10 **k.** 9.7832 − 10 **l.** 6.8055 − 10 **m.** 22,003.92 **n.** 1022.8219 **o.** 0.00098469 **p.** 0.00000017 **q.** 64106.2 **r.** 0.000425 **s.** 0.0105

Exercises **1.** 0.3909 **3.** 0.5705 **5.** 0.0294 **7.** 3.9405 **9.** 1.3139 **11.** 3.5877 **13.** 9.8062 − 10, or −0.1938 **15.** 7.5403 − 10, or −2.4597 **17.** 7.34 **19.** 8.30 **21.** 83,600 **23.** 0.613 **25.** 0.00973 **27.** 0.000613 **29.** 6.34 **31.** 0.613 **33.** 2.5378 **35. a.** 904 **b.** 8^{1107} **c.** $\pm 3.1622777\ (\pm\sqrt{10})$ **37.** $10^{3 \log 2} = 8$ **39.** $10^{\log 4 + \log 2} = 8$

Mixed Review **41.** $P(x) = (x^2 + 5x + 6)(x - 1) + 0$

LESSON 12-6

Try This **a.** 3.6592 **b.** 8.3779 − 10 or −1.6221 **c.** 2856 **d.** 0.0005955

Exercises **1.** 1.6194 **3.** 0.4689 **5.** 2.8130 **7.** 9.1538 − 10 **9.** 7.6291 − 10 **11.** 9.2494 − 10 **13.** 2.7786 **15.** 2.9031 **17.** 224.5 **19.** 14.53 **21.** 70,030 **23.** 0.09245 **25.** 0.5343 **27.** 0.007295 **29.** 9.8445 − 10 **31.** Values found by interpolation are slightly less. **33.** 0.8268

Mixed Review **35.** 3 or 1 **37.** 0 **39.** Yes **41.** Yes **43.** $f^{-1}(x) = x^2 - 3$

Log and Exponent Functions **1.** −0.5213902 or -5.2139×10^{-1}; an error occurs. Negative numbers do not have logarithms. **3.** $f(f(f(f(x))))$, where $f(x) = \log(x)$, $f(f(f(f(x))))$, where $f(x) = 10^x$

LESSON 12-7

Try This **a.** 2.8074 **b.** 1.2925 **c.** 3 **d.** 125 **e.** 8.75 **f.** 2 **g.** Approximately 10 years **h.** 34 dB **i.** 60 dB **j.** ≈ 8.4

Exercises **1.** 3 **3.** 3.3219 **5.** $\frac{5}{2}$ **7.** −3, −1 **9.** 1.4037 **11.** 2.7095 **13.** 3.6067 **15.** 5.6456 **17.** 1 **19.** 1 **21.** $\sqrt{41}$ **23.** 1, 10^{16} **25.** $\pm\frac{\sqrt{2}}{4}$ **27.** 22.5 years **29.** 64 dB **31.** 120 dB **33.** ≈ 8.3 **35.** $\approx 6.3 \times 10^7 I_0$ **37.** 7.8 **39.** $\pm 4\sqrt{39}$ **41.** No solution **43.** 100, $\frac{1}{100}$ **45.** $-\frac{1}{2}$ **47.** $t = \frac{\log_b y - \log_b k}{a}$ **49.** $n = \log_V c - \log_V P$, or $\log_V \frac{c}{P}$ **51.** $y = xa^{2x}$ **53.** 10, 100 **55.** 5 **57.** $\left\{x \mid x < \frac{\log 0.8}{\log 0.5} \approx 0.3219\right\}$ **59.** 88 **61.** 4

Mixed Review **63.** 4 **65.** $f^{-1}(x) = 5x + 5$ **67.** $3 = \log_{10} 1000$ **69.** $\frac{1}{2} = \log_{81} 9$ **71.** $8^1 = 8$ **73.** $2^6 = 64$ **75.** None **77.** 1, 2, −2

LESSON 12-8

Try This

a.

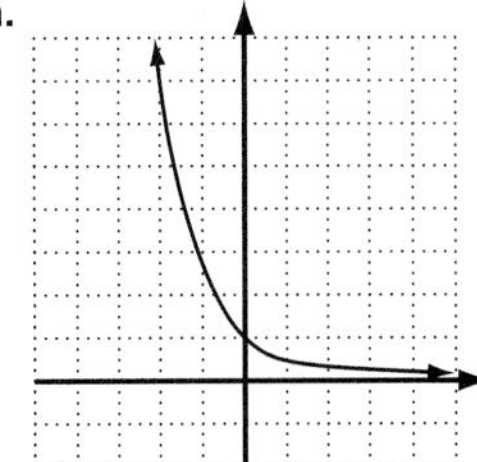

b.

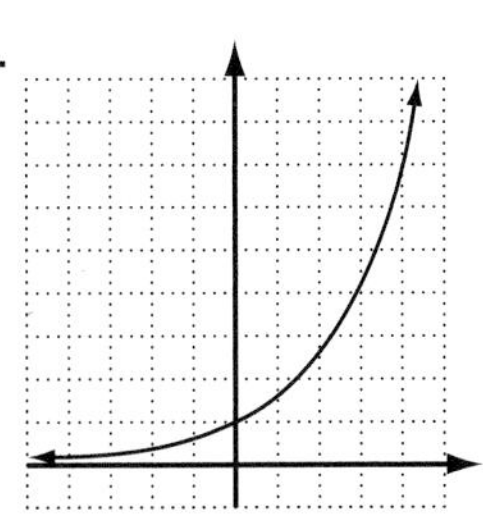

c. 0.693147 **d.** 4.605170 **e.** −2.599375 **f.** −0.000100 **g.** (1) 0.0514 (2) 500,000 **h.** 3.5 **i.** 3 **j.** 4.7385 **k.** 0.4342 **l.** 6.937 **m.** −0.783 **n.** 2.8076

Exercises These answers have been found using Table 3. If you use a calculator, there may be some variance in the last decimal place. **7.** 0.6313 **9.** −3.9739 **11.** 0.7561 **13.** −1.5465 **15.** 8.4119 **17.** −7.4872 **19.** −2.5256 **21.** 13.7953 **23.** $k \approx 0.03145$; $P \approx 2{,}216{,}518$ **25.** 125 grams **27.** 248,000 years **29.** 7997 years **31.** −0.0048 **33.** 3.8697 **35.** −0.2614 **37.** $t = \frac{\ln P - \ln P_0}{k}$ **39. a.** \$1.1255 **b.** \$1.126825 **c.** \$1.1274746 **d.** 1.1274969 is the maximum **41.** $e \approx 1.444667861$

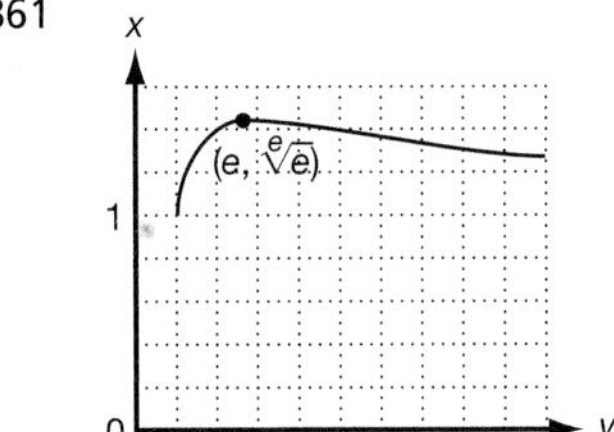

43. By Theorem 12-7, $\log_a b = \frac{\log_b b}{\log_b a} = \frac{1}{\log_b a}$ **45.** By Theorem 12-7, $\log_M a = \frac{\log_b a}{\log_b M}$, so $(\log_b M)(\log_M a) = \log_b a$. Then, by Theorem 12-5, $\log_M a^{\log_b M} = \log a$. Then, by definition of logarithms, $a^{\log_b M} = M^{\log_b a}$. Now raise both sides to the power, $\log_b a$, and the result follows.

Mixed Review **47.** Yes, no, no **49.** 26

Preparing for Standardized Tests **1.** (D) **3.** (B) **5.** (B)

CHAPTER 12 WRAP UP

1. $y = \frac{1}{3}x + \frac{1}{3}$ **2.** $x = 3y^2 + 2y - 1$ **3.** (1, 4), (8, −3), (−5, −1)

4. (3, 2), (7, 5), (−4, 6) **5.** Yes **6.** No **7.** $g^{-1}(x) = x^2 - 4x + 4$, $x \geq 2$ **8.** $h^{-1}(x) = 2x + 2$ **9.** Set of all real numbers, set of all positive numbers; (0, 1)

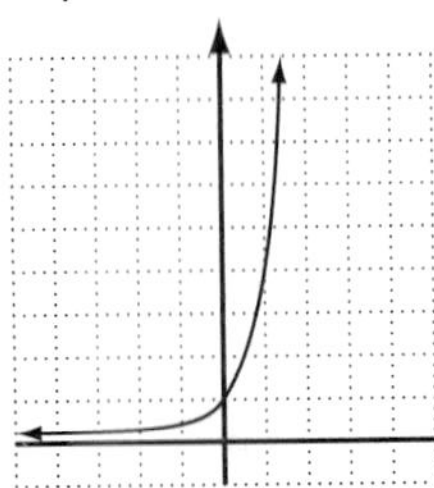

10.

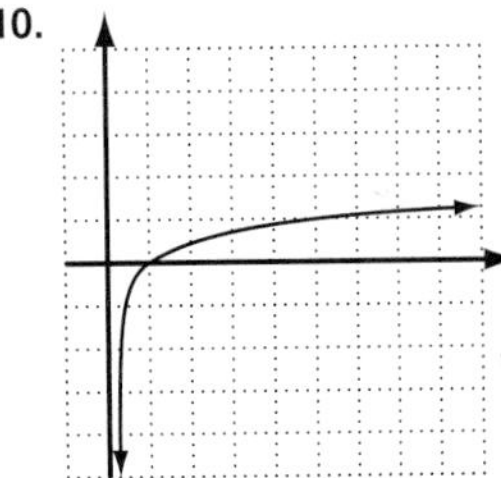

11. $2.3 = \log_7 x$ **12.** $\frac{1}{3} = \log_8 2$ **13.** $3^4 = 81$ **14.** $8^t = M$

15. 4 **16.** $\frac{1}{2}$ **17.** 3 **18.** t **19.** $\log_b\left[\frac{c\sqrt{ac}}{d^4}\right]$

20. $\frac{1}{3}(2\log M - \log N)$ **21.** 1.255 **22.** 0.544 **23.** −0.602

24. 0.2385 **25.** 1.4183 **26.** 7.9063 − 10 **27.** 0.7649

28. 5.87 **29.** 0.00230 **30.** 214 **31.** 1.2730 **32.** 14.55

33. $-\frac{1}{5}$ **34.** −3 **35.** 9 **36.** 258 **37.** 14.2 years **38.** 0.4700

39. 7.3778 **40.** 3.1610

CHAPTERS 1–12 CUMULATIVE REVIEW

1. 10 **3.** −4 **5.** $-5 \leq x$ **7.** $x > 60$ **9.** $x - 6 = 0$ **11.** $\left(-\frac{1}{2}, -\frac{1}{2}\right)$ **13.** 5 liters of A and 19 liters of B

15.

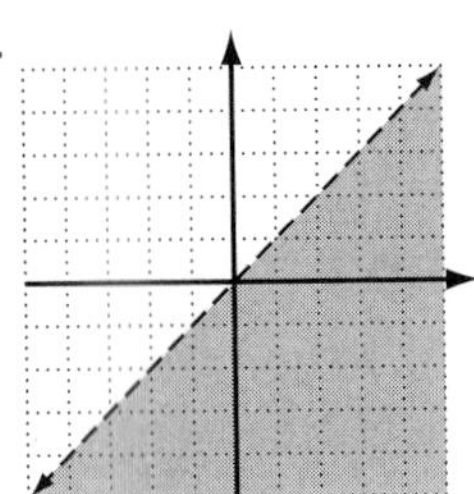

17. $4z^2 + 16yz + 16y^2$
19. $a^6 + 6a^4b + 12a^2b^2 + 8b^3$

21. $(a^8 + 1)(a^4 + 1)(a^2 + 1)(a + 1)(a - 1)$
23. $(y + 5)(y^2 - 5y + 25)$ **25.** $(x - 4)(2x + 3)(2x - 3)$

27. $\frac{1}{3}, 6$ **29.** $\frac{x^2(y - 3)}{y^2(x - 1)}$ **31.** $x^3 + 3x^2 + x - 9$

33. $x = \frac{1}{2}, x = -\frac{2}{7}$ **35.** −5 **37.** $4y\sqrt{3y}$ **39.** $\frac{\sqrt{6}}{3}$

41. $\frac{\sqrt{2}(\sqrt[3]{12})|x|}{6}$ **43.** $x = 5$ **45.** $\frac{-1 + 5i}{13}$ **47.** $-\frac{3}{4}, 2$

49. $\frac{-1 \pm i\sqrt{5}}{2}$ **51.** $x^2 - 2x - 2 = 0$ **53.** Both axes **55.** Even

57. Neither **59. a.** $-\frac{3}{2}$ **b.** $\frac{2 \pm \sqrt{5}}{3}$

61. Center: (0, 0); vertices: $(\sqrt{6}, 0), (-\sqrt{6}, 0)$; foci: $(\sqrt{22}, 0), (-\sqrt{22}, 0)$; asymptotes $y = \frac{2\sqrt{6}}{3}x$, $y = \frac{-2\sqrt{6}}{3}x$

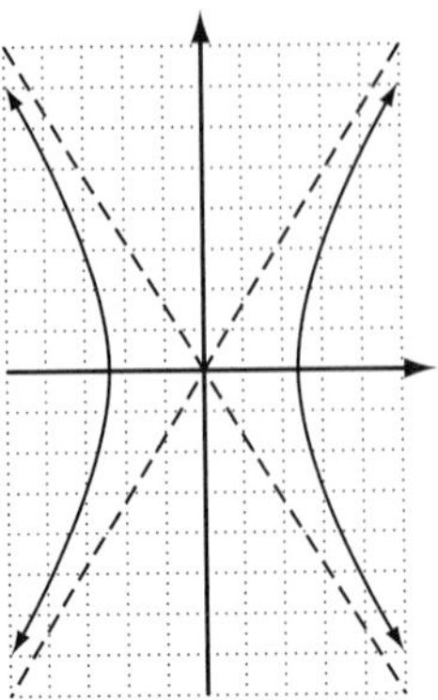

63. $(-3, -2), \left(\frac{17}{5}, \frac{6}{5}\right)$ **65.** 62 **67.** $\frac{1}{2}, -1, 2 + i, 2 - i$

69. $f^{-1}(x) = \frac{x + 3}{2}$ **71.** 64 **73.** $\log_a 12x$ **75.** 0.021 **77.** 1

79. 3.465

Chapter 13

Skills & Concepts You Need for Chapter 13

1. −10 **2.** −48 **3.** (−1, 4) **4.** $\left(3, 7, -\frac{1}{2}\right)$ **5.** (−2, 5, −3)

LESSON 13-1

Try This **a.** 3 × 2 **b.** 2 × 2 **c.** 3 × 3 **d.** 1 × 2 **e.** 2 × 1 **f.** 1 × 1 **g.** (−8, 2) **h.** (−1, 2, 3)

Exercises **1.** 2 × 3 **3.** 5 × 2 **5.** $\left(\frac{3}{2}, \frac{5}{2}\right)$ **7.** $\left(\frac{1}{2}, \frac{3}{2}\right)$

9. $\left(\frac{1}{2}, 2, 1\right)$ **11.** (1, −3, −2, −1) **13.** Answers may vary. Since both multiplication and subtraction (addition with inverses) are row-equivalent operations, the result is a row-equivalent matrix. **15.** $(x, y, z, w, n) = (2, -2, 3, -29, 9)$

Mixed Review **17.** $\frac{a + b}{a^2 + ab + b^2}$ **19.** 3.141 **21.** 5.9562

LESSON 13-2

Try This **a.** (1) $\begin{bmatrix} -2 & -6 \\ 13 & 0 \end{bmatrix}$ (2) $\begin{bmatrix} -2 & -6 \\ 13 & 0 \end{bmatrix}$ (3) $\begin{bmatrix} 4 & -1 \\ 6 & -3 \end{bmatrix}$

b. $\begin{bmatrix} -1 & 4 & -7 \\ -2 & -4 & 8 \end{bmatrix}$ **c.** $\begin{bmatrix} -6 & 6 \\ 1 & -4 \\ -7 & 5 \end{bmatrix}$ **d.** $\begin{bmatrix} -2 & 1 & -5 \\ -6 & -4 & 3 \end{bmatrix}$

e. $\begin{bmatrix} -1 & -3 & 5 \\ 2 & 0 & 0 \\ -6 & 10 & -7 \end{bmatrix}$ **f.** $\begin{bmatrix} 3 & 2 & 3 \\ 10 & 4 & 2 \end{bmatrix}$ **g.** $\begin{bmatrix} 11 & -2 & -7 \\ -3 & 13 & -5 \\ 7 & 2 & -6 \end{bmatrix}$

Exercises **1.** 2 × 2 **3.** 2 × 3 **5.** $\begin{bmatrix} -2 & -3 \\ 6 & -4 \end{bmatrix}$

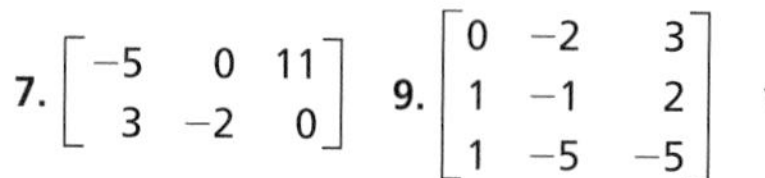

7. $\begin{bmatrix} -5 & 0 & 11 \\ 3 & -2 & 0 \end{bmatrix}$ **9.** $\begin{bmatrix} 0 & -2 & 3 \\ 1 & -1 & 2 \\ 1 & -5 & -5 \end{bmatrix}$ **11.** Cannot be added

13. $\begin{bmatrix} 4 & 7 \\ 2 & -2 \end{bmatrix}$ **15.** Cannot be subtracted **17.** $\begin{bmatrix} 2 & 2 & -7 \\ -1 & -1 & 4 \\ 5 & 1 & 3 \end{bmatrix}$

19. Cannot be subtracted **21.** $\begin{bmatrix} 3 & 3 & -7 \\ 5 & -2 & -1 \end{bmatrix}$

23. $\begin{bmatrix} 3 & -5 & 2 \\ -1 & 0 & 4 \\ 2 & 3 & 5 \end{bmatrix}$ **25.** $\begin{bmatrix} -2 & 7 & -7 \\ 0 & -0 & -3 \\ 0 & 0 & -6 \end{bmatrix}$

27. Cannot be subtracted

29. $(G + H) + M = (M + H) + G = \begin{bmatrix} -3 & 3 & 1 \\ 2 & -1 & -2 \\ -1 & -8 & 0 \end{bmatrix}$

31. Let $A = \begin{bmatrix} a_{11} & \cdots & a_{1n} \\ \vdots & & \vdots \\ a_{m1} & \cdots & a_{mn} \end{bmatrix}$ $B = \begin{bmatrix} b_{11} & \cdots & b_{1n} \\ \vdots & & \vdots \\ b_{m1} & \cdots & b_{mn} \end{bmatrix}$

$$A - B = \begin{bmatrix} a_{11} - b_{11} & \cdots & a_{1n} - b_{1n} \\ \vdots & & \vdots \\ a_{m1} - b_{m1} & \cdots & a_{mn} - b_{mn} \end{bmatrix}$$

$$= \begin{bmatrix} a_{11} + (-b_{11}) & \cdots & a_{1n} + (-b_{1n}) \\ \vdots & & \vdots \\ a_{m1} + (-b_{m1}) & \cdots & a_{mn} + (-b_{mn}) \end{bmatrix} = A + (-B)$$

Mixed Review **33.** 1.183 **35.** $\pm\frac{\sqrt{10}}{2}$ **37.** −5, 3

LESSON 13-3

Try This **a.** 14 **b.** −2 **c.** $-2x + 12$ **d.** (3, 1) **e.** $\left(-\frac{10}{41}, -\frac{13}{41}\right)$ **f.** 93 **g.** 60 **h.** 100 **i.** (1, 3, −2) **j.** $\left(\frac{1}{3}, \frac{4}{5}, -\frac{1}{15}\right)$

Exercises **1.** 3 **3.** 36 **5.** −10.3 **7.** 0 **9.** (2, 0) **11.** (−4, −5) **13.** $\left(\frac{1}{3}, -\frac{2}{3}\right)$ **15.** −10 **17.** −3 **19.** −11 **21.** (2, −1, 4) **23.** (1, 2, 3) **25.** $\left(\frac{3}{2}, \frac{13}{14}, \frac{33}{14}\right)$ **27.** Sample: If the number of variables does not equal the number of equations, the matrix of coefficients will not be a square matrix. Only a square matrix has a determinant, and Cramer's rule uses determinants. **29.** $3y^2 + 2y$ **31.** 2 **33.** −34

35. $\left(\frac{15 - 4\pi}{-3\sqrt{3} - \pi^2}, \frac{4\sqrt{3} + 5\pi}{-3\sqrt{3} - \pi^2}\right)$ **37.** Since a given $n \times n$ matrix can only have one value for its determinant, the determinant is a function. Its domain is the set of $n \times n$ matrices and its range is the set of real numbers.

39. $\begin{vmatrix} 1 & x & x^2 \\ 1 & y & y^2 \\ 1 & z & z^2 \end{vmatrix} = \begin{vmatrix} y & y^2 \\ z & z^2 \end{vmatrix} - \begin{vmatrix} x & x^2 \\ z & z^2 \end{vmatrix} + \begin{vmatrix} x & x^2 \\ y & y^2 \end{vmatrix}$

$= yz^2 - zy^2 - (xz^2 - zx^2) + (xy^2 - yx^2)$
$= yz^2 - zy^2 - xz^2 + zx^2 + xy^2 - yx^2$
$= (x - y)(y - z)(z - x)$

41. Answers may vary. **a.** $\begin{vmatrix} 2 & w \\ -1 & l \end{vmatrix}$ or $\begin{vmatrix} 2l & -w \\ 1 & 1 \end{vmatrix}$ **b.** $\begin{vmatrix} a^2 & b \\ -b & 1 \end{vmatrix}$ or $\begin{vmatrix} a & -1 \\ b^2 & a \end{vmatrix}$

Mixed Review **43.** 8 **45.** 512 **47.** $y^3 - 2y^2 + 5$

LESSON 13-4

Try This **a.** $\begin{bmatrix} 5 & -10 & 5x \\ 20 & 5y & 5 \\ 0 & -25 & 5x^2 \end{bmatrix}$ **b.** $\begin{bmatrix} -3t & 3t & -12t & -3xt \\ -3yt & -9t & 6t & -3yt \\ -3t & -12t & 15t & -3yt \end{bmatrix}$

c. $\begin{bmatrix} 12 \\ 13 \\ 5 \\ 16 \end{bmatrix}$ **d.** $\begin{bmatrix} 0 & 26 \\ -8 & 3 \\ -13 & 33 \\ -7 & 32 \end{bmatrix}$ **e.** [8 5 4] **f.** $\begin{bmatrix} 2 & 8 & 6 \\ -29 & -34 & -7 \end{bmatrix}$

g. Undefined **h.** $\begin{bmatrix} 1 & 4 & 8 \\ -1 & 8 & 8 \end{bmatrix}$ **i.** $\begin{bmatrix} 3 & 4 & -2 \\ 2 & -2 & 5 \\ 6 & 7 & -1 \end{bmatrix}\begin{bmatrix} x \\ y \\ z \end{bmatrix} = \begin{bmatrix} 5 \\ 3 \\ 0 \end{bmatrix}$

j. $\begin{bmatrix} 5 & 7 & 0 \\ 3 & -2 & 1 \\ -2 & 3 & -1 \end{bmatrix}\begin{bmatrix} x \\ y \\ z \end{bmatrix} = \begin{bmatrix} 19 \\ 1 \\ -12 \end{bmatrix}$

k. $\begin{bmatrix} 3 & 0 & 2 & -7 \\ 0 & 1 & -2 & 0 \\ 5 & 5 & 0 & -3 \\ 0 & 0 & 10 & -3 \\ 1 & 0 & -1 & -1 \end{bmatrix}\begin{bmatrix} v \\ w \\ x \\ y \end{bmatrix} = \begin{bmatrix} 13 \\ 0 \\ -5 \\ 15 \\ 2 \end{bmatrix}$

l. $\begin{bmatrix} 4 & 0 & 0 & 0 \\ 4 & 1 & 0 & 0 \\ 4 & 2 & 1 & 0 \\ 4 & 3 & 2 & 1 \end{bmatrix}\begin{bmatrix} w \\ x \\ y \\ z \end{bmatrix} = \begin{bmatrix} -1 \\ -3 \\ -6 \\ -10 \end{bmatrix}$

Exercises **1.** $\begin{bmatrix} -2 & -4 \\ -8 & -6 \end{bmatrix}$ **3.** $\begin{bmatrix} 14 & -14 \\ -14 & 14 \end{bmatrix}$ **5.** $\begin{bmatrix} t & 3t \\ 2t & 6t \end{bmatrix}$

7. $\begin{bmatrix} 2 & -9 & -6 \\ 3 & -3 & -4 \\ -2 & 2 & -1 \end{bmatrix}$ **9.** [−22] **11.** [−36] **13.** $\begin{bmatrix} 1 & 3 \\ -6 & 17 \end{bmatrix}$

15. $\begin{bmatrix} 0 & 0 \\ 0 & 0 \end{bmatrix}$ **17.** [−14 −11 −3] **19.** [−13 −1 −4]

21. $\begin{bmatrix} 3 & 3 \\ -1 & -1 \end{bmatrix}$ **23.** $\begin{bmatrix} -5 & 4 & 3 \\ 5 & -9 & 4 \\ 7 & -18 & 17 \end{bmatrix}$ **25.** $\begin{bmatrix} -7 \\ -18 \end{bmatrix}$

27. Not possible **29.** $\begin{bmatrix} 3 & -2 & 4 \\ 2 & 1 & -5 \end{bmatrix}\begin{bmatrix} x \\ y \\ z \end{bmatrix} = \begin{bmatrix} 17 \\ 13 \end{bmatrix}$

31. $\begin{bmatrix} 1 & -1 & 2 & -4 \\ 2 & -1 & -1 & 1 \\ 1 & 4 & -3 & -1 \\ 3 & 5 & -7 & 2 \end{bmatrix}\begin{bmatrix} x \\ y \\ z \\ w \end{bmatrix} = \begin{bmatrix} 12 \\ 0 \\ 1 \\ 9 \end{bmatrix}$

33. $\begin{bmatrix} 13 & 5 & 0 \\ 24 & 18 & 18 \\ 18 & 17 & 15 \end{bmatrix}$; $\begin{bmatrix} -4 & -1 & 0 \\ -9 & -5 & 9 \\ 2 & -2 & 4 \end{bmatrix}$ **35.** $\frac{1}{72}\begin{bmatrix} 3 & -12 & 27 \\ 30 & -36 & 14 \end{bmatrix}$

37. Yes; 5 rows and 6 columns **39.** If A is $m \times n$, B is $n \times m$; AB is $m \times m$ and BA is $n \times n$.

41. $A + B = \begin{bmatrix} a+e & c+g \\ b+f & d+h \end{bmatrix}$, $B + A = \begin{bmatrix} a+e & c+g \\ b+f & d+h \end{bmatrix}$

43. $A - B = \begin{bmatrix} a & c \\ b & d \end{bmatrix} - \begin{bmatrix} e & g \\ f & h \end{bmatrix} = \begin{bmatrix} a-e & c-g \\ b-f & d-h \end{bmatrix}$,

$A + (-B) = \begin{bmatrix} a & c \\ b & d \end{bmatrix} + \begin{bmatrix} -e & -g \\ -f & -h \end{bmatrix} = \begin{bmatrix} a-e & c-g \\ b-f & d-h \end{bmatrix}$

45. $k(A + B) = k\begin{bmatrix} a+e & c+g \\ b+f & d+h \end{bmatrix} = \begin{bmatrix} ka+ke & kc+kg \\ kb+kf & kd+kh \end{bmatrix}$,

$kA + kB = \begin{bmatrix} ka & kc \\ kb & kd \end{bmatrix} + \begin{bmatrix} ke & kg \\ kf & kh \end{bmatrix} = \begin{bmatrix} ka+ke & kc+kg \\ kb+kf & kd+kh \end{bmatrix}$

Mixed Review **47.** $x^4 - 6x^2y + 9y^2$ **49.** $\frac{4m^2\sqrt[3]{z}}{9n^4z^5}$

51. $\frac{1}{2}, -2, 2i, -2i$ **53.** 25 m, 13 m

LESSON 13-5

Try This **a.** No, $AB = \begin{bmatrix} 1 & 0 \\ 0 & -1 \end{bmatrix}$ **b.** Yes, $AB = BA = I$

c. Does not exist **d.** $\begin{bmatrix} \frac{2}{5} & -\frac{3}{5} \\ \frac{1}{5} & \frac{1}{5} \end{bmatrix}$ **e.** $\begin{bmatrix} \frac{1}{6} & -\frac{1}{6} \\ \frac{1}{10} & \frac{1}{10} \end{bmatrix}$

Exercises **1.** Yes **3.** No **5.** A **7.** $\begin{bmatrix} 2 & -5 \\ -1 & 3 \end{bmatrix}$ **9.** $\begin{bmatrix} -3 & 5 \\ 5 & -8 \end{bmatrix}$

11. $\begin{bmatrix} 0 & 1 \\ -1 & 0 \end{bmatrix}$ **13.** $\begin{bmatrix} \frac{1}{4} & 0 \\ 0 & 1 \end{bmatrix}$ **15.** $\frac{1}{\frac{1}{8}}\begin{bmatrix} \frac{1}{4} & 0 \\ -1 & \frac{1}{2} \end{bmatrix}$ or $\begin{bmatrix} 2 & 0 \\ -8 & 4 \end{bmatrix}$

17. $\frac{1}{xy}\begin{bmatrix} y & 0 \\ 0 & x \end{bmatrix}$ or $\begin{bmatrix} \frac{1}{x} & 0 \\ 0 & \frac{1}{y} \end{bmatrix}$, $xy \neq 0$ **19.** $\begin{bmatrix} \frac{1}{x} \end{bmatrix}$, $x \neq 0$

21. $AB^{-1} = \begin{bmatrix} -20 & 4 \\ -9 & 85 \end{bmatrix}^{-1} = \frac{-1}{1664} \cdot \begin{bmatrix} 85 & -4 \\ 9 & -20 \end{bmatrix}$

$B^{-1}A^{-1} = \frac{1}{52}\begin{bmatrix} 11 & -10 \\ 3 & 2 \end{bmatrix} \cdot \frac{-1}{32}\begin{bmatrix} 5 & -4 \\ -3 & -4 \end{bmatrix} = \frac{-1}{1664} \cdot \begin{bmatrix} 85 & -4 \\ 9 & -20 \end{bmatrix}$

23. Let $A = \begin{bmatrix} 0 & 0 \\ a & b \end{bmatrix}$ or $\begin{bmatrix} a & b \\ 0 & 0 \end{bmatrix}$ or $\begin{bmatrix} 0 & a \\ 0 & b \end{bmatrix}$ or $\begin{bmatrix} a & 0 \\ b & 0 \end{bmatrix}$.

Then $|A| = 0$ and A^{-1} does not exist. **25.** Let $A = \begin{bmatrix} a & b \\ ka & kb \end{bmatrix}$

or $\begin{bmatrix} a & ka \\ b & kb \end{bmatrix}$. Then $|A| = akb - bka = 0$ and A^{-1} does not exist.

Mixed Review **27.** $(a + 5b + c)(a + 5b - c)$ **29.** $\frac{b^4}{a^8}$

31. $\frac{8x^3z^3}{y^6}$ **33.** $\frac{3}{5}$

LESSON 13-6

Try This **a.** $A^{-1} = \begin{bmatrix} -\frac{1}{2} & \frac{1}{2} & \frac{1}{2} \\ 1 & 0 & -1 \\ \frac{3}{2} & -\frac{1}{2} & -\frac{1}{2} \end{bmatrix}$ **b.** A^{-1} does not exist.

c. $\left(-\frac{3}{22}, \frac{5}{22}\right)$ **d.** $\left(-\frac{14}{5}, -\frac{24}{5}, -\frac{4}{5}\right)$

Exercises **1.** $A^{-1} = \begin{bmatrix} -1 & 1 & 0 \\ -1 & 0 & 1 \\ 6 & -2 & -3 \end{bmatrix}$ **3.** $A^{-1} = \begin{bmatrix} -\frac{4}{3} & -\frac{5}{3} & 1 \\ -\frac{4}{3} & -\frac{8}{3} & 1 \\ \frac{1}{3} & \frac{2}{3} & 0 \end{bmatrix}$

5. $A^{-1} = \begin{bmatrix} -\frac{1}{2} & \frac{1}{2} & \frac{1}{2} \\ 1 & 0 & -1 \\ \frac{3}{2} & -\frac{1}{2} & -\frac{1}{2} \end{bmatrix}$ **7.** (2, 2) **9.** (−2, 3)

11. (3, −3, −2) **13.** $A^{-1} = \begin{bmatrix} \frac{1}{x} & 0 & 0 \\ 0 & \frac{1}{y} & 0 \\ 0 & 0 & \frac{1}{z} \end{bmatrix}$, $x, y, z \neq 0$

15. $X = \begin{bmatrix} -7 & -6 \\ 12 & 10 \end{bmatrix}$ **17.** By definition of the inverse of a matrix, $A^{-1}A = I$ and $(A^{-1})(A^{-1})^{-1} = I$

$$A^{-1}A = A^{-1}(A^{-1})^{-1}$$
$$A(A^{-1}A) = A[A^{-1}(A^{-1})^{-1}]$$

Apply associative property of multiplication of matrices.

$$(AA^{-1})A = (AA^{-1})(A^{-1})^{-1}$$
$$IA = I(A^{-1})^{-1}$$
$$A = (A^{-1})^{-1}$$

19. $\begin{bmatrix} -\frac{7}{4} & -1 & -\frac{1}{2} \\ -\frac{13}{4} & -3 & -\frac{9}{2} \\ \frac{5}{4} & 0 & -\frac{3}{2} \end{bmatrix}$

Mixed Review **21.** (−4, 9) **23.** $\frac{40 + 5\sqrt{6}}{58}$ **25.** $\frac{u\sqrt[3]{9uv^2}}{3v^2}$

27. $1 < x$ **29.** 80, 78, 86

LESSON 13-7

Try This **a.** *Profit:* A: \$1467; B: \$1507.50; C: \$2137.50

Exercises **1.** A: \$428.75; B: \$818.75; C: \$968.75; D: \$180 **3.** Hawks 29, Eagles 32, Angels 31, Tornadoes 36, Cyclones 43, Zephyrs 38, Jays 40, Dynamos 37 **5.** Item 1: cost \$5.00, total \$35.00; Item 2: cost \$10.00, total \$80.00; Item 3: cost \$8.50, total \$85.00 **7.** The square of the matrix is

$$\begin{bmatrix} 14 & 8 & 6 & 7 \\ 8 & 6 & 5 & 6 \\ 6 & 5 & 17 & 8 \\ 7 & 6 & 8 & 9 \end{bmatrix}.$$

The element a_{12} represents the two-flight routes between Peoria and Detroit.

$a_{12} = 0 \cdot 1 + 1 \cdot 0 + 3 \cdot 2 + 2 \cdot 1.$

$0 \cdot 1$ indicates that there is no two-flight route with Peoria as the intermediate stop. $1 \cdot 0$ indicates that there is no route with Detroit as the intermediate stop. $3 \cdot 2$ indicates that there are 6 routes with St. Louis as the intermediate stop, and $2 \cdot 1$ indicates that there are two routes with Denver as the intermediate stop.

Mixed Review **9.** $-5 \leq x \leq 5$ **11.** $s \geq 90$

Preparing for Standardized Tests

1. (D) **3.** (A) **5.** (D) **7.** (A) **9.** (C)

Application

1. a. PLAY BALL **b.** SEND MONEY **3.** 9 −34 73 −4 5 8 44 65 34 20 −28 77 **5.** PROCEED CAREFULLY

CHAPTER 13 WRAP UP

1. 2×3 **2.** 3×1 **3.** $(1, -2)$ **4.** $\left(\frac{41}{22}, -\frac{16}{11}, -\frac{45}{22}\right)$

5. $\begin{bmatrix} -2 & 0 \\ 1 & -4 \end{bmatrix}$ **6.** $\begin{bmatrix} -4 & 10 \\ 7 & 0 \end{bmatrix}$ **7.** 14 **8.** 6 **9.** $\left(\frac{13}{6}, -\frac{1}{2}\right)$

10. $\left(\frac{46}{17}, \frac{14}{17}\right)$ **11.** −1 **12.** −2 **13.** (2, 3, 1) **14.** $\left(\frac{25}{22}, -\frac{17}{11}, -\frac{26}{11}\right)$

15. $\begin{bmatrix} 9 & 0 \\ -6 & 3 \end{bmatrix}$ **16.** $\begin{bmatrix} -12 & 0 \\ 8 & -4 \end{bmatrix}$ **17.** $\begin{bmatrix} -6 & -3 & 3 \\ 5 & 2 & -4 \end{bmatrix}$

18. $\begin{bmatrix} -5 & -1 & 7 \\ 2 & 4 & -3 \end{bmatrix}$ **19.** Does not exist

20. $\begin{bmatrix} 5 & 2 & -4 \\ -3 & -4 & -2 \\ 6 & 7 & 5 \end{bmatrix}\begin{bmatrix} x \\ y \\ z \end{bmatrix} = \begin{bmatrix} 0 \\ 6 \\ 15 \end{bmatrix}$ **21.** $\begin{bmatrix} 2 & -3 \\ -1 & 2 \end{bmatrix}$

22. Does not exist **23.** $\begin{bmatrix} \frac{2}{3} & -\frac{1}{6} & -\frac{1}{6} \\ 0 & -\frac{1}{2} & \frac{1}{2} \\ -\frac{1}{3} & \frac{1}{3} & \frac{1}{3} \end{bmatrix}$ **24.** $\begin{bmatrix} -\frac{1}{2} & \frac{3}{2} & -\frac{1}{2} \\ \frac{3}{2} & -\frac{7}{2} & \frac{1}{2} \\ \frac{1}{2} & -\frac{1}{2} & \frac{1}{2} \end{bmatrix}$

25. $(1, -2)$ **26.** $(6, -2)$ **27.** Store A: \$15.70; Store B: \$11.90; Store C: \$16.60

Chapter 14

Skills & Concepts You Need for Chapter 14

1. 20 **2.** 60 **3.** 15 **4.** 125 **5.** 32 **6.** $-\frac{1}{30}$ **7.** 5, 8, 11 **8.** 2, 11, 26 **9.** −3, 9, −27 **10.** $\frac{1}{2}, \frac{1}{4}, \frac{1}{8}$

LESSON 14-1

Try This **a.** $a_1 = 1, a_2 = 3, a_3 = 7, a_{10} = 1023, a_{15} = 32{,}767$ **b.** $a_1 = -1, a_2 = 4, a_3 = -9, a_{10} = 100, a_{15} = -225$ **c.** 0, 4, 8, 12, 16 **d.** 4, 2, 0, −2, −4 **e.** $a_n = 2n$ **f.** $a_n = (-1)^n(n)$ **g.** $a_n = n^3$ **h.** $a_n = 2^{n-1}$ **i.** $S_1 = \frac{1}{2}, S_2 = \frac{3}{4}, S_3 = \frac{7}{8}, S_4 = \frac{15}{16}$ **j.** $3 + \frac{5}{2} + \frac{7}{3} = 7\frac{5}{6}$ **k.** $4 + 24 + 124 + 624 = 776$ **l.** $\sum_{n=1}^{5} 2n$ **m.** $\sum_{n=1}^{\infty} (-1)^{n+1}(n+1)$

Exercises **1.** 4, 7, 10, 13; 31; 46 **3.** $\frac{1}{2}, \frac{2}{3}, \frac{3}{4}, \frac{4}{5}; \frac{10}{11}; \frac{15}{16}$ **5.** −1, 0, 3, 8; 80; 195 **7.** $2, 2\frac{1}{2}, 3\frac{1}{3}, 4\frac{1}{4}; 10\frac{1}{10}; 15\frac{1}{15}$ **9.** 2, 5, 17, 65, 257 **11.** $8, 6, 5, 4\frac{1}{2}, 4\frac{1}{4}$ **13-19.** Answers may vary. **13.** $a_n = 2n - 1$ **15.** $a_n = \frac{n+1}{n+2}$ **17.** $a_n = 3^{n/2}$ **19.** $a_n = -3n + 2$ **21.** $S_1 = \frac{1}{3}, S_2 = \frac{1}{2}, S_3 = \frac{7}{12}, S_4 = \frac{5}{8}$ **23.** $S_1 = 4, S_2 = 11, S_3 = 21, S_4 = 34$ **25.** $\frac{1}{2} + \frac{1}{4} + \frac{1}{6} + \frac{1}{8} + \frac{1}{10} = \frac{137}{120}$ **27.** $2^1 + 2^2 + 2^3 + 2^4 + 2^5 = 62$ **29.** $\log 7 + \log 8 + \log 9 + \log 10 = \log(7 \cdot 8 \cdot 9 \cdot 10) = \log 5040$ **31.** $\sum_{n=1}^{6} \frac{n}{n+1}$ **33.** $\sum_{n=1}^{6} (-1)^n 2^n$ **35.** $\sum_{n=2}^{\infty} (-1)^n n^2$ **37.** $\frac{3}{2}, \frac{3}{2}, \frac{3}{2}, \frac{3}{2}, \frac{3}{2}$ **39.** 0, 0.693, 1.792, 3.178, 4.787 **41.** 1.645751 **43.** $1 - \frac{1}{n+1}$

Mixed Review **45.** $\begin{bmatrix} 15 & 14 & 20 \\ 8 & 2 & 22 \\ 9 & 32 & 26 \end{bmatrix}$ **47.** $\begin{bmatrix} 13 & 33 & 27 \\ 4 & 4 & 16 \\ 31 & 33 & 69 \end{bmatrix}$ **49.** Not possible

LESSON 14-2

Try This **a.** $a_1 = 2, d = 1$ **b.** $a_1 = 1, d = 3$ **c.** $a_1 = 19, d = -5$ **d.** $a_1 = 10, d = -\frac{1}{2}$ **e.** 50 **f.** a_{72} **g.** $a_1 = 7, d = 12$; 7, 19, 31, 43, . . . **h.** 3, 10, 17, 24 **i.** 20,100 **j.** 112,101 **k.** 225 **l.** 455

Selected Answers

Exercises **1.** $a_1 = 2, d = 5$ **3.** $a_1 = 7, d = -4$ **5.** $a_1 = \frac{3}{2}, d = \frac{3}{4}$ **7.** $a_{12} = 46$ **9.** $a_{17} = -41$ **11.** a_{27} **13.** a_{102} **15.** $a_1 = 8, d = -3; 8, 5, 2, -1, \ldots$ **17.** 2, 7, 12, 17, 22 **19.** 2550 **21.** 670 **23.** 432 **25.** 855 **27.** 465 **29.** $S_n = n^2$ **31.** 16 means, $d = \frac{49}{17} = 2\frac{15}{17}$; $1, 3\frac{15}{17}, 6\frac{13}{17}, 9\frac{11}{17}, \ldots, 47\frac{2}{17}, 50$ **33.** $a_1 = p - 5q, d = 3p + 2q$ **35.** \$151,679.65 **37.** $\frac{1}{8}, \frac{1}{11}, \frac{1}{14}, \frac{1}{17}$

39. $S_n = a_1 + a_2 + a_3 + \cdots + a_{n-2} + a_{n-1} + a_n$
Group terms as follows:
$S_n = (a_1 + a_n) + (a_2 + a_{n-1}) + (a_3 + a_{n-2}) + \cdots$
If n is odd, the middle term $a_{\left(\frac{n+1}{2}\right)}$ will be left over.
Now $a_2 = a_1 + d$ and $a_{n-1} = a_n - d$, so
$(a_2 + a_{n-1}) = (a_1 + a_n)$.
Likewise the sums of all the pairs are equal,
so $S_n = (a_1 + a_n) + (a_1 + a_n) + \cdots$. If n is even, there are $\frac{n}{2}$ pairs, so $S_n = \frac{n}{2}(a_1 + a_n)$. If n is odd, there are $\frac{n-1}{2}$ pairs, so

$$S_n = \frac{n-1}{2}(a_1 + a_n) + a_{\left(\frac{n+1}{2}\right)}$$
$$= \frac{n-1}{2}(a_1 + a_n) + \frac{1}{2}(a_1 + a_n)$$
$$= \frac{n}{2}(a_1 + a_n)$$

41. $x + d = y$, or $x = y - d$; $z = y + d$;
$x + y + z = y - d + y + y + d = 3y$

Mixed Review **43.** $y > -\frac{4}{3}$ and $y < 4$ **45.** -30

47. $\begin{bmatrix} \frac{1}{30} & -\frac{2}{5} & \frac{1}{6} \\ -\frac{1}{6} & 0 & \frac{1}{6} \\ \frac{11}{30} & \frac{3}{5} & -\frac{1}{6} \end{bmatrix}$ **49.** $f^{-1}(x) = x^3 - 1$ **51.** $f^{-1}(x) = \log_3 x$

53. $\log_7 5 = x$ **55.** $\log_5 x = 7$

LESSON 14-3

Try This **a.** 5 **b.** -3 **c.** $-\frac{1}{4}$ **d.** $\frac{1}{3}$ **e.** -9375 **f.** 10 or -10 **g.** \$507.89 **h.** 11,718 **i.** $\frac{341}{256}$ **j.** 363 **k.** $\frac{65}{27}$

Exercises **1.** $-\frac{1}{3}$ **3.** -1 **5.** $\frac{1}{x}$ **7.** 243 **9.** 1250 **11.** 3, ± 12, 48 **13.** $\frac{1}{4}, \pm\frac{1}{8}, \frac{1}{16}, \pm\frac{1}{32}, \frac{1}{64}$ **15.** \$1015.79 **17.** 762 **19.** $\frac{547}{18}$ **21.** $\frac{1 - x^8}{1 - x}$ **23.** $\frac{63}{32}$ **25.** 21,844 **27. a.** $\frac{1}{256}$ ft **b.** $26\frac{169}{256}$ ft **29. a.** \$5866.60 **b.** \$1296.05 **31. a.** 6 **b.** $2\sqrt{3}$ **c.** $\frac{\sqrt{6}}{6}$ **d.** $\sqrt{3}$ **33.** Yes **35. a.** $\frac{a_n}{a_{n-1}} = r$, so $\frac{a_n^2}{a_{n-1}^2} = r^2$; hence, $a_1^2, a_2^2, \ldots,$ is geometric, with ratio r^2. **b.** $\frac{a_n}{a_{n-1}} = r$, so $\frac{a_n^{-3}}{a_{n-1}^{-3}} = r^{-3}$; thus $a_1^{-3}, a_2^{-3}, \ldots$ is geometric, with ratio r^{-3}. **37.** \$1,529,908.60 **39.** Let $y = xr$ and $z = xr^2$. The differences are the same; the terms make up an arithmetic sequence with $d = \frac{1 + r}{2xr(1 - r)}$.

Mixed Review **41.** (5, 0), (3, 4), (3, -4) **43.** 9 cm

LESSON 14-4

Try This **a.** No **b.** No **c.** Yes **d.** $\frac{3}{2}$ **e.** $\frac{16}{5}$

Exercises **1.** No **3.** Yes **5.** Yes **7.** Yes **9.** 8 **11.** 2 **13.** $\frac{160}{9}$ **15.** $\frac{7}{9}$ **17.** $\frac{7}{33}$ **19.** $\frac{170}{33}$ **21.** 24 m **23.** 512 cm^2 **25.** $\frac{1}{3}$ decimal, or $\frac{1}{11}$ binary **27.** B

Mixed Review **29.** 1 positive; 0, 2, or 4 negative **31.** $-1, -5, 4, 2i, -2i$

33.

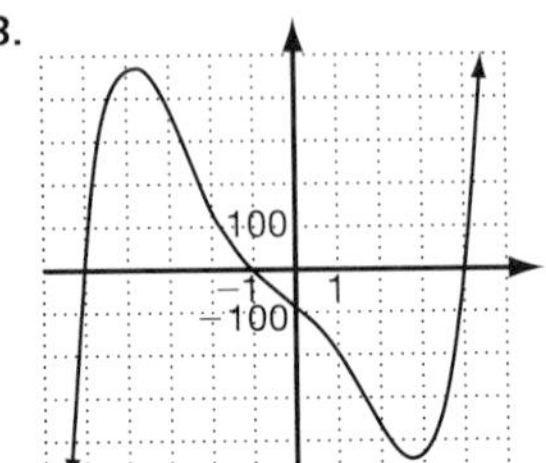

35. 27, 37, 47; 137

LESSON 14-5

Try This **a.** Show that the statement is true for $n = 1$: $1 = \frac{1(1 + 1)}{2}$; $1 = 1$. Assume the statement is true for $n = k$: $1 + 2 + 3 + 4 + \cdots + k = \frac{k(k + 1)}{2}$. Show the statement is true for $n = k + 1$: $1 + 2 + 3 + 4 + \cdots + k + k + 1 =$ $\frac{k(k + 1)}{2} + k + 1 = \frac{k(k + 1)}{2} + \frac{2(k + 1)}{2} = \frac{k(k + 1) + 2(k + 1)}{2}$ $= \frac{(k + 1)(k + 2)}{2} = \frac{(k + 1)[(k + 1) + 1]}{2}$ **b.** Show that the statement is true for $n = 1$: $2^1 - 1 = 2^{1+1} - 1 - 2$; $1 = 1$.
Assume the statement is true for $n = k$:
$1 + 3 + 7 + 15 + \cdots + (2^k - 1) = 2^{k+1} - k - 2$.
Show the statement is true for $n = k + 1$:
$1 + 3 + 7 + 15 + \cdots + (2^k - 1) + (2^{k+1} - 1)$
$= 2^{k+1} - k - 2 + 2^{k+1} - 1 = 2 \cdot 2^{k+1} - k - 1 - 2$
$= 2^{(k+1)+1} - (k + 1) - 2$.

Exercises **1.** True for $n = 1$: $1 + 2 = \frac{1}{2} \cdot 1(1 + 5)$; $3 = 3$.
Assume true for $n = k$; show true for $n = k + 1$.
$3 + 4 + 5 + \cdots + (k + 2) + (k + 3) = \frac{k(k + 5)}{2} + k + 3$
$= \frac{k(k + 5) + 2(k + 3)}{2} = \frac{k^2 + 7k + 6}{2} = \frac{(k + 1)(k + 6)}{2}$
$= \frac{1}{2}(k + 1)[(k + 1) + 5]$

3. True for $n = 1$: $-(1 + 1) = -\frac{1}{2} \cdot 1(1 + 3)$; $-2 = -2$.
Assume true for $n = k$; show true for $n = k + 1$.
$-2 - 3 - 4 - \cdots - (k + 1) - (k + 2)$
$= \frac{-k(k + 3)}{2} - (k + 2) = \frac{-k(k + 3) - 2(k + 2)}{2}$

$= \frac{-(k^2 + 5k + 4)}{2} = \frac{-(k + 1)(k + 4)}{2}$

$= -\frac{1}{2}(k + 1)[(k + 1) + 3]$

5. True for $n = 1$: $1^2 = \frac{1(1 + 1)(2 \cdot 1 + 1)}{6}$; $1 = 1$.
Assume true for $n = k$; show true for $n = k + 1$.
$1^2 + 2^2 + 3^2 + \cdots + k^2 + (k + 1)^2$
$= \frac{k(k + 1)(2k + 1)}{6} + (k + 1)^2 = \frac{(k + 1)(2k^2 + 7k + 6)}{6}$
$= \frac{(k + 1)(k + 2)(2k + 3)}{6} = \frac{(k + 1)(k + 2)[2(k + 1) + 1]}{6}$

7. True for $n = 1$: $\frac{1}{1(1 + 1)} = \frac{1}{1 + 1}$; $\frac{1}{2} = \frac{1}{2}$.
Assume true for $n = k$; show true for $n = k + 1$.
$\frac{1}{1 \cdot 2} + \frac{1}{2 \cdot 3} + \cdots + \frac{1}{k(k + 1)} + \frac{1}{(k + 1)(k + 2)}$
$= \frac{k}{k + 1} + \frac{1}{(k + 1)(k + 2)} = \frac{k(k + 2)}{(k + 1)(k + 2)} + \frac{1}{(k + 1)(k + 2)}$
$= \frac{(k + 1)^2}{(k + 1)(k + 2)} = \frac{(k + 1)}{(k + 2)} = \frac{(k + 1)}{[(k + 1) + 1]}$

9. True for $n = 1$: $5 - 1 = \frac{1(9 - 1)}{2}$; $4 = 4$.
Assume true for $n = k$; show true for $n = k + 1$.
$4 + 3 + 2 + \cdots + (5 - k) + [5 - (k + 1)]$
$= \frac{k(9 - k)}{2} + (4 - k) = \frac{-k^2 + 7k + 8}{2}$
$= \frac{(k + 1)(-k + 8)}{2} = \frac{1}{2}(k + 1)[9 - (k + 1)]$

11. True for $n = 1$: $2 \cdot 1 + 3 = 1(1 + 4)$; $5 = 5$.
Assume true for $n = j$; show true for $n = j + 1$.
$\sum_{k=1}^{j}(2k + 3) + [2(j + 1) + 3] = j(j + 4) + (2j + 5)$
$= j^2 + 6j + 5 = (j + 1)[(j + 1) + 4]$ **13.** Proving that the proposition is true for 1 is like knocking over the first domino. Proving that if the proposition is true for k, then it is true for $k + 1$ is like knowing that knocking over a given domino guarantees that the next domino will also fall.

15. True for $n = 1$: $1^5 = \frac{1^2 \cdot 2^2 \cdot 3}{12}$; $1 = 1$.
Assume true for $n = j$; show true for $n = j + 1$.
$\sum_{k=1}^{j} k^5 + (j + 1)^5 = \frac{j^2(j + 1)^2(2j^2 + 2j - 1)}{12} + (j + 1)^5$
$= \frac{(j + 1)^2[2j^4 + 2j^3 - j^2 + 12(j + 1)^3]}{12}$
$= \frac{(j + 1)^2(2j^4 + 14j^3 + 35j^2 + 36j + 12)}{12}$
$= \frac{(j + 1)^2(j + 2)^2(2j^2 + 6j + 3)}{12}$
$= \frac{(j + 1)^2(j + 2)^2(2(j + 1)^2 + 2(j + 1) - 1)}{12}$

Mixed Review **17.** $2, -2, 2i, -2i, -1$ **19.** $10\sqrt{2}$ **21.** $5, -5$ **23.** $3, -3, 3i, -3i$

LESSON 14-6

Problems **1.** They needed a 25% raise the following year. **3.** The values are $a = 4$, $b = 5$, and $c = 6$ or $a = -4$, $b = -5$, and $c = -6$. **5.** This person had 12 items correct on the test.

CHAPTER 14 WRAP UP

1. $0, \frac{1}{3}, \frac{2}{4}, \frac{3}{5}; \frac{9}{11}; \frac{14}{16}$ **2.** $0, 1\frac{1}{2}, 2\frac{2}{3}, 3\frac{3}{4}; 9\frac{9}{10}; 14\frac{14}{15}$
3. $2, -2, -\frac{2}{3}, -\frac{2}{5}, -\frac{2}{7}$ **4.** $n^2 - 1$ **5.** $\frac{n + 1}{n}$ **6.** $3 + 9 + 27$
7. $\sum_{n=1}^{6}(4n)(-1)^{n+1}$ **8.** $a_1 = 3$, $d = 1\frac{1}{2}$; and $a_{10} = 16\frac{1}{2}$ **9.** a_{15}
10. 7, 12, 17 **11.** 465 **12.** 330 **13.** −2 **14.** 256 **15.** a_8
16. 36, 18 **17.** $3\frac{15}{16}$ **18.** −1641 **19.** No **20.** Yes **21.** 40
22. $8\frac{1}{3}$ **23.** True for $n = 1$: $3 \cdot 1 - 2 = \frac{1(3 \cdot 1 - 1)}{2}$; $1 = 1$.
Assume true for $n = k$; show that the statement is true for $n = k + 1$: $1 + 4 + 7 + \cdots + (3k - 2) + [3(k + 1) - 2]$
$= \frac{k(3k - 1)}{2} + [3(k + 1) - 2] = \frac{3k^2 - k + 6k + 2}{2}$
$= \frac{3k^2 + 5k + 2}{2} = \frac{(k + 1)(3k + 2)}{2} = \frac{(k + 1)[3(k + 1) - 1]}{2}$

Chapter 15

Skills & Concepts You Need for Chapter 15 **1.** $\frac{1}{12}$
2. $\frac{1}{495}$ **3.** $\frac{11}{850}$ **4.** $9x^2 + 6x + 1$ **5.** $4 - 12x + 9x^2$
6. $x^3 - 3x^2 + 3x - 1$ **7.** $x^4 + 8x^3 + 24x^2 + 32x + 16$

LESSON 15-1

Try This **a.** 24 **b.** 64 **c.** 6 **d.** 120 **e.** 720 **f.** 720 **g.** 362,880 **h.** 18! **i.** 10 · 9! **j.** 11 · 10 · 9 · 8! **k.** 210 **l.** 5040 **m.** 56 **n.** 55,440 **o.** 151,200 **p.** 2880

Exercises **1.** 24 **3.** 720 **5.** 336 **7.** 720 **9.** 24 **11.** 5040 **13.** 720 **15.** 40,320 **17.** 120 **19.** 1 **21.** 9 · 8! **23.** $a \cdot (a - 1)!$ **25.** 27 · 26 · 25 · 24 · 23 · 22! **27.** 24 **29.** 604,800 **31.** 380 **33.** 336 **35.** 120, 60 **37.** ${}_6P_4 = 360$ **39.** 20,160 **41.** 9 · 9 · 8 · 7 · 6 · 5 · 4, or 544,320 **43.** Answers may vary. **a.** 11! **b.** $69! \approx 1.7 \times 10^{98}$ **45.** 8 **47.** 11 **49.** We can factor a 2 from each factor. There are n factors, thus $2^n[1 \cdot 2 \cdot 3 \cdot \ldots \cdot (n)] = 2^n n!$. **51.** For $n > 4$, $n!$ always contains a factor of 5 and 2, therefore $n!$ is divisible by 10, so it must end in a zero.

Mixed Review **53.** $\pm 3, \pm 6i$ **55.** 3.3 **57.** 5.55 **59.** 42 **61.** ≈ 0.5 **63.** $\approx \frac{4}{3}$ **65.** **a.** $E = 1000 + 0.06g$ **b.** \$1510

LESSON 15-2

Try This **a.** 26^5 **b.** (1) 2652 (2) 2704 **c.** 420 **d.** 210 **e.** 5040

Selected Answers

Exercises **1.** 1296; 360 **3.** 11,880 **5.** 648; 180 **7.** 648; 180 **9.** $80 \cdot 26 \cdot 9999 = 20,797,920$ **11.** 6 **13.** 34,650 **15.** 151,200 **17.** 180 **19.** (B) **21.** 24 **23.** 5040 **25. a.** 120 **b.** 625 **c.** 24 **d.** 6 **27.** 36
29. Multiply the left side of the equation by $(n-r)!$: $n \cdot (n-1) \cdot \cdots \cdot (n-r+1) \cdot (n-r)! = n!$ Multiply the right side of the equation by $(n-r)!$: $\frac{n!}{(n-r)!} \cdot (n-r)! = n!$
If $ac = bc$ and $a, b, c \neq 0$, then $a = b$, so the two forms are equivalent. **31.** 5040 **33.** $2n - 1$

35. $$_nP_r = \frac{n!}{(n-r)!} = \frac{n(n-1)(n-2)\ldots(n-r+1)(n-r)!}{(n-r)!} = n(n-1)(n-2)\ldots(n-r+1)$$

Mixed Review **37.** No, yes, yes
39. $P(x) = (x-1)(x+2)(x-3)(x+4)$; 1, −2, 3, −4

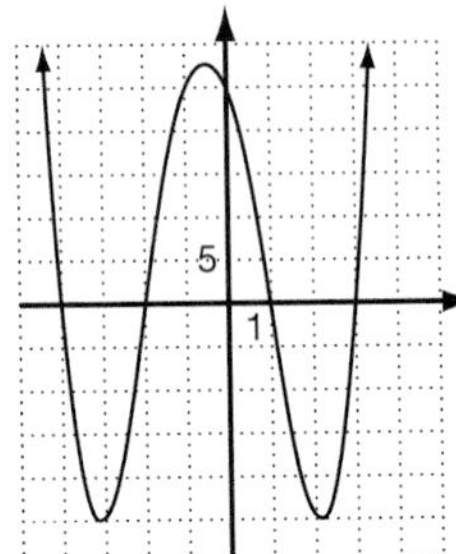

41. 16 **43.** $x^{5/2}$, x^3, $x^{7/2}$

LESSON 15-3

Try This **a.** (1) 1 (2) 4 (3) 6 (4) 4 (5) 1 **b.** 45 **c.** 45 **d.** n **e.** 792 **f.** $\sum_{r=0}^{9}\binom{9}{r} = \binom{9}{0} + \binom{9}{1} + \binom{9}{2} + \cdots + \binom{9}{9}$

Exercises **1.** 126 **3.** 1225 **5.** 495 **7.** $\frac{n(n-1)(n-2)}{6}$ **9.** 8855 **11.** 72 **13.** 28, 56 **15.** 1200 **17.** $\binom{58}{6} \cdot \binom{42}{4}$ **19.** 56 **21.** 1 **23.** $\frac{(n+1)n}{2}$ **25.** 4 **27.** 8 **29.** $\frac{n(n-1)}{2}$; $\frac{n(n-3)}{2}$

Mixed Review **31.** $\begin{bmatrix} 7 & 4 & 13 \\ 10 & 2 & 23 \\ 14 & 16 & 18 \end{bmatrix}$ **33.** −1

35. $\begin{bmatrix} 9 & 6 & 17 \\ 16 & 11 & 30 \\ 7 & 2 & 15 \end{bmatrix}$ **37.** $f^{-1}(x) = x^{3/2}, x \geq 0$

39. $f^{-1}(x) = \frac{1}{3}x - \frac{1}{2}$ **41.** 10 **43.** $-\frac{14}{3} \leq x \leq 2$ **45.** 12 m, 10 m

LESSON 15-4

Try This **a.** $-1512x^5$ **b.** $8064y^{10}$ **c.** $x^{10} - 5x^8 + 10x^6 - 10x^4 + 5x^2 - 1$ **d.** $16x^4 + 32\frac{x^3}{y} + 24\frac{x^2}{y^2} + 8\frac{x}{y^3} + \frac{1}{y^4}$ **e.** 2^{50} **f.** 2^{10}

Exercises **1.** $15a^4b^2$ **3.** $-745,472a^3$ **5.** $-1,959,552u^5v^{10}$ **7.** $m^5 + 5m^4n + 10m^3n^2 + 10m^2n^3 + 5mn^4 + n^5$ **9.** $x^{10} - 15x^8y + 90x^6y^2 - 270x^4y^3 + 405x^2y^4 - 243y^5$ **11.** $\binom{n}{0} - \binom{n}{1} + \binom{n}{2} - \binom{n}{3} + \cdots + \binom{n}{n}(-1)^n$ **13.** $99 + 70\sqrt{2}$ **15.** 128 **17.** 2^{26} **19.** $-7 - 4i\sqrt{2}$

21. $\sum_{r=0}^{n}\binom{n}{r}(-1)^r a^{n-r}b^r$ **23.** The product $(x+y)(x+y)(x+y)$ is $x^3 + x^2y + x^2y + x^2y + xy^2 + xy^2 + xy^2 + y^3$. There are 3 ways to select 1 term of the form x^2y. **25.** $-5 \pm 2\sqrt{2}$

27. $$\binom{n-1}{r-1} + \binom{n-1}{r} = \frac{(n-1)!}{(r-1)!(n-1-r+1)!} + \frac{(n-1)!}{r!(n-1-r)!} = \frac{(n-1)!}{(r-1)!(n-r)!} + \frac{(n-1)!}{r!(n-r-1)!}$$
$$= \frac{(n-1)!(r) + (n-1)!(n-r)}{(r)!(n-r)!} = \frac{(n-1)!(r+n-r)}{(r)!(n-r)!} = \frac{(n-1)!(n)}{r!(n-r)!} = \frac{(n)!}{r!(n-r)!} = \binom{n}{r}$$

Mixed Review **29.** ±16, ±8, ±4, ±2, ±1 **31.** $P(-3) = 625$; $P(-1) = 81$; $P(0) = 16$; $P(2) = 0$; $P(30) = 614,656$ **33.** $\frac{1}{4} - \frac{i}{4}$ **35.** 3,628,800 **37.** $10,000

LESSON 15-5

Try This **a.** $\frac{1}{2}$ **b.** $\frac{11}{850}$ **c.** $\frac{1}{6}$

Exercises **1.** $\frac{1}{4}$ **3.** $\frac{1}{13}$ **5.** $\frac{1}{2}$ **7.** $\frac{2}{13}$ **9.** $\frac{2}{7}$ **11.** 0 **13.** $\frac{11}{4165}$ **15.** $\frac{1}{18}$ **17.** $\frac{245}{1938}$ **19. a.** 2,598,960 **b.** $13 \cdot 48 = 624$ **c.** $\frac{624}{2,598,960} = \frac{1}{4165}$
21. a. $\binom{13}{1}\binom{4}{2}\binom{12}{3}\binom{4}{1}\binom{4}{1}\binom{4}{1} = 1,098,240$ **b.** 0.423

Mixed Review **23.** Vertex: (4, −3); line of symmetry: $x = 4$; focus: (4, −2); directrix: $y = -4$ **25.** 360,360 **27.** 504 **29.** $2500

LESSON 15-6

Try This **a.** $\frac{5}{6}$ **b.** $\frac{7}{13}$ **c.** $\frac{1}{4}$ **d.** $\frac{1}{12}, \frac{1}{18}$

Exercises **1.** $\frac{15}{22}$ **3.** $\frac{6}{11}$ **5.** $\frac{1}{2}$ **7.** $\frac{2}{3}$ **9.** $\frac{1}{2}$ **11.** $\frac{4}{13}$ **13.** $\frac{9}{13}$ **15.** $\frac{1}{36}$ **17.** $\frac{1}{8}$ **19.** $\frac{5}{24}$ **21.** $\frac{3}{7}$ **23. a.** 0.75 **b.** 0.30

25. S

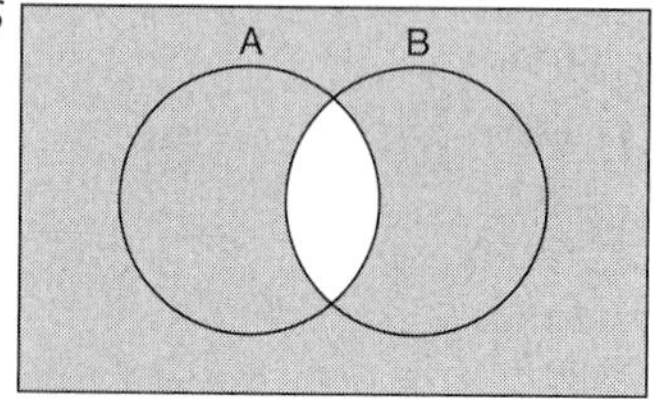

27. $\frac{1}{9{,}979{,}200}$ **29.** $\frac{1}{15}$

Mixed Review **31.** $(x+4)^2 = 4(y+3)$

33. $(x-4)^2 = 4(y+3)$ or $(y+3)^2 = -\frac{1}{2}(x-4)$

LESSON 15-7

Try This **a.** Theoretical probability is 0.375. **b.** Theoretical probability is 0.375. **c.** Theoretical probability is 0.625. **d.** 0.80

Exercises Answers may vary. Theoretical probabilities are given. **1.** ≈ 0.64 **3.** ≈ 0.563 **5.** ≈ 0.313 **7.** ≈ 0.06 **9.** ≈ 0.22 **11.** ≈ 0.55 **13.** ≈ 0.13 **15.** ≈ 0.14 **17.** ≈ 0.075 **19.** ≈ 0.08 **21.** Answers may vary. **23.** ≈ 0.427 **25.** 0.083 **27.** ≈ 0.34

Mixed Review **29.** $\frac{x-7}{x+7}$ **31.** $e^8 = u$ **33.** $\ln t = t + 1$

Binomial Probabilities

1. ≈ 0.23

3. $(p+(1-p))^n = \binom{n}{0}p^n(1-p)^0 + \binom{n}{1}p^{n-1}(1-p)^1 + \cdots + \binom{n}{n}p^0(1-p)^n$ but $p + (1-p) = 1$, so $(p+(1-p))^n = 1^n = 1$ Thus the sum of the terms of the binomial expansion is 1. The probability of r successes in a sample of size n, for $r = 0$ to $r = n$, is thus 1.

LESSON 15-8

Try This **a.** ≈ 0.29 **b.** ≈ 0.08 **c.** ≈ 0.94

Exercises **1.** ≈ 0.64 **3.** ≈ 0.38 **5.** ≈ 0.52 **7.** ≈ 0.47 **9.** ≈ 0.504 **11–13.** Answers may vary. **15.** ≈ 0.4 **17.** ≈ 0.016 **19.** ≈ 0.21 **21.** ≈ 0.33

Mixed Review **23.** $\frac{3-a}{a(a+3)}$ **25.** 36

Application

1. 00011 10010 11101 01100 **3.** 01100 11011 11011 01100 **5.** No error **7.** 0.017 **9.** 0.0000019 **11.** 0.976

CHAPTER 15 WRAP UP

1. 24 **2.** 24 **3.** 720 **4.** 40,320 **5.** 1 **6.** 1 **7.** $14 \cdot 13!$ **8.** 210 **9.** 1,814,400 **10.** 1296 **11.** 3360 **12.** 5040 **13.** 3003 **14.** 10 **15.** 120 **16.** $-48{,}384x^5$ **17.** $32x^5 - 320x^4 + 1280x^3 - 2560x^2 + 2560x - 1024$

18. 256 **19.** $\frac{25}{102}$ **20.** $\frac{1}{9}$ **21.** $\frac{4}{13}$ **22.** $\frac{9}{25}$ **23.** ≈ 0.65 **24.** ≈ 0.58

Chapter 16

Skills & Concepts You Need for Chapter 16

1. 0.9609 **2.** 0.7218 **3.** 6.0934 – 10 or −3.9066 **4.** 5.1733 – 10 or 4.8267 **5.** 0.6152 **6.** −3.2806 **7.** 2.5572

8. $\frac{1}{2} + \frac{2}{2} + \frac{3}{2} + \frac{4}{2} + \frac{5}{2} + \frac{6}{2} + \frac{7}{2} + \frac{8}{2} = 18$

9. $3 + 9 + 27 + 81 + 243 = 363$

10. $-\frac{3}{4} + -\frac{1}{4} + \frac{3}{4} + \frac{11}{4} = \frac{10}{4} = 2.5$

LESSON 16-1

Try This **a.**

Stem	Leaf
12	2, 6, 6, 1, 5, 0, 9, 7, 3, 8, 6, 5, 3
13	2, 2, 5, 7, 2, 2, 2, 1
14	3, 8, 5, 3, 8, 4, 3
15	4, 4, 3, 3
16	4, 4
17	3

b.

Stem	Leaf
1	77
2	98, 93, 89
3	89, 09, 91, 93, 12, 85, 31, 38, 54, 21
4	39, 66, 86, 38, 41
5	01
6	65, 11

c.

Interval	Freq (f)	Rel f
14–15	3	0.08
16–17	2	0.05
18–19	2	0.05
20–21	4	0.11
22–23	5	0.13
24–25	3	0.08
26–27	4	0.11
28–29	2	0.05
30–31	1	0.03
32–33	4	0.11
34–35	3	0.08
36–37	2	0.05
38–39	2	0.05
40–41	1	0.03

Exercises **1.** The number 8 must also be used as a stem.

3.

Stem	Leaf
4	9, 9, 9, 6, 8
5	6, 6, 5, 8, 9, 7, 6, 5, 4, 3, 8, 6
6	3, 1, 0, 3, 0, 8, 5, 7, 3, 1, 4, 4

Selected Answers

5.

Stem	Leaf
12	5, 5
13	6, 6, 9, 8, 6
14	8, 7, 6, 2, 8
15	8, 2, 4, 6
16	4, 9, 4, 5, 8
17	2, 4, 9, 4, 6, 4
18	3, 9, 5, 9
19	0, 6, 2
20	6, 7
21	5, 2, 3, 5
22	4, 5
23	9, 8
24	
25	4

7.

Interval	Freq (f)	Rel f
24.6–25.0	2	0.07
25.1–25.5	2	0.07
25.6–26.0	7	0.25
26.1–26.5	2	0.07
26.6–27.0	5	0.18
27.1–27.5	4	0.14
27.6–28.0	4	0.14
28.1–28.5	1	0.04
28.6–29.0	1	0.04

9.

Interval	Freq (f)	Rel f
61–65	2	0.05
66–70	7	0.17
71–75	5	0.12
76–80	9	0.21
81–85	1	0.02
86–90	13	0.31
91–95	0	0.00
96–100	4	0.10
101–105	1	0.02

11. A stem-and-leaf diagram can be constructed quickly but it is not as informative as a frequency distribution. However, a frequency distribution can take longer to construct. **13.** 0.3

Mixed Review **15.** Center: $(-1, -3)$; vertices: $(-1, -8)$, $(-1, 2)$; foci: $(-1, -3 - \sqrt{41})$, $(-1, -3 + \sqrt{41})$; asymptotes: $y + 3 = \pm\frac{5}{4}(x + 1)$

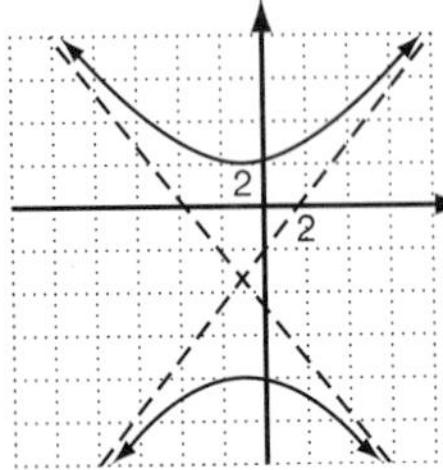

17. 302,400 **19. a.** $k = 18; y = \frac{18}{x}$ **b.** $k = 8; y = \frac{8}{x}$ **c.** $k = 28; y = \frac{28}{x}$

LESSON 16-2

Try This **a.** 189.4 pounds **b.** 78 **c.** 31.5

d.

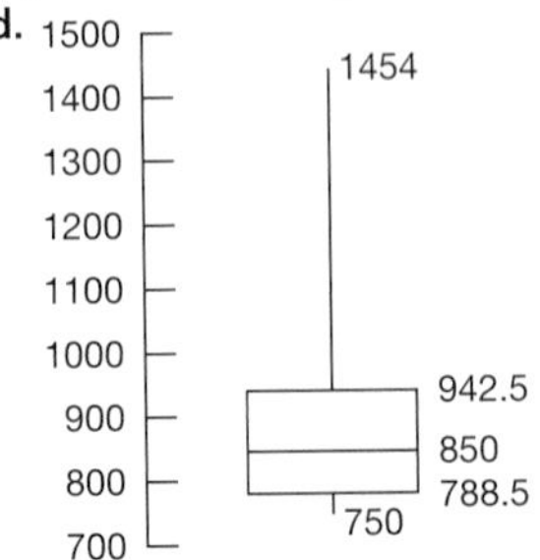

Exercises **1.** Mean 830.6, median 794, mode 794
3. Mean 99.97, median 98.7, mode 98.6

5. **7.**

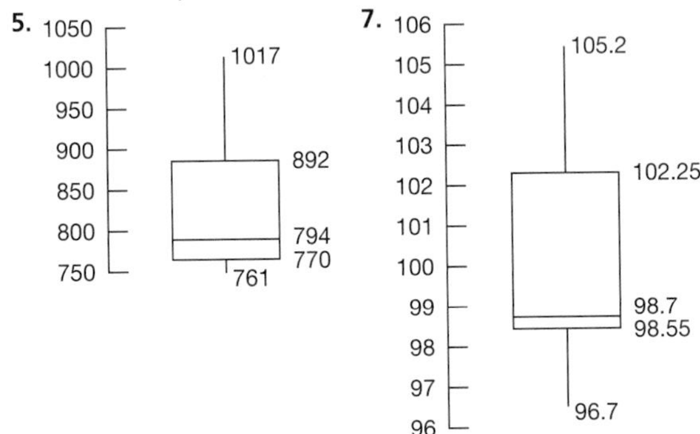

9. Sometimes **11.**

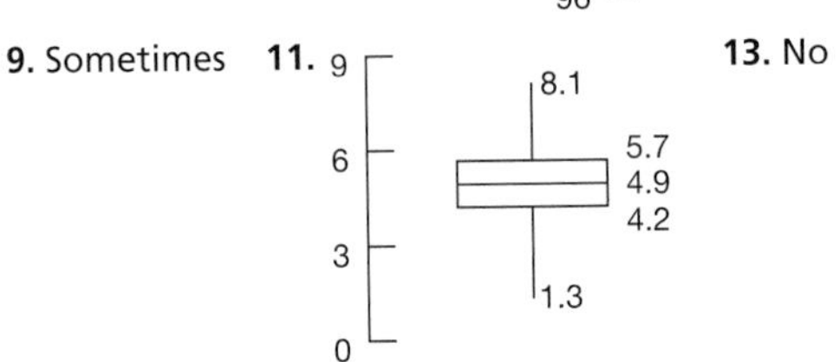

13. No

15. 886.72; $\approx 13.8\%$

Mixed Review **17.** Center: $(1, 2)$; vertices: $(-1, 2)$, $(3, 2)$, $(1, 1)$, $(1, 3)$; foci: $(1 - \sqrt{3}, 2)$, $(1 + \sqrt{3}, 2)$
19. $f(x) = x^4 - 6x^3 + 7x^2 + 36x - 78$

LESSON 16-3

Try This **a.** 5, 1.3 **b.** 73.4 **c.** 8.57

Exercises **1.** Range = 1642, mean deviation = 537.7, variance = 366,337.49, standard deviation = 605.3
3. Range = 5.9, mean deviation = 1.68, variance = 4.01, standard deviation = 2.00 **5.** Range = 34, mean deviation = 9.9, variance = 120.4, standard deviation = 10.97 **7.** Set A: mean deviation = 6, standard deviation = 6.4. Set B: mean deviation = 366, standard deviation = 422.63. **9.** The calculations are equal.

Mixed Review **11.** $\frac{4}{3}$ **13.** $(1, -2)$

LESSON 16-4

Try This **a.** 16% **b.** 84% **c.** −1.25 **d.** 2.5 **e.** −0.4 **f.** 0 **g.** 0.9505 **h.** 0.7580 **i.** 0.0062 **j.** ≈ 11 times in 100

Exercises **1.** ≈ 34% **3.** ≈ 2.5% **5.** 1.7 **7.** −0.75 **9.** 0.0367 **11.** 0.0274 **13.** 0.9980 **15.** 0.0446 **17.** 0.2743 **19.** 1.32 **21.** −1.25 **23.** 0.35 **25.** 0.2257 **27.** 0.2511 **29.** 0.9817 **31.** 0.0990 **33.** 0.7745 **35.** 0.6915 **37.** 0.0062 **39.** D **41.** ≈ 0.675 **43. a.** 5000, 50 **b.** ≈ 0.9544

Mixed Review **45.** $y^4 - 2y^3x + \frac{3}{2}y^2x^2 - \frac{1}{2}yx^3 + \frac{1}{16}x^4$

47. $15p^4q^2$, q^6 **49.** 125 m

51. $f(x) = x^4 + 8x^3 + 24x^2 + 32x + 16$

LESSON 16-5

Try This **a.** No **b.** Answers may vary. For example, for an audience of 120 people, choose every twelfth person as they exit the theater. **c.** Answers may vary. For example, use a random number table to generate the last four digits of telephone numbers for prefixes in your community.
d. Answers may vary. (1) This sample is likely to be biased against irradiation. (2) This sample might be representative. (3) This sample might be biased in favor of irradiation.
e. Answers may vary. For a sample of 200 voters, interview the following: 80 voters under age 35; 40 voters age 35–44; 40 voters age 45–54; 30 voters age 55–64; 10 voters age 65 or older.

Exercises **1.** Not a random sample because each student at the high school did not have an equal chance of participating **3.** Not a random sample because each student did not have a chance to be selected **5.** Not a random sample because there are 99 possible selections for the first number, 100 for the second, and 101 for the third **7.** The scientist could have given each mouse a number from 1 to 30, then used a random number table to select 5 of these numbers. **9.** This is only representative of people who walk past the county court building. This may be biased because not everyone will walk past the building. **11.** This is only representative of individuals who attend wrestling meets. **13.** This is representative of people who live in densely populated areas. It would be biased because it does not include voters living in rural areas. **15.** By randomly selecting 33 people from Kent County, 133 people from New Castle County, and 34 from Sussex County. **17.** Assign each of the 20,000 people a number, then use a random number generator to select 12 people. **19.** Roosevelt won by a landslide. Poorer people could not afford the luxuries of telephones, clubs, or mail, and many were illiterate. They favored Roosevelt but were not represented in the poll.

Mixed Review **21.** $(y + 1)^3$ **23.** 4 oz of Happy Trail Mix and 8 oz of Mountain Top Trail Mix

LESSON 16-6

Try This **a.** We expect 15 6s and 75 other numbers. $\chi^2 = \frac{16}{15} + \frac{16}{75} = \frac{96}{75} = 1.28$ **b.** No. $\chi^2 = 11.58$, which is greater than 9.21, the table value for 3 possible outcomes at the 1% level. **c.** $\chi^2 = 11.36$; it is significant at both the 5% and 1% levels. We would conclude that there is a difference between the pairs of lanes at these levels, and reject the null hypothesis.

Exercises **1.** $\frac{49}{55} \approx 0.89$ **3.** $\frac{9441}{80} = 118.0125$

5.

8	64	$\frac{64}{12}$
4	16	$\frac{16}{15}$
0	0	$\frac{0}{18}$
3	9	$\frac{9}{21}$
−4	16	$\frac{16}{21}$
−8	64	$\frac{64}{18}$
−1	1	$\frac{1}{15}$
−2	4	$\frac{4}{12}$ $\chi^2 \approx 11.546$

7. A **9.** $\chi^2 \approx 31.83$; we reject the null hypothesis at the 1% level of significance. **11.** No. For Example 1, $\chi^2 \approx 0.28$ using proportions. **13. a.** Small expected values have too much effect on the value of χ^2. **b.** We can group the data so that expected values are greater than 5.

Mixed Review **15.** $\frac{9}{4}$

Application **1.** Math 2.41, Science 2.27, History 2.77, English 2.58, Social Studies 2.38, Languages 2.60, Total 2.51 **3.** No, they are not symmetric about the mean. **5.** You could show histograms, give median and mode grades, and break down the data further to see why the grades deviated from expected grades.

CHAPTER 16 WRAP UP

1.

Stem	Leaf
4	9
5	3, 0
6	7, 3, 3, 5
7	3, 7, 8, 1, 4, 6, 2, 3, 4, 7, 0, 2
8	2, 0, 1, 0, 0, 0, 3
9	2, 3, 6, 0, 1

2.

Interval	Freq (f)	Rel f
30–39	14	0.4375
40–49	13	0.40625
50–59	1	0.03125
60–69	3	0.09375
70–79	0	0
80–89	1	0.03125

3. Mean 934.72, mode 720, median 720

Selected Answers

4. 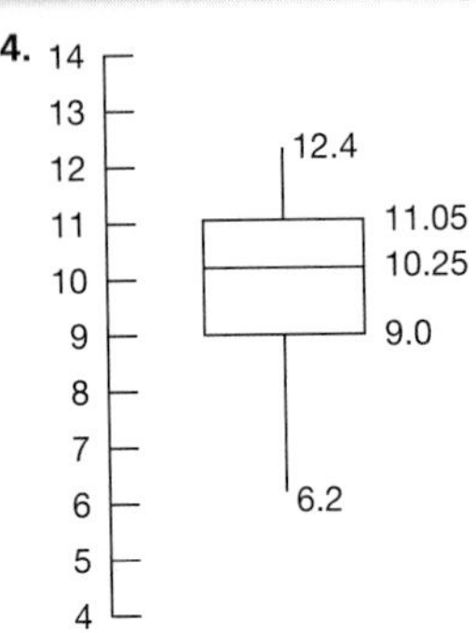

5. 13 **6.** 13.7 **7.** 195.8 **8.** 27.8 **9.** 16% **10.** −0.8 **11.** 0.1056 **12.** No. This is not random because students are not chosen independently. **13.** Assign each of the 200 doctors a number from 1 to 200, then randomly select five of those numbers. **14.** To select a stratified random sample of 200 students, you would randomly choose 56 freshmen, 72 sophomores, 48 juniors, and 24 seniors. **15.** $\chi^2 = 3.30625$ **16.** $3.30625 < 3.84$, so we accept the null hypothesis. **17.** $\chi^2 = 31.63 > 12.6$, so we reject the null hypothesis.

Chapter 17

Skills & Concepts You Need for Chapter 17

1. 19, 9 **2.** $3t^2 - 10t - 8$ **3.** $24(a - 2b)(a + 2b)$ **4.** $3xy(x - 3y)(x - 2y)$ **5.** $-\frac{a+2}{2}$ **6.** $\frac{2}{x}$ **7.** $\frac{-2c^2 + 7dc + c - d}{(2c - 1)(2c + 1)}$ **8.** 3, −4 **9.** $\frac{2}{3}$, −4 **10.** $\frac{1 \pm i\sqrt{11}}{2}$ **11.** $\frac{-1 \pm \sqrt{5}}{2}$ **12.** $f(-x) = (-x)^3 - (-x) = -x^3 + x = -(x^3 - x) = -f(x)$ **13.** $g(-x) = 2(-x)^2 - (-x)^4 = 2x^2 - x^4 = g(x)$

LESSON 17-1

Try This **a.** $\sin\theta = \frac{4}{5}$, $\cos\theta = \frac{3}{5}$, $\tan\theta = \frac{4}{3}$ **b.** $r = 12\sqrt{2}$ ft **c.** $\cot\theta \approx 1.33$, $\sec\theta = 1.25$, $\csc\theta \approx 1.67$ **d.** $\sin\theta = \frac{15}{17}$, $\tan\theta = \frac{15}{8}$, $\csc\theta = \frac{17}{15}$, $\sec\theta = \frac{17}{8}$, $\cot\theta = \frac{8}{15}$

Exercises **1.** $\sin\theta = \frac{7}{25}$, $\cos\theta = \frac{24}{25}$, $\tan\theta = \frac{7}{24}$ **3.** $\sin\theta = \frac{8}{17}$, $\cos\theta = \frac{15}{17}$, $\tan\theta = \frac{8}{15}$ **5.** $a = 3$ **7.** $b = 2$ **9.** $\cot\theta \approx 3.43$, $\sec\theta \approx 1.04$, $\csc\theta \approx 3.57$ **11.** $\cot\theta \approx 1.88$, $\sec\theta \approx 1.13$, $\csc\theta \approx 2.13$ **13.** $\sin\theta = \frac{\sqrt{3}}{2}$, $\sec\theta = 2$, $\cos\theta = \frac{1}{2}$, $\csc\theta = \frac{2\sqrt{3}}{3}$, $\cot\theta = \frac{\sqrt{3}}{3}$ **15.** $\cos\theta = \frac{\sqrt{3}}{2}$, $\tan\theta = \frac{\sqrt{3}}{3}$, $\cot\theta = \sqrt{3}$, $\sec\theta = \frac{2\sqrt{3}}{3}$, $\csc\theta = 2$ **17.** $\sin\theta = \frac{1}{2}$, $\cos\theta = \frac{\sqrt{3}}{2}$, $\tan\theta = \frac{\sqrt{3}}{3}$, $\cot\theta = \sqrt{3}$, $\sec\theta = \frac{2\sqrt{3}}{3}$, $\csc\theta = 2$ **19.** $\sin\theta = \frac{\sqrt{2}}{2}$, $\cos\theta = \frac{\sqrt{2}}{2}$, $\tan\theta = 1$, $\cot\theta = 1$, $\sec\theta = \sqrt{2}$, $\csc\theta = \sqrt{2}$

21. $40\sqrt{3}$ m; add observer's height **23.** $5\sqrt{3}$

Mixed Review **25.** $13\sqrt{13} - 7\sqrt[4]{7}$ **27.** $\sqrt[20]{a^8b^{15}}$ **29.** 128 **31.** π

LESSON 17-2

Try This **a.** First **b.** Third **c.** Fourth **d.** Third **e.** First **f.** First **g.** $\sin\theta = -\frac{1}{2}$, $\cos\theta = \frac{\sqrt{3}}{2}$, $\tan\theta = -\frac{\sqrt{3}}{3}$ **h.** Cosine and secant values are positive; the other four function values are negative. **i.** $\sin 180° = 0$, $\cos 180° = -1$, $\tan 180° = 0$, $\sin 270° = -1$, $\cos 270° = 0$, $\tan 270°$ is undefined. **j.** 30° **k.** 30° **l.** $-\frac{1}{2}$, $-\frac{\sqrt{3}}{2}$, $\frac{\sqrt{3}}{3}$ **m.** $-\frac{\sqrt{2}}{2}$, $\frac{\sqrt{2}}{2}$, −1 **n.** 0, −1, 0

Exercises **1.** First **3.** Third **5.** First **7.** Second **9.** Second **11.** Fourth **13.** $\sin\theta = -\frac{3}{5}$; $\cos\theta = -\frac{4}{5}$; $\tan\theta = \frac{3}{4}$ **15.** $\sin\theta = -\frac{3}{5}$; $\cos\theta = \frac{4}{5}$; $\tan\theta = -\frac{3}{4}$ **17.** $\sin\theta = \frac{\sqrt{3}}{2}$; $\cos\theta = -\frac{1}{2}$; $\tan\theta = -\sqrt{3}$ **19.** All function values are positive. **21.** The cosine and secant function values are positive; the other four are negative. **23.** All function values are positive.

25.

θ	$\cot\theta$	$\sec\theta$	$\csc\theta$
0°	—	1	—
90°	0	—	1
180°	—	−1	—
270°	0	—	−1

27. 30° **29.** 45° **31.** 45° **33.** 0 **35.** Undefined **37.** Undefined **39.** $-\frac{\sqrt{2}}{2}$ **41.** $-\frac{\sqrt{3}}{2}$ **43.** $\frac{\sqrt{3}}{3}$ **45.** $-\sqrt{2}$ **47.** 1 **49.** $-\frac{\sqrt{3}}{2}$, $-\frac{1}{2}$, $\sqrt{3}$ **51.** 0 , −1 , 0 **53.** $\sin 30° = 0.500$, $\cos 30° \approx 0.866$, $\tan 30° \approx 0.577$, $\csc 30° = 2.000$, $\sec 30° \approx 1.155$, $\cot 30° \approx 1.732$ **55.** $\sin 120° \approx 0.866$, $\cos 120° = -0.500$, $\tan 120° \approx -1.732$, $\csc 120° \approx 1.155$, $\sec 120° = -2.000$, $\cot 120° \approx -0.577$ **57.** $\sin\theta \approx 0.866$, $\cos\theta = 0.5$, $\tan\theta \approx 1.732$, $\csc\theta \approx 1.155$, $\sec\theta = 2$, $\cot\theta \approx 0.577$ **59.** $\sin\theta = -\frac{8}{17}$, $\cos\theta = -\frac{15}{17}$, $\tan\theta = \frac{8}{15}$, $\csc\theta = -\frac{17}{8}$, $\sec\theta = -\frac{17}{15}$, $\cot\theta = \frac{15}{8}$ **61.** $\sin\theta = -\frac{5}{13}$, $\cos\theta = \frac{12}{13}$, $\tan\theta = -\frac{5}{12}$, $\csc\theta = -\frac{13}{5}$, $\sec\theta = \frac{13}{12}$, $\cot\theta = -\frac{12}{5}$ **63.** 18.75 in.

Mixed Review **65.** No **67.** $\pm\frac{1}{5}$ **69.** $\frac{7}{13}$ **71.** $\frac{11}{26}$

LESSON 17-3

Try This **a.** $\frac{5}{4}\pi$ **b.** $\frac{5}{3}\pi$ **c.** $-\frac{7}{4}\pi$ **d.** 240° **e.** 450° **f.** −144° **g.** 57.6 cm **h.** 6 radians **i.** 2 **j.** $\sqrt{3}$ **k.** $\sqrt{2}$ **l.** 377 cm/s **m.** 3.6 radians/s

Exercises **1.** $\frac{\pi}{6}$ **3.** $\frac{5\pi}{9}$ **5.** $\frac{5\pi}{12}$ **7.** $\frac{2\pi}{3}$ **9.** $-\frac{16\pi}{9}$ **11.** $-\frac{17\pi}{36}$ **13.** 57.3° **15.** 1440° **17.** 135° **19.** 20.9 cm **21.** 5.7 **23.** $\sqrt{3}$ **25.** $\frac{2\sqrt{3}}{3}$ **27.** 1 **29.** $\frac{\sqrt{3}}{3}$ **31.** 0 **33.** ≈ 54 m/min **35.** ≈ 9.4 cm/s **37.** ≈ 66,659 mi/h **39.** ≈ 1429 radians/h **41.** ≈ 11.4 mi/h **43. a.** ≈ 53.33 grads **b.** 170 grads **c.** 25 grads **d.** ≈ 142.86 grads **45.** ≈ 111.6 km; ≈ 69.8 mi **47.** Yes, for all angles **49.** ≈ 25,000 mi

Mixed Review **51.** No **53.** $f^{-1}(x) = x^{1/3}$ **55.** $f^{-1}(x) = \sqrt[4]{x^2 + 1}, x \geq 1$ **57.** e **59.** $\frac{10}{9}$

LESSON 17-4

Try This **a.** 0.2644 **b.** 0.4699 **c.** 0.6383 **d.** −0.9868 **e.** 52°50′ **f.** 37°27′ **g.** 43.917° **h.** ≈ 0.6264 **i.** ≈ 1.900 **j.** ≈ 21°15′ **k.** ≈ 31°47′

Exercises **1.** 0.2306 **3.** 0.5519 **5.** 0.5467 **7.** 1.127 **9.** −0.7969 **11.** 0.6383 **13.** 0.5392 **15.** 3.689 **17.** 81°10′ **19.** 45°50′ **21.** 13°40′ **23.** 46°39′ **25.** 67°3′ **27.** −48°57′ **29.** 412°33′ **31.** 45.42° **33.** 76.88° **35.** −68.78° **37.** 225.55° **39.** ≈ 0.4775 **41.** ≈ 0.5889 **43.** ≈ 0.4494 **45.** ≈ 39°43′ **47.** ≈ 45°44′ **49.** ≈ 74°53′ **51.** ≈ 0.2095π **53.** ≈ 1.1922222π **55.** ≈ 74.694267° **57.** ≈ 2172.0382° **59.** ≈ 1477.08° **61.** ≈ 135.576° **63.** ≈ 0.5708 **65.** ≈ −0.5528 **67.** ≈ −22.4013 **69.** ≈ 0.0864 **71.** ≈ −0.0089 **73.** Find the reciprocal of 1.706 using the $\frac{1}{x}$ key, and then press the inv and cos, or $\cos^{-1}$ keys. **75.** $\sin\theta \approx \theta$ for small angles. **77.** ≈ 61.63944° **79.** 8.65689×10^5 mi is the diameter.

Mixed Review **81.** Yes, yes **83.** Yes, no **85.** $(-1, -2, 3)$ **87.** All real numbers **89.** 242 **91.** 0.05556, or $\frac{1}{18}$

LESSON 17-5

Try This **a.** 3 **b.** D: The set of all real numbers; R: $-1 \leq \sin x \leq 1$ **c.** Yes; 2π **d.** Odd **e.** 2π **f.** $\{y \mid y \geq 1 \text{ or } y \leq -1\}$

g.

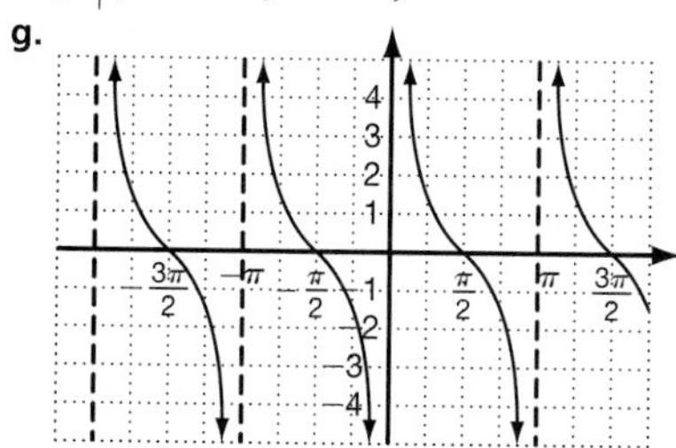

h. π **i.** Domain: $\{x \mid x \neq k\pi, k \text{ an integer}\}$; Range: All real numbers **j.** Odd

Exercises **1.** No **3.** Yes **5.** Yes **7.** 4

9.

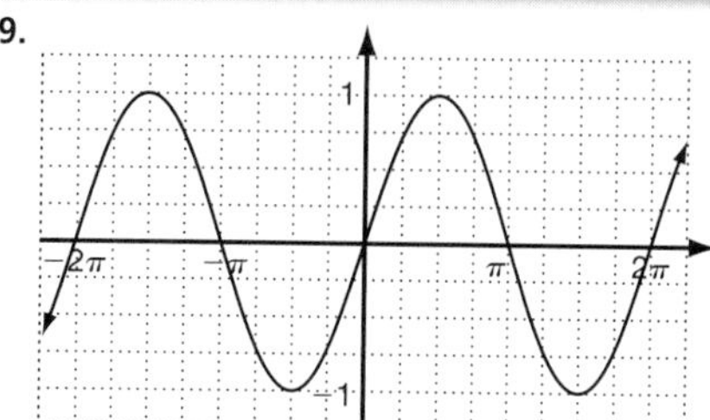

11.

−1	$-\frac{\sqrt{3}}{2}$	$-\frac{\sqrt{2}}{2}$	$-\frac{1}{2}$	0	$\frac{1}{2}$	$\frac{\sqrt{2}}{2}$	$\frac{\sqrt{3}}{2}$	1
−1	−0.866	−0.707	−0.5	0	0.5	0.707	0.866	1

13.

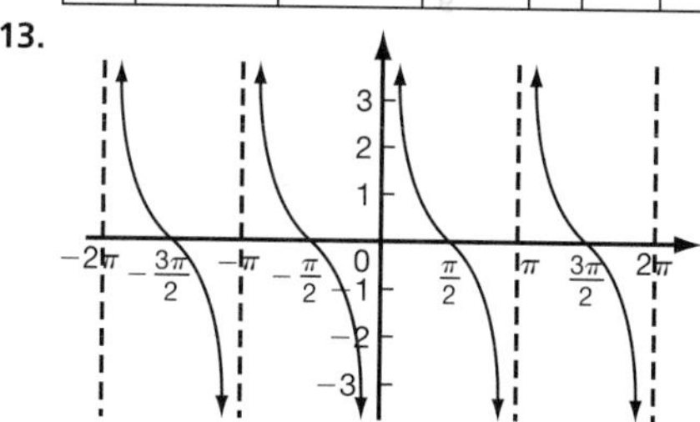

15.

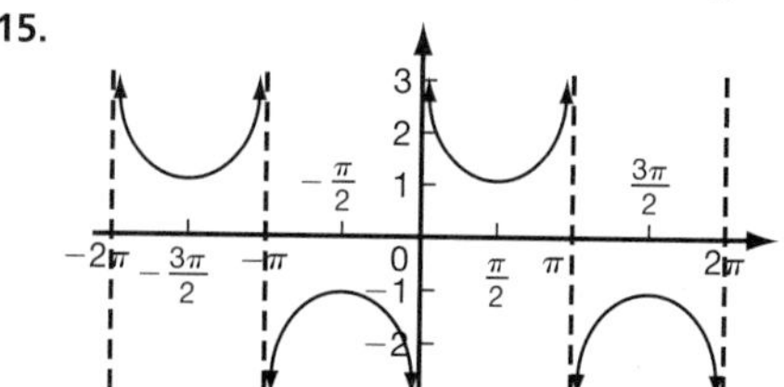

17.

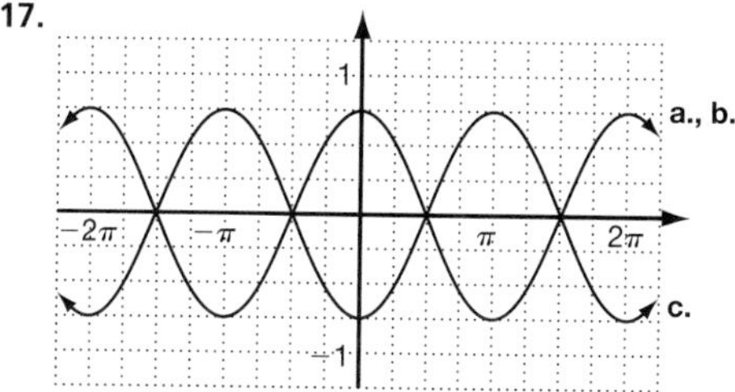

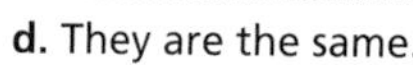

d. They are the same.

19.

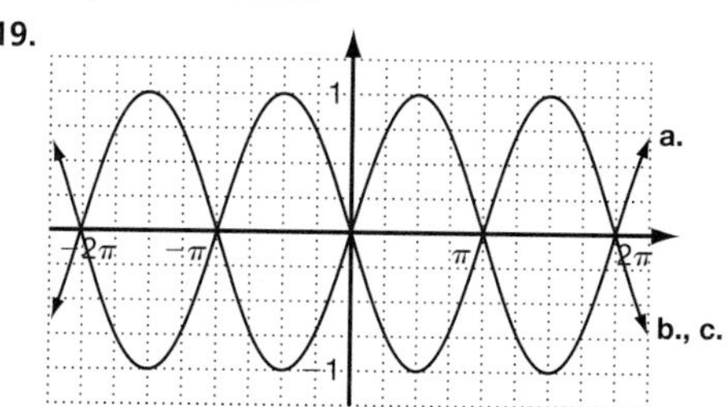

d. They are the same.

21. The sin and tan functions; the cos and cot functions **23. a.** If the graph of tan x were reflected across the y-axis and then translated to the right a distance of $\frac{\pi}{2}$, the graph of cot x

could be obtained. There are other ways to describe the relation. **b.** If the graph of sec x were translated to the right $\frac{\pi}{2}$ units, the graph of csc x would be obtained. There are other descriptions. **25.** $\left\{x \mid -\frac{\pi}{2} + 2k\pi < x < \frac{\pi}{2} + 2k\pi, k \text{ an integer}\right\}$

27.

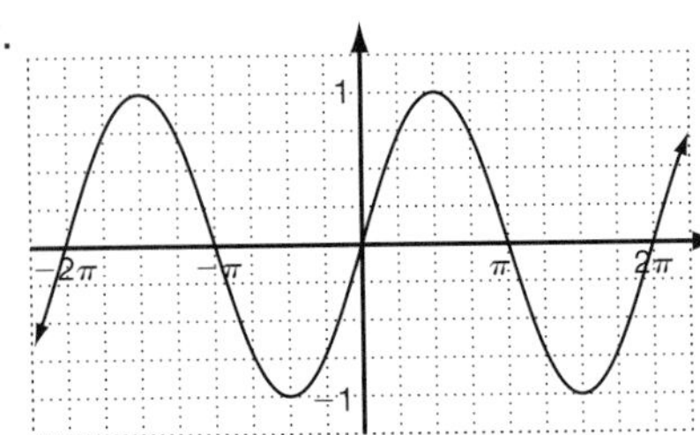

Mixed Review **29.** Odd **31.** Even **33.** 10

LESSON 17-6

Try This **a.** $\cos\theta \equiv \cot\theta \cdot \sin\theta$ **b.** $\sin^2\theta \equiv 1 - \cos^2\theta$ **c.** $\sin\theta \equiv \pm\sqrt{1 - \cos^2\theta}$ **d.** $\sec^2\theta - \tan^2\theta \equiv 1$; $\tan^2\theta \equiv \sec^2\theta - 1$ **e.** $\sec\theta \equiv \pm\sqrt{1 + \frac{\sin^2\theta}{\cos^2\theta}}$
f. $\cos\left(0 - \frac{\pi}{2}\right) = \cos\left(-\frac{\pi}{2}\right) = 0 = \sin 0$
g. $\cot\left(\theta + \frac{\pi}{2}\right) \equiv -\tan\theta$

Exercises **1.** $\cos\theta \equiv \frac{\sin\theta}{\tan\theta}$ **3.** $\csc\theta \equiv \pm\sqrt{1 + \cot^2\theta}$
5. $\cot\theta \equiv \pm\sqrt{\csc^2\theta - 1}$ **7.** $\tan\theta \equiv \pm\sqrt{\frac{1}{\cos^2\theta} - 1}$
9. $\sin\left(\frac{\pi}{4} - \frac{\pi}{2}\right) = \sin\left(-\frac{\pi}{4}\right) = -\frac{\sqrt{2}}{2} = -\cos\frac{\pi}{4}$
11. $\sin\left(\frac{\pi}{2} - \frac{5\pi}{4}\right) = \sin\left(-\frac{3\pi}{4}\right) = -\frac{\sqrt{2}}{2} = \cos\frac{5\pi}{4}$
13. $\tan\left(\theta - \frac{\pi}{2}\right) \equiv -\cot\theta$ **15.** $\sec\left(\frac{\pi}{2} - \theta\right) \equiv \csc\theta$
17. $\sin 25° \approx 0.4226$, $\cos 25° \approx 0.9063$, $\tan 25° \approx 0.4663$, $\cot 25° \approx 2.145$, $\sec 25° \approx 1.103$, $\csc 25° \approx 2.366$ **19.** $-\sin\theta$ **21.** $-\cos\theta$ **23.** $\cos\theta$ **25.** $-\cos\theta$ **27.** 0.92388 **29.** 0.92388 **31.** 0.38268 **33. a.** $\sin\theta \equiv \cos\left(\frac{\pi}{2} - \theta\right)$, $\cos\theta \equiv \sin\left(\frac{\pi}{2} - \theta\right)$, $\tan\theta \equiv \cot\left(\frac{\pi}{2} - \theta\right)$, $\cot\theta \equiv \tan\left(\frac{\pi}{2} - \theta\right)$, $\sec\theta \equiv \csc\left(\frac{\pi}{2} - \theta\right)$, $\csc\theta \equiv \sec\left(\frac{\pi}{2} - \theta\right)$ **b.** The function of an angle is equal to the cofunction of its complement, just as in right triangle trigonometry.
35. $\theta = 60°$; $\frac{1 - \cos 60°}{\sin 60°} = \frac{\sin 60°}{1 + \cos 60°}$; $\frac{\frac{1}{2}}{\frac{\sqrt{3}}{2}} = \frac{\frac{\sqrt{3}}{2}}{\frac{3}{2}}$; $\frac{\sqrt{3}}{3} = \frac{\sqrt{3}}{3}$
37. $x = \frac{\pi}{4}$; $\sec\frac{\pi}{4} - \sin\frac{\pi}{4}\tan\frac{\pi}{4} = \cos\frac{\pi}{4}$; $\sqrt{2} - \frac{\sqrt{2}}{2} \cdot 1 = \frac{\sqrt{2}}{2}$; $\frac{\sqrt{2}}{2} = \frac{\sqrt{2}}{2}$

Mixed Review **39.** $(x^2 + 25)(x + 5)(x - 5)$
41. $(x + 4)(x + 5)(x + 6)$ **43.** $x^3 - x^2 + x - 1$

45. $\frac{-3125l^{10}n^6\sqrt[3]{n^2}}{16{,}807m^{15}}$
47. $\sin\alpha = \frac{12}{13}$, $\cos\alpha = \frac{5}{13}$, $\tan\alpha = \frac{12}{5}$, $\cot\alpha = \frac{5}{12}$, $\csc\alpha = \frac{13}{12}$, $\sec\alpha = \frac{13}{5}$, $\sin\theta = \frac{5}{13}$, $\cos\theta = \frac{12}{13}$, $\tan\theta = \frac{5}{12}$, $\cot\theta = \frac{12}{5}$, $\csc\theta = \frac{13}{5}$, $\sec\theta = \frac{13}{12}$
49. $a = \sqrt{2}$, $b = 2$

LESSON 17-7

Try This **a.** A = 2

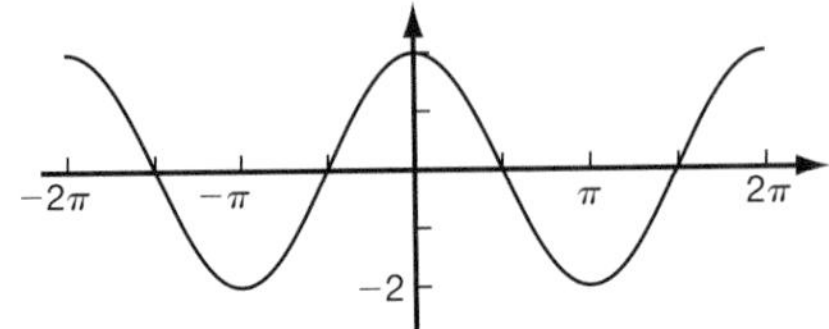

b. The period is π.

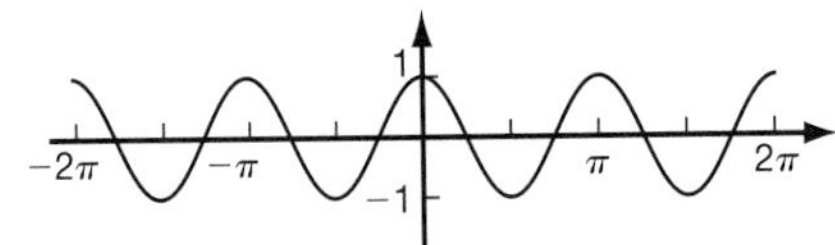

c. $A = 3$; The period is π.

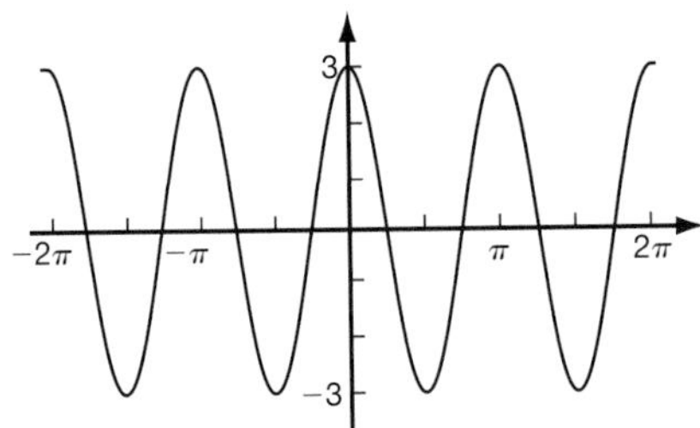

Exercises **1.** $A = \frac{1}{2}$ **3.** $A = 3$ **5.** $A = \frac{1}{3}$ **7.** $A = 4$
9. $A = 2$ **11.** The period is $\frac{2\pi}{3}$. **13.** The period is 4π. **15.** The period is 6π. **17.** The period is π. **19.** $A = 2$, period $= \pi$ **21.** $A = \frac{1}{2}$, period $= \pi$ **23.** $A = 2$, period $= 4\pi$ **25.** $A = \frac{1}{2}$, period $= \pi$ **27.** $A = \frac{1}{2}$, period $= \pi$ **31.** $y = -4\sin\left(\frac{1}{3}\theta\right)$ **33.** $A = \frac{1}{2}$, period $= 4\pi$

Mixed Review **35.** No, yes, no, yes, no

LESSON 17-8

Try This **a.** $\cos x + 1$ **b.** $\sin\theta$ **c.** $\sin x$ **d.** $\cot x = -4$ or $\cot x = 3$

Exercises **1.** $\sin^2 x - \cos^2 x$ **3.** $\sin x - \sec x$ **5.** $\sin\theta + \cos\theta$ **7.** $\cot x - \tan x$ **9.** $1 - 2\sin y\cos y$ **11.** $\sec^2\theta + 2\tan\theta$ **13.** $\cos x(\sin x + \cos x)$ **15.** $(\sin y - \cos y)(\sin y + \cos y)$

17. $\cos^2 x$ **19.** $\sin^2\theta - \cos^2\theta$ **21.** $3(\cot y + 1)^2$
23. $(\csc^2\theta + 5)(\cot^2\theta)$ **25.** $\tan x$ **27.** $\frac{2}{9}\cos\theta\cot\theta$
29. $\cos x - 1$ **31.** $\cos x + 1$ **33.** $\tan x = -7$ or $\tan x = 3$
35. $\sin\theta = \frac{3}{4}$ or $\sin\theta = -\frac{1}{2}$ **37.** $\tan\theta = 3 \pm \sqrt{13}$
39. No solution **41.** $\csc x = \frac{3 + \sqrt{41}}{4}$
43. $\frac{1}{\sin\theta} - \cos\theta\frac{\cos\theta}{\sin\theta} = \frac{1 - \cos^2\theta}{\sin\theta} = \frac{\sin^2\theta}{\sin\theta} = \sin\theta$
45. $\frac{(1 - \sin\theta)}{\cos\theta} = \frac{(1 - \sin\theta)(1 + \sin\theta)}{\cos\theta(1 + \sin\theta)} = \frac{(1 - \sin^2\theta)}{\cos\theta(1 + \sin\theta)}$
$= \frac{\cos^2\theta}{\cos\theta(1 + \sin\theta)} = \frac{\cos\theta}{1 + \sin\theta}$
47. No; $\sin\left(\frac{\pi}{2} + \frac{\pi}{2}\right) = \sin\pi = 0$, $\sin\frac{\pi}{2} + \sin\frac{\pi}{2} = 1 + 1 = 2$
49. $4 - |\tan y|$ **51.** $\frac{\cos x}{|1 - \sin x|}$
Mixed Review **53.** $(x + 2)^4$ **55.** $\frac{2\pi}{5}$ **57.** $\frac{7\pi}{6}$ **59.** 315° **61.** 30°

CHAPTER 17 WRAP UP

1. 20 cm **2.** $\sin\theta = \frac{1}{2}$, $\cos\theta = \frac{\sqrt{3}}{2}$, $\cot\theta = \sqrt{3}$, $\sec\theta = \frac{2\sqrt{3}}{3}$, $\csc\theta = 2$ or $\sin\theta = -\frac{1}{2}$, $\cos\theta = -\frac{\sqrt{3}}{2}$, $\cot\theta = \sqrt{3}$, $\sec\theta = \frac{-2\sqrt{3}}{3}$, $\csc\theta = -2$ **3.** First **4.** Third **5.** Second
6. Third **7.** $\sin\theta = -\frac{4}{7}$, $\cos\theta = \frac{\sqrt{33}}{7}$, $\tan\theta = \frac{-4\sqrt{33}}{33}$, $\cot\theta = -\frac{\sqrt{33}}{4}$, $\sec\theta = \frac{7\sqrt{33}}{33}$, $\csc\theta = -\frac{7}{4}$
8. 30° **9.** 30° **10.** 40° **11.** Undefined **12.** 1 **13.** $\frac{\sqrt{2}}{2}$ **14.** $\frac{\pi}{4}$
15. $\frac{5\pi}{6}$ **16.** $\frac{3\pi}{2}$ **17.** $-\frac{\pi}{3}$ **18.** 210° **19.** −60° **20.** 720°
21. $\sqrt{2}$ **22.** $\sqrt{3}$ **23.** 1 **24.** $\frac{1}{2}$ radians/s **25.** 0.1449
26. 0.8526 **27.** 0.5147 **28.** 0.6730 **29.** 24°35′ **30.** 47°48′
31.

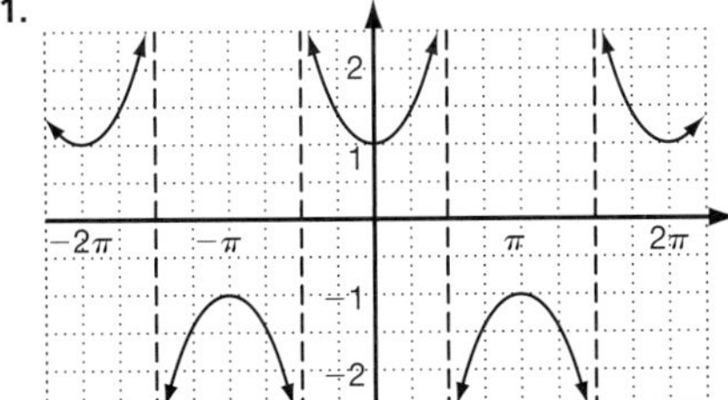

32. $1 = \frac{\frac{\sqrt{2}}{2}}{\frac{\sqrt{2}}{2}}$ **33.** $\sin\left(\frac{\pi}{2} - \frac{\pi}{4}\right) = \sin\frac{\pi}{4} = \frac{\sqrt{2}}{2} = \cos\frac{\pi}{4}$
34. $\cot\theta \equiv \pm\sqrt{\csc^2\theta - 1}$ **35.** $\csc\theta \equiv \pm\sqrt{\frac{1}{1 - \cos^2\theta}}$
36. $\cot\left(\theta - \frac{\pi}{2}\right) \equiv -\tan\theta$ **37.** $\sin 15° = 0.2588$
38. $\cos 15° = 0.9659$ **39.** $\tan 15° = 0.2679$
40. $\cot 15° = 3.732$ **41.** $\sec 15° = 1.035$ **42.** $\csc 15° = 3.864$

43. $A = 3$

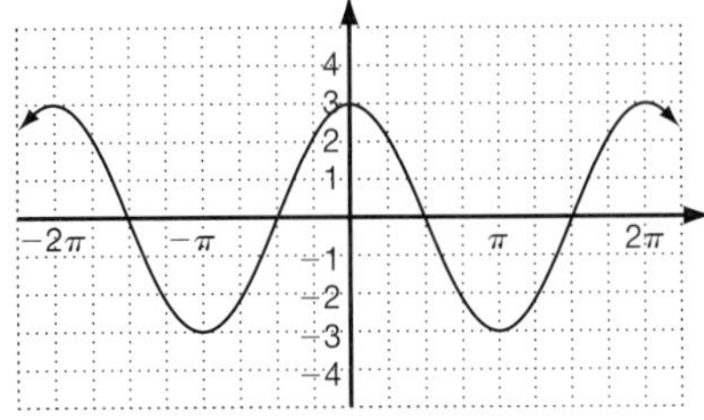

44. The period is π.

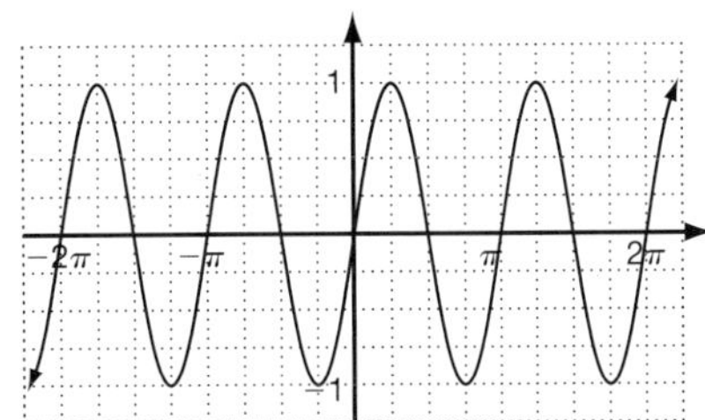

45. $\csc\theta$ **46.** $\frac{1 \pm \sqrt{7}}{3}$

Chapter 18

Skills & Concepts You Need for Chapter 18

1. 81 **2.** $9|c|$ **3.** $\frac{\sqrt[3]{100mn^2}}{5n}$ **4.** $-\frac{63 + 4\sqrt{15}}{33}$ **5.** $\sqrt{a^2 + b^2}$ **6.** 13
7. $f^{-1}(x) = \frac{1}{3}x + \frac{2}{3}$ **8.** $f^{-1}(x) = x^2 - 4x + 1$ **9.** $\pm\sqrt{\frac{\sin^2\theta}{1 - \sin^2\theta}}$
10. $\frac{\pm\sqrt{1 - \cos^2\theta}}{\cos\theta}$ **11.** $\pm\frac{\sqrt{\csc^2\theta - 1}}{\csc^2\theta - 1}$ **12.** $\frac{1}{\cot\theta}$
13. $\pm\sqrt{\sec^2\theta - 1}$

LESSON 18-1

Try This **a.** $\frac{1}{2}$ **b.** $\frac{\sqrt{2} - \sqrt{6}}{4}$ **c.** $\frac{\sqrt{6} - \sqrt{2}}{4}$ **d.** $\frac{\sqrt{2} + \sqrt{6}}{4}$
e. $-2 - \sqrt{3}$

Exercises **1.** $\cos A\cos B + \sin A\sin B$ **3.** $\frac{\sqrt{2} + \sqrt{6}}{4}$
5. $\frac{\sqrt{2} - \sqrt{6}}{4}$ **7.** $-\frac{\sqrt{3}}{2}$ **9.** $\frac{-\sqrt{2} - \sqrt{6}}{4}$ **11.** $-\frac{\sqrt{2}}{2}$
13. $\sin P\cos Q + \cos P\sin Q$ **15.** $\frac{\tan P - \tan Q}{1 + \tan P\tan Q}$
17. $\frac{\sqrt{2} + \sqrt{6}}{4}$ **19.** $2 - \sqrt{3}$ **21.** $\frac{\sqrt{6} - \sqrt{2}}{4}$ **23.** $2 + \sqrt{3}$
25. $\frac{\sqrt{6} - \sqrt{2}}{4}$ **27.** $\frac{\sqrt{2}}{2}$ **29.** $2 + \sqrt{3}$ **31.** $2 - \sqrt{3}$
33. $\cos 3\pi = -1$ **35.** $\cos(A - B)$ **37.** $2\cos\alpha\cos\beta$
39. $\tan(A - B)$ **41.** $\tan 52° = 1.280$ **43.** $2\sin\alpha\cos\beta$
45. $-\frac{\sqrt{3}}{2}$ **47.** $\frac{\cot\alpha\cot\beta - 1}{\cot\beta + \cot\alpha}$

Selected Answers

49. $\sin\frac{\pi}{2}\cos x - \cos\frac{\pi}{2}\sin x = 1 \cdot \cos x - 0 \cdot \sin x = \cos x$

51. $\cos\frac{\pi}{2}\cos x + \sin\frac{\pi}{2}\sin x = 0 + \sin x = \sin x$

53. 1.2071; 0.9659

55. $\cos 2\theta = \cos\theta\cos\theta - \sin\theta\sin\theta$
$= \cos^2\theta - \sin^2\theta$
$\sin 2\theta = \sin\theta\cos\theta + \cos\theta\sin\theta$
$= 2\sin\theta\cos\theta$

$\tan 2\theta = \frac{\tan\theta + \tan\theta}{1 - \tan\theta\tan\theta} = \frac{2\tan\theta}{1 - \tan^2\theta}$ **57.** -0.5351

59. $\sin(\sin x)\cos(\sin y) + \cos(\sin x)\sin(\sin y)$

61. $\sin x\cos y\cos z + \cos x\sin y\cos z + \cos x\cos y\sin z - \sin x\sin y\sin z$

Mixed Review **63.** $-m$ **65.** $\frac{5\sqrt{6}}{6}$ **67.** 0.3488 **69.** 0.8420 **71.** 243 **73.** 1102.5 m

LESSON 18-2

Try This **a.** $\frac{24}{25}$ **b.** $\sin 2\theta = \frac{120}{169}$, $\cos 2\theta = -\frac{119}{169}$, $\tan 2\theta = -\frac{120}{119}$, second quadrant **c.** Answers may vary. $\cos^3\theta - 3\sin^2\theta\cos\theta$ or $\cos\theta - 4\sin^2\theta\cos\theta$ or $2\cos^3\theta - \cos\theta - 2\sin^2\theta\cos\theta$ **d.** $\frac{\sqrt{2+\sqrt{3}}}{2}$ **e.** 1

Exercises **1.** $\frac{24}{25}, -\frac{7}{25}, -\frac{24}{7}$, II **3.** $\frac{24}{25}, \frac{7}{25}, \frac{24}{7}$, I

5. $\frac{24}{25}, -\frac{7}{25}, -\frac{24}{7}$, II **7.** $\frac{\sqrt{2+\sqrt{3}}}{2}$ **9.** $2 + \sqrt{3}$ or $\sqrt{7 + 4\sqrt{3}}$

11. $\frac{\sqrt{2+\sqrt{2}}}{2}$ **13.** $\frac{\sqrt{2+\sqrt{2}}}{2}$ **15.** $\sqrt{2} - 1$ or $\sqrt{3 - 2\sqrt{2}}$

17. $\cos x$ **19.** $\sin 4x$ **21.** 1 **23.** 1 **25.** $\sin 2x$

27. $8\sin\theta\cos^3\theta - 4\sin\theta\cos\theta$, or $4\sin\theta\cos^3\theta - 4\sin^3\theta\cos\theta$, or $4\sin\theta\cos\theta - 8\sin^3\theta\cos\theta$; $\cos^4\theta - 6\cos^2\theta\sin^2\theta + \sin^4\theta$, or $8\cos^4\theta - 8\cos^2\theta + 1$, or $1 - 8\sin^2\theta\cos^2\theta$

29. $\frac{1}{8}(3 + 4\cos 2\theta + \cos 4\theta)$

Mixed Review **31.** $f^{-1}(x) = \sqrt{x^3 - 1}$ **33.** $f^{-1}(x) = \ln x$

35.

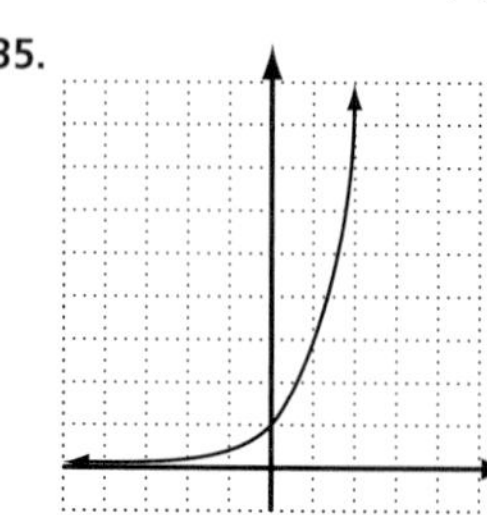

LESSON 18-3

Try This

a. $\cot^2 x - \cos^2 x \equiv \cos^2 x\cot^2 x$

$\frac{\cos^2 x}{\sin^2 x} - \cos^2 x$	$\cos^2 x\frac{\cos^2 x}{\sin^2 x}$
$\frac{\cos^2 x - \cos^2 x\sin^2 x}{\sin^2 x}$	
$\frac{\cos^2 x(1 - \sin^2 x)}{\sin^2 x}$	
$\frac{\cos^2 x\cos^2 x}{\sin^2 x}$	

b. $\frac{\sin 2\theta + \sin\theta}{\cos 2\theta + \cos\theta + 1} \equiv \tan\theta$

$\frac{2\sin\theta\cos\theta + \sin\theta}{2\cos^2\theta + \cos\theta}$	$\frac{\sin\theta}{\cos\theta}$
$\frac{\sin\theta(2\cos\theta + 1)}{\cos\theta(2\cos\theta + 1)}$	
$\frac{\sin\theta}{\cos\theta}$	

Exercises

1. $\csc x - \cos x\cot x \equiv \sin x$

$\frac{1}{\sin x} - \cos x\frac{\cos x}{\sin x}$	$\sin x$
$\frac{1 - \cos^2 x}{\sin x}$	
$\frac{\sin^2 x}{\sin x}$	
$\sin x$	

3. $\frac{1 + \cos\theta}{\sin\theta} + \frac{\sin\theta}{\cos\theta} \equiv \frac{\cos\theta + 1}{\sin\theta\cos\theta}$

$\frac{1 + \cos\theta}{\sin\theta} \cdot \frac{\cos\theta}{\cos\theta} + \frac{\sin\theta}{\cos\theta} \cdot \frac{\sin\theta}{\sin\theta}$	$\frac{\cos\theta + 1}{\sin\theta\cos\theta}$
$\frac{\cos\theta + \cos^2\theta + \sin^2\theta}{\sin\theta\cos\theta}$	
$\frac{\cos\theta + 1}{\sin\theta\cos\theta}$	

5. $\frac{1 - \sin x}{\cos x} \equiv \frac{\cos x}{1 + \sin x}$

$\frac{1 - \sin x}{\cos x} \cdot \frac{\cos x}{\cos x}$	$\frac{\cos x}{1 + \sin x} \cdot \frac{1 - \sin x}{1 - \sin x}$
$\frac{\cos x - \sin x\cos x}{\cos^2 x}$	$\frac{\cos x - \cos x\sin x}{1 - \sin^2 x}$
	$\frac{\cos x - \sin x\cos x}{\cos^2 x}$

7. $\frac{1 + \tan\theta}{1 + \cot\theta} \equiv \frac{\sec\theta}{\csc\theta}$

$\frac{1 + \frac{\sin\theta}{\cos\theta}}{1 + \frac{\cos\theta}{\sin\theta}}$	$\frac{\frac{1}{\cos\theta}}{\frac{1}{\sin\theta}}$
$\frac{\frac{\cos\theta + \sin\theta}{\cos\theta}}{\frac{\sin\theta + \cos\theta}{\sin\theta}}$	$\frac{\sin\theta}{\cos\theta}$
$\frac{\sin\theta}{\cos\theta}$	

9. $\dfrac{\sin x + \cos x}{\sec x + \csc x} \equiv \dfrac{\sin x}{\sec x}$

$\dfrac{\sin x + \cos x}{\dfrac{1}{\cos x} + \dfrac{1}{\sin x}}$	$\dfrac{\sin x}{\dfrac{1}{\cos x}}$
$\dfrac{\sin x + \cos x}{\dfrac{\sin + \cos x}{\cos x \sin x}}$	$\cos x \sin x$
$\cos x \sin x$	

11. $\dfrac{1 + \tan \theta}{1 - \tan \theta} + \dfrac{1 + \cot \theta}{1 - \cot \theta} \equiv 0$

$\dfrac{1 + \dfrac{\sin \theta}{\cos \theta}}{1 - \dfrac{\sin \theta}{\cos \theta}} + \dfrac{1 + \dfrac{\cos \theta}{\sin \theta}}{1 - \dfrac{\cos \theta}{\sin \theta}}$	0
$\dfrac{\dfrac{\cos \theta + \sin \theta}{\cos \theta}}{\dfrac{\cos \theta - \sin \theta}{\cos \theta}} + \dfrac{\dfrac{\sin \theta + \cos \theta}{\sin \theta}}{\dfrac{\sin \theta - \cos \theta}{\sin \theta}}$	
$\dfrac{\cos \theta + \sin \theta}{\cos \theta - \sin \theta} + \dfrac{\sin \theta + \cos \theta}{\sin \theta - \cos \theta}$	
$\dfrac{\cos \theta + \sin \theta}{\cos \theta - \sin \theta} - \dfrac{\cos \theta + \sin \theta}{\cos \theta - \sin \theta}$	

13. $\dfrac{1 + \cos 2\theta}{\sin 2\theta} \equiv \cot \theta$

$\dfrac{1 + 2\cos^2 \theta - 1}{2 \sin \theta \cos \theta}$	$\dfrac{\cos \theta}{\sin \theta}$
$\dfrac{\cos \theta}{\sin \theta}$	

15. $\sec 2\theta \equiv \dfrac{\sec^2 \theta}{2 - \sec^2 \theta}$

$\dfrac{1}{\cos 2\theta}$	$\dfrac{\dfrac{1}{\cos^2 \theta}}{2 - \dfrac{1}{\cos^2 \theta}}$
$\dfrac{1}{2\cos^2 \theta - 1}$	$\dfrac{\dfrac{1}{\cos^2 \theta}}{\dfrac{2\cos^2 \theta - 1}{\cos^2 \theta}}$
	$\dfrac{1}{2\cos^2 \theta - 1}$

17. $\dfrac{\sin(\alpha + \beta)}{\cos \alpha \cos \beta} \equiv \tan \alpha + \tan \beta$

$\dfrac{\sin \alpha \cos \beta + \cos \alpha \sin \beta}{\cos \alpha \cos \beta}$	$\dfrac{\sin \alpha}{\cos \alpha} + \dfrac{\sin \beta}{\cos \beta}$
	$\dfrac{\sin \alpha \cos \beta + \cos \alpha \sin \beta}{\cos \alpha \cos \beta}$

19. $\dfrac{\tan \theta + \sin \theta}{2 \tan \theta} \equiv \cos^2 \dfrac{\theta}{2}$

$\dfrac{\dfrac{\sin \theta}{\cos \theta} + \sin \theta}{2\dfrac{\sin \theta}{\cos \theta}}$	$\dfrac{1 + \cos \theta}{2}$
$\dfrac{\dfrac{\sin \theta + \sin \theta \cos \theta}{\cos \theta}}{2\dfrac{\sin \theta}{\cos \theta}}$	
$\dfrac{\sin \theta + \sin \theta \cos \theta}{2 \sin \theta}$	
$\dfrac{1 + \cos \theta}{2}$	

21. $\cos^4 x - \sin^4 x \equiv \cos 2x$

$(\cos^2 x - \sin^2 x)(\cos^2 x + \sin^2 x)$	$\cos^2 x - \sin^2 x$
$\cos^2 x - \sin^2 x$	

23. $\dfrac{\tan 3\theta - \tan \theta}{1 + \tan 3\theta \tan \theta} \equiv \dfrac{2 \tan \theta}{1 - \tan^2 \theta}$

$\tan(3\theta - \theta)$	$\tan 2\theta$
$\tan 2\theta$	

25. $\sin(\alpha + \beta)\sin(\alpha - \beta) \equiv \sin^2 \alpha - \sin^2 \beta$

$(\sin \alpha \cos \beta + \cos \alpha \sin \beta)(\sin \alpha \cos \beta - \cos \alpha \sin \beta)$

$\sin^2 \alpha \cos^2 \beta - \cos^2 \alpha \sin^2 \beta$

$\sin^2 \alpha(1 - \sin^2 \beta) - (1 - \sin^2 \alpha)(\sin^2 \beta)$

$\sin^2 \alpha - \sin^2 \alpha \sin^2 \beta - \sin^2 \beta + \sin^2 \alpha \sin^2 \beta$

$\sin^2 \alpha - \sin^2 \beta$

27. $\cos(\alpha + \beta) + \cos(\alpha - \beta) \equiv 2 \cos \alpha \cos \beta$

$(\cos \alpha \cos \beta - \sin \alpha \sin \beta) + (\cos \alpha \cos \beta + \sin \alpha \sin \beta)$

$2 \cos \alpha \cos \beta$

29. Answers may vary. **31.** $\sin \theta = \cos \phi$

33. $$\frac{E_1 + E_2}{2} = \frac{\sqrt{2}E_t \cos\left(\theta + \frac{\pi}{p}\right) + \sqrt{2}E_t \cos\left(\theta - \frac{\pi}{p}\right)}{2}$$

$$= \sqrt{2}E_t \frac{\cos \theta \cos \frac{\pi}{p} - \sin \theta \sin \frac{\pi}{p} + \cos \theta \cos \frac{\pi}{p} + \sin \theta \sin \frac{\pi}{p}}{2}$$

$$= \sqrt{2}E_t \cos \theta \cos \frac{\pi}{p}$$

Similarly for $\dfrac{E_1 - E_2}{2}$

Mixed Review

35.

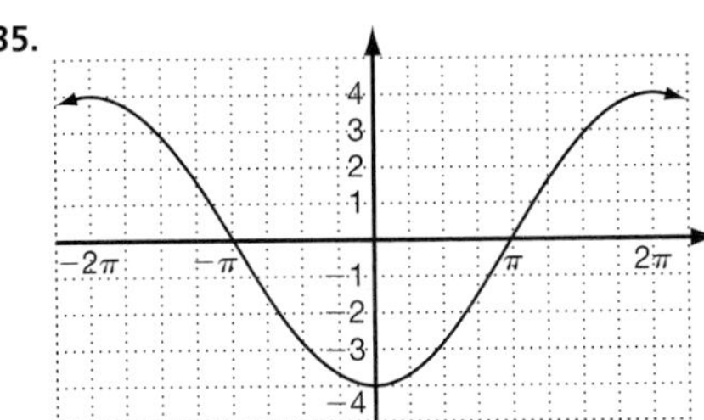

37. 4 **39.** 5 ft

Selected Answers

LESSON 18-4

Try This **a.** Not a function

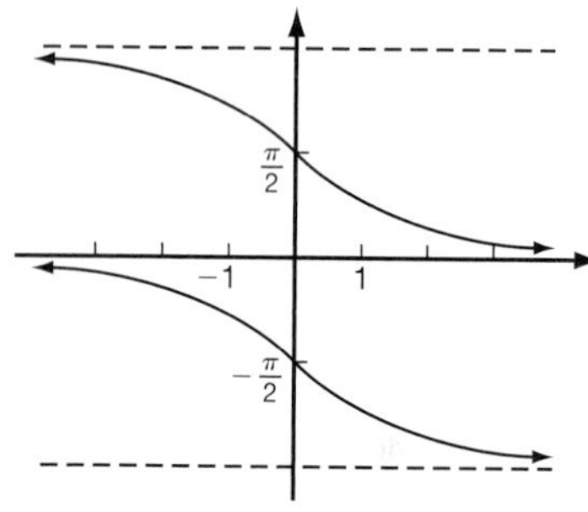

b. $\frac{\pi}{4} + 2k\pi, \frac{7\pi}{4} + 2k\pi$ **c.** $\frac{\pi}{3} + 2k\pi, \frac{2\pi}{3} + 2k\pi$
d. $25° + k \cdot 360°, 155° + k \cdot 360°$ **e.** $\frac{3\pi}{4} + k\pi$ **f.** $\frac{\pi}{3}$ **g.** $\frac{3\pi}{4}$
h. $\frac{3\pi}{4}$ **i.** $-\frac{\pi}{4}$

Exercises **1.** $\frac{\pi}{4} + 2k\pi, \frac{3\pi}{4} + 2k\pi$ **3.** $\frac{\pi}{4} + 2k\pi, -\frac{\pi}{4} + 2k\pi$
5. $\frac{5\pi}{4} + 2k\pi, -\frac{\pi}{4} + 2k\pi$ **7.** $\frac{3\pi}{4} + 2k\pi, \frac{5\pi}{4} + 2k\pi$ **9.** $\frac{\pi}{3} + k\pi$
11. $\frac{\pi}{4} + k\pi$ **13.** $\frac{5\pi}{6} + k\pi$ **15.** $\frac{3\pi}{4} + k\pi$ **17.** $0 + 2k\pi$
19. $\frac{\pi}{2} + 2k\pi$ **21.** $23° + k \cdot 360°, 157° + k \cdot 360°$
23. $39° + k \cdot 360°, 141° + k \cdot 360°$ **25.** $36°58' + k \cdot 360°, 323°02' + k \cdot 360°$ **27.** $21°25' + k \cdot 360°, 338°35' + k \cdot 360°$
29. $20°10' + k \cdot 180°$ **31.** $38°20' + k \cdot 180°$
33. $31° + k \cdot 360°, 329° + k \cdot 360°$ **35.** $9°10' + k \cdot 360°, 170°50' + k \cdot 360°$ **37.** $\frac{\pi}{4}$ **39.** $\frac{\pi}{3}$ **41.** $-\frac{\pi}{3}$
43. The principal values of the inverse function Arccos are restricted to the range $\{y|0 \leq y \leq \pi\}$, which does *not* include $-\frac{\pi}{4}$. **45.** $-\frac{\pi}{3}$ **47.** $\frac{3\pi}{4} + k\pi$ (k an integer)
49. $2k\pi$ (k an integer) **51.** $\frac{\pi}{2} + 2k\pi$ (k an integer) **53.** The semicircle to the right of the y-axis from (and including) $-\frac{\pi}{2}$ to (and including) $\frac{\pi}{2}$ **55.** The semicircle to the right of the y-axis from (not including) $-\frac{\pi}{2}$ to (not including) $\frac{\pi}{2}$
57. 0.2356 radians **59.** 2.6675 radians **61.** −0.3869 radians
63. a. $\approx 66°$ **b.** If $r = R$, the angle must be 0°. **65.** $-\frac{\pi}{3}$
67. $\frac{\sqrt{3}}{2}$ **69.** $-\frac{\pi}{2}$

Mixed Review **71.** 1.66 **73.** ±1.468

LESSON 18-5

Try This **a.** $\frac{\pi}{6}, \frac{5\pi}{6}, \frac{7\pi}{6}, \frac{11\pi}{6}$, plus $2k\pi$ **b.** $\frac{\pi}{6}, \frac{5\pi}{6}, \frac{7\pi}{6}, \frac{11\pi}{6}$
c. 75°30′, 284°30′, 120°, 240° **d.** 90°, 120°, 240°, 270°

Exercises **1.** $\frac{4\pi}{3}, \frac{5\pi}{3}$ or 240°, 300° **3.** $\frac{\pi}{6}, \frac{5\pi}{6}, \frac{7\pi}{6}, \frac{11\pi}{6}$ or 30°, 150°, 210°, 330° **5.** $\frac{\pi}{6}, \frac{5\pi}{6}, \frac{3\pi}{2}$ or 30°, 150°, 270° **7.** 0 , 2π or 0°, 360° **9.** $\frac{\pi}{6}, \frac{5\pi}{6}$ or 30°, 150° **11.** B **13.** $\frac{\pi}{4}, \frac{\pi}{2}, \frac{5\pi}{4}, \frac{3\pi}{2}$ **15.** $0, \frac{2\pi}{3}, \pi, \frac{4\pi}{3}, 2\pi$ **17.** $\frac{\pi}{6}, \frac{\pi}{3}, \frac{5\pi}{6}, \frac{5\pi}{3}$ **19.** $0, \frac{\pi}{2}, \pi, \frac{3\pi}{2}, 2\pi$
21. $0, \frac{\pi}{2}, \pi, \frac{3\pi}{2}, 2\pi$ **23.** $\frac{2\pi}{3}, \frac{4\pi}{3}, \frac{3\pi}{2}$ **25.** $\frac{\pi}{4}, \frac{3\pi}{4}, \frac{5\pi}{4}, \frac{7\pi}{4}$
27. $\frac{\pi}{6}, \frac{5\pi}{6}$ **29.** $\frac{7\pi}{12}, \frac{23\pi}{12}$ **31.** $\frac{7\pi}{4}$ **33.** 60°, 120°, 240°, 300°
35. 60°, 240° **37.** 30°, 60°, 120°, 150°, 210°, 240°, 300°, 330°

Mixed Review **39.** Zeros: $3i, -3i, 1, -2$; x-intercepts: $1, -2$
41. $P(x) = (x^2 + 9)(x + 2)(x - 1)$

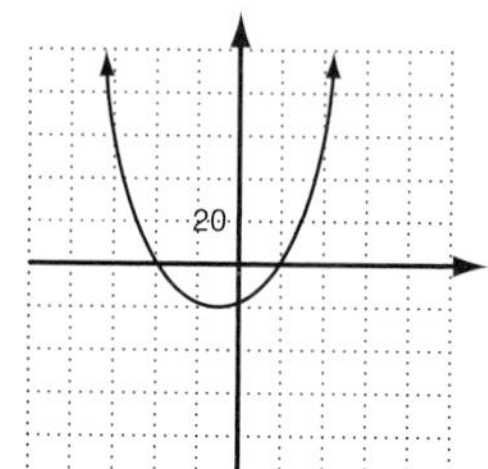

43. $\pm 3, \pm 4i$ **45.** 30,240 **47.** 126

LESSON 18-6

Try This **a.** $a \approx 38.43, b \approx 54.88$ **b.** $\angle A \approx 56°19'$, $\angle B \approx 33°41', c \approx 7.211$ **c.** ≈ 75.8 m **d.** ≈ 28°30′
e. 240.3 ft **f.** 136 km; 63.4 km

Exercises **1.** $\angle B = 53°50', b = 37.2, c = 46.1$
3. $\angle A = 77°20', a = 436.5, c = 447.4$ **5.** $\angle B = 72°40'$, $a = 4.24, c = 14.2$ **7.** $\angle A = 20°40', b = 0.0130, c = 0.0139$
9. $\angle A = 33°30', a = 0.0247, b = 0.0373$ **11.** $a = 3.57$, $\angle A = 63°20', \angle B = 26°40'$ **13.** $c = 21.6, \angle A = 33°40'$, $\angle B = 56°20'$ **15.** Apply the Pythagorean Theorem, $16^2 + b^2 = 20^2$. Then $b = 12, \angle B = 36°50'; \angle A = 53°10'$.
17. 9.59 ft **19.** 171.5 ft **21.** 10°20′ **23.** 60°20′ **25.** 274 ft
27. 610 ft **29.** 201 km **31.** 29.5 cm **33.** 96.7 cm
35. 7.92 km **37.** 3.45 km **39.** Area $= \frac{ab}{2}, \frac{a}{c} = \sin A$, $a = c \sin A$. Substituting, area $= \frac{bc}{2} \sin A$.
41. $d \approx \sqrt{h^2 + 2(3963)h}$, where d and h are in miles; 38.7 miles

Mixed Review **43.** $\pm\frac{7}{5}i$

LESSON 18-7

Try This **a.** $m\angle B = 87, b \approx 9.94, c \approx 7.84$ **b.** $m\angle A = 59$, $a \approx 221.05, c \approx 225.55$ **c.** No solution **d.** $\angle B \approx 36°52'$, $\angle C \approx 90°, c \approx 5$ **e.** $m\angle A \approx 43, m\angle C \approx 104, c \approx 35.6$, or $m\angle A \approx 137, m\angle C \approx 10, c \approx 6.4$ **f.** $m\angle A \approx 124, m\angle C \approx 18$, $a \approx 26.9$ **g.** ≈ 8.452

Exercises **1.** $m\angle C = 50, a \approx 18.4, c \approx 16.3$ **3.** $m\angle C = 96$,

$b \approx 15.2$, $c \approx 20.3$ **5.** $m\angle C = 17$, $a \approx 26.3$, $c \approx 10.5$ **7.** $m\angle A = 121$, $a \approx 33.4$, $c \approx 14.0$ **9.** $\angle B = 68°50'$, $a \approx 32.3$, $b \approx 32.3$ **11.** $\angle A \approx 12°20'$, $\angle C \approx 17°40'$, $c \approx 4.25$ **13.** $\angle A \approx 20°20'$, $\angle B \approx 99°40'$, $b \approx 34.1$ **15.** $\angle B \approx 56°20'$, $\angle C \approx 87°40'$, $c \approx 40.8$ or $\angle B \approx 123°40'$, $\angle C \approx 20°20'$, $c \approx 14.2$ **17.** $\angle C \approx 44°40'$, $\angle B \approx 19°$, $b \approx 6.25$ **19.** $\angle B \approx 44°20'$, $\angle A \approx 74°30'$, $a \approx 33.3$ **21.** 30 **23.** ≈ 0.0868 **25.** $\approx 5.438\ m^2$ **27.** ≈ 76.3 m **29.** ≈ 50.8 ft **31.** ≈ 1467 km **33.** 10.6 km or 2.43 km **35.** Let the diagonals intersect to form four triangles, and the diagonals have lengths of $(a + b)$ and $(c + d)$. Area $= \frac{1}{2}bd \sin \theta + \frac{1}{2}ac \sin \theta + \frac{1}{2}ad \sin (180° - \theta) + \frac{1}{2}bc \sin (180° - \theta) = \frac{1}{2}(bd + ac + ad + bc) \sin \theta = \frac{1}{2}(a + b)(c + d) \sin \theta$

Mixed Review **37.** $\frac{36b^2d^2\sqrt[3]{d^2}}{a^4c^4}$ **39.** 1 **41.** 54 **43.** $-209{,}715$ **45.** $f(x) = x^4 + 10x^2 - 96$

LESSON 18-8

Try This **a.** $a = 40.5$, $\angle B = 22°10'$, $\angle C = 35°50'$ **b.** $\angle A = 108°10'$, $\angle B = 22°20'$, $\angle C = 49°30'$

Exercises **1.** $c \approx 12.0$, $\angle A \approx 20°40'$, $\angle B \approx 24°20'$ **3.** $a \approx 14.9$, $\angle B \approx 23°40'$, $\angle C \approx 126°20'$ **5.** $a \approx 24.8$, $\angle B \approx 20°40'$, $\angle C \approx 26°20'$ **7.** $b \approx 74.8$, $\angle A \approx 95°30'$, $\angle C \approx 11°50'$ **9.** *sometimes* ($\angle A \leq 90°$) **11.** $\angle A \approx 42°50'$, $\angle B \approx 61°$, $\angle C \approx 76°10'$ **13.** $\angle A \approx 44°$, $\angle B \approx 52°40'$, $\angle C \approx 83°20'$ **15.** $\angle A \approx 37°20'$, $\angle B \approx 37°20'$, $\angle C \approx 105°20'$ **17.** $\angle A \approx 24°10'$, $\angle B \approx 30°40'$, $\angle C \approx 125°10'$ **19.** 912 km **21.** 87.4 ft **23.** 52°50′, 85°30′, 41°40′ **25. a.** 15.73 ft **b.** 120.6 ft^2 **27.** $a^2 + b^2 + c^2 = 2abc\left(\frac{\cos A}{a} + \frac{\cos B}{b} + \frac{\cos C}{c}\right)$ **29.** Area $= \frac{1}{2}a^2 \sin \theta$; $\theta = 90°$

Mixed Review **31.** 2 **33.** 2 **35.** 10 **37.** Q: $4x^3 + 4x^2 + 2x + 5$, R: 1 **39.** $(x^4 + 4y^2)(x^2 + 2y)(x^2 - 2y)$ **41.** $2(c - 15)(c + 1)$

LESSON 18-9

Try This **a.** $1 - i$ **b.** $2(\cos 60° + i \sin 60°)$ **c.** 20 cis 55° **d.** $2 \text{ cis } \frac{\pi}{4}$ **e.** 32 cis 270° **f.** 16 cis 120° **g.** $1 + i, -1 - i$ **h.** $\sqrt{3} + i, -\sqrt{3} + i, -2i$

Exercises **1.** $\frac{3\sqrt{3}}{2} + \frac{3}{2}i$ **3.** $-2\sqrt{2} + 2i\sqrt{2}$ **5.** $-10i$ **7.** $\frac{5\sqrt{2}}{2} - \frac{5\sqrt{2}}{2}i$ **9.** $2 + 2i$ **11.** $2\sqrt{3} + 2i$ **13.** $-2 - 2i$ **15.** $\sqrt{2} \text{ cis } \frac{3\pi}{4}$ or $\sqrt{2}$ cis 135° **17.** $2 \text{ cis } \frac{\pi}{6}$ or 2 cis 30° **19.** $20 \text{ cis } \frac{11\pi}{6}$ or 20 cis 330° **21.** $2 \text{ cis } \frac{\pi}{2}$ or 2 cis 90° **23.** $5 \text{ cis } \pi$ or 5 cis 180° **25.** $4 \text{ cis } \frac{3\pi}{2}$ or 4 cis 270° **27.** 4 cis 0 **29.** 40 cis 0 **31.** $8 \text{ cis } \frac{2\pi}{3}$ **33.** $\text{cis } \frac{\pi}{2}$ **35.** $\frac{\sqrt{2}}{2} \text{ cis } \frac{7\pi}{12}$ **37.** $2 \text{ cis } \frac{3\pi}{2}$ **39.** $8 \text{ cis } \pi$ or 8 cis 180° **41.** $64 \text{ cis } \pi$ or 64 cis 180° **43.** $8 \text{ cis } \frac{3\pi}{2}$ or 8 cis 270° **45.** $-8 - 8i\sqrt{3}$ **47.** $-8 - 8i\sqrt{3}$ **49.** i **51.** 1 **53.** $\sqrt{2}$ cis 60° and $\sqrt{2}$ cis 240°, or $\sqrt{2} \text{ cis } \frac{\pi}{3}$ and $\sqrt{2} \text{ cis } \frac{4\pi}{3}$ **55.** cis 30°, cis 150°, and cis 270°, or $\text{cis } \frac{\pi}{6}$, $\text{cis } \frac{5\pi}{6}$, and $\text{cis } \frac{3\pi}{2}$ **57.** 2 cis 0°, 2 cis 90°, 2 cis 180°, and 2 cis 270°, or 2 cis 0, $2 \text{ cis } \frac{\pi}{2}$, $2 \text{ cis } \pi$, and $2 \text{ cis } \frac{3\pi}{2}$

59. $(1 + 0i)^3 = (\text{cis } 0)^3 = \text{cis } 0 = 1$,
$\left(-\frac{1}{2} + \frac{\sqrt{3}}{2}i\right)^3 = (\text{cis } 120°)^3 = \text{cis } 0 = 1$,
$\left(-\frac{1}{2} - \frac{\sqrt{3}}{2}i\right)^3 = (\text{cis } 240°)^3 = \text{cis } 0 = 1$

61. cis 0°, cis 90°, cis 180°, cis 270°, or ± 1, $\pm i$

63.
$$\left|\frac{z}{w}\right| = \left|\frac{r_1}{r_2} \text{ cis } (\theta_1 - \theta_2)\right| = \left|\frac{r_1}{r_2} \cos (\theta_1 - \theta_2) + \frac{r_1}{r_2} i \sin (\theta_1 - \theta_2)\right| = \sqrt{\frac{r_1^2}{r_2^2} \cos^2 (\theta_1 - \theta_2) + \frac{r_1^2}{r_2^2} \sin^2 (\theta_1 - \theta_2)} = \sqrt{\frac{r_1^2}{r_2^2}} = \frac{r_1}{r_2}$$
$$\left|\frac{z}{w}\right| = \left|\frac{r_1 \text{ cis } \theta_1}{r_2 \text{ cis } \theta_2}\right| = \left|\frac{r_1 \cos \theta_1 + r_1 i \sin \theta_1}{r_2 \cos \theta_2 + r_2 i \sin \theta_2}\right| = \frac{\sqrt{r_1^2 \cos^2 \theta_1 + r_1^2 \sin^2 \theta_1}}{\sqrt{r_2^2 \cos^2 \theta_2 + r_2^2 \sin^2 \theta_2}} = \frac{\sqrt{r_1^2}}{\sqrt{r_2^2}} = \frac{r_1}{r_2}$$

65. 1 **67.** $\begin{bmatrix} -i & 0 \\ 0 & i \end{bmatrix}$

Mixed Review **69.** 720° **71.** 105° **73.** $\frac{5\pi}{12}$ **75.** $-\frac{\pi}{2}$ **77.** $2, -3, \pm\sqrt{2}$ **79. a.** 41.7 mg **b.** 13.9 mg **c.** 3.9 mg

Application **1.** < 4000 mi **3.** $\frac{25{,}000}{3006} \approx 8.32$, so 9 stations are needed. **5.** 203.6 mi, 611.5 mi

CHAPTER 18 WRAP UP

1. $\cos x \cos y - \sin x \sin y$ **2.** $2 - \sqrt{3}$ **3.** $\frac{\sqrt{2} + \sqrt{6}}{4}$ **4.** $\frac{\sqrt{2} - \sqrt{6}}{4}$ **5.** $2 - \sqrt{3}$ **6.** $\sin 2\theta = \frac{24}{25}$, $\cos 2\theta = \frac{7}{25}$, $\tan 2\theta = \frac{24}{7}$, Quadrant I **7.** $\sin 2\theta = \frac{24}{25}$, $\cos 2\theta = -\frac{7}{25}$, $\tan 2\theta = -\frac{24}{7}$, Quadrant II **8.** $\frac{1}{2}\sqrt{2 + \sqrt{3}}$, or $\frac{\sqrt{2} + \sqrt{6}}{4}$ **9.** $\frac{\sqrt{2 - \sqrt{2}}}{2}$

10. $\tan 2\theta \equiv \frac{2 \tan \theta}{1 - \tan^2 \theta}$

$\tan (\theta + \theta)$	$\frac{2 \tan \theta}{1 - \tan^2 \theta}$
$\frac{\tan \theta + \tan \theta}{1 - \tan \theta \tan \theta}$	
$\frac{2 \tan \theta}{1 - \tan^2 \theta}$	

11. $\frac{\pi}{6} + 2k\pi$, $\frac{5\pi}{6} + 2k\pi$, k an integer **12.** $\frac{3\pi}{4} + 2k\pi$, $\frac{5\pi}{4} + 2k\pi$, k an integer **13.** $-\frac{\pi}{4}$ **14.** $\frac{\pi}{6}$ **15.** $0, \pi, 2\pi$ **16.** $\frac{\pi}{6}, \frac{5\pi}{6}, \frac{\pi}{2}, \frac{3\pi}{2}$ **17.** $\angle B = 47°30'$,

$b = 1310$, $c = 1780$ **18.** $\angle A = 58°10'$, $\angle B = 31°50'$, $b = 4.55$ **19.** $\angle A = 38°50'$, $b = 37.9$, $c = 48.6$ **20.** 86.9 ft **21.** 3708.8 mi **22.** $m\angle C = 60$, $a = 16.3$, $c = 22.0$ **23.** $m\angle A = 34$, $a = 0.619$, $c = 0.514$ **24.** $\angle B = 49°30'$, $\angle C = 58°30'$, $c = 4.48$ **25.** $\angle A = 19°10'$, $\angle C = 25°50'$, $b = 7.96$ **26.** $\angle A = 33°30'$, $\angle B = 62°10'$, $\angle C = 84°20'$ **27.** 20.4 **28.** $-\sqrt{2} + i\sqrt{2}$ **29.** $\sqrt{2}$ cis $\frac{\pi}{4}$ or $\sqrt{2}$ cis 45° **30.** $-1 + i\sqrt{3}$ **31.** $\sqrt[6]{2}$ cis 15°, $\sqrt[6]{2}$ cis 135°, $\sqrt[6]{2}$ cis 255°

CHAPTERS 1–18 CUMULATIVE REVIEW

1. 19 **3.** -7 **5.** $a > 2$ **7.** $-5, x, 13$ **9.** $\$0.138m + \$1620$; \$1758 **11.** $(-1, 3, 6)$ **13.** $4x^3y + 5x^2y - 8xy - 10y$ **15.** $3(2x - 11y)^2$ **17.** $2(x + 2)(x - 2)(x + 3)$ **19.** 8, 1 **21.** $\frac{a - 3}{5a + 2}$ **23.** $-5, 3$ **25.** $3|x|\sqrt{10x}$ **27.** $|x + 3|$ **29.** $-1 - \sqrt{35}$ **31.** $-28 - 44i$ **33.** $\frac{\sqrt{2}}{3}, -\frac{\sqrt{2}}{3}$ **35.** $64, -\frac{343}{8}$ **37.** x-axis **39.** Neither **41.** (1, 3), $x = 1$, max: 3

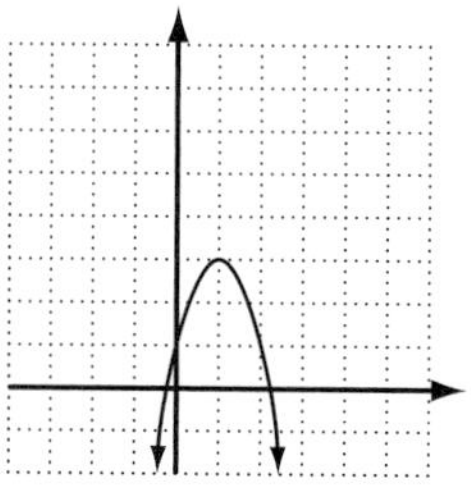

43. Center: $(-1, -3)$, radius: 2 **45.** Q: $x^2 + 3x + 9$, R: 0 **47.** $\frac{1}{2}, \frac{1 + \sqrt{5}}{2}, \frac{1 - \sqrt{5}}{2}$ **49.** $x = 2y^2 + 3$ **51.** $\log_{10} 3 = 0.4771$ **53.** $\log_x z = y$ **55.** 1

57. $\begin{bmatrix} -3 & 6 & 30 \\ 9 & -12 & 24 \\ 0 & 15 & -3 \end{bmatrix}$ **59.** $\begin{bmatrix} -\frac{3}{16} & \frac{13}{48} & \frac{7}{24} \\ \frac{1}{64} & \frac{1}{192} & \frac{19}{96} \\ \frac{5}{64} & \frac{5}{192} & -\frac{1}{96} \end{bmatrix}$ **61.** (2, 2)

63. -41 **65.** $\frac{27}{4}$ **67.** 120 **69.** $16a^4 + 96a^3y + 216a^2y^2 + 216ay^3 + 81y^4$ **71.** $\frac{2}{3}$

73. Answers may vary.

Interval	Tally	Frequency
13–15	I	1
16–18	II	2
19–21		0
22–24	~~IIII~~ II	7
25–27	II	2
28–30	III	3
31–33	III	3
34–36	I	1

75.

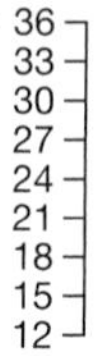

77. 4.6 **79.** 5.6 **81.** III **83.** II **85.** $\frac{5\pi}{9}$

87.

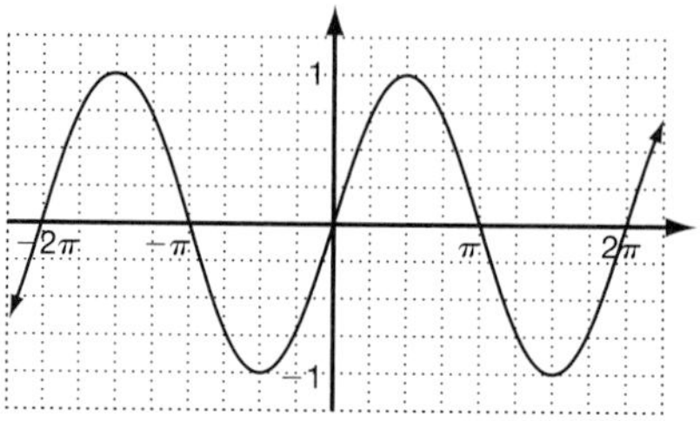

89. $A = \frac{1}{2}$, period $= \pi$

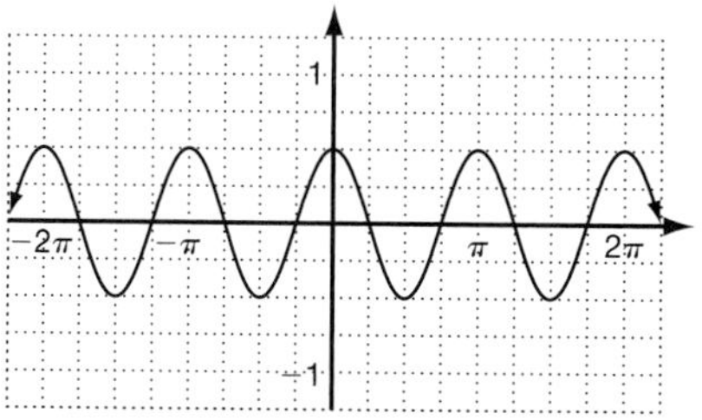

91. $2 \cos \alpha \cos \beta$

93.
$$\frac{1 - \cos x}{\sin x} \equiv \frac{\sin x}{1 + \cos x}$$
$$\frac{(1 - \cos x)(1 + \cos x)}{(\sin x)(1 + \cos x)} \quad \frac{(\sin x)(\sin x)}{(1 + \cos x)(\sin x)}$$
$$(1 - \cos x)(1 + \cos x) \quad (\sin x)(\sin x)$$
$$1 - \cos^2 x \quad \sin^2 x$$
$$\sin^2 x$$

95. $0, \pi, 2\pi$ **97.** $\angle A = 65°40'$, $\angle B = 24°20'$, $b = 4.2$ **99.** $\angle A = 12°20'$, $\angle C = 17°40'$, $c = 4.25$ **101.** 2 cis $\frac{7\pi}{6}$ **103.** $-10i$

Index

Index

STAFF CREDITS

The people who helped produce Prentice Hall ***Algebra 2 with Trigonometry***—representing editorial, editorial services, design services, market research, marketing, marketing services, project office, on-line services/multimedia development, production services, and publishing processes—are listed below.

Scott F. Andrews, Barbara Bertell, Gail Davidson, Jo DiGiustini, Deborah Faust, Barbara J. Goodchild, Kerri Hoar, Catherine Maglio, Tim McDonald, Sandra Morris, Paul W. Murphy, Greg Oles, Judi Pinkham, Sydney Schuster, Stuart Wallace, Stewart Wood, Carol Zacny

ADDITIONAL CREDITS

Charles Carpenter, Delphine Dupee, Sue Gerould, Simone Haber, Angela Husband, Al Jacobson, Lidia Martinez, Marsha Novak, Nancy Smith

Cover Design: Studio Montage

Cover Image: Superstock

Book Design: Thompson Steele

Photography:

Chapter 1: Page 3, Stone/Joseph Pobereskin; **13,** Archive Photos; **25,** Robert Holmes/Corbis; **30,** Stone; **33,** Stone/Joseph Pobereskin; **37,** Carolyn A. McKeone/Photo Researchers, Inc.

Chapter 2: Page 61, Berry Medley/Medley of Photography; **67,** Stone/Kerrick James Photo; **69,** Berry Medley/Medley of Photography; **80,** Stone/Chris Cheadle; **93,** Michael Newman/PhotoEdit; **100,** Erik Simonsen/Image Bank.

Chapter 3: Page 105, Omni-Photo Communications; **127,** Tony Freeman/PhotoEdit; **143,** Omni-Photo Communications; **144,** Volvo Cars of North America, Inc.; **151,** Grace Davies/Omni-Photo Communications; **153,** Harvey Lloyd/The Stock Market; **154,** Grantpix/Photo Researchers, Inc.

Chapter 4: Page 159, Stone/Terry Vine; **170,** Stone/Martine Mouchy; **182,** Stone/Terry Vine; **194,** Alon Reininger/Contact Press Images/Picturequest.

Chapter 5: Page 205, Stone/Baron Wolman; **206,** Stone/Ian Shaw; **208,** Stone/Baron Wolman; **218,** Stone/Jon Riley; **234,** Wil Blanche/Omni-Photo Communications; **236,** Hans Reinhard/Photo Researchers, Inc.

Chapter 6: Page 243, Stone/Ed Pritchard; **270,** W. Lynn Seldon Jr./Omni-Photo Communications; **272,** Network Prod./The Image Works; **275,** Stone/Ed Pritchard; **276,** Al Tielemans/Duomo; **278,** Tony Freeman/PhotoEdit; **281,** Stone/Joel Rogers; **285,** Susan Van Etten/PhotoEdit.

Chapter 7: Page 291, Stone; **299,** David R. Frazier Photolibrary, Inc.; **300,** Stone; **319,** Susan G. Drinker/The Stock Market; **320,** 1994 Kip Peticolas/Fundamental Photographs; **334,** The Stock Market.

Acknowledgments

Chapter 8: Page 341, Harald Sund/Image Bank; **349,** Jeff Hunter/Image Bank; **359,** Eric Meola/Image Bank; **366,** Harald Sund/Image Bank; **370,** Frank Siteman/PhotoEdit.

Chapter 9: Page 383, Stone/Kevin Schafer; **384l,** Stone/Kevin Schafer; **384m,** Stone/Davies & Star; **384r,** Stone/John Warden; **387,** Stone/Robin Smith; **411,** William Hart/PhotoEdit; **415,** Bob Daemmrich/The Image Works; **419,** Stone/Don Smetzer; **422,** Eastcott/Momatiuk/The Image Works.

Chapter 10: Page 429, NASA; **434,** PhotoDisc, Inc.; **438,** NASA; **448,** Courtesy of St. Louis Science Center; **452,** Young-Wolff/PhotoEdit; **457,** Jeff Greenburg/PhotoEdit; **470,** Norm Thomas 1987/Photo Researchers, Inc.; **471,** PhotoEdit; **473,** Michael Newman/PhotoEdit.

Chapter 11: Page 479, 500, Stone/George Kavanagh; **501,** Leonard de Selva/Corbis; **510,** Richard Haynes.

Chapter 12: Page 515, Spencer Grant/Liaison Agency; **546,** Neal Preston/Corbis; **548,** Spencer Grant/Liaison Agency; **555,** Alexander Tsiaras/Stock Boston.

Chapter 13: Page 567, David Young-Wolff/PhotoEdit; **598,** Stone/Jake Rajas; **600,** David Young-Wolff/PhotoEdit; **604,** Corbis.

Chapter 14: Page 611, Picture Perfect; **612,** Peter Skinner/Photo Researchers, Inc.; **622,** James L. Amos/Corbis; **624,** Ben Simmons/The Stock Market; **632,** Richard Mega/Fundamental Photographs; **636,** Picture Perfect; **638,** Najlah Feanny/Stock Boston.

Chapter 15: Page 643, Stone; **651,** Jonathan Nourok/PhotoEdit; **655, 678,** The Granger Collection, New York; **683,** Stone.

Chapter 16: Page 689, Paul J. Sutton/Duomo; **695,** AP/Wide World Photos; **697,** Stone/Neil Selkirk; **700,** Peter Hvizdak/The Image Works; **707,** F. Stuart Westmoreland/Photo Researchers, Inc.; **712,** Hulton Getty/Liaison Agency; **718,** Paul J. Sutton/Duomo.

Chapter 17: Page 727, Leonard Lessin/Peter Arnold, Inc.; **740,** Richard Haynes; **745,** NASA; **746,** Roger Wilmshurst/Frank Lane Picture/Corbis; **747,** Fredrik D. Bodin/Stock Boston; **770,** Leonard Lessin/Peter Arnold, Inc.; **775,** Bill Aron, MR/PhotoEdit.

Chapter 18: Page 781, Rafael Macia, 1995/Photo Researchers, Inc.; **800,** Pete Saloutos, 1996/The Stock Market; **808,** Rafael Macia, 1995/Photo Researchers, Inc.; **809,** AP/Wide World Photos; **815,** NASA; **816,** Sylvester Allred/Visuals Unlimited; **820,** Stone/Pete Seaward; **827,** Steven E. Sutton/Duomo.